AN INTRODUCTION TO
BRAIN AND BEHAVIOR

AN INTRODUCTION TO
BRAIN AND BEHAVIOR

Second Edition

BRYAN KOLB
University of Lethbridge

IAN Q. WHISHAW
University of Lethbridge

WORTH PUBLISHERS

Senior Sponsoring Editor: Laura Pople
Development Editor: Barbara Brooks
Assistant Editor: Danielle Storm
Marketing Manager: Carlise Stembridge
Project Editor: Georgia Lee Hadler
Manuscript Editor: Patricia Zimmerman
Production Manager: Sarah Segal
Media and Supplements Editor: Danielle Pucci
Text Design: Michael Mendelsohn, Vicki Tomaselli
Cover Design: Vicki Tomaselli
Photo Editor: Patricia Marx
Senior Illustration Coordinator: Bill Page
Illustrations: DragonFly Media Group and Northeastern Graphic, Inc.
Composition: Northeastern Graphic, Inc.
Printing and Binding: RR Donnelley

Cover art: Copyright 2004, Doak Heyser

ISBN: 0716711877; EAN: 9780716711872

Library of Congress Cataloging-in-Publication Data
Kolb, Bryan, 1947–
    An introduction to brain and behavior / Bryan Kolb, Ian Q. Whishaw.—2nd ed.
    p. cm.
    Includes bibliographical references and index.
    ISBN 0-7167-1187-7
    1. Brain—Textbooks. 2. Human behavior—Physiological aspects—Textbooks. 3.
Neurophysiology—Textbooks. I. Whishaw, Ian Q., 1939– II. Title.

QP376.K635 2005
612.8′2—dc22

                                                            2004061245

First printing 2005

Worth Publishers
41 Madison Avenue
New York, NY 10010
www.worthpublishers.com

About the Authors

BRYAN KOLB received his Ph.D. from the Pennsylvania State University in 1973. He conducted postdoctoral work at the University of Western Ontario and the Montreal Neurological Institute. He moved to the University of Lethbridge in 1976, where he is currently Professor of Psychology and Neuroscience and holds a Board of Governors Chair in Neuroscience. His current research examines how neurons of the cerebral cortex change in response to various factors, including hormones, experience, psychoactive drugs, neurotrophins, and injury, and how these changes are related to behavior in the normal and diseased brain. Kolb is a Killam Fellow (Canada Council), a Fellow of the Canadian Psychological Association (CPA), the American Psychological Association, the American Psychological Society, and the Royal Society of Canada. He is a recipient of the Hebb Prize from CPA and from the Canadian Society for Brain, Behaviour, and Cognitive Science (CSBBCS) and is a former president of the CSBBCS. He is one of the theme leaders in the Canadian Stroke Network. He is an adjunct professor at the University of British Columbia and University of Calgary, as well as the Hotchkiss Brain Institute in Calgary, Alberta.

IAN Q. WHISHAW received his Ph.D. from the University of Western Ontario in 1971. He moved to the University of Lethbridge in 1970, where he is currently Professor of Psychology and Neuroscience and holds a Board of Governors Chair in Neuroscience. He has held visiting appointments at the University of Texas, University of Michigan, Cambridge University, and the University of Strasbourg, France. He is a Fellow of Clair Hall, Cambridge, and a member of the Hotchkiss Brain Institute in Calgary, Alberta. His current research examines how the precise details of movements are influenced by injury or disease to the motor systems of rodents and humans and how animals and humans move through real and mental space. Whishaw is a Fellow of the Canadian Psychological Association, the American Psychological Association, and the Royal Society of Canada, and the Institute for Scientific Information includes him in its list of most cited neuroscientists. He is a recipient of a Bronze medal from the Canadian Humane Society, a recipient of the Ingrid Speaker medal for research, and President of NeuroDetective, Inc.

To the first neuron, our ancestors, our families, and students who read this book

Contents in Brief

Contents

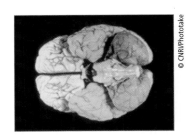

© CNRI/Phototake

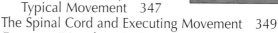
Corbis

CHAPTER 11
What Causes Emotional and Motivated Behavior?   388

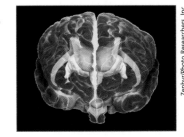

CHAPTER 12
Why Do We Sleep and Dream?   438

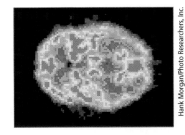

Zephyr/Photo Researchers, Inc.

Hank Morgan/Photo Researchers, Inc.

© Randy Faris/Corbis

Preface

Throughout this book, we examine the nervous system with a focus on function, on how our behavior and our brains interact. We structured the first edition of *An Introduction to Brain and Behavior* on key questions that students and neuroscientists ask about the brain:

- Why do we have a brain?
- How is the nervous system organized?
- How do drugs affect our behavior?
- How does the brain learn?
- How does the brain think?

As it was then, our goal in the present edition is to bring coherence to a vast subject by helping students understand the big picture. Asking fundamental questions about the brain has another benefit: it piques students' interest in the subject that they are studying and challenges them to join us on the journey of discovery that is brain science.

Scientific understanding of the brain and human behavior continues to grow at an exponential pace. We want to communicate the excitement of recent breakthroughs in brain science and to relate some of our own experiences in studying the brain for the past 40 years, both to make the field's developing core concepts and latest revelations understandable and meaningful and to take uninitiated students to the frontiers of physiological psychology.

We feature the relation between the brain and behavior in every chapter. For example, when we first describe how neurons communicate in Chapter 5, we also describe how plasticity in connections between neurons can serve as the basis of learning. Later, in Chapter 13, which is directed to the question of how we learn and remember, we explore how interactions among different parts of the brain enable our more complex behaviors.

Emphasis on Evolution, Genetics, and Psychopharmacology

To make sure that this book conveys the excitement of current neuroscience as researchers understand it, we emphasize evolution, genetic research, contemporary research methods, and psychopharmacology throughout. After all, evolution results from the complex interplay of genes and environment. This ongoing interplay influences a person's brain and behavior from earliest infancy through old age.

We cover the evolution of the brain in depth in Chapters 1 and 2 and return to this perspective of neuroscience in an evolutionary context in almost every chapter. Examples include

- evolution of the synapse in Chapter 5
- evolution of the visual pathways in Chapter 8
- how natural selection might promote overeating in Chapter 11
- evolutionary theories of sleeping and dreaming in Chapter 12
- evolution of sex differences in spatial cognition and language in Chapter 14
- links between our evolved reactions to stress and the development of anxiety disorders in Chapter 15

CHAPTER-BY-CHAPTER HIGHLIGHTS

Chapter 1 now has a context-setting section titled "Why Study Brain and Behavior?" that includes an index of disorders and the chapters in which they are covered (Table 1-1).

Chapter 2 adds function to structure, incorporating the standard terminology of central and peripheral (somatic and autonomic) nervous systems, and explores the central nervous system from the bottom up (spinal cord to forebrain), including a section on the "Evolutionary Development of the Nervous System."

Chapter 3 coverage of genetic research includes information on knockout technology, genomics, and proteomics and an expanded discussion of protein function.

Chapter 4 explains chemical and electrical events across the cell membrane concurrently; a Focus on New Research box titled "Opening the Voltage-Sensitive Gates" explains current thinking on how gated channels work and how they evolved.

Chapter 5 expands coverage of neuropeptide transmitters, the relation between neuromodulatory activating systems and psychological disorders, and the activity of dendritic spines in learning and adaptation at the neural level.

Chapter 6 features two new sections, "A Caution about Linking Correlation to Causation" and "Drugs and Brain Development," and a Focus on New Research box titled "Hormones and the Range of a Behavior" examines how genes and hormones might interact in sexual behaviors.

Chapter 7 begins with a Focus on New Research box titled "The Neural Basis of Drug Cravings," which describes the role of mesolimbic nuclei in addiction; text coverage of psychopharmacology, depression, and hormones is updated and expanded.

Chapter 8 broadens coverage of the nature of sensation and perception and of the tectopulvinar pathway; a Focus on New Research box titled "Testing Vision in Nonhuman Subjects" describes state-of-the-art research on optomotor responses.

Chapter 9 sharpens the coverage of sound waves as the physical stimulus for hearing, updates the treatment of inner and outer hair-cell function in audition, and adds new coverage on lateralization of the insular cortex function for language.

Chapter 10 extends the integration of clinical examples with anatomy and physiology coverage; a new section, "Feeling and Treating Pain," expands and updates pain coverage; a Focus on New Research box explores current explanations for "Tickling."

Chapter 11 begins with a Focus on New Research box titled "The Pain of Rejection," which demonstrates how physical and social pain have a common neurobiological basis; a new Focus on Disorders box titled "Weight-Loss Strategies" outlines the challenge to researchers evaluating the effectiveness of various diet plans; a new section, "The Chemical Senses," explains olfaction and gustation.

Chapter 12 updates coverage of research on genetic and neuronal control of circadian rhythms, dream content, and the possible contribution of sleeping to aspects of memory; a Focus on New Research box titled "Synchronizing Biorhythms at the Molecular Level" describes the search for a "chime" that synchronizes daily biorhythms.

Chapter 13 reports on the links between practicing motor skills and overall enhanced learning ability in a Focus on New Research box titled "Movement, Learning, and Neuroplasticity"; investigates similarities imaged in the brains of patients with psychogenic amnesia and in those whose amnesia results from brain trauma in a new section, "What Is Special about Personal Memories?"; and updates the neurobiology of emotional memory and the long-term effects of psychoactive drugs on learning and memory.

Chapter 14 updates converging research evidence obtained with the use of multiple imaging techniques on neural activity during thinking; adds coverage on brain activation in social cognition; and revisits a classic debate in the Focus on New Research box titled "Pay Attention!"

Chapter 15, reorganized and updated, integrates and expands on the research and treatment methods described in the preceding chapters and features three Focus on New Research boxes: "Neuropsychoanalysis," "Treating Behavioral Disorders with TMS," and "Antidepression Action in Neurogenesis."

The **Epilogue** places neuroscience in an evolutionary context and revisits the eight principles of nervous system function first presented in Chapter 2 as a means for students to synthesize and integrate the information that they have learned.

The **Appendix** frames the debate concerning the use of animals in research on the brain and behavior and contrasts the arguments that favor the use of animals in research with those against the practice.

The foundations of genetic research are introduced in depth in Chapter 3, where knockout technology is introduced. Chapter 5 includes discussions of metabotropic receptors and DNA and of learning and genes. The role of genes in development is integral to Chapter 6, as is the topic of genes and drug action in Chapter 7. Chapter 8 explains the genetics of color vision, and the genetics of sleep disorders is a major topic in Chapter 12. Chapter 15 considers the role of genetics in understanding the causes of behavioral disorders.

You'll find the newest research methods explained throughout the book, with PET in Chapter 9, fMRI in Chapters 11 and 14, TMS in Chapter 14, ERP in Chapter 4, and animal testing in Chapter 8. New to this edition, Focus on New Research comprises 18 boxes that showcase new and interesting developments on topics relevant to each chapter. In Chapter 6, for example, we investigate sexually dimorphic birds to see the relative roles of genes and hormones on sex differences in brain and behavior. In Chapter 11, we compare brain activation in response to physical and emotional pain and find their effects to be surprisingly similar.

Chapter 7 deals with drugs and behavior, and we turn to this topic in many other chapters as well. You will find coverage of drugs and information transfer in Chapter 4, drugs and cellular communication in Chapter 5, drugs and motivation in Chapter 11, drugs and sleep disorders in Chapter 12, neuronal changes with drug use in Chapter 13, and drugs as treatments for a range of disorders in Chapter 15.

Scientific Background Provided

We describe the journey of discovery that is neuroscience in a way that students just beginning to study the brain and behavior can understand. We have found that this course can sometimes prove daunting, largely because understanding brain function requires information from all the basic sciences. If we are ultimately interested in how the brain understands language or music, for example, the properties of sound waves and the functioning of the ear become relevant because the ear is where auditory information enters the brain.

These encounters with basic science can be both a surprise and a shock to introductory students, who often come to the course lacking the necessary background. Our approach provides all the background that students require to understand an introduction to brain science. We provide the philosophical and anatomical background needed to understand modern evolutionary theory, offer a short introduction to chemistry before describing the chemical activities of the brain, and briefly discuss electricity before exploring the brain's electrical activity.

Similarly, we review basic psychological facts such as behavioral development in Chapter 6 and the forms of learning and memory in Chapter 13. In these ways, the student is able to tackle brain science with greater confidence. Students in social science disciplines often remark on the amount of biology and chemistry in the book, whereas an equal number of students in biological sciences remark on the amount of psychology. We must be doing something right!

Clinical Focus Maintained

We repeatedly emphasize that neuroscience is a human science—that everything in this book is relevant to our lives. Neuroscience helps us understand how we learn, how we develop, and how we can help people who suffer from sometimes deadly and destructive brain and behavioral disorders. We have found that emphasizing the clinical aspects of neuroscience is especially useful in motivating introductory students and in demonstrating to them the relevance of our field.

Clinical material helps to make neurobiology particularly relevant to those who are going on to careers in psychology, social work, or other professions related to mental health, as well as to students pursuing careers in the biological sciences. For this reason, we not only integrate clinical information throughout this textbook and feature it in Focus on Disorders boxes but also expand on it at the end in Chapter 15.

As in the first edition, the placement of some topics in *Brain and Behavior* is novel relative to traditional treatments. For example, we include brief descriptions of brain diseases close to discussions of basic processes that may be associated with those diseases. The integrated coverage of Parkinson's disease in Chapter 5 is an example.

This strategy helps first-time students repeatedly see the close links between what they are learning and real-life problems. The integration of real-life problems, especially behavioral disorders, into every chapter is further accomplished by our many Focus on Disorders boxes. These boxes typically employ interesting case studies to highlight specific disorders that are related to a chapter's content.

In this new edition, which has been extensively reviewed for accuracy, we cover more than 75 disorders, from addiction to Tourette's syndrome, all indexed in Table 1-1 on page 4 for easy reference. On the basis of the reactions of students and the advice of teachers, we have completely revamped our capstone Chapter 15 to integrate and expand on the research and treatment methods described in the preceding chapters' coverage of neurological and psychiatric disorders, including a discussion of causes and classifications of abnormal behavior. Certainly the most common questions from students who contact us, sometimes years after they have completed our courses, concern the major behavioral disorders that people are likely to encounter in their lifetimes and that are now reviewed in Chapter 15.

Another area of emphasis in this book is on questions that relate to the biological basis of behavior. For us, the excitement of neuroscience is in understanding how the brain explains what we do, whether it be talking, sleeping, seeing, or learning. Readers will therefore find nearly as many illustrations about behavior as there are illustrations about the brain. This emphasis on explaining behavior's biological basis is another reason that we have included at least three Focus on Disorders boxes in each of the first 14 chapters.

SUMMARY OF METHODS OF STUDYING BRAIN AND BEHAVIOR

TECHNIQUE	CHAPTER IN WHICH AN EXAMPLE IS DISCUSSED
Behavioral studies	
Clinical investigations of individual cases	11, 15
Neurosurgical studies of patients at surgery	9
Neuropsychological analyses of groups of patients	14
Neuropsychological analyses of laboratory animals	13
Ethological studies of behavior	6
Cognitive psychology and psychophysics	14
Developmental studies	6
Behavioral genetics	6
Brain imaging	
Positron emission tomography (PET)	8
Functional magnetic resonance imaging (fMRI)	14
Magnetic resonance spectroscopy (MRS)	15
Brain stimulation	
Electrical stimulation	10
Transcranial magnetic stimulation (TMS)	14
Brain recording	
Electroencephalography	5
Magnetoencephalography	14
Event-related potentials	5
Long-term enhancement	5
Single-cell recording	4
Brain anatomy	
Cytological measures (i.e., measuring cell morphology)	3
Histological measures (i.e., measuring cell characteristics)	3
Tracing neural connections	4
Synaptic measures	13
Clinical investigations	15

Research Methods Integrated

We believe that research methods are best understood in the context of their use. Thus we continue in this edition to integrate research methods throughout the book rather than segregating them within a separate chapter. In describing how a neuron works, we explore how scientists record the electrical activity of the neuron. When we describe how humans think, we examine the techniques of medical imaging used by researchers to see the brain in the act of thinking. And, when answering the question of what motivates behavior, we delve into the research methods of producing brain lesions or electrically stimulating the brain.

In these ways, the uses of a particular method are made more meaningful to students. We include coverage of nearly two dozen contemporary methods, listed in the accompanying table. Many research methods are illustrated visually in the book and in animations on the accompanying CD-ROM.

Throughout the book, further visual reinforcement is provided by 25 illustrated Experiments, linked to text discussions of research on neurotransmission, brain development, learning, thinking, and many other topics. The Experiments help students understand how neuroscientists conduct research in context by presenting the scientific method visually, from hypothesis to experimental procedures to results to conclusions.

To take students to the cutting edge of neuroscience research, the Focus on New Research boxes emphasize not only new research methods but also the findings and applications that come from them. In Chapter 8, for instance, we explore how new methods for investigating visual functions in rodents allow researchers to ask new questions about the organization of the visual system in laboratory animals and how experiences can alter this function. We also show that developing such new techniques for studying laboratory animals can be applied to the study and benefit of humans.

Abundant Chapter Pedagogy

In addition to the innovative teaching devices just described, you will find numerous other in-text pedagogical aids. Every chapter begins with both an Outline and a Focus vignette that draws students into the topic by connecting brain and behavior to relevant clinical or research experience. Within the chapters, end-of-section Reviews help students remember major points, illustrations in the margins help them visualize or review concepts, and terms are defined in the margins to reinforce their importance.

Each chapter ends with a Summary consisting of topical key questions and their answers, a list of Review Questions that aid in the study and preparation for tests, and provocative questions For Further Thought that explore interesting implications of chapter content. A list of Key Terms, including the page numbers on which those terms are defined; an annotated list of Recommended Readings; and Neuroscience Interactive, a list of on-line sources that can broaden a student's understanding of chapter topics, round out the end-of-chapter resources.

Superb Visual Reinforcement

Our most important learning aid, which you can see by simply paging through this book, continues to be an expansive and, we believe, exceptional set of illustrations. Hand in hand with our words, these illustrations describe and illuminate the world of the brain.

The illustrations in every chapter are consistent and reinforce one another. For example, throughout the book, we consistently color code diagrams that illustrate each aspect of the neuron and those that depict each structural region in the brain. We often include micrographic images to show what a particular neural structure actually looks like when viewed through a microscope. You will also find these images on our Powerpoint presentations and integrated as labeling exercises in our study guide and testing materials.

Teaching Through Metaphors, Examples, and Principles

We've developed this book in a style that students enjoy, because, if a textbook is not enjoyed, it has little chance of teaching well. We heighten students' interest in the material that they are reading particularly through abundant use of metaphors and examples. Students read about patients whose brain injuries are sources of insight into brain function, and we examine car engines, robots, and prehistoric flutes for the same purpose. Frequent comparative biology examples help students understand how much we humans have in common with creatures as far distant from us as sea slugs.

We also facilitate learning by reemphasizing main points and by distilling sets of principles about brain function that can serve as a framework to guide the student's thinking. Thus, Chapter 2 concludes by introducing eight key principles that explain how the various parts of the nervous system work together. These principles form the basis of many later discussions in the book.

The Epilogue, which is new to this edition, revisits the eight principles through a summary of major points extracted from the book's preceding 15 chapters. Students will find that reading and rereading the Epilogue can help them understand and remember the broader themes and messages of the book. It will also help students put the key information in each chapter into a meaningful context as they synthesize the information that they have learned into an integrated theory of how the brain works.

Big-Picture Emphasis

One challenge in writing an introductory book on any topic is deciding what to include and what to exclude. We decided to organize discussions to focus on the bigger picture. A prime example is the discussion of general principles of nervous system function introduced in Chapter 2, echoed throughout the book, and revisited in the Epilogue. Although any such set of principles may be a bit arbitrary, it nevertheless gives students a useful framework for understanding the brain's activities.

Similarly, in Chapters 6 through 15, we tackle behavioral topics in a more general way than most contemporary books do. For instance, in Chapter 11, we revisit the experiments and ideas of the 1960s as we try to understand why animals behave in the way that they do, after which we consider emotional and motivated behaviors as diverse as eating and anxiety attacks. Another example of our focus on the larger picture is the discussion of learning and memory in Chapter 13, which is presented alongside a discussion of recovery from brain damage.

We believe that this broader focus helps students grasp the larger problems that behavioral neuroscience is all about. Broadening our focus, however, has required us to leave out some details that might be found in other textbooks. But, to us, discussions of larger problems and issues in the study of brain and behavior are of greater interest to the student who is new to this field and are more likely to be remembered.

As in the first edition, we have been selective in our citation of the truly massive literature on the brain and behavior because we believe that numerous citations can sometimes disrupt the flow of a textbook and distract students from the task of mastering what they read. We provide citations to classic works by including the names of the researchers, sometimes with a thumbnail portrait, and by mentioning where the research was performed. In areas where there is controversy or new breakthroughs, we also include detailed citations to current papers, citing papers from the years 2004 and 2005 when possible. A References section listing all the literature used in developing this textbook is provided at the end of the book.

Supplements

Materials of various kinds, for students and instructors and thoroughly checked for accuracy, are available to supplement our book.

For Students

Revised! *Foundations of Behavioral Neuroscience* **CD-ROM** Created by Uri Hasson, New York University, and Yehuda Shavit, Hebrew University of Jerusalem, and produced by the Open University of Israel and CADRE Design, this innovative CD comprises five modules: Neural Communication, Central Nervous System, Vision, Movement, and Research Methods. References to this CD (and to the book's companion Web site, described next) appear in the margins of each chapter, pointing to places where the text discussion is enhanced by a video clip or an animation. The CD-ROM features: rotating three-dimensional models of the human brain and eye; 25 or so video clips; animations of key physiological mechanisms; interactive examples of neuroimaging technologies, including MRI and CT; and a number of pedagogical features, including a clickable glossary, search engine, and multiple-choice questions.

In the revised CD, each module is enhanced by a "Test Yourself" component. Written by Paul Currie, Barnard College, these additional assessment questions and drag-and-drop activities offer students an opportunity to test their understanding of the material presented in each module. Customized for *An Introduction to Brain and Behavior*, Second Edition, the CD also includes quizzes and flashcards for every chapter of the textbook. On completion of any testing component, students will receive instant feedback. Instructors who assign the CD material as homework can view their student's results by quiz, student, or question (through an on-line gradebook accessible through the companion Web site) or can get weekly results by e-mail.

Revised! *An Introduction to Brain and Behavior,* **Second Edition, Companion Web Site** Created by Joe Morrissey, Binghamton University, and available at www.worth-publishers.com/kolb, the companion Web site is an online educational setting for students that provides a virtual study guide, 24 hours a day, 7 days a week. Best of all, the resources are free and do not require any special access codes or passwords. Tools on the site include: chapter outlines and summaries; learning objectives; annotated Web links; interactive flashcards; research exercises; selections from *PsychQuest* and *Psych-Sim 5.0* by Thomas Ludwig, Hope College; and online quizzes with immediate feedback and instructor notification.

For the instructor, the site offers online testing (with access to a quiz gradebook for viewing student results), a syllabus posting service, PowerPoint presentation files, electronic versions of illustrations in the book (through Worth Publishers' Image and Lecture Gallery), and links to additional tools including the WebCT E-pack and Blackboard course cartridge.

Revised! *Study Guide* Written by Terrence J. Bazzett, State University of New York at Geneseo, this revised *Study Guide* is carefully crafted, with the use of a variety of engaging exercises and tools, to enhance student interest in the material presented in the textbook. To aid learning and retention, each chapter includes a review of key concepts, terms, practice tests, short-answer questions, illustrations for identification and labeling, Internet activities, CD-ROM questions, and crossword puzzles. Students who have completed the tests and exercises can better organize and apply what they have studied.

Making Sense of Psychology on the Web Written by Connie Varnhagen, University of Alberta, and useful for the novice as well as the experienced Internet user, this brief book helps students to become discriminating Web users and researchers. The guide includes a CD-ROM containing the award-winning Research Assistant HyperFolio, innovative software that enables students to clip bits and pieces of Web sites and other electronic resources (snippets of text, illustrations, video clips, audio clips, and more) and compile them into worksheets and an easily accessible electronic "filing cabinet."

Scientific American Explores the Hidden Mind: A Collector's Edition On request, this Reader is free of charge when packaged with the textbook. In the past decade, we have learned more about the brain and how it creates the mind than we have in the entire preceding century. In a special collector's edition, *Scientific American* provides a must-have compilation of updated feature articles that explore and reveal the mysterious inner workings of our minds and brains.

Improving the Mind and Brain: A Scientific American Special Issue On request, this Reader is free of charge when packaged with the textbook. This new single-topic issue from *Scientific American* magazine features the latest findings from the most distinguished researchers in the field.

Ronald J. Comer's *Psychological Disorders,* **a** *Scientific American* **Reader** On request, this Reader is free of charge when packaged with the textbook. Drawn from *Scientific American,* this full-color collection of articles enhances coverage of the disorders covered in the physiological psychology course. The selections have been hand-picked by Worth author and clinical psychologist Ronald Comer, who provides a preview and discussion questions for each article.

For Instructors

Revised! *Instructor's Resources* **Debora Baldwin, University of Tennessee, Knoxville, has revised the** *Instructor's Resources.* They feature chapter-by-chapter learning objectives and chapter overviews, detailed lecture outlines, thorough chapter summaries, chapter key terms, in-class demonstrations and activities, springboard topics for discussion and debate, ideas for research and term-paper projects, homework assignments and exercises, and suggested readings for students (from journals and periodicals). Course-planning suggestions and a guide to videos and Internet resources also are included.

Assessment Tools

Revised! Test Bank Prepared by Robert Sainsbury, University of Calgary, the revised Test Bank includes a battery of more than 1500 multiple-choice and short-answer test questions as well as diagram exercises tied to the major illustrations in each chapter. Each item is keyed to the page in the textbook on which the answer can be found. The questions include a wide variety of applied, conceptual, and factual questions that have been thoroughly reviewed and edited for accuracy.

Diploma Computerized Test Bank The Test Bank is also available on a dual-platform CD-ROM. Instructors are guided step by step through the process of creating a test and can quickly add an unlimited number of questions, edit, scramble, or resequence items, and format a test. The accompanying gradebook enables them to record students' grades throughout the course and to sort student records and view detailed analyses of test items, curve tests, generate reports, add weights to grades, and more. The CD-ROM is the access point for Diploma Online Testing, allowing instructors to create and administer secure exams over a network and over the Internet, as well as Blackboard- and WebCT-formatted versions of each item in the Test Bank.

Online Quizzing, Powered by Questionmark This supplement is accessed through the companion Web site at www.worthpublishers.com/kolb. Instructors can easily and securely quiz students on-line by using prewritten multiple-choice questions for each chapter. Students receive instant feedback and can take the quizzes multiple times. Using the online quiz gradebook, instructors can view results by quiz, student, or question or they can obtain weekly results by e-mail.

Presentation

Chapter Illustrations and Outline PowerPoint Slides Available at www.worthpublishers.com/kolb, these PowerPoint slides can be either used directly or customized to fit an instructor's needs. There are two prebuilt, customizable slide sets for each chapter of the book—one featuring chapter text and the other featuring all chapter figures, tables, and illustrations.

New! Enhanced Lecture PowerPoint Slides Available at www.worthpublishers.com/kolb, this slide set was created by Kevin Peters, Trent University, a longtime adopter, and is based on his personal experience of teaching with *An Introduction to Brain and Behavior.* These customized slides focus on key terms and themes and feature tables, illustrations, and figures from both the textbook and outside sources.

Worth Publishers' Image and Lecture Gallery Available at www.worthpublishers. com/ilg, the Image and Lecture Gallery is a convenient way to access electronic versions of lecture materials. Instructors can browse, search, and download illustrations from every book published by Worth Publishers, as well as prebuilt PowerPoint presentations that contain all chapter illustrations or chapter section headings in text form. Users can also create personal folders on a personalized home page for easy organization of the materials.

Overhead Transparencies This set of more than 100 full-color transparencies consists of key illustrations, figures, and tables from the textbook and is available for use in classroom presentations.

Video

New! Worth Publishers' Neuroscience Video Collection Edited by Ronald J. Comer, Princeton University, and available on VHS, DVD, and CD-ROM (in MPEG format), this all-new video collection consists of dozens of video segments, each from 1 to 10 minutes in length. Clinical documentaries, television news reports, and archival footage constitute only a small part of the exciting source material for each video. Each segment has been created to provide illustrations that can help bring the lecture to life, engaging students and enabling them to apply neuroscience theory to the real world. This collection offers powerful and memorable demonstrations such as the links between the brain and behavior, neuroanatomical animations, cutting-edge neuroscience research, brain assessment in action, important historical events, interviews, and a wide sampling of brain phenomena and brain dysfunction. A special cluster of segments reveal the range of research methods used to study the brain. The accompanying Faculty Guide offers a description of each segment so that instructors can make informed decisions about how to best use the videos to enhance their lectures.

The Brain and Behavior Video Segments Available on VHS, this special collection includes targeted selections from the revised edition of the highly praised *Scientific American Frontiers* series. Hosted by Alan Alda, these video clips provide instructors with an excellent tool to show how neuroscience research is conducted. The 10–12-minute modules focus on the work of Steve Sumi, Renee Baillargeon, Car Rosengren, Laura Pettito, Steven Pinker, Barbara Rothbaum, Bob Stickgold, Irene Pepperberg, Marc Hauser, Linda Bartoshuk, and Michael Gazzaniga.

The Mind **Video Teaching Modules, Second Edition** Edited by Frank J. Vattano, Colorado State University, with the consultation of Charles Brewer, Furman University, and David Myers in association with WNET, these 35 brief, engaging video clips dramatically enhance and illustrate lecture topics and are available on VHS and DVD. This completely revised collection of short clips contains updated segments on language processing, infant cognitive development, heredity factors in alcoholism, and living without memory (featuring a dramatic new interview with Clive Wearing). The accompanying Faculty Guide offers descriptions for each module as well as suggestions in regard to how they might be incorporated into class presentations.

The Brain **Video Teaching Modules, Second Edition** Edited by Frank J. Vattano, Thomas L. Bennet, and Michelle Butler, all of Colorado State University, and available on VHS and DVD, this collection is a great source of classroom discussion ideas. It includes 32 short clips that provide vivid examples of brain development, function, disorders, and research. The Second Edition contains 10 new and 13 revised modules with added material, new audio, and new graphics. Individual segments range from 3 to 15 minutes in length, providing flexibility in highlighting specific topics. The accompanying Faculty Guide offers descriptions for each module as well as suggestions in regard to how they might be incorporated into class presentations.

Course-Management Aids

On-line Course Materials (WebCT and Blackboard) As a service for adopters who use WebCT or Blackboard course-management systems, the various resources for this textbook are available in the appropriate format for their systems. The files can be customized to fit specific course needs or they can be used as is. Course outlines, prebuilt quizzes, links, activities, and a whole array of materials are included, eliminating hours of work for instructors. For more information, please visit our Web site at www.worth-publishers.com/mediaroom and click "course management."

Acknowledgments

Although, as authors, our names are on the cover of this book, we did not write the book alone, although we are certainly responsible for any errors. Once again, the staff at Worth Publishers and W. H. Freeman and Company played a major role, right from the beginning until the end. We especially want to thank Buck Rogers, with whom we originally conceived this book's first edition; Susan Brennan, for insisting that we write it; and Jessica Bayne, who cheerfully kept us at it and guided us and the Worth staff to produce a first edition far more elegant than we had originally imagined. We would also like to thank John Woolsey and Mike Demaray, who originated the comprehensive and beautiful illustrations.

Senior sponsoring editor Laura Pople encouraged and enlightened us as we planned this revision. Her keen editorial sense is the force behind our New Research boxes and our integrated approach in Chapter 15. Assistant editor Danielle Storm ably managed the reviewing program and facilitated the movement of chapters into the production process.

Barbara Brooks, who developed the second edition, did a truly amazing job. She brought a fresh perspective to the book and forced us to rethink what we did 5 years earlier in the development of the first edition and why. She made what could have been a tedious process of revising the book into something rather fun. It is safe to say that much of the improvement of this second edition is due solely to her and we are truly grateful.

Manuscript editor Patty Zimmerman once again made sure that the details came out right. Project editor Georgia Lee Hadler organized the final editing, kept us on task as we got down to proofreading, and made sure that we met the publication schedule. Managing editor Tracey Kuehn, photo editor Trish Marx, and production manager Sarah Segal ensured the book's quality and timely publication. Danielle Pucci managed the outstanding media and print supplements program.

Our colleagues, too, played a major role in developing this edition. We are especially indebted to those reviewers who provided extensive comments on selected chapters and illustrations: Barry Anton, University of Puget Sound; R. Bruce Bolster, University of Winnipeg; James Canfield, University of Washington; Edward Castaneda, Arizona State University; Darragh P. Devine, University of Florida; Kenneth Green, California State University, Long Beach; Eric Jackson, University of New Mexico; Sheri Mizumori, University of Washington; Michael Nelson, University of Missouri, Rolla; Joshua S. Rodefer, University of Iowa; Charlene Wages, Francis Marion University; Doug Wallace, Northern Illinois University; Patricia Wallace, Northern Illinois University; and Edie Woods, Madonna University. Sheri Mizumuri deserves special mention here as she not only read the entire manuscript and had fresh ideas that proved invaluable, but she was truly amazing at spotting tiny errors that had passed by both us and others who read the manuscript.

We also wish to acknowledge those whose advice helped to shape our first edition: Patrick Ament, Central Missouri State University; Trevor Archer, University of Goteborg; Giorgio Ascoli, George Mason University; Brian Auday, Gordon College; Aldo Badiani, University of Michigan; Debora Baldwin, University of Tennessee, Knoxville; Terry Bazzett, State University of New York, Geneseo; Kent Berridge, University of Michigan; Gayle Brosnan-Waters, Vanguard University; John Bruno, Ohio State University; Rebecca Chesire, University of Hawaii, Manoa; Paul Currie, Barnard College; Darragh Devine, University of Florida; Shelly Dickinson, Reed College; Sherry Dingman, Marist College; D. L. Dodson, Lebanon Valley College; Betty Dorr, Fort Lewis College; Steven Dworkin, University of North Carolina, Wilmington; Marcia Earhard, Dalhousie University; Gregory Ervin, Brigham Young University; Thor Eysteinsson, University of Iceland; Rick Gilmore, Pennsylvania State University; Karen Glendenning, Florida State University; Dennis Goff, Randolph-Macon Women's College; Ed Green, University of Miami; Kenneth Green, California State University, Long Beach; Stuart Hall, University of Montana; Andrew Harver, University of North Carolina, Charlotte; Harold Herzog, Western Carolina University; Jonathan Hess, University of Illinois, Springfield; Theresa Jones, University of Washington; Wesley Jordan, St. Mary's College of Maryland; Stephen Kiefer, Kansas State University; Jeansok Kim, Yale University; Mark Kristal, State University of New York, Buffalo; Paul Kulkosky, University of Southern Colorado; Charles Kutscher, Syracuse University; Daniel Leger, University of Nebraska, Lincoln; Michael Markham, Florida International University; Richard Marshall, University of Texas, Austin; William Meil, Indiana University of Pennsylvania; Garrett Milliken, College of Charleston; Daniel Moriarty, University of San Diego; Tony Nunez, Michigan State University; Joseph Porter, Virginia Commonwealth University; Julio Ramirez, Davidson College; Michael Renner, West Chester University; Tony Robertson, Malaspina University College; Robin Roof, Eastern Michigan University; Neil Rowland, University of Florida; Robert Schneider, Metropolitan State College; Katherine Schultz, University of Winnipeg; Susan Sesack, University of Pittsburgh; Fred Shaffer, Truman State University; Cheryl Sisk, Michigan State University; Leslie Skeen, University of Delaware; R. W. Skelton, University of Victoria; Laura Smale, Michigan State University; Robert Spencer, University of Colorado, Boulder; Rodney Swain, University of Wisconsin, Milwaukee; Susan Swithers, Purdue University; Anne Jane Tierney, Colgate University; C. Robin Timmons, Drew University; Keith Trujillo, California State University, San Marcos; Lawrence Wichlinski, Carleton College; Diane Witt, Binghamton University; Xiaojuan Xu, Grand Valley State University; William Yates, University of Pittsburgh; and Mark Zrull, Appalachian State University. We especially want to thank Robert Sainsbury of the University of Calgary, who tried the book out with his students and provided invaluable feedback.

Finally, we must thank our families, for putting up with what turned out to be a bigger project than even we bargained for, and our students, technicians, and postdoctoral fellows, who kept our research programs moving forward when we were engaged in revising the book.

Bryan Kolb and Ian Q. Whishaw

What Are the Origins of Brain and Behavior?

Traumatic Brain Injury

Each year a reported 80,000 people in the United States of America experience long-term disability from complications related to head trauma (Brain Injury Association, 2002). Traumatic brain injuries are the leading cause of both death and disability among children and teenagers (Cassidy et al., 2004). What is it like to be brain injured? Fred Linge, a clinical psychologist with a degree in brain research, wrote this description 12 years after his traumatic brain injury occurred:

A variety of mechanical forces cause traumatic brain injuries as a result of a blow to the head.

The damage at the site of impact is called a coup (shown in pink).

Direction of blow   **Direction of blow**

The pressure resulting from a coup produce a countercoup on the opposite side of the brain (shown in blue).

Movement of the brain may shear nerve fibers, causing microscopic lesions, especially in frontal and temporal lobes. Blood trapped in the skull (hematoma) and swelling (edema) cause pressure on the brain.

> In the second it took for my car to crash head-on, my life was permanently changed, and I became another statistic in what has been called "the silent epidemic."
>
> During the next months, my family and I began to understand something of the reality of the experience of head injury. I had begun the painful task of recognizing and accepting my physical, mental, and emotional deficits. I couldn't taste or smell. I couldn't read even the simplest sentence without forgetting the beginning before I got to the end. I had a hair-trigger temper that could ignite instantly into rage over the most trivial incident.
>
> During the first year, I could not take too much stimulation from other people. My brain would simply overload, and I would have to go off into my room to get away. Noise was hard for me to take, and I wanted the place to be kept quiet, which was an impossibility in a small house with three youngsters in it. I remember laying down some impossible rules for all of us. For example, I made rules that everybody had to be in bed by 9:30 PM, that all lights had to be out, and that no noise of any kind was permitted after that time. No TV, radios, or talking was allowed. Eventually the whole family was in an uproar.
>
> Two years after my injury, I wrote a short article: "What Does It Feel Like to Be Brain Damaged?" At that time, I was still intensely focusing on myself and my own struggle. (Every head-injured survivor I have met seems to go through this stage of narcissistic preoccupation, which creates a necessary shield to protect them from the painful realities of the situation until they have a chance to heal.) I had very little sense of anything beyond the material world and could only write about things that could be described in factual terms. I wrote, for example, about my various impairments and how I learned to compensate for them by a variety of methods.
>
> At this point in my life, I began to involve myself with other brain-damaged people. This came about in part after the publication of my article. To my surprise, it was reprinted in many different publications, copied, and handed out to thousands of survivors and families. It brought me an enormous outpouring of letters, phone calls, and personal visits that continue to this day. Many were struggling as I had struggled, with no diagnosis, no planning, no rehabilitation, and most of all, no hope. . . . The catastrophic effect of my injury was such that I was shattered and then remolded by the experience, and I emerged from it a profoundly different person with a different set of convictions, values, and priorities. (Linge, 1990)

The diffuse effects of traumatic brain injury make diagnosis very difficult, which is why brain injuries have been collectively called a "silent epidemic." Victims of severe traumatic brain injury can suffer serious repercussions in their everyday lives. Like Fred Linge, many have difficulty returning to their former levels of functioning, including carrying out the jobs that they held before injury.

Traumatic brain injury results from a blow to the head that subjects the brain to a variety of forces shown on the accompanying illustration:

■ The force exerted on the skull at the site of the blow causes a *contusion* (bruising) known as a "coup" (French for a strike or blow).

■ The blow may force the brain against the opposite side of the skull, producing an additional contusion called a "countercoup."

■ The movement of the brain may cause a twisting or shearing of nerve fibers, resulting in microscopic *lesions* (damage to the nervous system). Such lesions may be found throughout the brain, but they are most common at the front and sides.

■ The bruises and strains caused by the impact may produce bleeding *(hemorrhage)*. The blood trapped within the skull acts as a growing mass *(hematoma),* which exerts pressure on surrounding brain regions.

■ Like blows to other parts of the body, blows to the brain produce *edema* (swelling), a collection of fluid in and around damaged tissue. Edema is another source of pressure on the brain.

People who sustain traumatic brain injury often lose consciousness because the injury affects nerve fibers in lower parts of the brain associated with waking. The severity of coma can indicate the severity of the injury. Traumatic brain injuries resulting from motor vehicle accidents are particularly severe because the head is moving when the blow is struck, thereby increasing the velocity of the impact.

In the years after his injury, Fred Linge made an immense journey. Before the car crash, he gave less thought to the relation between his brain and his behavior than he did to tying his shoes. At the end of his journey, adapting to his injured brain and behavior dominated his life. He became a consultant and advisor to other people who also had suffered brain injury.

The purpose of this book is to take you on a journey toward understanding the link between brain and behavior: how the brain is organized to create and monitor behavior and what happens when the brain is not functioning properly. Much of the evidence comes from studying three sources: the evolution of brain and behavior in diverse animal species, how the brain is related to behavior in normal people, and changes in people who suffer brain damage or other brain abnormalities. The knowledge emerging from the results of these studies is changing how we think about ourselves, how we structure education and our social interactions, and how we aid those with brain injury, disease, and disorder.

In this chapter, we answer the question, What are the origins of brain and behavior? We begin by defining both brain and behavior and outlining the nervous system's basic structure. We then take a historical look at three major theories concerning the relation between brain and behavior. From this background, we explore the evolution of brain and behavior, showing how the brain and complex behavior emerged and changed as animals evolved. Finally, we consider how the human brain has adapted to its most complex function—culture.

WHY STUDY BRAIN AND BEHAVIOR?

The brain is a physical object, a living tissue, a body organ. Behavior is action, momentarily observable, but fleeting. Brain and behavior differ greatly but are linked.

The brain was once thought to play little or no role in behavior, and so the study of brain function was seen as a biological pursuit not central to psychology. Even today, many students view the brain as peripheral to understanding human behavior.

Linking Brain Function to Brain Injury

The case history of Phineas Gage is a source of early insight into how the brain controls behavior (MacMillan, 2000). Gage was a 25-year-old dynamite worker on a railroad bed construction site who in 1848 survived an explosion that blasted an iron tamping bar (about a meter long and 3 centimeters wide) through the front of his head (see photograph). Surprisingly, quite a few people have survived similar injuries, even from tamping bars, but Gage's physician, John M. Harlow, wrote an account of Gage's accident and this account helped propel Gage to fame.

Gage had been of average intelligence and very industrious and dependable. He was described as "energetic and persistent in executing all of his plans of operation." But,

Reconstruction of Gage's brain injury with the use of modern imaging techniques. From "The Return of Phineas Gage: Clues about the Brain from the Skull of a Famous Patient," by H. Damasio, T. Grabowski, R. Frank, A. M. Galaburda, and A. R. Damasio, 1994, *Science, 20,* p. 1102.

Department of Neurology and Image Analysis Facility, University of Iowa.

after the accident, his behavior changed completely. Harlow, in describing the case, wrote:

> The equilibrium or balance, so to speak, between his intellectual faculties and animal propensities seems to have been destroyed. He is fitful, irreverent, indulging at times in the grossest profanity, manifesting but little deference to his fellows, impatient of restraint or advice when it conflicts with his desires, at times perniciously obstinate, yet capricious and vacillating, devising many plans of operation, which are no sooner arranged than they are abandoned in turn for others appearing more feasible. A child in his intellectual capacity and manifestations, he has the animal passions of a strong man. (Blumer and Benson, 1975, p. 153)

The remarkable feature of Gage's frontal-lobe injury is that he did not display obvious motor or memory impairments; his brain injury mainly affected his personality. Harlow provided evidence that the frontal lobes were locations of foresight and planning.

Although the tamping bar and Gage's skull have been preserved, Gage's precise injury could not be described, because no autopsy was performed after his death and so the actual damage produced by the tamping bar could not be determined. Measurements from Gage's skull and modern imaging techniques have been used to reconstruct the accident and determine the probable location of the lesion. The frontal cortex of both hemispheres appears to have been damaged.

Yet the brain and behavior have evolved together: one is responsible for the other, which is responsible for the other, which is responsible for the other, and so on and on. A classic example of the control exerted by the brain on behavior is illustrated in "Linking Brain Function to Brain Injury."

Nearly 150 years after French neurologist Jean Charcot first autopsied patients who died of brain diseases and related their symptoms to their pathology, the accumulated research suggests three reasons for linking the study of brain and behavior:

1. A growing list of behavioral disorders can be explained and possibly cured by understanding the brain. Indeed, more than 2000 disorders may in some way be

related to brain abnormalities. As indexed in **Table 1-1**, throughout this book, especially in the "Focus" sections, we detail relations between brain disorders and behavioral disorders.

2. The brain is the most complex living organ on Earth and is found in many different groups of animals. Students of the brain want to understand its place in the biological order of our planet. Chapter 1 describes the basic structure and evolution of the brain, especially the human brain, and Chapters 3 through 5 describe the function of brain cells—cells that are common to all animals that possess a nervous system.

3. How the brain produces both behavior and human consciousness is a major unanswered scientific question. Many scientists and students study the brain from the philosophical perspective of understanding humanity. Many chapters in this book touch on the relation between psychological questions related to brain and behavior and philosophical questions related to humanity. For example, in Chapters 13 and 14, we address questions related to how we learn and how we think.

None of us can predict the ways in which knowledge about the brain and behavior may prove useful. One former psychology major wrote to tell us that she took our course only because she was unable to register in a preferred course. She felt that, although our course was interesting, it was "biology and not psychology." After graduating and getting a job in a social agency, she found to her delight that, by understanding the links

Table 1-1 Index of Disorders Discussed in Chapters 1 through 15

Addiction 7	Brain tumors 3*	Insomnia 12	Phenylketonuria 15
ADHD 15	Carbon monoxide poisoning 8*	Korsakoff's syndrome 13*	Posttraumatic stress disorder 7
Affective disorders 11*, 15	Cerebral aneurysm 9*	Learning disabilities 1*, 6	Presbyopia 8*
Agenesis of the frontal lobe 11*	Cerebral palsy 6*, 10	Lou Gehrig's disease 4*	Psychosis 7
Agnosia 8	Closed head injury 1*	Mania 15	Quadripelegia 10
Alzheimer's disease 5, 13*, 15	Contralateral neglect 14	Meningitis 2*	Restless legs syndrome 12
Amnesia 13	Dementia 15	Mental retardation 6	Schizophrenia 5, 6*, 7, 15
Androgen insensitivity syndrome 11*	Demoic acid poisoning 7	Migraine 8*	Scotoma 8
Androgenital syndrome 11*	Depression 5, 7, 11*, 15	Missile wound 1	Seasonal affective disorder 12*
Anencephaly 6	Down's syndrome 3	MPTP poisoning 5*	Sleep apnea 12*
Anorexia nervosa 11	Drug-induced psychosis 7*	Multiple sclerosis 3*, 15	Spinal-cord injury 10, 11
Anxiety disorders 11*, 15	Encephalitis 2*	Myasthenia gravis 4*	Split-brain syndrome 14
Aphasia 9	Environmental deprivation 6*	Myopia 8*	Stroke 2*, 15
Apraxia 10	Epilepsy 4, 9*, 15	Narcolepsy 12	Synesthesia 14*
Arteriovenous malformations 9*	Fetal alcohol syndrome 7*	Obesity 11	Tay-Sachs disease 3
Asperger's syndrome 15	Frontal leucotomy 11	Obsessive compulsive disorder 5, 7	Tourette's syndrome 5, 10*
Ataxia 8	Hemianopia 8	Panic disorder 11*	Traumatic brain injury 1*, 15
Autism 10*	Huntington's chorea 3*	Paraplegia 10*	
Bell's palsy 2*	Hyperopia 8*	Parkinson's disease 5*, 15	
Bipolar disorder 15	Insanity 1*		

Note: Name of disorder is followed by chapter number(s).
* Disorder is subject of "Focus on Disorders."
Abbreviations: ADHD, attention deficit hyperactivity disorder; MPTP, methylphenyltetrahydropyridine.

between brain and behavior, she had insight into the disorders of many of her clients and treatment options for them. So let's begin, by defining first the brain, then behavior, and finally how they evolved together.

What Is the Brain?

For his postgraduate research, our friend Harvey chose to study the electrical activity that the brain gives off. He said that he wanted to live on as a brain in a bottle after his body died. He expected that his research would allow his bottled brain to communicate with others who could "read" his brain's electrical signals. Harvey mastered the techniques of brain electrical activity but failed in his objective, not only because the goal was technically impossible but also because he lacked a full understanding of what "brain" means.

Brain is the Anglo-Saxon word for the tissue that is found within the skull, and it is this tissue that Harvey wanted to put into a bottle. The brain has two almost symmetrical halves called **hemispheres,** one on the left and one on the right. So, just as your body is symmetrical, having two arms and two legs, so is the brain. **Figure 1-1A** shows the left hemisphere of a typical human brain oriented in the upright human skull. If you make a fist with your right hand and hold it up, the fist can represent the positions of the brain's broad divisions, or lobes, within the skull, with the thumb pointing toward the front (Figure 1-1B).

The entire outer layer of the human brain consists of a thin, folded layer of nerve tissue, the **cerebral cortex,** detailed in the sectional view in Figure 1-1A. The word *cortex,* Latin for the bark of a tree, is apt, considering the cortex's heavily folded surface and its location in covering most of the rest of the brain. The grooves of the cortex are called sulci and the bumps are called gyri. Unlike the bark on a tree, they are not random folds but demarcate functional zones. Later on, we'll provide their names and functions. The cortex of each hemisphere is divided into four lobes, named after the skull bones beneath which they lie.

Hemisphere. Literally, half a sphere, referring to one side of the cerebral cortex or one side of the cerebellum.

Cerebral cortex. Outer layer of brain-tissue surface composed of neurons; the human cerebral cortex contains many folds.

◎ On the *Foundations of Behavioral Neuroscience* CD, visit the module on the central nervous system. Go to the overview and look at the three-dimensional view of the human cortex for a hands-on view of what this organ looks like. (See the Preface for information about this CD.)

Figure 1-1

The Human Brain **(A)** The cerebral cortex of the nearly symmetrical hemispheres of the brain is divided into four lobes. The cerebral cortex is a thin sheet of nerve tissue that is folded many times to fit inside the skull, as shown in the sectional view. **(B)** Your right fist can serve as a guide to the orientation of the brain's left hemispheres and lobes.

(A)

Lobes define broad divisions of the cerebral cortex.

The brain is made up of two hemispheres, left and right.

Sectional view

Bumps in the brain's folded surface are called gyri, and cracks are called sulci.

Cerebral cortex is the brain's thin outer "bark" layer.

Top

Parietal lobe

Frontal lobe

Front

Occipital lobe

Temporal lobe

Back

Bottom

Glauberman/Photo Researchers

(B)

Your right hand, if made into a fist, represents the positions of the lobes of the left hemisphere of your brain.

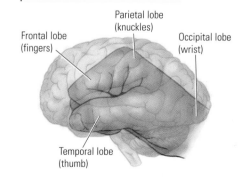

Parietal lobe (knuckles)

Frontal lobe (fingers)

Occipital lobe (wrist)

Temporal lobe (thumb)

Temporal lobe. Cortex lying below the lateral fissure, beneath the temporal bone at the side of the skull.

Frontal lobe. Cerebral cortex anterior to the central sulcus and beneath the frontal bone of the skull.

Parietal lobe. Cerebral cortex posterior to the central sulcus and beneath the parietal bone at the top of the skull.

Occipital lobe. Cerebral cortex at the back of the brain and beneath the occipital bone.

Neuron. A specialized cell engaged in information processing.

Spinal cord. Part of the central nervous system encased within the vertebrae or spinal column.

Central nervous system (CNS). The brain and spinal cord.

Peripheral nervous system (PNS). All the neurons in the body located outside the brain and spinal cord.

Sensory neuron. Neuron that carries incoming information from sensory receptors into the spinal cord and brain.

Motor neuron. Neuron that carries information from the spinal cord and brain to make muscles contract.

◉ Use the *Foundations* CD to look at how these nerve networks work in our brains. The overview of the brain in the central nervous system module includes a rotatable, three-dimensional view of the brain that will help you visualize how all these parts fit together.

The forward-pointing **temporal lobe** is located at the side of the brain, approximately the same place as the thumb on your upraised fist. Immediately above your thumbnail, your fingers correspond to the location of the **frontal lobe,** so called because it is located at the front of the brain, beneath the frontal bone of the skull. The **parietal lobe** is located beneath the parietal bone at the top of the skull, behind the frontal lobe and above the temporal lobe. The area at the back of each hemisphere beneath the occipital bone constitutes the **occipital lobe**.

Harvey clearly wanted to preserve not just his brain but his *self*—his consciousness, his thoughts, his intelligence. This meaning of the term *brain* refers to something other than the organ found inside the skull. It refers to the brain as that which exerts control over behavior.

This meaning of *brain* is what we intend when we talk of someone being "the brain" or when we speak of the computer that guides a spacecraft as being the vessel's "brain." The term *brain,* then, signifies both the organ itself and the fact that this organ controls behavior. Why could Harvey not manage to preserve his control-exerting self inside a bottle? Read on to learn one answer to this question.

Gross Structure of the Nervous System

Just like every other organ of the body, the brain is composed of billions of cells that come in a variety of shapes and sizes. **Neurons** (sometimes called nerve cells) are the cells that most directly control behavior. Neurons have long processes called axons and dendrites that allow them to communicate with one another, with sensory receptors on the body, with muscles, and with internal body organs.

The nervous system consists of two main subdivisions: the central nervous system and the peripheral nervous system. Most of the connections between the brain and the rest of the body are made through the **spinal cord,** which descends through a canal in the backbone. Together, the brain and spinal cord make up the **central nervous system** (CNS), as shown in **Figure 1-2.** Thus the CNS is encased in bone, the brain by the skull and the spinal cord by the vertebrae. It is "central" both because it is physically located as the core of the nervous system and because it is the core structure mediating behavior.

All the nerve processes radiating out beyond the brain and spinal cord as well as all the neurons outside the brain and spinal cord constitute the **peripheral nervous system** (PNS) (see Figure 1.2). An extensive network of **sensory neurons** in the PNS connect to receptors on the body's surface, internal organs, and muscles to gather sensory information for the CNS. **Motor neurons** in the PNS convey information from the CNS to move muscles of the face, body, and limbs. Motor neurons also govern the workings of your body's internal organs, autonomic functions, such as the beating of your heart, the contractions of your stomach, and the movement of your diaphragm to inflate and deflate your lungs.

To return to the question of Harvey's brain-in-a-bottle experiment, the effect of placing the brain or even the entire CNS in a bottle would be to separate it from the PNS and thus to separate it from the sensations and movements mediated by the PNS. How would the brain function without sensory information and without the ability to produce movement?

In the 1920s, Edmond Jacobson (1932) wondered what would happen if our muscles completely stopped moving, a question relevant to Harvey's experiment. Jacobson believed that, even when we think we are entirely motionless, we still make subliminal movements related to our thoughts. The muscles of the larynx subliminally move when we "think in words," for instance, and we make subliminal movements of our eyes when we imagine or visualize a scene. So, in Jacobson's experiment, people practiced "total" relaxation and were later asked what the experience was like. They reported a condition of "mental emptiness," as if the brain had gone blank.

In 1957, Woodburn Heron investigated the effects of sensory deprivation, including feedback from movement, by having each subject lie on a bed in a bare, soundproof room and remain completely still. Tubes covered the subjects' arms so that they had no sense of touch, and translucent goggles cut off their vision. The subjects reported that the experience was extremely unpleasant, not just because of the social isolation but also because they lost their normal focus in this situation. Some subjects even hallucinated, as if their brains were somehow trying to create the sensory experiences that they suddenly lacked. Most asked to be released from the study before it ended.

Findings from these experiments suggest that the CNS needs ongoing sensory stimulation, including the stimulation that comes from movement, if it is to maintain its intelligent activity. Thus, when we use the term *brain* to mean an intelligent, functioning organ, we should probably refer to an active brain that is connected to the rest of the nervous system. Unfortunately for Harvey, that a brain in a bottle, disconnected from the PNS, would continue to function normally seems very unlikely.

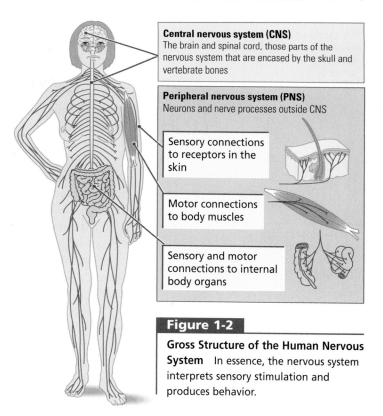

Central nervous system (CNS)
The brain and spinal cord, those parts of the nervous system that are encased by the skull and vertebrate bones

Peripheral nervous system (PNS)
Neurons and nerve processes outside CNS

Sensory connections to receptors in the skin

Motor connections to body muscles

Sensory and motor connections to internal body organs

Figure 1-2

Gross Structure of the Human Nervous System In essence, the nervous system interprets sensory stimulation and produces behavior.

What Is Behavior?

Irenäus Eibl-Eibesfeldt began his textbook, *Ethology: The Biology of Behavior*, published in 1970, with the following definition: "Behavior consists of patterns in time." These patterns can be made up of movements, vocalizations, or changes in appearance, such as the movements associated with smiling. The expression "patterns in time" can even include thinking. Although we cannot directly observe someone's thoughts, techniques exist for monitoring changes in the brain's electrical and biochemical activity that may be associated with thought. So thinking, too, forms patterns in time.

The behavioral patterns of some animals are relatively fixed; that is, most of their behaviors are inherited ways of responding. The behavioral patterns of other animals are both inherited and learned. If all members of a species display the same behavior under the same circumstances, that species has probably inherited a nervous system evolved to produce that relatively fixed behavioral pattern automatically. In contrast, if each member of a species displays a somewhat different response in a similar situation, that species has inherited a much more flexible nervous system that is capable of changes in behavior due to learning.

An example of the difference between a relatively fixed behavioral pattern and a more flexible one is seen in the eating behavior of two different animal species—crossbills and roof rats—as illustrated in **Figure 1-3**. A crossbill is a bird with a beak that seems to be awkwardly crossed at the tips; yet this beak is exquisitely evolved to eat certain kinds of pine cones. When eating these pine cones, crossbills use largely

A crossbill's beak is *specifically designed* to open pine cones. This behavior is innate.

A baby roof rat must learn from its mother how to eat pine cones. This behavior is learned.

Figure 1-3

Innate and Learned Behaviors Some animal behaviors are largely innate and fixed (*top*), whereas others are largely learned (*bottom*). This learning is a form of cultural transmission. *Top*: Adapted from *The Beak of the Finch* (p. 183), by J. Weiner, 1995, New York: Vintage. *Bottom*: Adapted from "Cultural Transmission in the Black Rat: Pinecone Feeding," by J. Terkel, 1995, *Advances in the Study of Behavior, 24*, p. 122.

◉ Visit the *Brain and Behavior* Web site (**www.worthpublishers.com/kolb**) and go to the Chapter 1 Web links to view a timeline on the history of brain research.

fixed *behavioral patterns that* are inherited and do not require much modification through learning.

If the shape of a crossbill's beak is changed even slightly by trimming, the bird is no longer able to eat preferred pine cones until its beak grows back. Roof rats, in contrast, are rodents with sharp incisor teeth that appear to have evolved to cut into anything. But roof rats can eat pine cones efficiently only if they are taught to do so by an experienced mother.

The behavior described here is limited to pine-cone eating, and we do not intend to imply that all behavior displayed by crossbills is fixed or that all behavior displayed by roof rats is learned. A central goal of research is to distinguish between behaviors that are inherited and those that are learned and to understand how the nervous system produces each type of behavior.

The complexity of behavior varies considerably in different species. Generally, animals with smaller, simpler nervous systems have a narrow range of behaviors. Animals with complex nervous systems have more behavioral options. We humans believe that we are the animal species with the most complex nervous system and the greatest capacity for learning new responses.

Species that have evolved greater complexity have not thrown away their simpler nervous systems, however. Rather, complexity emerges in part because new nervous system structures are added to old ones. For this reason, although human behavior depends mostly on learning, we, like other species, still possess many inherited ways of responding. The sucking response of a newborn infant is an inherited eating pattern in humans, for example.

In Review

Brain and behavior are linked, and behavioral disorders can be explained and possibly cured by understanding the brain. Understanding how the brain produces both behavior and consciousness remains a major unanswered scientific question. Students of the brain want to understand its place in the biological order of our planet. The brain consists of nearly symmetrical left and right cerebral hemispheres, each with a folded outer layer called the cortex, which is divided into four lobes: temporal, frontal, parietal, and occipital. The brain and spinal cord together make up the central nervous system. All the nerve fibers radiating out beyond the brain and spinal cord as well as all the neurons outside the brain and spinal cord form the peripheral nervous system. Nerves of the PNS carry sensory information to the CNS and motor instructions from the CNS to muscles and tissues of the body. A simple definition of behavior is any kind of movement in a living organism. Although all behaviors have both a cause and a function, they vary in complexity and in the degree to which they are inherited, or automatic, and the degree to which they depend on learning.

PERSPECTIVES ON BRAIN AND BEHAVIOR

Returning to the central question in the study of brain and behavior, how the two are related, we now describe three classic theories about the cause of behavior along with a major proponent of each school of thought—mentalism, dualism, and materialism—as it relates to behavioral neuroscience. You will recognize familiar "common sense" ideas that you might have about behavior as being derived from one or another of these long-standing theories.

Aristotle and Mentalism

Aristotle
(384–322 BC)

The hypothesis that the mind (or soul or psyche) is responsible for behavior can be traced back more than 2000 years to ancient Greece. In classical mythology, Psyche was a mortal who became the wife of the young god Cupid. Venus, Cupid's mother, opposed his marriage to a mortal, and so she harassed Psyche with countless, almost impossible tasks.

Psyche performed the tasks with such dedication, intelligence, and compassion that she was made immortal, thus removing Venus's objection to her. The ancient Greek philosopher Aristotle was alluding to this story when he suggested that all human intellectual functions are produced by a person's **psyche**. The psyche, Aristotle argued, is responsible for life, and its departure from the body results in death.

Aristotle's account of behavior had no role for the brain, which he thought existed to cool the blood. To him, the nonmaterial psyche was responsible for human thoughts, perceptions, and emotions and for such processes as imagination, opinion, desire, pleasure, pain, memory, and reason. The psyche was an entity independent of the body. Aristotle's view that a nonmaterial psyche governs our behavior was adopted by Christianity in its concept of the soul and has been widely disseminated throughout the world.

Mind is an Anglo-Saxon word for memory and, when "psyche" was translated into English, it became mind. The philosophical position that a person's mind, or psyche, is responsible for behavior is called **mentalism,** meaning "of the mind." Because the mind is nonmaterial, it cannot be studied with scientific methods. Just the same, mentalism has had an influence on modern behavioral science because many terms—*sensation, perception, attention, imagination, emotion, motivation, memory,* and *volition* among them—are still employed as labels for patterns of behavior today, and matters related to these behaviors are the focus of contemporary research in psychology.

François Gerard,
Psyche and Cupid (1798)

Psyche. Synonym for mind, an entity once proposed to be the source of human behavior.

Mind. Proposed nonmaterial entity responsible for intelligence, attention, awareness, and consciousness.

Mentalism. Of the mind; an explanation of behavior as a function of the nonmaterial mind.

Mind–body problem. Quandary of explaining a nonmaterial mind in command of a material body.

Dualism. Philosophical position that holds that both a nonmaterial mind and the material body contribute to behavior.

Descartes and Dualism

René Descartes
(1596–1650)

In the first book on brain and behavior, *Treatise on Man,* René Descartes (1596–1650), a French physiologist, mathematician, and philosopher, proposed a new explanation of behavior in which the brain played an important role. Descartes placed the seat of the mind in the brain and linked the mind to the body. He saw mind and body as separate but interconnected. In the first sentence of *Treatise on Man* (1664), he stated that mind and body "must be joined and united to constitute people. . . ."

To Descartes, most of the activities of the body and brain, including sensation, motion, digestion, breathing, and sleeping, could be explained by the mechanical and physical principles current in seventeenth-century Europe. The mind, on the other hand, is nonmaterial, separate from the body, and responsible for rational behavior. Descartes's proposal that an entity called the mind directs a machine called the body was the first serious attempt to explain the role of the brain in controlling intelligent behavior. The problem of how a nonmaterial mind and a physical brain might interact has come to be called the **mind–body problem,** and the philosophical position that behavior is controlled by two entities, a mind and a body, is called **dualism.**

Figure 1-4, an illustration from *Treatise on Man*, shows how, to Descartes, the mind receives information from the body. When a hand touches a ball, for example,

Figure 1-4

Dualism Descartes argued that the pineal body in the brain receives different messages from a hand holding a flute and from a hand touching a ball. The mind, resident in the pineal body, interprets these messages and so learns about the flute and ball. From *Treatise on Man*, by R. Descartes, 1664. Reprint and translation (p. 60), 1972, Cambridge, MA: Harvard University Press.

the mind learns through the brain that a ball exists, where the ball is located, and what its size and texture are. The mind also directs the body to touch the ball, but again it does so through the brain. The mind can command the brain to make the body carry out a great variety of actions, such as running, changing breathing rate, or throwing the ball across the room. The rational mind, then, depends on the brain both for information and to control behavior.

Descartes was also aware of the many new machines being built, including clocks, water wheels, and gears. He saw mechanical gadgets on public display in parks. In the water gardens in Paris, one device caused a hidden statue to approach and spray water when an unsuspecting stroller walked past it. The statue's actions were triggered when the person stepped on a pedal hidden in the sidewalk.

Influenced by these mechanical devices, Descartes used mechanical analogies, for example, to describe how we automatically make decisions about distances and angles on the basis of visual information and to explain why, when we focus directly on an object, we are less aware of what surrounds it. He also considered in detail "mechanical" physiological functions, such as digestion, respiration, and the roles of nerves and muscles. To explain how the mind controls the body, Descartes suggested that the mind resides in a small structure in the center of the brain called the *pineal body*, which is located beside fluid-filled cavities called *ventricles*.

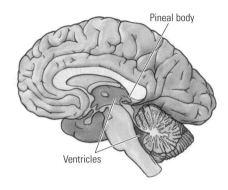

Pineal body

Ventricles

According to Descartes, the pineal body directs fluid from the ventricles through nerves and into muscles. When the fluid expands those muscles, the body moves. In Descartes's theory, then, the mind regulates behavior by directing the flow of ventricular fluid to the appropriate muscles. Note that, for Descartes, mind and body were separate entities, and the pineal body was only a structure through which the mind works.

Many problems in detail and logic corrupt Descartes's theory. We now know that people who have a damaged pineal body or even no pineal body at all still display normal intelligent behavior. The pineal body plays a role in behavior related to biological rhythms, but it does not govern human behavior. We now know that fluid is not pumped from the brain into muscles when they contract. Placing an arm in a bucket of water and contracting the arm's muscles does not cause the water level in the bucket to rise, as it should if the volume of the muscle increased because fluid had been pumped into it. We now also know that there is no obvious way that a nonmaterial entity can influence the body, because doing so requires the spontaneous creation of energy, which violates the physical law of conservation of matter and energy.

Nevertheless, Descartes proposed scientific tests of his theory. To determine if an organism possesses a mind, Descartes proposed two tests: the language test and the action test. To pass the language test, an organism must use language to describe and reason about things that are not physically present. The action test requires the organism to display behavior that is based on reasoning and is not just an automatic response to a particular situation. Descartes also assumed that animals are unable to pass the tests. A good deal of experimental work that we will describe is directed toward determining if he was right. For example, studies of sign language taught to apes are partly intended to find out whether apes can describe and reason about things that are not present and so pass the language test. "Origins of Spoken Language" on page 11 summarizes the contemporary view on language in animals.

Descartes's theory led to a number of unfortunate results. On the basis of it, some people argued that young children and the mentally insane must lack minds, because they often fail to reason appropriately. We still use the expression "he's lost his mind" to describe someone who is "mentally ill." Some proponents of this view also reasoned that, if someone lacked a mind, that person was simply an inhuman machine not due normal respect or kindness. Cruel treatment of animals, children, and the mentally ill

○ Visit the *Brain and Behavior* Web site (**www.worthpublishers.com/kolb**) and go to the Chapter 1 Web links to read a detailed history of the origins of the mind–body question.

Origins of Spoken Language

Language is such a striking characteristic of our species that it was once thought to be a trait unique to humans. Nevertheless, evolutionary theory predicts that language is unlikely to have appeared suddenly and full-blown in modern humans. Language must have antecedents in other species, especially the species most closely related to us.

Great Ape Trust of Iowa

The first attempt to teach human vocal language to chimps was an abject failure. Not until 1971, when Beatrice and Alan Gardner taught a version of American Sign Language to a chimpanzee named Washoe, was it realized that nonverbal forms of language might have preceded verbal language. To test this hypothesis, Sue Savage-Rumbaugh and coworkers began teaching a pygmy chimpanzee named Malatta a symbolic language called Yerkish. (The pygmy chimpanzee, or *bonobo,* is a species thought to be an even closer relative of humans than the common chimp.)

Malatta and her son Kanzi were caught in the wild, and Kanzi accompanied his mother to class. It turned out that, even though he was not specifically trained, Kanzi learned more Yerkish than his mother did. Remarkably, Kanzi also displayed clear evidence of understanding quite complex human speech.

Realizing that chimps in the wild have a rich vocal repertoire and are especially vocal in producing food peeps in association with food, Jared Taglialatela and coworkers (2003) recorded the vocalizations made by Kanzi when he was interacting with people and eating different kinds of foods. From video records of many interactions with humans, the scientists selected vocalizations associated with "banana," "grape," "juice," and "yes." Spectral analyses of the sounds associated with the semantic context or meaning of each condition were evaluated to determine whether the peeps uttered by Kanzi were similar in similar situations and distinct in different situations.

The analyses revealed that the peeps were indeed similar for vocalizations that occurred within a specific semantic context and structurally different between the different contexts. Although Kanzi is a language competent chimp, the finding that he uses "chimpanzeeish" in specific situations in his interactions with humans provides further support for the idea that human language may be derived from more primitive forms of communication used by human ancestors.

has been justified by Descartes's theory for centuries. It is unlikely that Descartes himself intended these interpretations. He was reportedly very kind to his own dog, named Monsieur Grat.

Darwin and Materialism

By the mid–nineteenth century, another theory of brain and behavior was emerging. This theory was the modern perspective of **materialism**—the idea that rational behavior can be fully explained by the working of the brain and the rest of the nervous system, without any need to refer to an immaterial mind that controls our actions. This perspective became especially prominent because it is supported scientifically by the evolutionary theories of Alfred Russel Wallace and Charles Darwin.

Materialism. Philosophical position that holds that behavior can be explained as a function of the nervous system without explanatory recourse to the mind.

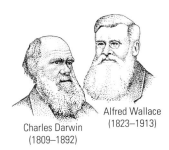

Charles Darwin
(1809–1892)

Alfred Wallace
(1823–1913)

◉ Visit the *Brain and Behavior* Web site
(**www.worthpublishers.com/kolb**)
and go to the Chapter 1 Web links to view
more research about Charles Darwin.

Natural selection. Darwin's theory
for explaining how new species evolve
and existing species change over time.
Differential success in the reproduction
of different characteristics (phenotypes)
results from the interaction of organisms
with their environment.

Species. Group of organisms that can
interbreed.

Wallace and Darwin independently arrived at the same conclusion—the idea that all living things are related. Each outlined this view in papers presented at the Linnaean Society of London in July 1858. Darwin further elaborated on the topic in his book titled *On the Origin of Species by Means of Natural Selection,* published in 1859. This book presented a wealth of supporting detail, which is why Darwin is mentioned more often as the founder of modern evolutionary theory.

Both Darwin and Wallace had looked carefully at the structure of plants and animals and at animal behavior. Despite the diversity of living organisms, both men were struck by the myriad characteristics common to so many species. For example, the skeleton, muscles, and body parts of humans, monkeys, and other mammals are remarkably similar.

Such observations led first to the idea that living organisms must be related, an idea widely held even before Wallace and Darwin. But, more importantly, these same observations led to Darwin's explanation of how the great diversity in the biological world could have evolved from common ancestry. Darwin's principle of natural selection proposes that animals have traits in common because these traits are passed from parents to their offspring.

Natural selection is Darwin's theory for explaining how new species evolve and existing species change over time. A **species** is a group of organisms that can breed among themselves but not with members of other species. Individual organisms within any species vary extensively in their characteristics, or *phenotypes,* with no two members of the species being exactly alike. Some are big, some are small, some are fat, some are fast, some are lightly colored, and some have large teeth. Those individual organisms whose characteristics best help them to survive in their environment are likely to leave more offspring than are less-fit members. This unequal ability of individual members to survive and reproduce leads to a gradual change in a species' population, with characteristics favorable for survival in that particular habitat becoming more prevalent in succeeding generations.

Neither Darwin nor Wallace understood the basis of the great variation in plant and animal species. The underlying principles of that variation were discovered by another scientist, Gregor Mendel, beginning about 1857, through experiments that he did with pea plants. Mendel deduced that heritable factors, which we now call *genes,* are related to the various physical traits displayed by the species.

Members of a species that have a particular gene or combination of genes will express that trait. If the genes for a trait are passed on to offspring, the offspring also will have the same trait. New traits appear because new gene combinations are inherited from parents, because existing genes change or mutate, because suppressed genes are reexpressed, because expressed genes are suppressed, or because genes or parts of genes are deleted or duplicated.

Thus, the unequal ability of individual organisms to survive and reproduce is related to the different genes that they inherit from their parents and pass on to their offspring. By the same token, similar characteristics within or between species are usually due to similar genes. For instance, genes that produce the nervous system in different kinds of animal species tend to be very similar.

Darwin's theory of natural selection has three important implications for the study of the brain and behavior:

1. Because all animal species are related, so too must be their neurons and their brains. Today, brain researchers study animals as different as slugs, fruit flies, rats, and monkeys, knowing that they can often extend their findings to human beings.
2. Because all species of animals are related, so too must be their behavior. Darwin was particularly interested in this subject. In his book titled *On the Expression of*

the Emotions in Man and Animals, he argued that emotional expressions are similar in humans and other animals because we inherited these expressions from a common ancestor. Evidence for such inheritance is illustrated in **Figure 1-5**, which shows that smiling is common to people throughout the world. That people in different parts of the world display the same behavior suggests that the trait is inherited rather than learned.

3.   Both the brain and behavior changed bit by bit in animals that evolved to greater complexity, as humans obviously did. In the following section, we will trace the steps in which the human nervous system evolved from a simple, netlike arrangement of nerve fibers, to a spinal cord connected to that net, and finally to a nervous system with a brain that controls behavior.

Evidence that the brain controls behavior is today so strong that the idea has the status of a theory: *the brain theory.* Donald O. Hebb in his influential book titled *The Organization of Behavior,* published in 1949, described the brain theory as follows:

> Modern psychology takes completely for granted that behavior and neural function are perfectly correlated, that one is completely caused by the other. There is no separate soul or life force to stick a finger into the brain now and then and make neural cells do what they would not otherwise. (Hebb, 1949, p. xiii)

Some people reject the idea that the brain is responsible for behavior because they think it denies religion. The biological explanation of brain and behavior, however, is neutral with respect to religious beliefs. Fred Linge, the brain-injured man whose experience begins this chapter, has strong religious beliefs, as do the other members of his family. They used their religious strength to aid in his recovery. Yet, despite their religious beliefs, they realize that Linge's brain injury was the cause of his change in behavior and that the process of recovery that his brain underwent is the cause of his restored health. Similarly, many behavioral scientists hold strong religious beliefs and see no contradiction between those beliefs and their use of the scientific method to examine the relations between the brain and behavior.

Figure 1-5

Inherited Behavior   Part of the evidence supporting Darwin's suggestion that emotional expression is inherited is the finding that people from all parts of the world display the same emotional expressions that they also recognize in others, as is illustrated by these smiles.

In Review

We have considered three perspectives on how behavior arises. Mentalism is the view that behavior is a product of an intangible entity called the mind (psyche); the brain has little importance. Dualism is the notion that the mind acts through the brain to produce language and rational behavior, whereas the brain alone is responsible for the "lower" kinds of actions that we have in common with other animal species. Materialism, the view that all behavior, language and reasoning included, can be fully accounted for by brain function, guides contemporary research on the brain and behavior.

EVOLUTION OF BRAIN AND BEHAVIOR

The study of living organisms shows that not all have nervous systems or brains and that nervous systems and behavior built up and changed bit by bit as animals evolved. We will trace the evolution of the human brain and behavior by describing (1) those animals that first developed a nervous system and muscles with which to move and (2) how the nervous system became more complex as the brain evolved to mediate complex behavior.

The popular interpretation of human evolution is that we are descended from apes. Actually, apes are not our ancestors, although we *are* related to them through a

Common ancestor. Forebear from which two or more lineages or family groups arise and so is ancestral to both groups.

common ancestor, a forebear from which two or more lineages or family groups arise. To demonstrate the difference, consider the following story.

Two people named Joan Campbell were introduced at a party, and their names afforded a good opening for a conversation. Although both belong to the Campbell lineage (family line), one Joan is not descended from the other. The two women live in different parts of North America, one in Texas and the other in Ontario, and both their families have been in those locations for many generations.

Nevertheless, after comparing family histories, the two Joans discovered that they have ancestors in common. The Texas Campbells are descended from Jeeves Campbell, brother of Matthew Campbell, from whom the Ontario Campbells are descended. Jeeves and Matthew had both boarded the same fur-trading ship when it stopped for water in the Orkney Islands north of Scotland before sailing to North America in colonial times.

The Joan Campbells' common ancestors, then, were the mother and father of Jeeves and Matthew. Both the Texas and the Ontario Campbell family lines are descended from this same man and woman. If the two Joan Campbells were to compare their genes, they would find similarities that correspond to their common lineage.

In much the same way, humans and apes are descended from common ancestors. But, unlike the Joan Campbells, we do not know who those distant relatives were. By comparing the brain and behavioral characteristics of humans and related animals and by comparing their genes, however, scientists are tracing our lineage back farther and farther to piece together the story of our origins. In the following sections, we will trace some of the main evolutionary events that led up to human brains and human behavior.

Origin of Brain Cells and Brains

The earth formed about 4.5 billion years ago, and the first life forms arose about a billion years later. About 700 million years ago, animals evolved the first brain cells, and, by 250 million years ago, the first brain had evolved. A humanlike brain first developed only about 3 million to 4 million years ago, and our modern human brain has been around for only the past 100,000 to 200,000 years. As evolutionary history goes, that is a short time span. Although life evolved very early in the history of our planet, brain cells and the brain are recent adaptations, and large complex brains, such as ours, appeared only an eye blink ago in evolutionary terms.

Classification of Life

Since the first living organism appeared, the divergence of life on Earth has been enormous. Millions of species have evolved, and millions have gone extinct. As many as 30 million to 100 million species currently inhabit the planet. Scientists have described only a small number of these species, about 1.5 million. The rest remain to be found, named, and classified.

Taxonomy, the branch of biology concerned with naming and classifying species, groups organisms according to their common characteristics and their relationships to one another. As shown in **Figure 1-6**, the broadest unit of classification is a kingdom, with more subordinate groups being phylum, class, order, family, genus, and species. We humans belong to the animal kingdom, the chordate phylum, the mammalian class, the primate order, the Hominidae family, the *Homo* genus, and the *sapiens* species. Animals are usually identified by their genus and species name. So we humans are called *Homo sapiens,* meaning "wise humans."

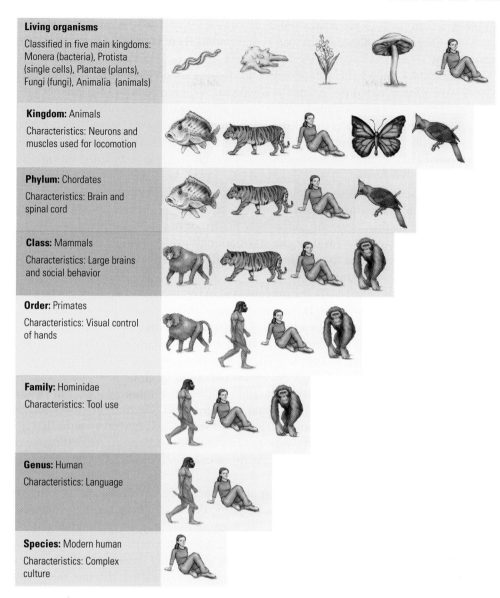

Living organisms

Classified in five main kingdoms: Monera (bacteria), Protista (single cells), Plantae (plants), Fungi (fungi), Animalia (animals)

Kingdom: Animals

Characteristics: Neurons and muscles used for locomotion

Phylum: Chordates

Characteristics: Brain and spinal cord

Class: Mammals

Characteristics: Large brains and social behavior

Order: Primates

Characteristics: Visual control of hands

Family: Hominidae

Characteristics: Tool use

Genus: Human

Characteristics: Language

Species: Modern human

Characteristics: Complex culture

Figure 1-6

Taxonomy of Modern Humans
Taxonomy classifies comprehensive groups of living organisms into increasingly specific subordinate groups. Modern humans are the only surviving species of the genus that included numerous extinct species of humanlike animals.

This taxonomic hierarchy is useful in helping us trace the evolution of brain cells and the brain. Brain cells and muscles first evolved in animals, allowing them to move. The brain as an organ first evolved in chordates, allowing more complex movements; a large brain with many different functions first evolved in mammals; a brain capable of producing complex tools first evolved in apes; and a brain capable of written language and complex culture first evolved in *Homo sapiens*. Although the most complex brain and patterns of behavior have evolved in the human lineage, large brains and complex behaviors have also evolved in some other lineages. Highly social dolphins have large brains and some birds, such as the Galápagos woodpecker finch, use simple tools.

Galápagos woodpecker finch

Evolution of Animals with Nervous Systems

A nervous system is not essential for life. In fact, most organisms in both the past and the present have done without one. Of the five main taxonomic kingdoms of living organisms illustrated at the top of Figure 1-6, only one, Animalia, contains species with nervous systems. Taxonomists have so far identified about 1 million animal species and

Cladogram. Phylogenetic tree that branches repeatedly, suggesting a classification of organisms based on the time sequence in which evolutionary branches arise.

Nerve net. Simple nervous system that has no brain or spinal cord but consists of neurons that receive sensory information and connect directly to other neurons that move muscles.

Bilateral symmetry. Body plan in which organs or parts present on both sides of the body are mirror images in appearance. For example, the hands are bilaterally symmetrical, whereas the heart is not.

Segmentation. Division into a number of parts that are similar; refers to the idea that many animals, including vertebrates, are composed of similarly organized body segments.

Ganglia. Collection of nerve cells that function somewhat like a brain.

Chordates. Group of animals that have both a brain and a spinal cord.

Homeobox gene cluster. A group of genes that specify the segmental organization of the nervous system of insects and vertebrates and so are thought to have arisen in a common ancestor to these lineages.

organized them into 15 phyla (the plural of *phylum*). Differences among the nervous systems of these phyla illustrate the evolutionary markers of increasing nervous system complexity.

Figure 1-7A shows the animal phyla in a chart called a **cladogram** (from the Greek word *clados,* meaning "branch"). Cladograms display groups of related organisms as branches on a tree; branch order represents how the groups are related evolutionarily, as well as the traits that distinguish them. A cladogram is read from left to right, with the most recently evolved organism or trait located at the right. The branches for animals that possess neurons and muscle tissue diverge at the far right in Figure 1-7A.

Neurons and muscles underlie the new forms of movement that distinguish the animal kingdom. The simpler animal groups that branch off before this evolutionary milestone have neither. Neurons and muscle tissue became more complex, as did the behaviors that they control, as new groups of animals evolved. Animals without neurons and muscles continue to exist and evolve, but we will follow the evolution of animals with neurons and muscles.

As illustrated in Figure 1-7B, the nervous system representative of older phyla, such as jellyfishes and sea anemones, is extremely simple. It consists of a diffuse **nerve net,** with no structure that resembles a brain. (Compare the human nervous system illustrated in Figure 1-2. Now imagine that the brain and spinal cord have been removed).

In moving to the right in Figure 1-7B, we find that species in somewhat more recently evolved phyla, such as flatworms, are more complexly structured. These organisms have heads and tails, and their bodies have **bilateral symmetry** (one-half of the body is the mirror image of the other) and **segmentation** (the body is composed of similarly organized parts). These animals also have segmented nervous systems that resemble the human nervous system, with sensory and motor neurons projecting from each segment. Bilateral symmetry and segmentation are two important structural features of the human nervous system.

Species in still more recently evolved phyla, such as clams, snails, and octopuses, have clusters of neurons called **ganglia** in particular body parts. Ganglia resemble primitive brains and function somewhat like them in that they are command centers. In some phyla, encephalization, meaning "in the head," becomes distinctive. For example, insects, have ganglia in the head that are sufficiently large to merit the term brain. One phylum, the **chordates,** of which humans are members, displays the greatest degree of encephalization.

Chordates get their name from the *notochord,* a flexible rod that runs the length of the back. In humans, the notochord is present only in the embryo; by birth, bony vertebrae encase the spinal cord. Although the nervous systems of prechordates, such as fruit flies, and chordates, such as humans, have many anatomical differences, the nervous systems of both are formed under the instruction of similar sets of **homeobox gene clusters.** These groups of genes specify the segmented organization of the nervous system of insects and vertebrates and so are thought to have arisin in a common ancestor to these lineages. Thus, the nervous systems of diverse animals are much more similar than their superficial anatomical differences suggest.

The Chordate Nervous System

Figure 1-8 pictures representatives of seven of the nine classes to which the approximately 38,500 chordate species belong. Wide variation exists in the nervous systems of chordates, but the basic pattern of a net that is bilaterally symmetrical, segmented, with

(A)

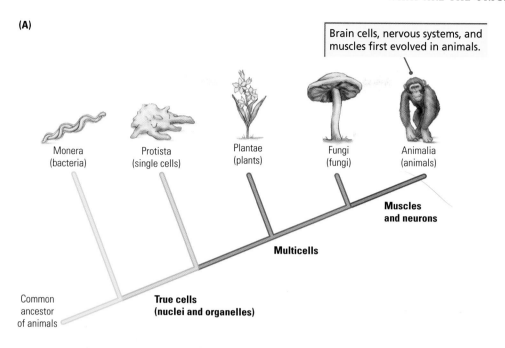

Brain cells, nervous systems, and muscles first evolved in animals.

(B)

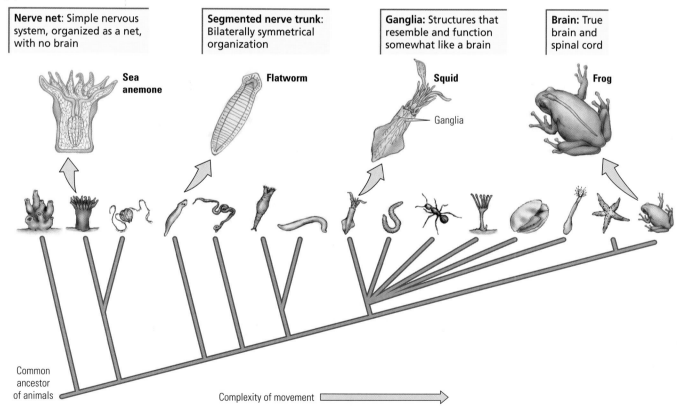

Figure 1-7

Evolution of the Nervous System   **(A)** This cladogram relates the evolutionary sequence connecting the five main kingdoms. **(B)** This cladogram shows the evolutionary relationships among the nervous systems of the 15 animal phyla, from a nerve net, to a segmented nervous system, to ganglia and nerve trunks, and finally to a brain and spinal cord.

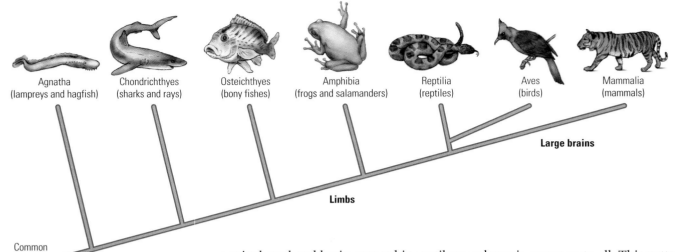

Agnatha (lampreys and hagfish) — Chondrichthyes (sharks and rays) — Osteichthyes (bony fishes) — Amphibia (frogs and salamanders) — Reptilia (reptiles) — Aves (birds) — Mammalia (mammals)

Large brains

Limbs

Common ancestor

Figure 1-8

Representative Classes of Chordates
This cladogram illustrates the evolutionary relationship among animals having a brain and a spinal cord. Brain size increased with the development of limbs in amphibia. Birds and mammals are the most recently evolved chordates, and large brains relative to body size are found in both classes.

◉ To view a closeup of the cerebellum, go to the brainstem and subcortical structures section of the central nervous system module on the *Foundations* CD.

Cerebellum. Major structure of the hindbrain specialized for motor coordination. In large-brained animals, it may also have a role in the coordination of other mental processes.

a spinal cord and brain encased in cartilage or bone is common to all. This pattern is found even in the earliest chordate species. Two additional features distinguish the chordate nervous system:

1. The nervous system is "crossed," that is, one hemisphere of the brain receives most sensory signals from the opposite side of the body and sends motor commands mainly to the opposite side of the body (left hemisphere controls right body and vice versa). In prechordate animals, the nervous system does not cross over. The reason that the chordate nervous system is crossed is not fully understood, but crossed pathways allow for greater control of movements of the limbs than for those of the trunk. Possibly, this crossed anatomical pathway permits each hemisphere to hold one side of the body still while moving the limbs on the other side.

2. The chordate spinal cord lies behind the heart and gut, but the prechordate nervous system lies in front of these structures. Some anatomists speculate that this shift of the chordate nervous system toward the back was a key adaptation in allowing the nervous system to grow larger.

The evolution of more complex behavior in chordates is closely related to the evolution of the cerebral hemispheres, or *cerebrum,* and of the **cerebellum** (Latin, meaning "little brain"). The relative differences between these two brain regions in different classes of chordates are illustrated in **Figure 1-9**. The behaviors controlled by these regions include new forms of locomotion on land, complex movements of the mouth and hands for eating, improved learning ability, and highly organized social behavior.

The cerebrum and the cerebellum are proportionately small and smooth in the earliest-evolved classes (e.g., fish, amphibians, and reptiles). In later-evolved chordates, especially the birds and mammals, these structures become much more prominent. Finally, in many large-brained mammals, both structures are extensively folded, which greatly increases their surface area while allowing them to fit into a small skull (just as folding a piece of paper enables it to occupy a small container such as an envelop).

Increased size and folding become particularly pronounced in the dolphins and primates, animals with the largest brains relative to their body size. Because relatively large brains with a complex cortex and cerebellum have evolved in a number of animal lineages, humans are neither unique nor special in these respects. We humans are distinguished, however, in belonging to a lineage having large brains and are unique in having the largest brain of all animals.

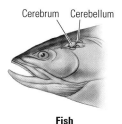 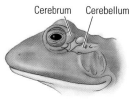 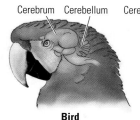 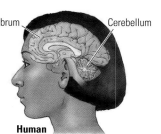

Cerebrum Cerebellum   Cerebrum Cerebellum   Cerebrum Cerebellum   Cerebrum   Cerebellum

Fish   **Frog**   **Bird**   **Human**

Figure 1-9

Brain Evolution   The brains of representative chordates have many structures in common, illustrating a single basic brain plan across chordate species.

In Review

Brain cells and nervous systems are relatively recent developments in the evolution of life on Earth. Because they evolved only once, in the animal kingdom, a similar basic pattern exists in the nervous systems of all animals. The nervous system becomes more complex with the evolution of chordates, and this increase in complexity closely parallels increasingly complex behavior. Particular animal lineages, such dolphins and primates, are characterized by especially large brains and complex behaviors. These evolutionary developments in chordates are closely tied to their bilateral symmetry, segmented spinal cord, brain encased in cartilage or bone, crossed nervous system pathways, migration of the nervous system toward the back of the body, and growth of the cerebral cortex and cerebellum.

HUMAN EVOLUTION

Anyone can see similarities among humans, apes, and monkeys, but some people believe that humans are far too different from monkeys and apes to have an ancestor in common with them. These skeptics have reasoned that the absence of a "missing link," or intermediate ancestor, further argues against the possibility of common descent. In the past century, however, so many intermediate forms between humans and other apes have been found in the fossil record that entire books are required to describe them. Here we consider only the brains and behaviors of some of the more prominent ancestors that link apes to us and to the human brain and behavior.

○ Visit the *Brain and Behavior* Web site (**www.worthpublishers.com/kolb**) and go to the Chapter 1 Web links to view a tutorial about human evolution.

Humans: Members of the Primate Order

The human relationship to apes and monkeys places us in the *primate order,* a subcategory of mammals that includes not only apes and monkeys, but lemurs, tarsiers, and marmosets as well (**Figure 1-10**). In fact, we humans are only 1 of about 275 species in the primate order. Primates have excellent color vision, with the eyes positioned at the front of the face to enhance depth perception, and they use this highly developed sense to deftly guide their hand movements.

Female primates usually have only one infant per pregnancy, and they spend a great deal more time caring for their young than most other animals do. Associated with their skillful movements and their highly social nature, primates' brains are on average larger than those of animals in other orders of mammals, such as rodents (mice, rats, beavers, squirrels) and carnivores (wolves, bears, cats, weasels).

Humans are members of the suborder apes, which includes gibbons, orangutans, gorillas, and chimpanzees as well (see Figure 1-10). Apes are arboreal animals, with limber shoulder joints that allow them to brachiate (swing from one handhold to another) in

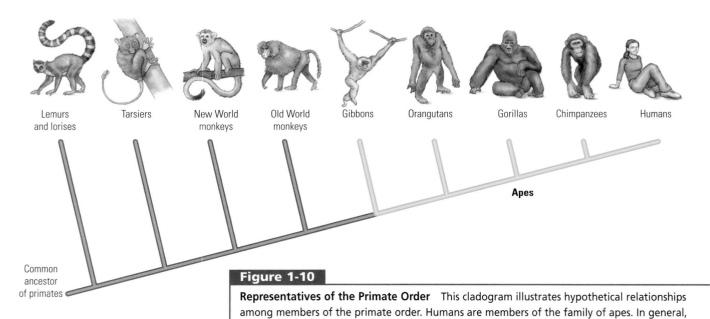

Lemurs and lorises   Tarsiers   New World monkeys   Old World monkeys   Gibbons   Orangutans   Gorillas   Chimpanzees   Humans

Apes

Common ancestor of primates

Figure 1-10

Representatives of the Primate Order   This cladogram illustrates hypothetical relationships among members of the primate order. Humans are members of the family of apes. In general, brain size increases across the groupings, with humans having the largest primate brains.

Hominid. General term referring to primates that walk upright, including all forms of humans, living and extinct.

trees, a trait retained by humans, although they generally do not live in trees. Apes are distinguished as well by their intelligence and large brains, traits that humans exemplify.

Among the apes, we are most closely related to the chimpanzee, having had a common ancestor between 5 million and 10 million years ago. The family to which humans belong is called Hominidae. In the past 5 million years, many **hominids,** primates that walk upright, evolved in our lineage. Some extinct hominid species lived at the same time as one another. At present, however, we are the only surviving hominid species.

Australopithecus: **Our Distant Ancestor**

One of our hominid ancestors is probably *Australopithecus* (from the Latin word *austral,* meaning "southern," and the Greek word *pithekos,* meaning "ape") or a primate very much like it. **Figure 1-11** shows reconstructions of the animal's face and body. The name *Australopithecus* was coined by an Australian, Raymond Dart, for the skull of a child that he found in a box of fossilized remains from a limestone quarry near Taung, South Africa, in 1924. (The choice of a name to represent his native land is probably not accidental.) We now know that many species of *Australopithecus* existed, some at the same time.

The skull of the "Taung child" did not belong to the earliest species, which lived more than 4 million years ago. These early hominids were among the first primates to show a distinctly human characteristic: they walked upright. Scientists have deduced their upright posture from the shape of their back, pelvic, knee, and foot bones and from a set of fossilized footprints that a family of australopiths left behind, walking through freshly fallen volcanic ash some 3.6 million to 3.8 million years ago. The footprints feature the impressions of a well-developed arch and an unrotated big toe more like that of humans than of apes.

Figure 1-11

Australopithecus *Australopithecus* (*top*) walked upright with free hands, as do modern humans, but its brain was the size of a modern-day ape's, about one-third the size of the human brain. Figure comparison (*bottom*) based on the most complete *Australopithecus* skeleton yet found, a young female about 1 meter tall popularly known as Lucy, who lived 3 million years ago.

Homo sapiens   "Lucy"

The evolutionary lineage from *Australopithecus* to humans is not known precisely, in part because many *Australopithecus*

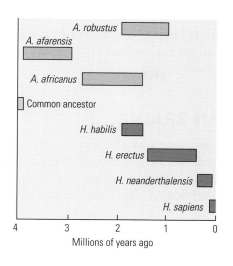

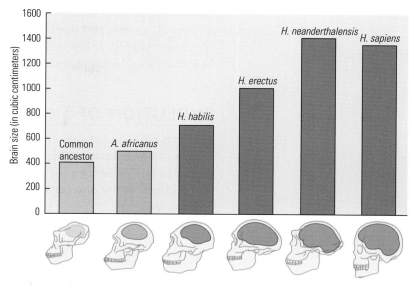

species evolved, some contemporaneously. One possible lineage is shown on the left in **Figure 1-12.** A common ancestor gave rise to the *Australopithecus* lineage, and one member of this group gave rise to the *Homo* lineage.

The last of the australopith species disappears from the fossil record about 1 million years ago after coexisting with other hominids for some time. Also illustrated in Figure 1-12, at the right, is the large increase in brain size that evolved in the hominid lineage. The brain of *Australopithicus* was about the same size of that of nonhuman apes, but succeeding members of the human lineage display a steady increase in brain size.

The First Humans

The oldest fossils designated as genus *Homo,* or human, are those found by Mary and Louis Leakey in the Olduvai Gorge in Tanzania in 1964, dated at about 2 million years. The primates that left these skeletal remains had a strong resemblance to *Australopithecus,* but Mary Leakey argued that their dental pattern is more similar to that of modern humans than to that of australopiths. More important, they made simple stone tools. The Leakeys named the species *Homo habilis* (meaning "handy human") to signify that its members were toolmakers. Again, the precise relationships in the *Homo* lineage are not known, because a number of early *Homo* species lived at the same time.

The first humans whose populations spread beyond Africa migrated into Europe and into Asia. This species was *Homo erectus* ("upright human"), so named because of the mistaken notion that its predecessor, *H. habilis,* had a stooped posture. *Homo erectus* first shows up in the fossil record about 1.6 million years ago and lived until perhaps as recently as 100,000 to 30,000 years ago. Its brain was bigger than that of any previous hominid, overlapping in size the measurements of present-day human brains (see Figure 1-12, right). *H. erectus* also made more sophisticated tools than did *H. habilis.*

Modern humans, *Homo sapiens,* appeared in Asia and North Africa within about the past 200,000 years and in Europe within the past 100,000 years. Most anthropologists think that they migrated from Africa originally. Until about 30,000 years ago in Europe and 18,000 ago in Asia, they coexisted with other hominid species. The Asiatic species, *Homo floresienses,* found on the Indonesian island of Flores was, at about three feet tall, an especially small subspecies of *Homo erectus* (Morwood et al., 2004).

In Europe, for example, *H. sapiens* coexisted with Neanderthals, named after Neander, Germany, where the first Neanderthal skulls were found. Neanderthals had

Figure 1-12

The Origins of Humans   (*Left*) The human lineage and a lineage of extinct *Australopithecus* probably arose from a common ancestor about 4 million years ago. Thus the ancestor of the human lineage *Homo* was likely an animal similar to *Australopithecus africanus.* (*Right*) Brain size across this proposed lineage has increased nearly threefold.

AFRICA

brains as large as or larger than those of modern humans, used tools similar to those of early *H. sapiens,* and possibly had a similar hunting culture. We do not know how *H. sapiens* completely replaced other human species, but perhaps they had advantages in tool making, language use, or social organization.

EVOLUTION OF THE HUMAN BRAIN

Scientists who study brain evolution propose that a relative increase in the size and complexity of brains in different species enabled the evolution of more complex behavior. In this section, we consider the relation between brain size and behavior across different species. We also consider leading hypotheses about how the human brain became so large.

Brain Size and Behavior

In his book titled *The Evolution of the Brain and Intelligence,* published in 1973, Harry Jerison uses the *principle of proper mass* to sum up the idea that species exhibiting more complex behaviors will possess relatively larger brains than will species whose behaviors are less complex. Jerison also developed an index of brain size to compare different species' brains, even though they differ in body size. He calculated that, as body size increases, the size of the brain increases at about two-thirds the increase in body weight.

Using this index, plus an average brain-volume-to-body-weight ratio as a base, we can quantify the expected brain size for a mammal of any given weight. The diagonal line in **Figure 1-13** plots expected brain size. Body size is on the *x*-axis, and brain size is on the *y*-axis. The shaded polygon surrounding the diagonal line encompasses the actual brain-to-body-size ratios of all mammals.

Animals that lie below the diagonal line have brains that are below the average expected ratio for an animal of that size, whereas animals that lie above the diagonal have brains that are larger than expected for an animal of that size. Notice that the rat's brain is a little smaller and the elephant's brain is a little larger than the ratio predicts. Notice also that a modern human is located farther from the diagonal than any

Figure 1-13

Brain-to-Body-Size Ratios of Some Familiar Mammals The axes use logarithmic units to encompass the wide range of body and brain sizes. The shaded polygon includes the brain and body sizes of all mammals. Adapted from *The Evolution of the Brain and Intelligence* (p. 175), by H. J. Jerison, 1973, New York: Academic Press.

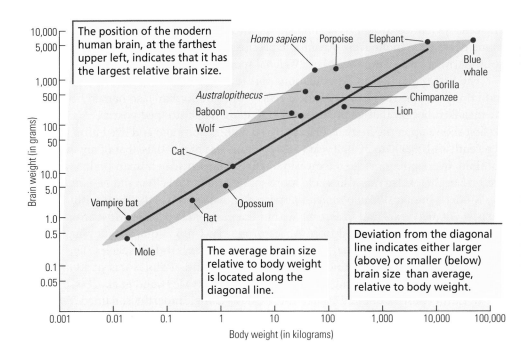

other animal, indicating a brain that is relatively larger for its body size than that of any other animal.

Using the ratio of actual brain size to expected brain size, Jerison also developed an **encephalization quotient** (EQ), a numerical value for the brain size of each species. The top half of **Figure 1-14** lists the EQs for several familiar animals. Notice that a rat has an EQ about one-half that of a cat, which is representative of the average mammal on the diagonal in Figure 1-13.

Crows have an EQ similar to that of monkeys, and dolphins have an EQ comparable to that of *Homo erectus*. People who study crows would agree that they are intelligent birds, whereas dolphins are both highly intelligent and highly social mammals. The bottom half of Figure 1-14 lists the EQs for a number of large-brained species in the primate lineage.

Underlying Jerison's principle of proper mass is the idea that a larger brain is needed for increasingly complex behavior. We can see some obvious relations between larger brains and more complex behavior, or movements, as we progress up the chordate ladder from older to more recent classes of animals, with limb use as an example (see Figure 1-8). Among older chordates, cyclostomes, such as the lamprey, move by making snake-like, side-to-side body movements, whereas the more recent fish species have fins that enable more complex movements. In amphibians, fins evolved into limbs used in an even more complex way than fins, to enable walking on land.

Birds and mammals use their limbs for still more complex movements, both for locomotion and for handling objects. Being a primate is associated with many other limb innovations, including extensive tool making. Each increase in behavioral complexity is associated with increases in brain size.

Why the Hominid Brain Enlarged

The evolution of modern humans—from the time when humanlike creatures first appeared until the time when humans like ourselves first existed—spans about 5 million years. As illustrated by the relative size differences of skulls pictured in **Figure 1-15**, much of this evolution entailed changes in brain size, which were accompanied by changes in behavior.

The nearly threefold increase in brain size from apes (EQ 2.5) to modern humans (EQ 7.0) has been a subject of extensive research and equally extensive speculation. One line of evidence points to a series of rapid climate changes as a spur for behavioral adaptation. Most likely, each new hominid species appeared after climate changes produced new environments. Populations of existing hominids were isolated, enabling a rapid selection for traits adaptive in each new environment.

The first of these climate changes was triggered about 8 million years ago. Before that time, most of Africa was rich forest inhabited by monkeys and apes, among other abundant plant and animal species. Then a massive tectonic event (a deformation of the earth's crust) produced the Great Rift Valley, which runs from south to north across the eastern part of the African continent.

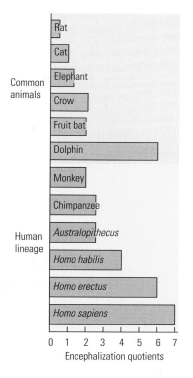

Figure 1-14

Comparative Encephalization Quotients The EQs of some familiar animals are compared in the top half of the chart, and members of the primate lineage are ranked in the bottom half.

Encephalization quotient (EQ). Jerison's measure of brain size obtained from the ratio of actual brain size to the expected brain size, according to the principle of proper mass, for an animal of a particular body size.

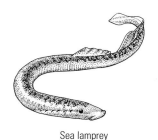

Sea lamprey

Figure 1-15

The Course of Human Evolution The relative size of the hominid brain has increased nearly threefold, illustrated here by comparing *Australopithecus afarensis* (left), *Homo erectus* (center), and modern *Homo sapiens* (right). A missing part of the *Australopithecus* skull, shown in blue, has been reconstructed. From *The Origin of Modern Humans* (p. 165), by R. Lewin, 1998, New York: Scientific American Library.

K. O'Farrell/Concepts

This reshaping of the African landmass left a wet jungle climate to the west and a much drier savannah climate to the east. To the west, the apes continued unchanged in their former habitat. But, in the drier eastern region, apes evolved rapidly into upright hominids in response to the selective pressures of a mixture of tree-covered and grassy regions that formed their new home.

Upright posture has a number of adaptive advantages, including being an efficient, rapid means of locomotion across grass-covered areas. Such an upright posture may have evolved in *Australopithecus* because these arboreal animals were forced to spend more time on the ground moving between clumps of trees. Upright posture may also have helped hominids to regulate their body temperature by reducing the amount of body surface directly exposed to the sun and to improve their ability to scan the environment for opportunities and threats; it may have been useful for tree climbing as well.

Just before the appearance of *Homo habilis* 2 million years ago, the African climate rapidly grew even drier, with spreading grasslands and even fewer trees. Anthropologists speculate that the hominids that evolved into *Homo habilis* adapted to this new habitat by becoming scavengers on the dead of the large herds of grazing animals that then roamed the open grasslands.

The appearance of *Homo erectus* may have been associated with a further change in climate, a rapid cooling that lowered sea levels (by trapping more water as ice) and opened up land bridges into Europe and Asia. At the same time, the new hominid species upgraded their hunting skills and the quality of their tools for killing, skinning, and butchering animals. Archeologists hypothesize a number of migrations of hominids from Africa into other parts of the world, with modern humans being the last of these migrants.

A wide array of hypotheses seeks to explain why the modern human brain is so large. One hypothesis contends that the primate life style favors an increasingly complex nervous system. A second links brain growth to changes in hominid physiology. And a third proposes that a slowed rate of maturation in a species favors larger brains. We will now examine all these points of view.

THE PRIMATE LIFE STYLE

That the primate life style favors a larger brain can be illustrated by examining how primates forage for food. Foraging is important for all animals, but some foraging activities are simple, whereas others are complex. Eating grass or vegetation is not difficult; if there is lots of vegetation, an animal need only munch and move on. Vegetation eaters do not have especially large brains. Among the apes, gorillas, which are mainly vegetation eaters, have relatively small brains (see Figure 1-13). In contrast, apes that eat fruit, such as chimpanzees, have relatively large brains.

The relation between fruit foraging and larger brain size can be seen in a study by Katharine Milton (1993), who examined the feeding behavior and brain size of two South American (New World) monkeys that have the same body size—the spider monkey and the howler monkey. As is illustrated in **Figure 1-16**, the spider monkey obtains nearly three-quarters of its nutrients from eating fruit and has a brain twice as large as that of the howler monkey, which obtains less than half of its nutrients from fruit.

What is so special about eating fruit that favors a larger brain? The answer is not that fruit contains a brain-growth factor, although fruit *is* a source of sugar that the brain depends on for energy. The answer is that foraging for fruit is a complex activity. Unlike plentiful vegetation within easy reach on the ground, fruit grows on trees, and only on certain trees, in certain seasons. Among the many kinds of fruit, some are better for eating than others, and many different animals and insects compete for a fruit crop. Moreover, after a fruit crop has been eaten, it takes time for a new crop to grow. Each of these factors poses a challenge for an animal that eats mostly fruit.

Good sensory skills, such as color vision, are needed to recognize ripe fruit in a tree, and good motor skills are required to reach and manipulate it. Good spatial skills are needed to navigate to trees that contain fruit. Good memory skills are required to remember where fruit trees are, when the fruit will be ripe, and in which trees the fruit has already been eaten.

Fruit eaters have to be prepared to deal with competitors, including members of their own species, who also want the fruit. To keep track of ripening fruit, having friends who can help search also benefits a fruit eater. As a result, successful fruit-eating animals tend to have complex social relations and a means of communicating with others of their species. In addition, having a parent who can teach fruit-finding skills is helpful to a fruit eater; so being both a good learner and a good teacher is useful.

We humans are fruit eaters and we are descended from fruit eaters, and so we are descended from animals with large brains. In our evolution, we also exploited and elaborated fruit-eating skills to obtain other temporary and perishable types of food as we scavenged, hunted, and gathered. These new food-getting efforts required navigating long distances, and they required recognition of a variety of food sources. At the same time, they required making tools for digging up food, killing animals, cutting skin, and breaking bones.

These tasks also require cooperation and a good deal of learned behavior. Humans distinguish themselves from apes in displaying a high degree of male–male, female–female, and male–female cooperation in matters not related to sexual activity (Schuiling, 2003). The elaboration of all these life-style skills necessitated more brain cells over time. Added up, more brain cells produce an even larger brain.

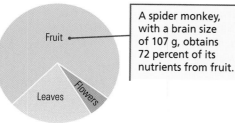

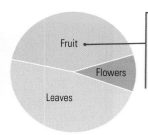

Spider monkey diet

A spider monkey, with a brain size of 107 g, obtains 72 percent of its nutrients from fruit.

Fruit · Leaves · Flowers

Howler monkey diet

A howler monkey, with a brain size of 50 g, obtains only 42 percent of its nutrients from fruit.

Fruit · Flowers · Leaves

Figure 1-16

Picky Eaters Katharine Milton examined the feeding behavior and brain size of two South American (New World) monkeys that have the same body size but different brain sizes and diets.

CHANGES IN HOMINID PHYSIOLOGY

Researchers have attempted to relate physical differences between humans and other apes to the evolution of a larger brain in humans. One adaptation that may have given a special boost to greater brain size in our human ancestors was a new form of brain cooling. Dean Falk (1990), a neuropsychologist who studies brain evolution, developed her **radiator hypothesis** from her car mechanic's remark that, to increase the size of a car's engine you have to also increase the size of the radiator that cools it.

Falk reasoned that, if the brain's radiator, the circulating blood, adapted into a more effective cooling system, the brain could increase in size. Brain cooling is so important because the human brain works so hard. Although your brain makes up less than 2 percent of your body weight, it uses 25 percent of your body's oxygen and 70 percent of its glucose. As a result of all this metabolic activity, your brain generates a great deal of heat and is at risk of overheating under conditions of exercise or heat stress.

Falk argues that, unlike australopith skulls, *Homo* skulls contain holes through which cranial blood vessels passed. These holes suggest that *Homo* species had a much more widely dispersed blood flow from the brain than did earlier hominids, and this more widely dispersed blood flow would have greatly enhanced brain cooling.

Radiator hypothesis. Idea that selection for improved brain cooling through increased blood circulation in the brains of early hominids enabled the brain to grow larger.

Neoteny. Process in which maturation is delayed, and so an adult retains infant characteristics; idea derived from the observation that newly evolved species resemble the young of their common ancestors.

Figure 1-17

Neoteny The shape of an adult human's head more closely resembles the shape of the head of a juvenile chimpanzee (*left*) than the shape of the head of an adult chimp (*right*), leading to the hypothesis that we humans may be neotenic descendants of our more apelike common ancestors.

A second adaptation, identified by Hansell Stedman and his colleagues (2004), stems from a genetic mutation associated with marked size reductions in individual facial muscle fibers and entire masticatory muscles. The Stedman team speculates that smaller masticatory muscles in turn led to smaller and more delicate bones in the head. Smaller bones in turn allowed for changes in diet and an increase in brain size.

Stedman and his colleagues estimate that this mutation occurred 2.4 million years ago, coinciding with the appearance of the first humans. The methodology used by Stedman, in which human and ape genes are compared, will likely lead to future insights into other differences between humans and apes, including those in brain size and function.

NEOTENY

When a species' rate of maturation slows down, a process called **neoteny,** juvenile stages of predecessors become the adult features of descendants. Maturation is delayed and the adult retains some infant characteristics. Because the head of an infant is large relative to body size, neoteny would lead to adults with larger skulls to house larger brains.

Many features of human anatomy besides a large brain-size-to-body-size ratio link us with the juvenile stages of other primates. These features include a small face, a vaulted cranium, an unrotated big toe, an upright posture, and a primary distribution of hair on the head, armpits, and pubic areas.

Figure 1-17 illustrates that the head shape of a baby chimpanzee is more similar to an adult human than it is to the head shape of an adult chimpanzee.

Humans also retain some behaviors of primate infants, including play, exploration, and an intense interest in novelty and learning. Neoteny is common in the animal world. Domesticated dogs are neotenic wolves, and sheep are neotenic goats.

Another aspect of neoteny related to human brain development is that a slowing down of human maturation would have allowed more time for brain cells to be produced (McKinney, 1998). Most brain cells in humans develop just before and after birth; so an extended prenatal and neonatal period would prolong the stage of life in which most brain cells are developing. This prolonged stage would, in turn, enable increased numbers of brain cells to develop.

In Review

Constant changes in the environment eliminate some animal species and create new opportunities for others to evolve. Among certain groups of animals, adaptations to these changes include an increase in brain size. Thus, the large human brain evolved in response to a number of pressures and opportunities, including changes in climate, the appearance of new food resources to exploit, physiological adaptations, and neoteny.

STUDYING BRAIN AND BEHAVIOR IN MODERN HUMANS

The evolutionary approach that we've been using to explain how the large human brain evolved is based on comparisons *between* species. Special care attends extending evolutionary principles to physical comparisons *within* species, especially biological comparisons within or among groups of modern humans. We will illustrate the difficulty of within-species comparisons by considering misguided attempts to correlate human brain size with intelligence. Then we turn to another aspect of studying the brain and behavior in modern humans—the fact that, unlike the behavior of other animal species, so much of modern human behavior is culturally learned.

Fallacies of Human Brain-Size Comparisons

We have documented parallel changes in brain size and behavioral complexity through the many species that form the human lineage. Some people have proposed that, because brain-size differences between species are related to behavioral complexity, similar comparisons might be made between individual members of a single species. For example, some investigators have attempted to show that people with the largest brains display the most intelligent behavior. Stephen Jay Gould, in his 1981 book titled *The Mismeasure of Man,* reviewed many of these attempts to correlate human brain size with intelligence and was critical of this research because of its faulty logic and methods.

For one thing, determining how to measure the size of a person's brain is difficult. If a tape measure is simply placed around a person's head, it is impossible to factor out the thickness of the skull. There is also no agreement about whether volume or weight is a better measure of brain size. And, no matter which indicator we use, we must consider body size. For instance, the human brain varies in weight from about 1000 grams to more than 2000 grams, but people also vary in body mass. To what extent should we factor in body mass in deciding if a particular brain is large or small? And how should we measure the mass of the body, given that a person's total weight can fluctuate widely?

Age and health affect the brain's mass as well. People who suffer brain injury in early life often have smaller brains and behavioral impairments. If we wait until after death to measure a brain, the cause of death, the water content of the brain, and the time elapsed since death will all affect the results.

Even if the problems of measurement could be solved, the question of what is causing what remains. Exposure to a complex environment can promote growth in existing brain cells. So, if larger brains are found to correlate with higher intelligence, does the complex problem solving cause the greater brain mass or does the greater brain mass enable the more complex behavior?

As if these factors were not perplexing enough, we must also consider what is meant by intelligence. When we compare the behavior of *different* species, we are comparing **species-typical behavior**—in other words, behavior displayed by all members of a species. For example, lampreys do not have limbs and cannot walk, whereas salamanders do have limbs and can walk; so the difference in brain size between the two species can be correlated with this trait.

When we compare behavior *within* a species, however, we are usually comparing how well one individual member performs a certain task in relation to other members— for example, how well one salamander walks relative to how well another salamander walks. In addition, for humans, individual performance on a task is influenced by many factors unrelated to inherent ability, such as opportunity, interest level, training, motivation, and health.

People vary enormously in their individual abilities, depending on the particular task. One person may have superior verbal skills but mediocre spatial abilities, whereas another person may be adept at solving spatial puzzles but struggles with written work, and still another may excel at mathematical reasoning and be average in everything else. Which of these people should we consider the most intelligent? Should certain skills get greater weight as measures of intelligence? Clearly, it is difficult to say.

Species-typical behavior. Behavior that is characteristic of all members of a species.

Figure 1-18

Brain Weight and Intelligence in Dogs
A within-species comparison of intelligence rankings and brain size among breeds of dogs yields a correlation of 0.009, which indicates no relationship at all. A correlation of 1.0 indicates a perfectly positive or negative relationship. Intelligence rankings are from *The Intelligence of Dogs,* by S. Coren, 1994, Toronto: The Free Press. Size measures are from "Brain Weight–Body Weight Scaling in Dogs and Cats," by R. T. Bronson, 1979, *Brain, Behavior and Evolution, 16,* 227–236.

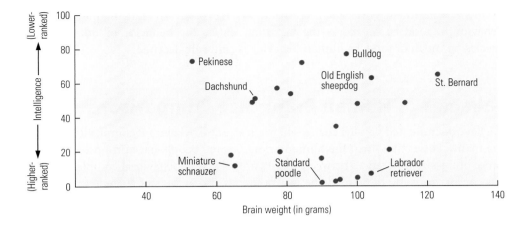

Given these questions, it is not surprising that brain size and intelligence within the human species, and between the sexes for that matter, do not seem particularly related. The brains of people who virtually everyone agrees are very intelligent have been found to vary in size from the low end to the high end of the range for our species. The brilliant physicist Albert Einstein had a brain of average size. Women's brains weigh about 10 percent less than men's brains on average, roughly equivalent to the average difference in female and male body size, but the two sexes do not differ in measures of average intelligence.

The lack of correlation between brain size and intelligence within a single species is not limited to humans. **Figure 1-18** plots the average brain size in different breeds of dogs against each breed's level of intelligence as ranked by dog experts. The brain sizes, which range from less than 50 grams to nearly 130 grams, were not adjusted for the breeds' body sizes, because such adjustments are not made in studies of humans. The results are all over the map, indicating no relation at all between the overall size of a breed's brain and that breed's intelligence ranking.

Differences of some kind must exist in the brains of individual persons because people differ in behavior and talents. Neuroscientists are not yet sure what structural or functional measures are related to behavioral traits. Gross brain size is not very likely to be one of them, however. Researchers who study this question believe that measures of the relative size and function of particular brain regions will prove more helpful.

Culture

The most remarkable thing that our brains have allowed us to develop is an extraordinarily rich **culture,** the complex learned behaviors passed on from generation to generation. Here is a list, in alphabetical order, of major categories of behavior that are part of human culture:

> Age-grading, athletic sports, bodily adornment, calendar [use], cleanliness training, community organization, cooking, cooperative labor, cosmology, courtship, dancing, decorative art, divination, division of labor, dream interpretation, education, eschatology, ethics, ethnobotany, etiquette, faith healing, family feasting, fire making, folklore, food taboos, funeral rites, games, gestures, gift giving, government, greetings, hair styles, hospitality, housing, hygiene, incest taboos, inheritance rules, joking, kin groups, kinship nomenclature, language, law, luck, superstitions, magic, marriage, mealtimes, medicine, obstetrics, penal sanctions, personal names, population policy, postnatal

Culture. Learned behaviors that are passed on from one generation to the next through teaching and learning.

care, pregnancy usages, property rights, propitiation of supernatural beings, puberty customs, religious ritual, residence rules, sexual restrictions, soul concepts, status differentiation, surgery, tool making, trade, visiting, weaving, and weather control. (Murdock, 1965)

Not all the items in this list are unique to humans. Many other animal species display elements of some of these behaviors. For example, many other animals display age grading (any age-related behavior or status), courtship behavior, rudimentary tool use, and elements of language. Despite such behavioral similarities across species, humans clearly have progressed much further in the development of culture than other animals have. For humans, every category of activity on Murdock's list requires extensive learning from other members of the species, and exactly how each behavior is performed can differ widely from one group of people to another.

A human brain must function adequately to acquire these complex cultural skills. When its functioning is inadequate, a person may be unable to learn even basic elements of culture. "Learning Disabilities" describes how incapacitating it can be to have a brain that has difficulty in learning to read.

Because of steady growth in cultural achievements, the behavior of *Homo sapiens* today is completely unlike that of *Homo sapiens* living 100,000 years ago. The earliest surviving art, such as carvings and paintings, dates back only some 30,000 years; agriculture appears still more recently, about 10,000 to 15,000 years ago; and reading and writing, the foundations of our modern literate and technical societies, were invented only about 7000 years ago.

St. Ambrose, who lived in the fourth century, is reported to be the first person who could read silently. Most forms of mathematics, another basis of modern technology, were invented even more recently than reading and writing were. And many of our skills in using mechanical devices are still more recent in origin.

Learning Disabilities

Focus on Disorders

Children absorb their society's culture, and acquiring language skills seems virtually automatic for most. Yet some people have lifelong difficulties in mastering language-related tasks, difficulties classified by educators under the umbrella of *learning disabilities.*

Perhaps the most common learning disability is impairment in learning to read, or *dyslexia* (from Greek words suggesting "bad" and "reading"). Not surprisingly, children with dyslexia have difficulty learning to write as well as to read. In 1895, James Hinshelwood, an eye surgeon, examined some schoolchildren who were having reading problems, but he could find nothing wrong with their vision. Hinshelwood was the first person to suggest that these children were impaired in brain areas associated with the use of language.

In more recent times, Norman Geshwind and Albert Galaburda (1985) proposed how such impairment might come about. These researchers were struck by the finding that dyslexia is far more common in boys than in girls. Perhaps, they reasoned, excessive amounts of the hormone testosterone, which produces male physical characteristics early in development, might also produce abnormal development in language areas of the brain. Pursuing this hypothesis, they examined postmortem the brains of a small sample of people who had experienced dyslexia. They found abnormal collections of neurons, or "warts," in the language areas of the left hemisphere. This relation between structural abnormalities in the brain and learning difficulties is further evidence that an intact brain is necessary for normal human functioning.

These examples highlight a remarkable feature of the modern human brain: it performs so many tasks in our modern world that were not directly selected for in our early hominid evolution. The brains of early *Homo sapiens* certainly did not evolve to help program computers or travel to distant planets. And yet the same brains are capable of both these complex tasks and more. Apparently, the things that the human brain did evolve to do contained all the elements necessary for adapting to far more sophisticated skills. Thus, the human brain evolved a capacity allowing it to be highly flexible in accommodating the variety of knowledge and achievements of modern culture.

The acquisition of complex culture was a gradual, step-by-step process, with one achievement leading to another. Among our closest relatives, chimpanzees also have culture in the sense that some groups display tool-using skills that others have not acquired. In her book titled *The Chimpanzees of Gombe,* primatologist Jane Goodall describes the process by which symbolic concepts, a precursor of language, might have developed in chimpanzees. She uses the concept of "fig" as an example, explaining how a chimp might progress from knowing a fig only as a tangible here-and-now entity to having a special vocal call that represents this concept symbolically. Goodall writes:

> We can trace a pathway along which representations of . . . a fig become progressively more distant from the fig itself. The value of a fig to a chimpanzee lies in eating it. It is important that he quickly learn to recognize as *fig* the fruit above his head in a tree (which he has already learned to know through taste). He also needs to learn that a certain characteristic odor is representative of *fig*, even though the fig is out of sight. Food calls made by other chimpanzees in the place where he remembers the fig tree to be located may also conjure up a concept of *fig*. Given the chimpanzees' proven learning ability, there does not seem to be any great cognitive leap from these achievements to understanding that some quite new and different stimulus (a symbol) can also be representative of *fig*. Although chimpanzee calls are, for the most part, dictated by emotions, cognitive abilities are sometimes required to interpret them. And the interpretations themselves may be precursors of symbolic thought. (Goodall, 1986, pp. 588–589)

Presumably, in our own distant ancestors, the repeated acquisition of concepts, as well as the education of children in those concepts, gradually led to the acquisition of language and other aspects of a complex culture. The study of the human brain, then, is not just the study of the structure of a body organ. It is also the study of how that organ acquires sophisticated cultural skills—that is, of how the human brain fosters behavior in today's world.

In Review

Care must be taken in extending evolutionary principles of the brain and behavior. What is true for comparisons across different species may not be true for comparisons within a species. For instance, although a larger brain correlates with more complex behavior in comparisons of different species, brain size and intelligence are not particularly related in comparisons of individual members within a species such as modern humans. We humans are distinguished in the animal kingdom by the amount of our behavior that is culturally learned. We have progressed much further in the development of culture than other species have.

SUMMARY

■ *What is the use of studying brain and behavior?* The study of brain and behavior leads us to an understanding of our origins, to an understanding of human nature, and to an understanding of the causes of many behavioral disorders and their treatment.

■ *What is the brain and what is behavior?* Behavior can be defined as any kind of movement in a living organism. As such, a behavior has both a cause and a function. The flexibility and complexity of behavior vary greatly among different species. Humans are capable of highly flexible and complex behaviors. Located inside the skull, the brain is the organ that exerts control over behavior. The brain seems to need ongoing sensory and motor stimulation to maintain its intelligent activity.

■ *How is the nervous system structured?* The nervous system is composed of the central nervous system, which includes the brain and the spinal cord, and the peripheral nervous system, through which the brain and spinal cord communicate with sensory receptors, with muscles and other tissues, and with the internal organs.

■ *How has Western tradition viewed the relation between the brain and behavior?* There have been three major explanations: mentalism, dualism, and materialism. In antiquity, Aristotle believed that the brain has no role in behavior, but rather that behavior is the product of an intangible entity called the psyche, or mind. Descartes modified mentalism in the European Renaissance, proposing the dualist explanation that only rational behavior is produced by the mind, whereas other behaviors are produced mechanically by the brain. Finally, 150 years ago, Darwin's proposal that all living organisms are descended from a common ancestor led materialists to conclude that the source of *all* behavior is the brain.

■ *How did brain cells and the nervous system evolve?* Brain cells and the nervous system evolved in some groups of animals over millions of years. The evolutionary stages through which the human brain evolved can be traced through the human lineage to their common ancestors. The nervous system evolved only in the animal kingdom, and a true brain and spinal cord evolved only in the chordate phylum. Mammals are a class of chordates characterized by especially large brains relative to body size.

■ *What species were the early ancestors of modern humans?* One of our early hominid ancestors was probably *Australopithecus,* or a primate very much like it, who lived in Africa several million years ago. From an australopith species, more humanlike species likely evolved. Among them are *Homo habilis* and *Homo erectus.* Modern humans, *Homo sapiens,* did not appear in Asia and North Africa until about 200,000 to 100,000 years ago.

■ *How did the human brain evolve?* The human brain evolved through the lineage of hominid species that are the ancestors of modern humans. Since *Australopithecus,* the hominid brain has increased in size almost threefold. Environmental challenges and opportunities that favored the natural selection of more complex behavior patterns, changes in physiology, and neoteny stimulated brain evolution in humans.

■ *What are some important considerations in studying the brain and behavior of modern humans?* Principles learned in studying the evolution of the brain and behavior across species may not apply to the brain and behavior within a single species, such as *Homo sapiens.* As animals evolved, a larger brain was associated with more complex behavior; yet, within our species, the most able and intelligent people do not necessarily have the largest brains. In the study of modern humans, the great extent to which our behavior is not inherent in our nervous systems but rather is culturally learned must be recognized.

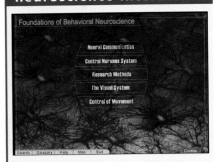

There are many resources available for expanding your learning online:

■ **www.worthpublishers.com/kolb**

Try the Chapter 1 quizzes and flashcards to test your mastery of the chapter material. You'll also be able to link to other sites that will reinforce what you've learned.

■ **http://neurolab.jsc.nasa.gov/ timeline.htm**

Review a timeline of the pioneers in brain study from René Descartes to Roger Sperry in the Spotlight on Neuroscience, National Aeronautics and Space Administration (NASA).

■ **http://serendip.brynmawr.edu/ Mind/Table.html**

Visit this site by R. H. Wozniak of Bryn Mawr College to learn more about the philosophical underpinnings of dualism and materialism and to read a detailed history of the origins of the mind–body question and the rise of experimental psychology.

On your *Foundations* CD-ROM, you'll be able to begin learning about the anatomy of the brain in the module on the Central Nervous System. This module is composed of a rotatable, three-dimensional brain as well as a number of sections of the brain that you can move through with the click of a mouse. In addition, the Research Methods module contains various computer tomographic and magnetic resonance images of the brain, including a video clip of a coronal MRI scan.

KEY TERMS

bilateral symmetry, p. 16
central nervous system (CNS), p. 6
cerebellum, p. 18
cerebral cortex, p. 5
chordates, p. 16
cladogram, p. 16
common ancestor, p. 14
culture, p. 28
dualism, p. 9
encephalization quotient (EQ), p. 23
frontal lobe, p. 6
ganglia, p. 16

hemisphere, p. 5
homeobox gene cluster, p. 16
hominid, p. 20
materialism, p. 11
mentalism, p. 9
mind, p. 9
mind–body problem, p. 9
motor neuron, p. 6
natural selection, p. 12
neoteny, p. 26
nerve net, p. 16
neuron, p. 6
occipital lobe, p. 6

parietal lobe, p. 6
peripheral nervous system (PNS), p. 6
psyche, p. 9
radiator hypothesis, p. 25
segmentation, p. 16
sensory neuron, p. 6
species, p. 12
species-typical behavior, p. 27
spinal cord, p. 6
temporal lobe, p. 6

REVIEW QUESTIONS

1. Summarize the ideas of Aristotle, Descartes, and Darwin regarding the relation between the brain and behavior.

2. How would you go about tracing your own lineage by using the taxonomic system described in this chapter?

3. Recall the number of species of living organisms in each taxonomic subgrouping. What do you think accounts for the apparent relation between numbers of species and brain size?

4. Brain size is one way of accounting for behavioral complexity in interspecies comparisons but not for intraspecies comparisons. What is the reasoning behind this distinction?

5. How does the existence of culture increase the difficulty of understanding human brain function?

FOR FURTHER THOUGHT

Darwin's principle of natural selection is based on the existence of a broad range of individual differences within a species. There are large individual differences in brain size among modern humans. Under what conditions could a new human species with a still-larger brain evolve?

RECOMMENDED READING

Campbell, N. A. (2003). *Biology,* 4th ed. Menlo Park, CA: Benjamin Cummings. This introductory biology textbook provides a comprehensive overview of the structure and function of living organisms.

Coren, S. (1994). *The intelligence of dogs.* Toronto: The Free Press. This very popular book includes a number of tests that are supposed to tell you how smart your dog is. The book also provides comparisons of intelligence for different dog breeds as rated by dog trainers. Check your dog out against other breeds by using easy-to-perform tests. Remember, if your dog is not well trained, it might not do well on the tests.

Darwin, C. (1965). *The expression of the emotions in man and animals.* Chicago: University of Chicago Press. (Original work published 1872.) If a dog growls at you, is the dog angry? Darwin thought so. Darwin's only book on psychology is one in which he argues that the expression of emotions is similar in animals, including humans, which suggests the inheritance of emotions from a common ancestor. This view is becoming popular today, but Darwin proposed it more than 130 years ago.

Darwin, C. (1963). *On the origin of species by means of natural selection, or the preservation of favored races in the struggle for life.* New York: New American Library. (Original work published 1859.) This book is the most important one ever written in biology. Darwin extensively documents the evidence for his theory of natural selection. The book is an enjoyable account of natural life, and one chapter, titled "Instincts," describes behavior in both wild and domesticated animals.

Goodall, J. (1986). *The chimpanzees of Gombe.* Cambridge, MA: Harvard University Press. Goodall's three-decade-long study of wild chimpanzees, begun in 1960, rates as one of the most scientifically important studies of animal behavior ever undertaken. Learn about chimpanzee family structure and chimpanzee behavior, and look at the beautiful photographs of chimpanzees engaged in various behaviors.

Gould, S. J. (1981). *The mismeasure of man.* New York: Norton. Gould criticizes and repudiates extensive literature of the nineteenth and twentieth centuries that claims that differences in human intelligence and differences in the intelligence of the sexes are due to differences in brain size. The appealing feature of this book is that Gould is highly critical of the methodology of the proponents of the brain-size hypothesis while also giving reasons derived from modern genetics for criticizing their position.

Lorenz, K. Z. (1981). *The foundations of ethology.* New York: Springer Verlag. Learn how to study animals and learn how they behave from one of the founders of ethology, the study of animal behavior.

Martin, R. D. (1990). *Primate origins and evolution: A phylogenetic reconstruction.* Princeton, NJ: Princeton University Press. Martin provides a detailed description of the origins and the evolution of primates. This book is an excellent primate reference.

Weiner, J. (1995). *The beak of the finch.* New York: Vintage. This book is a marvelous study of evolution in action. Weiner documents how the populations of Galápagos finches are affected by changes in the availability of certain kinds of food. Careful measurements of the finches' beaks demonstrate that certain beak sizes and shapes are favored when certain kinds of food are available; however, when the appropriate food becomes unavailable, populations of birds with differently shaped beaks become favored.

How Does the Nervous System Function?

Focus on New Research: Optimizing Connections in the Brain

An Overview of Brain Function and Structure

The Brain's Primary Functions

Basic Brain Terminology

The Brain's Surface Features

Focus on Disorders: Meningitis and Encephalitis

Focus on Disorders: Stroke

The Brain's Internal Features

Microscopic Inspection: Cells and Fibers

Neuroanatomy and Functional Organization of the Nervous System

Evolutionary Development of the Nervous System

The Central Nervous System

The Somatic Nervous System

Focus on Disorders: Magendie, Bell, and Bell's Palsy

The Autonomic Nervous System

Eight Principles of Nervous System Function

Principle 1: The Sequence of Brain Processing Is "In ⟶ Integrate ⟶ Out"

Principle 2: Sensory and Motor Divisions Exist Throughout the Nervous System

Principle 3: Many of the Brain's Circuits Are Crossed

Principle 4: The Brain Is Both Symmetrical and Asymmetrical

Principle 5: The Nervous System Works Through Excitation and Inhibition

Principle 6: The Central Nervous System Functions on Multiple Levels

Principle 7: Brain Systems Are Organized Both Hierarchically and in Parallel

Principle 8: Functions in the Brain Are Both Localized and Distributed

Left: **Carolina Biological Supply/Phototake**. *Middle:* **Corbis**.
Right: **CNRI/Phototake**.

CHAPTER

Optimizing Connections in the Brain

As stated in Chapter 1, compared with other mammals, primates have evolved a larger brain than would be predicted from their body size. Overall, scientists believe that this increase in brain size is due to an expansion of existing structures rather than to the production of entirely new structures. As the brain has enlarged with evolution, so, too, have the number of connections among different brain regions.

Connections take up space. When the fraction of the neocortex that is occupied by connections is factored out from cell bodies, synapses, and other brain constituents, we find that roughly 60 percent of the volume in the neocortex is taken up by axons and dendrites, as shown in the accompanying illustration. The amount of space required by these connections poses an important problem of economy: if brain regions have extensive interconnections with one another, the increase in brain size could be larger if the regions were distant than if they were adjacent. Connections between distant regions would have to be in fiber bundles that would traverse some distance and take up space, whereas adjacent regions could connect directly and save space. Direct connections would reduce brain size, and, as we learned in Chapter 1, increasing brain size has complications because, for example, it is necessary to provide more blood and to keep the brain cooled (recall the radiator hypothesis of brain evolution).

Recent studies have directly examined whether evolution favors economy of connective distance as a factor in locating different brain regions. Several principles can be extracted from this research:

1. *Brain structures do not enlarge in isolation.* There is a correlated evolution of different brain regions and, especially, the cerebral hemispheres and cerebellum. Thus, as the neocortex enlarges with evolution, so, too, does the cerebellum. Furthermore, as sensory areas have expanded in the course of evolution, so have associated motor areas.

2. *Evolution selects for developmental processes that minimize the length of neural connections.* The shorter the connections between regions, the faster the transmission, the less space taken up by fiber tracts, and the less likelihood of errors in making these connections in the course of development.

3. *When all possible connections between different brain regions are considered, adjacent areas have more connections than do areas that are not adjacent.* For example, Klyachko and Stevens (2003) examined all possible permutations of connections in 11 areas in the frontal lobe of the rhesus monkey. They calculated 39.9 million possible arrangements of connections, but the actual arrangement observed in rhesus monkeys was optimal, and any deviation increased axonal volume.

We can conclude that the best predictor of the function of any given brain region is probably the function of the adjacent areas. Areas that are adjacent are heavily interconnected and so presumably have interdependent functions.

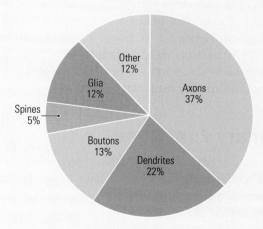

This estimate of the volume of neocortex made up of different components shows that the wires (axons and dendrites) account for nearly 60 percent of the volume.

This chapter builds on the foundation laid in Chapter 1 for studying brain and behavior. Here we consider the biology of the nervous system and how its basic components function. We focus first on the brain and then elaborate on how the brain works in concert with the rest of the nervous system. This focus on function suggests eight basic principles of nervous system organization that are given in detail in the concluding section. These "big ideas" apply equally to the micro- and macro- views of the nervous system presented in this chapter and the following ones on neu- robiology and to the broader picture of behavior that emerges in later chapters.

AN OVERVIEW OF BRAIN FUNCTION AND STRUCTURE

When buying a new car, people like to open the hood and examine the engine, the part of the car responsible for most of its behavior—and misbehavior. In doing so, we see a maze of tubes, wires, boxes, and fluid reservoirs. All most of us can do is gaze, because what we

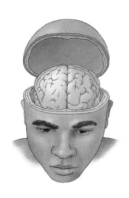

see simply makes no sense, except in the most general way. We know that the engine burns gasoline to make the car move and somehow generates electricity to run the radio and lights. But this tells us nothing about what all the engine's many parts do. What we need is information about how such a system works.

When it comes to behavior, the brain is the engine. In many ways, examining a brain for the first time is similar to looking under the hood of a car. We have a vague sense of what the brain does but no sense of how the parts that we see ac- complish these tasks. We may not even be able to identify the parts. In fact, at first glance, the outside of a brain may look more like a mass of folded tubes divided down the middle than like a structure with many interconnected pieces.

What can you make of the human brain shown in **Figure 2-1**? Can you say anything about how it works? At least car engines have parts with regular shapes that are recogniz- ably similar, which is not true of mammals' brains. When we compare the brain of a cat with that of a human, as shown in **Figure 2-2**, for example, we see enormous differences not just in overall size but also in the structure and relative sizes of the parts. In fact, some parts present in one brain are totally absent in the other. What is it that these parts do that makes one animal stalk mice and another read textbooks?

The Brain's Primary Functions

Perhaps the simplest summary of brain function is that it produces behavior, or move- ment, as you learned in Chapter 1. To produce behavior as we search, explore, and manipulate our environments, the brain must have information about the world— about the objects around us, their size, shape, and movement, for instance. Without

Figure 2-1

Human Brain in Situ When the skull is opened the gyri (bumps) and sulci (cracks) of the cerebral hemispheres are visible, but their appearance offers little information about their function.

Figure 2-2

Mammalian Brains On the outside, the brains of a rat, cat, monkey, and human differ dramatically in size and in general appearance. The rat brain is smooth, whereas the other brains have furrows of varying patterns in the cerebral cortex. The cerebellum, located above the brainstem, is wrinkled in all these species. The brainstem is the route by which most information enters and exits the brain. The olfactory bulb, which controls the perception of smells, is relatively larger in cats and rats but is not visible in monkeys and humans, because it is small and lies on the underside of the brain. Photographs courtesy of Wally Welker/University of Wisconsin Comparative Mammalian Brain Collection.

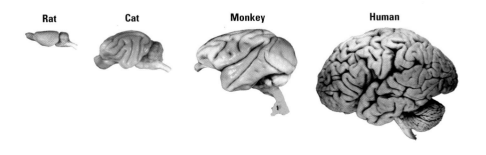

Rat Cat Monkey Human

such information, the brain cannot orient and direct the body to produce an appropriate response to stimulation.

The need for such information is especially true when the required response is some complex behavior, such as catching a ball. The organs of the nervous system are designed to admit information from the world and convert this information into biological activity that produces subjective experiences of reality. The brain thus produces what we believe is reality in order for us to move. These subjective experiences of reality are essential to carrying out any complex task.

This view of the brain's primary purpose may seem abstract, but it is central to understanding how the brain functions. Consider the task of answering a telephone. The brain directs the body to pick up the phone when the nervous system responds to vibrating molecules of air by creating the subjective experience of a ring. We perceive this sound and react to it as if it actually existed, when in fact the sound is merely a fabrication of the brain.

That fabrication is produced by a chain reaction that takes place when vibrating air molecules hit the eardrum. Without the nervous system, especially the brain, there is no such thing as sound. Rather, there is only the movement of air molecules.

There is more to a telephone ring than just the movement of air molecules however. Our creation of reality is based not only on the sensory information received but also on the cognitive processes each of us might use to interact with the incoming information. A telephone ringing when we are expecting a call has a different meaning from its ringing when we are not expecting a call, such as at 3:00 AM.

The subjective reality created by the brain can be better understood by comparing the realities of two different kinds of animals. You are probably aware that dogs perceive sounds that humans do not. This difference in perception does not mean that a dog's nervous system is better than ours or that our hearing is poorer. Rather, the perceptual world created by a dog brain simply differs from that created by a human brain. Neither subjective experience is "right." The difference in experience is merely due to two different systems for processing physical stimuli.

The same differences exist in visual perceptions. Dogs see very little color, whereas our world is rich with color because our brains create a different reality. Such subjective differences exist for good reason: they allow different animals to exploit different features of their environments. Dogs use their hearing to detect the movements of mice in the grass; early humans probably used color vision for identifying ripe fruit in trees. Evolution, then, equips each species with a view of the world that helps it survive.

These sensory examples show how a brain helps guide an organism's behavior. To make this link between sensory processing and behavior, the brain must also have a system for accumulating, integrating, and using knowledge. Whenever the brain collects sensory information, it is essentially creating knowledge about the world, knowledge that it can use to produce more-effective behaviors. The knowledge currently being created in one sensory domain can be compared both with past knowledge and with knowledge gathered in other domains.

We can now identify the brain's three primary functions:

1. Creating a sensory reality
2. Integrating information
3. Producing behavior

Each function requires specific neural systems to create the sensory world, to produce movement (behavior), and to integrate the two.

As introduced in Chapter 1, the central nervous system (CNS) consists of the brain and the spinal cord, and the peripheral nervous system (PNS) encompasses everything else. The CNS–PNS distinction, diagrammed in **Figure 2-3A**, is based on anatomy. In a functional organization, little changes, but the focus shifts to how the parts of the

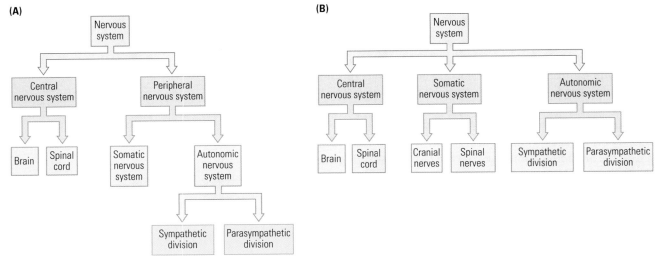

(A)

(B)

Figure 2-3

Parsing the Nervous System The nervous system can be conceptualized anatomically **(A)** and functionally **(B)**. The functional approach employed in this book focuses on how the parts of the nervous system interact.

○ Visit the *Brain and Behavior* Web site (**www.worthpublishers.com/kolb**) and go to the Chapter 2 Web links to view an index listing the roots of neuroanatomical terms.

Somatic nervous system (SNS). Part of the PNS that includes the cranial and spinal nerves to and from the muscles, joints, and skin that produce movement, transmit incoming sensory input, and inform the CNS about the position and movement of body parts.

Autonomic nervous system (ANS). Part of the PNS that regulates the functioning of internal organs and glands.

system work together (Figure 2-3B). That is, the major divisions of the PNS, the somatic and autonomic nervous systems, step up to constitute, along with the CNS, a three-part functional scheme:

■ The CNS includes the brain and the spinal cord.
■ The **somatic nervous system** (SNS), all the spinal and cranial nerves to and from the muscles, joints, and skin, produces movement and transmits incoming sensory information, including the position and movement of body parts, to the CNS.
■ The **autonomic nervous system** (ANS) balances the body's internal organs to "rest and digest" through the parasympathetic (calming) nerves or to "fight or flee" or engage in vigorous activity through the sympathetic (arousing) nerves.

Basic Brain Terminology

The place to start our structural overview is to "open the hood" by observing the brain snug in its home within the skull. Figure 2-1 shows a brain viewed from this perspective. The features that you see are part of what is called the brain's "gross anatomy," not because they are ugly, but because they constitute a broad overview. The hundreds, even thousands, of discrete brain regions make the task of mastering brain terminology seem daunting. Many structures have several names, and terms are often used interchangeably. This peculiar nomenclature arose because research on brain and behavior spans several centuries and includes scientists of many nationalities and languages.

When the first anatomists began to examine the brain with the primitive tools of their time, they made many erroneous assumptions about how the brain works, and the names that they chose for brain regions are often manifestations of those errors. For instance, they named one region of the brain the *gyrus fornicatus* because they thought that it had a role in sexual function. In fact, most of this region has nothing to do with sexual function. Another area was named the *red nucleus* because it appears reddish in fresh tissue. This name denotes nothing of the area's potential functions, which turn out to be the control of limb movements.

As time went on, the assumptions and tools of brain research changed, but the naming continued to be haphazard and inconsistent. Early investigators named structures after themselves or objects or ideas. They used different languages, especially

Latin, Greek, and English. More recently, investigators have often used numbers or letters, but even this system lacks coherence, because the numbers may be used in combination with letters, which may be either Greek or Latin. When we look at current brain terminology, then, we see a mixture of all these naming systems.

Many nervous system structures include information about anatomical location. Table 2-1 summarizes these location-related terms. Notice in Figure 2-4A that structures found on top of the human brain or on the top of another structure within the brain are *dorsal*; structures located toward the bottom of the human brain or one of its parts are *ventral*. Structures found toward the brain's midline are *medial*, whereas those located toward the sides are *lateral*. (Your, heart, for example, is medial; your hips are lateral.)

Figure 2-4B contrasts anatomical directions relative to the body orientations of a human and a dog. Now compare how these directionals are applied to the human brain in Figure 2-4A. Structures located toward the front of the brain are *anterior*, whereas those located toward the back of the brain are *posterior*. Sometimes the terms *rostral* and *caudal* are used instead of *anterior* and *posterior*, respectively. And, occasionally, the terms *superior* and *inferior* are used to refer to structures that are located dorsally or ventrally. These terms do *not* label structures according to their importance, just their location. It is also common to combine terms. For example, a structure may be described as *dorsolateral*, which means that it is located "up and to the side."

Table 2-1	Anatomical Locations
Term	Meaning with respect to the nervous system
	toward the front or the head
Caudal	Located near or toward the tail
Dorsal	On or toward the back or, in reference to brain nuclei, located above
Frontal	"Of the front" or, in reference to brain sections, a viewing orientation from the front
Inferior	Located below
Lateral	Toward the side of the body
Medial	Toward the middle, specifically the body's midline; sometimes written as *mesial*
Posterior	Located near or toward the tail
Rostral	"Toward the beak"; located toward the front
Sagittal	Parallel to the length (from front to back) of the skull; used in reference to a plane
Superior	Located above
Ventral	On or toward the belly or the side of the animal in which the belly is located or, in reference to brain nuclei, located below

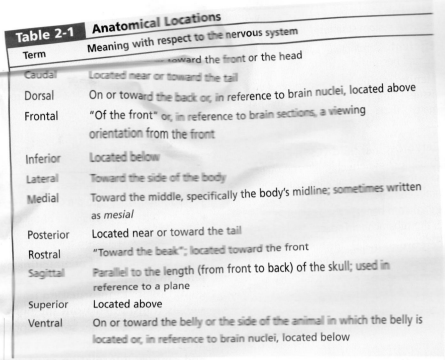

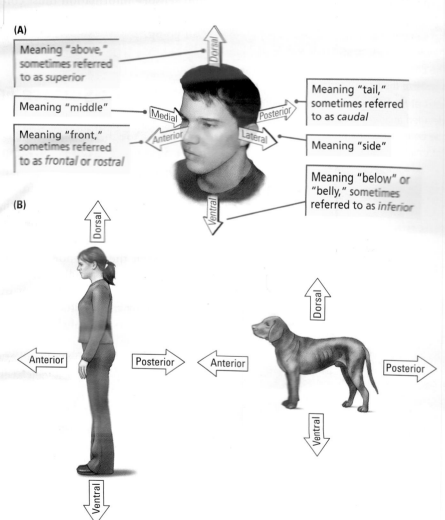

Figure 2-4

Anatomical Orientation Because humans walk upright, anatomical directions relative to the head and brain, shown in part A, take a shift compared with the head orientation of a four-legged animal, shown in part B. **(A)** The concepts "dorsal" and "ventral" take a 90° turn counterclockwise when they reach the level of the human brain. Similarly, *posterior* and *caudal* (both mean "tail") refer to a slightly different orientation for the vertically situated human head. **(B)** Anatomical directions relative to body orientation.

Afferent. Conducting toward a central nervous system structure.

Efferent. Conducting away from a central nervous system structure.

Meninges. Three layers of protective tissue—dura mater, arachnoid, and pia mater—that encase the brain and spinal cord.

Cerebrospinal fluid (CSF). Clear solution of sodium chloride and other salts that fills the ventricles inside the brain and circulates around the brain and spinal cord beneath the arachnoid layer in the subarachnoid space.

Cerebrum. Major structure of the forebrain, consisting of two virtually identical hemispheres (left and right).

On the *Foundations of Behavioral Neuroscience* CD, visit the module on the central nervous system to better visualize the brain's surface features. To look at the various structures go to the detailed anatomy view in the section on the cortex. (See the Preface for more information about this CD.)

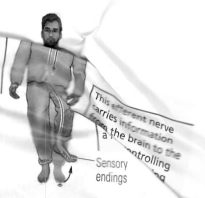

carries information from sensory receptors in skin to the brain.

This efferent nerve carries information from the brain to the ... controlling ...

Sensory endings

Figure 2-5

Information Flow Afferent sensory nerves carry information into the CNS; efferent motor nerves carry information out of the CNS.

The direction of neural information flow also is important. **Afferent** (incoming) refers to information coming into the CNS or one of its parts, whereas **efferent** (outgoing) refers to information leaving the CNS or one of its parts. Thus, the sensory signals transmitted from the body into the brain are afferent, and efferent signals from the brain trigger some response (**Figure 2-5**). The words are similar but easy to keep straight. The letter "a" in *afferent* comes alphabetically before the "e" in *efferent*, and sensory information must come into the brain *before* an outward-flowing signal can trigger a response. Therefore, *afferent* means "incoming" and *efferent* means "outgoing."

The Brain's Surface Features

Return to the brain in the open skull. The first thing that you encounter is not the brain but rather a tough, triple-layered covering, the **meninges**, illustrated in **Figure 2-6**. The outer *dura mater* (from Latin, meaning "hard mother") is a tough double layer of fibrous tissue that encloses the brain and spinal cord in a kind of loose sack. In the middle is the *arachnoid* layer (from Greek, meaning "like a spider's web"), a very thin sheet of delicate connective tissue that follows the brain's contours. The inner layer, or *pia mater* (from Latin, meaning "soft mother"), is a moderately tough membrane of connective-tissue fibers that cling to the brain's surface.

Between the arachnoid layer and pia mater flows **cerebrospinal fluid** (CSF), a colorless solution of sodium chloride and other salts. The cerebrospinal fluid cushions the brain so that it can move or expand slightly without pressing on the skull. The symptoms of meningitis, an infection of the meninges and CSF, are described in "Meningitis and Encephalitis" on page 42.

After removing the meninges, we can lift the brain from the skull and examine its parts. As we look at the brain in the dorsal view at the top of **Figure 2-7**, it appears to have two major parts, each wrinkly in appearance, resembling a walnut meat taken whole from its shell. They are the left and right hemispheres of the **cerebrum**, the most recently evolved structure of the central nervous system.

From the opposite, ventral view shown in the second panel in Figure 2-7, the hemispheres of the smaller "little brain," or *cerebellum*, are visible. Both the cerebrum and the cerebellum are visible in the lateral and medial views shown in the

Figure 2-6

Cerebral Security A triple-layered covering, the meninges, encases the brain and spinal cord, and the cerebrospinal fluid (CSF) cushions them.

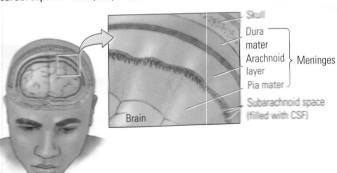

Skull
Dura mater
Arachnoid layer } Meninges
Pia mater
Subarachnoid space (filled with CSF)
Brain

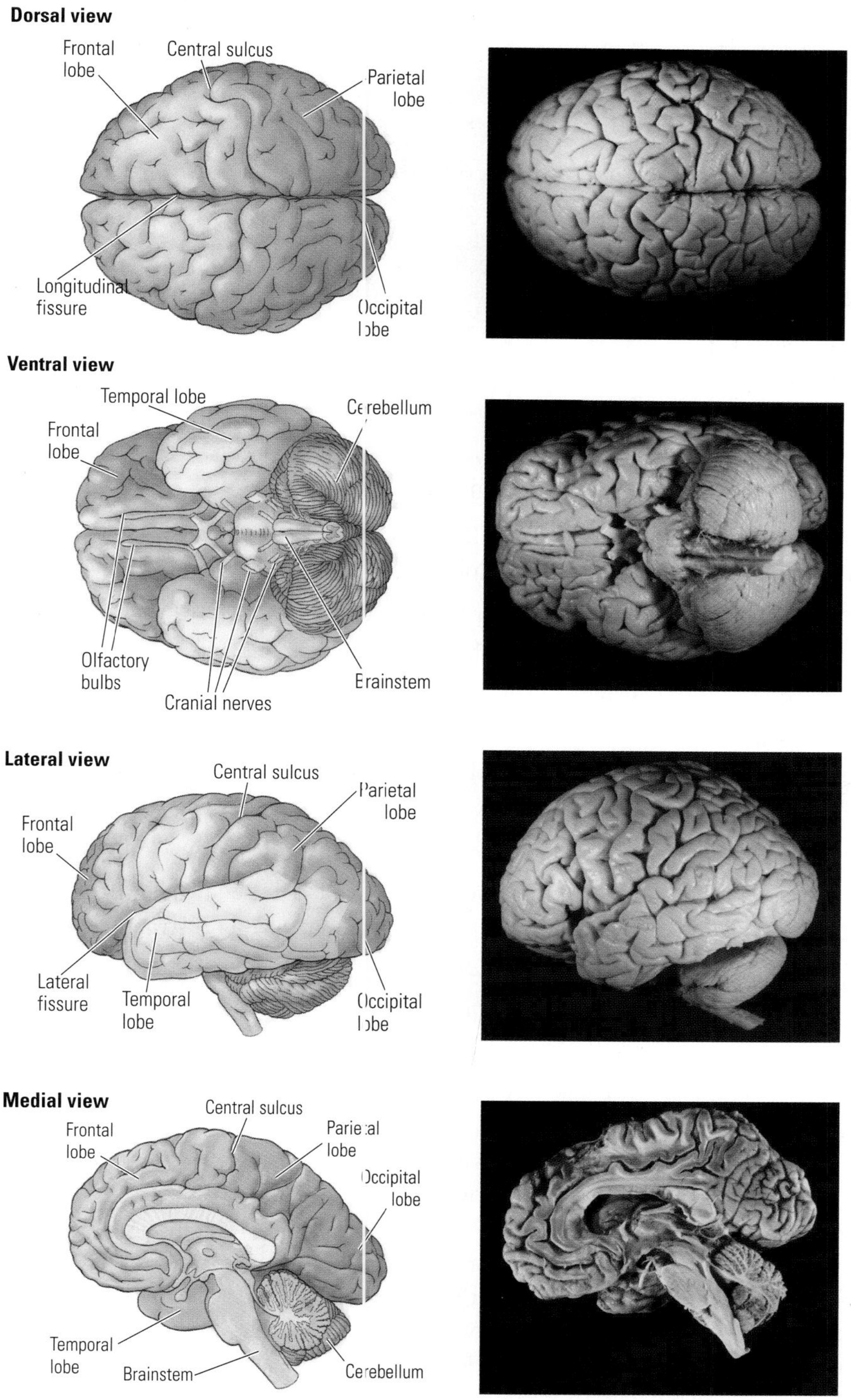

Dorsal view

- Frontal lobe
- Central sulcus
- Parietal lobe
- Longitudinal fissure
- Occipital lobe

Ventral view

- Temporal lobe
- Frontal lobe
- Cerebellum
- Olfactory bulbs
- Cranial nerves
- Brainstem

Lateral view

- Central sulcus
- Frontal lobe
- Parietal lobe
- Lateral fissure
- Temporal lobe
- Occipital lobe

Medial view

- Central sulcus
- Frontal lobe
- Parietal lobe
- Occipital lobe
- Temporal lobe
- Brainstem
- Cerebellum

Figure 2-7

Views of the Human Brain   Locations of the lobes of the cerebral hemispheres are shown in these top, bottom, side, and midline views, as are the cerebellum and the three major sulci. Photographs courtesy of Yakolev Collection/AFIP.

🔘 Visit the central nervous system module on the *Foundations* CD to examine, locate, and rotate the parts of the brain. To view the three-dimensional models, go to the overview and look in the section on the subdivisions of the CNS.

bottom panels of Figure 2-7. These structures appear wrinkled in large-brained animals because their outer surface, or cortex, is a relatively thin sheet of tissue that is crinkled up to fit into the skull, as described in Chapter 1 (see also Figure 2-2).

Thus, much of the cortex is invisible from the brain's surface. All we can see are bumps, or **gyri** (singular: gyrus), and cracks, or **sulci** (singular: sulcus). Some sulci are so very deep that they are called *fissures*. The longitudinal fissure between the cerebral

Gyrus (pl. gyri). A groove in brain matter, usually a groove found in the neocortex or cerebellum.

Sulcus (pl. sulci). A small cleft formed by the folding of the cerebral cortex.

Meningitis and Encephalitis

Various harmful microorganisms can invade the layers of the meninges, particularly the pia mater and the arachnoid layer, as well as the CSF flowing between them, and cause infections called *meningitis*. One symptom, inflammation, places pressure on the brain. Because the space between meninges and skull is slight, unrelieved pressure can lead to delirium and, if the infection progresses, to drowsiness, stupor, and even coma.

Usually, the earliest symptom of meningitis is severe headache and a stiff neck (cervical rigidity). Head retraction (tilting the head backward) is an extreme form of cervical rigidity. Convulsions, a common symptom in children, indicate that the brain also is affected by the inflammation.

Infection of the brain itself is called *encephalitis*. Some of the many forms of encephalitis have great historical significance. Early in the past century, in World War I, a form of encephalitis called sleeping sickness *(encephalitis lethargica)* reached epidemic proportions.

Its first symptom is sleep disturbance. People sleep all day and become wakeful, even excited, at night. Subsequently, they show symptoms of Parkinson's disease—severe tremors and difficulty in controlling body movements. Many are completely unable to make any voluntary movements, such as walking or even combing their hair. Survivors of

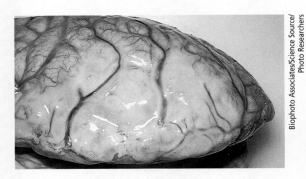

Biophoto Associates/Science Source/Photo Researchers

Pus is visible over the anterior surface of this brain infected with meningitis.

sleeping sickness were immortalized by the neurologist Oliver Sacks in the book and movie *Awakenings*.

The cause of these encephalitis symptoms is death of a brain area known as the substantia nigra ("black substance"), which you will learn about later in this chapter. Other forms of encephalitis may have different effects on the brain. For example, Rasmussen's encephalitis attacks one cerebral hemisphere in children. In most cases, the only effective treatment is radical: the removal of the entire affected hemisphere.

Surprisingly, some young children who lose a hemisphere adapt rather well. They may even complete college, literally with half a brain. But retardation is a more common outcome of hemispherectomy after encephalitis.

Brainstem. Central structures of the brain including the hindbrain, midbrain, thalamus, and hypothalamus.

Stroke. Sudden appearance of neurological symptoms as a result of severe interruption of blood flow.

White matter. Areas of the nervous system rich in fat-sheathed neural axons.

Gray matter. Areas of the nervous system composed predominantly of cell bodies and blood vessels.

Ventricle. A cavity in the brain that contains cerebral spinal fluid.

hemispheres and the lateral fissure at the side of the brain are both shown in various views in Figure 2-7, along with the central sulcus at the top of the cerebrum.

If we now look at the bottom of the brain, the ventral view in Figure 2-7, we see something completely different. In the midst of the wrinkled cerebrum and cerebellum emerges a smooth whitish structure with little tubes attached. This central set of structures is the **brainstem,** and the little tubes signify the cranial nerves that run to and from the brain.

One final gross feature is obvious: the brain appears to be covered in blood vessels. Like the rest of the body, the brain receives blood through arteries and sends it back through veins to the kidneys and lungs for cleaning and oxygenation. The cerebral arteries emerge from the neck to wrap around the outside of the brainstem, cerebrum, and cerebellum, finally piercing the brain's surface to nourish its inner regions.

Three major arteries feed blood to the cerebrum—namely, the anterior, middle, and posterior cerebral arteries shown in **Figure 2-8**. Because the brain is very sensitive

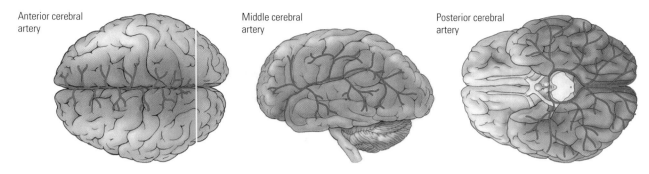

Anterior cerebral artery   Middle cerebral artery   Posterior cerebral artery

Figure 2-8

Major Cerebral Arteries   Each major artery feeds a different region of the cerebrum.

to loss of blood, a blockage or break in a cerebral artery is likely to lead to the death of the affected region, a condition known as **stroke.** Because the three cerebral arteries service different parts of the brain, strokes disrupt different brain functions, depending on the artery affected (see "Stroke" on page 44).

The Brain's Internal Features

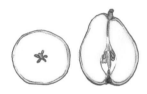

The simplest way to examine the inside of something is to cut it in half. The orientation in which we cut makes a difference in what we see, however. Consider what happens when we slice through a pear. If we cut from side to side, we cut across the core; if we cut it from top to bottom, we cut parallel to the core. Our impression of what the inside of a pear looks like is clearly influenced by the way in which we slice it. The same is true of the brain.

We can reveal the brain's inner features by slicing it downward through the middle, parallel to the front of the body, as shown in **Figure 2-9A.** The result, shown in Figure 2-9B, is known as a *frontal section* because we can now see the inside of the brain from the front. It is immediately apparent that the interior is not homogeneous.

Both light and dark regions of tissue are visible, and though these regions may not be as distinctive as the parts of a car's engine, they nevertheless represent different brain components. The light regions, called **white matter,** are mostly nerve fibers with fatty coverings that produce the white appearance, much as fat droplets in milk make it appear white. In the darker regions, called **gray matter,** capillary blood vessels and cell bodies predominate.

A second feature apparent at the middle of our frontal section are two wing-shaped cavities. The brain contains four such fluid-filled **ventricles,** which are shown in place

Ⓞ Use the *Foundations* CD to examine a three-dimensional model of the ventricular system in the section on subcortical structures in the central nervous system module.

Figure 2-9

Frontal Section Through the Brain The brain is **(A)** cut through the middle parallel to the front of the body and then **(B)** viewed at a slight angle. This frontal section displays white matter, gray matter, and the lateral ventricles. A large bundle of fibers, the corpus callosum, visible above the ventricles joins the two hemispheres.

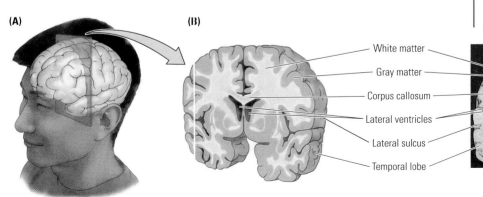

(A)   **(B)**

White matter
Gray matter
Corpus callosum
Lateral ventricles
Lateral sulcus
Temporal lobe

Glauberman/Photo Researchers

Stroke

A severe interruption of blood flow to the brain kills brain cells and causes the sudden appearance of the neurological symptoms of stroke. In the United States, someone suffers a stroke approximately every minute, producing more than a half million new stroke victims every year. Worldwide, stroke is the second leading cause of death.

Even with the best and fastest medical attention, most who endure stroke suffer some residual motor, sensory, or cognitive deficit. For every ten people who have a stroke, two die, six are disabled to varying degrees, and two recover to a degree but still endure a diminished quality of life. One in ten who survive risks further stroke.

Consequences of stroke are significant for victims, their families, and their life styles. Consider Mr. Anderson, a 45-year-old electrical engineer who took his three children to the movies one Saturday afternoon in 1998 and collapsed. Rushed to the hospital, he was diagnosed as having a massive stroke of the middle cerebral artery of his left hemisphere. The stroke has impaired Mr. Anderson's language and his motor control on the right side ever since.

Seven years after his stroke, Mr. Anderson remained unable to speak, but he could understand simple conversations. Severe difficulties in moving his right leg required him to use a walker. He could not move the fingers of his right hand and so had difficulty feeding himself, among other tasks. Mr. Anderson will probably never return to his engineering career or be able to drive or to get around on his own.

Like Mr. Anderson, most stroke survivors require help to perform everyday tasks. Their caregivers are often female relatives who give up their own careers and other pursuits. Half of these caregivers develop emotional illness, primarily depression or anxiety or both, after a year's time. Lost income

Canadian Stroke Network

In this CT scan of a brain with a stroke, the dark area of the right is the area that has been damaged by the loss of blood flow.

and stroke-related medical bills have a significant effect on the family's standard of living.

Although we tend to speak of stroke as a single disorder, two major types of strokes have been identified. In the more common and often less severe *ischemic stroke,* a blood vessel is blocked (such as by a clot). The more severe *hemorrhagic stroke* results from a burst vessel bleeding into the brain.

The hopeful news is that ischemic stroke can be treated acutely with a drug called tissue plasminogen activator (t-PA) that breaks up clots and allows a return of normal blood flow to an affected region. (Unfortunately, no treatment exists for hemorrhagic stroke, where the use of clot-preventing t-PA would be disastrous.) The results of clinical trials showed that, when patients are given t-PA within 3 hours of suffering an ischemic stroke, the number who make a nearly complete recovery increases by 32 percent compared with those who are given a placebo (Chiu et al., 1998). In addition, impairments are reduced in the remaining patients who survive the stroke.

One difficulty is that many people are unable to get to a hospital soon enough for treatment with t-PA. Most stroke victims do not make it to an emergency room until about 24 hours after symptoms appear, too late for treatment with t-PA. Apparently, most people fail to realize that stroke is an emergency.

Other drugs producing an even better outcome than does t-PA will likely become available in the future. It is hoped that these drugs will extend the 3-hour window for administering treatment after a stroke. There is also intense interest in developing treatments in the postacute period that will stimulate the brain to initiate repairative processes. Such treatment will facilitate the patient's functional improvement (see a review by Teasell et al., 2002).

in **Figure 2-10**. Cells that line the ventricles make the cerebrospinal fluid that fills them. The ventricles are connected; so the CSF flows from the two lateral ventricles (also visible in Figure 2-9) to the third and fourth ventricles that lie on the brain's midline and into the canal that runs the length of the spinal cord. The CSF is also found in the space between the lower layers of the meninges wrapping around the brain and spinal cord.

Although the functions of the ventricles are not well understood, researchers think that the ventricles play an important role in maintaining brain metabolism. The cerebral spinal fluid may allow certain compounds access to the brain, and it probably helps the brain excrete metabolic wastes. In the event of head or spinal trauma, CSF cushions the blow.

Another way to cut through the brain is perpendicular to front to back. The result is a side view, or *sagittal* section (**Figure 2-11A**). If we make our cut down the brain's midline, we divide the cerebrum into its two hemispheres, revealing several distinctive brain components (Figure 2-11B). One is a long band of white matter that runs much of the length of the cerebral hemispheres. This band, the **corpus callosum,** contains about 200 million nerve fibers that join the two hemispheres and allow communication between them.

Figure 2-11B clearly shows that the cortex covers the cerebral hemispheres above the corpus callosum, whereas below it are various internal structures. Owing to their location below the cortex, these structures are known as *subcortical* regions. These older brain regions generally control basic physiological functions, whereas the newer cortical structures process motor, sensory, perceptual, and cognitive functions.

Recall from Chapter 1 that bilateral symmetry and segmentation are two important structural features of the human nervous system. If you were to compare the left and right hemispheres in sagittal section, you would be struck by their symmetry. The brain, in fact, has two of nearly every structure, one on each side. The few one-of-a-kind structures, such as the third and fourth ventricles, are found along the brain's midline. Another one-of-a-kind example is the pineal gland, mentioned in Chapter 1 as the seat of the mind in Descartes's theory about how the brain works.

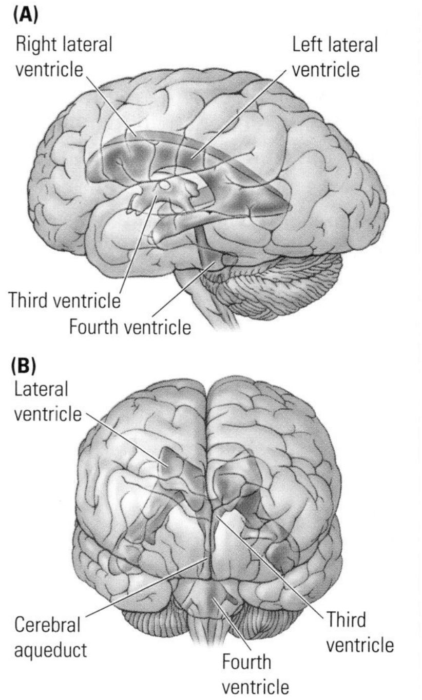

Microscopic Inspection: Cells and Fibers

Although the parts of a car engine are all large enough to be seen with the naked eye, the fundamental units of the brain—its cells—are so small that they can be viewed only with the aid of a microscope. By using a microscope, we quickly discover that the brain has two main types of cells: *neurons* and *glia*, illustrated in **Figure 2-12**. The human brain contains about 80 billion neurons and 100 billion glia. Neurons carry out the brain's major functions, whereas glia aid and modulate the neurons' activities—for example, forming the fatty covering, or insulation, over neurons. Both neurons and glia come in many forms, each determined by the work done by particular cells. We examine the structures and functions of neurons and glia in Chapter 3.

(A)

Right lateral ventricle

Left lateral ventricle

Third ventricle
Fourth ventricle

(B)
Lateral ventricle

Cerebral aqueduct

Third ventricle

Fourth ventricle

Figure 2-10

Cerebral Ventricles The four ventricles are interconnected. There are two symmetrical lateral ventricles, one in each hemisphere, and the third and fourth cerebral ventricles, each of which lies in the midline of the brain.

Corpus callosum. Fiber system connecting the two cerebral hemispheres.

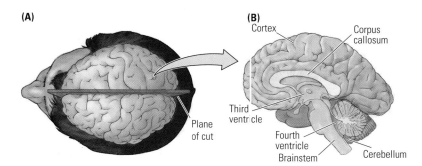

(A)

Plane of cut

(B)

Cortex

Corpus callosum

Third ventricle

Fourth ventricle

Brainstem

Cerebellum

Figure 2-11

Sagittal Section Through the Brain The brain is **(A)** cut from front to back and then **(B)** viewed from the side. This medial sagittal section separates the hemispheres, allowing a view of the midline structures of the brain, including the subcortical structures that lie below the corpus callosum.

Figure 2-12

Brain Cells A prototypical neuron (left) and glial cell (right) show that both have branches emanating from the cell body. This branching organization increases the surface area of the cell membrane. The neuron is called a pyramidal cell because the cell body is shaped somewhat like a pyramid; the glial cell is called an astrocyte because of its star-shaped appearance.

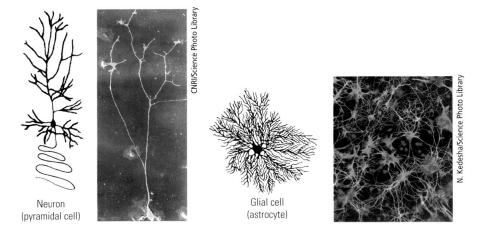

Neuron
(pyramidal cell)

Glial cell
(astrocyte)

We can see the internal structures of the brain in much more detail by dyeing their cells with special stains (**Figure 2-13**). For example, if we use a dye that selectively stains cell bodies, we can see that the distribution of cells within the gray matter of the cerebral cortex is not homogeneous but rather forms layers, as shown in Figure 2-13A and C. Each layer contains similarly staining cells. Stained subcortical regions are seen to be composed of clusters, or **nuclei,** of similar cells.

Although layers and nuclei are very different in appearance, both form functional units within the brain. Whether a particular brain region has layers or nuclei is largely an accident of evolution. By using a stain that selectively dyes the fibers of neurons, as shown in Figure 2-13B and D, we can see the borders of the subcortical nuclei more clearly. In addition, we can see that the cell bodies stained in the right-hand panels of Figure 2-13 lie in regions adjacent to the regions with most of the fibers.

A key feature of neurons is that they are connected to one another by fibers known as *axons.* When axons run along together, much like the wires that run from a car engine to the dashboard, they form a **nerve** or a **tract.** By convention, the term *tract* is usually used to refer to collections of nerve fibers found within the brain and spinal cord, whereas bundles of fibers located outside these CNS structures are typically referred to simply as *nerves.* Thus, the pathway from the eye to the brain is known as the optic nerve, whereas the pathway from the cerebral cortex to the spinal cord is known as the corticospinal tract.

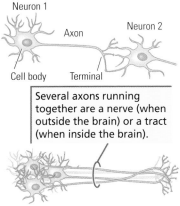

Neuron 1

Axon

Neuron 2

Cell body   Terminal

Several axons running together are a nerve (when outside the brain) or a tract (when inside the brain).

Figure 2-13

Cortical Layers and Glia Brain sections from the left hemisphere of a monkey (midline is to the left in each image). Cells are stained with **(A)** a selective cell-body stain (Nissl stain) for neurons and **(B)** a selective fiber stain, staining for insulating glial cells, or *myelin.* The images reveal very different pictures of the brain at a microscopic level. Closer up **(C and D)**, notice the difference in appearance between these higher-power micrographs through the gray- and white-matter sections of different cortical regions.

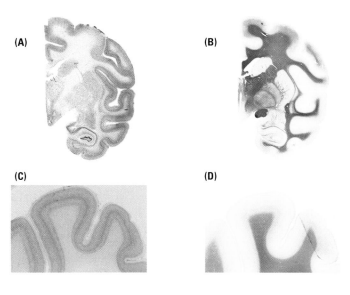

(A)

(B)

(C)

(D)

In Review

Inside the skull and under the meninges, we find two main brain structures: the cerebrum and the cerebellum. Both are separated into roughly symmetrical hemispheres that have many gyri and sulci covering their surfaces. At the base of the brain, we see the brainstem, of which the cerebellum is a part. Cutting open the brain, we observe the fluid-filled ventricles, the corpus callosum that connects the two cerebral hemispheres, and the cortex and subcortical regions below it. We also see that brain tissue is of two main types: white matter and gray matter.

Nucleus (pl. nuclei). A group of cells forming a cluster that can be identified with special stains to form a functional grouping.

Nerve. Large collection of axons coursing together outside the central nervous system.

Tract. Large collection of axons coursing together within the central nervous system.

NEUROANATOMY AND FUNCTIONAL ORGANIZATION OF THE NERVOUS SYSTEM

When we look under the hood, we can make some pretty good guesses about what each part of a car engine does. The battery must provide electrical power to run the radio and lights, for example, and, because batteries need to be charged, the engine must contain some mechanism for charging them. We can take the same approach to deduce the functions of the parts of the brain. For example, the part of the brain connected to the optic nerve coming from each eye must have something to do with vision. Similarly, brain structures connected to the auditory nerve coming from each ear must have something to do with hearing.

From these simple observations we can begin to understand how the brain is organized. The real test of inferences about the brain comes in analyzing actual brain function: how this seeming jumble of parts produces behaviors as complex as human thought. The place to start is the brain's anatomy.

Evolutionary Development of the Nervous System

The developing brain is less complex than the mature adult brain and provides a clearer picture of its basic structural plan. As detailed in Chapter 7, the biological similarity of embryos of vertebrate species as diverse as amphibians and mammals is striking in the earliest stages of development. The brain of a young vertebrate embryo begins as a sheet of cells that folds into a hollow tube and develops into three regions: forebrain, midbrain, and hindbrain.

These three regions of the primitive developing brain are recognizable as a series of three enlargements at the end of the embryonic spinal cord (**Figure 2-14A**). The adult brain of a fish, amphibian, or reptile is roughly equivalent to this three-part brain. The *prosencephalon* (front brain) is responsible for olfaction, the *mesencephalon* (middle brain) is the seat of vision and hearing, and the *rhombencephalon* (hindbrain) controls movement and balance. The spinal cord is considered part of the hindbrain.

In mammals, the prosencephalon develops further to form the cerebral hemispheres, the cortex and subcortical structures known collectively as the *telencephalon* (endbrain), and the *diencephalon* (between brain) containing the thalamus, among other structures (Figure 2-14B). The hindbrain also develops further into the *metencephalon* (across brain), which includes the enlarged cerebellum, and the *myelencephalon* (spinal brain), including the medulla and the spinal cord.

The human brain is a more complex mammalian brain, possessing especially large cerebral hemispheres while retaining most of the features of other mammalian

(A) Vertebrate

Prosencephalon
Mesencephalon
Rhombencephalon
Spinal cord

(B) Mammalian embryo

Telencephalon
Diencephalon
Mesencephalon
Myelencephalon
Spinal cord
Metencephalon

(C) Fully developed human brain

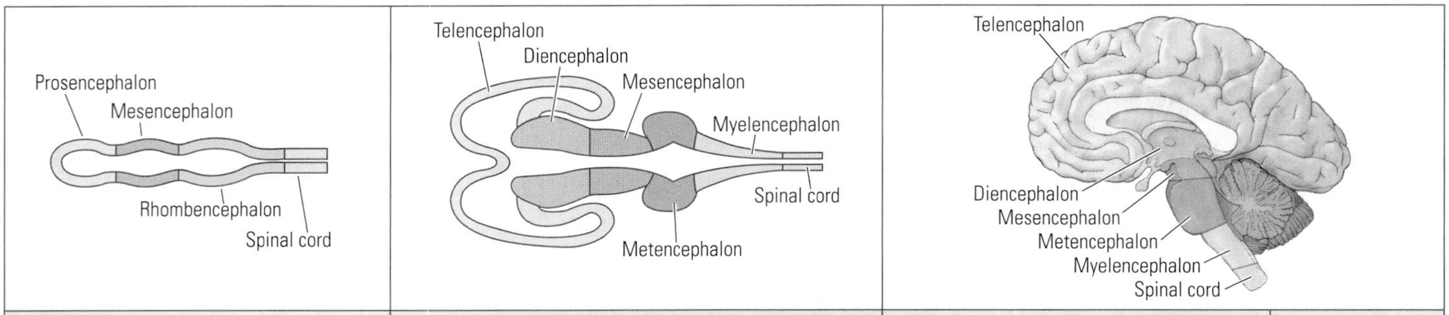

Telencephalon
Diencephalon
Mesencephalon
Metencephalon
Myelencephalon
Spinal cord

Prosencephalon (forebrain)	Telencephalon (end brain)	Neocortex, basal ganglia, limbic system olfactory bulb, lateral ventricles	Forebrain
	Diencephalon (between brain)	Thalamus, hypothalamus, pineal body, third ventricle	
Mesencephalon (midbrain)	Mesencephalon	Tectum, tegmentum, cerebral aqueduct	Brainstem
Rhombencephalon (hindbrain)	Metencephalon (across-brain)	Cerebellum, pons, fourth ventricle	
	Myelencephalon (spinal brain)	Medulla oblongata, fourth ventricle	
Spinal cord	Spinal cord	Spinal cord	Spinal cord

Figure 2-14

Stages in Brain Evolution and Development The forebrain grows dramatically in the evolution of the mammalian brain.

brains (Figure 2-14C). Most behaviors are not the product of a single locus in the brain but rather of many brain areas and levels. These several nervous system layers do not simply replicate function; rather, each region adds a different dimension to the behavior. This hierarchical organization affects virtually every behavior in which humans engage.

The Central Nervous System

With its literally thousands of parts, learning the name of a particular CNS structure is pointless without also learning something about its function. In this section, therefore, we focus on the names and functions of the major components of the CNS outlined in Table 2-2: the spinal cord, the brainstem, and the forebrain.

These three subdivisions reinforce the concept of *levels of function,* with newer levels partly replicating the work of older ones. A simple analogy to this evolutionary progress is learning to read. When you began to read, you learned simple words and sentences. As you progressed, you mastered new, more challenging words and longer, more complicated sentences, but you still retained the simpler skills that you had learned first. Much later, you encountered Shakespeare, with a complexity and subtlety of language unimagined in grade school, taking you to a new level of reading comprehension.

Each new level of training adds new abilities that overlap and build on previously acquired skills. Yet all the functional levels deal with reading. Likewise, in the course of natural selection, the brain has evolved functional levels that overlap one another in purpose but allow for a growing complex-

Table 2-2   Anatomical Divisions of the Central Nervous System

Anatomical division	Functional division	Principal structures
Forebrain	Forebrain	Cerebral cortex
		Basal ganglia
		Limbic system
Brainstem	Diencephalon	Thalamus
		Hypothalamus
	Midbrain	Tectum
		Tegmentum
	Hindbrain	Cerebellum
		Pons
		Medulla oblongata
		Reticular formation
Spinal cord	Spinal nerves	Cervical nerves
		Thoracic nerves
		Lumbar nerves
		Sacral nerves

ity of behavior. For instance, the brain has functional levels that control movements. With the evolution of each new level, the complexity of movement becomes increasingly refined. We expand on the principle of evolutionary levels of function later in this chapter.

THE SPINAL CORD

Although producing movement is one function of the brain, it is ultimately the spinal cord that controls most body movements. To understand how important the spinal cord is, think of the old saying "running around like a chicken with its head cut off." When a chicken's head is lopped off to provide dinner for the farmer's family, the chicken is still capable of running around the barnyard until it collapses from loss of blood. The chicken accomplishes this feat because the spinal cord can act independently of the brain.

You can demonstrate movement controlled by the spinal cord in your own body by tapping your patellar tendon, just below your kneecap (the patella). Your lower leg kicks out and, try as you might, it is very hard to prevent the movement from occurring. Your brain, in other words, has trouble inhibiting the reaction. This type of automatic movement is known as a *spinal reflex,* a topic that we return to in Chapter 10.

THE BRAINSTEM

The brainstem begins where the spinal cord enters the skull and extends upward to the lower areas of the forebrain. The brainstem receives afferent nerves from all of the body's senses, and it sends efferent nerves to control all of the body's movements except the most complex movements of the fingers and toes. The brainstem, then, both produces movements and creates a sensory world.

In some animals, such as frogs, the entire brain is largely equivalent to the brainstem of mammals or birds. And frogs get along quite well, demonstrating that the brainstem is a fairly sophisticated piece of machinery. If we had only a brainstem, we would still be able to create a world, but it would be a far simpler, sensorimotor world, more like what a frog experiences.

The brainstem can be divided into three regions: **hindbrain, midbrain,** and **diencephalon,** sometimes called the "between brain" because it borders upper and lower parts of the brain. In fact, the "between brain" status of the diencephalon can be seen in a neuroanatomical inconsistency: some anatomists place it in the brainstem and others place it in the forebrain. The left side of **Figure 2-15** illustrates the location of these three brainstem regions under the cerebral hemispheres, and the right side of the figure compares the shape of the brainstem regions to the lower part of your arm held upright. The hindbrain is long and thick like your forearm, the midbrain is short and compact like your wrist, and the diencephalon at the end is bulbous like your hand forming a fist.

The hindbrain and midbrain are essentially extensions of the spinal cord; they developed first as simple animals evolved a brain at the anterior end of the body. It makes

Hindbrain. Evolutionarily the oldest part of the brain; contains the pons, medulla, reticular formation, and cerebellum structures that coordinate and control most voluntary and involuntary movements.

Midbrain. Central part of the brain that contains neural circuits for hearing and seeing as well as orienting movements.

Diencephalon. The "between brain" that contains the hypothalamus, thalamus, and epithalamus; thought to coordinate many basic instinctual behaviors, including temperature regulation, sexual behavior, and eating.

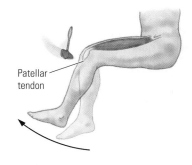

Patellar tendon

🔘 On the *Foundations* CD, visit the module on the central nervous system for a detailed, three-dimensional view of the brainstem.

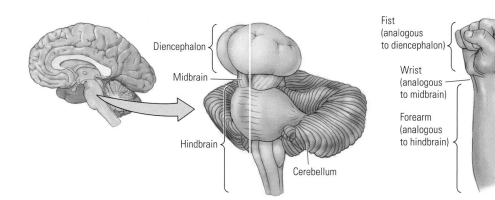

Diencephalon

Midbrain

Hindbrain

Cerebellum

Fist (analogous to diencephalon)

Wrist (analogous to midbrain)

Forearm (analogous to hindbrain)

Figure 2-15

Brainstem Structures   Medial view of the brain at left shows the relation of the brainstem to the cerebral hemisphere. Brainstem structures perform both sensory and motor functions.

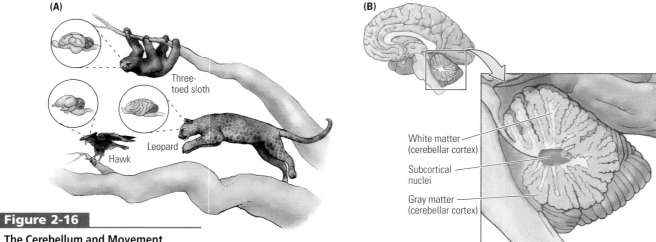

(A)

Three-toed sloth

Leopard

Hawk

(B)

White matter (cerebellar cortex)

Subcortical nuclei

Gray matter (cerebellar cortex)

Figure 2-16

The Cerebellum and Movement
(A) Their relatively large cerebellums enable fine, coordinated movements such as flight and landing in birds and prey-catching in cats. Slow-moving animals like the sloth have relatively smaller cerebellums. **(B)** Like the cerebrum, the cerebellum has a cortex with gray and white matter and subcortical nuclei.

Figure 2-17

Hindbrain The principal structures of the hindbrain integrate both voluntary and involuntary body movement.

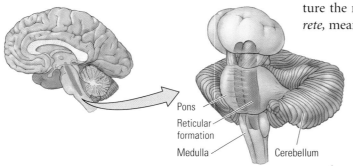

Pons

Reticular formation

Medulla

Cerebellum

sense, therefore, that these lower brainstem regions should retain a division between structures having sensory functions and those having motor functions, with sensory structures located dorsally and motor ones ventrally.

Each brainstem region performs more than a single task. Each contains various subparts, made up of groupings of nuclei that serve different purposes. All three regions, in fact, have both sensory and motor functions. However, the hindbrain is especially important in motor functions, the midbrain in sensory functions, and the diencephalon in integrative tasks. Here we consider the central functions of these three regions; later chapters contain more detailed information about them.

The Hindbrain The hindbrain controls various motor functions ranging from breathing to balance to fine movements, such as those used in dancing. Its most distinctive structure, and one of the largest structures of the human brain, is the cerebellum. The size of the cerebellum increases with the physical speed and dexterity of a species, as shown in **Figure 2-16A**. Animals that move relatively slowly (such as a sloth) have relatively small cerebellums for their body size, whereas animals that can perform rapid, acrobatic movements (such as a hawk or a cat) have very large cerebellums. The cerebellum, which resembles a cauliflower when viewed in sagittal section in Figure 2-16B, is important in controlling complex movements and apparently has a role in a variety of cognitive functions as well.

As we look below the cerebellum at the rest of the hindbrain, shown in **Figure 2-17**, we find three subparts: the *reticular formation,* the *pons,* and the *medulla.* Extending the length of the entire brainstem at its core, the **reticular formation** is a netlike mixture of neurons (gray matter) and nerve fibers (white matter) that gives this structure the mottled appearance from which its name derives (from the Latin *rete,* meaning "net"). The reticular formation has a variety of functions that are localized along its length into small patches, each with a special function in stimulating the forebrain, such as in awakening from sleep. Not surprisingly, the reticular formation is sometimes also called the *reticular activating system.*

The pons and medulla contain substructures that control many vital movements of the body. Nuclei within the pons receive inputs from the cerebellum and actually bridge it (the Latin word *pons* means "bridge") to the rest of the brain. At the rostral tip of the spinal cord, the medulla's nuclei control such vital functions as the regulation of breathing and the cardiovascular system. For this reason, a blow to the back of the head can kill you—your breathing stops if the control centers in the hindbrain are injured.

The Midbrain   In the midbrain, shown in **Figure 2-18**, the sensory component, the **tectum,** is located dorsally, whereas a motor structure, the **tegmentum,** is ventral (*tectum* meaning roof and *tegmentum* meaning floor). The tectum receives a massive amount of sensory information from the eyes and ears. The optic nerve sends a large bundle of nerve fibers to the *superior colliculus,* whereas the *inferior colliculus* receives much of its input from auditory pathways. (*Collis* in Latin means hill; thus the colliculi appear to be four little hills on the upper surface of the midbrain.) The colliculi function not only to process sensory information but also produce **orienting movements** related to sensory inputs, such as turning your head to see the source of a sound.

This orienting behavior is not as simple as it may seem. To produce it, the auditory and visual systems must share some sort of common "map" of the external world so that the ears can tell the eyes where to look. If the auditory and visual systems had different maps, it would be impossible to use the two systems together. In fact, the colliculi also have a tactile map. After all, if you want to look at the source of an itch on your leg, your visual and tactile systems need a common representation of where that place is.

Lying ventral to the tectum, the tegmentum (shown in cross section in Figure 2-18) is not a single structure but rather is composed of many nuclei, largely with movement-related functions. Several of its nuclei control eye movements. The so-called *red nucleus* controls limb movements, and the *substantia nigra* is connected to the forebrain, a connection especially important in initiating movements. The *periacqueductal gray matter,* made up of cell bodies that surround the acqueduct joining the third and fourth ventricles, contains circuits controlling species-typical behaviors (e.g., female sexual behavior). These nuclei also play an important role in the modulation of pain by opiates.

The Diencephalon   The diencephalon, shown in sagittal section at the top left in **Figure 2-19**, has more anatomical structures than the hindbrain and midbrain have, owing to its roles in integrating both motor and sensory functions. The two principal structures of the diencephalon are the hypothalamus and the thalamus. Both are visible on the ventral view in Figure 2-7, where the thalamus is just to the left of the tip of the brainstem, and the hypothalamus is to the left of the thalamus.

The **hypothalamus** is composed of about 22 small nuclei, as well as nerve-fiber systems that pass through it. Attached to the base of the hypothalamus is the pituitary gland, shown at the bottom left in Figure 2-19. Although constituting only about 0.3 percent of the brain's weight, the hypothalamus takes part in nearly all aspects of behavior, including feeding, sexual behavior, sleeping, temperature regulation, emotional behavior, hormone function, and movement.

The hypothalamus is organized more or less similarly in different mammals, largely because the control of feeding, temperature, and so on, is carried out similarly. But there are sex differences in the structures of some parts of the hypothalamus, which are probably due to differences between males and females in activities such as sexual behavior and parenting. A critical function of the hypothalamus is to control the body's production of hormones, which is accomplished by interactions with the pituitary gland.

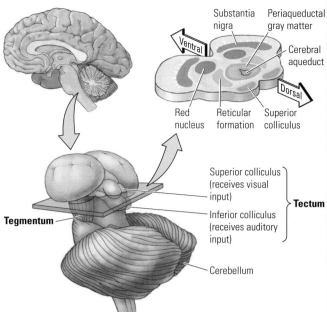

Figure 2-18

Midbrain   Structures in the midbrain are critical in producing orienting movements, species-specific behaviors, and the perception of pain.

Reticular formation. Midbrain area in which nuclei and fiber pathways are mixed, producing a netlike appearance; associated with sleep–wake behavior and behavioral arousal.

Tectum. Roof (area above the ventricle) of the midbrain; its functions are sensory processing, particularly visual and auditory, and producing orienting movements.

Tegmentum. Floor (area below the ventricle) of the midbrain; a collection of nuclei with movement-related, species-specific, and pain-perception functions.

Orienting movement. Movement related to sensory inputs, such as turning the head to see the source of a sound.

Hypothalamus. Diencephalon structure that contains many nuclei associated with temperature regulation, eating, drinking, and sexual behavior.

Diencephalon

Thalamus

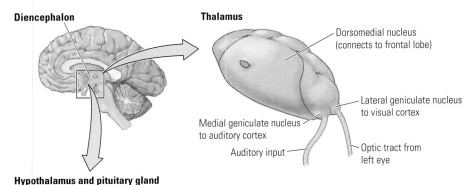

Dorsomedial nucleus
(connects to frontal lobe)

Lateral geniculate nucleus
to visual cortex

Medial geniculate nucleus
to auditory cortex

Auditory input

Optic tract from
left eye

Hypothalamus and pituitary gland

Hypothalamus

Pituitary stalk

Pituitary gland

Figure 2-19

Diencephalon The connections of only 3 of the 20-odd thalamic nuclei are shown for the right thalamus, but each nucleus connects to a discrete region of cortex. Lying below (hypo) the thalamus, at the base of the brain, the hypothalamus and pituitary lie above the roof of the mouth. The pituitary gland lies adjacent to the optic chiasm, where the left and right optic tracts (originating from the eyes) cross over en route to the occipital lobe.

The other principal structure of the diencephalon, the **thalamus,** is much larger than the hypothalamus. Like the hypothalamus, the thalamus contains about 20 nuclei, although the thalamic nuclei are much larger than those in the hypothalamus. Perhaps most distinctive among the functions of the thalamus is its role as a kind of gateway for channeling sensory information traveling to the cerebral cortex.

All sensory systems send inputs to the thalamus for information integration and relay to the appropriate area in the cortex. The optic nerve, for example, sends information through a large bundle of fibers to a region of the thalamus, the *lateral geniculate nucleus,* shown on the right in Figure 2-19. In turn, the lateral geniculate nucleus processes some of this information and then sends it to the visual region of the cortex. The routes to the thalamus may be somewhat indirect; for example, the route for olfaction traverses several synapses before entering the dorsomedial nucleus of the thalamus. Analogous sensory regions of the thalamus receive auditory and tactile information, which is subsequently relayed to the respective auditory and tactile cortical regions.

Some thalamic regions have motor functions or perform an integrative task. One region with an integrative function is the *dorsomedial thalamic nucleus* (see Figure 2-19). It has connections to most of the frontal lobe of the cortex. We return to the thalamic sensory nuclei in Chapters 8 through 10, where we examine how sensory information is processed. Other thalamic regions are considered in Chapters 11 and 13, where we explore motivation and memory.

Ⓞ For a three-dimensional view of the hypothalamus and thalamus, visit the central nervous system module on the *Foundations* CD. To examine the structures, go to the overview and look in the section on subcortical structures.

THE FOREBRAIN

The **forebrain,** whose major internal and external structures are shown in **Figure 2-20,** is the largest region of the mammalian brain. Each of its three principal structures has multiple functions. To summarize briefly, the **neocortex,** another name for the cerebral cortex, regulates a host of mental activities ranging from perception to planning; the **basal ganglia** control voluntary movement; and the **limbic system** regulates emotions and behaviors that create and require memory. You will encounter each of these forebrain structures in detail later in this book.

Extending our analogy between the brainstem and your forearm, imagine that the "fist" of the brainstem (the diencephalon) is thrust inside a watermelon. The watermelon represents the forebrain, with the rind being the cortex and the fruit inside being the limbic system and the basal ganglia. By varying the size of the watermelon, we can vary the size of the brain, which in a sense is what evolution has done. The forebrain varies considerably in size across species (see Figure 2-2).

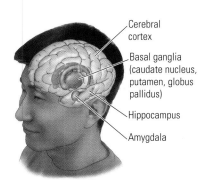

Cerebral
cortex

Basal ganglia
(caudate nucleus,
putamen, globus
pallidus)

Hippocampus

Amygdala

Figure 2-20

Forebrain Structures The major structures of the forebrain integrate sensation, emotion, and memory to enable advanced cognitive functions such as thinking, planning, and language.

The Cortex   There are actually two types of cortex, the old and the new. The neocortex (new bark) has six layers of gray matter on top of a layer of white matter. The neocortex is the tissue that is visible when we view the brain from the outside, as in Figure 2-7. The neocortex is unique to mammals, and its primary function is to create and respond to a perceptual world.

The older cortex, sometimes called *limbic cortex,* has three or four layers of gray matter on top of a layer of white matter. This tissue is not easily observed on the outside surface of the human brain, except where it forms the *cingulate cortex,* a region visible in medial views lying just above the corpus callosum (see the medial view in Figure 2-7). The limbic cortex is more primitive than the neocortex. It is found in the brains of other chordates in addition to mammals, especially in birds and reptiles.

The limbic cortex is thought to play a role in controlling motivational states. Although anatomical and functional differences exist between the neocortex and the limbic cortex, the distinctions are not critical for most discussions in this book. Therefore, we will usually refer to both types of tissue simply as cortex.

Measured by volume, the cortex makes up most of the forebrain, comprising 80 percent of the human brain overall. It is the brain region that has expanded the most during mammalian evolution. The human neocortex has a surface area as large as 2500 square centimeters but a thickness of only 1.5 to 3.0 millimeters. This area is equivalent to about four pages of this book. (In contrast, a chimpanzee has a cortical area equivalent to about one page.)

The pattern of sulci and gyri formed by the folding of the cortex varies across species. Some species, such as rats, have no sulci or gyri, whereas carnivores have gyri that form a longitudinal pattern (look back at the cat brain in Figure 2-2). In primates, the sulci and gyri form a more diffuse pattern.

As you know, the human cortex consists of two nearly symmetrical hemispheres, the left and the right, which are separated by the longitudinal fissure. Each hemisphere is subdivided into the four lobes, corresponding to the skull bones overlying each hemisphere, introduced in Chapter 1: frontal, temporal, parietal, and occipital. Unfortunately, bone location and brain function are unrelated. As a result, the lobes of the cortex are rather arbitrarily defined regions that include many different functional zones.

Nonetheless, we can attach some gross functions to each lobe. The three posterior lobes have sensory functions: the occipital lobe is visual; the parietal lobe is tactile; and the temporal lobe is visual, auditory, and gustatory. In contrast, the frontal lobe is motor and is sometimes referred to as the brain's "executive" because it integrates sensory and motor functions and formulates plans of action.

Fissures and sulci often establish the boundaries of cortical lobes. For instance, in humans, the central sulcus and lateral fissure form the boundaries of each frontal lobe. They also form the boundaries of each parietal lobe, but in this case the lobes lie posterior to the central sulcus. The lateral fissure demarcates each temporal lobe as well, forming its dorsal boundary. The occipital lobes are not so clearly separated from the parietal and temporal lobes, because no large fissure marks their boundaries. Traditionally, the occipital lobes are defined on the basis of other anatomical features, which are presented in Chapter 8.

The layers of the cortex have several distinct characteristics:

■ Different layers have different cell types.
■ The density of cells in each layer varies, ranging from virtually no cells in layer I (the top layer) to very dense cell packing in layer IV (**Figure 2-21**).
■ Other differences in appearance relate to the functions of cortical layers in different regions. These visible differences led neuroanatomists of the early twentieth century to

Thalamus. Diencephalon structure through which information from all sensory systems is integrated and projected into the appropriate region of the neocortex.

Forebrain. Evolutionarily the newest part of the brain; coordinates advanced cognitive functions such as thinking, planning, and language; contains the limbic system, basal ganglia, and the neocortex.

Neocortex (cerebral cortex). Newest, outer layer (new bark) of the forebrain and composed of about six layers of gray matter that creates our reality.

Basal ganglia. Group of nuclei in the forebrain that coordinates voluntary movements of the limbs and the body; located just beneath the neocortex and connected to the thalamus and to the midbrain.

Limbic system. Disparate forebrain structures lying between the neocortex and the brainstem that form a functional system controlling affective and motivated behaviors and certain forms of memory; includes cingulate cortex, amygdala, hippocampus, among other structures.

⊙ Visit the module on the central nervous system on the *Foundations* CD to view a three-dimensional model of the cortex, along with photographs of cortical sections.

⊙ Visit the *Brain and Behavior* Web site (**www.worthpublishers.com/kolb**) and go to the Chapter 2 Web links to see how the cortex looks in other animals.

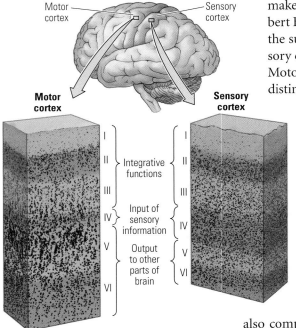

Figure 2-21

Layering in the Neocortex   As this comparison of cortical layers in the sensory and motor cortices shows, layer IV is relatively thick in the sensory cortex and relatively thin in the motor cortex. Afferents go to layer IV (from the thalamus) as well as to layers II and III. Efferents go to other parts of the cortex and to the motor structures of the brain.

Cytoarchitectonic map. Map of the neocortex based on the organization, structure, and distribution of the cells.

make maps of the cortex, like the one in **Figure 2-22A** that was developed by Albert Brodmann in about 1905. Because these maps are based on cell characteristics, the subject of cytology, they are called **cytoarchitectonic maps.** For example, sensory cortex in the parietal lobe, shown in red in Figure 2-21, has a distinct layer IV. Motor cortex in the frontal lobe, shown in blue in the same illustration, has a more distinctive layer V. Layer IV is an afferent layer, whereas layer V is efferent. It makes sense that a sensory region would have a large input layer, whereas a motor region would have a large output layer.

Chemical differences in the cells in different cortical layers can be revealed by staining the tissue. Some regions are rich in one chemical, whereas others are rich in another. These differences are presumably related to functional specialization of different areas of the cortex.

The one significant difference between the organization of the cortex and the organization of other parts of the brain is its range of connections. Unlike most brain structures that connect to only selective brain regions, the cortex is connected to virtually all other parts of the brain. The cortex, in other words, is the ultimate meddler. It takes part in everything. This fact not only makes it difficult to identify specific functions of the cortex but also complicates our study of the rest of the brain because the cortex's role in other brain regions must always be considered.

To illustrate, consider your perception of clouds. You have no doubt gazed up at clouds on a summer's day and imagined sailing ships, elephants, faces, and countless other objects. Although a cloud does not really look exactly like an elephant, you can concoct an image of one if you impose your frontal cortex—that is, your imagination—on the sensory inputs. This kind of cortical activity is known as *top-down processing* because the top level of the nervous system, the cortex, is influencing how information is processed in lower regions—in this case, the midbrain and hindbrain.

The cortex influences many behaviors besides the perception of objects. It influences our cravings for foods, our lust for things (or people), and how we interpret the meaning of abstract concepts, words, and images. The cortex is the ultimate creator of our reality, and one reason that it serves this function is that it is so well connected.

The Basal Ganglia   A collection of nuclei that lie within the forebrain just below the white matter of the cortex, the basal ganglia consist of three principal structures: the *caudate nucleus,* the *putamen,* and the *globus pallidus,* all shown in **Figure 2-23.** Together with the thalamus and two closely associated structures, the *substantia nigra* and *subthalamic nucleus,* the basal ganglia form a system that functions primarily to control certain aspects of voluntary movement.

Figure 2-22

Brain Maps   **(A)** In his cytoarchitectonic map of the cortex, Brodmann defined areas by the organization and characteristics of the cells. **(B)** This schematic map shows the regions associated with the simplest sensory perceptions of touch, vision, and audition. As we shall see, the areas of the cortex that process sensory information are far greater than these basic areas.

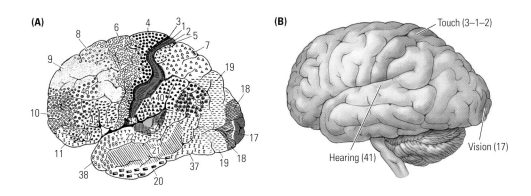

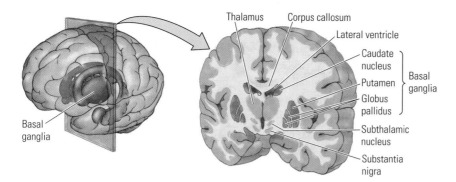

Figure 2-23

Basal Ganglia   This frontal section of the cerebral hemispheres shows the basal ganglia relative to surrounding structures. Two associated structures, the substantia nigra and subthalamic nucleus, instrumental in controlling and coordinating movement, also are illustrated.

We can observe the functions of the basal ganglia by analyzing the behavior that results from the many diseases that interfere with the normal functioning of these nuclei. People afflicted with Parkinson's disease, one of the most common disorders of movement in the elderly, take short, shuffling steps, display bent posture, and often require a walker to get around. Many have an almost continual tremor of the hands and sometimes of the head as well. (We return to this disorder in Chapters 5 and 10.) Another disorder of the basal ganglia is Tourette's syndrome, characterized by various motor tics, involuntary vocalizations (including curse words and animal sounds), and odd, involuntary movements of the body, especially of the face and head.

Neither Parkinson's disease nor Tourette's syndrome is a disorder of *producing* movements, as in paralysis. Rather they are disorders of *controlling* movements. The basal ganglia, therefore, must play a role in the control and coordination of movement patterns, not in activating the muscles.

The Limbic System   In the 1930s, psychiatry was dominated by the theories of Sigmund Freud, who emphasized the roles of sexuality and emotion in understanding human behavior. At the time, regions controlling these behaviors had not been identified in the brain, but a group of brain structures, collectively called the limbic system, as yet had no known function. It was a simple step to thinking that perhaps the limbic system played a central role in sexuality and emotion.

One sign that this hypothesis might be right came from James Papez, who discovered that people with rabies have infections of limbic structures, and one of the symptoms of rabies is emotionality. We now know that such a simple view of the limbic system is inaccurate. In fact, the limbic system is not a unitary system at all, and, although some limbic structures have roles in emotion and sexual behaviors, limbic structures serve other functions, too, including memory and motivation.

The principal structures of the limbic system are shown in **Figure 2-24**. They include the *amygdala,* the *hippocampus,* and the *limbic,* or *cingulate, cortex,* which lies in the cingulate gyrus between the cerebral hemispheres. Removal of the amygdala produces truly startling changes in emotional behavior. For example, a cat with the amygdala removed will wander through a colony of monkeys, completely undisturbed by their hooting and threats. No self-respecting cat would normally be caught anywhere near such bedlam.

The hippocampus, the cingulate cortex, and associated structures have roles in certain memory functions, as well as in the control of navigation in space. Many limbic structures also are believed to be at least partly responsible for the rewarding properties of psychoactive drugs. As we shall see in Chapter 7, repeated exposure to drugs such as amphetamine or nicotine produces both chemical and structural changes in the cingulate cortex and hippocampus, among other structures.

◉ Visit the central nervous system module on the *Foundations* CD for a three-dimensional view of the basal ganglia. To see the model, go to the overview and look in the section on subcortical structures.

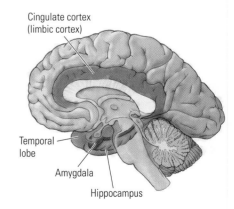

Figure 2-24

Limbic System   This medial view of the right hemisphere illustrates the principal structures of the limbic system that play roles in emotional and sexual behaviors and memory.

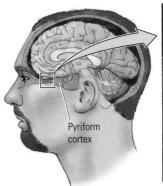
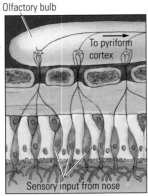

The Olfactory System At the very front of the brain lie the *olfactory bulbs,* the organs responsible for our sense of smell. The olfactory system is unique among the senses, as **Figure 2-25** shows, because it is almost entirely a forebrain structure (see also the ventral view in Figure 2-7). Recall that the other sensory systems project most of their inputs from the sensory receptors to the midbrain and thalamus. Olfactory input takes a less direct route: the olfactory bulb sends most of its inputs to a specialized region, the *pyriform cortex,* at the bottom of the brain before progressing to the dorsal medial thalamus, which then provides a route to the frontal cortex.

Compared with the olfactory bulbs of animals such as rats and dogs, which depend more heavily on the sense of smell than we do, the human olfactory bulb is relatively small. Nonetheless, it is still sensitive and plays an important role in various aspects of our feeding and sexual behavior. We return to the olfactory system in Chapter 11.

Figure 2-25

Sense of Smell The relatively small olfactory bulb of humans lies at the base of the human brain and is connected to receptor cells that lie in the nasal cavity.

The Somatic Nervous System

The somatic nervous system (SNS) is monitored and controlled by the CNS—the cranial nerves by the brain and the spinal nerves by the spinal cord.

THE CRANIAL NERVES

The linkages provided by the **cranial nerves** between the brain and various parts of the head and neck as well as various internal organs are illustrated and tabulated in **Figure 2-26.** Cranial nerves can have afferent functions, such as sensory inputs to the brain from the eyes, ears, mouth, and nose, or they can have efferent functions, such as motor

Figure 2-26

Cranial Nerves Each of the 12 pairs of cranial nerves has a different function. A common mnemonic device for learning the order of the cranial nerves is, On old Olympus's towering top, a Finn and German vainly skip and hop. The first letter of each word (except the last *and*) is, in order, the first letter of the name of each nerve.

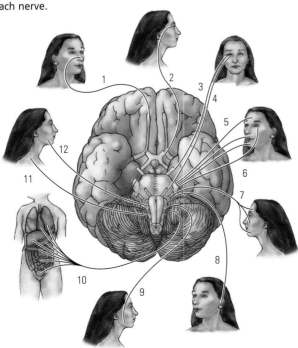

Cranial nerve	Name	Function
1	Olfactory	Smell
2	Optic	Vision
3	Oculomotor	Eye movement
4	Trochlear	Eye movement
5	Trigeminal	Masticatory movements and facial sensation
6	Abducens	Eye movement
7	Facial	Facial movement and sensation
8	Auditory vestibular	Hearing and balance
9	Glossopharyngeal	Tongue and pharynx movement and sensation
10	Vagus	Heart, blood vessels, viscera, movement of larynx and pharynx
11	Spinal accessory	Neck muscles
12	Hypoglossal	Tongue muscles

control of the facial muscles, tongue, and eyes. Some cranial nerves have both sensory and motor functions, such as the modulation of both sensation and movement in the face.

The 12 pairs of cranial nerves are known both by their numbers and by their names (see Figure 2-26). One set of 12 controls the left side of the head, whereas the other set controls the head's right side. This arrangement makes sense for innervating duplicated parts of the head (such as the eyes), but it is not so clear why separate nerves should control the right and left sides of a singular structure (such as the tongue). Yet that is how the cranial nerves work. If you have ever received novocaine for dental work, you know that usually just one side of your tongue becomes anesthetized because the dentist injects the drug into only one side of your mouth. The rest of the skin and muscles on each side of the head are similarly controlled by cranial nerves located on that same side.

We consider many of the cranial nerves in some detail in later chapters in discussions on topics such as vision, hearing, and responses to stress. For now, you simply need to know that cranial nerves form part of the somatic nervous system, providing inputs to the brain from the head's sensory organs and muscles and controlling head and facial movements. The cranial nerves also contribute to maintaining autonomic functions by connecting the brain and internal organs and by influencing other autonomic responses, such as salivation.

THE SPINAL NERVES

The spinal cord lies inside the bony spinal column, which is made up of a series of small bones called **vertebrae,** categorized into five regions from top to bottom: *cervical, thoracic, lumbar, sacral,* and *coccygeal,* as diagrammed in **Figure 2-27A.** You can think of

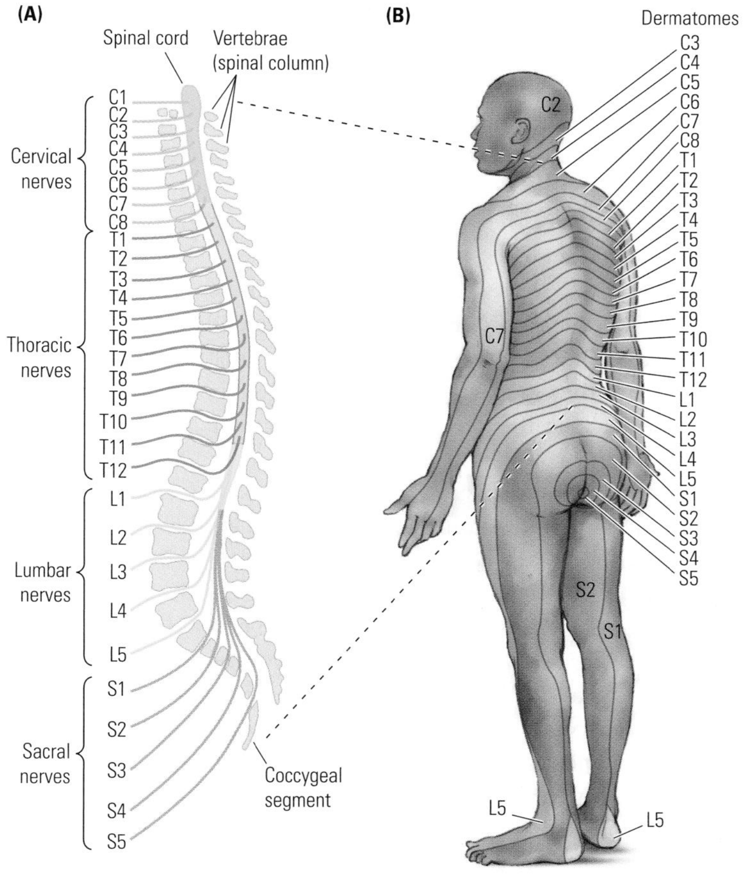

Cranial nerve. One of a set of 12 nerve pairs that control sensory and motor functions of the head, neck, and internal organs.

Vertebrae. The bones, or segments, that form the spinal column.

Figure 2-27

Spinal Segments and Dermatomes
(A) The spinal column, illustrated in sagittal view showing the five spinal-cord segments: cervical (C), thoracic (T), lumbar (L), sacral (S), and coccygeal.
(B) Each spinal segment corresponds to a dermatome supplied with afferent peripheral nerve fibers by a single spinal-cord dorsal root and identified by the segment number (examples are C5 and L2).

Dermatome. Area of the skin supplied with afferent nerve fibers by a single spinal-cord dorsal root.

Law of Bell and Magendie. The general principle that sensory fibers are located dorsally and ventral fibers are located ventrally.

○ Go to the *Foundations* CD and find the spinal-cord area of the central nervous system module. There you can see a detailed illustration of the spinal cord.

each vertebra within these five groups as a very short segment of the spinal column. The corresponding spinal-cord segment within each vertebral region functions as that segment's "minibrain."

This arrangement may seem a bit odd, but it has a long evolutionary history. Think of a simpler animal, such as a snake, which evolved long before humans did. A snake's body is a tube divided into segments. Within that tube is another tube, this one of neurons of the spinal cord, which also is segmented. Each of the snake's nervous system segments receives fibers from sensory receptors in the part of the body adjacent to it, and that nervous system segment sends fibers back to the muscles in that body part. Each segment, therefore, works independently.

A complication arises in animals lsuch as humans, who have limbs that may originate at one spinal-segment level but extend past other segments of the spinal column. Your shoulders, for example, may begin at C3 (cervical segment 3), but your arms hang down well past the sacral segments. So, unlike the snake, which has spinal-cord segments that connect to body segments fairly directly adjacent to them, human body segments are schematically in more of a patchwork pattern, as shown in Figure 2-27B, but make sense if the arms are extended as they are if we walk on "all fours."

Regardless of their complex pattern, however, the segments of our bodies still correspond to segments of the spinal cord. Each of these body segments is called a **dermatome** (meaning "skin cut"). A dermatome has both a sensory nerve, which sends information from the skin, joints, and muscles to the spinal cord, and a motor nerve, which controls the movements of the muscles in that particular segment of the body.

These sensory and motor nerves, known as *spinal nerves,* are functionally equivalent to the cranial nerves of the head. Whereas the cranial nerves receive information from sensory receptors in the eyes, ears, facial skin, and so forth, the spinal nerves receive information from sensory receptors in the rest of the body. Similarly, whereas the cranial nerves move the muscles of the eyes, tongue, and face, the peripheral nerves move the muscles of the limbs and trunk.

SNS Connections   Like the central nervous system, the somatic nervous system is bilateral (two sided). Just as the cranial nerves control functions on the same side of the head on which they are found, the spinal nerves on the left side of the spinal cord control the left side of the body, and those on the right side of the spinal cord control the body's right side.

Figure 2-28 shows the spinal column in cross section. Look first at the nerve fibers entering the spinal cord's dorsal side (in the body of a normally upright animal such as a human, the dorsal side means the back, as illustrated in Figure 2-4). These dorsal fibers are afferent: they carry information from the body's sensory receptors. The fibers collect together as they enter a spinal-cord segment, and this collection of fibers is called a *dorsal root.*

Fibers leaving the spinal cord's ventral side (*ventral* here means the front) are efferent, carrying information from the spinal cord to the muscles. They, too, bundle together as they exit the spinal cord and so form a *ventral root.* As you can see in the cross section at the top of the drawing in Figure 2-28, the outer part of the spinal cord consists of white matter, or CNS nerve tracts. These tracts are arranged so that, with some exceptions, dorsal tracts are sensory and ventral tracts are motor. The inner part of the cord, which has a butterfly shape, is gray matter composed largely of cell bodies.

The observation that the dorsal spinal cord is sensory and the ventral side is motor is one of the nervous system's very few established laws, the **law of Bell and Magendie.** Combined with an understanding of the spinal cord's segmental organization, this law enables neurologists to make quite accurate inferences about the location of spinal-cord

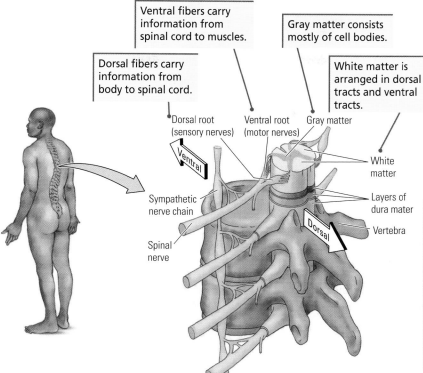

Ventral fibers carry information from spinal cord to muscles.

Dorsal fibers carry information from body to spinal cord.

Gray matter consists mostly of cell bodies.

White matter is arranged in dorsal tracts and ventral tracts.

Dorsal root (sensory nerves)

Ventral root (motor nerves)

Gray matter

Ventral

White matter

Sympathetic nerve chain

Dorsal

Layers of dura mater

Vertebra

Spinal nerve

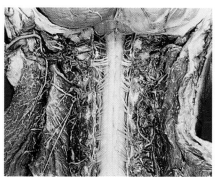

Bassett/Visuals Unlimited

Figure 2-28

Spinal-Cord Connections The spinal cord runs inside the vertebral column. The sympathetic nerve chain, which is part of the autonomic nervous system, lies outside the spinal column. As in the brain, spinal gray matter is made up largely of cell bodies, whereas the white matter is made up of fiber tracts that ascend dorsally (superiorly) and descend ventrally (inferiorly) to and from the brain, respectively. Note that you are viewing the spine from the back in this diagram. A photograph shows the exposed spinal column from this dorsal view.

damage or disease on the basis of changes in sensation or movement that patients experience. For instance, if a person experiences numbness in the fingers of the left hand but can still move the hand fairly normally, one or more of the dorsal nerves in spinal-cord segments C7 and C8 must be damaged. In contrast, if sensation in the hand is normal but the person cannot move the fingers, the ventral roots of the same segments must be damaged. The topic of diagnosing spinal-cord injury or disease is further discussed in "Magendie, Bell, and Bell's Palsy" on page 60.

So far we have emphasized the segmental organization of the spinal cord, but the spinal cord must also somehow coordinate inputs and outputs across different segments. For example, many body movements require the coordination of muscles that are controlled by different segments, just as many sensory experiences require the coordination of sensory inputs to different parts of the spinal cord. How is this coordination of spinal-cord activities accomplished? The answer is that the spinal-cord segments are interconnected in such a way that adjacent segments can operate together to direct rather complex coordinated movements.

The integration of spinal-cord activities does not require the brain's participation, which is why the headless chicken can run around in a reasonably coordinated way. Still, a close working relation must exist between the brain and the spinal cord. Otherwise, how could we consciously plan and execute our voluntary actions? Somehow information must be relayed back and forth, and examples of this information sharing are numerous. For instance, tactile information from sensory nerves in the skin travels not just to the spinal cord but also to the cerebral cortex through the thalamus. Similarly, the cerebral cortex and other brain structures can control movements because of their connections to the ventral roots of the spinal cord. So, even though the brain and spinal cord can function independently, the two are intimately connected in their functions.

Magendie, Bell, and Bell's Palsy

François Magendie, a volatile and committed French experimental physiologist, reported in a three-page paper in 1822 that he had succeeded in cutting the dorsal and ventral roots of puppies, animals in which the roots are sufficiently segregated to allow such surgery. Magendie found that cutting the dorsal roots caused loss of sensation, whereas cutting the ventral roots caused loss of movement.

Eleven years earlier, a Scotsman named Charles Bell had proposed functions for these nerve roots on the basis of anatomical information and the results of somewhat inconclusive experiments on rabbits. Although Bell's findings were not identical with Magendie's, they were similar enough to ignite a controversy. Bell hotly disputed Magendie's claim to the discovery of dorsal and ventral root functions. As a result, the principle of sensory and motor segregation in the nervous system has been given both researchers' names: the law of Bell and Magendie.

Magendie's conclusive experiment on puppies was considered extremely important because it enabled neurologists for the first time to localize nervous system damage from the symptoms that a patient displays. Bell went on to describe an example of such localized, cranial motor-nerve dysfunction that still bears his name—Bell's palsy, which is a facial paralysis that occurs when the motor part of the facial nerve

on one side of the head becomes inflamed (see the accompanying photograph).

The onset of Bell's palsy is typically sudden. Often the stricken person wakes up in the morning and is shocked to discover that the face is paralyzed on one side. He or she cannot open the mouth on that side of the head or completely close the eye on that side. Most people fully recover from Bell's palsy, although it may take several months. But, in rare instances, such as that of Jean Chretien, the former prime minister of Canada, paralysis of the mouth is permanent.

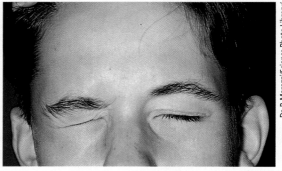

Dr. P. Marazzi/Science Photo Library/ Photo Researchers

A young man suffering from Bell's palsy, a paralysis of the facial nerve that causes weakness over one side of the face. He was photographed during an involuntary tic (a nervous reaction) that affects the right side of the face, causing his right eye to close tightly.

The Autonomic Nervous System

The internal autonomic nervous system (ANS) is a hidden partner in controlling behavior. Even without our conscious awareness, it stays on the job to keep the heart beating, the liver releasing glucose, the pupils of the eyes adjusting to light, and so forth. Without the ANS, which regulates the internal organs and glands by connections through the SNS to the CNS, life would quickly cease. Although it is possible to learn to exert some conscious control over some of these vegetative activities, such conscious interference is unnecessary. One important reason is that the ANS must keep working during sleep when conscious awareness is off-duty.

The two divisions of the ANS, **sympathetic** and **parasympathetic,** work in opposition. The sympathetic system arouses the body for action, for example, by stimulating the heart to beat faster and inhibiting digestion when we exert ourselves during exercise or times of stress; that is, the familiar "fight or flight" response. The parasympathetic

Sympathetic system. Part of the autonomic nervous system; arouses the body for action, such as mediating the involuntary fight or flight response to alarm by increasing heart rate and blood pressure.

Parasympathetic system. Part of the autonomic nervous system; acts in opposition to the sympathetic system—for example, preparing the body to rest and digest by reversing the alarm response or stimulating digestion.

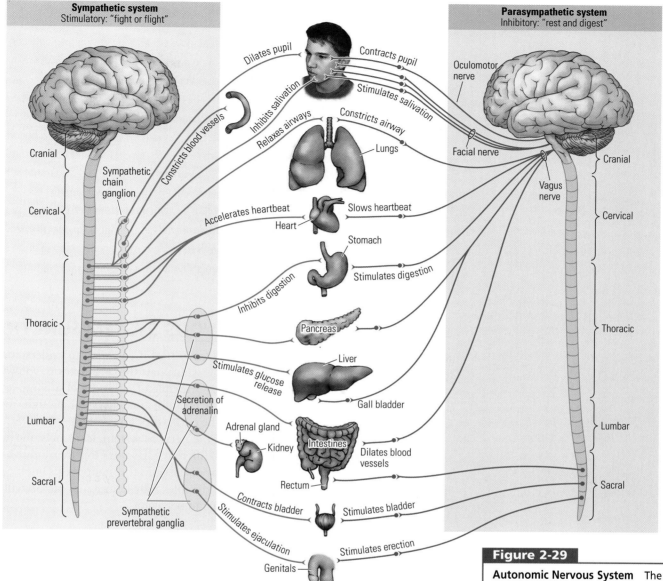

Sympathetic system
Stimulatory: "fight or flight"

Parasympathetic system
Inhibitory: "rest and digest"

Dilates pupil / Contracts pupil

Inhibits salivation / Stimulates salivation

Oculomotor nerve

Cranial

Sympathetic chain ganglion

Constricts blood vessels

Relaxes airways / Constricts airway

Facial nerve

Lungs

Cervical

Accelerates heartbeat / Slows heartbeat

Heart

Vagus nerve

Cranial

Stomach

Inhibits digestion / Stimulates digestion

Cervical

Thoracic

Pancreas

Stimulates glucose release

Liver

Thoracic

Secretion of adrenalin

Gall bladder

Adrenal gland

Lumbar

Kidney / Intestines / Dilates blood vessels

Lumbar

Sacral

Rectum

Sympathetic prevertebral ganglia

Contracts bladder / Stimulates bladder

Sacral

Stimulates ejaculation / Stimulates erection

Genitals

Figure 2-29

Autonomic Nervous System The pathways of the two divisions of the autonomic nervous system exert opposing effects on the organs that they innervate. All autonomic fibers connect at "stops" en route from the CNS to their target organs. (*Left*) Arousing sympathetic fibers connect to a chain of ganglia near the spinal cord. (*Right*) Calming parasympathetic fibers connect to individual parasympathetic ganglia near the target organs.

system calms the body down, for example, by slowing the heartbeat and stimulating digestion to allow us to "rest and digest" after exertion and during quiet times.

Like the SNS, the ANS interacts with the rest of the nervous system. Activation of the sympathetic system starts in the thoracic and lumbar spinal-cord regions. But the spinal nerves do not directly control the target organs. Rather, the spinal cord is connected to *autonomic control centers,* which are collections of neural cells called ganglia. The ganglia control the internal organs.

The sympathetic ganglia are located near the spinal cord, forming a chain that runs parallel to the cord, as illustrated on the left in **Figure 2-29.** The parasympathetic system also is connected to the spinal cord—specifically, to the sacral region—but the greater part of it derives from three cranial nerves: the *vagus nerve,* which calms most of the internal organs, and the *facial* and *oculomotor nerves,* which control salivation and pupil dilation, respectively. In contrast with the sympathetic system, the parasympathetic system connects with ganglia that are near the target organs, as shown on the right in Figure 2-29.

In Review

Traditional discussions of the nervous system that focus on anatomy distinguish between the central nervous system, which consists of the brain and spinal cord, and the peripheral nervous system, which encompasses everything else. We focus instead on a functional categorization in which the CNS interacts with the divisions of the PNS: the somatic nervous system that includes the spinal and cranial nerves of the head and body and the autonomic nervous system that controls the body's internal organs. Each nervous system segment can be further subdivided into functionally distinct subsections such as the forebrain, hindbrain, and spinal cord of the CNS. Similarly, within each CNS subsection, we find more functional subregions, such as the limbic system and the basal ganglia of the forebrain. Finally, each functional system can be further divided into areas that have their own unique functions, such as the caudate nucleus, putamen, and globus pallidus of the basal ganglia. An effective process for learning the anatomy of the nervous system is to work from the general to the more specific in each category and, in each case, to remember to associate structure with function.

EIGHT PRINCIPLES OF NERVOUS SYSTEM FUNCTION

Knowing the parts of a car engine is the place to start if you want to understand how an engine works. But even though you know which part the carburetor is, you will not understand its function until you grasp the principle of air and fuel mixing, igniting and powering the cylinders. Knowing the parts, unfortunately, is not enough. You also need some guiding principles about how the parts work together.

Now that you know the basic parts of the nervous system, learning some general principles will help you understand how its different parts work together. **Table 2-3** lists eight principles that form the basis for many discussions throughout this book. Spending the time needed to understand these principles fully before moving on will place you at an advantage in your study of brain and behavior.

Principle 1: The Sequence of Brain Processing Is "In → Integrate → Out"

The parts of the brain make a great many connections with one another. Recall, for example, that meddling cerebral cortex that appears to be connected to everything. This connectivity of the brain is the key to its functioning.

Table 2-3	Principles of Nervous System Functioning
1. Information-processing sequence in the brain is "in ⟶ integrate ⟶ out."	
2. Sensory and motor functions throughout the nervous system are separated.	
3. Inputs and outputs to the brain are crossed.	
4. Brain anatomy and function display both symmetry and asymmetry.	
5. The nervous system operates by a juxtaposition of excitation and inhibition.	
6. The nervous system has multiple levels of function.	
7. Brain components operate both in parallel and hierarchically.	
8. Functions in the brain are both localized in specific regions and distributed.	

Sensory and motor systems interact constantly to control an organism's interaction with its environment. The fundamental points of connection between neurons, known as *synapses,* allow cells in different brain regions to influence one another. Chapter 5 explains the organization of the synapse. The key point here is that most neurons have afferent (incoming) connections with tens or sometimes hundreds of thousands of other neurons, as well as efferent (outgoing) connections to neurons and many other cell types.

CREATING NEW INFORMATION

Figure 2-30 charts a basic example of creating new information in the brain through the sense of vision, beginning with receptor cells, neurons located in the retina of the eye. Different receptor cells are most receptive to light of a particular wavelength: red, green, or blue. In the brain, neurons receive inputs from one or more of these color-sensitive receptors.

A neuron might be able to receive inputs from only one receptor type, from two receptor types, or from all three. A neuron receiving input only from green-type receptor cells "knows" only about green and forwards only green information. In contrast, a neuron receiving input from both green- and red-type receptors "knows" about two colors and forwards a very different message, as would a neuron receiving input from all three receptor types.

The neurons that receive more than one kind of input sum the information that they get. In a sense, they *create* new information that did not previously exist. This summation is the "integration operation" of the brain.

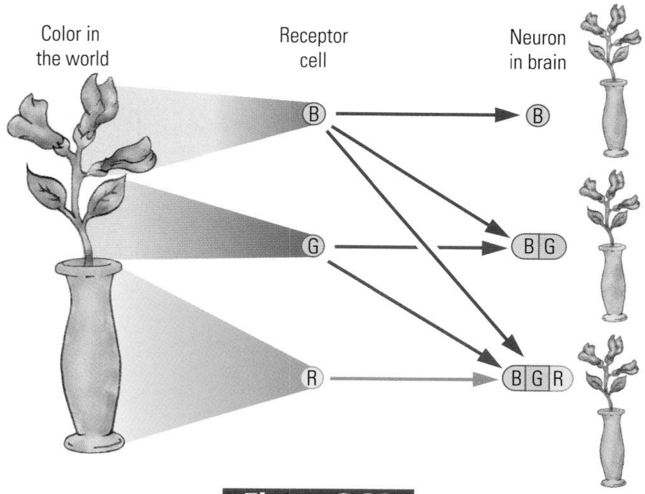

SUMMATION OF INPUTS

The top panel in **Figure 2-31** shows how multiple connections enable neurons to integrate information at the cellular level and thus create new information. The inputs to a neuron at any given moment are summed up, and the signal sent by that neuron to other neurons incorporates this summation.

Summation is more than just adding up equally weighted inputs. Some inputs have a greater influence than do others on the receiving neuron, and the simultaneous occurrence of certain inputs may have effects that far exceed their simple sum. The summation of information, then, can transform information before it's passed on to other neurons. This transformation makes the summation process partly one of creating new information.

The same principle holds for the functioning of nuclei within the brain or of a layer of brain tissue, as illustrated in the middle panel of Figure 2-31. The inputs to each neuron in a nucleus are not identical, and so there are internal (intrinsic) connections between the neurons. Several areas of the nucleus might each send different information to another area, which integrates that information and sends a combined message along to several other areas.

This process is much like the summation of information in a single neuron, but, in this case, summation takes place in a collection of neurons. As a result of summation, the output of all the cells in the nucleus is changed. Once again, there is information integration.

The logical extension of this discussion is to view the entire brain as an organ that receives inputs, creates information, and produces behavior, as illustrated in the bottom panel of Figure 2-31. To the animal whose brain is engaged in this process, the creation of information from inputs represents reality. The more complex the brain

Color in the world   Receptor cell   Neuron in brain

Figure 2-30

Integrating Information   Receptor cells B (blue), G (green), and R (red), or "input," each code information about one hue and pass it along to neurons B, B/G, and B/G/R in the brain. The neurons sum (integrate) this information to send a new message (output) that we perceive as color.

O For an animation of how neurons integrate information, go to the section on neural integration in the neural communication module on the *Foundations* CD.

Figure 2-31

Levels of Neural Processing (*Top*) At the cellular level, each of neurons 1 through 5 sends some message to neuron 6, which essentially now "knows" what neurons 1 through 5 signaled. This "knowledge" is a form of integration. The output from neuron 6 is sent to neurons 7 and 8, whose activity is affected by the "knowledge" of neuron 6. (*Center*) At the level of brain nuclei, areas A through C signal area X, which can integrate (combine) the information from areas A through C. The integrated information is then sent to areas Y and Z. (*Bottom*) At the macro level, the world provides information to the brain, which produces behavior.

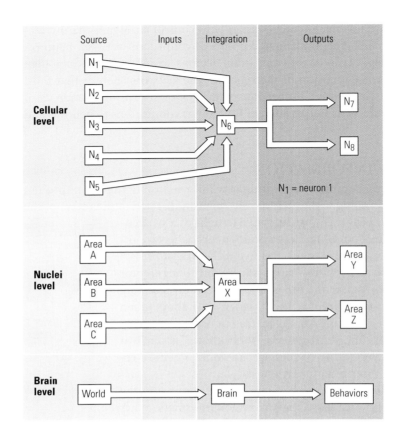

circuitry, the more complex the reality that can be created and, subsequently, the more complex the thoughts that can be expressed. The emergence of thought that enables consciousness may be the brain's ultimate act of integration.

Principle 2: Sensory and Motor Divisions Exist Throughout the Nervous System

The segregation of sensory and motor functions described by the Bell and Magendie law exists throughout the nervous system. However, distinctions between motor and sensory functions become subtler in the forebrain.

SENSORY AND MOTOR DIVISIONS AT THE PERIPHERY

The spinal nerves, as diagrammed in Figure 2-28, are either sensory or motor in function. Some cranial nerves are exclusively sensory; some are exclusively motor; and some have two parts, one sensory and one motor, much like spinal nerves serving the skin and muscles.

SENSORY AND MOTOR DIVISIONS IN THE BRAIN

Essentially extensions of the spinal cord, the lower brainstem regions—hindbrain and midbrain—retain the spinal-cord division, with sensory structures located dorsally and motor ones ventrally. Recall that an important function of the midbrain is to orient the body to stimuli. This orientation requires both sensory input and motor output. The midbrain's colliculi, which are located dorsally in the tectum, are the sensory component, whereas the tegmentum, which is ventral (below the colliculi), is a motor structure that plays a role in controlling various movements, including orienting ones. Brainstem structures are illustrated in Figures 2-15 through 2-18.

Distinct sensory nuclei are present in the thalamus, too, although they are no longer located dorsally. Because all sensory information reaches the forebrain through the thalamus, it is not surprising to find separate nuclei associated with vision, hearing, and touch. Separate thalamic nuclei also control movements. Other nuclei have neither sensory nor motor functions but rather connect to cortical areas, such as the frontal lobe, that perform more integrative tasks.

Finally, sensory and motor functions are divided in the cortex as well. This division exists in two ways. First, there are separate sensory and motor cortical regions. Some primarily process a particular sensory input, such as vision, hearing, or touch. Others control detailed movements of discrete body parts, such as the fingers. Second, the entire cortex can be viewed as being organized around the sensory and motor distinction. For instance, layer IV of the cortex always receives sensory inputs, whereas layers V and VI always send motor outputs, as shown in Figure 2-21. Layers I, II, and III integrate sensory and motor operations.

Principle 3: Many of the Brain's Circuits Are Crossed

A most peculiar organizational feature of the brain is that most of its inputs and outputs are "crossed," as shown in **Figure 2-32**. Each hemisphere receives sensory stimulation from the *opposite (contralateral)* side of the body and controls muscles on the opposite side as well. Crossed organization explains why people who experience strokes (blood clots or bleeding) in the left cerebral hemisphere may have difficulty in sensing stimulation to the right side of the body or in moving body parts on the right side. The opposite is true of people with strokes in the right cerebral hemisphere.

The human visual system is crossed in a more complicated way than are systems for other parts of the body or for animals with eyes on the sides of their head, such as the rat shown on the left in Figure 2-32. Two eyes facing forward instead of sideward inevitably see much the same thing, except on the far sides of the field of vision. The problem with this arrangement is that, to see an object with both eyes, information about it must go to the same place in the brain. Duplicate information cannot be sent to two different places.

Figure 2-32 (right) shows how the human brain solves this problem by dividing each eye's visual field into a left half and a right half. The information that either eye

◉ For an animation and illustration of how the visual system is crossed, go to the section on the optic chiasm in the visual system module on the *Foundations* CD.

Figure 2-32

Crossed Neural Circuits These schematic representations of a rat and a human brain in dorsal view show the projection of visual and somatosensory input to contralateral (opposite-side) areas of the cortex and the crossed projection of the motor cortex to the contralateral side of the body. The brain splits the visual input from each eye in two: input from the right side of the world as seen by both eyes goes to the left hemisphere, and input from the left side of the world as seen by both eyes goes to the right hemisphere. For simplicity, these diagrams show neural activity as going directly to and from the brain; in reality, intricate neural connections en route to the sensory areas and between the brain's left and right sides knit our perceptual world together. (*Left*) Because the eyes of rats are laterally placed, most of the input from each eye travels to the opposite hemisphere. (*Right*) The frontally placed eyes of humans create a far narrower visual field than that which the rat perceives.

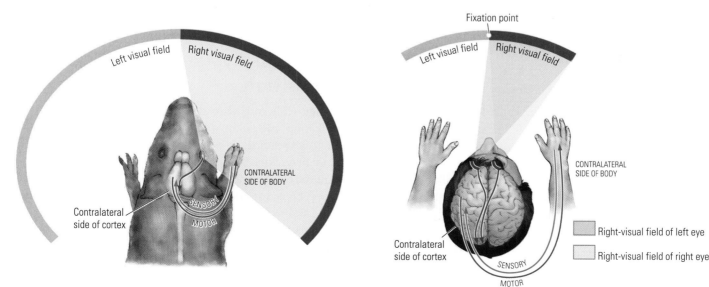

receives from the left half of its visual field is sent to the right side of the brain, and the information that either eye receives from the right half of its visual field is sent to the left side of the brain.

A crossed nervous system must join the two sides of the perceptual world together somehow. To do so, innumerable neural connections link the left and right sides of the brain. The most prominent connecting cable is the corpus callosum, which joins the left and right cerebral hemispheres with about 200 million nerve fibers (see Figure 2-9B).

Two important exceptions to the crossed-circuit principle are in the olfactory and somatic systems. Olfactory information does not cross but rather projects directly into the same *(ipsilateral)* side of the brain. Further, the cranial and peripheral nerves do not cross but are connected ipsiliaterally.

Principle 4: The Brain Is Both Symmetrical and Asymmetrical

Although the left and the right hemispheres look like mirror images, they also have some asymmetrical features. Asymmetry is essential for integrative tasks, language and body control among them.

Consider speaking. If a language zone existed in both hemispheres, each connected to one side of the mouth, we would have the strange ability to talk out of both sides of our mouths at once. This would not make talking easy, to say the least. One solution is to locate language control of the mouth on one side of the brain only. Organizing the brain in this way allows us to speak with a single voice.

A similar problem arises in controlling the body's movement in space. We would not want the left and the right hemispheres each trying to take us to a different place. Again, the problem can be solved if a single brain area controls this sort of spatial processing.

In fact, processes such as language and spatial navigation *are* localized on only one side of the brain. Language is usually on the left side, and spatial functions are usually on the right. The brains of many species have both symmetrical and asymmetrical features. The control of singing is located in one hemisphere in the bird brain. Like human language, birdsong is usually located on the left side. It seems likely that the control of song by two sides of the brain would suffer the same problems as the control of language and that birds and humans independently evolved the same solution—namely, to place the control only on one side of the brain.

Principle 5: The Nervous System Works Through Excitation and Inhibition

Imagine that the telephone rings while you are reading this page. You stop reading, get up, walk to the telephone, pick it up, and talk to a friend who convinces you that going to a movie would be more fun than reading. To carry out this series of actions, not only must your brain initiate certain behaviors, it must also stop other behaviors. When you were talking, for example, you were not engaged in reading. To walk and talk, you had to first stop reading. Producing behavior, then, requires both initiating some actions and stopping others.

In talking about the nervous system, we refer to the initiation of an activity as **excitation** and the cessation of an activity as **inhibition.** Recall, for example, that the sympathetic and parasympathetic systems produce opposite actions. The sympathetic system excites the heart, whereas the parasympathetic inhibits it.

Excitation. A process by which the activity of a neuron or brain area is increased.

Inhibition. A process by which the activity of a neuron or brain area is decreased or stopped.

The juxtaposition of excitation and inhibition is central to how the nervous system produces behavior. The same principle that governs behavior governs the activity of individual neurons. Neurons can pass on information to other neurons either by being active or by being silent. That is, they can be "on" or "off." Some neurons in the brain function primarily to excite other neurons, whereas others function to inhibit other neurons. These excitatory and inhibitory effects are produced by various neurochemicals.

Just as individual neurons can act to excite or inhibit other neurons, brain nuclei (or layers) can do the same to other nuclei (or layers). These actions are especially obvious in the motor systems. Inhibiting reading and initiating walking to the telephone, for example, result from the on and off actions of specific motor-system nuclei.

Now imagine that one of the nuclei that normally inhibits some movement is injured. The injury creates an inability to inhibit that particular response. This symptom can be seen in people with frontal-lobe injury who are often unable to inhibit talking at inappropriate times or cursing. Recall the story of Phineas Gage in Chapter 1. In contrast, people with injury to excitatory areas cannot initiate movement. Injury in an area that normally initiates speech can leave a person unable to talk at all.

Thus, brain injury can produce either a *loss* of behavior or a *release* of behavior. Behavior is lost when the damage prevents excitatory instructions; behavior is released when the damage prevents inhibitory instructions.

Principle 6: The Central Nervous System Functions on Multiple Levels

John Hughlings-Jackson
(1835–1911)

Similar sensory and motor functions are carried out in various parts of the CNS—that is, the spinal cord, brainstem, and forebrain. But why are multiple areas with overlapping functions needed? It seems simpler to put all the controls for a certain function in a single place. Why bother with duplication? It turns out that, as the brain evolved, new areas were added but old ones were retained, as described in "Optimizing Connections in the Brain" at the beginning of this chapter. The simplest solution has been to add new structures on top of existing ones.

We see this "descent with modification" solution in the evolution from primitive vertebrates to amphibians to mammals. Primitive vertebrates, such as lampreys, make only whole-body movements to swim—movements controlled by the spinal cord and hindbrain. Amphibians developed legs and corresponding neural control areas in the brainstem. Land mammals later developed new capacities with their limbs, such as independent limb movements and fine digit movements. These movements, too, required new control areas, which were selected for in the forebrain. We therefore find three distinct areas of motor control in mammals: the spinal cord, the brainstem, and the forebrain.

A century ago, John Hughlings-Jackson suggested that the addition of new brain structures in the course of evolution could be viewed as adding new levels of nervous system control. The lowest level is the spinal cord, the next level is the brainstem, and the highest level is the forebrain. These levels are not autonomous, however. To move the arms, the brainstem must use circuits in the spinal cord. Similarly, to make independent movements of the arms and fingers, such as in tying a shoelace, the cortex must use circuits in both the brainstem and the spinal cord. Each new level offers a refinement and elaboration of the motor control provided by one or more lower levels.

○ Visit the *Brain and Behavior* Web site (**www.worthpublishers.com/kolb**) and go to the Web links for additional information about the evolution of the brain.

Binding problem. A theoretical problem with the integration of sensory information. Because a single sensory event is analyzed by multiple parallel channels that do not converge on a single region, there is said to be a problem in binding together the segregated analyses into a single sensory experience.

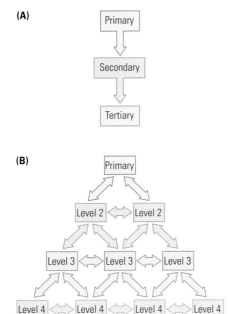

(A)

Primary

↓

Secondary

↓

Tertiary

(B)

Primary

Level 2 ⟷ Level 2

Level 3 ⟷ Level 3 ⟷ Level 3

Level 4 ⟷ Level 4 ⟷ Level 4 ⟷ Level 4

Figure 2-33

Models of Neural Information Processing **(A)** Simple serial hierarchical model of cortical processing similar to that first proposed by Alexandre Luria, who conceptualized information as being organized by the brain into three levels: primary, secondary, and tertiary. **(B)** In Daniel Felleman and David van Essen's distributed hierarchical model, multiple levels exist in each of several processing streams. Areas at each level interconnect.

We can observe the operation of functional levels in the behavior of people with brain injuries. Someone whose spinal cord is disconnected from the brain cannot voluntarily move a limb, because the brain has no way to control the movement. But the limb can still move automatically to withdraw reflexively from a noxious stimulus, because the circuits for moving the muscles are still intact in the spinal cord. Similarly, if the forebrain is not functioning but the brainstem is still connected to the spinal cord, a person can still move, but the movements are relatively simple: there is limited limb use and no digit control.

The principle of multiple levels of function can also be applied to the cortex in mammals, which evolved by adding new areas, mostly sensory-processing ones. The newer areas essentially added new levels of control that provide more and more abstract analysis of inputs. Consider the recognition of an object, such as a car. The simplest level of analysis recognizes the features of this object such as its size, shape, and color. A higher level of analysis recognizes this object as a car. And an even higher level of analysis recognizes it as Susan's car with a dent in the fender. Probably the highest functional levels are cortical regions that substitute one or more words for the object (SUV for an automobile, for instance) and can think about the car in its absence.

When we consider the brain as a structure composed of multiple levels of function, these levels clearly must be extensively interconnected to integrate their processing and create unified perceptions or movements. The nature of this connectivity in the brain leads to the next principle of brain function: the brain has both parallel and hierarchical circuitry.

Principle 7: Brain Systems Are Organized Both Hierarchically and in Parallel

The brain and spinal cord are semiautonomous areas organized into functional levels, and, even within a single level, more than one area may take part in a given function. How then, with these different systems and levels, do we eventually obtain a unified conscious experience? Why, when we look at Susan's car, do we not have the sense that one part of the brain is processing features such as shape while another part is processing color? Or why, when we tie our shoelaces, are we not aware that different levels of motor control are at work to move our arms and fingers and coordinate their actions?

These questions are part of the **binding problem,** which focuses on how the brain ties together its various activities into a whole perception or behavior. The solution to the binding problem must somehow be related to the ways in which the parts of the nervous system are connected. The two alternative possibilities for "wiring" the nervous system are serial or parallel circuits.

A *serial circuit* hooks up in a linear series all the regions concerned with a given function, as shown in **Figure 2-33A.** Consider seeing Susan's car again. In a serial system, the information from the eyes would go first to a region (or regions) that performs the simplest analysis—for example, the detection of specific properties, such as color and shape. This information would then be passed on to another region that sums up the information and identifies a car. The information would next proceed to yet another region that compares this car with stored images and identifies it as Susan's car. Notice how the perceptual process entails the hierarchical flow of information sequentially through the serial circuit from simple to complex.

One difficulty with hierarchical models, however, is that functionally related structures in the brain are not always linked in a linear series. Although the brain has many serial connections, many expected connections are missing. For example, within the visual system, not all cortical regions are connected to one another. The simplest explanation is that the unconnected regions must have very different functions, as we shall see in Chapter 8.

Another solution to the binding problem is to imagine multiple hierarchical systems that operate in parallel but are also interconnected. Figure 2-33B illustrates the flow of information in such a *distributed* hierarchy. If you trace the information flow from the primary area to levels 2, 3, and 4, you can see the parallel pathways. These multiple parallel pathways are also connected to each other. However, the connections are more selective than those that exist in a purely serial circuit.

The visual system provides a good example of such parallel hierarchical pathways. Let's return once again to Susan's car. As we look at the car door, one set of visual pathways processes information about its nature, such as its color and shape, whereas another set of pathways processes information about door-related movements, such as those required to open it.

These two visual systems are independent of each other, with no connections between them. Yet your perception when you pull the door open is not one of two different representations—the door's size, shape, and color on the one hand, and the opening movements on the other. When you open the door, you have the impression of unity in your conscious experience.

Interestingly, the brain is organized into multiple parallel pathways in all its subsystems. Yet our conscious experiences are always unified. We will return to this conundrum, as well as to the binding problem, at the end of this book. For now, keep in mind that your commonsense impressions of how the brain works may not always be correct.

Principle 8: Functions in the Brain Are Both Localized and Distributed

In our consideration of brain organization, we have so far assumed that functions can be localized in specific parts of the brain. This assumption makes intuitive sense, but it turns out to be controversial. One of the great debates in the history of brain research has been about what aspects of different functions are actually localized in specific brain regions.

Perhaps the fundamental problem is that of defining a function. Consider language, for example. Language includes the comprehension of spoken words, written words, signed words (as in American Sign Language), and even touched words (as in Braille). Language also includes processes of producing words orally, in writing, and by signing, as well as constructing whole linguistic compositions, such as stories, poems, songs, and essays.

Because the function that we call language has many aspects, it is not surprising that these aspects reside in widely separated areas of the brain. We see evidence of this widespread distribution in language-related brain injuries. People with injuries in different locations may selectively lose the abilities to produce words, understand words, read words, write words, and so forth. Specific language-related abilities, therefore, are found in specific locations, but language itself is distributed throughout a wide region of the brain.

Memory provides another example of this same distributed pattern. Memories can be extremely rich in detail and can include sensual material, feelings, words, and much more. Like language, then, aspects of memory are located in many brain regions distributed throughout a vast area of the brain.

Because many functions are both localized and distributed in the brain, damage to a small brain region produces only *focal symptoms*. Massive brain damage is required to completely remove some function. For instance, a relatively small injury could impair some aspect of language functioning, but it would take a very widespread injury to completely remove all language abilities. In fact, one of the characteristics of dementing diseases, such as Alzheimer's, is that people can endure widespread deterioration of the cortex yet maintain remarkably normal language functions until late stages of the disease.

In Review

Knowing the parts of a brain and some general notions of what they might do is only the beginning. Learning how the parts work together allows us to proceed to a closer look, in the chapters that follow, at how the brain produces behavior. We have identified eight principles about nervous system functioning for review on a regular basis, with an eye toward understanding the general concept rather than simply memorizing the principle. The balance created by the whole nervous system through excitation and inhibition, balance within the functioning brain, and balance within individual cells all work together to produce behavior.

SUMMARY

▥ *How can we view the nervous system for functional analysis?* In contrast with a two-part anatomical organization, the human nervous system can be viewed as composed of three semiautonomous functional divisions. The central nervous system includes the brain and the spinal cord. The somatic nervous system consists of the spinal nerves that enter and leave the spinal column, going to and from muscles, skin, and joints in the body and of the cranial nerves that link the CNS to the head, neck, and internal organs. The autonomic nervous system controls the body's internal organs. Its sympathetic (arousing) and parasympathetic (calming) divisions work in opposition to each other. The law of Bell and Magendie states that tracts and nerves entering a dorsal structure carry sensory information to and from receptors in the body, whereas nerves entering and leaving on the ventral side carry motor information to the periphery.

▥ *What gross external and internal features constitute the brain?* Under the tough, protective meninges that covers the brain lie its two major structures—the larger cerebrum, the most recently evolved structure of the nervous system, and the smaller cerebellum. Both structures are divided into symmetrical hemispheres covered with gyri (bumps) and sulci (cracks). At the base of the brain, where it joins the spinal cord, the brainstem is visible, as are the cranial nerves. A frontal section through the brain reveals the fluid-filled ventricles inside it, as well as the white matter, gray matter, and reticular matter that make up its tissue. Apparent in sagittal section are the corpus callosum, which joins the two hemispheres, and beneath it the subcortical structures that control more basic neural functions in concert with the SNS and ANS.

▥ *What are the basic structures and functions of the brainstem?* The brainstem consists of the hindbrain, midbrain, diencephalon, and cerebellum. Within the hindbrain, the reticular formation activates the forebrain, the pons serves as a bridge from the cerebellum to the rest of the brain, and the medulla controls such vital functions as breathing. In the midbrain, the tectum, a dorsal structure, processes information from the eyes and ears and produces orienting movements related to these sensory inputs. Ventral to the tectum, the nuclei of the tegmentum orchestrate movement-related functions. The diencephalon, or between brain, consists mainly of the thalamus and the hypothalamus. The thalamus collects sensory inputs from the cranial nerves and brainstem and sends this information to the cortex, whereas the hypothalamus integrates the autonomic nervous system with the central control of species-typical behaviors such as sexual activity and feeding.

▪ *What are the important structures and functions of the forebrain?* The forebrain is the largest, most anterior region of the brain. Its wrinkled outer surface is the neocortex. Sulci, especially deep ones called fissures, form the anatomical boundaries of the four lobes on each cerebral hemisphere: frontal, parietal, temporal, and occipital. The cells of the cortex form six distinctive layers based on their specialized sensory, motor, or integrative functions. Extensive interconnections to other brain regions are essential to the directing role of the cortex in top-down neural processing. The basal ganglia, lying just below the white matter of the cortex, interact with the brainstem, primarily in directing movement. Also important in the forebrain are the structures of the limbic system. The amygdala regulates emotional behavior, whereas the hippocampus and the cingulate cortex both have roles in memory, in motivation, and in orienting and navigating the body in space.

▪ *How does the somatic nervous system work?* The cranial nerves of the somatic nervous system link the muscles of the face and some internal organs to the brain. Some cranial nerves are sensory, some are motor, and some combine both functions. The spinal nerves transmit afferent sensory input from the skin, muscles, and joints of the body to the CNS. Efferent connections to the skeletal muscles give the SNS control over the body's movements on the side where the nerves are located. The spinal cord functions as a kind of minibrain for the peripheral (spinal) nerves that enter and leave its five spinal regions. Each region works relatively independently, although CNS fibers interconnect them and coordinate their activities.

▪ *How does the autonomic nervous system work?* The ANS acts either to activate (sympathetic division) or to inhiibit (parasympathetic division) the body's internal organs through two parallel divisions that balance out internal acitivity. The parasympathetic division directs the organs to "rest and digest," whereas the sympathetic division prepares for "fight or flight."

▪ *What basic principles govern nervous system functioning?* Knowing how the parts of the nervous system work together helps us to understand how the brain produces behavior. Here are eight guiding principles:

1. The sequence of processing within the brain is "in → integrate → out." The term *integrate* refers to the creation of new information as cells, nuclei, and brain layers sum the inputs that they receive from different sources.
2. Sensory and motor functions are separated throughout the nervous system, not just in the periphery but in the brain as well.
3. Most brain circuits are *crossed,* meaning that the right cerebral hemisphere is connected to the left side of the body, whereas the left hemisphere is connected to the body's right side.
4. The brain, though largely symmetrical, also has asymmetrical organization appropriate for controlling tasks such as language and spatial navigation.
5. The nervous system works through a combination of excitatory and inhibitory signals.
6. The nervous system operates on multiple levels of function, which range from older or more primitive to higher functional levels that evolved more recently. Tasks are often duplicated among these multiple levels.

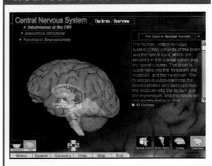

neuroscience interactive

There are many resources available for expanding your learning online:

■ **www.worthpublishers.com/kolb**
Try the Chapter 2 quizzes and flashcards to test your mastery of the chapter material. You'll also be able to link to some other sites that will reinforce what you've learned.

■ **www.brainmuseum.org/evolution/ index.html**
Link to brain atlases that include photographs, stained sections, and movie clips from humans, monkeys, and even a dolphin. Note the differences among the brains (the increasing complexity as you move from mouse to human) as well as the similarities (try to find brain nuclei that are the same across species).

■ **www.williamcalvin.com/1990s/ 1998SciAmer.htm**
Read an article about the theory of brain evolution from *Scientific American.*

On your *Foundations* CD-ROM, you'll be able to view an entire module on the Central Nervous System. This module includes a rotatable, three-dimensional brain and many sections of the brain through which you can move with the click of a mouse. In addition, the Research Methods module includes various computer tomographic and magnetic resonance images of the brain, including a video clip of a coronal MRI scan.

7. Brain circuits are organized to process information both hierarchically and in parallel.
8. Functions exemplified by memory and language are both localized and distributed in the brain.

KEY TERMS

afferent, p. 40
autonomic nervous system (ANS), p. 38
basal ganglia, p. 53
binding problem, p. 68
brainstem, p. 42
cerebrospinal fluid (CSF), p. 40
cerebrum, p. 40
corpus callosum, p. 45
cranial nerve, p. 57
cytoarchitectonic map, p. 54
dermatome, p. 58
diencephalon, p. 49
efferent, p. 40

excitation, p. 66
forebrain, p. 53
gray matter, p. 42
gyrus (pl. gyri), p. 41
hindbrain, p. 49
hypothalamus, p. 51
inhibition, p. 66
law of Bell and Magendie, p. 58
limbic system, p. 53
meninges, p. 40
midbrain, p. 49
neocortex (cerebral cortex), p. 53
nerve, p. 47
nucleus (pl. nuclei), p. 47

orienting movement, p. 51
parasympathetic system, p. 60
reticular formation, p. 51
somatic nervous system (SNS), p. 38
stroke, p. 42
sulcus (pl. sulci), p. 41
sympathetic system, p. 60
tectum, p. 51
tegmentum, p. 51
thalamus, p. 53
tract, p. 47
ventricle, p. 42
vertebra, p. 54
white matter, p. 42

REVIEW QUESTIONS

1. What are the three primary functions of the brain?
2. What features of the brain are visible from the outside?
3. Contrast the anatomical and functional divisions of the nervous system.
4. Expand the Bell and Magendie law to include the entire nervous system.
5. In what sense is the nervous system crossed?
6. In what sense is the activity of the nervous system a summation of excitatory and inhibitory processes?
7. What does it mean to say that the nervous system is organized into levels of function?

FOR FURTHER THOUGHT

In the course of studying the effects of the removal of the entire cerebral cortex on the behavior of dogs, Franz Goltz noticed that the dogs were still able to walk, smell, bark, sleep, withdraw from pain, and eat. He concluded that functions must not be localized in the cerebrum, reasoning that only widely distributed functions could explain how the dogs still performed all these behaviors despite so much lost brain tissue. On the basis of the principles introduced in this chapter, how would you explain why the dogs behaved so normally in spite of having lost about one-quarter of the brain?

RECOMMENDED READING

Diamond, M. C., Scheibel, A. B., & Elson, L. M. (1985). *The human brain coloring book.* New York: Barnes & Noble. Although a coloring book might seem an odd way to learn neuroanatomy, many students find this book to be a painless way to study the relations between brain structures.

Jerison, H. J. (1991). *Brain size and the evolution of mind*. New York: American Museum of Natural History. What is the mind and why do we have language? These questions and many more are discussed by the leading expert in brain evolution. This monograph is a fascinating introduction to the issues surrounding why the brain grew larger in the primate evolutionary branch and what advantage a large brain might confer in creating a richer sensory world.

Heimer, L. (1995). *The human brain and spinal cord: Functional neuroanatomy and dissection guide* (2nd ed.). New York: Springer Verlag. If coloring books aren't your thing, then Heimer's dissection guide to the human brain will provide a more traditional, as well as sophisticated, guide to human brain anatomy.

Luria, A. R. (1973). *The working brain*. Harmondsworth, England: Penguin. Luria was a Russian neurologist who studied thousands of patients over a long career. He wrote a series of books outlining how the human brain functions, of which *The Working Brain* is the most accessible. In fact, *The Working Brain* is really the first human neuropsychology book. Although many of the details of Luria's ideas are now outdated, his general framework for how the brain is organized is substantially correct.

Zeki, S. (1993). *A vision of the brain*. London: Blackwell Scientific. Humans are visual creatures. Zeki's book uses the visual system as a way of introducing the reader to how the brain is organized. It is entertaining and introduces the reader to Zeki's ideas about how the brain functions.

What Are the Units of Nervous System Function?

Programming Behavior

In the search to discover how a nervous system produces behavior, robots may help provide answers. Robots, after all, engage in goal-oriented actions, just as animals do. A robot's computer must guide and coordinate those actions, doing much the same work that an animal's nervous system does.

Barbara Webb's little cricket robot, constructed from Lego blocks, wires, and a motor and shown in the accompanying photograph, illustrates this interesting use of electronic technology. Although far more cumbersome than nature's model, Webb's robot is designed to mimic a female cricket that listens for and travels to the source of a male's chirping song. These behaviors are not as simple as they may seem.

In approaching a male, a female cricket must avoid open, well-lit places where a predator could detect her. In addition, a female cricket must often choose between competing males, preferring, for example, the male that makes the longest chirps. All these behaviors must be "wired into" a successful cricket robot, making sure that one behavior does not interfere with another. In simulating cricket behavior in a robot, Webb is duplicating the rules of a cricket's nervous system, which are "programmed" by its genes.

Is the idea of comparing a living cricket's nervous system to a manufactured robot's computer-driven parts disturbing? In their attempts to explain behavior, remember, scientists, like philosophers, frequently search for analogies among the things they know. Descartes compared the nervous system to simpler mechanical devices, such as a water pump or a clock. Today's comparison to computerized robots is just a contemporary analogy.

Robots help neuroscientists to learn more about the brain and behavior. Researchers such as Webb switch back and forth between studying the nervous system and the behaviors that it enables and writing computer programs and building robots designed to simulate those behaviors. When the animal under study and the computerized robot respond in exactly the same way, researchers can be fairly sure that they understand how some part of the nervous system works.

At the present time, the construction of robots that display principles of nervous system function is important to the area of science called artificial intelligence (AI), which attempts to produce machines that can think. At some time in the future, robots may even help neuroscientists evaluate the correctness of a complete theory of how the brain works. Scientists who believe they have a complete understanding of brain function might validate their theory by building a robot whose behavior is indistinguishable from a human being's.

Robert P. Carr/Burce Coleman Inc. (animal); Barbara Webb (model)

Rules obtained from the study of crickets' behavior can be programmed into robots to be tested. From "A Cricket Robot," by B. Webb, 1996, *Scientific American, 214*(12), p. 99.

Computer software runs on programmed instructions written in lines of code. In the living cell, genes are coded to make proteins, the building bocks of cells and of interaction among cells. Genes thus intimately participate in the production of behavior, but only indirectly. Genes located in the chromosomes of each cell determine the proteins that a particular cell will make. Thus, genes are blueprints for proteins, with each gene containing the code for one protein.

A gene's workings, however, can go awry, sometimes with devastating consequences for behavior. Many of the neurological disorders described in this book are caused by errors in protein manufacture due to errors in genes passed from parent to child, which is why we explore the process of genetic transmission in this chapter.

So one function of living cells is to act as organic factories that produce proteins. Nerve cells allow us to respond to stimuli in the environment, process that information, and act. These cells are of different types, each distinctive in its structure and function. Just as we can explore the function of a robot by examining its overall structure, so we can investigate the overall structure of a cell as a source of insight into its work.

This chapter also investigates the internal structures of cells, the organelles that perform various tasks. If you think of a cell as nature's microscopic robot, the organelles become the miniaturized components that allow the cell to do its job. Ultimately, the genes of female and male crickets determine their behavior. Think of the challenge of programming into a robot all the instructions needed to carry out its every task. Yet a cell, nature's tiny robot, contains all the instructions that it requires packed away in its chromosomes.

CELLS OF THE NERVOUS SYSTEM

If Barbara Webb's little robot mysteriously arrived in a box on your doorstep, could you guess what it is designed to do? The robot's wheels imply that it is meant to move, and the gears next to the wheels suggest that it can vary its speed or perhaps change directions by varying the speed of one wheel relative to the other. The robot's many exposed wires show that it is not intended to go into water. And, because this robot has no lights or cameras, you can infer that it is not meant to see. The structure of the robot suggests its function. So it is with cells.

There are problems in examining the cells of the nervous system for insights into their function. These cells are very small, are packed tightly together, and have the consistency of jelly. To see a brain cell, you must first distinguish it from surrounding cells, stain it to make it visible, and then magnify it by using a microscope. Anatomists have developed ways of removing most of the water from the brain by soaking it in formaldehyde, after which the brain can be sliced thin and stained with various dyes that either color its cells completely or color some of the cells' components. Now the cells can be placed under a microscope for viewing. Anatomists can also "culture" brain cells in a dish where living cells can be viewed and studied more simply than they can when they are in a living brain.

There remains, however, the problem of making sense of what you see. Different brain samples can yield different images, and different people can interpret those images in different ways. So began a controversy between two great scientists over what neurons really are. One was the Italian Camillo Golgi and the other the Spaniard Santiago Ramón y Cajal. Both men were awarded the Nobel Prize for medicine in 1906.

Imagine that you are Camillo Golgi hard at work in your laboratory staining and examining cells of the nervous system. You immerse a thin slice of brain tissue in a solution containing silver nitrate and other chemicals, a technique used at the time

---

○ Visit the *Brain and Behavior* Web site (**www.worthpublishers.com/kolb**) and go to the Chapter 3 Web links to view an article on robotics and artificial intelligence.

○ Use the *Foundations of Behavioral Neuroscience* CD to learn about different ways to look at the brain. In the module on research methods, you'll find a section on histology that includes samples of six common stains for brain sections. (See the Preface for more information about this CD.)

Cell body (soma). Core region of the cell containing the nucleus and other organelles for making proteins.

Dendrite. Branch of a neuron that consists of an extension of the cell membrane, thus greatly increasing the area of the cell.

Axon. "Root," or single fiber, of a neuron that carries messages to other neurons.

to produce black-and-white photographic prints. A contemporary method, shown in **Figure 3-1**, produces a color-enhanced microscopic image that resembles the images Golgi saw.

The image is beautiful and intriguing, but what do you make of it? To Golgi, this structure suggested that the nervous system is composed of a network of interconnected fibers. He thought that information, like water running through pipes, somehow flowed around this "nerve net" and produced behavior. His theory was not implausible, given what he saw.

But Santiago Ramón y Cajal came to a different conclusion. He studied the brain tissue of chick embryos because he assumed that their nervous systems would be simpler and easier to understand than would an adult nervous system. **Figure 3-2** shows one of the images that he rendered from the neural cells of a chick embryo. Cajal concluded that the nervous system is made up of discrete cells that begin life with a rather simple structure that becomes more complex with age. When mature, these cells consist of a main body with extensions projecting from it.

The structure looks something like a radish, with branches coming out of the top and roots coming out of the bottom. Cajal's belief that these complexly shaped cells are the functional units of the nervous system is now universally accepted. The idea proposed by Cajal, that neurons are the units of brain function, is called the *neuron hypothesis.*

Figure 3-2 shows the three basic subdivisions of a neuron. The core region is called the **cell body** or **soma** (Greek, meaning "body"). Most of a neuron's branching extensions are called **dendrites** (from Greek for "tree"), but the main "root" is called the **axon** (Greek for "axle"). A neuron has only one axon, but most neurons have many dendrites. Some small neurons have so many dendrites that they look like a garden hedge.

The nervous system is composed not only of neurons but also of cells called glia (the name comes from the Greek word for "glue"; see Figure 2-12). Neurons are the functional units that enable us to receive information, process it, and act. Glial cells help the neurons out, binding them together (some *do* act as glue) and providing support, nutrients, and protection, among other functions detailed later in the chapter. The human nervous system contains about 100 billion neurons and perhaps 10 times as many glial cells. No, no one has counted them all. Scientists have estimated the total number by counting the cells in a small sample of brain tissue and then multiplying by the brain's volume (**Figure 3-3**).

How can we explain how 100 billion cells cooperate, make connections, and produce behavior? Fortunately, examining how one cell works can be a source of insight that we can generalize to other cells. Brain cells really are like robots built to a common plan, depending on their particular type. As you learn to recognize some of the different types of neurons and glial cells in your body, you will also see how their specialized structures contribute to their functions.

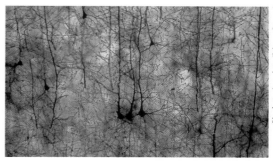

Biophoto Associates/Science Source/ Photo Researchers

Figure 3-1

Histological Preparation Tissue preparation revealing human pyramidal cells stained by using the Golgi technique.

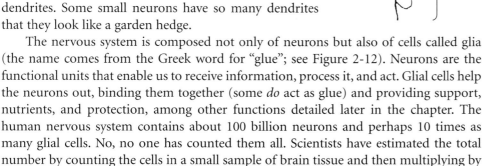

Dendrites

Cell body

Axon

Figure 3-2

Drawing of a Neuron by Cajal Dendrites gather information from other neurons, the soma (cell body) integrates the information, and the axon sends the information to other cells. Note that there is only one axon, though it may have branches, called collaterals. Adapted from *Histologie du système nerveux de l'homme et des vertebres*, by S. Ramón y Cajal, 1909–1911, Paris: Maloine.

Figure 3-3

Estimating Cell Count The researcher first obtains a thin slice of brain tissue from a rat (*left*) and then selects a region of the cortex for cell counting (*middle*). Multiplying the number of cells in this part of the tissue by the volume of the cortex yields an estimate of the total number of cells. The cells pictured at the right are stained with cresyl violet, which adheres to protein molecules in the cell body, giving it a blue color.

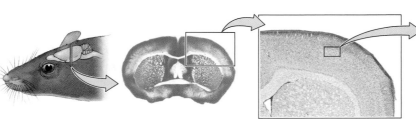

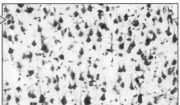

⊙ Go to the Web links for Chapter 3 on the *Brain and Behavior* Web site (**www.worthpublishers.com/kolb**) to read more about the history of the neuron hypothesis.

Neurons

As the information-processing units of the nervous system, neurons must do many things. They must acquire information from sensory receptors, pass that information on to other neurons, and make muscles move to produce behaviors. They must encode memories and produce our thoughts and emotions as well. At the same time, they must regulate all the many body processes to which we seldom give a thought, such as breathing, heartbeat, body temperature, and the sleep–wake cycle. This is a tall order but easily accomplished by our microscopic neurons.

Some scientists think that a specific function is sometimes assigned to a single neuron. For example, Fernando Nottebohm and his colleagues (1994) studied how birds produce songs and proposed that a single neuron may be responsible for each note sung. For most behavior in most species, however, scientists think that neurons work together in groups of many hundreds to many thousands to produce some aspect of a behavior.

According to this view, the loss of a neuron or two would be no more noticeable than the loss of one or two voices from a cheering crowd. It is the crowd that produces the overall sound, not each individual person. In much the same way, although neuroscientists say that neurons are the information-processing units of the brain, they really mean that large teams of neurons serve this function.

Scientists also speak informally about *the* structure of a particular neuron, as if that structure never changes. If fresh brain tissue is kept alive in a dish of salty water and viewed occasionally through a microscope, the neurons reveal themselves to be surprisingly active, both producing new dendrite branches and losing old ones. In fact, when they are watched over a period of time in the brain or in a dish, they seem to be continuously growing and shrinking and changing their shape.

For some neurons, these physical changes result from coding and storing our experiences and memories. Neural changes of all kinds are possible because of a special property that neurons possess. Even in a mature, fully grown neuron, the cell's genetic blueprints can be "reopened," allowing the neuron to alter its structure and function by producing new proteins.

Another important property of neurons is their longevity. At a few locations in the nervous system, the ongoing production of new neurons does take place throughout life, and some behavior does depend on the production of new neurons. But most of your neurons are with you for life and are never replaced. If the brain or spinal cord is damaged, for example, the neurons that are lost may not be replaced, and functional recovery is poor.

THE NEURON'S BASIC STRUCTURE AND FUNCTION

Figure 3-4 displays the basic features of neurons in detail. The surface area of the cell is increased immensely by its extensions into dendrites and an axon (Figure 3-4A and B). The dendritic area is further increased by many small protrusions called **dendritic spines** (Figure 3-4C). A neuron may have from 1 to 20 dendrites, each may have from one to many branches, and the spines on the branches may number in the many thousands. Because dendrites collect information from other cells, their surface area corresponds to how much information the neuron can gather.

Each neuron has but a single axon (Figure 3-4D). Axons carry messages to other neurons. It begins at one end of the cell body at an expansion known as the **axon**

Figure 3-4

Major Parts of a Neuron Note here how different stains highlight different aspects of the neuron. **(A)** A typical neuron stained with the use of the Golgi technique to reveal its dendrites and cell body. **(B)** A drawing of a neuron illustrates its basic structures. **(C)** An electron micrograph captures the synapse between an axon from another neuron and a dendritic spine. **(D)** A high-power light-microscopic view inside the cell body.

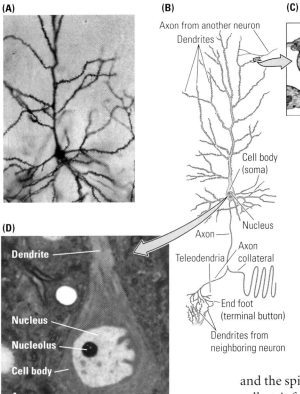

hillock (little hill). The axon may branch out into one or many **axon collaterals,** which usually emerge from it at right angles (see Figure 3-4B).

As shown in detail in Figure 3-4B, the lower tip of an axon may divide into a number of smaller branches (*teleodendria,* or end branches). At the end of each teleodendrion is a knob called an **end foot** or *terminal button.* The end foot is very close to a dendritic spine or some other part of another neuron, although it does not touch it (see Figure 3-4C). This "almost connection," which includes the surfaces of the end foot and the neighboring dendritic spine as well as the space between them, is called a **synapse.**

Chapter 4 describes how neurons communicate; here we simply generalize about function by examining shape. Imagine looking at a river system from an airplane. You see many small streams merging to make creeks, which join to form tributaries, which join to form the main river channel. As the river reaches its delta, it breaks up into a number of smaller channels again before discharging its contents into the sea.

The general shape of a neuron is somewhat similar to such a river system, and the neuron works in a broadly similar way. It collects information from many different sources on its dendrites, channels that information onto its axon, and then sends the information along its teleodendria to its end feet. At the end feet, the information is released onto a target surface. This flow of information from the dendrites through the cell body and then along the axon to the end feet is illustrated in **Figure 3-5.**

A neuron receives a great deal of information on its hundreds to thousands of dendritic spines, but it has only one axon, and so it must also act as a decision-making device. As described in Chapter 2, the message that it sends must be an averaged, or summary, response to all the incoming information. Because it produces a summary response, the neuron is also a computational device. Chapter 4 describes in detail how these decision-making processes take place.

TYPES OF NEURONS

The nervous system contains neurons in an array of shapes and sizes, structured differently because of their specialized tasks. Some appear quite simple and others very complex. With a little practice in looking into a microscope, you can quickly learn to recognize three neuron types by their features and functions. *Sensory neurons* (**Figure 3-6A**) are designed to bring information into the brain from sensory receptors, *interneurons* (Figure 3-6B) to process it within the brain, and *motor neurons* (Figure 3-6C) to carry it out of the brain to the body's muscles.

Sensory Neurons These neurons are the simplest structurally. A **bipolar neuron** found in the retina of the eye has a single short dendrite on one side of its cell body and a single short axon on the other side. It brings sensory information from the retina's light receptors to the neurons that will carry visual information into the visual centers of the brain.

A bit more complicated is the **somatosensory neuron** that brings sensory information from the

Dendritic spine. Protrusion from a dendrite that greatly increases its surface area and is the usual point of dendritic contact with axons.

Axon hillock. Juncture of soma and axon where the action potential begins.

Axon collateral. Branch of an axon.

End foot. Knob at the tip of an axon that conveys information to other neurons; also called a terminal button.

Synapse. Junction between one neuron and another neuron, usually between an end foot of the axon of one neuron and a dendritic spine of the other neuron.

Bipolar neuron. Neuron with one axon and one dendrite.

Somatosensory neuron. Brain cell that brings sensory information from the body into the spinal cord.

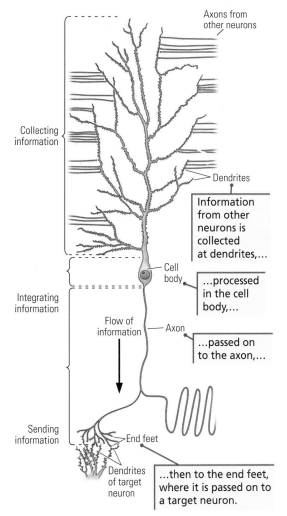

Axons from other neurons

Collecting information

Dendrites

Information from other neurons is collected at dendrites,...

Cell body

...processed in the cell body,...

Integrating information

Flow of information

Axon

...passed on to the axon,...

Sending information

End feet

Dendrites of target neuron

...then to the end feet, where it is passed on to a target neuron.

Figure 3-5

Information Flow in a Neuron The sequence of information processing in a neuron is in → integrate → out. Neurons act as decision-making devices by summing incoming information and incorporating this summation into the messages that they send.

Figure 3-6

Neuron Shape and Function The appearance of different kinds of neurons is distinctive (note that these cells are not drawn to scale). Sensory neurons **(A)** collect information from a source and pass it on to an interneuron. **(B)** The many branches of interneurons collect information from many sources. Motor neurons **(C)** are distinctively large and pass this information on to command muscles to move.

(A) Sensory neurons

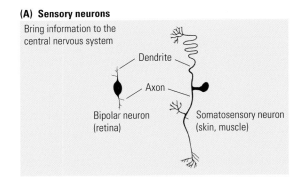

Bring information to the central nervous system

Bipolar neuron (retina)

Somatosensory neuron (skin, muscle)

(B) Interneurons

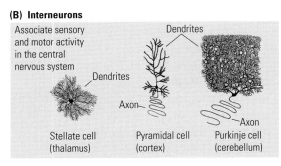

Associate sensory and motor activity in the central nervous system

Stellate cell (thalamus)

Pyramidal cell (cortex)

Purkinje cell (cerebellum)

(C) Motor neurons

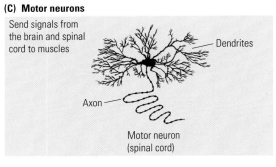

Send signals from the brain and spinal cord to muscles

Motor neuron (spinal cord)

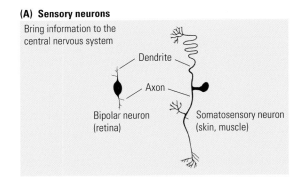 To learn more about synapses, visit the section on the structure of a neuron in the neural communications module on the *Foundations* CD. You can also view an animation showing a simple neural network in the section on neural integration.

body into the spinal cord. Structurally, the somatosensory dendrite connects directly to its axon, and so the cell body sits to one side of this long pathway.

Interneurons Generally called *association cells* because they link sensory and motor activity, **interneurons** include pyramidal cells and Purkinje cells. A specific association cell, the *stellate cell* (meaning star shaped), is characteristically small, with many dendrites extending around the cell body. Its axon is difficult to see among the maze of dendrites.

A **pyramidal cell** has a long axon, a pyramid-shaped cell body, and two sets of dendrites, one set projecting from the apex of the cell body and the other from its sides. Pyramidal cells carry information from the cortex to the rest of the brain and spinal cord.

A **Purkinje cell** (named for its discoverer) is a distinctive pyramidal cell with extremely branched dendrites that form a fan shape. It carries information from the cerebellum to the rest of the brain and spinal cord. A major difference between animals with small brains and animals with large brains is that large-brained animals have more interneurons.

Motor Neurons To collect information from many sources, motor neurons have extensive networks of dendrites, large cell bodies, and long axons that connect to muscles. Motor neurons are located in the lower brainstem and spinal cord. All outgoing neural information must pass through them to reach the muscles.

NEURAL CONNECTIONS

Neurons are "networkers" that produce behavior, and the appearance of each neuron tells us something about the connections that it must make. Figure 3-6 illustrates the relation between form and function of neurons but does not illustrate actual size. Generally, neurons that project for long distances, such as somatosensory neurons, pyramidal neurons, and motor neurons, are very large relative to other neurons. In general, neurons with large cell bodies have extensions that are very long, whereas neurons with small cell bodies have short extensions.

Long extensions carry information to distant parts of the nervous system; short extensions are engaged in local processing. For example, the tips of the dendrites of some sensory neurons are located in your big toe, whereas the target of their axons is at the base of your brain. These sensory neurons send information over a distance as long as 2 meters, or more. The axons of some pyramidal neurons must reach from the cortex as far as the lower spinal cord, a distance that can be as long as a meter. The imposing size of this pyramidal cell body therefore is in accord with the work that it must do in providing nutrients and other supplies for its axons and dendrites.

THE LANGUAGE OF NEURONS: EXCITATION AND INHIBITION

Neurons are in constant communication. Their basic language may remind you of how digital devices such as computers work. That is, neurons either *excite* other neurons (turn them on) or *inhibit* other neurons (turn them off). Like computers, neurons send "yes" or "no" signals to one another; the "yes" signals are the excitatory signals, and the "no" signals are the inhibitory signals. Recall that excitation and inhibition are subjects of one of the principles discussed in Chapter 2. Each neuron receives thousands of excitatory and inhibitory signals every second.

The neuron's response to all those inputs is democratic: it *sums* them. A neuron is spurred into action only if its excitatory inputs exceed its inhibitory inputs. If the reverse is true and inhibitory inputs exceed excitatory inputs, the neuron does not activate.

We can apply the principle of the excitation and inhibition of neuron action to the workings of the cricket robot described at the beginning of this chapter. Suppose we could insert a neuron between the microphone for sound detection on each side of this robot and the motor on the *opposite* side. **Figure 3-7A** shows how the two neurons would be connected. It would take only two rules to instruct the robot to seek out a chirping male cricket:

Rule 1: Each time that a microphone detects a male cricket's song, an excitatory message is sent to the opposite wheel's motor, activating it. This rule ensures that the robot turns toward the cricket each time that it hears a chirp.

Rule 2: The message sent should be proportional to the intensity of the sound. This rule means that, if the chirp is coming from the robot's left side, it will be detected as being louder by the microphone on the left, which will make the right wheel turn a little faster, swinging the robot to the left. The opposite would happen if the sound came from the right. If the sound comes from straight ahead, both microphones will detect it equally, and the robot will move directly forward. This rule ensures that the robot travels in the correct direction.

To make the robot in a more "intelligent" way requires more neurons. Figure 3-7B shows how we could mimic the idea of sensory and motor neurons. The robot now has two sound-detecting sensory neurons receiving input from its microphones. When activated, each of these sensory neurons excites a motor neuron that turns on one of the two wheel motors. But now we add sensory neurons coming from photoreceptors on the robot that detect light. These light-detecting sensory neurons, when activated, inhibit the motor neurons leading to the wheels and so prevent the robot from moving toward a male until it is dark and "safe."

Interneuron. Association neuron interposed between a sensory neuron and a motor neuron; thus, in mammals, interneurons constitute most of the neurons of the brain.

Pyramidal cell. Distinctive neuron found in the cerebral cortex.

Purkinje cell. Distinctive neuron found in the cerebellum.

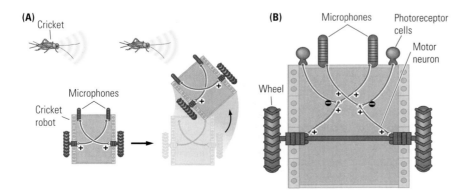

Figure 3-7

Excitation and Inhibition
(A) Excitatory inputs from the chirping of a male cricket, picked up by the cricket robot's microphones, activate the robot's wheels to orient toward the chirp. **(B)** In a slightly more complex cricket robot, sensory neurons from the speaker excite motor neurons, but inhibitory input from photoreceptors turn the motor neurons off.

Glial cell. Nervous system cell that provides insulation, nutrients, and support, as well as aiding in the repair of neurons.

Tumor. Mass of new tissue that grows uncontrolled and independent of surrounding structures.

Ependymal cell. Glial cell that makes and secretes cerebral spinal fluid; found on the walls of the ventricles of the brain.

This arrangement gives the robot some interesting properties. For example, at dusk the excitatory signals from sound and weak inhibitory signals from the dim light might conflict. The robot might make small "intention" movements that orient it to the male while not actually searching for it. A researcher might want to examine the behavior of a real female cricket to see if it acts in the same way under these conditions.

This arrangement illustrates the function of sensory and motor neurons and the principle of excitation and inhibition, but bear in mind that it contains only six neurons and each neuron has only one connection with another neuron. We have not even placed interneurons in the robot. Imagine how infinitely more complex a human nervous system is with its hundred billion neurons, most of which are interneurons, each with thousands of connections.

Still, this simple example serves a valuable purpose. It shows the great versatility of function possible from the dual principles of excitation and inhibition. From the simple yes-or-no language of neurons emerges enormous possibilities for behavior.

Glial Cells

Imagine how much more efficient your robot would be if you could add components that enhance the functioning of your simulated neurons. Some could attach the neurons to the appropriate parts of the robot; others could insulate the neurons to prevent them from short-circuiting one another. The insulating components might also increase the speed of signals along the robot's wired pathways. Still other auxiliary components could lubricate moving parts or eliminate debris, keeping your robot clean and shiny. Does all this sound too good to be true? Not really. All these functions are served by glial cells in your nervous system.

Glial cells are often described as the support cells of the nervous system. Although they do not transmit much information themselves, they help neurons carry out this task. Most neurons form only early in life, but glial cells are constantly replacing themselves. ("Brain Tumors" describes the results of uncontrolled glial cell growth.) Table 3-1 lists the five major classes of glia. Each has a characteristic structure and function.

EPENDYMAL CELLS

On the walls of the ventricles, the cavities inside your brain, are **ependymal cells** that produce and secrete the cerebrospinal fluid that fills the ventricles. Cerebral spinal fluid is constantly being formed and flows through the ventricles toward the base of the brain, where it is absorbed into the blood vessels. Cerebrospinal fluid serves several purposes. It acts as a shock absorber when the brain is jarred; it provides a medium through which waste products are eliminated; it may play a role in brain cooling; and it may be a source of nutrients for certain parts of the brain located adjacent to the ventricles.

As CSF flows through the ventricles, it passes through some narrow passages, especially the fourth

Table 3-1	Types of Glial Cells	
Type	**Appearance**	**Features and function**
Ependymal cell		Small, ovoid; secretes cerebrospinal fluid (CSF)
Astrocyte		Star shaped, symmetrical; nutritive and support function
Microglial cell		Small, mesodermally derived; defensive function
Oligodendroglial cell		Asymmetrical; forms myelin around axons in brain and spinal cord
Schwann cell		Asymmetrical; wraps around peripheral nerves for form myelin

Brain Tumors

Focus on Disorders

One day while she was watching a movie in a neuro-psychology class, R. J., a 19-year-old college sophomore, collapsed on the floor and began twitching, displaying symptoms of a brain seizure. The instructor helped her to the university clinic, where she recovered, except for a severe headache. She reported that she had suffered from severe headaches on a number of occasions.

A few days later, computer tomography (CT) was used to scan her brain; the scan showed a tumor over her left frontal lobe. She underwent surgery to have the tumor removed and returned to classes after an uneventful recovery. She successfully completed her studies, finished law school, and has been practicing law for more than 15 years without any further symptoms.

A **tumor** is a mass of new tissue that undergoes growth that is uncontrolled and independent of surrounding structures. No region of the body is immune, but the brain is a common site. Brain tumors do not grow from neurons but rather from glia or other supporting cells. The rate of growth depends on the type of cell affected.

Some tumors, such as R. J.'s, are benign and not likely to recur after removal; others are malignant, likely to progress, and apt to recur after removal. Both kinds of tumors can pose a risk to life if they develop in sites from which they are difficult to remove.

The earliest symptoms are usually due to increased pressure on surrounding brain structures and can include headaches, vomiting, mental dullness, changes in sensory and motor abilities, and seizures such as that experienced by R. J. Many symptoms depend on the precise location of the tumor. The three major types of brain tumors are classified according to how they originate:

1. *Gliomas* arise from glial cells. They constitute roughly half of all brain tumors. Gliomas that arise from astrocytes are usually slow growing, not often malignant, and relatively easy to treat. In contrast, gliomas that arise from blast or germinal cells (precursor cells that grow into glial

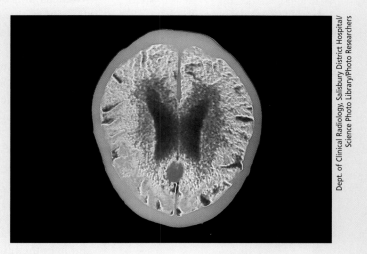

The red area in this colored CT scan is a meningioma, a noncancerous tumor arising from the arachnoid membrane covering the brain. A meningioma may grow large enough to compress the brain but usually does not invade brain tissue.

Dept. of Clinical Radiology, Salisbury District Hospital/ Science Photo Library/Photo Researchers

cells; see Chapter 7) are much more often malignant, grow more quickly, and often recur after treatment.

2. *Meningiomas,* the type of tumor that R. J. had, attach to the meninges and so grow entirely outside the brain, as shown in the accompanying CT scan. These tumors are usually well encapsulated, and, if located in places that are accessible, recovery after surgery is good.

3. The *metastatic tumor* becomes established by a transfer of tumor cells from one region of the body to another (which is what the term *metastatic* means). Typically, metastatic tumors are present in multiple locations, making treatment difficult. Symptoms of the underlying condition often first appear when the tumor cells reach the brain.

Treatment for a brain tumor is usually surgery, which also is one of the main means of diagnosing the type of tumor. If possible, the entire tumor is removed. Radiotherapy (treatment with X-rays) is useful for destroying developing tumor cells. Chemotherapy, although common for treating tumors in other parts of the body, is less successful in the treatment of brain tumors because getting the chemicals across the blood–brain barrier is difficult.

Hydrocephalus. Buildup of pressure in the brain and, in infants, swelling of the head caused if the flow of CSF is blocked; can result in retardation.

Astrocyte. Glial cell with a star-shaped appearance that provides structural support to neurons in the central nervous system and transports substances between neurons and capillaries.

Microglia. Form of glial cell that scavenges debris in the nervous system.

ventricle, which runs through the brainstem (see Figure 2-10). If the fourth ventricle is fully or partly blocked, the fluid flow is restricted. Because CSF is continuously being produced, this blockage causes a buildup of pressure that begins to expand the ventricles, which in turn push on the surrounding brain.

If such a blockage develops in a newborn infant, before the skull bones are fused, the pressure on the brain is conveyed to the skull and the baby's head consequently swells. This condition, called **hydrocephalus** (literally, water brain), can cause severe mental retardation and even death. To treat it, doctors insert one end of a tube, called a shunt, into the blocked ventricle and the other end into a vein. The shunt allows the CSF to drain into the bloodstream.

ASTROGLIA

Astrocytes (star-shaped glia shown in Figure 2-12), also called *astroglia,* provide structural support within the central nervous system. Their extensions attach to blood vessels and to the brain's lining, creating scaffolding that holds neurons in place. These same extensions provide pathways for the movement of certain nutrients between blood vessels and neurons. Astrocytes also secrete chemicals that keep neurons healthy and help them heal if injured.

At the same time, astrocytes play an important role in contributing to a protective partition between blood vessels and the brain, the *blood–brain barrier.* As shown in

Figure 3-8, the end feet of astrocytes attach to the cells of blood vessels, causing the blood-vessel cells to bind tightly together. These tight junctions prevent an array of substances, including many toxins, from entering the brain through the blood-vessel walls.

The molecules (smallest units) of these substances are too large to pass between the blood-vessel cells unless the blood–brain barrier is somehow compromised. But the downside to the blood–brain barrier is that many useful drugs, including antibiotics such as penicillin, cannot pass through to the brain either. As a result, brain infections are very difficult to treat.

Figure 3-8

Function of Astrocytes
Astrocyte processes attach to neurons and to blood vessels to provide support between different structures in the brain, stimulate the cells on blood vessels to form tight junctions and so form the blood–brain barrier, and transport chemicals excreted by neurons to blood vessels.

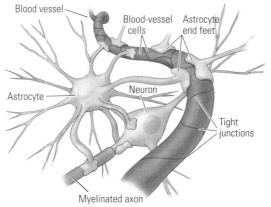

Yet another important function of astrocytes is to enhance brain activity. When you engage a part of your brain for some behavior, the brain cells of that area require more oxygen and glucose. In response, the blood vessels in the area dilate, allowing greater oxygen- and glucose-carrying blood flow. But what triggers the blood vessels to dilate? This is where the astrocytes come in. They convey signals from the neurons to the blood vessels, stimulating them to expand and so provide more fuel.

Astrocytes also contribute to the process of healing damaged brain tissue. If the brain is injured by a blow to the head or penetrated by some sharp object, astrocytes form a scar to seal off the damaged area. Although the scar tissue is beneficial in healing the injury, it can unfortunately act as a barrier to the regrowth of damaged neurons. Some experimental approaches to repairing brain tissue seek to get the axons and dendrites of CNS neurons to grow around or through a glial scar.

MICROGLIA

Unlike other glial cells, which originate in the brain, **microglia** originate in the blood as an offshoot of the immune system and migrate throughout the brain. Microglia monitor the health of brain tissue. When brain cells are damaged, microglia invade

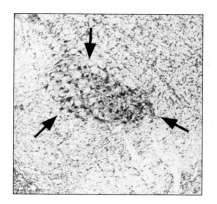 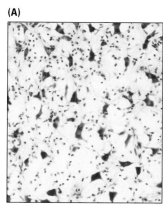 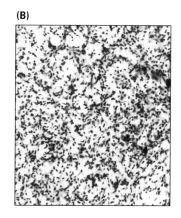

(A) **(B)**

Figure 3-9

Detecting Brain Damage
Arrows on the micrograph at the left indicate a brain area called the red nucleus in a rat. **(A)** Closeup of cresyl violet–stained neurons in the healthy red nucleus. **(B)** After exposure to a neurotoxin, only microglia remain.

the area to provide growth factors that aid in repair and to engulf and remove foreign matter and debris, an immune process called *phagocytosis.* Damage to the brain can be detected in a postmortem examination because, as illustrated in **Figure 3-9**, microglia will be left where neurons were once located.

OLIGODENDROGLIA AND SCHWANN CELLS

Two kinds of glial cells insulate the axons of neurons. Like the rubber insulation on electrical wires, this **myelin** prevents adjacent neurons from short-circuiting each other's activity. **Oligodendroglia** myelinate axons in the brain and spinal cord by sending out large, flat branches that enclose and separate adjacent axons (the prefix *oligo* means "few" and here refers to the fact that these glia have few branches in comparison with astrocytes; see Table 3-1).

Schwann cells provide myelin to axons in the peripheral nervous system. Each Schwann cell wraps itself repeatedly around a part of an axon, forming a structure somewhat like a bead on a string. In addition to the myelination, Schwann cells and oligodendroglia contribute to a neuron's nutrition and function by absorbing chemicals that the neuron releases and releasing chemicals that the neuron absorbs.

In Chapter 4 you will learn how myelin speeds up the flow of information along a neuron. Neurons that are heavily myelinated send information much faster than neurons having little or no myelin. Most neurons that must send messages over long distances, including sensory and motor neurons, are heavily myelinated.

If myelin is damaged, a neuron may be unable to send any messages over its axons. In **multiple sclerosis** (MS), myelin is damaged, and the functions of the neurons whose axons it encases are disrupted. "Multiple Sclerosis" on page 86 describes the course of the disease.

GLIAL CELLS AND NEURON REPAIR

A deep cut on your body, on your arm or leg for instance, may cut the axons connecting your spinal cord to muscles and to sensory receptors as well. Severed motor-neuron axons will render you unable to move the affected part of your body, whereas severed sensory fibers will result in loss of sensation from that body part. Cessation of both movement and sensation is **paralysis.** Over a period of weeks to months after motor and sensory axons are severed, movement and sensation will return. The human body can repair this kind of nerve damage, and so the paralysis is not permanent.

Both microglia and Schwann cells play a part in repairing damage to the peripheral nervous system. When a PNS axon is cut, it dies. Microglia remove all the debris

Myelin. Glial coating that surrounds axons in the central and peripheral nervous systems.

Oligodendroglia. Glial cell in the central nervous system that myelinates axons.

Schwann cell. Glial cell in the peripheral nervous system that forms the myelin on sensory and motor axons.

Multiple sclerosis (MS). Nervous system disorder that results from the loss of myelin (glial-cell covering) around neurons.

Paralysis. Loss of sensation and movement due to nervous system injury.

Multiple Sclerosis

Focus on Disorders

One day J. O., who had just finished university requirements to begin work as an accountant, noticed a slight cloudiness in her right eye; the cloudiness did not go away when she wiped her eye. The area of cloudiness grew over the next few days. Her optometrist suggested that she see a neurologist, who diagnosed optic neuritis, a symptom that could be a flag for multiple sclerosis.

Although we do not yet understand what causes MS, we do know that it is characterized by a loss of myelin, both on pathways bringing sensory information to the brain and on pathways taking commands to muscles. This loss of myelin occurs in patches, and scarring is frequently left in the affected areas.

Eventually, a hard scar, or *plaque,* may form in the affected areas, which is why the disease is called sclerosis (from the Greek word meaning "hardness"). Associated with the loss of myelin is impairment in neuron function, causing characteristic MS symptoms of sensory loss and difficulty in moving. Fatigue, pain, and depression are common related symptoms. Bladder dysfunction, constipation, and sexual dysfunction all complicate the condition. Multiple sclerosis greatly affects a person's emotional, social, and vocational functioning. As yet, it has no cure.

J. O.'s eye cleared over the next few months, and she had no further symptoms until after the birth of her first child 3 years later, when she felt a tingling in her right hand that spread up her arm, until gradually she lost movement in the arm. Movement was restored 5 months later. Then 2½ years later, after her second child was born, she felt a tingling in her left big toe that spread along the sole of her foot and then up to her leg, eventually leading again to loss of movement. J. O. received corticosteroid treatment, which helped, but the condition rebounded when she stopped treatment. Then it subsided and eventually disappeared.

Since then, J. O. has had no major outbreaks of motor impairment, but she still feels occasional tingling in her trunk, some weakness in her left leg, and brief periods of tingling and numbness in different body parts that last a couple of weeks before clearing. The feeling is very similar to the numbness in the face after a dentist gives a local anesthetic.

Although she suffers no depression, J. O. reports enormous fatigue, takes daily long naps, and is ready for bed early in the evening. Her sister and a female cousin have experienced similar symptoms. Computer tomographic scans on both J. O. and her sister revealed scarring in the spinal cord, a condition that helped confirm an MS diagnosis for them. One of J. O.'s grandmothers had been confined to a wheelchair, although the source of her problem was never diagnosed.

J. O. occasionally wears a brace to support her left knee and sometimes wears a collar to support her neck. She makes every effort to reduce stress to a minimum, but otherwise she lives a normal life that includes exercise and even vigorous sports such as water skiing.

J. O.'s extremely strange symptoms, which are often difficult to diagnose, are typical of multiple sclerosis. The first symptoms usually appear in adulthood, and their onset is quite sudden and swift. These initial symptoms may be loss of sensation in the face, limbs, or body or loss of control over movements or loss of both sensation and control. Motor symptoms usually appear first in the hands or feet.

Often there is remission of early symptoms, after which they may not appear again for years. In some of its forms, however, the disease may progress rapidly over a period of just a few years until the person is reduced to bed care. In cases in which the disease is fatal, the average age of death is between 65 and 84.

left by the dying axon. Meanwhile, the Schwann cells that provided its myelin first shrink and then divide, forming numerous smaller glial cells along the path that the axon formerly took. The neuron then sends out axon sprouts that search for and follow the path made by the Schwann cells.

Eventually, one sprout reaches the intended target, and this sprout becomes the new axon; all other sprouts retract. The Schwann cells envelop the new axon, forming new myelin and restoring normal function, as shown in **Figure 3-10**. In the PNS, then, Schwann cells serve as signposts to guide axons to their appropriate end points. Axons can get lost, however, as sometimes happens after surgeons reattach a severed limb. If axons destined to innervate one finger end up innervating another finger instead, the wrong finger will move when a message is sent along that neuron.

Unfortunately, glial cells do not provide much help in allowing neurons in the central nervous system to regrow, and they may actually inhibit regrowth. When the CNS is damaged, as happens, for example, when the spinal cord is cut, function does not return, even though the distance that damaged fibers must bridge is short. That recovery should take place in the peripheral nervous system but not in the central nervous system is both a puzzle and a challenge in attempts to help people with brain and spinal-cord injury.

The absence of recovery after spinal-cord injury is especially frustrating, because the spinal cord contains many axon pathways, just like those found in the PNS. Researchers investigating how to encourage the regrowth of CNS neurons have focused on the spinal cord. They have placed tubes across an injured area, trying to get axons to regrow through the tubes. They have also inserted immature glial cells into injured areas to facilitate axon regrowth, and they have used chemicals to stimulate the regrowth of axons. Some success has been obtained with each of these techniques, but none is as yet sufficiently advanced to treat people with spinal-cord injuries.

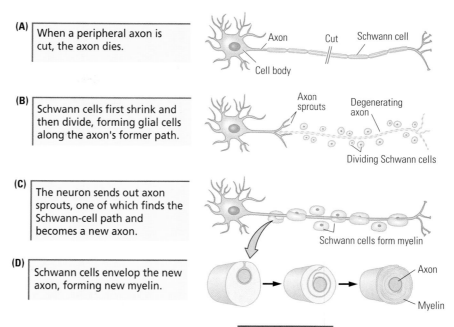

(A) When a peripheral axon is cut, the axon dies.

(B) Schwann cells first shrink and then divide, forming glial cells along the axon's former path.

(C) The neuron sends out axon sprouts, one of which finds the Schwann-cell path and becomes a new axon.

(D) Schwann cells envelop the new axon, forming new myelin.

Figure 3-10

Neuron Repair Schwann cells aid the regrowth of axons in the peripheral nervous system.

In Review

The two classes of nervous system cells are neurons and glia. The three types of neurons are sensory neurons, interneurons, and motor neurons. They are the information-conducting units of the nervous system and either excite or inhibit one another through their connecting synapses. The five types of glial cells are ependymal cells, astrocytes, microglia, oligodendroglia, and Schwann cells. Their function is to nourish, insulate, support, and repair neurons.

INTERNAL STRUCTURE OF A CELL

What is it about the structure of neurons that gives them their remarkable ability to receive, process, store, and send a seemingly limitless amount of information? To answer this question, we must look inside a neuron to see what its components are and understand what these components do. The internal features of a neuron can be colored with stains and examined under a light microscope that produces an image by reflecting light waves through the tissue. If the neurons are very small, they can be viewed with an electron microscope, in which electrons take the place of the photons of the light microscope. Just as we can take apart a robot to see how its pieces work, we can view the parts of a cell and take apart a cell to understand how its pieces function.

Because a cell is so small, it is sometimes hard to imagine that it, too, has components. Yet packed inside are hundreds of interrelated parts that do the cell's work. This feature is as true of neurons as it is of any other cell type. A primary function of a cell is to act as a miniature "factory" of work centers that manufacture and transport the proteins that are the cell's products.

To a large extent, the characteristics of cells are determined by their proteins. Time and again, when we ask how a cell performs a certain function, the answer lies in the structure of a certain protein. Each cell can manufacture hundreds to thousands of proteins, which variously take part in building the cell and in communicating with other cells; when their structures contain errors, they are implicated in many kinds of brain disease. In the following sections, we explain how the different parts of a cell contribute to protein manufacture, describe what a protein is, and detail some major functions of proteins.

Reviewing some basic chemistry is useful for understanding this story. The smallest unit of a protein, or any other chemical substance, is the molecule. Molecules, and the even smaller atoms that make them up, are the basic units of a cell factory's inputs and outputs. Our journey into the interior of a cell therefore begins with a look at these basic components. If you already understand the structure of water and you know what a salt is and what ions are, this section will serve as a brief review.

Elements and Atoms

Of the earth's 92 naturally occurring *elements,* substances that cannot be broken down into other substances, the 10 listed in **Table 3-2** account for most of an average living cell's composition. Three elements—oxygen, carbon, and hydrogen—account for more than 90 percent of the cell, with the other 7 elements constituting most of the remainder. Cells also contain many other elements that, although important, are present in extremely small quantities.

Chemists represent each element with a symbol, many of which are simply the first one or two letters of the element's English name. Examples are the symbols O for oxygen, C for carbon, and H for hydrogen. Other symbols, however, come from the element's Latin name: K, for instance, is the symbol for potassium, called *kalium* in Latin, and Na is the symbol for sodium, in Latin called *natrium.*

An *atom* is the smallest quantity of an element that retains the properties of that element. An atom has a nucleus

Table 3-2	Chemical Composition of the Brain		
Name of element	Symbol	Percentage of weight	Nucleus and electrons (not to scale)
Hydrogen	H	9.5	
Carbon	C	18.5	
Oxygen	O	65	
Nitrogen	N	3.5	
Calcium	Ca	1.5	
Phosphorus	P	1.0	
Potassium	K	0.4	
Sulfur	S	0.2	
Sodium	Na	0.2	
Chlorine	Cl	0.2	

that contains neutrons and protons (**Figure 3-11**). The *neutrons* are neutral in charge, but the *protons* carry a positive charge (+).Orbiting particles called *electrons,* each of which carries a negative charge (−), surround the nucleus. The basic structures of a cell's most common atoms are shown in the right-hand column of Table 3-2.

Ordinarily, an atom has an equal number of positive and negative charges and so is electrically neutral. But elements that are chemically reactive can easily lose or gain one or more electrons. When an atom gives up an electron, it becomes positively charged; when it takes on an extra electron, it becomes negatively charged.

In either case, the charged atom is now an *ion.* An ion formed by losing one electron is represented by the element's symbol and a plus sign. For example, the symbol K^+ represents a potassium ion, and Na^+ represents a sodium ion. An ion formed by losing two electrons is represented by the element's symbol followed by two positive charges (Ca^{2+} for a calcium ion). Some ions that are important for cell function have gained electrons rather than lost them. Such an ion is represented by the element's symbol followed by a negative sign (for example, Cl^- representing an ion of chlorine, called a chloride ion). The positive and negative charges of ions allow them to interact, a property that is central to cell function.

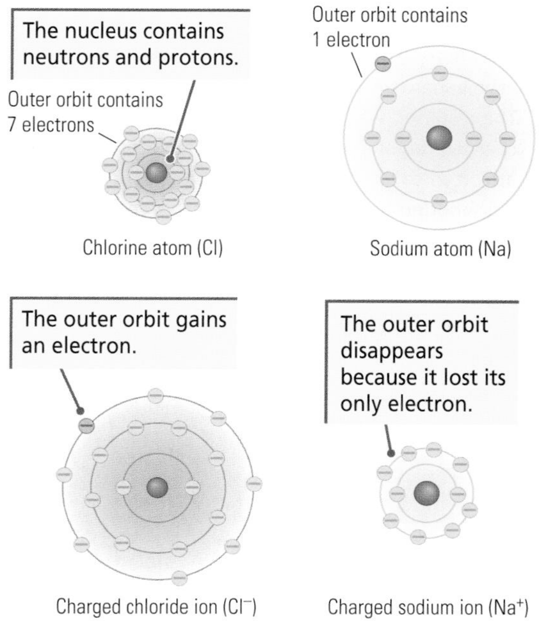

The nucleus contains neutrons and protons.

Outer orbit contains 7 electrons

Outer orbit contains 1 electron

Chlorine atom (Cl)

Sodium atom (Na)

The outer orbit gains an electron.

The outer orbit disappears because it lost its only electron.

Charged chloride ion (Cl^-)

Charged sodium ion (Na^+)

Figure 3-11

Ion Formation Ions are formed by the addition or loss of electrons.

Na^+	sodium ion
K^+	potassium ion
Ca^{2+}	calcium ion
Cl^-	chlorine ion

Molecules

When atoms bind together, they form *molecules,* the smallest units of a substance that contain all that substance's properties. For example, a water molecule (H_2O) is the smallest unit of water that still retains the properties of water. Breaking down water any further would divide it into its two component elements, the gases hydrogen and oxygen.

Atomic symbols specify a substance's formula. For example, the formula H_2O indicates that a water molecule is a union of two hydrogen atoms and one oxygen atom. Similarly, NaCl, the formula for table salt (sodium chloride), shows that this substance consists of one sodium atom and one chlorine atom, whereas KCl, the formula for potassium chloride, another kind of salt, says that this substance is composed of one potassium atom and one chlorine atom. Water, salts, and ions play prominent parts in the cell's functions, as you will learn throughout the next few chapters.

Salts break into their constituent ions in water. When salts such as NaCl and KCl are formed, the sodium or potassium atom gives up an electron to the chlorine atom. Therefore these salts are composed of negatively and positively charged ions tightly held together by their electrical attraction.

In contrast, the atoms that constitute a water molecule are held together by *shared* electrons. As you can see in **Figure 3-12A**, the electrons provided by the H atoms spend some of their time orbiting the O atom. In this particular case, the electron sharing is not equal. The shared electrons spend more time orbiting O than they do H, which gives the oxygen region of the molecule a slight negative charge and leaves the hydrogen regions with a slight positive charge. Water, therefore, is a *polar molecule,* meaning that it has opposite charges on opposite ends (just as the earth does at the North and South Poles).

Because water molecules are polar, they are electrically attracted to ions and to one another. A slightly positively charged hydrogen ion of one water molecule is attracted to the slightly negatively charged oxygen ion of a nearby molecule. This attracting force is called a *hydrogen bond* (Figure 3-12B). Each water molecule can form hydrogen bonds with a maximum of four neighbors. The attraction of water molecules for one another

Figure 3-12

Chemistry of Water **(A)** Two hydrogen (H) atoms share electrons with one oxygen (O) atom. The resulting water molecule is polar. **(B)** The charged regions of a polar water molecule are attracted to oppositely charged parts of neighboring water molecules. Each water molecule can hydrogen bond to a maximum of four partners.

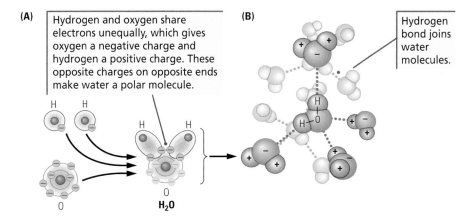

(A) Hydrogen and oxygen share electrons unequally, which gives oxygen a negative charge and hydrogen a positive charge. These opposite charges on opposite ends make water a polar molecule.

(B) Hydrogen bond joins water molecules.

H_2O

is also described by the term *hydrophilic,* or water loving (from the Greek *hydro,* meaning "water," and *philia,* meaning "love"). Other polar molecules also are hydrophilic—they, too, are attracted to water molecules.

Hydrogen bonding gives water some interesting properties, such as high surface tension (small insects can walk across water), strong cohesion (water droplets cling together), and a high boiling point (the temperature at which liquid water vaporizes). Water can also break down, or dissolve, salts.

An example of dissolving is what happens to sodium chloride, or table salt, in water. As already stated, NaCl is formed by electrical attraction when sodium atoms give up electrons to chlorine atoms and the resulting positively and negatively charged ions (Na^+ and Cl^-) join together to form a crystal (**Figure 3-13A**). Salt cannot retain its crystal shape in water, however. As shown in Figure 3-13B, the polar water molecules muscle their way between the Na^+ and Cl^- lattice, surrounding and separating the ions. The result is salty water. Sodium chloride is one of the dissolved salts found in the fluid that exists inside and outside cells. Many other salts, such as KCl (potassium chloride) and $CaCl_2$ (calcium chloride) are found there as well.

Parts of a Cell

We have compared a cell to a miniature factory, with work centers that cooperate to make and ship the cell's products—proteins. We now continue this analogy as we investigate the internal parts of a cell and how they function, beginning here with a quick overview of the cell's internal structure. **Figure 3-14** displays many cellular components.

A factory's outer wall separates it from the rest of the world and affords some security. Likewise, a cell's double-layered outer wall, or *cell*

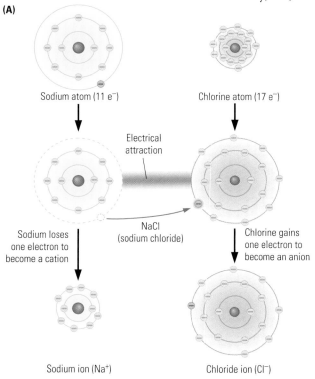

(A)

Sodium atom (11 e⁻)   Chlorine atom (17 e⁻)

Electrical attraction

NaCl (sodium chloride)

Sodium loses one electron to become a cation

Chlorine gains one electron to become an anion

Sodium ion (Na^+)   Chloride ion (Cl^-)

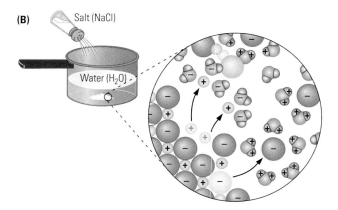

(B) Salt (NaCl)

Water (H_2O)

Figure 3-13

Salts Dissolve **(A)** Crystals of table salt are formed by the electrical attraction of sodium and chlorine. The positively charged sodium ion (Na^+) is short one electron, whereas the chlorine gains an electron and so has a negative charge (Cl^-). **(B)** Weakly bound polar water molecules surround Na^+ ions and Cl^- ions, dissolving the salt. The positive part of the water molecule is attracted to the negative Cl^- ion, and the negative part of the water molecule is attracted to the positive Na^+ ion.

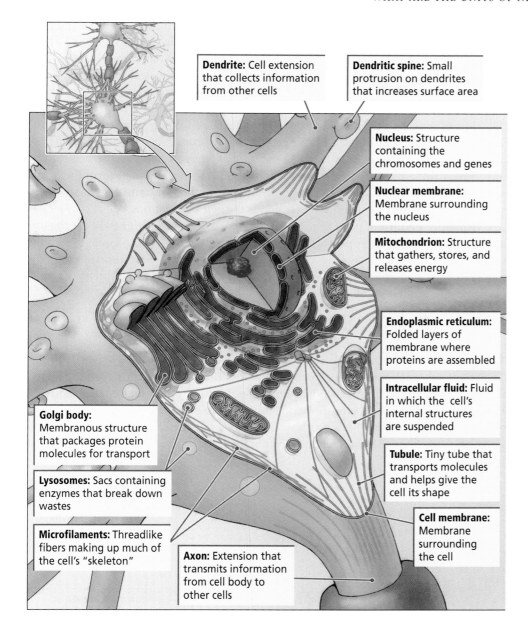

Dendrite: Cell extension that collects information from other cells

Dendritic spine: Small protrusion on dendrites that increases surface area

Nucleus: Structure containing the chromosomes and genes

Nuclear membrane: Membrane surrounding the nucleus

Mitochondrion: Structure that gathers, stores, and releases energy

Endoplasmic reticulum: Folded layers of membrane where proteins are assembled

Intracellular fluid: Fluid in which the cell's internal structures are suspended

Tubule: Tiny tube that transports molecules and helps give the cell its shape

Cell membrane: Membrane surrounding the cell

Golgi body: Membranous structure that packages protein molecules for transport

Lysosomes: Sacs containing enzymes that break down wastes

Microfilaments: Threadlike fibers making up much of the cell's "skeleton"

Axon: Extension that transmits information from cell body to other cells

Figure 3-14

Typical Nerve Cell   This view inside a neuron reveals its organelles and other internal components.

membrane separates it from its surroundings and allows it to regulate what enters and leaves its domain. The cell membrane surrounds the neuron's cell body, dendrites and their spines, and the axon and its terminals and so forms a boundary around a continuous intracellular compartment.

Very few substances can enter or leave a cell, because the cell membrane is almost impenetrable. Proteins made by the cell are embedded in the cell membrane to facilitate the transport of substances into and out of the cell. Some proteins thus serve as the cellular factory's gates.

Although the neurons and glia of the brain appear to be tightly packed together, they, like all cells, are separated by *extracellular fluid* composed mainly of water with dissolved salts and many other chemicals. A similar fluid is found inside a cell as well. The important point is that the concentrations of substances inside and outside the cell are different. The fluid inside a cell is known as the *intracellular fluid.*

Within the cell are other membranes that surround its interior compartments (see Figure 13-14), similar to the work areas demarcated by the inner walls of a factory. In

⊙ The section on the cell body in the neural communication module on the *Foundations* CD further details the internal structure of a neuron.

each inner compartment, the cell concentrates chemicals that it needs while keeping out unneeded ones. The prominent *nuclear membrane* surrounds the cell's *nucleus,* where the genetic blueprints for the cell's proteins are stored, copied, and sent to the "factory floor." The *endoplasmic reticulum* (ER) is an extension of the nuclear membrane where the cell's protein products are assembled in accord with instructions from the nucleus.

When those proteins are assembled, they are packaged and sent throughout the cell. Parts of the cell called the *Golgi bodies* provide the packaging rooms where the proteins are wrapped, addressed, and shipped. Other cell components are called *tubules,* of which there are a number of kinds. Some *(microfilaments)* reinforce the cell's structure, others aid in the cell's movements, and still others *(microtubules)* form the transportation network that carries the proteins to their destinations, much as roads allow a factory's trucks and forklifts to deliver goods to their destinations.

Two other important parts of the cellular factory shown in Figure 3-14 are the *mitochondria,* the cell's power plants that supply its energy needs, and *lysosomes,* sacklike vesicles that transport incoming supplies and move and store wastes. Interestingly, more lysosomes are found in old cells than in young ones. Cells apparently have trouble disposing of their garbage, just as we do.

With this brief overview of the cell's internal structure in mind, you can now examine its parts in more detail, beginning with the cell membrane.

THE CELL MEMBRANE: BARRIER AND GATEKEEPER

The cell membrane separates the intracellular from the extracellular fluid and so allows the cell to function as an independent unit. The structure of the membrane, shown in **Figure 3-15A**, also regulates the movement of substances into and out of the cell. One of these substances is water. If too much water enters a cell, it will burst, and, if too much water leaves a cell, it will shrivel. The cell membrane helps ensure that neither will happen.

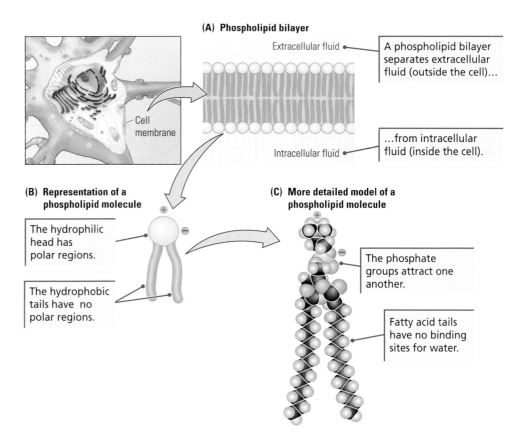

Figure 3-15

Structure of the Cell Membrane
(A) The membrane's bilayer. **(B)** Detail of a phospholipid molecule's polar head and electrically neutral tails. **(C)** Space-filling model shows why the phosphate head's polar regions (positive and negative poles) are hydrophilic, whereas its fatty acid tail, having no polar regions, is hydrophobic.

(A) Phospholipid bilayer

Extracellular fluid

A phospholipid bilayer separates extracellular fluid (outside the cell)...

Cell membrane

...from intracellular fluid (inside the cell).

Intracellular fluid

(B) Representation of a phospholipid molecule

The hydrophilic head has polar regions.

The hydrophobic tails have no polar regions.

(C) More detailed model of a phospholipid molecule

The phosphate groups attract one another.

Fatty acid tails have no binding sites for water.

The cell membrane also regulates the differing concentrations of salts and other chemicals on its inner and outer sides. This regulation is important because, if the concentrations of chemicals within a cell become unbalanced, the cell will not function normally. What properties of a cell membrane allow it to regulate water and salt concentrations within the cell? One is its special molecular construction. These molecules, called *phospholipids*, are named for their structure, shown close up in Figure 3-15B.

The phosopholipid molecule's "head" contains the element phosphorus (P) bound to some other atoms, and its two "tails" are lipids, or fat molecules. The head region is polar, with a slight positive charge in one location and a slight negative charge in another, like water molecules. The tails consist of hydrogen and carbon atoms that are tightly bound to one another by their shared electrons; hence there are no polar regions in the fatty tail. Figure 3-15C shows a chemical model of the phosopholipid molecule.

The polar head and the nonpolar tails are the underlying reasons that a phospholipid molecule can form membranes. The heads are hydrophilic and so are attracted to one another and to polar water molecules. The nonpolar tails have no such attraction for water. They are *hydrophobic*, or water hating (the suffix *phobic* comes from the Greek word *phobia*, meaning "fear"). Quite literally, then, the head of a phospholipid loves water and the tails hate it. To avoid water, the tails of phospholipid molecules point toward each other, and the hydrophilic heads align with one another and point outward to the intracellular and extracellular fluid. In this way, the cell membrane consists of a bilayer (two layers) of phospholipid molecules (see Figure 3-15A).

The bilayer cell membrane is flexible while still forming a remarkable barrier to a wide variety of substances. It is impenetrable to intracellular and extracellular water, because polar water molecules cannot pass through the hydrophobic tails on the interior of the membrane. Ions in the extracellular and intracellular fluid also cannot penetrate this membrane, because they carry charges and thus cannot pass the phospholipid heads. In fact, only a few small molecules, such as oxygen (O_2), can pass through a phospholipid bilayer.

Recall that the cell-membrane barrier is punctuated with embedded protein "gates" that receive its supplies, dispose of its wastes, and ship its products. Before we describe these mechanisms in detail, we consider how proteins are manufactured and transported within the cell.

THE NUCLEUS: SITE OF GENE TRANSCRIPTION

In our factory analogy, the nucleus is the cell's executive office where the blueprints for making proteins are stored, copied, and sent to the factory floor. These blueprints are called *genes*, segments of DNA that encode the synthesis of particular proteins. Genes are contained within the *chromosomes*, the double-helix structures that hold an organism's entire DNA sequence. (The name *chromosome* means "colored body," referring to the fact that chromosomes can be readily stained with certain dyes.)

The chromosomes are like a book of blueprints for making a complex building, whereas a gene is like one page of the book containing the plan for a door or a corridor between rooms. Each chromosome contains thousands of genes. The location of the chromosomes in the nucleus of the cell, the appearance of a chromosome, and the structure of the DNA in a chromosome are shown in **Figure 3-16**.

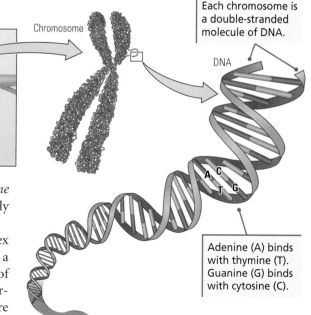

Figure 3-16

A Chromosome The nerve-cell nucleus contains paired chromosomes of double-stranded DNA molecules bound together by a sequence of nucleotide bases.

Each chromosome is a double-stranded molecule of DNA.

Chromosome

DNA

A C
T G

Adenine (A) binds with thymine (T). Guanine (G) binds with cytosine (C).

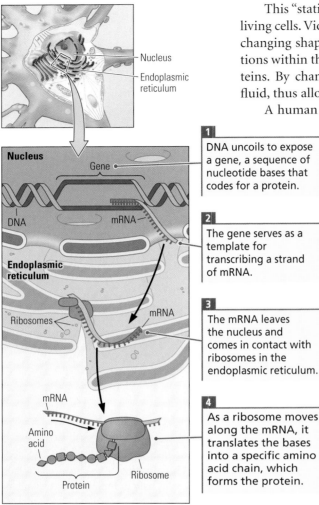

1

DNA uncoils to expose a gene, a sequence of nucleotide bases that codes for a protein.

2

The gene serves as a template for transcribing a strand of mRNA.

3

The mRNA leaves the nucleus and comes in contact with ribosomes in the endoplasmic reticulum.

4

As a ribosome moves along the mRNA, it translates the bases into a specific amino acid chain, which forms the protein.

Figure 3-17

Protein Synthesis The flow of information in a cell is from DNA to mRNA to protein (peptide chain).

⊙ For an animation showing protein synthesis in action, visit the Chapter 3 Web links on the *Brain and Behavior* Web site at (**www.worthpublishers.com/kolb**).

This "static" picture of chromosomes does not represent the way that they look in living cells. Video recordings of the cell nucleus show that chromosomes are constantly changing shape and moving in relation to one another so as to occupy the best locations within the nucleus for collecting the building blocks of proteins and making proteins. By changing shape, chromosomes expose different genes to the surrounding fluid, thus allowing the processes of protein formation to begin.

A human somatic (body) cell has 23 pairs of chromosomes, or 46 in all (in contrast, the 23 chromosomes within a reproductive cell are not paired). Each chromosome is a double-stranded molecule of *deoxyribonucleic acid* (DNA), which is capable of replicating and determining the inherited structure of a cell's proteins. The two strands of a DNA molecule coil around each other, as shown in Figure 3-16. Each strand possesses a variable sequence of four *nucleotide bases,* the constituent molecules of the genetic code: *adenine* (A), *thymine* (T), *guanine* (G), and *cytosine* (C).

Adenine on one strand always pairs with thymine on the other, whereas guanine on one strand always pairs with cytosine on the other. The two strands of the DNA helix are bonded together by the attraction that these paired bases have for each other. Sequences of hundreds of nucleotide bases within the chromosomes spell out the genetic code—for example, ATGCCG, and so forth.

Now you are ready to understand exactly how genes work. Recall that a gene is a segment of a DNA strand that encodes the synthesis of a particular protein. The code is contained in the sequence of the nucleotide bases, much as a sequence of letters spells out a word. The sequence of bases "spells out" the particular order in which *amino acids,* the constituent molecules of proteins, should be assembled to construct a certain protein.

To initiate the process, the appropriate gene segment of the DNA strands first unwinds. The exposed sequence of nucleotide bases on one of the DNA strands then serves as a template to attract free-floating molecules called nucleotides. The nucleotides thus attached form a complementary strand of *ribonucleic acid* (RNA), the single-stranded nucleic acid molecule required for protein synthesis. This process, called *transcription,* is shown in steps 1 and 2 of **Figure 3-17**. (To transcribe means "to copy," as one would copy a piece of text in a word-processing program.)

The RNA produced through transcription is much like a single strand of DNA except that the base *uracil* (U, which also is attracted to adenine) takes the place of thymine. The transcribed strand of RNA is called *messenger RNA* (mRNA) because it carries the genetic code out of the nucleus to the endoplasmic reticulum, where proteins are manufactured. The sequence for this process is

$$DNA \rightarrow mRNA \rightarrow protein$$

THE ENDOPLASMIC RETICULUM: SITE OF PROTEIN SYNTHESIS

Steps 3 and 4 in Figure 3-17 show that the ER consists of membranous sheets folded to form numerous channels. A distinguishing feature of the ER is that it may be studded with *ribosomes,* protein structures that act as catalysts in the building of proteins. When an mRNA molecule reaches the ER, it passes through a ribosome, where its genetic code is "read."

In this process, called *translation,* a particular sequence of nucleotide bases in the mRNA is translated into a particular sequence of amino acids. (To translate means to convert one language into another, in contrast with transcription, in which the language remains the same.) *Transfer RNA* (tRNA) assists in translation. *Proteins* are just long chains of amino acids, folded up to form specific shapes.

The flow of information contained in the genetic code is conceptually quite simple: a DNA strand is transcribed into an mRNA strand, and the mRNA strand is translated by ribosomes into a molecular chain of amino acids. As shown in **Figure 3-18**, each group of three consecutive nucleotide bases along an mRNA molecule encodes one particular amino acid. These sequences of three bases are called *codons*. For example, the base sequence uracil, guanine, guanine (UGG) encodes the amino acid tryptophan (Trp), whereas the base sequence uracil, uracil, uracil (UUU) encodes the amino acid phenylalanine (Phe). Codons also direct the placement of particular amino acids into a polypeptide chain.

Humans require 20 different amino acids for the synthesis of proteins. All 20 are structurally similar, as illustrated in **Figure 3-19A**. Each consists of a central carbon atom (C) bound to a hydrogen atom (H), an *amino group* (NH^{3+}), a *carboxyl group* (COO^{2-}), and a *side chain* (represented by the letter R). The side chain, which varies in chemical composition from one amino acid to another, helps to give different protein molecules their distinctive biochemical properties.

Amino acids are linked together by a special bond called a *peptide bond* (Figure 3-19B). A series of amino acids is called a *polypeptide chain* (meaning "many peptides"). Just as a remarkable number of words can be made from the 26 letters of the English alphabet, a remarkable number of peptide chains can be made from the 20 different amino acids. These amino acids can form 400 (20 × 20) different dipeptides (two-peptide combinations), 8000 (20 × 20 × 20) different tripeptides (three-peptide combinations), and almost countless polypeptides.

A polypeptide chain and a protein are related, but they are not the same. The relation is analogous to that between a ribbon and a bow of a particular size and shape that can be made from the ribbon. Long polypeptide chains have a strong tendency to twist into a helix (a spiral) or to form pleated sheets, which, in turn, have a strong tendency to fold together to form more-complex shapes as shown in **Figure 3-20**. A folded-up polypeptide chain constitutes a protein. In addition, two or more polypeptide chains may combine to form a single protein. Many proteins are globular (round)

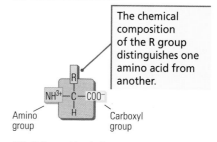

(A) Amino acid structure

The chemical composition of the R group distinguishes one amino acid from another.

Amino group / Carboxyl group

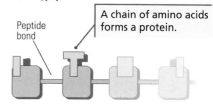

(B) Polypeptide chain

A chain of amino acids forms a protein.

Peptide bond

Figure 3-18

Transcription and Translation In protein synthesis (see Figure 3-17), a strand of DNA is transcribed into mRNA. Each sequence of three bases in the mRNA strand (a codon) encodes one amino acid. Directed by the codons, the amino acids link together to form a polypeptide chain. The amino acids illustrated are tryptophan (Trp), phenylalanine (Phe), glycine (Gly), and serine (Ser).

Figure 3-19

Properties of Amino Acids **(A)** Each amino acid consists of a central carbon atom (C) attached to an amine group (NH^{3+}), a carboxyl group (COO^-), and a distinguishing side chain (R). **(B)** The amino acids are linked by peptide bonds to form a polypeptide chain.

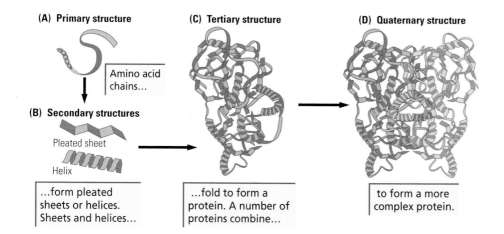

(A) Primary structure

Amino acid chains...

(B) Secondary structures

Pleated sheet

Helix

...form pleated sheets or helices. Sheets and helices...

(C) Tertiary structure

...fold to form a protein. A number of proteins combine...

(D) Quaternary structure

to form a more complex protein.

Figure 3-20

Four Levels of Protein Structure Whether a polypeptide chain forms a pleated sheet or a helix and its ultimate three-dimensional shape are determined by the sequence of amino acids in the primary structure.

Channel. Opening in a protein embedded in the cell membrane that allows the passage of ions.

Gate. Protein embedded in a cell membrane that allows substances to pass through the membrane on some occasions but not on others.

Pump. Protein in the cell membrane that actively transports a substance across the membrane.

in shape and others are fibrous, but, within these broad categories, countless variations are possible. A protein's shape and ability to change shape and to combine with other proteins are central to the protein's function.

GOLGI BODIES AND MICROTUBULES: PROTEIN PACKAGING AND SHIPMENT

Any one neuron may use as many as 10,000 protein molecules. Some proteins are destined to be incorporated into the structure of the cell. They become part of the cell membrane, the nucleus, the ER, and so forth. Other proteins remain in the intracellular fluid, where they act as enzymes—protein catalysts that facilitate the cell's chemical reactions. Still other proteins are excreted by the cell as "messenger molecules" and so allow the cell to communicate with other cells. Getting all these different proteins to the right destinations is the task of the cell components that package, label, and ship them. These components operate much like a postal service.

To reach their appropriate destinations, the protein molecules that have been synthesized in the cell must first be wrapped in membranes and given labels that indicate where they are to go. This wrapping and labeling takes place in the organelles called Golgi bodies. The packaged proteins are then loaded onto motor molecules that "walk" along the many microtubules radiating through the cell, thus carrying the protein to its destination. The work of exporting proteins is illustrated in **Figure 3-21**.

If a protein is destined to remain within the cell, it is unloaded into the intracellular fluid. If it is to be incorporated into the cell membrane, it is carried to the membrane, where it inserts itself. Suppose that a particular protein is to be excreted at the cell membrane. In this process, called *exocytosis,* the membrane, or *vesicle,* in which the protein is wrapped first fuses with the membrane of the cell. Now the protein inside the vesicle can be expelled into the extracellular fluid. Many excreted proteins travel to other cells to induce chemical reactions and so serve as messenger molecules.

THE CELL MEMBRANE REVISITED: CHANNELS, GATES, AND PUMPS

Knowing something about the structure of proteins will help you to understand other ways that substances can travel across what would otherwise be an impermeable cell membrane. Recall that some of the proteins that cells manufacture are carried to the cell membrane, where they become embedded. Hydrophobic parts of a protein molecule affix themselves within the cell membrane while hydrophilic parts of the protein

Figure 3-21

Protein Export Exporting a protein entails packaging, transport, and its function at the destination.

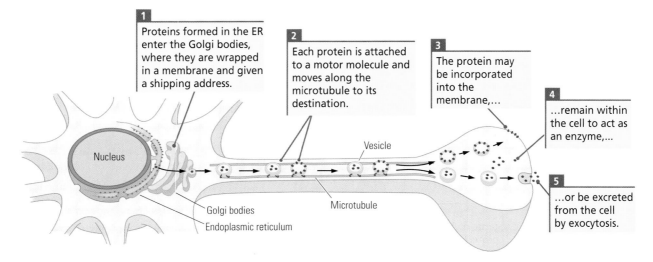

1 Proteins formed in the ER enter the Golgi bodies, where they are wrapped in a membrane and given a shipping address.

2 Each protein is attached to a motor molecule and moves along the microtubule to its destination.

3 The protein may be incorporated into the membrane,...

4 ...remain within the cell to act as an enzyme,...

5 ...or be excreted from the cell by exocytosis.

Nucleus

Vesicle

Golgi bodies

Microtubule

Endoplasmic reticulum

stick out into the intra- and extracellular fluid. In this way, membrane protein molecules span the cell membrane.

These membrane proteins play a number of important roles, one of which is transporting substances across the membrane. We will consider how three such membrane proteins work: channels, gates, and pumps. In each case, notice how the function of the particular protein is an emergent property of its shape.

Both the *shape* of a protein and its ability to *change* shape are emergent properties of the precise sequence of amino acids that compose the protein molecule. Some proteins change shape when other chemicals bind to them, others change shape as a function of temperature, and still others change shape in response to changes in electrical charge. The ability of a protein molecule to change shape is analogous to a lock in a door. When a key of the appropriate size and shape is inserted into the lock and turned, the locking device activates and changes shape, allowing the door to be closed or opened.

An example of a shape-changing protein is the enzyme hexokinase, illustrated in **Figure 3-22**. The surface of this protein molecule has a groove, called a *receptor,* which is analogous to a keyhole. When another molecule—in this case, glucose—enters the receptor area, it induces a slight change in the shape of the protein, causing the hexokinase to embrace the glucose. Either small molecules or other proteins can bind to the receptors of proteins and cause them to change shape. Changes in shape then allow the proteins to serve some new function.

A cell-membrane protein's shape or its ability to change shape enable substances to cross the cell membrane. Some membrane proteins create **channels** through which substances can pass. Different-sized channels in different proteins allow the passage of different substances. **Figure 3-23A** illustrates a protein with a particular shape forming a small channel in the cell membrane that is large enough for potassium (K^+) ions, but not other ions, to pass through. Other protein channels allow sodium ions or chloride ions to pass into or out of the cell.

Figure 3-23B shows a protein molecule that acts as a **gate** to regulate the passage of substances across the cell membrane by changing its shape in response to some trigger, as the protein hexokinase does in Figure 3-22. The protein allows the passage of substances when its shape forms a channel and prevents the passage of substances when its shape leaves the channel closed. Thus a part of this protein acts as a gate.

Changes in the shape of a protein can also allow it to act as a **pump**. Figure 3-23C shows a protein that, when Na^+ and K^+ ions bind to it, changes its shape to carry ("pump") the substances across the membrane, exchanging the Na^+ on one side of the membrane for the K^+ on the other side of the membrane.

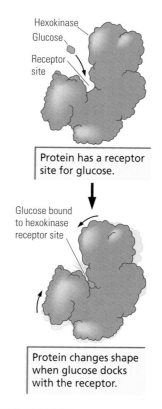

Hexokinase
Glucose
Receptor site

Protein has a receptor site for glucose.

Glucose bound to hexokinase receptor site

Protein changes shape when glucose docks with the receptor.

Figure 3-22

Receptor Binding When substances bind to a protein's receptors, the protein changes shape, which may change its function.

◉ For more information about how substances are transported across the membrane, visit the section on membrane potential in the neural communication module on the *Foundations* CD.

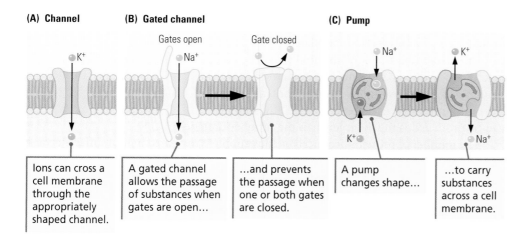

(A) Channel

K^+

Ions can cross a cell membrane through the appropriately shaped channel.

(B) Gated channel

Gates open
Na^+

Gate closed

A gated channel allows the passage of substances when gates are open...

...and prevents the passage when one or both gates are closed.

(C) Pump

Na^+
K^+

K^+
Na^+

A pump changes shape...

...to carry substances across a cell membrane.

Figure 3-23

Transmembrane Proteins Channels, gates, and pumps are embedded in the cell membrane.

Channels, gates, and pumps play an important role in allowing substances to enter and leave a cell. This passage of substances is critical in explaining how neurons send messages. Chapter 4 explores the topic of neuron communication in detail.

In Review

Chemical elements within cells combine to form molecules that in turn organize into the constituent parts of the cell, including the cell membrane, nucleus, endoplasmic reticulum, Golgi bodies, tubules, and vesicles. Important products of the cell are proteins, which serve many functions including acting at the cell membrane as channels, gates, and pumps to allow substances to cross the membrane. Simply put, the sequence of events in building a protein is: DNA makes mRNA and mRNA makes protein. When formed, the protein molecules are wrapped by the Golgi bodies and transported to their designated sites in the neuron, to its membrane, or for export from the cell by microtubules.

GENES, CELLS, AND BEHAVIOR

Genes are the blueprints for proteins, proteins are essential to the function of cells, and cells produce behavior. That sequence of connections sounds simple enough. But exactly how one connection leads to another is one of the big challenges for future research. If you choose a career in neuroscience research, you will most likely be working out some aspect of this relation.

Just as the replacement of a malfunctioning part of a robot restores its function, the identification and replacement of an abnormal gene could provide a cure for the brain and behavioral abnormalities that it produces. Genetic research, then, promises a revolutionary effect not only on the study of the brain and behavior but also on the search for new ways to treat genetic disorders. For these reasons, we will focus on human genetics in the rest of this chapter.

To review, genes are chromosome segments that encode proteins, and proteins serve as enzymes, membrane channels, and messenger molecules. This knowledge does not tell you much about the ultimate structure and function of a cell, because so many genes and proteins take part. The eventual function of a cell is an emergent property of all its many constituent parts.

Similarly, knowing that behaviors result from the activity of neurons does not tell you much about the ultimate form that behaviors will take, because so many neurons participate in them. Your behavior is an emergent property of the action of all your billions of neurons. The challenge for future research is to be able to explain how genes, proteins, cells, and behavior are related.

Understanding the contributions of genes alone is a tremendous challenge. The field of study directed toward understanding how genes produce proteins is called *genomics.* Humans have up to 20,000 genes, about half of which contribute to building the brain. Although each gene is a code for one protein, the number of proteins that can be produced is much larger than the number of genes.

The number of proteins produced by the genome is increased in four different ways:

1. Most gene pairs have a number of variants, or alleles, and each allele will produce a slightly different protein, as explained in the next section. In addition, in an individual organism, one of the gene variants from one parent may be imprinted so that it is expressed, whereas the other variant is not.

○ You can learn more about genetics by exploring the Chapter 3 Web links on the *Brain and Behavior* Web site (**www.worthpublishers.com/kolb**).

2. Enzymes in the nucleus can edit the mRNA that carries the message from a gene to produce a protein, resulting in still more protein variants.

3. Once formed, protein molecules can be cleaved by enzymes, producing two or more different proteins.

4. As we have described, protein molecules can merge to form still different proteins. The mergers may include thousands of proteins that form interactions that collaborate to produce biological functions.

In principle, then, there is no upper limit on the number of proteins that could be manufactured by a cell, but the number of proteins required for normal cell function is likely fewer than 100,000. Knowing what functions each of those proteins has would greatly advance our understanding of how the brain is constructed and produces behavior. The field of study directed toward understanding what all these proteins do is called *proteomics.*

Thus, although the Human Genome Project has cataloged the human genome (all the genes in our species) and the genomes of many other species also have been described, identifying the function of every gene and describing the emergent properties of their proteins and their interactions will take a long time. Interestingly, genome size and chromosome number seem unrelated to the complexity of the organism (**Table 3-3**). "Knocking out Genes" on page 100 describes one technique developed by genomics researchers.

Even though neuroscientists cannot yet explain human behavior in relation to genes and neurons, we know the severe behavioral consequences of about 2000 genetic abnormalities that affect the nervous system. For example, an error in a gene could produce a protein that should be a K^+ channel but will not allow K^+ to pass, it may produce a pump that will not pump, or it may produce a protein that the transportation system of the cell refuses to transport.

With thousands of different proteins in a cell, a genetic mutation that results in an abnormality of any one protein could have a beneficial effect, it could have little noticeable effect, or it could have severe negative consequences. Studying genetic abnormalities is one source of insight into how genes, neurons, and behaviors are linked. Such studies may also help us to reduce the negative effects of these abnormalities, perhaps someday even eliminating them completely.

⊙ On the *Brain and Behavior* Web site (**www.worthpublishers.com/kolb**) visit the Chapter 3 Web links for the latest updates on the Human Genome Project.

Chromosomes and Genes

Recall that the nucleus of each human somatic cell contains 23 pairs of chromosomes, or 46 in all. One member of each pair of chromosomes comes from the mother, and the other member comes from the father. The chromosome pairs are numbered from

Table 3-3	Genome Size and Chromosome Number in Selected Species	
Species	**Genome size (base pairs)**	**Chromosome number**
Ameba	670,000,000,000	Several hundred
Lily	90,000,000,000	12
Mouse	3,454,200,000	20
Human	2,850,000,000	23
Carp	1,700,000,000	49
Chicken	1,200,000,000	39
Housefly	900,000,000	6
Tomato	655,000,000	12

Knocking Out Genes

A small, common nematode that is found in soil and lives on bacteria, *Caenorhabditis elegans*, or *C. elegans*, was the first animal genome sequenced. It has 19,757 genes that code for proteins. To discover what these proteins do, Ravi Kamath and colleagues (2003) developed a method for selectively "knocking out" each gene and observing the resulting phenotype (expressed traits) of the worms thus produced.

Their method capitalizes on the way in which cells have evolved to protect themselves from invasion by the double-stranded RNA (dsRNA) of viruses. If dsRNA is introduced into the cell, a mechanism called RNA-mediated interference (RNAi) inactivates the gene that would produce that sequence of RNA. Thus, a cell so infected will not produce the affected mRNA sequence, and its resulting protein will not be made.

C. elegans is remarkable in that, if it eats a dsRNA, gene silencing can be produced by the knockout method. Kamath

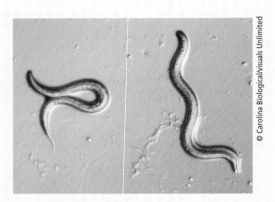

© Carolina Biological/Visuals Unlimited

Caenorhabditis elegans is a small roundworm about 1 millimeter long that lives in the soil. It was the first species to have all of its neurons, synapses, and its genome described.

and colleagues infected different strains of bacteria with different RNAi and examined the phenotype of the offspring of worms that had particular genes inactivated. In all, they were able to inactivate 86 percent of *C. elegans*'s genes. What do the resulting phenotypes of these offspring tell us about the function of its genes? Kamath and colleagues were able to classify identified genes into a number of groups, including the following two:

■   Ancient genes, those also found in more phylogenetically primitive animals. Deletion of one of these genes is lethal, suggesting that they are essential for life in all animals.

■   Animal genes, those also found in many species including mice and humans. Deletion of these genes results in abnormalities in body shape or movement. *C. elegans* with these genetic deletions could thus serve as animal models for human genetic disorders.

One use of knockout methodology identifies genes with specific interesting properties. Kaveh Ashrafi and colleagues (2003) described a screen for fat-regulatory genes in *C. elegans*. These researchers included a fluorescent dye, in addition to the dsRNA, in the worm's diet. This dye allowed fat droplets in the intestinal cells of living worms to be visualized by measuring fluorescence intensity with a light meter.

The scientists identified 305 genes that reduce the amount of body fat on inactivation and 112 genes that increase it. Many of these genes have been identified in humans and so might be new targets for understanding human fat regulation and for identifying new antiobesity drugs.

1 to 23, with chromosome 1 being the largest and chromosome 22 being next to the smallest (chromosome 21 is the smallest; **Figure 3-24**).

Chromosome pairs 1 through 22 are called *autosomes*, and they contain the genes that contribute to most of our physical appearance and behavioral functions. The 23rd pair comprises the *sex chromosomes*, which eventually produce our physical and behavioral sexual characteristics. There are two types of sex chromosomes, referred to as X and Y because of their appearance. Female mammals have two X chromosomes, whereas males have an X and a Y.

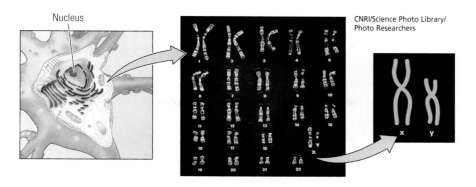

Nucleus

CNRI/Science Photo Library/
Photo Researchers

Figure 3-24

Human Chromosomes   The nucleus of a human cell contains 23 chromosomes derived from the father and 23 from the mother. Sexual characteristics are determined by the 23rd pair, the sex chromosomes.

Because your chromosomes are "matched" pairs, a cell contains two copies of every gene, one inherited from your mother, the other from your father. These two matching copies of a gene are called **alleles.** The term "matched" here does not necessarily mean identical. The nucleotide sequences in a pair of alleles may be either identical or different. If they are identical, the two alleles are **homozygous** (*homo* means "the same"). If they are different, the two alleles are **heterozygous** (*hetero* means "different").

The nucleotide sequence that is most common in a population is called the **wild-type** allele, whereas a less frequently occurring sequence is called a **mutation.** Mutant genes often determine genetic disorders.

Genotype and Phenotype

The actions of genes give rise to what we call physical or behavioral *traits,* but these actions are not always straightforward. A gene may be "imprinted" by one parent so that it is not expressed, even though present. The actions of a protein manufactured by one gene may be suppressed or modified by other genes. Developmental age or experiential factors also may influence gene expression. For these reasons, as well as others, some genes are not expressed as traits or may be expressed only incompletely.

The proteins and genes that contribute to human skin color provide a good example. The color expressed depends on the precise complement of a number of different genes. And environmental factors such as exposure to sunlight may modify gene expression. Genes and expressed traits can thus be very different, and so scientists distinguish between them:

Genotype refers to the full set of all the genes that an organism possesses.

Phenotype refers to the appearance of an organism that results from the interaction of genes with one another and with the environment (*pheno* comes from the Greek word meaning "show").

The extent of phenotypic variation, given the same genotype, can be dramatic. For example, in strains of genetically identical mice, some develop a brain with no corpus callosum, the large band of fibers that connects the two hemispheres (**Figure 3-25**). This abnormality is similar to a disorder in humans. The absence of a corpus callosum has a genetic cause, but something happens in the development of the brain that determines whether the trait is expressed in a particular mouse. Although the precise causal factors are not known, they affect the embryo at about the time at which the corpus callosum should form.

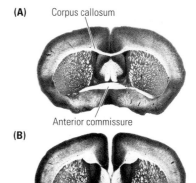

(A)   Corpus callosum

Anterior commissure

(B)

Figure 3-25

Genetic Expression   Identical sections through the brains of genetically identical mice reveal distinctly different phenotypes. The mouse in part A has a corpus callosum, whereas the mouse in part B does not. Adapted from "Defects of the Fetal Forebrain in Acallosal Mice," by D. Wahlsten and H. W. Ozaki, in *Callosal Agenesis* (p. 126), edited by M. Lassonde and M. A. Jeeves, 1994, New York: Plenum Press.

Allele. Alternate form of a gene; a gene pair contains two alleles.

Homozygous. Having two identical alleles for a trait.

Heterozygous. Having two different alleles for the same trait.

Wild type. Refers to a normal (most common in a population) phenotype or genotype.

Mutation. Alteration of an allele that yields a different version of that allele.

This example illustrates the importance of distinguishing between genotype and phenotype. Having identical genes does not mean that those genes will be identically expressed. By the same token, even if we knew everything about the structure and function of our own genes, it would be impossible to predict how much of our behavior is due to our genotype, because so much of our behavior is phenotypical.

Dominant and Recessive Alleles

If both alleles in a pair of genes are homozygous, the two encode the same protein, but, if the two alleles in a pair are heterozygous, they encode two different proteins. Three possible outcomes attend the heterozygous condition when these proteins express a physical or behavioral trait: (1) only the allele from the mother may be expressed; (2) only the allele from the father may be expressed; or (3) both alleles may be expressed simultaneously.

A member of a gene pair that is routinely expressed as a trait is called a *dominant* allele; a routinely unexpressed allele is *recessive.* Alleles can vary considerably in their dominance. In complete dominance, only the allele's own trait is expressed in the phenotype. In incomplete dominance, the expression of the allele's own trait is only partial. In *codominance,* both the the allele's own trait and that of the other allele in the gene pair are expressed completely.

The concept of dominant and recessive alleles was first introduced by Gregor Mendel, a nineteenth-century monk who studied pea plants in his monastery garden (see Chapter 1). Mendel showed that organisms possess discrete units of heredity, which we now call genes. Each gene makes an independent contribution to the offspring's inheritance, even though that contribution may not always be visible in the offspring's phenotype. When paired with a dominant allele, a recessive allele is often not expressed. Still, it can be passed on to future generations and influence their phenotypes when not masked by the influence of some dominant trait.

Genetic Mutations

As you know, the mechanism for reproducing genes and passing them on to offspring is fallible. Errors can arise in the nucleotide sequence when reproductive cells make gene copies. The new versions of the genes are mutations. The number of potential genetic mutations is enormous.

A mutation may be as small as a change in a single nucleotide base. Because the average gene has more than 1200 nucleotide bases, an enormous number of mutations can potentially occur on a single gene. For example, the *BRCA1* gene, found on chromosome 17, predisposes women to breast cancer, and more than 100 different mutations have already been found on this gene. Thus, in principle, there are more than 100 different ways in which to inherit a predisposition to breast cancer.

A change in a nucleotide or the addition of a nucleotide in a gene sequence can be either beneficial or disruptive. An example of a mutation that is both causes sickle-cell anemia, a condition in which blood cells have an abnormal sickle shape that offers some protection against malaria, but they also have poor oxygen-carrying capacity, thus weakening the person who possesses them.

Other genetic mutations are more purely beneficial in their results, and still others are seemingly neutral to the functioning of the organism that carries them. Most mutations, however, have a negative effect. If not lethal, they produce in their carriers debilitating physical and behavioral abnormalities.

A mutation may have a specific effect on one particular trait or it can have widespread effects. Most mutant genes responsible for human hereditary disorders cause multiple symptoms. The abnormal protein produced by the gene takes part in many different chemical reactions, and so the affected person may have an abnormal appearance as well as abnormal function.

Mendel's Principles Apply to Genetic Disorders

Some disorders caused by mutant genes clearly illustrate Mendel's principles of dominant and recessive alleles. One is **Tay-Sachs disease,** caused by a dysfunctional protein that acts as an enzyme known as HexA (hexosaminidase A), which fails to break down a class of lipids (fats) in the brain. Symptoms usually appear a few months after birth. The baby begins to suffer seizures, blindness, and degenerating motor and mental abilities. Inevitably, the child dies within a few years. The Tay-Sachs mutation appears with high frequency among certain ethnic groups, including Jews of European origin and French Canadians.

The dysfunctional Tay-Sachs enzyme is caused by a recessive allele. Distinctive inheritance patterns result from recessive alleles, because two copies of the allele (one from the mother and one from the father) are needed for the disorder to develop. A baby can inherit Tay-Sachs disease only when *both* parents carry the recessive Tay-Sachs allele.

Because both parents have survived to adulthood, they must also both possess a corresponding dominant normal allele for that particular gene pair. The egg and sperm cells produced by this man and woman will therefore contain a copy of one or the other of these two alleles. Which allele is passed on is determined completely by chance.

This situation gives rise to three different potential gene combinations in any child produced by two Tay-Sachs carriers, as diagrammed in **Figure 3-26A**. The child may have two normal alleles, in which case he or she will be spared the disorder and cannot pass on the disease. The child may have one normal and one Tay-Sachs allele,

Tay-Sachs disease. Inherited birth defect caused by the loss of genes that encode the enzyme necessary for breaking down certain fatty substances; appears 4 to 6 months after birth and results in retardation, physical changes, and death by about age 5.

Figure 3-26

Inheritance Patterns   **(A)** Recessive condition: If a parent has one mutant allele, that parent will not show symptoms of the disease but will be a carrier. If both parents carry a mutant allele, each of their offspring stands a 1 in 4 chance of developing the disease. **(B)** Dominant condition: A person with a single allele will develop the disease. If this person mates with a normal partner, offspring have a 50-50 chance of developing the disease. If both parents are carriers, both will develop the disease, and offspring have a 75 percent chance of developing it.

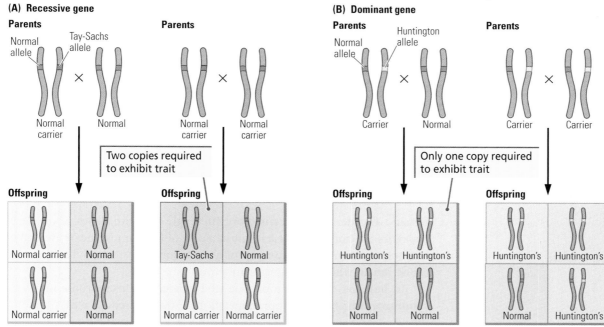

Huntington's chorea. Autosomal genetic disorder that results in motor and cognitive disturbances; caused by an increase in the number of CAG (cytosine-adenine-guanine) repeats on chromosome 4.

Down's syndrome. Chromosomal abnormality resulting in mental retardation and other abnormalities, usually caused by an extra chromosome 21.

in which case he or she, like the parents, will be a carrier of the disorder. Or the child may have two Tay-Sachs alleles, in which case he or she will develop the disease.

In the recessive condition, the chance of a child of two carriers being normal is 25 percent, the chance of being a carrier is 50 percent, and the chance of having Tay-Sachs disease is 25 percent. If only one of the parents is a Tay-Sachs carrier and the other is normal, then any of their children has a 50-50 chance of being either normal or a carrier. Such a couple has no chance of conceiving a baby with Tay-Sachs disease.

Fortunately, a blood test can detect whether a person carries the recessive Tay-Sachs allele. This allele operates independently of the dominant allele, just as Mendel described. As a result, it still produces the defective HexA enzyme, and so the person who carries it has a higher-than-normal lipid accumulation in the brain.

Because this person also has a normal allele that produces a functional enzyme, the abnormal lipid accumulation is not enough to cause Tay-Sachs disease. People found to be carriers can make informed decisions about conceiving children. If they avoid having children with another Tay-Sachs carrier, none of their children will have the disorder, although some will probably be carriers.

The one normal allele that a carrier of Tay-Sachs possesses produces enough functional enzyme to enable the brain to operate in a satisfactory way. It would *not* be the case if the normal allele were dominant, however, as happens with the genetic disorder **Huntington's chorea.** In Huntington's chorea, an abnormal version of a protein known as huntingtin builds up in nervous system cells. In some way, this protein causes the death of brain cells, especially cells in the basal ganglia and the cortex, as discussed further in "Huntington's Chorea."

Symptoms can begin anytime from infancy to old age, but they most often start in midlife. These symptoms include abnormal involuntary movements, which is why the disorder is called a chorea (from the Greek, meaning "dance"). Other symptoms are memory loss and eventually a complete deterioration of behavior, followed by death. The abnormal *huntingtin* allele is dominant to a normal allele, and so only one defective allele is needed to cause the disorder.

Figure 3-26B illustrates the inheritance patterns associated with a dominant allele that produces a disorder such as Huntington's chorea. If one parent carries the defective allele, offspring have a 50 percent chance of inheriting the disorder. If both parents have the defective allele, the chance of inheriting it increases to 75 percent. Because the abnormal *huntingtin* allele is usually not expressed until midlife, after the people who possess it have already had children, it can be passed from generation to generation even though it is lethal.

As with the Tay-Sachs allele, there is now a test for determining if a person possesses the allele that causes Huntington's chorea. If a person is found to have the allele, he or she can elect not to procreate. A decision not to have children in this case will reduce the incidence of the abnormal *huntingtin* allele in the human gene pool.

Chromosome Abnormalities

Genetic disorders are not caused only by single defective alleles. Some nervous system disorders are caused by aberrations in a part of a chromosome or even an entire chromosome. Changes in the number of chromosomes, even a doubling of chromosomes is one way in which new species are produced.

In humans, one condition due to a change in chromosome number is **Down's syndrome,** which affects approximately 1 in 700 children. Down's syndrome is usually the result of an extra copy of chromosome 21. One parent (usually the mother) passes on two of these chromosomes to the child, rather than the normal single chromosome.

Huntington's Chorea

Focus on Disorders

Woody Guthrie, whose protest songs made him a spokesman for farm workers during the Great Depression of the 1930s, is revered as one of the founders of American folk music. His best-known song is "This Land Is Your Land." Bob Dylan, who gave his first concert wearing Woody Guthrie's suit, was instrumental in reviving Woody's popularity in the 1960s.

Guthrie died in 1967 after struggling with the symptoms of what was eventually diagnosed as Huntingon's chorea. His mother had died of a similar condition, although her illness was never diagnosed. Two of Guthrie's five children, from two marriages, developed the disease, and his second wife, Marjorie, became active in promoting its study.

Huntington's chorea is devastating, characterized by memory impairment, abnormal uncontrollable movements, and marked changes in personality, eventually leading to virtually total loss of normal behavioral, emotional, and intellectual functioning. Fortunately, it is rare, with an incidence of only 5 to 10 victims in 100,000 people; it is most common in people of European ancestry.

The symptoms of Huntington's chorea result from the degeneration of neurons in the basal ganglia and cortex. Those symptoms can appear at any age but typically start in midlife. In 1983, the gene, called the *huntingtin* gene, responsible for Huntington's chorea was located on chromosome 4 and, 10 years later, its abnormality was identified as an expanded region of the huntingtin protein that it encodes, a region characterized by many repeats of the codon CAG. (Normally, people have fewer than 30 CAG repeats.)

The CAG nucleotide sequence encodes the amino acid glutamine. As a result, the huntingtin protein produced by the defective *huntingtin* gene contains many repeats of glutamine in its polypeptide chain. As the number of repeats increases

Woody Guthrie.

beyond 30, the onset of the disease is earlier and earlier. Thus the disease can begin from very early to very late in life, depending on the number of repeats. Typically, non-Europeans have fewer CAG repeats than do Europeans, which accounts for their decreased susceptibility to Huntington's chorea.

The area of CAG repeats is also prone to expansion in transmission from the father, when it can double or even triple in size. In inheritance from the mother, the area of repeats remains stable. Despite our current insights into its causes, many unanswered questions about Huntington's chorea remain. One is why symptoms take so long to develop even with many CAG repeats. A possible answer is that the extra glutamine segments in the abnormal huntingtin protein cause it to fold in abnormal ways, rendering it resistant to removal from the cell. Another question is why the abnormal huntingtin protein causes cell death only in certain regions of the brain. As yet, researchers also know little about how the progress of the disease might be stopped, but finding ways to remove the abnormal protein is one possibility.

Combining these two chromosomes with one from the other parent yields three chromosomes 21, an abnormal number called a *trisomy* (**Figure 3-27**).

Although chromosome 21 is the smallest human chromosome, its trisomy severely alters a person's phenotype. People with Down's syndrome have characteristic facial features and short stature. They also endure heart defects, susceptibility to respiratory infections, and mental retardation. They are prone to developing leukemia

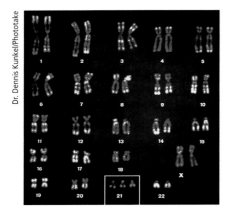

Figure 3-27

Chromosome Aberration (*Top*) Down's syndrome, also known as trisomy 21, is caused by an extra copy of chromosome 21. (*Bottom*) Chris Burke, who lives with Down's syndrome, played a leading role on the television series *Life Goes On* in the 1990s.

and Alzheimer's disease. Although people with Down's syndrome usually have a much shorter-than-normal life span, some live to middle age or beyond. Improved education for children with Down's syndrome shows that they can learn to compensate greatly for the brain changes that cause mental handicaps.

Genetic Engineering

Despite enormous advances in understanding the structure and function of genes, there remains a huge gap in understanding how genes produce behavior. Nevertheless, geneticists have invented a number of methods to influence the traits that genes express. The most recent of these methods, as well as the most direct avenue for the study of gene expression, is *genetic engineering.* In its simplest form, genetic engineering entails either removing a gene from a genome or adding a gene to it. In so-called *transgenic animals,* a gene added to the genome is passed along and expressed in subsequent generations.

Probably the oldest means of influencing genetic traits is the selective breeding of animals and plants. Beginning with the domestication of wolves into dogs more than 15,000 years ago, many species of animals have been domesticated by selectively breeding males and females that display particular traits. For example, the selective breeding of dogs has produced breeds that can run fast, haul heavy loads, retrieve prey, dig for burrowing animals, climb rocky cliffs in search of sea birds, herd sheep and cattle, or sit on an owner's lap and cuddle.

Selective breeding is an effective way to alter gene expression. As is described by Heidi Parker and her colleagues (2004) in regard to the dog genome, insights into the relations between genes and the different behaviors displayed by different dog breeds are possible.

Maintaining spontaneous mutations is another method of affecting genetic traits. By using this method, researchers create whole populations of animals possessing some unusual trait that originally arose as an unexpected mutation in only one or a few individual animals. In laboratory colonies of mice, for example, large numbers of spontaneous mutations have been discovered and maintained.

There are strains of mice that have abnormal movements, such as reeling, staggering, and jumping. Some have diseases of the immune system; others have sensory deficits and are blind or cannot hear. Many of these genetic abnormalities can also be found in humans. As a result, the neural and genetic bases of the altered behavior in the mice can be studied systematically to develop treatments for human disorders.

More direct approaches to manipulating the expression of genetic traits include altering early embryonic development. One such method is *cloning.* One form of cloning can produce an offspring that is nearly genetically identical with another animal.

To clone an animal, scientists begin with a cell nucleus containing DNA, usually from a living animal, place it into an egg from which the nucleus has been removed, and, after stimulating the egg to start dividing, implant the new embyro into the uterus of a female. Because each individual animal that develops from these cells is genetically identical with the donor of the nucleus, clones can be used to preserve valuable traits, to study the relative influences of heredity and environment, or to produce new tissue or organs for transplant to the donor.

Dolly, a female sheep, was the first mammal to be cloned (**Figure 3-28**). It must be noted that cloned animals are not always normal. Dolly died at quite a young age for a sheep and displayed a number of symptoms characteristic of premature aging.

In genetic engineering, genes can be introduced into an embryo or removed from it. For example, the introduction of a new gene can allow goats to produce medicines in their milk, and those medicines can be extracted from the milk to treat human diseases (Niemann et al., 2003). It is also possible to produce *chimeric animals,* which have genes from two different species. A cell from one species is introduced into the early embryonic stage of a different species. The resulting animal has cells with genes from both parent species and behaviors that are a product of those gene combinations.

The chimeric animal displays an interesting mix of the behaviors of the parent species. For example, chickens that have received Japanese quail cells in early embryogenesis display some aspects of quail crowing behavior rather than chicken crowing behavior, thus providing evidence for the genetic basis of some bird vocalization (Balaban et al., 1988). The chimeric preparation provides an investigative tool for studying the neural basis of crowing because quail neurons can be distinguished from chicken neurons when examined under a microscope.

One application of genetic engineering is in the study and treatment of human genetic disorders. For instance, researchers have introduced into a line of mice the human gene that causes Huntington's chorea (Lione et al., 1999). The mice express the abnormal *huntingtin* allele and display symptoms similar to the disorder in humans. This mouse line is being used to study potential therapies for this disorder in humans.

As described at the beginning of this section (see "Knocking Out Genes" on page 100), *knockout technology* can be used to inactivate a gene so that a line of mice fails to express it (Eells, 2003). That line of mice can then be used to study possible therapies for human disorders caused by the loss of a single protein due to a mutant gene. Remarkably interesting knockout animals can be bred.

It is potentially possible to knock out genes that are related to certain kinds of memory, such as emotional memory, social memory, or spatial memory. Such technology provides a useful way of investigating the neural basis of memory. So genetic research is directed not only toward finding cures for genetic abnormalities in brain and behavior, but also toward studying normal brain function.

AP Photo/John Chadwick

Figure 3-28

A Clone and Her Offspring   Dolly (*right*) was cloned in 1996, when a team of researchers in Scotland implanted a nucleus from a mammary-gland cell of an adult sheep into another ewe's unfertilized egg from which the nucleus had been removed. The resulting embryo was implanted into a third sheep's uterus. Dolly subsequently mated and bore a lamb (*left*).

Ⓞ To learn more about creating knockout mice, visit the *Brain and Behavior* Web site (**www.worthpublishers.com/kolb**) and go to the Web links for Chapter 3.

In Review

Researchers in genomics study how genes produce proteins, whereas those studying proteomics seek to understand what individual proteins do. Each of our 46 chromosomes contains thousands of genes, and each gene contains the code for one protein. The genes that we receive from our mothers and fathers may include slightly different versions (alleles) of particular genes, which will be expressed in slightly different proteins. Abnormalities in a gene, caused by mutations, can result in an abnormally formed protein that, in turn, results in the abnormal function of cells. Recessive or dominant alleles can result in neurological disorders such as Tay-Sachs disease and Huntington's chorea, respectively. Genetic engineering is a new science in which the genome of an animal is altered. The genetic composition of a cloned animal is identical with that of a parent or sibling; transgenic animals contain new or altered genes; and knockouts have genomes from which a gene has been deleted. The study of alterations in the nervous systems or in the behavior of animals produced by these manipulations can be a source of insight into how genes produce proteins and how proteins contribute to the structure and function of the nervous system.

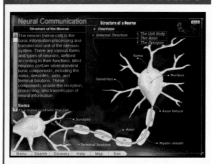
SUMMARY

▥ *What kinds of cells are found in the nervous system?* The nervous system is composed of two kinds of cells: neurons, which transmit information, and glia, cells that support brain function. Sensory neurons send information from the body's sensory receptors to the brain, motor neurons send commands enabling muscles to move, and interneurons link sensory and motor activities in the CNS. Like neurons, glial cells can be grouped by structure and function. Ependymal cells produce cerebrospinal fluid; astrocytes structurally support neurons, help to form the blood–brain barrier, and seal off damaged brain tissue; microglia aid in the repair of brain cells; and oligodendroglia and Schwann cells myelinate axons in the central and peripheral nervous systems, respectively.

▥ *What is the basic external structure of a neuron?* A neuron is composed of three basic parts: a cell body, or soma; branching extensions called dendrites designed to receive information; and a single axon that passes information along to other cells. A dendrite's surface area is greatly increased by numerous dendritic spines; an axon may have branches called axon collaterals, which are further divided into teleodendria, each ending at a terminal button, or end foot. A synapse is the "almost connection" between a terminal button and the membrane of another cell.

▥ *How is a cell internally structured?* A surrounding cell membrane protects the cell and regulates what enters and leaves it. Within the cell are a number of compartments, also enclosed in membranes. These compartments include the nucleus (which contains the cell's chromosomes and genes), the endoplasmic reticulum (where proteins are manufactured), the mitochondria (where energy is gathered and stored), the Golgi bodies (where protein molecules are packaged for transport), and lysosomes (which break down wastes). A cell also contains a system of tubules that aid its movements, provide structural support, and act as highways for transporting substances.

▥ *Why are proteins important to cells?* To a large extent, the work of cells is carried out by proteins. The nucleus contains chromosomes, which are long chains of genes, each encoding a specific protein needed by the cell. Proteins perform diverse tasks by virtue of their diverse shapes. Some act as enzymes to facilitate chemical reactions; others serve as membrane channels, gates, and pumps; and still others are exported for use in other parts of the body.

▥ *How do genes work?* A gene is a segment of a DNA molecule and is made up of a sequence of nucleotide bases. Through a process called transcription, a copy of a gene is produced in a strand of mRNA. The mRNA then travels to the endoplasmic reticulum, where a ribosome moves along the mRNA molecule, and is translated into a sequence of amino acids. The resulting chain of amino acids is a polypeptide. Polypeptides fold and combine to form protein molecules with distinctive shapes that are used for specific purposes in the body.

▥ *What do we inherit genetically from our parents?* From each parent, we inherit one of each of the chromosomes in our 23 chromosome pairs. Because chromosomes are "matched" pairs, a cell contains two alleles of every gene. Sometimes the two alleles of a pair are homozygous (the same), and sometimes they are heterozygous (different). An allele may be dominant and expressed as a trait; recessive and not expressed; or codominant, in which case both it and the other allele in the pair are expressed in the individual organism's phenotype. One allele of each gene is designated the wild type, or most common one in a population, whereas the other alleles of that gene are called mutations. A person might inherit any of these alleles from a parent, depending on that parent's genotype.

▨ *What is the relation among genes, cells, and behavior?* Comprehending the links among genes, cells, and behavior is the ultimate goal of research, but as yet these links are only poorly understood. The structure and function of a cell are properties of all its many genes and proteins, just as behavior is a property of the actions of billions of nerve cells. It will take years to learn how such a complex system works. In the meantime, the study of genetic abnormalities is a potential source of insight.

▨ *What causes genetic abnormalities?* Genes can potentially undergo many mutations, in which their codes are altered by one or more changes in the nucleotide sequence. Most mutations are harmful and may produce abnormalities in nervous system structure and behavioral function. Genetic research seeks to prevent the expression of genetic and chromosomal abnormalities and to find cures for those that are expressed.

KEY TERMS

allele, p. 101	ependymal cell, p. 82	oligodendroglial cell, p. 85
astrocyte, p. 84	gate, p. 96	paralysis, p. 85
axon, p. 76	glial cell, p. 82	pump, p. 96
axon collateral, p. 79	heterozygous, p. 101	Purkinje cell, p. 81
axon hillock, p. 79	homozygous, p. 101	pyramidal cell, p. 81
bipolar neuron, p. 79	Huntington's chorea, p. 104	Schwann cell, p. 85
cell body (soma), p. 76	hydrocephalus, p. 84	soma (cell body), p. 76
channel, p. 96	interneuron, p. 81	somatosensory neuron,
dendrite, p. 76	microglial cell, p. 84	p. 79
dendritic spine, p. 79	multiple sclerosis (MS),	synapse, p. 79
Down's syndrome, p. 104	p. 85	Tay-Sachs disease, p. 103
end foot (terminal button),	mutation, p. 101	tumor, p. 82
p. 79	myelin, p. 85	wild type, p. 101

REVIEW QUESTIONS

1. Describe five kinds of neurons and five kinds of glia and their functions.

2. Describe the functions of the different parts of a cell.

3. Why can so many nervous system diseases be due to faulty genes?

FOR FURTHER THOUGHT

People often compare the "machine of the day" to the nervous system. Why can we never understand our nervous system by comparing it to a computer and how it works?

RECOMMENDED READING

Alberts, B., Bray, D., Lewis, J., Raff, M., Roberts, K., & Watson, J. D. (2002). *Molecular biology of the cell* (4th ed.). New York: Garland. This standard text provides a comprehensive description of the cells and cell function in living organisms.

Levitan, I. B., & Kaczmarek, L. K. (2002). *The neuron: Cell and molecular biology* (3rd ed). Oxford: Oxford University Press. An extremely readable text describing the function of the neuron. The coverage is comprehensive, and the text is enjoyable to read, accompanied by numerous illustrations that assist in explanation.

How Do Neurons Transmit Information?

Left: **Dr. David Scott/Phototake.** *Middle:* **Mason Morfit/ FPG International/PictureQuest.** *Right:* **CNRI/Phototake.**

Epilepsy

J.D. worked as a disc jockey for a radio station and did so for parties in his off-hours. One evening he set up on the back of a truck at a rugby field to emcee a jovial and raucous rugby party. Between musical sets, he made introductions, told jokes, and exchanged toasts and jugs of beer with the partyers.

About one o'clock in the morning, J. D. suddenly collapsed, making unusual jerky motions, and then passed out. He was rushed to a hospital emergency room, where he gradually recovered. The attending physician noted that he was not drunk, released him to his friends, and recommended a series of neurological tests for the next day. Subsequent state-of-the-art brain scans indicated no obvious brain injury or tumor.

The key to diagnosing J. D.'s problem lay in an older technology based on the small electrical signals given off by the brain. Sensitive recording machines, such as the electroencephalograph developed in the 1930s, can detect those signals. When the electrical activity in J. D.'s brain was recorded while a strobe light was flashed before his eyes, the electroencephalogram displayed a series of abnormal electrical patterns characteristic of epilepsy, graphed in the accompanying illustration.

The doctor prescribed Dilantin (diphenylhydantoin), an anesthetic agent given in low doses, and advised J. D. to refrain from drinking. He was required to give up his driver's license to prevent the possibility that an attack while driving could cause an accident. And he lost his job at the radio station. After 3 months of uneventful drug treatment, he was taken off medication and his driver's license was restored. Eventually J. D. convinced the radio station that he could resume work, and, in the past 10 years, he has been seizure-free.

One person in 20 will experience an epileptic seizure in his or her lifetime. Synchronous stimuli can trigger a seizure; thus a strobe light is often used in diagnosis. Some epileptic seizures are *symptomatic*—they can be linked to a specific cause, such as infection, trauma, tumor, or other damage to a part of the brain. *Idiopathic* seizures (related to the individual person) appear to arise spontaneously. Their cause is poorly understood.

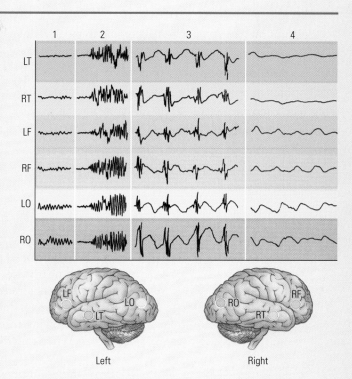

EEG patterns recorded during the stages of a grand mal seizure: (1) normal pattern before the seizure; (2) onset of seizure; (3) clonic phase in which the person makes rhythmic movements in time with the large, abnormal electrical discharges; (4) period of coma after the seizure ends. Color dots on the approximate recording sites of the cortex are coded to the recordings. Abbreviations: LT and RT, left and right temporal; LF and RF, left and right frontal; LO and RO, left and right occipital. Adapted from *Fundamentals of Human Neuropsychology* (p. 80), by B. Kolb and I. Q. Whishaw, 1980, San Francisco: W. H. Freeman and Company.

Three symptoms are found in many kinds of epilepsy:

1. The victim often experiences an aura, or warning, of an impending seizure, which may take the form of a sensation, such as odors or sounds, or may simply be a "feeling."
2. The victim may lose consciousness and later be unaware that the seizure ever happened.
3. The seizure is often accompanied by abnormal movements such as repeated chewing or shaking, twitches that start in a limb and spread across the body, and, in some cases, a total loss of muscle tone and postural support, causing the person to collapse.

Seizures may be categorized according to the severity of these symptoms. In *petit mal* (from the French for "little bad") *seizures,* there is usually a brief loss of awareness and small or brief abnormal movements. In contrast, *grand mal* ("big bad") *seizures* entail severe abnormalities of movement, collapse, and loss of consciousness.

If seizures occur repeatedly and cannot be controlled by drug treatment, surgery may be performed. The goal of surgery is to remove damaged or scarred tissue that serves as the focal point of a seizure. Removing this small area prevents seizures from starting and spreading to other brain regions.

Figure 4-1, perhaps the most reproduced drawing in behavioral neuroscience, is nearly 350 years old. Taken from René Descartes's book titled *Treatise on Man,* it illustrates the first serious attempt to explain how information travels through the nervous system. Descartes proposed that the carrier of information is cerebrospinal fluid flowing through nerve tubes.

When the fire burns the man's toe, Descartes reasoned, it stretches the skin, which tugs on a nerve tube leading to the brain. In response to the tug, a valve in a ventricle of the brain opens and CSF flows down the tube, filling the leg muscles and causing them to contract and pull the toe back from the fire. The flow of fluid through other tubes to other muscles of the body (not shown in Figure 4-1) causes the head to turn toward the painful stimulus and the hands to rub the injured toe.

As discussed in Chapter 1, Descartes's theory was inaccurate, yet it is remarkable because he isolated the three basic questions that underlie a behavioral response:

1.   How do our nerves detect a sensory stimulus and inform the brain about it?
2.   How does the brain decide what response should be made?
3.   How does the brain command muscles to move to produce a behavioral response?

Descartes was trying to explain the very same things that we want to explain today. If not by stretched skin tugging on a nerve tube that initiates the message, the message must still be initiated somehow. If not by the opening of valves to initiate the flow of CSF to convey information, the information must still be sent. If not by the filling of muscles with fluid that produces movements, some other mechanism must still cause muscles to contract.

What all these mechanisms in fact are is the subject of this chapter. We examine how neurons convey information from the environment throughout the nervous system and ultimately activate muscles to produce movement. Then we describe how researchers use electrical activity to study brain function. We begin by explaining the electrical activity of the nervous system.

Figure 4-1

Descartes's Theory of Information Flow   From Descartes, 1664.

ELECTRICITY AND NEURONS

The first hints about how the nervous system conveys its messages came in the eighteenth century after the discovery of electricity. You have extensive experience with electricity, which powers the lights in your home and the batteries that run so many gadgets. In technical terms, **electricity** is a flow of electrons from a body that contains a higher charge (more electrons) to a body that contains a lower charge (fewer electrons), and this electron flow can perform work.

The body with the higher electrical charge is the **negative pole,** because electrons are negatively charged and this body has more of them. The body with the lower electrical charge is the **positive pole. Electrical potential,** measured in **volts,** describes the difference in charge between the two poles. (The term *potential* is used because the electrons on the negative pole have the potential to flow to the positive pole. The negatively charged electrons are attracted to the positive pole because opposite charges attract.)

Each wall socket in your house has a positive and a negative pole. Similarly, if you look at a battery, you will see that one of its poles is marked "−" for negative and the other "+" for positive. The poles are separated by an insulator, a substance through which electrons cannot flow. Therefore, a flow, or **current,** of electrons streams from the negative (−) to the positive (+) pole only if the two poles are connected by a conducting medium, such as a bare wire. If a wire, or **electrode,** from each pole is brought into contact with biological tissue, current will flow from the wire connected to the negative pole into the tissue and then from the tissue into the wire connected to the positive pole.

Electrons can accumulate on many substances, including our bodies, which is why you sometimes get a shock from touching a metal object after walking on a carpet. From the carpet, you accumulate relatively loose electrons, which give your body a greater negative charge than that of objects around you. In short, you become a negative pole.

Electrons normally leave your body as you walk around, because the earth acts as a positive pole. If you are wearing rubber-soled shoes, however, you retain electrical potential because the rubber acts as an insulator. If you then touch a metal object, such as a water fountain, electrons that are equally distributed on your body suddenly rush through the contact area of your fingertips. In fact, if you watch your fingertips just before they touch the water fountain, you will see a small spark as the electrons are transferred. These electrons leaving your fingertips give you the shock.

Combing your hair is another way to accumulate electrons. If you then hold a piece of paper near the comb, the paper will bend in the comb's direction. The negative charges on the comb have pushed the paper's negative charges to the back side of the paper, leaving the front side positively charged. Because unlike charges attract, the paper bends toward the comb.

Discoveries on the nature of electricity quickly led to proposals that electricity plays a role in conducting information in the nervous system. In the next section, we describe a few milestones that lead from this idea to an understanding of how the nervous system really conveys information.

Electricity. The flow of electrons.

Negative pole. The source of electrons.

Positive pole. Location to which electrons flow.

Electrical potential. An electrical charge; the ability to do work through the use of stored potential electrical energy.

Volt. A measure of a difference in electrical potential.

Current. The flow of electrons from a region of higher negative charge to a region of lower negative charge; the flow of various ions across the neuron membrane.

Electrode. An insulated wire or a saltwater-filled glass tube that is used to stimulate or record from neurons.

⊙ Visit the *Brain and Behavior* Web site (**www.worthpublishers.com/kolb**) and go to the Chapter 4 Web links for an introductory review of bioelectricity.

Early Clues to Electrical Activity in the Nervous System

In 1731, Stephen Gray performed an experiment similar to the comb experiment just described. He rubbed a rod with a piece of cloth to accumulate electrons on the rod. Then he touched the charged rod to the feet of a boy suspended on a rope and brought a metal foil to the boy's nose. The foil bent on approaching the boy's nose, being attracted to it, and, as foil and nose touched, electricity passed from the rod, through the boy, to the foil.

Electrical stimulation. Passing an electrical current from the tip of an electrode through tissue, resulting in changes in the electrical activity of the tissue.

⊙ Visit the *Foundations of Behavioral Neuroscience* CD and find the area on electrical brain stimulation in the module on research methods. You'll see a model of an electrical stimulator and a video clip of the self-stimulation of a rat. (See the Preface for more information about this CD.)

Yet the boy was completely unaware that the electricity had passed through his body. Therefore, Gray speculated that electricity might be the messenger in the nervous system. Although this conclusion was not precisely correct, two other lines of evidence implicated electrical activity in the nervous system's flow of information. One of these lines of evidence consisted of the results of electrical-stimulation studies, the other of the results of electrical-recording studies.

ELECTRICAL-STIMULATION STUDIES

When eighteenth-century Italian scientist Luigi Galvani observed that frogs' legs hanging on a wire in a market twitched during a lightning storm, he surmised that sparks of electricity from the storm were activating the muscles. Investigating this possibility, he found that, if an electrical current is applied to a dissected nerve, the muscle to which the nerve is connected contracts. Galvani concluded that the electricity flows along the nerve to the muscle. This observation provoked a huge debate among scientists concerning what he had actually found, and this debate pointed them in the direction of understanding how nerves conduct information.

Many other researchers used Galvani's technique of **electrical stimulation** to produce muscle contraction. The technique requires a battery or other source of electrons that delivers an electrical current. **Figure 4-2A** illustrates such an electrical stimulator that transforms the 120-volt current from a wall socket into a current ranging from 2 to 10 volts, which will not damage cells.

Timers allow the stimulator to deliver either a single pulse of current lasting about $\frac{1}{100}$ of a second or a series of these brief pulses. Wire leads connected to the stimulator's negative and positive poles carry the electrical current. One lead is attached to a stimulating electrode, which is usually a wire (or a specially constructed glass tube) insulated except for the tip that comes in contact with the cells to be stimulated. The other lead (called the reference), attached to the positive pole, is placed on some other part of the body. When the stimulator is on, the flow of electricity out of the tip of the electrode onto the cells is enough to produce a physiological response.

In the mid-nineteenth century, two Prussian scientists, Gustave Theodor Fritsch and Eduard Hitzig, demonstrated that electrical stimulation of the neocortex causes movement. They studied several animal species, including rabbits and dogs, and may even have stimulated the neocortex of a person whom they were treating for head injuries on a Prussian battlefield. They observed movements of the arms and legs of their subjects in response to the stimulation of the neocortex.

In 1874, Robert Bartholow, a Cincinnati physician, wrote the first report describing the effects of human brain stimulation. His patient, Mary Rafferty, had a skull defect

Figure 4-2

Electrical Activity in Animal Tissue
(A) In electrical stimulation, current (electrons) leaves the stimulator through a wire lead (red) that attaches to an electrode. From the uninsulated tip of the electrode, the current enters the tissue and, in doing so, stimulates it. A second lead (green) is connected to a reference electrode into which the current flows back to the stimulator. The reference electrode contacts a relatively large surface area that spreads out the current and therefore does not excite the tissue here. **(B)** In electrical recording, a voltmeter measures electrical current.

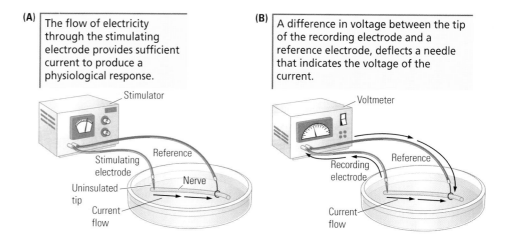

(A) The flow of electricity through the stimulating electrode provides sufficient current to produce a physiological response.

(B) A difference in voltage between the tip of the recording electrode and a reference electrode, deflects a needle that indicates the voltage of the current.

that exposed part of her neocortex. Bartholow stimulated her exposed brain tissue to examine the effects. In one of his observations he wrote:

> Passed an insulated needle into the left posterior lobe so that the non-insulated portion rested entirely in the substance of the brain. The reference was placed in contact with the dura mater. When the circuit was closed, muscular contraction in the right upper and lower extremities ensued. Faint but visible contraction of the left eyelid, and dilation of the pupils, also ensued. Mary complained of a very strong and unpleasant feeling of tingling in both right extremities, especially in the right arm, which she seized with the opposite hand and rubbed vigorously. Notwithstanding the very evident pain from which she suffered, she smiled as if much amused. (Bartholow, 1874)

Bartholow's report was not well received. An uproar after its publication forced him to leave Cincinnati. Nevertheless, he had demonstrated that the brain of a conscious person could be stimulated electrically to produce movement of the body.

Wilder Penfield
(1891–1976)

In the twentieth century, brain stimulation became a standard part of many neurosurgical procedures. In particular, after the method had been perfected in experimental animal studies, Wilder Penfield, a neurosurgeon at the Montreal Neurological Institute, used electrical stimulation to map the neocortex of surgery patients in the 1950s. The maps that he produced allowed him to determine the function of various neocortical regions and so to minimize the removal of undamaged tissue. Penfield especially wanted to locate language areas in the neocortex to be able to spare them during surgery.

ELECTRICAL-RECORDING STUDIES

Another line of evidence that the flow of information in the brain is partly electrical in nature came from the results of recording experiments with the use of a **voltmeter,** a device that measures the flow and the strength of electrical voltage. As illustrated in Figure 4-2B, the voltmeter has one wire connected to a recording electrode and a second connected to a reference electrode, much as an electrical stimulator does. Any difference in voltage between the tip of the recording electrode and the reference causes a current to flow through the voltmeter, deflecting a needle that indicates the voltage of the current.

Richard Caton, a Scottish physician who lived in the late nineteenth and early twentieth centuries, was the first to attempt to measure the electrical currents of the brain with a sensitive voltmeter. He reported that, when he placed electrodes on the skull of a human subject, he could detect fluctuations in his voltmeter recordings. Today this type of brain recording, the **electroencephalogram** (EEG), is a graph of the brain's electrical activity, and the electroencephalograph is a standard tool for measuring brain activity.

Hermann von Helmholtz
(1821–1894)

The results of electrical-recording studies provided evidence that neurons send electrical messages, but concluding that nerve tracts carry conventional electrical currents through the body proved problematic. Hermann von Helmholtz, a nineteenth-century German scientist, developed a procedure for measuring the speed of information flow in a nerve. He stimulated a nerve leading to a muscle and measured the time that it took the muscle to contract. The time was extremely long. The nerve conducted information at the rate of only 30 to 40 meters per second, whereas electricity flows along a wire at the much faster speed of light (3×10^8 meters per second).

The flow of information in the nervous system, then, is much too slow to be a flow of electricity. And there is another problem. When current is passed between electrodes

---

Voltmeter. A device that measures the difference in electrical potential between two bodies.

Electroencephalogram (EEG). Graph that records electrical activity through the skull or from the brain and represents graded potentials of many neurons.

○ On the *Foundations* CD, find the EEG section in the module on research methods. Investigate a model of an electroencephalograph and view EEG recordings.

Figure 4-3

Wave Effect Waves created by dropping a stone in water do not entail the forward movement of the water but rather differences in pressure that change the height of the surface of the water.

placed on the brain to produce movement in a limb, the electrical current flows directly between those electrodes. So how do muscles that are a considerable distance away from the electrodes come to move?

To explain the electrical signals of a neuron, Julius Bernstein suggested in 1886 that neurons have an electrical charge that can change and move and that the electrical charge has a chemical basis. This suggestion led to the idea that modifications of a neuron's charge travel along the axon as a wave. Successive waves constitute the message that the neuron conveys.

Notice that it is not the *charge* but the *wave* that travels along the axon. To understand the difference, consider other kinds of waves. If you drop a stone into a pool of water, the contact made by the stone hitting the water produces a wave that travels away from the site of impact, as shown in **Figure 4-3**. The water itself does not travel. Only the change in pressure moves, changing the height of the surface of the water and creating the wave effect.

Similarly, when you speak, you induce pressure waves in air, and these waves carry the "sound" of your voice to a listener. If you flick a towel, a wave travels to the other end of the towel. Just as waves through the air send a spoken message, waves of chemical change travel along an axon to deliver a neuron's message.

Modern Tools for Measuring a Neuron's Electrical Activity

We do not feel waves of neural activity traveling around our bodies because the waves that carry nervous system messages are very small and are restricted to the surfaces of neurons. Still, we can measure such waves and determine how they are produced, by using electrical-stimulation and -recording techniques. If an electrode connected to a voltmeter is placed on a single axon, the electrode can detect a change in electrical charge on that axon's membrane as the wave passes, as illustrated in **Figure 4-4**.

As simple as this process may seem, it was successfully carried out only after a few other discoveries had been made. The procedure requires a neuron large enough to record, a recording device sufficiently sensitive to detect a very small electrical impulse, and an electrode small enough to place on the surface of a single neuron. The discovery of the giant axon of the squid, the invention of the oscilloscope, and the development of microelectrodes met all these requirements.

THE GIANT AXON OF THE SQUID

The neurons of most animals, including humans, are tiny, on the order of 1 to 20 micrometers (1–20 μm) in diameter, too small to be seen by the eye and too small to perform experiments on easily. British zoologist J. Z. Young, when dissecting the North Atlantic squid, *Loligo,* noticed that it has truly giant axons, as much as a millimeter (1000 μm) in diameter. **Figure 4-5** illustrates *Loligo* and the giant axons leading to its body wall, or mantle, which contracts to propel the squid through the water.

Voltmeter

Incoming signal

Electrical charge

Outgoing signal

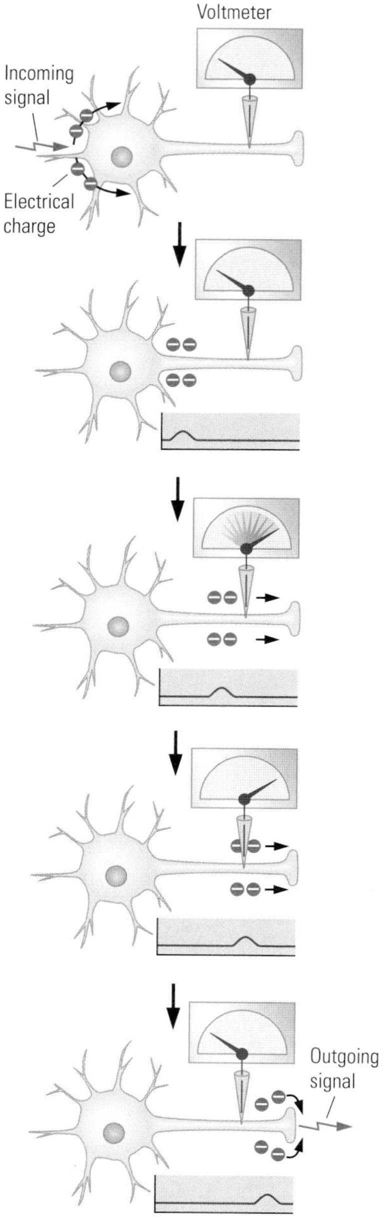

Figure 4-4

Wave of Information Neurons can convey information as a wave induced by stimulation on the cell body traveling down the axon to its terminal. A voltmeter detects the passage of the wave.

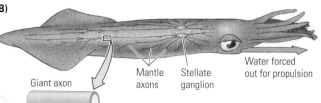

Figure 4-5

Laboratory Specimen (A) The North Atlantic squid propels itself both with fins and by contracting its mantle to force water out for propulsion. (B) The stellate ganglion projects giant axons to contract the squid's mantle.

Loligo is not a giant squid. It is only about a foot long. But its axons are giants as axons go. Each axon is formed by the fusion of many smaller axons. Because larger axons send messages faster than smaller axons do, these giant axons allow the squid to jet propel away from predators.

Andrew Huxley (b. 1917)

Alan Hodgkin (1914–1988)

In 1936, Young suggested to Alan Hodgkin and Andrew Huxley, two neuroscientists at Cambridge University in England, that *Loligo*'s axons were large enough to use for electrical-recording studies. A giant axon could be dissected out of the squid and kept functional in a bath of salty liquid that approximates body fluids. In this way, Hodgkin and Huxley easily studied the neuron's electrical activity.

THE OSCILLOSCOPE

Hodgkin and Huxley's experiments were made possible by the invention of the **oscilloscope.** You are familiar with one form of oscilloscope, a conventional television set. An oscilloscope can also be used as a sensitive voltmeter to measure the very small and rapid changes in electrical currents that come from an axon.

The important component of an oscilloscope is its glass vacuum tube. In the tube, from which air is removed, a beam of negatively charged electrons is projected onto the tube's phosphorus-painted screen. When the electrons hit the paint, the phosphorus glows momentarily. Moving the beam of electrons around leaves a visible trace on the screen that lasts a second or so.

The trace is produced by changing the charge on two pairs of metal plates. The members of each pair are positioned opposite one another on the inner surface of the tube, as shown in **Figure 4-6A**. Changing the charges on the vertical pair of plates, located on the tube's sides, pushes the electron beam away from the negative pole toward the positive pole, which leaves a horizontal line on the screen.

Oscilloscope. A device that measures the flow of electrons to measure voltage.

On the *Foundations* CD, find the section on the membrane potential in the module on neural communication. In the animations showing resting potential and action potential, you will view output from an oscilloscope used for neural recording. Note that the oscilloscope changes in electrical potential when the cell is stimulated.

(A)

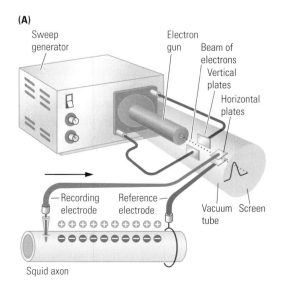

(B)

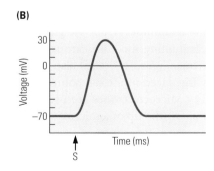

Figure 4-6

Oscilloscope Recording (A) Changes in electrical current across the cell membrane deflect the electron beam in the oscilloscope's vertical plane. (B) The graph of a trace, where S stands for stimulation. The horizontal axis measures time, and the vertical axis measures voltage. The voltage of the axon shown in part A is represented as −70 mV.

⊙ To see a model and a video clip demonstrating how microelectrodes are used, visit the section on microelectrodes in the research methods module on the *Foundations* CD.

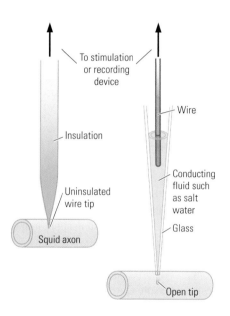

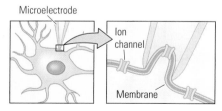

Figure 4-7

Uses of Microelectrodes (*Top, not to scale*) A squid axon is larger than the tip of either a wire (*left*) or a glass (*right*) microelectrode. Both types of electrodes can be placed on an axon or into it. (*Bottom*) One way to use a microelectrode is to record from only a small piece of an axon by pulling the membrane up into the glass electrode through suction.

One metal plate of the horizontal pair is located at the top of the tube; the other is located at the bottom. One horizontal plate is connected to the recording electrode and the other to a reference electrode. Any electrical change between these two electrodes drives the beam of electrons up and down, leaving a vertical line on the screen.

To visualize how recordings are made with an oscilloscope, imagine aiming a hose at a brick wall. The spray of water is analogous to the beam of electrons. Moving the hose horizontally leaves a horizontal spray on the wall, whereas moving the hose vertically leaves a vertical spray. The water line on the wall is analogous to the phosphorus line traced by the oscilloscope's electron beam.

If you move the hose horizontally at a constant rate across the wall and then block the water temporarily and start again, each horizontal sweep provides a measure of time. Now imagine that someone bumps your arm upward as you make a horizontal sweep, deflecting the trace as it sweeps across the wall. The time during which the trace is deflected away from the horizontal baseline indicates how long the bump lasted, and the height of the deflection indicates the size of the bump.

An oscilloscope operates in a very similar way. The charge on the vertical poles is controlled by a timer, whereas the horizontal poles are connected to the preparation from which the recording is being made. A vertical deflection of the trace, either up or down, indicates a change in electrical activity on the preparation. Measuring the duration of this deflection tells how long the electrical change lasts, whereas measuring the size of the deflection tells you the magnitude of the change.

The advantage of using an oscilloscope instead of a voltmeter with a mechanical needle is that an oscilloscope can record extremely small and rapid events, such as those that take place in an axon. The scales used when recording from an axon, graphed in Figure 4-6B, are *milliseconds* (1 ms = one-one thousandth of a second) and *millivolts* (1 mV = one-one thousandth of a volt). Today, computers that measure small electrical currents have replaced the oscilloscope.

MICROELECTRODES

The final ingredient needed to measure a neuron's electrical activity is a set of electrodes small enough to place on or into an axon. Such *microelectrodes* can also be used to deliver an electrical current to a single neuron. One way to make a microelectrode is to etch the tip of a piece of thin wire to a fine point and insulate the rest of the wire. The tip is placed on or into the neuron, as illustrated at the top of **Figure 4-7**.

Microelectrodes can also be made from a thin glass tube. If the middle of the tube is heated while the ends of the tube are pulled, the middle stretches as it turns molten, and eventually breaks, producing two pieces of glass tubing, each tapered to a very fine tip. The tip of a glass microelectrode can be as small as 1 μm, even though it still remains hollow. When the glass tube is then filled with salty water, which provides the conducting medium through which an electrical current can travel, it acts as an electrode. Figure 4-7 (top) also shows a glass microelectrode containing a salt solution. A wire placed in the salt solution connects the electrode to an oscilloscope.

Microelectrodes are used to record from an axon in a number of different ways. Placing the tip of a microelectrode on an axon provides an extracellular measure of the electrical current from a very small part of the axon. If a second microelectrode is used as the reference, one tip can be placed on the surface of the axon and the other inserted into the axon. This technique provides a measure of voltage across the cell membrane.

A still more refined use of a glass microelectrode is to place its tip on the neuron's membrane and apply a little back suction until the tip becomes sealed to a patch of the membrane, as shown in the bottom panels of Figure 4-7. This technique is analogous to placing a soda straw against a piece of plastic wrapping and sucking back to grasp the plastic. This method allows a recording to be made only from the small patch of membrane that is sealed within the perimeter of the microelectrode tip.

Using the giant axon of the squid, an oscilloscope, and microelectrodes, Hodgkin and Huxley recorded the electrical voltage on an axon's membrane and explained the nerve impulse. The basis of this electrical activity is the movement of intracellular and extracellular ions, which carry positive and negative charges. So to understand Hodgkin and Huxley's results, you first need to understand the principles underlying the movement of ions.

How the Movement of Ions Creates Electrical Charges

As you learned in Chapter 3, the intracellular and extracellular fluid of a neuron is filled with various charged ions, including positively charged Na^+ (sodium) and K^+ (potassium), and negatively charged Cl^- (chloride) ions. These fluids also contain numerous negatively charged protein molecules (A^- for short). Positively charged ions are called *cations,* and negatively charged ions are called *anions.* Three factors influence the movement of anions and cations into and out of cells: *diffusion, concentration gradient,* and *charge.*

Because molecules move constantly, they spontaneously tend to spread out from where they are more concentrated to where they are less concentrated. This spreading out is **diffusion.** Requiring no work, diffusion results from the random motion of molecules as they move and bounce off one another to gradually disperse in a solution. When diffusion is complete, a dynamic equilibrium, with an equal number of molecules everywhere, is created.

Smoke from a fire gradually diffuses into the air of a room, until every bit of air contains the same number of smoke molecules. Dye poured into water diffuses in the same way—from its point of contact to every part of the water in the container. Recall from Chapter 3 that salts placed in water dissolve into ions surrounded by water molecules. Carried by the random motion of the water molecules, the ions diffuse throughout the solution to equilibrium, when every part of the container has exactly the same concentration.

Concentration gradient describes the relative concentration of a substance in space. As illustrated in **Figure 4-8A,** drop a little ink into a beaker of water, and the dye starts out concentrated at the site of contact and then spreads. The ink diffuses from a point of higher concentration to points of lower concentration until it is equally distributed, and all the water in the beaker is the same color.

A similar process takes place when a salt solution is placed into water. The salt concentration is initially high in the location where it enters the water, but it then diffuses from that location until its ions are in equilibrium. You are familiar with other kinds of gradients. For example, a car parked on a hill will roll down the grade if it is taken out of gear.

Because ions carry an electrical charge and similar charges repel each other, ion movement can be described either by a concentration gradient or a **voltage gradient,** the difference in charge between two regions that allows a flow of current if the two regions are connected. Ions will move down a voltage gradient from an area of higher charge to an area of lower charge, just as they move down a concentration gradient from an area of higher concentration to an area of lower concentration. Figure 4-8B illustrates this process: when salt is dissolved in water, its diffusion can be described as either movement down a concentration gradient (for sodium and chloride ions) or movement down a voltage gradient (for the positive and negative charges). In a container such as a beaker, which allows unimpeded movement of ions, the positive and negative charges eventually balance.

Diffusion. Movement of ions from an area of higher concentration to an area of lower concentration through random motion.

Concentration gradient. Differences in concentration of a substance among regions of a container that allows the substance to diffuse from an area of higher concentration to an area of lower concentration.

Voltage gradient. Difference in charge between two regions that allows a flow of current if the two regions are connected.

◉ Visit the module on neural communication on the *Foundations* CD. In the section on the membrane potential you'll see an animation of action potential showing how electrical and concentration gradients mediate ionic movement through a membrane. Note the changes on the oscilloscope as ions flow into and out of the cell.

Figure 4-8

Moving to Equilibrium   (A) A concentration gradient. When you drop a small amount of ink into a beaker of water, the ink will flow away from the point of contact, where it has a higher concentration, into areas of lower concentration until it is equally distributed in the beaker. **(B)** An electrostatic gradient. Pouring a salty solution into water frees its positive and negative ions to flow down their electrostatic gradients until positive and negative charges are everywhere equal.

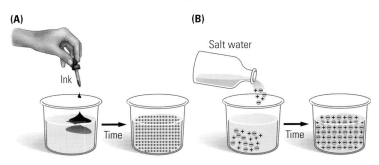

(A)   Ink

(B)   Salt water

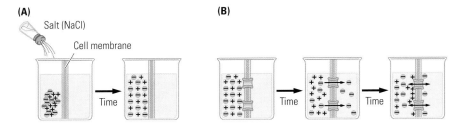

(A)
Salt (NaCl)
Cell membrane
Time

(B)
Time   Time

Figure 4-9

Modeling the Cell Membrane
(A) Impermeable membrane. When salt dissolves in water, positive and negative ions diffuse but cannot cross the solid barrier. **(B)** Semipermeable membrane. If the barrier has a hole through which Cl⁻ can pass but Na⁺ cannot pass, half of the container will become positively charged and the other half negatively charged. The voltage difference will be greatest across the membrane.

A lack of impediment is not the case in intracellular and extracellular fluid, because the semipermeable cell membrane acts as a partial barrier to the movement of ions between a cell's interior and exterior. As described in Chapter 3, a cell membrane is composed of a phospholipid bilayer, with the hydrophobic tails of one layer pointing inward toward those of the other layer and the hydrophilic heads pointing outward. This membrane is impermeable to salty solutions because the salt ions, which are surrounded by water molecules, will not pass through the membrane's hydrophobic tails.

An imaginary experiment illustrates how a cell membrane influences the movement of ions in this way. **Figure 4-9A** shows a container of water divided in half by a solid membrane. If we place a few grains of salt (NaCl) in the left half of the container, the salt dissolves and the ions diffuse down their concentration and voltage gradients until the water is in equilibrium. In the left side of the container, there is no longer a gradient for either sodium or chloride ions, because the water everywhere is equally salty. There are no gradients for these ions on the other side of the container either, because the membrane prevents the ions from entering that side. But there *are* concentration and voltage gradients for both sodium and chloride ions *across* the membrane—that is, from the salty side to the fresh-water side.

Recall that protein molecules embedded in a cell membrane form channels that act as pores to allow certain kinds of ions to pass through the membrane. Returning to our imaginary experiment, we place a couple chloride channels in the membrane that divides the container of water, as illustrated at the left in Figure 4-9B. Chloride ions will now cross the membrane and move down their concentration gradient on the side of the container that previously had no chloride ions, shown in the middle of Figure 4-9B. The sodium ions, in contrast, will not be able to cross the membrane. (Although sodium ions are smaller than chloride ions, sodium ions have a greater tendency to stick to water molecules and so they are bulkier and will not pass through a small chloride channel.)

If the only factor affecting the movement of chloride ions were the chloride concentration gradient, the efflux (outward flow) of chloride from the salty to the unsalty side of the container would continue until chloride ions were in equilibrium on both sides. But this is not what actually happens. Because the chloride ions carry a negative charge, they are attracted back toward the positively charged sodium ions (opposite charges attract). Consequently, the concentration of chloride ions remains higher in the left side of the container than in the right, as illustrated on the right Figure 4-9B.

The efflux of chloride ions down the chloride *concentration* gradient is counteracted by the influx (inward flow) of chloride ions down the chloride *voltage* gradient. At some point, equilibrium is reached in which the concentration gradient of chloride ions is balanced by the voltage gradient of chloride ions. In brief:

$$\text{concentration gradient} = \text{voltage gradient}$$

At this equilibrium, there is a differential concentration of the chloride ions on the two sides of the membrane, the difference in ion concentration produces a difference in charge, and so a voltage exists across the membrane. The left side of the container is positively charged because some chloride ions have migrated, leaving a preponderance of positive (Na⁺) charges. The right side of the container is negatively charged because some chloride ions (Cl⁻) have entered that chamber where no ions were before. The charge is highest on the surface of the membrane, the area at which positive and negative ions accumulate, and is much the same as what happens in a real cell.

In Review

Even several hundred years ago, experimental results implicated electrical activity in the nervous system's flow of information. But not until the mid–twentieth century did scientists solve all the technical problems in measuring the changes in electrical charge that travel like a wave along an axon's membrane. Their solutions included recording from the giant axons of the North Atlantic squid, using an oscilloscope to measure small changes in voltage and obtaining microelectrodes small enough to place on or into an axon. The electrical activity of axons entails the diffusion of ions that move both down a concentration gradient (from an area of relatively high concentration to an area of lower concentration) and down a voltage gradient (from an area of relatively high charge to an area of lower charge). The flow of ions in the nervous system is also affected by the semipermeable membrane and ion channels in cell membranes, which may open (facilitating ion movement), close (impeding that movement), or pump ions across the membrane.

ELECTRICAL ACTIVITY OF A MEMBRANE

Specific aspects of the cell membrane's electrical activity interact to convey information throughout the nervous system. The movement of ions across neural membranes creates the electrical activity that enables this information to flow.

Resting Potential

Figure 4-10A graphs the voltage difference recorded when one microelectrode is placed on the outer surface of an axon's membrane and another is placed on its inner surface. In the absence of stimulation, the difference is about 70 mV. Although the charge on the

Figure 4-10

Resting Potential   The electrical charge across a cell membrane produced by differences in ion concentration.

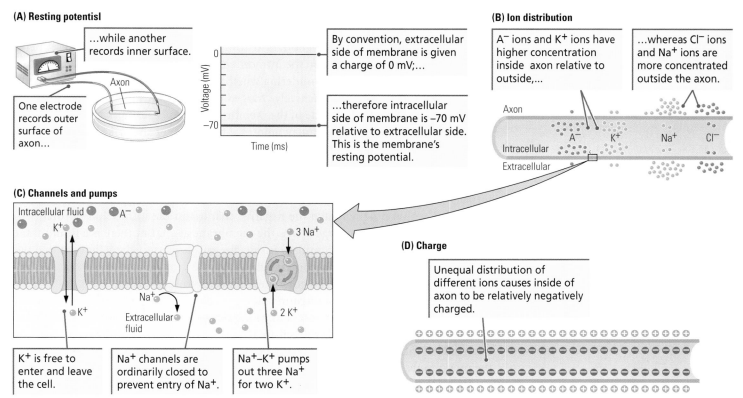

(A) Resting potentisl

One electrode records outer surface of axon... ...while another records inner surface.

Axon

By convention, extracellular side of membrane is given a charge of 0 mV;...

...therefore intracellular side of membrane is –70 mV relative to extracellular side. This is the membrane's resting potential.

Voltage (mV)

Time (ms)

(B) Ion distribution

A^- ions and K^+ ions have higher concentration inside axon relative to outside,...

...whereas Cl^- ions and Na^+ ions are more concentrated outside the axon.

Axon

Intracellular

Extracellular

A^- K^+ Na^+ Cl^-

(C) Channels and pumps

Intracellular fluid A^-

K^+

$3\ Na^+$

Na^+

Extracellular fluid

$2\ K^+$

K^+

K^+ is free to enter and leave the cell.

Na^+ channels are ordinarily closed to prevent entry of Na^+.

Na^+–K^+ pumps out three Na^+ for two K^+.

(D) Charge

Unequal distribution of different ions causes inside of axon to be relatively negatively charged.

Resting potential. Electrical charge across the cell membrane in the absence of stimulation; a store of energy produced by a greater negative charge on the intracellular side relative to the extracellular side.

○ On the *Foundations* CD, visit the section on the membrane potential in the module on neural communication. Here you can view an animation of resting potential. Note that the oscilloscope changes in electrical potential when the cell is stimulated.

outside of the membrane is actually positive, by convention it is given a charge of zero. Therefore, the inside of the membrane at rest is −70 mV *relative* to the extracellular side.

If we were to continue to record for a long period of time, the charge across the membrane would remain much the same. The difference in charge on the inside and outside of the membrane creates an electrical potential; however, the charge can change, given certain changes in the membrane. The charge is thus a store of *potential* energy called the membrane's **resting potential.** (We might use the term *potential* in the same way to talk about the financial potential of someone who has money in the bank—that person can spend that money at some future time.)

The resting potential, then, is a store of energy that can be used at a later time. Most of your body's cells have a resting potential, but it is not identical on every axon. A resting potential can vary from −40 to −90 mV on axons of different animal species.

Four charged particles take part in producing the resting potential: ions of sodium (Na^+) and potassium (K^+), chloride ions (Cl^-), and large protein molecules (A^-). As Figure 4-10B shows, these charged particles are distributed unequally across the axon's membrane, with more protein anions and K^+ ions in the intracellular fluid and more Cl^- and Na^+ ions in the extracellular fluid. Let us consider how the unequal concentrations arise and how each contributes to the membrane's resting potential.

Large protein anions are manufactured inside cells. No membrane channels are large enough to allow these proteins to leave the cell; so they remain in the intracellular fluid, and their charge contributes to the negative charge on the inside of the cell membrane. The negative charge of protein anions alone is sufficient to produce a transmembrane voltage or resting potential. Because most cells in the body manufacture these large, negatively charged protein molecules, most cells have a charge across the cell membrane.

To balance the negative charge created by large protein anions in the intracellular fluid, cells accumulate positively charged K^+ ions to the extent that about 20 times as many potassium ions cluster inside the cell as outside it. Potassium ions cross the cell membrane through open potassium ion channels, as shown in Figure 4-10C. With this high concentration of potassium ions inside the cell, however, the potassium ion concentration gradient across the membrane limits the number of K^+ ions entering the cell. In other words, some potassium ions do not enter the cell, because the internal concentration of K^+ ions is much higher than the external K^+ concentration.

A few residual K^+ ions are enough to contribute to the charge across the membrane, adding to the negativity on the intracellular side of the membrane relative to the extracellular side. You may be wondering whether you read the last sentence correctly. If there are 20 times as many positively charged potassium ions inside the cell as there are outside, why should the inside of the membrane have a *negative* charge? Should not all those K^+ ions in the intracellular fluid give the inside of the cell a positive charge instead? No, because not quite enough potassium ions are able to enter the cell to balance the negative charge of the protein anions.

Think of it this way: if the number of potassium ions that could accumulate on the intracellular side of the membrane were unrestricted, the positively charged potassium ions inside would exactly match the negative charges on the intracellular protein anions. There would be no charge across the membrane at all. But there *is* a limit on the number of K^+ ions that accumulate inside the cell because, when the intracellular potassium ion concentration becomes higher than the extracellular concentration, further K^+ influx is opposed by the potassium concentration gradient.

The equilibrium of the potassium voltage gradient and the potassium concentration gradient results in some potassium ions remaining outside the cell. Only a few potassium ions staying outside the cell are needed to maintain a negative charge on the inner side of the membrane. As a result, potassium ions contribute to the charge across the membrane.

Recall that sodium (Na^+) and chloride (Cl^-) ions also take part in producing the resting potential. If positively charged sodium ions were free to move across the membrane, they would diffuse into the cell and eliminate the transmembrane charge produced by the unequal distribution of potassium ions inside and outside the cell. This diffusion does not happen, because sodium ion channels on the cell membrane are ordinarily closed (see Figure 4-10C), blocking the entry of most sodium ions. Still, given enough time, sufficient sodium could leak into the cell to neutralize its membrane potential. The cell membrane has a different mechanism to prevent this neutralization from happening.

When Na^+ ions do leak into the neuron, they are immediately escorted out again by the action of a *sodium–potassium pump,* a protein molecule embedded in the cell membrane (see Figure 4-10C). A membrane's many thousands of pumps continually exchange three intracellular Na^+ ions for two K^+ ions. The K^+ ions are free to leave the cell through open potassium channels, but closed sodium channels slow the reentry of the Na^+ ions. In this way, Na^+ ions are kept out to the extent that about 10 times as many sodium ions reside on the extracellular side of the axon membrane as on the membrane's intracellular side. The difference in Na^+ concentrations also contributes to the resting potential of the membrane.

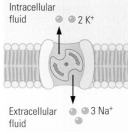

Intracellular fluid 2 K^+

Extracellular fluid 3 Na^+

Sodium–potassium pump

Now consider the chloride ions. Unlike sodium ions, Cl^- ions move in and out of the cell through open channels in the membrane. The equilibrium at which the chloride concentration gradient equals the chloride voltage gradient is approximately the same as the membrane's resting potential, and so chloride ions ordinarily contribute little to the resting potential. At this equilibrium point, there are about 12 times as many Cl^- ions outside the cell as inside it.

As summarized in Figure 4-10D, the unequal distribution of anions and cations leaves a neuron's intracellular fluid negatively charged at about -70 mV relative to the fluid outside the cell. Three aspects of the semipermeable cell membrane contribute to this resting potential:

1. Large negatively charged protein molecules remain inside the cell.
2. Gates keep out positively charged Na^+ ions, and channels allow K^+ and Cl^- ions to pass more freely.
3. Na^+–K^+ pumps extrude Na^+ from the intracellular fluid.

Graded Potentials

Recall that the charges on the inside and the outside of the cell membrane can change. If the concentration of any of the ions across the cell membrane changes, the membrane voltage will change. The resting potential provides an energy store that can be used somewhat like the water in a dam, where small amounts can be released by opening gates for irrigation or to generate electricity.

Conditions under which ion concentrations across the cell membrane change produce **graded potentials,** relatively small voltage fluctuations that are restricted to the vicinity on the axon where ion concentrations change. Just as a small wave produced in the middle of a large, smooth pond decays before traveling much distance, graded potentials produced on a membrane decay before traveling very far. But an isolated axon will not undergo a spontaneous change in charge. For a graded potential to arise, an axon must somehow be stimulated.

Stimulating an axon electrically through a microelectrode mimics the way in which the membrane voltage changes to produce a graded potential in the living cell. If the voltage applied to the inside of the membrane is negative, the membrane potential increases

Graded potential. Small voltage fluctuation in the cell membrane restricted to the vicinity on the axon where ion concentrations change to cause a brief increase (hyperpolarization) or decrease (depolarization) in electrical charge across the cell membrane.

Figure 4-11

Graded Potentials **(A)** Stimulation (S) that increases relative membrane voltage produces a hyperpolarizing graded potential. **(B)** Stimulation that decreases relative membrane voltage produces a depolarizing graded potential.

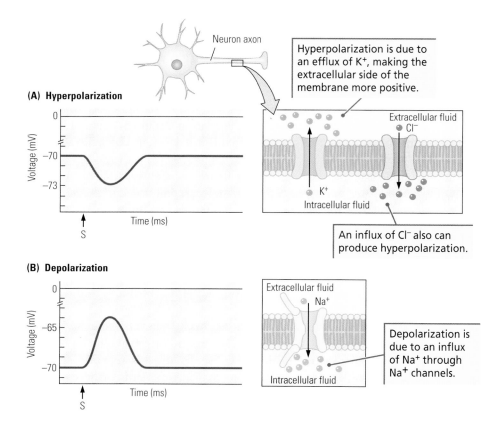

(A) **Hyperpolarization**

Hyperpolarization is due to an efflux of K⁺, making the extracellular side of the membrane more positive.

An influx of Cl⁻ also can produce hyperpolarization.

(B) **Depolarization**

Depolarization is due to an influx of Na⁺ through Na⁺ channels.

Hyperpolarization. Increase in electrical charge across a membrane, usually due to the inward flow of chloride ions or the outward flow of potassium ions.

Depolarization. Decrease in electrical charge across a membrane, usually due to the inward flow of sodium ions.

Action potential. Large, brief, reversal in polarity of an axon.

Threshold potential. Voltage on a neural membrane at which an action potential is triggered by the opening of Na⁺ and K⁺ voltage-sensitive channels; about −50 millivolts relative to extracellular surround.

Voltage-sensitive channel. Gated protein channel that opens or closes only at specific membrane voltages.

---

in negative charge by a few millivolts. As illustrated in **Figure 4-11A**, it may change from a resting potential of −70 mV to a new, slightly greater potential of −73 mV.

This change is a **hyperpolarization** because the charge (polarity) of the membrane increases. Conversely, if positive voltage is applied inside the membrane, its potential decreases by a few millivolts. As illustrated in Figure 4-11B, it may change from a resting potential of −70 mV to a new, slightly smaller potential of −65 mV. This change is a **depolarization** because the membrane charge decreases. Graded potentials are usually brief, lasting only milliseconds.

Hyperpolarization and depolarization typically occur on the soma (cell-body) membrane and on the dendrites of neurons. These areas contain channels that can open and close, causing the membrane potential to change (see Figure 4-11). Three channels, for sodium, potassium, and chloride ions, underlie graded potentials.

For the membrane to become hyperpolarized, its extracellular side must become more positive, which can be accomplished with an efflux of K⁺ ions or an influx of Cl⁻ ions. Evidence that potassium channels have a role in hyperpolarization comes from the fact that the chemical *tetraethylammonium* (TEA), which blocks potassium channels, also blocks hyperpolarization. But, if potassium channels are ordinarily open, how can a greater-than-normal efflux of K⁺ ions take place? Apparently, even though potassium channels are open, there is still some resistance to the outward flow of potassium ions. Reducing this resistance enables hyperpolarization.

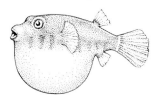

Puffer fish

Depolarization, on the other hand, can be produced by an influx of sodium ions and is produced by the opening of normally closed sodium channels. The involvement of sodium channels in depolarization is indicated by the fact that the chemical *tetrodotoxin,* which blocks sodium channels, also blocks depolarization. The puffer fish, which is considered a delicacy in some countries, especially Japan,

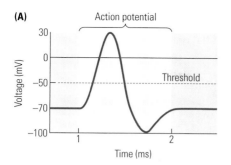

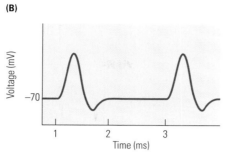

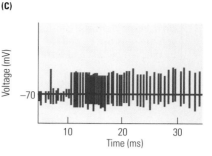

Figure 4-12

Measuring Action Potentials The time scale on the horizontal axis is compressed to chart **(A)** the phases of a single action potential, **(B)** each action potential as a discrete event, and **(C)** the ability of a membrane to produce many action potentials in a short time.

secretes this potentially deadly poison; so skill is required to prepare this fish for dinner. The fish is lethal to the guests of careless cooks because its toxin impedes the electrical activity of neurons.

The Action Potential

An **action potential** is a brief but extremely large reversal in the polarity of an axon's membrane that lasts about 1 ms. **Figure 4-12A** illustrates the magnitude of the voltage change associated with an action potential. The voltage across the membrane suddenly reverses, making the intracellular side positive relative to the extracellular side, and then abruptly reverses again, after which the resting potential is restored. Because the duration of the action potential is so brief, many action potentials can occur within a second, as illustrated in Figure 4-12B and C, where the time scales are compressed. An action potential occurs when a large concentration of first Na^+ ions and then K^+ ions crosses the membrane rapidly.

The change in membrane polarity that underlies an action potential occurs only when electrical stimulation causes the membrane potential to drop to about −50 mV relative to the charge outside the membrane. At this voltage level, or **threshold potential,** the membrane undergoes a remarkable further change in charge with no additional stimulation. The relative voltage of the membrane drops to zero and then continues to depolarize until the charge on the inside of the membrane is as great as +30 mV—a total voltage change of 100 mV. Then the membrane potential reverses again, becoming slightly hyperpolarized—a reversal of a little more than 100 mV. After this second reversal, the membrane slowly returns to its resting potential.

Experimental results reveal that the voltage that produces an action potential is due to a brief influx of sodium ions followed by a brief efflux of potassium ions. If an axon membrane is stimulated to produce an action potential while the solution surrounding the axon contains TEA (to block potassium channels), a smaller-than-normal action potential due entirely to a sodium influx is recorded. Similarly, if an axon's membrane is stimulated to produce an action potential while the solution surrounding the axon contains tetrodotoxin (to block sodium channels), a slightly different action potential due entirely to the efflux of potassium is recorded. **Figure 4-13** illustrates these experimental results, showing that the action potential on an axon normally consists of the summed current changes caused first by the inflow of sodium and then by the outflow potassium ions.

THE ROLE OF VOLTAGE-SENSITIVE ION CHANNELS

What cellular mechanisms underlie the movement of Na^+ and K^+ ions to produce an action potential? The answer lies in the behavior of a class of sodium and potassium ion channels that are sensitive to the membrane's voltage. These **voltage-sensitive channels**

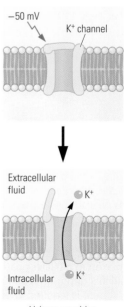

Voltage-sensitive
potassium channel

(A)

An action potential is produced by changes in voltage-sensitive K⁺ and Na⁺ channels, which can be blocked by TEA and tetrotoxin, respectively.

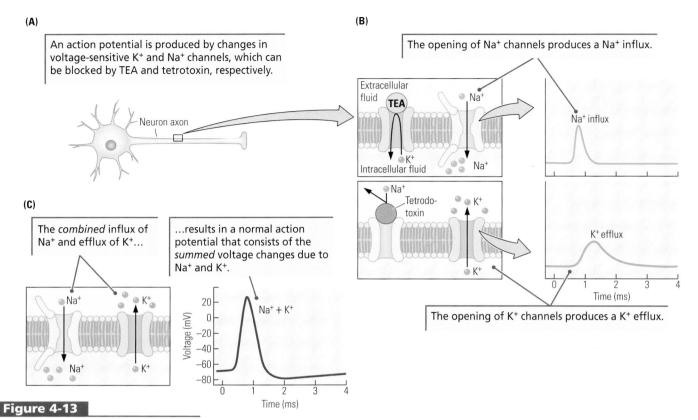

(B)

The opening of Na⁺ channels produces a Na⁺ influx.

(C)

The *combined* influx of Na⁺ and efflux of K⁺...

...results in a normal action potential that consists of the *summed* voltage changes due to Na⁺ and K⁺.

The opening of K⁺ channels produces a K⁺ efflux.

Figure 4-13

Physiology of the Action Potential
Experiments demonstrate that the action potential on an axon results from an inward flow of sodium ions followed by an outward flow of potassium ions.

◉ You can use the *Foundations* CD to review the action potential animation described on page 119. Note the ionic changes associated with this phenomenon and the oscilloscope readout for the action potential.

Absolutely refractory. Refers to the state of an axon in the repolarizing period during which a new action potential cannot be elicited (with some exceptions), because gate 2 of sodium channels, which is not voltage-sensitive, is closed.

Relatively refractory. Refers to the state of an axon in the later phase of an action potential during which increased electrical current is required to produce another action potential; a phase during which potassium channels are still open.

are closed when an axon's membrane is at its resting potential, and so ions cannot pass through them. When the membrane reaches threshold voltage, the configuration of the voltage-sensitive channels alters, enabling them to open and let ions pass through them. Thus, these "gated" channels can open to permit the flow of ions or close to restrict the flow of ions.

Voltage-sensitive channels are attuned to the threshold voltage of −50 mV. Voltage-sensitive sodium channels are more sensitive than the potassium channels, and so the voltage change due to sodium ion influx occurs slightly before the voltage change due to potassium ion efflux. "Opening the Voltage-Sensitive Gates" explains current thinking about how gated channels work and how they evolved.

ACTION POTENTIALS AND REFRACTORY PERIODS

Although action potentials can occur as many as hundreds of times a second, their frequency has an upper limit. If the axon membrane is stimulated during the depolarizing phase of the action potential, another action potential will not occur. The axon will also not produce another action potential when it is repolarizing, or **absolutely refractory.** (Exceptions do exist: some CNS neurons can discharge again during the repolarizing phase.)

If, on the other hand, the axon membrane is stimulated during hyperpolarization, another action potential can be induced, but the stimulation must be more intense than that which initiated the first action potential. During this phase, the membrane is **relatively refractory.** Because of refractory periods, there is about a 5-ms limit on how frequently action potentials can occur. In other words, an axon can produce action potentials at a maximum rate of about 200 per second.

Refractory periods are due to the way that gates of the voltage-sensitive sodium and potassium channels open and close. Sodium channels have two gates, and potassium

Opening the Voltage-Sensitive Gates

The cell membrane is studded with ion channels that regulate the transport of sodium, potassium, and calcium ions into and out of the cell. Each of these complex proteins contains a pore (channel) through which an appropriate ion can pass. Some ion channels also have a voltage-sensitive structure (a gate) that opens in response to changes in the cell-membrane voltage.

All voltage-sensitive channels (Na^+, Ca^{2+}, K^+) have a similar structure, suggesting that they all have a common origin but evolved to specialize for allowing different ions to cross the cell membrane. Potassium voltage-sensitive channels consist of four protein subunits, with six membrane-spanning regions. One of them, region 4, is positively charged.

Youxing Jiang and his colleagues (2003) modeled a potassium voltage-sensitive channel, shown in the accompanying diagram. Their goal was to understand how its pore opens in response to voltage changes on the membrane. They suggested that transmembrane region 4 twists, with a movement like that of a canoe paddle, in response to membrane-voltage changes to thus open the pore.

Until recently researchers hypothesized that voltage-sensitive sodium, potassium, and calcium channels are

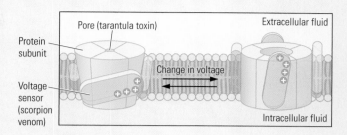

Adapted from Jiang et al., 2004.

unique to organisms that have a nervous system, where they play a role in electrical signaling in neurons. Vanessa Ruta and her colleagues (2003) found that an archaebacterium (ancient bacterium) from a deep oceanic thermal vent also has voltage-sensitive potassium channels. Both the archaebacterium's and the neuron's voltage-sensitive potassium channels are affected in the same way by two neurotoxins. Scorpion venom blocks the voltage sensor, and tarantula toxin blocks the pore. Because archaebacteria do not have nervous systems and are located far from scorpions and tarantulas, voltage channels that play a general role in transmembrane transportation must have been co-opted by animals having a nervous system in the course of evolution to play a role in nervous system information transmission.

channels have one gate. **Figure 4-14** illustrates the position of these gates before, during, and after the various phases of the action potential.

During the resting potential, gate 1 of the sodium channel depicted in Figure 4-14 is closed and only gate 2 is open. At the threshold level of stimulation, gate 1 also opens. Gate 2, however, closes very quickly after gate 1 opens. This sequence produces a brief period during which both gates are open followed by a brief period during which gate 2 is closed. When gate 1 opens, the membrane depolarizes and, when gate 2 closes, depolarization ends. The opening of the K^+ channels repolarizes and eventually hyperpolarizes the membrane.

Both sodium gates eventually regain their resting potential positions, with gate 1 closed and gate 2 open. But, while gate 2 of the Na^+ channel is closed, the membrane is absolutely refractory. Because the potassium channels close more slowly than the sodium channels do, the hyperpolarization produced by a continuing efflux of potassium ions makes the membrane relatively refractory for a period of time after the action potential has passed. The refractory periods have very practical uses in conducting information, as you will see next, when we consider the nerve impulse.

A lever-activated toilet provides an analogy for some of the changes in polarity that take place during an action potential. Pushing the lever slightly produces a slight flow of

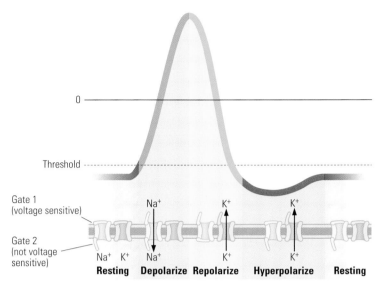

Figure 4-14

Phases of an Action Potential
Initiated by changes in voltage-sensitive sodium and potassium channels, an action potential begins with a depolarization (gate 1 of the sodium channel opens and then gate 2 closes). The slower-opening potassium-channel gate contributes to repolarization and hyperpolarization until the resting membrane potential is restored.

Nerve impulse. Propagation of an action potential on the membrane of an axon.

Node of Ranvier. The part of an axon that is not covered by myelin.

water, which stops when the lever is released. This activity is analogous to a graded potential. A harder lever press brings the toilet to threshold and initiates flushing, a response that is out of all proportion to the lever press. This activity is analogous to the action potential. During the flush, the toilet is absolutely refractory, meaning that another flush cannot be induced at this time. During the refilling of the bowl, in contrast, the toilet is relatively refractory, meaning that reflushing is possible but harder to bring about. Only after the cycle is over and the toilet is once again "resting," can the usual flush be produced again.

The Nerve Impulse

Suppose you place two recording electrodes at a distance from each other on an axon membrane and then electrically stimulate an area adjacent to one of these electrodes. That electrode would immediately record an action potential. A similar recording would register on the second electrode in a flash. Apparently, an action potential has arisen near this electrode also, even though this second electrode is some distance from the original point of stimulation.

Is this second action potential simply an echo of the first that passes down the axon? No, it cannot be, because the size and shape of the action potential are exactly the same at the two electrodes. The second is not just a faint, degraded version of the first but is equal in magnitude. Somehow the full action potential has moved along the axon. This propagation of an action potential along an axon is called a **nerve impulse.**

Why does an action potential move? Remember that the total voltage change during an action potential is 100 mV, far beyond the 20-mV change needed to bring the membrane from its resting state of −70 mV to the threshold level of −50 mV. Consequently, the voltage change on the part of the membrane at which an action potential first occurs is large enough to bring adjacent parts of the membrane to a threshold of −50 mV.

When the membrane of an adjacent part of the axon reaches −50 mV, the voltage-sensitive channels at that location pop open to produce an action potential there as well. This second occurrence, in turn, induces a change in the voltage of the membrane still farther along the axon, and so on and on, down the axon's length. **Figure 4-15** illustrates this process. The nerve impulse occurs because each action potential propagates another action potential on an adjacent part of the axon membrane. The word *propagate* means "to give birth," and that is exactly what happens. Each successive action potential gives birth to another down the length of the axon.

Two main factors ensure that a single nerve impulse of a constant size travels down the axon:

1. Voltage-sensitive channels produce refractory periods. Although an action potential can travel in either direction on an axon, refractory periods prevent it from reversing direction and returning to the point from which came. Thus refractory periods create a single, discrete impulse that travels only in one direction.

2. All action potentials generated as a nerve impulse travels are of the same magnitude. An action potential depends on energy expended at the site where it occurs, and the same amount of energy is expended at every site along the membrane where a nerve impulse is propagated. As a result, there is no such thing as a dissipated action potential. Simply stated, an action potential is either generated completely or it is not generated at all, which means that a nerve impulse always maintains a constant size.

The domino effect

To summarize the action of a nerve impulse, think of the voltage-sensitive channels along the axon as a series of dominoes. When one domino falls, it knocks over its neighbor, and so on down the line. The "wave" cannot return the way that it has come. There is also no decrement in the size of the fall. The last domino travels exactly the same distance and falls just as hard as the first one did.

Essentially this "domino effect" happens when voltage-sensitive channels open. The opening of one channel produces a voltage change that triggers its neighbor to open, just as one domino knocks over the next. When gate 2 on a voltage-sensitive sodium channel closes, that channel is inactivated, much as a domino is temporarily inactivated after it falls over. Both channel and domino must be reset before they can work again. Finally, the channel-opening response does not grow any weaker as it moves along the axon. The last channel opens exactly like the first, just as the domino action stays constant to the end of the line. Because of this behavior of voltage-sensitive channels, a single nerve impulse of constant size moves in only one direction along an axon.

Saltatory Conduction and Myelin Sheaths

Because the giant axons of squid are so large, they can transmit nerve impulses very quickly, much as a large-diameter pipe can deliver a lot of water at a rapid rate. But large axons take up substantial space, and so a squid cannot accommodate many of them or its body would become too bulky. For us mammals, with our many axons producing repertoires of complex behaviors, giant axons are out of the question. Our axons must be extremely slender because our complex behaviors require a great many of them.

Our largest axons are only about 30 μm wide; so the speed with which they convey information should not be especially fast. And yet, like most vertebrate species, we are hardly sluggish creatures. We process information and generate responses with impressive speed. How do we manage to do so if our axons are so thin? The vertebrate nervous system has evolved a solution that has nothing to do with axon size.

Glial cells play a role in speeding nerve impulses in the vertebrate nervous system. Schwann cells in the human peripheral nervous system and oligodendroglia in the central nervous system wrap around each axon, insulating it except for a small, exposed gap between each glial cell (Figure 4-16). As described in Chapter 3, this insulation is referred to as myelin or as a myelin sheath, and insulated axons are said to be myelinated.

Action potentials cannot occur where myelin is wrapped around an axon. For one thing, the myelin creates an insulating barrier to the flow of ionic current. For another, regions of an axon that lie under myelin have few channels through which ions can flow, and, as you know, such channels are essential to generating an action potential.

But axons are not totally encased in myelin. Unmyelinated gaps on the axon between successive glial cells are richly endowed with voltage-sensitive channels. These tiny gaps in the myelin sheath, the **nodes of Ranvier,** are sufficiently close to one another that an action potential occurring at one node can trigger the opening of voltage-sensitive gates at an adjacent node. In this way, a relatively slow action potential jumps at the speed of light from node to node, as shown in

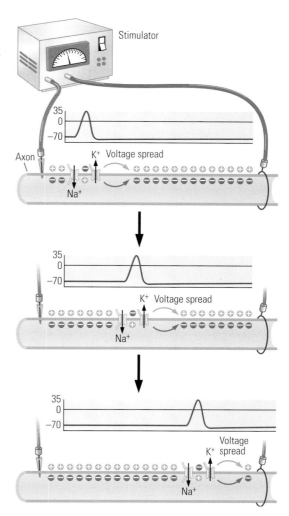

Figure 4-15

Propagating an Action Potential
Voltage sufficient to open Na$^+$ and K$^+$ channels spreads to adjacent sites of the membrane, inducing voltage-sensitive gates to open. Here, voltage changes are shown on only one side of the membrane.

Figure 4-16

Myelination An axon is myelinated by **(A)** oligodendroglia in the CNS and **(B)** Schwann cells in the PNS. Each glial cell is separated by a gap, or node of Ranvier.

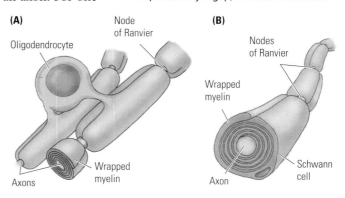

Figure 4-17

Saltatory Conduction
(A) Unmyelinated nodes of Ranvier are rich in voltage-sensitive channels. **(B)** In saltatory conduction, the action potential jumps from node to node.

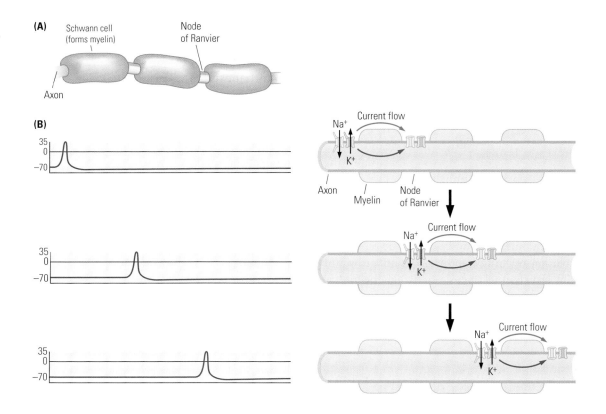

Figure 4-17. This flow of energy is called **saltatory conduction** (from the Latin verb *saltare*, meaning "to dance").

Jumping from node to node greatly speeds the rate at which an action potential can travel along an axon. On larger, myelinated mammalian axons, nerve impulses can travel at a rate as high as 120 meters per second, compared with only about 30 meters per second on smaller, uninsulated axons. Think of how a "wave" of consecutively standing spectators travels around a football stadium. As one person rises, the adjacent person rises, producing the wave effect. This wave is like conduction along an unmyelinated axon. Now think of how much faster the wave would complete its circuit around the field if only spectators in the corners rose to produce it, which is analogous to a nerve impulse that travels by jumping from one node of Ranvier to the next. The quick reactions of which humans and other mammals are capable are due in part to this saltatory conduction in their nervous systems.

⊙ On the *Foundations* CD, visit the module on neural communications. In the section on conduction of the action potential you can watch an animation showing the role of the myelin sheath in conduction. Note the role of the nodes of Ranvier in this process.

In Review

Microelectrodes connected to a voltmeter and placed on either side of an axon membrane will record a voltage difference across the membrane due to the unequal distribution of ions inside and outside the cell. The semipermeable membrane prevents the efflux of large protein anions, and it pumps sodium ions out of the cell. Although potassium ions and chloride ions are relatively free to cross the membrane through their respective channels, the equilibrium at which their concentration gradient matches their voltage gradient contributes to the relative transmembrane difference of −70 mV in charge. Some sodium and potassium channels sensitive to the membrane's voltage open when the membrane is electrically stimulated, allowing a brief free flow of ions across the membrane and stimulating an action potential, a brief reversal of charge on the membrane. The voltage change

Saltatory conduction. Propagation of an action potential at successive nodes of Ranvier; saltatory means "jumping" or "dancing."

associated with an action potential is sufficiently large to stimulate adjacent parts of the axon membrane to the threshold for propagating the action potential along the length of an axon as a nerve impulse. Along a myelinated axon, a nerve impulse travels by saltatory conduction, jumping from one node of Ranvier to the next and greatly increasing the speed at which a nerve impulse travels.

Excitatory postsynaptic potential (EPSP). Brief depolarization of a neuron membrane in response to stimulation, making the neuron more likely to produce an action potential.

Inhibitory postsynaptic potential (IPSP). Brief hyperpolarization of a neuron membrane in response to stimulation, making the neuron less likely to produce an action potential.

HOW NEURONS INTEGRATE INFORMATION

John C. Eccles
(1903–1997)

A neuron is more than just an axon connected to microelectrodes by some curious scientist who stimulates it with electrical current. A neuron has an extensive dendritic tree covered with spines, and, through these dendritic spines, it can have more than 50,000 connections to other neurons. Nerve impulses traveling to each of these synapses from other neurons bombard the receiving neuron with all manner of inputs. In addition, a neuron has a cell body between its dendritic tree and its axon, and this cell body, too, can receive connections from many other neurons.

How does the neuron integrate this enormous array of inputs into a nerve impulse? In the 1960s, John C. Eccles and his students performed experiments that helped to answer this question. Rather than recording from the giant axon of a squid, the researchers recorded from the cell bodies of large motor neurons in the vertebrate spinal cord. They did so by refining the stimulating and recording techniques developed for the study of squid axons.

A spinal-cord motor neuron has an extensive dendritic tree with as many as 20 main branches that subdivide numerous times and are covered with dendritic spines. Motor neurons receive input from multiple sources, including the skin, joints, muscles, and brain, which is why they are ideal for studying how a neuron responds to diverse inputs. Each motor neuron sends its axon directly to a muscle, as you would expect for neurons that produce movement. "Myasthenia Gravis" on page 132 explains what happens when muscle receptors lose their sensitivity to motor-neuron messages.

Excitatory and Inhibitory Postsynaptic Potentials

To study the activity of motor neurons, Eccles inserted a microelectrode into a vertebrate spinal cord until the tip was located in or right beside a motor neuron's cell body. He then placed stimulating electrodes on the axons of sensory fibers entering the spinal cord. By teasing apart the fibers of the incoming sensory nerves, he was able to stimulate one fiber at a time.

Figure 4-18 diagrams the experimental setup that Eccles used. He found that stimulating some of the fibers produced a depolarizing graded potential (reduced the charge) on the membrane of the motor neuron to which these fibers were connected. Eccles called these potentials **excitatory postsynaptic potentials** (EPSPs). Because they reduce the charge on the membrane toward the threshold level, they increase the probability that an action potential will result.

In contrast, when Eccles stimulated other incoming sensory fibers, he produced a hyperpolarizing graded potential (increased the charge) on the receiving motor-neuron membrane. Eccles called these potentials **inhibitory postsynaptic potentials** (IPSPs). Because they increase the charge on the membrane away from the threshold level, they decrease the probability that an action potential will result.

Figure 4-18

Eccles's Experiment To demonstrate how input onto neurons influences their excitability, a recording is made from a motor neuron while either an excitatory (*left*) or an inhibitory (*right*) input is delivered. Stimulation (S) of the excitatory pathway produces a membrane depolarization, or EPSP. Stimulation of the inhibitory pathway produces a membrane hyperpolarization, or IPSP.

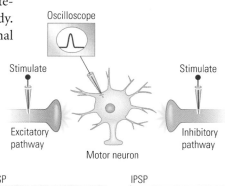

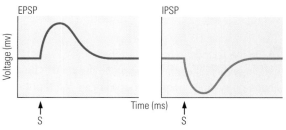

Myasthenia Gravis

R. J. was 22 years old in 1941 when she noticed that her eyelid drooped. She consulted her physician, but he was unable to explain her condition or give her any help. Over the next few years, she experienced some difficulty in swallowing, general weakness in her limbs, and terrific fatigue.

Many of the symptoms would disappear for days and then suddenly reappear. R. J. also noted that, if she got a good night's sleep, she felt better but, if she performed physical work or became stressed, the symptoms got worse. About 3 years after the symptoms first appeared she was diagnosed with myasthenia gravis, a condition that affects the communication between motor neurons and muscles.

A specialist suggested that R. J. undergo a new treatment in which the thymus gland is removed. She underwent the surgery and, within the next 5 years, all her symptoms gradually disappeared. She has been symptom free for more than 60 years.

In myasthenia gravis, the receptors of muscles are insensitive to the chemical messages passed from axon terminals. Consequently, the muscles do not respond to commands from motor neurons. Myasthenia gravis is rare, with a prevalence of 14/100,000, and the disorder is more common in women than in men.

The age of onset is usually in the 30s to 40s for women and after age 50 for men. In about 10 percent of cases, the condition is limited to the eye muscles, but, for the vast majority of patients, the condition gets worse. At the time when R. J. contracted the disease, about a third of myasthenia gravis patients died from the disease or from complications such as respiratory infections.

Why is removal of the thymus gland sometimes an effective treatment? A gland of the immune system, the thymus

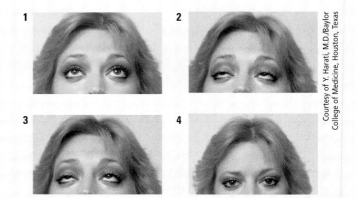

Courtesy of Y. Harati, M.D./Baylor College of Medicine, Houston, Texas

This myasthenia gravis patient was asked to look up (photograph 1). Her eyelids quickly became fatigued and drooped (photographs 2 and 3). Photograph 4 shows her eyelids open normally after a few minutes rest.

takes part in producing antibodies to foreign material and viruses that enter the body. In myasthenia gravis, the thymus may start to make antibodies to the end-plate receptors on muscles. Blocked by these antibodies, the receptors can no longer produce a normal response to acetylcholine, the chemical transmitter at the muscle synapse; so Na^+ and K^+ do not move through the end-plate pore and the muscle does not receive the signal to contract. Disorders in which the immune system makes antibodies to a person's own body are called *autoimmune diseases*.

Myasthenia gravis has now been modeled almost completely in animals and has become a model for studying other autoimmune diseases. A variety of contemporary treatments besides removal of the thymus include thyroid removal and drug treatments, such as those that increase the release of acetylcholine at muscle receptors. As a result, most myasthenia gravis patients today live out their normal life spans.

○ On the *Foundations* CD, visit the module on neural communication. In the section on synaptic transmission, you can view animations of EPSP and IPSP.

Both EPSPs and IPSPs last only a few milliseconds, after which they decay and the neuron's resting potential is restored. EPSPs are associated with the opening of sodium channels, which allows an influx of Na^+ ions. IPSPs are associated with the opening of potassium channels, which allows an efflux of K^+ ions (or with the opening of chloride channels, which allows an influx of Cl^- ions).

Although the size of a graded potential is proportional to the intensity of the stimulation, an action potential is not produced on the motor neuron's cell-body membrane even when an EPSP is strongly excitatory. The reason is simple: the cell-body membrane of most neurons does not contain voltage-sensitive channels. The stimulation must reach the axon hillock, the area of the cell where the axon begins. This area is rich in voltage-sensitive channels.

Summation of Inputs

Remember that a motor neuron has thousands of dendritic spines, allowing for myriad inputs to its membrane, both EPSPs and IPSPs. How do these incoming graded potentials interact? For example, what happens if there are two EPSPs in succession? Does it matter if the time between them is increased or decreased? And what is the result when an EPSP and an IPSP arrive together? Answers to such questions provide an understanding of how the thousands of inputs to a neuron might influence its activities.

If one excitatory pulse of stimulation is delivered and is followed some time later by a second excitatory pulse, one EPSP is recorded and, after a delay, a second identical EPSP is recorded, as shown at the top of **Figure 4-19**. These two EPSPs are independent and do not interact. If the delay between them is shortened so that the two occur in rapid succession, however, a single large EPSP is produced, as also shown in Figure 4-19.

Here the two excitatory pulses are summed (added together to produce a larger depolarization of the membrane than either would induce alone). This relation between two EPSPs occurring closely together in time is called **temporal summation.** The bottom half of Figure 4-19 illustrates that equivalent results are obtained with IPSPs. Therefore, temporal summation is a property of both EPSPs and IPSPs.

Now let us use two recording electrodes to see the effects of spatial relations on the summation of inputs. What happens when inputs to the cell body's membrane are located close together, and what happens when the inputs are spaced farther apart?

If two EPSPs occur at the same time but on widely separated parts of the membrane (**Figure 4-20A**), they do not influence each other. If two EPSPs occurring close together in

Temporal summation. Graded potentials that occur at approximately the same time on a membrane are summated.

Figure 4-19

Temporal Summation (*Top*) Two depolarizing pulses of stimulation (S$_1$ and S$_2$) separated in time produce two EPSPs similar in size. Pulses close together in time partly sum. Simultaneous EPSPs sum as one large EPSP. (*Bottom*) Two hyperpolarizing pulses (S$_1$ and S$_2$) widely separated in time produce two IPSPs similar in size. Pulses in close temporal proximity partly sum. Simultaneous IPSPs sum as one large IPSP.

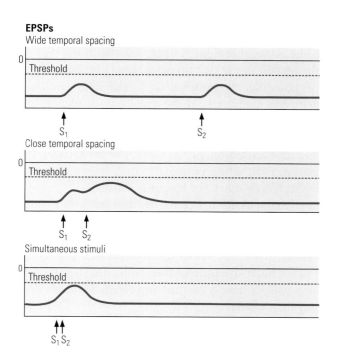

EPSPs
Wide temporal spacing

Close temporal spacing

Simultaneous stimuli

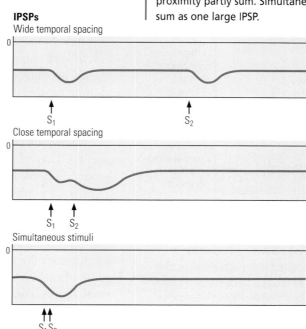

IPSPs
Wide temporal spacing

Close temporal spacing

Simultaneous stimuli

(A)

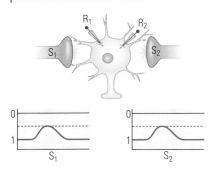

EPSPs produced at the same time, but on separate parts of the membrane, do not influence each other.

Figure 4-20

Spatial Summation Illustrated here for EPSPs, the process for IPSPs is equivalent.

(B)

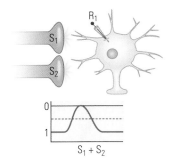

EPSPs produced at the same time, and close together, add to form a larger EPSP.

time are also close together in location, however, they add to form a larger EPSP (Figure 4-20B). This **spatial summation** indicates that two separate inputs occurring very close to each other in space sum. Similarly, two IPSPs produced at the same time sum if they occur at approximately the same place on the cell-body membrane but not if they are widely separated.

Summation is thus a property of both EPSPs and IPSPs in any combination. The interactions between EPSPs and IPSPs are understandable when you consider that it is the influx and efflux of ions that are being summed. The influx of sodium ions accompanying one EPSP is added to the influx of sodium ions accompanying a second EPSP if the two occur close together in time and space. If the two influxes of sodium ions are remote in time or in space or in both, no summation is possible.

The same is true regarding effluxes of potassium ions. When they occur close together in time and space, they sum; when they are far apart in either or both of these ways, there is no summation. The patterns are identical for an EPSP and an IPSP. The influx of sodium ions associated with the EPSP is added to the efflux of potassium ions associated with the IPSP, and the difference between them is recorded as long as they are spatially and temporally close together. If, on the other hand, they are widely separated in time or in space or in both, they do not interact and there is no summation.

A neuron with thousands of inputs responds no differently from one with only a few inputs. It democratically sums all inputs that are close together in time and space. The cell-body membrane, therefore, always indicates the summed influences of multiple inputs. Because of this temporal and spatial summation, a neuron can be said to analyze its inputs before deciding what to do. The ultimate decision is made at the axon hillock.

The Axon Hillock

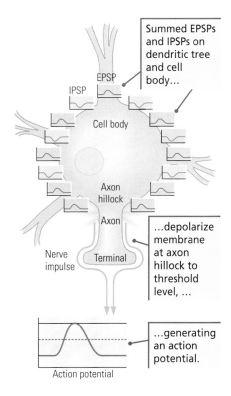

Figure 4-21

Triggering an Action Potential If the summated EPSPs and IPSPs on the dendritic tree and cell body of a neuron change the membrane to threshold level at the axon hillock, an action potential travels down the axon membrane.

The axon hillock, shown emanating from the cell body in **Figure 4-21**, is rich in voltage-sensitive channels. These channels, like those on the squid axon, open at a particular membrane voltage. The actual threshold voltage varies with the type of neuron, but, to keep things simple, we will stay with a threshold level of −50 mV.

To produce an action potential, the summed IPSPs and EPSPs on the cell-body membrane must depolarize the membrane at the axon hillock to −50 mV. If that threshold voltage is only briefly obtained, just one or a few action potentials may occur. If the threshold level is maintained for a longer period, however, action potentials will follow one another in rapid succession, just as quickly as the gates on the voltage-sensitive channels can recover. Each action potential is then repeatedly propagated to produce a nerve impulse that travels down the length of the axon.

Do all graded potentials equally influence the voltage-sensitive channels at the axon hillock? Not necessarily. Remember that neurons often have extensive dendritic trees. EPSPs and IPSPs on the distant branches of dendrites may have less influence than that of EPSPs and IPSPs that are closer to the axon hillock. Inputs close to the axon hillock are usually much more dynamic in their influence than those occurring some distance away, which usually have a modulating effect. As in all democracies, some inputs have more say than others.

To summarize the relation between EPSPs, IPSPs, and action potentials, imagine a brick standing on end a few inches away from a wall. It can be tilted back and forth over quite a wide range. If it is tilted too far in one direction, it falls against the wall, whereas, if it is tilted too far in the other direction, it topples over completely. Movements toward the wall are like IPSPs (inhibitory inputs). No matter how much these inputs sum, the brick never falls. Movements away from the wall are like EPSPs (excitatory inputs). If their sum reaches some threshold point, the brick topples over. With sufficient excitation, then, the brick falls, which is analogous to generating an action potential.

Spatial summation. Graded potentials that occur at approximately the same location on a membrane are summated.

In Review

Stimulation at synapses produces graded potentials on a neuron's cell body and dendrites. Graded potentials that decrease the charge on the cell membrane, moving it toward the threshold level, are called excitatory postsynaptic potentials because they increase the likelihood that an action potential will occur. Graded potentials that increase the charge on the cell membrane, moving it away from the threshold level, are called inhibitory postsynaptic potentials because they decrease the likelihood that an action potential will result. EPSPs and IPSPs that occur close together in time and space are summed. In this way, a neuron integrates information that it receives from other neurons. If summed inputs are sufficiently excitatory to bring the axon hillock to a threshold level, an action potential is triggered and then propagated as it travels along the cell's axon as a nerve impulse.

◉ Visit the module on neural communication on the *Foundations* CD. In the section on neural integration you can watch an animation showing the process of spatial and temporal summation.

INTO THE NERVOUS SYSTEM AND BACK OUT

The nervous system allows us to respond to sensory stimuli by detecting them in the environment and sending messages about them to the brain. The brain interprets the information, triggering responses that contract muscles and cause movements of the body. Until now, we have been dealing with only the middle of this process—how neurons convey information to one another, integrate that information, and generate action potentials. We have not explored the beginning and end of the journey.

To fill in those missing pieces, we now explain how a sensory stimulus initiates a nerve impulse and how a nerve impulse produces a muscular contraction. You will see that ion channels are again important but that these channels are different from those described so far. You will first see how they differ as we examine the production of action potentials by sensory stimuli.

How Sensory Stimuli Produce Action Potentials

We receive information about the world through tactile sensations (body senses such as touch and pain), auditory sensations (hearing), visual sensations (sight), and chemical sensations (taste and olfaction). Each sensory modality has one or more separate functions. For example, the body senses include touch, pressure, joint sense, pain, and temperature. Receptors for audition and balance are modified touch receptors. The visual system has receptors for light and for different colors. And taste and olfactory senses are sensitive to many chemical compounds. Some of these receptors are organelles attached to a sensory neuron's dendrite, whereas other receptors are part of the neuron's membrane.

To process all these different kinds of sensory inputs requires a remarkable array of different sensory receptors. But one thing that neurons related to these diverse

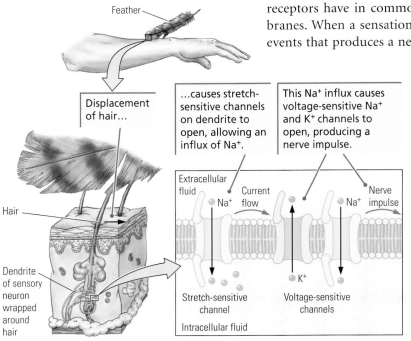

Figure 4-22

Tactile Stimulation A hair's touch receptor activated by a feather results in a nerve impulse heading to the brain.

receptors have in common is the presence of ion channels on their cell membranes. When a sensation stimulates these ion channels, it initiates the chain of events that produces a nerve impulse.

Touch provides an example. Each hair on the human body is very sensitive to touch, allowing us to detect an even very slight displacement. You can demonstrate this sensitivity to yourself by selecting a single hair on your arm and bending it. If you are patient and precise in your experimentation, you will discover that some hairs are sensitive to displacement in one direction only, whereas others respond to displacement in any direction. What enables this very finely tuned sensitivity?

The dendrites of sensory neurons are specialized to conduct nerve impulses, and one of these dendrites is wrapped around the base of each hair on your body, as shown in **Figure 4-22**. When a hair is mechanically displaced, the dendrite encircling it is stretched, initiating the opening of a series of **stretch-sensitive channels** in the dendrite's membrane. When these channels open, they allow an influx of Na$^+$ ions sufficient to depolarize the dendrite to its threshold level. At threshold, the voltage-sensitive sodium and potassium channels open to initiate the nerve impulse.

Other kinds of sensory receptors have similar mechanisms for transforming the energy of a sensory stimulus into nervous system activity. The receptors for hearing and balance have hairs that, when displaced, likewise activate stretch-sensitive channels. In the visual system, light particles strike chemicals in the receptors in the eye, and the resulting chemical change activates ion channels in the membranes of relay neurons. An odorous molecule in the air that lands on an olfactory receptor and fits itself into a specially shaped compartment opens chemical-sensitive ion channels. When tissue is damaged, injured cells release a chemical called bradykinin that activates bradykinin-sensitive channels on a pain nerve.

In later chapters, we consider the details of how sensory receptors change, or *transduce,* energy from the external world into action potentials. The point here is that, in all our sensory systems, ion channels begin the process of information conduction.

How Nerve Impulses Produce Movement

What happens at the end of the neural journey? How, after sensory information has traveled to the brain and been interpreted, is a behavioral response that includes the contraction of muscles generated? Behavior, after all, is movement, and, for movement to take place, muscles must contract. If motor neurons fail to work, movement becomes impossible and muscles atrophy (see "Lou Gehrig's Disease").

You know that motor neurons send nerve impulses through their axons to muscles. The motor-neuron axons, in turn, generate action potentials in muscle cells, which are instrumental in making the muscle contract. So the question is, How does an action potential on a motor-neuron axon produce an action potential on a muscle?

The axon of each motor neuron makes one or a few contacts (synapses) with its target muscle, similar to those that neurons make with one another (**Figure 4-23**). The part of the muscle membrane that is contacted by the axon terminal is a specialized

Stretch-sensitive channel. Ion channel on a tactile sensory neuron that activates in response to stretching of the membrane, initiating a nerve impulse.

Lou Gehrig's Disease

Baseball legend Lou Gehrig played for the New York Yankees from 1923 until 1939. He was a member of numerous World Series championship teams, set a host of individual records, some of which still stand today, and was immensely popular with fans, who knew him as the "Iron Man." His record of 2130 consecutive games was untouched until 1990, when Cal Ripkin, Jr., played his 2131st consecutive game.

In 1938, Gehrig started to lose his strength. In 1939, he played only eight games and then retired from baseball. Eldon Auker, a pitcher for the Detroit Tigers, described Lou's physical decline: "Lou seemed to be losing his power. His walking and running appeared to slow. His swing was not as strong as it had been in past years."

Eldon was not describing the symptoms of normal aging but rather the symptoms of amyotrophic lateral sclerosis

(ALS), a diagnosis shortly to be pronounced by Lou's physician. ALS was first described by Jean-Martin Charcot in 1869, but, after Lou Gehrig developed the condition, it was commonly called Lou Gehrig's disease. Gehrig died in 1941 at the age of 38.

ALS affects about 6 of every 100,000 people and strikes most commonly between the ages of 50 and 75, although its onset can be as early as the teenage years. About 10 percent of victims have a family history of the disorder. The disease begins with general weakness, at first in the throat or upper chest and in the arms and legs. Gradually, walking becomes difficult and falling common. The patient may lose use of the hands and legs, have trouble swallowing, and have difficulty speaking. The disease does not usually affect any sensory systems, cognitive functions, bowel or bladder control, or even sexual function. Death is often within 5 years of diagnosis.

ALS is due primarily to the death of motor neurons, which connect the rest of the nervous system to muscles, allowing movement. Neurons in the brain that connect primarily with motor neurons also can be affected. The technical term, amyotrophic lateral sclerosis, describes its consequences on both muscles (*amyotrophic* means "muscle weakness") and on the spinal cord (*lateral sclerosis* means "hardening of the lateral spinal cord") where motor neurons are located.

Several theories have been advanced to explain why motor neurons suddenly start to die in ALS victims. Perhaps this cell death is caused by the atrophy of microtubules that carry proteins down the motor-neuron axons, perhaps by a buildup of toxic chemicals within the motor neurons, perhaps by toxic chemicals released from other neurons. No one knows for sure. Recent evidence suggests that ALS can result from head trauma that activates the cell's DNA to produce signals that initiate the neuron's death, a phenomenon known as programmed cell death (Przedborski, 2004). At the present time, there is no cure for ALS, although some newly developed drugs appear to slow its progression and offer some hope for future treatments.

Baseball Hall of Fame Library, Cooperstown, N.Y.

Lou Gehrig jumping over Yankee teammate Joe DiMaggio's bat.

Figure 4-23

Muscle Contraction
(A) In this microscopic view of a motor-neuron axon collaterals contacting muscle end plates, the dark patches are end plates and the axon terminals are not visible.
(B) An axon terminal contacts an end plate. **(C)** The neurotransmitter acetylcholine attaches to receptor sites on transmitter-sensitive end-plate channels, opening them. These large channels allow the simultaneous influx of sodium ions and efflux of potassium ions, generating a current sufficient to activate voltage-sensitive channels that trigger an action potential on the muscle, causing it to contract.

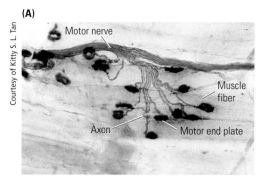

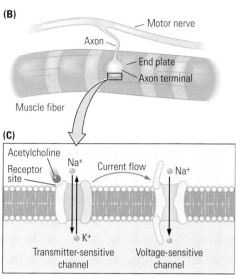

area called an **end plate,** shown in Figure 4-23A and B. The axon terminal releases onto the end plate a chemical transmitter called **acetylcholine** (ACh) that activates skeletal muscles.

This transmitter does not enter the muscle but rather attaches to **transmitter-sensitive channels** on the end plate (Figure 4-23C). When these channels open in response to ACh, they allow a flow of ions across the muscle membrane sufficient to depolarize it to the threshold for its action potential. At threshold, adjacent voltage-sensitive channels open. They, in turn, produce an action potential on the muscle fiber, which is the basis for muscular contraction.

The transmitter-sensitive channels on muscle end plates are somewhat different from the channels on axons and dendrites. A single end-plate channel is larger than two sodium and two potassium channels on a neuron combined. When transmitter-sensitive channels open, they allow both sodium ions and potassium ions to flow through the same pore. The number of channels that open depends on the amount of transmitter released. Therefore, to generate a sufficient depolarization on the end plate to activate neighboring voltage-sensitive channels requires the release of an appropriate amount of acetylcholine.

A wide range of neural events can be explained by the actions of membrane channels. Some channels generate the transmembrane charge. Others mediate graded potentials. Still others trigger the action potential. Sensory stimuli activate channels on neurons to initiate a nerve impulse, and the nerve impulse eventually activates channels on motor neurons to produce muscle contractions.

These various channels and their different functions probably evolved over a long period of time in the same way that new species of animals and their behaviors evolve. So far, not all the different channels that neural membranes possess have been described, but you will learn about some additional channels in subsequent chapters.

End plate. On a muscle, the receptor–ion complex that is activated by the release of the neurotransmitter acetylcholine from the terminal of a motor neuron.

Acetylcholine (ACh). The first neurotransmitter discovered in the peripheral and central nervous systems; activates skeletal muscles.

Transmitter-sensitive channel. Receptor complex that has both a receptor site for a chemical and a pore through which ions can flow.

In Review

The way in which a sensory stimulus initiates a nerve impulse is surprisingly similar for all our sensory systems. The membrane of a receptor cell contains a mechanism for transducing sensory energy into changes in ion channels that, in turn, allow ion flow to alter the voltage of the membrane to the point that voltage-sensitive channels open, initiating a nerve impulse. Muscle contraction also depends on ion channels. The axon terminal of a motor neuron releases the chemical transmitter acetylcholine onto the end plate of a muscle-cell membrane. Transmitter-sensitive channels on the end plate open in response, and the subsequent flow of ions depolarizes the muscle membrane to the threshold for its action potential. This depolarization, in turn, activates neighboring voltage-sensitive channels, producing an action potential on the muscle fiber, which brings about contraction of the muscle.

STUDYING THE BRAIN'S ELECTRICAL ACTIVITY

Our description of how a sensory stimulus initiates a flow of information in the nervous system that eventually results in some behavioral response should not mislead you into thinking that neurons are active only when something in the environment triggers them. The results of brain-wave recording studies show that electrical activity is always going on in the brain. The nervous system is electrically active during vigorous exercise, during rest, during daydreaming and sleep, and even under anesthesia. In each case, moreover, it is active in a different way.

The various electrical patterns associated with different kinds of behaviors are sufficiently distinctive to allow some fairly accurate assessments of what a person is doing at any given time. The ability to read the brain's electrical activity has not progressed to the point at which researchers can tell what someone is thinking, but it is getting close. Investigators can tell whether someone is awake or asleep and whether the brain is working normally.

As a result, measures of brain activity have become very important for studying brain function, for medical diagnosis, and for monitoring the effectiveness of therapies used to treat brain disorders. Three major techniques for studying the brain's electrical activity are single-cell recording, which tracks action potentials, and electroencephalographic recording and event-related potential recording, both of which record graded potentials. In part, these techniques are used to record the electrical activity at different parts of the neurons. The activity of those parts is influenced by specialized ion channels.

Rapid-acting, voltage-dependent sodium channels are located on the axon hillock and axon of most neurons, and so action potentials that depend on the presence of these channels are best recorded at these parts of a neuron. The electrical behavior of cell bodies and dendrites tends to be much more varied than that of axons, and electroencephalograms and event-related potentials are recorded from these parts of the neuron. Most dendrites do not have rapid voltage-dependent sodium channels and so do not produce action potentials, but some do have them and thus produce action potentials.

Single-Cell Recordings

While recording the activity of single neurons in the limbic region of the rat brain, James Ranck (see Taube & Bassett, 2003) noticed that the action potentials of a single, especially interesting neuron had a remarkable relation to the rat's behavior, summarized in **Figure 4-24**. Whenever the rat faced in a particular direction, the neuron vigorously fired; that is, it generated action potentials. When the rat turned somewhat away from this direction, the neuron fired more slowly. And, when the rat's position was opposite this neuron's favored direction, the neuron did not fire at all.

Ranck called this type of neuron a **head-direction cell.** In studying it further, he found that it displays still more remarkable behavior. If a rat is taken to another room, the neuron maintains its directional selectivity. Even when the rat is picked up and pointed in different directions, the neuron still behaves just as it does when the rat turns by itself.

Who would have predicted that a neuron in the brain would behave in such a way? This discovery serves as an excellent example of the power of single-cell recording techniques to provide information about how different regions of the brain work. We humans also may have head-direction cells to help us locate where we are in relation to some reference point, such as home. We can keep track of both our active and our passive movements to maintain a "sense of direction" no matter how many times we turn

Head-direction cell. A neuron in the hippocampus that discharges when an animal faces in a particular direction.

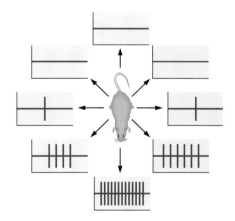

Figure 4-24

Single-Cell Recording Head-direction cells help the rat determine its location in space. Located in the limbic system, these cells fire when the rat faces in a given direction—in this case, the bottom of the page. The firing rate of a single cell decreases as the rat is rotated from the cell's preferred direction. Each of the eight surrounding traces of neural activity shows the cell's relative rate of firing when the rat faces in the direction indicated by the corresponding arrow.

or are turned. The hippocampal formation, in which head-direction cells are found, presumably regulates this sense of direction.

The technique of single-cell recording has come a long way in the decades since Hodgkin and Huxley's pioneering experiments on giant axons in squid. We can now record the activity of single neurons in freely moving mammals by permanently implanting microelectrodes into their brains. The massive amount of information obtained during cell recordings is stored and analyzed on a computer. Nevertheless, the basic recording procedure has not changed that much.

Small, insulated wire microelectrodes, with their uninsulated tips filed to a fine point, are preferred to glass microelectrodes. An oscilloscope is still used to visualize the behavior of the cell, but, in addition, the cell's activity is played into a loudspeaker so that cell firing can be heard as a beep or pop. The head-direction cell that Ranck recorded went "beep beep" extremely rapidly when the rat pointed in the preferred direction, and it was silent when the rat turned completely away.

Many hundreds of single-cell recording studies have been conducted to discover the types of stimuli that cause neurons to fire. Neurons fire in response to stimuli as simple as lights or tones and as complex as the face of a particular person or the sound of a particular voice. Single neurons have also been found to have a wide range of firing patterns. They may discharge in proportion to the intensity of a stimulus, fire rhythmically with it, or fire when the stimulus starts or stops. Remarkably, single cells also communicate by their silence. The cells in the pathway between the eye and the brain, for example, have a very high discharge rate when an animal is in the dark. Many of these cells decrease their rate of firing in response to light.

You will encounter other examples of the link between behavior and single-cell activity in later chapters. It is impossible to fully understand how a region of the brain works without understanding what the individual cells in that region are doing, and this knowledge is acquired through single-cell recording techniques. Such studies must usually be done with animals, because only in exceptional circumstances, such as brain surgery or as a treatment for disease, is it possible to implant electrodes into the brain of a person for the purposes of recording single-cell activity.

EEG Recordings

Recall your encounter with EEGs at this beginning of this chapter in connection with epilepsy. In the early 1930s, Hans Berger discovered that electrical activity in the brain could be recorded simply by placing electrodes onto the skull. Popularly known as "brain waves," recording this electrical activity produces an "electrical record from the head," or an electroencephalogram. EEGs reveal some remarkable features of the brain's electrical activity. The EEGs in **Figure 4-25** illustrate three:

1. The living brain's electrical activity is never silent even when a person is asleep or anesthetized.
2. An EEG recorded from the cortex has a large number of patterns, some of which are rhythmical.
3. The EEG changes as behavior changes.

When a person is aroused, excited, or even just alert, the EEG pattern has a low amplitude (the height of the brain waves) and a fast frequency (the number of brain waves per second), as shown in Figure 4-25A. This pattern is typical of an EEG taken from anywhere on the skull of an alert subject, not only human subjects but other animals, too. In contrast, when a person is calm and relaxing quietly, especially with

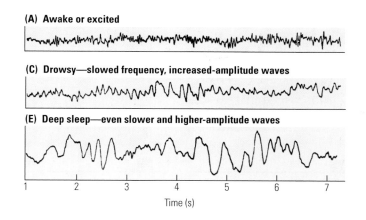

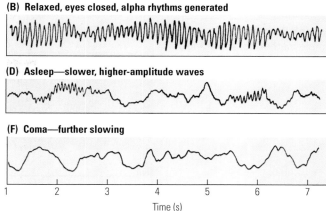

(A) Awake or excited

(B) Relaxed, eyes closed, alpha rhythms generated

(C) Drowsy—slowed frequency, increased-amplitude waves

(D) Asleep—slower, higher-amplitude waves

(E) Deep sleep—even slower and higher-amplitude waves

(F) Coma—further slowing

Time (s)

Time (s)

Figure 4-25

Characteristic EEG Recordings
Wave patterns reflect different states of consciousness in humans. Adapted from *Epilepsy and the Functional Anatomy of the Human Brain* (p. 12), by W. Penfield and H. H. Jasper, 1954, Boston: Little, Brown.

eyes closed, the rhythmical brain waves shown in Figure 4-25B often emerge. These **alpha rhythms** are extremely regular, with a frequency of approximately 11 cycles per second and amplitudes that wax and wane as the pattern is recorded. In humans, alpha rhythms are generated in the region of the visual cortex at the back of the brain. If a relaxed person is disturbed or opens his or her eyes, the alpha rhythms abruptly stop.

Not everyone displays alpha rhythms, and some people display them much better than others. You can buy a little voltmeter for monitoring your own alpha rhythms. A lead from one pole of the voltmeter is attached to the skull with a paste that conducts an electrical current, and the reference wire is pasted to the ear lobe. You can then relax with eyes closed, trying to make the voltmeter "beep." Each wave of the alpha rhythm, if sufficiently large, produces a beep. Many people can quickly learn to turn alpha waves on and off by using this procedure. A generation ago, beeping EEG voltmeters were promoted as a way of quickly learning how to reach a meditative state.

The EEG is a sensitive indicator of behaviors beyond simple arousal and relaxation. Figure 4-25C through E illustrates EEG changes as a person goes from drowsiness to sleep and finally into deep sleep. EEG rhythms become progressively less frequent and larger in amplitude. Still slower waves appear during anesthesia, after brain trauma, or when a person is in a coma (illustrated in Figure 4-25F). In brain death, the EEG becomes a flat line.

These distinctive brain-wave patterns make the EEG a reliable tool for monitoring sleep stages, estimating the depth of anesthesia, evaluating the severity of head injury, and searching for other brain abnormalities. The brief periods of unconsciousness and involuntary movements that characterize epileptic seizures, described at the beginning of this chapter, are associated with very abnormal spike-and-wave patterns in the EEG. The important point here is that EEG recording provides a useful tool both for research and for diagnosing brain abnormalities.

An EEG measures the summed graded potentials from many thousands of neurons. Neurons of the neocortex provide an especially good source of EEG waves because these cells are lined up in layers and have a propensity to produce graded potentials in a rhythmical fashion. EEG waves are usually recorded with a special kind of oscilloscope called a polygraph (meaning "many graphs"), illustrated in **Figure 4-26**.

Each channel on a polygraph is equivalent to one oscilloscope. Instead of measuring electrical activity with a beam of electrons, the polygraph electrodes are connected to magnets, which are in turn connected to pens. A motor pulls a long sheet of paper at a constant rate beneath the pens, allowing the patterns of electrical activity to be written on the paper. Because the graded potentials being measured have quite low

On the *Foundations* CD, find the EEG section in the module on research methods. Here you can review the model of an electroencephalograph described on page 115 (margin note).

Alpha rhythm. Rhythmical EEG wave with a frequency of 11 cycles per second.

Figure 4-26

Polygraph Recording EEG
A simple method for recording electrical activity of the human brain.

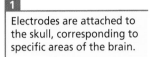
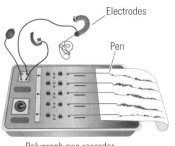
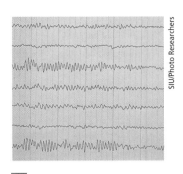

Electrodes

Pen

Polygraph pen recorder

1 Electrodes are attached to the skull, corresponding to specific areas of the brain.

2 Polygraph electrodes are connected to magnets, which are connected to pens...

3 ...that produce a paper record of electrical activity in the brain. This record indicates a relaxed person.

frequencies, the pens can keep up with them. To read this record, the experimenter simply observes its changing patterns.

Recently, computers have been programmed to read EEG waves. Many channels of EEG activity are fed into the computer, which then matches active areas with specific regions of the brain. The computer screen can display a representation of the brain, with changes in color representing brain activity.

Because the EEG is recorded as a subject is engaged in some behavior or problem-solving activity, the computer display can show an on-line display of brain activity in real time. The computer-assisted analysis is useful for finding how the brain processes sensory information, solves problems, and makes decisions. It is also useful in clinical diagnosis—for example, for charting the progress of abnormal electrical activity associated with epilepsy.

Miniaturized computer-based polygraphs about the size of an audiocassette recorder can be worn on a belt. They store the EEG record of a freely moving person for later replay on a chart polygraph or computer. One possible future use of miniaturized EEG recording devices is to enable brain-wave patterns to control the cursor on a computer. This technology would be very helpful to people who are paralyzed. If they could learn to control their EEGs sufficiently to command a cursor, they would be able to use the computer to communicate with others.

Event-Related Potentials

Brief changes in an EEG signal in response to a discrete sensory stimulus are called **event-related potentials** (ERPs), which are largely the graded potentials on dendrites that a sensory stimulus triggers. You might think that they should be easy to detect, but they are not. The problem is that ERPs are mixed in with so many other electrical signals in the brain that they are difficult to spot just by visually inspecting an EEG record. One way to detect ERPs is to produce the stimulus repeatedly and average the recorded responses. Averaging tends to cancel out any irregular and unrelated electrical activity, leaving in the EEG record only the potentials that the stimulus generated.

To clarify this procedure, imagine throwing a small stone into a lake of choppy water. Although the stone produces a splash, that splash is hard to see among all the ripples and waves. This splash made by a stone is analogous to an event-related potential caused by a sensory stimulus. Like the splash surrounded by choppy water, the ERP is hard to detect because of all the other electrical activity around it. A solution is to throw

Event-related potential (ERP). Brief change in slow-wave brain activity in response to a sensory stimulus.

a number of stones exactly the same size, always hitting the same spot in the water and producing the same splash over and over. If a computer is then used to calculate an average of the water's activity, random wave movements will tend to average one another out, and you will see the splashes produced by the stones as clearly as if a single stone had been thrown into a pool of calm water.

Figure 4-27 shows an ERP record (top) that results when a person hears a tone. Notice that the EEG record is very irregular when the tone is first presented. But, after averaging over 100 stimulus presentations, a distinctive wave pattern appears, as shown in the bottom panel of Figure 4-27. This ERP pattern consists of a number of negative (N) and positive (P) waves that occur over a period of a few hundred milliseconds after the stimulus.

The waves are numbered in relation to the time at which they occur. For instance, in Figure 4-27, N_1 is a negative wave occurring about 100 ms after the stimulus, whereas P_2 is a positive wave occurring about 200 ms after the stimulus. Not all these waves are unique to this particular stimulus. Some are common to any auditory stimulus that might be presented. Other waves, however, correspond to important differences in this specific tone. ERPs to spoken words even contain distinctive peaks and patterns that differentiate such similar words as "cat" and "rat."

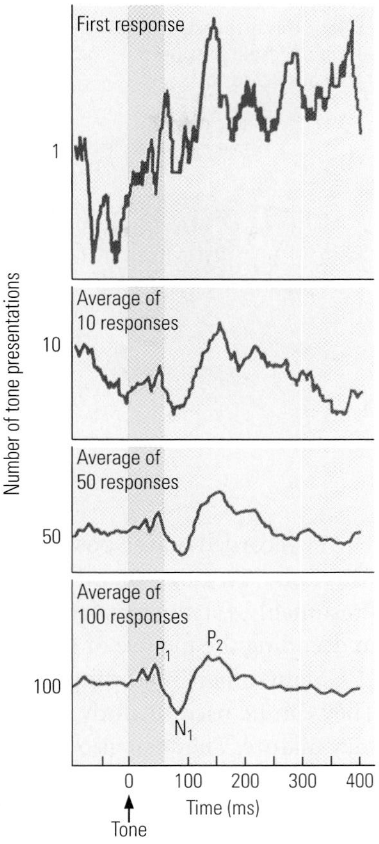

Among the many practical reasons for using ERPs to study the brain, one advantage is that the technique is noninvasive. Electrodes are placed on the surface of the skull, not into the brain. Therefore, ERPs can be used to study humans, including college students—the most frequently used subjects.

Another advantage is cost. In comparison with other techniques, such as brain scans, ERPs are inexpensive. Additionally, with modern technology, ERPs can be recorded from many brain areas simultaneously, by pasting an array of electrodes (sometimes more than 100) onto different parts of the skull. Because certain brain areas respond only to certain kinds of sensory stimuli (e.g., auditory areas respond to sounds and visual areas to sights), the relative responses at different locations can be used to map brain function.

Figure 4-28 shows a multiple-recording method that uses 64 electrodes simultaneously to detect ERPs at many cortical sites. Computerized averaging techniques reduce the masses of information obtained to simpler comparisons between electrode sites. For example, if the focus of interest is P_2, the computer can display a graph of the skull showing only the amplitude of P_2. A computer can also convert the averages at different sites into a color code, creating a graphic representation that shows the brain regions that are most responsive.

ERPs can be used not only to detect which areas of the brain are processing particular stimuli but also to study the order in which different regions play a role. This second use of ERPs is important because, as information travels through the brain, we want to know the route that it takes on its journey. In Figure 4-28, the subject is viewing a picture of a rat that appears repeatedly in the same place on a computer screen.

Figure 4-27

Detecting ERPs In the averaging process for an auditory ERP, a tone is presented at time 0, and EEG activity in response is recorded. After many successive presentations of the tone, the averaged EEG wave sequence develops a distinctive shape that becomes extremely clear after averaging 100 responses, as shown in the bottom panel. Positive (P_1 and P_2) and negative (N_1) waves that appear at different times after the stimulus presentation are used for analysis.

For more information on ERPs, visit the *Brain and Behavior* Web site and go to the Chapter 4 Web links.

Figure 4-28

Multiple recording method As the subject at the left—very likely a college student volunteer—looks at a rat displayed on a computer screen, researchers view a two-dimensional display of the electrode sites (*center*). Brain images of the ERPs (*right*) in the resting condition and 200 ms after stimulation in the viewing condition.

Electrodes attached to the scalp of research subject are connected to...

Electrodes in geodesic sensor net

...computer display of electrical activity, showing a large positive (P_2) wave at posterior right side of the head.

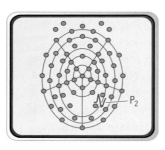

This electrical activity can be converted into a color representation showing the hot spot for the visual stimulus.

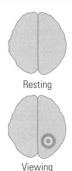

Resting

Viewing

The P_2 recorded on the posterior right side of the head is larger than P_2 occurring anywhere else, meaning that this region is a "hot spot" for processing the visual stimulus. Presumably, for this particular subject, the right posterior part of the brain is central in decoding the picture of the rat 200 ms after it is presented.

Many other interesting research areas can be investigated with the use of ERPs. They can be used to study how children learn and process information differently as they mature. They can also be used to examine how a person with a brain injury compensates for the impairment by using other, undamaged regions of the brain. ERPs can even help reveal which brain areas are most sensitive to the aging process and therefore contribute most to declines in behavioral functions among the elderly. All these areas can be addressed with this simple, inexpensive research tool.

In Review

Neuroscientists use three major techniques to study the brain's electrical activity. Single-cell recording monitors a single neuron. Many hundreds of single-cell studies have been conducted to determine what the firing patterns of particular neurons are and what stimuli trigger them. The electrical activity of the brain can be recorded simply by placing electrodes onto the skull and obtaining an electroencephalogram. EEGs show that the brain's electrical activity never ceases, even under anesthesia, that this activity can be rhythmical, and that different patterns of brain waves are often associated with different behaviors. Finally, researchers can study event-related potentials, the brief changes in an EEG in response to a discrete sensory stimulus, such as a tone or a flash of light. ERPs allow scientists to determine which areas of the brain are processing various kinds of stimuli and in which order those areas come into play.

SUMMARY

■ *What two kinds of research provided early clues that electrical activity is somehow implicated in the nervous system's flow of information?* The two kinds of research that provided these early clues were electrical-stimulation studies and electrical-recording studies. The results of early electrical-stimulation studies, which date as far back as the eighteenth century, showed that stimulating a nerve with electrical current sometimes induces the contraction of a muscle. The results of early electrical-recording studies, in which the brain's electrical current was measured with a voltmeter, showed that electrical activity is continually occurring within the nervous system.

▨ *What technical problems had to be overcome to measure the electrical activity of a single neuron?* To measure the electrical activity of a single neuron, researchers first had to find neurons with axons large enough to study. They also had to develop both a recording device sufficiently sensitive to detect very small electrical impulses and an electrode tiny enough to be placed on or into a neuron. These problems were overcome by studying the giant axons of squid, the invention of the oscilloscope, and the development of microelectrodes.

▨ *How is the electrical activity of neurons generated?* The electrical activity of neurons is generated by the flow of electrically charged ions across the cell membrane. These ions flow both down a concentration gradient (from an area of relatively high concentration to an area of lower concentration) and down a voltage gradient (from an area of relatively high voltage to an area of lower voltage). The distribution of ions is affected as well by the opening and closing of ion channels in neural membranes.

▨ *What are graded potentials and how do they change the resting potential of a neuron's membrane?* In an undisturbed neuron, the intracellular side of the membrane has an electrical charge of about −70 mV relative to the extracellular side. This charge, called the resting potential, is due to an unequal distribution of ions on the membrane's two sides. Large negatively charged protein anions are too big to leave the neuron, and the cell membrane actively pumps out positively charged sodium ions. In addition, unequal distributions of potassium cations and chloride anions contribute to the resting potential. Then, when the neuron is stimulated, ion channels in the membrane are affected, which in turn changes the distribution of ions, suddenly increasing or decreasing the transmembrane voltage by a small amount. A slight increase in the voltage is called hyperpolarization, whereas a slight decrease is called depolarization. Both conditions are known as graded potentials.

▨ *What is an action potential and how is it related to a nerve impulse?* An action potential is a brief but large change in the polarity of an axon membrane triggered when the transmembrane voltage drops to a threshold level of about −50 mV. The transmembrane voltage suddenly reverses (with the intracellular side becoming positive relative to the extracellular side) and then abruptly reverses again, after which the resting potential is gradually restored. These reversals are due to the behavior of voltage-sensitive channels—sodium and potassium channels that are sensitive to the membrane's voltage. When an action potential is triggered at the axon hillock, it can propagate along the axon as a nerve impulse. Nerve impulses travel more rapidly on myelinated axons because of saltatory conduction: the action potentials jump between the nodes separating the glial cells that form the axon's myelin sheath.

▨ *How do neurons integrate information?* The summated inputs to neurons from other cells can produce both excitatory postsynaptic potentials and inhibitory postsynaptic potentials. EPSPs and IPSPs are summed both temporally and spatially, which integrates the incoming information. If the resulting sum moves the voltage of the membrane at the axon hillock to the threshold level, an action potential will be produced on the axon.

▨ *How do nerve impulses travel into the nervous system and back out?* Sensory-receptor cells in the body contain mechanisms for transducing sensory energy into energy changes in ion channels. These changes, in turn, alter the transmembrane voltage to

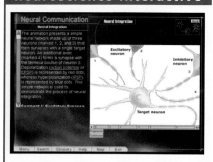

the point at which voltage-sensitive channels open, triggering an action potential and propagating a nerve impulse. After traveling through the nervous system and being processed by the brain, nerve impulses may produce the muscular contractions that enable behavioral responses. Ion channels again come into play at this end of the pathway because the chemical transmitter acetylcholine, released at the axon terminal of a motor neuron, activates channels on the end plate of a muscle-cell membrane. The subsequent flow of ions depolarizes the muscle-cell membrane to the threshold for its action potential. This depolarization, in turn, activates voltage-sensitive channels, producing an action potential on the muscle fiber.

■ *What techniques do researchers use to study the brain's electrical activity?* Single-cell recordings trace action potentials from single neurons in the brain. Electroencephalograms record graded potentials of brain cells, usually from electrodes on the surface of the scalp. Recording event-related potentials, also from the scalp, show the brief changes in an EEG signal in response to a particular sensory stimulus.

KEY TERMS

absolutely refractory, p. 126
acetylcholine (ACh), p. 138
action potential, p. 124
alpha rhythm, p. 141
concentration gradient,
  p. 119
current, p. 113
diffusion, p. 119
depolarization, p. 124
electrical potential, p. 113
electrical stimulation,
  p. 114
electricity, p. 113
electrode, p. 113
electroencephalogram
  (EEG), p. 115

end plate, p. 138
event-related potential
  (ERP), p. 142
excitatory postsynaptic
  potential (EPSP), p. 131
graded potential, p. 123
head-direction cell, p. 139
hyperpolarization, p. 124
inhibitory postsynaptic
  potential (IPSP), p. 131
negative pole, p. 113
nerve impulse, p. 128
node of Ranvier, p. 128
positive pole, p. 113
relatively refractory, p. 126
oscilloscope, p. 117

resting potential, p. 122
saltatory conduction,
  p. 130
spatial summation, p. 135
stretch-sensitive channel,
  p. 136
temporal summation,
  p. 133
threshold potential, p. 124
transmitter-sensitive
  channel, p. 138
volt, p. 113
voltage gradient, p. 119
voltage-sensitive channel,
  p. 124
voltmeter, p. 115

REVIEW QUESTIONS

1. Explain the contributions of the membrane, channels, and four types of ions to a cell's resting potential.

2. The transduction of sensory energy into neural activity at a sensory receptor, the nerve impulse, and the activation of a muscle can all be explained by a common principle. Explain that principle.

3. Name and describe how three techniques for monitoring brain activity measure the electrical activity of the brain.

FOR FURTHER THOUGHT

The brain is in a constant state of electrical excitation, which requires a substantial amount of energy to sustain. Why do you suppose this constant electrical activity is needed?

RECOMMENDED READING

Posner, M. I., & Raichle, M. E. (1994). *Images of mind*. New York: W. H. Freeman and Company. This book will introduce you to the field of imaging psychology. For the past 300 years, scientists have studied people with brain injuries as a source of insight into the relation between the brain and human behavior. This book describes how computerized electroencephalographic recordings (EEGs), scans produced by computerized axial tomography (CAT), scans produced by positron emission tomography (PET), magnetic resonance imaging (MRI), and functional MRI allow neuropsychologists to look at the structure and function of the living brain.

Valenstein, E. S. (1973). *Brain control*. New York: Wiley. When scientists discovered that they could implant stimulating electrodes into the brains of animals to elicit behavior and to generate what seemed to be pleasure or pain, it was not long before psychiatrists experimented with the same techniques in humans in an attempt to control human brain disease. A renowned scientist, Valenstein writes about the application of brain-control techniques to humans in an engaging and insightful manner, bringing his own scientific knowledge to bear on the procedures and the ethics of this field.

How Do Neurons Communicate and Adapt?

The Basis of Neural Communication in a Heartbeat

Discoveries about how neurons communicate actually stem from experiments designed to study what controls an animal's heart rate. If you are excited or exercising, your heartbeat quickens; if you are resting, it slows. Heartbeat rate changes to match energy expenditure—that is, to meet the body's nutrient and oxygen needs. Heartbeat undergoes a most dramatic change when you dive beneath water: it almost completely stops. This drastic slowing, called *diving bradycardia,* conserves the body's oxygen when you are not breathing. Bradycardia (*brady,* meaning "slow," and *cardia,* meaning "heart") is a useful survival strategy. This energy-conserving response under water is common to many animals. But what controls it?

To find out, in 1921 Otto Loewi conducted a now classic experiment. As shown in the Procedure section of **Experiment 5-1**, he first maintained a frog's heart in a salt bath and then electrically stimulated the vagus

Kevin Schafer

A puffin (genus *Fratercula,* Latin for "little brother"), beak laden with food, returns to her chick. Puffins fish by diving underwater, propelling themselves by flapping their short stubby wings, as if flying. During these dives, their hearts display the diving bradycardia response, just as our hearts do.

nerve, the cranial nerve that leads from the brain to the heart (see Figure 2-26). At the same time, Loewi channeled some of the fluid bath from the container with the stimulated heart through a tube to another container where a second heart was immersed but not electrically stimulated.

Loewi recorded the beating rates of both hearts. His findings are represented in the Results section of Experiment 5-1. The electrical stimulation decreased the beating rate of the first heart, but, more important, the second heartbeat also slowed. This finding suggested that the fluid transferred from the first to the second container carried the message "slow down."

But where did the message come from originally? Loewi reasoned that a chemical released from the stimulated vagus nerve must have diffused into the fluid in sufficient quantity to influence the second heart. The experiment therefore demonstrated that the vagus nerve contains a chemical that tells the heart to slow its rate of beating.

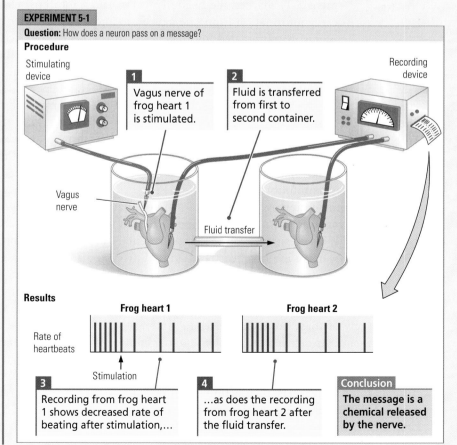

EXPERIMENT 5-1

Question: How does a neuron pass on a message?

Procedure

Stimulating device

Recording device

1 Vagus nerve of frog heart 1 is stimulated.

2 Fluid is transferred from first to second container.

Vagus nerve

Fluid transfer

Results

Frog heart 1   Frog heart 2

Rate of heartbeats

Stimulation

3 Recording from frog heart 1 shows decreased rate of beating after stimulation,...

4 ...as does the recording from frog heart 2 after the fluid transfer.

Conclusion

The message is a chemical released by the nerve.

Loewi subsequently identified the messenger chemical as acetylcholine (ACh), the chemical transmitter described in Chapter 4 that activates skeletal muscles. Yet here ACh acts to inhibit, or slow heartbeat down. And, yes, ACh is the chemical message that slows the heart in diving bradycardia. Apparently, the heart adjusts its rate of beating in response to at least two different messages: an excitatory message that says "speed up" and an inhibitory message that says "slow down."

In this chapter we describe how neurons communicate through excitatory and inhibitory signals: the chemicals that carry the neuron's signal and the receptors on which those chemicals act. In the final part of the chapter, we explore the neural bases of learning—that is, the ability of neural synapses to adapt as a result of the organism's experience.

A CHEMICAL MESSAGE

Otto Loewi
(1873–1961)

Loewi's successfully performed heartbeat experiment (see Experiment 5-1) marked the beginning of research into how chemicals carry information from one neuron to another. In further experiments, he stimulated another nerve to the heart, the accelerator nerve, and obtained a speeded-up heart rate. As before, the fluid that bathed the accelerated heart increased the rate of beating of a second heart that was not electrically stimulated. Loewi identified the chemical that carries the message to speed up heart rate in frogs as **epinephrine** (EP), also known as *adrenaline.*

Adrenaline (Latin) and epinephrine (Greek) are the same substance, produced by the adrenal glands located atop the kidneys. Adrenaline is the name more people know, in part because a drug company used it as a trade name, but EP is common parlance in the neuroscience community.

Further experimentation eventually demonstrated that the chemical that accelerates heart rate in mammals is **norepinephrine** (NE, also *noradrenaline*), a chemical closely related to EP. The results of Loewi's complementary experiments showed that ACh from the vagus nerve inhibits heartbeat, and NE from the accelerator nerve excites it.

Messenger chemicals released by a neuron onto a target to cause an excitatory or inhibitory effect are now referred to as **neurotransmitters.** Outside the central nervous system, many of these same chemicals, EP among them, circulate in the bloodstream as *hormones.* As detailed in Chapter 7, under control of the hypothalamus, the pituitary gland directs hormones to excite or inhibit targets such as the organs and glands in the autonomic nervous system. In part because hormones travel through the bloodstream to distant targets, their action is slower than that of CNS neurotransmitters prodded by the lightening-quick nerve impulse.

Later in the chapter, you will learn how groups of neurons project neurotransmitter systems throughout the brain to modulate, or temper, aspects of behavior. In the next section, we examine the synapse, the site where excitatory and inhibitory neurochemicals take effect. The three Focus on Disorders boxes in this chapter tell the fascinating

Acetylcholine (ACh)   Epinephrine (EP)

Epinephrine (EP, or adrenaline). Chemical messenger that acts as a hormone to mobilize the body for fight or flight during times of stress and as a neurotransmitter in the central nervous system.

Norepinephrine (NE, or noradrenaline). Neurotransmitter found in the brain and in the parasympathetic division of the autonomic nervous system.

Neurotransmitter. Chemical released by a neuron onto a target with an excitatory or inhibitory effect.

story of how damage to one such neurotransmitter system results in a specific neurological disorder, beginning with "Parkinson's Disease" on page 152.

Structure of Synapses

Loewi's discovery about the regulation of heart rate by chemical messengers was the first of two important findings that form the foundation for current understanding of how neurons communicate. The second had to wait nearly 30 years, for the invention of the electron microscope, which enabled scientists to see the structure of a synapse.

The electron microscope, shown on the right in **Figure 5-1**, uses some of the principles of both an oscilloscope and a light microscope, shown at the left. The electron microscope works by projecting a beam of electrons through a very thin slice of tissue. The varying structure of the tissue scatters the beam onto a reflective surface where it leaves an image, or shadow, of the tissue.

The resolution of an electron microscope is much higher than that of a light microscope because electron waves are smaller than light waves and so there is much less scatter when the beam strikes the tissue. If the tissue is stained with substances that reflect electrons, very fine structural details can be observed. Compare the images at the bottom of Figure 5-1.

The first good electron micrographs, made in the 1950s, revealed the structure of a synapse for the first time. In the center of the micrograph in **Figure 5-2A**, the upper part of the synapse is the axon end terminal; the lower part is the dendrite. Note the

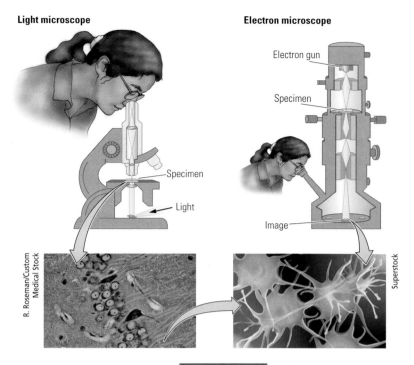

Light microscope

Specimen

Light

Electron microscope

Electron gun

Specimen

Image

R. Roseman/Custom Medical Stock

Superstock

Figure 5-1

Microscopic Advance Whereas a light microscope (*left*) can be used to see the general features of a cell, an electron microscope (*right*) can be used to examine the details of a cell's organelles.

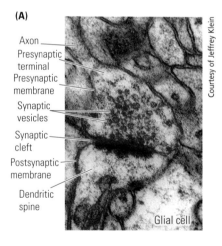

(A)

Axon
Presynaptic terminal
Presynaptic membrane
Synaptic vesicles
Synaptic cleft
Postsynaptic membrane
Dendritic spine

Glial cell

Courtesy of Jeffrey Klein

Figure 5-2

Chemical Synapse **(A)** Electron photomicrograph of a synapse. Surrounding the centrally located synapse are glial cells, axons, dendrites, and other synapses. **(B)** Characteristic parts of a synapse. Neurotransmitter, contained in vesicles, is released from storage granules and travels to the presynaptic membrane where it is expelled into the synaptic cleft through the process of exocytosis. The neurotransmitter then crosses the cleft and binds to receptor proteins on the postsynaptic membrane.

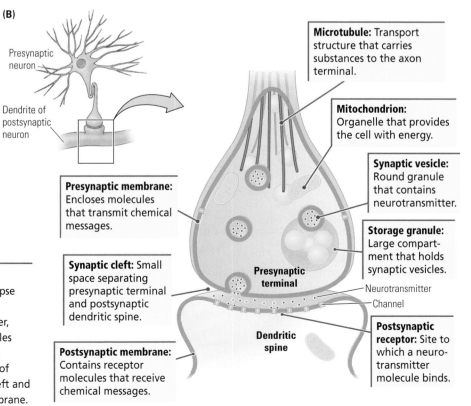

(B)

Presynaptic neuron

Dendrite of postsynaptic neuron

Microtubule: Transport structure that carries substances to the axon terminal.

Mitochondrion: Organelle that provides the cell with energy.

Synaptic vesicle: Round granule that contains neurotransmitter.

Storage granule: Large compartment that holds synaptic vesicles.

Presynaptic terminal

Neurotransmitter
Channel

Postsynaptic receptor: Site to which a neurotransmitter molecule binds.

Presynaptic membrane: Encloses molecules that transmit chemical messages.

Synaptic cleft: Small space separating presynaptic terminal and postsynaptic dendritic spine.

Postsynaptic membrane: Contains receptor molecules that receive chemical messages.

Dendritic spine

Parkinson's Disease

Case VI: The gentleman . . . is seventy-two years of age. He has led a life of temperance, and has never been exposed to any particular situation or circumstance which he can conceive likely to have occasioned, or disposed to this complaint: which he rather seems to regard as incidental on his advanced age, than as an object of medical attention. . . . About eleven or twelve, or perhaps more, years ago, he first perceived weakness in the left hand and arm, and soon after found the trembling to commence. In about three years afterwards the right arm became affected in a similar manner: and soon afterwards the convulsive motions affected the whole body and began to interrupt speech. In about three years from that time the legs became affected. Of late years the action of the bowels had been very much retarded. (James Parkinson, 1817/1989)

In his 1817 essay from which this case study is taken, James Parkinson reported similar symptoms in six patients, some of whom he observed only in the streets near his clinic. Shaking was usually the first symptom, and it typically began in a hand. Over a number of years, the shaking spread to include the arm and then other parts of the body. As the disease progressed, patients had a propensity to lean forward and walk on the forepart of their feet. They also tended to run forward to prevent themselves from falling.

In the later stages of the disease, patients had difficulty eating and swallowing. They drooled and their bowel movements slowed. Eventually, the patients lost all muscular control and were unable to sleep because of the disruptive tremors.

More than 50 years after James Parkinson first described this debilitating set of symptoms, French neurologist Jean Charcot named them Parkinson's disease in recognition of the accuracy of Parkinson's observations. Three major findings have helped researchers understand the neural basis of Parkinson's disease.

The first came in 1919 when Constantin Tréatikoff studied the brains of nine Parkinson patients on autopsy and found that the substantia nigra, an area of the midbrain described in Chapter 2, had degenerated. In the brain of one patient who had experienced symptoms of Parkinson's disease on one side of the body only, the substantia nigra had degenerated on the side opposite that of the symptoms. These observations clearly implicated the substantia nigra in the disorder.

The other two major findings about the neural basis of Parkinson's disease came almost half a century later when methods for analyzing the brain for neurotransmitters had been developed. One was the discovery that a single neurotransmitter, **dopamine,** is related to the disorder, and the other was that axons containing dopamine connect the substantia nigra to the basal ganglia.

The examination of the brains of six Parkinson patients during autopsies showed that the dopamine level in the basal ganglia was reduced to less than 10 percent of normal (Ehringer & Hornykiewicz, 1960). Confirming the role of dopamine in this disorder, Urban Ungerstedt found in 1971 that injecting a neurotoxin called 6-hydroxydopamine into rats selectively destroyed neurons containing dopamine and produced the symptoms of Parkinson's disease as well.

The results of these studies and many others, including anatomical ones, show that (1) the substantia nigra contains dopamine neurons and (2) the axons of these neurons project to the basal ganglia. The death of these neurons and the loss of the neurotransmitter from their terminals create the symptoms of Parkinson's disease.

Researchers do not yet know exactly why dopamine neurons start to die in the substantia nigra of patients who have the idiopathic form of Parkinson's disease. (*Idiopathic* refers to a condition related to the individual person, not to some external cause such as a neurotoxin.) Discovering why idiopathic Parkinsonism arises is an important area of ongoing research.

round granular substances in the terminal. They are the **synaptic vesicles** containing the neurotransmitter.

The dark patches on the dendrite consist mainly of protein receptor molecules that receive chemical messages. Dark patches on the axon terminal membrane are protein molecules that serve largely as channels and pumps to release the transmitter or to recapture it once it is released. The terminal and the dendrite are separated by a small space, the **synaptic cleft.**

You can also see on the micrograph that the synapse is sandwiched by many surrounding structures. These structures include glial cells, other axons and dendritic processes, and other synapses. The surrounding glia contribute to chemical neurotransmission in a number of ways—by supplying the building blocks for the synthesis of neurotransmitters or mopping up excess neurotransmitter molecules, for example.

The drawing in Figure 5-2B details the process of neurotransmission at a **chemical synapse,** the junction where messenger molecules are released from one neuron to excite the next neuron. In this example, the **presynaptic membrane** forms the axon terminal, the **postsynaptic membrane** forms the dendritic spine, and the space between the two is the synaptic cleft. Within the axon terminal are specialized structures, including mitochondria, the organelles that supply the cell's energy needs; **storage granules,** large compartments that hold several synaptic vesicles; and microtubules that transport substances, including the neurotransmitter, to the terminal.

Chemical synapses are the rule in mammalian nervous systems, but they are not the only kind of synapse. Rare in mammals but commonly found in other animals, the **electrical synapse** (also known as a gap junction) is a fused presynaptic and postsynaptic membrane that allows an action potential to pass directly from one neuron to the next. This fusion prevents the brief delay in information flow—about 5 ms per synapse—of chemical transmission. For example, the crayfish's electrical synapses activate its tail flick, a response that allows it to escape quickly from a predator.

Why, if chemical synapses transmit messages more slowly, do mammals depend on them almost exclusively? The benefits outweigh the drawback of slowed communication. Probably the greatest benefit is the flexibility that chemical synapses allow in controlling whether a message is passed from one neuron to the next.

Neurotransmission in Four Steps

The four-step process of chemically transmitting information across a synapse is illustrated in **Figure 5-3** and explained in this section. In brief, the neurotransmitter must be

1. synthesized and stored in the axon terminal;
2. transported to the presynaptic membrane and released in response to an action potential;
3. able to activate the receptors on the target cell membrane located on the postsynaptic membrane; and
4. inactivated or it will continue to work indefinitely.

NEUROTRANSMITTER SYNTHESIS AND STORAGE

Neurotransmitters are derived in two general ways. Some are synthesized in the axon terminal from building blocks derived from food. **Transporters,** protein molecules that pump substances across the cell membrane, absorb the required precursor chemicals from the blood supply. (Sometimes transporter proteins absorb the neurotransmitter ready-made.) Mitochondria in the axon terminal provide the energy needed both to synthesize precursor chemicals into the neurotransmitter and to wrap them in membranous vesicles.

Dopamine (DA). Amine neurotransmitter that plays a role in coordinating movement, in attention and learning, and in behaviors that are reinforcing.

Synaptic vesicle. Organelle consisting of a membrane structure that encloses a quantum of neurotransmitter.

Synaptic cleft. Gap that separates the presynaptic membrane from the postsynaptic membrane.

Chemical synapse. Junction where messenger molecules are released when stimulated by an action potential.

Presynaptic membrane. Membrane on the transmitter-output side of a synapse.

Postsynaptic membrane. Membrane on the transmitter-input side of a synapse.

Storage granule. Membranous compartment that holds several vesicles containing a neurotransmitter.

Electrical synapse. Fused presynaptic and postsynaptic membrane that allows an action potential to pass directly from one neuron to the next.

Transporter. Protein molecule that pumps substances across a membrane

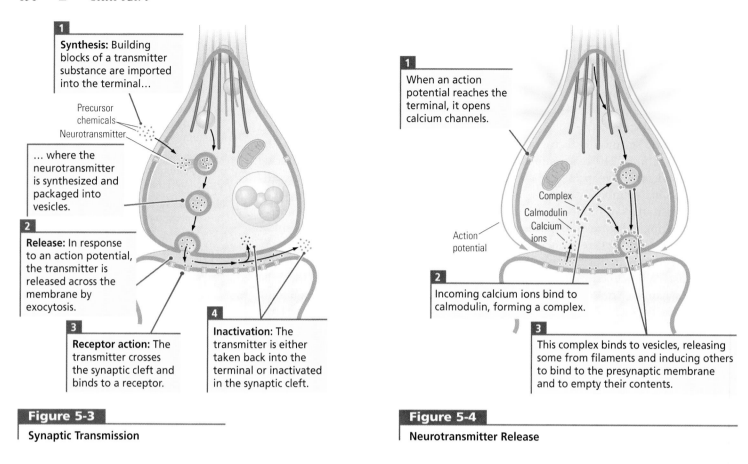

Figure 5-3

Synaptic Transmission

1

Synthesis: Building blocks of a transmitter substance are imported into the terminal...

Precursor chemicals

Neurotransmitter

... where the neurotransmitter is synthesized and packaged into vesicles.

2

Release: In response to an action potential, the transmitter is released across the membrane by exocytosis.

3

Receptor action: The transmitter crosses the synaptic cleft and binds to a receptor.

4

Inactivation: The transmitter is either taken back into the terminal or inactivated in the synaptic cleft.

Figure 5-4

Neurotransmitter Release

1

When an action potential reaches the terminal, it opens calcium channels.

Complex

Calmodulin

Calcium ions

Action potential

2

Incoming calcium ions bind to calmodulin, forming a complex.

3

This complex binds to vesicles, releasing some from filaments and inducing others to bind to the presynaptic membrane and to empty their contents.

Other neurotransmitters, as described in Chapter 3, are synthesized in the cell body according to instructions contained in the neuron's DNA, packaged in membranes on the Golgi bodies, and transported on microtubules to the axon terminal. Cell-derived neurotransmitters may also be manufactured within the presynaptic terminal from mRNA that is similarly transported to the terminal.

Regardless of their origin, neurotransmitters in the axon terminal can usually be found in three locations, depending on the type of neurotransmitter in the terminal. Some vesicles are warehoused in granules, as mentioned earlier. Other vesicles are attached to microfilaments in the terminal, and still others are attached to the presynaptic membrane, ready to release their content into the synaptic cleft. After the contents of a vesicle have been released from the presynaptic membrane, other vesicles move into place at that membrane location, ready for release when needed.

RELEASE OF THE NEUROTRANSMITTER

When an action potential is propagated on the presynaptic membrane, voltage changes on the membrane set the release process in motion. Calcium cations (Ca^{2+}) play an important role. The presynaptic membrane is rich in voltage-sensitive calcium channels, and the surrounding extracellular fluid is rich in Ca^{2+}. As illustrated in **Figure 5-4**, the action potential's arrival opens these calcium channels, allowing an influx of calcium ions into the axon terminal.

The incoming Ca^{2+} binds to the protein *calmodulin*, and the resulting complex takes part in two chemical reactions: one releases vesicles bound to the presynaptic membrane, and the other releases vesicles bound to filaments in the axon terminal. The vesicles released from the presynaptic membrane empty their contents into the synaptic cleft

○ You can use your *Foundations of Behavioral Neuroscience* CD to better visualize the structure and function of the axon terminal. Go to the section on synaptic transmission in the neural communication module and watch the animation. Note how the internal components work as a unit to release neurotransmitter substances across the synapse. (See the Preface for more information about this CD.)

through the process of exocytosis, described in Chapter 3. The vesicles that were formerly bound to the filaments then migrate to the presynaptic membrane to replace the vesicles that just emptied their contents.

ACTIVATION OF RECEPTOR SITES

After the neurotransmitter has been released from vesicles on the presynaptic membrane, it diffuses across the synaptic cleft and binds to specialized protein molecules embedded in the postsynaptic membrane. These **transmitter-activated receptors** have binding sites for the transmitter substance, or *ligand*. The postsynaptic cell may be affected in one of three ways, depending on the type of neurotransmitter and the kind of receptors on the postsynaptic membrane. The transmitter may

1. depolarize the postsynaptic membrane and so have an excitatory action on the postsynaptic neuron;
2. hyperpolarize the postsynaptic membrane and so have an inhibitory action on the postsynaptic neuron; or
3. initiate other chemical reactions that modulate either effect, inhibitory or excitatory, or that influence other functions of the receiving neuron.

In addition to interacting with the postsynaptic membrane's receptors, a neurotransmitter may interact with receptors on the presynaptic membrane. That is, it may influence the cell that just released it. Presynaptic receptors that a neurotransmitter may activate are called **autoreceptors** ("self-receptors") to indicate that they receive messages from their own axon terminals.

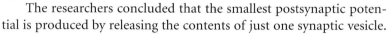

How much neurotransmitter is needed to send a message? In the 1950s, Bernard Katz and his colleagues provided an answer. Recording electrical activity from the postsynaptic membranes of muscles, they detected small, spontaneous depolarizations they called *miniature postsynaptic potentials*. The potentials varied in size, but each size appeared to be a multiple of the smallest potential.

The researchers concluded that the smallest postsynaptic potential is produced by releasing the contents of just one synaptic vesicle.

Bernard Katz (1911–2003)

They called this amount of neurotransmitter a **quantum**. To produce a postsynaptic potential that is large enough to initiate a postsynaptic action potential requires the simultaneous release of many quanta from the presynaptic cell.

The results of subsequent experiments show that the number of quanta released from the presynaptic membrane in response to a single action potential depends on two factors: (1) the amount of Ca^{2+} that enters the axon terminal in response to the action potential and (2) the number of vesicles docked at the membrane, waiting to be released. Both these factors are relevant to synaptic activity during learning, which we consider at the end of the chapter.

DEACTIVATION OF THE NEUROTRANSMITTER

Chemical transmission would not be a very effective messenger system if a neurotransmitter lingered within the synaptic cleft, continuing to occupy and stimulate receptors. If this happened, the postsynaptic cell could not respond to other messages sent by the presynaptic neuron. Therefore, after a neurotransmitter has done its work, it is quickly removed from receptor sites and from the synaptic cleft.

Deactivation is accomplished in at least four ways. One way is diffusion: some of the neurotransmitter simply diffuses away from the synaptic cleft and is no longer available to bind to receptors. The second way is degradation by enzymes in the synaptic

Transmitter-activated receptor. Protein embedded in the membrane of a cell that has a binding site for a specific neurotransmitter.

Autoreceptor. "Self-receptor" in a neural membrane that responds to the transmitter that the neuron releases.

Quantum (pl. quanta). Quantity, equivalent to the contents of a single synaptic vesicle, that produces a just observable change in postsynaptic electric potential.

Reuptake. Deactivation of a neurotransmitter when membrane transporter proteins bring the transmitter back into the presynaptic axon terminal for subsequent reuse.

cleft. In the third way, membrane transporter proteins may bring the transmitter back into the presynaptic axon terminal for subsequent reuse, a process called **reuptake.** The by-products of degradation by enzymes also may be taken back into the terminal to be used again in the cell. Fourth, some neurotransmitters are taken up by neighboring glial cells. Potentially, the glial cells can also store transmitter for reexport to the axon terminal.

Interestingly, an axon terminal has chemical mechanisms that enable it to respond to the frequency of its own use. If the terminal is very active, the amount of neurotransmitter made and stored there increases. If the terminal is not often used, however, enzymes located within the terminal may break down excess transmitter. The by-products of this breakdown are then reused or excreted from the neuron. Axon terminals may even send messages to the neuron's cell body requesting increased supplies of the neurotransmitter or the molecules with which to make it.

Varieties of Synapses

So far, we have considered a generic chemical synapse, with features that most synapses possess. In the nervous system, synapses vary widely, each relatively specialized in location, structure, function, and target. **Figure 5-5** illustrates this diversity on a single hypothetical neuron.

You have already encountered two kinds of synapses in Chapter 4. One is the *axo-dendritic synapse* detailed in Figure 5-2, in which the axon terminal of a neuron ends on a dendrite or dendritic spine of another neuron. The other synapse familiar to you

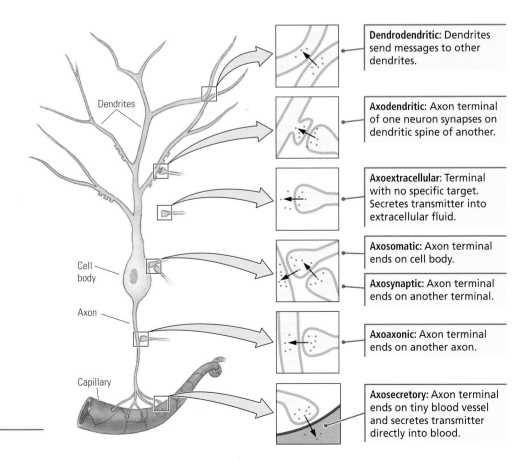

Dendrodendritic: Dendrites send messages to other dendrites.

Axodendritic: Axon terminal of one neuron synapses on dendritic spine of another.

Axoextracellular: Terminal with no specific target. Secretes transmitter into extracellular fluid.

Axosomatic: Axon terminal ends on cell body.

Axosynaptic: Axon terminal ends on another terminal.

Axoaxonic: Axon terminal ends on another axon.

Axosecretory: Axon terminal ends on tiny blood vessel and secretes transmitter directly into blood.

Dendrites

Cell body

Axon

Capillary

Figure 5-5

The Versatile Synapse

is the *axomuscular synapse,* in which an axon synapses with a muscle end plate to stimulate movement (see Figure 4-23B). In addition, Figure 5-5 illustrates the *axosomatic synapse,* an axon terminal ending on a cell body; the *axoaxonic synapse,* an axon terminal ending on another axon; and the *axosynaptic synapse,* an axon terminal ending on another presynaptic terminal—that is, at the synapse between some other axon and its target.

Axoextracellular synapses have no specific targets but instead secrete their transmitter chemicals into the extracellular fluid. In the *axosecretory synapse,* a terminal synapses with a tiny blood vessel called a capillary and secretes its transmitter directly into the blood. Finally, synapses are not limited to axon terminals. Dendrites also may send messages to other dendrites through *dendrodendritic synapses.*

This wide variety of connections makes the synapse a versatile chemical delivery system. Synapses can deliver transmitters to highly specific sites or to diffuse locales. Through connections to the dendrites, cell body, or axon of a neuron, transmitters can control the actions of that neuron in different ways.

Through axosynaptic connections, they can also provide exquisite control over another neuron's input to a cell. By excreting transmitters into extracellular fluid or into the blood, axoextracellular and axosecretory synapses can modulate the function of large areas of tissue or even of the entire body. Recall that many transmitters secreted by neurons act as hormones circulating in your blood, with widespread influences on your body.

Excitatory and Inhibitory Messages

A neurotransmitter can influence the function of a neuron in a remarkable number of ways. In its direct actions in influencing a neuron's electrical excitability, however, a neurotransmitter acts in only one of two ways: either to increase or to decrease the probability that the cell with which it comes in contact will produce an action potential. Thus, despite the wide variety of synapses, they all convey messages of only these two types: excitatory or inhibitory. For simplicity, *Type I synapses* are excitatory in their actions, whereas *Type II synapses* are inhibitory. Each type has a different appearance and is located on different parts of the neurons under its influence.

As shown in **Figure 5-6**, Type I synapses are typically located on the shafts or the spines of dendrites, whereas Type II synapses are typically located on a cell body. In addition, Type I synapses have round synaptic vesicles, whereas the vesicles of Type II synapses are flattened. The material on the presynaptic and postsynaptic membranes is denser in a Type I synapse than it is in a Type II, and the Type I cleft is wider. Finally, the active zone on a Type I synapse is larger than that on a Type II synapse.

The different locations of Type I and Type II synapses divide a neuron into two zones: an excitatory dendritic tree and an inhibitory cell body. You can think of excitatory and inhibitory messages as interacting from two different perspectives.

Viewed from an inhibitory perspective, you can picture excitation coming in over the dendrites and spreading to the axon hillock to trigger an action potential. If the message is to be stopped, it is best stopped by applying inhibition on the cell body, close to the axon hillock where the action potential originates. In this model of excitatory–inhibitory interaction, inhibition blocks excitation in a "cut 'em off at the pass" strategy.

Figure 5-6

Excitatory and Inhibitory Zones
Excitatory Type I synapses occupy the spines and dendritic shafts of the neuron, and inhibitory Type II synapses are found on the cell body.

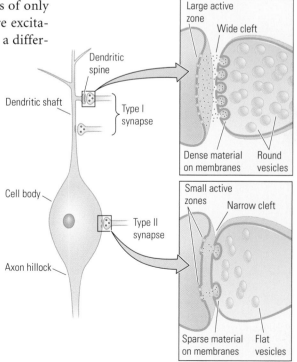

Dendritic spine

Dendritic shaft

Type I synapse

Large active zone

Wide cleft

Dense material on membranes

Round vesicles

Cell body

Type II synapse

Axon hillock

Small active zones

Narrow cleft

Sparse material on membranes

Flat vesicles

○ On the *Foundations* CD, find the area on synaptic transmission in the neural communication module. In the sections on excitatory and inhibitory synapses, watch the animations to learn more about excitatory and inhibitory messages.

Another way to conceptualize excitatory–inhibitory interaction is to picture excitation overcoming inhibition. If the cell body is normally in an inhibited state, the only way to generate an action potential at the axon hillock is to reduce the cell body's inhibition. In this "open the gates" strategy, the excitatory message is like a racehorse ready to run down the track, but first the inhibitory starting gate must be removed.

In Chapter 2, you met the nineteenth-century English neurologist John Hughlings-Jackson, who recognized both the role of inhibition and the release of behavior seen in human neurological disorders when inhibitory messages are blocked. Characteristic symptoms are "released" when a normal inhibitory influence is lost. The tremors of Parkinson's disease, a prime example, must be caused by rhythmically active neurons that are ordinarily under inhibition. An involuntary unwanted movement such as a tremor is called a *dyskinesia* (from the Greek *dys*, meaning "bad," and *kinesia*, meaning "movement").

Evolution of Complex Neurotransmission Systems

Considering all the biochemical steps required for getting a message across a synapse and the variety of synapses, you may well wonder why—and how—such a complex communication system ever evolved. This arrangement must make up for its complexity in the considerable behavioral flexibility that it affords the nervous system. Flexible behavior is a decided evolutionary advantage.

How did *chemical* transmitters come to dominate this complex communication system? If you think about the feeding behaviors of simple single-celled creatures, the origin of chemical secretions for communication is not that hard to imagine. The earliest unicellular creatures secreted juices onto bacteria to immobilize and prepare them for ingestion. These digestive juices were probably expelled from the cell body by exocytosis, in which a vacuole or vesicle attaches itself to the cell membrane and then opens into the extracellular fluid to discharge its contents. The prey thus immobilized is captured through the reverse process of endocytosis.

The mechanism of exocytosis for digestion parallels its use to release a neurotransmitter for communication. Quite possibly the digestive processes of single-celled animals were long ago adapted into processes of neural communication in more complex organisms.

In Review

In mammals, the principal form of communication between neurons is chemical. Chemical neurotransmission appears to be an adaptation of processes used by single-celled organisms to immobilize, ingest, and digest food. When an action potential is propagated on an axon terminal, a chemical transmitter is released from the presynaptic membrane into the synaptic cleft. There the transmitter diffuses across the cleft and binds to receptors on the postsynaptic membrane, after which the transmitter is deactivated. The nervous system has evolved a variety of synapses, between axon terminals and dendrites, cell bodies, muscles, other axons, and even other synapses. One variety of synapse releases chemical transmitters into extracellular fluid or into the bloodstream as hormones, and still another connects dendrites to other dendrites. Chemical synapses, though slower and more complex than electrical synapses, more than compensate by greatly increasing behavioral flexibility. Even though synapses vary in both structure and location, they all do one of only two things: excite their targets or inhibit them.

VARIETIES OF NEUROTRANSMITTERS

Subsequent to the discovery that excitatory and inhibitory chemicals control heart rate, many researchers of the 1920s thought that the brain must work under much the same dual-type control. They reasoned that there must be excitatory and inhibitory brain cells and that norepinephrine and acetylcholine were the transmitters through which these neurons worked. They could never have imagined what we know today: the human brain may employ approximately 100 neurotransmitters, which may be excitatory at one location and inhibitory in another, and more than one neurotransmitter may be active at a single synapse.

Although neuroscientists are now certain of only about 50 substances that act as neurotransmitters, discovery in this field continues. Few scientists are willing to put an upper limit on the eventual number of transmitters that will be found. In this section, you will learn how neurotransmitters are identified and how they fit within three broad categories based on their chemical structure. The functional aspects of neurotransmitters interrelate and are intricate, with no simple one-to-one relation between a single neurotransmitter and a single behavior.

○ Visit the *Brain and Behavior* Web site (**www.worthpublishers.com/kolb**) and go to the Chapter 5 Web links for information about current research on neurotransmitters.

Identifying Neurotransmitters

Among the many thousands of chemicals in the nervous system, which are neurotransmitters? **Figure 5-7** presents four identifying criteria:

1. The chemical must be synthesized in the neuron or otherwise be present in it.
2. When the neuron is active, the chemical must be released and produce a response in some target.
3. The same response must be obtained when the chemical is experimentally placed on the target.
4. A mechanism must exist for removing the chemical from its site of action after its work is done.

The criteria for identifying a neurotransmitter are fairly easy to apply when examining the somatic nervous system, especially at an accessible nerve–muscle junction with only one main neurotransmitter, acetylcholine. But identifying chemical transmitters in the central nervous system is not so easy. In the brain and spinal cord, thousands of synapses are packed around every neuron, preventing easy access to a single synapse and its activities. Consequently, for many of the substances thought to be CNS neurotransmitters, the four criteria have been met only to varying degrees. A suspect chemical that has not yet been shown to meet all the criteria is called a *putative* (supposed) *transmitter.*

Researchers trying to identify new CNS neurotransmitters use microelectrodes to stimulate and record from single neurons. A glass microelectrode is small enough to be placed on specific targets on a neuron. It can be filled with a chemical of interest and, when a current is passed through the electrode, the chemical can be ejected into or onto the neuron to mimic the release of a neurotransmitter onto the cell.

New staining techniques can identify specific chemicals inside the cell. Methods have also been developed for preserving nervous system tissue in a saline bath while experiments are performed to determine how the neurons in the tissue communicate. The use of "slices of tissue" simplifies the investigation by allowing the researcher to view a single neuron through a microscope while stimulating it or recording from it.

Figure 5-7

Criteria for Identifying Neurotransmitters

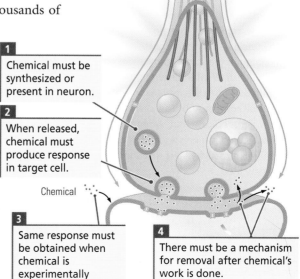

1 Chemical must be synthesized or present in neuron.

2 When released, chemical must produce response in target cell.

Chemical

3 Same response must be obtained when chemical is experimentally placed on target.

4 There must be a mechanism for removal after chemical's work is done.

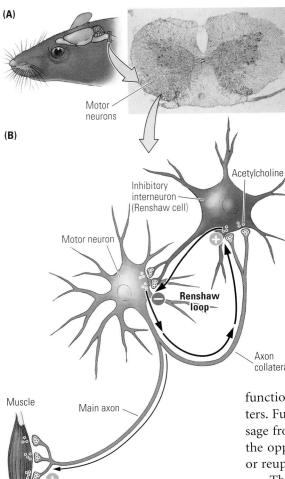

(A)

Motor
neurons

(B)

Acetylcholine

Inhibitory
interneuron
(Renshaw cell)

Motor neuron

Renshaw
loop

Axon
collateral

Muscle

Main axon

Acetylcholine

Figure 5-8

Renshaw Loop **(A)** Location of spinal-cord motor neurons that project to the muscles of the rat's forelimb. **(B)** Circular connections of a motor neuron in a Renshaw loop, with its main axon going to a muscle and its axon collateral remaining in the spinal cord to synapse with a Renshaw interneuron there. The terminals of both the main axon and the collateral contain ACh. The plus and minus signs indicate that, when the motor neuron is highly excited, it can modulate its activity level through the Renshaw loop.

Small-molecule transmitters. Class of quick-acting neurotransmitters synthesized in the axon terminal from products derived from the diet.

Acetylcholine was the first substance identified as a CNS neurotransmitter. A logical argument that predicted its presence even before experimental proof was gathered greatly facilitated the process. All the motor-neuron axons leaving the spinal cord use ACh as a transmitter. Each of these axons has an axon collateral within the spinal cord that synapses on a nearby CNS interneuron. The interneuron, in turn, synapses back on the motor neuron's cell body. This circular set of connections, called a *Renshaw loop* after the researcher who first described it, is shown in **Figure 5-8**.

Because the main axon to the muscle releases acetylcholine, investigators suspected that its axon collateral also might release ACh. It seemed unlikely that two terminals of the same axon would use different transmitters. Knowing what chemical to look for made it easier to find and obtain the required proof that ACh is in fact a neurotransmitter in both locations. The loop made by the axon collateral and the interneuron in the spinal cord forms a feedback circuit that enables the motor neuron to inhibit itself from becoming overexcited if it receives a great many excitatory inputs from other parts of the CNS. Follow the positive and negative signs in Figure 5-8B to see how the Renshaw loop works.

Today the term "neurotransmitter" is used more broadly than it was when researchers began to identify these chemicals. The term applies to substances that carry a message from one neuron to another by influencing the voltage on the postsynaptic membrane. And chemicals that have little effect on membrane voltage but rather share a message-carrying function, such as changing the structure of a synapse, also qualify as neurotransmitters. Furthermore, neurotransmitters can communicate not only by delivering a message from the presynaptic to the postsynaptic membrane but by sending messages in the opposite direction as well. These reverse-direction messages influence the release or reuptake of transmitters.

The definition of what a transmitter is and the criteria used to identify one have also become increasingly flexible because neurotransmitters are so diverse and active in such an array of ways. Different kinds of neurotransmitters typically coexist within the same synapse, complicating the question of what exactly each contributes in relaying or modulating a message. To find out, researchers have to apply various transmitter "cocktails" to the postsynaptic membrane. And some transmitters are gases that act so differently from a classic neurotransmitter such as acetylcholine that it is hard to compare the two.

Classifying Neurotransmitters

Some order can be imposed on the diversity of neurotransmitters by classifying them into three groups on the basis of their chemical composition: (1) small-molecule transmitters, (2) neuropeptides, and (3) transmitter gases.

SMALL-MOLECULE TRANSMITTERS

The first neurotransmitters identified are the quick-acting **small-molecule transmitters** such as acetylcholine. Typically, they are synthesized from dietary nutrients and packaged ready for use in axon terminals. When a small-molecule transmitter has been released from a terminal button, it can be quickly replaced at the presynaptic membrane.

Because small-molecule transmitters or their main components are derived from the food that we eat, their level and activity in the body can be influenced by diet. This fact is important in the design of drugs that act on the nervous system. Many neuroactive drugs are designed to reach the brain by the same route that small-molecule transmitters or their precursor chemicals do.

Table 5-1 lists some of the best-known and most extensively studied small-molecule transmitters. In addition to acetylcholine, four amines (related by a chemical structure that contains an amine, or NH, group) and four amino acids are included in this list. A few other substances are sometimes also classified as small-molecule transmitters. In the future, researchers are likely to find more.

Figure 5-9 illustrates how acetylcholine molecules are synthesized and broken down. As you know, ACh is present at the junction of neurons and muscles, including the heart, as well as in the CNS. The molecule is made up of two substances, *choline* and *acetate*.

Choline is among the breakdown products of fats, such as egg yolk, and acetate is a compound found in acidic foods, such as vinegar. As depicted in Figure 5-9, inside the cell, acetyl coenzyme A (acetyl CoA) carries acetate to the synthesis site, and the transmitter is synthesized as a second enzyme, choline acetyltransferase (ChAT), transfers the acetate to choline to form ACh. After ACh has been released into the synaptic cleft and diffuses to receptor sites on the postsynaptic membrane, a third enzyme, acetylcholinesterase (AChE), reverses the process by detaching acetate from choline. These breakdown products can then be taken back into the presynaptic terminal for reuse.

Some of the transmitters grouped together in Table 5-1 also share common biochemical pathways to synthesis and so are related. You are familiar with the amines dopamine (DA), norepinephrine (NE), and epinephrine (EP). To review, DA loss has a role in Parkinson's disease, EP is the excitatory transmitter at the heart of the frog, and NE is the excitatory transmitter at the heart of mammals.

Figure 5-10 charts the biochemical sequence that synthesizes these amines in succession. The precursor chemical is tyrosine, an amino acid abundant in food. (Hard

Table 5-1	Small-Molecule Neurotransmitters
Acetylcholine (ACh)	
Amines	
Dopamine (DA)	
Norepinephrine (NE)	
Epinephrine (EP)	
Serotonin (5-HT)	
Amino acids	
Glutamate (Glu)	
Gamma-aminobutyric acid (GABA)	
Glycine (Gly)	
Histamine	

Figure 5-9

Chemistry of Acetylcholine
Two enzymes combine the dietary precursors of ACh within the cell and a third breaks them down in the synapse for reuptake.

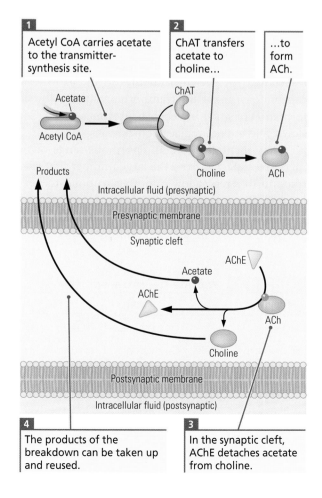

1 Acetyl CoA carries acetate to the transmitter-synthesis site.

2 ChAT transfers acetate to choline...

...to form ACh.

4 The products of the breakdown can be taken up and reused.

3 In the synaptic cleft, AChE detaches acetate from choline.

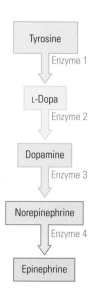

Figure 5-10

Sequential Synthesis of Three Amines
A different enzyme is responsible for each successive molecular modification in this biochemical sequence

Rate-limiting factor. Any enzyme that is in limited supply, thus restricting the pace at which a chemical can be synthesized.

Glutamate. Amino acid neurotransmitter that excites neurons.

Gamma-aminobutyric acid (GABA). Amino acid neurotransmitter that inhibits neurons.

Neuropeptide. A multifunctional chain of amino acids that acts as a neurotransmitter; synthesized from mRNA on instructions from the cell's DNA.

cheese and bananas are good sources.) The enzyme tyrosine hydroxylase (enzyme 1 in Figure 5-10) changes tyrosine into L-dopa, which is sequentially converted by other enzymes into dopamine, norepinephrine, and, finally, epinephrine.

An interesting fact about this biochemical sequence is that the supply of the enzyme tyrosine hydroxylase is limited. Consequently, so is the rate at which dopamine, norepinephrine, and epinephrine can be produced, regardless of how much tyrosine is present or ingested. This **rate-limiting factor** can be bypassed by orally ingesting L-dopa, which is why L-dopa is a medication used in the treatment of Parkinson's disease, as described in "Awakening with L-Dopa."

Two amino acid transmitters, **glutamate** and **gamma-aminobutyric acid** (GABA), also are closely related. GABA is formed by a simple modification of the glutamate molecule, as shown in **Figure 5-11**. These two transmitters are the workhorses of the brain because so many synapses use them.

In the forebrain and cerebellum, glutamate is the main excitatory transmitter and GABA is the main inhibitory transmitter. (The amino acid glycine is a much more common inhibitory transmitter in the brainstem and spinal cord.) Type I excitatory synapses, described earlier, thus have glutamate as a neurotransmitter and Type II inhibitory synapses have GABA as a neurotransmitter. Interestingly, glutamate is widely distributed in CNS neurons, but it becomes a neurotransmitter only if it is appropriately packaged in vesicles in the axon terminal.

PEPTIDE TRANSMITTERS

More than 50 amino acid chains of various lengths form the families of the peptide transmitters listed in **Table 5-2**. As you learned in Chapter 3, these molecular chains are amino acids connected by peptide bonds, which accounts for the name. **Neuropeptides** are made through the translation of mRNA from instructions contained in the neuron's DNA.

In some neurons, peptide transmitters are made in the axon terminal, but most are assembled on the neuron's ribosomes, packaged in a membrane by Golgi bodies, and transported by the microtubules to the axon terminals. The entire process of neuropeptide synthesis and transport is relatively slow compared with the nearly readymade formation of small-molecule neurotransmitters. Consequently, peptide transmitters act slowly and are not replaced quickly.

Neuropeptides have an enormous range of functions in the nervous system, as might be expected from the large number that exist there. They act as hormones that respond to stress, allow a mother to bond to her infant, regulate eating and drinking and pleasure and pain, and they probably contribute to learning. Opium and related synthetic chemicals such as morphine, long known to produce both euphoria and pain reduction, appear to mimic the actions of three peptides: met-enkephalin,

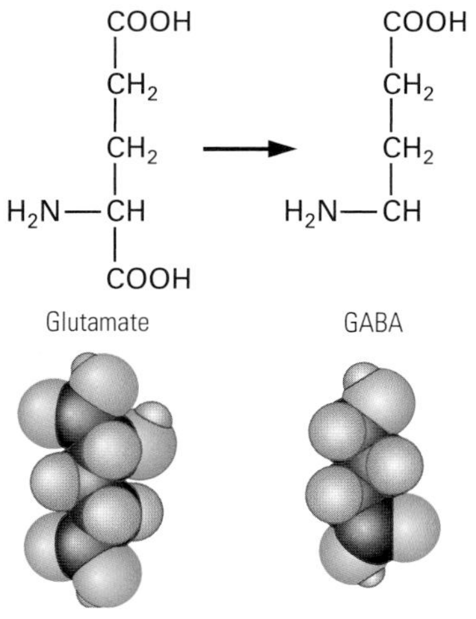

Figure 5-11

Amino Acid Transmitters *(Top)* Removal of a carboxyl (COOH) group from the bottom of the glutamate molecule produces GABA. *(Bottom)* Their different shapes thus allow these amino acid transmitters to bind to different receptors.

Table 5-2	Peptide Neurotransmitters
Family	**Example**
Opioids	Enkephaline, dynorphin
Neurohypophyseals	Vasopressin, oxytocin
Secretins	Gastric inhibitory peptide, growth-hormone-releasing peptide
Insulins	Insulin, insulin growth factors
Gastrins	Gastrin, cholecystokinin
Somatostatins	Pancreatic polypeptides

Awakening with L-Dopa

He was started on L-dopa in March 1969. The dose was slowly raised to 4.0 mg a day over a period of three weeks without *apparently* producing any effect. I first discovered that Mr. E. was responding to L-dopa by accident, chancing to go past his room at an unaccustomed time and hearing regular footsteps inside the room. I went in and found Mr. E., who had been chair bound since 1966, walking up and down his room, swinging his arms with considerable vigor, and showing erectness of posture and a brightness of expression completely new to him. When I asked him about the effect, he said with some embarrassment: "Yes! I felt the L-dopa beginning to work three days ago—it was like a wave of energy and strength sweeping through me. I found I could stand and walk by myself, and that I could do everything I needed for myself—but I was afraid that you would see how well I was and discharge me from the hospital." (Sacks, 1976)

In this case history, neurologist Oliver Sacks describes administering L-dopa to a patient who acquired postencephalitic Parkinsonism as an aftereffect of severe influenza in the 1920s. The relation between the influenza and symptoms of Parkinson's disease suggests that the flu virus entered the brain and selectively attacked dopamine neurons in the substantia nigra. L-Dopa, by increasing the amount of DA in remaining synapses, relieved the patient's symptoms.

Two separate groups of investigators had quite independently given L-dopa to Parkinson patients beginning in

The movie *Awakenings* recounts the L-dopa trials conducted by Oliver Sacks and described in his book of the same title.

1961 (Birkmayer & Hornykiewicz, 1961; Barbeau, Murphy, & Sourkes, 1961). Both research teams knew that the chemical is catalyzed into dopamine at DA synapses (see Figure 5-10), but they did not know if it could relieve the symptoms of Parkinsonism. The L-dopa turned out to dramatically reduce the muscular rigidity that the patients suffered, although it did not relieve their tremors.

L-Dopa has since become a standard treatment for Parkinson's disease. Its effects have been improved by administering drugs that prevent L-dopa from being broken down before it gets to dopamine neurons in the brain. L-Dopa is not a cure. Parkinson's disease still progresses during treatment and, as more and more dopamine synapses are lost, the treatment becomes less and less effective and eventually begins to produce dyskinesia. When these side effects eventually become severe, the L-dopa treatment must be discontinued.

---

leu-enkephalin, and beta-endorphin. (The term *enkephalin* derives from the phrase "in the cephalon," meaning "in the brain or head," whereas the term *endorphin* is a shortened form of "endogenous morphine.")

A part of the amino acid chain in each of these three peptide transmitters is structurally similar to the others, as illustrated for two of these peptides in **Figure 5-12**. Presumably, opium mimics this part of the chain. The discovery of naturally occurring opium-like peptides suggested that one or more of them might take part in the management of pain. Opioid

Met-enkephalin

Leu-enkephalin

Tyr Gly Gly Phe Leu

Figure 5-12

Opioid Peptides Parts of the amino acid chains of some neuropeptides are similar in structure and are similar to drugs such as opium and morphine, which mimic their functions.

Nitric oxide (NO). Acts as a chemical neurotransmitter gas—for example, to dilate blood vessels, aid digestion, and activate cellular metabolism.

Carbon monoxide (CO). Acts as a neurotransmitter gas in the activation of cellular metabolism.

Ionotropic receptor. Embedded membrane protein with two parts: a binding site for a neurotransmitter and a pore that regulates ion flow to directly and rapidly change membrane voltage.

Metabotropic receptor. Embedded membrane protein, with a binding site for a neurotransmitter but no pore, linked to a G protein that can affect other receptors or act with second messengers to affect other cellular processes.

G proteins. Family of guanyl nucleotide–binding proteins coupled to metabotropic receptors that, when activated, bind to other proteins.

Figure 5-13

Ionotropic Receptor When activated, these embedded proteins bring about direct, rapid changes in membrane voltage.

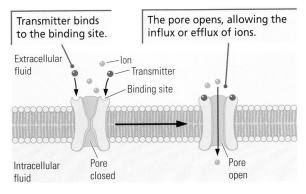

Transmitter binds to the binding site.

The pore opens, allowing the influx or efflux of ions.

Extracellular fluid — Ion — Transmitter — Binding site

Intracellular fluid — Pore closed — Pore open

On your *Foundations* CD, find the section on the membrane potential in the module on neural communication. Review ionic flow across the cell membrane. Imagine this flow being associated with ionotropic-receptor stimulation to induce action potentials and neural signals.

---

peptides, however, appear to be in a number of locations and perform a variety of functions in the brain, including the inducement of nausea. Therefore opium-like drugs are still preferred for pain management.

Unlike small-molecule transmitters, neuropeptides do not bind to ion channels, and so they have no direct effects on the voltage of the postsynaptic membrane. Instead, peptide transmitters activate synaptic receptors that indirectly influence cell structure and function. Because peptides are amino acid chains that are degraded by digestive processes, they generally cannot be taken orally as drugs, as the small-molecule transmitters can.

TRANSMITTER GASES

The gases **nitric oxide** (NO) and **carbon monoxide** (CO) are the most unusual neurotransmitters yet identified. As soluble gases, they are neither stored in synaptic vesicles nor released from them; instead, they are synthesized in the cell as needed. After synthesis, each gas diffuses away, easily crossing the cell membrane and immediately becoming active.

Nitric oxide serves as a chemical messenger in many parts of the body. It controls the muscles in intestinal walls, and it dilates blood vessels in brain regions that are in active use, allowing these regions to receive more blood. Because it also dilates blood vessels in the sexual organs, NO is active in producing penile erections. Viagra, a drug used to treat erectile dysfunction acts by enhancing the action of NO. Both NO and CO activate metabolic processes in cells, including those modulating the production of other neurotransmitters.

Receptors for Direct and Indirect Effects

When a neurotransmitter is released from a synapse, it crosses the synaptic cleft and binds to a receptor. What happens next depends on the receptor type. Each of the two general classes of receptor proteins has a different effect. One directly changes the electrical potential of the postsynaptic membrane, whereas the other induces cellular change indirectly.

Ionotropic receptors allow the movement of ions across a membrane (the suffix *tropic* means "to move toward"). As **Figure 5-13** illustrates, an ionotropic receptor has two parts: (1) a binding site for a neurotransmitter and (2) a pore or channel. When the neurotransmitter attaches to the binding site, the receptor changes shape, either opening the pore and allowing ions to flow through it or closing the pore and blocking the flow of ions. Because the binding of the transmitter to the receptor is quickly followed by the opening or closing of the receptor pore that affects the flow of ions, ionotropic receptors bring about very rapid changes in membrane voltage. Ionotropic receptors are usually excitatory in that they trigger an action potential.

Structurally, ionotropic receptors are similar to the voltage-sensitive channels discussed in Chapter 4. Their membrane-spanning subunits form the "petals" of the pore that lies in the center. Within the pore is a shape-changing segment that allows the pore to open or close, regulating the flow of ions through it.

In contrast, a **metabotropic receptor** has a binding site for a neurotransmitter but lacks its own pore through which ions can flow. Through a series of steps, activated metabotropic receptors indirectly produce changes in nearby ion channels or in the cell's metabolic activity (i.e., in activity that requires an expenditure of energy, which is what the term *metabolic* means).

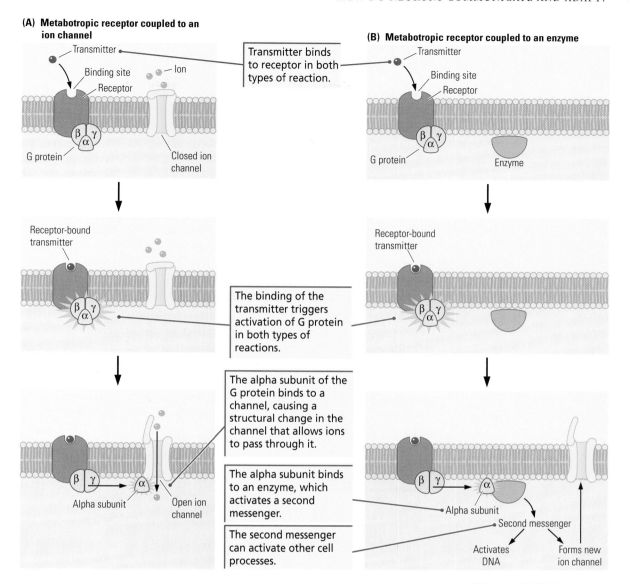

(A) Metabotropic receptor coupled to an ion channel

Transmitter
Binding site
Ion
Receptor
G protein
β γ α
Closed ion channel

Transmitter binds to receptor in both types of reaction.

(B) Metabotropic receptor coupled to an enzyme

Transmitter
Binding site
Receptor
G protein
β γ α
Enzyme

Receptor-bound transmitter

β γ α

The binding of the transmitter triggers activation of G protein in both types of reactions.

Receptor-bound transmitter

β γ α

The alpha subunit of the G protein binds to a channel, causing a structural change in the channel that allows ions to pass through it.

β γ α
Alpha subunit
Open ion channel

The alpha subunit binds to an enzyme, which activates a second messenger.

The second messenger can activate other cell processes.

β γ α
Alpha subunit
Second messenger
Activates DNA
Forms new ion channel

Figure 5-14

Metabotropic Receptors When activated, these embedded membrane proteins trigger associated G proteins, thereby exerting indirect effects **(A)** on nearby ion channels or **(B)** in the cell's metabolic activity.

Figure 5-14A shows the first of these two indirect effects. The metabotropic receptor consists of a single protein that spans the cell membrane, its binding site facing the synaptic cleft. Receptor proteins are each coupled to one of a family of guanyl nucleotide-binding proteins, **G proteins** for short, shown on the inner side of the cell membrane in Figure 5-14A.

A G protein consists of three subunits: alpha, beta, and gamma. The alpha subunit detaches when a neurotransmitter binds to the G protein's associated metabotropic receptor. The detached alpha subunit can then bind to other proteins within the cell membrane or within the cytoplasm of the cell.

If the alpha subunit binds to a nearby ion channel in the membrane as shown at the bottom of Figure 5-14A, the structure of the channel changes, modifying the flow of ions through it. If the channel is open, it may be closed by the alpha subunit or, if closed, it may opened. Changes in the channel and the flow of ions across the membrane influence the membrane's electrical potential.

The binding of a neurotransmitter to a metabotropic receptor can also trigger more-complicated cellular reactions, summarized in Figure 5-14B. All of these reactions begin when the detached alpha subunit binds to an enzyme. The enzyme in turn

Second messenger. Activated by a neurotransmitter (the first messenger), a chemical that carries a message to initiate a biochemical process.

activates a **second messenger** (the neurotransmitter is the first messenger) that carries instructions to other structures inside the cell. As illustrated in at the bottom of Figure 5-14B, the second messenger can

◼ bind to a membrane channel, causing the channel to change its structure and thus alter ion flow through the membrane;
◼ initiate a reaction that causes protein molecules within the cell to become incorporated into the cell membrane, for example, resulting in the formation of new ion channels; or
◼ instruct the cell's DNA to initiate the production of a new protein.

In addition, metabotropic receptors allow for the possibility that a single neurotransmitter's binding to a receptor can activate an escalating sequence of events called an *amplification cascade*. The cascade effect causes many downstream proteins (second messengers or channels or both) to be activated or deactivated. Ionotropic receptors do not have such a widespread "amplifying" effect.

No one neurotransmitter is associated with a single receptor type or a single influence on the postsynaptic cell. Typically, a transmitter may bind either to an ionotropic receptor and have an excitatory effect on the target cell or to a metabotropic receptor and have an inhibitory effect. Recall that acetylcholine has an excitatory effect on skeletal muscles, where it activates an ionotropic receptor, but an inhibitory effect on the heart, where it activates a metabotropic receptor. In addition, each transmitter may bind with several different kinds of ionotropic or metabotropic receptors. Elsewhere in the nervous system, for example, acetylcholine may activate a wide variety of either receptor type.

In Review

Neurotransmitters are identified with the use of four experimental criteria: synthesis, release, receptor action, and inactivation. The broad classes of chemically related neurotransmitters are small-molecule transmitters, peptide transmitters, and transmitter gases. All the classes are associated with both ionotropic and metabotropic receptors. An ionotropic receptor contains a pore or channel that can be opened or closed to regulate the flow of ions through it, which, in turn, directly brings about voltage changes on the cell membrane. Metabotropic receptors activate second messengers to indirectly produce changes in the function and structure of the cell. The approximately 100 likely neurotransmitters active in the nervous system are each associated with many different ionotropic and metabotropic receptors.

NEUROTRANSMITTER SYSTEMS AND BEHAVIOR

When researchers began to study neurotransmission at the synapse a half century ago, you'll recall, they reasoned that any given neuron would contain only one transmitter at all its axon terminals. New methods of staining neurochemicals, however, reveal that this hypothesis, called Dale's law after its originator, is an oversimplification.

A single neuron may use one transmitter at one synapse and a different transmitter at another synapse, as David Sulzer (1998) and his coworkers have shown. Moreover, different transmitters may coexist in the same terminal or synapse. Neuropeptides have been found to coexist in terminals with small-molecule transmitters, and more than one small-molecule transmitter may be found in a single synapse. In some cases, more than one transmitter may even be packaged within a single vesicle.

All such findings make for a bewildering number of combinations of neurotransmitters and receptors for them. They caution as well against the assumption of a simple cause–effect relation between a neurotransmitter and a behavior. What are the functions of so many combinations? Neuroscientists do not have a complete answer. Fortunately, neurotransmission can be simplified by concentrating on the dominant transmitter located within any given axon terminal. The neuron and its dominant transmitter can then be related to a function or behavior.

We now consider some of the links between neurotransmitters and behavior. We begin by exploring the two parts of the peripheral nervous system: somatic and autonomic. Then we investigate neurotransmission in the central nervous system.

Neurotransmission in the Somatic Nervous System

Motor neurons in the brain and spinal cord send their axons to the body's skeletal muscles, including the muscles of the eyes and face, trunk, limbs, fingers, and toes. Without these somatic nervous system neurons, movement would not be possible. Motor neurons are also called **cholinergic neurons** because acetylcholine is their main neurotransmitter. (The term *cholinergic* applies to any neuron that uses ACh as its main transmitter.) At a skeletal muscle, cholinergic neurons are excitatory and produce muscular contractions.

Just as a single main neurotransmitter serves the SNS, so does a single main receptor, an ionotropic, transmitter-activated channel called a **nicotinic ACh receptor** (nAChr). When ACh binds to this receptor, the receptor's pore opens to permit ion flow, thus depolarizing the muscle fiber. The pore of a nicotinic receptor is large and permits the simultaneous efflux of potassium ions and influx of sodium ions. The molecular structure of nicotine, a chemical found in tobacco, activates the nAChr in the same way that ACh does, which is how this receptor got its name. The molecular structure of nicotine is sufficiently similar to ACh that nicotine acts as a ligand, fitting into acetylcholine receptor binding sites.

Although acetylcholine is the primary neurotransmitter at skeletal muscles, other neurotransmitters also are found in these cholinergic axon terminals and are released onto the muscle along with ACh. One of these neurotransmitters is a neuropeptide called *calcitonin-gene-related peptide* (CGRP) that acts through second messengers to increase the force with which a muscle contracts.

Neurotransmission in the Autonomic Nervous System

The complementary divisions of the ANS, sympathetic and parasympathetic, regulate the body's internal environment (see Figure 2-29). Recall from Chapter 2 that the sympathetic division rouses the body for action, producing the *fight-or-flight response*. Heart rate is turned up, digestive functions are turned down. The parasympathetic division calms the body down, producing an essentially opposite *rest-and-digest response*. Digestive functions are turned up, heart rate is turned down, and the body is made ready to relax.

Figure 5-15 shows the neurochemical organization of the ANS. Both ANS divisions are controlled by acetylcholine neurons that emanate from the CNS at two levels

Cholinergic neuron. Neuron that uses acetylcholine as its main neurotransmitter.

Nicotinic ACh receptor (nAChr). Ionotropic receptor at which acetylcholine and the drug nicotine act as ligands to activate the flow of ions through the receptor pore.

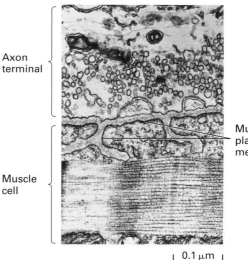

Axon terminal

Muscle plasma membrane

Muscle cell

0.1 μm

Nicotinic Acetylcholine Receptor From J. E. Heuser and T. Reese, 1977, in E. R. Kandel, ed., *The Nervous System*, vol. 1, *Handbook of Physiology*, Oxford University Press, p. 266.

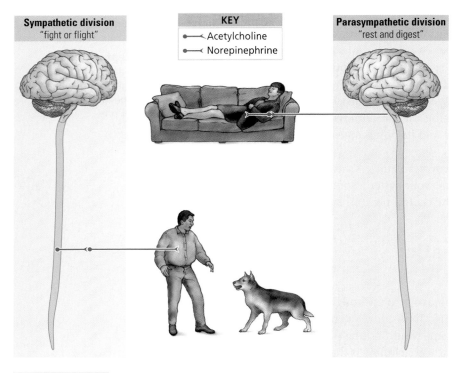

Sympathetic division
"fight or flight"

KEY
● ─< Acetylcholine
● ─< Norepinephrine

Parasympathetic division
"rest and digest"

Figure 5-15

Neurochemistry of the ANS All the neurons leaving the spinal cord have acetylcholine as a neurotransmitter. (*Left*) In the sympathetic division, these ACh neurons activate NE neurons, which stimulate organs required for fight or flight and suppress the activity of organs used to rest and digest. (*Right*) In the parasympathetic division, ACh neurons from the spinal cord activate acetylcholine neurons in the ANS, which suppress activity in organs used for fight or flight and stimulate organs used to rest and digest.

Activating system. Neural pathways that coordinate brain activity through a single neurotransmitter; cell bodies are located in a nucleus in the brainstem and axons are distributed through a wide region of the brain.

of the spinal cord. The CNS neurons synapse with parasympathetic neurons that also contain acetylcholine, and with sympathetic neurons that contain norepinephrine. In other words, ACh neurons in the central nervous system synapse with sympathetic NE neurons to prepare the body's organs for fight or flight. Cholinergic (ACh) neurons in the CNS synapse with autonomic ACh neurons in the parasympathetic system to prepare the body's organs to rest and digest.

Whether acetylcholine synapses or norepinephrine synapses are excitatory or inhibitory on a particular body organ depends on that organ's receptors. During sympathetic arousal, norepinephrine turns up heart rate and turns down digestive functions because NE receptors on the heart are excitatory, whereas NE receptors on the gut are inhibitory. Similarly, acetylcholine turns down heart rate and turns up digestive functions because its receptors on these organs are different. Acetylcholine receptors on the heart are inhibitory, whereas those on the gut are excitatory. The activity of neurotransmitters, excitatory in one location and inhibitory in another, allows the sympathetic and parasympathetic divisions to form a complementary autonomic regulating system that maintains the body's internal environment under differing circumstances.

Neurotransmission in the Central Nervous System

Some CNS neurotransmitters take part in specific behaviors that occur only periodically, each month or each year perhaps. For instance, neuropeptide transmitters act as hormones specifically to prepare female white-tail deer for the fall mating season (luteinizing hormone). Come winter, a different set of biochemicals facilitates the development of the deer fetus. The mother gives birth in the spring, and yet another set of highly specific neuropeptide hormones such as oxytocin, which enables her to recognize her own fawn, and prolactin, which enables her to nurse, takes control.

Some of the same neuropeptides serve similar, specific hormonal functions in humans. Others, such as neuropeptide growth hormones, have much more general functions in regulating growth, and neuropeptide corticosteroids mediate general responses to stress.

In contrast, regulating more general, routine, and continuously occurring (vegetative) behaviors is mainly the work of small-molecule transmitters. For example, GABA and glutamate, the most common neurotransmitters in the brains of all animals, regulate neural excitability. Our minute-to-minute fluctuations in arousal levels are mediated in part by the changing activity of these two neurotransmitters.

Each of four small-molecule transmitters—acetylcholine, dopamine, norepinephrine, and serotonin—participates in its own neural **activating system** that coordinates wide areas of the brain to act in concert. The cell bodies of each system's neurons are located in a restricted region of the brainstem, and their axons are distributed widely throughout the brain. You can envision the activating systems as being analogous to the power supply to a house. A branch of the power line goes to each room, but the electrical devices powered in each room differ.

Figure 5-16 shows a cross section of a rat brain stained for the enzyme acetylcholinesterase, which breaks ACh down in synapses, as depicted earlier in Figure 5-9. The darkly stained areas of the neocortex have high AChE concentrations, indicating the presence of cholinergic terminals. High concentrations of acetylcholine in the basal ganglia and basal forebrain also render these stained structures very dark in Figure 5-16. The terminals emanate from neurons that are clustered in a rather small area just in front of the hypothalamus. Such an anatomical organization, in which a few neurons send axons to widespread brain regions, suggests that these neurons play a role in synchronizing activity throughout the brain.

Referred to by the transmitters that their neurons contain, the four major activating systems are the cholinergic, dopaminergic, noradrenergic, and serotonergic. **Figure 5-17** maps the location of each system's nuclei, with arrow shafts mapping the pathways of axons and arrowheads indicating axon-terminal locales. The activating systems are

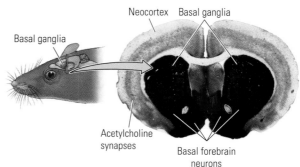

Figure 5-16

Cholinergic Activation   The drawing (*left*) shows the location of the transverse-section micrograph (*right*), stained to reveal AChE. Cholinergic neurons of the basal forebrain are located in the lower part of the section, adjacent to the two white circles (which are fibers in the anterior commissure). These neurons project to the neocortex, and the darkly stained bands in the cortex show areas rich in cholinergic synapses. The dark central parts of the section, also rich in cholinergic neurons, are the basal ganglia.

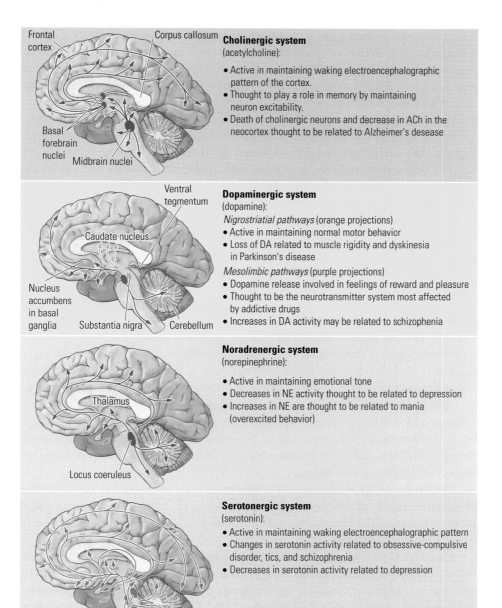

Cholinergic system
(acetylcholine):

- Active in maintaining waking electroencephalographic pattern of the cortex.
- Thought to play a role in memory by maintaining neuron excitability.
- Death of cholinergic neurons and decrease in ACh in the neocortex thought to be related to Alzheimer's desease

Dopaminergic system
(dopamine):

Nigrostriatial pathways (orange projections)
- Active in maintaining normal motor behavior
- Loss of DA related to muscle rigidity and dyskinesia in Parkinson's disease

Mesolimbic pathways (purple projections)
- Dopamine release involved in feelings of reward and pleasure
- Thought to be the neurotransmitter system most affected by addictive drugs
- Increases in DA activity may be related to schizophenia

Noradrenergic system
(norepinephrine):

- Active in maintaining emotional tone
- Decreases in NE activity thought to be related to depression
- Increases in NE are thought to be related to mania (overexcited behavior)

Serotonergic system
(serotonin):

- Active in maintaining waking electroencephalographic pattern
- Changes in serotonin activity related to obsessive-compulsive disorder, tics, and schizophrenia
- Decreases in serotonin activity related to depression

Figure 5-17

Major Activating Systems   Each system's cell bodies are gathered into nuclei (large round circles) in the brainstem. The axons project diffusely through the brain and synapse on target structures. Each activating system is associated with one or more behaviors or diseases.

Alzheimer's disease. Degenerative brain disorder; first appears as progressive memory loss and later develops into generalized dementia.

Schizophrenia. Behavioral disorder characterized by delusions, hallucinations, disorganized speech, blunted emotion, agitation or immobility, and a host of associated symptoms.

similarly organized in that the cell bodies of their neurons are clustered together in only a few nuclei in the brainstem, whereas the axons are widely distributed in the forebrain, brainstem, and spinal cord.

As summarized on the right in Figure 5-17, each activating system is associated with a number of behaviors. With the exception of dopamine's clear link to Parkinson's disease, however, associations between activating systems and brain disorders are much less certain than are their links to behaviors. All these systems are subjects of extensive ongoing research.

The difficulty in making definitive correlations between activating systems and behavior or activating systems and disorder is that the axons of these systems connect to almost every part of the brain. One likely relation is the activating systems' modulatory roles in many behaviors and disorders. We will detail some of the documented relations between the systems and behavior and disorders here and in many subsequent chapters.

CHOLINERGIC SYSTEM

The cholinergic system plays a role in normal waking behavior, evidenced by its contribution to the electroencephalographic activity recorded from the cortex and hippocampus in an alert, mentally active person. Cholinergic activation is also thought to play a role in memory. As detailed in Chapter 13, people who suffer from the degenerative **Alzheimer's disease,** which starts with minor forgetfulness and progresses to major memory dysfunction, show a loss of these cholinergic neurons at autopsy. One treatment strategy currently being pursued for Alzheimer's is to develop drugs that stimulate the cholinergic system to enhance alertness.

The brain abnormalities associated with Alzheimer's disease are not limited to the cholinergic neurons, however. Autopsies reveal extensive damage to the neocortex and other brain regions. As a result, what role the cholinergic neurons play in the progress of the disorder is not yet clear. Perhaps their destruction causes degeneration in the cortex or perhaps the cause-and-effect relation is the other way around, with cortical degeneration being the cause of cholinergic cell death. Then, too, the loss of cholinergic neurons may be just one of many neural symptoms of Alzheimer's disease.

⊙ Learn more about Parkinson's disease at the *Brain and Behavior* Web site (**www.worthpublishers.com/kolb**). Here you can find links to current research as well as foundations supporting investigations of this disorder.

DOPAMINERGIC SYSTEM

The *nigrostriatial dopaminergic system* plays a role in coordinating movement. As described throughout this chapter in relation to Parkinsonism, when DA neurons in the substantia nigra are lost, the result is a condition of extreme rigidity. Opposing muscles contract at the same time, making it difficult for an affected person to move. Parkinson patients also exhibit rhythmic tremors, especially of the limbs, which signals a release of formerly inhibited movement. Although Parkinson's disease usually arises for no known cause, it can actually be triggered by the ingestion of certain drugs, as described in "The Case of the Frozen Addict." Those drugs may act as selective neurotoxins that kill dopamine neurons.

Dopamine in the *mesolimbic DA system* may be the neurotransmitter most affected by addictive drugs, as described in Chapters 7 and 11. Many drugs that people abuse act by stimulating the mesolimbic part of the system, where dopamine release triggers feelings of reward or pleasure.

Excessive DA activity has a role in **schizophrenia,** a behavioral disorder characterized by delusions, hallucinations, disorganized speech, blunted emotion, agitation or immobility, and a host of associated symptoms. Schizophrenia is one of the most common and debilitating psychiatric disorders, affecting 1 in 100 people. We examine its possible causes in Chapter 7 and its neurobiology in Chapter 15.

The Case of the Frozen Addict

Focus on Disorders

Patient 1: During the first 4 days of July 1982, a 42-year-old man used 4½ grams of a "new synthetic heroin." The substance was injected intravenously three or four times daily and caused a burning sensation at the site of injection. The immediate effects were different from heroin, producing an unusual "spacey" high as well as transient visual distortions and hallucinations. Two days after the final injection, he awoke to find that he was "frozen" and could move only in "slow motion." He had to "think through each movement" to carry it out. He was described as stiff, slow, nearly mute, and catatonic during repeated emergency room visits from July 9 to July 11. He was admitted to a psychiatric service on July 15, 1982, with a diagnosis of "catatonic schizophrenia" and was transferred to our neurobehavioral unit the next day. (Ballard et al., 1985, p. 949)

This patient was one of seven young adults hospitalized at about the same time in California. All showed symptoms of severe Parkinson's disease that appeared very suddenly after drug injection and are extremely unusual in people their age. All reportedly injected a synthetic heroin that was being sold on the streets in the summer of 1982.

An investigation by J. William Langston and his colleagues (Bjorklund, Lindvall, & Langston, 1992) found that the heroin contained a contaminant called MPTP (1-methyl-4-phenyl-1,2,3,6-tetrahydropyridine) resulting from poor preparation during its synthesis. The results of experimental studies in rodents showed that MPTP was not itself responsible for the patients' symptoms but was metabolized into MPP^+ (1-methyl-4-phenylpyridinium), a neurotoxin.

In one autopsy of a suspected case of MPTP poisoning, the victim suffered a selective loss of dopamine neurons in the substantia nigra. The rest of the brain was normal. Injection of MPTP into monkeys produced similar symptoms and a similar selective loss of DA neurons in the substantia nigra. Thus, the combined clinical and experimental evidence indicates that Parkinson's disease can be induced by a toxin that selectively kills dopamine neurons in the brainstem.

In 1988, Patient 1 received an experimental treatment at University Hospital in Lund, Sweden. Dopamine neurons taken from human fetal brains at autopsy were implanted into the caudate and putamen. Extensive work with rodents and nonhuman primates in a number of laboratories had demonstrated that fetal neurons, which have not yet developed dendrites and axons, can survive transplantation and grow into mature neurons that can secrete neurotransmitters.

Patient 1 had no serious postoperative complications and was much improved 24 months after the surgery. He could dress and feed himself, visit the bathroom with help, and make trips outside his home. He also responded much better to medication. The transplantation of fetal neurons to treat Parkinson's disease continues to be an area of active research worldwide.

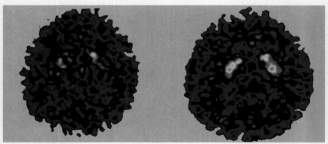

Positron emission tomographic (PET) images of Patient 1's brain before the implantation of fetal dopamine neurons (*left*) and 12 months after this operation (*right*). The increased area of red and gold shows that the transplanted neurons are producing DA. From "Bilateral Fetal Mesencephalic Grafting in Two Patients with Parkinsonism Induced by 1-Methyl-4-phenyl-1,2,3,6-tetrahydropyradine (MPTP)," by H. Widner, J. Tetrud, S. Rehngrona, B. Snow, P. Brundin, B. Gustavii, A. Bjorklund, O. Lindvall, and J. W. Langston, 1992, *New England Journal of Medicine, 327,* p. 151.

Dr. Hakan Widner, M.D., PhD., Lord University, Sweden

Noradrenergic neuron. From *adrenaline,* Latin for epinephrine; a neuron containing norepinephrine.

Obsessive-compulsive disorder (OCD). Behavioral disorder characterized by compulsively repeated acts (such as hand washing) and repetitive, often unpleasant, thoughts (obsessions).

Learning. Relatively permanent change in behavior that results from experience.

NORADRENERGIC SYSTEM

The term **noradrenergic** is derived from *adrenaline,* the Latin name for epinephrine. Norepinephrine (noradrenalin) may play a role in learning by stimulating neurons to change their structure. It may also facilitate normal development of the brain and play a role in organizing movements.

In the main, behaviors and disorders related to the noradrenergic system concern the emotions and have been difficult to identify. Some symptoms of depression may be related to decreases in the activity of noradrenergic neurons, whereas some of the symptoms of mania (excessive excitability) may be related to increases in the activity of these same neurons.

SEROTONERGIC SYSTEM

The serotonergic system is active in maintaining a waking EEG in the forebrain when we move and thus plays a role in wakefulness, as does the cholinergic system. Serotonin also plays a role in learning, as described in the next section. Some symptoms of depression may be related to decreases in the activity of serotonin neurons, and drugs commonly used to treat depression act on serotonin neurons. Consequently, two forms of depression may exist, one related to norepinephrine and another related to serotonin.

The results of some research suggest that some symptoms of schizophrenia also may be related to increases in serotonin activity, which implies that there may be different forms of schizophrenia as well. Increased serotonergic activity is also related to symptoms observed in **obsessive-compulsive disorder** (OCD), a condition in which a person compulsively repeats acts (such as hand washing) and has repetitive and often unpleasant thoughts (obsessions).

In Review

Although neurons can synthesize more than one neurotransmitter, they are usually identified by the principal neurotransmitter in their axon terminals. Although there is no one-to-one relation between any neurotransmitter and any behavior, some neurotransmitters take part in specific behaviors that may occur only periodically, such as acting as hormones to stimulate reproduction. Other CNS neurotransmitters continuously monitor vegetative behaviors. Neural activating systems modulate aspects of behavior. Acetylcholine produces muscular contractions in the SNS, and acetylcholine and norepinephrine regulate the complementary divisions of the ANS. The CNS contains not only widely dispersed glutamate (excitatory) and GABA (inhibitory) neurons but also activating systems of acetylcholine, norepinephrine, dopamine, and serotonin. These neuromodulatory systems are associated both with specific aspects of behavior and with specific neurological disorders.

ROLE OF SYNAPSES IN LEARNING AND MEMORY

Experience actually alters the synapse, because not only are synapses versatile in structure and function, they are also adaptable, or *plastic:* they can change. The synapse, therefore, provides a potential site for the neural basis of **learning,** a relatively permanent change in behavior that results from experience. Structural changes in synapses underlie the three simple learning behaviors examined in this section. In Chapter 13, we take up learning and memory again. And Experiments and Focus boxes throughout the

Donald O. Hebb
(1904–1985)

book often revisit **neuroplasticity,** the nervous system's adaptability and potential for self-repair.

Donald O. Hebb (1949) was not the first to suggest that learning is mediated by structural changes in synapses. But the change that he envisioned in his book titled *The Organization of Behavior* was novel half a century ago. Hebb theorized: "When an axon of cell A is near enough to excite a cell B and repeatedly or persistently takes part in firing it, some growth process or metabolic change takes place in one or both cells such that A's efficiency, as one of the cells firing B, is increased" (Hebb, 1949, p. 62).

Hebb's proposal was untestable when he developed it but has been supported through the succeeding decades as research methods have advanced. Eric Kandel (1976) and many other neuroscientists have demonstrated that learning does often require the joint firing of two neurons, which increases the efficiency of their synapses. A synapse that physically adapts in this way is called a *Hebb synapse* today.

Increased efficiency at the Hebb synapse is the structural basis for new behavior, or learning. To explain the neurological basis of simple kinds of learning, Kandel and others have studied an animal with a relatively simple nervous system. Their subject, the marine snail *Aplysia californica* shown in **Figure 5-18**, is an ideal subject for learning experiments. Slightly larger than a softball and lacking a shell, *Aplysia* has roughly 20,000 neurons, some of which are quite accessible to researchers, who can isolate and study circuits having very few synapses.

When threatened, *Aplysia* defensively withdraws its more vulnerable body parts—the gill (through which it extracts oxygen from the water to breathe) and the siphon (a spout above the gill that excretes seawater and waste). By touching or shocking the snail's appendages, researchers can produce enduring changes in its defensive behaviors. These behavioral responses can then be used to study underlying changes in the snail's nervous system.

At the microscopic level, the physical structure of synapses adapts as a response to learning. The learned responses that we will now describe—habituation, sensitization, and associative learning—employ neural mechanisms of which you already know. Learned responses also underlie behaviors that you will recognize.

Neuroplasticity. The nervous system's potential for neurophysical or neurochemical change that enhances its adaptability to environmental change and its ability to compensate for injury.

Habituation. Learning behavior in which a response to a stimulus weakens with repeated stimulus presentations.

Jeff Rotman

Figure 5-18

Aplysia Californica

Habituation Response

In **habituation,** the response to a stimulus weakens with repeated presentations of that stimulus. If you are accustomed to living in the country and then move to a city, you might at first find the sounds of traffic and people extremely loud and annoying. With time, however, you stop noticing most of the noise most of the time. You have habituated to it.

Habituation develops with all our senses. When you first put on a shoe, you "feel" it on your foot, but very shortly it is as if the shoe is no longer there. You have not become insensitive to sensations, however. When people talk to you, you still hear them; when someone steps on your foot, you still feel the pressure. Your brain has habituated to the customary, "background" sensations.

Aplysia habituates to waves in the shallow tidal zone where it lives. These snails are constantly buffeted by the flow of waves against their bodies, and they learn that waves are just the background "noise" of daily life. They do not flinch and withdraw every time a wave passes over them. They habituate to this stimulus.

A sea snail that is habituated to waves remains sensitive to other touch sensations. Prodded with a novel object, it responds by withdrawing its siphon and gill. The animal's reaction to repeated presentations of the same novel stimulus forms the basis for **Experiment 5-2**, studying its habituation response.

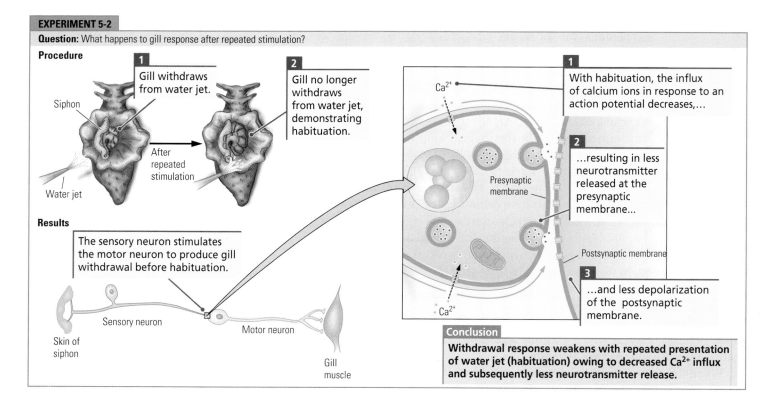

EXPERIMENT 5-2

Question: What happens to gill response after repeated stimulation?

Procedure

1 Gill withdraws from water jet.

Siphon

Water jet

After repeated stimulation

2 Gill no longer withdraws from water jet, demonstrating habituation.

Ca^{2+}

1 With habituation, the influx of calcium ions in response to an action potential decreases,...

Presynaptic membrane

2 ...resulting in less neurotransmitter released at the presynaptic membrane...

Postsynaptic membrane

Ca^{2+}

3 ...and less depolarization of the postsynaptic membrane.

Results

The sensory neuron stimulates the motor neuron to produce gill withdrawal before habituation.

Sensory neuron

Motor neuron

Skin of siphon

Gill muscle

Conclusion

Withdrawal response weakens with repeated presentation of water jet (habituation) owing to decreased Ca^{2+} influx and subsequently less neurotransmitter release.

NEURAL BASIS OF HABITUATION

The Procedure section of Experiment 5-2 shows the setup for studying what happens to the withdrawal response of *Aplysia*'s gill after repeated stimulation. A gentle jet of water is sprayed on the siphon while movement of the gill is recorded. If the jet of water is presented to *Aplysia*'s siphon as many as 10 times, the gill-withdrawal response is weaker some minutes later when the animal is again tested with the water jet. The decrement in the strength of the withdrawal is habituation, which can last as long as 30 min.

The Results section of Experiment 5-2 starts by showing a simple representation of the pathway that mediates *Aplysia*'s gill-withdrawal response. For purposes of illustration, only one sensory neuron, one motor neuron, and one synapse are shown, even though, in actuality, about 300 neurons may take part in this response. The jet of water stimulates the sensory neuron, which in turn stimulates the motor neuron responsible for the gill withdrawal. But exactly where do the changes associated with habituation take place? In the sensory neuron? In the motor neuron? Or in the synapse between the two?

Habituation does *not* result from an inability of either the sensory or the motor neuron to produce action potentials. In response to direct electrical stimulation, both the sensory neuron and the motor neuron retain the ability to generate action potentials even after habituation. Electrical recordings from the motor neuron show that, accompanying the development of habituation, the excitatory postsynaptic potentials in the motor neuron become smaller.

The most likely way in which these EPSPs decrease in size is that the motor neuron is receiving less neurotransmitter from the sensory neuron across the synapse. And, if less neurotransmitter is being received, then the changes accompanying habituation must be taking place in the presynaptic axon terminal of the sensory neuron.

CALCIUM CHANNELS HABITUATE

Kandel and his coworkers measured neurotransmitter output from a sensory neuron and verified that less neurotransmitter is in fact released from a habituated neuron than from a nonhabituated one. Recall that the release of a neurotransmitter in response to an action potential requires an influx of calcium ions across the presynaptic membrane. As habituation takes place, that calcium ion influx decreases in response to the voltage changes associated with an action potential. Presumably, with repeated use, calcium channels become less responsive to voltage changes and more resistant to the passage of calcium ions.

Why this happens is not yet known. At any rate, the neural basis of habituation lies in the presynaptic response. Its mechanism, which is summarized in the right-hand closeup of Experiment 5-2, is a reduced sensitivity of calcium channels and a consequent decrease in the release of a neurotransmitter. This reduced sensitivity of calcium channels in response to voltage changes produces habituation, as summarized in the Conclusion section of the experiment.

Sensitization Response

A sprinter crouched in her starting blocks is often hyperresponsive to the starter's gun; its firing triggers in her a very rapid reaction. The stressful, competitive context in which the race takes place helps to sensitize her to this sound. **Sensitization,** an enhanced response to some stimulus, is the opposite of habituation. The organism becomes hyperresponsive to a stimulus rather than accustomed to it.

Sensitization occurs within a context. Sudden, novel stimulation heightens our general awareness and often results in larger-than-normal responses to all kinds of stimulation. If you are suddenly startled by a loud noise, you become much more responsive to other stimuli in your surroundings, including some to which you had been previously habituated.

The same thing happens to *Aplysia*. Sudden, novel stimuli can heighten a snail's responsiveness to familiar stimulation. When attacked by a predator, for example, the snail becomes acutely aware of other changes in its environment and hyperresponds to them. In the laboratory, a small electric shock to *Aplysia*'s tail mimics a predatory attack and effects sensitization, as illustrated in the Procedure section of **Experiment 5-3**. A single electric shock to the tail of *Aplysia* enhances its gill-withdrawal response for a period that lasts from minutes to hours.

NEURAL BASIS OF SENSITIZATION

The neural circuits participating in sensitization are a little more complex than those that take part in a habituation response. To simplify the picture, the Results section of Experiment 5-3 shows only one of each kind of neuron: the sensory and motor neurons already described that produce the gill-withdrawal response and an interneuron that is responsible for sensitization.

An interneuron that receives input from a sensory neuron in the tail (and so carries information about the shock) makes an axoaxonic synapse with a siphon sensory neuron. The interneuron's axon terminal contains serotonin. Consequently, in response to a tail shock, the tail sensory neuron activates the interneuron, which in turn releases serotonin onto the axon of the siphon sensory neuron. Information from the siphon still comes through the siphon sensory neuron to activate the motor neuron leading to the gill muscle, but the gill-withdrawal response is amplified by the action of the interneuron in releasing serotonin onto the presynaptic membrane of the sensory neuron.

Sensitization. Learning behavior in which the response to a stimulus strengthens with repeated presentations of that stimulus because the stimulus is novel or because the stimulus is stronger than normal—for example, after habituation has occurred.

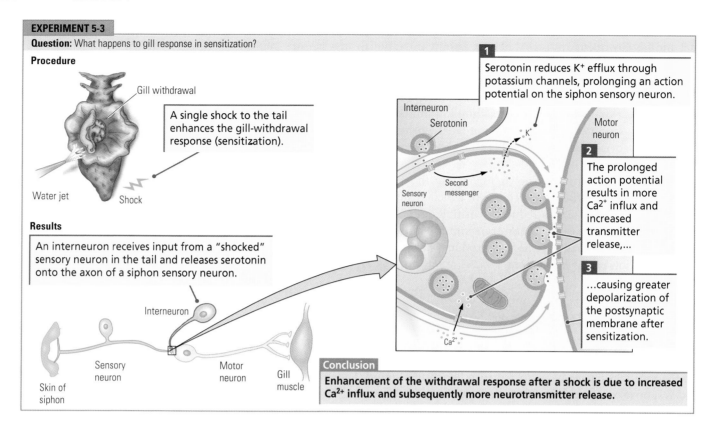

EXPERIMENT 5-3

Question: What happens to gill response in sensitization?

Procedure

Gill withdrawal

A single shock to the tail enhances the gill-withdrawal response (sensitization).

Water jet

Shock

1 Serotonin reduces K⁺ efflux through potassium channels, prolonging an action potential on the siphon sensory neuron.

Interneuron

Serotonin

Motor neuron

Sensory neuron

Second messenger

2 The prolonged action potential results in more Ca²⁺ influx and increased transmitter release,...

3 ...causing greater depolarization of the postsynaptic membrane after sensitization.

Ca²⁺

Results

An interneuron receives input from a "shocked" sensory neuron in the tail and releases serotonin onto the axon of a siphon sensory neuron.

Interneuron

Sensory neuron

Motor neuron

Gill muscle

Skin of siphon

Conclusion

Enhancement of the withdrawal response after a shock is due to increased Ca²⁺ influx and subsequently more neurotransmitter release.

At the molecular level, the serotonin released from the interneuron binds to a metabotropic serotonin receptor on the axon of the siphon sensory neuron. This binding activates second messengers in the sensory neuron. Specifically, the serotonin receptor is coupled through its G protein to the enzyme adenyl cyclase. This enzyme increases the concentration of the second messenger cyclic adenosine monophosphate (cAMP) in the presynaptic membrane of the siphon sensory neuron.

Through a number of chemical reactions, cAMP attaches a phosphate molecule (PO_4) to potassium (K^+) channels, and the phosphate renders the K^+ channels less responsive. The closeup on the right side of the Results section in Experiment 5-3 sums it up. In response to an action potential traveling down the axon of the siphon sensory neuron (such as one generated by a touch to the siphon), the K^+ channels on that neuron are slower to open. Consequently, potassium ions cannot repolarize the membrane as quickly as is normal, and so the action potential lasts a little longer than it usually would.

POTASSIUM CHANNELS SENSITIZE

The longer-lasting action potential prolongs the inflow of Ca^{2+} into the membrane. The increased concentration of Ca^{2+} in turn results in more neurotransmitter being released from the sensory synapse onto the motor neuron that leads to the gill muscle. This increased release of neurotransmitter produces a larger-than-normal gill-withdrawal response. The gill withdrawal may also be enhanced by the fact that the second messenger cAMP may mobilize more synaptic vesicles, making more neurotransmitter ready for release into the sensory–motor synapse.

Sensitization, then, is the opposite of habituation at the synaptic level as well as at the behavioral level. In sensitization, more calcium influx results in more transmitter being released, whereas, in habituation, less calcium influx results in less neurotransmitter being released. The structural basis of cellular memory in these two forms of learning is different, however. In sensitization, the change takes place in potassium channels, whereas, in habituation, the change takes place in calcium channels.

Long-Term Potentiation and Associative Learning

The findings from studies of habituation and sensitization in *Aplysia* show that physical changes in synapses do underlie simple forms of learning. In this section, we look at experiments that demonstrate how adaptive synapses participate in learning in the mammalian brain. Such **associative learning,** a response elicited by linking unrelated stimuli together—by learning that A goes with B—is very common.

Associating a telephone number with a person, an odor with a food, or a sound with a musical instrument are everyday examples of associative learning. Your learning that learning takes place at synapses is another example. The phenomenon that underlies associative learning entails a neural change in which an excitatory signal crossing a synapse is enhanced long after use.

NEURAL BASIS OF ASSOCIATIVE LEARNING

We begin in the forebrain structure called the hippocampus (see Figure 2-20). The limbic cortex of the mammalian hippocampus has only three layers, rather than the six layers in the neocortex. The neurons in one of these limbic layers are packed closely together, which aligns their dendrites and cell bodies. This arrangement allows summed EPSPs from many of these neurons—sums known as *field potentials*—to be recorded quite easily with extracellular electrodes.

Both the relatively simple circuitry of the hippocampus and the ease of recording large field potentials there make it an ideal structure for studying the neural basis of learning. In 1973, Timothy Bliss and Terje Lømø demonstrated that repeated electrical stimulation of the *perforant pathway* entering the hippocampus produces a progressive increase in field-potential size recorded from hippocampal cells. This enhancement in the size of the field potentials lasts for a number of hours to weeks or even longer. Bliss and Lømø called it **long-term potentiation** (LTP).

The fact that LTP lasts for some time after stimulation suggests two things:

1. At the synapse, a change must take place that allows the field potential to become larger and remain larger.
2. The change at the synapse might be related to everyday learning experiences.

Long-term potentiation can be recorded at many synapses in the nervous system, but the hippocampus, because of its simple structure, continues to be a favorite location for study. **Figure 5-19A** illustrates the experimental procedure for a typical synapse. The presynaptic neuron is stimulated electrically while the electrical activity produced by the stimulation is recorded from the postsynaptic neuron. The inset in Figure 5-19A shows the EPSP produced by a single pulse of electrical stimulation.

In a typical experiment, a number of test stimuli are given to estimate the size of the induced EPSP. Then a strong burst of stimulation, consisting of a few hundred pulses of electrical current per second, is administered. Then the test pulse is given again. Figure 5-19B illustrates that the increased amplitude of the EPSP remains larger for as long as 90 min after the high-frequency burst of stimulation.

Associative learning. Linkage of two or more unrelated stimuli to elicit a behavioral response.

Long-term potentiation (LTP). In response to stimulation at a synapse, changed amplitude of an excitatory postsynaptic potential that lasts for hours to days or longer and plays a part in associative learning.

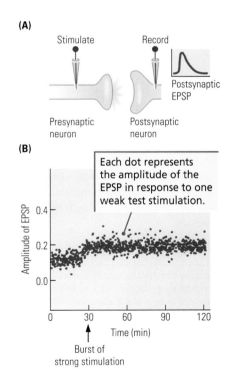

Figure 5-19

Recording Long-Term Potentiation (A) In this experimental setup, the presynaptic neuron is stimulated with a test pulse and the EPSP is recorded from the postsynaptic neuron. **(B)** After a period of intense stimulation, the amplitude of the EPSP produced by the test pulse increases.

The high burst of stimulation has produced a long-lasting change in the response of the postsynaptic neuron: LTP has occurred. For the EPSP to increase in size, either more neurotransmitter must be released from the presynaptic membrane or the postsynaptic membrane must become more sensitive to the same amount of transmitter. So the question is, What mechanism enables this change?

NEUROCHEMISTRY OF LTP

To examine the possible synaptic changes underlying LTP, we turn to the results of some experiments concerning glutamate at the terminals of hippocampal neurons. Glutamate acts on two different types of receptors on the postsynaptic membrane, NMDA (*N*-methyl-D-aspartate) and AMPA (alpha-amino-3-hydroxy-5-methylisoazole-4-proprionic acid) receptors. As **Figure 5-20A** shows, AMPA receptors ordinarily mediate the responses produced when glutamate is released from a presynaptic membrane. NMDA receptors usually do not respond to glutamate, because their pores are blocked by magnesium ions (Mg^{2+}).

However, NMDA receptors are *doubly gated channels* that can open to allow the passage of calcium ions if two events take place at approximately the same time:

1. The postsynaptic membrane is depolarized by strong electrical stimulation, displacing the magnesium ion from the NMDA pore (Figure 5-20B).
2. NMDA receptors are activated by glutamate from the presynaptic membrane (Figure 5-20C).

With the doubly gated NMDA channels open, calcium ions enter the postsynaptic neuron and act through second messengers to initiate the cascade of events associated with LTP. These events include increased responsiveness of AMPA receptors to glutamate, formation of new AMPA receptors, and even retrograde messages to the presynaptic terminal to enhance glutamate release.

Hippocampal NMDA receptors thus mediate a change that in every way meets the criteria for a Hebb synapse. The synapse changes with use. The familiar part of the story is that calcium ions take part, just as in learning in *Aplysia*. The NMDA receptor change is associative in that two different stimuli—the initial strong electrical stimula-

Figure 5-20

Glutamate's Lasting Effects   Enhanced glutamate prompts a neurochemical cascade that underlies synaptic change and LTP.

(A) Weak electrical stimulus

Because the NMDA receptor pore is blocked by a magnesium ion, release of glutamate by a weak electrical stimulation activates only the AMPA receptor.

(B) Strong electrical stimulus (depolarizing EPSP)

A strong electrical stimulation can depolarize the postsynaptic membrane sufficiently that the magnesium ion is removed from the NMDA receptor pore.

(C) Weak electrical stimulus

Now glutamate, released by weak stimulation, can activate the NMDA receptor to allow Ca^{2+} influx, which, through a second messenger, increases the function or number of AMPA receptors or both.

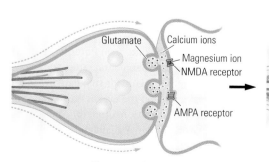

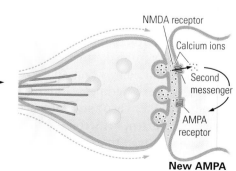

tion and the weaker test stimulus—activating two different mechanisms are linked. Remember that the NMDA receptor is doubly gated. In order for calcium ions to pass through its pore, the magnesium block must be removed by depolarization of the membrane, and then glutamate must bind to the receptor.

The demonstration of LTP occurring at a synapse when a weak stimulus is paired with a stronger one provides a model that underlies real-life associative learning. Normally, the strong stimulation comes from an interesting feature of the action potentials produced by certain neurons. When these neurons fire, the nerve impulse travels from the axon hillock not only down the axon but also back up the dendritic tree (in many other neurons, the action potential travels only down the axon). This dendritic action potential creates a depolarization of the postsynaptic membrane that is adequate to remove the Mg^{2+} block in NMDA receptors.

When the Mg^{2+} blocks are removed, the release of glutamate into any synapse on the dendrite can activate NMDA receptors and thus produce LTP. The real-life corollary of weak stimulation may be an environmental event that triggers glutamate-releasing activity into a synapse at the same time as the postsynaptic membrane is being depolarized. Thus, if one behavioral event causes the hippocampal cells to discharge at the same time as some other event causes the release of glutamate onto the dendrites of those cells, LTP would occur. A specific example will help you see how this process relates to associative learning in mammals.

Suppose that, as a rat walks around, a hippocampal cell fires when the rat reaches a certain location. The stimulus that produces this firing may be the sight of a particular object, such as a light. The neural signal about the light will be carried by the visual system to the neocortex and then from the visual neocortex to memory storage in the hippocampal cell, the putative site of learning.

Now suppose that, during an excursion to this place where the light is located, the rat encounters a tasty piece of food. Input concerning that food can be carried from the taste area of the neocortex to the same hippocampal cell that fires in response to the light. As a result, the taste and odor input associated with the food arrives at the cell at the time that it is firing in response to the light.

Because the cell is firing, the Mg^{2+} block is removed, and so LTP can take place. Subsequently, the sight of the light will fire this hippocampal cell, but so will the odor of this particular food. The hippocampal cell, in other words, stores an association between the food and the light. If the rat were to smell the odor of this food on the snout of another rat that had eaten it, the hippocampal cell would discharge. Because the discharge of this cell is also associated with a particular light and location in the environment, would the rat go to that location, expecting once again to find food there?

Bennett Galef and his coworkers (1990) in fact demonstrated that a rat that smells the odor of a particular food on the breath of a demonstrator rat will go to the appropriate location to obtain the food. This social transmission of food-related information is an excellent example of associative learning. Although the behavior can be disrupted by lesions in the hippocampus, it has not yet been demonstrated that learning this food-and-place association is mediated by LTP in synapses, because it is technically difficult to locate the appropriate synapses and record from them in a freely moving animal.

Long-term potentiation is not the only change in a neuron that can underlie learning. Learning can also be mediated by a neuron that becomes less active in response to repeated stimulation. This process is called *long-term depression* or LTD. The neural basis of LTD may be quite similar to that of LTP in that both require NMDA receptors. In neurons that display LTD, the influx of Ca^{2+} may result not in increased responsiveness or increased numbers of AMPA receptors but rather in decreased responsiveness or decreased numbers of AMPA receptors.

⊙ For more information about the role of long-term potentiation in learning, visit the Chapter 5 Web links on the *Brain and Behavior* Web site (**www.worth publishers.com/kolb**).

Learning at the Synapse

The neural changes associated with learning must be long-lasting enough to account for a relatively permanent change in an organism's behavior. The changes at synapses described in the preceding sections develop quite quickly, but they do not last indefinitely, as memories often do. How, then, can synapses be responsible for the relatively long term changes in learning and memory?

Repeated stimulation produces habituation and sensitization or associative behaviors that can persist for months. Brief training produces short-term learning, whereas longer training periods produce more enduring learning. If you cram for an exam the night before, you usually forget the material quickly, but, if you study a little each day for a week, your learning tends to endure. What underlies this more persistent form of learning? It would seem to be more than just a change in the release of glutamate, and, whatever the change is, it must be long-lasting.

Craig Bailey and Mary Chen (1989) found that the number and size of sensory synapses change in well-trained, habituated, and sensitized *Aplysia*. Relative to a control neuron, the number and size of synapses decrease in habituated animals and increase in sensitized animals, as represented in **Figure 5-21**. Apparently, synaptic events associated with habituation and sensitization can also trigger processes in the sensory cell that result in the loss or formation of new synapses.

Craig Bailey

Mary Chen

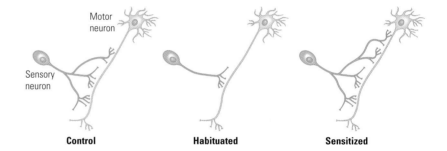

Motor neuron

Sensory neuron

Control   **Habituated**   **Sensitized**

Figure 5-21

Physical Basis of Memory   Relative to a control neural connection (*left*), the number of synapses between *Aplysia*'s sensory neuron and a motor neuron decline as a result of habituation (*center*) and increase as a result of sensitization (*right*). Such structural changes may underlie enduring memories.

A mechanism through which these processes can take place begins with calcium ions that mobilize second messengers to send instructions to nuclear DNA. The transcription and translation of nuclear DNA, in turn, initiate structural changes at synapses. "Dendritic Spines, Small but Mighty" summarizes experimental evidence about structural changes in dendritic spines. The second messenger cAMP probably plays an important role in carrying instructions regarding these structural changes to nuclear DNA. The evidence for cAMP's involvement comes from studies of fruit flies.

In the fruit fly, *Drosophila*, two genetic mutations can produce the same learning deficiency. Both render the second messenger cAMP inoperative, but in opposite ways. One mutation, called *dunce*, lacks the enzymes needed to degrade cAMP, and so the fruit fly has abnormally high levels. The other mutation, called *rutabaga*, reduces levels of cAMP below the normal range for *Drosophila* neurons.

Significantly, fruit flies with either of these mutations are impaired in acquiring habituated and sensitized responses because their levels of cAMP cannot be regulated. New synapses seem to be required for learning to take place, and the second messenger cAMP seems to be needed to carry instructions to form them. **Figure 5-22** summarizes these research findings.

Experiment 5-4 asks whether neural stimulation that produces LTP causes structural changes in neurons. To investigate this question, German researchers Florian Engert and Tobias Bonhoeffer (1999) took slices of the hippocampus from the brains of rats and maintained them in a culture where they subjected the neurons to stimulation.

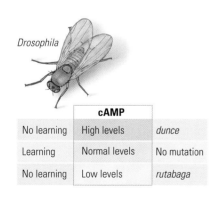

Drosophila

	cAMP	
No learning	High levels	*dunce*
Learning	Normal levels	No mutation
No learning	Low levels	*rutabaga*

Figure 5-22

Genetic Disruption of Learning   Two mutations in the fruit fly, *Drosophila*, inactivate the second messenger cAMP by moving its level above or below the concentration range at which it can be regulated.

Dendritic Spines, Small but Mighty

Dendritic spines, illustrated in Experiment 5-4, contain an astounding variety of protein molecules. Research now suggests that spines are the paramount example of biological nanotechnology (Tashiro & Yuste, 2003).

To mediate learning, each spine must be able to act independently, undergoing changes that its neighbors do not undergo. Spines may appear and disappear on a dendrite in a matter of seconds, and they may even extend or move along a dendrite to search out and contact a presynaptic axon terminal. When forming part of a synapse, they can change in size and shape and even divide.

Dendritic spines are from about 1 to 3 μm long and less than 1 μm in diameter and protrude from the dendrite shaft. Each neuron may have many thousands of spines, and the human cerebral cortex may contain a total of 10^{14} dendritic spines. Characteristically, spines have an expanded head connected to a narrow shaft, but they may take an array of shapes. The heads of spines serve as biochemical compartments and can generate huge electrical potentials.

The mechanisms that allow spines to appear and change in shape include a number of different cytoskeletal filaments linked to the membrane receptors. The influx of calcium or other actions of the dendritic receptors can lead to the assembly of larger filaments; some can change the length of the spine, others can change its width, and still others can cause it to divide.

The activation of receptors can induce mRNA within the spine to produce more of these structural proteins. In addition, second messengers within the spine can carry signals to the cell's DNA to send more mRNA addressed to just the signaling spine. Understanding the workings of spines will eventually assist in understanding learning and adaptation at the neural level.

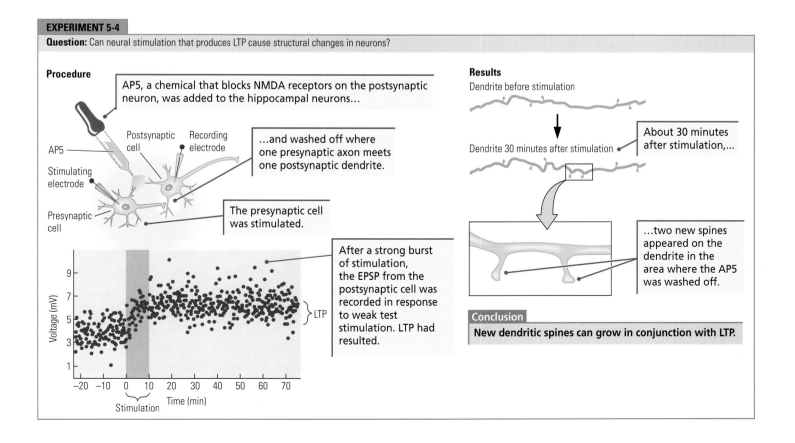

EXPERIMENT 5-4

Question: Can neural stimulation that produces LTP cause structural changes in neurons?

Procedure

AP5, a chemical that blocks NMDA receptors on the postsynaptic neuron, was added to the hippocampal neurons…

AP5

Stimulating electrode

Postsynaptic cell   Recording electrode

Presynaptic cell

…and washed off where one presynaptic axon meets one postsynaptic dendrite.

The presynaptic cell was stimulated.

After a strong burst of stimulation, the EPSP from the postsynaptic cell was recorded in response to weak test stimulation. LTP had resulted.

Voltage (mV)

LTP

Stimulation   Time (min)

Results

Dendrite before stimulation

Dendrite 30 minutes after stimulation

About 30 minutes after stimulation,…

…two new spines appeared on the dendrite in the area where the AP5 was washed off.

Conclusion

New dendritic spines can grow in conjunction with LTP.

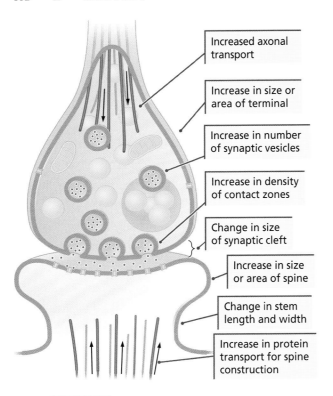

Increased axonal transport

Increase in size or area of terminal

Increase in number of synaptic vesicles

Increase in density of contact zones

Change in size of synaptic cleft

Increase in size or area of spine

Change in stem length and width

Increase in protein transport for spine construction

Figure 5-23

Neural Bases of Learning Locations on a synapse where structural changes may subserve learning

○ Learn more about the confocal microscope in the research methods section of your *Foundations* CD. You'll see a diagram of the apparatus as well as video clips of cells taken with a confocal microscope.

In their setup, illustrated in the Procedure section of Experiment 5-4, they injected the fluorescent molecule calcein through the recording electrode into the postsynaptic cell to color it green and allow them to view it through a microscope. Then they stimulated the presynaptic hippocampal neuron sufficiently to depolarize the cell membrane and remove the Mg^{2+} block from NMDA receptors.

Except for the part being stimulated, the presynaptic neuron was washed with AP5, a drug that blocks NMDA receptors. A second microelectrode was inserted into the axons of other neurons that had synapsed with the first cell. The axons were then stimulated electrically, and the EPSPs produced by that stimulation were recorded from the postsynaptic cell.

The graph at the center of Experiment 5-4 shows the amplitude changes in EPSPs recorded from the postsynaptic neuron. Each dot represents the size of an EPSP in response to a single test stimulus. Left of zero on the time scale, a number of weak test stimuli are given to determine the sizes of the EPSPs, followed by an intense 10-min burst of electrical stimulation. Then, in response to the stimulation, EPSPs with larger amplitudes are recorded, indicating that LTP has occurred.

Using a *confocal* microscope (similar to a light microscope except that the light comes from a laser), the experimenters observed the changes to the dendrite. The Results section of Experiment 5-4 sketches these changes. About 30 min after stimulation, two new spines appeared on the dendrite. No spines appeared on other parts of the neuron that were still subjected to the AP5 block. This experiment concludes that new dendritic spines can grow in conjunction with LTP. The implication is that they adapt to support long-term interneural communication and may provide the neural basis for brain plasticity and learning.

In this experiment, the axon terminals could not be seen, but presumably new terminals arose to connect the stimulated axons to the new dendritic spines, thus forming new synapses. Note that the new spines appeared about 30 min after LTP, and so these new connections were not required for LTP. The new synapses, however, are probably required for LTP to endure.

In Review

The neural basis for learning and memory resides at the synapse. *Aplysia's* synaptic function mediates two forms of learning: habituation and sensitization. Presynaptic voltage-sensitive calcium channels mediate habituation by growing less sensitive with use. Metabotropic serotonin receptors on a sensory neuron can change the sensitivity of presynaptic potassium channels and so increase Ca^{2+} influx to mediate sensitization. At the same time, these receptors can produce fewer or more synapses to provide a structural, physical basis for long-term habituation and sensitization and for changes in behavior. Mammals also demonstrate structural synaptic changes related to associative learning. Clearly, many changes in the synapses of neurons can mediate learning, but associative learning takes place only if requisite events take place at nearly the same time and thus become linked. Because associative learning has a neural basis, measurements of synaptic structure and neurochemistry may suggest relations between synaptic change, experience, and behavior. **Figure 5-23** summarizes synaptic structures that can be measured and related to learning and behavior.

SUMMARY

▪ *What early experiments provided the key to understanding how neurons communicate with one another?* In the 1920s, Otto Loewi suspected that nerves to the heart secrete a chemical that regulates its rate of beating. His subsequent experiments with frogs showed that acetylcholine slows heart rate, whereas epinephrine increases it. This observation provided the key to understanding the basis of chemical neurotransmission.

▪ *What is the basic structure of a synapse that passes information from one neuron to another neuron?* A synapse consists of the first neuron's axon terminal (surrounded by a presynaptic membrane), a synaptic cleft (a tiny gap between the two neurons), and a postsynaptic membrane on the second neuron. Systems for the chemical synthesis of excitatory or inhibitory neurotransmitters are located in the presynaptic neuron's axon terminal or soma, whereas systems for storing the neurotransmitter are in its axon terminal. Receptor systems on which that neurotransmitter acts are located on the postsynaptic membrane.

▪ *What are the major stages in the function of a neurotransmitter?* The four major stages in neurotransmitter function are (1) synthesis and storage, (2) release from the axon terminal, (3) action on postsynaptic receptors, and (4) inactivation. After synthesis, the neurotransmitter is wrapped in a membrane to form synaptic vesicles in the axon terminal. When an action potential is propagated on the presynaptic membrane, voltage changes set in motion the attachment of vesicles to the presynaptic membrane and the release of neurotransmitter by exocytosis. One synaptic vesicle releases a quantum of neurotransmitter into the synaptic cleft, producing a miniature potential on the postsynaptic membrane. To generate an action potential on the postsynaptic cell requires the simultaneous release of many quanta of transmitter. After a transmitter has done its work, it is inactivated by such processes as diffusion out of the synaptic cleft, breakdown by enzymes, and reuptake of the transmitter or its components into the axon terminal (or sometimes uptake into glial cells).

▪ *What are the three major varieties of neurotransmitters, and in what kinds of synapses do they participate?* Small-molecule transmitters, neuropeptides, and transmitter gases are broad classes of the perhaps 100 neurotransmitters. Neurons containing these transmitters make a variety of connections with various parts of other neurons, as well as with muscles, blood vessels, and extracellular fluid. Functionally, neurons can be both excitatory and inhibitory, and they can participate in local circuits or in general brain systems. Excitatory synapses, known as Type I, are usually located on a dendritic tree, whereas inhibitory synapses, known as Type II, are usually located on a cell body.

▪ *What are the two general classes of receptors for neurotransmitters?* Each neurotransmitter may be associated with both ionotropic and metabotropic receptors. An ionotropic receptor quickly and directly produces voltage changes on the postsynaptic cell membrane as its pore opens or closes to regulate the flow of ions through the cell membrane. Slower-acting, metabotropic receptors activate second messengers to indirectly produce changes in the function and structure of the cell.

▪ *How are the principal neurotransmitter systems related to behavior?* Because neurotransmitters are multifunctional, scientists find it impossible to isolate single-neurotransmitter–single-behavior relations. Rather, systems of neurons that employ the same principal neurotransmitter influence various general aspects of behavior. For instance, acetylcholine, the main neurotransmitter in the somatic motor system, controls movement of the skeletal muscles, whereas, in the autonomic system, acetylcholine and norepinephrine are the main transmitters controlling the body's internal organs. The central nervous system contains not only widely dispersed glutamate and GABA

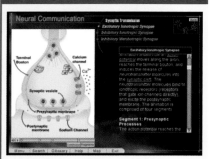

neuroscience interactive

There are many resources available for expanding your learning online:

■ **www.worthpublishers.com/kolb**
Try the Chapter 5 quizzes and flashcards to test your mastery of the chapter material. You'll also be able to link to other sites that will reinforce what you've learned.

■ **www.pdf.org**
Link to this site to learn more about Parkinson's disease and current research to find a cure.

On your *Foundations* CD-ROM, you'll find that the module on Neural Communication provides important reinforcement of what you've learned. In addition, the Research Methods module contains coverage of some of the technological techniques referred to in this chapter, including the confocal microscope.

neurons but also neural activating systems that employ acetylcholine, norepinephrine, dopamine, or serotonin as their main neurotransmitter. All these systems ensure that wide areas of the brain act in concert, and each is associated with various classes of behaviors and disorders.

■ *How do changes in synapses effect learning?* Changes in synapses underlie learning and memory. In habituation, a form of learning in which a response weakens as a result of repeated stimulation, calcium channels become less responsive to an action potential and, consequently, less neurotransmitter is released when an action potential is propagated. In sensitization, a form of learning in which a response strengthens as a result of stimulation, changes in potassium channels prolong the duration of the action potential, resulting in an increased influx of calcium ions and, consequently, release of more neurotransmitter. With repeated training, new synapses can develop, and both these kinds of learning can become relatively permanent. In associative learning, when two events take place together, the formation of new synapses can record their relation for the long term.

■ *What structural changes in synapses may be related to learning?* In *Aplysia,* the number of synapses connecting sensory neurons and motor neurons decreases in response to repeated sessions of habituation. Similarly, in response to repeated sessions of sensitization, the number of synapses connecting the sensory and the motor neurons increases. Presumably, these changes in synapse number are related to long-term learning. The results of experiments on the mammalian hippocampus show that the number of synapses can change rapidly in cultured preparations. About 30 min after long-term potentiation has been induced, new dendritic spines appear, suggesting that new synapses are formed during LTP. Possibly the formation of new synapses can similarly be responsible for new learning.

KEY TERMS

activating system, p. 168
Alzheimer's disease, p. 170
associative learning, p. 177
autoreceptor, p. 155
carbon monoxide (CO),
   p. 164
chemical synapse, p. 153
cholinergic neuron, p. 167
dopamine (DA), p. 153
electrical synapse, p. 153
epinephrine (EP), p. 150
gamma-aminobutyric acid
   (GABA), p. 162
glutamate, p. 162
G protein, p. 164
habituation, p. 173
ionotropic receptor, p. 164
learning, p. 172

long-term potentiation
   (LTP), p. 177
metabotropic receptor,
   p. 164
neuropeptides, p. 167
neuroplasticity, p. 173
neurotransmitter, p. 150
nicotinic ACh receptor
   (nAChr), p. 167
nitric oxide (NO), p. 164
noradrenergic neuron,
   p. 172
norepinephrine (NE),
   p. 150
obsessive-compulsive
   disorder (OCD), p. 172
postsynaptic membrane,
   p. 153

presynaptic membrane,
   p. 153
quantum (pl. quanta),
   p. 155
rate-limiting factor, p. 162
reuptake, p. 156
schizophrenia, p. 170
second messenger, p. 166
sensitization, p. 175
small-molecule
   transmitters, p. 156
storage granule, p. 153
synaptic cleft, p. 153
synaptic vesicle, p. 153
transmitter-activated
   receptor, p. 155
transporter, p. 153

REVIEW QUESTIONS

1. Explain how neurotransmitters are synthesized, stored, released, and broken down.

2. How many kinds of neurotransmitters are there? Describe the problem in proving that a chemical found in a neuron is a neurotransmitter.

3. What are the two main kinds of transmitter-activated receptors and how do they differ in function?

4. Choose a neurotransmitter-activating system and describe its organization.

5. Which mechanisms are the same and which are different in the various kinds of learning discussed in this chapter?

FOR FURTHER THOUGHT

Speculate about how the origins of synaptic systems in the brain parallel the evolution of species. Why are such potential relations important?

RECOMMENDED READING

Cooper, J. R., Bloom, F. E., & Roth, R. H. (2002). *The biochemical basis of neuropharmacology.* New York: Oxford University Press. This readable and up-to-date account of the chemical systems in the brain is a good reference. The book describes the various kinds of brain neurotransmitters and the kinds of synapses and chemical systems in which they are found.

How Does the Brain Develop and Adapt?

Left: **Oliver Meckes/Ottawa/Photo Researchers.** *Middle:* **Photodisc.**
Right: **R. E. Steiner/Photo Researchers.**

Metamorphosis

A fertilized monarch butterfly egg first develops through a larval stage to begin life as a caterpillar. After a time, the caterpillar spins itself a cocoon. Inside, as a seemingly inert pupa, it undergoes a transformation, emerging from the cocoon as an adult butterfly. These rigidly demarked stages of development, collectively called *metamorphosis,* are noted on the accompanying sketch.

Consider how formidable metamorphosis is. The developing larva fashions a caterpillar's body, including a nervous system that produces crawly, caterpillar-like movements and controls a feeding apparatus designed for munching leaves. During metamorphosis, this original nervous system is reconstructed to control the flight, feeding, and reproductive behaviors of a butterfly.

The addition of flying is remarkable because this behavior requires entirely different muscles from those used in crawling. And where the caterpillar's main challenge is to find food as it inches slowly around in a limited area, adult monarch butterflies fly hundreds to thousands of miles in their annual migration and must navigate to a specific geographical location. A caterpillar would seem to need a major brain overhaul to control the completely reconfigured body and new behaviors that go with being a butterfly.

We humans do not metamorphose into a different life form in the course of our development, but we do "morph" through a variety of stages nonetheless. Like the monarch, we begin life as a fertilized egg that develops a body and a nervous system. When we are born, however, we are not able to fend for ourselves. Human offspring are virtually helpless for an extended time after birth. The behavioral demands on the brain of a newborn include relatively simple actions such as searching for a nipple from which to feed and recognizing it and signaling hunger or discomfort to caregivers by crying out.

Soon a human infant develops a variety of new behaviors such as crawling and, later, walking, eating solid foods, using tools, and learning a language. At school age, the child's brain becomes able to formulate increasingly complex ideas, solve challenging problems, and remember large quantities of information. Not a metamorphosis but clearly a transformation.

Brain maturation does not end at college graduation but continues well into the 20s. As the adult brain begins to age, it starts to lose cells and grows fewer new ones. Eventually the cumulative loss forces the middle-aged brain to reconfigure some of its parts to forestall the effects of aging.

In old age, the progressive loss of neurons and connections can be delayed, or even prevented, by keeping the brain active. If new connections are being formed by life-long learning and cognitive stimulation, there is a reduction in synaptic loss—a "use it or lose it" scenario. In fact, even if neurons are lost in aging, at least some neuron loss may be compensated by increasing synapses on the remaining neurons.

Brain development, then, is lifelong, a continuous process central to human functioning. Changes in the brain allow us to adapt to the environment throughout our life cycle. Behavioral development depends on brain development.

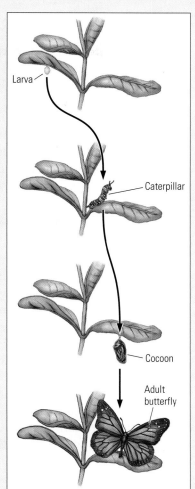

Larva

Caterpillar

Cocoon

Adult butterfly

H ow did the brain evolve from a small and simple organ into a large and highly complex one? When we consider the many kinds of neurons and glia located in specific nuclei, cortical layers, and so on, we wonder, How is this complicated architecture accomplished? Considering how many influences on brain development there are, how do the vast majority of people end up normal?

PERSPECTIVES ON BRAIN DEVELOPMENT

We can shed light on nervous system development by viewing its architecture from different vantage points—*structural, functional,* and *environmental.* In this chapter, we consider the neurobiology of development first, explore the behavioral correlates of developing brain functions next, and then explore how experiences and environments influence neuroplasticity over the life span.

To understand how scientists go about studying the interconnected processes of brain and behavioral development, think about all the architectural parallels between how the brain is constructed and how a house is built.

Mr. Higgins Builds a House

Mr. Higgins finds a picture of his dream house in a magazine and decides to build it himself. He orders a blueprint that outlines the structure so that everyone who works on its construction is building the same house. Mr. Higgins quickly discovers that houses, like brains, go through several stages of development.

The construction phase begins with the laying of a concrete foundation. At this point, however, Mr. Higgins starts to realize that the blueprint is not as detailed as it first appeared. It specifies where the walls, pipes, and electrical outlets will be, but it does not always say exactly what materials to use where. Thus, the choice of a particular kind of plywood or a particular type of nail or screw is often more or less random within limits. Similarly, the blueprint specifies connections between certain circuits in the power box and certain fixtures or outlets, but it does not detail the precise route that the connecting wires should take.

Mr. Higgins also finds that the blueprint does not specify the precise order in which tasks should be done. He knows that the foundation has to be finished first, the subfloor next, and the walls framed after that. But what comes then is largely left to his discretion.

Given the number of options open to him, Mr. Higgins realizes that his home will undoubtedly be unique, different from anyone else's conception of the blueprint. He also discovers that outside events can influence how his house will turn out. A severe storm may cause damage or delay the process. Changes in the quality of construction materials will change the quality of the building, for better or worse.

Neuropsychologists recognize much the same process at work in "building" a brain. Like a house, a brain is constructed in levels, each one with a different function (**Figure 6-1**). Whereas house plans are drawn in the form of a blueprint, the plans for a brain are encoded in genes.

As Mr. Higgins learned, architects do not specify every detail in a blueprint; nor do genes include every instruction for how a brain is assembled and wired. The brain is just too complex to be encoded entirely and precisely in genes. For this reason, the fate of billions of brain cells is left partly open, especially in regard to the massive undertaking of forming appropriate connections between cells.

If the structure and fate of each brain cell are not specified in advance, what controls brain development? Many factors are at work, including special molecules, such

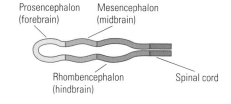

Prosencephalon (forebrain)   Mesencephalon (midbrain)

Rhombencephalon (hindbrain)   Spinal cord

Figure 6-1

Three-Chambered Architecture Recall from Figure 2-14 that the human brain evolved from the expansion of the three-chambered vertebrate nervous system shown here—hindbrain, midbrain, forebrain—to a five-chambered mammalian brain.

as hormones. Like house building, brain development is influenced by events in the environment in the construction phase and by the quality of the materials used.

Experiences both in the womb and after birth can change the way in which the brain develops. Similarly, if the brain is injured or affected by poisons or drugs, brain development may be compromised because the building materials are compromised. We return to enviornmental influences later, after examining the major stages in brain development and the interconnected processes of brain and behavioral development.

Linking Brain and Behavioral Development

Brain and behavior develop apace. Scientists thus reason that these two lines of development are closely linked. Events that alter behavioral development should similarly alter the brain's structural development and vice versa.

As the brain develops, neurons become more and more intricately connected, and these increasingly complex interconnections underlie increasingly complex behavior. These observations enable neuroscientists to study the relation between brain and behavioral development from three different perspectives:

1. Structural development can be studied and correlated with the emergence of behavior.
2. Behavioral development can be analyzed and predictions can be made about what underlying circuitry must be emerging.
3. Factors that influence both brain structure and behavioral development, such as language or injury, can be studied.

PREDICTING BEHAVIOR FROM BRAIN STRUCTURE

We can look at the structural development of the nervous system and correlate it with the emergence of specific behaviors. For example, we can link the development of certain brain structures to motor development of, say, grasping or crawling in infants. As brain structures mature, their functions emerge and develop, manifested in behaviors that we can observe.

Neural structures that develop quickly—the visual system, for instance—exhibit their functions sooner than structures that develop more slowly, as do those for speech. Because the human brain continues to develop well past adolescence, you should not be surprised that some abilities emerge or mature rather late. Certain cognitive behaviors controlled by the frontal lobes, for example, are among the last to develop.

Perhaps the best example is the ability to understand the nuances of social interaction, which is a function of the frontal lobes. One way to test a person's understanding of social interaction is illustrated in **Figure 6-2**. The person looks at a cartoon scene and is asked to mimic the facial expression appropriate for the face that is blank.

This ability does not emerge until midadolescence, and so adults have no difficulty with this task, but children are very poor at producing the correct expression. Not that children have trouble *producing* facial expressions; they do so spontaneously at a very early age. What they lack is an adultlike ability to *interpret* expressions, because brain structures that play an important role in this ability are late to mature. Children therefore may make social gaffes and are often unable to grasp all the nuances of a social situation or interaction.

Behaviors that seem simple to us adults, such as a wink or a flirtatious look, are incomprehensible to children. Children, then, are not miniature adults who

Figure 6-2

Testing Social Development Until midadolescence, the nuances of social perception present children with great difficulty. In this test, the task is to mimic the facial expression that is socially appropriate for the blank face in the drawing. Adapted from "Developmental Changes in the Recognition and Comprehensional Expression: Implications for Frontal Lobe Function," by B. Kolb, B. Wilson, and L. Taylor, 1992, *Brain and Cognition,* 20, p. 77.

simply need to learn the "rules" of adult behavior. The brain of a child is very different from that of an adult, and the brains of children at different ages are really not comparable either.

CORRELATING BRAIN STRUCTURE AND BEHAVIOR

We can turn our sequence of observations around, scrutinizing behavior for the emergence of new abilities, and then inferring underlying neural maturation. For example, as language emerges in the young child, we expect to find corresponding changes in neural structures that control language. In fact, such changes are what neuroscientists do find.

At birth, children do not speak, and even extensive speech training would not enable them to do so. The neural structures that control speech are not yet mature enough. As language emerges, we can conclude that the speech-related structures in the brain are undergoing the necessary maturation.

The same reasoning can be applied to frontal-lobe development. As frontal-lobe structures mature through adolescence and into early adulthood, we look for related changes in behavior, but we can also do the reverse: because we observe new abilities emerging in the teenage years and even later, we infer that they must be controlled by late-maturing neural structures and connections.

INFLUENCES ON BRAIN AND BEHAVIOR

The third way to study interrelations between brain and behavioral development is to identify and study factors that influence both. From this perspective, the mere emergence of a certain fully developed brain structure is not enough; we must also know the events that shape how that structure functions and produces certain kinds of behaviors. Some of the events that influence brain function are sensory experience, injuries, and the actions of hormones and genes.

Logically, if behavior is influenced by one of these factors, then structures in the brain that are changed by that factor are responsible for the behavioral outcomes. For example, we might study how the abnormal secretion of a hormone affects both a certain brain structure and a certain behavior. We can then infer that, because the observed behavioral abnormality results from the abnormal functioning of the brain structure, that structure must normally play some role in controlling the behavior.

In Review

Brain development is variable and is influenced by an interaction of the genetic blueprint and the pre- and postnatal experiences that the developing brain encounters. Development can be approached from three different perspectives: structural brain development correlated with the emergence of behavior, behavioral development analyzed to predict what underlying neural circuitry must be emerging, and external and internal influences factored into brain and behavioral development. In this last approach, the idea is that events that alter behavioral development, such as an injury to the brain or fluctuating hormone levels, should similarly alter structural development.

Neural plate. Thickened region of the ectodermal layer that gives rise to the neural tube.

Neural tube. Structure in the early stage of brain development from which the brain and spinal cord develop.

NEUROBIOLOGY OF DEVELOPMENT

Some 2000 years ago, the Roman philosopher Seneca proposed that a human embryo is an adult in miniature, and thus the task of development is simply to grow bigger. This idea, known as *preformation,* was so appealing that it was widely believed for centuries to be true. Even with the development of the microscope, the appeal of preformation proved so strong that biologists claimed to see microscopic horses in horse semen.

By the middle of the nineteenth century, the idea of preformation began to wane as people realized that embryos look nothing like the adults that they become. In fact, it was obvious that the embryos of different species more closely resemble one another than their respective parents. **Figure 6-3** shows the striking similarity in the early embryos of species as diverse as salamanders, chickens, and humans.

Early in development, all vertebrate species have a similar-looking primitive head, a region with bumps or folds, and all possess a tail. Only as an embryo develops does it acquire the distinctive characteristics of its species. The similarity of young embryos is so great that many nineteenth-century biologists saw it as evidence for Darwin's view that all vertebrates arose from a common ancestor millions of years ago.

Although the embryonic nervous systems are not shown in Figure 6-3, they are as similar structurally as their bodies. **Figure 6-4** details the three-chambered brain of a young vertebrate embryo: forebrain, midbrain, and hindbrain. The remaining neural tube forms the spinal cord. How do these three regions develop? We can trace the events as the embryo matures.

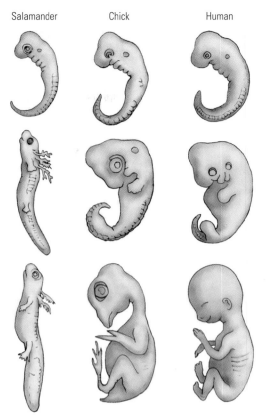

Salamander   Chick   Human

Figure 6-3

Embryos and Evolution
The physical similarity of embryos of different species is striking in the earliest stages of development, as these salamander, chick, and human embryos show. This similarity led to the conclusion that embryos are not simply miniature versions of adults.

Gross Development of the Human Nervous System

When an egg is fertilized by a sperm, the resulting human zygote consists of just a single cell. But this cell soon begins to divide, and by the 15th day, the emerging embryo resembles a fried egg, as shown in **Figure 6-5**. It is made of several sheets of cells with a raised area in the middle called the *embryonic disc*, which is essentially the primitive body.

By day 21, 3 weeks after conception, primitive neural tissue, known as the **neural plate,** occupies part of the outermost layer of embryonic cells. The neural plate first folds to form the *neural groove,* as detailed in **Figure 6-6**. The neural groove then curls to form the **neural tube,** much as a flat sheet of paper can be curled to make a cylinder.

Prenatal Stages
Zygote = fertilization to 2 weeks
Embryo = 2 to 8 weeks
Fetus = 9 weeks to birth

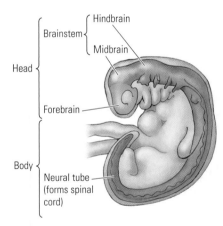

Head { Brainstem { Hindbrain / Midbrain } Forebrain

Body { Neural tube (forms spinal cord)

Figure 6-4

Basic Vertebrate Nervous System
Forebrain, midbrain, and hindbrain are visible in the human embryo at about 28 days, as is the remaining neural tube, which will form the spinal cord.

Day 1: Fertilization   **Day 2: Division**   **Day 15**

      Embryonic disc

Figure 6-5

From Fertilization to Embryo   Development begins at fertilization (day 1), with the formation of the zygote. On day 2, the zygote begins to divide. On day 15, the raised embryonic disk begins to form. Adapted from *The Developing Human: Clinically Oriented Embryology* (4th ed., p. 61), by K. L. Moore, 1988, Philadelphia: Saunders.

Figure 6-6

Neural Tube Forms   A long depression, the neural groove, first forms in the neural plate. By day 21, the primitive brain and neural groove are visible. On day 23, the neural tube is forming as the neural plate collapses inward along the length of the dorsal surface of the embryo. The embryo is shown in a photograph at 24 days.

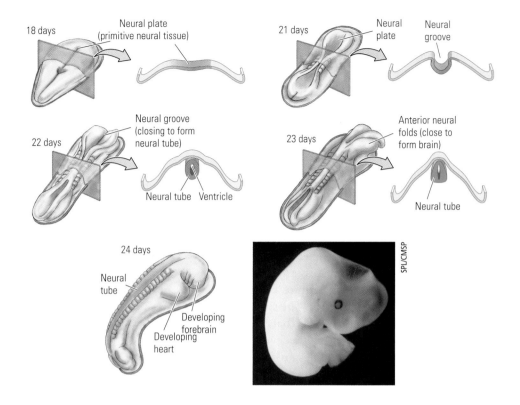

○ Visit the *Brain and Behavior* Web site (**www.worthpublishers.com/kolb**) and go to the Chapter 6 Web links to view images of human embryos at various stages of development.

Figure 6-7

Neural-Tube Development   Scanning electron micrographs show the neural tube closing in a mouse embryo.
Reproduced with the permission of Dr. R. E. Poelman, Laboratory of Anatomy, University of Leyden.

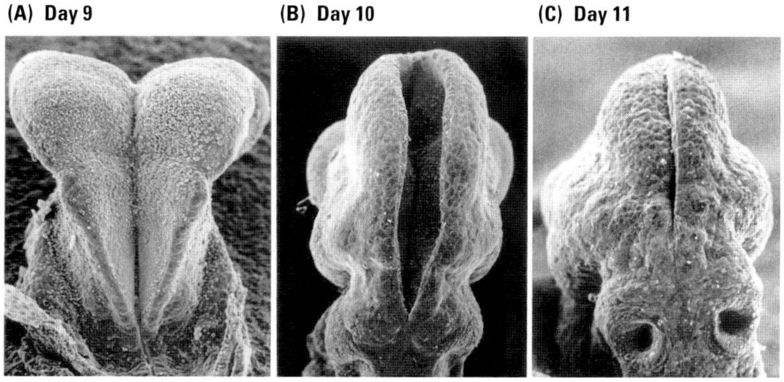

(A) Day 9   **(B) Day 10**   **(C) Day 11**

Micrographs of the neural tube closing in a mouse embryo can be seen in **Figure 6-7**. The cells that form the neural tube can be thought of as the "nursery" for the rest of the nervous system. The open region in the center of the tube remains open and matures into the brain's ventricles and the spinal canal.

The body and the nervous system change rapidly in the next 3 weeks of development. By 7 weeks (49 days), the embryo begins to resemble a miniature person. **Figure 6-8** shows that the brain looks distinctly human by about 100 days after conception, but it does not begin to form gyri and sulci until about 7 months. By the end of the 9th month, the fetal brain has the gross appearance of the adult human brain, even though its cellular structure is different.

Another developmental process, shown in **Figure 6-9**, is sexual differentiation. Although the genitals begin to form in the 7th week after conception, they appear identical in the two sexes at this early stage. There is not yet any *sexual dimorphism*, or structural difference between the sexes. Then, about 60 days after conception, male and female genitals start to become distinguishable.

What does sexual differentiation have to do with brain development? The answer is hormonal. Sexual differentiation is stimulated by the presence of the hormone testosterone in male embryos and by its absence in female embryos. Testosterone changes the genetic activity of certain cells, most obviously those that form the genitals, but neural cells also respond to this hormone, and so certain regions of the embryonic brain also may begin to show sexual dimorphism, beginning about 60 days after conception.

Prenatal exposure to gonadal hormones acts to shape male and female brains differently because these hormones activate different genes in the neurons of the two sexes. As we shall see, experience affects male and female brains differently; therefore genes and experience are shaping the brain very early in life.

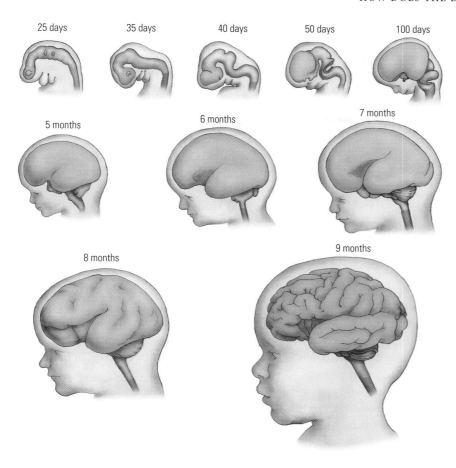

Figure 6-8

Prenatal Brain Development The developing human brain undergoes a series of embryonic and fetal stages. You can identify the various nervous system parts by color (review Figure 6-4) as they develop in the course of gestation. Adapted from "The Development of the Brain," by W. M. Cowan, 1979, *Scientific American, 241*(3), p. 116.

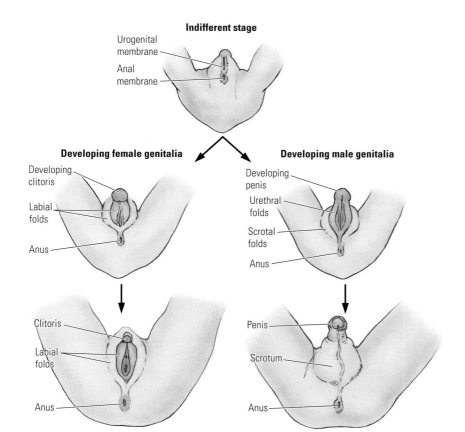

Figure 6-9

Sexual Differentiation in the Human Infant Early in development (indifferent stage), male and female human embryos are identical. In the absence of testosterone, the female structure emerges (*left*). In response to testosterone, the genitalia begin to develop into the male structure at about 60 days (*right*). Parallel changes take place in the embryonic brain in response to the absence or presence of testosterone.

Neural stem cell. A self-renewing, multipotential cell that gives rise to any of the different types of neurons and glia in the nervous system.

Ventricular zone. Lining of neural stem cells surrounding the ventricles in adults.

Progenitor cell. Precursor cell derived from a stem cell; it migrates and produces a neuron or a glial cell.

Neuroblast. Product of a progenitor cell that gives rise to any of the different types of neurons.

Glioblast. Product of a progenitor cell that gives rise to different types of glial cells.

Origins of Neurons and Glia

The presence of **neural stem cells** lining the neural tube, the nursery for the brain, has only recently been confirmed in adults. The stem-cell layer is identified as a region, from two to three cells thick, immediately adjacent to the ependymal lining of the lateral ventricles (see a review by Morshead & van der Kooy, 2004).

A stem cell has an extensive capacity for self-renewal. It divides and produces two stem cells, both of which can divide again. In adulthood, one stem cell dies after division, leaving a constant number of dividing stem cells. In an adult, the neural stem cells line the ventricles and thus form what is called the **ventricular zone.**

If lining the ventricles were all that stem cells did throughout the decades of a human life, they would seem like odd kinds of cells to possess. But stem cells have a function beyond self-renewal: they give rise to so-called **progenitor cells** (precursor cells). These progenitor cells also can divide and, as shown in **Figure 6-10**, they eventually produce nondividing cells known as **neuroblasts** and **glioblasts.** In turn, neuroblasts and glioblasts mature into neurons and glia. Neural stem cells, then, give rise to all the many specialized cell types in the central nervous system.

Sam Weiss and his colleagues (1996) discovered that stem cells remain capable of producing neurons and glia not just into early adulthood but even in an aging brain. This important discovery implies that neurons that die in an adult brain should be replaceable. But neuroscientists do not yet know how to instruct stem cells to carry out this replacement process.

One possibility is to make use of signals that the brain normally uses to control stem-cell production in the adult brain. For example, when female mice are pregnant, the level of the neuropeptide prolactin increases, and this increase stimulates the brain to produce more neurons (Shingo et al., 2003). Perhaps these naturally occurring hormonal signals will provide a way to replace lost neurons in the injured brain.

An important question in the study of brain development is how undifferentiated cells are stimulated to form stem cells, progenitor cells, neuro- and glioblasts, and finally neurons and glia. In other words, how does a stem cell "know" to become a neuron rather than a skin cell? Recall from Chapter 3 that each human cell has 23 chromosome pairs containing the approximately 20,000 genes of the human genome. In each cell, certain genes are "turned on" by a signal, and those genes then produce a particular cell type.

"Turned on" means that a formerly dormant gene becomes activated, which results in the cell making a specific protein. You can easily imagine that certain proteins are needed to produce skin cells, whereas other proteins are needed for neurons. The specific signals for turning on genes are largely unknown, but these signals are probably chemical.

Thus, the chemical environment of a cell in the brain is different from that of a cell that forms skin, and so different genes in these cells are activated, producing different proteins and different cell types. The different chemical environments needed to trigger this cellular differentiation could be caused by the activity of other neighboring cells or by chemicals, such as hormones, that are transported in the bloodstream.

You can see that the differentiation of stem cells into neurons must require a series of signals and the

Figure 6-10

Origin of Brain Cells Cells in the brain begin as multipotential stem cells, which develop into precursor cells, which produce blasts, which finally develop into specialized neurons or glia.

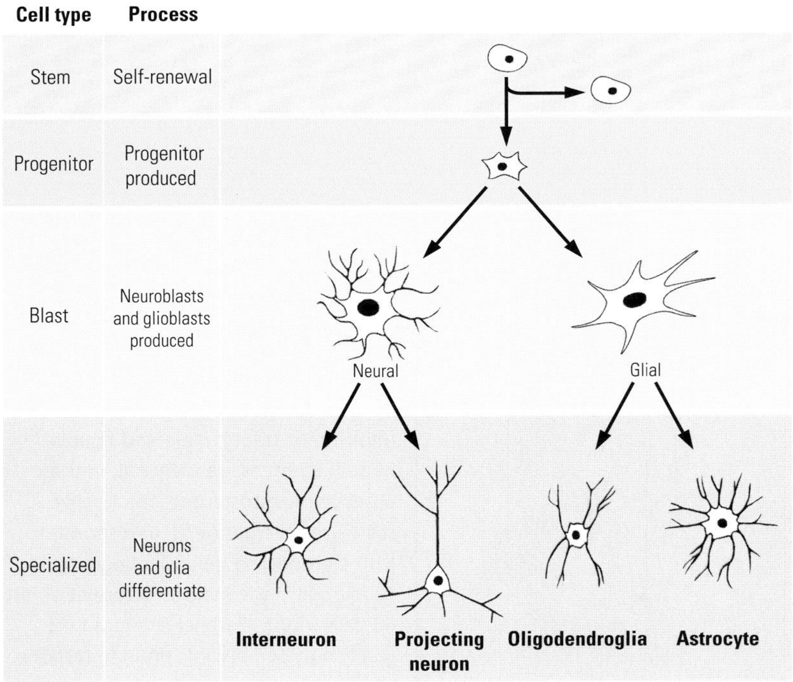

Cell type	Process
Stem	Self-renewal
Progenitor	Progenitor produced
Blast	Neuroblasts and glioblasts produced
Specialized	Neurons and glia differentiate

Neural

Glial

Interneuron **Projecting neuron** **Oligodendroglia** **Astrocyte**

resulting activation of genes. A chemical signal must induce the stem cells to produce progenitor cells, and then another chemical signal must induce the progenitor cells to produce either neuroblasts or glioblasts. Finally, a chemical signal, or perhaps even a set of signals, must induce the genes to make a particular type of neuron.

One class of compounds that signal cells to develop in particular ways are called **neurotrophic factors.** By removing stem cells from the brain of an animal and placing those cells in solutions that keep them alive, researchers can study how neurotrophic factors function. When one compound, known as *epidermal growth factor* (EGF), is added to the cell culture, it stimulates stem cells to produce progenitor cells. Another compound, *basic fibroblast growth factor* (bFGF), stimulates progenitor cells to produce neuroblasts.

At this point, the destiny of a given neuroblast is not predetermined. The blast can become any type of neuron if it receives the right chemical signal. The body relies on a "general-purpose neuron" that, when exposed to certain neurotrophic factors, matures into the specific type of cell that the nervous system requires in a particular location.

This flexibility makes brain development simpler than it would be if each different type of cell, as well as the number of cells of each type, had to be precisely specified in an organism's genes. In the same way, building a house from "all purpose" two-by-fours that can be cut to any length as needed is easier than specifying in a blueprint a precise number of precut pieces of lumber that can be used only in a certain location.

Neurotrophic factor. A chemical compound that acts to support growth and differentiation in developing neurons and may act to keep certain neurons alive in adulthood.

⊚ For more information on development of the brain and nervous system, as well as their effect on behavior, visit the Chapter 6 Web links on the *Brain and Behavior* Web site (**www.worth publishers.com/kolb**).

Growth and Development of Neurons

In human brains, approximately 10 billion (10^{10}) cells are needed to form just the cortex that blankets a single hemisphere. To produce such a large number of cells, about 250,000 neurons must be born per minute at the peak of prenatal brain development. But, as Table 6-1 shows, this rapid formation of neurons and glia is just the first step in the growth of a brain. These cells must travel to their correct locations (a process called *migration*), they must differentiate into the right type of neuron or glial cell (see Figure 6-10), and the neurons must grow dendrites and axons and subsequently form synapses.

Recall that the brain must also prune back unnecessary cells and connections, sculpting itself according to the experiences and needs of the particular person. We consider each of these stages in brain development next, focusing on the development of the cerebral cortex, because more is known about cortical development than about the development of any other area of the human brain. However, the principles derived from our examination of the cortex apply to neural growth and development in other brain regions as well.

Table 6-1	Stages of Brain Development
1. Cell birth (neurogenesis; gliogenesis)	
2. Cell migration	
3. Cell differentiation	
4. Cell maturation (dendrite and axon growth)	
5. Synaptogenesis (formation of synapses)	
6. Cell death and synaptic pruning	
7. Myelogenesis (formation of myelin)	

NEURAL GENERATION, MIGRATION, AND DIFFERENTIATION

In humans, as in other vertebrates, the brain begins as part of the neural tube, the part that contains the cells from which the brain will form. **Figure 6-11** shows that the generation of the cells that will eventually form the cortex begins about 7 weeks after conception and is largely complete by 20 weeks. In other words, *neurogenesis* (the process of forming neurons) is largely finished after about 5 months of gestation, approximately the time at which prematurely born infants have some chance of surviving.

During the next 5 months, until just after full-term birth, the fetal brain is especially delicate and extremely vulnerable to injury, teratogens (chemicals that cause malformations), and trauma, including anoxia, as explained in "Cerebral Palsy" on page 196.

Focus on Disorders

Cerebral Palsy

We met Patsy when she took our introductory course on brain and behavior. She walked with a peculiar shuffle; her handwriting was almost illegible; and her speech was at times almost unintelligible. Patsy had cerebral palsy, and she earned an A in the course.

William Little, an English physician, first noticed in 1853 that difficult or abnormal births could lead to later motor difficulties in children. The disorder that Little described was cerebral palsy, although it has also been called Little's disease. Cerebral palsy is common worldwide, with an incidence estimated to be 1.5 in every 1000 births. Among surviving babies who weigh less than 2.5 kilograms at birth, the incidence is much higher—about 10 in every 1000.

The most common cause of cerebral palsy is birth injury, especially due to anoxia, a lack of oxygen. Anoxia may result from a defect in the placenta, the organ that allows oxygen and nutrients to pass from mother to child, or it may be caused by an entanglement of the umbilical cord during birth, which may reduce the oxygen supply to the infant. Other causes include infections, hydrocephalus, seizures, and prematurity. All produce a defect in the immature brain, either before, during, or just after birth.

Most children with cerebral palsy appear normal in the first few months of life but, as the nervous system develops, the motor disturbances become progressively more noticeable. The most common symptom, which afflicts about half of those affected, is spasticity, or exaggerated contraction of muscles when they are stretched. Not surprisingly, spasticity often interferes with other motor functions. For example, people with cerebral palsy may have an odd gait, sometimes dragging one foot.

A second common symptom is dyskinesia, involuntary extraneous movements such as tremors and uncontrollable jerky twists, called athetoid movements, which often occur in activities such as walking. A third common symptom is rigidity, or resistance to passive movement. For example, a patient's fingers may resist being moved passively by an examiner, even though the patient is able to move the fingers voluntarily. In addition to having these motor symptoms, people with cerebral palsy are at risk for retardation, although many, Patsy included, function at a high intellectual level and earn college and postgraduate degrees.

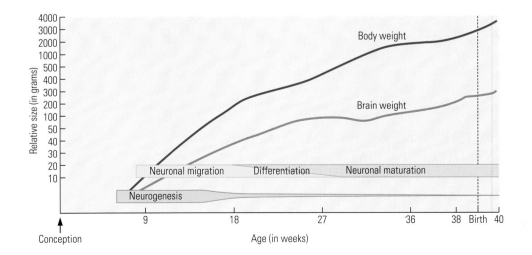

Figure 6-11

Development of the Human Cerebral Cortex The cortex begins to form about 6 weeks after conception, with neurogenesis largely complete by 20 weeks. Neural migration and cell differentiation begin at about 8 weeks and are largely complete by about 29 weeks. Neuron maturation, including axon and dendrite growth, begins at about 20 weeks and continues until well after birth. Both brain weight and body weight increase rapidly and in parallel during the prenatal period. Adapted from "Pathogenesis of Late-Acquired Leptomeningeal Heterotopias and Secondary Cortical Alterations: A Golgi Study," by M. Marin-Padilla, in *Dyslexia and Development: Neurobiological Aspects of Extraordinary Brains* (p. 66), edited by A. M. Galaburda, 1993, Cambridge, MA: Harvard University Press.

Apparently, the developing brain can more easily cope with injury earlier, during the time of neuron generation, than it can during the final stages of cell migration or cell differentiation, which is the first stage in cell maturation. One reason may be that, once neurogenesis has stopped, it is very hard to start it again. If neurogenesis is still progressing, it may be possible to make more neurons to replace injured ones or perhaps existing neurons can be allocated differently.

The same is true in supplying the lumber for a house. If some of the lumber is damaged in milling, the damaged pieces can be replaced easily. But, if the lumber is damaged in transit or on site, it is not so easy to replace, especially if the mill is closed. Replacement is even more difficult if the lumber has already been cut to size for a specific use.

Cell migration begins shortly after the first neurons are generated, but it continues for about 6 weeks after neurogenesis is complete. At this point, the process of cell differentiation, in which neuroblasts become specific types of neurons, begins. Cell differentiation is essentially complete at birth, although neuron maturation, which includes the growth of dendrites, axons, and synapses, goes on for years and, in some parts of the brain, may continue throughout adulthood.

As you learned in Chapter 2, the cortex is organized into layers that are distinctly different from one another in their cellular makeup. How is this arrangement of differentiated areas created during development? Pasko Rakic and his colleagues have been finding answers to this question for more than three decades. Apparently, the ventricular zone contains a primitive map of the cortex that predisposes cells formed in a certain ventricular region to migrate to a certain cortical location. For example, one region of the ventricular zone may produce cells destined to migrate to the visual cortex, whereas another region produces cells destined to migrate to the frontal lobes.

But how do the cells know where these different parts of the cortex are located? They follow a path made by **radial glial cells.** Each of these path-making cells has a fiber that extends from the ventricular zone to the surface of the cortex, as illustrated in **Figure 6-12A**. The close-up view in Figure 6-12B shows that neural cells from a given region of the ventricular zone need only follow the glial road and they will end up in the right location.

The advantage of this system is that, as the brain grows, the glial fibers stretch but they still go to the same place. Figure 6-12A also shows a nonradially migrating cell that is moving perpendicularly to the radial glial fibers. Although most cortical neurons follow the radial glial fibers, a small number appear to migrate by seeking some type of chemical signal. Researchers do not yet know why these cells function differently.

Cortical layers develop from the inside out, much like adding layers to a tennis ball. The neurons of innermost layer VI migrate to their locations first, followed by those destined for layer V, and so on, as successive waves of neurons pass earlier-arriving neurons to assume progressively more exterior positions in the cortex. The formation of the cortex is a bit like building a house from the ground up until you reach the roof. The materials needed to build higher floors must pass through lower floors to get to their destinations.

One thing that facilitates the building of a house is that each new story has a blueprint-specified dimension, such as 8 feet high. How do neurons determine how thick a cortical layer should be? This is a tough question, especially when you consider that the layers of the cortex are not all the same thickness.

Probably the answer is partly related to timing. Cells destined for a certain layer are generated at a certain time in the ventricular zone, and so they migrate together in that particular time frame. The mechanisms that govern this timing are not yet understood, however.

In addition, some local environmental signals—chemicals produced by other cells—likely influence the way in which cells form layers in the cortex. These intercellular signals progressively restrict the

Radial glial cell. Path-making cell that a migrating neuron follows to its appropriate destination.

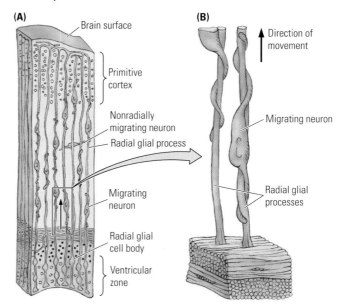

Figure 6-12

Neural Migration Neuroscientists hypothesize that the map for the cortex is represented in the ventricular zone. **(A)** Radial glial fibers extend from the ventricular zone to the cortical surface. **(B)** Neurons migrate along the radial glial fibers, which take them from the protomap in the ventricular zone to the respective region in the cortex. Adapted from "Neurons in Rhesus Monkey Cerebral Cortex: Systematic Relation Between Time of Origin and Eventual Disposition," by P. Rakic, 1974, *Science, 183,* p. 425.

(A)
Brain surface
Primitive cortex
Nonradially migrating neuron
Radial glial process
Migrating neuron
Radial glial cell body
Ventricular zone

(B)
Direction of movement
Migrating neuron
Radial glial processes

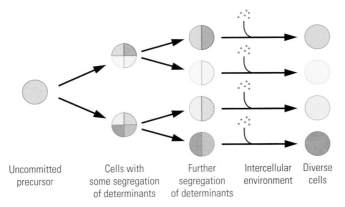

Uncommitted precursor | Cells with some segregation of determinants | Further segregation of determinants | Intercellular environment | Diverse cells

Figure 6-13

Cellular Commitment As diagrammed in Figure 6-10, precursor cells have an unlimited cell-fate potential but, as they develop, the interaction of genes, maturation, and environmental influences increasingly steer them toward a particular cell type.

◉ You can use your *Foundations of Behavioral Neuroscience* CD to review the structure of dendrites. Visit the module on neural communication and look at the overview of a neuron's structure. (See the Preface for more information about this CD.)

choice of traits that a cell can express, as illustrated in **Figure 6-13.** Thus, the emergence of distinct types of cells in the brain does not result from the unfolding of a specific genetic program. Instead, it is due to the interaction of genetic instructions, timing, and signals from other cells in the local environment.

NEURAL MATURATION

After neurons migrate to their final destinations and differentiate into specific neuron types, they begin to mature in two ways. Maturing neurons grow dendrites to provide the surface area for synapses with other cells, and they extend their axons to appropriate targets to initiate synapse formation.

Two events take place in the development of a dendrite: dendritic arborization (branching) and the growth of dendritic spines. As illustrated in **Figure 6-14,** dendrites begin as individual processes protruding from the cell body. Later, they develop increasingly complex extensions that look much like the branches of trees visible in winter; that is, they undergo arborization. The dendritic branches then begin to form spines, which are the location of most synapses on the dendrites.

Although dendritic development begins prenatally in humans, it continues for a long time after birth, as Figure 6-14 shows. Dendritic growth proceeds at a slow rate, on the order of micrometers per day. Contrast this rate with that of the development of axons, which grow on the order of a millimeter per day, about a thousand times as fast. The disparate developmental rates of axons and dendrites are important because the faster-growing axon can contact its target cell before the dendrites of that cell are completely formed. In this way, the axon may play a role in dendritic differentiation and, ultimately, in neuron function—for example, as part of the visual, motor, or language circuitry of the brain.

Axon-appropriate connections may be millimeters or even centimeters away in the developing brain, and the axon must find its way through a complex cellular terrain to make them. Axon connections present a significant engineering problem for the developing brain. Such a task could not possibly be specified in a rigid genetic program. Rather, genetic–environmental interaction is at work again as the formation of axonic connections is guided by various molecules that attract or repel the approaching axon tip.

Santiago Ramón y Cajal was the first to describe this developmental process a century ago. He called the growing tips of axons **growth cones. Figure 6-15A** shows that,

Figure 6-14

Neural Maturation In postnatal differentiation of the human cerebral cortex—shown here around Broca's area, which controls speaking—the neurons begin with simple dendritic fields that become progressively more complex until a child reaches about 2 years of age. Thus brain maturation parallels the development of a behavior—that is, the emergence of language. Adapted from *Biological Foundations of Language* (pp. 160–161), by E. Lenneberg, 1967, New York: Wiley.

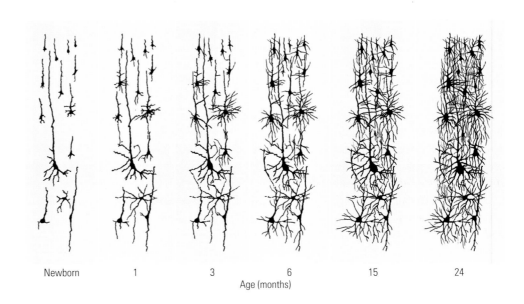

Newborn | 1 | 3 | 6 | 15 | 24
Age (months)

(A)

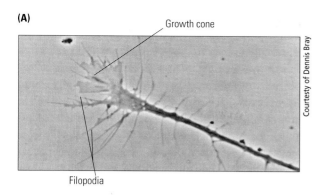

Growth cone

Filopodia

Courtesy of Dennis Bray

(B)

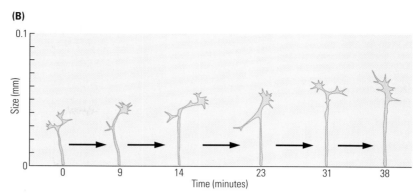

as these growth cones extend, they send out shoots, analogously to fingers reaching out to find a pen on a cluttered desk. When one shoot, known as a **filopod** (plural, *filopodia*), reaches an appropriate target, the others follow. Figure 6-15B charts the growth of a hypothetical axon tip and its growth-cone extensions over time.

Growth cones are responsive to two types of cues:

1. **Cell-adhesion molecules (CAMs)** are cell-manufactured molecules that either lie on the cell surface or are secreted into the intercellular space. Some CAMs provide a surface to which growth cones can adhere, hence their name, whereas others serve to attract or repel growth cones.

2. **Tropic molecules,** to which growth cones respond, are produced by the targets being sought by the axons. (*Tropic* molecules, which guide axons, should not be confused with the *trophic* molecules, discussed earlier, that support the growth of neurons and their processes.) Tropic molecules essentially tell growth cones to "come over here." They likely also tell other growth cones seeking different targets to "keep away."

Although Ramón y Cajal predicted tropic molecules more than 100 years ago, they have proved difficult to find. Only one group, **netrins** (from Sanskrit for "to guide"), has been identified so far. Given the enormous number of connections in the brain and the great complexity in wiring them, many other types of tropic molecules are likely to be found.

SYNAPTIC DEVELOPMENT

The number of synapses in the human cerebral cortex is staggering, on the order of 10^{14}. This huge number could not possibly be determined by a genetic program that assigns each synapse a specific location. Instead, only the general outlines of neural connections in the brain are likely to be genetically predetermined. The vast array of specific synaptic contacts is then guided into place by a variety of environmental cues and signals.

A human fetus displays simple synaptic contacts in the fifth gestational month. By the seventh gestational month, synaptic development on the deepest cortical neurons is extensive. After birth, the number of synapses increases rapidly. In the visual cortex, synaptic density almost doubles between age 2 months and age 4 months and then continues to increase until age 1 year.

CELL DEATH AND SYNAPTIC PRUNING

If you wanted to make a statue, you could start either with grains of sand and glue them together to form the desired shape or with a block of stone and chisel the unwanted pieces away. Sculptors consider the second route much easier. They start with more than they need and eliminate the excess. So does the brain, and it is the value of cell

Figure 6-15

Seeking a Path   **(A)** At the tip of this axon, nurtured in a culture, a growth cone sends out filopodia seeking specific molecules to guide the axon's growth direction. **(B)** Growth in the axon tip and its growth cones over time.

Growth cone. Growing tip of an axon.

Filopod. Process at the end of a developing axon that reaches out to search for a potential target or to sample the intercellular environment.

Cell-adhesion molecule (CAM). A chemical molecule to which specific cells can adhere, thus aiding in migration.

Tropic molecule. Signaling molecule that attracts or repels growth cones.

Netrins. The only class of tropic molecules yet isolated.

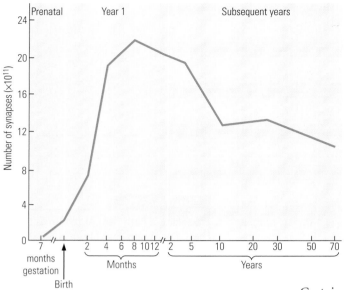

Figure 6-16

Synaptic Pruning An estimate of the synapses in the human visual cortex as a function of age shows that the total rises rapidly, peaking at about 1 year; declines until about 10 years of age; and levels off until early adulthood, when it gradually begins to drop again over the remaining life span. Adapted from "Synaptogenesis in Human Cerebral Cortex," by P. R. Huttenlocher, in *Human Behavior and the Developing Brain* (p. 142), edited by G. Dawson and K. W. Fischer, 1994, New York: Guilford Press.

Neural Darwinism. Hypothesis that the processes of cell death and synaptic pruning are, like natural selection in species, the outcome of competition among neurons for connections and metabolic resources in a neural environment.

Apoptosis. Cell death that is genetically programmed.

death and synaptic pruning. The "chisel" in the brain could be of several forms, including a genetic signal, experience, reproductive hormones, and even stress.

For example, as already stated, the number of synapses in the visual cortex increases rapidly after birth, reaches a peak at about 1 year, and begins to decline as the brain apparently prunes out unnecessary or incorrect synapses. The graph in **Figure 6-16** plots this rise and fall in synaptic density. Pasko Rakic estimated that, at the peak of synapse loss in humans, as many as 100,000 synapses may be lost per second. We can only wonder what the behavioral consequence of this rapid synaptic loss might be. It is probably no coincidence that children, especially toddlers and adolescents, seem to change moods and behaviors quickly.

How does the brain accomplish this elimination of neurons? The simplest explanation is competition, sometimes referred to as **neural Darwinism.** Charles Darwin believed that one key to evolution is the production of variation in the traits that a species possesses. Certain traits can then be selected by the environment for their favorableness in aiding survival. According to a Darwinian perspective, then, more animals are born than can survive to adulthood, and environmental pressures "weed out" the less-fit ones. Similar pressures cause neural Darwinism.

What exactly is causing this weeding out of cells in the brain? It turns out that, when neurons form synapses, they become somewhat dependent on their targets for survival. In fact, deprived of synaptic targets, they eventually die. This neuron death occurs because target cells produce neurotrophic factors, which we encountered earlier, that are absorbed by the axon terminals and function to regulate neuronal survival. Nerve growth factor (NGF), for example, is made by cortical cells and absorbed by cholinergic neurons in the basal forebrain.

If many neurons are competing for a limited amount of a neurotrophic factor, only some of those neurons can survive. The death of neurons deprived of a neurotrophic factor is different from the cell death caused by injury or disease. When neurons are deprived of a neurotrophic factor, certain genes seem to be "turned on," resulting in a message for the cell to die. This programmed process is called **apoptosis.**

Apoptosis accounts for the death of overabundant neurons, but it does not account for the pruning of synapses from cells that survive. In 1976, French neurobiologist Jean-Pierre Changeux proposed a theory for synapse loss that also is based on competition. According to Changeux, synapses persist into adulthood only if they have become members of functional neural networks. If they have not, they are eventually eliminated from the brain.

An example will help explain this mechanism of synaptic pruning. Consider neural input to the midbrain from the eyes and ears. The visual input goes to the superior colliculus, and the auditory input goes to the inferior colliculus (see Figure 2-18). Some errant axons from the auditory system will likely end up in the visual midbrain and form synapses with the same cells as those connected to axons coming from the visual pathway.

However, the auditory axons are not part of functional networks in this location. Whereas inputs from an eye are apt to be active at the same time as one another, inputs from an ear are unlikely to be active along with the visual ones. The presence of simultaneous electrical activity in a set of visually related synapses leads to the formation of a neural circuit comprising those synapses.

In contrast, the errant auditory inputs, because they are not active at the same time as the visual inputs, become unstable and are eventually eliminated. We can speculate that environmental factors such as hormones, drugs, and experience would influence the formation of active neural circuits and thus influence the processes of synapse stabilization and pruning. In fact, as you will see shortly, experience can have truly massive effects on the organization of the nervous system.

Richard Tees   Janet Werker

In addition to outright errors in synapse formation that give rise to synaptic pruning, more-subtle changes in neural circuits may trigger the same process. An instance of such a change accounts for the findings of Janet Werker and Richard Tees (1992), who studied the ability of infants to discriminate speech sounds taken from widely disparate languages, such as English, Hindi (from India), and Salish (a Native American language). Their results show that young infants can discriminate speech sounds of different languages without previous experience, but their ability to do so declines in the first year of life. One explanation of this declining ability is that synapses encoding speech sounds not normally encountered in the infant's daily environment are not active simultaneously with other speech-related synapses. As a result, they become unstable and are eliminated.

Synapse elimination is extensive. Peter Huttenlocher (1994) estimated it to be 42 percent of all synapses in the human cortex. Synapse elimination is much less extensive in smaller-brained animals, however. In the rat cortex, it is about 10 percent, and, in the cat cortex, about 30 percent. The reason for these differences may be that, the larger the brain, the more difficult it is to make precise connections and so the greater the need for excess synapses and the consequent synaptic pruning.

Synaptic pruning may also allow the brain to adapt more flexibly to environmental demands. Human cultures are probably the most diverse and complex environments with which any animal must cope. Perhaps the flexibility in cortical organization that is achieved by the mechanism of selective synaptic pruning is a necessary precondition for successful development in this kind of environment.

Synaptic pruning may also be a precursor related to different perceptions that people develop about the world. Consider, for example, the obvious differences in "Eastern" and "Western" philosophies about life, religion, and culture. Given the obvious differences to which people in the East and West are exposed as their brains develop, we can only imagine how differently their individual perceptions and cognitions may be. Considered together as a species, however, we humans are far more alike than we are different.

Glial Development

The birth of astrocytes and oligodendrocytes begins after most neurogenesis is complete and continues throughout life. As you know from Chapter 3, oligodendroglia form the myelin that surrounds axons in the spinal cord and brain. Although CNS axons can function before they are myelinated, normal adult function is attained only after myelination is complete. Consequently, myelination is a useful rough index of cerebral maturation.

In the early 1920s, Paul Flechsig noticed that myelination of the cortex begins just after birth and continues until at least 18 years of age. He also noticed that some cortical regions were myelinated by age 3 to 4 years, whereas others showed virtually no myelination at that time. **Figure 6-17** shows one of Flechsig's cortical maps with areas shaded according to earlier or later myelination. Flechsig hypothesized that the earliest-maturing areas control simple movements or sensory analyses, whereas the latest-myelinating areas control the highest mental functions.

◉ On your *Foundations* CD, you can review the myelination of axons and how it affects neural transmission. To view an animation of this process, go to the area on the conduction of the action potential in the module on neural communication.

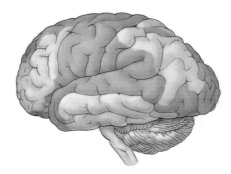

Figure 6-17

Progress of Myelination In this cortical map, based on Flechsig's research, the light-colored zones are very late to myelinate, which led Flechsig to propose that their functions are qualitatively different—specifically, more complex—from those that mature earlier.

In Review

The first neural stem cell heralds brain development in the 3-week-old human embryo. Beginning as a sheet of cells that folds to become the neural tube, nervous system formation then proceeds rapidly; by about 100 days after conception, the brain begins to take a recognizably human form. Neurons and glia develop through a series of seven stages: birth, migration, differentiation, maturation, synaptic formation, cell death, and myelination. Neurons begin to process simple information before they are completely mature, but behavioral development is constrained by the maturation of central nervous system structures and circuits. For example, although infants and children are capable of complex movements, not until myelination is complete in adolescence are adult levels of coordination and fine motor control reached.

CORRELATING BEHAVIOR WITH BRAIN DEVELOPMENT

It is reasonable to predict that, as a particular brain area matures, a person exhibits behaviors corresponding to that particular mature brain structure. The strongest advocate of this view has been Eric Lenneberg, who, in 1967, published a seminal book titled *Biological Foundations of Language*. A principal theme is that children's acquisition of language is tied to the development of critical language areas in the cerebral cortex.

This idea immediately stimulated debate about the merits of correlating brain and behavioral development. Now, some 40 years later, the relation is widely accepted, although the influence of environmental factors such as experience and learning on behavior is still considered critical. That is, psychologists believe that behaviors cannot emerge until the neural machinery for them has developed, but, when that machinery is in place, related behaviors develop quickly through stages and are shaped significantly by experience. The new behaviors then alter brain structure by the processes of neural Darwinism presented earlier.

Researchers have studied these interacting changes in the brain and behavior, especially in regard to the emergence of motor skills, language, and problem solving in children. We now explore each of these developments.

Motor Behaviors

The development of locomotion skills is easy to observe in human infants. At first, babies are unable to move about independently but, eventually, they learn to crawl and then to walk. Other motor skills develop in less obvious but no less systematic ways. For example, Tom Twitchell (1965) studied and described how the ability to reach for objects and grasp them progresses in a series of stages, illustrated in **Figure 6-18**.

Shortly after birth, infants are capable of flexing the joints of an arm in such a way that they can scoop something toward their bodies, but, newborns do not seem to direct their arm movements toward any specific thing. Then, between 1 and 3 months of age, a baby begins to orient a hand toward an object that the hand has touched and gropes to hold that object. For example, if the baby's hand touches a stick, the fingers will flex to grasp it. At this stage, however, all the fingers flex together. At this time babies also begin to make spontaneous hand and digit movements, a kind of "motor babbling" (Wallace & Whishaw, 2003).

Between 8 and 11 months, infants' grasping becomes more sophisticated as the "pincer grasp," employing the index

Figure 6-18

Development of the Grasping Response of Infants Adapted from "The Automatic Grasping Response of Infants," by T. E. Twitchell, 1965, *Neuropsychologia, 3,* p. 251.

2 months

Orients hand toward an object and gropes to hold it.

4 months

Grasps appropriately shaped object with entire hand.

10 months

Uses pincer grasp with thumb and index finger opposed.

finger and the thumb, develops. The pincer grasp is a significant development because it allows babies to make the very precise finger movements needed to manipulate small objects. What we see, then, is a sequence in the development of grasping: first scooping, then grasping with all the fingers, and then grasping by using independent finger movements.

If the development of increasingly well coordinated grasping depends on the emergence of certain neural machinery, anatomical changes in the brain should accompany the emergence of these motor behaviors. Probably many such changes take place, especially in the development of dendritic arborizations. And a correlation between myelin formation and the ability to grasp has been found (Yakovlev & Lecours, 1967). In particular, a group of axons from motor-cortex neurons become myelinated at about the same time that reaching and grasping with the whole hand develop. Another group of motor-cortex neurons, which are known to control finger movements, become myelinated at about the time that the pincer grasp develops.

We can now make a simple prediction. If specific motor-cortex neurons are essential for adultlike grasping movements to emerge, the removal of those neurons should make an adult's grasping ability similar to that of a young infant, which is in fact what happens. One of the classic symptoms of damage to the motor cortex is the permanent loss of the pincer grasp, as you will learn in Chapter 10.

Visit the Chapter 6 Web links on the *Brain and Behavior* Web site to see other examples of motor development in childhood.

Language Development

The acquisition of speech follows a gradual series of developments that has usually progressed quite far by the age of 3 or 4. According to Lenneberg, children reach certain important speech milestones in a fixed sequence and at constant chronological ages. These milestones are summarized in **Table 6-2**.

Although language skills and motor skills generally develop in parallel, the capacity for language depends on more than just the ability to make controlled movements of the mouth, lips, and tongue. Precise movements of the muscles controlling these body parts develop well before children can speak. Furthermore, even when children have sufficient motor skill to articulate most words, their vocabularies do not rocket ahead but rather progress gradually.

A small proportion of children (about 1 percent) have normal intelligence and normal motor-skill development, and yet their speech acquisition is markedly delayed. Such children may not begin to speak in phrases until after age 4, despite an apparently normal environment and the absence of any obvious neurological signs of brain damage. Because the timing of the onset of speech appears universal in the remaining 99 percent of children across all cultures, something different is likely to occur in the brain maturation of a child with late language acquisition. But it is hard to specify what that difference is.

Because the age of language onset is usually between 1 and 2 and language acquisition is largely complete by age 12, the best strategy is to consider how the cortex is different before and after these two milestones. By age 2, cell division and migration are complete in the language zones of the cerebral cortex. The major changes that take place between the ages of 2 and 12 are in the interconnections of neurons and the myelination of the speech zones.

The changes in dendritic complexity in these areas are among the most impressive in the brain. Recall from Figure 6-14 that the axons and dendrites of the speech zone called Broca's area are simple at birth but grow dramatically more dense between 15 and 24 months of age. This neural development correlates with an equally dramatic change in language ability, given that a baby's vocabulary starts to expand rapidly at about age 2 (see Table 6-2).

We can therefore infer that language development may be constrained, at least in part, by the maturation of language areas in the cortex. Individual differences in the

Table 6-2	**Developmental Milestones for Basic Language Functions**
Approximate age	**Basic social and language functions**
Birth	Comforted by sound of human voice; most common utterances are discomfort and hunger cries
6 weeks	Responds to human voice and makes cooing and pleasure noises; cries to gain assistance
2 months	Begins to distinguish different speech sounds; cooing becomes more guttural, or "throaty"
3 months	Orients head to voices; makes a vocal response to others' speech; begins babbling, or chanting various syllabic sounds in a rhythmic fashion
4 months	Begins to vary pitch of vocalizations; imitates tones
6 months	Begins to imitate sounds made by others
9 months	Begins to convey meaning through intonation, using patterns that resemble adult intonations
12 months	Starts to develop a vocabulary; a 12-month-old may have a vocabulary of 5 to 10 words that will double in the next 6 months
24 months	Vocabulary expands rapidly and can consist of approximately 200 to 300 words; names most common everyday objects; most utterances are single words
36 months	Has vocabulary of 900 to 1000 words; 3- to 4-word simply constructed sentences (subject and verb); can follow two-step commands
4 years	Has a vocabulary of more than 1500 words; asks numerous questions; sentences become more complex
5 years	Typically has a vocabulary of approximately 1500 to 2200 words; discusses feelings; the average 5- to 7-year-old has acquired a slow but fluent ability to read; handwriting likely to be slow
6 years	Speaks with a vocabulary of about 2600 words; understands from 20,000 to 24,000 words; uses all parts of speech
Adult	Has 50,000+ word vocabulary by 12 years old

Adapted from "Development of the Child's Brain and Behavior," by B. Kolb and B. Fantie, in *Handbook of Clinical Child Neuropsychology* (2nd ed., p. 29), edited by C. R. Reynolds and E. Fletcher-Janzen, 1997, New York: Plenum.

speed of language acquisition may be accounted for by differences in this neural development. Children with early language abilities may have early maturation of the speech zones, whereas children with delayed language onset may have later speech-zone maturation.

Development of Problem-Solving Ability

The first person to try to identify discrete stages of cognitive development was Swiss psychologist Jean Piaget (1952). He realized that he could infer children's understanding of the world by observing their behavior. For example, a baby who lifts a cloth to retrieve a hidden toy is showing an understanding that objects continue to exist even when out of sight. This understanding, the concept of *object permanence*, is revealed by the behavior of the infant in the upper photographs of **Figure 6-19**.

An absence of understanding also can be seen in children's behavior, as shown by the actions of the 5-year-old girl in the lower photographs of Figure 6-19. She was shown two identical beakers with identical volumes of liquid in each and then watched

Doug Goodman/Monkmeyer

Courtesy of Don and Sandy Hockenbury

Figure 6-19

Stages of Cognitive Development
(*Top*) The infant shows that she understands object permanence—that things continue to exist when they are out of sight. (*Bottom*) This girl does not yet understand the principle of conservation of volume. Beakers with identical volumes but different shapes seem to her to hold different amounts of liquid.

as one beaker's liquid was poured into a taller, narrower beaker. When asked which beaker contained more liquid, she pointed to the taller beaker, not understanding that the amount of liquid remains constant despite the difference in appearance. Children display an understanding of this principle, the *conservation of liquid volume,* at about age 7.

By studying children engaged in such tasks, Piaget concluded that cognitive development is a continuous process. Children's strategies for exploring the world and their understanding of it are constantly changing. These changes are not simply the result of acquiring specific pieces of new knowledge. Rather, at certain points in development, fundamental changes take place in the organization of a child's strategies for learning about the world and for solving problems. With these developing strategies comes new understanding.

Piaget identified four major stages of cognitive development, which are summarized in **Table 6-3**:

▨ Stage I is the sensorimotor period, from birth to about 18 to 24 months of age. During this time, babies learn to differentiate themselves from the external world, come to realize that objects exist even when out of sight, and gain some understanding of cause-and-effect relations.

▨ Stage II, the preoperational period, extends from ages 2 to 6 years. Children gain the ability to form mental representations of things in their world and to represent those things in words and drawings.

▨ Stage III is the period of concrete operations, typically from ages 7 to 11 years. Children are able to mentally manipulate ideas about material (concrete) things such as volumes of liquid, dimensions of objects, and arithmetic problems.

▨ Stage IV, the period of formal operations, is attained sometime after age 11. Children are now able to reason in the abstract, not just in concrete terms.

If we take Piaget's stages as rough approximations of qualitative changes that take place in children's thinking as they grow older, we can ask what neural changes might

◉ Visit the Chapter 6 Web links on the *Brain and Behavior* Web site (**www.worthpublishers.com/kolb**) for more information on Piaget's stages of cognitive development.

Table 6-3	Piaget's Stages of Cognitive Development	
Typical age range	Description of stage	Developmental phenomena
Birth to 18–24 months	*Stage I: Sensorimotor* Experiences the world through senses and actions (looking, touching, mouthing)	Object permanence Stranger anxiety
About 2–6 years	*Stage II: Preoperational* Represents things with words and images but lacks logical reasoning	Pretend play Egocentrism Language development
About 7–11 years	*Stage III: Concrete operational* Thinks logically about concrete events; grasps concrete analogies and performs arithmetical operations	Conservation Mathematical transformations
About 12+ years	*Stage IV: Formal operational* Reasons abstractly	Abstract logic Potential for mature moral reasoning

underlie them. One place to look for brain changes is in the relative rate of brain growth.

After birth, brain and body do not grow uniformly but rather tend to increase in mass during irregularly occurring periods commonly called **growth spurts.** In his analysis of brain-weight-to-body-weight ratios, Herman Epstein (1979) found consistent spurts in brain growth between 3 and 10 months (accounting for an increase of 30 percent in brain weight by the age of 1½ years) as well as from the ages of 2 to 4, 6 to 8, 10 to 12, and 14 to 16+ years. The increments in brain weight were from about 5 to 10 percent in each of these 2-year periods.

Brain growth takes place without a concurrent increase in the number of neurons, and so it is most likely due to the growth of glial cells and synapses. Although synapses themselves would be unlikely to add much weight to the brain, the growth of synapses is accompanied by increased metabolic demands, which cause neurons to become larger, new blood vessels to form, and new astrocytes to be produced.

We would expect such an increase in the complexity of the cortex to generate more-complex behaviors, and so we might predict significant, perhaps qualitative, changes in cognitive function during each growth spurt. The first four brain-growth spurts identified by Epstein coincide nicely with the four main stages of cognitive development described by Piaget. Such correspondence suggests significant alterations in neural functioning with the onset of each cognitive stage.

At the same time, differences in the rate of brain development or perhaps in the rate at which specific groups of neurons mature may account for individual differences in the age at which the various cognitive advances identified by Piaget emerge. Although Piaget did not identify a fifth stage of cognitive development in later adolescence, the presence of a growth spurt then implies one.

One difficulty in linking brain-growth spurts to cognitive development is that growth spurts are superficial measures of changes taking place in the brain. We need to know at a deeper level what neural events are contributing to brain growth and just where they are taking place.

A way to find out is to observe children's attempts to solve specific problems that are diagnostic of damage to discrete brain regions in adults. If children perform a particular task poorly, then whatever brain region regulates the performance of that task in adults must not yet be mature in children. Similarly, if children can perform one task but not another, the tasks apparently require different brain structures, and these structures mature at different rates.

Bill Overman and Jocelyn Bachevalier (Overman, Bachevalier, Turner, & Peuster, 1992) used this logic to study the development of forebrain structures required for

learning and memory in young children and in monkeys. The Procedure section of **Experiment 6-1** shows the three intelligence-test items presented to their subjects. The first task was simply to learn to displace an object to obtain a food reward. When the subjects had learned this *displacement* task, they were trained in two more tasks believed to measure the functioning of the temporal lobes and the basal ganglia, respectively.

Growth spurt. Sporadic period of sudden growth that lasts for a finite time.

Bill Overman

In the *nonmatching-to-sample* task, the subjects were shown an object that they could displace to receive a food reward. After a brief (15-second) delay, two objects were presented: the first object and a novel object. The subjects then had to displace the novel object to obtain the food reward. Nonmatching to sample is thought to measure object recognition, which is a function of the temporal lobes. The subject can find the food only by recognizing the original object and *not* choosing it.

In the third task, *concurrent discrimination,* the subjects were presented with a pair of objects and had to learn that one object in that pair was always associated with a food reward, whereas the other object was never rewarded. The task was made more difficult by sequentially giving the subjects 20 different object pairs. Each day, they were presented with one trial per pair. Concurrent discrimination is thought to measure trial-and-error learning of specific object information, which is a function of the basal ganglia.

Adults easily solve both the nonmatching and the concurrent tasks but report that the concurrent task is more difficult because it requires remembering far more information. The key question developmentally is whether there is a difference in the age at which children (or monkeys) can solve these two tasks.

It turns out that children can solve the concurrent task by about 12 months of age, but not until about 18 months of age can they solve what most adults believe to be the easier nonmatching task. These results imply that the basal ganglia, the critical area for the concurrent-discrimination task, mature more quickly than the temporal lobe, which is the critical region for the nonmatching-to-sample task.

A Caution about Linking Correlation to Causation

Throughout this section, we have described research that implies that changes in the brain cause changes in behavior. Neuroscientists assert that, by looking at behavioral development and brain development in parallel, they can make some inferences regarding the causes of behavior. Bear in mind, however, that just because two things correlate (take place together) does not prove that one of them causes the other.

The correlation–causation problem raises red flags in studies of brain and behavior, because research in behavioral neuroscience, by its very nature, is often based on such correlations. Nevertheless, correlational studies, especially developmental correlational studies, have proved to be a powerful tool as sources of insight into fundamental principles of brain and behavior.

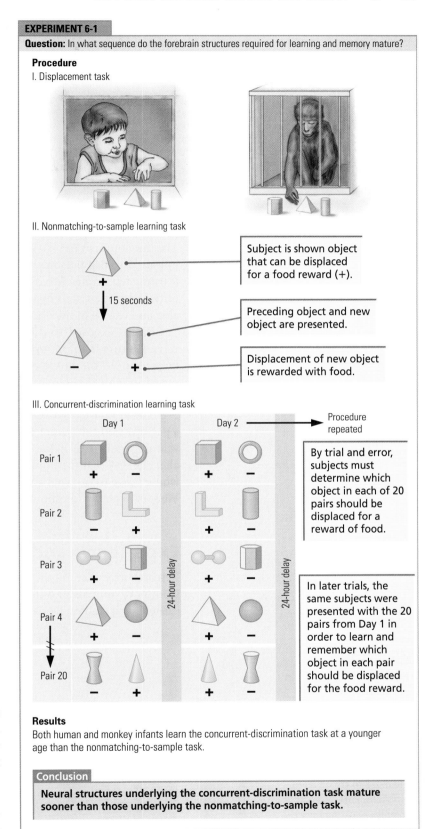

EXPERIMENT 6-1

Question: In what sequence do the forebrain structures required for learning and memory mature?

Procedure

I. Displacement task

II. Nonmatching-to-sample learning task

Subject is shown object that can be displaced for a food reward (+).

15 seconds

Preceding object and new object are presented.

Displacement of new object is rewarded with food.

III. Concurrent-discrimination learning task

Day 1   Day 2   Procedure repeated

Pair 1
Pair 2
Pair 3
Pair 4
Pair 20

24-hour delay

By trial and error, subjects must determine which object in each of 20 pairs should be displaced for a reward of food.

In later trials, the same subjects were presented with the 20 pairs from Day 1 in order to learn and remember which object in each pair should be displaced for the food reward.

Results

Both human and monkey infants learn the concurrent-discrimination task at a younger age than the nonmatching-to-sample task.

Conclusion

Neural structures underlying the concurrent-discrimination task mature sooner than those underlying the nonmatching-to-sample task.

Adapted from "Object Recognition Versus Object Discrimination: Comparison Between Human Infants and Infant Monkeys," by W. H. Overman, J. Bachevalier, M. Turner, and A. Peuster, 1992, *Behavioral Neuroscience, 106,* p. 18.

In Review

Children develop increasingly mature motor, language, and cognitive behaviors in predictable sequences. These behavioral developments correlate with neural changes in the brain, and neuroscientists infer that the two are probably related. For example, as the cortex and basal ganglia develop, different motor abilities and cognitive capacities emerge. Although correlation does not prove causation, correlational research has proved to be powerful in predicting basic relations between brain development and behavioral milestones.

BRAIN DEVELOPMENT AND THE ENVIRONMENT

The development of behaviors is shaped not only by the emergence of brain structures but also by each person's environment and experiences. Recall from the discussion of learning in Chapter 5 that neuroplasticity refers to the lifelong changes in the structure of the brain that accompany experience. Neuroplasticity suggests that the brain is pliable and can be molded into different forms, at least at the microscopic level.

Brains exposed to different environmental experiences are molded in different ways. Culture is an important aspect of the human environment, and so culture must help to mold the human brain. As noted earlier, we would therefore expect people raised in widely different cultures to acquire differences in brain structure that have lifelong effects on their behavior.

The brain is plastic in response not only to external events but also to events within a person's body, including the effects of hormones, injury, and abnormal genes. The developing brain early in life is especially responsive to these internal factors, which in turn alter the way that the brain reacts to external experiences. In this section, we explore a whole range of external and internal environmental influences on brain development. We start with the question of exactly how experience manages to alter brain structure.

Experience and Cortical Organization

Researchers can study the effects of experience on the brain and behavior by placing laboratory animals in different environments and observing the results. In one of the earliest such studies, Donald Hebb (1947) took a group of young laboratory rats home and let them grow up in his kitchen. A control group grew up in standard laboratory cages at McGill University.

Figure 6-20

Hebb-Williams Maze In this version of the maze, a rat is placed in the start box (S) and must learn to find the food in the goal box (G). Investigators can reconfigure the walls of the maze to create new problems. Rats raised in complex environments solve such mazes much more quickly than do rats raised in standard laboratory cages.

The "home rats" had many experiences that the caged rats did not, including being chased with a broom by Hebb's less-than-enthusiastic wife. Subsequently, Hebb gave both groups a rat-specific "intelligence test" that consisted of learning to solve a series of mazes, collectively known as *Hebb-Williams mazes*. A sample maze is shown in **Figure 6-20**. The home rats performed far better on these tasks than the caged rats did. Hebb therefore concluded that intelligence must be influenced by experience.

On the basis of his research, Hebb reasoned that people reared in "stimulating" environments will maximize their intellectual development, whereas people raised in "impoverished" environments will not reach their intellectual potential. Although Hebb's reasoning may seem logical, the problem lies in defining in what ways environments may be stimulating or impoverished.

People living in slums, for example, with few formal educational resources, are not in what we would normally call an enriched setting, but that does not necessarily mean that the environment offers no cognitive stimulation or challenge. To the contrary, people raised in this setting are better adapted for survival in a slum than are people raised in upper-class homes. Does this adaptability make them more intelligent in a certain way?

In contrast, slum dwellers are not likely to be well adapted for college life, which was probably closer to what Hebb had in mind when he referred to such an environment as limiting intellectual potential. Indeed, it was Hebb's logic that led to the development of preschool television programs, such as *Sesame Street,* that offer enrichment for children who would otherwise have little preschool exposure to reading.

The idea that early experience can change later behavior seems sensible enough, but we are left with the question of why experience should make such a difference. As discussed in Chapter 5, one reason is that experience changes the structure of neurons, which is especially evident in the cortex. Neurons in the brains of animals raised in complex environments, such as that shown in **Figure 6-21A**, are larger and have more synapses than do those of animals reared in barren cages. Representative neurons are compared in Figure 6-21B.

Presumably, the increased number of synapses results from increased sensory processing in a complex and stimulating environment. The brains of animals raised in complex settings also display more (and larger) astrocytes. Although complex-rearing studies do not address the effects of human culture directly, predictions about human development are easily made on the basis of their findings. We know that experience can modify the brain, and so we can predict that different experiences might modify the brain differently, which seems to be the case in language development.

Recall that exposure to different languages in infancy alters a child's subsequent ability to discriminate language-specific speech sounds. A similar process is likely to take place for music. People exposed to Western music since childhood usually find Eastern music peculiar, even nonmusical, on first encountering it when they are adults. Presumably, cells in the language- and music-analysis systems of the auditory cortex are altered by early experience and lose much of their plasticity in adulthood.

This loss of plasticity does not mean that the adult human brain becomes fixed and unchangeable, however. Doubtless the brains of adults are influenced by exposure to new environments and experiences, although probably more slowly and less extensively than the brains of children are. Findings from animal studies have shown plasticity in the adult brain. In fact, there is evidence that the brain is affected by experience well into old age, which is good news for those of us who are no longer children.

Figure 6-21

Enriched Environment, Enhanced Development **(A)** A complex housing environment for a group of about six rats. The animals have an opportunity to move about and to interact with toys that are changed weekly.
(B) Representative neurons from the parietal cortex of a laboratory-housed rat (*left*) and a complex-environment-housed rat (*right*). The neuron on the right is more complex and has about 25 percent more dendritic space for synapses.

(A)

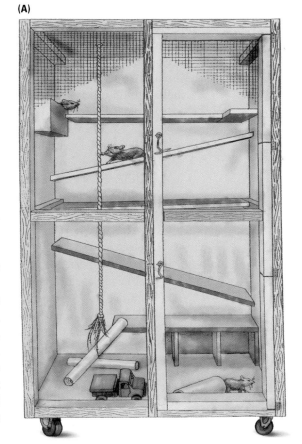

(B)

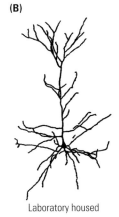

Laboratory housed

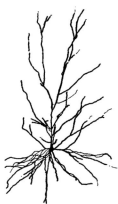

Complex-environment housed

Chemoaffinity hypothesis. Proposal that neurons or their axons and dendrites are drawn toward a signaling chemical that indicates the correct pathway.

Amblyopia. A condition in which vision in one eye is reduced as a result of disuse; usually caused by a failure of the two eyes to point in the same direction.

Experience and Neural Connectivity

If experience can influence the structure of the cerebral cortex after a person is born, can it also sculpt the brain prenatally? It can. This prenatal influence of experience is very clearly illustrated in studies of the developing visual system.

Consider the problem of connecting the eyes to the rest of the developing visual system. A simple analogy will help. Imagine that students in a large lecture hall are each viewing the front of the room (the visual field) through a small cardboard tube, such as an empty paper-towel roll. If each student looks directly ahead, he or she will see only a small bit of the visual field.

This analogy essentially illustrates how the photoreceptor cells in the eyes act. Each cell sees only a small bit of the visual field. The problem is to put all the bits together to form a complete picture. To do so, receptors (analogously to students sitting side by side) that see adjacent views must send their information to adjacent regions in the various parts of the brain's visual system, such as the midbrain. How do they accomplish this feat?

Roger Sperry (1963) suggested that specific molecules exist in different cells in the various regions of the midbrain, giving each cell a distinctive chemical identity. Each cell, in other words, has an identifiable biochemical label. This idea is called the **chemoaffinity hypothesis.** Presumably, incoming axons seek out a specific chemical, such as the tropic factors discussed earlier, and consequently land in the correct general region of the midbrain.

Many experiments have shown this process to take place prenatally as the eye and brain are developing. But the problem is that chemical affinity "directs" incoming axons only to a general location. To return to our two adjacent retinal cells, how do they now place themselves in the *precisely* correct position?

This is where postnatal experience comes in: fine-tuning of neural placement is believed to be activity dependent. Because adjacent receptors tend to be activated at the same time, they tend to form synapses on the same neurons in the midbrain, after chemoaffinity has drawn them to a general midbrain region. This process is shown in **Figure 6-22.** Neurons A and G are unlikely to be activated by the same stimulus, and so they seldom fire synchronously. Neurons A and B, in contrast, are apt to be activated by the same stimuli, as are B and C. Through this simultaneous activity over time, cells eventually line up correctly in the connections that they form.

Now consider what happens to axons coming from different eyes. Although the neural inputs from the two eyes may be active simultaneously, cells in the same eye are more likely to be active together than are cells in different eyes. The net effect is that inputs from the two eyes tend to organize themselves into neural bands, called *columns*, that represent the same region of space in each eye, as shown in **Figure 6-23.** The formation of these segregated cortical columns therefore depends on the patterns of coinciding electrical activity on the incoming axons.

If experience is abnormal—if one eye were covered during a crucial time in development, for example—then the neural connections will not be guided appropriately by experience. In fact, this is exactly what happens to a child who has a "lazy eye." Visual input from the lazy eye does not contribute to the fine-tuning of neural connections as it should, and so the details of those connections do not develop normally, much as if the eye had been covered. The resulting loss of sharpness in vision known as **amblyopia.**

The importance of coinciding electrical activity and the formation of neural columns in the brain are demonstrated beautifully in a clever experiment by Martha Constantine-Paton (Constantine-Paton & Law, 1978). She knew that, because the optic nerves of frogs are completely crossed, the optic tectum on each side has input from only one eye. She wondered what would

Figure 6-22

Neural Connectivity in the Visual System Neurons A through G project from the retina to the tectum in the midbrain. The activities of adjacent neurons (C and D, say) are more likely to coincide than are the activities of widely separated neurons such as A and G. As a result, adjacent retinal neurons are more likely to establish permanent synapses on the same tectal neurons. By using chemical signals, axons grow to the approximate location in the tectum (*top*). The connections are made more precise over time by the correlated activity (*bottom*).

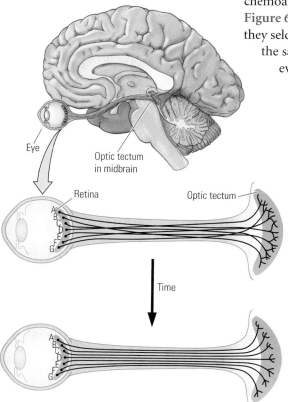

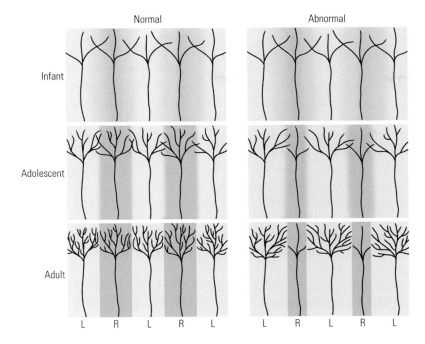

Figure 6-23

Ocular-Dominance Columns In the postnatal development of the cat brain, axons enter the cortex where they grow large terminal arborizations. In infancy, the projections of both eyes overlap (L, left eye; R, right eye). In adulthood, a nonoverlapping pattern of terminal arborizations from each of the eyes, shown at the bottom left, is normal. If one eyelid of a kitten is sewn shut during a critical week of development, the terminations from that eye retract and those from the open eye expand, as shown at the right.

(A)

From Martha Constantine-Paton and Margaret I. Law, "Eye Specific Termination Bands in Tecta of Three-Eyed Frogs," *Science*, November 10, 1978, vol. 202, pp. 639–641. ©1978 by the American Association for the Advancement of Science.

(B)

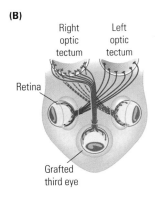

Figure 6-24

Three-Eyed Frog **(A)** A third eye was grafted prenatally into this frog. **(B)** The third eye forms connections with one optic tectum—in this case, the right. Because the connections of the third eye are shared with the frog's left eye, these two eyes compete for synaptic space, leading to the formation of alternating bands of connections.

happen if a third eye were transplanted in the embryonic frog head. This eye would probably send connections to one of the tecta, which would now have to accommodate to the new input.

This accommodation is exactly what happened, as shown in **Figure 6-24**. The third eye sent connections to one of the tecta, in competition with the ungrafted eye sending axons there. This competition resulted in the formation of one neural column for each eye. We can only imagine what this frog made of the world with its three eyes.

To summarize, the details of neural connections are modified by experience. An organism's genetic blueprint is vague in regard to exactly which connections in the brain go to exactly which neurons. Experience fine-tunes neural connectivity.

Critical Periods for Experience and Brain Development

At particular times in the course of brain development, specific experiences are especially important for development to be normal. In kittens, for example, the effect of suturing one eye closed has the most disruptive effect on cortical organization between

Critical period. Developmental "window" during which some event has a long-lasting influence on the brain; often referred to as *sensitive period*.

Imprinting. Process that predisposes an animal to form an attachment to objects or animals at a critical period in development.

30 and 60 days after birth. A time span during which brain development is most sensitive to a specific experience is often called a **critical period.**

The absence of appropriate sensory experience during a critical period may result in abnormal brain development, leading to abnormal behavior that endures even into adulthood. Richard Tees offered an analogy to help explain the concept of critical periods. He pictured the developing animal as a little train traveling past an environmental setting, perhaps the Rocky Mountains. All the windows are closed at the beginning of the journey (prenatal development), but, at particular stages of the trip, the windows in certain cars open, exposing the occupants (different parts of the brain) to the outside world. Some windows open to expose the brain to specific sounds, others to certain smells, others to particular sights, and so on.

This exposure affects the brain's development and, in the absence of any exposure through an open window, that development is severely disturbed. As the journey continues, the windows become harder to open until, finally, they are permanently closed. This closure does not mean that the brain can no longer change, but changes become much harder to induce.

Now, imagine two different trains, one headed through the Rocky Mountains and another, the Orient Express, traveling across eastern Europe. The "views" from the windows are very different, and the effects on the brain are correspondingly different. In other words, not only is the brain altered by the experiences that it has during a critical period, but the particular kinds of experiences encountered matter, too.

An extensively studied behavior that relates to the concept of critical periods is **imprinting,** a critical period during which an animal learns to restrict its social preferences to a specific class of objects, usually the members of its own species. In birds, such as chickens or waterfowl, the critical period for imprinting is often shortly after hatching. Normally, the first moving object that a young hatchling sees is a parent or sibling, and so the hatchling's brain appropriately imprints to its own species.

This appropriate imprinting is not inevitable, however. Konrad Lorenz (1970) demonstrated that, if the first animal or object that baby goslings encounter is a person, the goslings imprint to that person as though he or she were their mother. **Figure 6-25** shows a flock of goslings that imprinted to Lorenz and followed him wherever he went. This incorrect imprinting has long-term consequences for the hatchlings, which will often direct their subsequent sexual behavior toward humans.

A Barbary dove that had become imprinted to Lorenz directed its courtship toward his hand and even tried to copulate with the hand if it were held in a certain orientation.

Interestingly, birds imprint not just to humans but to inanimate objects, especially moving objects. Chickens have been induced to imprint to a milk bottle sitting on the back of a toy train moving around a track. But the brain is not entirely clueless when it comes to selecting a target to which to imprint. Given a choice, young chicks will imprint on a real chicken over any other stimulus.

Its rapid acquisition and permanent behavioral consequences suggest that, during imprinting, the brain makes a rapid change of some kind, probably a structural change, given the permanence of the new behavior. Gabriel Horn and his colleagues at Cambridge University (1985) tried

Thomas D. McAvoy/*Time* Magazine

Figure 6-25

Strength of Imprinting Ethologist Konrad Lorenz followed by goslings that imprinted on him. Because he was the first object that the geese encountered after hatching, he became their "mother."

to identify what changes in the brains of chicks during imprinting. The results of Horn's electron microscopic studies show that the synapses in a specific region of the forebrain, the IMHV, enlarge with imprinting. Imprinting, then, seems to be a good model for studying brain plasticity during development, in part because the changes are rapid, related to specific experience, and localized in the brain.

Abnormal Experience and Brain Development

If complex experiences can stimulate brain growth and influence later behavior, severely restricted experiences seem likely to retard both brain growth and behavior. To study the effects of such restrictions, Donald Hebb and his colleagues placed young Scottish terriers in the dark with as little stimulation as possible and compared their behavior with that of dogs raised in a normal environment.

When the dogs raised in the barren environment were later removed from that environment, their behavior was very unusual. They showed virtually no reaction to people or other dogs, and they appeared to have lost the sensation of pain. Even sticking pins in them produced no response. When given a dog version of the Hebb-Williams intelligence test for rats, these dogs performed very poorly and were unable to learn some tasks that dogs raised in more stimulating settings could learn easily.

The results of subsequent studies have shown that depriving young animals specifically of visual input or even of maternal contact has devastating consequences for their behavioral development and, presumably, for the development of the brain. For instance, Austin Riesen and his colleagues (Riesen, 1982) extensively studied animals raised in the dark and found that, even though the animals' eyes still work, they may be functionally blind after early visual deprivation. The absence of visual stimulation results in the atrophy of dendrites on cortical neurons, which is essentially the opposite of the results observed in the brains of animals raised in complex and stimulating environments.

Not only does the absence of specific sensory inputs adversely affect brain development, so do more-complex abnormal experiences. In the 1950s, Harry Harlow began the first systematic laboratory studies of analogous deprivation in laboratory animals. Harlow showed that infant monkeys raised without maternal (or paternal) contact have grossly abnormal intellectual and social behaviors in adulthood.

Harlow separated baby monkeys from their mothers shortly after birth and raised them in individual cages. Perhaps the most stunning effect was that, in adulthood, these animals were totally unable to establish normal relations with other animals. Unfortunately, Harlow did not analyze the brains of the deprived monkeys. We would predict atrophy of cortical neurons, especially in the frontal-lobe regions known to be related to normal social behavior.

The importance of the environment in brain development cannot be overemphasized. Children exposed to barren environments or to abuse or neglect will be at a serious disadvantage later in life. Proof can be seen in the retarded intellectual development of children raised in dreadful circumstances, as described in "Romanian Orphans" on page 214. Although it is often argued that children can succeed in school and in life *if they really want to,* it is clear that abnormal developmental experiences can alter the brain irrevocably. As a society, we cannot be complacent about the environments to which our children are exposed.

Exposure to stress is another type of early experience that appears to have a major effect on a child's later behavior. Stress can actually alter the expression of certain genes such as those related to the transport of serotonin back across the presynaptic membrane. Such alteration in serotonin activity can severely alter how the brain responds to stressful experiences later in life.

Romanian Orphans

In the 1970s, the Communist regime governing Romania outlawed all forms of birth control and abortion. The natural result was thousands of unwanted pregnancies. More than 100,000 unwanted children were placed in orphanages where the conditions were appalling.

The children were housed and clothed but had virtually no environmental stimulation. In most instances, they were confined to cots. There were few, if any, playthings and virtually no personal interaction with caregivers. Bathing often consisted of being hosed down with cold water. After the Communist government fell and the outside world was able to intervene, hundreds of these children were rescued and placed in adoptive homes throughout the world, especially in the United States, Canada, and the United Kingdom.

Several studies of the fate of these severely deprived children document their poor physical state on arrival in their new homes. They were malnourished; they had chronic respiratory and intestinal infections; and they were severely developmentally impaired. A British study by Michael Rutter and his colleagues (Rutter, 1998) found them to be two standard deviations below age-matched children for weight, height, and head circumference. Assessments with the use of

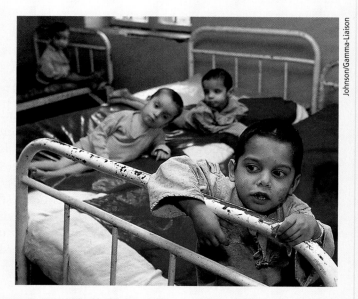

The conditions depicted in this photograph are those found in the warehousing of Romanian orphans in the 1970s and 1980s. Findings from studies on this population have shown that the lack of stimulation hampered normal brain development.

scales of motor and cognitive development showed most of the children to be in the retarded range.

The improvement in these children in the first 2 years after placement in their adoptive homes was nothing short of

Stress early in life may predispose people to develop various behavioral disorders, including depression (Sodhi & Sanders-Bush, 2004). Early stress can also leave a lasting imprint on brain structure: the amygdala is enlarged and the hippocampus is reduced in size (Salm et al., 2004). Such changes have been associated with the development of depressive and anxiety disorders (see Chapters 7 and 11).

Hormones and Brain Development

The determination of sex is largely genetic. In mammals, the Y chromosome present in males controls the process by which an undifferentiated primitive gonad develops into testes, as illustrated in Figure 6-9. The testes subsequently secrete testosterone, which stimulates the development of male reproductive organs and, in puberty, the appearance of male secondary sexual characteristics such as facial hair and the deepening of the voice.

Gonadal hormones also influence the development of neurons. Testosterone is released in males during a brief period in the course of prenatal brain development, and it subsequently acts to alter the brain, much as it alters the sex organs. This process is called **masculinization.**

Masculinization. Process by which exposure to androgens (male hormones) alters the brain, rendering it identifiably male.

spectacular. Average height and weight became nearly normal, although head circumference remained below normal. (Head circumference can be taken as a very rough measure of brain size.)

Many of the children were now in the normal range of motor and cognitive development. A significant number, however, were still considered retarded. Why were there individual differences in recovery from the past deprivation?

The key factor in predicting recovery was age at adoption. Those children adopted before 6 months of age did significantly better than those adopted later. In a Canadian study by Elenor Ames (1997), Romanian orphans who were adopted before 4 months of age had an average Stanford-Binet IQ of 98 when tested at 4½ years of age. In comparison, age-matched Canadian controls had an average IQ of 109. Findings from brain-imaging studies showed the Romanian children adopted at an older age to have smaller-than-normal brains.

Although there are no formal studies of large groups of these children as they approached adolescence, anecdotal reports of individual children who were adopted at an older age indicate continuing problems in adolescence. Some of these youngsters confronted significant learning disabilities in school, suffered from hyperactivity, and did not develop normal patterns of social interaction.

The inescapable conclusion emerging from the Romanian orphanage experience is that the human brain may be able to recover from a brief period of extreme deprivation in early infancy, but periods longer than 6 months produce significant abnormalities in brain development that cannot be overcome completely. This conclusion is supported by the case study of an American girl named Genie, who experienced severe social and experiential deprivation as well as chronic malnutrition at the hands of her psychotic father (see Curtis, 1978). She was discovered at the age of 13, after spending much of her life in a closed room, during which time she was punished for making any noise. After her rescue, she, too, showed rapid growth and cognitive development, although her language development remained severely retarded.

To summarize, studies of the Romanian orphans, of orphans from other highly impoverished settings, and of cases such as that of Genie make it clear that the developing brain requires stimulation for normal development. Although the brain may be able to catch up after a short period of deprivation, more than a few months of severe deprivation results in a smaller-than-normal brain and associated behavioral abnormalities, especially in cognitive and social skills.

Just as testosterone does not affect all body organs, it does not affect all regions of the brain. It does, however, affect many brain regions and in many different ways. For instance, it affects the number of neurons formed in certain brain areas, reduces the number of neurons that die, increases cell growth, increases or reduces dendritic branching, increases or reduces synaptic growth, and regulates the activity of synapses.

Although we have emphasized the role of testosterone in brain development, estrogen also likely influences postnatal brain development. Goldstein and colleagues found sex differences in the volume of cortical regions that are known to have differential levels of receptors for testosterone and estrogen, respectively, as diagrammed in **Figure 6-26** (Goldstein et al., 2001). Clearly, hormones alter brain development: a male brain and a female brain are not the same.

Testosterone's effects on brain development were once believed to be unimportant, because this hormone was thought to primarily influence regions of the brain related to sexual behavior but not regions of "higher" functions. We now know that this belief is false. Testosterone changes the structure of cells in many regions of the cortex, with diverse behavioral consequences that include influences on cognitive processes.

Figure 6-26

Sex Differences in Brain Volume
Cerebral areas related to sex differences in the distribution of estrogen (blue) and androgen (pink) receptors in the developing brain correspond to areas of relatively larger cerebral volumes in adult women and men. After Goldstein et al., 2001.

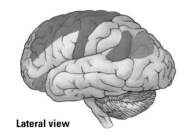

Lateral view

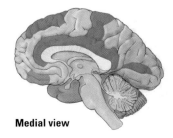

Medial view

Consider the example described earlier in Experiment 6-1. Jocelyn Bachevalier trained infant male and female monkeys in the concurrent-discrimination task, in which the subject has to learn which of two objects in a series of object pairs conceals a food reward. In addition, Bachevalier trained the animals in another task, known as *object-reversal learning.* The task is to learn that one particular object always conceals a food reward, whereas another object never does. After this pattern has been learned, the reward contingencies are reversed so that the particular object that has always been rewarded is now never rewarded, whereas the formerly unrewarded object now conceals the reward. When this new pattern has been learned, the contingencies are reversed again, and so on, for five reversals.

Bachevalier found that 2½-month-old male monkeys were superior to female monkeys on the object-reversal task, but females did better on the concurrent task. Apparently, the different brain areas required for these two tasks mature at different rates in male and female monkeys. Bachevalier later tested additional male monkeys whose testes had been removed at birth and so were no longer exposed to testosterone. These animals performed like females on the tasks, implying that testosterone was influencing the rate of brain development in areas related to certain cognitive behaviors.

Bachevalier and her colleague Bill Overman (Overman et al., 1996) then repeated the experiment, this time using as their subjects children from 15 to 30 months old. The results were the same: boys were superior at the object-reversal task and girls were superior at the concurrent task. There were no such male–female differences in performance among older children (32–55 months of age). Presumably, by this older age, the brain regions required for each task had matured in both boys and girls. At the earlier age, however, gonadal hormones seemed to be influencing the rate of maturation in certain regions of the brain, just as they had in the baby monkeys.

Although the biggest effects of gonadal hormones may be during early development, their role is by no means finished in infancy. Gonadal hormones (including both testosterone and estrogen, which is produced in large quantities by the ovaries in females) continue to influence the structure of the brain throughout an animal's life. In fact, removal of the ovaries in middle-aged laboratory rats leads to marked growth of dendrites and the production of more glial cells in the cortex. This finding of widespread neural change in the cortex associated with loss of estrogen has implications for the treatment of postmenopausal women.

Gonadal hormones also affect how the brain responds to events in the environment. For instance, among rats housed in complex environments, males show more dendritic growth in neurons of the visual cortex than do females (see Juraska, 1990). In contrast, females housed in this setting show more dendritic growth in the hippocampus than do males. Apparently, the same experience can affect the male and female brain differently owing to the mediating influence of gonadal hormones.

This finding means that, as females and males develop, their brains continue to become more and more different from each other, much like coming to a fork in a road. Once having chosen to go down one path, your direction of travel is forever changed as the roads diverge and become increasingly farther apart.

To summarize, gonadal hormones alter the basic development of neurons, shape the nature of experience-dependent changes in the brain, and influence the structure of neurons throughout our lifetimes. These neural effects of sex hormones need to be considered by those who believe that behavioral differences between males and females are solely the result of environmental experiences.

In part, it is true that environmental factors exert a major influence. But one reason that they do may be that male and female brains are different to start with, and even the same events, when experienced by structurally different brains, may lead to different effects on the brain. In our view, the important task is not to deny the presence of sex

Hormones and the Range of a Behavior

Focus on New Research

Songbirds such as finches have an especially interesting brain dimorphism (two different forms) related to singing. Males sing and females do not. This behavioral sex difference is directly related to a neural birdsong circuit that is present in males but not in females.

Robert Agate and his colleagues (2003) studied the brain of a rare strain of zebra finch, a gynandromorph that exhibits physical characteristics of both sexes, as shown in the accompanying photograph. Genetic analysis shows that cells on one half of the brain and body are genetically female and cells on the other half are genetically male.

Because both sides of the bird body and brain were exposed to the same hormones in the bloodstream during prenatal development, the effect of male and female genes on the birdsong circuit can be examined to determine how the

Robert Agate

This zebra finch is a rare gynandromph, as can be seen by the female plumage on one side of the body and the male plumage on the other side.

genes and hormones might interact. Two hypotheses result:

1. If the sex difference in the birdsong circuit were totally related to the presence of hormones prenatally, then both sides of the brain should be equally masculine or feminine.

2. If the genetic sex of the cells were important to sexual differentiation, then the two sides of the brain would be different. In this case, the normal role of the hormone might be to enhance the genetic effect rather than to produce the sex difference.

Agate's results confirm the second hypothesis: the neural song circuit was masculine on the male side of the brain. Such a structural difference could be explained only by a genetic difference in the brain that was at least partly independent of the effects of the hormones.

---

differences in brain organization and function, but rather to understand the degree to which those neurological differences contribute to observed differences in behavior.

Another key question related to hormonal influences on brain development is whether there might be sex differences in brain organization that are independent of hormonal action. In other words, are differences in the action of sex-chromosome genes unrelated to sex hormones? Although little is known about such genetic effects in humans, the results of recent studies in birds make it clear that genetic effects on brain cells may indeed contribute to sex differentiation. See "Hormones and the Range of a Behavior."

◎ For more information on the role hormones play in brain development and cognitive functioning, visit the Chapter 6 Web links on the *Brain and Behavior* Web site (**www.worth publishers.com/kolb**).

Injury and Brain Development

If the brain is damaged in the course of development, is it irrevocably altered? In the 1930s, Donald Hebb studied children with major birth-related injuries to the frontal lobes and found that such children had severe and permanent behavioral abnormalities in adulthood. He concluded that severe brain damage early in life can alter the subsequent development of the rest of the brain, leading to chronic behavioral disorders.

To what extent have other studies confirmed Hebb's conclusion? There are few anatomical studies of humans with early brain injuries, but we can make some general predictions from the study of laboratory animals. In general, early brain injuries do produce abnormal brains, especially at certain critical periods in development.

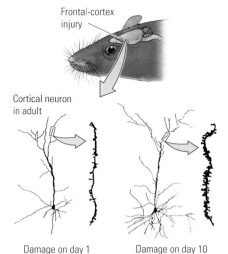

Frontal-cortex injury

Cortical neuron in adult

Damage on day 1   Damage on day 10

Figure 6-27

Time-Dependent Effects
In the rat, damage to the frontal cortex on the day of birth leads to the development of cortical neurons with simple dendritic fields and a sparse growth of spines in the adult (*left*). In contrast, damage to the frontal cortex at 10 days of age leads to the development of cortical neurons with expanded dendritic fields and denser spines than normal in adults (*right*). Adapted from "Possible Anatomical Basis of Recovery of Function After Neonatal Frontal Lesions in Rats," by B. Kolb and R. Gibb, 1993, *Behavioral Neuroscience, 107,* p. 808.

For humans, the worst time appears to be in the last half of the intrauterine period and the first couple of months after birth. Rats that suffer injuries at a comparable time have significantly smaller brains than normal, and their cortical neurons show a generalized atrophy relative to normal brains, as illustrated in **Figure 6-27**. Behaviorally, these animals appear cognitively retarded, deficient in a wide range of skills.

The effect of injury to the developing brain is not always devastating, however. For example, researchers have known for more than 100 years that children with brain injuries in the first couple of years after birth almost never have the severe language disturbances common to adults with equivalent injuries. Animal studies help explain why.

Whereas damage to the rat brain in the developmental period comparable to the last few months of gestation in humans produces widespread cortical atrophy, damage at a time in the development of the rat brain that is roughly comparable to age 6 months to 2 years in humans actually produces more dendritic development in rats, as seen on the right in Figure 6-27. Furthermore, these animals show dramatic recovery of functions, implying that the brain has a capacity during development to compensate for injury.

Drugs and Brain Development

The U.S. National Institute on Drug Abuse (NIDA) estimates that about 25 percent of all live births in the United States today are exposed to nicotine in utero. Similar statistics on alcohol consumption by pregnant mothers are not available, but the effects of alcohol consumption in the etiology of fetal alcohol effects are well documented, as detailed in Chapter 7.

NIDA also estimates that 5.5 percent of all expectant mothers, approximately 221,000 pregnant women each year in the United States, use an illicit drug at least once in the course of their pregnancies. And what about caffeine? More than likely most children were exposed to caffeine (from coffee, tea, cola drinks, and chocolate) in utero.

The precise effects of drug intake on brain development are poorly understood, but the overall conclusion from current knowledge is that children with prenatal exposure to a variety of psychoactive drugs have an increased likelihood of later drug use (Malanga & Kosofsky, 2003). Many experts suggest that, although, again, poorly studied, childhood disorders such as learning disabilities and hyperactivity may be related to prenatal exposure to drugs such as nicotine or caffeine or both. Malanga and Kosofsky note poignantly that "society at large does not yet fully appreciate the impact that prenatal drug exposure can have on the lives of its children."

Other Kinds of Abnormal Brain Development

The nervous system need not be damaged by external forces to develop abnormally. For instance, many genetic abnormalities are believed to result in abnormalities in the development and, ultimately, the structure of the brain. *Spina bifida,* a condition in which the genetic blueprint goes awry and the neural tube does not close completely, leads to an incompletely formed spinal cord. After birth, children with spina bifida usually have serious motor problems because of this spinal-cord abnormality.

Imagine what would happen if some genetic abnormality caused the front end of the neural tube not to close properly. Because the front end of the neural tube forms

○ Visit the *Brain and Behavior* Web site (**www.worthpublishers.com/kolb**) and go to the Chapter 6 Web links to learn more about abnormal brain development.

the brain, this failure would result in gross abnormalities in brain development. Such a condition exists and is known as **anencephaly.** Infants affected by this condition die soon after birth.

Abnormal brain development can be much subtler than anencephaly. For example, if cells do not migrate to their correct locations and these mispositioned cells do not subsequently die, they can disrupt brain function and may lead to disorders ranging from seizures to schizophrenia. In a variety of conditions, neurons fail to differentiate normally. In certain cases, the neurons fail to produce long dendrites or spines. As a result, connectivity in the brain is abnormal, leading to mental retardation.

The opposite condition also is possible: neurons continue to make dendrites and form connections with other cells to the point at which these neurons become extraordinarily large. The functional consequences of all the newly formed connections can be devastating. Excitatory synapses in the wrong location effectively short-circuit a neuron's function.

A curious consequence of abnormal brain development is that behavioral effects may emerge only as the brain matures and the maturing regions begin to play a greater role in behavior. This consequence is especially true of frontal-lobe injuries. The frontal lobes continue to develop into early adulthood, and often not until adolescence do the effects of frontal-lobe abnormalities begin to be noticed.

Schizophrenia is a disease characterized by its slow development, usually not becoming obvious until late adolescence. As detailed in Chapter 15, the schizophrenic brain has many abnormalities, some of which are in the frontal lobes. "Schizophrenia" on page 220 relates the progress and possible origin of the disease.

> **Anencephaly.** Failure of the forebrain to develop.

Mental Retardation

Mental retardation, or developmental disability, refers to impairment in cognitive functioning that accompanies abnormal brain development. Impairment may range in severity from mild, allowing an almost normal life style, to severe, requiring constant care. As summarized in **Table 6-4**, mental retardation can result from chronic malnutrition, genetic abnormalities such as Down's syndrome, hormonal abnormalities, brain injury, or neurological disease. Different causes produce different abnormalities in brain organization, but the critical similarity across all types of retardation is that the brain is not normal.

A study by Dominique Purpura (1974) is one of the few systematic investigations of the brains of developmentally disabled children. Purpura used Golgi stain to examine the neurons of children who had died from accident or disease unrelated to the nervous system. When he examined the brains of children with various forms of retardation, he found that dendrite growth was stunted and the spines were very sparse relative to dendrites from children of normal intelligence, as illustrated in **Figure 6-28**.

The simpler structure of these neurons is probably indicative of a marked reduction in the number of connections in the brain, which presumably caused the developmental disability. Variation in both the nature and the extent of neuronal abnormality in different children would lead to different behavioral syndromes.

Table 6-4	**Causes of Mental Retardation**	
Cause	**Example mechanism**	**Example condition**
Genetic abnormality	Error of metabolism	Phenylketonuria (PKU)
	Chromosomal abnormality	Down's syndrome
Abnormal embryonic development	Exposure to a toxin	Fetal alcohol syndrome
Prenatal disease	Infection	Rubella (also called German measles)
		Retardation
Birth trauma	Anoxia (oxygen deprivation)	Cerebral palsy
Malnutrition	Abnormal brain development	Kwashiorkor
Environmental abnormality	Sensory deprivation	Children in Romanian orphanages

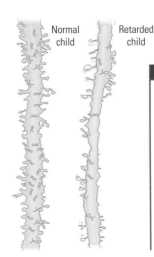

Normal child   Retarded child

Figure 6-28

Neural Contrast

Representative dendritic branches from cortical neurons in a child of normal intelligence (*left*) and a developmentally disabled child (*right*), whose neurons are smaller and have far fewer spines. Adapted from "Dendritic Spine 'Dysgenesis' and Mental Retardation," by D. P. Purpura, 1974, *Science, 186*, p. 1127

Schizophrenia

When Mrs. T. was 16 years old, she began to experience her first symptom of schizophrenia: a profound feeling that people were staring at her. These bouts of self-consciousness soon forced her to end her public piano performances. Her self-consciousness led to withdrawal, then to fearful delusions that others were speaking about her behind her back, and finally to suspicions that they were plotting to harm her. At first Mrs. T.'s illness was intermittent, and the return of her intelligence, warmth, and ambition between episodes allowed her to complete several years of college, to marry, and to rear three children. She had to enter a hospital for the first time at age 28, after the birth of her third child, when she began to hallucinate.

Now, at 45, Mrs. T. is never entirely well. She has seen dinosaurs on the street and live animals in her refrigerator. While hallucinating, she speaks and writes in an incoherent, but almost poetic way. At other times, she is more lucid, but even then the voices she hears sometimes lead her to do dangerous things, such as driving very fast down the highway in the middle of the night, dressed only in a nightgown. . . . At other times and without any apparent stimulus, Mrs. T. has bizarre visual hallucinations. For example, she saw cherubs in the grocery store. These experiences leave her preoccupied, confused, and frightened, unable to perform such everyday tasks as cooking or playing the piano. (Gershon & Rieder, 1992, p. 127)

It has always been easier to identify schizophrenic behavior than to define what schizophrenia is. Perhaps the one universally accepted criterion for its diagnosis is the absence of other neurological disturbances or affective (mood) disorders that could cause a person to lose touch with reality—a definition by default. Some textbooks emphasize bizarre hallucinations and disturbances of thought, much like those displayed by Mrs. T. However, the symptoms of schizophrenia are heterogeneous, suggesting that the biological abnormalities vary from person to person.

In 1913, Emil Kraepelin first proposed that schizophrenia follows a progressively deteriorating course with a dismal final outcome. This opinion was dominant throughout most of the twentieth century. Today, a consensus is emerging that Kraepelin's view is probably incorrect. Most patients appear to stay at a fairly stable level after the first few years

In Review

The brain is especially plastic during its development and can therefore be molded by experience into different forms, at least at the microscopic level. Not only is the brain plastic in response to external events, it may be changed as well by internal events, including the effects of hormones, injury, abnormal genes and drugs. The sensitivity of the brain to experience varies with time. At critical periods in development, specific parts of the brain are particularly sensitive to experience and environment. If experiences are abnormal, then the brain's development is abnormal, possibly leading to such disorders as schizophrenia or various degrees of developmental disability.

HOW DO ANY OF US DEVELOP A NORMAL BRAIN?

When we consider the complexity of the brain, the less-than-precise process of brain development, and the number of factors that can influence it, we are left marveling at how so many of us end up with brains that pass for normal. After all, we must all have

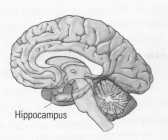 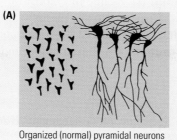 

(A) Organized (normal) pyramidal neurons

(B) Disorganized (schizophrenic) pyramidal neurons

Hippocampus

Examples from the hippocampus of pyramidal-cell orientation in **(A)** a normal brain and **(B)** a schizophrenic brain, where the orientations of these pyramidal neurons are highly disorganized. (Adapted from "A Neurohistologic Correlate of Schizophrenia" by J. A. Kovelman and A. B. Scheibel, 1984, *Biological Psychiatry, 19,* p. 1613.)

of displaying schizophrenic symptoms, with little evidence of a decline in neuropsychological functioning. The symptoms come and go, much as for Mrs. T., but the severity is relatively constant after the first few episodes.

Numerous studies have investigated the brains of schizophrenia patients, both in autopsies and in MRI and CT scans. Although the results vary, most neuroscientists agree that the brains of people who develop schizophrenia are lighter in weight than normal and have enlarged ventricles. Research findings also suggest that schizophrenic brains have smaller frontal lobes (or at least a reduction in the number of neurons in the prefrontal cortex) and thinner parahippocampal gyri.

One of the most interesting discoveries is that of Joyce Kovelman and Arnold Scheibel (1984), who found abnormalities in the orientation of neurons in the hippocampi of schiz-ophrenics. Rather than the consistently parallel orientation of neurons in this region characteristic of normal brains, the schizophrenic brains have a more haphazard organization, as shown in the accompanying drawing.

Evidence is increasing that the abnormalities observed in schizophrenic brains are associated with disturbances of brain development. William Bunney and his colleagues (1997) suggested that at least a subgroup of schizophrenia sufferers experience either environmental insults or some type of abnormal gene activity in the fourth to sixth month of fetal development. These events are thought to result in abnormal cortical development, particularly in the frontal lobes. Later in adolescence, as the frontal lobes approach maturity, the person begins to experience symptoms deriving from this abnormal prenatal development.

had neurons that migrated to wrong locations, made incorrect connections, and were exposed to viruses or other harmful substances. If the brain were as fragile as it might seem, to end up with a normal brain would be almost impossible.

Apparently, animals have evolved a substantial capacity to repair minor abnormalities in brain development. Most people have developed in the range that we call "normal" because the human brain's plasticity and regenerative powers overcome minor developmental deviations. Recall that one stage in brain development consists of cell death and synaptic pruning. By initially overproducing neurons and synapses, the brain has the capacity to correct any errors that might have arisen accidentally.

These same plastic properties of the brain later allow us to cope with the ravages of aging. Neurons are dying throughout our lifetimes and, by age 50, we ought to be able to see significant effects of all of this cell loss, especially considering the cumulative results of exposure to environmental toxins, drugs, closed head injuries, and so on. But this is not what happens. Although teenagers may not believe it, very few 50-year-olds are demented. By most criteria, the 50-year-old who has been intellectually active throughout adulthood is likely to be much wiser than the 18-year-old whose brain has lost relatively few neurons.

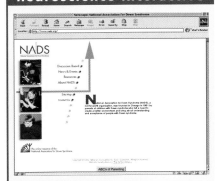

neuroscience interactive

Many resources are available for expanding your learning online:

▓ **www.worthpublishers.com/kolb**
Try the Chapter 6 quizzes and flashcards to test your mastery of the chapter material. You'll also be able to link to other sites that will reinforce what you've learned.

▓ **www.embryo.soad.umich.edu**
Link here to see a remarkable collection of human embryos through magnetic resonance microscopy.

▓ **www.nads.org**
Investigate current research about Down's syndrome at the National Association for Down's Syndrome.

▓ **www.ucpa.org**
Learn more about cerebral palsy at the home page of United Cerebral Palsy.

On your *Foundations* CD-ROM, you can visit the module on Neural Communication for an important review on the neural structure.

Clearly, we must have some mechanism to compensate for loss and minor injury to our brain cells. This capacity for plasticity and change, for learning and adapting, is a most important characteristic of the human brain during development and throughout life. We return to learning and memory in Chapter 13.

SUMMARY

▓ *What are the stages of neural development?* Human brain maturation is a long process, lasting well into the 20s. Neurons, the units of brain function, develop a phenotype, migrate, and, as their processes elaborate, establish connections with other neurons even before birth. The developing brain produces many more neurons and connections than it needs and then prunes back in toddlerhood and again in adolescence to a stable adult level maintained by some neurogenesis throughout the life span.

▓ *How does behavior develop?* Throughout the world, across the cultural spectrum, from newborn to child to adolescent and through adulthood, we develop through similar behavioral stages. As infants develop physically, motor behaviors emerge in a predictable sequence from gross, poorly directed movements toward objects to controlled pincer grasps to pick up objects as small as pencils by about 11 months. Cognitive behaviors also develop through a series of testable stages of logic and problem solving. Researchers such as Jean Piaget have identified and characterized four or more distinct stages of cognitive development, each of which can be identified by special behavioral tests.

▓ *How do behavioral and neural maturation relate to one another?* Behaviors emerge as the neural systems that produce them develop. Cognitive behavior follows a similar developmental sequence from the rudimentary to the complex. The hierarchical relation between brain structure and function can be inferred by matching the median developmental timetables of neurodevelopment with observed behavior. Motor behaviors emerge in synchrony with the maturation of motor circuits in the cerebral cortex, basal ganglia, and cerebellum, as well as in the connections from these areas to the spinal cord. Similar correlations between emerging behaviors and neuronal development can be seen in the maturation of cognitive behavior, as circuits in the frontal and temporal lobes mature in early adulthood.

▓ *What factors influence neural maturation and plasticity?* The brain is most plastic during its development, and the structure of neurons and their connections can be molded by various factors throughout development. The brain's sensitivity to factors such as external events, quality of environment, drugs, gonadal hormones, and injury, varies over time: at critical periods in the course of development, different brain regions are particularly sensitive to different events.

▓ *How sensitive is the developing brain to injury?* Perturbations of the brain in the course of development from, say, anoxia, trauma, or toxins can significantly alter brain development and result in severe behavioral abnormalities including retardation and cerebral palsy. The brain does have a substantial capacity to repair or correct minor abnormalities, however, allowing most people to develop normal behavioral repertoires and to maintain brain function throughout life.

KEY TERMS

amblyopia, p. 210

anencephaly, p. 219

apoptosis, p. 200

cell-adhesion molecule
  (CAM), p. 199

chemoaffinity hypothesis,
  p. 210

critical period, p. 212

filopod, p. 199

glioblast, p. 194

growth cone, p. 199

growth spurt, p. 206

imprinting, p. 212

masculinization, p. 214

netrin, p. 199

neural Darwinism, p. 200   neuroblast, p. 194   radial glial cell, p. 197
neural plate, p. 196   neurotrophic factor, p. 195   tropic molecule, p. 199
neural stem cell, p. 194   progenitor (precursor)   ventricular zone, p. 194
neural tube, p. 190   cell, p. 194

REVIEW QUESTIONS

1. Describe the gross development of the nervous system. Summarize and explain the steps in brain development.

2. What roles do neurochemicals, genetics, and experience play in development?

3. How does behavioral development relate to neural development?

4. How does experience affect brain development?

FOR FURTHER THOUGHT

1. Experience plays an important role in brain development. How might interaction between sex and environment account for the broad spectrum of sexual identity in adulthood?

2. How can the principles of behavioral neurodevelopment help to explain why each brain is unique?

RECOMMENDED READING

Edelman, G. M. (1987). *Neural Darwinism: The theory of neuronal group selection.* New York: Basic Books. Edelman applies the Darwinian concept of survival of the fittest to the nervous system's shedding of neurons in the course of development and throughout a person's lifetime. Although not universally accepted, the ideas in the book are amusing to read.

Greenough, W. T., & Chang, F. F. (1988). Plasticity of synapse structure and pattern in the cerebral cortex. In A. Peters and E. G. Jones (Eds.), *Cerebral cortex: Vol. 7. Development and maturation of the cerebral cortex* (pp. 391–440). New York: Plenum. Greenough is one of the world leaders in the study of experience-dependent change in the nervous system. This chapter not only provides a nice historical review, but also lays out seminal ideas on the developmental plasticity of the nervous system.

Hebb, D. O. (1949). *The organization of behavior.* New York: Wiley. Although 1949 may seem like a long time ago for a book to be still relevant today, Hebb's book may be the most important single volume on brain and behavior. It was the first serious attempt to outline a neuropsychological theory of how the brain could produce behavior and, especially, thought. Development is an important theme in the book because Hebb believed that experience plays an essential role in developing the cognitive and neural structures necessary for adulthood. This book is mandatory reading for any student going on to graduate school in behavioral neuroscience.

Meany, M. J. (2001). Maternal care, gene expression, and the transmission of individual differences in stress reactivity across generations. *Annual Review of Neuroscience, 24,* 1161–1192. Meany is a leading researcher on the role of maternal behavior in brain and behavioral development. This review brings together a wide range of findings showing how the effects of experience can cross generations through alterations in gene expression.

Michel, G. F., & Moore, C. L. (1995). *Developmental psychobiology.* Cambridge, MA: MIT Press. Most neural development books are thin on behavioral development, but this book strikes a nice balance in its analysis of both brain and behavioral development.

Purves, D., & Lichtman, J. W. (1985). *Principles of neural development.* Sunderland, MA: Sinauer. Although not primarily about the development of the cortex, the book provides sufficient background to enable a thorough understanding of the principles that guide nervous system development.

How Do Drugs and Hormones Influence the Brain and Behavior?

Left: **Dr. Dennis Kunkel/Phototake.** *Middle:* **Edward Holub/Corbis.** *Right:* **Pascal Goetgheluck/Photo Researchers, Inc.**

The Neural Basis of Drug Cravings

Exposure to drug paraphernalia and other prominent drug-related cues induce intense craving in addicts and thereby influence drug taking. What is the neural basis of this craving? Where in the brain does it take place? Can craving be prevented or reversed? The answers may be found in the brain's *mesolimbic dopamine system.*

Mesolimbic dopamine (DA) neurons are located in the medial part of the midbrain called the *ventral tegmental area* (VTA), and the axons of these neurons project to a part of the basal ganglia called the *nucleus accumbens,* as shown in **Figure 7-1**. Several lines of evidence associate the nucleus accumbens with addictive behavior. If rewarding stimuli are presented to a rat, as many as 80% of the neurons in the VTA discharge, and DA is released from their synapses in the nucleus accumbens. The use of probes in the nucleus accumbens that measure DA level reveals that the neuronal discharge is associated with a brief DA surge.

The injection of DA into the nucleus accumbens of rats through a small cannula appears to be rewarding because these rats will push a bar to receive the injection. They will also push a bar to receive electrical stimulation of the VTA, which also excites dopamine neurons to release DA into the nucleus accumbens. Many addictive drugs likewise increase DA release or potentiate its action in the nucleus accumbens.

Paul Phillips and his colleagues (2003) examined whether the cues that signal a cocaine reward to cocaine-addicted rats can produce a release of DA from dopamine terminals in the nucleus accumbens and whether such release is related to drug-seeking behavior. The rats learned that, when a light flashed, they could press a bar to activate an indwelling cannula and receive an injection of cocaine. Thus, the light was the cue.

The experimenters implanted into the rats' nucleus accumbens a carbon-fiber microelectrode that chemically reacts with DA to produce an electrical signal if DA levels increase. They found that the light cue produced a brief DA release in drug-addicted rats but *not* in control rats. In association with the DA release, the rat addicts approached the bar and pressed it to receive a cocaine injection.

Electrical stimulation of the VTA produced the same brief release in the addicted rats and was followed by cocaine seeking behavior as well. These results suggest that learned associations to drug-related cues actually empower those cues alone to activate DA release in the VTA and that this release is associated with drug-seeking behavior. Thus, the release of DA in the VTA, which is normally associated with natural interest in food, sexual activity, or other rewarding stimuli, may also be the neural corollary of behaviors related to drug craving.

This poses a major difficulty in developing treatments for addiction: that natural rewards and addiction are dependent on the same neurons. The same brain events that cue drug craving, including DA release in the nucleus accumbens, are associated with many everyday stimuli, including aversive, novel, and intense stimuli, and even actions that result in monetary rewards (Zink, Pagnoni, Martin-Skurski, Chappelow, & Berns, 2004). For this reason, addictions are extremely difficult to treat. Attempts range from counseling to therapy with drugs, from cognitive-behavior therapy, remarkably, even to psychosurgery in which the nucleus accumbens is destroyed by a lesion.

Even when treatment is successful, a person may never really be free from drug cravings. Nevertheless, understanding the neural changes associated with the acquisition of an addiction holds great promise for the development of effective therapies.

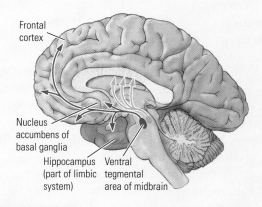

Frontal cortex

Nucleus accumbens of basal ganglia

Hippocampus (part of limbic system)

Ventral tegmental area of midbrain

Figure 7-1

Mesolimbic Dopamine Pathways Axons of neurons in the midbrain ventral tegmental area project to the nucleus accumbens, frontal cortex, and hippocampus.

Psychopharmacology. Study of how drugs affect the nervous system and behavior.

Psychoactive drug. Substance that acts to alter mood, thought, or behavior and is used to manage neuropsychological illness.

Psychopharmacology is the study of how drugs affect the nervous system and behavior. In this chapter, we group various drugs by their major behavioral effects. You will learn that the effects of drugs depend on how they are taken, in what quantities, and under what circumstances.

We begin by looking at the major ways that drugs are administered, what routes they take to reach the central nervous system, and how they are eliminated from the body. We consider how drugs act on neurons and why different people may respond differently to the same dose of a drug. Many principles related to drugs also apply to the action of hormones, the chapter's final topic.

Before we examine how drugs produce their effects on the brain for good or for ill, we must raise a caution: the sheer number of neurotransmitters, receptors, and possible sites of drug action is astounding. Psychopharmacology research has made important advances on some principles of drug action, but neuroscientists do not know everything there is to know about any drug. To illustrate, consider some unexpected effects produced by a drug long considered safe.

THE DOMOIC ACID MYSTERY

Japanese and Chinese fishermen discovered long ago that seaweed can be used as a medicine. They may have observed that flies die after alighting on seaweed washed up on the shore, and so they tried rubbing seaweed onto their skin as an insect repellent. It worked. They also found that, when eaten, seaweed kills intestinal worms, and so they used seaweed extracts to get rid of worms in children.

These folk remedies led scientists to analyze the chemical composition of the seaweed *Chondria armata.* They identified two chemically similar insecticidal compounds in it: domoic acid and kainic acid. Purified doses of these acids were given to large numbers of children as a treatment for worms, with no reported side effects. Physicians therefore concluded that these substances were nontoxic to humans. Unfortunately, they were wrong.

On November 22, 1987, two people in Moncton, New Brunswick, Canada, were hospitalized after suffering from gastroenteritis and mental confusion. Soon more reports of the illness came from Quebec, and, by December 9, five people had died. In all, more than 200 cases of this mysterious disorder were reported.

The severity of symptoms varied greatly, but the worst cases included marked confusion and memory loss. For some who survived, memory impairment was permanent. Autopsies revealed extensive cell loss in the hippocampus, in the amygdala and surrounding cortex, and in the thalamus (Hynie & Todd, 1990).

The only experience common to the victims was that all had eaten mussels. To find out whether the mussels were the source of the illness, scientists injected mussel extracts into mice. Soon after, the mice started scratching behind one ear and then convulsed and died. Apparently, these mussels did contain a toxin, but the curious scratching behavior indicated that the toxin was unlike any other known shellfish poison.

Chemical analysis of the mussels showed that they contained high levels of domoic acid. Investigators were surprised. How did the mussels become contaminated with domoic acid, and why was it suddenly acting like a poison?

To answer the first question, the investigators traced the source of the mussels to two Prince Edward Island cultured-mussel farms. Cultured-mussel farming began in 1975 and by the 1980s had grown into a large, successful industry, producing as much as 3.2 million pounds of mussels annually. Mussel farmers release mussel sperm and eggs into the water, where the resulting zygotes attach themselves to long ropes suspended there. The mussels feed by siphoning from 2 to 6 liters of water per hour to extract small sea organisms called phytoplankton.

More than 90 percent of the phytoplankton that the Prince Edward Island mussels consumed were single-cell diatoms called *Nitzschia pungens*. When analyzed, the diatoms were found to contain domoic acid. Because there had been no evidence of domoic acid in diatoms before 1987, a search for the origins of the contamination began. Apparently, a drought in 1987 produced a buildup of domoic acid–containing seaweed in the streams and along the shoreline. By feeding on seaweed, the diatoms had accumulated large quantities of domoic acid, which was then passed up the food chain to the mussels as they fed on the diatoms.

But the discovery that domoic acid was the toxic agent in this episode only partly solved the mystery. Remember that domoic acid had been thought harmless. It had been widely used to rid children of worms. How had it now resulted in sickness, brain damage, and death? And why were only some people affected? Surely, more than 200 people had eaten the contaminated mussels. In the following sections, where domoic acid poisoning is used to illustrate some of the principles of drug action, you will find the answers to these questions. In addition, you will learn how the domoic acid story has led to other insights into brain function.

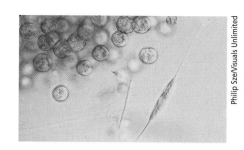

Diatoms, in a variety of shapes, form the very base of the food chain. *Nitzschia pungens,* the circular organisms in this photograph, are ubiquitous in the ocean and are frequently present in great numbers in fresh water.

PRINCIPLES OF PSYCHOPHARMACOLOGY

Drugs are chemical compounds administered to bring about some desired change in the body. Drugs are usually used to diagnose, treat, or prevent illness, to relieve pain and suffering, or to improve some adverse physiological condition. In this chapter, we focus on **psychoactive drugs**—substances that act to alter mood, thought, or behavior and are used to manage neuropsychological illness.

Many psychoactive drugs are taken for nonmedical reasons or recreationally, by some to the point that they become *substances of abuse.* Such drug taking impairs the user's functioning, promotes craving, and may produce addiction. Like domoic acid, some psychoactive drugs can also act as toxins, producing sickness, brain damage, or death.

Drug Routes into the Nervous System

To be effective, a psychoactive drug has to reach its nervous system target. The way that a drug enters and passes through the body to reach that target is called its *route of administration.* Many drugs are administered orally because oral administration is a natural and safe way to consume a substance. Drugs can also be inhaled into the lungs, administered through rectal suppositories, absorbed from patches applied to the skin, or injected into the bloodstream, into a muscle, or even into the brain.

Figure 7-2 illustrates the various routes of drug administration. These different routes pose different barriers between the drug and its target. Taking a drug by mouth is easy and convenient, but not all drugs can pass the barriers of the digestive-tract contents and walls. Generally, there are fewer barriers between a drug and its target if the drug is inhaled rather than swallowed. Drugs that are administered as gases or aerosols penetrate the cell linings of the respiratory tract easily and are absorbed across these membranes into the bloodstream nearly as quickly as they are inhaled. Presumably such drugs of abuse as nicotine, cocaine, and marijuana, when administered as a gas or smoke, are absorbed in a similar way.

Figure 7-2

Routes of Drug Administration

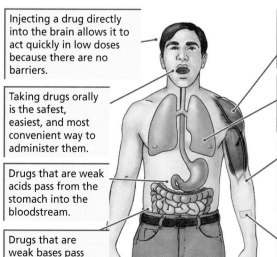

Injecting a drug directly into the brain allows it to act quickly in low doses because there are no barriers.

Taking drugs orally is the safest, easiest, and most convenient way to administer them.

Drugs that are weak acids pass from the stomach into the bloodstream.

Drugs that are weak bases pass from the intestines to the bloodstream.

Drugs injected into muscle encounter more barriers than do drugs inhaled.

Drugs inhaled into the lungs encounter few barriers en route to the brain.

Drugs injected into the bloodstream encounter the fewest barriers to the brain but must be hydrophilic.

Drugs contained in adhesive patches are absorbed through the skin and into the bloodstream.

Philip Sze/Visuals Unlimited

Our largest organ, the skin, has three layers of cells and is designed to be a protective body coat. Some small-molecule drugs (e.g., nicotine) penetrate the skin's barrier almost as easily as they penetrate the cell lining of the respiratory tract, whereas large-molecule drugs do not. There are still fewer obstacles if a drug is injected directly into the blood. The fewest obstacles are encountered if a psychoactive drug is injected directly into the brain.

Figure 7-2 also summarizes the characteristics of drugs that allow them to pass through various barriers to reach their targets. Let us look more closely at the barriers that a drug taken orally must pass to get to the brain. Oral administration is the most complex route. To reach the bloodstream, an ingested drug must first be absorbed through the lining of the stomach or small intestine. If the drug is liquid, it is absorbed more readily. Drugs taken in solid form are not absorbed unless they can be dissolved by the stomach's gastric juices.

In either form, liquid or solid, absorption is affected by the physical and chemical properties of the drug, as well as by the presence of other stomach or intestinal contents. In general, if a drug is a weak acid, such as alcohol, it is readily absorbed across the stomach lining. If it is a weak base, it cannot be absorbed until it passes through the stomach and into the intestine—a process that may destroy it.

After it has been absorbed by the stomach or intestine, the drug must next enter the bloodstream. This part of the journey requires additional properties. Because blood has a high water concentration, a drug must be hydrophilic to be carried in the blood. A hydrophobic substance will be blocked from entering the bloodstream. After it is in the blood, a drug is then diluted by the approximately 6 liters of blood that circulate through an adult's body.

To reach its target, a drug must also travel from the blood into the extracellular fluid, which requires that its molecules be small enough to pass through the pores of capillaries, the tiny vessels that carry blood to the body's cells. Even if the drug makes this passage, it may encounter still other obstacles. For one thing, the sheer volume of water in the body's extracellular fluid (roughly 35 liters) will dilute the drug even further. For another, the drug is at risk of being modified or destroyed by various metabolic processes taking place in cells.

Considering the many obstacles that psychoactive drugs encounter on their journey from mouth to brain, it is clear why inhaling a drug or injecting it into the bloodstream has advantages. These alternative routes of administration bypass the obstacle of the digestive tract. In fact, with each obstacle eliminated en route to the brain, the dosage of a drug can be reduced by a factor of 10 without reducing its effects.

For example, 1 milligram (mg), equal to 1000 micrograms (μg), of *amphetamine,* a psychomotor stimulant, produces a noticeable behavioral change when ingested orally. If inhaled into the lungs or injected into the blood, thereby circumventing the stomach, a dose of just one-tenth of a milligram (100 μg) produces the same results. Similarly, if amphetamine is injected into the cerebrospinal fluid, thus bypassing both the stomach *and* the blood, 10 μg is enough to produce an identical outcome, as is merely 1 mcg if dilution in the cerebrospinal fluid also is skirted and the drug is injected directly onto target neurons.

This math is well known to sellers and users of illicit drugs. Drugs that can be prepared to be inhaled or injected intravenously are much cheaper per dose because the amount required is so much smaller than that needed for an effective oral dose.

REVISITING THE BLOOD–BRAIN BARRIER

As you know, the passage of drugs across capillaries in the brain is made much more difficult by the *blood–brain barrier,* which prevents the passage of most substances. The brain has a rich capillary network. In fact, none of its neurons is farther than about 50 μm (one-millionth of a meter) away from a capillary.

ⓞ For more information on the routes of drug administration, visit the Chapter 7 Web links on the *Brain and Behavior* Web site (**www.worthpublishers. com/kolb**).

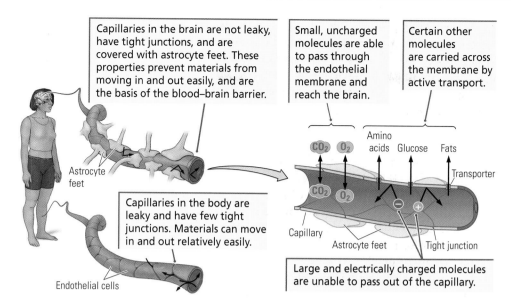

Capillaries in the brain are not leaky, have tight junctions, and are covered with astrocyte feet. These properties prevent materials from moving in and out easily, and are the basis of the blood–brain barrier.

Small, uncharged molecules are able to pass through the endothelial membrane and reach the brain.

Certain other molecules are carried across the membrane by active transport.

Capillaries in the body are leaky and have few tight junctions. Materials can move in and out relatively easily.

Astrocyte feet

Endothelial cells

Amino acids   Glucose   Fats

CO_2 O_2

Transporter

CO_2 O_2

Capillary

Astrocyte feet

Tight junction

Large and electrically charged molecules are unable to pass out of the capillary.

Figure 7-3

Blood–Brain Barrier   Capillaries in most of the body allow for the passage of substances between capillary cell membranes, but those in the brain, stimulated by the actions of astrocytes, form the tight junctions of the blood–brain barrier.

Figure 7-3 shows the structure of brain capillaries and why they are impermeable to many substances. As you can see on the left side of Figure 7-3, like all capillaries, brain capillaries are composed of a single layer of *endothelial cells*. In the walls of capillaries in most parts of the body, endothelial cells are not fused together, and so substances can pass through the clefts between the cells. In contrast, in the brain (at least in most parts of it), endothelial cell walls are fused to form "tight junctions," and so molecules of most substances cannot squeeze between them.

Figure 7-3 also shows that the endothelial cells of brain capillaries are surrounded by the end feet of astrocyte glial cells attached to the capillary wall, covering about 80 percent of it. The glial cells provide a route for the exchange of food and waste between capillaries and the brain's extracellular fluid and from there to other cells, shown on the right in Figure 7-3. They may also play a role in maintaining the tight junctions between endothelial cells and in making capillaries dilate to increase blood flow to areas of the brain in which neurons are very active.

You may wonder why endothelial cells form tight junctions only in *most* parts of the brain, not in *all* of it. Astrocytes attached to the capillaries appear to be responsible for the tight junctions formed by the endothelial cells. The cells of capillary walls in a few brain regions lack tight junctions, and so these regions, shown in **Figure 7-4**, lack a blood–brain barrier. One is the pituitary gland of the hypothalamus. The pituitary is a source of many hormones that are secreted into the blood system, and their release is triggered in part by other hormones carried to the pituitary by the blood.

The absence of a blood–brain barrier in the area postrema of the lower brainstem allows toxic substances in the blood to trigger a vomiting response. The pineal gland also lacks a blood–brain barrier, enabling hormones to reach it and modulate the day–night cycles that this structure controls.

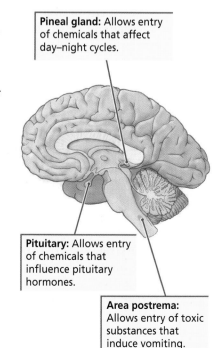

Pineal gland: Allows entry of chemicals that affect day–night cycles.

Pituitary: Allows entry of chemicals that influence pituitary hormones.

Area postrema: Allows entry of toxic substances that induce vomiting.

Figure 7-4

Barrier-Free Brain Sites   The pituitary gland is a target for many blood-borne hormones, the pineal gland is a target for hormones that affect circadian rhythms, and the area postrema initiates vomiting in response to noxious substances.

To carry out its work, the rest of the brain needs oxygen and glucose for fuel and amino acids to build proteins, among other substances. These fuel molecules must routinely travel from the blood to brain cells, just as carbon dioxide and other waste products must routinely be excreted from brain cells into the blood. Molecules of these vital substances cross the blood–brain barrier in two ways:

1. Small molecules such as oxygen and carbon dioxide, which are not ionized and so are fat soluble, can pass right through the endothelial membrane.
2. Molecules of glucose, amino acids, and other food components can be carried across the membrane by active-transport systems, such as sodium–potassium pumps—proteins specialized for the transport of a particular substance.

When a substance has passed from the capillaries into the brain's extracellular fluid, it can move readily into neurons and glia.

The blood–brain barrier serves a number of purposes. Because the electrical activity of neurons depends on certain extracellular concentrations of ions, it is important that ionic substances not cross the blood–brain barrier and upset the brain's electrical activity. It is also important that neurochemicals from the rest of the body not pass into the brain and disrupt the communication between neurons.

In addition, the blood–brain barrier protects the brain from the effects of many circulating hormones and from various toxic and infectious substances. Injury or disease can sometimes rupture the blood–brain barrier, letting pathogens through. For the most part, however, the brain is very well protected from substances potentially harmful to its functioning.

The blood–brain barrier has special relevance for understanding drug actions on the nervous system. A drug can reach the brain only if its molecules are small and not ionized, enabling them to pass through endothelial cell membranes, or if the drug has a chemical structure that allows it to be carried across the membrane by an active-transport system. Because very few drug molecules are small or have the correct chemical structure, very few can gain access to the CNS. Because the blood–brain barrier works so well, it is extremely difficult to find new drugs to use as treatments for brain diseases.

To summarize, drugs that can make the entire trip from the mouth to the brain have some special chemical properties. The most effective ones are small molecules, weak acids, water and fat soluble, potent in small amounts, and not easily degraded. Domoic acid meets all these criteria. Because it is a weak acid, it is easily absorbed through the stomach. It is potent in small amounts, and so it survives dilution in the bloodstream and extracellular fluid. Finally, it is a small molecule similar in structure to those of nutrients that are transported across the blood–brain barrier and so it, too, is transported.

HOW THE BODY ELIMINATES DRUGS

After a drug has been administered, the body soon begins to break it down (catabolize) and remove it. Drugs are catabolized throughout the body, broken down in the kidneys and liver, as well as in the intestine by bile. They are excreted in urine, feces, sweat, breast milk, and exhaled air. Drugs that are developed for therapeutic purposes are usually designed not only to increase their chances of reaching their targets but also to enhance their survival time in the body.

The body has trouble removing some ingested substances, making them potentially dangerous, because they can build up in the body and become poisonous. For instance, certain toxic metals, such as mercury, are not easily eliminated; when they accumulate, they can produce severe neurological conditions. When researchers studied the medical histories of patients with severe domoic acid poisoning, they found that all had preexisting kidney problems. This finding suggests that the kidneys play an important role in eliminating domoic acid. Because these patients' kidneys did not function normally, domoic acid reached toxic levels in their bodies.

Agonist. Substance that enhances the function of a synapse.

Antagonist. Substance that blocks the function of a synapse.

Individual Differences in Response to Psychoactive Drugs

The vast differences among individual responses to drugs are due to differences in age, sex, body size, metabolic rate, and other factors that affect sensitivity to a particular substance. For instance, larger people are generally less sensitive to a drug than smaller people are, because their greater volume of body fluids dilutes drugs more.

Females are about twice as sensitive to drugs as males on average. This difference is due in part to their relatively smaller body size, but it is also due to hormonal differences. Old people may be twice as sensitive to drugs as young people are. The elderly often have less-effective barriers to drug absorption as well as less-effective processes for metabolizing and eliminating drugs from their bodies.

Individual differences in sensitivity to domoic acid were observed among people who ate toxic mussels. Only 1 in 1000 became ill, and only some of those who were ill suffered severe memory impairment, with even fewer dying. The three patients with impaired memory were men aged 69, 71, and 84. All who died were men older than 68. Apparently, domoic acid is either more readily absorbed or more poorly excreted or both in older men. The results of subsequent studies of mice confirmed the greater sensitivity of older animals to the toxic effects of domoic acid.

Drug Action at Synapses: Agonists and Antagonists

Drugs take effect by initiating chemical reactions in the body or by influencing the body's ongoing chemical activities. As you know, many chemical reactions take place in the nervous system's neurons, especially at synapses. Most drugs that have psychoactive effects do so by influencing these chemical reactions at synapses. So, to understand how drugs work, we must explore the ways in which they modify synaptic actions.

Figure 7-5 summarizes the seven major steps in neurotransmission at a synapse. Synthesis of the neurotransmitter can take place in the cell body, the axon, or the terminal. The neurotransmitter is then held in storage granules or in vesicles or in both until it is released from the terminal's presynaptic membrane.

The amount of transmitter released into the synapse is regulated in relation to experience. When released, the transmitter acts on a receptor embedded in the postsynaptic membrane. It is then either destroyed or taken back up into the presynaptic terminal for reuse. The synapse also has mechanisms for degrading excess neurotransmitter and removing unneeded by-products from the synapse.

Each of these steps in neurotransmission includes a chemical reaction that a drug can potentially influence in one of two ways: either by increasing the effectiveness of neurotransmission or by diminishing it. **Agonists** are drugs that increase the effectiveness of neurotransmission, whereas **antagonists** decrease its effectiveness. Agonists and antagonists can work in a variety of ways, but their end results are always the same. To illustrate, consider the acetylcholine synapse between motor neurons and muscles.

Figure 7-5

Points of Influence In principle, a drug can modify seven major chemical processes, any of which results in reduced or enhanced synaptic transmission.

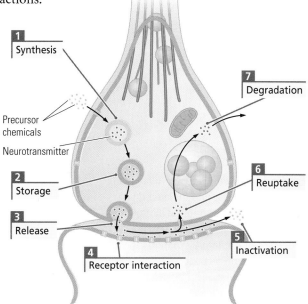

1 Synthesis

Precursor chemicals

Neurotransmitter

2 Storage

3 Release

4 Receptor interaction

5 Inactivation

6 Reuptake

7 Degradation

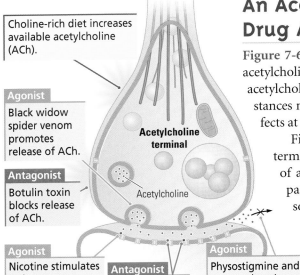

Choline-rich diet increases available acetylcholine (ACh).

Agonist
Black widow spider venom promotes release of ACh.

Antagonist
Botulin toxin blocks release of ACh.

Acetylcholine terminal

Acetylcholine

Agonist
Nicotine stimulates ACh receptors.

Antagonist
Curare blocks ACh receptors.

Agonist
Physostigmine and organophosphates block the inactivation of ACh.

Figure 7-6

Acetylcholine Agonists and Antagonists Drugs affect ACh transmission by affecting its synthesis, release, or binding to the postsynaptic receptor and by affecting its breakdown or inactivation.

○ On your *Foundations of Behavioral Neuroscience* CD, find the area on synaptic transmission in the module on neural communication. Review the processes of excitatory synaptic function and consider drugs that act as agonists, such as those that affect acetylcholine. (See the Preface for more information about this CD.)

An Acetylcholine Synapse: Examples of Drug Action

Figure 7-6 shows how selected drugs and toxins act as agonists or antagonists at the acetylcholine synapse. Acetylcholine agonists excite muscles, making them rigid, whereas acetylcholine antagonists inhibit muscles, rendering them flaccid. Some of these substances may be new to you, but you have probably heard of others. Knowing their effects at the synapse allows you to understand the behavioral effects that they produce.

Figure 7-6 shows two toxins that influence the release of ACh from the axon terminal. Black widow spider venom is an agonist because it promotes the release of acetylcholine to excess. A black widow spider bite contains enough toxin to paralyze an insect but not enough to paralyze a person, but a victim may feel some muscle weakness.

Botulin toxin, the poisonous agent in tainted foods such as canned goods that have been improperly processed, acts as an antagonist because it blocks the release of ACh. The effects of botulin toxin can last from weeks to months. A severe case can result in the paralysis of both movement and breathing and so cause death.

Despite being a poison, botulin toxin has medical uses. If injected into a muscle, it can selectively paralyze that muscle. This selective action makes it useful in blocking excessive and enduring muscular twitches or contractions, including the contraction that makes movement difficult for people with cerebral palsy. Under the trade name Botox, botulin toxin is also used cosmetically to paralyze facial muscles that cause facial wrinkling.

Figure 7-6 also shows two drugs that act on receptors for acetylcholine. As you learned in Chapter 5, nicotine's molecular structure is similar enough to that of ACh to allow nicotine to fit into the receptors' binding sites where it acts as an agonist. *Curare* acts as an antagonist by occupying cholinergic receptors and so preventing acetylcholine from binding to them.

When curare binds to these receptors, it does not cause them to function; instead, it blocks them. After having been introduced into the body, curare acts quickly, and it is cleared from the body in a few minutes. Large doses, however, arrest movement and breathing for a sufficient period of time to result in death.

Early European explorers of South America discovered that the Indians along the Amazon River killed small animals by using arrowheads coated with curare prepared from the seeds of a plant. The hunters themselves did not become poisoned when eating the animals, because ingested curare cannot pass from the gut into the body. Many curare-like drugs have been synthesized. Some are used to briefly paralyze large animals so that they can be examined or tagged for identification. You have probably seen this use of these drugs in wildlife programs on television. Skeletal muscles are more sensitive to curare-like drugs than are respiratory muscles; so an appropriate dose will paralyze an animal's movement temporarily but still allow it to breathe.

The fifth drug action shown in Figure 7-6 is that of physostigmine, a drug that inhibits cholinesterase, the enzyme that breaks down acetylcholine. Physostigmine therefore acts as an agonist to increase the amount of ACh available in the synapse. Physostigmine is obtained from an African bean and is used as a poison by native peoples in Africa.

Large doses can be toxic because they produce excessive excitation of the neuromuscular synapse and so disrupt movement and breathing. In small doses, however, physostigmine is used to treat myasthenia gravis, a condition of muscular weakness in which muscle receptors are less than normally responsive to acetylcholine (recall "Myasthenia Gravis" on page 132). The action of physostigmine is short lived, lasting only a few minutes or, at most, a half hour. But another class of compounds called *organophosphates* bind irreversibly to acetylcholinesterase and consequently are extremely toxic. Many insecticides and chemical weapons are organophosphates. Insects use glutamate as a neurotransmitter at the nerve–muscle junction but, elsewhere in their nervous systems, they have numerous nicotine receptors. Thus, organophosphates poison insects by acting centrally, but they poison chordates by acting peripherally as well.

Hundreds of other drugs can act on ACh neuromuscular synapses, and thousands of additional substances can act on other kinds of synapses. A few that are neurotoxins are listed in **Table 7-1**. Despite their varied effects, all these substances act either as agonists or as antagonists. If you understand the opposing actions of agonists and antagonists, you will also understand how some drugs can be used as antidotes for poisoning by other drugs.

If a drug or toxin that is ingested affects neuromuscular synapses, will it also affect acetylcholine synapses in the brain? That depends on whether the substance can cross the blood–brain barrier. Some of the drugs that act on ACh synapses at the muscles can also act on ACh synapses in the brain. For example, physostigmine and nicotine can readily pass the blood–brain barrier and affect the brain, whereas curare cannot. Thus, whether a cholinergic agonist or antagonist has psychoactive action depends on the size and structure of its molecules, which determine whether that substance can reach the brain.

Table 7-1	Some Neurotoxins, Their Sources, and Their Actions	
Substance	**Origin**	**Action**
Tetrodotoxin	Puffer fish	Blocks membrane permeability to Na^+ ions
Magnesium	Natural element	Blocks Ca^{2+} channels
Reserpine	Tree	Destroys storage granules
Colchicine	Crocus plant	Blocks microtubules
Caffeine	Coffee bean	Blocks adenosine receptors, blocks Ca^{2+} channels
Spider venom	Black widow spider	Stimulates ACh release
Botulin toxin	Food poisoning	Blocks ACh release
Curare	Plant berry	Blocks ACh receptors
Rabies virus	Infected animal	Blocks ACh receptors
Ibotenic acid	Mushroom	Similar to domoic acid/mimics glutamate
Strychnine	Plant	Blocks glycine
Apamin	Bees and wasps	Blocks Ca^{2+} channels

In Review

Drugs are substances used to treat physical or mental disorders. Psychoactive drugs, substances that produce changes in behavior by acting on the nervous system, are one subject of psychopharmacology, the study of how drugs affect the nervous system and behavior. Drugs encounter various barriers on the journey between their entry into the body and their action at a CNS target. Perhaps the most important obstacle is the blood–brain barrier, which generally allows only substances needed for nourishing the brain to pass from the capillaries into the CNS. Most drugs that have psychoactive effects do so by crossing the blood–brain barrier and influencing chemical reactions at brain synapses. Drugs that influence communication between neurons do so by acting either as agonists (increasing) or as antagonists (decreasing) the effectiveness of neurotransmission. There are, however, great individual differences in people's responses to drugs due to differences in age, sex, body size, and other factors that affect sensitivity to a particular substance. The body eliminates drugs through feces, urine, sweat glands, the breath, and breast milk.

CLASSIFICATION OF PSYCHOACTIVE DRUGS

Drugs with similar chemical structures can have quite different effects, whereas drugs having different structures can have very similar effects. Hence classifications based on a drug's chemical structure have not been very successful. Classification schemes based on

Barbiturate. Drug that produces sedation and sleep.

Antianxiety agent. Drug that reduces anxiety; minor tranquillizers such as benzodiazepines and sedative-hypnotic agents are of this type.

Tolerance. Lessening of response to a drug over time.

Cross-tolerance. Response to a novel drug is reduced because of tolerance developed in response to a related drug.

To learn more about the variety of psychoactive drugs, visit the Chapter 7 Web links on the *Brain and Behavior* Web site (**www.worthpublishers. com/kolb**).

Table 7-2	**Classification of Psychoactive Drugs**

I. Sedative hypnotics and antianxiety agents

  Barbiturates (anesthetic agents), alcohol

  Benzodiazepines: diazepam (Valium)

II. Antipsychotic agents

  Phenothiazines: chlorpromazine

  Butyrophenones: haloperidol

III. Antidepressants

  Monoamine oxydase (MAO) inhibitors

  Tricyclic antidepressants: imipramine (Tofranil)

  Atypical antidepressants: fluoxetine (Prozac)

IV. Mood stabilizers

  Lithium

V. Narcotic analgesics

  Morphine, codeine, heroin

VI. Psychomotor stimulants

  Cocaine, amphetamine, caffeine, nicotine

VII. Psychedelics and hallucinogens

  Anticholinergics: atropine

  Noradrenergics: mescaline

  Serotonergics: LSD (lysergic acid diethylamide), psilocybin

  Tetrahydrocannabinol: marijuana

receptors in the brain also have been problematic, because a single drug can act on many different receptors. The same problem arises with classification systems based on the neurotransmitter that a drug affects, because many drugs act on many different transmitters.

The classification that we use, summarized in **Table 7-2**, is based on the most pronounced behavioral or psychoactive effect that a drug produces. That breakdown divides drugs into seven classes, with each class containing from a few to many thousands of different chemicals in its subcategories.

Drugs that are used to treat neuropsychological illnesses are listed again in **Table 7-3**, along with the dates that they were discovered and the names of their discoverers. You may be surprised to know that their therapeutic actions were all originally discovered by accident. Subsequently, scientists and pharmaceutical companies developed many forms of each drug in an effort to increase its effectiveness and reduce its side effects. At

Table 7-3	**Drugs Used for the Treatment of Mental Illness**			
Illness	Drug class	Representative drug	Common trade name	Discoverer
Schizophrenia	Phenothiazines	Chlorpromazine	Largactile Thorazine Haldol	Jean Delay and Pierre Deniker (France), 1952
	Butyrophenone	Haloperidol		Paul Janssen (Belgium), 1957
Depression	Monoamine oxidase (MAO) inhibitors	Iproniazid	Marsilid	Nathan S. Kline and J. C. Saunders (United States), 1956
	Tricyclic antidepressants	Imipramine	Tofranil	Roland Kuhn (Switzerland), 1957
	Selective serotonin reuptake inhibitors	Fluoxetine	Prozac	Eli Lilly Company, 1986
Bipolar disorder	Lithium (metallic element)			John Cade (Australia), 1949
Anxiety disorders	Benzodiazepines	Chlordiazepoxide	Librium Valium	Leo Sternbach (Poland), 1940
	Meprobamate		Miltown Equanil	Frank Berger and William Bradley (Czechoslovakia), 1946

the same time, experimental researchers attempted to explain each drug's action on the nervous system—explanations that are as yet incomplete. We will consider the actions of some of these drugs as we describe the classification system outlined in Table 7-2.

Antianxiety Agents and Sedative Hypnotics

The effects of antianxiety drugs and sedative hypnotics differ, depending on their dose. At low doses they reduce anxiety, at medium doses they sedate, and at high doses they produce anesthesia or coma. At very high doses they can kill (**Figure 7-7**).

Most common among this diverse group of drugs are alcohol, barbiturates, and benzodiazepines. Alcohol is well known to most people because it is so widely consumed. Its potentially devastating effects on developing fetuses are explored in "Fetal Alcohol Syndrome," on page 236. **Barbiturates** are sometimes prescribed as a sleeping medication, but they are now mainly used to induce anesthesia before surgery. *Benzodiazepines* are also known as *minor tranquilizers* or **antianxiety agents.** An example is the widely prescribed drug Valium.

Benzodiazepines are often used by people who are having trouble coping with a major life stress, such as a traumatic accident or a death in the family. Whereas both alcohol and barbiturates can induce sleep, anesthesia, and coma at doses only slightly higher than those that produce sedation, the dose of benzodiazepines that produces sleep and anesthesia is substantially higher than that which is needed to relieve anxiety.

A characteristic feature of sedative hypnotics is that they cause weaker and weaker responses in the user who takes repeated doses. A larger dose is then required to maintain the drug's initial effect. This lessening of response to a drug over time is called **tolerance. Cross-tolerance** develops when the tolerance developed for one drug is carried over to a different drug.

Cross-tolerance suggests that the two drugs are similar in their actions on the nervous system. Alcohol, barbiturates, and benzodiazepines show cross-tolerance, suggesting that they affect a common nervous system target. This common target is now known to be the receptor sites for the major inhibitory neurotransmitter GABA. Neurons that contain GABA are widely distributed in the nervous system and function to inhibit the activity of other neurons (see Chapter 5).

One of the receptors affected by GABA is the GABA$_A$ receptor. As illustrated at the left in **Figure 7-8**, this receptor contains a chloride channel. Excitation of the receptor produces an influx of Cl– ions through its pore. Remember that an influx of Cl– ions increases the concentration of negative charges inside the cell membrane, hyperpolarizing it and making it less likely to initiate or propagate an action potential. The inhibitory effect of GABA, therefore, is to decrease a neuron's rate of firing.

The GABA$_A$ receptor is a target for sedative hypnotics because it has not only a binding site for GABA but two other binding sites as well. One of these sites accepts alcohol and barbiturates (the sedative-hypnotic site), whereas the other accepts benzodiazepines (the antianxiety site). Drugs binding to the sedative-hypnotic site directly increase the influx of chloride ions and so act like GABA. Consequently, the higher the dose of these drugs, the greater their inhibitory effect on neurons.

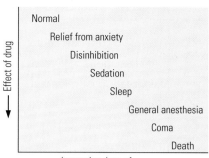

Normal
Relief from anxiety
Disinhibition
Sedation
Sleep
General anesthesia
Coma
Death

Effect of drug →

Increasing dose of sedative-hypnotic drug ⟶

Figure 7-7

Effects of Sedatives This continuum of behavioral sedation shows how increasing doses of sedative-hypnotic drugs can affect behavior.

Figure 7-8

Drug Effects at the GABA$_A$ Receptor Sedative hypnotics, antianxiety agents, and GABA each have different binding sites.

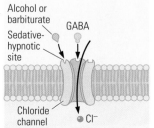

Alcohol or barbiturate
Sedative-hypnotic site
GABA
Chloride channel
Cl–

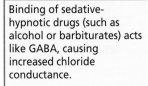

Binding of sedative-hypnotic drugs (such as alcohol or barbiturates) acts like GABA, causing increased chloride conductance.

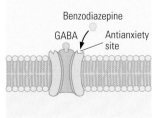

Benzodiazepine
GABA
Antianxiety site

Binding of antianxiety drugs (benzodiazepines) enhances binding effects of GABA.

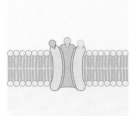

Because of their different actions, these drugs should never be taken together. Combined doses can cause coma or death.

Fetal Alcohol Syndrome

The term **fetal alcohol syndrome** (FAS) was coined in 1973 to describe a pattern of physical malformation and mental retardation observed in some children born of alcoholic mothers. Children with FAS may have abnormal facial features, such as unusually wide spacing between the eyes. They also have a range of brain abnormalities, from small brains with abnormal gyri to abnormal clusters of cells and misaligned cells in the cortex.

Related to these brain abnormalities are certain behavioral symptoms that FAS children tend to have in common. They display varying degrees of learning disabilities and lowered intelligence test scores, as well as hyperactivity and other social problems.

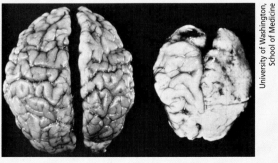

(*Top*) Effects of fetal alcohol syndrome are not merely physical; many FAS children are severely retarded. (*Bottom*) The convolutions characteristic of the brain of a normal child (*left*) are grossly underdeveloped in the brain of a child who suffered from fetal alcohol syndrome (*right*).

The identification of FAS stimulated widespread interest in the effects of alcohol consumption by pregnant women. The offspring of approximately 6 percent of alcoholic mothers suffer from pronounced FAS. In major cities, the incidence of FAS is about 1 in 700 births. Its incidence increases to as many as 1 in 8 births on one Native American reservation in Canada.

FAS is not an all-or-none syndrome. Alcohol-induced abnormalities can vary from hardly noticeable physical and psychological effects to the full-blown FAS syndrome. The severity of effects is thought to be related to when, how much, and how frequently alcohol is consumed in the course of pregnancy. Apparently, the effects are worse if alcohol is consumed in the first 3 months of pregnancy, which, unfortunately, may be a time when many women do not yet realize that they are pregnant.

Severe FAS is also more likely to coincide with binge drinking, which produces high blood-alcohol levels. Other factors related to a more severe outcome are poor nutritional health of the mother and the mother's use of other drugs, including the nicotine in cigarettes.

A major question raised by FAS is how much alcohol is too much to drink during pregnancy. The answer to this question is complex, because the effects of alcohol on a fetus depend on so many factors. To be completely safe, it is best not to drink at all in the months preceding pregnancy and during it. This conclusion is supported by findings that as little as one drink of alcohol per day during pregnancy can lead to a decrease in intelligence test scores of children.

Fetal alcohol syndrome in both its full-blown and milder forms has important lessons for us. Alcohol is a widely used drug. When taken in moderation, it is thought to have some health benefits; yet it does pose risks, although those risks are completely preventable if alcohol is used appropriately.

A major problem is that women who are most at risk for bearing FAS babies are poor and not well educated, with alcohol-consumption problems that predate pregnancy and little access to prenatal care. It is often difficult to inform these women about the dangers that alcohol poses to a fetus and to encourage them to abstain from drinking while they are pregnant.

The effect of antianxiety drugs is different. Excitation of the antianxiety site enhances the binding of GABA to its receptor site (Figure 7-8, center), which means that the availability of GABA determines the potency of an antianxiety drug. Because GABA is very quickly reabsorbed by the neurons that secrete it and by surrounding glial cells, GABA concentrations are never excessive, making it hard to overdose on antianxiety drugs.

Scientists do not know what natural substances bind to the GABA$_A$ receptor binding sites other than GABA. A. Leslie Morrow and her coworkers (1999) suggest that a natural brain hormone, allopregnanolone, may bind to the sedative-hypnotic site. Allopregnanolone is produced by the pituitary gland. An additional mechanism by which alcohol may have its sedative effects is by facilitating the production of allopregnanolone, which in turn activates the sedative-hypnotic site of the GABA$_A$ receptor, thus producing sedation. An explanation of the less-potent effect of alcohol on human males than on females is that females have higher levels of allopregnanolone, thus making them more sensitive to the effects of alcohol.

Because of their different actions on the GABA$_A$ receptor, sedative-hypnotic and antianxiety drugs should never be taken together (Figure 7-8, right). A sedative hypnotic acts like GABA, but, unlike GABA, it is not quickly absorbed by surrounding cells. Thus, by remaining at the binding site, its effects are enhanced by an antianxiety drug. The cumulative action of the two drugs will therefore exceed the individual action of either one. Even small combined doses of antianxiety and sedative-hypnotic drugs can produce coma or death.

Drugs that act on GABA receptors may affect the development of the brain. Fetal alcohol syndrome is an example of a developmental disorder due to effects of alcohol that is ingested by a mother on the subsequent development and behavior of a fetus.

Antipsychotic Agents

The term *psychosis* is applied to neuropsychological conditions such as schizophrenia, characterized by hallucinations (false sensory perceptions) or delusions (false beliefs). The use of antipsychotic drugs, also called **major tranquilizers** or **neuroleptics,** has greatly improved the functioning of schizophrenia patients and contributed to reducing the number housed in institutions, as **Figure 7-9** graphs. The success of antipsychotic agents is an important therapeutic achievement because the incidence of schizophrenia is high, about 1 in every 100 people.

Although major tranquilizers have been widely used for 50 years, their therapeutic actions are still not understood. They have an immediate effect in reducing motor activity, and so they alleviate the excessive agitation of some schizophrenia patients. In fact, one of their negative side effects can be to produce symptoms reminiscent of Parkinson's disease, in which control over movement is impaired. After a short period of use they can reduce the symptoms of schizophrenia. With prolonged use, neuroleptics can cause dyskinesia, including rhythmical movements of the mouth, hands, and other body parts. The effects are usually reversible if the person stops taking the drug.

At least part of the action of antipsychotic drugs is to block the D$_2$ receptor for dopamine. This action led to the **dopamine hypothesis of schizophrenia,**

Fetal alcohol syndrome (FAS). Pattern of physical malformation and mental retardation observed in some children born of alcoholic mothers.

Major tranquilizer (neuroleptic). Drug that blocks the D$_2$ receptor; used mainly for treating schizophrenia.

Dopamine hypothesis of schizophrenia. Proposal that schizophrenic symptoms are due to excess activity of the neurotransmitter dopamine.

⊙ On your *Foundations* CD, find the area on synaptic transmission in the module on neural communication. Review the process of inhibitory synaptic function and consider drugs that, like GABA, act as antagonists in the CNS.

Figure 7-9

Trends in Resident Care　The dramatic decrease in the number of resident patients in state and municipal mental hospitals in the United States began after 1955, when psychoactive drugs were introduced into widespread therapeutic use. Adapted from *A Primer of Drug Action* (p. 276), by R. M. Julien, 1995, New York: W. H. Freeman and Company.

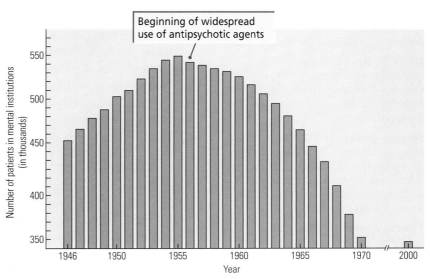

Beginning of widespread use of antipsychotic agents

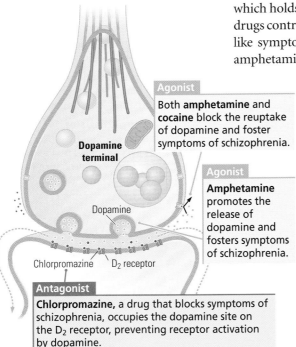

Agonist

Both **amphetamine** and **cocaine** block the reuptake of dopamine and foster symptoms of schizophrenia.

Agonist

Amphetamine promotes the release of dopamine and fosters symptoms of schizophrenia.

Dopamine terminal

Dopamine

Chlorpromazine   D₂ receptor

Antagonist

Chlorpromazine, a drug that blocks symptoms of schizophrenia, occupies the dopamine site on the D₂ receptor, preventing receptor activation by dopamine.

Figure 7-10

Drug Effects at D₂ Receptors   That chlorpromazine can lessen schizophrenia symptoms, whereas the abuse of amphetamine or cocaine can produce them, suggests that excessive activity at the dopamine receptor is related to schizophrenia.

Monoamine oxidase (MAO) inhibitor. Antidepressant drug that blocks the enzyme monoamine oxidase from degrading neurotransmitters such as dopamine, noradrenaline and serotonin.

Tricyclic antidepressant. First-generation antidepressant drug with a chemical structure characterized by three rings that blocks serotonin reuptake transporter proteins.

Second-generation antidepressant. Drug whose action is similar to tricyclics (first-generation antidepressants) but more selective in its action on the serotonin reuptake transporter proteins; also called *atypical antidepressant.*

Selective serotonin reuptake inhibitor (SSRI). Tricyclic antidepressant drug that blocks the reuptake of serotonin into the presynaptic terminal.

which holds that some forms may be related to excessive DA activity, which antipsychotic drugs control. Other support for the dopamine hypothesis comes from the schizophrenia-like symptoms of chronic users of amphetamine, a stimulant. As **Figure 7-10** shows, amphetamine is a DA agonist that fosters the release of DA from the presynaptic membrane of DA synapses and blocks the reuptake of DA from the synaptic cleft. If amphetamine causes schizophrenia-like symptoms by increasing DA activity, perhaps naturally occurring schizophrenia is related to excessive DA action, too.

Even though such drug effects lend support to the dopamine hypothesis of schizophrenia, experimental studies have been unable to find clear evidence of dopamine-related differences in the brains of normal people and those of schizophrenia patients. The brains of patients with schizophrenia do not contain a greater number of DA synapses, release more DA from presynaptic membranes, or possess more D₂ receptors. Consequently, the cause of schizophrenia and the mechanism by which antipsychotic agents work currently remain unclear.

Antidepressants

Major depression—a mood disorder characterized by prolonged feelings of worthlessness and guilt, the disruption of normal eating habits, sleep disturbances, a general slowing of behavior, and frequent thoughts of suicide—is very common. At any given time, about 6 percent of the adult population suffers from it, and, in the course of a lifetime, 30 percent may experience at least one episode that lasts for months or longer. Depression affects twice as many women as men.

Most people recover from depression within a year of its onset, but, if the illness is left untreated, the incidence of suicide is high, as discussed in "Major Depression" on page 240. Of all psychological disorders, major depression is one of the most treatable, and cognitive and intrapersonal therapies are as effective as drug therapies (Comer, 2004). Three different types of drugs have antidepressant effects: the **monoamine oxidase (MAO) inhibitors;** the **tricyclic antidepressants,** so called because of their three-ringed chemical structure; and the **second-generation antidepressants,** sometimes called atypical antidepressants, that include fluoxetine (Prozac). Second-generation antidepressants do not have a three-ringed structure, but they are similar to the tricyclics in their actions.

Antidepressants are thought to act by improving chemical neurotransmission at serotonin, noradrenaline, histamine, and acetylcholine synapses, and perhaps at dopamine synapses as well. **Figure 7-11** shows their action at a serotonin synapse, the synapse on which most research is focused. As you can see, MAO inhibitors and the tricyclic and second-generation antidepressants have different mechanisms of action in increasing the availability of serotonin.

Monoamine oxidase is an enzyme that breaks down serotonin within the axon terminal. The inhibition of MAO by a MAO inhibitor therefore provides more serotonin for release with each action potential. The tricyclic antidepressants and the second-generation antidepressants block the reuptake transporter that takes serotonin back into the axon terminal. The second-generation antidepressants are thought to be especially selective in blocking serotonin reuptake, and, consequently, some are also called **selective serotonin reuptake inhibitors** (SSRIs). Because the transporter is blocked, serotonin remains in the synaptic cleft for a longer period, thus prolonging its action on postsynaptic receptors.

There is, however, a significant problem in understanding how antidepressants function. Although these drugs begin to affect synapses very quickly, their antidepressant actions take weeks to develop. No one is sure why. Of interest in this respect is the fact that Prozac increases the production of new neurons in the hippocampus, a limbic structure in the temporal lobes. The hippocampus is vulnerable to stress-induced damage, and its restoration by Prozac has been proposed to underlie the drug's antidepressant effects (Santarelli et al., 2003). We consider these effects in detail in Chapter 15.

About 20 percent of patients with depression fail to respond to antidepressant drugs. Accordingly, depression can likely have many other causes including the dysfunction of other transmitter systems and even damage to the brain, including the frontal lobes. Some people cannot tolerate the side effects of antidepressants, which can include increased anxiety, sexual dysfunction, sedation, dry mouth, blurred vision, and memory impairment.

Although many scientists hoped that the second-generation antidepressants would produce fewer side effects than do tricyclic antidepressants, that hope has not been fully realized. In fact, how SSRIs act on the brain is unclear, although slight modifications in the molecular structure of an antidepressant can change its affinity for different brain targets so that it can, for example, affect noradrenaline or dopamine synapses or even affect corticotropin-releasing factor, a stress hormone implicated in depression.

For instance, advertisements for Prozac, one of the more selective antidepressant compounds, suggest that this drug can be used to treat not only depression but also obsessive-compulsive disorder (OCD). The major symptoms of OCD are obsessive thoughts (ideas that people cannot get out of their heads) and compulsive behaviors (ritual-like actions that they endlessly perform). Although OCD is related to guilt and anxiety, as is depression, it is usually classified as an anxiety disorder, a separate condition from depression.

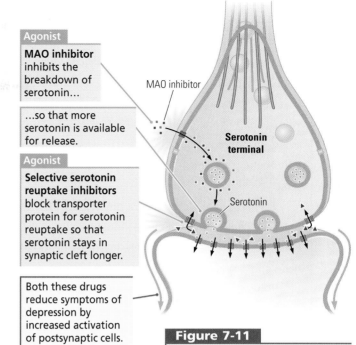

Agonist

MAO inhibitor inhibits the breakdown of serotonin...

...so that more serotonin is available for release.

Agonist

Selective serotonin reuptake inhibitors block transporter protein for serotonin reuptake so that serotonin stays in synaptic cleft longer.

Both these drugs reduce symptoms of depression by increased activation of postsynaptic cells.

Figure 7-11

Drug Effects at Serotonin Receptors Different antidepressant drugs act on the serotonin synapse in different ways to increase the availability of serotonin.

Narcotic Analgesics

The term **narcotic analgesics** describes a group of drugs that have sleep-inducing (narcotic) and pain-relieving (analgesic) properties. Many of these drugs are derived from *opium,* an extract of the seeds of the opium poppy, *Papaver somniferum,* which is shown in **Figure 7-12**. Opium has been used for thousands of years to produce euphoria, analgesia, sleep, and relief from diarrhea and coughing.

In 1805, German chemist Friedrich Sertürner synthesized two pure substances from the poppy plant: codeine and morphine. Codeine is often an ingredient in prescription cough medicine and pain relievers. Morphine, named for Morpheus, the Greek god of dreams, is a very powerful pain reliever. Despite decades of research, no other drug has been found that exceeds morphine's effectiveness as an analgesic.

Opium antagonists such as *nalorphine* and *naloxone* block the actions of morphine and so are useful in treating morphine overdoses. Heroin, another opiate drug, is synthesized from morphine. It is more fat soluble than morphine and penetrates the blood–brain barrier more quickly, allowing it to produce very rapid relief from pain. Although heroin is a legal drug in some countries, it is illegal in others, including the United States.

Narcotic analgesic. Drug like morphine, with sleep-inducing (narcotic) and pain-relieving (analgesic) properties.

Figure 7-12

Potent Poppy Opium is obtained from the seeds of the opium poppy (*left*). Morphine (*center*) is extracted from opium, and heroin (*right*) is in turn synthesized from morphine.

Major Depression

P. H. was a 53-year-old high school teacher who, although popular with his students, was feeling less and less satisfaction from his work. His marriage was foundering because he was becoming apathetic and no longer wanted to socialize or go on holidays with his wife. He was having great difficulty getting up in the morning and arriving at school on time.

P. H. eventually consulted a physician with a complaint of severe chest pains, which he thought signified that he was about to have a heart attack. He informed his doctor that a heart attack would be a welcome relief because it would end his problems. The physician concluded that P. H. was suffering from depression and referred him to a psychiatrist.

The psychiatrist arranged for P. H. to come in once a week for counseling and gave him a prescription for an MAO inhibitor. The psychiatrist informed P. H. that many foods contain tyramine, a chemical that can raise blood pressure to dangerous levels, and, because the action of this chemical increases when taking MAO inhibitors, he should avoid foods that contain tyramine. The psychiatrist gave him a list of foods to be avoided and especially warned him against eating cheese or drinking wine, the standard advice given to patients for whom MAO inhibitors were prescribed.

A few days later, P. H. opened a bottle of wine, took a two-pound block of cheese out of the refrigerator, and began to consume them. That evening he suffered a massive left-hemisphere stroke that left him unable to speak or to walk. It seemed clear that P. H. had attempted to commit suicide.

Because of their dangers, MAO inhibitors are now seldom prescribed.

Since the 1950s, depression has been treated with antidepressant drugs, a variety of cognitive-behavior therapies (CBTs), and electroconvulsive therapy (ECT), a treatment in which electrical current is passed briefly through one hemisphere of the brain. Of the drug treatments available, tricyclic antidepressants, including the selective serotonin reuptake inhibitors (SSRIs), are now favored because they are safer and more effective than MAO inhibitors.

Although drugs are often useful in the treatment of depression, their widespread prescription is associated with considerable controversy and debate (Medwar & Hardon, 2004). For example, prompted in part by complaints from family members that drug treatments have caused suicide, especially in children, the U.S. Food and Drug Administration has advised physicians to monitor the side effects of SSRIs including fluoxetine (Prozac), sertraline (Zoloft), and paroxetine (Paxil, Seroxat). The issue of suicide is complex in part because many of these drugs have not been approved by the FDA for children.

Nevertheless, findings from a number of studies show no difference in the rate of suicide between groups receiving serotonin reuptake inhibitors and a placebo (Khan, Khan, Kolts, & Brown, 2003). At best, these findings suggest that drug treatment is not effective in preventing suicide in this suicide-prone population and that other suicide-prevention measures should be used.

○ Visit the Chapter 7 Web links on the *Brain and Behavior* Web site (**www.worthpublishers.com/kolb**) to read more about current events and controversies surrounding antidepressants.

Among the opioids prescribed for clinical use in pain management are morphine, hydromorphone, levorphanol, oxymorphone, methadone, meperidine, oxycodone, and fentanyl (Inturrisi, 2002). The opioids are potently addictive; so, in addition to using illegally manufactured and distributed drugs such as heroin, drug abusers often obtain and abuse opioid drugs intended for pain management. People who suffer from chronic pain and who use opioids for pain relief also can become addicted, although such addictions are not common.

What are the effects of opiate drugs on the CNS? Candace Pert and Solomon Snyder (1973) provided an important answer to this question by injecting radioactive opiates into the brain and identifying special receptors to which the opiates bound. But what were these receptors doing in the brain? Opiates, such as morphine, after all, are not naturally occurring brain chemicals. This question was answered by Scottish pharmacologists John Hughes and Hans Kosterlitz (1977), who identified two short peptides that had opioid properties and appeared to be neurotransmitters (see Figure 5-12). They called these opiate-like transmitters **endorphins,** an abridgement of the phrase *endo*genous m*orphin*e-like substances.

We now know that there are endorphin-containing neurons in many brain regions and that morphine is similar enough to endorphins to mimic their action in the brain. Researchers have extensively studied whether endorphins can be used as drugs to relieve pain. The answer is so far mixed.

Although synthetic endorphins do alleviate pain, they also cause other effects, including nausea, and they are difficult to deliver to the brain. Consequently, morphine remains a preferred pain treatment. Morphine acts on three opioid-receptor classes: mu, delta, and kappa receptors. Findings from studies on mice in which the genes that produce these receptors have been knocked out show that the mu receptor is critical both for morphine's effects on pain and for its addictive properties. Thus, the objectives of pain research in producing an analgesic that does not produce addiction may be difficult to realize.

> **Endorphin.** Peptide hormone that acts as a neurotransmitter and may be associated with feelings of pain or pleasure; mimicked by opioid drugs such as morphine, heroin, opium, and codeine.

Figure 7-13

Behavioral Stimulant Cocaine (*left*) is obtained from the leaves of the coca plant (*center*). Crack cocaine (*right*) is chemically altered to form "rocks" that vaporize when heated at low temperatures.

Stimulants

This diverse group of drugs increases the activity of neurons in a number of ways. Stimulants are subdivided into three groups: behavioral stimulants, general stimulants, and psychedelics.

BEHAVIORAL STIMULANTS

Behavioral stimulants are drugs that increase motor behavior as well as elevate a person's mood and level of alertness. Two examples are cocaine and amphetamine. Cocaine is a powder extracted from the Peruvian coca shrub, shown in **Figure 7-13**. The indigenous people of Peru have chewed coca leaves through the generations to increase their stamina in the harsh environment of the high elevations at which they live.

Refined cocaine can either be sniffed ("snorted") or injected. Cocaine users who do not like to inject cocaine intravenously or cannot afford it in powdered form, sniff or smoke "rocks," a potent, highly concentrated form also called "crack." Crack is chemically altered so that it vaporizes at low temperatures, and the vapors are inhaled.

Figure 7-14

Warning Label Cocaine was once an ingredient in a number of invigorating beverages, including Coca-Cola.

Cocaine was originally popularized as an antidepressant by Viennese psychoanalyst Sigmund Freud. In an 1884 paper titled "In Praise of Coca," Freud (1974) concluded: "The main use of coca will undoubtedly remain that which the Indians have made of it for centuries: it is of value in all cases where the primary aim is to increase the physical capacity of the body for a given short period of time and to hold strength in reserve to meet further demands—especially when outward circumstances exclude the possibility of obtaining the rest and nourishment normally necessary for great exertion."

Sigmund Freud
(1856–1939)

Cocaine was once widely used in the manufacture of soft drinks and wine mixtures, which were promoted as invigorating tonics. It is the origin of the trade name Coca-Cola, because this soft drink once contained cocaine, as suggested by the advertisement in **Figure 7-14**. The addictive properties of cocaine soon became apparent, however.

Amphetamine. Drug that releases the neurotransmitter dopamine into its synapse and, like cocaine, blocks dopamine reuptake.

Psychedelic drug. Drug that can alter sensation and perception; lysergic acid dielthylmide, mescalin, and psilocybin are examples.

Freud had recommended cocaine to a close friend who, in an attempt to relieve excruciating pain after the amputation of his thumb, had become addicted to morphine. The euphoric effects of cocaine helped the friend withdraw from the morphine, but soon he required larger and larger doses of cocaine. Eventually, he experienced euphoric episodes followed by a sudden crash after each injection. He continued to use larger and larger doses. Similar experiences by others led to an escalating negative view of cocaine use.

Freud also recommended that cocaine could be used as a local anesthetic. Cocaine did prove valuable as a local anesthetic, and many derivatives, such as Novocaine, are used for this purpose today.

Amphetamine is a synthetic compound that was discovered in attempts to synthesize the neurotransmitter epinephrine. Both amphetamine and cocaine are dopamine agonists that act first by blocking the dopamine reuptake transporter. Interferring with the reuptake mechanism leaves more DA available in the synaptic cleft. Amphetamine also stimulates the release of DA from presynaptic membranes. Both mechanisms increase the amount of DA available in synapses to stimulate DA receptors.

Amphetamine was first used as a treatment for asthma. A form of amphetamine, Benzedrine, was sold in inhalers as a nonprescription drug through the 1940s. Soon people discovered that they could open the container and ingest its contents to obtain an energizing effect. In 1937, an article in the *Journal of the American Medical Association* reported that Benzedrine tablets improved performance on mental-efficiency tests. This information was quickly disseminated among students, who began to use the drug as an aid to study for examinations.

Amphetamine was widely used in World War II to help keep troops and pilots alert (and is still used by the U.S. Air Force for this purpose today) and to improve the productivity of wartime workers. It is also used as a weight-loss aid. Many over-the-counter compounds marked as stimulants or weight-loss aids have amphetamine-like pharmacological actions.

In the 1960s, drug users discovered that they could obtain an immediate pleasurable "rush," often described as a whole-body orgasm, by the intravenous injection of amphetamine. People who took amphetamine in this way and were called "speed freaks" would inject the drug every few hours for days, remaining in a wide-awake, excited state without eating. They would then crash in exhaustion and hunger and, after a few days of recovery, would begin the cycle again. One explanation for repeated injections was to prevent the depressive crash that occurred when the drug wore off.

Today, an amphetamine derivative, methamphetamine (also known as meth, speed, crank, smoke, or crystal ice) is in widespread use. About 2 percent of the U.S. population have used it. The widespread use of methamphetamine is related to its ease of manufacture in illicit laboratories and to its potency, thus making it a relatively inexpensive, yet potentially devastating, drug (Anglin, Burke, Perrochet, Stamper, & Dawud-Noursi, 2000).

GENERAL STIMULANTS

General stimulants are drugs that cause a general increase in the metabolic activity of cells. Caffeine, a widely used stimulant, inhibits an enzyme that ordinarily breaks down the second messenger cyclic adenosine monophosphate (cAMP), discussed in relation to learning at the synapse in Chapter 5. The resulting increase in cAMP leads to an increase in glucose production within cells, thus making more energy available and allowing higher rates of cellular activity.

PSYCHEDELICS

Psychedelic drugs alter sensory perception and cognitive processes. There are four major types of psychedelics:

Peyote cactus

Marijuana leaf

Psilocybe mushroom

1. Acetylcholine psychedelics either block or facilitate transmission at acetylcholine synapses in the brain.
2. Norepinephrine psychedelics include mescaline, obtained from the peyote cactus, which is legal in the United States for use by Native Americans for religious practices.
3. Tetrahydrocannabinol (THC), the active ingredient in marijuana, is obtained from the hemp plant *Cannabis sativa*. There is growing evidence that cannabis acts on endogenous THC receptors called the CB1 and CB2 receptors thought by scientists to be the receptors for an endogenous neurotransmitter called anandamide. Surprisingly, results from a number of lines of research suggest that anandamide plays a role in enhancing forgetting. The idea is that anandamide prevents memory systems of the brain from being overwhelmed by the information to which the brain is exposed each day. Thus, THC use may have a detrimental effect on memory.
4. Serotonin psychedelics likely achieve part of their psychedelic action by affecting serotonin neurons. Lysergic acid diethylamide (LSD) and psilocybin (obtained from a certain mushroom) stimulate postsynaptic receptors of some serotonin synapses and block the activity of other serotonin neurons through serotonin autoreceptors. Psychedelics may stimulate other transmitter systems, including norepinephrine receptors.

In Review

Classifying psychoactive drugs by their principal behavioral effects yields seven major categories: sedative hypnotics and antianxiety agents, antipsychotic agents, antidepressants, mood stabilizers, narcotic analgesics, psychomotor stimulants, and stimulants that have psychedelic and hallucinogenic effects. Researchers are still learning how these drugs act on the nervous system. Sedative hypnotics and antianxiety agents, including alcohol, barbiturates, and benzodiazepines, affect receptor sites for the neurotransmitter GABA. Although the therapeutic actions of antianxiety agents are still not understood, one of those actions is to block a certain kind of DA receptor. Antidepressants, including the SSRIs and MAO inhibitors, are thought to act by improving chemical transmission in serotonin, noradrenaline, histamine, and acetylcholine receptors. The narcotic analgesics derived from opium produce their effects by binding to special receptors for naturally occurring brain chemicals called endorphins. Cocaine and amphetamine are psychomotor stimulants that act as DA agonists, making more DA available in synapses. As scientists continue to study the actions of psychoactive drugs, they will also learn much more about neuropsychological disorders and possible treatments.

DRUGS, EXPERIENCE, CONTEXT, AND GENES

Many behaviors trigger very predictable results. When you strike the same piano key repeatedly, you hear the same note each time. When you flick a light switch over and over again, the same bulb goes on exactly as before. This cause-and-effect consistency of many things in our world does not extend to psychoactive drugs.

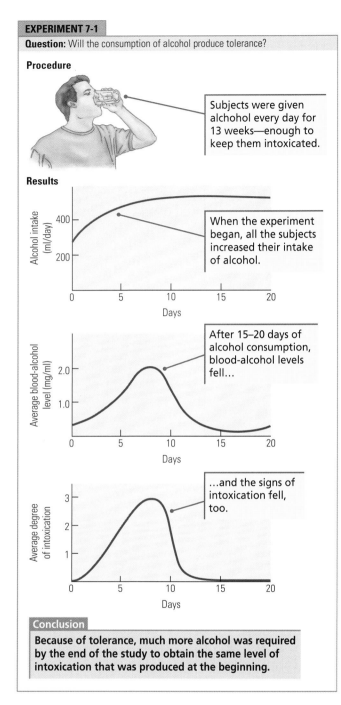

EXPERIMENT 7-1

Question: Will the consumption of alcohol produce tolerance?

Procedure

Subjects were given alchohol every day for 13 weeks—enough to keep them intoxicated.

Results

When the experiment began, all the subjects increased their intake of alcohol.

After 15–20 days of alcohol consumption, blood-alcohol levels fell...

...and the signs of intoxication fell, too.

Conclusion

Because of tolerance, much more alcohol was required by the end of the study to obtain the same level of intoxication that was produced at the beginning.

Adapted from "An Experimental Study of the Etiology of 'Rum Fits' and Delirium Tremens," by H. Isbell, H. F. Fraser, A. Winkler, R. E. Belleville, and A. J. Eisenman, 1955, *Quarterly Journal of Studies on Alcohol, 16,* pp. 1–21.

A drug will not produce the same effects every time that it is taken, for several reasons. For one thing, a drug may be taken in different contexts with different accompanying behaviors, which cause the brain to respond to it differently. The actions of a drug on one person may be quite different from its actions on someone else because a person's experience and the influence of genes also determine drug reactions. Finally, with repeated use by the same person, the effect of a drug can be dramatically different from the effect obtained with the first use. The reasons are tolerance and sensitization: many drugs produce an enduring change in the brain that, in time, can be quite substantial and can alter what subsequent doses do. In the following sections, we consider a number of ways in which repeated use of drugs changes the brain and behavior.

Tolerance

Two college freshman roommates, B. C. and A. S., went to a party, then to a bar, and by 3 AM were in a restaurant ordering pizza. A. S. decided that he wanted to watch the chef make his pizza, and off he went to the kitchen. A long and heated argument ensued between A. S., the chef, and the manager.

The two roommates then got into A. S.'s car and were leaving the parking lot when a police officer, called by the manager, drove up and stopped them. A. S. failed a breathalyzer test, which estimates body-alcohol content, and was taken into custody; but, surprisingly, B. C. passed the test, even though he had consumed the same amount of alcohol as A. S. had. Why this difference in their responses to the drinking bout?

The reason for the difference could be that B. C. had developed greater tolerance for alcohol than A. S. had. Isbell and coworkers (1955) showed how such tolerance comes about. These researchers gave volunteers in a prison enough alcohol daily in a 13-week period to keep them in a constant state of intoxication. Yet they found that the subjects did not stay drunk for 3 months straight.

When the experiment began, all the subjects showed rapidly rising levels of blood alcohol and behavioral signs of intoxication, as shown in the Results section of **Experiment 7-1**. Between the 12th and 20th days of alcohol consumption, however, blood alcohol and the signs of intoxication fell to very low levels, even though the subjects maintained a constant alcohol intake. Interestingly, too, although blood-alcohol levels and signs of intoxication fluctuated in subsequent days of the study, one did not always correspond with the other. A relatively high blood-alcohol level was sometimes associated with a low outward appearance of intoxication. Why?

These results were likely the products of three different kinds of tolerance:

1. In the development of *metabolic tolerance,* the number of enzymes needed to break down alcohol in the liver, blood, and brain increases. As a result, any alcohol that is consumed is metabolized more quickly, and so blood-alcohol levels are reduced.
2. In the development of *cellular tolerance,* the activities of brain cells adjust to minimize the effects of alcohol present in the blood. This kind of tolerance can help

explain why the behavioral signs of intoxication may be very low despite a relatively high blood-alcohol level.

3. *Learned tolerance,* too, can help explain a drop in the outward signs of intoxication. As people learn to cope with the daily demands of living while under the influence of alcohol, they may no longer appear to be drunk.

That learning plays a role in tolerance to alcohol may surprise you, but this role has been confirmed in many studies. In an early description of the effect, Wenger and his coworkers (1981) trained rats to walk on a narrow conveyor belt to prevent electric shock to their feet from a grid over which the belt slid. One group of rats received alcohol after training in walking the belt, whereas another group received alcohol before training. A third group received training only, and a fourth group received alcohol only.

After several days of exposure to their respective conditions, all groups were given alcohol before a walking test. The rats that had received alcohol before training performed well, whereas those that had received training and alcohol separately performed just as poorly as those that had never had alcohol before or those that had not been trained. Apparently, animals can acquire the motor skills needed to balance on a narrow belt despite alcohol intoxication. Over time, in other words, they can learn to compensate for being drunk.

The results of these experiments are relevant to our story of A. S. and B. C. A. S. came from a large city and worked for long hours assisting his father with his plumbing business. He seldom attended parties and was unaccustomed to the effects of alcohol. B. C., in contrast, came from a small town, where he was the acclaimed local pool shark. He was accustomed to "sipping a beer" both while waiting to play and during play, which he did often. B. C.'s body, then, was prepared to metabolize alcohol, and his experience in drinking while engaging in a skilled sport had prepared him to display controlled behavior under the influence of alcohol. Enhanced metabolism and controlled behavior are manifestations of tolerance to alcohol.

Tolerance can develop not only to alcohol but also to many other drugs, such as barbiturates, amphetamine, and narcotics. In humans, for instance, a dose of 100 mg of morphine is sufficient to cause profound sedation and even death in some first-time users, but those who have developed tolerance to this drug have been known to take 4000 mg without adverse effects. Similarly, long-time users of amphetamine may take doses 100 or more times as great as the doses that they initially took to produce the same effect. In other words, with repeated administration of a drug, the effect produced by that drug may progressively diminish owing to metabolic tolerance, cellular tolerance, and learned tolerance.

Sensitization

Repeated exposure to the same drug does not always result in tolerance. Tolerance resembles habituation (recall the learning experiments in Chapter 5). The drug taker may experience the opposite reaction, an *increased* responsiveness to successive equal doses, called *sensitization.* Whereas tolerance generally develops with repeated use of a drug, sensitization is much more likely to develop with occasional use.

To demonstrate drug sensitization, Terry Robinson and Jill Becker (1986) isolated rats in observation boxes and recorded their reactions to an injection of amphetamine, especially reactions such as increases

Terry Robinson

Jill Becker

EXPERIMENT 7-2

Question: Does the injection of a drug always produce the same behavior?

Procedure 1

In the Robinson and Becker study, animals were given periodic injections of the same dose of amphetamine. Then the researchers measured the number of times each rat reared in its cage.

Procedure 2

In the Whishaw study, animals were given different numbers of swims after being injected with Flupentixol. Then the researchers measured their speed to escape to a platform in a swimming pool.

Agonist
Amphetamine

Release enhanced

Dopamine

Reuptake transporter blocked

Antagonist
Flupentixol

Receptor blocked

Flupentixol

Results 1

Number of incidents of rearing (y-axis: 12, 24)
Number of injections (x-axis: 1, 3, 5, 9)

Results 2

Time to platform (s) (y-axis: 3, 60)
Number of trials (x-axis: 1, 4, 8, 12)

Conclusion 1

Sensitization, as indicated by increased rearing, develops with periodic repeated injections.

Conclusion 2

Sensitization is also dependent on the occurrence of the behavior. The number of swims, not the spacing of swims or the treatment, causes an increase in the time it takes for the rat to reach the platform.

(*Left*) Adapted from "Enduring Changes in Brain and Behavior Produced by Chronic Amphetamine Administration: A Review and Evaluation of Animal Models of Amphetamine Psychosis," by T. E. Robinson and J. B. Becker, 1986, *Brain Research Reviews, 397,* pp. 157–198. (*Right*) Adapted from "Training-Dependent Decay in Performance Produced by the Neuroleptic *cis*(Z)-Flupentixol on Spatial Navigation by Rats in a Swimming Pool," by I. Q. Whishaw, G. Mittelman, and J. L. Evenden, 1989, *Pharmacology, Biochemistry, and Behavior, 32,* pp. 211–220.

in sniffing, rearing, and walking, which are typical rat responses to this drug. Every 3 or 4 days, the investigators repeated the procedure, shown in the Procedure 1 section of **Experiment 7-2**. The graph in the Results 1 section of the experiment shows that the behavior of the rats was more vigorous each time they received the drug.

This increased response on successive tests was not due to the animals becoming comfortable with the test situation. Control animals that received no drug did not display a similar escalation in sniffing, rearing, and walking. Moreover, the sensitization to amphetamine was enduring. Even when two injections of amphetamine were separated by months, the animals still showed an increased response to the drug. It is noteworthy also that a single exposure to the drug produced sensitization.

Remember that amphetamine is a DA agonist and acts both by stimulating the release of DA from the axon terminals of dopamine neurons and by blocking its reuptake into those terminals. Which of these two actions might underlie sensitization to amphetamine? One possibility is that sensitization is due to the release of DA. Perhaps with each successive dose of amphetamine, more DA is released, causing a progressively increasing behavioral response to the drug.

This explanation was confirmed by another experiment on rats, some of which had been sensitized to amphetamine and others of which had never been given the drug (Casteñeda, Becker, & Robinson, 1988). The basal ganglia, which are rich in DA synapses, were removed from the brain of each rat and placed in a fluid-filled container. Then the tissue was treated with amphetamine. An analysis of the fluid that bathed the tissue showed that the basal ganglia from sensitized rats released more DA than did the basal ganglia of nonsensitized rats. This increased release of DA can explain sensitization to amphetamine.

Sensitization also develops to drugs with depressant effects, such as the major tranquilizer Flupentixol, which is a DA antagonist that blocks DA receptors. Procedure 2, on the right in Experiment 7-2, shows the effect of Flupentixol on the swimming behavior of rats in another study (Whishaw, Mittleman, & Evenden, 1989). The researchers trained the rats to swim a short distance to a platform in a swimming pool. When the rats were able to reach the platform within 1 to 2 seconds, they were given an injection of Flupentixol that remained active through a single day's testing.

On the first few swims after the injection of the drug, the rats swam normally, but then they began to slow down. After about 12 swims, they simply sank

Ian Whishaw

when placed in the water and had to be removed to prevent them from drowning. This effect was not just the result of administering 12 successive swimming trials on the same day. If the rats were both injected with the drug *and* given only one swim trial each day for 12 days, the same results were obtained. On the first few days, the rats swam normally, but thereafter they began to slow down until, by the 12th day, they sank when placed into the water. Thus, it was not the drug alone, but the swimming experience under the influence of the drug that was critical to the drug's effect on performance.

Sensitization to the drug depended on the number of swims, regardless of the spacing between swims or the number of drug injections. Presumably, Flupentixol blocks DA synapses in the brain more effectively after sensitization in a way that accounts for these results.

Sensitization can be very selective with respect to the behavior affected, and it is detected only if tests are always given under the same conditions. For example, if rats are given amphetamine in their home cage on a number of occasions before a sensitization experiment starts, their behavior in the test situation does not reveal their previous drug experience. Sensitization develops as if the animals were receiving the drug for the first time.

Furthermore, sensitization is difficult to achieve in an animal that is tested in its home cage. Fraioli and coworkers (1999) gave amphetamine to two groups of rats and recorded the rats' behavioral responses to successive injections. One group of rats lived in the test apparatus; so, for that group, home was the test box. The other group of rats was taken out of its normal home cage and placed in the test box for each day's experimentation. The "home" group showed no sensitization to amphetamine, whereas the "out" group displayed robust sensitization.

At least part of the explanation of the "home–out" effect is that the animals are accustomed to engaging in a certain repertoire of behaviors in their home environment, and so it is difficult to get them to change that behavior even in response to a drug. It is likewise difficult to condition new behavior to their familiar home cues.

When animals are placed in novel environments and receive spaced injections of a drug, however, their response to the drug may increase, showing sensitization. Presumably, humans, too, show sensitization to a drug when they periodically take it in novel contexts where new cues can be readily associated with the novel cognitive and physiological effects of the drug.

Addiction and Dependence

B. G. started smoking when she was 13 years old. Now a university lecturer, she has one child and is aware that smoking is not good for her own health or for the health of her family. She has quit smoking many times without success. Recently, she used a nicotine patch taped to her skin. The patch provides the nicotine without the smoke.

After successfully abstaining from cigarettes for more than 6 months with this treatment, she began to smoke again. Because the university where she works has a no-smoking policy, she has to leave the campus and stand across the street from the building in which she works to smoke. Her voice has developed a rasping sound, and she has an almost chronic "cold." She says that she used to enjoy smoking but does not any more. Concern about quitting dominates her thoughts.

B. G. has a drug problem. She is one of approximately 25 to 35 percent of North Americans who smoke. Most begin smoking between the ages of 15 and 35, and each consumes an average of about 18 cigarettes a day, nearly a pack-a-day habit. Like B. G.,

Substance abuse. Use of a drug for the psychological and behavioral changes that it produces aside from its therapeutic effects.

Addiction. Desire for a drug manifested by frequent use of the drug, leading to the development of physical dependence in addition to abuse; often associated with tolerance and unpleasant, sometimes dangerous, withdrawal symptoms on cessation of drug use. Also called *substance dependence.*

Withdrawal symptoms. Physical and psychological behaviors displayed by an addict when drug use ends.

Psychomotor activation. Increased behavioral and cognitive activity; at certain levels of consumption, the drug user feels energetic and in control.

⊙ Visit the *Brain and Behavior* Web site (**www.worthpublishers.com/kolb**) and go to the Chapter 7 Web links to learn more about substance abuse and addiction.

most smokers realize that smoking is a health hazard, have experienced unpleasant side effects from it, and have attempted to quit but cannot. B. G. is exceptional only in her white-collar occupation. Today, most smokers are found within blue-collar occupations rather than among professional workers.

Substance abuse is a pattern of drug use in which people rely on a drug chronically and excessively, allowing it to occupy a central place in their lives. A more advanced state of abuse is *substance dependence,* popularly known as **addiction.** Addicted people are physically dependent on a drug in addition to abusing it. They have developed tolerance for the drug, and so an addict requires increased doses to obtain the desired effect.

Users may also experience unpleasant, sometimes dangerous **withdrawal symptoms** if they suddenly stop taking the abused drug. These symptoms can include muscle aches and cramps, anxiety attacks, sweating, nausea, and, for some drugs, even convulsions and death. Withdrawal symptoms from alcohol or morphine can begin within hours of the last dose and tend to intensify over several days before they subside.

Although B. G. abuses the drug nicotine, she is not physically dependent on it. She smokes approximately the same number of cigarettes each day (she has not developed tolerance to nicotine) and she does not get sick if she is deprived of cigarettes (she does not suffer severe sickness on withdrawal from nicotine but does display some physical symptoms—irritability, anxiety, and increases in appetite and insomnia). B. G. illustrates that the power of psychological dependence can be as influential as the power of physical dependence.

Many different kinds of abused or addictive drugs—including sedative hypnotics, antianxiety agents, narcotics, and stimulants—have a common property: they produce **psychomotor activation** in some part of their dose range. That is, at certain levels of consumption, these drugs make the user feel energetic and in control. This common effect has led to the hypothesis that all abused drugs may act on the same target in the brain. One proposed target is dopamine neurons, because their stimulation is associated with psychomotor activity. Recall "The Neural Basis of Drug Cravings" at the beginning of this chapter, describing an experiment illustrating one relation between DA and drug consumption.

Three lines of evidence support a central role for DA in drug abuse:

1. Animals will press a bar for electrical stimulation of the mesolimbic dopamine system in the brain, and they will no longer press it if the dopamine system is blocked or damaged. This finding suggests that the release of DA is somehow rewarding.
2. Abused drugs seem to cause the release of DA or to prolong its availability in synaptic clefts. Even drugs that have no primary action on DA synapses have been found to increase its level. Apparently, when activated, many brain regions that contain no DA neurons themselves may stimulate DA neurons elsewhere in the brain.
3. Drugs such as major tranquilizers, that block DA receptors or decrease its availability at DA receptors, are not abused substances.

Explaining Drug Abuse

Why do people become addicted to drugs? According to an early explanation, habitual users of a drug experience psychological or physiological withdrawal symptoms when the effects of the drug wear off. They feel anxious, insecure, or just plain sick in the absence of the drug, and so they take the drug again to alleviate those symptoms. In this way, they get "hooked" on the drug.

Although this dependency hypothesis may account for part of drug-taking behavior, it has shortcomings as a general explanation. For example, an addict may abstain from a drug for months, long after any withdrawal symptoms have abated, and yet still be drawn back to using the drug. In addition, some drugs, such as the tricyclic antidepressants, produce withdrawal symptoms when discontinued, but these drugs are not abused.

Researchers currently see addiction as a series of stages. The first stage is the activation of *pleasure* by the consequences of drug taking. Using the drug produces in the person a positive subjective sensation. In other words, the user *likes* the experience.

In the second stage, pleasure is linked through *associative learning* with mental representations of drug cues, the objects, acts, places, and events related to taking the drug. This associative learning may be achieved through *classical conditioning* (also called *Pavlovian conditioning*). You may recall from your introductory psychology course that classical conditioning consists of learning to associate some formerly neutral stimulus (such as the sound of a bell for a dog) with a stimulus (such as food in the mouth) that elicits some involuntary response (such as salivation).

The pairing of the two stimuli continues until the formerly neutral stimulus is alone able to trigger the involuntary reaction. In drug use, the sight of the drug and the drug-taking context and equipment are repeatedly paired with administering the drug, which produces a pleasurable reaction. Soon the visual cues alone are enough to elicit pleasure.

The third stage is attributing **incentive salience** to the cues associated with drug use. In other words, those cues become highly desired and sought-after incentives in their own right. Stimuli that signal the availability of these incentives also become attractive. For instance, acts that led to the drug-taking situation in the past become attractive, as do acts that the drug taker predicts will lead again to the drug.

Drug users may even begin to collect objects that remind them of the drug. Pipe collecting by pipe smokers and decanter collecting by drinkers are examples. In this sequence of events, then, a number of repetitions of the drug-taking behavior lead from liking that act to seeking it out or wanting it, regardless of its current consequences.

A number of findings are in keeping with this explanation of drug addiction. For one thing, ample evidence reveals that abused drugs initially have a pleasurable effect. There is also evidence that a habitual user continues to use his or her drug of choice even though taking it no longer produces any pleasure. Heroin addicts sometimes report that they are miserable, that their lives are in ruins, and that the drug is not even pleasurable anymore, but they still want it. Furthermore, desire for the drug is often greatest just when the addicted person is maximally high on the drug, not when he or she is withdrawing from it.

To account for all the facts about drug abuse and addiction, Terry Robinson and Kent Berridge (1993) proposed the **incentive-sensitization theory.** This perspective is also called the *wanting-and-liking theory* because, according to Robinson and Berridge, wanting and liking are produced by the effect of a drug on two different brain systems, as illustrated in **Figure 7-15**. Robinson and Berridge define *wanting* as equivalent to craving for a drug, whereas *liking* is defined as the pleasure that drug taking produces.

They propose that the road to drug dependence begins at the initial experience when the drug affects a neural system associated with "pleasure." At this time, the user may experience liking the substance. With repeated use, liking the drug may decline from its initial level. Now the user may also begin to show tolerance to the drug's effects and so may begin to increase the dosage to increase liking.

The drug also affects a different neural system—that associated with wanting. With each use, the user increasingly associates the cues related to drug use—for example, an injection needle, the room in which the drug is taken, people with whom the drug is taken—with the drug-taking experience. The user makes this association because he or she has become classically conditioned to all the cues associated with drug taking.

Incentive salience. Quality acquired by drug cues that become highly desired and sought-after incentives in their own right.

Incentive-sensitization theory. When a drug is associated with certain cues, the cues themselves elicit desire for the drug; also called *wanting-and-liking theory*.

Figure 7-15

Incentive-Sensitization Theory When first used, a psychoactive drug produces moderate wanting and liking. With repeated use, tolerance for liking develops, and consequently the expression of liking decreases. In contrast, the system that mediates wanting sensitizes, and wanting the drug increases. Wanting is associated with drug cues.

Peter Dokus/Stone

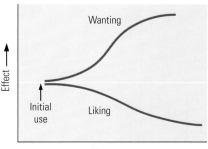

According to Robinson and Berridge, later encounters with these wanting cues, rather than the expected liking (the pleasure from the drug), initiates wanting.

How can the wanting-and-liking theory explain B. G.'s behavior in regard to smoking? B. G. reports that her most successful period of abstinence from cigarettes coincided with moving to a new town. She stopped smoking for 6 months and, during that time, felt as if she were free and in command of her life again. The wanting-and-liking theory would argue that her ability to quit at this time was increased because she was separated from the many cues that had previously been associated with smoking.

Then one night after going out to dinner, B. G. and a few of her new colleagues went to a bar, where some of them began to smoke. B. G. reported that her desire for a cigarette became overpowering. Before the evening was over, she bought a package of cigarettes and smoked more than half of it.

On leaving the bar, she left the remaining cigarettes on the table, intending that this episode would be only a one-time lapse. Shortly thereafter, however, she resumed smoking. The wanting-and-liking theory suggests that her craving for a cigarette was strongly conditioned to certain social cues that she encountered again on her visit to the bar, which is why the wanting suddenly became overwhelming.

The neural basis for liking and wanting are not completely understood. Robinson and Berridge believe that liking may be due to the activity of opioid neurons, whereas wanting may be due to activity in the mesolimbic dopamine system. In these dopamine pathways, recall, the axons of DA neurons in the midbrain project to the nucleus accumbens, the frontal cortex, and the limbic system (see Figure 7-1).

When cues that have previously been associated with drug taking are encountered, the mesolimbic system becomes active, producing the subjective experience of wanting. That desire for the drug is not a conscious act. Rather, the craving derives from unconsciously acquired associations between drug taking and various cues related to it.

We can extend the wanting-and-liking explanation of drug addiction to many other life situations. Cues related to sexual activity, food, and even sports can induce a state of wanting, sometimes in the absence of liking. We frequently eat when prompted by the cue of other people eating, even though we may not be hungry and derive little pleasure from eating at that time.

Behavior on Drugs

Ellen is a healthy, attractive, intelligent 19-year-old university freshman. In her high-school health class, she learned about the sexual transmission of HIV and other diseases. More recently, in her college orientation, senior students presented a seminar about the dangers of having unprotected sexual intercourse and provided the freshmen in her residence with free condoms and "safe sex" literature.

It is certain that Ellen knows the facts about unprotected sexual intercourse and is cognizant of the associated dangers. Indeed, she holds negative attitudes toward having unprotected sexual intercourse, does not intend to have unprotected sexual intercourse, and has always practiced safe sex. She and her former boyfriend were always careful to use latex condoms during intercourse.

At a homecoming party in her residence, Ellen has a great time, drinking and dancing with her friends and meeting new people. She is particularly taken with Brad, a sophomore at her college, and the two of them decide to go back to her room to order a pizza. One thing leads to another, and Ellen and Brad have sexual intercourse without using a condom. The next morning, Ellen wakes up, dismayed and surprised at her behavior, and very concerned that she may be pregnant or may have contracted a sexually transmitted disease. She is terrified that she may have contracted AIDS (MacDonald, Zanna, & Fong, 1998).

What happened to Ellen? What is it about drugs, especially alcohol, that makes people do things that they would not ordinarily do? Ellen is not alone in engaging in risky behavior under the influence of alcohol. Alcohol is associated with many harmful behaviors that are costly both to individual people and to society. These behaviors include not only unprotected sexual activity but also drinking and driving, date rape, spousal or child abuse, and other forms of aggression and crime.

An early and still widely held explanation of the effects of alcohol is the **disinhibition theory.** It holds that alcohol has a selective depressant effect on the cortex, the region of the brain that controls judgment, while sparing subcortical structures, those areas of the brain responsible for more-primitive instincts, such as desire. Stated differently, alcohol presumably depresses learned inhibitions based on reasoning and judgment while releasing the "beast" within.

This theory often excuses alcohol-related behavior with such statements as, "She was too drunk to know better," or "The boys had a few too many and got carried away." Does such disinhibition explain Ellen's behavior? Not really. Ellen had used alcohol in the past and managed to practice safe sex despite the effects of the drug. The disinhibition theory cannot explain why her behavior was different on this occasion. If alcohol is a disinhibitor, why is it not *always* so?

Craig MacAndrew and Robert Edgerton (1969) questioned the disinhibition theory along just these lines in their book titled *Drunken Comportment.* They cite many instances in which behavior under the influence of alcohol changes from one context to another. People who engage in polite social activity at home when consuming alcohol may become unruly and aggressive when drinking in a bar.

Even their behavior at the bar may be inconsistent. For example, while drinking one night at a bar, Joe becomes obnoxious and gets into a fight; but on another occasion he is charming and witty, even preventing a fight between two friends, whereas on a third occasion he becomes depressed and only worries about his problems. McAndrew and Edgerton also cite examples of cultures in which people are *dis*inhibited when sober only to become inhibited after consuming alcohol and cultures in which people are inhibited when sober and become *more* inhibited when drinking. How can all these differences in alcohol's effects be explained?

MacAndrew and Edgerton suggest that behavior under the effects of alcohol represents "time out" from the rules of daily life that would normally apply. This time out takes into consideration learned behavior that is specific to the culture, group, and setting. Time out can help explain Ellen's decision to sleep with Brad. In our culture, alcohol is used to facilitate social interactions, and so behavior while intoxicated represents time out from more-conservative rules regarding dating. But time-out theory has more difficulty explaining Ellen's lapse in judgment regarding safe sex. Ellen had never practiced unsafe sex before and had never made it a part of her time-out social activities. So why did she engage in it with Brad?

Tara MacDonald

Tara MacDonald and her coworkers (1998) suggest an explanation for alcohol-related lapses in judgment like Ellen's. **Alcohol myopia** (nearsightedness) is the tendency for people under the influence of alcohol to respond to a restricted set of immediate and prominent cues while ignoring more remote cues and potential consequences. Immediate and prominent cues are very strong and obvious and are close at hand.

In an altercation, the person with alcohol myopia will be quicker than normal to throw a punch because the cue of the fight is so strong and immediate. Similarly, at a raucous party, the myopic drinker will be more eager than usual to join in because the immediate cue of boisterous fun dominates the person's view. In regard to Ellen and Brad, once they arrived at Ellen's room, the sexual cues of the moment were far more immediate than concerns about long-term safety. As a result, Ellen

Disinhibition theory. Explanation holding that alcohol has a selective depressant effect on the cortex, the region of the brain that controls judgment, while sparing subcortical structures responsible for more-primitive instincts, such as desire.

Alcohol myopia. "Nearsighted" behavior displayed under the influence of alcohol: local and immediate cues become prominent, and remote cues and consequences are ignored.

responded to those immediate cues and behaved as she normally would not. Such alcohol myopia can explain many other lapses in judgment that lead to risky behavior, including aggression, date rape, and reckless driving under the influences of alcohol.

Why Doesn't Everyone Abuse Drugs?

Observing that some people are more prone to drug abuse and dependence than other people are, scientists have wondered if this difference might be genetically based. Three lines of evidence suggest a genetic contribution.

1. The results of twin studies show that, if one of two twins abuses alcohol, the other is more likely to abuse it if those twins are identical (have the same genetic makeup) than if they are fraternal (have only some of their genes in common).
2. The results of studies of people adopted shortly after birth reveal that they are more likely to abuse alcohol if their biological parents were alcoholic, even though they have had almost no contact with those parents.
3. Although most animals do not care for alcohol, the selective breeding of mice, rats, and monkeys can produce strains that consume large quantities of it.

There are problems with all these lines of evidence, however. Perhaps identical twins show greater concordance for alcohol abuse because they are exposed to more similar environments than fraternal twins are. And perhaps the link between alcoholism in adoptees and their biological parents has to do with nervous system changes due to prebirth exposure to the drug. Finally, the fact that animals can be selectively bred for alcohol consumption does not mean that human alcoholics have a similar genetic makeup. The evidence for a genetic basis of alcohol abuse will become compelling only when a gene or set of genes related to alcoholism is found.

Another avenue of research into individual differences associated with drug abuse has been to search for personality traits that drug abusers tend to have in common. One such trait is unusual risk taking. Consider Frenchman Bruno Gouvy, the daredevil who was the first person to jump out of a helicopter and surf the sky on a snowboard (**Figure 7-16**). He also set a world speed record on a monoski and was the first person to snowboard down Mont Blanc, the highest peak in Europe. He set a windsurfing record across the Mediterranean Sea and a free-fall speed record after jumping out of a plane. In an attempt to snowboard down three major peaks in one day, he hit black ice and fell 3000 feet to his death.

Do people who love high-risk adventure have a genetic predisposition toward risk taking that will also lead them to experiment with drugs (Comings et al., 1996)? In an attempt to find out if certain behavioral traits are related to drug abuse, Pier Vincenzo Piassa and his coworkers (1989) gave rats an opportunity to self-administer amphetamine. Some rats were very quick to become amphetamine "junkies," giving themselves very large doses, whereas other rats avoided the drug.

By examining the behavior of the rats in advance of the drug-taking opportunity, the researchers were able to identify characteristics associated with becoming an amphetamine user. In particular, those rats that ran around the most when placed in an open area, thus seeming less cautious and self-restrained than other rats, were also the most likely to become addicted. Perhaps, the researchers concluded, such behavioral traits make some rats more prone to drug use.

Although research on the characteristics that might influence becoming a drug user continues, no unequivocal evidence suggests that

Figure 7-16

Bruno Gouvy in Flight

Redneck/Liaison

a specific gene determines substance abuse. Nor is there unequivocal evidence that differences in the dopamine system make some people more prone to drug abuse than others. And, even if a particular substance-abuse gene or genes could be found, that genetic factor would not provide a full explanation of drug addiction. Identical twins have all their genes in common, and yet, when one becomes a drug abuser, the other does not necessarily become one, too. Clearly, learning also plays an important role in developing drug abuse and addiction.

Can Drugs Cause Brain Damage?

Table 7-1 on page 233 shows that many substances produced by plants and animals, including domoic acid, the causative agent in mussel poisoning, can act as neurotoxins. Given the widespread use of psychoactive drugs in our society, it is important to ask whether these substances can do the same. In this section, we examine the evidence that commonly used psychoactive drugs can act as neurotoxins and investigate the processes by which they might have toxic effects.

SOLVING THE DOMOIC ACID MYSTERY

Let us first consider how domoic acid acts as a toxin on the nervous system. The chemical structure of domoic acid is similar to that of the neurotransmitter glutamate. Because of its structural similarity to glutamate, domoic acid is referred to as a *glutamate analogue.* It is also a glutamate agonist because, like glutamate, it binds to glutamate receptors and affects them in the same way.

Domoic acid   Kainic acid

As described in Chapter 5, each neurotransmitter can attach to a number of different types of receptors. Domoic acid acts to stimulate one of the three types of glutamate receptors, the *kainate receptor,* so named because kainate, a chemical used in fertilizer, binds very potently to it. Domoic acid, it turns out, binds to the kainate receptor even more potently than does kainate itself. (Because receptors are usually named for the compound that most potently binds to them, had domoic acid been discovered earlier, the kainate receptor would have been called the domoic acid receptor.)

The distribution of the different glutamate receptor subtypes in the brain varies from region to region. Kainate receptors are especially numerous in the hippocampus. If domoic acid reaches these receptors in high enough concentrations, it overexcites the receptors, initiating a series of biochemical reactions that results in the death of the postsynaptic neuron. Consequently, domoic acid is more toxic to the hippocampus than it is to other brain regions.

Figure 7-17 shows a section through the brain of a rat that has been given an injection of domoic acid. The brain is colored with a silver stain that accumulates in damaged neurons. Tissue in the hippocampus exhibits the greatest amount of damage, although there is also sparse damage elsewhere in the brain.

It may seem surprising that a chemical that mimics a neurotransmitter can cause memory problems and brain damage. To understand how domoic acid can act as a neurotoxin requires that we temporarily turn to a different story, that of monosodium glutamate (MSG). The plot of this second story eventually links up with the plot of the domoic acid story.

In the late 1960s, there were many reports that MSG, a salty-tasting, flavor-enhancing food additive, produced headaches in some people. In the process of investigating why this effect happened, scientists placed large doses of MSG on cultured neurons and noticed that the neurons died. Subsequently, they injected monosodium glutamate into the brains of experimental animals, where it also produced neuron death.

> Domoic acid produces hippocampal damage, as shown by a dark silver stain that highlights degeneration.

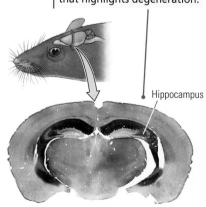

Hippocampus

Figure 7-17

Neurotoxicity Domoic acid damage is not restricted to the hippocampus; it can be seen to a lesser extent in many other brain regions. Micrograph from NeuroScience Associates.

These findings raised the question of whether large doses of the neurotransmitter glutamate, which MSG resembles structurally, might also be toxic to neurons. It turned out that it is. This finding suggested that a large dose of *any* substance that acts like glutamate might be toxic.

Now the toxic action of domoic acid can be explained. Domoic acid in large quantities excessively stimulates the glutamate receptors of certain brain cells, and this activation is related to neuronal death. Glutamate-receptor activation results in an influx of Ca^{2+} into the cell, and the influx of excessive Ca^{2+} may through second messengers activate a "suicide gene" in a cell's DNA. Such apoptosis, as you learned in Chapter 6, may be a mechanism by which the brain disposes of sick cells.

This is not to say that people should totally avoid MSG, which is similar in chemical structure to glutamate. Only very large doses of these substances are harmful, just as glutamate itself is not harmful except in large doses. Glutamate, in fact, is an essential chemical in the body.

Recent findings show that we even have taste-bud receptors for glutamate on our tongues, in addition to our receptors for sweet, salty, bitter, and sour. The glutamate taste-bud receptor, mGluR4, most likely functions to encourage us to eat foods containing glutamate, especially high-protein foods such as meat. Clearly, glutamate in doses typically found in food is required by the body and is not toxic. Only excessive doses of glutamate or its analogues cause harm.

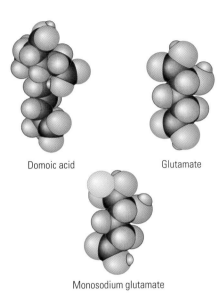

Domoic acid　　　　Glutamate

Monosodium glutamate

POTENTIAL HARMFULNESS OF RECREATIONAL DRUGS

What about the many recreational drugs that affect the nervous system? Are any of them potentially harmful? The answer is not always easy to determine, as Una McCann and her coworkers (1997) found in their review of research.

For one thing, there is the problem of sorting out the effects of the drug itself from the effects of other factors related to taking the drug. For instance, although chronic alcohol use can be associated with damage to the thalamus and limbic system, producing severe memory disorders, it is not the alcohol itself that seems to cause this damage but rather related complications of alcohol abuse, including vitamin deficiencies due to poor diet. For example, not only do alcoholics obtain reduced amounts of thiamine (vitamin B_1) in their diets, but alcohol also interferes with the absorption of thiamine by the intestine. Thiamine plays a vital role in maintaining cell-membrane structure.

Similarly, there are many reports of people who suffer some severe psychiatric disorder subsequent to their abuse of certain recreational drugs, but, in most cases, it is difficult to determine whether the drug initiated the condition or just aggravated an existing problem. It is also hard to determine exactly whether the drug itself or some contaminant in the drug is related to a harmful outcome. Recall the development of Parkinson's disease after the use of synthetic heroin, described in Chapter 5, which was caused by a contaminant (MPTP) rather than by the heroin itself.

A number of cases of chronic use of marijuana have been associated with psychotic attacks, as "Drug-Induced Psychosis" describes. But the marijuana plant contains at least 400 chemicals, 60 or more of which are structurally related to its active ingredient tetrahydrocannabinol. Clearly, it is almost impossible to determine whether the psychotic attacks are related to THC or to some other ingredient contained in marijuana or to aggravation of an existing condition.

There is growing evidence that some recreational drugs can cause brain damage and cognitive impairments. MDMA, also called *ecstasy,* is a widely used synthetic amphetamine. Although MDMA is structurally related to amphetamine, it produces hallucinogenic effects and is referred to as a "hallucinogenic amphetamine." Findings from animal studies show that doses of MDMA approximating those taken by human users result in the degeneration of very fine serotonergic nerve terminals.

Drug-Induced Psychosis

At age 29, R. B. S. was a chronic marijuana smoker. For years, he had been selectively breeding a particularly potent strain of marijuana in anticipation of the day when it would be legalized. R. B. S. made his living as a pilot, flying small freight aircraft into coastal communities in the Pacific Northwest.

One evening, R. B. S. experienced a sudden revelation that he was no longer in control of his life. Convinced that he was being manipulated by a small computer that had been implanted into his brain when he was 7 years old, he confided in a close friend, who urged him to consult a doctor. R. B. S. insisted that he had undergone the surgery when he participated in an experiment at a local university. He also claimed that all the other children who participated in the experiment had been murdered.

The doctor told R. B. S. that it was unlikely that he had a computer implanted in his brain, but called the psychology department at the university and got confirmation that children had in fact taken part in an experiment conducted years before. The records of the study had long since been destroyed. R. B. S. believed that this information completely vindicated his story. His delusional behavior persisted and cost him his pilot's license.

The delusion seemed completely compartmentalized in R. B. S.'s mind. When asked why he could no longer fly, he intently recounted the story of the implant and the murders, asserting that its truth had cost him the medical certification needed for a license. Then he happily discussed other topics in a normal way.

R. B. S. was suffering from a mild focal psychosis: he was losing contact with reality. In some cases, this loss of contact is so severe and the capacity to respond to the environment is so impaired and distorted that the person can no longer function in the world. People in a state of psychosis may experience hallucinations (false sensory perceptions) or delusions (false beliefs) or they may withdraw into a private world isolated from people and events around them.

Phil Schermeister/Stone

Cannabis sativa is an annual herb that reaches a height between 3 and 15 feet. Hemp grows in a wide range of altitudes, climates, and soils and has myriad practical uses.

A variety of drugs can produce psychosis, including LSD, amphetamine, cocaine, and, as shown by this case, marijuana. The active ingredient in marijuana is Δ-9-tetrahydrocannabinol (THC). At low doses, THC has mild sedative-hypnotic effects, similar to those of alcohol. At high doses, it can produce euphoria and hallucinations.

The marijuana that R. B. S. used so heavily comes from the leaves of the hemp plant *Cannabis sativa,* perhaps the oldest cultivated nonfood plant. Humans have used hemp for thousands of years to make rope, paper, cloth, and a host of products. And marijuana has beneficial medical effects: THC alleviates nausea and vomiting associated with chemotherapy in cancer and AIDS patients, controls the brain seizures symptomatic of epilepsy, reduces intraocular pressure in patients with glaucoma, and relieves the symptoms of some movement disorders. But marijuana's psychedelic effect has, to date, prevented its legalization in the United States.

There is little cross-tolerance between THC and other drugs, which suggests that THC has its own brain receptor. THC may mimic a naturally occurring substance called anandamide, which acts on a THC receptor that naturally inhibits adenyl cyclase, part of one of the second-messenger systems active in sensitization (see Chapter 5).

R. B. S.'s heavy marijuana use certainly raises the suspicion that the drug had some influence on his delusional condition. Henquet et al. (2004) report that cannabis use moderately increases the risk of psychotic symptoms in young people and has a much stronger effect in those with evidence of predisposition for psychosis. There is no evidence that marijuana use produces brain damage. It is possible that R. B. S.'s delusions might have eventually occurred anyway, even if he had not used marijuana. Furthermore, marijuana contains about 400 compounds besides THC, any of which could trigger psychotic symptoms. Approximately 10 years after his initial attack, R. B. S.'s symptoms subsided, and he returned to flying.

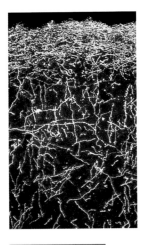

Figure 7-18

Drug Damage Treatment with MDMA changes the density of serotonin axons in the neocortex of a squirrel monkey: (*left*) normal monkey; (*right*) monkey 18 months after treatment. From "Long-Lasting Effects of Recreational Drugs of Abuse on the Central Nervous System," by U. D. McCann, K. A. Lowe, and G. A. Ricaurte, 1997, *The Neurologist, 3*, p. 401.

In rodents, these terminals regrow within a few months after drug use is stopped, but, in monkeys, the terminal loss may be permanent, as shown in **Figure 7-18**. Memory impairments have been reported in users of MDMA, which may be a result of similar neuronal damage (Morgan, 1999). But researchers still want to know if people's use of MDMA is associated with the same loss of serotonergic terminals as it is in rodents and monkeys. Answering this question is complicated by the fact that many MDMA users have also used other drugs. In addition, the types of anatomical analysis used with other animals cannot be used with humans.

The finding that MDMA can be toxic to neurons has led to investigations into whether amphetamine itself also is toxic. The results of studies in rodents have shown that high doses of amphetamine can result in the loss of DA terminals. One form of amphetamine—methamphetamine, one of the most widely used recreational drugs—has been found to produce both brain damage, as revealed by brain-imaging studies, and impaired memory performance, as indicated by neuropsychological tests (Thompson et al., 2004). The subjects used in this study had been using the drug for about 10 years, and so the study does not produce evidence that a single or only a few uses of the drug have similar detrimental brain and behavioral effects but that in some way repeated use can permanently damage neurons.

The psychoactive properties of cocaine are similar to those of amphetamine, and its possible deleterious effects have been subjected to intense investigation. The results of many studies show that cocaine use is related to the blockage of cerebral blood flow and other changes in blood circulation. Whether cocaine causes these abnormalities or aggravates preexisting conditions is not clear.

Phencyclidine (PCP), or "angel dust," is an NMDA-receptor blocker that was originally developed as an anesthetic. Its use was discontinued after about half of treated patients were found to display psychotic symptoms for as long as a week after coming out of anesthesia. PCP users report perceptual changes and the slurring of speech after small doses, with high doses producing perceptual disorders and hallucinations. Some of the symptoms can last for weeks. The mechanisms by which PCP produces enduring behavioral changes are unknown, but John Olney and his colleagues (1971) reported that, after rats are given a related drug (MK-801), they undergo abnormal changes in neurons, as well as loss of neurons. This finding suggests that the altered behavior of PCP users may be related to neuron damage.

Some drugs that produce altered perceptual experiences and changes in mood do not appear linked to brain damage. For instance, LSD, a drug believed to act on serotonergic neurons, produces hallucinations but does not seem to cause enduring brain changes in rats. Similarly, although opiates produce mood changes, the results of long-term studies of opiate users have not revealed persistent cognitive impairments or brain damage.

In Review

Behavior may change in a number of ways with the repeated use of a drug. These changes include tolerance, in which a behavioral response decreases; sensitization, in which a behavioral response increases; and substance dependence, or addiction, in which the desire to use a drug increases as a function of experience with it. Today, many researchers believe that it is not so much avoidance of withdrawal symptoms that keeps people using a drug as it is a set of powerful learned incentives associated with drug taking. Individual differences in experience and genetic makeup, as well as the context in which a drug is taken, influence that drug's effects on behavior. Disinhibited behavior while a person is under the influence of alcohol can often be explained by the concepts of time out and alcohol myopia. Scientists are still investigating the potential deleterious effects on the brain of different psychedelic drugs. So far, their findings have been mixed, with some drugs producing brain damage and others apparently not doing so.

HORMONES

In 1849, European scientist A. A. Berthold performed the first experiment to demonstrate the existence and function of *hormones,* chemicals released by an endocrine gland. *Endocrine glands* are cell groups in the body that secrete hormones into the bloodstream to circulate to a body target and affect it. Berthold removed the testes of a rooster and found that the rooster no longer crowed; nor did it engage in sexual or aggressive behavior. Berthold then reimplanted one testis in the rooster's body cavity. The rooster began crowing and displaying normal sexual and aggressive behavior again. The reimplanted testis did not establish any nerve connections, and so Berthold concluded that it must release a chemical into the rooster's circulatory system to influence the animal's behavior.

That chemical, we now know, is *testosterone,* the sex hormone secreted by the testes and responsible for the distinguishing characteristics of the male. The effect that Berthold produced by reimplanting the testis can be mimicked by administering testosterone to a castrated rooster, or capon. The hormone is sufficient to make the capon behave like a rooster with testes.

Testosterone's influence on the rooster illustrates some of the ways that this hormone produces male behaviors. Testosterone also initiates changes in the size and appearance of the mature male body. In a rooster, for example, testosterone produces the animal's distinctive plumage and crest, and it activates other sex-related organs.

Hormones, like other drugs, are used to treat or prevent disease. People take synthetic hormones as a replacement therapy because of the removal of glands that produce those hormones or because of their malfunction. People also take hormones, especially sex hormones, to counteract the effects of aging, and they take them to increase physical strength and endurance and to gain an advantage in sports.

As many as 100 hormones in the human body are classified as either steroids or peptides. **Steroid hormones** are synthesized from cholesterol and are lipid (fat) soluble. Steroids diffuse away from their site of synthesis in glands, including the gonads, adrenal cortex, and thyroid, easily crossing the cell membrane. They enter target cells in the same way and act on the cells' DNA to increase or decrease the production of proteins. **Peptide hormones,** such as insulin and growth hormone, are made by cellular DNA in the same way that other proteins are made, and they influence their target cell's activity by binding to metabotropic receptors on the cell membrane, generating a second messenger that affects the cell's physiology.

Hormones fall into one of three main groups with respect to their behavioral functions, and they may function in more than one of these groups:

1. Hormones that maintain **homeostasis,** a state of internal metabolic balance and regulation of physiological systems in an organism, form one group. (The term *homeostasis* comes from the Greek words *homeo,* meaning "the same place," and *stasis,* meaning "standing.") Homeostatic mineralocorticoids (e.g., aldosterone) control the concentration of water in blood and cells; control the levels of sodium, potassium, and calcium in the body; and promote digestive functions.

2. **Gonadal (sex) hormones** control reproductive functions. They instruct the body to develop as male (e.g., testosterone) or female (e.g., estrogen), influence sexual

Normal rooster

Rooster who has had gonads removed

Steroid hormone. Fat-soluble chemical messenger synthesized from cholesterol.

Peptide hormone. Chemical messenger synthesized by cellular DNA that acts to affect the target cell's physiology.

Homeostasis. State of internal metabolic balance and regulation of physiological systems in an organism.

Gonadal (sex) hormone. One of a group of hormones, such as testosterone, that control reproductive functions and bestow sexual appearance and identity as male or female.

Glucocorticoid. One of a group of steroid hormones, such as cortisol, secreted in times of stress; important in protein and carbohydrate metabolism.

behavior and the conception of children, and, in women, control the menstrual cycle (e.g., estrogen and progesterone), the birthing of babies, and the release of breast milk (e.g., prolactin, oxytocin).

3. Hormones activated in psychologically challenging events or emergency situations prepare the body to cope by fighting or fleeing. **Glucocorticoids** (cortisol and corticosterone are examples), a group of steroid hormones secreted in times of stress, are important in protein and carbohydrate metabolism, controlling sugar levels in the blood and the absorption of sugar by cells.

Hierarchical Control of Hormones

Figure 7-19 shows that the control and action of hormones are organized into a four-level hierarchy consisting of the brain, the pituitary and remaining endocrine glands, and the target cells affected by the hormones. As detailed in Chapter 11, the brain, mainly the hypothalamus, releases neurohormones that stimulate the pituitary to pump hormones into the circulatory system. The pituitary hormones, in turn, influence the endocrine glands to release appropriate hormones into the bloodstream. These hormones then act on various targets in the body, also providing feedback to the brain about the need for more or less hormone release.

Although many questions remain about how hormones produce complex behavior, they not only affect body organs but also target the brain and activating systems there. Almost every neuron in the brain contains receptors on which various hormones can act. In addition to influencing sex organs and physical appearance in a rooster, testosterone may have neurotransmitter-like effects on the brain cells that it targets, especially neurons that control crowing, male sexual behavior, and aggression.

In these neurons, testosterone is transported into the cell nucleus, where it activates genes. The genes, in turn, trigger the synthesis of proteins needed for cellular processes that produce the rooster's male behaviors. Thus, the rooster receives not only a male body but a male brain as well.

Figure 7-19

Hormonal Hierarchy

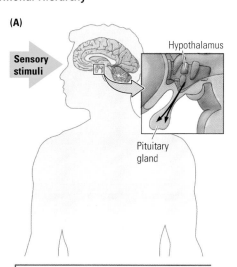

(A)

In response to sensory stimuli and cognitive activity, the hypothalamus produces neurohormones that enter the anterior pituitary through veins and the posterior pituitary through axons.

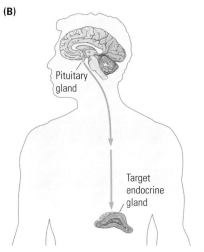

(B)

On instructions from these releasing hormones, the pituitary sends hormones into the bloodstream to target endocrine glands.

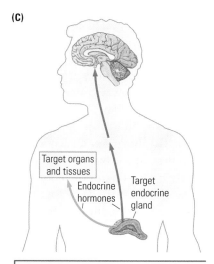

(C)

In response to pituitary hormones, the endocrine glands release their own hormones that stimulate target organs, including the brain. In response, the hypothalamus and the pituitary decrease hormone production.

The diversity of testosterone's functions clarifies why the body uses hormones as messengers: their targets are so widespread that the best possible way of reaching all of them is to travel in the bloodstream, which goes everywhere in the body. In subsequent chapters, we will take up the story of hormones again, as we examine motivation and the relation between learning and memory.

Homeostatic Hormones

The body's internal environment must remain within relatively constant parameters in order for us to function. An appropriate balance of sugars, proteins, carbohydrates, salts, and water is required in the bloodstream, in the extracellular compartments of muscles, in the brain and other body structures, and within all body cells. Homeostasis of the internal environment must be maintained regardless of a person's age, activities, or conscious state. As children or adults, at rest or in strenuous work, when we have overeaten or when we are hungry, to survive, we need a relatively constant internal environment. Thus, the homeostatic hormones are essential to life itself.

Insulin is a homeostatic hormone. The normal concentration of glucose in the bloodstream varies between 80 and 130 milligrams per 100 milliliters of blood. One group of cells in the pancreas releases insulin, which causes blood sugar to fall by instructing the liver to start storing glucose rather than releasing it and by instructing cells to increase glucose uptake. The resulting decrease in glucose then decreases the stimulation of pancreatic cells so that they stop producing insulin.

Diabetes mellitus is caused by a failure of these pancreatic cells to secrete enough or any insulin. As a result, blood-sugar levels can fall (hypoglycemia) or rise (hyperglycemia). In hyperglycemia, blood-glucose levels rise because insulin does not instruct cells of the body to take up that glucose. Consequently, cell function, including neural function, can fail through glucose starvation, even in the presence of high levels of glucose in the blood. In addition, chronic high blood-glucose levels cause damage to the eyes, kidneys, nerves, heart, and blood vessels. In hypoglycemia, inappropriate diet can lead to to low blood sugar, which can be so severe as to cause fainting.

Gonadal Hormones

We are prepared for our adult reproductive roles by the gonadal hormones that give us our sexual appearance, mold our identity as male or female, and allow us to engage in sex-related behaviors. Sex hormones begin to act on us even before we are born and continue their actions throughout our lives (see Chapters 6, 11, and 13).

For males, sex hormones produce the male body and male behaviors. The Y chromosome of males contains a gene called the sex-determining region or *SRY* gene. If cells in the undifferentiated gonads of the early embryo contain an *SRY* gene, they will develop into a testes and, if they do not, they will develop into an ovary. In the male, the testes produce the hormone testosterone, which in turn masculinizes the body, producing the male body and genital organs and the male brain.

The **organizational hypothesis** proposes that actions of hormones during development alter tissue differentiation. Thus, testosterone masculinizes the brain early in life by being taken up in brain cells where it is converted into estrogen by the enzyme aromatase. Estrogen then acts on estrogen receptors to initiate a chain of events that include the activation of certain genes in the cell nucleus. These genes then contribute to the masculinization of brain cells and their interactions with other brain cells.

Hormones play a somewhat lesser role in producing the female body, but they control menstrual cycles, regulate many facets of pregnancy and birth, and stimulate milk

Organizational hypothesis. Proposal that actions of hormones during development alter tissue differentiation; for example, testosterone masculinizes the brain.

production for breast-feeding babies. It might seem surprising that estrogen, a hormone usually associated with the female, masculinizes the male brain. Estrogen does not have the same effect on the female brain, because females have a blood enzyme that binds to estrogen and prevents its entry into the brain.

Hormones contribute to surprising differences in the brain and in cognitive behavior. The male brain is slightly larger than the female brain after corrections are made for body size, and the right hemisphere is somewhat larger than the left in males. The female brain has a higher rate both of cerebral blood flow and of glucose utilization. There are also a number of differences in brain size in different regions of the brain including nuclei in the hypothalamus that are related to sexual function, parts of the corpus callosum that are larger in females, and a somewhat larger language region in the female brain.

Three lines of evidence, summarized by Elizabeth Hampson and Doreen Kimura (1992), support the conclusion that sex-related cognitive differences result from these brain differences. These cognitive differences also depend in part on the continuing circulation of the sex hormones. The evidence:

1. The results of spatial and verbal tests given to females and males in many different settings and cultures show that males tend to excel in the spatial tasks and females in the verbal ones.
2. The results of similar tests given to female subjects in the course of the menstrual cycle show fluctuations in test scores with various phases of the cycle. During the phase in which the female sex hormones estradiol (metabolized from estrogen) and progesterone are at their lowest levels, women do comparatively better on spatial tasks, whereas, during the phase in which levels of these hormones are high, women do comparatively better on verbal tasks.
3. Tests comparing premenopausal and postmenopausal women, women in various stages of pregnancy, and females and males with varying levels of circulating hormones all provide some evidence that hormones affect cognitive function.

These sex-hormone–related differences in cognitive function are not huge. A great deal of overlap in performance scores exists between males and females. Yet statistically the differences seem reliable. Similar influences of sex hormones on behavior are found in other species. The example of the rooster described earlier shows the effects of testosterone on that animal's behavior. Findings from a number of studies demonstrate that motor skills in female humans and other animals improve at estrus, a time when progesterone levels are high.

Stress Hormones

Life is stressful. "Stress" is a term borrowed from engineering to describe a process in which an agent exerts a force on an object. Applied to humans and other animals, a *stressor* is a stimulus that challenges the body's homeostasis and triggers arousal.

Stress responses are not only physiological, but also behavioral, and include both arousal and attempts to reduce stress. A stress response can outlast a stress-inducing incident and may even occur in the absence an obvious stressor. Living with constant stress can be debilitating.

Surprisingly, the body's response is the same whether the stressor is exciting, sad, or frightening. Robert Sapolsky (1992) uses the vivid image of a hungry lion chasing down a zebra to illustrate the stress response. The chase elicits very different reactions in the two animals, but their physiological stress responses are exactly the same.

The stress response begins when the body is subjected to a stressor, and especially when the brain perceives a stressor and responds with arousal. The response consists of two separate sequences, one fast and the other slow.

To learn more about hormones and the body's hormonal response to stress, visit the Chapter 7 Web links on the *Brain and Behavior* Web site (**www.worth publishers.com/kolb**).

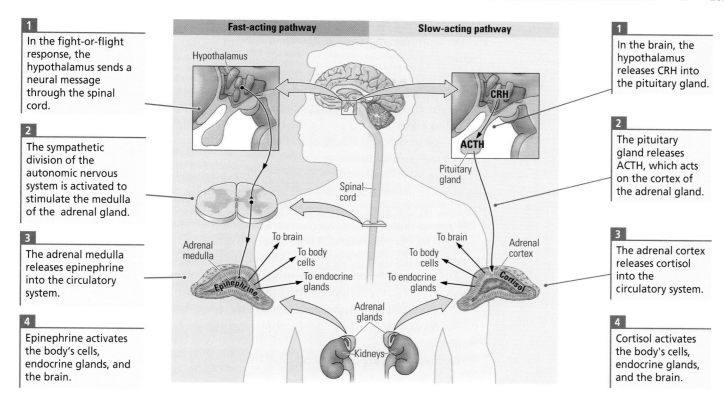

1
In the fight-or-flight response, the hypothalamus sends a neural message through the spinal cord.

2
The sympathetic division of the autonomic nervous system is activated to stimulate the medulla of the adrenal gland.

3
The adrenal medulla releases epinephrine into the circulatory system.

4
Epinephrine activates the body's cells, endocrine glands, and the brain.

1
In the brain, the hypothalamus releases CRH into the pituitary gland.

2
The pituitary gland releases ACTH, which acts on the cortex of the adrenal gland.

3
The adrenal cortex releases cortisol into the circulatory system.

4
Cortisol activates the body's cells, endocrine glands, and the brain.

Figure 7-20

Activating a Stress Response   Two pathways to the adrenal gland control the body's response to stress. The fast-acting pathway primes the body immediately for fight or flight. The slow-acting pathway both mobilizes the body's resources to confront a stressor and repairs stress-related damage.

The left side of **Figure 7-20** shows the fast response. The sympathetic division is activated to prepare the body and its organs for "fight or flight," and the parasympathetic division for "rest and digest" is turned off (see Figure 2-29). In addition, the sympathetic division stimulates the medulla on the interior of the adrenal gland to release epinephrine. The epinephrine surge (often called the adrenaline surge after epinephrine's original name) prepares the body for a sudden burst of activity. Among its many functions, epinephrine stimulates cell metabolism so that the body's cells are ready for action.

The hormone controlling the slow response is the steroid cortisol, a glucocorticoid released from the outer layer (cortex) of the adrenal gland, as shown on the right side of Figure 7-20. The cortisol pathway is activated more slowly, taking from minutes to hours. Cortisol has a wide range of functions, which include turning off all bodily systems not immediately required to deal with a stressor. For example, cortisol turns off insulin so that the liver starts releasing glucose, thus temporarily producing an increase in energy supply. It also shuts down reproductive functions and inhibits the production of growth hormone. In this way, the body's energy supplies can be concentrated on dealing with the stress.

Ending a Stress Response

Normally, stress responses are brief. The body mobilizes its resources, deals with the challenge physiologically and behaviorally, and then shuts down the stress response. Just as the brain is responsible for turning on the stress reaction, it is also responsible for turning it off. Consider what can happen if the stress response is not shut down:

- The body continues to mobilize energy at the cost of energy storage.
- Proteins are used up, resulting in muscle wasting and fatigue.
- Growth hormone is inhibited, and so the body cannot grow.
- The gastrointestinal system remains shut down, reducing the intake and processing of food to replace used resources.

Posttraumatic stress disorder (PTSD). Syndrome characterized by physiological arousal symptoms related to recurring memories and dreams related to a traumatic event—for months or years after the event.

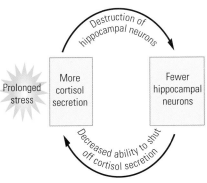

Figure 7-21

Vicious Cycle Unrelieved stress promotes an excessive release of cortisol that causes damage to neurons in the hippocampus. The damaged neurons are unable to detect cortisol and therefore cannot signal the adrenal gland to stop producing it. The result is a feedback loop in which the enhanced secretion of cortisol further damages hippocampal neurons.

■ Reproductive functions are inhibited.

■ The immune system is suppressed, contributing to the possibility of infection or disease.

Sapolsky (2003) argued that the hippocampus plays an important role in turning off the stress response. The hippocampus contains a high density of cortisol receptors, and it has axons that project to the hypothalamus. Consequently, the hippocampus is well suited to detecting cortisol in the blood and instructing the hypothalamus to reduce blood-cortisol levels.

There may, however, be a more insidious relation between the hippocampus and blood-cortisol levels. Sapolsky and his coworkers observed wild-born vervet monkeys that had become agricultural pests in Kenya and had therefore been trapped and caged. They found that some of the monkeys became sick and died of a syndrome that appeared to be related to stress. Those that died seemed to have been subordinate animals housed with particularly aggressive, dominant monkeys.

Autopsies showed high rates of gastric ulcers, enlarged adrenal glands, and pronounced hippocampal degeneration that was especially noticeable in the CA3 region of the hippocampus. The hippocampal damage may have been due to prolonged high cortisol levels produced by the unremitting stress of being caged with the aggressive monkeys.

Cortisol levels are usually regulated by the hippocampus, but, if these levels remain elevated because a stress-inducing situation continues, the high cortisol levels eventually damage the hippocampus. The damaged hippocampus is then unable to do its work of reducing the level of cortisol. Thus, a vicious cycle is set up in which the hippocampus undergoes progressive degeneration and cortisol levels are not controlled.

Remember that domoic acid, the agent in mussel poisoning, damages the hippocampus because it mimics the effects of high levels of the neurotransmitter glutamate. Prolonged high cortisol levels may damage the hippocampus by mimicking the excitotoxicity of domoic acid. By stimulating some hippocampal cells, cortisol causes them to release glutamate. If this stimulation is excessive, the sustained release of glutamate may be toxic to other hippocampal cells.

The cycle of prolonged stress, elevated cortisol levels, and damage to the hippocampus is illustrated in **Figure 7-21**. Because stress-response circuits in monkeys are very similar to those in humans, the possibility exists that excessive stress in humans also can lead to damaged hippocampal neurons. Because the hippocampus is thought to play a role in memory, stress-induced damage to the hippocampus is postulated to result in impaired memory as well as in **posttraumatic stress disorder** (PTSD). Posttraumatic stress disorder is characterized by physiological arousal symptoms related to recurring memories and dreams related to a traumatic event—for months or years after the event. People with PTSD feel as if they are reexperiencing the trauma, and the accompanying physiological arousal enhances their belief of impending danger.

Research has not led to a clear-cut answer concerning whether the cumulative effects of stress damage the human hippocampus. For example, research on women who were sexually abused in childhood and were diagnosed as suffering from posttraumatic stress disorder yields some reports of no changes in memory or in hippocampal volume, as measured with brain-imaging techniques, compared with other reports of memory impairments and reductions in hippocampal volume (Liberson & Phan, 2003). That such different results can be obtained in what appear to be similar studies can be explained in a number of ways.

First, how much damage to the hippocampus must occur to produce a stress syndrome is not certain. Second, brain-imaging techniques may not be sensitive to subtle changes in hippocampal cell function or moderate cell loss. Third, large individual and environmental differences influence how people respond to stress. Finally, preexisting injury to the hippocampus or other brain regions could influence the probability of developing posttraumatic stress disorder (Gilbertson et al., 2002).

Humans are long lived and have many life experiences that complicate simple extrapolations from a single stressful event. Nevertheless, changes to the brain induced by prolonged stress complicate the treatment of stress-related disorders and suggest that it is important to treat stress so that brain and body injury do not occur.

In Review

Hormones are hierarchically controlled by sensory experiences, the brain, the pituitary gland, and the endocrine glands that produce and secrete them through the bloodstream to targets throughout the body. Hormones are of two types, steroid and peptide, and can be classified into three groups: (1) homeostatic hormones regulate body nutrients and metabolic processes; (2) gonadal hormones regulate sexual behavior, pregnancy, and child bearing; and (3) stress hormones regulate the body's responses to challenging events. Because these hormones often have such widespread targets, traveling through the bloodstream is an effective way to deliver their chemical messages.

SUMMARY

▪ *How do psychoactive drugs work?* Psychoactive drugs—substances that alter mood, thought, or behavior—produce their effects by acting on receptors or on chemical processes in the nervous system, especially on processes of neural transmission at synapses. They act either as agonists to stimulate neuronal activity or as antagonists to depress it. Psychopharmacology is the study of drug effects on the brain and behavior.

▪ *How does a drug enter the body, reach its target, and leave the body?* Drugs, chemicals taken to bring about some desired change in the body, are administered by mouth, by inhalation, by absorption through the skin, and by injection. To reach a target in the nervous system, a drug must pass a through numerous barriers posed by digestion, dilution, the blood–brain barrier, and cell membranes. Drugs are diluted by body fluids as they pass through successive barriers, metabolized in the body, and excreted through sweat glands and in feces, urine, breath, and breast milk.

▪ *How do people respond to drugs?* A drug does not have a uniform action on every person. Physical differences—in body weight, sex, age, or genetic background—influence the effects of a given drug on a given person, as do behaviors, such as learning, and environmental context.

▪ *How are psychoactive drugs classified?* Psychoactive drugs are classified into seven groups according to their major behavioral effects, as sedative hypnotics and antianxiety agents, antipsychotic agents, antidepressants, mood stabilizers, narcotic analgesics, psychomotor stimulants, and stimulants that have psychedelic and hallucinogenic effects. Each group contains natural or synthetic drugs or both, and they may produce their actions in different ways.

▪ *How does the repeated use of drugs and their use in different contexts affect behavior?* A common misperception about drugs is that their actions are specific and consistent. But the body and brain rapidly become tolerant to many drugs, and so the dose must be increased to produce a constant effect. Alternatively, people may become sensitized to a drug, in which case the same dose produces increasingly greater effects. Learning also plays an important role in a person's behavior under the influence of a drug.

▪ *Why do people become addicted to drugs?* Addiction develops in a number of stages as a result of repeated drug taking. Initially, drug taking produces pleasure, or liking, but, with repeated use, it becomes conditioned to associated objects, events, and places. Eventually, those conditioned cues acquire incentive salience, causing the drug user to seek them out, which leads to more drug taking. The subjective experience associated with prominent cues and drug seeking promotes craving for the drug. As addiction proceeds, the subjective experience of liking decreases while that of wanting increases.

▪ *Does the effect of a drug depend on the drug-taking situation?* The influence of drugs on behavior varies widely with the situation and as a person learns appropriate drug-related behaviors. Some drugs, such as alcohol, can produce behavioral myopia such that a person is primarily influenced by prominent cues in the environment. These cues may encourage the person to act in ways in which he or she would not normally behave.

▪ *Why doesn't everyone abuse drugs?* Considering how many people use tobacco, drink alcohol, use recreational drugs, or abuse prescription drugs, it is probably rare to find someone who has not used a drug when it was available. Nevertheless, some people do seem vulnerable to drug use and addiction. Individual differences in genetics could be influential, but drug availability and peer influences are likely more influential. Because the neural mechanisms that are implicated in addiction are the same neural systems responsible for wanting and liking more generally, anyone is likely to be a potential drug abuser.

▪ *Can the repeated use of drugs produce brain damage?* Excessive use of alcohol can be associated with damage to the thalamus and hypothalamus, but the cause of the damage is poor nutrition rather than the direct actions of alcohol. Cocaine can harm brain circulation, producing brain damage by reduced blood flow or by bleeding into neural tissue. The drug "ecstasy," or MDMA, can result in the loss of fine axon collaterals of serotonin neurons and in the associated impairments in cognitive function. Psycedelic drugs such as marijuana and LSD can be associated with psychotic behavior, but whether this behavior is due to the direct effects of the drugs or to the aggravation of preexisting conditions is not clear.

▪ *What are hormones?* Steroid and peptide hormones are produced by endocrine glands and circulate in the bloodstream to affect a wide variety of targets. Hormones are under the hierarchical control of sensory events, the brain, the pituitary gland, and the endocrine glands, which all interact to regulate hormone levels. Homeostatic hormones regulate the balance of sugars, proteins, carbohydrates, salts, and other substances in the body. Sex hormones regulate the physical features and behaviors associated with reproduction and the care of offspring. Stress hormones regulate the body's ability to cope with arousing and challenging situations. Failures to turn stress responses off after a stressor has passed can contribute to susceptibility to posttraumatic stress disorder and other psychological and physical diseases.

KEY TERMS

addiction, p. 248

agonist, p. 231

alcohol myopia, p. 251

amphetamine, p. 242

antagonist, p. 231

antianxiety agent, p. 234

barbiturate, p. 234

cross-tolerance, p. 234

disinhibition theory,
　p. 251

dopamine hypothesis of
　schizophrenia, p. 237

endorphin, p. 241

fetal alcohol syndrome
　(FAS), p. 237

glucocorticoid, p. 258

gonadal (sex) hormone,
　p. 257

homeostasis, p. 257

incentive salience, p. 249

incentive-sensitization
　theory, p. 249

major tranquilizer, p. 237

monoamine oxidase
　(MAO) inhibitor,
　p. 238

narcotic analgesic, p. 239

organizational hypothesis,
　p. 259

peptide hormone, p. 257

REVIEW QUESTIONS

1. What problems are encountered in an effort to make a psychoactive drug a "magic bullet" targeting the CNS?

2. Describe how the blood–brain barrier works.

3. Describe the seven categories of drugs.

4. Distinguish between the dependency hypothesis and the wanting-and-liking theory of drug addiction.

5. Distinguish between the disinhibition, time-out, and alcohol-myopia explanations of behavior under the effects of drugs.

6. Describe the hierarchical control of hormones.

7. Describe some proposed effects of prolonged stress responses on the body and brain.

FOR FURTHER THOUGHT

A traditional view is that drugs cause people to behave in certain ways. Discuss contemporary views of how drugs can influence our behavior.

Because many drugs work by affecting the function of synapses, the effect that they produce must be similar to some naturally produced behavior. Discuss this idea in relation to a drug of your choice.

RECOMMENDED READING

Becker, J. B., Breedlove, S. M., & Crews, D. (2002). *Behavioral endocrinology.* Cambridge, MA: MIT Press. A book consisting of a number of chapters on hormones, each written by an expert.

Cooper, J. R., Bloom, F. E., & Roth, R. H. (1996). *The biochemical basis of neuropharmacology.* New York: Oxford University Press. A summary of how synapses respond to drugs. Consists of a general description of how synapses work and summarizes the structure and function of a number of different neurochemical synapses.

Feldman, R. S., Meyer, J. S., & Quenzer, L. F. (1997). *Principles of neuropsychopharmacology.* Sunderland, MA: Sinauer. A comprehensive but advanced book about how various drugs affect the nervous system. An outstanding reference on contemporary neuropsychopharmacology.

Julien, R. M. (2001). *A primer of drug action.* New York: Worth Publishers. As the name suggests, this book is an extremely readable introduction to how drugs affect the nervous system and produce changes in behavior, mood, and cognitive function.

Sapolsky, R. M. (1994). *Why zebras don't get ulcers.* New York: W. H. Freeman and Company. A readable popular summary of everything you would like to know about stress. The theme of the book is that stress affects the brain and contributes to a great many medical conditions—including heart disease, depression, sexual and reproductive problems, and hormonal disorders—to aging, and to death; finally, of course, it affects zebras.

How Do We Sense, Perceive, and See the World?

Migraines and a Case of Blindsight

Born in a small English town in 1940, D. B. had a medically uneventful childhood until he began to experience recurring headaches at about age 14. Before each headache, D. B. received a warning in the form of a visual aura: the sensation of an oval-shaped area containing a flashing light appeared just to the left of center in his field of vision. In the next few minutes, the oval enlarged, and, after about 15 min, the flashing light vanished and D. B. was blind in the region of the oval.

D. B. described the oval as an opaque white area surrounded by a rim of color. A headache on the right side of his head followed. The headache could persist for as long as 48 hours, but usually D. B. fell asleep before that much time elapsed. When he awakened, the headache was gone and his vision was normal again.

Karl Lashley

D. B., a well-studied patient in visual neuroscience, and Karl Lashley, a pioneer of research in this field, both suffered severe migraines. The term *migraine* (derived from a Greek word meaning "half of the skull") refers to recurrent headaches that are usually localized to one side of the head. Migraines vary in severity, frequency, and duration and are often accompanied by nausea and vomiting. Migraine is perhaps the most common of all neurological disorders, afflicting some 5 to 20 percent of the population at some time in their lives.

D. B. and Karl Lashley suffered from classic migraine, common to many sufferers, which is preceded by an aura that usually lasts from 20 to 40 min. Lashley carefully described his visual aura, which began as a spot of flashing (scintillating) light and then slowly enlarged. Like D. B., Lashley had no sight in the scintillating area; and, as that area enlarged, Lashley could detect lines of different orientations in it.

Findings from blood-flow studies reveal that, during such an aura, a reduction of blood flow in the posterior occipital cortex spreads at a rate of about 2 millimeters per minute. The aura may gradually expand to fill an entire side of the person's field of vision but rarely, if ever, crosses over to the opposite visual field. At its maximum, the person can see nothing on that side of the world. Vision then returns, although most people feel dizzy and often nauseated for a while.

Although D. B. and Lashley had visual auras, auras may also be auditory or tactile; in some cases, they may result in an inability to move or to talk. After the aura passes, most people suffer a severe headache that results from a dilation of cerebral blood vessels. The headache is usually on one side of the head, just as the aura is on one side of the field of vision. Left untreated, these migraine headaches may last for hours or even days.

D. B.'s attacks continued at intervals of about 6 weeks for 10 years. After one attack, he did not totally regain his vision but was left with a small blind spot, or *scotoma,* illustrated in the accompanying series of photographs. In some attacks, D. B. also began to experience occasional loss of skin sensation along the left side of his body. Like his visual symptoms, these tactile auras disappeared after the headache was gone.

When D. B. was 26 years old, a neurologist found that a collection of abnormal blood vessels at the back of his right

X = Fixation point

In the development of a migraine scotoma as described by Karl Lashley, a person looking at the small "x" (shown in white in the photograph at the far left) first sees a small patch of lines. Information in the world is not visible at that location. The striped area continues to grow outward, leaving an opaque area (scotoma) where the stripes had been. Within 15 to 20 minutes, the visual field is almost completely blocked by the scotoma. Normal vision returns shortly thereafter.

occipital lobe was causing the migraine attacks. (In case you suffer from migraines, we hasten to point out that this cause is unusual.) By the time D. B. was 30, the migraines became more severe and began to interfere with his family and social life, as well as his job.

Because no drug treatment was effective, D. B. had the malformed blood vessels surgically removed in 1973. The operation relieved his pain and generally improved his life, but a part of his right occipital lobe was deprived of blood and died. As a result, D. B. became blind in the left half of his visual field; that is, as he looks at the world through either eye, he is unable to see anything to the left of the midline.

D. B. came to the attention of Lawrence Weizkrantz, a world-renowned visual neuroscientist at Oxford University, who made a remarkable discovery about D. B.'s blindness. Although D. B. could not identify objects in his blind area, he could very accurately "guess" if a light had blinked on there. He could even say where the light that he did not "see" was located.

Apparently, even though D. B. could not consciously perceive a light in his blind region, his brain knew when a light had blinked and *where* it had appeared. This phenomenon is referred to as *blindsight*. D. B.'s brain, in other words, knew more than he was consciously aware of.

What applies to D. B. applies to everyone. You are consciously aware of only part of the visual information that your brain is processing. This selectivity is an important working principle behind human sensation and perception. Weizkrantz was able to detect it in the visual system because of D. B.'s injury.

Vision is not unique in this regard. We are also unaware of much of the processing that takes place in other sensory pathways for hearing, balance and touch, taste, and smell. But vision is the focus of this chapter. The ability to lose conscious visual perception while retaining unconscious vision leads to this chapter's major question: How do we "see" the world?

The function of the visual system is to convert light energy into neural activity that has meaning for us. In this chapter, we begin an exploration of how this conversion takes place with a general summary of sensation and perception—what it really means to experience the sensory information transmitted by our environment. In an overview of the visual system's anatomy, we then consider the anatomical structure of the eyes, the connections between the eyes and the brain, and the sections of the brain that process visual information.

Turning next to the experience of sight, we focus on how neurons respond to visual input, enabling the brain to perceive different features, such as color and shape. "Testing Vision in Nonhuman Species" on p. 270 describes one technique that researchers have developed to study how the brain perceives movement. At the chapter's end, we explore the culmination of vision—to *understand* what we see: How do we infuse light energy with meaning, to grasp the meaning of written words or to see the beauty in a painting?

THE NATURE OF SENSATION AND PERCEPTION

As we look at the world, we naturally assume that what we see is what is really "out there." Cameras and videos reinforce this impression, seeming to re-create the very same visual world that we experience first hand. But our version of the world, whether we see it directly or view it reproduced, is always a creation of the brain. What we see is not an objective reproduction of what is "out there" but rather a subjective construction of reality that the brain manufactures.

With this in mind, we can make a distinction between sensation and perception. *Sensation* is the registration of physical stimuli from the environment by the sensory organs, whereas *perception* is the interpretation of sensations by the brain. Our version of reality is our perception of the sensory world.

Sensory Experience and Sensory Reality

Compared with humans, dogs have very limited color vision. Compared with dogs, humans have an olfactory system that smells in black and white. Dogs smell in technicolor.

Which sensory system, dog or human, truly represents the world? Neither. Human brains and dog brains create species-specific sensations. Each is merely one version of "reality" among many. These sensory experiences are not genuine reproductions of the world; rather, they exist only in the mind of the perceiver.

In fact, the version of the world that we experience is not even constant in our own minds. As dusk falls, for example, our color perception shifts so that red now appears black even as green remains green. You can observe this color shift in the petals of a red rose and its green leaves. As light fails, the red rose becomes blackish, but the green leaves stay green.

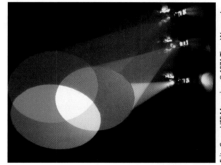

It is not that red has suddenly vanished from the external world. Rather, it is that your visual system can no longer create this color as light levels drop. But add light—say, by shining a flashlight on the rose—and the petals will immediately look red again. Visual artists from illustrators to filmmakers exploit such properties of visual perception in their work.

The mind creates not just the visual world but the world of all the senses. Consider hearing. There is an old philosophical question about whether a tree falling in the forest makes a sound if no one is there to hear it. The answer is no. A falling tree makes sound waves but no sound.

Sound as we perceive it does not exist without a brain to create it. The only reason that we experience sound is that the information from the ear goes to a region of the brain that converts the neural activity into what we then perceive to be sound. The brain might just as well convert that neural activity into some other subjective sensation. Imagine the ear being connected to the visual system. The sound of the tree falling would become a visual experience rather than an auditory one, because the visual system would not know that the information came from the ear.

It is hard to imagine just what the noise of a tree falling would "look" like, but we would not experience sound. Sound is the product of the particular auditory processing system that we possess. Without that system, there is no sound as we know it. Some people have the capacity, known as *synesthesia*, to join sensory experiences across modalities. To such a person, a particular sound will also produce a color or taste, as we detail in Chapter 14.

If the sensory world is merely a creation of the brain, it follows that different brains might create different sensory experiences, even among members of the same species. To demonstrate, consider the color red. We perceive red because certain cells in our eyes are activated by certain wavelengths of light that we call red or green. (How this works will be explained shortly.) If we did not have these cells, we could not experience red. In fact, about 5 percent of all human males lack the cells. They are therefore red–green color-blind and cannot tell these two colors apart.

Color blindness is just one extreme of normal human variation in color perception. More subtle variations also exist. For instance, Joris Winderickx and her colleagues

Testing Vision in Nonhuman Subjects

A challenge in studying sensory and perceptual systems in nonhumans is to determine their capacities without the benefit of verbal communication. Thus, if we wish to know what a cat or dog or rat sees, we cannot simply show them an eye chart and have them recite the letters. Rather, we have to figure out a way to "speak" the animal's language.

One way to ask animals about their perceptual capacities is to use reward. For example, animals can be trained to seek rewards that are associated with certain visual stimuli and not with others, but this training may take weeks and is not likely to work with young animals that do not yet have the cognitive capacities to learn such reward-based tasks. These drawbacks can be problematic because researchers often want quick answers to questions related to sensory capacities, and developmental neuroscientists would like to track the development of sensory capacities.

Glen Prusky and Rob Douglas have been designing tests to circumvent these problems. In one test, they take advantage of the optomotor responses (eye movements generated to stabilize moving information on the retina) that all animals show spontaneously from a young age. If a moving grating passes in front of you, it is very difficult to prevent your eyes from following the moving vertical lines. In fact, both humans and nonhumans track the lines not only with

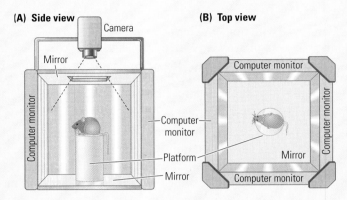

(A) In a three-dimensional optomotor testing apparatus, a mouse is placed on a platform positioned in the middle of an arena created by a quadrangle of computer monitors. Line gratings drawn on the screens are extended vertically with floor and ceiling mirrors. A video camera monitors the animal's behavior from above. **(B)** The mouse is surrounded by line gratings and allowed to move freely on the platform. Adapted from Prusky and Douglas (2004).

(1992) asked men who were not red–green color-blind to mix red and green lights together to match a series of yellow lights (in the mixing of colors of light, red and green make yellow). The men varied in the amounts of red versus green that they used to match the different yellows, but these variations were consistent for each man. Some of the men required relatively more red to match the yellows, others required relatively more green. We could say that the second group, compared with the first, had a slightly rosier view of the world to begin with.

Winderickx found two forms of the receptor cell that detects red; about 60 percent of men have one form, 40 percent have the other. The difference between these two forms is small but significant and results from a small difference in the gene that encodes the red-detecting receptor. The Winderickx study provided the first evidence that normal variation in our mental world is traceable to normal variation in our genes.

Analyzing Sensory Information

D. B., who was not consciously aware of the presence of a light in his blind area yet could indicate where the light was, illustrates another point about sensory experiences. Clearly, the brain must process visual information in multiple ways. Some processing allows us to consciously analyze visual stimuli, whereas other information processing happens unconsciously.

the eyes but also by moving the head. If the thickness of the lines is made smaller and smaller, there will be a point at which we can no longer perceive the individual lines, and the optomotor response stops.

Thus, we can measure an animal's visual acuity, the equivalent of asking people to read smaller and smaller print, by varying the size of the moving lines. This response is natural and requires no training. Indeed, scientists have known for more than 50 years that, if an animal is placed inside a cylinder that has stripes and the cylinder is then rotated, the animal will show the optomotor response.

Such tests have proved difficult to administer, however, because the investigator needs many cylinders, each with different-width lines, and it is difficult to change the cylinders quickly. Prusky and Douglas (2004) solved this problem by constructing a virtual three-dimensional cylinder as shown in the illustration.

Four flat-screen computer monitors are arranged to form a quadrangle. The animal is placed on a small platform in the center of the quadrangle, and a small camera tracks its behavior. A line grating is generated by computer and appears to be moving around the subject. The subject responds by tracking the movement with its head and neck. Because the moving grating is computer generated, the width of the lines can be changed instantly. This feature makes it possible to determine the precise point at which the animal no longer perceives the lines, because the animal stops tracking at this point.

There is one other clever feature of this task. As the animal moves around on the platform, the distance between its eyes and computer grating will vary. This feature is important because, if the animal moves closer, lines that were not visible may now be seen. The trick is to make the lines smaller if the animal moves toward them and bigger if it moves away. With the use of coordinates of head location obtained from the camera, the precise position of the animal can be calculated by the computer and the virtual world changes. (To see this feature in action, go to www.CerebralMechanics.com and try it for yourself.)

The Prusky and Douglas task thus provides a quick way for an animal and investigator to communicate. Furthermore, rodent infants can be tested as soon as their eyes are open, at about 2 weeks of age. This type of test could be used for human infants as well, especially if there is reason to believe that an infant has visual problems that need treatment.

To prove to yourself that your brain operates in both ways, imagine yourself seated at a desk writing an essay. As you work, you engage in many behaviors that require vision. You read books and write notes, you type on a computer, and you reach for and drink from a mug of coffee.

What exactly are you doing when you make these visually guided movements? What happens when you reach for your pen or your coffee mug? Before reading further, reach for objects of different sizes and shapes around you and observe what you do. First, your eyes orient to the object. Then, as your hand moves toward it, your fingers form the appropriate shape long before they get to the object. When you reach for a pen, your thumb and index finger assume a position as if to pinch the pen. When you reach for a mug, your hand is oriented vertically so that your fingers can grasp the handle.

These movements are illustrated in **Figure 8-1A.** You did not consciously think about this finger-and-hand positioning. It just happened. Reaching for the pen or the mug was conscious, but the shaping of your hand for the particular object was not. Although both movements are guided by

(A)

(B)

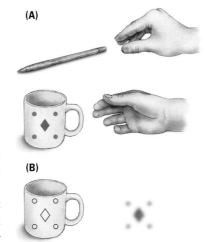

Figure 8-1

Visual Perception   Although you may consciously decide to reach for an object such as a pen or a mug **(A),** your hand forms the appropriate posture automatically, without your conscious awareness. The mug can be separated into two distinct visual representations **(B),** one for shape and another for color. Note that the color pattern is fuzzy, whereas the shape is sharp but appears only in shades of gray. These representations are meant to mimic the types of analysis that take place in two different brain regions as visual information about the mug is being processed. The mug does not actually exist in the brain as we perceive it.

visual information, different regions of the brain and different kinds of processing are required.

There is more. Consider your coffee mug. It has a shape and it has a color pattern. Yet you are not consciously aware of each of these attributes separately, as depicted in Figure 8-1B. Instead, you perceive the patterned mug to be a single object. It may therefore surprise you to learn that your brain produces this unified perception after analyzing color separately from shape, each analysis in a different neural location. Consequently, people can have brain damage that allows them to see the color of an object but to have no idea of what the object is, because its shape is indecipherable.

Conversely, a person with another sort of brain damage might see the shape of an object clearly but have no clue to its color. The brain essentially dissects the object, analyzes the various parts separately, and then produces what appears to be a unified perception of the whole. Yet there is no "picture" of the entire object in one place in the brain. How, then, do we perceive a single object if we have only multiple mental versions of it with which to work? You may recall from Chapter 2 that we referred to this conundrum as the *binding problem*. We will return to this fascinating question later.

In Review

We identified two key points about sensation and perception. First, our perceptions of the world are entirely a creation of the brain. Different species and, to a lesser extent, different individual members of a species have different perceptions of what the world is really like. Neither is right or wrong, but both are imaginary. Second, the brain does not analyze sensory information as though it were uniform. Rather, sensory information entering the brain is dissected and passed to specialized regions that analyze particular characteristics. We only have the impression that we perceive a unified sensory world. This binding problem is one of the puzzles of how the brain works. Before returning to that puzzle, we must first identify how the visual system breaks down visual stimuli.

ANATOMY OF THE VISUAL SYSTEM

Vision is our primary sensory experience. Far more of the human brain is dedicated to vision than to any of our other senses. Understanding the organization of the visual system is therefore key to understanding human brain function. To build this understanding, we begin by following the routes that visual information takes to the brain and within it. This exercise is a bit like traveling a road to discover where it goes. The first step is to consider what the visual system analyzes—namely, light.

Light: The Stimulus for Vision

Simply put, light is electromagnetic energy that we see. This energy comes either directly from a source, such as a lamp or the sun, that produces it or indirectly after having been reflected off one or more objects. In either case, light energy travels from the outside world, through the pupil, and into the eye, where it strikes a light-sensitive surface on the back of the eye called the **retina**. From this stimulation of receptors on the retina, we start the process of creating a visual world.

Retina. Light-sensitive surface at the back of the eye consisting of neurons and photoreceptor cells.

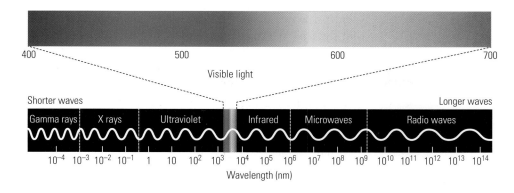

Figure 8-2

Visible Light The part of the electromagnetic spectrum visible to the human eye is restricted to a mere sliver of wavelengths.

A useful way to represent light is as a continuously moving wave. Not all light waves are the same length, however. **Figure 8-2** shows that, within the rather narrow range of electromagnetic energy visible to humans, the wavelength varies from about 400 nanometers (violet) to 700 nanometers (red). (A nanometer, abbreviated nm, is one-billionth of a meter.)

The range of visible light is constrained not by the properties of light waves but rather by the properties of our visual receptors. If our receptors could detect light in the ultraviolet or infrared range, we would see additional colors. In fact, bees detect light in both the visible and the ultraviolet range and so have a broader range of color perception than we do.

Structure of the Eye

How do the cells of the retina absorb light energy and initiate the processes leading to vision? To answer this question, we first consider the structure of the eye as a whole so that you can understand how it is designed to capture and focus light. Only then do we consider the photoreceptor cells.

The functionally distinct parts of the eye are shown in **Figure 8-3**. They include the *sclera,* the white part that forms the eyeball; the *cornea,* the eye's clear outer covering;

⊙ Visit the module on the visual system on your *Foundations of Behavioral Neuroscience* CD. In the section on the eye you can rotate the three-dimensional model to better understand the anatomy of the eye and the structure of the retina. (See the Preface for more information about this CD.)

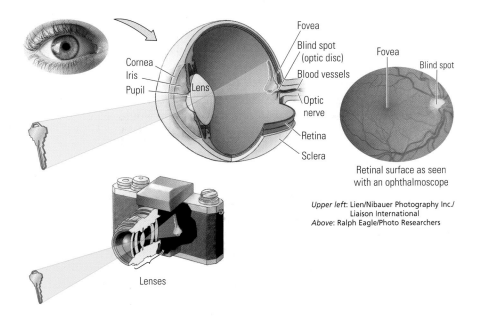

Upper left: Lien/Nibauer Photography Inc./ Liaison International
Above: Ralph Eagle/Photo Researchers

Figure 8-3

Visual Basics The cornea and lens of the eye, like the lens of a camera, focus light rays to project a backward, inverted image on the receptive surface—namely, the retina and film, respectively. The optic nerve conveys information from the eye to the brain. The fovea is the region of best vision and is characterized by the densest distribution of photoreceptor cells. The region in the eye where the blood vessels enter and the axons of the ganglion cells leave, called the optic disc, has no receptors and thus forms a blind spot. Note that there are few blood vessels around the fovea in the photograph of the retina at far right.

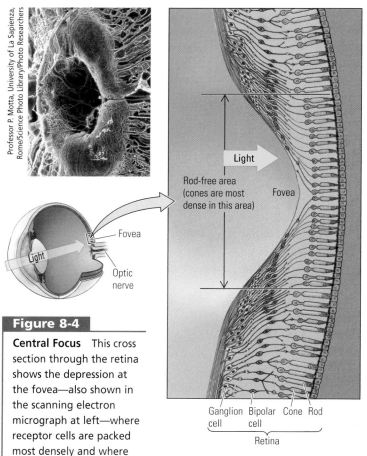

Light

Fovea

Optic
nerve

Light

Rod-free area
(cones are most
dense in this area)

Fovea

Ganglion   Bipolar   Cone Rod
cell   cell

Retina

Figure 8-4

Central Focus This cross
section through the retina
shows the depression at
the fovea—also shown in
the scanning electron
micrograph at left—where
receptor cells are packed
most densely and where
our vision is clearest.

Blind spot. Region of the retina where
axons forming the optic nerve leave the
eye and where blood vessels enter and
leave; this region has no photoreceptors
and is thus "blind."

the *iris,* which opens and closes to allow more or less light
in; the *lens,* which focuses light; and the *retina,* where light
energy initiates neural activity. As light enters the eye, it is
bent first by the cornea, travels through the hole in the iris
called the *pupil,* and is then bent again by the lens. The curvature of the cornea is fixed, and so the bending of light waves
there is fixed, whereas small muscles adjust the curvature of
the lens.

The shape of the lens adjusts to bend the light to greater
or lesser degrees. This ability allows near and far images to be
focused on the retina. When images are not properly focused,
we require a corrective lens, as discussed in "Optical Errors of
Refraction and Visual Illuminance."

Figure 8-4 includes a photograph of the retina, which
is composed of photoreceptors beneath a layer of neurons
connected to them. Although the neurons lie in front of
the photoreceptor cells, they do not prevent incoming light
from being absorbed by those receptors, because the neurons are transparent and the photoreceptors are extremely
sensitive to light. (The neurons in the retina are insensitive
to light and so are unaffected by the light passing through
them.)

Together, the photoreceptor cells and the neurons of the
retina perform some amazing functions. They translate light
into action potentials, discriminate wavelengths so that we
can distinguish colors, and work in a range of light intensi-
ties from very bright to very dim. These cells afford visual
precision sufficient for us to see a human hair lying on the page of this book from a
distance of 18 inches.

As in a camera, the image of objects projected onto the retina is upside down and
backward. This flip-flopped orientation poses no problem for the brain. Remember
that the brain is *creating* the outside world, and so it does not really care how the image
is oriented initially. In fact, the brain can make adjustments regardless of the orientation of the images that it receives.

In fact, if you were to put on glasses that invert visual images and kept those glasses
on for several days, the world would first appear upside down but then would suddenly
appear right side up again because your brain would correct the distortion (Held,
1968). Curiously, when you removed the glasses, the world would temporarily seem
upside down once more, because your brain at first would be unaware that you had
tricked it another time. Eventually, though, your brain would solve this puzzle, too, and
the world would flip back in the right orientation.

THE BLIND SPOT

Try this experiment. Stand with your head over a tabletop and hold a pencil in your
hand. Close one eye. Stare at the edge of the tabletop nearest you. Now hold the pencil in a horizontal position and move it along the edge of the table, with the eraser on
the table. Beginning at a point approximately below your nose, move the pencil slowly
along the table in the direction of the open eye.

When you have moved the pencil about 6 inches, the eraser will vanish. You have
found your **blind spot,** a small area of the retina that is also known as the *optic disc.* As
shown on the far right in Figure 8-3, the optic disc is the area where blood vessels enter
and exit the eye and where fibers leading from retinal neurons form the optic nerve that

Optical Errors of Refraction and Visual Illuminance

Focus on Disorders

The eye, like a camera, works correctly only when sufficient light passes through the lens and is focused on the receptor surface—the retina of the eye or the film in the camera. Too little light entering the eye or the camera produces a problem of *visual illuminance:* it is hard to see any image at all. If the focal point of the light is slightly in front of the receptor surface or slightly behind it, a *refractive error* causes objects to appear blurry.

Refractive errors in the eye are of two basic types. Most common in young people (afflicting about 50 percent of the population) is *myopia* (nearsightedness), an inability to bring distant objects into clear focus. Myopia is most commonly caused by the normally round eyeball being elongated instead. Myopia can also be caused by excessive curvature of the front of the cornea. In either case, the focal point of light falls short of the retina.

In *hyperopia* (farsightedness), a less common refractive error in which people are unable to focus on near objects, the focal point of light falls beyond the retina. Whereas the myopic eyeball may be too long, the hyperoptic eyeball may be too short. Farsightedness may also result because the lens is too flat and does not adequately refract light. As

people age, the lens loses its elasticity and consequently becomes unable to refract light from nearby objects correctly.

This form of hyperopia is called *presbyopia* (old sightedness). Presbyopia is so common that it is rare to find people older than 50 who do not need glasses to see up close, especially for reading. Fortunately, this error and other errors of refraction can be cured by corrective lenses.

An additional complication to the aging eye cannot be cured by corrective lenses. As we age, the eye's lens and cornea allow less light through, and so less light strikes the retina—a problem of visual illuminance. Don Kline (1994) estimated that, between ages 20 and 40, there is a drop of 50 percent in visual illuminance in dim lighting and a further drop of 50 percent over every 20 additional years. As a result, it becomes increasingly difficult to see in dim light, especially at night.

Corrective lenses do not compensate for this reduced visual illuminance; the only solution is to increase lighting. Night vision is especially problematic. Not surprisingly, statistics show a marked drop in the number of people driving at night in each successive decade after age 40.

Normal

Retina

Myopia

Hyperopia

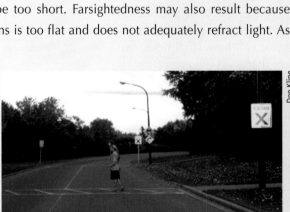

Don Kline

These photographs represent the drop in visual illuminance that occurs between age 20 (*left*) and age 60 (*right*).

Figure 8-5

Find Your Blind Spot Hold this book 30 centimeters (about 12 inches) away from your face. Shut your left eye and look at the cross with your right eye. Slowly bring the page toward you until the red dot disappears from the center of the yellow disc and is replaced by a yellow surface. The red spot is now in your blind spot and not visible. Your brain replaces the area with the surrounding yellow to fill in the image. Turn the book upside down to test your left eye.

Fovea. Region at the center of the retina that is specialized for high acuity; its receptive fields are at the center of the eye's visual field.

Rod. Photoreceptor specialized for functioning at low light levels.

Cone. Photoreceptor specialized for color and high visual acuity.

goes to the brain. There are therefore no photoreceptors in this part of the retina, and so you cannot see with it. **Figure 8-5** enables you to demonstrate your own blind spot.

Fortunately, your visual system solves the blind-spot problem by locating the optic disc in a different location in each of your eyes. The optic disc is lateral to the fovea in each eye, which means that it is left of the fovea in the left eye and right of the fovea in the right eye. Because the visual world of the two eyes overlaps, the blind spot of the left eye can be seen by the right eye and visa versa.

Thus, using both eyes together, you can see the whole visual world. People with blindness in one eye have a greater problem, however, because the sightless eye cannot compensate for the blind spot in the functioning eye. Still, the visual system compensates for the blind spot in several other ways, and so people who are blind in one eye have no sense of a hole in their field of vision.

The optic disc that produces a blind spot is of particular importance in neurology. It allows neurologists to indirectly view the condition of the optic nerve that lies behind it while providing a window onto events within the brain.

If there is an increase in intracranial pressure, such as occurs with a tumor or brain abscess (infection), the optic disc swells, leading to a condition known as *papilloedema* (swollen disc). The swelling occurs in part because, like all neural tissue, the optic nerve is surrounded by cerebrospinal fluid. Pressure inside the cranium can displace this fluid around the optic nerve, causing swelling at the optic disc.

Another reason for papilloedema is inflammation of the optic nerve itself, a condition known as *optic neuritis*. Whatever the cause, a person with a swollen optic disc usually loses vision owing to pressure on the optic nerve. If the swelling is due to optic neuritis, probably the most common neurological visual disorder, the prognosis for recovery is good.

THE FOVEA

Now try another experiment. Focus on the print at the left edge of this page. The words will be clearly legible. Now, while holding your eyes still, try to read the words on the right side of the page. It will be very difficult and likely impossible, even though you can see that words are there.

The lesson is that our vision is better in the center of the visual field than at the margins, or periphery. This difference is partly due to the fact that photoreceptors are more densely packed at the center of the retina, in a region known as the **fovea**. Figure 8-4 shows that the surface of the retina is depressed at the fovea. This depression is formed because many of the fibers of the optic nerve skirt the fovea to facilitate light access to its receptors.

Photoreceptors

The retina's photoreceptor cells convert light energy first into chemical energy and then into neural activity. When light strikes a photoreceptor, it triggers a series of chemical reactions that lead to a change in membrane potential. This change in turn leads to a change in the release of neurotransmitter onto nearby neurons.

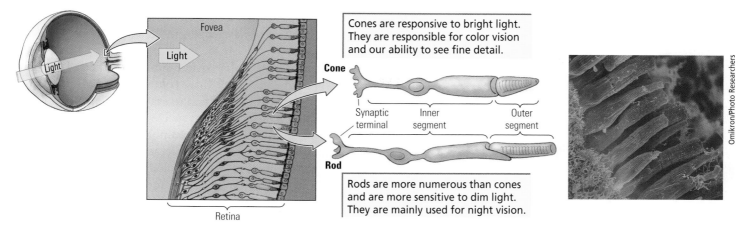

Cones are responsive to bright light. They are responsible for color vision and our ability to see fine detail.

Rods are more numerous than cones and are more sensitive to dim light. They are mainly used for night vision.

Omikron/Photo Researchers

Omikron/Photo Researchers

Rods and cones, the two types of photoreceptors, differ in many ways. As you can see in **Figure 8-6**, they are structurally different. Rods are longer than cones and cylindrically shaped at one end, whereas cones have a tapered end. **Rods,** which are more numerous than cones, are sensitive to low levels of brightness (luminance), especially in dim light, and are used mainly for night vision. **Cones** do not respond to dim light, but they are highly responsive in bright light. Cones mediate both color vision and our ability to see fine detail.

Rods and cones are not evenly distributed over the retina. The fovea has only cones, but their density drops dramatically at either side of the fovea. For this reason, our vision is not so sharp at the edges of the visual field, as demonstrated earlier.

A final difference between rods and cones is in their light-absorbing pigments. Although both rods and cones have pigments that absorb light, all rods have the same pigment, whereas cones have three different pigment types. Any given cone has one of these three cone pigments. The four different pigments, one in the rods and three in the cones, form the basis of our vision.

The three types of cone pigments absorb light over a range of frequencies, but their maximum absorptions are at about 419, 531, and 559 nm, respectively. The small range of wavelengths to which each cone pigment is maximally responsive is shown in **Figure 8-7**. Cones that contain these pigments are called "blue," "green," and "red," respectively, loosely referring to colors in their range of peak sensitivity.

Note, however, that, if you were to look at lights with wavelengths of 419, 531, and 559 nm, they would not appear blue, green, and red but rather violet, blue green, and yellow green, as you can see on the background spectrum in Figure 8-7. Remember, though, that you are looking at the lights with all three of your cone types and that each cone pigment is responsive to light across a range of frequencies, not just to its frequency of maximum absorption. So the terms blue, green, and red cones are not that far off the mark. Perhaps it would be more accurate to describe these three cone types as responsive to short, middle, and long visible wavelengths, referring to the relative length of light waves at which their sensitivities peak.

Not only does the presence of three different cone receptors contribute to our perception of color, so does the relative number and distribution of cone types across the retina. As **Figure 8-8** shows, the three cone types are distributed more or less randomly across the retina, making our ability to perceive different colors fairly constant across the visual field. Although there are approximately equal

Figure 8-6

Photoreceptor Cells   Both rods and cones are tubelike structures, as the scanning electron micrograph at the far right shows, but they differ, especially in the outer segment, which contains the light-absorbing visual pigment. Functionally, rods are especially sensitive to broad-spectrum luminance, and cones are sensitive to particular wavelengths of light.

Figure 8-7

Range and Peak Sensitivity   Our actual perception of color corresponds to the summed activity of the three types of cones, each type most sensitive to a narrow range of the spectrum. Note that rods, represented by the white curve, also have a preference for a range of wavelengths centered on 496 nm, but the rods do not contribute to our color perception; their activity is not summed with the cones in the color system.

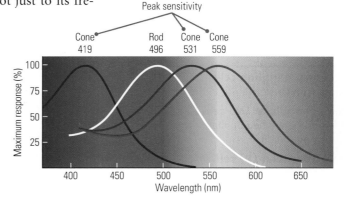

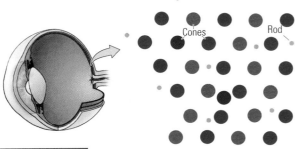

Figure 8-8

Retinal Receptors The retinal receptors form a mosaic of rods and three types of cones. This diagram represents the distribution near the fovea, where the cones outnumber the rods. There are fewer blue cones than red and green cones.

numbers of red and green cones, there are fewer blue cones, which means that we are not as sensitive to wavelengths in the blue part of the visible spectrum.

Other species that have color vision similar to that of humans also have three types of cones, with three color pigments. But, because of slight variations in these pigments, the exact frequencies of maximum absorption differ among different species. For humans, the exact frequencies are not identical with the numbers given earlier, which were an average across mammals. They are actually 426 and 530 nm for the blue and green cones, respectively, and 552 or 557 nm for the red cone. There are two peak sensitivity levels given for red because humans, as stated earlier, have two variants of the red cone. The difference in these two red cones appears minuscule, but recall that it does make a functional difference in color perception.

This functional difference between the two human variants of red cone becomes especially apparent in some women. The gene for the red cone is carried on the X chromosome. Because males have only one X chromosome, they have only one of these genes and so only one type of red cone. The situation is more complicated for women. Although most women have only one type of red cone, some have both, with the result that they are more sensitive than the rest of us to color differences at the red end of the spectrum. Their color receptors create a world with a richer range of red experiences. However, these women also have to contend with peculiar-seeming color coordination by others.

Retinal Neuron Types

Figure 8-9 shows that the photoreceptors in the retina are connected to two layers of retinal neurons. In the procession from the rods and cones toward the brain, the first layer contains three types of cells: *bipolar cells, horizontal cells,* and *amacrine cells.* Two cell types in the first neural layer are essentially linkage cells. The horizontal cells link photoreceptors with bipolar cells, whereas the amacrine cells link bipolar cells with cells of the second neural layer, the **retinal ganglion cells.** The axons of the ganglion cells collect in a bundle at the optic disc and leave the eye to form the optic nerve.

Figure 8-9

Retinal Cells The enlargement of the retina at the right shows the positions of the four types of neurons in the retina: bipolar, horizontal, amacrine, and ganglion cells. Notice that light must pass through both neuron layers to reach the photoreceptors.

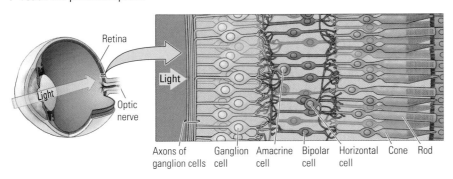

Axons of ganglion cells   Ganglion cell   Amacrine cell   Bipolar cell   Horizontal cell   Cone   Rod

Retinal ganglion cells are not all the same in regard to the brain cells to which they connect. They fall into two major categories, which in the primate retina are called M and P cells. The designations M and P derive from the distinctly different populations of cells in the visual thalamus to which these two classes of ganglion cells send their axons.

As shown in **Figure 8-10**, one of these populations consists of **magnocellular cells** (hence M), whereas the other consists of **parvocellular cells** (hence P). M cells, which are larger (*magno* means "large" in Latin), receive their input primarily from rods and so are sensitive to light but not to color. P cells, which are smaller (*parvo* means "small" in Latin), receive their input primarily from cones and so are sensitive to color.

M cells are found throughout the retina, including the periphery, where we are sensitive to movement but not to color or fine details. P cells are found largely in

Retinal ganglion cells. Neural cells of the retina that give rise to the optic nerve.

Magnocellular (M) cell. Large-celled visual-system neuron that is sensitive to moving stimuli.

Parvocellular (P) cell. Small-celled visual-system neuron that is sensitive to form and color differences.

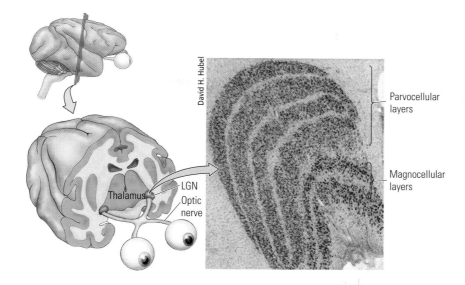

Parvocellular layers

Magnocellular layers

Thalamus
LGN
Optic nerve

Figure 8-10

Visual Thalamus The optic nerves connect with the lateral geniculate nucleus (LGN) of the thalamus. The LGN has six layers: two magnocellular layers that receive input mainly from rods and four parvocellular layers that receive input mainly from cones.

Optic chiasm. Junction of the optic nerves from each eye at which the axons from the nasal (inside—nearer the nose) halves of the retinas cross to the opposite side of the brain.

the region of the fovea, where we are sensitive to color and fine details. A distinction between these two categories of ganglion cells is maintained throughout the visual pathways, as you will see in the next section, where we follow the ganglion cell axons into the brain.

Visual Pathways

Imagine leaving your house and finding yourself on an unfamiliar road. Because the road is not on any map, the only way to find out where it goes is to follow it. You soon discover that the road divides in two, and so you must follow each branch sequentially to figure out its end point. Suppose you learn that one branch goes to a city, whereas the other goes to a national park. By knowing the end point of each branch, you can conclude something about their respective functions—that one branch carries people to work, whereas the other carries them to play, for example.

The same strategy can be used to follow the paths of the visual system. The retinal ganglion cells form the optic nerve, which is the road into the brain. This road travels to several places, each with a different function. By finding out where the branches go, we can begin to guess what the brain is doing with the visual input and how the brain creates our visual world.

Let us begin with the optic nerves, one exiting from each eye. As you know, they are formed by the axons of ganglion cells leaving the retina. Just before entering the brain, the optic nerves partly cross, forming the **optic chiasm** (from the shape of the Greek letter χ).

About half the fibers from each eye cross in such a way that the left half of each optic nerve goes to the left side of the brain, whereas the right halves go to the brain's right side, as diagrammed in **Figure 8-11**. The medial path of each retina, the *nasal retina*, crosses to the opposite side. The lateral path, the *temporal retina*, goes straight back on the same side. Because the light that falls on the right half of the retina actually comes from the left side of the

Figure 8-11

Crossing the Optic Chiasm This horizontal slice through the brain shows the visual pathway from each eye to the primary visual cortex of each hemisphere. Information from the blue side of the visual field goes to the two left halves of the retinas and ends up in the left hemisphere. Information from the red side of the visual field hits the right halves of the retinas and travels to the right side of the brain.

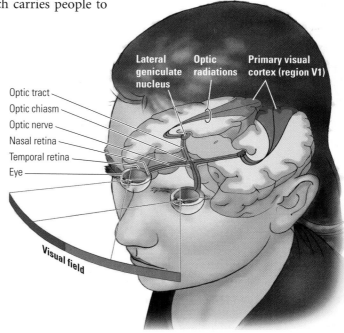

Optic tract
Optic chiasm
Optic nerve
Nasal retina
Temporal retina
Eye

Lateral geniculate nucleus
Optic radiations
Primary visual cortex (region V1)

Visual field

Figure 8-12

Flow of Visual Information into the Brain   The optic nerve has two principal branches: (1) the geniculostriate system through the LGN in the thalamus to the primary visual cortex and (2) the tectopulvinar system through the superior colliculus of the tectum to the pulvinar region of the thalamus and thus to the temporal and parietal lobes.

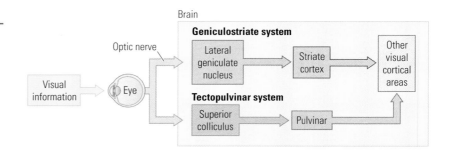

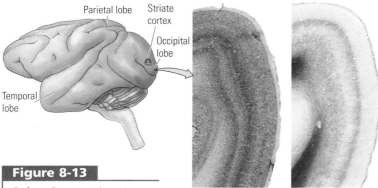

Figure 8-13

Striate Cortex   The primary visual cortex is referred to as striate cortex because it appears to have striations (stripes) when stained with either a cell-body stain (*left*) or a myelin stain (*right*) in these sections from a rhesus monkey brain.

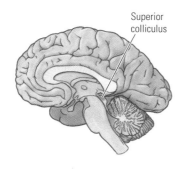

Geniculostriate system. Projections from the retina to the lateral geniculate nucleus to the visual cortex.

Striate cortex. Primary visual cortex in the occipital lobe; its striped appearance when stained gives it this name.

Tectopulvinar system. Projections from the retina to the superior colliculus to the pulvinar (thalamus) to the parietal and temporal visual areas.

visual field, information from the left visual field goes to the brain's right hemisphere, whereas information from the right visual field goes to the left hemisphere. Thus, half of each retina's visual field is represented on each side of the brain.

Having entered the brain, the axons of the ganglion cells separate, forming two distinct pathways, charted in **Figure 8-12.** All the axons of the P ganglion cells and some of the M ganglion cells form a pathway called the **geniculostriate system.** This pathway goes from the retina to the lateral geniculate nucleus (LGN) of the thalamus and then to layer IV of the primary visual cortex, which is in the occipital lobe.

As **Figure 8-13** shows, the primary visual cortex appears to have a broad stripe across it in layer IV and so is known as **striate cortex.** The term *geniculostriate* therefore means a bridge between the thalamus (geniculate) and the striate cortex. From the striate cortex, the axon pathway now splits, with one route going to vision-related regions of the parietal lobe and another route going to vision-related regions of the temporal lobe.

The second pathway leading from the eye is formed by the axons of the remaining M ganglion cells. These cells send their axons to the superior colliculus (located in the tectum of the midbrain; see Chapter 2). The superior colliculus sends connections to a region of the thalamus known as the pulvinar. This pathway is therefore known as the **tectopulvinar system** because it goes from the eye through the tectum to the pulvinar (see Figure 8-12). The pulvinar then sends connections to the parietal and temporal lobe.

To summarize, two principal pathways extend into the visual brain—namely, the geniculostriate and tectopulvinar systems. Each pathway eventually travels either to the parietal or the temporal lobe. Our next task is to determine the respective roles of the parietal lobe and the temporal lobe in creating our visual world.

Dorsal and Ventral Visual Streams

Identification of the temporal- and parietal-lobe visual pathways led researchers on a search for the possible functions of each. One way to examine these functions is to ask why evolution would produce two different destinations for the pathways in the brain. The answer is that each route must create visual knowledge for a different purpose.

David Milner and Mel Goodale (1995) proposed that these two purposes are to identify what a stimulus is (the "what" function) and to use visual information to control movement (the "how" function). Many authors have emphasized the role of the latter

David Milner   Mel Goodale

pathway as a "where" function. The problem is that "where" is a property of "what" a stimulus is as well as a cue for "how" to control movement to a place. We therefore will use the "what–how" distinction suggested by Milner and Goodale.

This "what" versus "how" distinction came from an analysis of where visual information goes when it leaves the striate cortex. **Figure 8-14** shows the two distinct visual pathways that originate in the striate cortex, one progressing to the temporal lobe and the other to the parietal lobe. The pathway to the temporal lobe has become known as the ventral stream, whereas the pathway to the parietal lobe has become known as the dorsal stream.

To understand how these two streams function, we need to return to the details of how the visual input from the eyes contributes to them. Both the geniculostriate and the tectopulvinar systems contribute to the dorsal and ventral streams.

GENICULOSTRIATE PATHWAY

The retinal ganglion-cell fibers from the two eyes distribute their connections to the two lateral geniculate nuclei (left and right) of the thalamus in what at first glance appears to be an unusual arrangement. As seen in Figure 8-11, the fibers from the left half of each retina go to the left LGN, whereas those from the right half of each retina go to the right LGN. But the fibers from each eye do not go to exactly the same place in the LGN.

Each LGN has six layers, and the projections from the two eyes go to different layers, as illustrated in anatomical context in Figure 8-10 and alone in **Figure 8-15**. Layers 2, 3, and 5 receive fibers from the ipsilateral eye (i.e., the eye on the same side), whereas layers 1, 4, and 6 receive fibers from the contralateral eye (i.e., the eye on the opposite side). This arrangement provides for combining the information from the two eyes and for segregating the information from the P and M ganglion cells.

Axons from the P cells go only to layers 3 through 6 (referred to as the parvocellular layers), whereas axons from the M cells go only to layers 1 and 2 (referred to as the magnocellular layers). Because the P ganglion cells are responsive to color and fine detail, layers 3 through 6 of the LGN must be processing information about color and form. In contrast, the M cells mostly process information about movement, and so layers 1 and 2 must deal with movement.

Before we continue, you should be aware that just as there are six layers of the LGN (numbered 1 through 6), there are also six layers of the striate cortex (numbered I through VI). That there happen to be six layers in each of these locations is an accident of evolution found in all primate brains. Let us now see where these LGN cells send their connections in the visual cortex.

You learned in Chapter 2 that layer IV is the main afferent (incoming) layer of the cortex. Layer IV of the visual cortex has several sublayers, two of which are known as IVCα and IVCβ. LGN layers 1 and 2 go to IVCα, and layers 3 through 6 go to IVCβ. As a result, a distinction between the P and M functions continues in the cortex.

As illustrated in **Figure 8-16**, input from the two eyes also remains separated in the cortex but through a different mechanism. The input from the ipsilaterally

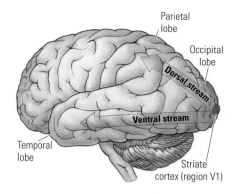

Figure 8-14

Visual Streaming   Visual information travels from the occipital visual areas to the parietal and temporal lobes, forming the dorsal and ventral streams, respectively.

Figure 8-15

Geniculostriate Pathway

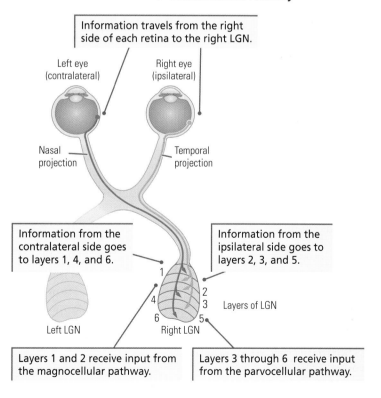

Information travels from the right side of each retina to the right LGN.

Left eye (contralateral)   Right eye (ipsilateral)

Nasal projection   Temporal projection

Information from the contralateral side goes to layers 1, 4, and 6.

Information from the ipsilateral side goes to layers 2, 3, and 5.

Layers of LGN

Left LGN   Right LGN

Layers 1 and 2 receive input from the magnocellular pathway.

Layers 3 through 6 receive input from the parvocellular pathway.

Figure 8-16

Maintaining Separate Visual Input
(*Left*) Information from the two eyes is segregated by layers in the lateral geniculate nucleus, and the lateral geniculate nucleus maintains this segregation in its projections to the visual cortex. Information from each eye travels to adjacent columns in cortical layer IV. (*Right*) A horizontal plane through V1 shows a zebralike effect of alternating ocular-dominance columns in the cortex. Photograph from "Functional Architecture of Macaque Monkey Visual Cortex," by D. H. Hubel and T. N. Weisel, 1977, *Proceedings of the Royal Society of London B, 198,* Figure 23.

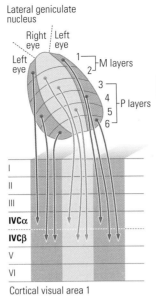

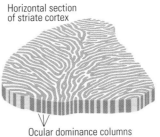

Ocular dominance columns

Cortical visual area 1

🔘 On your *Foundations* CD, find the primary visual cortex section in the visual system module to see the visual connections to the occipital lobe. Notice in particular how the lobe is layered in this region and how this layering parallels that seen in the LGN. If you would like additional information on the LGN, visit the section on the lateral geniculate nucleus.

Cortical column. Cortical organization that represents a functional unit six cortical layers deep and approximately 0.5 mm square and that is perpendicular to the cortical surface.

Primary visual cortex (V1). Striate cortex that receives input from the lateral geniculate nucleus.

Extrastriate (secondary visual) cortex. Visual cortical areas outside the striate cortex.

Blob. Region in the visual cortex that contains color-sensitive neurons, as revealed by staining for cytochrome oxidase.

connected LGN cells (that is, layers 2, 3, and 5) and the input from the contralaterally connected LGN cells (layers 1, 4, and 6) go to adjacent strips of cortex. These strips, which are about 0.5 millimeter across, are known as **cortical columns.** We return to the concept of cortical columns shortly.

In summary, the P and M ganglion cells of the retina send separate pathways to the thalamus, and this segregation remains in the striate cortex. The left and right eyes also send separate pathways to the thalamus, and these pathways, too, remain segregated in the striate cortex.

TECTOPULVINAR PATHWAY

As already noted, the tectopulvinar pathway is formed by the axons of the remaining M ganglion cells. These cells send their axons to the superior colliculus in the midbrain's tectum, which functions to detect the location of stimuli and to shift the eyes toward stimuli. The superior colliculus sends connections to the region of the thalamus known as the pulvinar.

The pulvinar has two main divisions: medial and lateral. The medial pulvinar sends connections to the parietal lobe, whereas the lateral pulvinar sends connections to the temporal lobe. One type of information that these connections are conveying is related to "where," which, as noted earlier, is important in both "what" and "how" functions.

The "where" function of the tectopulvinar system is useful in understanding blindsight in D. B. His geniculostriate system was disrupted but his tectopulvinar system was not, thus allowing him to identify the location of stimuli that he could not identify. Let us now look at how visual information proceeds from the striate cortex through the rest of the occipital lobe to the dorsal and ventral streams.

OCCIPITAL CORTEX

As shown in **Figure 8-17**, the occipital lobe is composed of at least six different visual regions, known as V1, V2, V3, V3A, V4, and V5. Region V1 is the striate cortex, which, as already mentioned, is sometimes also referred to as the **primary visual cortex.** The remaining visual areas of the occipital lobe are called the **extrastriate cortex** or *secondary visual cortex.* Because each of these occipital regions has a unique cellular structure (cytoarchitecture) and has unique inputs and outputs, we can infer that each must be doing something different from the others.

You already know that a remarkable feature of region V1 is its distinct layers, which extend throughout V1. These seemingly homogeneous layers are deceiving, however. When Margaret Wong-Riley and her colleagues (1993) stained the cortex for the enzyme cytochrome oxidase, which has a role in cell metabolism, they were surprised to

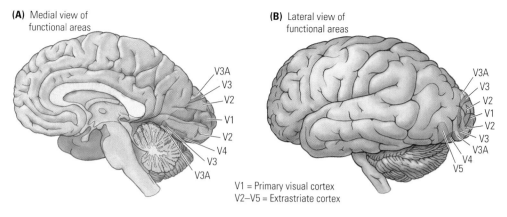

(A) Medial view of functional areas

(B) Lateral view of functional areas

V1 = Primary visual cortex
V2–V5 = Extrastriate cortex

Figure 8-17

Visual Regions of the Occipital Lobe

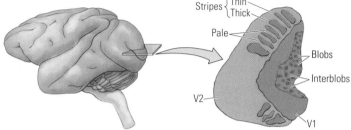

find an unexpected heterogeneity in region V1. So they sectioned the V1 layers in such a way that each cortical layer was in one plane of section, much like peeling off the layers of an onion and laying them flat on a table. The surface of each flattened layer can then be viewed from above.

As **Figure 8-18** illustrates, the heterogeneous cytochrome staining now appeared as random blobs in the layers of V1. In fact, these darkened regions have become known as **blobs,** and the less-dark regions separating them have become known as *interblobs*. Blobs and interblobs serve different functions. Neurons in the blobs take part in color perception, whereas neurons in the interblobs participate in form and motion perception. So, within region V1, input that arrives in the parvo- and magnocellular pathways of the geniculostriate system is segregated into three separate types of information: color, form, and movement.

This information is then sent to region V2, which lies next to region V1. Here the color, form, and movement inputs remain segregated. This segregation can again be seen through the pattern of cytochrome oxidase staining, but the staining pattern is different from that in region V1. **Figure 8-19** shows that region V2 has a pattern of thick and thin stripes that are intermixed with pale zones. The thick stripes receive input from the

Figure 8-18

Heterogeneous Layering The blobs in region V1 and the stripes in region V2 are illustrated in this drawing of a flattened section through the visual cortex. The blobs and stripes can be visualized by using a special stain for cytochrome oxidase, which is a marker for mitochondria.

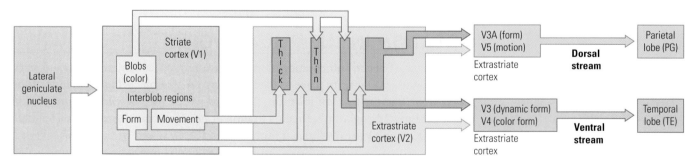

Figure 8-19

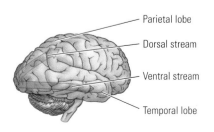

Charting the Dorsal and Ventral Streams The dorsal stream, which controls visual action, begins in region V1 and flows through region V2 to the other occipital areas and finally to the parietal cortex, ending in an area of the parietal lobe referred to as PG. The ventral stream, which controls object recognition, begins in region V1 and flows through region V2 to the other occipital areas and finally to the temporal cortex, ending in an area of the temporal lobe referred to as TE. The flow of information from the subregions of V1 (blobs and interblobs) is to the thick, thin, and pale zones of V2. Information in the thin and pale zones goes to regions V3 and V4 to form the ventral stream. That in the thick and pale zones goes to regions V3A and V5 to form the dorsal stream.

movement-sensitive neurons in region V1; the thin stripes receive input from V1's color-sensitive neurons; and the pale zones receive input from V1's form-sensitive neurons.

As diagrammed in Figure 8-19, the visual pathways proceed from region V2 to the other occipital regions and then to the parietal and temporal lobes, forming the dorsal and ventral streams. Although many parietal and temporal regions take part, the major regions are region G in the parietal lobe (thus called region PG) and region E in the temporal lobe (thus called region TE).

Within the dorsal and ventral streams, the function of the visual pathways becomes far more complex than a simple record of color, form, and movement. Rather, the color, form, and movement information is put together to produce a rich, unified visual world made up of complex objects, such as faces and paintings, and complex visuo-motor skills, such as catching a ball. The functions of the dorsal and ventral streams are therefore complex, but they can be thought of as consisting of "how" functions and "what" functions. "How" is action to be visually guided toward objects, whereas "what" identifies what an object is.

In Review

Vision begins when photoreceptors in the retina at the back of the eye convert light energy into neural activity in neighboring ganglion cells, the axons of which form the optic nerve leading to the brain. P ganglion cells receive input mostly from cones and carry information about color and fine detail, whereas M ganglion cells receive input mostly from rods and carry information about light but not color. Visual input takes two routes into the brain. The geniculostriate pathway travels through the LGN of the thalamus to layer IV of the striate cortex in the occipital lobe. The tectopulvinar pathway is from the tectum of the midbrain to the pulvinar of the thalamus and then to visual cortical areas. Both pathways contribute to the dorsal and ventral visual streams that project to the parietal and temporal lobes, respectively. The dorsal stream to the parietal lobe processes the visual guidance of movements (the how), whereas the ventral stream to the temporal lobe processes the visual perception of objects (the what).

LOCATION IN THE VISUAL WORLD

○ On your *Foundations* CD, find the area on the optic chiasm in the module on the visual system to better understand the concept of visual fields.

One aspect of visual information that we have not yet considered is location. As we move around, going from place to place, we encounter objects in specific locations. Indeed, if we had no sense of location, the world would be a bewildering mass of visual information. Our next task, then, is to look at how the brain constructs a spatial map from this complex array of visual input.

The coding of location begins in the retina and is maintained throughout all the visual pathways. To understand how this spatial coding is accomplished, you need to imagine your visual world as seen by your two eyes. Imagine the large red and blue rectangles in **Figure 8-20** as a wall. Focus your gaze on the black cross in the middle of the wall.

Visual field. Region of the visual world that is seen by the eyes.

Receptive field. Region of the visual world that stimulates a receptor cell or neuron.

All of the wall that you can see without moving your head is your **visual field.** The visual field can be divided into two halves, the left and right visual fields, by drawing a vertical line down the middle of the black cross. Now recall from Figure 8-11 that the left half of each retina looks at the right side of the visual field, whereas the right half of each retina looks at the visual field's left side. This means that input from the right visual field goes to the left hemisphere, whereas input from the left visual field goes to the right hemisphere.

Therefore the brain can easily determine whether visual information is located to the left or right of center. If input goes to the left hemisphere, the source must be in the right visual field; if input goes to the right hemisphere, the source must be in the left visual field. This arrangement tells you nothing about the precise location of an object in the left or right side of the visual field, however. To understand how precise spatial localization is accomplished, we must return to the retinal ganglion cells.

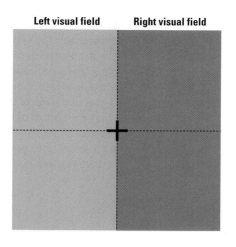

Left visual field   Right visual field

Figure 8-20

Visual Field Demonstration   As you focus on the cross at the center of the figure, the information at the left of this focal point forms the left visual field (red) and travels to the right hemisphere. The information to the right of the focal point forms the right visual field (blue) and travels to the left hemisphere. The visual field can be broken horizontally as well so that information above the focal point is in the upper visual field and that below the focal point is in the lower visual field.

Coding Location in the Retina

Look again at Figure 8-9 and you can see that each retinal ganglion cell receives input through bipolar cells from several photoreceptors. In the 1950s, Stephen Kuffler, a pioneer in studying the physiology of the visual system, made an important discovery about how photoreceptors and ganglion cells are linked. By shining small spots of light on the receptors, he found that each ganglion cell responds to stimulation on just a small circular patch of the retina. This patch became known as the ganglion cell's **receptive field.**

A ganglion cell's receptive field is therefore the region of the retina on which it is possible to influence that cell's firing. Stated differently, the receptive field represents the outer world as seen by a single cell. Each ganglion cell sees only a small bit of the world, much as you would if you looked through a narrow cardboard tube. The visual field is composed of thousands of such receptive fields.

Now let us consider how receptive fields enable the visual system to interpret the location of objects. Imagine that the retina is flattened like a piece of paper. When a tiny light is shone on different parts of the retina, different ganglion cells respond. For example, when a light is shone on the top-left corner of the flattened retina, a particular ganglion cell responds because that light is in its receptive field. Similarly, when a light is shone on the top-right corner, a different ganglion cell responds.

By using this information, we can identify the location of a light on the retina by knowing which ganglion cell is activated. We can also interpret the location of the light in the outside world because we know where the light must come from to hit a particular place on the retina. For example, light from above hits the bottom of the retina after passing through the eye's lens, whereas light from below hits the top of the retina. (Refer to Figure 8-3 to see why this is so.) Information at the top of the visual field will stimulate ganglion cells on the bottom of the retina, whereas information at the bottom of the field will stimulate ganglion cells on the top of the retina.

Location in the LGN and Cortical Region V1

Now consider the connection from the ganglion cells to the lateral geniculate nucleus. In contrast with the retina, the LGN is not a flat sheet; rather, it is a three-dimensional structure in the brain. We can compare it to a stack of cards, with each card representing a layer of cells.

Topographic map. A spatially organized neural representation of the external world.

Figure 8-21

Receptive Field Projection The information from a receptive field retains its spatial relation when it is sent to the lateral geniculate nucleus (LGN). In this example, information at the top of the visual field goes to the top of the LGN and information from the bottom of the visual field goes to the bottom of the LGN. Similarly, information from the left or right goes to the left or right of the LGN, respectively.

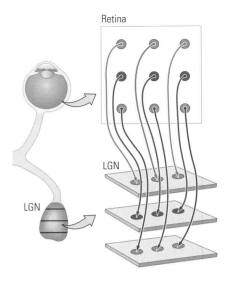

Figure 8-22

Topographic Organization of the Visual Cortex (V1) In the right occipital lobe, the area of left central vision (the fovea) is represented at the back of the brain, whereas the more peripheral visual areas are represented more anteriorly. The fovea also occupies a disproportionately large part of the cortex, which is why visual acuity is best in the central part of the visual field.

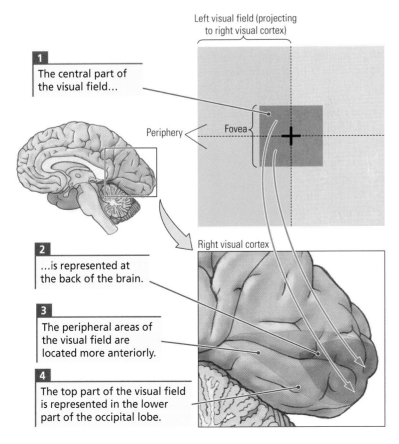

1 The central part of the visual field...

2 ...is represented at the back of the brain.

3 The peripheral areas of the visual field are located more anteriorly.

4 The top part of the visual field is represented in the lower part of the occipital lobe.

Left visual field (projecting to right visual cortex)

Periphery

Fovea

Right visual cortex

Figure 8-21 shows how the connections from the retina to the LGN can represent location. A retinal ganglion cell that responds to light in the top-left corner of the retina connects to the left side of the first card. A retinal ganglion cell that responds to light in the bottom-right corner of the retina connects to the right side of the last card. In this way, the location of left–right and top–bottom information is maintained in the LGN.

Like the ganglion cells, each of the LGN cells has a receptive field, which is the region of the retina that influences its activity. If two adjacent retinal ganglion cells synapse on a single LGN cell, the receptive field of that LGN cell will be the sum of the two ganglion cells' receptive fields. As a result, the receptive fields of LGN cells can be bigger than those of retinal ganglion cells.

The LGN projection to the striate cortex (region V1) also maintains spatial information. As each LGN cell, representing a particular place, projects to region V1, a topographic representation, or **topographic map,** is produced in the cortex. As illustrated in **Figure 8-22**, this representation is essentially a map of the visual world.

The central part of the visual field is represented at the back of the brain, whereas the periphery is represented more anteriorly. The upper part of the visual field is represented at the bottom of region V1, the lower part at the top of V1. The other regions of the visual cortex (such as V3, V4, and V5) also have topographical maps similar to that of V1. Thus the V1 neurons must project to the other regions in an orderly manner, just as the LGN neurons project to region V1 in an orderly way.

Within each visual cortical area, each neuron has a receptive field corresponding to the part of the retina to which the neuron is connected. As a rule of thumb, the cells in the cortex have much larger receptive fields than those of retinal ganglion cells. This increase in receptive-field size means that the receptive field of a cortical neuron must be composed of the receptive fields of many retinal ganglion cells, as illustrated in **Figure 8-23**.

There is one additional wrinkle to the organization of topographic maps. Jerison's principle of proper mass, which

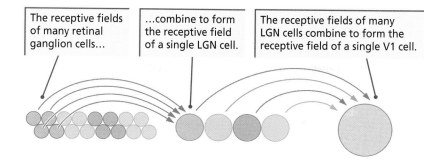

The receptive fields of many retinal ganglion cells...

...combine to form the receptive field of a single LGN cell.

The receptive fields of many LGN cells combine to form the receptive field of a single V1 cell.

Figure 8-23

Receptive Field Hierarchy The receptive fields of region V1 neurons are constructed from those of lateral geniculate (LGN) cells, which, in turn, are constructed from those of ganglion cells. The receptive field of a single ganglion cell is small. In this example, the receptive fields of the LGN cells are the summation of the fields of four ganglion cells. The receptive field of the V1 cell is the sum of the four LGN cells.

we applied to overall brain size in Chapter 1, states that the amount of neural tissue responsible for a particular function is equivalent to the amount of neural processing required for that function. Jerison's principle can be extended to regions within the brain as well. The visual cortex provides some good examples.

You can see in Figure 8-22 that not all parts of the visual field are equally represented in region V1. The small, central part of the visual field that is seen by the fovea is represented by a larger area in the cortex than the visual field's periphery, even though the periphery is a much larger part of the visual field. In accord with Jerison's principle, we would predict more processing of foveal information in region V1 than of peripheral information. This prediction makes intuitive sense because we can see more clearly in the center of the visual field than at the periphery. In other words, sensory areas that have more cortical representation provide a more detailed creation of the external world.

⊙ On the *Foundations* CD, find the section on the higher-order visual areas in the module on the visual system to investigate the location and anatomy of region V1.

The Visual Corpus Callosum

The creation of topographic maps based on the receptive fields of neurons is an effective way for the brain to code the location of objects. But, if the left visual field is represented in the right cerebral hemisphere and the right visual field is represented in the left cerebral hemisphere, how are the two halves of the visual field ultimately bound together in a unified representation of the world? After all, we have the subjective impression not of two independent visual fields, but rather of a single, continuous field of vision. The answer to how this unity is accomplished lies in the corpus callosum, which binds the two sides of the visual field at the midline.

Until the 1950s, the function of the corpus callosum was largely a mystery. Physicians had occasionally cut it to control severe epilepsy, as described in "Epilepsy" on page 111, or to reach a very deep tumor, but patients did not appear to be much affected by this surgery. The corpus callosum clearly linked the two hemispheres of the brain, but exactly which parts were connected was not yet known.

We now realize that the corpus callosum connects only certain brain structures. Whereas much of the frontal lobes have callosal connections, the occipital lobes have almost none, as shown in **Figure 8-24**. If you think about it, there is no reason for a neuron in the visual cortex that is "looking at" one place in the visual field to be concerned with what another neuron in the opposite hemisphere is "looking at" in another part of the visual field.

Cells that lie along the midline of the visual field are an exception, however. These cells would

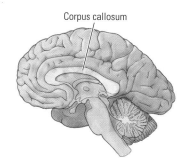

Corpus callosum

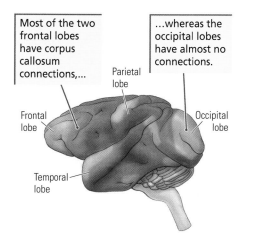

Most of the two frontal lobes have corpus callosum connections,...

...whereas the occipital lobes have almost no connections.

Parietal lobe

Frontal lobe

Occipital lobe

Temporal lobe

Figure 8-24

Callosal Connections The darker areas indicate regions of the cortex of a rhesus monkey that receive projections from the opposite hemisphere by means of the corpus callosum. Most of the occipital lobe has no such connections.

be "looking at" adjacent places in the field of vision, one slightly to the left of center and one slightly to the right. If connections existed between such cells, we could zip the two visual fields together by combining their receptive fields to cross at the midline, which is exactly what happens. Cortical cells with receptive fields that lie along the midline of your field of vision are connected to one another through the corpus callosum so that their receptive fields overlap the midline. The two fields thus become one.

In Review

The brain can determine the location of a particular stimulus because each neuron of the visual system connects to only a small part of the retina, known as that neuron's receptive field. Each receptive field, in turn, receives input from only a small part of the visual field, and so which part of the retina is stimulated effectively detects exactly where the light source is positioned in the environment. This location-detecting method is maintained at different levels in the visual system, from the ganglion cells of the retina to the neurons of the LGN in the thalamus to the neurons of the primary visual cortex. Inputs to different parts of cortical region V1 from different parts of the retina essentially form a topographic map of the visual world within the brain. Cells with receptive fields that lie along the midline of the field of vision are connected by the corpus callosum, binding the two sides of the visual world together as one.

NEURAL ACTIVITY

The pathways of the visual system are made up of individual neurons. By studying how these cells behave when their receptive fields are stimulated, we can begin to understand how the brain processes different features of the visual world beyond just the locations of light. To illustrate, we examine how neurons from the retina to the temporal cortex respond to shapes and colors. We then briefly consider how neurons in the dorsal stream behave.

Seeing Shape

Imagine that we have placed a microelectrode near a neuron somewhere in the visual pathway from retina to cortex and are using that electrode to record changes in the neuron's firing rate. This neuron occasionally fires spontaneously, producing action potentials with each discharge. Let us assume that the neuron discharges, on the average, once every 0.08 second. Each action potential is brief, on the order of 1 millisecond.

If we plot action potentials spanning a second, we see only spikes in the record because the action potentials are so brief. (Refer to Figure 4-12 for an illustration of this effect.) **Figure 8-25A** is a single-cell recording in which there are 12 spikes in the span of 1 second. If the firing rate of this cell increases, we will see more spikes (Figure 8-25B). If the firing rate decreases, we will see fewer spikes (Figure 8-25C). The increase in firing represents excitation of the cell, whereas the decrease represents inhibition. Excitation and inhibition, as you know, are the principal mechanisms of information transfer in the nervous system.

Now suppose we present a stimulus to the neuron by illuminating its receptive field in the retina, perhaps by shining a light stimulus on a blank screen within the cell's visual field. We might place before the eye a straight line positioned at a 45° angle. The cell

○ Visit the area on the primary visual cortex in the module on the visual system on your *Foundations* CD. In the section on the analysis of visual information you can learn more about how shape is perceived within the cortex. If you would like to see how the brain responds to shape in an MRI, go to the area on form perception in the section on higher order visual areas.

could respond to this stimulus either by increasing or decreasing its firing rate. In either case, we would conclude that the cell is creating information about the line.

Note that the same cell could show excitation to one stimulus, inhibition to another stimulus, and no reaction at all. For instance, the cell could be excited by lines oriented 45° to the left and inhibited by lines oriented 45° to the right. Similarly, the cell could be excited by stimulation in one part of its receptive field (such as the center) and inhibited by stimulation in another part (such as the periphery).

Finally, we might find that the cell's response to a particular stimulus is selective. Such a cell would be telling us about the importance of the stimulus to the animal. For instance, the cell might fire (be excited) when a stimulus is presented with food but not fire (be inhibited) when the same stimulus is presented alone. In each case, the cell is selectively sensitive to characteristics in the visual world.

Now we are ready to move from this hypothetical example to what visual neurons actually do when they process information about shape. Neurons at each level of the visual system have distinctly different characteristics and functions. Our goal is not to look at each neuron type but rather to consider generally how some typical neurons at each level differ from one another in their contributions to processing shape. We focus on neurons in three areas: the ganglion-cell layer of the retina, the primary visual cortex, and the temporal cortex.

PROCESSING IN RETINAL GANGLION CELLS

Cells in the retina do not actually see shapes. Shapes are constructed by processes in the cortex from the information that ganglion cells pass on about events in their receptive fields. Keep in mind that the receptive fields of ganglion cells are very small dots. Each ganglion cell responds only to the presence or absence of light in its receptive field, not to shape.

The receptive field of a ganglion cell has a concentric circle arrangement, as illustrated in **Figure 8-26A**. A spot of light falling in the central circle of the receptive

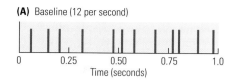
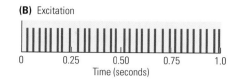
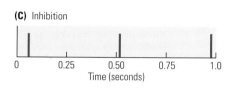

Figure 8-25

Recording Neural Stimulation When visually responsive neurons encounter a particular stimulus in their visual fields, they may show either excitation or inhibition. **(A)** At the baseline firing rate of a neuron, each action potential is represented by a spike. In a 1-second time period, there were 12 spikes. **(B)** Excitation is indicated by an increase in firing rate over baseline. **(C)** Inhibition is indicated by a decrease in firing rate under baseline.

Figure 8-26

On–Off Receptivity **(A)** In the receptive field of a retinal ganglion cell with an on-center and off-surround, a spot of light placed on the center causes excitation in the neuron, whereas a spot of light in the surround causes inhibition. When the light in the surround region is turned off, firing rate increases briefly (called an "offset" response). A light shining in both the center and the surround would produce a weak increase in firing in the cell. **(B)** In the receptive field of a retinal ganglion cell with an off-center and on-surround, light in the center produces inhibition, whereas light on the surround produces excitation, and light across the entire field produces weak inhibition.

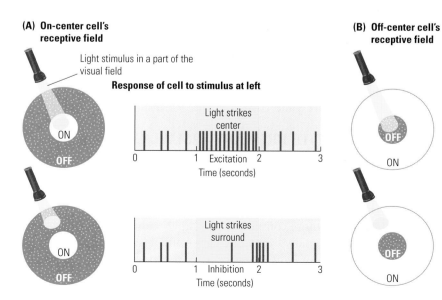
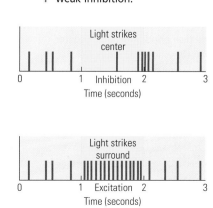

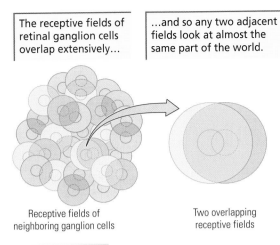

The receptive fields of retinal ganglion cells overlap extensively...

...and so any two adjacent fields look at almost the same part of the world.

Receptive fields of neighboring ganglion cells

Two overlapping receptive fields

Figure 8-27

Overlapping Receptive Fields

field excites some of these cells, whereas a spot of light falling in the surround (periphery) of the receptive field inhibits the cell. A spot of light falling across the entire receptive field causes a weak increase in the cell's rate of firing.

This type of neuron is called an *on-center cell.* Other ganglion cells, called *off-center cells,* have the opposite arrangement, with light in the center of the receptive field causing inhibition, light in the surround causing excitation, and light across the entire field producing weak inhibition (Figure 8-26B). The on–off arrangement of ganglion-cell receptive fields makes these cells especially responsive to very small spots of light.

This description of ganglion-cell receptive fields might mislead you into thinking that they form a mosaic of discrete little circles on the retina that do not overlap. In fact, neighboring retinal ganglion cells receive their inputs from an overlapping set of receptors. As a result, their receptive fields overlap, as illustrated in **Figure 8-27**. In this way, a small spot of light shining on the retina is likely to produce activity in both on-center and off-center ganglion cells.

How can on-center and off-center ganglion cells tell the brain anything about shape? The answer is that a ganglion cell is able to tell the brain about the amount of light hitting a certain spot on the retina compared with the average amount of light falling on the surrounding retinal region. This comparison is known as **luminance contrast.**

To understand how this mechanism tells the brain about shape, consider the hypothetical population of on-center ganglion cells represented in **Figure 8-28**. Their receptive fields are distributed across the retinal image of a light–dark edge. Some of the ganglion cells have receptive fields in the dark area, others have receptive fields in the light area, and still others have fields that straddle the edge of the light.

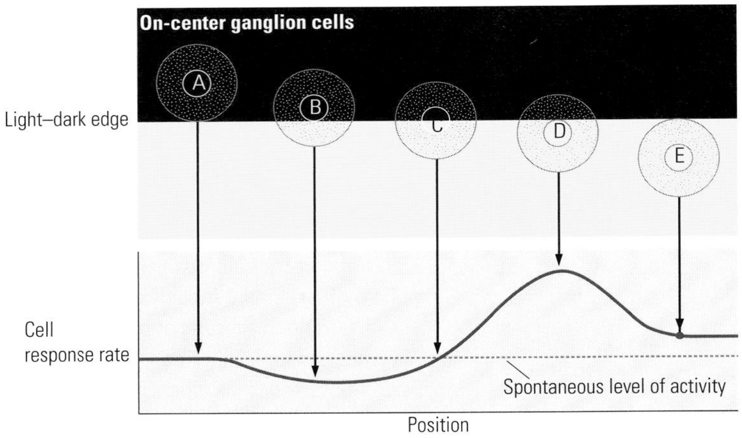

The ganglion cells with receptive fields in the dark or light areas are least affected because they experience either no stimulation or stimulation of *both* the excitatory and the inhibitory regions of their receptive fields. The ganglion cells most affected by the stimulus are those lying along the edge. Ganglion cell B is inhibited because the light falls mostly on its inhibitory surround, and ganglion cell D is excited because its entire excitatory center is stimulated but only part of its inhibitory surround is.

Consequently, information transmitted from retinal ganglion cells to the visual areas in the brain does not give equal weight to all regions of the visual field. Rather, it emphasizes regions containing differences in luminance. Areas with differences in luminance are found along edges. So retinal ganglion cells are really sending signals about edges, and edges are what form shapes.

On-center ganglion cells

Light–dark edge

Cell response rate

Spontaneous level of activity

Position

Figure 8-28

Activity at the Margins Responses of a hypothetical population of on-center ganglion cells whose receptive fields (A–E) are distributed across a light–dark edge. The activity of the cells along the edge is most affected relative to those away from the edge. Adapted from *Neuroscience* (p. 195), edited by D. Purves, G. J. Augustine, D. Fitzpatrick, L. C. Katz, A.-S. LaMantia, and J. O. McNamara, 1997, Sunderland, MA: Sinauer.

PROCESSING IN THE PRIMARY VISUAL CORTEX

Now consider cells in region V1, the primary visual cortex, that receive their visual inputs from LGN cells, which in turn receive theirs from retinal ganglion cells. Because each V1 cell receives input from multiple retinal ganglion cells, the receptive fields of the V1 neurons are much larger than those of retinal neurons. Consequently, the V1 cells respond to stimuli more complex than simply "light on" or "light off." In particular, these cells are maximally excited by bars of light oriented in a particular direction rather than by spots of light. These cells are therefore called *orientation detectors.*

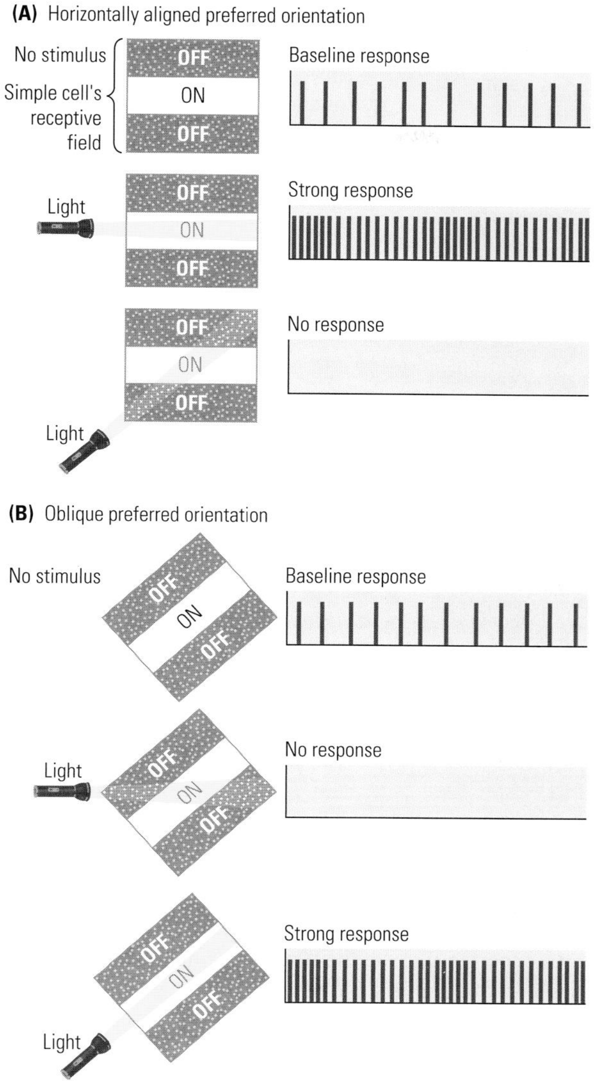

(A) Horizontally aligned preferred orientation

No stimulus — Simple cell's receptive field — OFF / ON / OFF — Baseline response

Light — OFF / ON / OFF — Strong response

OFF / ON / OFF — No response — Light

(B) Oblique preferred orientation

No stimulus — OFF / ON / OFF — Baseline response

Light — OFF / ON / OFF — No response

OFF / ON / OFF — Strong response — Light

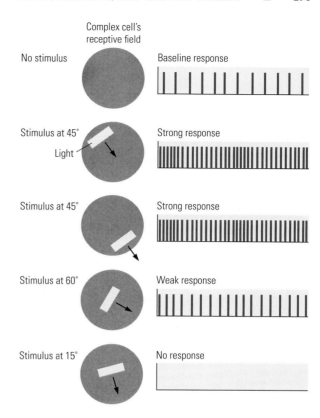

Complex cell's receptive field

No stimulus — Baseline response

Stimulus at 45° — Light — Strong response

Stimulus at 45° — Strong response

Stimulus at 60° — Weak response

Stimulus at 15° — No response

Figure 8-30

Receptive Field of a Complex Cell in the Visual Cortex   Complex cells respond to bars of light that move across their circular receptive fields at a particular angle. Unlike a simple cell's on–off response pattern, a complex cell shows the same response throughout the field, responding best when the bar is at a particular orientation. Its response is reduced or does not occur with the bar of light at other orientations.

Figure 8-29

Typical Receptive Fields for Simple Visual Cortex Cells
Simple cells respond to a bar of light in a particular orientation, such as horizontal **(A)** or oblique **(B)**. The position of the bar in the visual field is important, because the cell either responds (ON) or does not respond (OFF) to light in adjacent regions of the visual field.

Like the ganglion cells, some orientation detectors have an on–off arrangement in their receptive fields, but the arrangement is rectangular rather than circular. Visual cortex cells with this property are known as *simple cells*. Typical receptive fields for simple cells in the primary visual cortex are shown in **Figure 8-29**.

Simple cells are not the only kind of orientation detector in the primary visual cortex; several functionally distinct types of neurons populate region V1. For instance, *complex cells* such as those in **Figure 8-30** have receptive fields that are maximally excited by bars of light moving in a particular direction through the visual field. A *hypercomplex cell*, like a complex cell, is maximally responsive to moving bars but also has a strong inhibitory area at one end of its receptive field. As illustrated in **Figure 8-31**, a bar of light

If you would like to learn more about on-center and off-center ganglion cells, visit the physiological processes area of the eye section in the module on the visual system on your *Foundations* CD.

Luminance contrast. The amount of light reflected by an object relative to its surroundings.

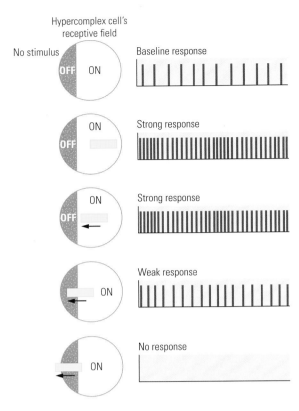

Hypercomplex cell's receptive field

No stimulus — Baseline response

OFF | ON

ON — Strong response

OFF

ON — Strong response

OFF

ON — Weak response

ON — No response

Figure 8-31

Receptive Field of a Hypercomplex Cell A hypercomplex cell responds to a bar of light in a particular orientation (e.g., horizontal) anywhere in the excitiatory (ON) part of its receptive field. If the bar extends into the inhibitory area (OFF), no response occurs.

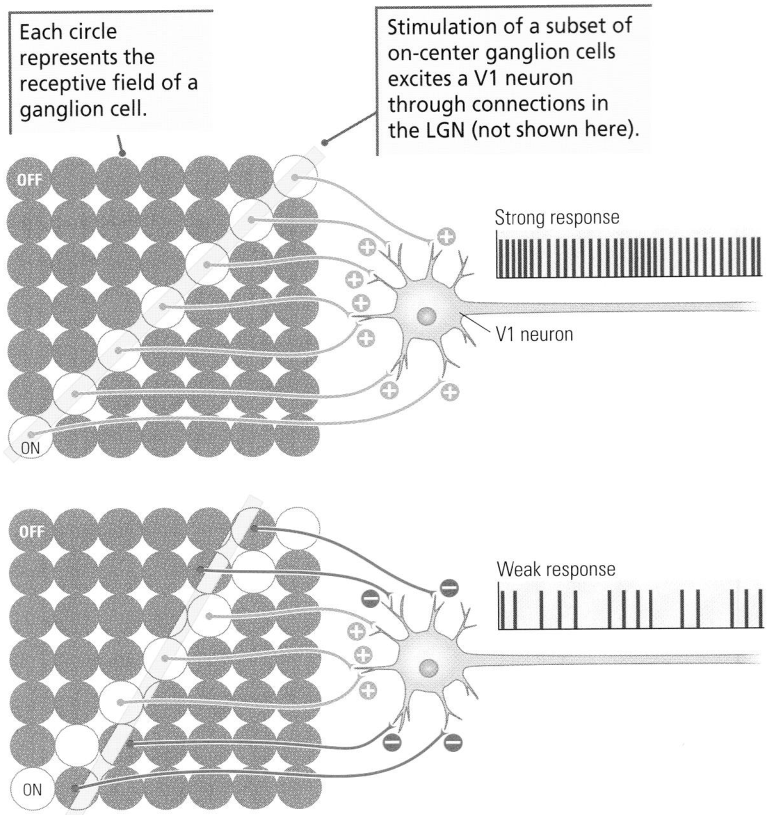

Each circle represents the receptive field of a ganglion cell.

Stimulation of a subset of on-center ganglion cells excites a V1 neuron through connections in the LGN (not shown here).

Strong response

OFF

ON

V1 neuron

OFF

Weak response

ON

Figure 8-32

V1 Receptivity A V1 cell responds to a row of ganglion cells in a particular orientation on the retina. The bar of light strongly activates a row of ganglion cells, each connected through the LGN to a V1 neuron. The activity of this V1 neuron is most affected by a bar of light at a 45° angle.

Ocular-dominance column.
Functional column in the visual cortex maximally responsive to information coming from one eye.

landing on the right side of the hypercomplex cell's receptive field excites the cell, but, if the bar lands on the inhibitory area to the left, the cell's firing is inhibited.

Note that each class of V1 neurons responds to bars of light in some way, yet this response results from input originating in retinal ganglion cells that respond maximally not to bars but to spots of light. How does this conversion from responding to spots to responding to bars take place? An example will help explain the process.

A thin bar of light falls on the retinal photoreceptors, striking the receptive fields of perhaps dozens of retinal ganglion cells. The input to a V1 neuron comes from a group of ganglion cells that happen to be aligned in a row, as in **Figure 8-32**. That V1 neuron will be activated (or inhibited) only when a bar of light hitting the retina strikes that particular row of ganglion cells. If the bar of light is at a slightly different angle, only some of the retinal ganglion cells in the row will be activated, and so the V1 neuron will be excited only weakly.

Figure 8-32 illustrates the connection between light striking the retina in a certain pattern and the activation of a simple cell in the primary visual cortex, one that responds to a bar of light in a particular orientation. Using the same logic, we can also diagram the retinal receptive fields of complex or hypercomplex V1 neurons. Try this as an exercise yourself by adapting the format in Figure 8-32.

A characteristic of cortical structure is that the neurons are organized into functional columns. **Figure 8-33** shows such a column, a 0.5-millimeter-diameter strip of

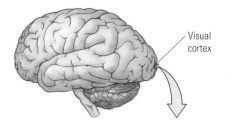
Visual cortex

Figure 8-33

Neural Circuit in a Column in the Visual Cortex In this stereoscopic (3D) view, the sensory inputs terminate on stellate cells in layer IV. These stellate cells synapse in layers III and V with pyramidal cells in the same vertical column of tissue. Thus the flow of information is vertical. The axons of the pyramidal cells leave the column to join with other columns or structures. Adapted from "The 'Module-Concept' in Cerebral Architecture," by J. Szentagothai, 1975, *Brain Research, 95*, p. 490.

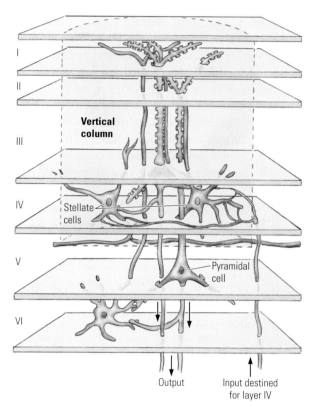

Vertical column

Stellate cells

Pyramidal cell

I

II

III

IV

V

VI

Output   Input destined for layer IV

Figure 8-34

Organization of Functional Columns in the Primary Visual Cortex **(A)** Cells with the same orientation preference are found throughout a column. Adjacent columns have orientation preferences that are slightly different from one another. **(B)** Ocular-dominance columns are arranged at right angles to the orientation columns, producing a three-dimensional organization of the visual cortex. The ocular-dominance columns alternate from left (L) to right (R) across the primary visual cortex, with two such alternations illustrated here.

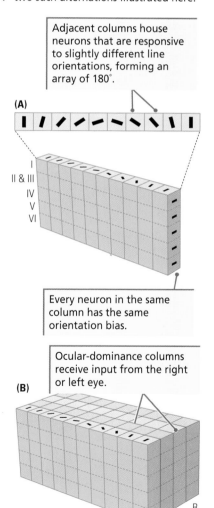

Adjacent columns house neurons that are responsive to slightly different line orientations, forming an array of 180°.

(A)

I
II & III
IV
V
VI

Every neuron in the same column has the same orientation bias.

Ocular-dominance columns receive input from the right or left eye.

(B)

R L R
R L

cortex that includes neurons and their connections. The pattern of connectivity in a column is vertical: inputs arrive in layer IV and then connect with cells in the other layers.

The neurons within a column have similar functions. For example, **Figure 8-34A** shows that neurons within the same column respond to lines oriented in the same direction. Adjacent columns house cells that are responsive to different line orientations.

Figure 8-34B shows the columns of input coming from each eye, discussed earlier, called **ocular-dominance columns.** So the visual cortex has both orientation columns housing neurons of similar sensitivity and ocular-dominance columns with input from one eye or the other.

PROCESSING IN THE TEMPORAL CORTEX

Finally, in regard to seeing shapes, consider neurons along the ventral stream in region E of the temporal lobe (see Figure 8-19). Rather than being responsive to spots or bars of light, these TE neurons are maximally excited by complex visual stimuli, such as faces or hands, and can be remarkably specific in their responsiveness. They may be responsive to particular faces seen head-on, to faces viewed in profile, to the posture of the head, or even to particular facial expressions.

How far does this specialized responsiveness extend? Would it be practical to have visual neurons in the temporal cortex specialized to respond to every conceivable feature

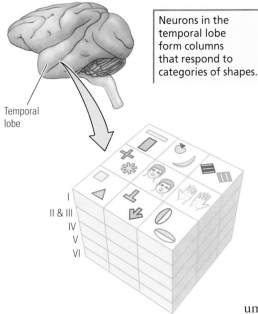

Neurons in the temporal lobe form columns that respond to categories of shapes.

Temporal lobe

I
II & III
IV
V
VI

Figure 8-35

Columnar Organization of Area TE
Neurons with similar but slightly different pattern selectivity cluster in vertical columns, perpendicular to the cortical surface.

of objects? Keiji Tanaka (1993) approached this question by presenting monkeys with many three-dimensional representations of animals and plants to find stimuli that are effective in activating particular neurons of the inferior temporal cortex.

Having identified stimuli that were especially effective, such as faces or hands, he then wondered which specific features of those stimuli are critical to stimulating the neurons. Tanaka found that most neurons in area TE require rather complex features for their activation. These features include a combination of characteristics such as orientation, size, color, and texture. Furthermore, neurons with similar, although slightly different, responsiveness to particular features tend to cluster together in columns, as shown in **Figure 8-35**.

Apparently, then, an object is not represented by the activity of a single neuron. Rather, objects are represented by the activity of many neurons with slightly varying stimulus specificity that are grouped together in a column. This finding is important because it provides an explanation for *stimulus equivalence,* recognizing an object as remaining the same despite being viewed from different orientations.

Think of how the representation of objects by multiple neurons in a column can produce stimulus equivalence. If each neuron in the column module varies slightly in regard to the features to which it responds but the effective stimuli largely overlap, the effect of small changes in incoming visual images will be minimized and we will continue to perceive an object as the same thing.

Another remarkable feature of neurons of the inferior temporal cortex in monkeys is that their stimulus specificity is altered by experience. If monkeys are trained to discriminate particular shapes to obtain a food reward, not only do they improve their discriminatory ability, but neurons in the temporal lobe also modify their preferred stimuli to fire maximally to some of the stimuli used in training. This result shows that the temporal lobe's role in visual processing is not determined genetically but is instead subject to experience, even in adults.

We can speculate that this experience-dependent characteristic evolved because it allows the visual system to adapt to different demands in a changing visual environment. Think of how different the demands on your visual recognition abilities are when you move from a dense forest to a treeless plain to a city street. The visual neurons of your temporal cortex can adapt to these differences (Tanaka, 1993). In addition, experience-dependent visual neurons ensure that people can identify visual stimuli that were never encountered as the human brain evolved.

Note that the preferred stimuli of neurons in the primary visual cortex are *not* modified by experience, which implies that the stimulus preferences of V1 neurons are genetically programmed. In any case, the functions of the V1 neurons provide the building blocks for the more complex and flexible characteristics of the inferior temporal cortex neurons.

Seeing Color

Scientists have long wondered how people are able to see a world so rich in color. Recall from Chapter 1 the hypothesis that color vision evolved in primates whose diets require them to identify ripe fruits or to avoid predators or other dangers. Another explanation has its roots in the Renaissance, when painters discovered that they could obtain the entire range of colors in the visual world by mixing only three colors of paint (red, blue, and yellow), the process of *subtractive color mixing.*

Although people at the time did not understand the basis of this three-color (trichromatic) mixing, we now know that color mixing is a property of the cones in the retina. The primary colors of light, unlike those used by painters, are red, blue, and green. Light of different wavelengths stimulates the three different types of cone receptors in different ways, and the ratio of the activity of these three receptor types creates our impression of different colors.

TRICHROMATIC THEORY

To see how the process works, look back at Figure 8-7. Light at 500 nanometers on the horizontal axis excites short-wavelength receptors to about 30 percent of their maximum, medium-wavelength receptors to about 65 percent of their maximum, and long-wavelength receptors to about 40 percent of their maximum. In contrast, a light at 600 nanometers excites these receptors to about 0, 25, and 75 percent of maximum, respectively.

According to the **trichromatic theory,** the color that we see—in this case, blue green at 500 nm and orange at 600 nm—is determined by the relative responses of the different cone types. If all three cone types are equally active, we see white.

The trichromatic theory predicts that, if we lack one type of cone receptor, we cannot process as many colors as we can with all three types, which is exactly what happens when a person is born with only two cone types. The colors that the person is unable to create depend on which receptor type is missing. The most common deficiency, as mentioned earlier in this chapter, is red–green color blindness, which afflicts about 5 percent of males and 0.5 percent of females. It is caused by the absence of either the medium-wavelength or the long-wavelength receptor. If a person is missing two types of cones, he or she cannot see any color.

Notice that the mere presence of cones in an animal's retina does not mean that the animal has color vision. It simply means that the animal has photoreceptors that are particularly sensitive to light. Many animals lack color vision as we know it, but the only animal with eyes known to have no cones at all is a fish, the skate.

As helpful as the trichromatic theory is in explaining color blindness, it cannot explain everything about human color vision—for example, the sense that, rather than three primary colors, there are actually four "basic" colors (red, green, yellow, and blue). A curious property of these four colors is that they seem to be linked as two pairs of opposites, a red-and-green pair and a yellow-and-blue pair. Why do we call these paired colors opposites?

You can see why by staring at one or more of these colors and then looking at a white surface. Try staring first at the red and blue box in **Figure 8-36** for about a minute and then at the white box next to it. When you shift your gaze to the white surface, you

Trichromatic theory. Explanation of color vision based on the coding of three primary colors: red, green, and blue.

○ Go to the section on the eye in the module on the visual system on your *Foundations* CD. In the section on color coding in the retina you can review the process of color vision and move the wavelength to different locations so that you can note the receptor ratios involved in processing them.

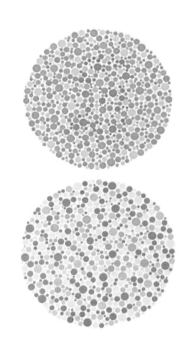

People with deficiencies in red–green color perception have difficulty seeing the numbers within the circles.

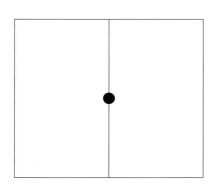

| Figure 8-36 |

Demostrating Opposing Color Pairs
Stare at the rectangle on the left for about 30 seconds. Then stare at the white box. You will experience an afterimage of green on the red side and of yellow on the blue side.

will experience a color afterimage in the color opposites of red and blue—that is, green and yellow. Conversely, if you stare at a green and yellow box and then shift to white, you will see a red and blue afterimage. These observations are not easily explained by the trichromatic theory.

OPPONENT-PROCESS THEORY

In 1874, Ewald Hering, a German physiologist, proposed an explanation of human color vision that also accounts for color afterimages. He argued that color vision is mediated by opponent processes in the retina. Remember that retinal ganglion cells have an on–off/center–surround organization. That is, stimulation to the center of the neuron's receptive field is either excitatory (in some cells) or inhibitory (in other cells), whereas stimulation to the periphery of the receptive field has the opposite effect (see Figure 8-26).

You can probably guess how this arrangement could be adapted to create color opponent-process cells. If excitation is produced by one wavelength of light and inhibition by another, cells would evolve that are excited by red and inhibited by green (or vice versa), as would cells that are excited by blue and inhibited by yellow (or vice versa). Red–green and blue–yellow would therefore be linked to each other as color opposites, just as Hering's **opponent-process theory** says.

In fact, about 60 percent of human retinal ganglion cells are color sensitive in this way, with the center responsive to one wavelength and the surround to another. The most common pairing, shown in **Figure 8-37**, is medium-wavelength (green) versus

Figure 8-37

Opponent-Color Contrast Response
A red–green color-sensitive retinal ganglion cell responds weakly to white-light illumination of its center and surround **(A)** because red and green cones absorb white light to similar extents, and so their inputs cancel out. The cell responds strongly to a spot of red light in its center **(B)**, as well as to red's paired wavelength, green, in the surround. It is inhibited by a small spot of green in its center **(C)**. The cell responds very strongly to simultaneous illumination of the center with red and the surround with green **(D)** and is completely inhibited by the simultaneous illumination of the center with green and the surround with red **(E)**.

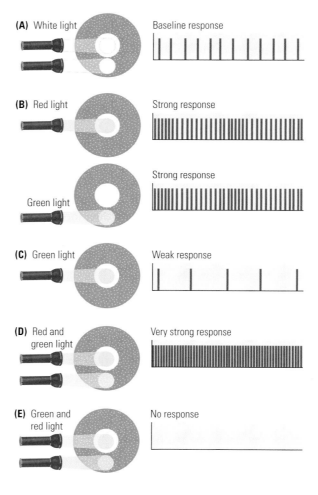

(A) White light — Baseline response

(B) Red light — Strong response

Green light — Strong response

(C) Green light — Weak response

(D) Red and green light — Very strong response

(E) Green and red light — No response

long-wavelength (red), but blue versus yellow cells also exist. Most likely, the reason that opponent-process cells evolved is to enhance the relatively small differences in spectral absorption of the three types of cones.

Cortical neurons in region V1 also respond to color in an opponent-process manner reminiscent of retinal ganglion cells. Recall that color inputs in the primary visual cortex go to the blobs that appear in sections stained for cytochrome oxidase (see Figure 8-18). These blobs are where the color-sensitive cells are found.

Figure 8-38 illustrates how the color-sensitive cells in the blobs are organized relative to the columns of orientation-sensitive cells and the ocular-dominance columns. The color-sensitive cells in the blobs are inserted amid the orientation and ocular-dominance columns. In this way, the primary visual cortex appears to be organized into modules that include ocular-dominance and orientation columns as well as blobs. You can think of it as being composed of several thousand modules, each analyzing color and contour for a particular region of the visual world. This organization allows the primary visual cortex to perform several functions concurrently.

How do neurons of the visual system beyond region V1 process color? You have already learned that cells in region V4 respond to color, but, in contrast with the cells in region V1, these V4 cells do not respond to particular wavelengths. Rather, they are responsive to different perceived colors, with the center of the field being excited by a certain color and the surround being inhibited.

Speculation swirls about the function of these V4 cells. One idea is that they are important for **color constancy,** the property of color perception whereby colors appear to remain the same relative to one another despite changes in light. For instance, if you were to look at a bowl of fruit through light-green glasses, the fruit would take on a greenish tinge, but bananas would still look yellow relative to red apples. If you removed all the fruit except the bananas and looked at them through the tinted glasses, the bananas would appear green because their color would not be relative to any other. Monkeys with V4 lesions lose color constancy, even though they can discriminate different wavelengths.

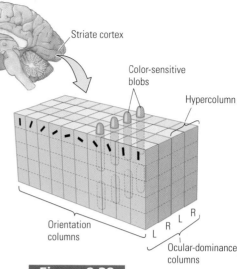

Figure 8-38

V1 Module   This module of striate cortex showing the orientation columns, ocular-dominance columns, and color-sensitive blobs is composed of two hypercolumns. Each hypercolumn consists of a full set (shown in red and blue) of orientation columns spanning 180° of preferred angle as well as a pair of blobs. All cells in the hypercolumn share the same receptive field.

Neural Activity in the Dorsal Stream

A striking characteristic of many cells in the visual areas of the parietal cortex is that they are virtually silent to visual stimulation when a person is under anesthesia. This is true of neurons in the posterior parietal regions of the dorsal stream. In contrast, cells in the temporal cortex do respond to visual stimulation even when a person is anesthetized.

The silence on the part of posterior parietal cortex neurons under anesthesia makes sense if their role is to process visual information for action. In the absence of action when a person is unconscious, there is no need for processing. Hence the cells are quiescent.

Cells in the dorsal stream are of many types, their details varying with the nature of the movement in which a particular cell is taking part. One interesting category of cells processes the visual appearance of an object to be grasped. For instance, if a monkey is going to pick up an apple, these cells respond even when the monkey is only looking at the apple. The cells do not respond when the monkey encounters the same apple in a situation where no movement is to be made.

Curiously, these cells respond if the monkey merely watches another monkey making movements to pick up the apple. Apparently, the cells have some sort of

For more information on the dorsal stream, visit the Chapter 8 Web links on the *Brain and Behavior* Web site (**www.worthpublishers.com/kolb**).

"understanding" of what is happening in the external world. But that understanding is always related to *action* performed with respect to visually perceived objects. These cells are what led David Milner and Mel Goodale (1995) to conclude that the dorsal stream is a "how" visual system.

In Review

The brain perceives color, form, and motion on the basis of information provided by retinal ganglion cells. Because luminance contrasts are located along the edges of shapes, ganglion cells send inputs to the brain that are the starting points for shape analysis. Neurons in the primary visual cortex then respond to more-complex properties of shapes, especially bars of light oriented in a certain direction. A V1 neuron's particular response pattern depends on the spatial arrangement of the ganglion cells to which it is connected. Visual analysis is completed in the temporal lobes, where neurons respond to complex visual stimuli, such as faces. Color analysis also begins in the retina, when light strikes the cone receptors connected to ganglion cells. According to the trichromatic theory, light of different wavelengths stimulates the three different types of cones in different ways, and the ratio of the activity of these three receptor types creates our impression of different colors. Color vision is also mediated by opponent processes in the retina. Ganglion cells are excited by one wavelength of light and inhibited by another, producing two pairs of what seem to be color opposites, which accounts for red-versus-green and yellow-versus-blue afterimages. In contrast with neurons in the ventral stream, the many types of neurons in the dorsal stream's parietal cortex all respond to visual information only when movement by the individual is to take place.

THE VISUAL BRAIN IN ACTION

Anatomical and physiological studies of brain systems leave one key question unanswered: How do all the cells in these systems act together to produce a particular function? One way to answer this question is to evaluate what happens when parts of the visual system are dysfunctional. Then we can see how these parts contribute to the workings of the whole. We will use this strategy to examine the neuropsychology of vision—the study of the visual brain in action.

Injury to the Visual Pathway Leading to the Cortex

Let us begin by seeing what happens when various parts of the visual pathway leading from the eye to the cortex are injured. For instance, destruction of the retina or optic nerve of one eye produces *monocular blindness,* the loss of sight in that eye. Partial destruction of the retina or optic nerve produces a partial loss of sight in one eye, with the loss restricted to the region of the visual field that has severed connections to the brain.

Injuries to the visual pathway beyond the eye also produce blindness. For example, complete cuts of the optic tract, the LGN, or region V1 of the cortex result in **homonymous hemianopia,** which is blindness of one entire side of the visual field, as

Homonymous hemianopia. Blindness of an entire left or right visual field.

Quadrantanopia. Blindness of one quadrant of the visual field.

Scotoma. Small blind spot in the visual field caused by a small lesion or migraines of the visual cortex.

shown in **Figure 8-39A.** We encountered this syndrome at the beginning of the chapter in the story of D. B., who had a lesion in region V1. Should a lesion in one of these areas be partial, as is often the case, the result is **quadrantanopia,** destruction of only a part of the visual field. This condition is illustrated in Figure 8-39B.

Figure 8-39C shows that small lesions in the occipital lobe often produce small blind spots, or **scotomas,** in the visual field. Unlike the blind spots described at the beginning of the chapter as symptomatic of migraine, brain-injured people are often totally unaware of scotomas. For one reason, the eyes are usually moving. We make tiny, involuntary eye movements almost constantly. Because of this usually constant eye motion, called *nystagmus,* a scotoma moves about the visual field, allowing the intact regions of the brain to perceive all the information in that field. If the eyes are temporarily held still, the visual system actually compensates for a scotoma through *pattern completion*—filling in the hole so to speak—so that the people and objects in the visual world are perceived as whole. The result is a seemingly normal set of perceptions.

The visual system may cover up a scotoma so successfully that its presence can be demonstrated to the patient only by "tricking" the visual system. This can be done by placing an object entirely within the scotoma and, without allowing the patient to shift gaze, asking what the object is. If the patient reports seeing nothing, the examiner moves the object out of the scotoma so that it suddenly "appears" in the intact region of the visual field, thus demonstrating the existence of a blind area.

This technique is similar to that illustrated in Figure 8-5 to demonstrate the presence of the blind spot that is due to the optic disc. When a person is looking at an object with only one eye, the brain compensates for the scotoma in the same way as it does for the optic-disc blind spot. As a result, the person does not notice the scotoma.

As you may have deduced by now, the type of blindness that a person suffers gives clues about where in the visual pathway the cause of the problem lies. If there is a loss of vision in one eye only, the problem must be in that eye or its optic nerve; if there is loss of vision in both eyes, the problem is most likely in the brain. Many people have difficulty understanding why a person with damage to the visual cortex has difficulty with both eyes. They fail to realize that it is the visual field, not the eye, that is represented in the brain.

Beyond region V1, the nature of visual loss caused by injury is considerably more complex. It is also very different in the ventral and dorsal streams. We therefore look at each of these pathways separately.

Injury to the "What" Pathway

While taking a shower, D. F., a 35-year-old woman, suffered carbon monoxide poisoning from a faulty gas-fueled water heater. The length of her exposure to the carbon monoxide is unclear, but, when her roommate found her,

◉ Visit the section on the higher-order visual areas in the visual system module of your *Foundations* CD to watch video clips from patients with damage to their visual cortex.

Figure 8-39

Consequences of Lesions in Region V1 The shaded areas indicate the regions of visual loss. **(A)** The effect of a complete lesion of V1 in the left hemisphere is hemianopia affecting the right visual field. **(B)** A large lesion of the lower lip of the calcarine fissure produces quadrantanopia that affects most of the upper-right visual quadrant. **(C)** A smaller lesion of the lower lip of the calcarine fissure results in a smaller scotoma.

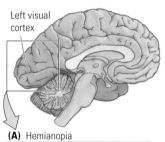

(A) Hemianopia

Injury

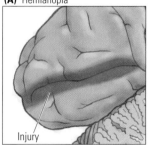

(B) Quadrantanopia

Injury

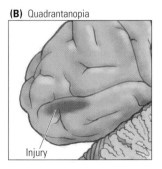

(C) Scotoma

Injury

Left visual field   Right visual field

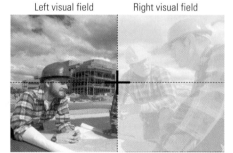

Left visual cortex

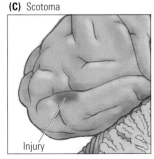

Jim Pickerell/Stock Connection/PictureQuest

Carbon Monoxide Poisoning

Brain damage from carbon monoxide (CO) poisoning is usually caused either by a faulty furnace or by motor vehicle exhaust fumes. CO gas is absorbed by the blood, resulting in swelling and bleeding of the lungs and anoxia (a loss of oxygen) in the brain. The cerebral cortex, hippocampus, cerebellum, and striatum are especially sensitive to CO-induced anoxia.

A curious characteristic of carbon monoxide poisoning is that only a small proportion of people who succumb to it have permanent neurological symptoms, and, among those who do have them, the symptoms are highly variable. The most common symptoms are cortical blindness and various forms of agnosia, as seen in D. F. In addition, many victims suffer language difficulties.

The peculiarities of the language difficulties are shown clearly in a young woman whose case was described by Norman Geschwind. Geschwind studied this patient for 9 years after her accidental poisoning; she required complete nursing care during this time. She never uttered spontaneous speech and did not comprehend spoken language. Nonetheless, she could repeat with perfect accuracy sentences that had just been said to her.

She could also complete certain well-known phrases. For example, if she heard "Roses are red," she would say "Roses are red, violets are blue, sugar is sweet, and so are you." Even odder was her ability to learn new songs. She did not appear to understand the content of the songs; yet, with only a few repetitions, she began to sing along with it and, eventually, she could sing the song spontaneously, making no errors in either words or melody.

Postmortem examination of this woman's brain found that, although she had extensive damage to the parietal and temporal lobes, as shown in the accompanying diagram, her speech areas were intact. Geschwind proposed that she could not comprehend speech, because the words that she heard did not arouse associations in other parts of her cortex. She could, however, repeat sentences because the internal connections of the speech regions were undamaged. Geschwind did not comment on whether this woman suffered from agnosia, but it seems likely that she did. The difficulty would be in diagnosing agnosia in a person who is unable to communicate.

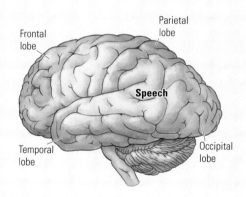

Areas damaged by carbon monoxide poisoning are shown in red in this postmortem diagram of the brain of Geschwind's patient.

the shower water was cold. Although carbon monoxide poisoning can cause several kinds of neurological damage, as discussed in "Carbon Monoxide Poisoning," the result in D. F. was an extensive lesion of the lateral occipital region, including cortical tissue in the ventral visual pathway.

The principal deficit that D. F. experienced was a severe inability to recognize objects, real or drawn, which is known as **visual-form agnosia** (see Farah, 1990). (*Agnosia* literally means "not knowing," and so a person with an agnosia has essentially no knowledge about some perceptual phenomenon.) A visual-form agnosia is an inability to recognize visual forms, whereas a color agnosia (*achromatopsia*) is an inability to recognize colors, and a face agnosia (*prosopagnosia*) is an inability to recognize faces.

Not only was D. F. unable to recognize objects, especially line drawings of objects, she could neither estimate their size or their orientation nor copy drawings of objects.

Visual-form agnosia. Inability to recognize objects or drawings of objects

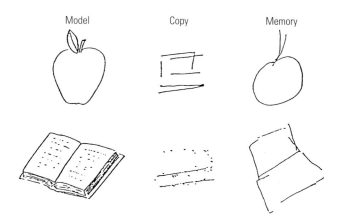

Model Copy Memory

Figure 8-40

Injury to the Ventral Stream Examples of the inability of D. F. to recognize and copy line drawings. She was not able to recognize either of the two drawings on the left. Nor, as the middle column shows, was she able to make recognizable copies of those drawings. She was, however, able to draw reasonable renditions from memory. But, when she was later shown her drawings, she had no idea what they were. Adapted from *The Visual Brain in Action* (p. 127), by A. D. Milner and M. A. Goodale, 1995, Oxford: Oxford University Press.

Yet, interestingly, as **Figure 8-40** illustrates, D. F. could draw reasonable facsimiles of objects from memory. But, when doing so, she did not recognize what she was drawing. D. F. clearly had a lesion that interfered with her ventral-stream "what" pathway.

Despite her inability to identify objects or to estimate their size and orientation, remarkably, D. F. still retained the capacity to appropriately shape her hand when reaching out to grasp something. (This capacity is illustrated in Figure 8-1.) Goodale, Milner, and their research colleagues (1991) have studied D. F. extensively for the past few years, and they have devised a way to demonstrate D. F.'s skill at reaching for objects.

The middle column in **Figure 8-41** shows the grasp patterns of a control subject (S. H.) when she picks up something irregularly shaped. S. H. grasps the object along one of two different axes that makes it easiest to pick up. When D. F. is presented with the same task, shown in the left-hand column, she is as good as S. H. at placing her index finger and thumb on appropriately opposed "grasp" points.

Clearly, D. F. remains able to use the structural features of objects to control her visually guided grasping movements, even though she is unable to "perceive" these same features. This result demonstrates that we are consciously aware of only a small part of the sensory processing that goes on in the brain. Furthermore, D. F.'s ability to use structural features of objects for guiding movement but not for perceiving shapes again shows us that the brain has separate systems for these two types of visual operations.

D. F.'s lesion is located quite far posteriorly in the ventral visual pathway. Lesions that are located more anteriorly produce other types of deficits, depending on the exact location. For example, J. I., whose case has been described by Oliver Sacks and Robert Wasserman (1987), was an artist who became color-blind owing to a cortical lesion presumed to be in region V4. His principal symptom was achromatopsia, mentioned earlier as an inability to distinguish any colors whatsoever. Yet J. I.'s vision appeared otherwise unaffected.

Similarly, L. M., a woman described by Josef Zihl and his colleagues (1983), lost her ability to detect movement after suffering a lesion presumed to be in region V5. In her case, objects either vanished when they moved or appeared frozen despite their movement. L. M. had particular difficulty pouring tea into a cup, because the fluid appeared to be frozen in midair. Yet she could read, write, and recognize objects, and she appeared to have normal form vision—until objects moved.

These varied cases demonstrate that cortical injuries in the ventral stream all somehow interfere with the determination of "what" things are

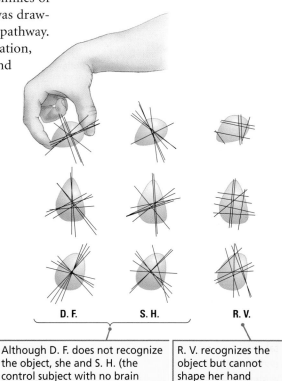

D. F. S. H. R. V.

| Although D. F. does not recognize the object, she and S. H. (the control subject with no brain damage) form their hands similarly to grasp it. | R. V. recognizes the object but cannot shape her hand appropriately to pick it up. |

Conclusion

The brain has different systems for visual object recognition and visual guidance of movement.

Figure 8-41

Grasp Patterns Representative "grasping" axes of three different shapes for patient D. F., who has visual-form agnosia, control subject S. H., and patient R. V., who suffered bilateral occipital parietal damage. Each line passes through the points where the index finger and thumb first made contact with the perimeter of the shape on individual trials in which the subjects were instructed to pick up the shape. Adapted from *The Visual Brain in Action* (p. 132), by A. D. Milner and M. A. Goodale, 1995, Oxford: Oxford University Press.

Optic ataxia. Deficit in the visual control of reaching and other movements.

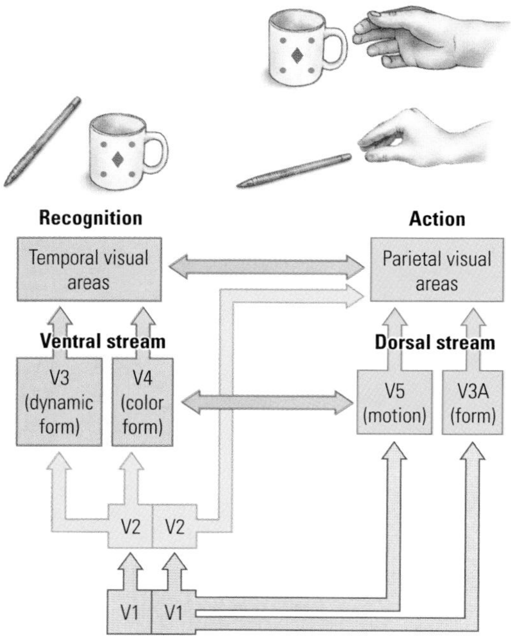

Figure 8-42

Summary of the What and How Visual Streams The dorsal stream, which takes part in visual action, begins in V1 and flows through V5 and V3A to the posterior parietal visual areas. Its role is to guide movements such as the hand postures for grasping a mug or pen. The ventral stream, which takes part in object recognition, begins in V1 and flows through V2 to V3 and V4 to the temporal visual areas. Its job is to identify objects in our visual world. The double-headed arrows show that information flows back and forth between the dorsal and ventral streams, between recognition and action.

or are like. In each case, the symptoms are somewhat different, however, which is thought to be indicative of damage to different subregions or substreams of the ventral visual pathway.

Injury to the "How" Pathway

In 1909, R. Balint described a rather peculiar set of visual symptoms associated with a bilateral parietal lesion. The patient had full visual fields and could recognize, use, and name objects, pictures, and colors normally. But he had a severe deficit in visually guided reaching, even though he could still make accurate movements directed toward his own body (presumably guided by tactile or proprioceptive feedback from his joints). Balint called this syndrome **optic ataxia.**

Since Balint's time, many descriptions of optic ataxia associated with parietal injury have been recorded. Goodale has studied several such patients, one of whom is a woman identified as R. V. In contrast with patient D. F.'s visual-form agnosia, R. V. had normal perception of drawings and objects, but she could not guide her hand to reach for objects.

The right-hand column in Figure 8-41 shows that, when she was asked to pick up the same irregularly shaped objects that D. F. could grasp normally, R. V. often failed to place her fingers on the appropriate grasp points, even though she could distinguish the objects easily. In other words, although R. V.'s perception of the features of an object was normal for the task of describing that object, her perception was not normal for the task of visually guiding her hand to reach for the object.

To summarize, people with damage to the parietal cortex in the dorsal visual stream can "see" perfectly well, yet they cannot accurately guide their movements on the basis of visual information. The guidance of movement is the function of the dorsal stream. In contrast, people with damage to the ventral stream cannot "see" objects, because the perception of objects is a ventral-stream function. Yet these same people can guide their movements to objects on the basis of visual information.

The first kind of patient, like R. V., has an intact ventral stream that analyzes the visual characteristics of objects. The second kind of patient, like D. F., has an intact dorsal stream that visually directs movements. By comparing the two types of cases, we can infer the visual functions of the dorsal and ventral streams.

In Review

As **Figure 8-42** shows, our visual experience is largely a result of visual processing in the ventral stream, but much of our visually guided behavior is a result of activity in the dorsal stream. An important lesson here is that we are conscious of only a small amount of what the brain actually does, even though we usually have the impression of being in control of all our thoughts and behaviors. Apparently, this impression of "free will" is partly an illusion.

SUMMARY

■ *How does the nervous system interpret sensory stimuli such as light waves to construct our perceptions—for example, vision?* D. B.'s surprising ability to locate lights shining in the blind side of his visual field makes clear that our sensory world is not unitary, despite what our conscious experience suggests. To understand the nature of sensation, and of vision in particular, we can dissect the visual system and examine how the parts work together to produce vision. Vision is but one of a half dozen senses that allow us to act in the world that we perceive.

▥ *How does the brain transform light energy into neural energy?* Like all sensory systems, vision begins with receptor cells. These photoreceptors transduce the physical energy, such as light waves, into neural activity. The visual receptors (rods and cones) are located in the retina at the back of the eye. Rods are sensitive to dim light, whereas cones are sensitive to bright light and are responsible for color vision. The three types of cones, each of which is maximally sensitive to a different wavelength of light, are often referred to as blue, green, and red cones. The name refers not to the color of light to which the cone responds but rather to the wavelength of light to which it is maximally sensitive.

▥ *How does visual information get from receptors in the retina to the brain?* Retinal ganglion cells receive input from photoreceptors through bipolar cells, and the axons of the ganglion cells send their axons out of the eye to form the optic nerve. The two categories of ganglion cells, P and M, each send a different kind of message to the brain. P cells receive input mostly from cones and convey information about color and fine detail. M cells receive input from rods and convey information about luminance and movement but not color. The optic nerve forms two distinct routes into the brain: the geniculostriate and tectopulvinar pathways. The geniculostriate pathway synapses first in the lateral geniculate nucleus of the thalamus and then in the primary visual cortex. The tectopulvinar pathway synapses first in the superior colliculus of the midbrain's tectum, then in the pulvinar of the thalamus, and finally in the visual cortex.

▥ *What are the pathways for visual information within the cortex?* Among the visual regions in the occipital cortex, regions V1 and V2 carry out multiple functions, whereas the remaining regions (V3, V3A, V4, and V5) are more specialized. Visual information flows from the thalamus to V1 and V2 and then divides to form two distinctly different pathways, or streams. The dorsal stream is concerned with the visual guidance of movements, whereas the ventral stream is concerned with the perception of objects.

▥ *How are neurons in the visual system organized?* At each step in the visual pathways, neurons produce distinctly different forms of activity. The sum of the neural activity in all regions produces our visual experience. Like all cortical regions, each functional column in the visual regions is a functional unit about 0.5 millimeter in diameter and extends to the depth of the cortex. Columns in the visual system are specialized for processes such as analyzing lines of a particular orientation or comparing similar shapes, such as faces.

▥ *How does the visual system interpret shapes?* Neurons in the ventral stream are selective for different characteristics of shapes. For example, cells in the visual cortex are maximally responsive to lines of different orientations, whereas cells in the inferior temporal cortex are responsive to different shapes, which in some cases appear to be abstract and in other cases have forms such as hands or faces.

▥ *How does the visual system interpret colors?* Cones in the retina are maximally responsive to different wavelengths of light, roughly corresponding to the perception of green, blue, and red. Retinal ganglion cells are opponent-process cells and have a center–surround organization such that cells are excited by one hue and inhibited by another (e.g., red versus green; blue versus yellow). Color-sensitive cells in the primary visual cortex, which are located in the blobs, also have opponent-process properties. Cells in region V4 also respond to the colors that we perceive rather than to particular

neuroscience interactive

Many resources are available for expanding your learning online:

■ **www.worthpublishers.com/kolb**
Try the Chapter 8 quizzes and flashcards to test your mastery of the chapter material. You'll also be able to link to other sites that will reinforce what you've learned.

To further enhance your understanding of the material in this chapter, you can visit the module on the Visual System on your *Foundations* CD-ROM. This section includes a three-dimensional model of the eye, illustrations of the substructures of the eye and the visual cortex, video clips of patients with visual disorders, and interactive activities to explore how the visual field and color vision are created.

wavelengths. Perceived color is influenced by the brightness of the world and by the color of nearby objects.

■ *What happens when the visual system is damaged?* Injury to the eye or optic nerve results in a complete or partial loss of vision in one eye. When the visual information enters the brain, information from the left and right visual fields goes to the right and left sides of the brain, respectively. As a result, damage to the visual areas on one side of the brain results in visual disturbance in both eyes. Specific visual functions are localized to different regions of the brain, and so localized damage to a particular region results in the loss of a particular function. For example, damage to region V4 produces a loss of color constancy, whereas damage to regions in the parietal cortex produces an inability to shape the hand appropriately to grasp objects.

■ *What is the difference between visual processing for "what" and visual processing for "how?"* Visual information is used for two distinctly different functions: identifying objects (the what) and moving in relation to the objects (the how). Visual information travels in the cortex from V1 to the temporal lobe, forming the ventral stream, and from V1 to the parietal lobe, forming the dorsal stream. The ventral stream produces our conscious awareness of visual information, including properties such as shape, movement, and color. In contrast, we are largely unconscious of the visual information processing in the dorsal stream, which is a type of "on-line" analysis that allows us to make accurate movements related to objects.

KEY TERMS

blind spot, p. 274
blob, p. 282
color constancy, p. 296
cone, p. 276
cortical column, p. 282
extrastriate (secondary) cortex, p. 282
fovea, p. 276
geniculostriate system, p. 280
homonymous hemianopia, p. 298
luminance contrast, p. 291

magnocellular (M) cell, p. 278
ocular-dominance column, p. 292
opponent-process theory, p. 296
optic ataxia, p. 302
optic chiasm, p. 279
parvocellular (P) cell, p. 278
primary visual cortex, p. 282
quadrantanopia, p. 298

receptive field, p. 284
retina, p. 272
retinal ganglion cell, p. 278
rod, p. 276
scotoma, p. 298
striate cortex, p. 280
tectopulvinar system, p. 280
topographic map, p. 286
trichromatic theory, p. 295
visual field, p. 284
visual-form agnosia, p. 300

REVIEW QUESTIONS

1. Describe the pathways that visual information follows through the brain.
2. Describe how the M and P cells differ and how they give rise to distinctly different pathways that eventually form the dorsal and ventral visual streams.
3. How do cells in the different levels of the visual system code different types of information?
4. Summarize what you believe to be the major point of this chapter.

FOR FURTHER THOUGHT

How does the visual system create a visual world? What differences between people and members of other species would contribute to different impressions of visual reality?

RECOMMENDED READING

Hubel, D. H. (1988). *Eye, brain, and vision.* New York: Scientific American Library. This book, written by a Nobel laureate for work on vision, is a general survey of how the visual system is organized. Like the other books in the Scientific American Library series, this one has beautiful illustrations that bring the visual system to life.

Milner, A. D., & Goodale, M. A. (1995). *The visual brain in action.* Oxford: Oxford University Press. Milner and Goodale have revolutionized our thinking of how the sensory systems are organized. This little book is a beautiful survey of neuropsychological and neurophysiological studies of the visual system.

Posner, M. I., & Raichle, M. E. (1997). *Images of the mind.* New York: Scientific American Library. This award-winning book is an introduction to the study of cognitive neuroscience, with an emphasis on visual cognitive neuroscience.

Weizkrantz, L. (1986). *Blindsight: A case study and implications.* Oxford: Oxford University Press. Weizkrantz's book about a single patient describes one of the most important case studies in neuropsychology. This book forced investigators to reconsider preconceived notions not only about how sensory systems work, but also about ideas such as consciousness.

Zeki, S. (1993). *A vision of the brain.* Oxford: Blackwell Scientific. Not only is Zeki's book a discussion of how he believes the visual system works, but it also has much broader implications for cortical functioning in general. Zeki is not afraid to be controversial, and the book does not disappoint.

How Do We Hear, Speak, and Make Music?

The Evolution of Language and Music

The finding that early modern humans (*Homo sapiens*) made music implies that music has been important in our evolution. Thomas Geissmann (2001) noted that, among most of the 26 species of singing primates, males and females sing duets. All singing primates are monogamous, suggesting that singing may somehow relate to sexual behaviors. Music may also play a role in primates' parenting behaviors.

The modern human brain is specialized for analyzing certain aspects of music in the right temporal lobe, which is complemented by specialization for analyzing aspects of speech in the left temporal lobe. Did music and language evolve simultaneously in our species? Possibly.

Neanderthals (*Homo neanderthalensis*) have long fascinated researchers. Neanderthals originated about 230,000 years ago and disappeared some 200,000 years later. During that time, they coexisted in Europe with *Homo sapiens*, whom they resembled in many ways.

In some locations, the two species may have even shared resources and tools. Researchers hypothesize that Neanderthal culture was significantly less developed than that of early modern humans. Neanderthals buried their dead with artifacts, which implies that they held spiritual beliefs, but no evidence reveals that they created visual art. In contrast, *Homo sapiens* began painting on cave walls some 30,000 years ago, near the end of the Neanderthal era. Anatomically, some skeletal analyses suggest that Neanderthals' physical language ability made them far less fluent speakers than their *Homo sapiens* contemporaries.

What about music? Behavioral scientists have shown that music plays as central a role in our social and emotional lives as language does. The evolutionary view of music and language as complementary behaviors has now cast serious doubt on the earlier view of Neanderthals as culturally "primitive."

Shown in **Figure 9-1** is the bone flute found in 1995 by Ivan Turk, a palenontologist at the Slovenian Academy of Sciences in Ljubljana. Turk was excavating a cave in northern Slovenia used by Neanderthals long ago as a hunting camp. Buried in the cave among a cache of stone tools was the leg bone of a young bear that looked as if it had been fashioned into a flute.

The bone had holes aligned along one of its sides that could not have been made by gnawing animals. Rather, the spacing resembles the hole positions on a modern flute. But the bone flute is at least 43,000 years old—perhaps as old as 82,000 years. All the evidence suggests that Neanderthals, not modern humans, made the instrument.

Bob Fink, a musicologist, analyzed the flute's musical qualities. He found that an eight-note scale similar to a do-re-mi scale could be played on the flute, but, compared with the scale most familiar in European music, one note was slightly off. That "blue note," a staple of jazz, is found in musical scales throughout Africa and India today.

The similarity between Neanderthal and contemporary musical scales encourages us to speculate about the brain that made this ancient flute. Like modern humans, Neanderthals probably had complementary hemispheric specialization for language and music. If so, their communication, social behaviors, and cultural systems may have been more advanced than scientists formerly reasoned.

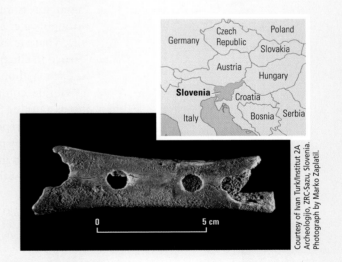

Courtesy of Ivan Turk/Institut 2A Archeologijo, ZRC-Sazu, Slovenia. Photograph by Marko Zaplatil.

Figure 9-1

Ancient Bone Flute   The alignment of the holes in this piece of bear femur found in a cave in northern Slovenia suggests that Neanderthals made a flute from it and made music with the flute.

Sound wave. Undulating displacement of molecules caused by changing pressure.

Frequency. Number of cycles that a wave completes in a given amount of time.

Hertz (Hz). Measure of frequency (repetition rate) of a sound wave; one hertz is equal to one cycle per second.

○ To further explore the relationship between evolution and music, visit the Chapter 9 Web links on the *Brain and Behavior* Web site (**www.worth publishers.com/kolb**).

Both language and music are universal among humans. The oral language of every known culture follows similar basic structural rules, and people in all cultures create and enjoy music. When we use language and music to communicate, what are we communicating, and why?

Music and language allow us both to organize and to interact socially. Like music, language probably improves parenting. Those who can communicate their intentions to one another and to their children presumably will be better parents.

Human social interaction is one of the most complex behaviors studied by ethologists. Consider groupings of teenage girls. Their social interactions are complex not only by virtue of the numbers of girls in groups but also by the rich set of rules—with rules about language and music high on the list—that each group invents to bond its members.

Humans' capacity for language and music are linked conceptually, because both are based on sound. Understanding how and why we engage in speech and music are the goals of this chapter. We first examine the physical nature of the energy that we perceive as sound and then how the human ear and nervous system function to detect and interpret it. We next examine the complementary neuroanatomy of human language and music processing. Finally, we investigate how two other species, birds and bats, interpret and utilize auditory stimuli.

SOUND WAVES: THE STIMULUS FOR AUDITION

When you strike a tuning fork, the energy of its vibrating prongs displaces adjacent air molecules. **Figure 9-2** shows how, as one prong moves to the left, the air molecules to the left compress (grow more dense) and the air molecules to the right become more rarefied (less dense). The opposite happens when the prong moves to the right. The undulating energy generated by this displacement of molecules causes waves of changing air pressure—**sound waves**—to emanate from the fork. Sound waves can move through water as well, and even through the ground.

What we experience as sound, as for our sight, is a creation of the brain, as you learned in Chapter 8. When a tree falls in the forest, it makes no sound unless someone hears it. Without a brain, sound does not exist. A falling tree merely makes molecules of air vibrate, compressing them and rarefying them into waves of changing air pressure, just as a tuning fork does.

We can represent waves of changing air pressure emanating from a falling tree or tuning fork by plotting air-molecule density against time at a single point, as shown in the top graph in **Figure 9-3**. The bottom graph shows how the energy from the right-hand prong of the fork moves to create the air-pressure changes associated with a single

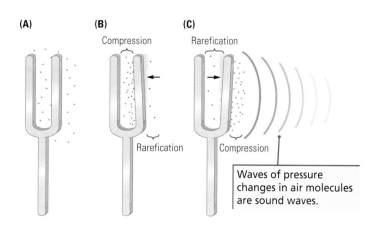

Figure 9-2

How a Tuning Fork Produces Sound Waves **(A)** When the fork is still, air molecules are distributed randomly around it. **(B)** When struck, the right arm of the fork moves to the left, causing air to be compressed on the leading edge and rarefied on the trailing edge. **(C)** The arm moves to the right, compressing the air to the right and rarefying the air to the left.

cycle. A *cycle* is one complete peak and valley on the graph—that is, the change from one maximum or minimum air-pressure level of the sound wave to the next maximum or minimum level, respectively.

PHYSICAL PROPERTIES OF SOUND WAVES

Light is electromagnetic energy that we see; sound is mechanical energy that we hear. Sound-wave energy, produced by the displacement of air molecules, has three physical attributes: frequency, amplitude, and complexity, summarized in **Figure 9-4**. The auditory system analyzes each property separately, just as the visual system analyzes color and form separately.

SOUND-WAVE FREQUENCY

Although sound waves travel at a fixed speed of 1100 feet per second, sound energy varies in wavelength (frequency). More precisely, **frequency** is the number of cycles that a wave completes in a given amount of time. Sound-wave frequencies are measured in cycles per second called **hertz** (Hz), named after the German physicist Heinrich Rudolph Hertz.

One hertz is 1 cycle per second; 50 Hz is 50 cycles per second; 6000 Hz is 6000 cycles per second; 20,000 Hz is 20,000 cycles per second; and so on. Sounds that we perceive as being low in *pitch* have slower wave frequencies (fewer cycles per second), whereas sounds that we perceive as being high pitched have faster wave frequencies (many cycles per second), as shown in the top panel of Figure 9-4.

Just as we can perceive light only at visible wavelengths, we can perceive sound waves in only a limited range of frequencies. These frequencies are plotted in **Figure 9-5**. Humans' hearing range is from about 20 to 20,000 Hz. Many animals communicate with sound, which means that their auditory systems are designed to interpret their species-typical sounds. After all, there is no point in making complicated songs or calls if other members of your species cannot hear them.

The range of sound-wave frequencies heard by different species varies extensively. Figure 9-5 shows that some species (such as frogs and birds) have rather narrow hearing ranges, whereas others (such as dogs, whales, and humans) have broad ranges. Some species use extremely high frequencies (bats are off the scale), whereas others use the low range (as do fish).

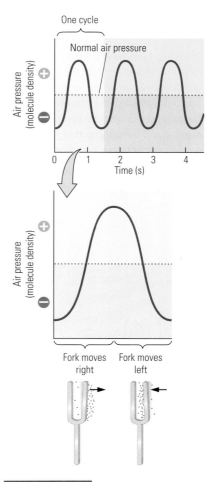

Figure 9-3

Visualizing a Sound Wave Air-molecule density plotted against time at a particular point relative to the right prong of the tuning fork. (Physicists call the resulting cyclical waves *sine waves*.)

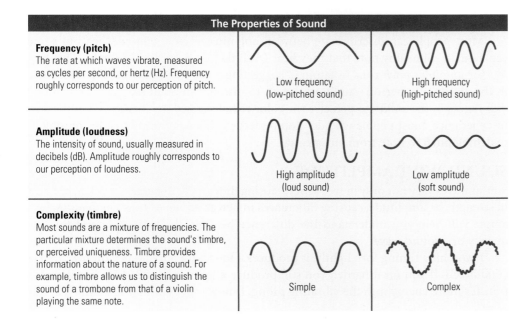

The Properties of Sound		
Frequency (pitch) The rate at which waves vibrate, measured as cycles per second, or hertz (Hz). Frequency roughly corresponds to our perception of pitch.	Low frequency (low-pitched sound)	High frequency (high-pitched sound)
Amplitude (loudness) The intensity of sound, usually measured in decibels (dB). Amplitude roughly corresponds to our perception of loudness.	High amplitude (loud sound)	Low amplitude (soft sound)
Complexity (timbre) Most sounds are a mixture of frequencies. The particular mixture determines the sound's timbre, or perceived uniqueness. Timbre provides information about the nature of a sound. For example, timbre allows us to distinguish the sound of a trombone from that of a violin playing the same note.	Simple	Complex

Figure 9-4

Physical Dimensions of Sound Waves The frequency, amplitude, and complexity of sound waves correspond to the perceptual dimensions of pitch, loudness, and timbre.

Figure 9-5

Hearing Ranges among Animals
Frogs and birds hear a relatively narrow range of frequencies; whales and dolphins have an extensive range, as do dogs. Although the human hearing range is fairly broad, we do not perceive many sound frequencies that other animals can both make and hear.

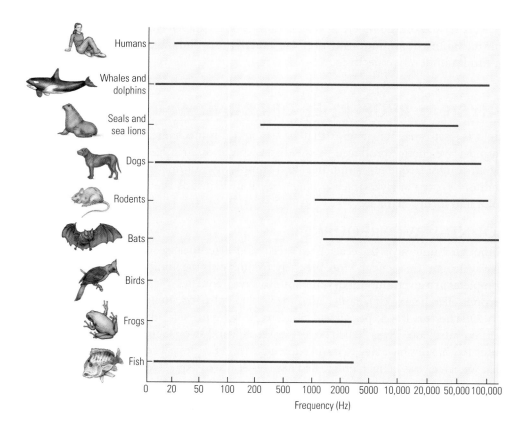

It is quite an achievement that the auditory systems of whales and dolphins are responsive to sound waves of such range. The characteristics at the extremes of these frequencies allow marine mammals to use them in different ways. Very-low-frequency sound waves travel long distances in water; whales produce them as a form of underwater communication over miles of distance. High-frequency sound waves create echoes and form the basis of sonar. Dolphins produce them in bursts, listening for the echoes that bounce back from objects and help the dolphins to navigate and locate prey.

As stated earlier, differences in the frequency of sound waves become differences in pitch when heard. Consequently, each note in a musical scale must have a different frequency because each has a different pitch. Middle C on the piano, for instance, has a frequency of 264 Hz.

Most people can discriminate between one musical note and another, but some can actually name any note that they hear (A, B flat, C sharp, and so forth). This *perfect* (or *absolute*) *pitch* runs in families, suggesting a genetic influence. The difference in the ability of a person's auditory system to distinguish pitch may be analogous to differences in the ability to perceive the color red, discussed in Chapter 8. On the side of experience, most people who develop perfect pitch also receive musical training in matching pitch to note from an early age.

SOUND-WAVE AMPLITUDE

Sound waves vary not only in frequency, causing differences in perceived pitch, but also in strength, or amplitude, causing differences in perceived *intensity*, or *loudness*. An example will help you understand the difference between the amplitude and the frequency of a sound wave.

If you hit a tuning fork lightly, it produces a tone with a frequency of, say, 264 Hz (middle C). If you hit it harder, you still produce a frequency of 264 Hz but you also transfer more energy into the vibrating prong. It now moves farther left and right but

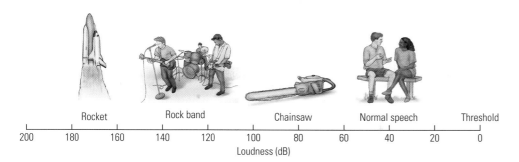

Rocket   Rock band   Chainsaw   Normal speech   Threshold

200   180   160   140   120   100   80   60   40   20   0

Loudness (dB)

Amplitude. Intensity of a stimulus; in audition, roughly equivalent to loudness, graphed by increasing the height of a sound wave.

at the same frequency. This greater energy is due to an increased *quantity* of air molecules compressed in each wave, even though the same middle C frequency (number of waves) is created every second.

This new dimension of energy in the sound wave is **amplitude,** the *magnitude* of change in air-molecule density. Increased compression of air molecules intensifies the energy in a sound wave, which "amps" the sound—makes it louder. Differences in amplitude are graphed by increasing the height of a sound wave, as shown in the middle panel of Figure 9-4.

Sound-wave amplitude is usually measured in *decibels* (dB), a measure of the strength of a sound relative to the threshold of human hearing as a standard, pegged at 0 dB. Normal speech sounds, for example, measure about 40 dB. Sounds that register more than about 70 dB we perceive as loud; those less than about 20 dB we perceive as quiet.

Because the human nervous system evolved to be sensitive to weak sounds, it is literally "blown away" by extremely strong ones. People regularly damage their hearing by exposure to very loud sounds (such as rifle fire at close range) or even by prolonged exposure to sounds that are only relatively loud (such as at a live concert). As a rule of thumb, sounds louder than 100 dB are likely to damage our hearing, especially if our exposure to them is prolonged.

Heavy-metal bands, among others, routinely play music that registers higher than 120 dB and sometimes as high as 135 dB. One researcher (Drake-Lee, 1992) found that rock musicians had a significant loss of sensitivity to sound waves, especially at about 6000 Hz. After a typical 90-min concert, this loss was temporarily far worse—as much as a 40-fold increase in sound pressure was needed to reach a musician's hearing threshold.

SOUND-WAVE COMPLEXITY

Sounds with a single frequency wave are *pure tones,* much like what you would get from a tuning fork or pitch pipe, but most sounds mix wave frequencies together in combinations and so are called *complex tones.* To better understand the blended nature of a complex tone, picture a clarinetist, such as Don Byron in **Figure 9-6**, playing a steady note. The upper graph in Figure 9-6 represents the sound wave produced by the clarinet.

Notice that the clarinet waveform has a more complex pattern than those of the simple waves described earlier in this chapter. Even when a musician plays a single note, the instrument is making

Christian Ducasse/Gamma-Liaison

Figure 9-6

Breaking Down a Complex Tone The wave shape of a single note from Don Byron's clarinet (*top*) and the component frequencies—the fundamental frequency (*middle*) and overtones (*bottom*)—that make up the complex tone. From *Stereo Review,* copyright 1977 by Diamandis Communications Inc.

Waveform from clarinet

Fundamental frequency

Simple waves that make up sound of clarinet

Overtones

1 2 3 4 5 6 7 8 9 10 11 12 13 14 15 16 17 18 19 20

a complex tone, not a pure tone. Using a mathematical technique known as Fourier analysis, we can break this complex tone into its many component pure tones, the numbered waves at the bottom of Figure 9-6.

The *fundamental frequency* (wave 1) is the rate at which the complex waveform pattern repeats. Waves 2 through 20 are *overtones,* a set of higher-frequency sound waves that vibrate at whole-number (integer) multiples of the fundamental frequency. Different musical instruments sound unique because they produce overtones of different amplitudes. Among the clarinet overtones, represented by the heights of the blue waves in Figure 9-6, wave 5 is low amplitude, whereas wave 2 is high amplitude.

Like primary colors, pure tones can be blended into complex tones in an almost infinite variety. In addition to emanating from musical instruments, complex tones emanate from the human voice, from birdsong, and from machines or repetitive mechanisms that give rise to rhythmic buzzing or humming sounds.

A key feature of complex tones, besides being made up of two or more pure tones, is some sort of periodicity. The fundamental frequency repeats at regular intervals. Sounds that are aperiodic, or random, we call *noise.*

Perception of Sound

The auditory system's task is to convert the physical properties of sound-wave energy into electrochemical neural activity that travels to the brain, which we then perceive as sound. Remember that the waves themselves make no sounds. The sounds that we hear, like the images that we see, are but a product of the brain.

To better understand the relation between the energy of sound-wave sensations and sound perceptions, think about what happens when you toss a pebble into a pond. Waves of water emanate from the point where the pebble enters the water. These waves produce no audible sound. But, if your skin were able to convert the energy of the water waves into neural activity that stimulated your auditory system, you would "hear" the waves when you placed your hand into the rippling water. When you removed your hand, the "sound" would stop.

The pebble hitting the water is much like a falling tree, and the waves that emanate from the pebble's point of entry are like the air-pressure waves that emanate from the place where the tree strikes the ground. The frequency of the waves determines the pitch of the sound heard by the brain, whereas the height (amplitude) of the waves determines the sound's loudness.

Our sensitivity to sound waves is extraordinary. At the threshold of human hearing, we can detect the displacement of air molecules of about 10 picometers (10^{-11} meter). We are rarely in an environment where we can detect such a small air-pressure change, because there is usually too much background noise. A very quiet rural setting is probably as close as we ever get to an environment suitable for testing the acuteness of our hearing. So, the next time you visit the countryside, take note of the sounds that you can hear. If there is no sound competition, you can often hear a single car engine miles away.

In addition to detecting very small changes in air pressure, the auditory system is also adept at simultaneously perceiving different sounds. As you sit reading this chapter, you are able to differentiate all sorts of sounds around you—traffic on the street, people talking next door, your computer's fan humming, footsteps in the hall. If you are listening to music, you detect the sounds of different instruments and voices.

You can perceive different sounds simultaneously because the different frequencies of air-pressure change associated with each sound wave stimulate different neurons in your auditory system. The perception of sounds is only the beginning of your auditory experience. Your brain interprets sounds to obtain information about events in your environment, and it analyzes a sound's meaning. These processes are clearly illustrated in your use of sound to communicate with other people through both language and music.

Properties of Language and Music As Sounds

Language and music differ from other auditory sensations in fundamental ways. Both convey meaning and evoke emotion. The analysis of meaning in sound is a considerably more complex behavior than simply detecting a sound and identifying it. The brain has evolved systems that analyze speech and musical sounds for meaning, in the left and right temporal lobes, respectively, as you learned at the beginning of this chapter.

Infants are receptive to speech and musical cues before they have any obvious utility, suggesting the innate presence of these skills. Humans have an amazing capacity for learning and remembering linguistic and musical information. We are capable of learning a vocabulary of tens of thousands of words, often in many languages, and we have a capacity for recognizing thousands of songs.

Language facilitates communication. We can organize our complex perceptual worlds by categorizing information with words. We can tell others what we think and know and imagine. Imagine the efficiency that gestures and spoken language added to the cooperative food hunting and gathering behaviors of early humans.

All these benefits of oral language seem obvious, but the benefits of music may seem less straightforward. In fact, music helps us to regulate our emotions and to affect the emotions of others. After all, when do people most commonly make music? We sing and play music to communicate with infants and put children to sleep. We play music to enhance social interactions and gatherings and when we feel romantic. We use music to bolster group identification—school songs or national anthems are examples.

Another characteristic that distinguishes speech and musical sounds from other auditory inputs is their delivery speed. Nonspeech and nonmusical noise produced at a rate of about 5 segments per second is perceived as a buzz. (A sound segment is a distinct unit of sound.)

Normal speed for speech is on the order of 8 to 10 segments per second, and we are capable of understanding speech at nearly 30 segments per second. Speech perception at these higher rates is truly amazing, because the speed of input far exceeds the auditory system's ability to transmit all the speech as separate pieces of information.

PROPERTIES OF LANGUAGE

Experience in listening to a particular language helps the brain to analyze rapid speech, which is one reason why people who are speaking languages with which you are unfamiliar often seem to be talking incredibly fast. Your brain does not know where the foreign words end and begin, making them seem to run together in a rapid-fire stream.

A unique characteristic of our perception of speech sounds is our tendency to hear variations of a sound as if they were identical, even though the sound varies considerably from one context to another. For instance, the English letter "d" is pronounced differently in the words "deep," "deck," and "duke," yet a listener perceives the pronunciations to be the same "d" sound. This auditory constancy is reminiscent of the visual system's capacity for object constancy described in Chapter 8.

The auditory system must therefore have a mechanism for categorizing sounds as being the same despite small differences in pronunciation. This mechanism, moreover, must be affected by experience, because different languages categorize speech sounds differently. A major obstacle to mastering a foreign language after the age of 10 is the difficulty of learning the categories of sound that are treated as equivalent.

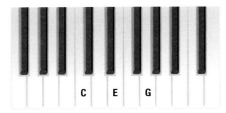

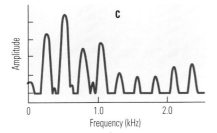

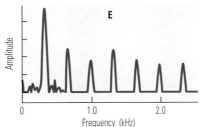

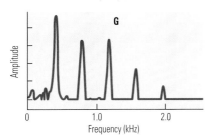

Figure 9-7

Fundamental Frequencies of Piano Notes The shapes of the sound waves of C, E, and G as played on a piano and recorded on a spectrograph. The first wave in each of these graphs is the fundamental frequency, and the secondary waves are the overtones.
Courtesy of D. Rendall.

Prosody. Melodical tone of the spoken voice.

PROPERTIES OF MUSIC

Like other sounds, the sounds of music differ from one another in the subjective properties that people perceive them to have. One property is *loudness,* the magnitude of the sound as judged by a person. Loudness, as you know, is related to the amplitude of a sound wave and is measured in decibels, but loudness is also subjective. What is "very loud" music for one person may be only "moderately loud" for another, whereas music that seems "soft" to one listener may not seem soft at all to someone else.

Another subjective property of musical sounds is *pitch,* the position of each tone on a musical scale as judged by the listener. Although pitch is clearly related to sound-wave frequency, there is more to it than that. Consider the note middle C as played on a piano. This note can be described as a pattern of sound frequencies, as is the clarinet note in Figure 9-6.

Like the note played on the clarinet, any musical note is defined by its fundamental frequency, which is the lowest frequency of the sound-wave pattern, or the rate at which the overall pattern is repeated. For middle C, the fundamental frequency is 264 Hz, as mentioned earlier. The sound waves, as measured by a spectrograph, are shown in **Figure 9-7**. Notice that, by convention, sound-wave spectrographs are measured in kilohertz (kHz), units of thousands of hertz. Thus, if we look at the fundamental frequency for middle C, it is the first large wave, which is at 0.264 kHz. The fundamental frequencies for G and E are 392 and 330, respectively.

An important feature of the human brain's analysis of music is that middle C is perceived as being the same note regardless of whether it is played on a piano or on a guitar, even though the sounds made by these instruments are very different. The right temporal lobe has a special function in extracting pitch from sound, whether the sound is speech or music. In speech, pitch contributes to the perceived melodical tone of a voice, or **prosody.**

A final property of musical sound is *quality,* the characteristics that distinguish a particular sound from all others of similar pitch and loudness. We can easily distinguish the sound of a violin from that of a trombone even though the same note is being played on both instruments at the same loudness. The quality of their sounds differs. The French word *timbre* is normally used to describe perceived sound quality.

In Review

Sound energy, the physical stimulus for the auditory system, is produced by changes in pressure waves that are converted into neural activity in the ear. Sound waves have three key qualities: frequency, amplitude, and complexity. Frequency is the rate at which the waves vibrate and roughly corresponds to the high or low pitch of the sound that we perceive. Amplitude, or wave height, is the magnitude of change in air-molecule pressure that the wave undergoes and roughly corresponds to perceived loudness. Complexity refers to the particular mixture of frequencies that create a sound's perceived uniqueness, or timbre. Combinations of these qualities allow the human auditory system to comprehend sounds as complex as language and music.

ANATOMY OF THE AUDITORY SYSTEM

Our next task is to understand how the nervous system analyzes sound waves. We begin by tracing the pathway taken by sound energy to and through the brain. The ear collects sound waves from the surrounding air and converts them into electrochemical neural energy, which then begins a long route through the brainstem to the auditory cortex.

Before we can trace the journey from the ear to the cortex, we need to ask what the auditory system is designed to do. Because sound waves have the properties of frequency, amplitude, and complexity, we can predict that the auditory system is structured to code these properties. In addition, most animals can tell where a sound comes from, and so there must be some mechanism for locating sound waves in space. Finally, many animals, including humans, not only analyze sounds for meaning but also make sounds themselves. Because the sounds that they produce are often the same as the ones that they hear, we can infer that the neural systems for sound production and analysis must be closely related.

In humans, the evolution of sound-processing systems for both language and music led to the enhancement of specialized cortical regions, especially in the temporal lobes. In fact, a major difference between the human and the monkey cortex is a marked expansion of auditory areas in humans.

Structure of the Ear

The ear is a biological masterpiece in three acts: the outer, middle, and inner ear, all illustrated in **Figure 9-8**. Both the *pinna,* the funnel-like external structure of the outer ear, and the *external ear canal,* which extends a short distance from the pinna inside

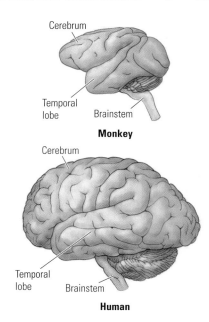

Monkey

Human

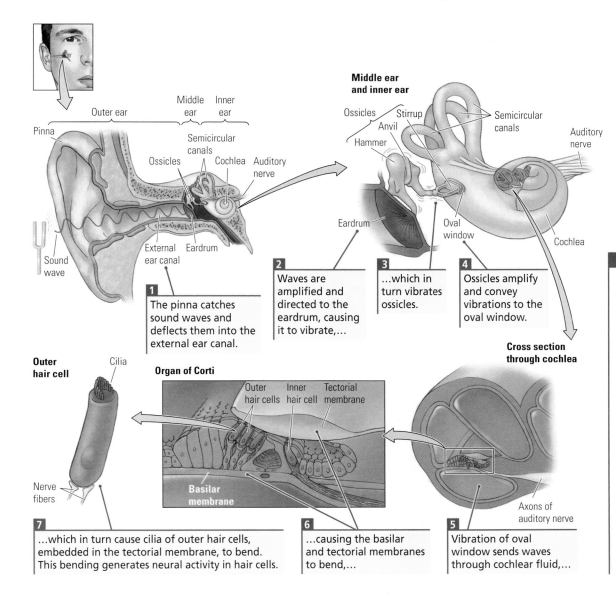

① The pinna catches sound waves and deflects them into the external ear canal.

② Waves are amplified and directed to the eardrum, causing it to vibrate,...

③ ...which in turn vibrates ossicles.

④ Ossicles amplify and convey vibrations to the oval window.

⑤ Vibration of oval window sends waves through cochlear fluid,...

⑥ ...causing the basilar and tectorial membranes to bend,...

⑦ ...which in turn cause cilia of outer hair cells, embedded in the tectorial membrane, to bend. This bending generates neural activity in hair cells.

Cross section through cochlea

Figure 9-8

Anatomy of the Human Ear Sound waves gathered into the outer ear are transduced from air pressure into mechanical energy in the middle-ear ossicles and into electrochemical activity in the inner-ear cochlea. Hair cells embedded in the basilar membrane (the organ of Corti) are tipped off by cilia. The cilia are displaced by movements of the basilar and tectorial membranes, leading to changes in the inner hair cells' membrane potentials and resultant activity of auditory (bipolar) neurons.

Ossicles. Bones of the middle ear: malleus (hammer), incus (anvil), and stapes (stirrup).

Cochlea. Inner-ear structure that contains the auditory receptor cells.

Basilar membrane. Receptor surface in the cochlea that transduces sound waves into neural activity.

Hair cell. Sensory neurons in the cochlea tipped by cilia; when stimulated by waves in the cochlear fluid, outer hair cells generate graded potentials in inner hair cells, which act as the auditory receptor cells.

the head, are made of cartilage and flesh. The pinna is designed to catch sound waves in the surrounding environment and deflect them into the external ear canal.

The external canal, because it narrows from the pinna, amplifies sound waves somewhat and directs them to the *eardrum* at its inner end. When sound waves strike the eardrum, it vibrates, the rate of vibration varying with the frequency of the waves. On the inner side of the eardrum, as depicted in Figure 9-8, is the middle ear, an air-filled chamber that contains the three smallest bones in the human body, connected to one another in a series.

These three **ossicles** are called the *hammer,* the *anvil,* and the *stirrup* because of their distinctive shapes. The ossicles attach the eardrum to the *oval window,* an opening in the bony casing of the **cochlea,** the inner-ear structure that contains the auditory receptor cells. These receptor cells and the cells that support them are collectively called the *organ of Corti,* shown in detail in Figure 9-8.

When sound waves vibrate the eardrum, those vibrations are transmitted to the ossicles. The ossicles' leverlike action conveys and amplifies the vibrations onto the membrane that covers the cochlea's oval window. As Figure 9-8 shows, the cochlea coils around itself and looks a bit like a snail shell. (The name *cochlea* derives from the Latin word for "snail.") Inside its bony exterior, the cochlea is hollow, as the cross-sectional drawing reveals.

The hollow cochlear compartments are filled with a lymphatic fluid, and floating in its midst is the thin **basilar membrane.** Embedded in a part of the basilar membrane are outer and inner **hair cells.** At the tip of each hair cell are several filaments called *cilia,* and the cilia of the outer hair cells are embedded in an overlying membrane, called the *tectorial membrane.* The inner hair cells loosely contact the tectorial membrane.

Pressure from the stirrup on the oval window makes the cochlear fluid move because a second membranous window in the cochlea (the *round window*) bulges outward as the stirrup presses inward on the oval window. In a chain reaction, the waves that travel through the cochlear fluid cause the basilar and tectorial membranes to bend, and the bending membranes stimulate the cilia at the tips of the outer hair cells. This stimulation generates receptor, or graded, potentials in the inner hair cells, which act as the auditory receptor cells. The change in the membrane potential of the inner hair cells varies the amount of neurotransmitter that they release onto auditory neurons that go to the brain.

The key question is how the conversion of sound waves into neural activity codes the various properties of sound that we perceive. In the late 1800s, German physiologist Hermann von Helmholtz proposed that sound waves of different frequencies cause different parts of the basilar membrane to resonate. Von Helmholtz was not precisely correct. Actually, *all* parts of the basilar membrane bend in response to incoming waves of any frequency. The key is where on the basilar membrane the *peak* displacement takes place.

This solution to the coding puzzle was not determined until 1960, when George von Békésy was able to observe the basilar membrane directly. He saw that a traveling wave moves along the membrane all the way from the oval window to the membrane's apex. The structure and function of the basilar membrane are easier to visualize if the cochlea is uncoiled and laid flat, as in **Figure 9-9.**

George von Békésy
(1899–1972)

The uncoiling structure in Figure 9-9A maps the frequencies to which each part of the basilar membrane is most responsive. When the oval window vibrates in response to the vibrations of the ossicles, shown in Figure 9-9B, it generates waves that travel through the cochlear fluid. Békésy placed little grains of silver along the basilar membrane and watched them jump in different places with different frequencies of incoming waves. Faster wave frequencies caused maximum peaks of displacement near the base of the basilar membrane, whereas slower wave frequencies caused maximum displacement peaks near the membrane's apex.

⊙ For additional information about the structure of the ear, visit the Chapter 9 Web links on the *Brain and Behavior* Web site (**www.worthpublishers.com/kolb**).

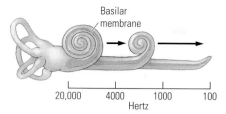

(A) Uncoiling of cochlea

Basilar membrane

20,000   4000   1000   100
Hertz

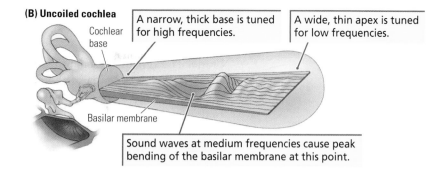

(B) Uncoiled cochlea

Cochlear base

A narrow, thick base is tuned for high frequencies.

A wide, thin apex is tuned for low frequencies.

Basilar membrane

Sound waves at medium frequencies cause peak bending of the basilar membrane at this point.

As a rough analogy, consider what happens when you shake a rope. If you shake it very quickly, the rope waves are very small and short and remain close to the hand in which you are holding the rope. But, if you shake the rope slowly with a broader movement, the longer waves reach their peak farther along the rope. The key point is that, although both rapid and slow shakes of the rope produce movement along the rope's entire length, the maximum displacement of the rope is found at one end or the other, depending on whether the wave movements are rapid or slow.

This same response pattern is true of the basilar membrane to sound-wave frequency. All sound waves cause some displacement along the entire length of the basilar membrane, but the amount of displacement at any point varies with the frequency of the sound wave. In the human cochlea, shown uncoiling in Figure 9-9A, the basilar membrane near the oval window is maximally affected by frequencies as high as about 20,000 Hz, whereas the most effective frequencies at the membrane's apex register less than 100 Hz.

Intermediate frequencies maximally displace points on the basilar membrane between its two ends, as shown in Figure 9-9B. When a wave of a certain frequency travels down the basilar membrane, hair cells at the point of peak displacement are stimulated, resulting in a maximal neural response in those cells. An incoming signal composed of many frequencies causes several different points along the basilar membrane to vibrate and excites hair cells at all these points.

Not surprisingly, the basilar membrane is much more sensitive to changes in frequency than the rope in our analogy is. This degree of sensitivity is achieved because the basilar membrane varies in thickness along its entire length. It is narrow and thick at the base, near the oval window, and wider and thinner at its tightly coiled apex. The combination of varying width and thickness enhances the effect of small differences in frequency on the basilar membrane. As a result, the cochlear receptors can code small differences in sound-wave frequency as neural impulses.

Auditory Receptors

Hair cells ultimately transform sound waves into neural activity. Figure 9-8 shows the anatomy of the hair cells; **Figure 9-10** illustrates how they are stimulated by sound waves. The human cochlea has two sets of hair cells: 3500 inner hair cells and 12,000 outer hair cells. Only the inner hair cells are the auditory receptors. This

Figure 9-9

Anatomy of the Cochlea **(A)** The frequencies to which the basilar membrane is maximally responsive are mapped as the cochlea uncoils. **(B)** Sound waves of different frequencies produce maximal displacement of the basilar membrane (shown uncoiled) at different locations.

Figure 9-10

Transducing Waves into Neural Activity Movement of the basilar membrane creates a shearing force in the cochlear fluid that bends the cilia, leading to the opening or closing of calcium channels in the outer hair cells. The influx of calcium ions leads to the release of transmitter by the inner hair cell, which stimulates an increase in action potentials in auditory neurons.

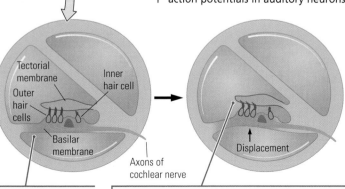

Cochlea

Tectorial membrane

Outer hair cells

Inner hair cell

Basilar membrane

Axons of cochlear nerve

Displacement

Movement of the basilar membrane in response to sound waves...

...creates a shearing force that bends cilia in contact with and near the overlying tectorial membrane. This bending generates neural activity in the hair cells from which the cilia extend.

total number of receptor cells is small, considering the number of different sounds that we can hear.

As diagrammed in Figure 9-10, the hair cells are anchored in the basilar membrane. The tips of the cilia of outer hair cells are attached to the overlying tectorial membrane, but the cilia of the inner hair cells do not touch that membrane. Nevertheless, the movement of the basilar and tectorial membranes causes the cochlear fluid to flow past the cilia of the inner hair cells, bending them back and forth. Animals with intact outer hair cells but no inner hair cells are effectively deaf. The outer hair cells function simply to sharpen the resolving power of the cochlea by contracting or relaxing and thereby changing the stiffness of the tectorial membrane.

How this function of the outer hair cells is controlled is puzzling. What stimulates these cells to contract or relax? The answer seems to be that the outer hair cells, through connections with axons in the auditory nerve, send a message to the brainstem auditory areas and receive a message back that causes the outer hair cells to alter tension on the tectorial membrane. In this way, the brain helps the hair cells to create an auditory world.

A final question remains: How does movement of the cilia alter neural activity? The neurons of the auditory nerve have a tonic rate of firing action potentials, and this rate is changed by how much neurotransmitter is released from the hair cells. It turns out that movement of the hair-cell cilia causes a change in polarization of the hair cell and a change in neurotransmitter release. Look at Figure 9-8 again and you'll notice that the cilia of a hair cell differ in height.

Movement of the cilia in the direction of the tallest results in depolarization, opening calcium channels and leading to the release of neurotransmitter onto the dendrites of the cells that form the auditory nerve, generating more nerve impulses. Movement in the direction of the shortest cilia hyperpolarizes the cell membrane and transmitter release decreases, thus decreasing activity in auditory neurons.

Hair cells are amazingly sensitive to the movement of their cilia. A movement sufficient to allow sound-wave detection is only about 0.3 nm, about the diameter of a large atom. We now can understand why our hearing is so incredibly sensitive.

Figure 9-11

Auditory Pathway Flowchart follows the primary route that auditory stimuli take from the cochlear nucleus through levels of processing in the hindbrain, midbrain, and auditory cortex. Auditory inputs cross to the hemisphere opposite the ear in the hindbrain and midbrain, then recross in the thalamus so that information from each ear reaches both hemispheres. Multiple nuclei process inputs en route to the auditory cortex.

Cochlea of left ear

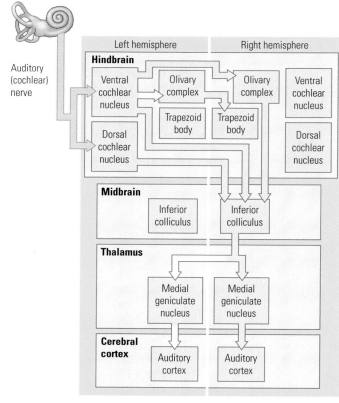

Pathways to the Auditory Cortex

The inner hair cells in the organ of Corti synapse with neighboring bipolar cells, the axons of which form the auditory (cochlear) nerve. The auditory nerve in turn forms part of the eighth cranial nerve, which governs hearing and balance (review Figure 2-26). Whereas ganglion cells in the eye receive inputs from many receptor cells, bipolar cells in the ear receive input from only a single hair-cell receptor.

The cochlear-nerve axons enter the brainstem at the level of the medulla and synapse in the *cochlear nucleus,* which has ventral and dorsal subdivisions. Two other nearby structures in the brainstem, the *superior olive* (a nucleus in the olivary complex) and the *trapezoid body,* each receive connections from the cochlear nucleus, as shown in **Figure 9-11**. The projections from the cochlear nucleus connect with cells on the same side of the brain as well as with cells on the opposite side. This arrangement mixes the inputs from the two ears to form the perception of a single sound.

Both the cochlear nucleus and the superior olive send projections to the *inferior colliculus* in the dorsal midbrain. Two distinct pathways emerge from the inferior colliculus, coursing to the **medial geniculate nucleus,** which lies in the thalamus. The ventral region of the medial geniculate nucleus projects to the **primary auditory cortex (area A1),** whereas the dorsal region projects to the auditory cortical regions adjacent to area A1.

In Chapter 8, you learned about two distinct visual pathways through the cortex: the ventral stream for object recognition and the dorsal stream for the visual control of movement. A similar what–how distinction exists in the auditory cortex (Romanski et al., 1999). Just as we can identify objects by their sound characteristics, we can direct our movements by the sound that we hear.

The role of sound in guiding movement is less familiar to sight-dominated people than it is to the blind. Nevertheless, the ability exists in us all. Imagine waking up in the dark and reaching to pick up a ringing telephone or to turn off an alarm clock. Your hand will automatically form the appropriate shape needed to carry out these movements just on the basis of the sound that you have heard.

That sound is guiding your movements much as a visual image guides them. Although relatively little is known about the auditory pathways in the cortex, one pathway appears to continue through the temporal lobe, much like the ventral visual pathway, and plays a role in identifying auditory stimuli. A second auditory pathway apparently goes to the posterior parietal region, where it forms a type of dorsal pathway for the auditory control of movement.

Medial geniculate nucleus. Major thalamic region concerned with audition.

Primary auditory cortex (area A1). Asymmetrical structures, found within Heschl's gyrus in the temporal lobes, that receive input from the ventral region of the medial geniculate nucleus.

Wernicke's area. Secondary auditory cortex (planum temporale) lying behind Heschl's gyrus at the rear of the left temporal lobe that regulates language comprehension; also called posterior speech zone.

Auditory Cortex

In the human cortex, the primary auditory cortex lies within Heschl's gyrus and is surrounded by secondary cortical areas, as shown in **Figure 9-12A**. The secondary cortex lying behind Heschl's gyrus is called the *planum temporale* (meaning "temporal plane").

In right-handed people, the planum temporale is larger on the left side of the brain than it is on the right, whereas Heschl's gyrus is larger on the right side than on the left. The cortex of the left planum forms a speech zone, known as **Wernicke's area** (the *posterior speech zone*), whereas the cortex of the larger, right-hemisphere Heschl's gyrus has a special role in the analysis of music.

These hemispheric differences mean that the auditory cortex is anatomically and functionally asymmetrical, a fundamental property of the nervous system that we encountered in Chapter 2. Although cerebral asymmetry is not unique to the auditory system, it is most obvious here because the auditory analysis of speech takes place only in the left hemisphere of right-handed people. About 70 percent of left-handed people have the same anatomical

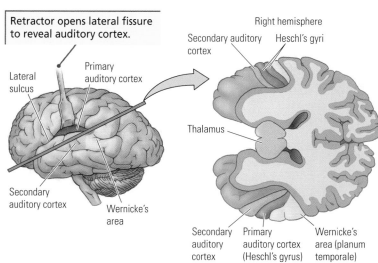

(A) Auditory cortex

Retractor opens lateral fissure to reveal auditory cortex.

Lateral sulcus

Primary auditory cortex

Secondary auditory cortex

Wernicke's area

Right hemisphere

Secondary auditory cortex   Heschl's gyri

Thalamus

Secondary auditory cortex   Primary auditory cortex (Heschl's gyrus)   Wernicke's area (planum temporale)

Left hemisphere

(B) Insula

Thalamus   Corpus callosum   Lateral ventricle

Gustatory cortex

Auditory cortex

Insula

Amygdala   Hippocampus

Figure 9-12

Human Auditory Cortex   **(A)** Diagram of the brain's left hemisphere shows the primary auditory cortex buried within Heschl's gyrus and adjacent secondary regions. In cross section, the posterior speech zone (Wernicke's area) is larger on the left. Heschl's gyrus is larger in the right hemisphere. **(B)** Frontal section showing the extent of the multifunctional insular cortex buried in the lateral fissure.

Lateralization. Process whereby functions become localized primarily on one side of the brain.

Insula. Located within the lateral fissure, multifunctional cortical tissue that contains regions related to language, to the perception of taste, and to the neural structures underlying social cognition.

○ To investigate cortical anatomy and the four lobes, visit the section on the cortex in the module on the central nervous system on your *Foundations of Behavioral Neuroscience* CD. You can also find information on the anatomy of the auditory system in the section on audition in the area on functional neuroanatomy. (See the Preface for more information about this CD.)

asymmetries as right-handers, an indication that speech organization is not related to hand preference. Language, which includes speech and other functions such as reading and writing, also is asymmetrical, although there are some right-hemisphere contributions to these broader functions.

The remaining 30 percent of left-handers fall into two distinct groups. The organization is opposite that of right-handers in about half of these people. The other half have some type of idiosyncratic bilateral representation of speech. That is, about 15 percent of all left-handed people have some speech functions in one hemisphere and some in the other hemisphere.

The localization of language on the side of the brain is often referred to as an example of **lateralization.** We return to lateralization later in this chapter and again in Chapter 14 in connection with thinking. Note here simply that, as a rule of thumb in neuroanatomy, if one hemisphere is specialized for one type of analysis, such as language in the left, the other hemisphere has a complementary function. In regard to audition, the right hemisphere appears to be lateralized for music.

Finally, as you can see in Figure 9-12B, the sulci of the temporal lobe enfold a large volume of cortical tissue. In particular, the cortical tissue buried in the lateral fissure, called the **insula,** is more extensive than the auditory cortex alone. The insular cortex not only has lateralized regions related to language but also contains areas controlling the perception of taste (the gustatory cortex) and areas linked to the neural structures underlying social cognition. We consider both of these topics in Chapter 11. As you might expect, injury to the insula can produce diverse deficits, such as disturbance of both language and taste.

In Review

Incoming sound-wave energy vibrates the eardrum, which in turn vibrates the tiny bones of the middle ear. The innermost ossicle presses on the inner ear's oval window and sets in motion the cochlear fluid. The motion of this fluid vibrates cilia on the outer hair cells in the cochlea by displacing the basilar membrane. This bending generates membrane potential changes in the inner hair cells that alter their neurotransmitter release and the subsequent activity of auditory neurons, thus converting sound waves into changes in neural activity. The frequencies of incoming sound waves are largely coded by the surface areas on the basilar membrane that are most displaced. The axons of bipolar cells of the cochlea form the auditory (cochlear) nerve, which enters the brain at the medulla as part of cranial nerve 8 and synapses on cells in the cochlear nucleus. The neurons of each cochlear nucleus and associated regions in the medulla then begin a pathway that courses to the opposite-side midbrain (inferior colliculus), then recrosses in the thalamus (medial geniculate nucleus), and ends in the left and right auditory cortex. As in the visual system, two different cortical auditory pathways exist, one for sound recognition (like the ventral visual stream) and one for sound localization (like the dorsal visual stream). The auditory cortex on the left and right are asymmetrical, with the planum temporale being larger on the left and Heschl's gyrus being larger on the right in the brains of right-handed people. This anatomical asymmetry is correlated to a functional asymmetry: the left temporal cortex analyzes language-related sounds, whereas the right temporal cortex analyzes music-related ones. Most left-handed people have a similar lateralization, although about 30 percent of left-handers have different patterns. The auditory cortext is part of the multifunctional cortex called the insula, which lies within the lateral fissure.

NEURAL ACTIVITY AND HEARING

We now turn to the ways in which the activities of neurons in the auditory system create our perception of sounds. Neurons at different levels in this system serve different functions. To get an idea of what individual hair cells and cortical neurons do, we consider how the auditory system codes sound-wave energy so that we perceive pitch, loudness, location, and pattern.

Hearing Pitch

Recall that our perception of pitch corresponds to the frequency (repetition rate) of sound waves, which is measured in hertz (cycles per second). Hair cells in the cochlea code frequency as a function of their location on the basilar membrane. The cilia of hair cells at the base of the cochlea are maximally displaced by high-frequency waves that we hear as high-pitched sounds, and those at the apex are displaced the most by low-frequency waves that we hear as low-pitched sounds.

This arrangement is a **tonotopic representation** (literally meaning "tone place"). Because the axons of the bipolar cells that form the cochlear nerve are each connected to only one hair cell, they contain information about the spot on the basilar membrane, from apex to base, that is being stimulated.

If we record from single fibers in the cochlear nerve, we find that, although each axon transmits information about only a small part of the auditory spectrum, the cells do respond to a range of sound-wave frequencies. In other words, each hair cell is maximally responsive to a particular frequency but also responds to nearby frequencies, even though the sound wave's amplitude must be greater (louder) for these nearby frequencies to generate a change in membrane potential.

This range of hair-cell responses to different frequencies at different amplitudes can be plotted to form a tuning curve, as in **Figure 9-13**. Such a sound-wave curve is reminiscent of the light-wave curves in Figure 8-7, which show the responsiveness of cones in the retina to different wavelengths of light. Each type of receptor cell is maximally sensitive to a particular wavelength, but it still responds somewhat to nearby wavelengths.

The axons of the bipolar cells in the cochlea project to the cochlear nucleus in an orderly manner. Those entering from the base of the cochlea connect with one location, those entering from the middle connect to another location, and those entering from the apex connect to yet another. As a result, the tonotopic representation of the basilar membrane is reproduced in the cochlear nucleus.

This systematic representation is maintained throughout the auditory pathways and can be found in cortical area A1, the primary auditory cortex. **Figure 9-14** shows the distribution of projections from the base and apex of the cochlea across area A1. Similar tonotopic maps can be constructed for each level of the auditory system.

Tonotopic representation. Property of audition in which sound waves are processed in a systematic fashion from lower to higher frequencies.

Figure 9-13

Tuning Curves The graphs represent two different axons in the cochlear nerve. Each is plotted by the frequency and amplitude of the sound-wave energy required to increase the firing rate of the neuron. The lowest point on each curve is the frequency to which that hair cell is most sensitive. The upper tuning curve is centered on a midrange frequency of 1000 Hz, whereas the lower tuning curve is centered on a frequency of 10,000 Hz, in the high range of human hearing.

Figure 9-14

Tonotopic Representation of Area A1 The anterior end of the primary auditory cortex corresponds to the apex of the cochlea and hence low frequencies, whereas the posterior end corresponds to the base of the cochlea and hence high frequencies. Heschl's gyrus is buried on the ventral side of the lateral fissure; so a retractor must be used to open the fissure to reveal the underlying auditory cortex.

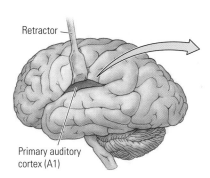

Retractor

Primary auditory cortex (A1)

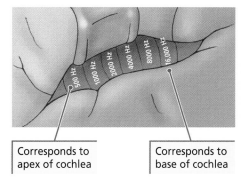

500 Hz | 1000 Hz | 2000 Hz | 4000 Hz | 8000 Hz | 16,000 Hz

Corresponds to apex of cochlea

Corresponds to base of cochlea

Cochlear implant. Electronic device implanted surgically into the inner ear to transduce sound waves into neural activity and allow deaf people to hear.

Cochlear implants bypass the normal route for sound-wave energy by electronically processing incoming stimulation directly to the correct locations on the basilar membrane.

To learn more about the development of the cochlear implant, visit the *Brain and Behavior* Web site (**www.worth publishers.com/kolb**) and go to the Web links for Chapter 9.

The systematic organization of tonotopic maps has enabled the development of **cochlear implants**—electronic devices surgically inserted in the inner ear to allow deaf people to hear (see Loeb, 1990). A miniature microphone-like processor detects the component frequencies of incoming sound waves and sends them to the appropriate place on the basilar membrane through tiny wires. The nervous system does not distinguish between stimulation coming from this artificial device and stimulation coming through the middle ear.

As long as appropriate signals go to the correct locations on the basilar membrane, the brain will "hear." Cochlear implants work very well, even allowing the deaf to detect the fluctuating pitches of speech. Their success corroborates the tonotopic representation of pitch in the basilar membrane.

One minor difficulty with the tonotopic theory of frequency detection is that the cochlea does not use this mechanism at the very apex of the basilar membrane, where hair cells, as well as the bipolar cells to which they are connected, respond to frequencies below about 200 Hz. At this location, *all* the cells respond to movement of the basilar membrane, but they do so in proportion to the frequency of the incoming wave. Higher rates of bipolar cell firing signal a relatively higher frequency, whereas lower rates of firing signal a lower frequency.

Why the cochlea uses a different system to differentiate pitches within this range of very-low-frequency sound waves is not clear. The reason probably has to do with the physical limitations of the basilar membrane. Although discriminating among low-frequency sound waves is not important to humans, animals such as elephants and whales depend on these frequencies to communicate. Most likely they have more neurons at this end of the basilar membrane than we humans do.

Detecting Loudness

The simplest way for cochlear (bipolar) cells to indicate sound-wave intensity is to fire at a higher rate when amplitude is greater, which is exactly what happens. More intense air-pressure changes produce more intense vibrations of the basilar membrane and therefore greater shearing of the cilia. This increased shearing leads to a greater amount of transmitter released onto bipolar cells. As a result, the bipolar axons fire more frequently, telling the auditory system that the sound is getting louder.

Detecting Location

The fact that each cochlear nerve synapses on both sides of the brain provides mechanisms for locating the source of a sound. In one mechanism, neurons in the brainstem compute the difference in a sound wave's arrival time at each ear. Such differences in arrival time need not be large to be detected. If two sounds presented through earphones are separated in time by as little as 10 microseconds, the listener will perceive that a single sound came from the leading ear.

This computation of left-ear–right-ear arrival times is carried out in the medial part of the superior olivary complex (see Figure 9-11). Because these hindbrain cells receive inputs from each ear, they are able to compare exactly when the signal from each ear reaches them.

Figure 9-15 shows how sound waves originating on the left reach the left ear slightly before they reach the right ear. As the sound source moves from the side of the head toward the middle, a person has greater and greater difficulty locating it. The reason is that the difference in arrival time becomes smaller and smaller until there is no difference at all. When we detect no difference, we infer that the sound is either directly in front of us or directly behind us.

To identify the location, we move our heads, making the sound waves strike one ear sooner. We have a similar problem distinguishing between sounds directly above and below us. Again, we solve the problem by tilting our heads, thus causing the sound waves to strike one ear before the other.

Another mechanism used by the auditory system to detect the source of a sound has to do not with the difference in arrival times of sound waves at the two ears, but instead with the sound's relative loudness on the left or the right. The basis of this mechanism is that higher-frequency sound waves do not easily bend around the head; so the head acts as an obstacle. As a result, higher-frequency sound waves on one side of the head are louder than on the other.

This difference is detected in the lateral part of the superior olive and the trapezoid body in the hindbrain. For sound waves coming from directly in front or behind or from directly above or below, the same problem of differentiation exists, requiring the same solution of tilting or turning the head.

Head tilting and turning take time. Although not usually important for humans, time is important for other animals, such as owls, that hunt by using sound. Owls need to know the location of a sound simultaneously in at least two directions (e.g., left and below or right and above).

Owls, like humans, can orient in the horizontal plane to sound waves (called *azimuth detection*) by using the different times at which sound waves reach the two ears. Additionally, the owl's ears have evolved to be slightly displaced in the vertical direction so that they can detect the sound waves' relative loudness in the vertical plane (called *elevation detection*). This solution allows owls to hunt entirely by sound in the dark (**Figure 9-16**). Bad news for mice.

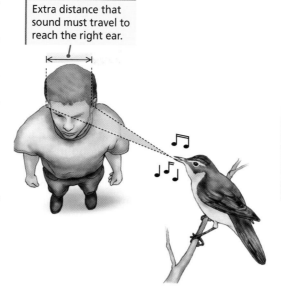

Extra distance that sound must travel to reach the right ear.

Figure 9-15

Locating a Sound Sound waves that originate on the left side of the body reach the left ear slightly before they reach the right ear, allowing us to locate the sound source. But the difference in arrival time is subtle, and the auditory system fuses the dual auditory stimuli so that we perceive a single, clear sound coming from the left.

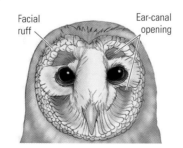

Facial ruff

Ear-canal opening

Figure 9-16

Hunting by Ear (*Left*) For an owl, differences in perceived loudness yield clues to the elevation of a sound source, whereas inter-ear time differences are used to detect the source's horizontal direction. This barn owl has aligned its talons with the body axis of the mouse that it is about to catch in the dark. (*Right*) The facial structure and external ears of the barn owl are formed by rows of tightly packed feathers, the facial ruff that extends from the relatively narrow skull down the length of the face to join below the beak. The ruff collects and funnels sound waves into ear-canal openings through feathered troughs formed by the ruff above and below the eyes. The owl's left ear is more sensitive to sound waves from the left and below, because the ear canal is higher on the left side and the trough is tilted down. The ear canal on the right is lower and the trough is tilted up, making the right ear more sensitive to sound waves from the right and above. Drawing adapted from "The Hearing of the Barn Owl," by E. I. Knudsen, 1981, *Scientific American, 245*(6), p. 115.

Art Wolfe/Tony Stone

Detecting Patterns in Sound

Music and language are perhaps the primary sound-wave patterns that humans recognize. Perceiving sound-wave patterns as meaningful units is thus fundamental to auditory analysis. Because music and language are lateralized in the right and left temporal lobes, respectively, we can guess that neurons in the right and left temporal cortex take part in pattern recognition and analysis of these two auditory experiences. Studying the activities of auditory neurons in humans is not easy, however.

Most of the knowledge that neuroscientists have comes from studies of how individual neurons respond in nonhuman primates. For instance, Peter Winter and Hans Funkenstein (1971) found that neurons in the auditory cortex of the squirrel monkey are specifically responsive to squirrel monkey vocalizations. More recently, Joseph Rauschecker and his colleagues (1995) discovered that neurons in the secondary auditory areas of rhesus monkeys are more responsive to mixtures of sound waves than to pure tones.

Other researchers also have shown that the removal of the temporal auditory cortex abolishes the ability to discriminate the vocalizations made by other members of the species (Heffner and Heffner, 1990). Interestingly, discrimination of species-typical vocalizations in monkeys seems more severely disrupted by injury to the left temporal cortex than to the right. This finding implies a possible functional asymmetry for the analysis of complex auditory material in nonhuman primates, as do the singing primates studied by Geissmann, cited at the beginning of this chapter.

In Review

Neurons in the cochlea form tonotopic maps that code sound-wave frequencies and are maintained throughout the levels of the auditory system. The same cells in the cochlea vary their firing rate, depending on sound-wave amplitude. Detecting the location of a sound is a function of neurons in the superior olive and trapezoid body of the brainstem. These neurons compute differences in sound-wave arrival time and loudness in the two ears. Understanding the sound-wave patterns of music and language requires pattern recognition, which is performed by cortical auditory neurons.

ANATOMY OF LANGUAGE AND MUSIC

This chapter began with the discovery of the Neanderthal flute and its evolutionary implications. The fact that Neanderthals made flutes implies not only that they processed musical sound-wave patterns but also that they made music. In the modern human brain, musical ability is generally a right-hemisphere specialization complementary to language ability, largely localized in the left hemisphere.

No one knows whether these complementary systems evolved together in the hominid brain, but it is certainly very possible that they did. Both language and music abilities are highly developed in the modern human brain. Although little is known about how language and music are processed at the cellular level, electrical stimulation and recording and blood-flow imaging studies have been sources of important insights into the regions of the cortex that process them. We investigate such studies next, focusing first on how the brain processes language.

Processing Language

More than 4000 human languages are spoken in the world today, and probably many others have gone extinct in past millennia. Researchers have wondered whether the brain has a single system for understanding and producing *any* language, regardless of its structure, or whether very different languages, such as English and Japanese, are processed in different ways. To answer this question, it helps to analyze languages to determine just how fundamentally similar they are, despite their obvious differences.

UNIFORMITY OF LANGUAGE STRUCTURE

Foreign languages often seem impossibly complex to nonspeakers. Their sounds alone may seem odd and difficult to make. If you are a native speaker of English, for instance, Asian languages, such as Japanese, probably sound peculiarly melodic and almost without obvious consonants to you, whereas European languages, such as German or Dutch, may sound heavily guttural.

Even within related languages, such as Spanish, Italian, and French, marked differences can make learning one of them challenging, even if the student already knows another. Yet, as real as all these linguistic differences may be, it turns out that they are superficial. The similarities among human languages, although not immediately apparent, are actually far more fundamental than their differences.

Noam Chomsky is usually credited with being the first linguist to stress similarities over differences in human language structure. In a series of books and papers written in the past 40 years, Chomsky made a very sweeping claim, as have researchers such as Steven Pinker (1997) more recently. They argue that all languages have common structural characteristics because of a genetically determined constraint on the nature of human language. Humans, apparently, have a built-in capacity for creating and using language.

When Chomsky first proposed this idea in the 1960s, it was greeted with skepticism, but it has since become clear that human language does indeed have a genetic basis. An obvious piece of evidence: language is universal in human populations. All people everywhere use language.

The complexity of language is not related to the technological complexity of a culture. The languages of technologically primitive peoples are every bit as complex and elegant as the languages of postindustrial cultures. Nor is the English of Shakespeare's time inferior or superior to today's English; it is just different.

Another piece of evidence that Chomsky adherents cite in favor of a genetic basis of human language is that humans learn language early in life and seemingly without effort. By about 12 months of age, children everywhere have started to speak words. By 18 months, they are combining words, and, by age 3 years, they have a rich language capability.

Perhaps the most amazing thing about language development is that children are not formally taught the structure of their language. As toddlers, they are not painstakingly instructed in the rules of grammar. In fact, their early errors—sentences such as "I goed to the zoo"—are seldom even corrected by adults. Yet children master language rapidly.

They also acquire language through a series of stages that are remarkably similar across cultures. Indeed, the process of language acquisition plays an important role in Chomsky's theory of the innateness of language, which is not to say that language development is not influenced by experience.

At the most basic level, for example, children learn the language that they hear spoken. In an English household, they learn English; in a Japanese home, they learn

Japanese. They also pick up the vocabulary and grammar (structure) of the people around them, which can vary from one speaker to another. Children go through a sensitive period for language acquisition, probably from about 1 to 6 years of age. If they are not exposed to language throughout this critical period, their language skills are severely compromised (see Chapter 6).

A third piece of evidence in favor of a genetic basis of language is the many basic structural elements that all languages have in common. Granted, every language has its own particular rules that specify exactly how the various parts of speech are positioned in a sentence (syntax), how words are inflected to convey different meanings, and so forth. But there are also overarching rules that apply to all human languages.

For instance, all languages employ grammar, the parts of speech that we call subjects, verbs, and direct objects. Consider the sentence "Jane ate the apple." "Jane" is the subject, "ate" is the verb, and "apple" is the direct object. Syntax is not specified by any universal rule but rather is a characteristic of the particular language. In English, the order is subject, verb, object; in Japanese, the order is subject, object, verb; in Gaelic, the order is verb, subject, object. Nonetheless, all languages have both syntax and grammar.

The existence of these structural pillars in all human languages can be seen in the phenomenon of *creolization*—the development of a new language from what was formerly a very rudimentary language, or *pidgin*. Creolization took place in the seventeenth-century Americas, when slave traders and the owners of colonial plantations brought together people from various African villages who lacked a common language. Because the new slaves needed to communicate, they quickly created a pidgin based on whatever language the plantation owners spoke—English, French, Spanish, or Portuguese.

The pidgin had a crude syntax (word order) but lacked a real grammatical structure. The children of the slaves who invented this pidgin were brought up by caretakers who spoke only pidgin to them. Yet, within a generation, these children had created their own creole, a language complete with a genuine syntax and grammar.

Clearly, the pidgin invented of necessity by adults was not a learnable language for children. Their innate biology shaped a new language similar in basic structure to all other human languages. All creolized languages seem to evolve in a similar way, even though the base languages are unrelated. This phenomenon could happen only if there were an innate, biolgical component to language development.

LOCALIZATION OF LANGUAGE APPARATUS IN THE BRAIN

Finding a universal basic language structure set researchers on a search for an innate brain system that underlies language use. By the late 1800s, it had become clear that language functions were at least partly localized—not just within the left hemisphere but to specific areas there. Clues that led to this conclusion began to emerge in the early part of the nineteenth century, when neurologists observed patients with frontal-lobe injuries who suffered language difficulties.

Paul Broca
(1824–1880)

Not until 1861, however, was the localization of certain language functions in the left hemisphere confirmed. Paul Broca examined a patient who had entirely lost his ability to speak except to say "tan" and to utter an oath. The man died shortly thereafter, and Broca examined his brain, finding a fresh injury to the left frontal lobe. On the basis of this case and several subsequent cases, Broca concluded that language functions are localized in the left frontal lobe in a region just in anterior to the central fissure. A person with damage in this area is unable to speak despite both an intact vocal apparatus and

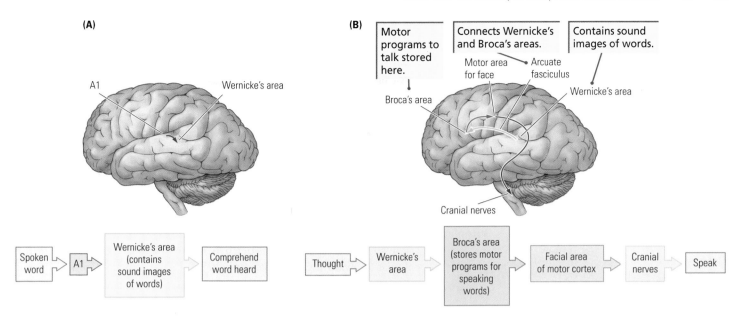

(A)

A1 — Wernicke's area

| Spoken word | → | A1 | → | Wernicke's area (contains sound images of words) | → | Comprehend word heard |

(B)

Motor programs to talk stored here. — Broca's area

Connects Wernicke's and Broca's areas. — Motor area for face — Arcuate fasciculus

Contains sound images of words. — Wernicke's area

Cranial nerves

| Thought | → | Wernicke's area | → | Broca's area (stores motor programs for speaking words) | → | Facial area of motor cortex | → | Cranial nerves | → | Speak |

normal language comprehension. The discovery of **Broca's area** was significant because it initiated the idea that the left and right hemispheres might have different functions.

Other neurologists at the time believed that Broca's area might be only one of several left-hemisphere regions that control language. In particular, neurologists suspected a relation between hearing and speech. Proving this suspicion correct, Karl Wernicke later described patients who had difficulty comprehending language after injury to the posterior region of the left temporal lobe identified as Wernicke's area in **Figure 9-17**.

We referred to Wernicke's area earlier as a speech zone (see Figure 9-12A). Damage to any speech area produces some form of **aphasia,** the general term for any inability to comprehend or produce language despite the presence of normal comprehension and intact vocal mechanisms. At one extreme, people who suffer *Wernicke's aphasia* can speak fluently, but their language is confused and makes little sense, as if they have no idea what they are saying. At the other extreme, a person with *Broca's aphasia* cannot speak despite normal comprehension and intact physiology.

Wernicke went on to propose a model for how the two language areas of the left hemisphere interact to produce speech, diagrammed in Figure 9-17A. He theorized that images of words are encoded by their sounds and stored in the left posterior temporal cortex. When we hear a word that matches one of those sound images, we recognize it, which is how Wernicke's area contributes to speech comprehension.

To *speak* words, Broca's area in the left frontal lobe must come into play, because the motor program to produce each word is stored in this area. Messages are sent to Broca's area from Wernicke's area through a pathway, the *arcuate fasciculus*, that connects the two regions. Broca's area in turn controls the articulation of words by the vocal apparatus, as diagrammed in Figure 9-17B.

Wernicke's model provided a simple explanation both for the existence of two major language areas in the brain and for the contribution of each area to the control of language. But the model was based on postmortem examinations of patients with brain lesions that were often extensive. Not until the pioneering studies of neurosurgeon Wilder Penfield, begun in the 1930s, were the language areas of the left hemisphere clearly and accurately mapped.

Figure 9-17

Neurology of Language In Wernicke's model of speech recognition, summarized in part A, stored sound images are matched to spoken words in the left posterior temporal cortex, shown in yellow. Speech is produced through the connection that the arcuate fasciculus makes between Wernicke's area and Broca's area, as summarized in part **B**.

⊙ For a closer look at the brain structures that control language on your *Foundations* CD, visit the language area in the brain overview section of the module on the central nervous system.

Broca's area. Anterior speech area in the left hemisphere that functions with the motor cortex to produce the movements needed for speaking.

Aphasia. Inability to speak or comprehend language despite the presence of normal comprehension and intact vocal mechanisms; *Broca's aphasia* is the inability to speak fluently despite the presence of normal comprehension and intact vocal mechanisms; *Wernicke's aphasia* is the inability to understand or to produce meaningful language even though the production of words is still intact.

AUDITORY AND SPEECH ZONES MAPPED BY BRAIN STIMULATION

It turns out, among Penfield's discoveries, that instead of Broca's area being the site of speech production and Wernicke's area the site of language comprehension, electrical stimulation of either region disrupts both processes. Penfield took advantage of the chance to map auditory and language areas of the brain when operating on patients undergoing elective surgery to treat intractable epilepsy. If you've read "Epilepsy" on page 111 you know that the goal of this surgery is to remove tissues where the abnormal discharges are localized.

A major challenge is to prevent injury to critical regions that serve important functions. To determine the location of these critical regions, Penfield used a tiny electrical current to stimulate the surface of the brain. By monitoring the response of the patient to stimulation in different locations, Penfield could map brain functions along the cortex.

Typically, two neurosurgeons perform the operation (**Figure 9-18A**), and a neurologist analyzes the electroencephalogram in an adjacent room. Because patients are awake, they can contribute during the procedure, and the effects of brain stimulation in specific regions can be determined in detail and mapped. Penfield placed little numbered tickets on different parts of the brain's surface where the patient noted that stimulation had produced some noticeable sensation or effect, producing the cortical map shown in Figure 9-18B.

When Penfield stimulated the auditory cortex, patients often reported hearing various sounds, a ringing sound like that of a doorbell, a buzzing noise, or a sound like that of birds chirping among them. This result is consistent with those of later studies of single-cell recordings from the auditory cortex in nonhuman primates. Findings in these later studies showed that the auditory cortex has a role in pattern recognition.

Penfield also found that stimulation in area A1 seemed to produce simple tones, ringing sounds, and so forth, whereas stimulation in the adjacent auditory cortex (Wernicke's area) was more apt to cause some interpretation of a sound, ascribing it to a familiar source such as a cricket, for instance. There was no difference in the effects of stimulation of the left or right auditory cortex, and the patients heard no words when the brain was stimulated.

Sometimes, however, stimulation of the auditory cortex produced effects other than the perception of sounds. Stimulation of one area, for example, might cause a patient to experience a sense of deafness, whereas stimulation of another area might produce a distortion of sounds actually being heard. As one patient exclaimed after a

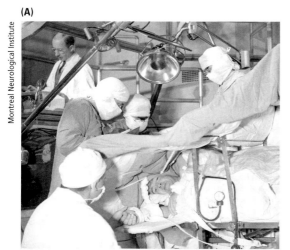

(A)

Montreal Neurological Institute

Figure 9-18

Mapping Cortical Functions   **(A)** The patient is fully conscious during neurosurgery, lying on his right side and kept comfortable with local anesthesia. The left hemisphere of his brain is exposed as Wilder Penfield stimulates discrete cortical areas. In the background, the neurologist monitors the electroencephalogram recorded from each stimulated area, which will help in identifying the eleptogenic focus. The anesthetist (seated) observes the patient's response to the cortical stimulation. **(B)** A drawing of the entire skull overlies a photograph of the patient's exposed brain during surgery. The numbered tickets identify the points that Penfield stimulated to map the cortex. At points 26, 27, and 28, a stimulating electrode produced interference with speech. Point 26 is presumably in Broca's area, 27 is the facial-control area in the motor cortex, and 28 is in Wernicke's area in this patient's brain.

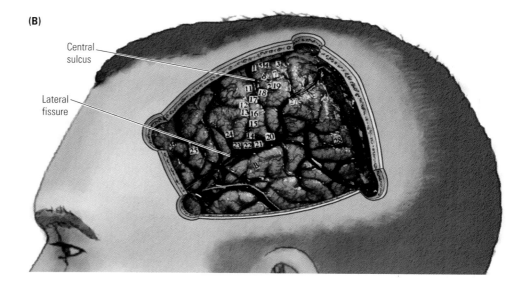

(B)

Central sulcus

Lateral fissure

certain region had been stimulated, "All that you said was mixed up!"

Penfield was most interested in the effects of brain stimulation not on simple sound-wave processing but on language. He and later researchers used electrical stimulation to identify four important cortical regions that control language. The two classic regions—Broca's area and Wernicke's area—are left-hemisphere regions. Located on both sides of the brain are the other two major regions of language use: the dorsal area of the frontal lobes and the areas of the motor and somatosensory cortex that control facial, tongue, and throat muscles and sensations. Although the effects on speech vary, depending on the region, stimulating any of them disrupts speech in some way.

Clearly, much of the left hemisphere takes part in audition, and **Figure 9-19** shows the areas of the left hemisphere that Penfield found engaged in some way in processing language. In fact, Penfield mapped cortical language areas in two ways, first by disrupting speech and then by eliciting speech. Not surprisingly, damage to any speech area produces some form of aphasia.

Disrupting Speech   Penfield expected that electrical current might disrupt ongoing speech by effectively "short-circuiting" the brain. He stimulated different regions of the cortex while the patient was in the process of speaking. In fact, the speech disruptions took several forms, including slurred speech, confusion of words, or difficulty in finding the right word. Such aphasias are detailed in "Left-Hemisphere Dysfunction."

Electrical stimulation of the **supplementary speech area** on the dorsal surface of the frontal lobes, shown in Figure 9-19, can even stop ongoing speech completely, a reaction that Penfield called *speech arrest*. Stimulation of other cortical regions well removed from the temporal and frontal speech areas has no effect on ongoing speech, with the exception of regions of the motor cortex that control movements of the face. This exception makes sense because talking requires movement of facial, tongue, and throat muscles.

Eliciting Speech   The second way that Penfield mapped language areas was to stimulate the cortex when a patient was *not* speaking to see if he could cause the person to utter a speech sound. Penfield did not expect to trigger coherent speech, because cortical stimulation is not physiologically normal and so probably would not produce actual words or word combinations. His expectation was borne out.

Stimulation of regions on both sides of the brain—for example, the supplementary speech areas—produces a sustained vowel cry, such as "Oh" or "Eee." Stimulation of the facial areas in the motor cortex and the somatosensory cortex produces some vocalization related to movements of the mouth and tongue. Stimulation outside these speech-related zones produces no such effects.

AUDITORY CORTEX MAPPED BY POSITRON EMISSION TOMOGRAPHY

Today, researchers use **positron emission tomography** (PET) to study the metabolic activity of brain cells engaged in processing language. PET imaging is based on a surprisingly old idea. In the late 1800s, Angelo Mosso was fascinated by the observation that pulsations in the living brain keep pace with the heartbeat. Mosso believed that the pulsations were related to changes in blood flow in the brain.

He later noticed that the pulsations appeared to be linked to mental activity. For example, when a subject was asked to perform a simple calculation, the increase in

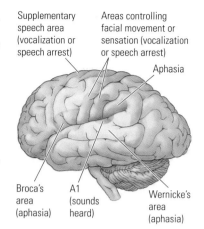

Supplementary speech area (vocalization or speech arrest)

Areas controlling facial movement or sensation (vocalization or speech arrest)

Aphasia

Broca's area (aphasia)

A1 (sounds heard)

Wernicke's area (aphasia)

Figure 9-19

Cortical Regions That Control Language   This map, based on Penfield's extensive study of patients who had surgery for the relief of intractable epilepsy, summarizes areas in the left hemisphere where direct stimulation may interfere with speech or produce vocalization. Adapted from *Speech and Brain Mechanisms* (p. 201), by W. Penfield and L. Roberts, 1956, London: Oxford University Press.

● Visit the Chapter 9 Web links on the *Brain and Behavior* Web site (**www. worthpublishers.com/kolb**) for current research on aphasia.

● For more information on positron emission tomography, visit the PET section in the module on research methods on your *Foundations* CD. There you will find a model of a PET camera and samples of PET scans.

Supplementary speech area. Speech-production region on the dorsal surface of the left frontal lobe.

Positron emission tomography (PET). Imaging technique that detects changes in blood flow by measuring changes in the uptake of compounds such as oxygen or glucose.

Focus on Disorders

Left-Hemisphere Dysfunction

Susan S., a 25-year-old college graduate and mother of two, suffered from epilepsy. When she had a seizure, which was almost every day, she would lose consciousness for a short period, during which she would often engage in repetitive behaviors, such as rocking back and forth. Such psychomotor seizures can usually be controlled by medication, but the drugs were ineffective for Susan. The attacks were very disruptive to her life because they prevented her from driving a car and restricted the types of jobs that she could hold.

So Susan decided to undergo neurosurgery to remove the region of abnormal brain tissue that was causing the seizures. This kind of surgery has a very high success rate. In her case, it entailed the removal of a part of the left temporal lobe, including most of the cortex in front of the auditory areas. Although it may seem to be a substantial amount of the brain to cut away, the excised tissue is usually abnormal; so any negative consequences are typically minor.

After her surgery, Susan did well for a few days, but then she suffered unexpected and unusual complications, which led to the death of the remainder of her left temporal lobe, including the auditory cortex and Wernicke's area. As a result, she was no longer able to understand language, except to respond to the sound of her name and to speak just one phrase: "I love you." Susan was also unable to read, showing no sign that she could even recognize her own name in writing.

To find ways to communicate with Susan, we tried humming nursery rhymes to her. She immediately recognized them and could say the words. We also discovered that her singing skill was well within the normal range and she had a considerable repertoire of songs.

Susan did not seem able to learn new songs, however, and she did not understand us if we "sang messages" to her. Apparently, Susan's musical repertoire was stored and controlled independently of her language system.

brain pulsations and, presumably, in blood flow, was immediate. But to demonstrate a relation between mental activity and blood flow within the brain requires a more quantifiable measure than just visual observation. Various procedures for measuring blood flow in the brain were devised in the twentieth century, one of which is described in "Arteriovenous Malformations." But not until the development of PET in the 1970s could blood flow in the brain of a human subject be measured safely and precisely (Posner and Raichle, 1997), confirming Mosso's observations.

A PET camera, like the one shown in **Figure 9-20,** is a doughnut-shaped array of radiation detectors that encircles a subject's head. A small amount of water, labeled with radioactive molecules, is injected into the bloodstream. The person injected with these molecules is in no danger, because the molecules, such as the radioactive isotope oxygen-15 (^{15}O), are very unstable. They break down in just a few minutes and are eliminated from the body quickly.

The radioactive ^{15}O molecules release tiny, positively charged, subatomic particles known as positrons (electrons with a positive charge). Positrons are emitted from an atom that is unstable because it is deficient in neutrons. The positrons are attracted to the negative charge of electrons in the brain, and the subsequent collision of these two particles leads to both of them being *annihilated*, thus creating energy.

This energy, in the form of two photons, leaves the head at the speed of light and is detected by the PET camera. The photons exit the head in exactly opposite directions from the site of positron–electron annilation at the same speed, and so their source can be identified. A computer identifies the coincident photons and locates the annihilation source.

The PET system enables the measurement of blood flow in the brain because the unstable radioactive molecules accumulate in the brain in direct proportion to the rate of local blood flow. Local blood flow, in turn, is related to neural activity because potassium

Figure 9-20

PET Scanner and Image In the image produced by a PET scan, shown at the far right, brightly colored yellow and red areas are regions of highest blood flow.

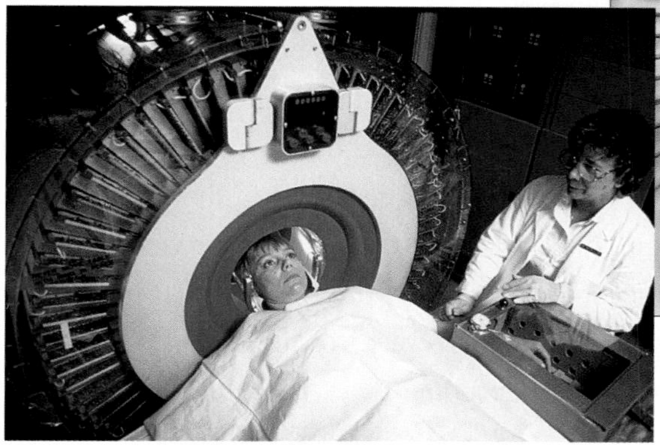

A small amount of radioactively labeled water is injected into a subject. Active areas of the brain use more blood and thus have more radioactive labels.

Annihilation photon detectors

Annihilation photons

Positrons from the radioactivity are released; they collide with electrons in the brain, and photons (a form of energy) are produced, exit the head, and are detected.

Hank Morgan/Science Source/Photo Researchers

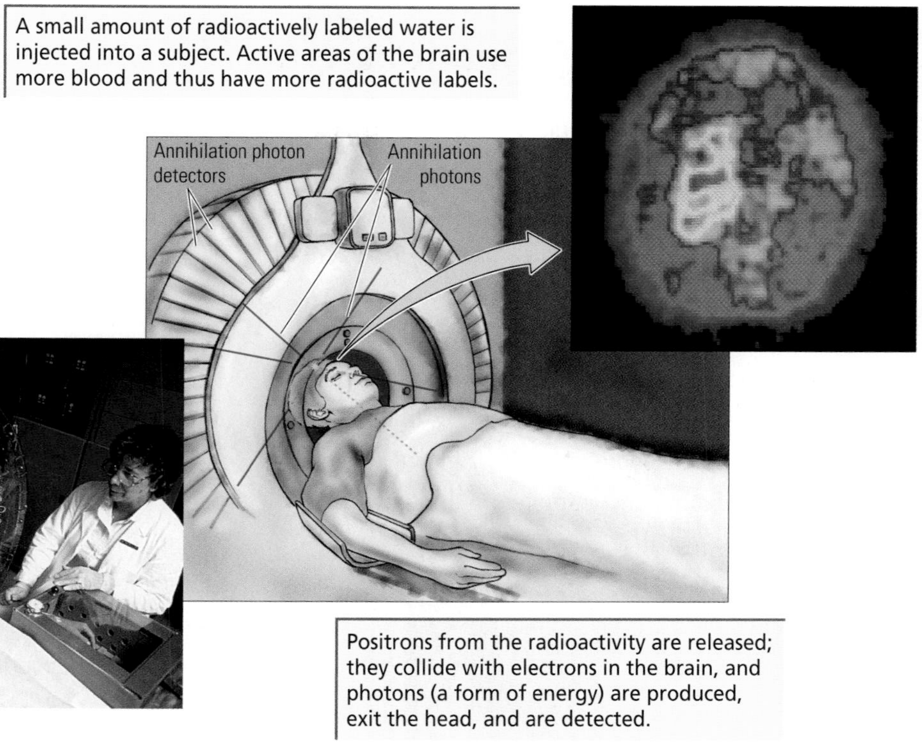

Alan Carruthers/Photo Researchers

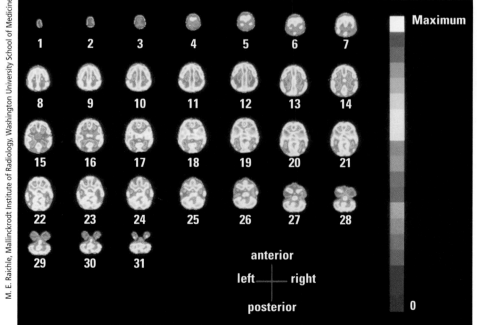

M. E. Raichle, Mallinckrodt Institute of Radiology, Washington University School of Medicine

Maximum

1 2 3 4 5 6 7

8 9 10 11 12 13 14

15 16 17 18 19 20 21

22 23 24 25 26 27 28

29 30 31

anterior

left —— right

posterior

0

Figure 9-21

Resting State PET images of blood flow obtained while a single subject rested quietly with eyes closed. Each scan represents a horizontal section, from the dorsal surface (1) to the ventral surface (31) of the brain.

ions released from stimulated neurons dilate adjacent blood vessels. The greater the blood flow, the higher the radiation counts recorded by the PET camera.

With the use of sophisticated computer imaging, blood flow in the brain when a person is at rest with closed eyes can be mapped (**Figure 9-21**). The map shows where the blood flow is highest in a series of frames. Even though the distribution of blood is not uniform, it is still difficult to conclude very much from such a map.

Arteriovenous Malformations

An arteriovenous malformation (also called an AV malformation or angioma) is a mass of enlarged and tortuous cortical blood vessels that form congenitally. AV malformations are quite common, accounting for as many as 5 percent of all cases of cerebrovascular disease.

Although angiomas may be benign, they often interfere with the functioning of the underlying brain and can produce epileptic seizures. The only treatment is to remove the malformation. This procedure carries significant risk, however, because the brain may be injured in the process.

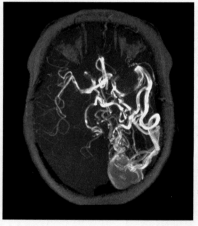

Simon Fraser/Royal Victoria Infirmary/Newcastle Upon Tyne/
Science Photo Library/Photo Researchers

MRI angiogram looking down on the surface of the brain of an 18-year-old girl with an angioma. The abnormal cerebral blood vessels (in white) formed a balloonlike structure (the blue area at lower right) that caused the death of brain tissue around it in the right occipital cortex.

Walter K. was diagnosed with an AV malformation when he was 26 years old. He had consulted a physician because of increasingly severe headaches, and a neurological examination revealed an angioma over his occipital lobe. A surgeon attempted to remove the malformation, but the surgery did not go well; Walter was left with a defect in the bone overlying his visual cortex. This bone defect made it possible to listen to the blood flow through the malformation.

Dr. John Fulton noticed that when Walter suddenly began to use his eyes after being in the dark, there was a prompt increase in the noise (known as a *bruit*) associated with blood flow. Fulton documented his observations by recording the sound waves of the *bruit* while Walter performed visual experiments.

For example, if Walter had his eyes closed and then opened them to read a newspaper, there was a noticeable increase in blood flow through the occipital lobe. If the lights went out, the noise of the blood flow subsided. Merely shining light into Walter's eyes had no effect; nor was there an effect when he inhaled vanilla or strained to listen to faint sounds.

Apparently, the *bruit* and its associated blood flow were triggered by mental effort related to vision. To reach this conclusion was remarkable, given that Fulton used only a stethoscope and a simple recording device for his study. Modern instrumentation, such as that of positron emission tomography, has shown that Fulton's conclusion was correct.

So PET researchers who are studying the link between blood flow and mental activity resort to a statistical trick. They subtract the blood-flow pattern when the brain is in a carefully selected control state, such as that depicted in the images in Figure 9-21, from the pattern of blood flow imaged when the subject is engaged in the experimental task under study. As illustrated in **Figure 9-22**, this subtraction process provides an image of the change in blood flow in the two states. The change can be averaged across subjects to yield a representative, average image difference that reveals which areas of the brain are selectively active during the task.

What happens when PET is used while subjects listen to sounds? Although there are many PET studies of auditory stimulation, a series conducted by Robert Zatorre and his colleagues (1992, 1995) serves as a good example. These researchers hypothesized that simple auditory stimulation, such as bursts of noise, would be analyzed by

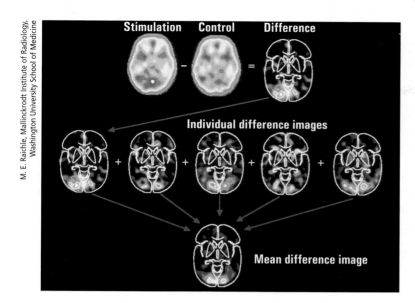

M. E. Raichle, Mallinckrodt Institute of Radiology, Washington University School of Medicine

Stimulation **Control** **Difference**

Individual difference images

Mean difference image

Figure 9-22

The Procedure of Subtraction In the upper row of scans, the control condition of resting while looking at a static fixation point is subtracted from the experimental condition of looking at a flickering checkerboard. The subtraction produces a different scan for each of the five experimental subjects shown in the middle row, but all show increased blood flow in the occipital region. The difference scans are averaged to produce the representative image at the bottom.

area A1, whereas more complex auditory stimulation, such as speech syllables, would be analyzed in adjacent secondary auditory areas.

The researchers also hypothesized that the performance of a speech-sound-discrimination task would selectively activate left-hemisphere regions. This selective activation is exactly what they found. **Figure 9-23A** shows increased activity in the primary auditory cortex in response to bursts of noise, whereas secondary auditory areas are activated by speech syllables (Figure 9-23B and C).

Both types of stimuli produced responses in both hemispheres, but there was greater activation in the left hemisphere for the speech syllables. These results imply that auditory area A1 analyzes all incoming auditory signals, speech and nonspeech, whereas the secondary auditory areas are responsible for some higher-order signal processing required for the analysis of language sound patterns.

As Figure 9-23C shows, the speech-sound-discrimination task yielded an intriguing additional result: during this task, Broca's area in the left hemisphere was activated as well. The involvement of this frontal-lobe region during auditory analysis may seem surprising. In Wernicke's model, Broca's area is considered the place where the motor programs needed to *produce* words are stored. It is not normally a region thought of as the site of speech-sound discrimination.

A possible explanation is that, to determine that the "g" in "bag" and "pig" is the same speech sound, the auditory stimulus must be related to how that sound is actually articulated. That is, the speech-sound perception requires a match with the motor behaviors associated with making that sound.

This role for Broca's area in speech analysis is confirmed further when investigators ask people to determine if a stimulus is a word or a nonword (e.g., "tid" versus "tin" or "gan" versus "tan"). In this type of study, information about how the words are articulated is irrelevant, and Broca's area would not need to be recruited. Imaging reveals that it is not.

Processing Music

Although Penfield did not study the effect of brain stimulation on musical analysis, many researchers study musical processing in brain-damaged patients. "Cerebral Aneurysms" describes one such case. Collectively, the results of these studies confirm

(A) Listening to bursts of noise

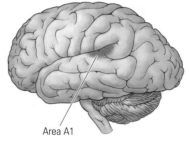

Area A1

(B) Listening to words

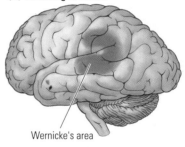

Wernicke's area

(C) Discriminating speech sounds

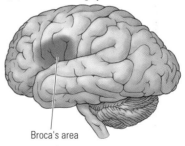

Broca's area

Figure 9-23

Selective Cortical Areas Activated in Different Language-Related Tasks
(A) Passively listening to noise bursts activates the primary auditory cortex. **(B)** Listening to words activates the posterior speech area, including Wernicke's area. **(C)** Making a phonetic discrimination activates the frontal region, including Broca's area.

Cerebral Aneurysms

C. N. was a 35-year-old nurse described by Isabelle Peretz and her colleagues (1994). In December 1986, C. N. suddenly developed severe neck pain and headache. A neurological examination revealed an aneurysm in the middle cerebral artery on the right side of her brain.

An *aneurysm* is a bulge in a blood-vessel wall caused by a weakening of the tissue, much like the bulge that appears in a bicycle tire at a weakened spot. Aneurysms in a cerebral artery are dangerous because, if they burst, severe bleeding and subsequent brain damage result.

In February 1987, C. N.'s aneurysm was surgically repaired, and she appeared to suffer few adverse effects. However, postoperative brain imaging revealed that a new aneurysm had formed in the same location but on the opposite side of the brain. This second aneurysm was repaired 2 weeks later.

After her surgery, C. N. had temporary difficulty finding the right word when she spoke, but, more important, her perception of music was deranged. She could no longer sing, nor could she recognize familiar tunes. In fact, singers sounded to her as if they were talking instead of singing. But C. N. could still dance to music.

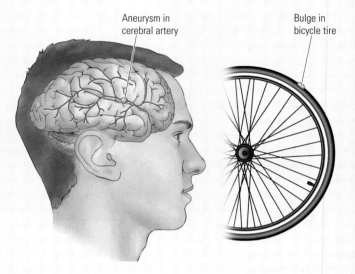

Because her music-related symptoms did not go away, she was given a brain scan. It revealed damage along the lateral fissure in both temporal lobes. The damage did not include the primary auditory cortex, nor did it include any part of the posterior speech zone. For these reasons, C. N. could still recognize nonmusical sound patterns and showed no evidence of language disturbance. This finding reinforces the hypothesis that nonmusical sounds and speech sounds are analyzed in parts of the brain separate from those that process music.

that musical processing is in fact largely a right-hemisphere specialization, just as language processing is largely a left-hemisphere one.

Maurice Ravel
(1875–1937)

An excellent example of right-hemisphere predominance for the processing of music is seen in a famous patient—French composer Maurice Ravel (1875–1937). "Bolero" is perhaps his best-known work. At the peak of his career, Ravel suffered a left-hemisphere stroke and developed aphasia. Yet many of Ravel's musical skills remained intact after the stroke because they were localized to the right hemisphere. He could still recognize melodies, pick up tiny mistakes in music that he heard being played, and even judge the tuning of pianos. His music perception was largely intact.

Interestingly, however, skills that had to do with music production were among those destroyed. Ravel could no longer recognize written music, play the piano, or compose. This dissociation of music perception and music production is curious. Apparently, the left hemisphere plays at least some role in certain aspects of music processing, especially those that have to do with making music.

To find out more about how the brain carries out the perceptual side of music processing, Zatorre and his colleagues (1994) conducted PET studies. When subjects listened simply to bursts of noise, Heschl's gyrus became activated (**Figure 9-24A**), but this was

(A) Listening to bursts of noise

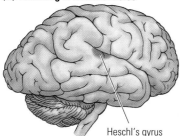

Heschl's gyrus

(B) Listening to melodies

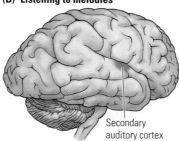

Secondary
auditory cortex

(C) Comparing pitches

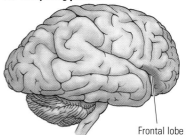

Frontal lobe

not the case when the subjects listened to melodies. As shown in Figure 9-24B, the perception of melody triggers major activation in the right-hemisphere auditory cortex lying in front of Heschl's gyrus, as well as minor activation in the same region of the left hemisphere (not shown).

In another test, subjects listened to the same melodies but this time were asked to indicate whether the pitch of the second note was higher or lower than that of the first note. During this task, which requires short-term memory of what has just been heard, blood flow in the right frontal lobe increased (Figure 9-24C). As with language, then, the frontal lobe plays a role in auditory analysis when short-term memory is required.

As noted earlier, the capacity for language appears to be innate. Sandra Trehub and her colleagues (1999) showed that music may be innate as well, as we hypothesized at the beginning of the chapter. Trehub found that infants show learning preferences for musical scales versus random notes. Like adults, children are very sensitive to musical errors, presumably because they are biased for perceiving regularity in rhythms. Thus, it appears that, at birth, the brain is prepared for hearing both music and language and, presumably, selectively attends to these auditory signals.

Figure 9-24

Selective Cortical Areas Activated in Different Music-Related Tasks
(A) Passively listening to noise bursts activates Heschl's gyrus. **(B)** Listening to melodies activates the secondary auditory cortex. **(C)** Making relative pitch judgments about two notes of each melody activates a right-frontal-lobe area.

In Review

The auditory system has complementary specialization in the cortex: left for language-related analyses and right for music-related ones. This asymmetry, however, appears to be relative, because there is good evidence that the left hemisphere plays a role in some aspects of music-related behaviors and that the right hemisphere has some language capabilities. The results of both electrical-stimulation and PET studies show that the left hemisphere contains several language-related areas. For instance, Wernicke's area identifies speech syllables and words, representations of which are stored in that location. Broca's area matches speech sounds to the motor programs necessary to articulate them, and, in this way, it plays a role in discriminating closely related speech-sound patterns. Additional regions of the frontal lobe play a role in the initiation of speech (supplementary speech area) and in the motor control of facial, tongue, and throat muscles (motor cortex). Damage to different regions of the left hemisphere produces different types of language disruptions (aphasias), whereas damage to the right hemisphere interferes with musical perception.

AUDITORY COMMUNICATION IN NONHUMAN SPECIES

Sound has survival value, as you know if you've ever crossed a busy intersection on foot. Audition is as important a sense to many animals as vision is to humans. Many animals also communicate with other members of their species by using sound, as humans do.

Here we consider just two types of auditory communication in nonhumans: birdsong and echolocation. Each strategy provides a model for understanding different aspects of brain–behavior relations in which the auditory system plays a role.

Birdsong

Of about 8500 living species of birds, about half are considered songbirds. Birdsong has many functions, including attracting mates (usually employed by males), demarcating territories, and announcing location or even mere presence. Although all birds of the same species have a similar song, the details of that song vary markedly from region to region, much as dialects of the same human language vary.

Figure 9-25 includes sound-wave spectrograms for the songs of male white-crowned sparrows that live in three different localities near San Francisco. Notice how the songs of birds are quite different from region to region. These regional differences are due to the fact that song development in young birds is influenced not just by genes but also by early experience and learning. In fact, young birds can acquire more elaborate songs than can other members of their species if the young birds have a good tutor (Marler, 1991).

Birdsong and human language have other broad similarities. Both appear to be innate yet are sculpted by experience. Both are diverse and can vary in complexity. Humans seem to have a basic template for language that is programmed into the brain, and a variety of specific structural forms are added to this template by experience. If a young bird is not exposed to song until it is a juvenile and then listens to recordings of birdsongs of different species, the young bird shows a general preference for the song of its own species. This preference must mean that a species-specific song template exists in the brain of each bird species. As for language, the details of this birdsong template are modified by experience.

Another broad similarity between birdsong and human language mentioned earlier is their great diversity. Among birds, this diversity can also be seen in the sheer number of songs that a species possesses. Species such as the white-crowned sparrow have but a single song; the marsh wren has as many as 150.

The number of syllables in birdsong also varies greatly, ranging from 30 for the canary to about 2000 for the brown thrasher. In a similar way, even though all modern human languages are equally complex, they vary significantly in the type and number of elements that they employ. For instance, the number of meaningful speech-sound patterns in human languages ranges from about 15 (for some Polynesian languages) to about 100 (for some dialects spoken in the Caucasus Mountains).

A final broad similarity between birdsong and human language lies in how they develop. In many bird species, song development is heavily influenced by experience

Figure 9-25

Birdsong Dialects Sound-wave spectrograms of male white-crowned sparrows found in three locales around San Francisco Bay are very similar, but the dialects differ from one another. Thus, like humans, birds raised in different regions have different dialects.

Adapted from "The Instinct to Learn," by P. Marler, 1991, in S. Carey and R. German (Eds.), *The Epigenesis of mind: Essays on biology and cognition* (p. 39), Hillsdale, NJ: Lawrence Erlbaum.

White-crowned sparrow

Point Reyes
Berkeley
San Francisco Bay
Sunset Beach

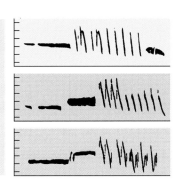

during a so-called sensitive period, just as it is in humans, as you learned in Chapter 6. Birds also go through stages in song development, just as humans go through stages in language development. Hatchlings make noises that attract the attention of their parents, usually for feeding, and human babies, too, emit cries to signal hunger, among other things.

The fledgling begins to make noises that Charles Darwin compared to the prespeech babbling of human infants. These noises, called *subsong*, are variable in structure and low in volume, and they are often produced as the bird appears to doze. Presumably, subsong, like human babbling, is a type of practice for the later development of adult communication after the bird has left the nest.

As a young bird matures, it starts to produce sound-wave patterns that contain recognizable bits of the adult song. Finally, the adult song emerges. In most species, the adult song remains remarkably stable, although a few species, such as canaries, can develop a new song every year.

The neurobiology of birdsong has been a topic of intense research, partly because it provides an excellent model of changes in the brain that accompany learning and partly because it can be a source of insight into how sex hormones influence behavior. Fernando Nottebohm and his colleagues first identified the major structures controlling birdsong in the late 1970s (Nottebohm & Arnold, 1976). These structures are illustrated in **Figure 9-26**.

The largest are the *higher vocal control center* (HVC) and the *nucleus robustus archistriatalis* (RA). The axons of the HVC connect to the RA, which in turn sends axons to the 12th cranial nerve. This nerve controls the muscles of the syrinx, the structure that actually produces the song.

The HVC and RA have several important, and some familiar, characteristics:

■ They are asymmetrical in some species, with the structures in the left hemisphere being larger than those in the right hemisphere. In many cases, this asymmetry is similar to the lateralized control of language in humans: if the left-hemisphere pathways are damaged, the birds stop singing, but similar injury in the right hemisphere has no effect on song.

■ Birdsong structures are sexually dimorphic (see "Hormones and the Range of a Behavior," on page 217). That is, they are much larger in males than in females. In canaries, they are five times as large in the male bird. This sexual difference is due to the hormone testosterone in males. Injection of testosterone into female birds causes the song-controlling nuclei to increase in size.

■ The size of the birdsong nuclei is related to singing skill. For instance, unusually talented singers among male canaries tend to have larger HVCs and RAs than do less-gifted singers.

■ The HVC and RA contain not only cells that produce birdsong but also cells responsive to hearing song, especially the song of a bird's own species.

The same structures therefore play a role in both song production and song perception. This avian neural anatomy is comparable to the overlapping roles of Broca's and Wernicke's areas in language perception and production in humans.

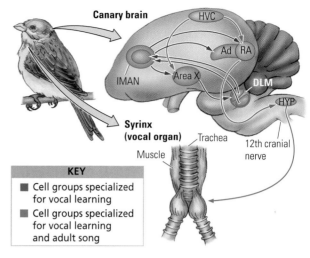

KEY

■ Cell groups specialized for vocal learning

■ Cell groups specialized for vocal learning and adult song

Figure 9-26

Avian Neuroanatomy Lateral view of the canary brain shows several nuclei that control song learning, the two critical ones being the higher vocal control center (HVC) and the nucleus robustus archistriatalis (RA). These areas are necessary both for adult singing and for learning the song. Other regions necessary for learning the song during development but not required for the adult song include the dorsal archistriatum (Ad), the lateral magnocellular nucleus of the anterior neostriatum (IMAN), area X of the avian striatum, and the medial dorsolateral nucleus of the thalamus (DLM).

Echolocation in Bats

Next to rodents, bats are the most numerous order of mammals. The two general groups, or suborders, of bats consist of the smaller echolocating bats (Microchiroptera) and the larger fruit-eating and flower-visiting bats (Megachiroptera), sometimes called flying

Echolocation. Ability to identify and locate an object by bouncing sound waves off the object.

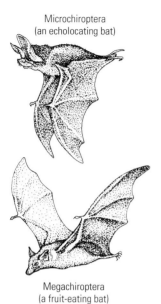

Microchiroptera
(an echolocating bat)

Megachiroptera
(a fruit-eating bat)

foxes. The echolocating bats interest us here because they use sound waves to navigate, to hunt, and to communicate. (Bats are not unique in using sound waves for these purposes. Dolphins are among the marine mammals that use a similar system in water.)

Most of the 680 species of echolocating bats feed on insects. Some others live on blood (vampire bats), and some catch frogs, lizards, fishes, birds, and small mammals. The auditory system of bats is specialized to use echolocation not only to locate targets in the dark but also to analyze the features of targets, as well as features of the environment in general. Through echolocation, a bat identifies prey, navigates through the leaves of trees, and locates surfaces suitable to land on. Perhaps a term analogous to *visualization,* such as "audification," would be more appropriate.

Echolocation works rather like sonar. The larynx of a bat emits bursts of sound waves at ultrasonic frequencies that bounce off objects and return to the bat's ears, allowing the animal to identify what is in the surrounding environment. The bat, in other words, navigates by the echoes that it hears, differentiating among the different characteristics of those echoes.

Objects that are moving, such as insects, have a moving echo. Smooth objects give a different echo from rough objects, and so on. A key component of this echolocation system is the analysis of differences in the return times of echoes. Close objects return echoes sooner than more distant objects do, and the textures of various objects' surfaces impose minute differences in return times.

A bat's cries are of short duration (ranging from 0.3 to 200 ms) and high frequency (from 12,000 to 200,000 Hz; see Figure 9-5). Most of this range lies at too high a frequency for the human ear to detect. Different bat species produce sound waves of different frequency that depend on the animal's ecology. Bats that catch prey in the open use different frequencies from those used by bats that catch insects in foliage and from those used by bats that hunt for prey on the ground.

The echolocation abilities of bats are impressive. The results of laboratory studies show that a bat with a 40-cm wing span can fly in total darkness through 14-by-14-cm openings in a grid of nylon threads only 80 μm thick, as shown in **Figure 9-27**. Bats in the wild can be trained to catch small food particles thrown up into the air in the dark. These echolocating skills make the bat a very efficient hunter. The little brown bat, for instance, can capture very small flying insects, such as mosquitoes, at the remarkable rate of two per second.

Researchers have considerable interest in the neural mechanisms of bat echolocation. Each bat species emits sound waves in a relatively narrow range of frequencies, and a bat's auditory pathway has cells specifically tuned to echoes in the frequency range of its species. For example, the mustached bat sends out sound waves ranging from 60,000 to 62,000 Hz, and its auditory system has a *cochlear fovea* (a maximally sensitive area in the organ of Corti) that corresponds to that frequency range. In this way, more neurons are dedicated to the frequency range used for echolocation than to any other range of frequencies.

Analogously, recall that our visual system dedicates more neurons to the retina's fovea, the area responsible for our most detailed vision. In the cortex of the bat's brain, several distinct areas process complex echo-related inputs. For instance, one area computes the distance of given targets from the animal, whereas another area computes the velocity of a moving target. This neural system makes the bat exquisitely adapted for nighttime navigation.

Figure 9-27

Born with Sonar A bat with a 40-cm wingspan can navigate through openings in a 14-by-14-cm mesh made of 80-μm nylon thread while flying in total darkness. The echolocating bat creates an accurate map of the world based entirely on auditory information.

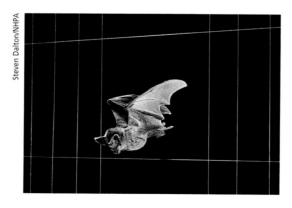

Steven Dalton/NHPA

In Review

The analysis of birdsong has identified several important principles of auditory functioning similar to those observed in human language, reinforcing the idea that many characteristics of human language may be innate. One principle underlying birdsong is that specialized structures in the avian brain produce and perceive vocal stimuli. Another is that these structures are influenced by early experience. Third, an innate template imposes an important constraint on the nature of the songs that a bird produces and perceives. Insect-eating bats employ high-frequency sound waves as biological sonar that allows them to navigate in the dark and to catch insects on the fly as well as to communicate with others of their species. An echolocating bat's auditory world is easily as rich as our visual world because it contains information about the shape and velocity of objects—information that our visual system provides. Humans do not hear nearly as well as bats, but we see much better.

SUMMARY

■ *What do language and music contribute to our auditory world?* Although we take language and music for granted, they play central roles in our mental lives as well as in our social lives. Both language and music provide a way to communicate with other people—and with ourselves. They also faciliate social identification, parenting, and cultural transmission.

■ *What is the nature of the stimulus that the brain perceives as sound?* The stimulus for the auditory system is the energy of sound waves that results from changes in air pressure. The ear transduces three fundamental physical qualities of sound-wave energy: frequency (repetition rate), amplitude (size), and complexity. Perceptually, neural networks in the brain then translate these energies into the pitch, loudness, and timbre of the sounds that we hear.

■ *How does the nervous system transduce changes in air pressure into our impression of sounds?* Beginning in the ear, a combination of mechanical and electrochemical systems transform sound waves into auditory perceptions—what we hear. Changes in air pressure are conveyed in a mechanical chain reaction from the eardrum to the bones of the middle ear to the oval window of the cochlea and the cochlear fluid that lies behind it in the inner ear. Movements of the cochlear fluid produce movements in specific regions of the basilar membrane, leading to changes in the electrochemical activity of the auditory receptors, the inner hair cells found on the basilar membrane that send neural impulses through the auditory nerve into the brain.

■ *How does the auditory system analyze sound waves?* The basilar membrane has a tonotopic organization. High-frequency sound waves maximally stimulate hair cells at their base, whereas low-frequency sound waves maximally stimulate hair cells at the apex, enabling cochlear neurons to code various sound frequencies. Tonotopic organization of sound-wave analysis is found at all levels of the auditory system, and the system also detects both amplitude and location. Sound amplitude is coded by the firing rate of cochlear neurons, with louder sounds producing higher firing rates than softer sounds do. Location is detected by structures in the brainstem that compute differences in the arrival times and the loudness of a sound in the two ears.

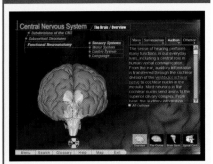

■ *What pathway does information travel from the auditory receptors to the neural cortex?* The hair cells of the cochlea synapse with bipolar neurons that form the cochlear nerve, which in turn forms part of the eighth cranial nerve. The cochlear nerve takes auditory information to three structures in the hindbrain: the cochlear nucleus, the superior olive, and the trapezoid body. Cells in these areas are sensitive to differences in both sound-wave intensity and arrival times in the two ears. In this way, they enable the brain to locate a sound. The auditory pathway continues from the hindbrain areas to the inferior colliculus of the midbrain, then to the medial geniculate nucleus in the thalamus, and finally to the auditory cortex. Like vision, dual pathways exist in the auditory cortex, one for pattern recognition and the other for controlling movements in auditory space. Cells in the cortex are responsive to specific categories of sounds, such as species-specific communication.

■ *How does the brain understand language and music?* Despite differences in speech-sound patterns and structures, all human languages have the same basic foundation of a syntax and a grammar. This fundamental similarity implies an innate template for creating language. The auditory areas of the cortex in the left hemisphere play a special role in analyzing language-related information, whereas those in the right hemisphere play a special role in analyzing music-related information. Among several language-processing areas in the left hemisphere, Wernicke's area identifies speech syllables and words and so is critically engaged in speech comprehension. Broca's area matches speech-sound patterns to the motor behaviors necessary to make them and so plays a major role in speech production. Broca's area also discriminates between closely related speech sounds. The primary auditory cortex of the right hemisphere plays a critical role in comprehending music. The right temporal lobe also analyzes prosody, the melodical qualities of speech.

■ *How does brain organization relate to the unique auditory worlds of other species?* Non-human species have evolved specialized auditory structures and behaviors. One example is birdsong. Regions of songbirds' brains are specialized for producing and comprehending song. In many species, these regions are lateralized to the left hemisphere, analogous in a way to how language areas are lateralized to the left hemisphere in most humans. The similarities between the development of song in birds and the development of language in humans, as well as similarities in the neural mechanisms underlying both the production and the perception of song and language, are striking. Both owls and bats can fly and catch prey at night by using only auditory information to guide their movement. Echolocating bats evolved a biological sonar that allows them to map of the objects in their world, just as humans map their visual worlds. This mainly auditory reality we humans can only try to imagine.

KEY TERMS

REVIEW QUESTIONS

1. What are the three physical properties of sound waves, and how does the auditory system code each one?

2. How does the auditory system code the location of a sound?

3. Why do all human languages have the same basic structure?

4. How is language perception organized in the brain?

5. How is blood flow measured in the brain, and what does it tell us about brain function?

6. Give a simple neurobiological explanation of how we understand and produce language.

7. What can we learn from birdsong that is relevant to human auditory function?

FOR FURTHER THOUGHT

1. Different species have different ranges of hearing. Why would such differences be adaptive?

2. What is special about language and music?

RECOMMENDED READING

Drake-Lee, A. B. (1992). Beyond music: Auditory temporary threshold shift in rock musicians after a heavy metal concert. *Journal of the Royal Society of Medicine, 85,* 617–619. Have you ever wondered what listening to loud music might be doing to your hearing? This paper looks at the effects of hearing loud music at a rock concert on hearing thresholds in the musicians. What is important to remember is that the musicians are standing beside the speakers, and so those in the front rows are likely to hear even louder music.

Gazzaniga, M. S. (1992). *Nature's mind.* New York: Basic Books. Michael Gazzaniga is an eminent cognitive neuroscientist who has an easy writing style. He has written several popular books, such as *Nature's Mind,* each of which is chock full of interesting ideas about how the brain works. This book is a pleasure to read and introduces the reader to Gazzaniga's ideas about why the brain is asymmetrically organized and what the fundamental differences between the hemispheres might be.

Luria, A. R. (1972). *The man with a shattered world.* Chicago: Regnery. Alexander Luria wrote many neuropsychology books in his long career, but this one is perhaps the most interesting and accessible to the nonspecialist. This book describes the effect of a bullet wound to the head of a university student who was recruited to defend Leningrad in World War II. The book has many anecdotes, often humorous, that show how the young man's mental world was severely altered by this traumatic experience. Reading this book can be a source of insight into what it is like to cope with brain damage.

Peretz, I. & Zatorre, R.J. (Eds.) (2001) The biological foundations of music. New York: New York Academy of Sciences. The origins, organization, and neural control of music is a fascinating topic. This book is a wonderful summary of what is known.

Pinker, S. (1997). *How the mind works.* New York: Norton. Steven Pinker gives us a provocative look at theories of how brain activity produces mental events. For those interested in cognitive neuroscience, this book is a good introduction to questions that we might ask in everyday life. For example, why does a face look more attractive with makeup? Or, why is the thought of eating worms disgusting?

How Does the Nervous System Respond to Stimulation and Produce Movement?

Left: **Dr. David Scott/Phototake.** *Middle:* **Corbis.** *Right:* **Dr. Scott T. Grafton/Visuals Unlimited.**

Portrait of an Artist

Kamala (the name means "lotus flower") is a female Indian elephant that lives at the zoo in Calgary, Canada. Her trunk, which is really just a greatly extended upper lip and nose, consists of about 2000 fused muscles. A pair of nostrils runs its length, and fingerlike projections are located at its tip. The skin of the trunk is soft and supple and is covered sparsely with sensory hairs.

Like all elephants, Kamala uses her trunk for many purposes—to gather food, scratch an ear, rub an itchy eye, or caress a baby. It can also be used to explore. Kamala raises her trunk to sniff the wind, lowers it to examine the ground for scents, and sometimes even pokes it into another elephant's mouth to investigate the food there.

Like other elephants, Kamala can inhale as much as 4 liters of water into her trunk, which she can then place in her mouth to drink or squirt over her body to bathe. She can also inhale dust or mud for bathing.

Kamala's trunk is a potential weapon. She can flick it as a threat, lash out with it in aggression, and throw things with it. Her trunk is both immensely strong and very agile. With it, Kamala can lift objects as large as an elephant calf or uproot entire trees. Yet this same trunk can grasp a single peanut from the palm of a proffered hand.

Kamala also uses her versatile trunk in one very unusual way (Onodera & Hicks, 1999). She is one of only a few elephants in the world that paints with its trunk. Like many artists, Kamala, pictured here at her easel, paints when it suits her. She has commemorated many important zoo events on canvas.

The idea of an elephant artist is not as far-fetched as it may at first seem. Other elephants, both in the wild and in captivity, pick up small stones and sticks and draw in the dust with them. But Kamala has gone well beyond this simple doodling. When given paints and a brush, she began to produce works of art, many of which have been sold to collectors. As have some other domesticated elephants, Kamala has achieved an international reputation as an artist (Komar & Melamid, 2004).

The Calgary Zoological Society

Born in 1975 in Sri Lanka's Yala National Park and orphaned as an infant, Kamala was adopted by the Calgary, Alberta, Zoological Society. Kamala began painting as part of an environmental enrichment program, and her paintings are widely sold to collectors.

A defining feature of animals is their ability to move. We humans display the most-skilled motor control of all animals, but members of many species display highly dexterous movements, as Kamala illustrates. This chapter explores how the nervous system produces movement.

We begin by considering how the control of movement is organized in the nervous system. Then we examine the various contributions of the neocortex, the brainstem, and the spinal cord to movements both gross and fine. Next we investigate how the basal ganglia and the cerebellum help to fine-tune our control of movement.

Finally, we turn to the role of the somatosensory system—the body senses of touch and balance. Although other senses, such as vision and hearing, play a part in enabling movement, body senses play a special role, as you will soon discover.

HIERARCHICAL CONTROL OF MOVEMENT

When Kamala paints a picture, her behaviors are sequentially organized. First, she looks at her canvas and her selection of paints, then, she considers what she wants to paint, and, finally, she executes her painting. These sequentially organized behaviors are dictated by the hierarchical organization of Kamala's nervous system. The major components of this nervous system hierarchy are the neocortex, the brainstem, and the spinal cord. All contribute to controlling the behaviors required to produce her artwork.

In the same way, your hierarchically organized nervous system controls every movement that you make. **Figure 10-1** shows the sequence of steps executed by the human nervous system in directing a hand to pick up a mug. The visual system must first inspect the cup to determine what part of it should be grasped. This information is then relayed from the visual cortex to cortical motor regions, which plan and initiate the movement, sending instructions to the part of the spinal cord that controls the muscles of the arm and hand.

As you grasp the handle of the cup, information from sensory receptors in the fingers travels to the spinal cord, and from there messages are sent to sensory regions of the cortex that control touch. The sensory cortex, in turn, informs the motor cortex that the cup is now being held. Other regions of the brain also participate in controlling the movement, as you learned in Chapter 2. For example, the basal ganglia help to produce the appropriate amount of force, and the cerebellum helps to regulate timing and corrects any movement errors.

Although at this point you probably will not remember all these various steps in controlling an everyday movement, refer to Figure 10-1 when you reach the end of this chapter as a way of reviewing what you have learned. The important concept to remember right now is simply the hierarchical organization of the entire system.

Recall, again from Chapter 2, that the idea that the nervous system is hierarchically organized originated with English neurologist John Hughlings-Jackson a century ago. He thought of the nervous system as being organized into a number of layers. Successively higher levels control more-complex aspects of behavior by acting through the lower levels. The

Figure 10-1

Sequentially Organized Movement
Movements such as reaching for a cup require the participation of broad areas of the nervous system. The brain tells the hand to reach, and the hand tells the brain that it has succeeded.

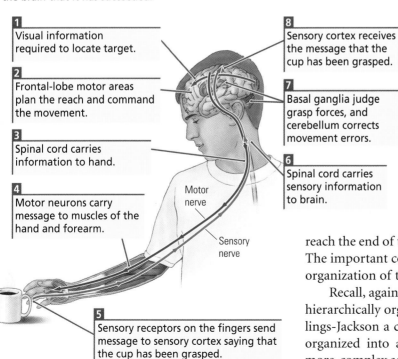

1 Visual information required to locate target.

2 Frontal-lobe motor areas plan the reach and command the movement.

3 Spinal cord carries information to hand.

4 Motor neurons carry message to muscles of the hand and forearm.

5 Sensory receptors on the fingers send message to sensory cortex saying that the cup has been grasped.

6 Spinal cord carries sensory information to brain.

7 Basal ganglia judge grasp forces, and cerebellum corrects movement errors.

8 Sensory cortex receives the message that the cup has been grasped.

Motor nerve

Sensory nerve

three major levels in Hughlings-Jackson's model are the same as those just mentioned for Kamala: the forebrain, the brainstem, and the spinal cord. Hughlings-Jackson also proposed that, within these divisions, further levels of organization could be found.

Hughlings-Jackson adopted the concept of hierarchical organization from evolutionary theory. He knew that the chordate nervous system had evolved gradually: the spinal cord had developed in worms; the brainstem in fish, amphibians, and reptiles; and the forebrain in birds and mammals.

Because each level of the nervous system had developed at different times, Hughlings-Jackson reasoned that each must have some functional independence. Consequently, if higher levels of the nervous system were damaged, the result would be regression to the simpler behaviors of "lower" animals, a phenomenon that Hughlings-Jackson called **dissolution.** The brain-damaged person would still possess a repertoire of behaviors, but they would be more typical of animals that had not yet evolved the destroyed brain structure.

A hierarchically organized structure such as the mammalian nervous system, however, does not operate piece by piece. It functions as a whole, with the higher regions working through and influencing the actions of the lower ones. In the control of movement, many parts of the nervous system participate, with some regions engaged in sensory control, others in planning and commanding the movement, and still others in actually carrying the action out. To understand how all these various regions work together to produce even a simple movement, such as picking up a mug, we will consider the major components of the hierarchy one by one, starting at the top with the forebrain.

The Forebrain and Initiating Movement

Complex movements consist of many components. Take painting a work of art. Your perceptions of what is appearing on the canvas must be closely coordinated with the brush strokes that your hand makes to achieve the desired effect.

The same high degree of control is necessary for many other complex behaviors. Consider playing basketball. At every moment, decisions must be made and actions must be performed. Dribble, pass, and shoot are different categories of movement, and each can be carried out in numerous ways. Skilled players choose among the categories effortlessly and execute the movements seemingly without thought.

One explanation of how we control movements that was popular in the 1930s centers on the concept of feedback. It holds that, after we perform an action, we wait for feedback about how well that action has succeeded, and then we make the next movement accordingly. But Karl Lashley (1951), in an article titled "The Problem of Serial Order in Behavior," found fault with this explanation.

Lashley argued that movements, such as those required for playing the piano, were performed too quickly to rely on feedback about one movement shaping the next movement. The time required to receive feedback about the first movement combined with the time needed to develop a plan for the subsequent movement and send a corresponding message to muscles was simply too long to permit piano playing. Lashley suggested that movements must be performed as **motor sequences,** with one movement module held in readiness while an ongoing sequence is being completed.

According to this view, all complex behaviors, including playing the piano, painting pictures, and playing basketball, require the selection and execution of multiple movement sequences. As one sequence is being executed, the next sequence is being

Dissolution. Hypothetical condition whereby disease or damage in the highest levels of the nervous system would produce not just loss of function but a repertory of simpler behaviors as seen in animals that have not evolved that particular brain structure.

Motor sequence. Movement modules preprogrammed by the brain and produced as a unit.

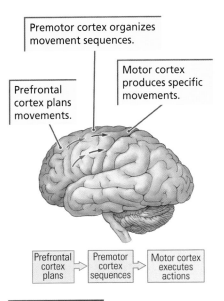

Prefrontal cortex plans movements.

Premotor cortex organizes movement sequences.

Motor cortex produces specific movements.

| Prefrontal cortex plans | → | Premotor cortex sequences | → | Motor cortex executes actions |

Figure 10-2

Initiating a Motor Sequence

prepared so that the second can follow the first smoothly. Interestingly, the act of speaking seems to bear out Lashley's view. When people use complex rather than simple sequences of words, they are more likely to pause and make "umm" and "ahh" sounds, suggesting that it is taking them more time than usual to organize their word sequences.

The frontal lobe of each hemisphere is responsible for planning and initiating motor sequences. The frontal lobe is divided into a number of different regions, including the three illustrated in **Figure 10-2**. From front to back, they are the prefrontal cortex, the premotor cortex, and the primary motor cortex.

At the top of this hierarchy, a function of the prefrontal cortex is to plan complex behaviors. Such a plan might be deciding to get up at a certain hour to arrive at work on time, deciding to stop at the library to return a book that is due, or deciding whether an action is right or wrong and thus whether it should be performed at all. Humans with prefrontal cortex injury often break social and legal rules not because they do not know them or the consequences of breaking them but because their decision making is faulty (Chapter 14). The prefrontal cortex does not specify the precise movements to be made. Like a business executive, it simply specifies the goal toward which movements should be directed.

To bring a plan to completion, the prefrontal cortex sends instructions to the premotor cortex, which produces the complex movement sequences appropriate to the task. If the premotor cortex is damaged, such sequences cannot be coordinated, and the goal cannot be accomplished. For example, the monkey on the right in **Figure 10-3** has a lesion in the dorsal part of its premotor cortex. It has been given the task of extracting a piece of food wedged in a hole in a table (Brinkman, 1984). If it simply pushes the food with a finger, the food will drop to the floor and be lost.

The monkey has to catch the food by holding a palm beneath the hole as the food is being pushed out. This brain injured animal is unable to make the two complementary movements together. It can push the food with a finger and extend an open palm, but it cannot coordinate these actions of its two hands, as the normal monkey on the left can. The premotor cortex also contains "mirror neurons" that discharge when the subject performs an action, such as reaching for food, or when the subject observes another individual performing the same movement. Mirror neurons allow a subject to make, observe, and represent movement sequences (Fadiga & Craighero, 2004).

The premotor cortex organizes movement sequences but does not specify how each movement is to be carried out. Those details are the responsibility of the primary motor cortex, which is responsible for executing skilled movements. To understand its role, consider some of the movements that we use to pick up objects.

Figure 10-3

Premotor Control On a task requiring both hands, the normal monkey can push the peanut out of a hole with one hand and catch it in the other but, 5 months after lesioning of the premotor cortex, the experimental monkey cannot. Adapted from "Supplementary Motor Area of the Monkey's Cerebral Cortex: Short- and Long-Term Effects after Unilateral Ablation and the Effects of Subsequent Callosal Section," by C. Brinkman, 1984, *Journal of Neuroscience, 4*, p. 925.

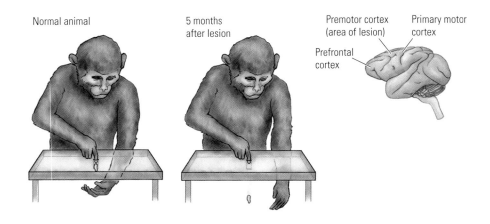

Normal animal

5 months after lesion

Premotor cortex (area of lesion)

Primary motor cortex

Prefrontal cortex

In using the pincer grip (**Figure 10-4A**), we hold an object between the thumb and index finger. This grip not only allows small objects to be picked up easily but also allows us to use whatever is held with considerable skill. In contrast, in using the power grasp (Figure 10-4B), we hold an object much less dexterously but with more power by simply closing the fingers around it.

Clearly, the pincer grip is a more demanding movement because the two fingers must be placed precisely on the object. People with damage to the primary motor cortex have difficulty correctly shaping their fingers to perform the pincer grip. They also have difficulty in performing many skilled movements of the hands, arms, or trunk (Lang & Schieber, 2004).

In summary, the frontal lobe in each hemisphere plans, coordinates, and executes precise movements. The regions of the frontal cortex that perform these functions are hierarchically related. After the prefrontal cortex has formulated a plan of action, it instructs the premotor cortex to organize the appropriate sequence of behaviors, and the movements themselves are executed by the motor cortex.

The hierarchical organization of frontal-lobe areas in producing movements is supported by findings from studies of cerebral blood flow, which serves as an indicator of neural activity. **Figure 10-5** shows the regions of the brain that were active as subjects in one such study performed different tasks (Roland, 1993).

Figure 10-4

Getting a Grip In a pincer grip **(A)**, an object is held between the thumb and index finger. In a power grasp, or whole-hand grip **(B)**, an object is held against the palm of the hand with the digits.

(A)

Blood flow increased in the hand area of the primary somatosensory and primary motor cortex when subjects used a finger to push a lever.

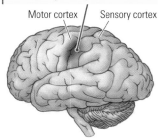

Motor cortex / Sensory cortex

(B)

Blood flow increased in the premotor cortex when subjects performed a sequence of movements.

Dorsal premotor cortex

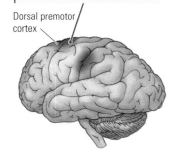

(C)

Blood flow increased in the prefrontal and temporal cortex when subjects used a finger to find a route through a maze.

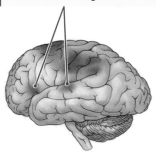

Figure 10-5

Hierarchical Control of Movement in the Brain
Adapted from *Brain Activation* (p. 63), by P. E. Roland, 1993, New York: Wiley-Liss.

As the subjects used a finger to push a lever, increased blood flow was limited to the primary somatosensory and primary motor cortex. As the subjects executed a sequence of finger movements, blood flow also increased in the premotor cortex. And, as the subjects used a finger to trace their way through a maze, a task that requires the coordination of movements in relation to a goal, blood flow increased in the prefrontal cortex as well.

Notice that blood flow did not increase throughout the entire frontal lobe as the subjects were performing these tasks. Blood flow increased only in those regions taking part in the required movements.

The Brainstem and Species-Typical Movement

Species-typical behaviors are actions displayed by every member of a species—the pecking of a robin, the hissing of a cat, or the breaching of a whale. In a series of studies, Swiss neuroscientist Walter Hess (1957) found that the brainstem controls

EXPERIMENT 10-1

Question: What are the effects of brainstem stimulation under different conditions?

Procedures

Results

Stimulating electrode in brainstem

Electrical stimulation alone produces restless behavior.

Electrical stimulation and the presence of a fist produces slight threat.

Electrical stimulation in the presence of a stuffed polecat (a type of weasel) produces vigorous threat.

Continued electrical stimulation in the presence of the stuffed polecat produces flight and screeching.

Conclusion

Stimulation of some brainstem sites produces behavior that depends on context, suggesting that an important function of the brainstem is to produce appropriate species-typical behavior.

Adapted from *The Collected Papers of Erich von Holst* (p. 121), translated by R. Martin, 1973, Coral Gables, FL: University of Miami Press.

species-typical behaviors. Hess developed the technique of implanting electrodes into the brains of cats and other animals and cementing them in place. These electrodes could then be attached to stimulating leads in the freely moving animal without causing the animal much discomfort.

By stimulating the brainstem, Hess was able to elicit almost every innate movement that the animal might be expected to make. A resting cat could be induced to suddenly leap up with an arched back and erect hair as though frightened by an approaching dog, for example. The movements elicited began abruptly when the stimulating current was turned on and ended equally abruptly when the stimulating current was turned off. The animal subjects performed such species-typical behaviors in a subdued manner when the stimulating current was low, but they increased in vigor as the stimulating current was turned up.

The actions varied, depending on the site that was stimulated. Stimulating some sites produced head-turning, others produced walking or running, and still others elicited displays of aggression or fear. The animal's reaction toward a particular stimulus could be modified accordingly. For instance, when shown a stuffed toy, a cat responded to electrical stimulation of some sites by stalking the toy and to stimulation of other sites with a fearful response and withdrawal.

Hess's experiments have been confirmed and expanded by other researchers with the use of many different animal species. For instance, **Experiment 10-1** shows the effects of brainstem stimulation on a chicken under various conditions (von Holst, 1973). Notice the effect of context: how the site stimulated interacts both with the presence of an object to which to react and with the stimulation's duration.

With stimulation of a certain site alone, the chicken displays only restless behavior. When a fist is displayed, the same stimulation elicits slightly threatening behavior. When the object displayed is then switched from a fist to a stuffed polecat, the chicken responds with vigorous threats. Finally, with continued stimulation in the presence of the polecat, the chicken flees, screeching.

Such experiments show that an important function of the brainstem is to produce species-typical adaptive behavior. Hess's classic experiments also gave rise to a sizable science-fiction literature in which "mind control" induced by brain stimulation figures centrally in the plot.

The brainstem also controls movements used in eating and drinking and in sexual behavior. Animals can be induced to display these survival-related behaviors when certain areas of the brainstem are stimulated. An animal can even be induced to eat nonfood objects, such as chips of wood, if the part of the brainstem that triggers eating is sufficiently stimulated. The brainstem is also important for maintaining posture, for standing upright, for making coordinated movements of the limbs, for swimming and walking, and for grooming the fur and making nests.

Grooming is a particularly complex movement pattern coordinated mainly by the brainstem (Aldridge, 2005). A grooming rat sits back on its haunches, licks its paws, wipes its nose with its paws, then wipes its paws across its face, and finally turns to lick the fur on its body. These movements are always performed in the same order. The next time you dry off after a shower or swimming, note the "grooming sequence" that you use. Humans' grooming sequence is very similar to the one that rats use.

The effects of damage to regions of the brainstem that organize movement sequences can be seen in the effects of **cerebral palsy.** A disorder primarily of motor function, cerebral palsy is caused by brain trauma in the course of fetal development or at birth (recall "Cerebral Palsy" on page 196). Trauma leading to cerebral palsy can sometimes happen in early infancy as well.

We examined E. S., a man who suffered a cold and infection when he was about 6 months old. Subsequently, he had great difficulty in coordinating his movements. As he grew up, his hands and legs were almost useless, and his speech was extremely difficult to understand. For most of his childhood, E. S. was considered retarded and was sent to a custodial school.

When he was 13 years old, the school bought a computer, and one of his teachers attempted to teach E. S. to use it by pushing the keys with a pencil that he held in his mouth. Within a few weeks, the teacher realized that E. S. was extremely intelligent and could communicate and complete school assignments on his computer. He was eventually given a motorized wheelchair that he could control with finger movements of his right hand.

Assisted by his computer and wheelchair, E. S. soon became almost self-sufficient and eventually attended college, where he achieved excellent grades and became a student leader. On graduation with a degree in psychology, he became a social worker and worked with children who suffered from cerebral palsy.

Clearly, a brain injury that causes cerebral palsy can be extremely damaging to movement while leaving sensory abilities and cognitive capacities unimpaired. Damage to the brainstem can also cause changes in cognitive function, such as occurs in **autism.** The severe symptoms of this disorder include greatly impaired social interaction, a bizarre and narrow range of interests, marked abnormalities in language and communication, and fixed repetitive movements (see "Autism").

The Spinal Cord and Executing Movement

On Memorial Day weekend in 1995, Christopher Reeve, a well-known actor who portrayed Superman in three films, was thrown from his horse at the third jump of a riding competition in Culpeper, Virginia. Reeve's spinal cord was severed near its upper end, at the C1–C2 level (see Figure 2-27). The injury left Reeve's brain intact and functioning and his remaining spinal cord intact and functioning, too, but his brain and spinal cord were no longer connected.

As a result, other than movements of his head and slight movement in his shoulders, Reeve's body was completely paralyzed. He was even unable to breathe without assistance. A generation ago such a severe injury would have been fatal, but modern and timely medical treatment allowed Reeve to survive.

Reeve, who died in October 2004 owing to complications from an infection, leveraged his celebrity to campaign for disabled people, fighting to prevent lifetime caps on insurance compensation for spinal-cord injuries, raising money for spinal-cord research, even testifying before Congress. Reeve's tireless pursuit toward recovery included regaining some ability to breathe on his own, recovering sensation over 70 percent of his body, and making stepping movements when assisted. His progress is a source of dramatic new insight into the possibilities for functional recovery after spinal-cord injury.

The spinal cord is sometimes viewed simply as a pathway for conveying information between the brain and the rest of the body. It does serve this function. If the spinal cord is severed, a person loses sensation and voluntary movements below the cut.

Cerebral palsy. Group of brain disorders that result from brain damage acquired perinatally.

Autism. Cognitive disorder with severe symptoms including greatly impaired social interaction, a bizarre and narrow range of interests, marked abnormalities in language and communication, and fixed, repetitive movements.

(*Top*) Christopher Reeve portraying Superman in a 1980 still from *Superman II.* (*Bottom*) As a result of his spinal-cord injury, Reeve had little movement below his neck but never stopped working toward the day that he would walk again. He is shown here with his wife, Dana, in 2002.

Autism

Leo Kanner and Hans Asperger first used the term *autism* (from the Greek *autos,* meaning "self") in the 1940s to describe children who seem to live in their own self-created worlds. Although some of these children were classified as mentally retarded, others' intellectual functioning was preserved.

An estimated 1 in 500 people has autism. Although it knows neither racial nor ethnic nor social boundaries, autism is four times as prevalent in boys as in girls. Many autistic children are noticeably different from birth. To avoid physical contact, these babies arch their backs and pull away from their caregivers or they become limp when held. But approximately one-third of autistic children develop normally until somewhere between 1 and 3 years of age. Then the autistic symptoms emerge.

Perhaps the most recognized characteristic of autism is a failure to interact socially with other people. Some autistic children do not relate to other people on any level. The attachments that they do form are to inanimate objects, not to other human beings.

Another common characteristic of autism is an extreme insistence on sameness. Autistic children vehemently resist even small modifications to their surroundings or their daily routines. Objects must always be placed in exactly the same locations, and tasks must always be carried out in precisely the same ways.

One reason for this insistence on sameness may be an inability to understand and cope with novel situations. Autistic children also have marked impairments in language development. Many do not speak at all, and others repeat words aimlessly with little attempt to communicate or convey meaning.

These children also exhibit what seem like endlessly repetitive body movements, such as rocking, spinning, or

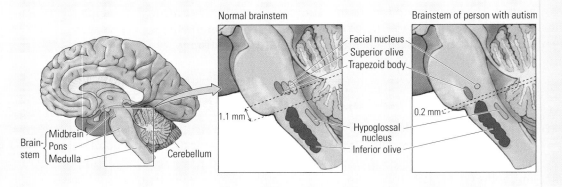

Autism affects the brainstem, where several nuclei in the posterior pons are reduced in size, including the facial nucleus, superior olive, and trapezoid body.

⊙ For additional information about current research on spinal-cord injury, visit the Chapter 10 Web links on the *Brain and Behavior* Web site (**www.worthpublishers.com/kolb**).

Paraplegia. Paralysis of the legs due to spinal-cord injury.

Quadriplegia. Paralysis of the legs and arms due to spinal-cord injury.

If the cut is low, **paraplegia** results: paralysis and loss of sensation are confined to the legs and lower body, as described in "Spinal-Cord Injury." A cut higher on the spinal cord, such as Christopher Reeve survived, entails paralysis and loss of sensation in the arms as well as the legs, a condition called **quadriplegia.**

In addition to its role in transmitting messages to and from the brain, the spinal cord is capable of producing many movements without any brain involvement. Movements that depend on the spinal cord alone are collectively called *spinal-cord reflexes.* Some of these automatic movements entail the limbs. For example, a light touch to the surface of the foot causes the leg to extend reflexively to contact the object that is touching it. This reflex aids the foot and leg in contacting the ground to bear weight in walking. Other reflexes result in limb withdrawal. For instance, a noxious stimulus applied to a hand causes the whole arm to reflexively pull back, thereby avoiding the injurious object.

flapping the hands. Some may engage as well in aggressive or self-injurious behavior. The severity of these symptoms varies. Some are severely impaired, whereas others learn to function quite well. Still others have exceptional abilities in music, art, or mathematics.

As might be expected of a disorder with the range of symptoms seen in autism, anatomical studies reveal abnormal structures and cells in a number of brain regions, including the limbic system and the cerebellum. Brain scans indicate that the cerebellum may be smaller in people with autism than in control subjects.

At birth, children with autism have relatively small heads compared with normal children, but, over the first year, 60 percent develop an excessive increase in head size, largely owing to an increase in the volume of the neocortex (Courchesne & Akshoomoff, 2003). Brain imaging also shows that the sulci in the frontal lobes of children with autism retain an immature organization (Levitt et al., 2003). Together these findings suggest that the normal sculpturing

of the brain in early infancy, in which there is normally a loss of cells, dendrites, and synapses to sculpture the adult brain, is abnormal in autistism.

An indication of a genetic influence on developing autism stems from the finding that both members of identical twin pairs are more likely than are those of fraternal twin pairs to develop the disorder. Patricia Roder (2000) suggested that one cause may be an abnormality in the gene that plays a central role in the development of the brainstem. She found that an area of the brainstem in the caudal part of the pons is small in people diagnosed autistic, as the accompanying diagram shows. Several nuclei in this area, including the nucleus that controls facial muscles, are either small or missing, which may lead to subtle facial abnormalities such as those shown in the photographs.

Evidence also reveals that a virus can trigger autism. Women have an increased risk of giving birth to an autistic child if they are exposed to rubella (German measles) in the first trimester of pregnancy. Researchers also suspect that industrial toxins can trigger autism, but the evidence remains uncertain.

Photos courtesy of Susan L. Hyman

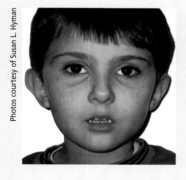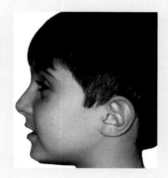

Although children with autism often are normal in appearance, some physical anomalies characterize the disorder. The corners of the mouth may be low compared with the upper lip, and the tops of the ears may flop over (*left*). The ears may be a bit lower than normal and have an almost square shape as well (*right*).

Spinal circuits can also produce more-complex reflexive movements. An example is the stepping reflex. If body weight is supported while the feet are in contact with a conveyor belt, the legs "walk" reflexively to keep up with the belt.

Each leg has its own neural circuit that allows it to step. When the limb is moved backward on the conveyor belt, causing the foot to lose support, the limb reflexively lifts off the belt and swings forward underneath the body. As the foot then touches the surface of the belt again, tactile receptors initiate the reflex that causes the foot to push against the surface and support the body's weight. In this way, several spinal reflexes work together to produce the complex movement of walking. Because this walking is reflexive, even a newborn baby will display it when held in the correct position on a conveyor belt.

One of the more complex reflexes that can be observed in other vertebrates is the **scratch reflex.** Here, an animal reflexively scratches a part of its body in response to a

Scratch reflex

Scratch reflex. Automatic response in which the hind limb reaches to remove a stimulus from the surface of the body.

Spinal-Cord Injury

Each year, on average, about 11,000 people in the United States and 1000 people in Canada suffer spinal-cord injury. Often the spinal cord is completely severed, leaving the victim with no sensation or movement from the site of the cut downward. Although 12,000 people annually incurring spinal-cord injury may seem like a large number, it is small relative to the number in these two countries who suffer other kinds of nervous system damage each year. Recall from Chapter 1, for example, that complications related to head trauma disable a reported 80,000 Americans in a year.

To increase public awareness about their condition and promote research into possible treatments, some, like Christopher Reeve, become activists. Canadian Rick Hansen, pictured here, is especially active. He may even have been a role model for Reeve.

Hansen, an athletic teenager, became a paraplegic as the result of a lower thoracic spinal injury in 1975. Twelve years later, to raise public awareness to the potential of people with disabilities, Rick wheeled himself 40,000 kilometers around the world, generating more than $24 million for the Man in Motion Legacy Trust Fund. To date, the Fund has contributed more than $100 million in support of spinal-cord research, rehabilitation, wheelchair sports, and public-awareness programs.

Courtesy of Nike/Rick Hansen Institute

Rick Hansen on the Man in Motion Tour in 1987.

Rick Hansen is currently executive director of the Rick Hansen Institute at the University of British Columbia. The Institute provides leadership and support for initiatives in the field of disability research, with a special focus on spinal-cord injury.

Research to find treatments for spinal-cord damage is a frustrating field. A severed spinal cord, like a severed electrical cord, entails just a single cut that leaves the machinery on both sides of it intact. If only the cut could somehow be bridged, function might be restored. Reconnecting a severed electrical cord is easy—just strip and reconnect the wires. Restoring a severed spinal cord is not so easy.

Among the factors preventing nerve fibers from growing across a cut in a spinal cord are the formation of scar tissue, a lack of a blood supply, and the absence of appropriate growth factors to stimulate neuron growth. Add to these factors the fact that normal tissue at the edge of the cut actively repels regrowth. Can these obstacles be overcome? From a theoretical and experimental perspective, spinal-cord regeneration and recovery do seem achievable.

The results of studies suggest that it may be possible to induce neural fibers to grow across a spinal-cord cut. For instance, if the spinal cord in chicks and other baby animals is cut in the first 2 weeks of life, the spinal cord regrows and apparently normal function returns. Presumably, if the mixture of growth factors that enables this regeneration can be identified and applied to the severed spinal cords of adults, the same regrowth could result.

Also encouraging is the finding that, when a nerve fiber in the peripheral nervous system is cut, it regrows no matter how old the injured person is. Schwann cells that form the severed axon's myelin are thought to produce the chemical environment that facilitates this regrowth. Results of experiments in which Schwann cells are implanted into a cut spinal cord have been positive, although no cure has as yet been effected.

Other investigators, who built little bridges across a severed spinal cord, also obtained some encouraging evidence of regrowth. Rats that had been unable to move their legs regained postural support and were able to step after receiving this treatment.

stimulus from the surface of the body. The complexity of the scratch reflex is revealed in the accuracy of the movement. Without direction from the brain, the tip of a limb, usually a hind limb, can be correctly directed to the part of the body that is irritated.

In humans and other animals with a severed spinal cord, spinal reflexes still function, even though the spinal cord is cut off from communication with the brain. As a result, the paralyzed limbs may display spontaneous movements or spasms. But the brain can no longer guide the timing of these automatic movements. Consequently, reflexes related to bladder and bowel control may need to be artificially stimulated by caregivers.

In Review

The motor system is organized hierarchically. The forebrain, especially the frontal lobe, is responsible for selecting plans of action, coordinating body parts to carry out those plans, and executing precise movements. The brainstem, in contrast, is responsible for species-typical movements, for survival-related actions, and for posture and walking. In addition to being a pathway between the brain and the rest of the body, the spinal cord is independently responsible for reflexive movements. Although lower-level functions in this hierarchical system can continue in the absence of higher-level ones, it is the higher levels that provide voluntary control over movements. Consequently, when the brain is disconnected from the spinal cord, movement can no longer be controlled at will.

ORGANIZATION OF THE MOTOR SYSTEM

If we compare how Kamala paints a picture with her trunk with how human artists paint with their hands, the achievement of the same goal by such different behavioral strategies may seem remarkable. But the use of different body parts for skilled movements is widespread among animals. Dolphins and seals are adept at using their noses to carry and manipulate objects, and many other animals, including domestic dogs, accomplish the same end by using their mouths. Birds' beaks are specially designed for getting food, for building nests, and sometimes even for making and using tools.

Tails also are useful appendages. Some marsupials and some species of New World primates use their tails to pick up and carry objects. Among horses, the lips are dexterous enough to manipulate a single blade of grass of the type that a horse prefers from a patch of vegetation. Although humans tend to rely primarily on their hands for manipulating objects, they can still learn to handle things with other body parts, such as the mouth or a foot, if they have to. Some people without arms become extremely proficient at using a foot for writing or painting or even for driving.

What properties of the motor system allow such versatility in carrying out skilled movements? In this section, you will find the answer to this question as we examine the organization of the motor cortex and its descending pathways to the brainstem and spinal cord, which in turn connects with the muscles of the body.

The Motor Cortex

In 1870, two Prussian physicians, Gustav Fritsch and Eduard Hitzig, electrically stimulated the neocortex of an anesthetized dog and produced movements of the mouth, limbs, and paws on the opposite side of the dog's body. They provided the first direct evidence that the neocortex controls movement. Later researchers confirmed the finding by

◉ For a review of the organization of movement and motor systems, visit the section on organization of the motor systems in the control of movement module on your *Foundations of Behavioral Neuroscience* CD. (See the Preface for more information about this CD.)

Homunculus. Representation of the human body in the sensory or motor cortex; also any topographical representation of the body by a neural area.

Topographic organization. Neural spatial representation of the body or areas of the sensory world perceived by a sensory organ.

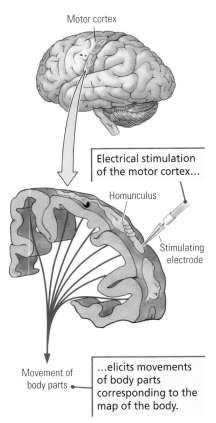

Motor cortex

Electrical stimulation of the motor cortex...

Homunculus

Stimulating electrode

Movement of body parts

...elicits movements of body parts corresponding to the map of the body.

Figure 10-6

Penfield's Homunculus Movements are topographically organized in the motor cortex. Stimulation of the dorsal medial regions of the cortex produces movements in the lower limbs. Stimulation in ventral regions of the cortex produces movements in the upper body, hands, and face.

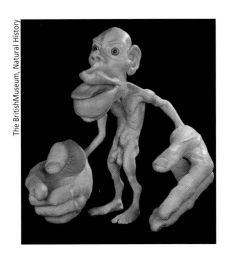

The BritishMuseum, Natural History

Figure 10-7

Homuncular Man An artist's representation illustrates the disproportionate areas of the sensory and motor cortices that control different parts of the body.

using a variety of animals as subjects, including primates such as monkeys and apes.

On the basis of this research background, beginning in the 1930s, Wilder Penfield used electrical stimulation to map the cortices of conscious human patients who were about to undergo neurosurgery with the aim of using the results to assist surgery (see Figure 9-18). He and his colleagues confirmed that movements in humans also are triggered mainly in response to stimulation of the primary motor cortex.

Penfield summarized his results by drawing cartoons of body parts to represent the areas of the primary motor cortex that produce movement in those parts. The result was a **homunculus** (little person) that could be spread out across the motor cortex, as illustrated in **Figure 10-6**. Because the body is symmetrical, an equivalent motor homunculus is represented in the cortex of each hemisphere, and each mainly controls movement in the opposite side of the body. Penfield also identified another, smaller motor homunculus in the dorsal premotor area of each frontal lobe, a region sometimes referred to as the *supplementary motor cortex*.

The most striking feature of the motor homunculus is the disproportionate relative sizes of its body parts, shown in **Figure 10-7**, compared with the relative sizes of actual parts of the human body. As you can see, the homunculus has very large hands with an especially large thumb. Its lips and tongue are especially prominent as well. In contrast, the trunk, arms, and legs, which constitute most of the area of a real body, are much smaller in relative size. These distortions illustrate the fact that large parts of the motor cortex regulate the hands, fingers, lips, and tongue, giving us precise motor control over these body parts. Areas of the body over which we have much less motor control have a much smaller representation in the motor cortex.

Another curious feature of the homunculus as laid out across the motor cortex is that the body parts are arranged much differently from those of an actual body. The area of the cortex that produces eye movements is located in front of the homunculus head on the motor cortex, as shown in the upper drawing in Figure 10-6. The head is oriented with the chin up and the forehead down, and the tongue is located below the forehead.

Such details aside, the homunculus shows at a glance that relatively larger areas of the brain control the parts of the body that we use to make the most skilled movements. It is thus a useful concept for understanding the **topographic organization** (functional layout) of the primary motor cortex.

The discovery of the topographical representation of the motor cortex suggested how movements might be produced. Information from other regions of the neocortex could be sent to the motor homunculus, and neurons in the appropriate part of the homunculus could then execute the movements called for. If finger movements are needed, for example, messages can be sent to the finger area of the motor cortex, triggering the required activity there. If this model of how the motor system works is correct, damage to any part of the homunculus would result in loss of movement in the corresponding part of the body.

Although the general idea underlying this model is correct, more-detailed mapping of the motor cortex and more-detailed studies of the effects of damage to it indicate that the picture is a bit more complex. When researchers investigated the motor cortex in nonhuman primates, with the use of smaller electrodes than those used by Penfield to examine his patients, they discovered as many as 10 motor homunculi (Galea & Darian-Smith, 1994). As many as 4 representations of the body may exist in the primary motor cortex, and a number of other representations may be found in the premotor cortex.

What each of these different homunculi does is still unclear. Perhaps each is responsible for a particular class of movements. Perhaps we select different parts of different homunculi for different movements, as a piano player selects different keys on a piano to play different cords. Whatever the functions turn out to be, they will have to be described by future research.

Corticospinal Tracts

The main pathways from the motor cortex to the brainstem and spinal cord are called the **corticospinal tracts.** (Recall from Chapter 2 that bundles of nerve fibers within the central nervous system are called *tracts;* outside the CNS they are called *nerves.* The term *corticospinal* indicates that these fiber bundles begin in the neocortex and terminate in the spinal cord.) The axons of the corticospinal tracts originate mainly in layer V pyramidal cells of the motor cortex. Axons also come from the premotor cortex and the sensory cortex.

The axons from the motor cortex descend into the brainstem, sending collaterals to a few brainstem nuclei and eventually emerging on the brainstem's ventral surface. There they form a large bump on each side of the brainstem surface. These bumps, known as *pyramids,* give the corticospinal tracts their alternate name, the *pyramidal tracts.*

At this point, most of the axons descending from the left hemisphere cross over to the right side of the brainstem. Likewise, most of the axons descending from the right hemisphere cross over to the left side of the brainstem. The rest of the axons stay on their original sides.

This division produces two corticospinal tracts, one uncrossed and the other crossed, entering each side of the spinal cord. **Figure 10-8** illustrates the division of tracts originating in the left-hemisphere cortex. The dual tracts on each side of the brainstem then descend into the spinal cord, forming the two spinal cord tracts.

In the cross section of the spinal cord in **Figure 10-9**, you can see the location of the two tracts on each side. Those fibers that cross to the opposite side of the brainstem descend the spinal cord in a lateral (side) position, giving them the name *lateral corticospinal tract.* Those fibers that remain on

Corticospinal tract. Bundle of nerve fibers directly connecting the cerebral cortex to the spinal cord, branching at the brainstem into an opposite-side lateral tract that informs movement of limbs and digits and a same-side ventral tract that informs movement of the trunk; also called pyramidal tract.

◉ On your *Foundations* CD, visit the section on the primary motor cortex in the module on the control of movement for a more detailed analysis of the motor homunculus. Notice the exaggerated body parts associated with fine motor control.

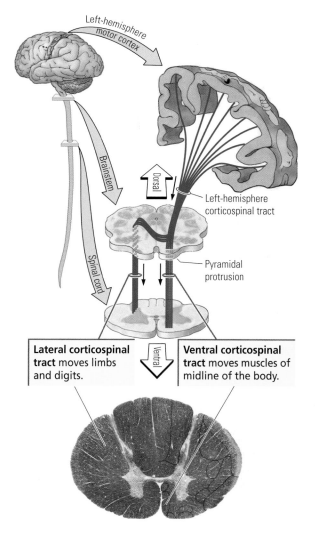

Figure 10-8

Corticospinal Tract   Nerve fibers from each hemisphere (only the tract from the left hemisphere is shown here) descend from the motor cortex to the brainstem, where they produce a protrusion (a pyramid) on the ventral surface. There the tract branches into the spinal cord. A lateral tract crosses the midline to the opposite side of the spinal cord, and a ventral tract remains on the same side. Fibers in the lateral tract are represented by the limbs and digits of the cortical homunculus and are destined to move muscles of the limbs and digits. Fibers of the ventral tract are represented by the midline of the homunculus and are destined to move muscles of the midline of the body. Photograph of spinal cord reproduced from *The Human Brain: Dissections of the Real Brain,* by T. H. Williams, N. Gluhbegovic, and J. Jew, on CD-ROM. Published by Brain University, brain-university.com 2000.

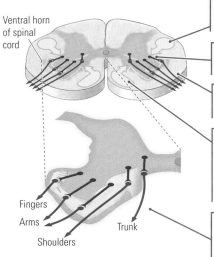

Ventral horn of spinal cord

Lateral corticospinal tract synapses with interneurons and motor neurons that innervate muscles of the limbs and digits.

Interneurons project to motor neurons.

Motor neurons project to muscles of the body.

Ventral corticospinal tract synapses with interneurons and motor neurons that innervate the trunk (midline of the body).

The interneurons and motor neurons of the spinal cord are envisioned as a homunculus representing the muscles that they innervate.

Fingers

Arms

Shoulders

Trunk

Figure 10-9

Motor-Tract Organization
The interneurons and the motor neurons of the ventral spinal cord are topographically arranged so that the more lateral neurons innervate the more distal parts of the limbs (those farther from the midline) and the more medial neurons innervate the more proximal muscles of the body (those closer to the midline).

○ On your *Foundations* CD, visit the section on descending motor tracts in the module on the control of movement for a visual overview of the corticospinal tracts.

their original side of the brainstem continue down the spinal cord in a ventral (front) position, giving them the name *ventral corticospinal tract.* As we will see, the two tracts eventually control different parts of the body.

Motor Neurons

The spinal-cord motor neurons that connect to muscles are located in the ventrolateral part of the spinal cord and jut out to form the spinal column's ventral horns. There are two kinds of neurons in the ventral horns. Interneurons lie just medial to the motor neurons and project onto them. The motor neurons send their axons to the muscles of the body. The fibers from the corticospinal tracts make synaptic connections with both the interneurons and the motor neurons, but all nervous system commands to the muscles are carried by the motor neurons.

Figure 10-9 shows that the more laterally located motor neurons project to muscles that control the fingers and hands, whereas intermediately located motor neurons project to muscles that control the arms and shoulders. The most medially located motor neurons project to muscles that control the trunk. Axons of the lateral corticospinal tract connect mainly with the lateral interneurons and motor neurons, and axons of the ventral corticospinal tract connect mainly to the medial interneurons and motor neurons. In other words, a homunculus of the body is represented again in the spinal cord.

To picture how the motor homunculus in the cortex is related to the motor neuron homunculus in the spinal cord, place your right index finger on top of your head above the index-finger region of the motor homunculus on the left side of the brain (see Figure 10-6). Following the axons of the cortical neurons downward, your route takes you through the brainstem, across its midline, and down the right lateral corticospinal tract.

The journey ends at the interneurons and motor neurons in the most lateral region of the spinal cord's right ventral horn—the horn on the opposite side of the nervous system from which you began. If you next follow the axons of these motor neurons, you will find that they synapse with muscles that move the index finger on that same right-hand side of the body. (By the way, the neurons that your brain is using to carry out this task are the same neurons whose pathway you are tracing.)

If you repeat the procedure by tracing the pathway from the trunk of the motor homunculus on the left side of the brain, you will follow the same route through the upper part of the brainstem. However, you will not cross over to the brainstem's opposite side. Instead, you will descend into the spinal cord on the left side, the same side of the nervous system on which you began, eventually ending up in the most medially located interneurons and motor neurons of the left side's ventral horn. In addition, some of these axons will also cross over to the other side of the spinal cord. Thus, if you follow the axons of these motor neurons, you will end up at their synapses with muscles that move the trunk on both sides of the body.

This exercise of the imagination should help you to remember the routes taken by the axons of the motor system. The limb regions of the motor homunculus contribute most of their fibers to the lateral corticospinal tract. Because these fibers have crossed over to the opposite side of the brainstem, they activate motor neurons that move the arm, hand, leg, and foot on the opposite side of the body.

In contrast, the trunk regions of the motor homunculus contribute their fibers to the ventral corticospinal tract. These fibers do not cross over at the brainstem, although some do cross over in the spinal cord. In short, the neurons of the motor homunculus in the left-hemisphere cortex control the trunk on both sides and the limbs on the body's right side. Similarly, neurons of the motor homunculus in the right-hemisphere cortex control the trunk on both sides of the body and the limbs on the body's left side (Kuypers, 1981). Thus, one hemisphere of the cortex controls the hands and fingers of the opposite side of the body and the trunk on both sides of the body. About a quarter of corticospinal neurons use glutamate as a neurotransmitter, another quarter use aspartate, and about half use both. At present, the specific motor functions mediated by these subpopulations of corticospinal neurons are unknown.

This description of motor-system pathways descending from the brain is highly simplified. There are actually about 26 pathways, including the corticospinal tracts. The other pathways carry instructions from the brainstem, such as information related to posture and balance, and control the autonomic nervous system. For all these functions, however, the motor neurons are the final common path.

Control of Muscles

The muscles with which spinal-cord motor neurons synapse control movement of the body. For example, the biceps and triceps of the upper arm control movement of the lower arm. Limb muscles are arranged in pairs, as shown in **Figure 10-10**. One member of a pair, the *extensor,* moves (extends) the limb away from the trunk. The other member of the pair, the *flexor,* moves the limb toward the trunk.

Connections between the interneurons and motor neurons of the spinal cord ensure that the muscles work together so that, when one muscle contracts, the other relaxes. Thus, the interneurons and motor neurons of the spinal cord not only relay instructions from the brain but also, through their connections, cooperatively organize the movement of many muscles. As you know, the neurotransmitter at the motor neuron–muscle junction is acetylcholine.

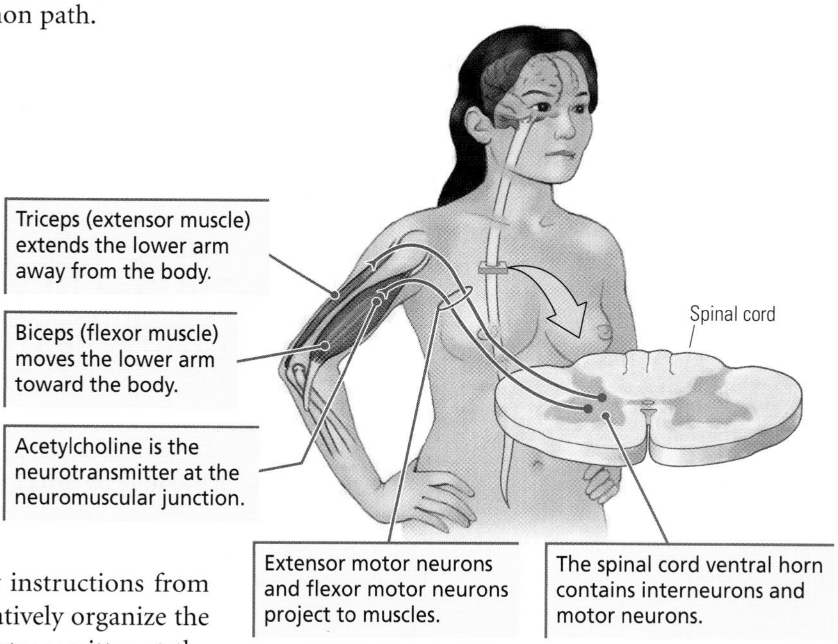

Triceps (extensor muscle) extends the lower arm away from the body.

Biceps (flexor muscle) moves the lower arm toward the body.

Acetylcholine is the neurotransmitter at the neuromuscular junction.

Spinal cord

Extensor motor neurons and flexor motor neurons project to muscles.

The spinal cord ventral horn contains interneurons and motor neurons.

Figure 10-10

Coordinating Movement

In Review

The motor cortex is topographically organized as a homunculus in which parts of the body that are capable of the most skilled movements (especially the mouth, fingers, and thumb) are regulated by larger cortical regions. Instructions regarding movement travel from the motor cortex through the corticospinal tracts to interneurons and motor neurons in the ventral horn of the spinal cord. A large part of the corticospinal-tract fibers cross to the opposite side of the spinal cord to form the lateral corticospinal tracts, and a smaller part stay on the same side to form the ventral corticospinal tracts. The ventral corticospinal tracts carry instructions for trunk movements, whereas the lateral corticospinal tracts carry instructions for arm and finger movements. The axons of motor neurons in the spinal cord then carry instructions to muscles.

Synergy. Innate pattern of movement coded by the motor cortex.

THE MOTOR CORTEX AND SKILLED MOVEMENTS

People everywhere perform skilled movements in remarkably similar ways. For instance, most people who reach for a small paperclip on a desk do so with the hand rotated so that the fingers are on the top and the thumb is on the bottom. They also use this pincer grip to hold the clip—that is, they grasp it between the thumb and index finger. These movements could be learned by watching other people, but we have no recollection of having, as children, spent any time observing and mastering such movement patterns.

In fact, even before 4 months of age, babies begin practicing finger movements by making them in the air; then they use the movements to touch themselves and their clothes (Wallace & Whishaw, 2003). Between 8 and 11 months of age, babies spontaneously begin to use the pincer grip to pick up tiny objects such as breadcrumbs. Most other primates also make use of the pincer grasp. All the evidence therefore suggests that, although we learn to make this skilled movement, the neurons and connections that enable the movement are innate. Basic similarities in the neural connections of the motor cortex and spinal cord are responsible for the basic patterns of movement that are common to the particular species.

These innate movement patterns are **synergies.** In primates, the pincer grip is one synergy and the power grasp is another. In this section, we describe how neurons produce synergies. We also explore how the motor cortices of other species produce their skilled movements, including the highly dexterous movements of an elephant's trunk.

○ To further investigate the role of the central nervous system in skilled movement, visit the section on the higher order motor cortex in the control of movement module on your *Foundations* CD. Here you can explore in detail the anatomy of the motor cortex.

Investigating Neural Control of Skilled Movements

In a study designed to investigate how the motor cortex controls movement, Edward Evarts (1968) used the simple procedure illustrated in the Procedure section of **Experiment 10-2.** He trained a monkey to flex its wrist in order to move a bar to which different weights could be attached. An electrode implanted in the wrist region of the motor cortex recorded the activity of neurons there.

Evarts discovered that these neurons began to discharge even before the monkey flexed its wrist, as shown in the Results section of Experiment 10-2. Apparently, they take part in planning the movement as well as initiating it. The neurons also continued to discharge as the wrist moved, confirming that they play a role in producing the movement. Finally, the neurons discharged at a higher rate when the bar was loaded with a weight. This finding shows that motor-cortex neurons increase the force of a movement by increasing their rate of firing, and its duration, as stated in the experiment's Conclusion.

Evarts's findings also revealed that the motor cortex has a role in specifying the direction of a movement. The neurons of the motor-cortex wrist area discharged when the monkey flexed its wrist inward but not when the wrist was extended back to its starting position. These on–off responses of the neurons, depending on whether the flexor or extensor muscle is being used, are a simple way of coding the direction in which the wrist is moving.

A generation later, Apostolos Georgopoulos and his coworkers (1999) used a method similar to that of Evarts to further examine the coding of movement direction. They trained monkeys to move a lever in different directions across the surface of a table. Recording from single cells in the arm region of the motor cortex, they found that each cell was maximally active when the monkey moved its arm in a particular direction.

Experiment 10-3 summarizes the results. As the monkey's arm moves in directions other than the one to which a particular cell maximally responds in the Procedure

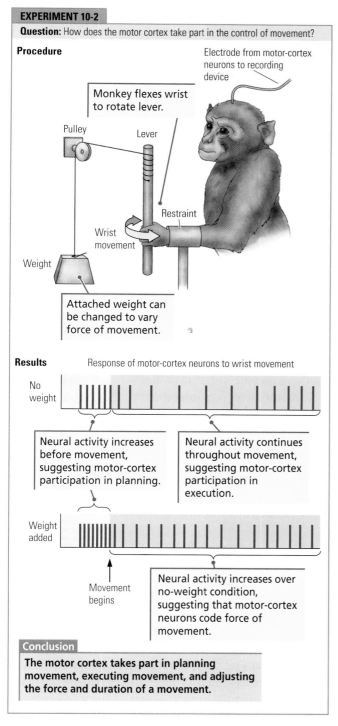

EXPERIMENT 10-2

Question: How does the motor cortex take part in the control of movement?

Procedure

Electrode from motor-cortex neurons to recording device

Monkey flexes wrist to rotate lever.

Pulley

Lever

Restraint

Wrist movement

Weight

Attached weight can be changed to vary force of movement.

Results Response of motor-cortex neurons to wrist movement

No weight

Neural activity increases before movement, suggesting motor-cortex participation in planning.

Neural activity continues throughout movement, suggesting motor-cortex participation in execution.

Weight added

Movement begins

Neural activity increases over no-weight condition, suggesting that motor-cortex neurons code force of movement.

Conclusion

The motor cortex takes part in planning movement, executing movement, and adjusting the force and duration of a movement.

Adapted from "Relation of Pyramidal Tract Activity to Force Exerted During Voluntary Movement," by E. V. Evarts, 1968, *Journal of Neurophysiology, 31,* p. 15.

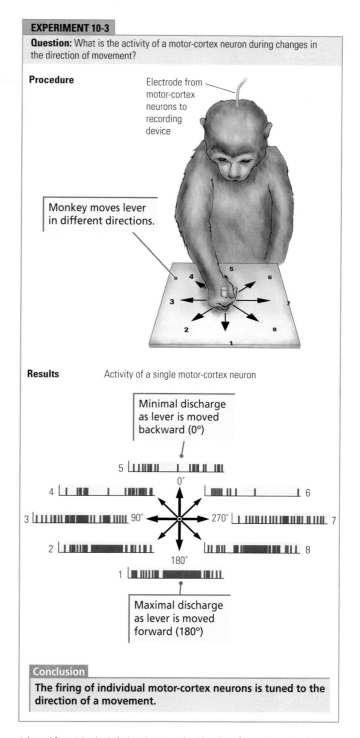

EXPERIMENT 10-3

Question: What is the activity of a motor-cortex neuron during changes in the direction of movement?

Procedure

Electrode from motor-cortex neurons to recording device

Monkey moves lever in different directions.

Results Activity of a single motor-cortex neuron

Minimal discharge as lever is moved backward (0°)

5

0°

4   6

3   90°   270°   7

2   8

180°

1

Maximal discharge as lever is moved forward (180°)

Conclusion

The firing of individual motor-cortex neurons is tuned to the direction of a movement.

Adapted from "On the Relations Between the Direction of Two-Dimensional Arm Movements and Cell Discharge in Primate Motor Cortex," by A. P. Georgopoulos, J. F. Kalaska, R. Caminiti, and J. T. Massey, 1982, *Journal of Neuroscience, 2,* p. 1530.

section, the cell decreases its activity in proportion to the displacement from the "preferred" direction, diagrammed in the Results section. For example, if a neuron discharges maximally as the arm moves directly forward, its discharge will be halved if the arm moves to one side, and discharge ceases altogether if the arm moves backward.

According to Georgopoulos and his coworkers, the motor cortex seems to calculate both the direction and the distance of movements. Each neuron in a large population of motor-cortex neurons could participate in producing a particular movement, just as

Baseball pitcher
winding up

findings from other studies suggest. But the discharge rate of a particular neuron depends on that movement's direction.

Georgopoulos and Evarts emphasize somewhat different views about how the motor cortex exerts control over movement. Both researchers believe that motor-cortex neurons plan and execute movements, but they disagree about what those planning and execution strategies entail. To better understand the difference between their hypotheses, imagine that you are preparing to pitch a ball to a catcher.

Does your throw require calculating which muscles to use and how much force to apply to each one? This position is that of Evarts. It is based on his findings about how neurons of the motor cortex change their rates of discharge in response not only to which muscle is needed (flexor or extensor, for instance) but also to how much force is required to make a particular movement.

Alternatively, perhaps your throw to the catcher simply requires determining where you want the ball to arrive. This position is that of Georgopoulos. He maintains that the cortex needs to specify only the spatial target of a movement—that is, its basic direction. Other brain structures, such as the brainstem and spinal cord, will look after the details of the throw.

Both theories are probably correct. Possibly, a subset of neurons codes force and another subset codes direction or, possibly, in some way cortical motor neurons can code both force and direction at the same time. Exactly what the code entails is still not understood. The "directional" hypothesis and the "force" hypothesis are both topics of current debate in the study of how the motor cortex controls movement (Crowe et al., 2004).

What investigators do agree on is that there is not a simple point-to-point correspondence between a part of the cortical topographic map and movement of a particular part of the body—for example, between a finger representation and a finger movement. Georgopoulos and his coworkers (1999) investigated the neural control of movement by recording from neurons in the motor cortices of monkeys that had been trained to make specific finger movements. They expected that, when a thumb or a certain finger moves, only the area of the motor cortex that represents that particular digit will be active.

But their expectations were not met. When one finger moved, not only were neurons in that finger's area of the motor cortex active but so were neurons in the cortical areas of other fingers. Apparently, the entire hand's representation in the motor cortex participates even in simple acts, such as moving one finger. Although this finding may seem surprising at first, it makes intuitive sense.

After all, to move one finger, some effort must be exerted to keep the other fingers still or to move them out of the way. There must be connections between all participating neurons to allow them to act in concert. These same connections would be necessary for sequential movements of the fingers, such as those used in playing the piano or painting a work of art. Furthermore, there are likely similar connections between the fingers, the arm, and the body that allow more-complex movements entailing many body segments to take place.

Control of Skilled Movements in Nonhuman Species

Humans are far from the only species that makes skilled movements. Kamala the elephant paints works of art with her trunk, and primates other than humans are very skilled with their hands, as we are. How is the motor cortex in other species organized to enable these skilled movement patterns?

The results of studies of a wide range of animals show that their motor cortices are organized to correspond to the skilled movements of their species. Just as in humans, larger parts of the motor cortex regulate body parts that carry out these movements. **Figure 10-11** shows cartoons representing the human homunculus and comparable drawings of four other animals—the rabbit, cat, monkey, and elephant.

As you can see, rabbits have a large motor-cortex representation for the head and mouth, cats for the mouth and front claws, and monkeys for the hands, feet, and digits. Although no one has mapped the motor cortex of an elephant, a disproportionately large area of its motor cortex is likely dedicated to regulating the trunk.

How did these specialized representations of the motor cortex evolve? One possibility is that they were adapted from the outside inward (Woolsey & Wann, 1976). Chance mutations caused an adaptive increase in the number of muscles in a particular part of the body, which led to more motor neurons in the spinal cord. Concurrent with this increase in motor neurons, the area of the motor cortex controlling those spinal-cord motor neurons increased. The larger motor-cortex representation, along with an increased possibility of making connections between these cortical neurons, led to an evolved capacity for making new and more-complex movements. That is, after the motor cortex had expanded, evolutionary pressure could then select for subregions to become specialized for new behaviors.

Let us apply this scenario to the development of the elephant's trunk. First, chance mutations led to the expansion of muscles in the elephant's lip and nose and the spinal-cord motor neurons needed to move them. These developments were retained because they were useful, perhaps because the trunk was stronger than in the elephant's ancestors. The area of the motor cortex coexpanded to represent the new muscles of the trunk. The cortical area for the trunk motor cortex expanded and differentiated to enable fine control of different trunk muscles that enabled selectively advantageous behaviors, such as feeding on new food sources.

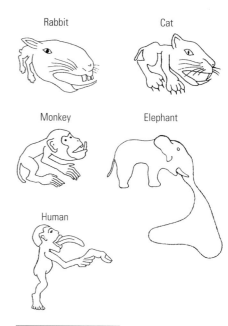

Figure 10-11

Motor-Control Cartoons The size of the cortical area regulating a body part in these motor-cortex representations corresponds to the skill required in moving that body part. The representation for the elephant is only surmised. Adapted from *Principles of Neural Science* (3rd ed., p. 373), by E. R. Kandel, J. H. Schwartz, and T. M. Jessel, 1991, New York: Elsevier.

How Motor-Cortex Damage Affects Skilled Movements

Scientists produced the first maps of the motor cortex in the 1930s. A number of researchers got slightly different results when they repeated the mapping procedures on the same subjects. These findings led to a debate.

Some scientists held that the map of the motor cortex was capable of changing—that areas controlling particular body parts might not always stay in exactly the same place and retain exactly the same dimensions. But other researchers felt that this view was unlikely. They argued that, given the enormous specificity of topographic maps of the motor cortex, these maps must surely be quite stable. If they appeared to change, it must be because the large electrodes used for stimulating and recording from cortical neurons must be producing inexact results.

As cortical-mapping procedures improved, however, and as smaller and smaller electrodes were used, it became clear that motor maps can indeed change. They can change as a result of sensory or motor learning (a topic to be explored in Chapter 13), and they can change when part of the motor cortex is damaged, as the following example shows.

A study by Randy Nudo and his coworkers (1996), summarized in the Procedure section of **Experiment 10-4**, illustrates change in a map of the motor cortex due to cortical damage. These researchers mapped the motor cortices of monkeys to identify the hand and digit areas. They then surgically removed a small part of the

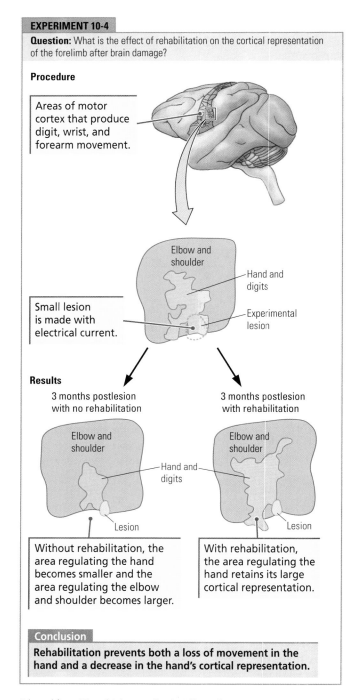

EXPERIMENT 10-4

Question: What is the effect of rehabilitation on the cortical representation of the forelimb after brain damage?

Procedure

Areas of motor cortex that produce digit, wrist, and forearm movement.

Elbow and shoulder

Hand and digits

Small lesion is made with electrical current.

Experimental lesion

Results

3 months postlesion with no rehabilitation

3 months postlesion with rehabilitation

Elbow and shoulder

Hand and digits

Elbow and shoulder

Lesion

Lesion

Without rehabilitation, the area regulating the hand becomes smaller and the area regulating the elbow and shoulder becomes larger.

With rehabilitation, the area regulating the hand retains its large cortical representation.

Conclusion

Rehabilitation prevents both a loss of movement in the hand and a decrease in the hand's cortical representation.

Adapted from "Neural Substrates for the Effects of Rehabilitative Training on Motor Recovery after Ischemic Infarct," by R. J. Nudo, B. M. Wise, F. SiFuentes, and G. W. Milliken, 1996, *Science*, *272*, p. 1793.

cortex that represents the digit area. After the surgery, the monkeys used the affected hand much less, relying mainly on the good hand.

Three months later, the researchers examined the monkeys. They found that the animals were unable to produce many movements of the lower arm, including the wrist, the hand, and the digits surrounding the area with the lesion. They also discovered that much of the area representing the hand and lower arm was gone from the cortical map. The shoulder, upper arm, and elbow areas had spread to take up what had formerly been space representing the hand and digits. The Results section of Experiment 10-4 shows this topographic change.

The experimenters wondered whether the change could have been prevented had they forced the monkeys to use the affected arm. To find out, they used the same procedure on other monkeys, except that, during the postsurgery period, they made the animals rely on the bad arm by binding the good arm in a sling.

Three months later, when the experimenters reexamined the motor maps of these monkeys, they found that the hand and digit area retained its large size, even though there was no neural activity in the spot with the lesion. Nevertheless, the monkeys had gained some function in the digits that had formerly been connected to the damaged spot. Apparently, the remaining digit area of the cortex was now controlling the movement of these fingers.

The property of the motor cortex that allows it to change as a result of experience, as you know, is plasticity. Thus, plasticity in the motor cortex underlies our ability to acquire new motor skills as well as our ability to recover from brain injury. Most likely plasticity is enabled by the formation of new connections among different parts of the homunculus in the motor cortex.

The motor-cortex reorganization that Nudo and his colleagues observed in monkeys probably explains some kinds of recovery from brain damage observed in humans. For instance, Paul Bucy and his coworkers (1964) studied a man whose corticospinal tract was surgically cut on one side of his nervous system to stop involuntary movement of his muscles. During the first 24 hours after the surgery, the side of his body contralateral to the cut was completely flaccid, and he was unable to make any movements on that side. (The impairment was on the side of the body opposite that of the cut because the corticospinal tract crossed to the other side just below the location of the cut.)

Then, gradually, there was some recovery of function. By the 10th day after the surgery, the patient could stand alone and walk with assistance. By the 24th day, he could walk unaided. Within 7 months, he could move his feet, hands, fingers, and toes with only slight impairment.

The explanation of this man's remarkable recovery is twofold. First, when the man died about 2½ years later, an autopsy revealed that approximately 17 percent of the corticospinal fibers were intact in the tract that had been cut. Apparently, the remaining fibers were able to take over much of the function formerly served by the entire pathway. Second, extensive reorganization likely took place in the map of the man's motor cortex, and so many cortical regions could use the fibers that had remained intact to send messages to motor neurons in the spinal cord.

In Review

Basic innate patterns of movement common to a particular mammalian species are organized in the motor cortex as synergies. The discharge patterns of motor-cortex neurons suggest that these neurons take part in planning and initiating movements as well as in carrying them out. Their discharge rate is related both to the force of muscle contraction and to the direction of a movement. Individual motor-cortex neurons are maximally responsive to movements in a particular direction. The topographic map of the motor cortex in a particular species is related to the species' body parts that are capable of making the most skillful movements. The relation between neurons in the motor cortex and the movement of specific muscles is plastic. Considerable change can take place in the cortical motor map and in recovery of function after injury to the motor cortex.

THE BASAL GANGLIA AND THE CEREBELLUM

The main evidence that the basal ganglia and the cerebellum perform motor functions is that damage to either structure impairs movement. Both structures also have extensive connections with the motor cortex, further suggesting their participation in movement. After an overview of the anatomy of the basal ganglia and cerebellum, we look at some of the symptoms that arise after they are damaged. Then we consider some experiments that illustrate the roles that these structures might play in controlling movement.

○ To further explore how the brain performs motor functions, visit the basal ganglia and cerebellum sections of the control of movement module on your *Foundations* CD. Look for details on what happens when there is damage to these regions.

The Basal Ganglia and Movement Force

Our control over movement is remarkable. We can manipulate objects as light as a needle, to sew, or swing objects as heavy as a baseball bat to drive a ball more than 100 yards. The brain areas that allow us to adjust the force of our movements in these ways include the basal ganglia, a collection of nuclei within the forebrain that make connections with the motor cortex and with the midbrain. As shown in **Figure 10-12**, a prominent structure in the basal ganglia is the caudate putamen, a large cluster of nuclei that extends as a "tail" into the temporal lobe, ending in the amygdala.

The basal ganglia receive inputs from two main sources:

1. All areas of the neocortex and limbic cortex, including the motor cortex, project to the basal ganglia.
2. The nigrostriatal dopaminergic activating system projects to the basal ganglia from the substantia nigra, a cluster of darkly pigmented cells in the midbrain.

Basal ganglia nuclei project back to both the motor cortex and the substantia nigra as well.

Two different, in many ways opposite, kinds of movement disorders result from damage to the basal ganglia. If cells of the caudate putamen are damaged, unwanted choreiform (writhing and twitching) movements result. For example, Huntington's chorea, in which cells of the caudate putamen are destroyed, is characterized by involuntary and exaggerated movements (see "Huntington's Chorea" on page 105). Other examples of involuntary movements related to caudate putamen damage are the

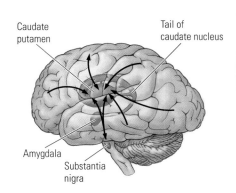

Caudate putamen
Tail of caudate nucleus
Amygdala
Substantia nigra

Figure 10-12

Basal Ganglia Connections The caudate putamen in the basal ganglia connects to the amygdala through the tail of the caudate nucleus. The basal ganglia also makes reciprocal connections with the substantia nigra, receives input from most regions of the cortex, and sends input into the frontal lobes through the thalamus.

Tourette's Syndrome

The neurological disorder Tourette's syndrome (TS) was first described in 1885 by Georges Gilles de la Tourette, a young French neurologist and friend of Sigmund Freud. Here is how de la Tourette described the symptoms as they appeared in Madame de D., one of his patients:

> Madame de D., presently age 26, at the age of 7 was afflicted by convulsive movements of the hands and arms. These abnormal movements occurred above all when the child tried to write, causing her to crudely reproduce the letters she was trying to trace. After each spasm, the movements of the hand became more regular and better controlled until another convulsive movement would again interrupt her work. She was felt to be suffering from over-excitement and mischief, and because the movements became more and more frequent, she was subject to reprimand and punishment. Soon it became clear that these movements were indeed involuntary and convulsive in nature. The movements involved the shoulders, the neck, and the face, and resulted in contortions and extraordinary grimaces. As the disease progressed, and the spasms spread to involve her voice and speech, the young lady made strange screams and said words that made no sense (Friedhoff & Chase, 1982).

The incidence of Tourette's syndrome is fewer than 1 in 1000 people. It is found in all racial groups and seems to be hereditary. The age range of onset is between 2 and 25 years. The most frequent symptoms are involuntary tics and involuntary complex movements, such as hitting, lunging, or jumping.

People with the syndrome may also suddenly emit cries and other vocalizations or inexplicably utter words that do not make sense in the context, including scatology and swearing. Tourette's syndrome is not associated with any other disorders, although much milder cases of tics may be related to it.

Tourette's syndrome is thought to be due to an abnormality of the basal ganglia, especially the right-hemisphere basal ganglia. It is one of the hyperkinetic disorders that can result from basal ganglia dysfunction. Its symptoms can be controlled with haloperidol, which blocks dopamine synapses in the basal ganglia.

Many people with TS function quite well, coping successfully with their symptoms. There are people with TS in all walks of life, even surgeons who must perform delicate operations. With the existence of the Tourette's Society in the past 20 years, public awareness of the disorder has increased. Children with TS are now less likely to be diagnosed as having a psychiatric condition, being hyperactive, or being troublemakers.

Hyperkinetic symptom. Symptom of brain damage that results in excessive involuntary movements, as seen in Tourette's syndrome.

Hypokinetic symptom. Symptom of brain damage that results in a paucity of movement, as seen in Parkinson's disease.

unwanted tics and vocalizations peculiar to Tourette's syndrome, which is discussed in "Tourette's Syndrome."

In addition to causing involuntary movements, or **hyperkinetic symptoms,** damage to the basal ganglia can result in a loss of motor ability, or **hypokinetic symptoms.** One hypokinetic disorder, Parkinson's disease, has been considered in several preceding chapters. It is caused by the loss of dopamine cells in the substantia nigra and is characterized by an inability to produce normal movements. The two different kinds of symptoms that arise subsequent to basal ganglia damage—hyperkinetic and hypokinetic symptoms—suggest that a major function of these nuclei is to modulate movement.

Steven Keele and Richard Ivry (1991) tried to relate the two opposing kinds of basal ganglia symptoms by suggesting that the underlying function of the basal ganglia is to generate the force required for each particular movement. According to this idea, some types of basal ganglia damage cause errors of too much force and so result in excessive movement, whereas other types of damage cause errors of too little force and so result in insufficient movement.

Keele and Ivry tested their hypothesis by giving healthy subjects as well as patients with various kinds of basal ganglia disorders a task that tested their ability to exert appropriate amounts of force. The subjects viewed a line on a television screen. By pushing a button with varying amounts of force, they could produce a second line to match the length of the first.

After a number of practice trials, the subjects were asked to press the button with the appropriate amount of force even when the first line was no longer visible as a guide. In contrast with control subjects, patients with basal ganglia disorders were unable to reliably do so. The force that they exerted was usually too little or too much, resulting in a line too short or too long.

What neural pathways enable the basal ganglia to modulate the force of movements? Basal ganglia circuits are quite complex, but one theory holds that two pathways affect the activity of the motor cortex: an inhibitory pathway and an excitatory pathway (Alexander & Crutcher, 1990). Both these pathways converge on an area of the basal ganglia called the internal part of the globus pallidus (GP_i), as charted in **Figure 10-13**.

The GP_i in turn projects into the the ventral thalamic nucleus, and the thalamus projects to the motor cortex. The thalamic projection modulates the size or force of a movement that the cortex produces and is influenced by the GP_i. The GP_i acts like the volume dial on a radio because its output determines whether a movement will be weak or strong.

The inputs to the GP_i are shown in red and green in Figure 10-13 to illustrate how they affect movement. If activity in the inhibitory pathway (red) is high relative to that in the excitatory pathway (green), inhibition of the GP_i will predominate, and the thalamus will be free to excite the cortex, thus amplifying movement force. If, on the other hand, activity in the excitatory pathway is high relative to that in the inhibitory pathway, excitation of the GP_i will predominate, and the thalamus will be inhibited, thus reducing input to the cortex and decreasing the force of movements.

The idea that the GP_i acts like a volume control over movement is currently receiving a great deal of attention as the basis for one type of treatment for Parkinson's disease. If the GP_i is surgically destroyed in Parkinson patients, muscular rigidity is reduced and the ability to make normal movements is improved. Also consistent with this "volume hypothesis," recordings made from cells of the globus pallidus show that they are excessively active in people with Parkinson's disease.

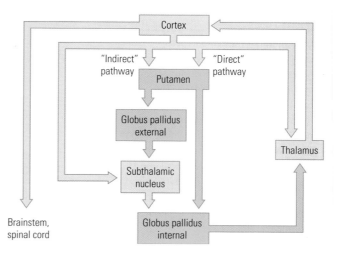

Figure 10-13

Regulating Movement Force Two pathways in the basal ganglia modulate cortically produced movements. On this flowchart, the green pathways are excitatory, and the red are inhibitory. The indirect pathway has an excitatory effect on the GP_i, whereas the direct pathway has an inhibitory effect. If activity in the indirect pathway dominates, the thalamus shuts down and the cortex is unable to produce movement. If direct-pathway activity dominates, the thalamus can become overactive, thus amplifying movement. Adapted from "Functional Architecture of Basal Ganglia Circuits: Neural Substrates of Parallel Processing," by R. E. Alexander and M. D. Crutcher, 1990, *Trends in Neuroscience, 13,* p. 269.

The Cerebellum and Movement Skill

Musicians have a saying: "Miss a day of practice and you're OK; miss two days and you notice; miss three days and the world notices." Apparently, some change must take place in the brain when practice of a motor skill is neglected. The cerebellum may be the part of the motor system that is affected. Whether the skill is playing a musical instrument, pitching a baseball, or typing on a computer keyboard, the cerebellum is critical for acquiring and maintaining motor skills.

The cerebellum, a large and conspicuous part of the motor system, sits atop the brainstem, clearly visible just behind the cerebral cortex. The cerebellum is divided into

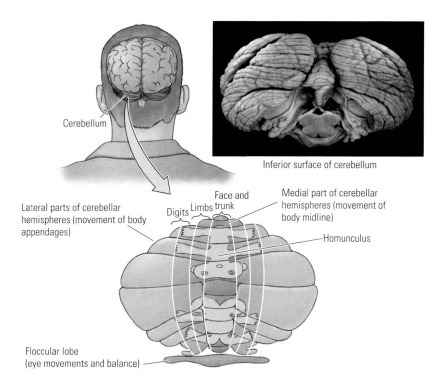

Figure 10-14

Cerebellar Homunculus The cerebellar hemispheres control body movements, and the flocculus controls eye movements and balance. The cerebellum is topographically organized: its more medial parts represent the midline of the body and its more lateral parts represent the limbs and digits. Photograph of cerebellum reproduced from *The Human Brain: Dissections of the Real Brain,* by T. H. Williams, N. Gluhbegovic, and J. Jew, on CD-ROM. Published by Brain University, brain-university.com 2000.

Cerebellum

Inferior surface of cerebellum

Lateral parts of cerebellar hemispheres (movement of body appendages)

Digits

Face and Limbs trunk

Medial part of cerebellar hemispheres (movement of body midline)

Homunculus

Floccular lobe (eye movements and balance)

two hemispheres, as is the cerebral cortex. A small lobe, the *flocculus,* projects from its ventral surface. Although smaller than the neocortex, the cerebellum has many more gyri and sulci than the neocortex, and it contains about one-half of all the neurons in the entire nervous system.

As **Figure 10-14** shows, the cerebellum can be divided into several regions, each specialized in a different aspect of motor control. At its base, the flocculus receives projections from the middle-ear vestibular system, described later in the chapter, and takes part in the control of balance. Many of its projections go to the spinal cord and to the motor nuclei that control eye movements.

Just as the motor cortex has a homuncular organization and a number of homunculi, the hemispheres of the cerebellum have at least two, as shown in Figure 10-14. The most medial part of each homunculus controls the face and the midline of the body. The more lateral parts are connected to areas of the motor cortex and are associated with movements of the limbs, hands, feet, and digits. The pathways from the hemispheres project to nuclei of the cerebellum, which in turn project to other brain regions, including the motor cortex.

To summarize the cerebellum's topographic organization, the midline of the homunculus is represented in its central part, whereas the limbs and digits are represented in the lateral parts. Tumors or damage to midline areas of the cerebellum disrupt balance, eye movement, upright posture, and walking but do not substantially disrupt other movements such as reaching, grasping, and using the fingers. For example, a person with medial damage to the cerebellum may, when lying down, show few symptoms. Damage to lateral parts of the cerebellum disrupts arm, hand, and finger movements much more than movements of the body's trunk.

Attempts to understand how the cerebellum controls movement have centered on two major ideas: that the cerebellum (1) plays a role in the timing of movements and (2) maintains movement accuracy. Keele and Ivry support the first idea. They suggest that underlying impairment in disorders of the cerebellum is a loss of timing.

Keele and Ivry (1991) maintain that the cerebellum acts as a clock or pacemaker to ensure that both movements and perceptions are appropriately timed. In a motor test of timing, subjects were asked to tap a finger to keep time with a metronome. After a number of taps, the metronome was turned off and the subjects were to maintain the beat. Those with damage to the cerebellum, especially to the lateral cerebellum, were impaired on the task.

In a perceptual test of timing, subjects were presented with two pairs of tones. The silent period between the first two tones was always the same length, whereas the silent period between the second two tones changed from trial to trial. The subjects had to judge whether the second silent period was longer or shorter than the first. Those with damage to the cerebellum were impaired on this task.

Apparently, the cerebellum can act like a clock to time perceptions as well as movements. Not all researchers believe that the cerebellum's major contribution to controlling movements is only one of timing, however. Tom Thach and his coworkers (1992) argued that another role for the cerebellum is to help make the adjustments needed to keep movements accurate.

The Thach team gathered evidence in support of this view by having subjects throw darts at a target, as shown in the Procedure section of **Experiment 10-5**. After a number of throws, which allowed the subjects to become reasonably accurate, the subjects put on glasses containing wedge-shaped prisms that displaced the apparent location of the target to the left. Now when the subjects threw a dart, it landed to the left of the intended target.

All subjects showed this initial distortion in aim. But then came an important difference, graphed in the Results section of Experiment 10-5. When normal subjects saw the dart miss the mark, they adjusted each successive throw until reasonable accuracy was restored. In contrast, subjects with damage to the cerebellum could not correct for this error. They kept missing the target far to the left time after time.

Next the control subjects removed the prism glasses and threw a few more darts. Again, another significant difference emerged. The first dart thrown by each normal subject was much too far to the right (owing to the previous adjustment that the subject had learned to make), but soon each adjusted once again until his or her former accuracy was regained.

In contrast, subjects with damage to the cerebellum showed no aftereffects from having worn the prisms, as if they had never compensated for the glasses to begin with. This experiment suggests that many movements that we make—whether throwing a dart, hitting a ball with a bat, writing neatly, or painting a work of art—depend on moment-to-moment learning and adjustments that are made by the cerebellum.

To better understand how the cerebellum improves motor skills by adjusting movements, imagine throwing a dart yourself. Suppose you aim at the bull's eye, throw the dart, and find that it misses the board completely. You then aim again, this time adjusting your throw to correct for the original error. Notice that there

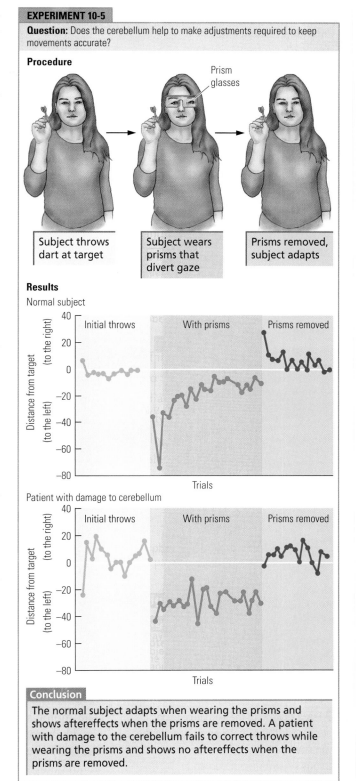

EXPERIMENT 10-5

Question: Does the cerebellum help to make adjustments required to keep movements accurate?

Procedure

Prism glasses

| Subject throws dart at target | Subject wears prisms that divert gaze | Prisms removed, subject adapts |

Results

Normal subject

Patient with damage to cerebellum

Conclusion

The normal subject adapts when wearing the prisms and shows aftereffects when the prisms are removed. A patient with damage to the cerebellum fails to correct throws while wearing the prisms and shows no aftereffects when the prisms are removed.

Adapted from "The Cerebellum and the Adaptive Coordination of Movement," by W. T. Thach, H. P. Goodkin, and J. G. Keating, 1992, *Annual Review of Neuroscience, 15,* p. 429.

Figure 10-15

Figure 10-15

Intention, Action, and Feedback A feedback circuit allows the cerebellum to correct movements to match intention. By comparing the message for the intended movement with the movement that was actually performed, the cerebellum can send an error message to the cortex to improve the accuracy of a subsequent movement.

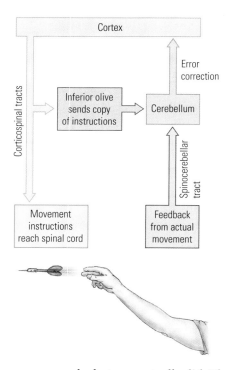

are actually two versions of your action: (1) the movement that you intended to make and (2) the actual movement as recorded by sensory receptors in your arm and shoulder.

If the intended movement is successfully carried out, you need make no correction on your next try. But if you miss, an adjustment is called for. One way in which the adjustment might be made is through the feedback circuit shown in **Figure 10-15**.

The cortex sends instructions to the spinal cord to throw a dart at the target. A copy of the same instructions is sent to the cerebellum through the inferior olive in the brainstem. When you then throw the dart, the sensory receptors in your arm and shoulder code the actual movement that you make and send a message about it back to the cerebellum through the spinocerebellar tract. This sensory pathway carries information about movements that have been made from the spinal cord to the cerebellum.

The cerebellum now has information about both versions of the movement: what you intended to do and what you actually did. The cerebellum can now calculate the error and tell the cortex how to correct the movement. When you next throw a dart, you incorporate that correction into your throw.

In Review

The basal ganglia contribute to motor control by adjusting the force associated with each movement. Consequently, damage to the basal ganglia results either in unwanted, involuntary hyperkinetic movements (too much force being exerted) or in such hypokinetic rigidity that movements are difficult to perform (too little force being exerted). The cerebellum contributes to the control of movement by improving movement skill. One way in which it may do so is by keeping track of the timing of movements. Another way is by making adjustments in movements to maintain their accuracy. In the latter case, the cerebellum compares an intended movement with an actual movement, calculates any necessary corrections, and informs the cortex.

ORGANIZATION OF THE SOMATOSENSORY SYSTEM

⊙ For a review of the somatosensory system, visit the somatosenses area of the brain-overview section in the central nervous system module on your *Foundations* CD.

The motor system is responsible for producing movements, but movement would quickly become impaired without sensation. The somatosensory system tells us what the body is up to and what's going on in the environment by providing information about bodily sensations, such as touch, temperature, pain, position in space, and movement of the joints.

In addition to helping us learn about the world, the somatosensory system allows us to distinguish what the world does to us from what we do to it. For example, when someone pushes you sideways, your somatosensory system tells you that you have been pushed. If you lunge to the side yourself, your somatosensory system tells you that you did the moving.

We are exploring the somatosensory system and the motor system in the same chapter because somatosensation has a closer relation to movement than the other senses do. If we lose sight or hearing or even both, we can still move around, and the same is true of other animals. Fish that inhabit deep, dark caves cannot see at all, yet they are able to move about normally. Animals, such as the butterfly, that cannot hear can still move very well. If an animal were to lose its body senses, however, its movements would quickly become so impaired that it would not be able to survive. Some aspects of somatosensation are absolutely essential to movement.

In considering the motor system, we started at the cortex and followed the motor pathways out to the spinal cord. This efferent (outward) route makes sense because it follows the direction in which instructions regarding movements flow. As we explore the somatosensory system, we will proceed in the opposite direction, because afferent sensory information flows inward from sensory receptors in various parts of the body through sensory pathways to the cortex.

Somatosensation is unique among sensory systems. It is not localized in the head as are vision, hearing, taste, and smell but rather is distributed throughout the entire body. Somatosensory receptors are found in all parts of the body, and neurons from these receptors carry information to the spinal cord.

Within the spinal cord, two somatosensory pathways project to the brain and, eventually, to the somatosensory cortex. One part of the somatosensory system, however, is confined to a single organ, the middle ear, which houses the vestibular system that contributes to our sense of balance and head movement. Before we detail its workings, we will investigate the anatomy of the somatosensory system and how it contributes to movement.

Somatosensory Receptors and Perception

Our bodies are covered with sensory receptors. They include our skin and body hair and are embedded in both surface layers and deeper layers of the skin and in muscles, tendons, and joints. Some receptors consist simply of the surface of a sensory neuron dendrite. Other receptors include a dendrite and other tissue, such as the dendrite attached to a hair or covered by a special capsule or attached by a sheath of connective tissue to adjacent tissue.

The density of sensory receptors, in the skin, muscles, tendons, and joints, varies greatly in different parts of the body. The variation in density is one reason why different parts of the body are more or less sensitive to stimulation. Body parts that are very sensitive to touch or capable of fine movements—including the hands, feet, lips, and eyes—have many more sensory receptors than other body parts do. Sensitivity to different somatosensory stimuli is also a function of the kinds of receptors that are found in a particular region.

Humans have two kinds of skin, hairy skin and **glabrous skin,** which is hairless and exquisitely sensitive to a wide range of stimuli. Glabrous skin, which includes the skin on the palms of the hands and feet, the lips, and the tongue, is much more richly endowed with receptors than hairy skin is. The need for heightened sensitivity in glabrous skin is due to the fact that it covers the body parts that we use to explore objects.

The touch sensitivity of skin is often measured with a two-point sensitivity test. This test consists of touching the skin with two sharp points simultaneously and observing how close together the points can be placed while still being detected as two points rather than one. On glabrous skin, we can detect the two points when they are as close as 3 mm apart.

Two-point sensitivity

Glabrous skin. Skin that does not have hair follicles but contains larger numbers of sensory receptors than do other skin areas.

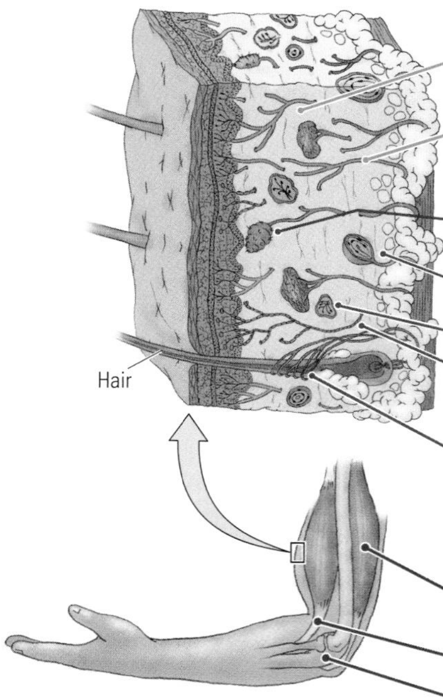

Nocioception (pain and temperature)	Adaptation	Damage to the dendrite or to surrounding cells releases chemicals that stimulate the dendrite to produce action potentials.
Free nerve endings for pain (sharp pain and dull pain)	Slow	
Free nerve endings for temperature (heat or coldness)	Slow	

Hapsis (fine touch and pressure)	Adaptation	Pressure on the various types of tissue capsules mechanically stimulates the dendrites within them to produce action potentials.
Meissner's corpuscle (touch)	Rapid	
Pacinian corpuscle (flutter)	Rapid	
Ruffini corpuscle (vibration)	Rapid	
Merkel's receptor (steady skin indentation)	Slow	
Hair receptors (flutter or steady skin indentation)	Slow	

Proprioception (body awareness)	Adaptation	Movements stretch the receptors to mechanically stimulate the dendrites within them to produce action potentials.
Muscle spindles (muscle stretch)	Rapid	
Golgi tendon organs (tendon stretch)	Rapid	
Joint receptors (joint movement)	Rapid	

Hair

Figure 10-16

Somatosensory Receptors Perceptions derived from the body senses of nocioception, hapsis, and proprioception depend on different receptors located in different parts of the skin, muscles, joints, and tendons.

On hairy skin, two-point sensitivity is much weaker. The two points seem to merge into one below a separation distance ranging from 2 to 5 cm, depending on exactly which part of the body is tested. You can confirm these differences in sensitivity on your own body by touching two sharp pencil points to a palm and to a forearm, varying the distances that you hold the points apart. Be sure not to look as you touch each surface.

Figure 10-16 illustrates a sampling of the various somatosensory receptors located in the skin. There may be as many as 20 or more kinds of somatosensory receptors in the human body, but they can all be classified into the three groupings in Figure 10-16, depending on the type of perception that they enable. These three types of perception and the receptors that mediate them are

■ **nocioception,** the perception of pain and temperature. Nociceptors consist of free nerve endings. When these endings are damaged or irritated, they secrete chemicals, usually peptides, which stimulate the nerve to produce an action potential. The action potential then conveys a message about pain or temperature to the central nervous system.

■ **hapsis,** the perception of objects that we grasp and manipulate or that contact the body—that is, the perception of fine touch and pressure. Haptic receptors are found both in superficial layers and in deep layers of the skin and are attached to body hairs as well. A haptic receptor consists of a dendrite attached to a hair or to connective tissue or a dendrite encased in a capsule of tissue. Mechanical stimulation of the hair, tissue, or capsule activates special channels on the dendrite, which in turn initiate an action potential. Differences in the tissue forming the capsule determine the kinds of mechanical energy conducted through the haptic receptor to the nerve. For example, pressure that squeezes the capsule of a Pacinian corpuscle is the necessary stimulus for initiating an action potential.

Nocioception. Perception of pain and temperature.

Hapsis. Perceptual ability to discriminate objects on the basis of touch.

■ **proprioception,** the perception of the location and movement of the body. Proprioceptors, which also are encapsulated nerve endings, are sensitive to the stretch of muscles and tendons and the movement of joints. In the Golgi tendon organ shown at the bottom of Figure 10-16, for instance, an action potential is triggered when the tendon moves, stretching the receptor attached to it.

Somatosensory receptors are specialized to tell us two things about a sensory event: when it occurs and whether it is still occurring. Information about when a stimulus occurs is handled by **rapidly adapting receptors.** These receptors respond to the beginning and the end of a stimulus and produce only brief bursts of action potentials. As shown in Figure 10-16, Meissner's corpuscles (which respond to touch), Pacinian corpuscles (which respond to fluttering sensations), and Ruffini corpuscles (which respond to vibration) are all rapidly adapting receptors.

In contrast, **slowly adapting receptors** detect whether a stimulus is still occurring. These receptors continue to respond as long as a sensory event is present. For instance, after you have put on an article of clothing and become accustomed to how it feels, only slowly adapting receptors (such as Merkel's receptors and hair receptors) remain active. The difference between a rapidly adapting and a slowly adapting receptor is due in part to the way in which each is stimulated and in part to the way in which ion channels in the membrane of the dendrite respond to mechanical stimulation.

Dorsal-Root Ganglion Neurons

The dendrites that carry somatosensory information belong to neurons whose cell bodies are located just outside the spinal cord in dorsal-root ganglia (see Figure 2-28). Their axons enter the spinal cord. As illustrated in **Figure 10-17**, such a *dorsal-root ganglion neuron* contains a single long dendrite, only the tip of which is responsive to sensory stimulation. This dendrite is continuous with the somatosensory neuron's axon.

Each segment of the spinal cord has one dorsal-root ganglion on each side containing many dorsal-root ganglion neurons, each of which responds to a particular kind of somatosensory information. In the spinal cord, the axons of dorsal-root ganglia neurons may synapse with other neurons or continue to the brain or both.

Proprioception. Perception of the position and movement of the body, limbs, and head.

Rapidly adapting receptor. Body sensory receptor that responds briefly to the onset of a stimulus on the body.

Slowly adapting receptor. Body sensory receptor that responds as long as a sensory stimulus is on the body.

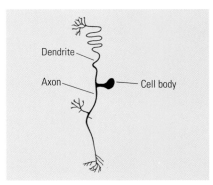

Dendrite

Axon — Cell body

Somatosensory neuron

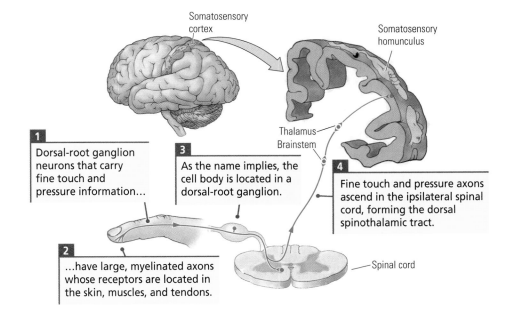

1 Dorsal-root ganglion neurons that carry fine touch and pressure information...

2 ...have large, myelinated axons whose receptors are located in the skin, muscles, and tendons.

3 As the name implies, the cell body is located in a dorsal-root ganglion.

4 Fine touch and pressure axons ascend in the ipsilateral spinal cord, forming the dorsal spinothalamic tract.

Somatosensory cortex

Somatosensory homunculus

Thalamus
Brainstem

Spinal cord

Figure 10-17

Haptic Dorsal-Root Ganglion Neuron
The dendrite and axon of this dorsal-root ganglion neuron are contiguous and carry sensory information from the skin to the central nervous system. The large myelinated dorsal-root axons travel up the spinal cord to the brain in the dorsal column, whereas the small axons synapse with neurons whose axons cross the spinal cord and ascend on the other side (shown in Figure 10-18).

Deafferentation. Loss of incoming sensory input usually due to damage to sensory fibers; also loss of any afferent input to a structure.

The axons of dorsal-root ganglion neurons vary in diameter and myelination. These structural features are related to the kind of information carried by the neurons. Proprioceptive (location and movement) information and haptic (touch and pressure) information are carried by dorsal-root ganglion neurons that have large, well-myelinated axons. Nocioceptive (pain and temperature) information is carried by dorsal-root ganglion neurons that have smaller axons with little or no myelination.

Because of their size and myelination, the larger neurons carry information much faster than the smaller neurons do. One explanation of why proprioceptive and haptic neurons are designed to carry messages quickly is that their information requires rapid responses. For instance, the nervous system must react to moment-to-moment changes in posture and to the equally rapid sensory changes that take place as we explore an object with our hands. In contrast, when the body is injured or cold, such rapid responding is not as essential, because these forms of stimulation usually continue for quite some time.

We can support the claim that sensory information is essential for movement by describing what happens when dorsal-root ganglion cells do not function. A clue comes from a visit to the dentist. If you have ever had a tooth "frozen" for dental work, you have experienced the very strange effect of losing sensation on one side of your face. Not only do you lose pain perception, you also seem to lose the ability to move your facial muscles properly, making it awkward to talk, eat, and smile. So, even though the anesthetic is blocking sensory nerves, your movement ability is affected as well.

In much the same way, damage to sensory nerves affects both sensory perceptions and motor abilities. John Rothwell and his coworkers (1982) described a patient, G. O., who was **deafferented** (lost afferent sensory fibers) by a disease that destroyed sensory dorsal-root ganglion neurons. G. O. had no somatosensory input from his hands. He could not, for example, feel when his hand was holding something. However, G. O. could still accurately produce a range of finger movements, and he could outline figures in the air even with his eyes closed. He could also move his thumb accurately through different distances and at different speeds, judge weights, and match forces by using his thumb.

Nevertheless, his hands were relatively useless to him in daily life. Although G. O. could drive his old car, he was unable to learn to drive a new one. He was also unable to write, to fasten shirt buttons, or to hold a cup.

He could begin movements quite normally, but, as he proceeded, the movement patterns gradually fell apart, ending in failure. Part of G. O.'s difficulties lay in maintaining muscle force for any length of time. When he tried to carry a suitcase, he would quickly drop it unless he continually looked down to confirm that it was there. Clearly, although G. O. had damage only to his sensory neurons, he suffered severe motor disability as well, including the inability to learn new motor skills.

Oliver Sacks

Abnormalities in movement also result from more-selective damage to neurons that carry proprioceptive information about body location and movement. Neurologist Oliver Sacks (1998) gave a dramatic example in his description of a patient, Christina, who suffered damage to proprioceptive sensory fibers throughout her body after taking megadoses of vitamin B_6. Christina was left with very little ability to control her movements and spent most of each day lying prone. Here is how she describes what a loss of proprioception means:

"What I must do then," she said slowly, "is use vision, use my eyes, in every situation where I used—what do you call it?—proprioception before. I've already noticed," she added, musingly, "that I may lose my arms. I think they are in one place, and I find they're in another. This proprioception is like the eyes of the body, the way the body sees itself. And if it goes, as it's gone with me, it's like the body's blind. My body can't see itself if it's lost its eyes, right? So I have to watch it—be its eyes." (Sacks, 1998, p. 46)

Clearly, although Christina's motor system is intact, she is almost completely immobilized without a sense of where her body is in space and what her body is doing. She tries to use her eyes to compensate for loss of proprioception, but visual monitoring is less than satisfactory. Just imagine what it would be like to have to look at each of your limbs in order to move them to appropriate locations, which explains why proprioception is so essential for movement (Cole, 1995).

Somatosensory Pathways to the Brain

As the axons of somatosensory neurons enter the spinal cord, they divide, forming two pathways to the brain. The haptic–proprioceptive axons ascend the spinal cord ipsilaterally (on the same side of the body on which they enter), whereas nociceptive fibers synapse with neurons whose axons cross to the contralateral side of the spinal cord before ascending to the brain. **Figure 10-18** shows these two routes through the spinal cord. The haptic–proprioceptive pathway is shown as a sold red line and the nocioceptive pathway as a dashed red line.

The haptic–proprioceptive axons are located in the dorsal portion of the spinal cord and form the **dorsal spinothalamic tract.** These axons synapse in the dorsal-column nuclei located at the base of the brain. Axons of neurons in the dorsal-column nuclei then cross over to the other side of the brainstem and ascend through the brainstem as part of a pathway called the *medial lemniscus.*

These axons synapse in the **ventrolateral thalamus.** The neurons of the ventrolateral thalamus send most of their axons to the somatosensory cortex, but some axons go to the motor cortex. Thus, three neurons are required to carry haptic–proprioceptive information to the brain: dorsal-root ganglia neurons, dorsal-column nuclei neurons, and thalamic neurons.

The nocioceptive axons, as already stated, take a different route to the brain. They synapse with neurons in the dorsal part of the spinal cord's gray matter. These neurons, in turn, send their axons to the ventral part of the other side of the spinal cord, where they form the **ventral spinothalamic tract.** This tract joins the medial lemniscus in the brainstem to continue on to the ventrolateral thalamus.

Some of the thalamic neurons receiving input from axons of the ventral spinothalamic tract also send their axons to the somatosensory cortex. So, again, three neurons are required to convey nocioceptive information to the brain: dorsal-root neurons, spinal-cord gray-matter neurons, and ventrolateral thalamic neurons.

Notice that the haptic-proprioceptive and the nocioceptive pathways enter the spinal cord together, separate in the spinal cord, and join up again in the brainstem. Thus, two separate pathways in the spinal

Dorsal spinothalamic tract. Pathway that carries fine-touch and pressure fibers.

Ventrolateral thalamus. Part of the thalamus that carries information about body senses to the somatosensory cortex.

Ventral spinothalamic tract. Pathway from the spinal cord to the thalamus that carries information about pain and temperature.

Figure 10-18

Dual Somatosensory Pathways to the Brain As neurons from the dorsal-root ganglia enter the spinal cord, the somatosensory pathways to the brain diverge.

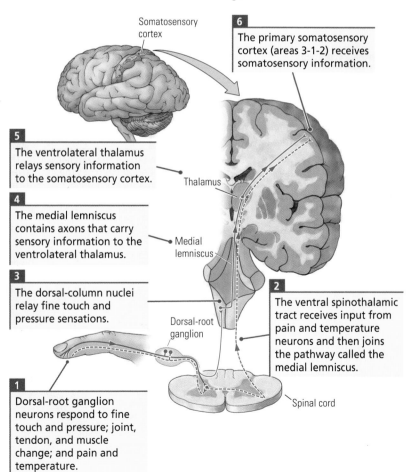

Somatosensory cortex

6 The primary somatosensory cortex (areas 3-1-2) receives somatosensory information.

5 The ventrolateral thalamus relays sensory information to the somatosensory cortex.

Thalamus

4 The medial lemniscus contains axons that carry sensory information to the ventrolateral thalamus.

Medial lemniscus

3 The dorsal-column nuclei relay fine touch and pressure sensations.

Dorsal-root ganglion

2 The ventral spinothalamic tract receives input from pain and temperature neurons and then joins the pathway called the medial lemniscus.

Spinal cord

1 Dorsal-root ganglion neurons respond to fine touch and pressure; joint, tendon, and muscle change; and pain and temperature.

cord convey somatosensory information. Because of this arrangement, unilateral damage in the spinal cord results in distinctive sensory losses to both sides of the body below the site of injury.

As is illustrated in **Figure 10-19**, there is loss of hapsis and proprioception on the side of the body on which the damage occurred and there is a loss of nocioception on the opposite side of the body. Unilateral damage to the dorsal roots or in the brainstem or the thalamus affects hapsis, proprioception, and nocioception equally, because these parts of the pathways for hapsis and proprioception and that for nocioception lie in close proximity.

Spinal Reflexes

Not only do somatosensory nerve fibers convey information to the cortex but they participate in behaviors mediated by the spinal cord and brainstem as well. Spinal-cord somatosensory axons, even those ascending in the dorsal columns, give off axon collaterals that synapse with interneurons and motor neurons on both sides of the spinal cord. The circuits made between sensory receptors and muscles through these connections mediate spinal reflexes.

The simplest spinal reflex consists of a single synapse between a sensory neuron and a motor neuron. **Figure 10-20** illustrates such a **monosynaptic reflex,** the knee jerk that affects the quadriceps muscle of the thigh, which is anchored to the leg bone by the patellar tendon. When the lower leg hangs free and this tendon is tapped with a small hammer, the quadriceps muscle is stretched, activating the stretch-sensitive sensory receptors embedded in it.

The sensory receptors then send a signal to the spinal cord through sensory neurons that synapse with motor neurons projecting back to the same thigh muscle. The discharge from the motor neurons stimulates the muscle, causing it to contract to resist the stretch. Because the tap is brief, the stimulation is over before the motor message ar-

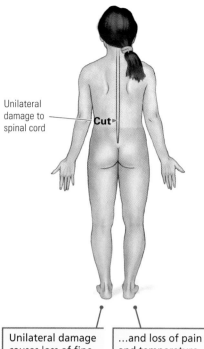

Unilateral damage to spinal cord

Cut ►

Unilateral damage causes loss of fine-touch and pressure sensation on the same side of the body below the cut...

...and loss of pain and temperature sensation on the opposite side of the body below the cut.

Figure 10-19

Effects of Unilateral Injury Damage to only one side of the spinal cord has different effects on fine-touch and pressure sensations compared with those on pain and temperature sensations.

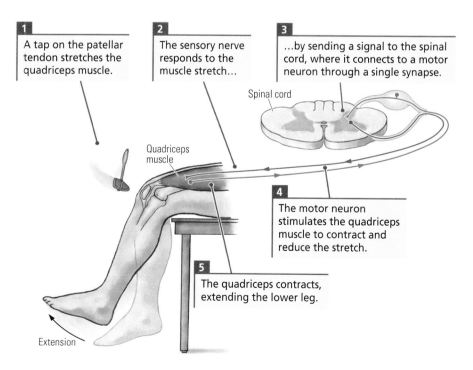

1 A tap on the patellar tendon stretches the quadriceps muscle.

2 The sensory nerve responds to the muscle stretch...

3 ...by sending a signal to the spinal cord, where it connects to a motor neuron through a single synapse.

Spinal cord

Quadriceps muscle

4 The motor neuron stimulates the quadriceps muscle to contract and reduce the stretch.

5 The quadriceps contracts, extending the lower leg.

Extension

Figure 10-20

Monosynaptic Reflex

rives; so the muscle contracts even though it is no longer stretched. This contraction pulls the leg up, thereby producing the reflexive knee jerk.

This very simple reflex entails monosynaptic connections between single sensory neurons and single motor neurons. Somatosensory axons from other receptors, especially those of the skin, make much more complex connections with both interneurons and motor neurons. These multisynaptic connections are responsible for more-complex spinal reflexes that include many muscles on both sides of the body.

Feeling and Treating Pain

One survey concerning complaints about pain reports that the average person will suffer the equivalent of 10 years of pain in his or her lifetime. Another survey reports that 36 percent—more than a third—of patients visiting a physician's office complain of chronic pain. Pain symptoms may be related to arthritis, myalgias (muscle pains), migraine, cancer, nociceptive pain (due to irritation of pain receptors), or neuropathic pain (due to irritation of pain nerves). People suffer pain as a result of acute injuries—including sprains, broken bones, cuts, burns—and stiffness due to exercise. Women may experience pain during menstruation, pregnancy, and childbirth.

People can also experience "central pain" in a part of their body that is not obviously injured. One kind of central pain, *phantom pain,* seems to occur in a limb, but the limb has been lost. People suffering pain would happily dispense with it. But pain is necessary, because the occasional person born without pain receptors experiences body deformities through failure to adjust posture and acute injuries through failure to avoid harmful situations.

Pain is a perception that results from the synthesis of a number of kinds of sensory information. There may be as many as eight different kinds of pain fibers, judging from the peptides and other chemicals released by pain fibers when irritated or damaged. Some of these chemicals irritate surrounding tissue, stimulating the tissue to release other chemicals to stimulate blood flow and to stimulate the pain fibers themselves. These reactions contribute to pain, redness, and swelling at the site of an injury.

In addition, haptic information contributes to the perception of pain. For example, people can accurately report the location and characteristics of various kinds of pain, but, in the absence of fine-touch and pressure information, pain is more difficult to identify and localize.

As described earlier, the ventral spinothalamic tract is the main pain pathway to the brain, but as many as four other pathways may carry pain information from the spinal cord to the brain. These pathways are both crossed and uncrossed and project to the reticular formation of the midbrain, where they may produce arousal, to the amygdala, where they may produce emotional responses, and to the hypothalamus, where they activate hormonal and cardiovascular responses. The fact of multiple pain pathways in the spinal cord makes it difficult to treat chronic pain by selectively cutting the ventrospinothalamic tract.

Circuits in the spinal cord also allow haptic–proprioceptive and nociceptive pathways to interact. Such interactions may be responsible for our very puzzling and variable responses to pain. For example, people who are engaged in combat or intense athletic competition may receive a serious injury to the body but start to feel the pain only much later.

A friend of ours, F. V., who was attacked by a grizzly bear while hiking, received 200 stitches to bind his wounds. When friends asked if it hurt to be bitten by a grizzly bear, he surprisingly answered no, explaining, "I had read the week before about someone

Monosynaptic reflex. Reflex requiring one synapse between sensory input and movement.

◉ To investigate recent research on pain and pain relief, visit the Chapter 10 Web links on the *Brain and Behavior* Web site (**www.worthpublishers.com/kolb**).

◉ On your *Foundations* CD, visit the area on the spinal reflexes in the control of movement module for more illustrations of the spinal cord and the spinal reflexes.

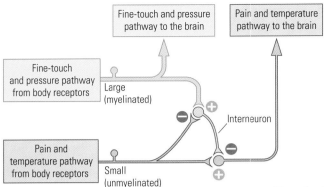

Figure 10-21

A Pain Gate An interneuron in the spinal cord receives excitatory input (plus sign) from the fine-touch and pressure pathway and inhibitor input (minus sign) from the pain and temperature pathway. The relative activity of the interneuron then determines whether pain and temperature information is sent to the brain. Adapted from *The Puzzle of Pain* (p. 154), by R. Melzack, 1973, New York: Basic Books.

Pain gate. Hypothetical neural circuit in which activity in fine-touch and pressure pathways diminishes the activity in pain and temperature pathways.

who was killed and eaten by a grizzly bear. So I was thinking that this bear was going to eat me unless I got away. I did not have time for pain. I was fighting for my life. It was not until the next day that I started feeling pain and fear."

Pain is puzzling in the variety of ways in which it can be lessened. The primacy of our friend's fear over his pain is related to the stress that he was under. Failure to experience pain in a fight-or-flight-situation may be related to the activation of endogenous brain opioids (see Chapter 5). Treatments for pain include opioid drugs (such as morphine), acupuncture (which entails the rapid vibration of needles embedded in the skin), and simply rubbing the area surrounding the injury. To explain in part how pain can be suppressed in so many different ways, Ronald Melzack and Patrick Wall (1965) proposed a "gate" theory of pain.

The essence of their idea is that activity due to haptic–proprioceptive stimulation can reduce pain, whereas the absence of such stimulation can increase pain. They argued that activity in the haptic–proprioceptive pathway can inhibit the pain pathway in the spinal cord through axon collaterals to spinal-cord interneurons. These neurons in turn inhibit pain neurons. For example, if the fine-touch and pressure pathway is active, it will excite the interneuron, which will in turn inhibit the second-order neurons in the pain and temperature pathway.

The action of this **pain gate** is charted in **Figure 10-21**. Notice that both the haptic–proprioceptive fibers and the nociceptive fibers synapse with the interneuron. Collaterals from the haptic–proprioceptive pathway excite the interneuron, whereas collaterals from the nociceptive pathway inhibit the interneuron. The interneuron, in turn, inhibits the neuron that relays pain information to the brain. Consequently, when the haptic–proprioceptive pathway is active, the pain gate partly closes, reducing the sensation of pain.

The gate theory can help explain how different treatments for pain work. For instance, when you stub your toe, you feel pain because the pain pathway to the brain is open. If you then rub the toe, activating the haptic–proprioceptive pathway, the flow of information in the pain pathway is reduced because the pain gate partly closes, which relieves the pain sensation.

Similarly, acupuncture may produce its pain-relieving effects because the vibrating needles used in this treatment selectively activate haptic and proprioceptive fibers, closing the pain gate. Interestingly, the interneurons in the pain gate may use opioid peptides as a neurotransmitter. If so, the gate theory can also explain how endogenous opoids reduce pain.

The gate theory even suggests an explanation for the "pins and needles" that we feel after sitting too long in one position. Loss of oxygen from reduced blood flow may first deactivate the large myelinated axons that carry touch and pressure information, leaving the small unmyelinated fibers that carry pain and temperature messages unaffected. As a result, "ungated" sensory information flows in the pain and temperature pathway, leading to the pins-and-needles sensation.

Melzack and Wall propose that pain gates may be located in the brainstem and cortex in addition to the spinal cord. These additional gates could help explain how other approaches to pain relief work. For example, researchers have found that feelings of severe pain can be lessened when people have a chance to shift their attention from the pain to other stimuli. Dentists have long used this technique by giving their patients something soothing to watch or listen to while undergoing painful work on their teeth.

This influence of attention on pain sensations may work through a cortical pain gate. Electrical stimulation in a number of sites in the brainstem also can reduce pain, perhaps by closing brainstem pain gates. Another way in which pain perceptions might be lessened is through descending pathways from the forebrain and the brainstem to the spinal-cord pain gate.

The presence of relatively complex neural circuits in the spinal cord, such as the pain gate, may be related both to the variable nature of pain and to some successful treatments and some problems in treating pain. In response to noxious stimulation, pain neurons in the spinal cord can undergo sensitization (see Experiment 5-3). In other words, successive pain experience can produce an escalating response to a similar noxious stimulus. Spinal-cord neurons thus learn to produce a larger pain signal.

One of the most successful treatments for pain is the injection of small amounts of morphine under the dura of the spinal cord. This epidural anesthesia is mediated by the action of morphine or other opioid drugs on pain neurons in the spinal cord. Although morphine is a very useful treatment for pain, the effects of morphine lessen with continued use. This form of habituation (see Experiment 5-2) may be related to changes that take place on the receptors of pain neurons in the spinal cord and brain.

The brain can also influence the pain signal that is sent to it from the spinal cord. Electrical stimulation in a region of the midbrain called the **periaqueductal gray matter** (PAG) is surprisingly effective in suppressing pain. The cell bodies of these neurons surround the cerebral aqueduct connecting the third and fourth ventricles (see Figure 2-18).

Neurons in the PAG excite brainstem-activating systems (including serotonin and noradrenaline neurons), which in turn project to the spinal cord, and inhibit neurons in the spinal cord that form the ascending pain pathways. Activation in these inhibitory circuits may explain in part why the sensation and perception of pain is lessened during sleep. Stimulation of the PAG by implanted microelectrodes is one way of treating pain that is resistant to all other therapies, including treatment with opioid drugs.

Many internal organs of the body, including the heart, the kidneys, and the blood vessels, have pain receptors, but the ganglion neurons carrying information from these receptors do not have their own pathway to the brain. Instead, these ganglion neurons synapse with spinal-cord neurons that receive nocioceptive information from the body's surface. Consequently, the neurons in the spinal cord that relay pain and temperature messages to the brain receive two sets of signals: one from the body's surface and the other from the internal organs.

These spinal-cord neurons cannot distinguish between the two sets of signals; nor can we. As a result, pain in body organs is often felt as **referred pain** coming from the surface of the body. For example, the pain in the heart associated with a heart attack may be felt as pain in the left shoulder and upper arm (**Figure 10-22**). Pain in the stomach is felt as pain in the midline of the trunk; pain in the kidneys is felt as pain in the lower back. Pain in blood vessels in the head is felt as diffuse pain that we call a headache (remember that the brain has no pain receptors).

The Vestibular System and Balance

The only localized part of the somatosensory system, the **vestibular system,** consists of two organs, one located in each middle ear. As **Figure 10-23A** shows, each vestibular organ is made up of two groups of receptors: the three *semicircular canals* and the *otolith organs,* which consist of the *utricle* and the *saccule.* These vestibular receptors do two jobs: (1) they tell us the position of the body in relation to gravity and (2) they signal changes in the direction and the speed of movements of the head.

You can see in Figure 10-23A that the semicircular canals are oriented in three different planes that correspond to the three dimensions in which we move. Each canal furnishes information about movement in its particular plane. The semicircular canals

Periaqueductal gray matter (PAG). Nuclei in the midbrain that surround the cerebral aqueduct joining the third and fourth ventricles; PAG neurons contain circuits for species-typical behaviors (e.g., female sexual behavior) and play an important role in the modulation of pain.

Referred pain. Pain felt on the surface of the body that is actually due to pain in one of the internal organs of the body.

Vestibular system. A set of receptors in the middle ear that indicate position and movement of the head

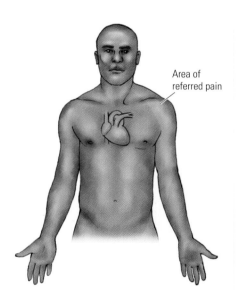

Area of referred pain

Figure 10-22

Referred Pain   During a heart attack, pain from receptors in the heart is felt in the left shoulder and upper arm.

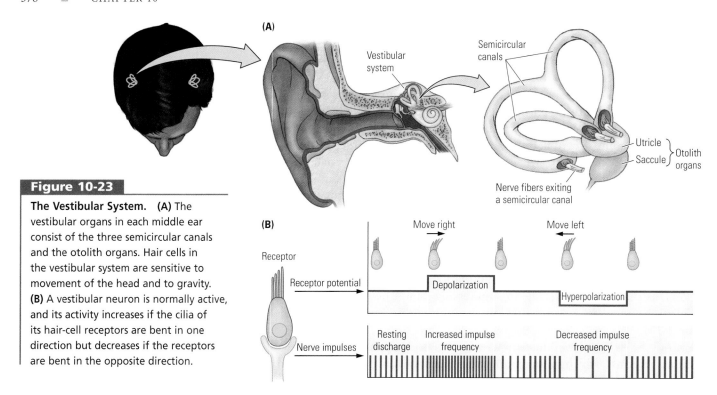

(A)

Vestibular system

Semicircular canals

Utricle

Saccule

Otolith organs

Nerve fibers exiting a semicircular canal

(B)

Receptor

Move right

Move left

Receptor potential

Depolarization

Hyperpolarization

Nerve impulses

Resting discharge

Increased impulse frequency

Decreased impulse frequency

Figure 10-23

The Vestibular System. **(A)** The vestibular organs in each middle ear consist of the three semicircular canals and the otolith organs. Hair cells in the vestibular system are sensitive to movement of the head and to gravity. **(B)** A vestibular neuron is normally active, and its activity increases if the cilia of its hair-cell receptors are bent in one direction but decreases if the receptors are bent in the opposite direction.

are filled with a fluid called *endolymph.* Immersed in the endolymph is a set of hair cells very much like the hair cells described in Chapter 9 that mediate hearing.

When the head moves, the endolymph also moves, pushing against the hair cells and bending the cilia at their tips. The force of the bending is converted into receptor potentials in the hair cells and action potentials that are sent over vestibular nerve axons to the brain. These axons are normally quite active: bending the hair cell cilia in one direction increases neurotransmitter release, consequently increasing vestibular nerve axon activity; bending them in the other direction decreases vestibular afferent axon activity.

These responses are diagrammed in Figure 10-23B. Typically, when the head turns in one direction, the message on the side of the body to which the turn is made is an increase in neural firing. The message on the body's opposite side is a decrease in firing.

The utricle and saccule are located just beneath the semicircular canals. They also contain hair cells, but these receptors are embedded in a gelatin-like substance that contains small crystals of the salt calcium carbonate called *otoconia.* When you tilt your head, the gelatin and otoconia press against the hair cells, bending them. The mechanical action of the hair bending modulates the rate of action potentials in vestibular afferent axons that convey messages about the position of the head in three-dimensional space.

The receptors in the vestibular system tell us about our location relative to gravity, about acceleration and deceleration of our movements, and about changes in movement direction. They also allow us to ignore the otherwise very destabilizing influence that our movements might have on us. For example, when you are standing on a bus, even slight movements of the vehicle could potentially throw you off balance, but they do not. Similarly, when you make movements yourself, you easily avoid tipping over, despite the constant shifting of your body weight. Your vestibular system enables you to keep from tipping over.

Here is an experiment that you can perform to illustrate the role of vestibular receptors in helping you to compensate for your own movements. If you hold your hand in front of you and shake it, your hand appears blurry. But, if you shake your head instead of your hand, the hand remains in focus. Compensatory signals from your vestibular system allow you to see the hand as stable even though you are moving around.

In Review

Body senses contribute to the perception of hapsis (touch and pressure), proprioception (location and movement), and nocioception (temperature and pain). Haptic–proprioceptive information is carried by the dorsal spinothalamic tract; nocioceptive information is carried by the ventral spinothalamic tract. The two systems interact in the spinal cord to regulate the perception of pain by a pain gate. In the midbrain, the periaqueductal gray matter effectively suppresses pain by activating neuromodulatory circuits that inhibit pain pathways. The only localized somatosensory system, the vestibular system, helps us keep our balance by signaling information about the head's position and our movement through space.

EXPLORING THE SOMATOSENSORY CORTEX

Not only do somatosensory neurons convey sensation to the brain but they also provide our perceptions—of things that we describe as pleasant or unpleasant, of the shape and texture of objects, of the effort required to complete tasks, and even of our spatial world. These perceptual abilities are mediated by the somatosensory cortex.

As illustrated in **Figure 10-24**, there are two main somatosensory areas in the cortex. The primary somatosensory cortex is the area that receives projections from the thalamus. It consists of Brodmann's areas 3-1-2 (all shaded red in the figure). The primary somatosensory cortex begins the process of constructing perceptions from somatosensory information. It mainly consists of the postcentral gyrus just behind the central fissure, which means that the primary somatosensory cortex is adjacent to the primary motor cortex. The secondary somatosensory cortex (Brodmann's areas 5 and 7, shaded orange and yellow in the figure), located in the parietal lobe just behind the primary somatosensory cortex, continues the construction of perceptions.

Secondary somatosensory cortex receives sensory information from the primary somatosensory cortex.

Primary somatosensory cortex receives sensory information from the body.

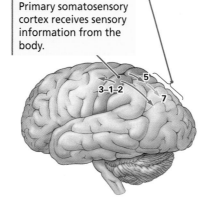

Figure 10-24

Somatosensory Cortex   Stimulation of the primary somatosensory cortex in the parietal lobe produces sensations that are referred to appropriate body parts by the motor cortex. Information from the primary somatosensory cortex travels to the secondary somatosensory cortex for further perceptual analysis and contribution to movement sequences mediated in the frontal lobes.

The Somatosensory Homunculus

In his studies of human patients undergoing brain surgery, Wilder Penfield electrically stimulated the somatosensory cortex and recorded the patients' responses. Stimulation at some sites elicited sensations in the foot, whereas stimulation of other sites produced

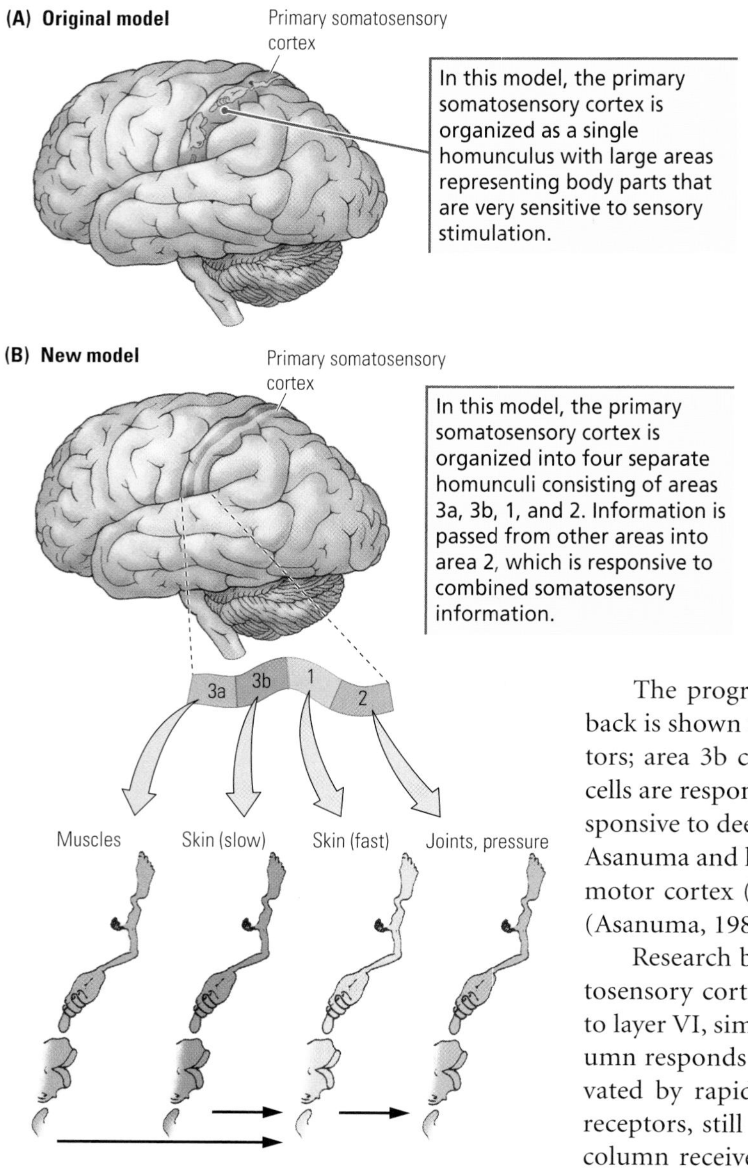

(A) Original model

Primary somatosensory cortex

In this model, the primary somatosensory cortex is organized as a single homunculus with large areas representing body parts that are very sensitive to sensory stimulation.

(B) New model

Primary somatosensory cortex

In this model, the primary somatosensory cortex is organized into four separate homunculi consisting of areas 3a, 3b, 1, and 2. Information is passed from other areas into area 2, which is responsive to combined somatosensory information.

3a   3b   1   2

Muscles   Skin (slow)   Skin (fast)   Joints, pressure

Figure 10-25

Two Models of Somatosensory Cortex Organization   **(A)** Penfield's single-homunculus model. **(B)** A four-homunculus model based on the stimulation of sensory receptors on the body surface and recording from the somatosensory cortex.

sensations in a hand, the trunk, or the face. By mapping these responses, Penfield was able to construct a somatosensory homunculus in the cortex, shown in **Figure 10-25A.**

Penfield's work half a century ago demonstrates, for example, that a dorsal-root ganglion neuron carrying fine-touch and pressure information from a finger through its connections sends information to the finger region of the somatosensory cortex. The sensory homunculus looks very similar to the motor homunculus in that the areas of the body most sensitive to sensory stimulation are accorded a relatively larger cortical area.

Using smaller electrodes and more-precise recording techniques in monkeys, Jon Kaas (1987) proposed that the somatosensory cortex does not consist of a single homunculus as proposed in Penfield's original model. He stimulated sensory receptors on the body and recorded the activity of cells in the sensory cortex. He found that the somatosensory cortex is actually composed of four representations of the body. Each is associated with a certain class of sensory receptors.

The progression of these areas across the human cortex from front to back is shown in Figure 10-25B. Area 3a cells are responsive to muscle receptors; area 3b cells are responsive to slow-responding skin receptors. Area 1 cells are responsive to rapidly adapting skin receptors, and area 2 cells are responsive to deep tissue pressure and joint receptors. In other studies, Hiroshi Asanuma and his coworkers found still another sensory representation in the motor cortex (area 4) in which cells respond to muscle and joint receptors (Asanuma, 1989).

Research by Vernon Mountcastle (1978) showed that cells in the somatosensory cortex are arranged in functional columns running from layer I to layer VI, similar to columns found in the visual cortex. Every cell in a column responds to a single class of receptors. Some columns of cells are activated by rapidly adapting skin receptors, others by slowly adapting skin receptors, still others by pressure receptors, and so forth. All neurons in a column receive information from the same local area of skin. In this way, neurons lying within a column seem to be an elementary functional unit of the somatosensory cortex.

The construction of perceptions from sensations depends on a hierarchical organization of the somatosensory cortex, with basic sensations being combined to form more-complex perceptions. This combining of information takes place as areas 3a and 3b project onto area 1, which in turn projects onto area 2. For example, whereas a cell in area 3a or 3b may respond to activity in only a certain area on a certain finger, cells in area 1 may respond to similar information from a number of different fingers.

At the next level of synthesis, cells in area 2 may respond to stimulation in a number of different locations on a number of different fingers, as well as to stimulation from different kinds of receptors. Thus, area 2 contains multimodal neurons that are responsive to movement force, orientation, and direction, all properties that we perceive when we hold an object in our hands and manipulate it.

With each successive relay of information, both the size of the pertinent receptive fields and the synthesis of somatosensory modalities increase. That the different kinds of somatosensory information are both separated and combined in the cortex raises the question of why both segregation and synthesis are needed. One reason that sensory in-

Tickling

Focus on New Research

Everyone knows the effects and consequences of tickling. The perception of tickling is a curious mixture of pleasant and unpleasant sensory stimulation. The tickle sensation is experienced not only by humans but also by other primates, cats, rats, and probably most mammals. Tickling is rewarding in that people and animals will solicit tickles from others, but it is also noxious because they will attempt to avoid the stimulation when it becomes too intense.

It is well known, and even described in ancient historical records, that a tickle stimulus is much more pronounced when produced by another person than when produced by ourselves. In other words, we find it hard, if not impossible, to tickle ourselves as others can tickle us. What accounts for the experience of a tickle and why can we not tickle ourselves?

Sarah Blakemore and her colleagues (1998) attempted to answer these questions by using a robot and brain-imaging techniques. They designed the robot so that, when operated by a human subject, it delivered one of two kinds of identical tactile stimuli to the palm of the subject's hand. In one condition, the robot faithfully delivered the stimulus that the subject commanded. In the other condition, the robot introduced an unpredictable delay in the stimulus.

The faithfully delivered stimulation was not perceived by the subject as tickles, but the unpredictable stimulus was. Thus, it is not the stimulation itself but its unpredictability that accounts in large part for the tickle perception.

Using the technique of functional magnetic resonance brain imaging (fMRI), which measures blood flow and hence brain activity, Blakemore and her colleagues found that the predictable and unpredictable sensory stimulation had different effects on the activity of a subject's sensory cortex. Even though the intensity of stimulation was the same in both conditions, the sensory cortex was much less responsive to the predictable than to the unpredictable stimulus. By extension, the sensory cortex is relatively unresponsive when we attempt to tickle ourselves in comparison with a tickle delivered by someone else.

Why are we less responsive to self-stimulation? Brain imaging of the cerebellum in the same two experimental conditions shows that the anterior cerebellum is less active during the predictable self-induced sensory stimulation compared with the unpredictable stimulation. The researchers propose, therefore, that, when we produce a movement to tickle ourselves, the cortex sends out a command to produce the movement and at the same time sends a signal to the cerebellum instructing it to ignore the associated sensory stimulation produced by the movement (see Figure 10-15).

If the sensation produced by the movement is predictable, feedback from the movement is muted by the cerebellum. If the sensory stimulation is not predictable, the cerebellum amplifies it. This brain circuitry, which is normally used to correct errors in our own movements, may thus underlie tickling. Perhaps the wriggly movements that we make in response to tickles are attempts to make the stimuli more predictable.

---

formation remains segregated at the level of the cortex could be that we often need to distinguish between different kinds of sensory stimuli coming from different sources. For example, we need to be able to tell the difference between tactile stimulation on the surface of the skin, which is usually produced by some external agent, and stimulation coming from muscles, tendons, and joints, which is likely produced by our own movements.

Yet, at the same time, we also often need to know about the combined sensory properties of a stimulus. For instance, when we manipulate an object, it is useful to "know" the object both in regard to its sensory properties, such as temperature and texture, and in regard to the movements that we make as we handle it. For this reason, the cortex provides for somatosensory synthesis, too. The tickle sensation seems rooted in an "other versus us" somatosensory distinction, as described in "Tickling."

⊙ For more information on the tickle sensation, visit the Chapter 10 Web links on the *Brain and Behavior* Web site (**www.worthpublishers.com/kolb**).

Effects of Damage to the Somatosensory Cortex

Suzanne Corkin

Damage to the primary somatosensory cortex impairs the ability to make even simple sensory discriminations and movements. Suzanne Corkin and her coworkers (1970) demonstrated this effect by examining patients with cortical lesions that included most of areas 3-1-2 in one hemisphere. The researchers mapped the sensory cortices of these patients before they underwent elective surgery for removal of a carefully defined piece of that cortex, including the hand area. The patients' sensory and motor skills in both hands were tested on three different occasions: before the surgery, shortly after the surgery, and almost a year afterward.

The tests included pressure sensitivity, two-point touch discrimination, position sense (reporting the direction in which a finger was being moved), and haptic sense (using touch to identify objects, such as a pencil, a penny, eyeglasses, and so forth). For all the sensory abilities tested, the surgical lesions produced a severe and seemingly permanent deficit in the contralateral hand. Sensory thresholds, proprioception, and hapsis were all greatly impaired.

The results of other studies in both humans and animals have shown that damage to the somatosensory cortex also impairs simple movements. For example, limb use in reaching for an object is impaired, as is the ability to shape the hand to hold an object (Leonard et al., 1991). Nevertheless, the somatosensory cortex is plastic, as is the motor cortex. It can dramatically reorganize itself after deafferentation.

In 1991, Tim Pons and his coworkers reported a dramatic change in the somatosensory maps of monkeys in which the ganglion cells for one arm had been deafferented a number of years earlier. The researchers had wanted to develop an animal model of damage to sensory nerves that could be a source of insight into human injuries, but they were interrupted by a legal dispute with an animal advocacy group. Years later, as the health of the animals declined, a court injunction allowed the mapping experiment to be conducted.

Pons and his coworkers discovered that the area of the somatosensory cortex that had formerly represented the arm no longer did so. Light touches on the lower face of a monkey now activated cells in what had formerly been the cortical arm region. As illustrated in **Figure 10-26**, the facial area in the cortex had expanded by as much as 10 to 14 mm, virtually doubling its original size by entering the arm area.

This massive change was completely unexpected. The stimulus–response patterns associated with the new expanded facial area of the cortex appeared indistinguishable from those associated with the original facial area. Furthermore, the trunk area, which bounded the other side of the cortical arm area, did not expand into the vacated arm area.

What could account for this expansion of the face area into the arm area? One possibility is that axons grew across the cortex from the face area into the arm area, but no evidence supports this possibility. Another possibility is that the thalamic neurons representing the facial area projected axon collaterals to the cortical neurons representing the arm area. These collaterals might be preexisting or they might be new growths subsequent to deafferentation.

There is evidence for preexisting collaterals that are not normally active, but these collaterals would probably not be able to extend far enough to account for all of the cortical reorganization. A third possibility is that, within the dorsal columns, facial-area neurons projected collaterals to arm-area neurons. These neurons are close together, and so the collaterals need travel only a millimeter or so.

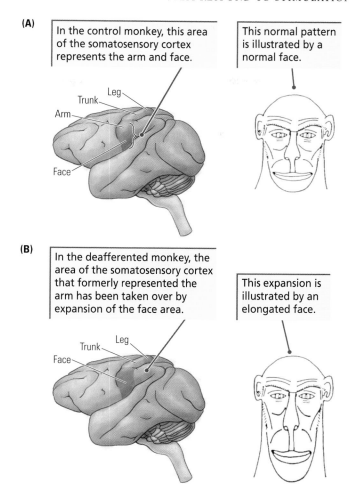

(A)

In the control monkey, this area of the somatosensory cortex represents the arm and face.

Leg
Trunk
Arm
Face

This normal pattern is illustrated by a normal face.

(B)

In the deafferented monkey, the area of the somatosensory cortex that formerly represented the arm has been taken over by expansion of the face area.

Leg
Trunk
Face

This expansion is illustrated by an elongated face.

Figure 10-26

Somatosensory Plasticity   Adapted from "Massive Cortical Reorganization after Sensory Deafferentation in Adult Macaques," by T. P. Pons, P. E. Garraghty, A. K. Ommaya, J. H. Kaas, and M. Mishkin, 1991, *Science, 252,* p. 1858.

Whatever the mechanism, the very dramatic cortical reorganization observed in this study eventually had far-reaching consequences for understanding other remarkable phenomena, including phantom-limb sensations. We will return to this story in Chapter 13, where we look at how the brain changes in response to experience.

The Somatosensory Cortex and Complex Movement

This chapter began by describing the remarkable painting skills of Kamala the elephant. Kamala first needs a plan—some idea of what she wants to paint. She must then execute the movements required to apply paint to her canvas, and she must use somatosensory information to confirm that she is producing the movements that she intends. So to paint or to perform virtually any complex movement, the motor system and the somatosensory system must work together. In this final section of the chapter, we explore that interaction.

The secondary somatosensory cortex plays an important role in confirming which movements have already taken place and in deciding which movements should follow. Damage to the secondary somatosensory cortex does not disrupt the plans for making movements, but it does disrupt how the movements are performed, leaving their execution fragmented and confused. The inability to complete a plan of action accurately

Apraxia. Inability to make voluntary movements in the absence of paralysis or other motor or sensory impairment, especially an inability to make proper use of an object

is called **apraxia** (from the Greek words for "no" and "action"). The following case highlights the symptoms of apraxia:

> A woman with a biparietal lesion [damage on both sides of the secondary somatosensory cortex] had worked for years as a fish-filleter. With the development of her symptoms, she began to experience difficulty in carrying on with her job. She did not seem to know what to do with her knife. She would stick the point in the head of a fish, start the first stroke, and then come to a stop. In her own mind she knew how to fillet fish, but yet she could not execute the maneuver. The foreman accused her of being drunk and sent her home for mutilating fish.
>
> The same patient also showed another unusual phenomenon that might possibly be apraxic in nature. She could never finish an undertaking. She would begin a job, drop it, start another, abandon that one, and within a short while would have four or five uncompleted tasks on her hands. This would cause her to do such inappropriate actions as putting the sugar bowl in the refrigerator, and the coffeepot inside the oven. (Critchley, 1953, pp. 158–159)

How does an intact secondary somatosensory cortex contribute to the organization of movement? Recall from Chapter 8 that visual information influences movement through the dorsal and ventral streams. The dorsal stream, working without conscious awareness, provides vision for action, as when we use the visual form of a cup to automatically shape a hand to grasp that cup. The ventral stream, in contrast, works with conscious awareness and provides the vision needed to identify objects.

As **Figure 10-27** illustrates, the secondary somatosensory cortex participates in both visual streams. The dorsal visual stream projects to the secondary somatosensory cortex and then to the prefrontal cortex. In this way, visual information is integrated with somatosensory information to produce movements that are appropriately shaped and directed for their targets.

Much less is known about how the secondary somatosensory cortex contributes to the ventral stream, but it is likely that somatosensory information about the identity of objects and completed movements is relayed by the ventral stream to the prefrontal cortex. The prefrontal cortex can then select the appropriate actions that should follow from those that are already complete. Consider the difference in the way we would reach for an empty glass versus a glass filled to the brim with hot liquid.

Close interaction between the somatosensory system and the motor system exists at all levels of the nervous system. It can be seen in the spinal cord, where sensory information contributes to spinal reflexes. It can also be seen in the brainstem, where various species-specific behaviors, such as attack, withdrawal, and grooming, require both appropriate patterns of movement and appropriate sensory information.

The close interrelation is found as well at the level of the neocortex, where skilled movements elicited by the motor regions of the frontal lobes require information about actions that have just taken place and about objects that have been or could be manipulated. In short, an interaction between the motor cortex, which decides what should be done, and the sensory cortex, which knows what has been done, is central to how the brain produces movement in the here and now.

Figure 10-27

Visual Aid The secondary somatosensory cortex contributes to information flow in dorsal (how) and ventral (what) visual streams

Information from the secondary somatosensory cortex contributes to the dorsal stream by specifing the movement used for grasping a target.

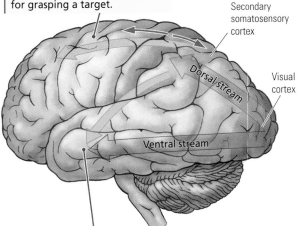

Secondary somatosensory cortex

Dorsal stream

Visual cortex

Ventral stream

Information from the secondary somatosensory cortex contributes to the ventral stream by providing information about object size and shape.

In Review

The primary somatosensory cortex, which is arranged as a series of homunculi, provides information to the secondary somatosensory cortex, which in turn contributes to the dorsal (how) and ventral (what) visual streams. Damage to the secondary somatosensory cortex produces apraxia, an inability to complete a series of movements. A person with this condition has trouble knowing both what action has just been completed and what action should follow in a movement sequence.

SUMMARY

■ *How is the motor system organized?* The organization of movement is hierarchical, with almost the entire brain contributing to it in some way. The forebrain plans, organizes, and initiates movements, whereas the brainstem coordinates regulatory functions, such as eating and drinking, and controls neural mechanisms that maintain posture and produce locomotion. Many reflexes are organized at the level of the spinal cord and occur without any involvement of the brain.

■ *How is the motor cortex organized?* Maps produced by stimulating the motor cortex show that it is organized topographically as a homunculus, with parts of the body capable of fine movements associated with large regions of motor cortex. Two pathways emerge from the motor cortex to the spinal cord. The lateral corticospinal tract consists of axons from the digit, hand, and arm regions of the motor cortex. The tract synapses with spinal interneurons and motor neurons located laterally in the spinal cord, on the side of the cord opposite the side of the brain on which the corticospinal tract started. The ventral corticospinal tract consists of axons from the trunk region of the motor cortex. This tract synapses with interneurons and motor neurons located medially in the spinal cord, on the same side of the cord as the side of the brain on which the corticospinal tract started. Interneurons and motor neurons of the spinal cord also are topographically organized, with more laterally located motor neurons projecting to digit, hand, and arm muscles and more medially located motor neurons projecting to trunk muscles.

■ *How do motor-cortex neurons produce movement?* Movements innate to a species are organized as synergies, or movement patterns. Motor-cortex neurons initiate movement, produce movement, control the force of movement, and indicate movement direction. Different species of animals have topographic maps in which areas of the body capable of the most-skilled movements have the largest motor-cortex representation. Disuse of a limb, such as that which might follow motor-cortex injury, results in shrinkage of that limb's representation in the motor cortex. This shrinkage of motor-cortex representation can be prevented, however, if the limb can be somehow forced into use.

■ *How do the basal ganglia and the cerebellum contribute to controlling movement?* Damage to the basal ganglia or to the cerebellum results in abnormalities of movement. This result tells us that both these brain structures somehow participate in movement control. The results of experimental studies suggest that the basal ganglia regulate the force of movements, whereas the cerebellum plays a role in movement timing and in maintaining the accuracy of movements.

■ *How is the somatosensory system organized?* The somatosensory system is distributed throughout the entire body and consists of more than 20 types of specialized receptors,

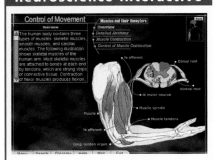

neuroscience interactive

Many resources are available for expanding your learning online:

■ **www.worthpublishers.com/kolb**

Try the Chapter 10 quizzes and flashcards to test your mastery of the chapter material. You'll also be able to link to other Web sites that will reinforce what you've learned.

■ **www.spinalinjury.net**

Go to this site to learn more about current research on spinal-cord injury.

■ **www.tsa-usa.org**

Learn more about Tourette's syndrome, an often misunderstood disorder, at the home page of the Tourette's Syndrome Association.

On your *Foundations* CD-ROM, you can visit the module on Control of Movement where you will find interactive illustrations to reinforce your understanding of key concepts.

each of which is sensitive to a particular form of mechanical energy. Each somatosensory receptor projecting from skin, muscles, tendons, or joints is associated with a dorsal-root ganglion neuron that carries the sensory information into the brain. Fibers carrying proprioceptive (location and movement) information and haptic (touch and pressure) information ascend the spinal cord as the dorsal spinothalamic tract. These fibers synapse in the dorsal-column nuclei at the base of the brain, at which point axons cross over to the other side of the brainstem to form the medial lemniscus, which ascends to the ventrolateral thalamus. Most of the ventrolateral thalamus cells project to the somatosensory cortex. Nocioceptive (pain and temperature) dorsal-root ganglion neurons synapse on entering the spinal cord. Their relay neurons cross the spinal cord to ascend to the thalamus as the ventral spinothalamic tract. Because there are two somatosensory pathways that take somewhat different routes, unilateral spinal-cord damage impairs proprioception and hapsis ipsilaterally below the site of injury and nocioception contralaterally below the site.

■ *How is somatosensory information represented in the neocortex?* The somatosensory system is represented topographically as a homunculus in the primary somatosensory region of the parietal cortex (areas 3-1-2) such that the most sensitive parts of the body are accorded the largest regions of neocortex. A number of homunculi represent different sensory modalities, and these regions are hierarchically organized. If sensory input from a part of the body is cut off from the cortex by damage to sensory fibers, adjacent functional regions of the sensory cortex can expand into the now-unoccupied region.

■ *How do the somatosensory system and the motor system interact?* The somatosensory system and the motor system are interrelated at all levels of the nervous system. At the level of the spinal cord, sensory information contributes to motor reflexes; in the brainstem, sensory information contributes to complex regulatory movements. At the level of the neocortex, sensory information is used to record just-completed movements, as well as to represent the sizes and shapes of objects. The somatosensory cortex contributes to the dorsal visual stream to direct hand movements to targets. The somatosensory cortex also contributes to the ventral visual stream to create representations of external objects.

KEY TERMS

apraxia, p. 384
autism, p. 349
cerebral palsy, p. 349
corticospinal tract, p. 355
deafferentation, p. 372
dissolution, p. 345
dorsal spinothalamic tract, p. 373
glabrous skin, p. 369
hapsis, p. 370
homunculus, p. 354
hyperkinetic symptom, p. 364

hypokinetic symptom, p. 364
monosynaptic reflex, p. 375
motor sequence, p. 345
nocioception, p. 370
pain gate, p. 376
paraplegia, p. 350
periaqueductal gray matter (PAG), p. 377
proprioception, p. 371
quadriplegia, p. 350
rapidly adapting receptor, p. 371

referred pain, p. 377
scratch reflex, p. 351
slowly adapting receptor, p. 371
synergy, p. 358
topographic organization, p. 354
ventral spinothalamic tract, p. 373
ventrolateral thalamus, p. 373
vestibular system, p. 377

REVIEW QUESTIONS

1. How are the somatosensory system and the motor system related?

2. Describe the pathways that convey somatosensory information to the brain.

3. Describe the pathways that convey motor instructions to the spinal cord.

4. What are the contributions of the cortex, the basal ganglia, and the cerebellum to movement?

5. Describe two theories of how the human motor cortex moves a hand to a target to grasp it.

6. Describe the changes that the somatosensory cortex and the motor cortex might undergo in response to injury to the cortex or to a limb.

FOR FURTHER THOUGHT

1. Why is the somatosensory system so much more intimately linked to movement than the other sensory systems are?

2. Why might the dorsal and ventral streams be separate systems for controlling hand movements?

RECOMMENDED READING

Asanuma, H. (1989). *The motor cortex.* New York: Raven Press. An excellent summary of the motor system by a scientist who made important advances in studying the role of the motor cortex in behavior.

Cole, J. (1995). *Pride and a daily marathon.* London: MIT Press. At the age of 19, Ian Waterman was struck down by a rare neurological condition that deprived him of joint position and proprioception. This book tells the story of how he gradually adapted to his strange condition by using vision and elaborate tricks to monitor his every movement and regain his life.

Melzack, R. (1973). *The puzzle of pain.* New York: Basic Books. For ages, physicians and scientists have attempted with little success to understand and control pain. Here, one of the world's leading researchers in the field of pain theory and treatment presents a totally readable book to unravel the mystery of pain.

Sacks, O. (1974). *Awakenings.* New York: Vintage Books. This prize-winning book presents a fascinating account of one of the mysteries of the motor system—how the great flu of the 1920s produced the Parkinsonism that developed as the aftermath of the "sleeping sickness." This story presents wonderful insights into the function of the motor system.

Porter, R., & Lemon, R. (1993). *Corticospinal function and voluntary movement.* Oxford: Clarendon Press. This book tells the story of the human brain's great pathway, the corticospinal tract.

What Causes Emotional and Motivated Behavior?

Left: **Dr. Dennis Kunkel/Phototake.** Middle: **Photodisc.** Right: **Zephyr/Photo Researchers.**

The Pain of Rejection

Focus on New Research

Sorrow, grief, and heartbreak are words that we use to describe a loss. Loss evokes painful feelings, as does the pain inflicted by social exclusion. Exclusion leads to "hurt" feelings. To discover whether painful or hurtful feelings are manifested in the brain's neural circuitry, Naomi Eisenberger and colleagues (2003) performed an experiment.

Participants were scanned in an fMRI apparatus while they played a virtual ball-tossing video game. Initially, the subjects believed that they were merely observing the game but, during the experimental phase, they became active participants. Within a few throws, the other "players" (actually computerized stooges) stopped throwing the ball to the participants, leading them to feel excluded.

The question the researchers asked is whether this emotional response activates the same neural systems that are normally activated when people feel physical pain. Two regions of the forebrain affected by physical pain are the anterior cingulate cortex, which becomes more active when physical pain is inflicted, and the orbital prefrontal cortex, which becomes more active when physical distress is low.

The Eisenberger team found that emotional pain activates the opposing reactions of these areas in exactly the same way. Participants' fMRI scans, recorded in the accompanying images, reveal that the anterior cingulate cortex may act to suppress the feelings of social distress, shown here in the fMRI scan on the left below, as does the orbital prefrontal cortex, shown in the scan on the right below.

These results suggest that the experience and regulation of both physical and social pain have a common neuroanatomical basis. Findings from this study are sources of two insights about the range of emotional feelings, or *affective states*:

1. The same pattern of brain activation accompanies both physical and emotional pain—in this case, "hurt feelings." Other investigators have shown parallel neural correlates for a range of pleasant feelings, including the craving for chocolate, winning the lottery, and sexual arousal.

2. Normalizing the activity of these brain regions likely provides a basis for both physical and mental restorative processes. Seeing the similarity in brain activation during both social and physical pain helps us to understand why social support can reduce physical pain, much as it soothes emotional pain.

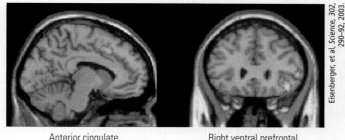

Anterior cingulate   Right ventral prefrontal

Eisenberger, et al, *Science*, 302, 290–92, 2003.

These fMRI scans showing activation in the anterior cingulate and orbital prefrontal cortex are the result of averaging many individual images and then using the subtraction process to produce a representative image (see Figure 9-22).

Emotion. Cognitive interpretation of subjective feelings.

Motivation. Behavior that seems purposeful and goal directed.

Knowing that the brain makes emotional experience real—more than mere metaphors of "hurt" or "pain"—how do we incorporate our thoughts and reasons for behaving as we do? Clearly, our subjective feelings and thoughts influence our actions. The cognitive interpretation of subjective feelings are **emotions**—anger, fear, sadness, jealousy, embarrassment, joy—but these feelings can operate outside our immediate awareness as well.

This chapter begins by exploring the causes of behaviors in which human beings and other animals engage. Sensory stimulation, neural circuits, and hormones are of primary importance in explaining behavior. We focus both on emotions and on the underlying reasons for **motivation**—behavior that seems purposeful and goal directed. Like emotion, motivated behavior is both inferred and subjective and can occur without awareness or intent.

Research on the neuroanatomy responsible for emotional and motivated behavior focuses on a neural circuit formed by the hypothalamus, the limbic system, and the frontal lobes. But behavior is influenced as much by the interaction of our social and natural environments and by evolution as it is by biology. To explain all this interaction in regard to how the brain controls behavior, we concentrate on the specific examples of feeding and sexual activity. Our exploration leads finally to the topic of reward, which plays another key role in explaining emotional and motivated behaviors.

IDENTIFYING THE CAUSES OF BEHAVIOR

We may think that the most obvious explanation for why we behave as we do is simply that we want to. This explanation assumes that we act in a state of free will—that we always have a choice. But the feeling of having free will is not a likely cause of behavior.

Consider Roger, a 25-year-old man whom we first met in the admissions ward of a large mental hospital. Roger approached us and asked if we had any snacks. We had chewing gum, which he accepted eagerly. We thought little about this encounter until 10 min later when we noticed Roger eating the flowers from the vase on a table. A nurse took the flowers away but said little to Roger.

Later, as we wandered about the ward, we encountered a worker replacing linoleum floor tiles. Roger was watching the worker and, as he did, he dipped his finger into the pot of gluing compound and licked the glue from his finger, as if he were sampling honey from a jar. When we asked Roger what he was doing, he said that he was really hungry and that this stuff was not too bad. It reminded him of peanut butter.

One of us tasted the glue and concluded not only that it did not taste like peanut butter but that it tasted awful. Roger was undeterred. We alerted a nurse, who quickly removed him from the glue. Later, we saw him eating another flower bouquet.

Neurological testing revealed that a tumor had invaded Roger's hypothalamus at the base of his brain. He was indeed hungry all the time and could likely consume more than 20,000 calories a day if allowed to do so.

Would you say that Roger had free will regarding his appetite and food preferences? Probably not. Roger seemed compelled to eat whatever he could find, driven by a ravenous hunger. In this case, the nervous system has produced behavior, not an act of free will. If the nervous system can produce one such behavior, it can likely produce many others.

Free will therefore does not adequately explain why we act as we do. If free will is not a satisfactory explanation of behavior, what explanation is? One possibility is the brain's inherent need for stimulation.

This need was first demonstrated in the early 1950s by psychologists Donald Hebb and Woodburn Heron (Hebb, 1955; Heron, 1957). They argued that people are motivated to interact with the environment to maintain at least a minimum level of brain stimulation, and they conducted a fascinating series of experiments that supports this view.

Behavior for Brain Maintenance

Hebb and his coworkers studied the effects of **sensory deprivation,** depriving people of nearly all sensory input. They wanted to see how well-fed, physically comfortable college students who were paid handsomely for their time would react if they did nothing, saw nothing, and heard or touched very little 24 hours a day. **Figure 11-1** shows the setting for this experiment.

Each man lay on a bed in a small sound-proofed room with his ears enveloped by a hollowed-out pillow that muffled the monotonous hums of a nearby fan and air conditioner. Cardboard tubes covered his hands and arms, cutting off his sense of touch, and a translucent visor covered his eyes, blurring the visual world. The subjects were given food on request and access to bathroom facilities. Otherwise, they were asked simply to enjoy the peace and quiet. For doing so, they would receive $20 a day, which was about four times what a student could earn even for a hard day's labor half a century ago.

Wouldn't you think the subjects would be quite happy to contribute to scientific knowledge in such a painless way? In fact, they were far from happy. Most subjects were content for perhaps 4 to 8 hours, but then they became increasingly distressed. They developed a need for stimulation of almost any kind. In one version of the experiment, the subjects could listen, on request, to a talk for 6-year-old children on the dangers of alcohol. Some of them requested to hear it 20 times a day. Few subjects lasted more than 24 hours in these conditions.

The results of sensory deprivation studies are curious. After all, the subjects' basic needs were being met, except perhaps the need for sexual gratification. (But Hebb assumed that, at the risk of insulting their virility, most of the young men in his study were accustomed to stretches of at least 3 or 4 days without engaging in sexual activity.)

So what was the cause of the subjects' distress? Why did they find sensory deprivation so aversive? The answer, Hebb and his colleagues concluded, must be that the brain has an inherent need for stimulation.

Psychologists Robert Butler and Harry Harlow (1954) came to a similar conclusion through a series of experiments that they conducted at about the same time that Hebb conducted his sensory-deprivation studies. Butler placed rhesus monkeys in a

Sensory deprivation. Experimental setup in which a subject is allowed only restricted sensory input; subjects generally have a low tolerance for deprivation and may even display hallucinations.

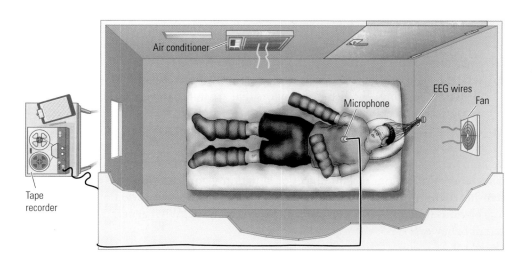

Tape recorder
Air conditioner
EEG wires
Microphone
Fan

Figure 11-1

Sensory Deprivation The subject lies on a bed in an environmental cubicle 24 hours a day, with time out only for meals and bathroom breaks. The room is always dimly lit. A translucent plastic visor restricts visual input; a U-shaped pillow and the noise of a fan and air conditioner limit the subject's auditory experience. In the experiment depicted here, the subject is wired for EEG recordings. The subject's sense of touch is restricted by cotton gloves and long cardboard cuffs. Adapted from "The Pathology of Boredom," by W. Heron, 1957, *Scientific American, 197*(4), p. 52.

University of Wisconsin

dimly lit room with a small door that could be opened to view an adjoining room. As shown in **Figure 11-2**, the researchers could vary the stimuli in the adjoining room so that the monkeys could view different objects or animals each time they opened the door.

Monkeys in these conditions spent a lot of time opening the door and viewing whatever was on display, such as toy trains in action. The monkeys were even willing to perform various tasks just for an opportunity to look through the door. The greater the amount of time during which they were deprived of a chance to look, the more time that they spent looking when finally given the opportunity.

These experiments, taken together with research on sensory deprivation undertaken by Hebb and colleagues, show that one reason that we engage in behavior is to stimulate the brain. In the absence of stimulation, the brain will seek it.

Figure 11-2

Brain Maintenance Monkeys quickly learn to solve puzzles or perform other tricks to gain access to a door that looks out into an adjacent room. A toy train is a strong visual incentive for the monkey peeking through the door; a bowl of fruit is less rewarding. Adapted from "Persistence of Visual Exploration in Monkeys," by R. A. Butler and H. F. Harlow, 1954, *Journal of Comparative and Physiological Psychology, 47,* p. 260.

Drives and Behavior

Surely stimulating the brain is not the only reason for behavior. Consider the behavior of a typical pet cat living in a house or apartment. It awakes in the morning, stretches, wanders to its feeding place, and has a drink of water and some food. Then it sits and cleans itself. Next, it wanders around and spots its favorite toy mouse, which it pounces on and throws in the air. It may pounce and throw again and again for a number of minutes.

Eventually, seemingly bored with the toy, the cat wanders about looking for attention. It sits on its owner's lap, starts to purr, and falls asleep. Shortly thereafter, it gets up and walks away, passes its food and mouse toy, and meows. It explores the apartment, sniffing here and there, before napping in a sunbeam. On waking, the cat returns to the food bowl, eats heartily, bats once at the toy in passing, and searches for its wool ball, which it chases for a while. Later, it stares out the window and eventually settles down for a long sleep.

This cat's seemingly unremarkable actions provide three clues to the causes of behavior:

1. The cat's response to a particular stimulus is not the same each time. Both the food and the toy mouse elicit behavior on some occasions but not on others.
2. The strength of the cat's behaviors varies. For instance, the mouse toy stimulates vigorous behavior at one time and none at another.
3. The cat engages not only in behaviors that satisfy obvious biological needs (eating, drinking, sleeping) but also in behaviors that are not so obviously necessary (playing, affection seeking, exploring).

These same patterns of behavior are typical of dogs or even of people. People can be amused by a puzzle or a book at one moment and completely bored by it the next. They also respond to a certain object or situation vigorously on some occasions and half-heartedly on others. And they engage in many behaviors that do not seem to have any obvious function, such as tapping their toes to music. What generates all these different behaviors?

As psychologists and biologists began to ponder the causes of behavior in the 1930s, they concluded that some sort of internal energy must drive it. This internal energizing factor had many names, including instincts and **drives.** (Actually, instincts and drives are not identical concepts but, for our purposes, it does not matter.)

The concept of drives gave rise to what became known as drive theories of behavior. Drive theorists assumed that, because animals perform many different behaviors, they must have many different drives—a sexual drive, a curiosity drive, a hunger drive, a thirst drive, and so on. According to drive theories, an animal engages in a particular behavior because its drive for it is high, and it ceases engaging in that behavior because its drive for it becomes low. Our cat, for example, played vigorously with the toy mouse when its play drive was high and ceased playing when its play drive diminished to zero.

Notice how drive theory suggests that the brain is somehow storing energy for behavior. That energy builds up until it reaches a level where it is released in action, thereby becoming a cause of behavior. Ethologists (scientists who study animal behavior) offer an interesting analogy to describe this process.

They compare behavior caused by drives to the flushing of a toilet. When the water reservoir of a toilet is full, depressing the handle leads to a "whoosh" of water that, once begun, cannot be stopped. When the reservoir is only partly full, depressing the handle still produces a flush, but a less vigorous one. If the reservoir is empty, no amount of handle pressing will cause the toilet to flush. Applying this analogy to our cat with the toy mouse, the cat will play vigorously if the play reservoir is full, less vigorously if it is partly full, and not at all if the reservoir is empty.

The "flush" model makes a couple assumptions about drive-induced behavior (**Figure 11-3**). It assumes that such a behavior, once started, will continue until all the energy in its reservoir is gone. Our cat keeps playing, although with decreasing vigor, until all the energy held in reserve for play is depleted.

The flush model also assumes separate stores of energy for different behaviors. For instance, cats have a drive to play, and they have a drive to kill. Engaging in one of these behaviors does not reduce the energy stored for the other. That is presumably why a cat may play with a mouse that it has caught for many minutes before finally killing it. The cat will pounce and attack the mouse repeatedly until all its energy for play is used up, and only then will it proceed to the next drive-induced behavior.

The flush model can be applied to many different kinds of actions and seems to make some intuitive sense. We do seem to behave as if there were a store of energy for various behaviors. For instance, males of most mammalian species typically have a refractory period subsequent to sexual intercourse when they no longer have interest in (or possibly energy for) sexual behavior. Later, the interest or energy returns. It is as though a pent-up sexual urge, once satisfied, vanishes for a time, awaiting a new energy buildup.

Drive. Hypothetical state of arousal that motivates an organism to engage in a particular behavior.

Androgen. Male hormone related to level of sexual interest.

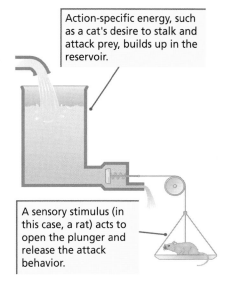

Action-specific energy, such as a cat's desire to stalk and attack prey, builds up in the reservoir.

A sensory stimulus (in this case, a rat) acts to open the plunger and release the attack behavior.

Figure 11-3

Flush Model of Motivation   According to drive theories, a reservoir of action-specific energy, once released, flows out and produces behavior. Each type of behavior is assumed to have its own store of energy. The greater the energy store, the longer the behavior persists. Without an energy store, there is no behavior.

Neural Circuits and Behavior

The problem with drive theories of behavior becomes clear when we try to relate drives to brain activity. Researchers once assumed that physiologists would quickly discover how the brain executes drives. Unfortunately, however, researchers were unable to establish a link between drives and brain activity.

As they searched inside the brain for drives, they found instead that behavioral change correlates with changes in hormones and cellular activity. For example, researchers studying the sexual drive found that a man's frequency of copulation is correlated with his levels of male hormones, called **androgens.** Unusually high androgen levels are related to very high sexual interest, whereas abnormally low androgen levels are linked to low sexual interest or perhaps no interest at all.

With knowledge of this correlation between sexual behavior and male hormones, the concept of sexual drive no longer seemed needed. Rather than searching for a sexual drive, researchers now sought to explain the action of androgens on neural circuits.

This physiological analysis provides more powerful explanations of behavior than does simply invoking the concept of drives. It allows us to say exactly what particular events in the brain can trigger a certain kind of behavior. For example, if an electrode is used to stimulate the brain cells activated by androgens, sexual behavior can be induced. In fact, such brain stimulation can produce amazing sexual activity in male rats, sometimes allowing 50 ejaculations over a couple of hours. Clearly, the activity of neurons is responsible for the behavior, not some hidden energy reservoir as drive theories presumed.

The idea of a neural basis for behavior has wide applications. For instance, we can say that Roger had such a voracious and indiscriminate appetite either because his brain circuits that initiated eating were excessively active or because his circuits that terminated eating were inactive. Similarly, we can say that Hebb's subjects were highly upset by sensory deprivation because their neural circuits that responded to sensory inputs were forced to be abnormally underactive. So the main reason why a particular thought, feeling, or action occurs lies in what is going on in brain circuits.

The Nature of Behavior: Why Cats Kill Birds

Although neural circuits are somewhat plastic as they form during brain development, they are not so easily changed later in life. It therefore follows that behaviors that are caused by these neural circuits also are going to be hard to modify. The killing of prey by cats is a good example.

One of the frustrating things about being a cat owner is that even well fed cats kill birds—often lots of birds. Most people are not too bothered when their cats kill mice, because they view mice as a nuisance. But birds are different. People enjoy watching birds in their yards and gardens. Many cat owners wonder why their pets keep killing birds.

To provide an answer, we can look to the activities of neural circuits. Cats must have a brain circuit that controls prey killing. When this circuit is active, a cat makes an appropriate kill. Viewed in an evolutionary context, it makes sense for cats to have such a circuit because, in the days when cats were not owned by doting human beings, they did not have food dishes that were regularly being filled.

Why does this prey-killing circuit become active when a cat does not need food? One explanation is that, to secure survival, the activity of circuits such as the prey-killing circuit have become rewarding in some way—they make the cat "feel good." As a result, the cat is likely to engage in the pleasure-producing behavior often, which helps to guarantee that it will usually not go hungry.

In the wild, after all, a cat that did not like killing would probably be a dead cat. The idea of behaviors such as prey killing being rewarding was first proposed by Steve Glickman and Bernard Schiff in the early 1960s. Because it is important to our understanding of the causes of behavior, we will return to it at the end of this chapter when we consider reward.

Killing behavior by cats is innate, not learned. It is triggered automatically in the presence of the right stimulus. The innateness of killing in cats is demonstrated by a motherless cat named Hunter that was found abandoned as a tiny kitten. Hunter was bottle fed and raised without a mother cat to "teach" her to hunt.

She did not need an education in hunting. She got her name from her innate and deadly skill at catching mice and other small prey. The prey-killing circuits in her brainstem worked without training. They no doubt were influenced by practice, however, because Hunter became more proficient at killing as she grew older. But the ultimate underlying cause of the behavior is a neural circuit that, when activated, produces stalking and killing responses.

Innate releasing mechanism (IRM).
Hypothetical mechanism that detects specific sensory stimuli and directs an organism to take a particular action.

In Review

Free will is a not an adequate explanation of behavior, because the nervous system can produce behaviors over which an organism has neither choice nor control. Researchers have investigated causes of behavior, including the apparent need of the brain to maintain at least a minimum level of stimulation, and the control exerted by the nervous system on behavior. The older idea of internal, energizing drives that build up and are released in behavior has given way to the more powerful explanation that behavior results from the hormone actions and neural circuits inside the brain that control how we think, act, and feel.

BIOLOGY, EVOLUTION, AND ENVIRONMENT

Why does the sight of a bird or a mouse trigger stalking and killing in a cat? Why does the female body stimulate sexual interest in men? We can address such questions by investigating the evolutionary and environmental influences on brain-circuit activity that contribute to behavior.

Evolutionary Influences on Behavior

The evolutionary explanation hinges on the concept of **innate releasing mechanisms** (IRMs), activators for inborn, adaptive responses that aid in an animal's survival. Innate releasing mechanisms help an animal to successfully feed, reproduce, and escape predators. The concept is best understood by analyzing its parts.

The term *innate* means that IRMs are present from birth rather than acquired through experience. The term also implies that the mechanisms have proved adaptive for the species and therefore have been maintained in the genome. The term *releasing* means that IRMs act as triggers to set free behaviors for which there are internal programs.

Let us return to our cat to illustrate. The brain of a cat must have a built-in mechanism that triggers appropriate stalking and killing in response to stimuli such as a bird or a mouse. Similarly, a cat must also have a built-in mechanism that triggers appropriate mating behavior in the presence of a suitable cat of the opposite sex. Although not all of a cat's behaviors are due to IRMs, you can probably think of other innate releasing mechanisms that cats possess, such as arching and hissing when encountering a threat. For all these IRMs, the animal's brain must have a set of norms against which it can match stimuli so as to trigger an appropriate response.

The existence of such innate, internalized norms is suggested in the following experiment. One of us (B. K.) and Arthur Nonneman allowed a litter of 6-week-old kittens to play in a room and become familiar with it. After this adjustment period, we introduced a two-dimensional image of an adult cat in a "Halloween posture," as shown in **Figure 11-4**.

(A)

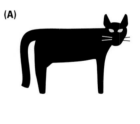

(B)

Figure 11-4

Innate Releasing Mechanism in Cats
Displaying the "Halloween cat" (*top*) stimulates cats to respond defensively, with raised fur, arched backs, and bared teeth. This behavior appears at about 6 weeks of age in kittens who have never seen such a posture before. The "Picasso" cat (*bottom*) evokes no response at all.

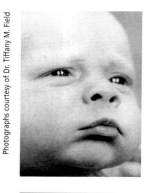

Photographs courtesy of Dr. Tiffany M. Field

Figure 11-5

Innate Releasing Mechanism in Humans Facial expressions made by young infants in response to expressions made by the experimenter. From "Discrimination and Imitation of Facial Expression by Neonates," by T. M. Field, R. Woodson, R. Greenberg, and D. Cohen, 1982, *Science, 218,* p. 180.

Evolutionary psychology. Discipline that seeks to apply principles of natural selection to understand the causes of human behavior.

The kittens responded with raised fur, arched backs, and bared teeth, all signs of being threatened by the image of the adult. Some even hissed at the model. These kittens had no experience with any adult cat except their mother, and there was no reason to believe that she had ever shown them this behavior. Rather, some sort of template of this posture must be prewired in the kitten brain. When the kittens saw the model that matched the preexisting template, a threat response was automatically triggered. This innate triggering mechanism is an IRM.

The IRM concept also applies to humans. In one study, Tiffany Field and her colleagues (1982) had an adult display to young infants various exaggerated facial expressions, such as happiness, sadness, and surprise. As **Figure 11-5** shows, the babies responded with very much the same expressions as the adults displayed. These newborns were too young to be imitating the adult faces intentionally. Rather, their responses must have been due to an IRM.

The babies must have had an innate ability to match these facial expressions to internal templates, which in turn triggered some prewired program to reproduce the expressions in their own faces. Such ability would have adaptive value if these facial expressions serve as important social signals for humans.

Evidence for a prewired motor program related to facial expressions also comes from the study of congenitally blind children. These children spontaneously produce the very same facial expressions that sighted people do, even though they have never seen them in others.

Although IRMs such as those just described are prewired into the brain, they can be modified by experience. For instance, our cat Hunter's stalking skills were not inherited fully developed at birth but rather matured functionally as she grew older. The same is true of many human IRMs, such as those for responding to sexually arousing stimuli.

Different cultures may emphasize different stimuli as arousing, and, even within a single culture, there is variation in what different people find sexually stimulating. Nonetheless, some human attributes are universally found to have sexually arousing value. An example is the hip-to-waist ratio of human females for most human males. This ratio is probably part of an IRM.

The IRM concept can be related to the Darwinian view of how the nervous system evolves. According to this view, natural selection favors behaviors that prove adaptive for an organism, and these behaviors are passed on to future generations. Because behavior patterns are produced by the activity of neurons in the brain, the natural selection of specific behaviors is really the selection of particular brain circuits.

Animals that survive long enough to reproduce and have healthy offspring are more likely to pass on the genes for making their brain circuits than are animals with traits that make them less likely to survive and successfully reproduce. Thus, cats with brain circuits that made them adept at stalking prey or responding fiercely to threats were more likely to survive and produce many offspring, passing on those adaptive brain circuits and behaviors to their young. In this way, the behaviors became widespread in the species over time.

Although the Darwinian view seems straightforward when considering how cats evolved brain circuits for stalking prey or responding to threats, it is less so when applied to many complex human behaviors. For instance, why have humans evolved the behavior of killing other members of their species? At first glance, this behavior would seem counterproductive to the survival of humans; so why has it endured?

A field of study called **evolutionary psychology,** which seeks to apply principles of natural selection to understand the causes of human behavior, is a source of insight. Consider how evolutionary psychologists account for homicide. When two men fight a duel, one common-sense explanation might be that they are fighting over grievances. But evolutionary psychologists would look at a duel differently, asking why a behavior pattern that risks people's lives is sustained in a population. Their answer is that fights are about social status.

Evolutionary psychologists assume that any behavior, including dueling, exists because the neural circuits producing it have been favored through natural selection. In this case, men who fought and won duels passed on their genes to future generations, whereas those who lost duels did not. Through time, therefore, the traits associated with successful dueling—strength, aggression, agility—became more prevalent among humans, and so, too, did dueling itself.

Martin Daly and Margot Wilson (1988) extended this type of analysis to further account for homicide. In their view, homicide may endure in our society despite its severe punishment because it is related to behaviors that were adaptive in the human past. Suppose, for example, that natural selection favored sexually jealous males who effectively intimidated their rivals and bullied their mates so as to guarantee their own paternity of any offspring produced by their mates. As a result, male jealousy would become a prevalent motive for interpersonal violence, including homicide.

Note that, in this view, homicide itself does not help a man produce more children. But men who are apt to commit homicides are more likely to engage in other behaviors (bullying and intimidation) that improve their social status and therefore their reproductive fitness. Homicide therefore is related to adaptive traits that have been selected through millennia.

The evolutionary psychology view is introduced here not to account for all human behavior and perhaps not even to account for homicide; rather, it demonstrates that evolutionary theory can generate hypotheses about how natural selection might have shaped the brain and behavior. In this way, evolutionary psychology can sometimes provide an additional and intriguing perspective on the neurological bases of behavior.

To learn more about evolutionary psychology, visit the Chapter 11 Web links on the *Brain and Behavior* Web site (**www.worthpublishers.com/kolb**).

The Chemical Senses

Just as chemical reactions play a central role in nervous system activity, chemical signals (chemosignals) play a central role in the motivated and emotional behavior of mammals. Mammals identify group members by odor, mark their territories with urine and other odorants, identify favorite and forbidden foods by taste, and form associations between odors, tastes, and emotional events. We thus consider the chemical senses here in the context of emotional and motivated behavior.

To learn more about the chemical senses, got to the Chapter 11 Web links on the *Brain and Behavior* Web site (**www.worthpublishers.com/kolb**).

OLFACTION

Odor is the most puzzling of the sensory systems. We can discriminate thousands of odors, yet we have great difficulty finding words to describe what we smell. We may like or dislike smells or compare one smell to another, but we lack a vocabulary for our olfactory perceptions.

Wine experts rely on olfaction to tell them about wines, but they must *learn* to use smell to do so. There are courses for training people in wine sniffing, courses that are typically one full day a week for a year, and most people who take such courses still have great difficulty in passing the final test. The degree of difficulty contrasts with that of vision and audition, which are designed to analyze specific qualities of the sensory input (such as pitch in audition or color in vision). In contrast, olfaction seem to be designed to determine whether information is familiar—for example, is a food or a friend—or to identify a signal such as a receptive mate.

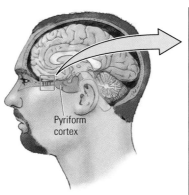

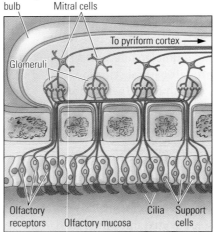

Olfactory bulb | Mitral cells

To pyriform cortex →

Glomeruli

Olfactory receptors | Olfactory mucosa | Cilia | Support cells

Figure 11-6

Olfactory Epithelium

Receptors for Smell The identification of chemosignals is conceptually similar to the identification of other sensory stimuli (light, sound, touch) except that, instead of converting physical energy such as light or sound waves into receptor potentials, scent interacts with chemical receptors. This constant chemical interaction appears to be tough on the receptors and so, in contrast with the receptors for light, sound, and touch, chemical receptors are constantly being replaced. The life of an olfactory receptor is about 60 days.

The receptor surface for olfaction is the olfactory epithelium, which lies in the nasal cavity, as illustrated in **Figure 11-6**. The epithelium is composed of receptor cells and support cells. Each receptor cell sends a process, which ends in 10 to 20 cilia, into a mucous layer known as the olfactory mucosa. Chemicals in the air that we breathe dissolve in the mucosa to interact with the cilia. If the receptors are affected by an olfactory chemosignal, metabotropic activation of a specific G protein leads to an opening of sodium channels and a change in membrane potential (see Chapter 5).

The receptor surface of the epithelium varies widely across species. In humans, the area is estimated to range from 2 to 4 cm²; in dogs, the area is about 18 cm²; and, in cats, it is about 21 cm². No wonder our sensitivity to odors is less acute than that of dogs and cats: they have 10 times as much receptor area as humans have. Roughly analogous to the tuning characteristics of cells in the auditory system, olfactory receptor neurons in vertebrates do not respond to specific odors but rather to a range of odors.

How does a limited number of receptor types allow us to smell many different odors? The simplest explanation is that any given odorant stimulates a unique pattern of receptors, and the summed activity, or pattern of activity, produces our perception of a particular odor. Analogously, the visual system enables us to identify many different colors with only three receptor types in the retina: the summed activity of the three cones leads to our rich color life.

A fundamental difference, however, is that there are far more receptors in the olfactory system than in the visual system. Richard Axel and Linda Buck won the Nobel Prize in medicine in 2004 for their discovery that a novel gene family (about 350 genes in humans) encodes a very large and diverse set of olfactory receptors. The combination of these receptors allows us to discriminate about 10,000 different smells.

Olfactory Pathways Olfactory receptor cells project to the olfactory bulb, ending in ball-like tufts of dendrites called glomeruli (see Figure 11-6). There they form synapses with the dendrites of mitral cells. The mitral cells send their axons from the olfactory bulb to a broad range of forebrain areas summarized in **Figure 11-7**. Although many of the olfactory targets, such as the amygdala and pyriform cortex, have no connection *through* the thalamus, as do other sensory systems, a thalamic connection (to the dorsomedial nucleus) does project to the orbitofrontal cortex. As we shall see, the orbitofrontal cortex plays a central role in a variety of emotional and social behaviors as well as in eating.

Accessory Olfactory System A unique class of odorants are **pheromones,** biochemicals released by one animal that act as chemosignals and can affect the physiology or behavior of another animal. For example, Karen Stern and Martha McClintock (1998)

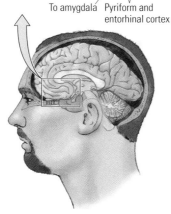

To thalamus and orbitofrontal cortex | To hypothalamus

Olfactory bulb

To amygdala | Pyriform and entorhinal cortex

Figure 11-7

Olfactory Pathways

Figure 11-8

Response to Pheromones (*Left*) A cat sniffs a urine-soaked cotton ball, (*middle*) raises its upper lip to close off the nasal passages, and (*right*) follows with the full gape response characteristic of flehmen, a behavior mediated by the accessory olfactory system. Photographs courtesy Arthur Nonneman and Bryan Kolb.

found that, when women reside together they begin to cycle together, a phenomenon referred to as the *Whitten effect*. Furthermore, the researchers found that the synchronization of menstrual cycles is conveyed by odors.

Pheromones appear to be able to affect more than sex-related behavior. A human chemosignal, androstadienone, has been shown to alter glucose utilization in the neocortex—that is, how the brain uses energy (Jacob et al., 2001). Thus, a chemosignal appears to affect cortical processes even though the signal was not actually detected consciously. The puzzle is why we would evolve such a mechanism and how it might actually affect cerebral functioning.

Pheromones are unique odors because they are detected by a special olfactory receptor system known as the *vomeronasal organ*, which is made up of a small group of sensory receptors that are connected by a duct to the nasal passage. The receptor cells in the vomeronasal organ send their axons to the accessory olfactory bulb, which lies adjacent to the main olfactory bulb. The vomeronasal organ connects primarily with the amygdala and hypothalamus by which it likely plays a role in reproductive and social behavior.

The vomeronasal organ probably does not participate in general olfactory behavior but rather in the analysis of pheromones such as those in urine. You may have seen bulls or cats engage in a behavior known as *flehmen*, which is illustrated in **Figure 11-8**. When exposed to novel cat or human urine, these animals raise their upper lip to close off the nasal passages and suck air into the mouth. The air flows through the duct on the roof of the mouth en route to the vomeronasal organ.

Curiously, cats respond to novel cat or human urine but do not respond to dog, rodent, or monkey urine or feces (Kolb & Nonneman, 1975). Damage to the orbitofrontal cortex eliminates the behavior, suggesting that the orbitofrontal cortex plays a key role in analyzing the pheromones in urine.

GUSTATION

Research reveals significant differences in taste preferences both between and within species. Humans and rats like sucrose and saccharin solutions, but dogs reject saccharin, and cats are indifferent to both, inasmuch as they do not detect sweetness at all. The failure of cats to taste sweetness may not be surprising; they are pure carnivores, and nothing that they normally eat is sweet.

Similarly, within the human species, clear differences in taste thresholds and preferences are obvious. An example is the preference for or dislike of bitter tastes—the flavor of brussels sprouts, for instance. People tend either to love them or hate them. Linda Bartoshuk (2000) showed absolute differences among adults: some perceive certain tastes as very bitter, whereas others are indifferent to them. Presumably, the latter group is more tolerant of brussels sprouts.

There are also differences in taste thresholds as we age. Children are much more responsive to tastes than adults and are often intolerant of spicy foods, because they

Pheromone. Odorant biochemical released by one animal that acts as a chemosignal and can affect the physiology or behavior of another animal.

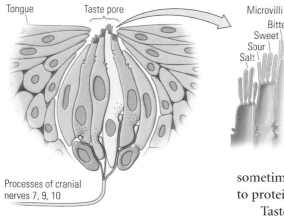

Figure 11-9

Anatomy of a Taste Bud   Adapted from Smith and Shepherd, 2003, p. 720.

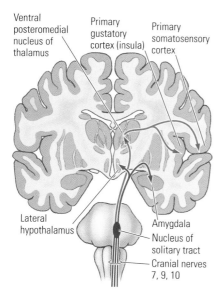

Figure 11-10

Gustatory Pathways

Reinforcer. In operant conditioning, any event that strengthens the behavior that it follows.

have more taste receptors than adults have. By age 20, humans have lost at least an estimated 50 percent of their taste receptors. No wonder children and adults have different food preferences.

Receptors for Taste   Taste receptors are found within taste buds located in several distinct subpopulations: on the tongue, under the tongue, on the soft palate on the roof of the mouth, on the sides of the mouth, and at the back of the mouth on the nasopharynx. Each of the five different taste-receptor types responds to a different chemical component of food. The four most familiar are sweet, sour, salty, and bitter. The fifth type, sometimes called the *umami* receptor, is specially sensitive to glutamate and perhaps to protein (see Chapter 5).

Taste receptors are grouped into taste buds, each containing several receptor types, as illustrated in **Figure 11-9**. Gustatory stimuli interact with the receptor tips, the *microvilli*, to open ion channels, leading to changes in membrane potential. The base of the taste bud is contacted by the branches of afferent nerves that come from cranial nerves 7 (facial nerve), 9 (glossopharyngeal nerve), or 10 (vagus nerve). You can review these cranial nerves in Figure 2-26.

Gustatory Pathways   Cranial nerves 7, 9, and 10 form the main gustatory nerve, the *solitary tract*. On entering the brainstem, the tract divides in two as illustrated in **Figure 11-10**. One route travels through the posterior medulla to the ventroposterior medial nucleus of the thalamus, which in turn sends out two pathways, one to the primary somatosensory cortex and the other to a region just rostral to the secondary somatosensory cortex in the gustatory cortex of the insula.

The gustatory region is dedicated to taste, whereas the primary somatosensory region is also responsive to tactile information and is probably responsible for localizing tastes on the tongue. The gustatory cortex sends a projection to the orbital cortex in a region near the input of the olfactory cortex. The mixture of olfactory and gustatory input in the orbital cortex likely gives rise to our perception of flavor.

The second pathway from the gustatory nerve projects through the pons to the hypothalamus and amygdala. Researchers hypothesize that this input plays some role in feeding behavior.

Environmental Influences on Behavior

B. F. Skinner (1904–1990)

Many psychologists have emphasized learning as a cause of behavior. No one would question that we modify our behavior as we learn, but B. F. Skinner went much further. He believed that behaviors are selected by environmental factors.

His argument is simple. Certain events function as rewards, or **reinforcers,** and, when a reinforcing event follows a particular response, similar responses are more likely to occur again. Skinner argued that reinforcement can be manipulated to encourage the display of complex forms of behavior.

The power of experience to shape behavior by pairing stimuli and rewards is typified by one of Skinner's experiments. A pigeon is placed in a box that has a small disc on one wall (the stimulus). If the pigeon pecks at the disc (the response), a food tray opens and the pigeon can feed (the reinforcement or reward). A pigeon quickly learns the association between the stimulus and the response, especially if the disc has a small spot on it. It pecks at the spot and, within minutes, it has mastered the response needed to receive a reward.

Now the response requirement can be made more complex. The pigeon might be required to turn 360° before pecking the disc to gain the reward. The pigeon can learn this response, too. Other contingencies might then be added, making the response requirements even more complex. For instance, the pigeon might be trained to turn in a clockwise circle if the disc is green, to turn in a counterclockwise circle if the disc is red, and to scratch at the floor if the disc is yellow.

If you suddenly came upon this complex behavior in a pigeon, you would probably be astounded. But, if you understood the experience that had shaped the bird's behavior, you would understand the cause. The rewards offered to the pigeon altered its behavior so that its responses were controlled by the color of the disc on the wall.

Skinner extended this type of analysis to include all sorts of behaviors that, at first, do not appear to be easily explained. For instance, he argued that various phobias could be accounted for by understanding a person's reinforcement history. An example is someone who was once terrified by a turbulent ride on a plane, thereafter avoiding air travel and manifesting a phobia of flying.

The avoidance of flying is rewarding because it lowers the person's anxiety level, and so the phobic behavior is maintained. Skinner also argued against the commonly held view that much of human behavior is under our own control. From Skinner's perspective, free will is only an illusion, because behavior is controlled not by the organism but rather by the environment through experience.

Although our intent is not to debate the pros and cons of Skinner's ideas here, we *can* conclude that many complex behaviors are learned. It is also true that learning takes place in a brain that has been selected for evolutionary adaptations. This combination of learning and inherited brain circuits can lead to some surprising results. A case in point can be seen, again, in pigeons.

Although a pigeon in a Skinner box can quickly learn to peck a disc to receive a bit of food, it cannot learn to peck a disc to escape from a mild electric shock to its feet. Why not? After all, the same simple pecking behavior is being rewarded. But apparently, the pigeon's brain is not prewired for this second kind of association. The bird is prepared to make the first association but not prepared to make the second, which makes adaptive sense.

For a pigeon, pecking is a behavior that in a natural environment is widely linked with obtaining food. Learning associations between pecking and food come easily to a pigeon. In contrast, learning to peck to prevent electric shock is not part of the brain circuitry that a pigeon is born with, and so mastering this association does not come easily to the bird. Typically, it flies away from noxious situations.

The specific nature of the behavior–consequence associations that animals are able to learn was first shown in 1966 by psychologist John Garcia. He observed that farmers in the western United States are constantly shooting at coyotes for attacking lambs; yet, despite the painful consequences, the coyotes never seem to learn to stop killing lambs in favor of safer prey. The reason, Garcia speculated, is that a coyote's brain is not prewired by adaptation to make this kind of association.

So Garcia proposed an alternative to deter coyotes from killing lambs—one that uses an association that a coyote's brain is prepared to make. This association is the connection between eating something that makes one sick and avoiding that food in the future. Garcia gave the coyotes a poisoned lamb carcass, which made them sick but did not kill them. With only one pairing of lamb and illness, most coyotes learned not to eat sheep for the rest of their lives.

Skinner box

Learned taste aversion. Acquired association between a specific taste or odor and illness; leads to an aversion to foods having that taste or odor.

Preparedness. Predisposition to respond to certain stimuli differently from other stimuli.

Many humans have similarly acquired food aversions because the taste of a certain food—especially a novel one—was subsequently paired with illness. This **learned taste aversion** is acquired even when the food that was eaten is in fact unrelated to the later illness. As long as the taste and the nausea are paired in time, the brain is prewired to make a connection between them.

For instance, one of us ate his first Caesar salad the night before coming down with a stomach flu. A year later, he was offered another Caesar salad and, to his amazement, felt ill just at the smell of it. Even though his earlier illness had not been due to the salad, he had formed an association between the novel flavor and illness.

This kind of strong and rapid associative learning makes adaptive sense. Having a brain that is prepared to make a connection between a novel taste and subsequent illness will help an animal avoid poisonous foods and so aid in its survival. Interestingly, a curious aspect of taste-aversion learning is that we are not even aware of having formed the association until we encounter the taste again.

The fact that the nervous system is often prewired to make certain associations but not to make others has led to the concept of **preparedness** in learning theories. This concept can help account for some quite complex behaviors. For example, if two rats are paired in a small box and exposed to a mild electric shock, they will immediately fight with one another, even though neither was responsible for the shock.

Apparently, the brain is prepared to make associations between injury and nearby objects or other animals. Perhaps you have occasionally felt your own temper flare toward someone who was near you when you were accidentally hurt or in pain for some reason unrelated to that person. The extent to which we might extend this idea to explain such human behaviors as bigotry and racism is an interesting topic for debate. But the point here is that environmental events are working on a brain that is prewired to make certain types of associations.

Inferring Purpose in Behavior: To Know a Fly

A pitfall in studying the causes of behavior is to infer purpose from an organism's actions. In other words, we have a tendency to assume that behavior is intentional. The problems in making this assumption are illustrated in a wonderful little book titled *To Know a Fly*, written by Vincent Dethier.

When a fly lands on a kitchen table, it wanders about, occasionally stomping its feet. Eventually, it finds a bit of food and sticks its proboscis (a trunklike extension) into the food and eats. The fly may then walk to a nearby place and begin to groom by rubbing its legs together quickly. Finally, it spends a long period motionless.

If you observed a fly engaged in these behaviors, it might appear to have been initially searching for food because it was hungry. When it found food, you might assume that it gorged itself until it was satisfied, and then it cleaned up and rested. In short, the fly's behavior might seem to you to have some purpose or intention.

Dethier studied flies for years to understand what a fly is actually doing when it engages in these kinds of behaviors. His findings have little to do with purpose or intention. When a fly wanders about a table, it is not deliberately searching; it is tasting things that it walks on.

As **Figure 11-11** shows, a fly's taste receptors are on its feet, rather than in its mouth as in humans. So tasting is automatic when a fly walks. An adult fly's nervous system has a built-in preference for sweet tastes and aversions to sour, salty, or bitter flavors. Therefore, when a fly encounters something sweet, it automatically lowers its proboscis and eats, or drinks if the sweet is liquid.

Figure 11-11

Feeding System of the Fly After having been sampled by taste buds on the fly's feet, food is taken in through the proboscis, after which it passes through the esophagus to the gut. Stretch receptors at the entrance to the gut determine when the esophagus is full. The recurrent nerve connects with the brain to signal cessation of eating.

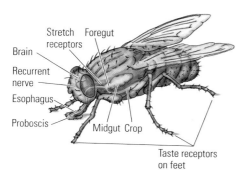

Brain
Stretch receptors
Foregut
Recurrent nerve
Esophagus
Proboscis
Midgut
Crop
Taste receptors on feet

The taste preferences of a fly are interesting. When humans are given very sweet foods, they normally eat less than they eat of foods that are not as sweet. In contrast, the sweeter the food is, the more a fly will consume. This taste preference can be measured by comparing how much a fly drinks of sugar solutions with different concentrations. The fly has a lower preference for weak sugar solutions and drinks less of them than very strong solutions.

The fly's preference for sweet tastes is so great that it will choose food that tastes very sweet over food that is less sweet but nutritionally better. For instance, when given a choice between regular glucose and an exceptionally sweet sugar called fucose that a fly cannot digest, the fly will always choose the fucose, presumably because it tastes better to a fly. In fact, given the opportunity, a fly will literally die of starvation by eating nothing but fucose, even though nutritious glucose is available only centimeters away.

Why does a fly stop eating? A logical possibility is that the amount of sugar in its blood rises to some threshold level. If this possibility were correct, injecting glucose into the circulatory system of a fly would prevent the fly from eating. But it is not what happens. Blood-glucose level has no effect on a fly's feeding. Furthermore, injecting food into the animal's stomach or intestine has no effect either. So what is left? The upper part of the digestive tract.

It turns out that flies have a nerve (the recurrent nerve) that extends from the neck to the brain and carries information about whether any food is present in the esophagus. If the recurrent nerve is cut, the fly is chronically "hungry" and never stops eating. Such flies become so full and fat that their feet no longer reach the ground, and they become so heavy that they cannot fly.

So what have we learned by studying the fly? The main message is that, even though a fly appears to act with a "purpose in mind," a series of very simple mechanisms actually control its behavior—mechanisms that are not remotely related to our concept of thought. A fly walks because it is tasting, it eats because its esophagus is devoid of food, and it stops when its esophagus has some food in it. When the nerve connecting the esophagus to the brain is cut, a fly will keep on eating even though the food is flattening its internal organs against the sides of its body.

Hunger is simply the activity of the nerve, not some drive concerning intention. Clearly, we should not assume that a behavior has a conscious purpose just because it appears to be the case. Behavior can have very subtle causes that do not include purpose, which raises the question, How do we know that any behavior is purposeful? That question turns out to be difficult to answer.

In Review

Behavior results from evolution and environment, and from the interaction of these two forces with neurobiological events. Learned behaviors can be selected and influenced by an individual organism's own unique experiences as well. The brain of a species is prewired to produce IRMs to specific sensory stimuli, and prewired brain circuits have been selected by evolution to prompt associations between certain environmental events. Further, human taste and smell receptors react chemically with olfactory and gustatory sensations. Their diverse pathways into the brain eventually merge in the orbitofrontal cortex, leading to the perception of flavor, the blending of smells and tastes in food. Pheromones are chemosignals that convey information about the sender and can influence the physiology of the reciever. In searching for the causes of behavior, then, be aware that behavior can have multiple causes, which can vary from one behavior to another, and may occur without intent.

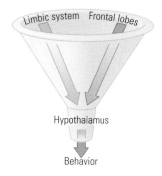

Figure 11-12

Funneling Signals   In this funnel model of control of motivated behaviors, inputs from the frontal lobes and limbic system are funneled through the hypothalamus, which controls the brainstem circuits to produce the behavioral patterns.

NEUROANATOMY OF MOTIVATED BEHAVIOR

Although the neural circuits that control behavior include regions at all levels of the brain, the critical structures are the hypothalamus and the associated pituitary gland, the limbic system, and the frontal lobes. In this section, we investigate the anatomical and functional organization of these major, functionally interrelated structures.

The hypothalamus receives much of its input from the limbic system and the frontal lobes, as illustrated in **Figure 11-12**, where the hypothalamus is represented by the neck of a funnel. The limbic system and the frontal lobes form the funnel's rim. The limbic and frontal regions project to the hypothalamus, which houses many of the basic circuits and **homeostatic mechanisms** (processes that keep critical body functions within a narrow, fixed range) for controlling behavior. To produce behavior, the hypothalamus sends axons to other brainstem circuits. Thus, although the hypothalamus plays a central role in controlling motivated behavior, it receives its instructions from the limbic system and the frontal lobes.

Regulatory and Nonregulatory Behavior

We seek mates, food, or sensory stimulation because of brain activity, but it is convenient to talk about such behavior as being "motivated." Like drives, however, motivated behaviors are not something that we can point to in the brain. Rather, motivations are inferences that we make about why someone, ourselves included, engages in a particular behavior. The two general classes of motivated behaviors are regulatory and nonregulatory. In this section we explore both categories before exploring the neuroanatomy of motivation.

Some Regulatory Behaviors

Temperature regulation

Eating and drinking

Salt consumption

Waste elimination

REGULATORY BEHAVIORS

We explored homeostatic mechanisms regulated by hormones in Chapter 7. **Regulatory behaviors,** those motivated by an organism's survival, are controlled by homeostatic mechanisms. By analogy, consider a house in which a thermostat is set at 18° Celsius, like the one in **Figure 11-13**. When the temperature falls below a certain tolerable range (say, to 16°C), the thermostat turns the furnace on. When the temperature rises above a certain tolerable level (say, to 20°C), the thermostat turns on the air conditioner.

Human body temperature is controlled in a somewhat similar manner by a "thermostat" in the hypothalamus that holds internal temperature at about 37°C, a temperature

Figure 11-13

Regulatory Mechanism   A thermostat controls temperature inside a house. An analogous mechanism could control temperature in the body.

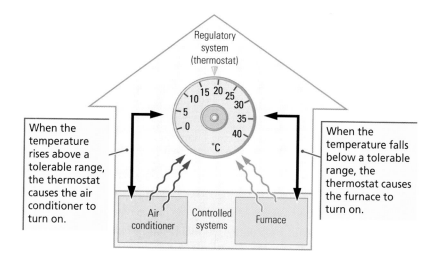

referred to as setpoint. Even slight variations cause us to engage in various behaviors to regain this setpoint. For example, when body temperature drops slightly, neural circuits that increase temperature are turned on. These neural circuits might induce an involuntary response such as shivering or a seemingly voluntary behavior such as moving closer to a heat source. Conversely, if body temperature rises slightly, we sweat or move to a cooler place.

Similar mechanisms control many other homeostatic processes, including the amount of water in the body, the balance of dietary nutrients, and the level of blood sugar. The control of many of these homeostatic systems is quite complex, requiring both neural and hormonal mechanisms. However, in some way, all of the body's homeostatic systems include the activity of the hypothalamus.

Imagine that specific cells are especially sensitive to temperature. When they are cool, they become very active; when they are warm, they become less active. These cells could function as a thermostat, telling the body when it is too cool or too warm. A similar set of cells could serve as a "glucostat," controlling the level of sugar in the blood, or as a "waterstat," controlling the amount of H_2O in the body. In fact, the body's real homeostatic mechanisms are slightly more complex than this imagined one, but they work in accord with the same general principle.

We evolved mechanisms to hold conditions such as temperature constant because the body, including the brain, is a chemical "soup" in which thousands of chemical reactions are taking place all the time. Maintaining constant temperature becomes critical. When temperature changes, even by such a small amount as 2 Celsius degrees, the rates at which chemical reactions take place change.

Such changes might be tolerable, within certain limits, if all the reaction times changed to the same extent. But they do not do so. Consequently, an increase of 2 degrees might increase one reaction by 10 percent and another by only 2 percent. Such uneven changes would wreak havoc with finely tuned body processes such as metabolism and the workings of neurons.

A similar logic applies to maintaining homeostasis in other body systems. For instance, cells require certain concentrations of water, salt, or glucose to function properly. If those concentrations were to fluctuate wildly, they would cause a gross disturbance of metabolic balance and a subsequent biological disaster.

NONREGULATORY BEHAVIORS

In contrast with regulatory behaviors, such as eating or drinking, **nonregulatory behaviors** are neither required to meet the basic needs of an animal nor controlled by homeostatic mechanisms. Thus, nonregulatory behaviors include everything else that we do—from sexual intercourse to parenting to such curiosity-driven activities as conducting psychology experiments. Some nonregulatory behaviors, such as sexual intercourse, entail the hypothalamus, but most of them probably do not. Rather, such behaviors entail a variety of forebrain structures, especially the frontal lobes. Presumably, as the forebrain evolved to a larger size, so did our range of nonregulatory behaviors.

Most nonregulatory behaviors are strongly influenced by external stimuli. As a result, sensory systems must play some role in controlling them. For example, the sexual behavior of most male mammals is strongly influenced by the pheromone emitted by receptive females. If the olfactory system is not functioning properly, we can expect abnormalities in sexual behavior. We will return to the topic of sexual behavior later in this chapter when we investigate it as an example of how a nonregulatory behavior is controlled. But first we will look at the brain structures taking part in motivated behaviors—both nonregulatory and regulatory ones.

Homeostatic mechanism. Process that maintains critical body functions within a narrow, fixed range.

Regulatory behavior. Behavior required to meet the basic needs of the animal.

Nonregulatory behavior. Behavior not required to meet the basic needs of the animal.

Some Nonregulatory Behaviors
Sexual behavior
Parental behavior
Aggression
Food preference
Curiosity
Reading

Pituitary gland. Endocrine gland attached to the bottom of the hypothalamus; its secretions control the activities of many other endocrine glands; known to be associated with biological rhythms.

Medial forebrain bundle (MFB). Tract that connects structures in the brainstem with various parts of the limbic system; forms the activating projections that run from the brainstem to the basal ganglia and frontal cortex.

◉ On your *Foundations of Behavioral Neuroscience* CD you can examine the hypothalamus in three dimensions. To view the model, visit the section on subcortical structures in the module on the central nervous system. (See the Preface for more information about this CD.)

The Hypothalamic Circuit's Regulatory Function

One function of the hypothalamus, as stated earlier, is to regulate our internal environment. It maintains homeostasis by acting on both the endocrine system and the autonomic nervous system (ANS). The hypothalamus also influences the selection of behaviors by the rest of the brain, especially by the limbic system, as you will discover later in the chapter when we consider emotional behavior. In these ways, the hypothalamus, although it constitutes less than 1 percent of the human brain's volume, controls an amazing variety of behaviors, ranging from heart rate to feeding to sexual activity.

HYPOTHALAMIC INVOLVEMENT IN HORMONE SECRETIONS

A principal function of the hypothalamus is to control the **pituitary gland,** which is attached to the hypothalamus by a stalk (**Figure 11-14A**). The optic nerves cross to form the optic chiasm right in front of the hypothalamus, and the optic tracts are just lateral to it (Figure 11-14B).

The hypothalamus can be divided into three regions: the lateral, the medial, and the periventricular, illustrated in frontal section in Figure 11-14B. The lateral hypothalamus is composed both of nuclei and of tracts running up and down the brain, connecting the lower brainstem to the forebrain. The principal tract, shown in **Figure 11-15**, is the **medial forebrain bundle** (MFB). The MFB, which connects structures in the brainstem

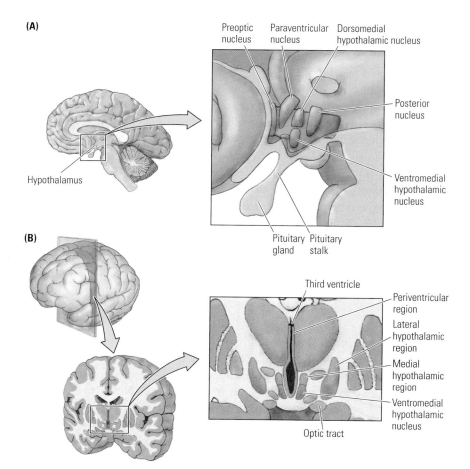

(A)

Preoptic nucleus
Paraventricular nucleus
Dorsomedial hypothalamic nucleus
Posterior nucleus
Ventromedial hypothalamic nucleus
Hypothalamus
Pituitary gland
Pituitary stalk

(B)

Third ventricle
Periventricular region
Lateral hypothalamic region
Medial hypothalamic region
Ventromedial hypothalamic nucleus
Optic tract

Figure 11-14

The Nuclei and Regions of the Hypothalamus **(A)** Medial view shows the relation between the hypothalamic nuclei and the rest of the brain. **(B)** In frontal section, the relation between the hypothalamus and the third ventricle can be seen. The three principal hypothalamic regions are the periventricular, lateral, and medial.

with various parts of the limbic system, forms the activating projections that run from the brainstem to the basal ganglia and frontal cortex.

Fibers that ascend from the dopamine- and noradrenaline-containing cells of the lower brainstem form a significant part of the MFB. Recall from Chapter 7 that dopamine is important in our experience of reward. Thus, the dopamine-containing fibers of the MFB contribute to the control of many motivated behaviors, including eating and sexual behaviors.

Each nucleus of the hypothalamus is anatomically distinct, but most have multiple functions. These multiple functions are due, in part, to the fact that the cells in different nuclei contain various peptide transmitters, each of which plays a role in different behaviors. For instance, the transmitters in the cells in the paraventricular nucleus may be vasopressin, oxytocin, or various combinations of other peptides (such as enkephalin and neurotensin).

The production of various neuropeptides hints at the special relation between the hypothalamus and the pituitary. The pituitary consists of distinct anterior and posterior glands, as shown in **Figure 11-16**. The posterior pituitary is composed of neural tissue and is essentially a continuation of the hypothalamus.

Neurons in the hypothalamus make peptides (e.g., oxytocin and vasopressin) that are transported down their axons to terminals lying in the posterior pituitary. If these neurons become active, they send action potentials to the terminals, causing the

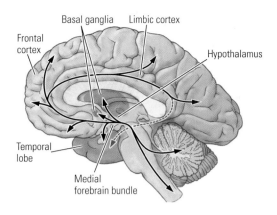

Figure 11-15

Medial Forebrain Bundle Major components of the MFB, a major pathway for fibers connecting various parts of the limbic system with the brainstem, are the activating projections that run from the brainstem to the basal ganglia and frontal cortex.

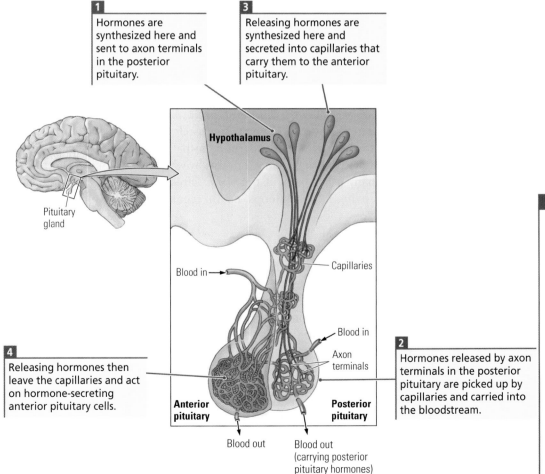

1

Hormones are synthesized here and sent to axon terminals in the posterior pituitary.

3

Releasing hormones are synthesized here and secreted into capillaries that carry them to the anterior pituitary.

4

Releasing hormones then leave the capillaries and act on hormone-secreting anterior pituitary cells.

2

Hormones released by axon terminals in the posterior pituitary are picked up by capillaries and carried into the bloodstream.

Figure 11-16

Hypothalamus and Pituitary Gland The pituitary has two divisions: the anterior and posterior. The anterior pituitary is connected to the hypothalamus by a system of blood vessels that carry hormones from the hypothalamus to the pituitary. The posterior pituitary receives input from axons of hypothalamic neurons. Both regions of the pituitary respond to hypothalamic input by producing hormones that travel in the bloodstream to stimulate target organs.

Releasing hormones. Peptides that are released by the hypothalamus and act to increase or decrease the release of hormones from the anterior pituitary.

Table 11-1	Major Hormones Produced by the Anterior Pituitary
Hormone	**Function**
Adrenocorticotrophic hormone (ACTH)	Controls secretions of the adrenal cortex
Thyroid-stimulating hormone (TSH)	Controls secretions of the thyroid gland
Follicle-stimulating hormone (FSH)	Controls secretions of the gonads
Luteinizing hormone (LH)	Controls secretions of the gonads
Prolactin	Controls secretions of the mammary glands
Growth hormone (GH)	Promotes growth throughout the body

terminals to release the peptides that are stored there. But rather than affecting another neuron, as occurs at most synapses, these peptides are picked up by capillaries in the posterior pituitary's rich vascular bed.

From there, they enter the body's bloodstream. The blood then carries the peptides to distant targets, where they have their effects. For example, vasopressin affects water resorption by the kidneys, and oxytocin controls both uterine contractions and the ejection of milk by mammary glands in the breasts. Peptides can have multiple functions, depending on the location of receptors. Thus, oxytocin not only controls milk ejection in females but also plays a more general role in several forms of affiliative behavior, including parental care, grooming, and sexual behavior in both men and women (Insel & Fernald, 2004).

The glandular tissue of the anterior pituitary synthesizes various hormones, the major ones being listed in **Table 11-1**. The hypothalamus controls the release of these anterior pituitary hormones by producing chemicals known as **releasing hormones.** Produced by hypothalamic cell bodies, releasing hormones are secreted into tiny blood vessels, or capillaries, that transport them to the anterior pituitary, as Figure 11-16 shows.

A releasing hormone can either stimulate or inhibit the release of an anterior pituitary hormone. For example, the hormone prolactin is produced by the anterior pituitary, but its release is controlled by a prolactin-releasing factor and a prolactin release–inhibiting factor, both synthesized in the hypothalamus. The release of hormones by the anterior pituitary in turn provides a means by which the brain can control what is taking place in many other parts of the body. Three factors control hypothalamic hormone-related activity: feedback loops, neural regulation, and responses based on experience.

Feedback Loops When the level of, say, thyroid hormone is low, the hypothalamus releases thyroid-stimulating hormone-releasing hormone (TSH-releasing hormone). The TSH-releasing hormone stimulates the anterior pituitary to release thyroid-stimulating hormone, which then acts on the thyroid gland to secrete more thyroid hormone.

There must, however, be some control over how much thyroid hormone is secreted, and so the hypothalamus has receptors to detect the level of thyroid hormone. When that level rises, the hypothalamus lessens its secretion of TSH-releasing hormone. This type of system is essentially a form of homeostatic control that works as a feedback mechanism, a system in which a neural or hormonal loop regulates the activity of neurons, initiating the neural activity or hormone release, as illustrated in **Figure 11-17A**.

The hypothalamus initiates a cascade of events that result in the secretion of hormones, but it pays attention to how much hormone is released. When a certain level is reached, it stops its hormone-stimulating signals. Thus, the feedback mechanism in the hypothalamus maintains a fairly constant circulating level of certain hormones.

Thyroid gland

Neural Control A second control over hormone-related activities of the hypothalamus requires regulation by other brain structures, such as the limbic system and the frontal lobes. Figure 11-17B diagrams this type of control in relation to the effects of oxytocin released from the paraventricular nucleus of the hypothalamus. As stated earlier, one function of oxytocin is to stimulate cells of the mammary glands to release milk. As an infant suckles the breast, the tactile stimulation causes hypothalamic cells to release oxytocin, which stimulates milk letdown. In this way, the oxytocin cells participate in a fairly simple reflex that is both neural and hormonal.

Other stimuli also can influence the release of oxytocin, however, which is where control by other brain structures comes in. For example, the sight, sound, or even thought of her baby can trigger a lactating mother to eject milk. Conversely, as diagrammed in Figure 11-17B, feelings of anxiety in a lactating woman can inhibit milk ejection. These excitatory and inhibitory influences exerted by cognitive activity imply that the cortex can influence neurons in the paraventricular region. Projections from the frontal lobes to the hypothalamus likely perform this role.

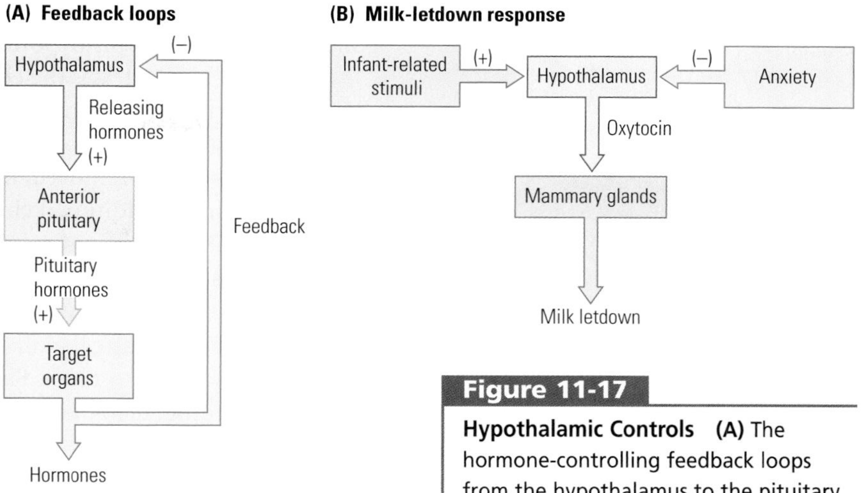

Experiential Responses A third way in which the hormone-related activities of the hypothalamus are controlled is by the brain's responses to experience. In response to experience, neurons in the hypothalamus undergo structural and biochemical changes just as cells in other brain regions do. In other words, hypothalamic neurons are like neurons elsewhere in the brain in that they can be changed by prolonged demands placed on them.

Such changes in hypothalamic neurons can affect the output of hormones. For instance, when a woman is lactating, the cells producing oxytocin increase in size to promote oxytocin release to meet the increasing demands of a growing infant for more milk. Through this control, which is mediated by experience, the baby is provided with sufficient milk over time.

HYPOTHALAMIC INVOLVEMENT IN GENERATING BEHAVIOR

So far, we have considered the role of the hypothalamus in controlling hormone systems, but equally important is its role in generating behavior. This function was first demonstrated by studies in which stimulating electrodes were placed into the hypothalami of various animals, ranging from chickens to rats and cats. When a small electric current was delivered through a wire electrode, an animal suddenly engaged in some complex behavior. The behaviors included eating and drinking; digging; and displaying fear, attack, predatory, or reproductive behavior.

The particular behavior depended on which of many sites in the hypothalamus was stimulated. All the behaviors were smooth, well integrated, and indistinguishable from normally occurring ones. Furthermore, all were goal directed.

The onset and termination of these behaviors depended entirely on the hypothalamic stimulation. For example, if an electrode in a certain location elicited feeding behavior, the animal would eat as soon as the stimulation was turned on and would continue to eat until the stimulation was turned off. If the food was removed, however, the animal would neither eat nor engage in other behaviors such as drinking. Recall

(A) Feedback loops

(B) Milk-letdown response

Figure 11-17

Hypothalamic Controls **(A)** The hormone-controlling feedback loops from the hypothalamus to the pituitary and its target organs. The hypothalamus releases hormones, which stimulate the anterior pituitary to release its hormones, which stimulate target organs such as the thyroid or adrenal gland to release their hormones. Those hormones act, in turn, to influence the hypothalamus to decrease its secretion of the releasing hormone. **(B)** Oxytocin stimulates the mammary glands to release milk. Oxytocin release from the hypothalamus is enhanced by infant-related stimuli and inhibited by maternal anxiety.

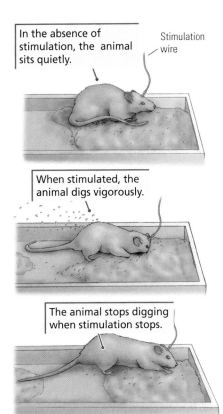

In the absence of stimulation, the animal sits quietly.

Stimulation wire

When stimulated, the animal digs vigorously.

The animal stops digging when stimulation stops.

Figure 11-18

Generating Behavior   When rats receive electrical stimulation to the hypothalamus, they produce goal-directed behaviors. This rat is stimulated to dig when and only when the electricity is turned on. Note also that, if the sawdust is removed (not shown in the bottom drawing), there is no digging.

that Roger ate continuously if foodlike materials were present, corresponding to the continuous activity of his hypothalamus caused by the tumor.

Figure 11-18 illustrates the effect of stimulation at a site that elicits digging. When there is no current, the animal sits quietly. When the current is turned on, the animal digs into the sawdust vigorously; when the current is turned off, the animal stops digging. If the sawdust is removed, there also is no digging.

Two important additional characteristics of the behaviors generated by hypothalamic stimulation are related to (1) the survival of the animal and the species and (2) reward. Animals apparently find the stimulation of these behaviors pleasant, as suggested by the fact that they willingly expend effort, such as pressing a bar, to trigger the stimulation. Recall that cats kill birds and mice because the act of stalking and killing prey is rewarding to them. Similarly, we can hypothesize that animals eat because eating is rewarding, drink because drinking is rewarding, and mate because mating is rewarding.

The Limbic Circuit's Organizing Function

We now turn our attention to parts of the brain that interact with the hypothalamus in generating motivated behaviors. These brain structures evolved as a ring of structures around the brainstem in early amphibians and reptiles. Nearly 150 years ago, Paul Broca was impressed by this evolutionary development and called these structures the "limbic lobe" (from the Latin word *limbus,* meaning "border" or "hem").

Known collectively as the limbic system today, these structures are actually a primitive cortex, as described in Chapter 2. In mammals, the limbic cortex encompasses the cingulate gyrus and the hippocampal formation, as shown in **Figure 11-19**. The hippocampal formation includes the **hippocampus,** a cortical structure that plays a role in species-specific behaviors, memory, and spatial navigation and is vulnerable to the effects of stress, and the *parahippocampal cortex* adjacent to it.

ORGANIZATION OF THE LIMBIC CIRCUIT

As anatomists began to study the limbic-lobe structures, connections between these structures and the hypothalamus became evident. It also became apparent that the limbic lobe has a role in emotion. For instance, in the 1930s, James Papez observed that people with rabies had radical abnormalities in their emotional behavior, and

Figure 11-19

Limbic Lobe   Encircling the brainstem, the limbic lobe as described by Broca consists of the cingulate gyrus and hippocampal formation (the hippocampus and parahippocampal cortex), the amygdala, the mammillothalamic tract, and the anterior thalamus.

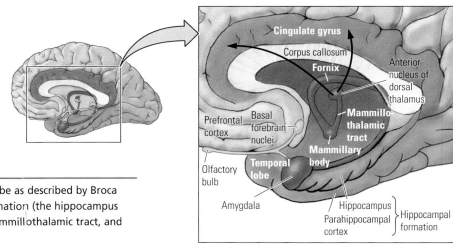

Cingulate gyrus
Corpus callosum
Fornix
Anterior nucleus of dorsal thalamus
Prefrontal cortex
Basal forebrain nuclei
Mammillo-thalamic tract
Mammillary body
Olfactory bulb
Temporal lobe
Amygdala
Hippocampus
Parahippocampal cortex
Hippocampal formation

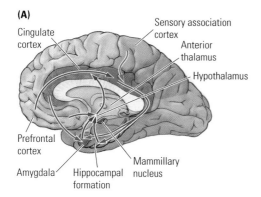

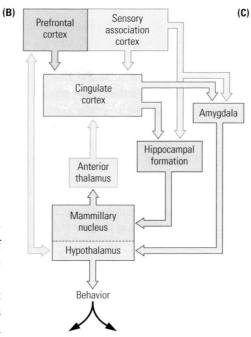

Figure 11-20

Limbic System **(A)** In this modern conception of the limbic system, an interconnected network of structures, the Papez circuit, controls emotional expression. **(B)** A schematic representation, coded to brain areas shown in part A by color, charting the major connections of the limbic system. **(C)** A reminder that parts A and B can be conceptualized as a funnel of outputs through the hypothalamus.

postmortems showed that the rabies had selectively attacked the hippocampus. (The definitive proof of rabies is still a postmortem examination of the hippocampus.)

On the basis of this finding, Papez concluded that the limbic lobe and associated subcortical structures provide the neural basis of emotion. He proposed a circuit, traced in **Figure 11-20A**, now known as the *Papez circuit,* whereby emotion could reach consciousness, which was presumed to reside in the cerebral cortex. Papez's limbic-circuit concept (also called the limbic system) was expanded by Paul MacLean in 1949 to include the amygdala and prefrontal cortex as well. Figures 11-19 and 11-20A show the amygdala lying adjacent to the hippocampus in the temporal lobe, with the prefrontal cortex lying just anterior.

Figure 11-20B charts the limbic circuit schematically. The hippocampus, amygdala, and prefrontal cortex all connect with the hypothalamus. The mammillary nucleus of the hypothalamus connects to the anterior thalamus, which in turn connects with the cingulate cortex, which then completes the circuit by connecting with the hippocampal formation, amygdala, and prefrontal cortex. This anatomical arrangement can be compared to the funnel in Figure 11-20C, which shows the hypothalamus as the spout leading to motivated behavior.

There is now little doubt that most structures of the limbic system, especially the amygdala and hypothalamus, take part in emotional behaviors, as detailed later in the chapter. But most limbic structures are now known to play an important role in various motivated behaviors as well as in emotion, especially in motivating species-typical behaviors such as feeding and sexual activity. The critical structures for such motivated behaviors, as well as for emotion, are the amygdala and the hypothalamus. Having already considered the hypothalamus, we now turn to the amygdala.

THE AMYGDALA

Named for the Greek word for "almond" because of its shape, the **amygdala** consists of three principal subdivisions: the corticomedial area, the basolateral area, and the central area. Like the hypothalamus, the amygdala receives inputs from all sensory systems. But, in contrast with the neurons of the hypothalamus, those of the amygdala require more-complex stimuli to be excited.

In addition, many amygdala neurons are *multimodal:* they respond to more than one sensory modality. In fact, some neurons in the amygdala respond to sight, sound, touch, taste, and smell stimuli. These cells must create a rather complex image of the sensory world.

○ To view a three-dimensional model of the hippocampus and the amygdala, visit the area on the limbic system in the section on functional neuroanatomy in the central nervous system module on your *Foundations* CD.

Hippocampus. Distinctive, three-layered subcortical structure of the limbic system lying in the medial region of the temporal lobe; plays a role in species-specific behaviors, memory, and spatial navigation and is vulnerable to the effects of stress.

Amygdala. Almond-shaped collection of nuclei located within the limbic system; plays a role in emotional and species-typical behaviors.

The amygdala sends connections primarily to the hypothalamus and the brainstem, where it influences neural activity associated with emotions and species-typical behavior. For example, when the amygdalae of epileptic patients are electrically stimulated before brain surgery, the patients become fearful and anxious. We observed a woman who responded with increased respiration and heart rate, saying that she felt as if something bad was going to happen, although she could not specify what.

Amygdala stimulation can also induce eating and drinking. We observed a man who drank water every time the stimulation was turned on. (There happened to be a pitcher of water on the table next to him.) Within 20 minutes, he had consumed about 2 liters of water. When asked if he was thirsty, he said, "No, not really. I just feel like drinking."

The amygdala's role in eating can be seen in patients with lesions in the amygdala. These patients, much as we saw in the effects of Roger's tumor, may be much less discriminating in their food choices, eating foods that were formerly unpalatable to them. Lesions of the amygdala may also give rise to hypersexuality.

The Frontal Lobes' Executive Function

The amygdala is intimately connected with the functioning of the frontal lobes that constitute all cortical tissue in front of the central sulcus. This large area is made up of several functionally distinct cortical regions. **Figure 11-21** shows the three main regions: the motor cortex, the premotor cortex, and the prefrontal cortex.

As you learned in Chapter 10, the motor cortex controls fine movements, especially of the fingers, hands, toes, feet, tongue, and face. The premotor cortex participates in the selection of appropriate movement sequences. For instance, a resting dog may get up in response to its owner's call, which serves as an environmental cue for a series of movements processed by one region of the premotor cortex. Or a dog may get up for no apparent reason and wander about the yard, which is a sequence of actions in response to an internal cue, this time processed by a different region of the premotor cortex.

Finally, the **prefrontal cortex** (which literally means "in front of the front") is anterior to the premotor cortex. It is made up of two primary areas: the dorsolateral region and the inferior region. Recall from Chapter 10 that the prefrontal cortex plays a role in specifying the goals toward which movement should be directed. In this role, it controls the processes by which we select movements that are appropriate for the particular time and place. This selection may be cued by internal information (such as memory and emotion) or it may be made in response to context (environmental information).

Like the amygdala, the frontal lobes, particularly the prefrontal cortex, receive highly processed information from all sensory areas. Many of the neurons in the prefrontal cortex, like those in the amygdala, are multimodal. As shown in **Figure 11-22**, the prefrontal cortex receives connections from the amygdala, the dorsomedial thalamus, the posterior parietal (sensory association) cortex, and the dopaminergic cells of the ventral tegmental area.

The dopaminergic input plays an important role in regulating how prefrontal neurons react to stimuli, including emotional ones. Abnormalities in this dopaminergic projection may account for some disorders, including schizophrenia, in which people have little emotional reaction to normally arousing stimuli (see Chapter 15).

Figure 11-22 also shows the areas to which the prefrontal cortex sends connections. The inferior prefrontal region projects axons to the amygdala and the hypothalamus in

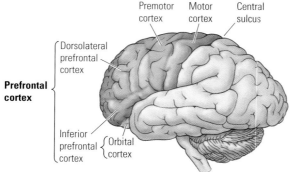

Premotor cortex   Motor cortex   Central sulcus

Dorsolateral prefrontal cortex

Prefrontal cortex

Inferior prefrontal cortex   Orbital cortex

Figure 11-21

Lateral View of the Gross Subdivisions of the Frontal Lobe

Prefrontal cortex. The cortex lying in front of the motor and premotor cortex of the frontal lobe; the prefrontal cortex is particularly large in the human brain.

particular. These axons provide a route for influencing the autonomic system, which controls changes in blood pressure, respiration, and so forth. The dorsolateral prefrontal region sends its connections primarily to the posterior parietal cortex, the cingulate cortex, the basal ganglia, and the premotor cortex. These connections provide a route for influencing movement as well as certain memory functions to be considered in Chapter 13.

As already stated, the prefrontal cortex takes part in the selection of behaviors appropriate to the particular time and place. This selection may be cued by internal information or it may be made in response to the environmental context. Disruption to this selection function can be seen in people with injury to the dorsolateral frontal lobe. They become overly dependent on environmental cues to determine their behavior. Like small children, they can be easily distracted by what they see or hear.

We have all experienced this kind of loss of concentration to some extent, but, for a frontal-lobe patient, the problem is exaggerated and persistent. Because the person becomes so absorbed in irrelevant stimuli, he or she is unable to act on internalized information most of the time.

A good example is J. C., whose bilateral damage to the dorsolateral prefrontal cortex resulted from having a tumor removed. J. C. would lie in bed most of the day fixated on television programs. He was aware of his wife's opinion of this behavior, but only the opening of the garage door when she returned home from work in the evening would stimulate him into action. Getting out of bed was controlled by this specific environmental cue and, without it, he seemed to lack motivation. Television completely distracted him from acting on internal knowledge of things that he could or should do.

Adapting behavior appropriately to the environmental context also is a function of the prefrontal cortex. Most people readily change their behavior to match the situation at hand. We behave in one way with our parents, in another with our friends, in another with our children, and in yet another with our coworkers. Each set of people creates a different context, and we shift our behaviors accordingly. Our tone of voice, our use of slang or profanity, and the content of our conversations are quite different in different contexts.

Even among our peers, we act differently, depending on who is present. We may be relaxed in the presence of some people and ill at ease with others. It is therefore no accident that the size of the frontal lobes is related to the sociability of a species' behavior. Social behavior is extremely rich in contextual information, and humans are highly social.

The control of behavior in context requires detailed sensory information, which is conveyed from all the sensory regions to the frontal lobes. This sensory input includes not only information from the external world but internal information from the ANS as well. People with damage to the inferior prefrontal cortex, which is common in traumatic brain injuries, have difficulty adapting their behavior according to the context, especially the social context. Consequently, they often make social gaffes.

In summary, the role of the frontal lobes in selecting behaviors is important in considering behavioral causes. The frontal lobes act much like a composer but, instead of selecting notes and instruments, they select our actions. Not surprisingly, the frontal lobes are sometimes described as housing executive functions, a concept that we will return to in Chapter 14 in considering the frontal lobe's role in planning. To grasp the full extent of frontal-lobe control of behavior, see "Agenesis of the Frontal Lobe" on page 414.

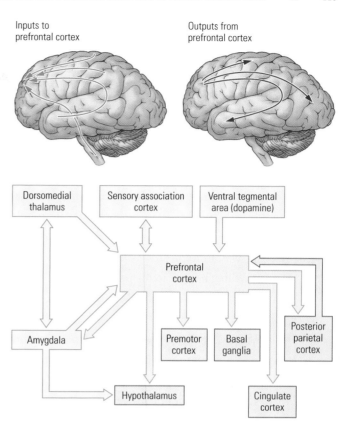

Inputs to prefrontal cortex

Outputs from prefrontal cortex

Figure 11-22

Prefrontal Connections The prefrontal cortex receives inputs from all of the sensory systems, the amygdala, the dorsal medial thalamus, and the dopamine-rich cells of the ventral tegmentum. The prefrontal cortex sends connections to the amygdala, premotor cortex, basal ganglia, posterior parietal cortex, and hypothalamus.

For additonal information about the frontal lobe, go to your *Foundations* CD and visit the area on the cortical lobes in the section on the cortex in the central nervous system module.

Agenesis of the Frontal Lobes

The role of the frontal lobes in motivated behavior is perhaps best understood by looking at J. P.'s case, described in detail by Stafford Ackerly (1964). J. P., who was born in December 1914, was a problem child. Early on, he developed the habit of wandering. Policemen would find him miles from home, as he had no fear of being lost. Severe whippings by his father did not deter him.

J. P.'s behavioral problems continued as he grew older, and, by adolescence, he was constantly in trouble. Yet J. P. also had a good side. When he started school, his first-grade teacher was so impressed with his polite manners that she began writing a letter to his parents to compliment them on having such a well-mannered child who was such a good influence in the class.

As she composed the letter, she looked up to find J. P. exposing himself to the class and masturbating. This contradiction of polite manners and odd behavior characterized J. P.'s conduct throughout his life. At one moment, he was charming and, at the next, he was engaged in socially unacceptable behavior.

He developed no close friendships with people of either sex, in large part because of his repeated incidents of public masturbation, stealing, excessive boastfulness, and wandering. He was a person of normal intelligence who seemed unaffected by the consequences of his behavior. Police officers, teachers, and neighbors all felt that he was willfully behaving in an asocial manner and blamed his parents for not enforcing strict enough discipline.

Perhaps as a result, not until he was 19 years old was J. P.'s true condition detected. To prevent J. P. from serving a prison term for repeated automobile theft, a lawyer suggested that J. P. undergo psychiatric evaluation. He was examined by a psychiatrist, who ordered a brain scan. The image revealed that J. P. lacked a right frontal lobe. Furthermore, his left frontal lobe was about 50 percent of normal size.

It is almost certain that he simply never developed frontal lobes. The failure of a structure to develop is known as *agenesis;* J. P. had agenesis of the frontal lobes. His case offers an unusual opportunity to study the role of the frontal lobes in motivated behavior.

Clearly, J. P. lacked the "bag of mental tricks" that most people use to come to terms with the world. Normally, behavior is affected both by its past consequences and by current environmental input. J. P. did not seem much influenced by either of these factors. As a result, the world was simply too much for him.

He always acted childlike and was unable to formulate plans for the future or to inhibit many of his behaviors. He acted on impulse. At home, he was prone to aggressive outbursts about small matters, especially with regard to his mother.

Curiously, he seemed completely unaware of his life situation. Even though the rest of his brain was working fairly well (his IQ was normal and his language skills were very good), the functional parts of his brain were unable to compensate for the absence of the frontal lobes.

In Review

Motivated behaviors appear to be goal directed and purposeful. Regulatory behavior is controlled by a homeostatic mechanism that works to keep a vital aspect of body function within a narrow, fixed range. Nonregulatory behaviors consist of everything else that we do. Many nonregulatory behaviors are partly controlled by external stimuli that serve as cues. Within the brain, the hypothalamus, the limbic system, and the frontal lobes house the major behavioral circuitry. The hypothalamus provides the simplest, largely homeostatic, control. The limbic system stimulates emotional reactions and species-typical behaviors, whereas the frontal lobes generate the rationale for behavior at the right time and place, taking factors such as external events and internal information into account.

STIMULATING EMOTION

Even though we all know what emotions are, it is easier to identify how emotions are expressed than it is to define them. The concept of emotion is difficult to define because emotion, like motivation, is intangible; it is an inferred state. The expression of emotions includes physiological changes, in heart rate, blood pressure, and hormone secretions. It also includes certain motor responses, especially the movements of the facial muscles that produce facial expression (see Figure 11-5).

The importance of emotion to our everyday lives cannot be underestimated. Emotion, for example, is the inspiration for artistic expression ranging from poetry to filmmaking to painting. Indeed, one reason that many people enjoy the arts is that they evoke emotions. We can therefore conclude that people find certain emotions pleasant. On the other hand, severe and prolonged negative emotions, especially anxiety and depression, can cause clinical disorders. Because so much of human life revolves around emotions, understanding them is central to understanding our humanness.

To explore the neural control of emotions, we must first specify the types of behavior that we want to explain. Think of any significant emotional experience that you had recently. Perhaps you had a serious disagreement with a close friend. Maybe you just became engaged to be married.

A common characteristic of such experiences is that they include autonomic responses such as rapid breathing, sweating, and dry mouth. They may also entail strong subjective feelings that we often label as anger, fear, or love. Finally, emotions typically entail thoughts or plans related to the experience, which may take the form of replaying conversations and events in your mind, anticipating what you might say or do under similar circumstances in the future, or planning your married life.

These three forms of experience suggest the influence of different neural systems. The autonomic component must include the hypothalamus and associated structures. The feelings are more difficult to localize but clearly include the amygdala and probably parts of the frontal lobes. And, finally, the cognitions are likely to be cortical.

What is the relation between our cognitive experience of an emotion and the physiological changes associated with it? One view is that the physiological changes (such as trembling and rapid heartbeat) come first, and the brain then interprets these changes as an emotion of some kind. This perspective implies that the brain (most likely the cortex) creates a cognitive response to autonomic information.

That response varies with the context in which the autonomic arousal occurs. For example, if we are frightened by a movie, we experience a weaker, more short-lived emotion than if we are frightened by a real-life encounter with a gang of muggers. Variations of this perspective have gone by many names, beginning with the *James-Lange theory,* named for its originators. All assume that the brain concocts a story to explain bodily reactions.

Two lines of evidence support the James-Lange theory and similar points of view. One is that the same autonomic responses can accompany different emotions. In other words, particular emotions are not tied to their own unique autonomic changes. This line of evidence leaves room for interpreting what a particular pattern of arousal means, even though particular physiological changes may suggest only a limited range of possibilities. The physiological changes experienced during fear and happiness are unlikely to be confused with one another, for instance.

The second line of evidence supporting the view that physiological changes are the starting point for emotions comes from people with reduced information about their own autonomic arousal, owing to spinal-cord injury, for example. Such people suffer a decrease in perceived emotion, the severity of which depends on how much sensory

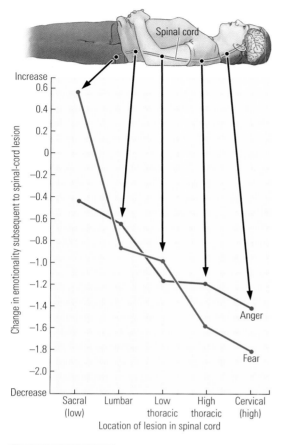

Figure 11-23

Losing Emotion Spinal injury reduces the experience of emotion. The extent of the loss of emotionality is greatest when the lesion is high on the spine.

Adapted from *Principles of Behavioral Neuroscience* (p. 339), by J. Beatty, 1995, Dubuque, IA: Brown & Benchmark.

Somatic marker hypothesis. Posits that "marker" signals arising from emotions and feelings act to guide behavior and decision making, usually in an unconscious process.

Klüver-Bucy syndrome. Behavioral syndrome, characterized especially by hypersexuality, that results from bilateral injury to the temporal lobe.

input they have lost. **Figure 11-23** illustrates this relation. It shows that people with the greatest loss of sensory input, which occurs with injuries at the uppermost end of the spinal cord, also have the greatest loss of emotional intensity. In contrast, people with low spinal injuries retain most of their visceral input and have essentially normal emotional reactions.

Antonio Damasio (1999) emphasized an important additional aspect of the link between emotion and cognitive factors in his **somatic marker hypothesis.** When Damasio studied patients with frontal-lobe injuries, he was struck by how they could be highly rational in analyzing the world yet still make decidedly irrational social and personal decisions. The explanation, he argued, is that the reasoning of people with frontal-lobe injury is no longer affected, either consciously or unconsciously, by the neural machinery that underlies emotion. Cut off from critical emotional input, many social and personal decisions are therefore rather poor.

To account for these observations, Damasio proposed that emotions are responses induced by either internal or external stimuli not normally attended to consciously. For example, if you encounter a bear as you walk down the street, presuming that you live in a place where this event could take place, the stimulus is processed rapidly without conscious appraisal. In other words, a sensory representation of the bear in the visual cortex is transmitted directly to brain structures, such as the amygdala, that initiate an emotional response.

This emotional response includes actions on structures in the forebrain and brainstem and ultimately on the autonomic nervous system. As mentioned earlier, the amygdala has connections to the frontal lobes, and so the emotional response can influence the frontal lobes' appraisal of the world. However, if the frontal lobes are injured, the emotional information is excluded from cognitive processing, and so the quality of emotion-related appraisals suffers. In other words, the response to the bear might be inappropriate.

To summarize, Damasio's somatic marker hypothesis proposes how emotions are normally linked to a person's thoughts, decisions, and actions. In a typical emotional state, certain regions of the brain send messages to many other brain areas and to most of the rest of the body through hormones and the ANS. These messages produce a global change in the organism's state, and this altered state influences behavior, usually in a nonconscious way.

The Amygdala and Emotional Behavior

In addition to controlling certain species-typical behaviors, the amygdala influences emotion (Davis et al., 2003). The role of the amygdala can be seen most clearly in monkeys whose amygdalae have been removed. In 1939, Heinrich Klüver and Paul Bucy reported an extraordinary result, now known as the **Klüver-Bucy syndrome,** that followed the removal of the amygdalae and anterior temporal cortices of monkeys. The principal symptoms include:

1. tameness and loss of fear;
2. indiscriminate dietary behavior (eating many types of formerly rejected foods);
3. greatly increased autoerotic, homosexual, and heterosexual activity, with inappropriate object choice (e.g., the sexual mounting of chairs);
4. tendency to attend to and react to every visual stimulus;
5. tendency to examine all objects by mouth; and
6. visual agnosia, an inability to recognize objects or drawings of objects (see Chapter 8).

Visual agnosia is due to damage to the ventral visual stream in the temporal lobe, but the other symptoms are related to the amygdala damage. The tameness and loss of fear after amygdalectomy is especially striking. Monkeys that normally show a strong aversion to stimuli such as snakes show no fear of them whatsoever. In fact, amygdalectomized monkeys may pick up live snakes and even put them in their mouths.

Although the Klüver-Bucy syndrome is not common in humans, because bilateral temporal lobectomies are rare, symptoms of the syndrome can be seen in people with certain forms of encephalitis, a brain infection (see "Meningitis and Encephalitis" on page 42). In some cases, an encephalitis centered on the base of the brain can damage both temporal lobes and produce many Klüver-Bucy symptoms, including especially indiscriminate sexual behavior and the tendency to examine objects by mouth.

The role of the amygdala in Klüver-Bucy syndrome points to its central role in emotion. So does electrical stimulation of the amygdala, which produces an autonomic response (such as increased blood pressure and arousal) as well as a feeling of fear. Although this production of fear by the brain in the absence of an obvious threat may seem odd, fear is important to a species' survival. To improve their chances of surviving, most organisms using fear as a stimulus minimize their contact with dangerous animals, objects, and places and maximize their contact with things that are safe.

The awareness of danger and safety has both an innate and a learned component, as Joe LeDoux (1996) emphasized. The innate component, much as in the IRMs, is the automatic processing of species-relevant sensory information—specifically, sensory inputs from the visual, auditory, and olfactory systems. The importance of olfactory inputs is not obvious to humans, whose senses are dominated by vision. But, for other animals, olfactory cues often predominate, and there is a major input of olfactory information directly into the amygdala (you can see this connection in the human brain in Figure 11-19).

Thus, a rat that has never encountered a ferret shows an immediate fear response to the odor of ferret. Other novel odors (such as peppermint or coffee) do not produce an innate fear reaction. The innate response triggers an autonomic activation that stimulates conscious awareness of danger.

In contrast, the learned component of fear consists of the avoidance of specific animals, places, and objects that the organism has come to associate with danger. The organism is not born with this avoidance behavior prewired. In a similar way, animals learn to increase contact with environmental stimuli that they associate with positive outcomes, such as food or sexual activity or, in the laboratory, drugs. Damage to the amygdala interferes with all these behaviors. The animal loses not only its innate fears but also its acquired fears and preferences for certain environmental stimuli.

To summarize, the amygdala is required for species survival. It influences autonomic and hormonal responses through its connections to the hypothalamus. It influences our conscious awareness of the positive and negative consequences of events and objects through its connections to the prefrontal cortex.

The Prefrontal Cortex and Emotional Behavior

At about the same time that Klüver and Bucy began studying their monkeys, Carlyle Jacobsen was studying the effects of frontal lobotomy on the cognitive capacities of two chimpanzees. A frontal lobotomy destroys a substantial amount of brain tissue as the result of inserting a sharp instrument into the frontal lobes and moving it back and forth.

In 1935, Jacobsen reported that one of the chimps that had been particularly neurotic before being subjected to this procedure, became more relaxed after it. Incredibly,

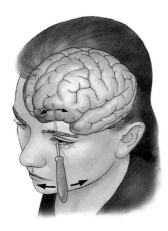

Figure 11-24

Transorbital Leukotomy In this procedure, a leukotome is inserted through the bone of the eye socket and the inferior frontal cortex is disconnected from the rest of the brain.

To learn more about the history of the frontal leukotomy and other psychosurgeries, visit the Chapter 11 Web links on the *Brain and Behavior* Web site (**www.worthpublishers.com/kolb**).

Psychosurgery. Any neurosurgical technique intended to alter behavior.

a leading Portuguese neurologist of the time, Egas Moniz, seized on this observation as a treatment for behavioral disorders in humans, and the frontal lobotomy was initiated as the first form of **psychosurgery.** One procedure is illustrated in **Figure 11-24.**

The use of psychosurgery, which refers to any neurosurgical technique intended to alter behavior, grew rapidly in the 1950s. In North America alone, nearly 40,000 people received frontal lobotomies as a treatment for psychiatric disorders. Not until the 1960s was there any systematic research into the effects of frontal lesions on social and emotional behavior. By this time, the frontal lobotomy had virtually vanished as a "treatment." There is now little doubt that prefrontal lesions in various species, including humans, have severe effects on social and emotional behavior.

Agnes is a case in point. We met Agnes at the psychiatric hospital where we met Roger, whose indiscriminate eating was described at the beginning of this chapter. At the time, Agnes, a 57-year-old woman, was visiting one of the nurses. Agnes had, however, once been a patient.

She had been subjected to a procedure known as a *frontal leukotomy* because her husband, an oil tycoon, felt that she was too gregarious. Evidently, he felt that her "loose lips" were a detriment to his business dealings. He convinced two psychiatrists that she would benefit from psychosurgery, and her life was changed forever.

To perform a leukotomy, as illustrated in Figure 11-24, a surgeon uses a special knife called a leukotome to sever the connections of a region of the inferior frontal cortex, including especially the orbital cortex (see Figure 11-21). The first thing that we noticed about Agnes was that she exhibited no outward sign of emotion. She had virtually no facial expression.

In our conversations with her, however, we quickly discovered that she had considerable insight into the changes brought about by the leukotomy. In particular, she indicated that she no longer had any feelings about things or most people, although, curiously, she was attached to her dog. She said that she often just felt empty and much like a zombie.

Her only moment of real happiness in the 30 years since her operation was the sudden death of her husband, whom she blamed for ruining her life. Unfortunately, Agnes had squandered her dead husband's considerable wealth as a consequence of her inability to plan or organize. This inability, we have seen, is another symptom of prefrontal injury.

The orbital region of the inferior prefrontal area has direct connections with the amygdala and hypothalamus. Stimulation of this area can produce autonomic responses, and, as we saw in Agnes, damage to this area can produce severe personality change characterized by apathy and loss of initiative or drive. The orbital cortex is likely responsible for the conscious awareness of emotional states that are produced by the rest of the limbic system, especially the amygdala.

Agnes's loss of facial expression is also fairly typical of frontal-lobe damage. In fact, people with frontal-lobe injuries or those who suffer from schizophrenia are usually impaired both at producing and perceiving facial expressions, including a wide range of expressions found in all human cultures—happiness, sadness, fear, anger, disgust, and surprise (Kolb & Taylor, 2000). As with J. P.'s agenesis, described earlier, it is difficult to imagine how such people can function effectively in our highly social world without being able to recognize the emotions of others.

Although facial expression is a key part of recognizing emotion, so is tone of voice, or *prosody*. Frontal-lobe patients are devoid of prosody, both in their own conversations and in understanding the prosody of others. The lost ability to comprehend or produce emotional expression in both faces and language partly explains the apathy of frontal-lobe patients. In some ways, they are similar to spinal-cord patients who have lost autonomic feedback and so can no longer feel the arousal associated with emotion.

Frontal-lobe patients can no longer either read emotion in other people's faces and voices or experience it in their own.

Some psychologists have proposed that our own facial expressions may provide us with important clues to the emotions that we are feeling. This idea has been demonstrated in experiments reviewed by Pamela Adelmann and Robert Zajonc (1989). In one such study, people were required to contract their facial muscles by following instructions about which parts of the face to move. Unbeknown to the participants, the movements produced happy and angry expressions. Afterward, they viewed a series of slides and reported how the slides made them feel.

They said that they felt happier when they were inadvertently making a happy face and angrier when the face that they were making was one of anger. Frontal-lobe patients presumably would have no such feedback from their own facial expressions, which could be a reason why their emotional experiences are dampened.

Emotional Disorders

As detailed in Chapter 7, a highly disruptive emotional disorder is major depression, characterized by abnormal regulation of feelings of sadness and happiness. A depressed person feels severely despondent for a prolonged time. Depression is common in our modern world, with a prevalence of at least 10 percent of the population.

Depression has a genetic component. It not only runs in families but also frequently tends to be found in both members of a pair of identical twins. The genetic component in depression implies a biological abnormality, but the cause remains unknown.

The strongest evidence supporting a biological cause of depression comes from the fact that about 70 percent of depressed people can be treated with one of several antidepressant drugs. This success rate has made antidepressants among the most widely prescribed classes of drugs in the world. As summarized in **Table 11-2**, antidepressants act on synapses (especially noradrenaline- and serotonin-containing synapses) by increasing the amount of available transmitter at them. The major projections of noradrenaline- and serotonin-containing cells to the limbic system imply that the activity of limbic regions, including the prefrontal cortex, is abnormal in depression (see Chapter 15).

Excessive anxiety is an even more common emotional problem than depression. Anxiety disorders, including posttraumatic stress disorder, phobias, and obsessive compulsive disorder, are estimated to affect from 15 to 35 percent of the population. Symptoms include persistent fears and worries in the absence of any direct threat, usually accompanied by various physiological stress reactions, such as rapid heartbeat, nausea, and breathing difficulty, as described in "Anxiety Disorders" on page 420. As with depression, the root cause of anxiety disorders is not known, but the effectiveness of drug treatments implies a biological basis.

Table 11-2	Types of Antidepressant Medications	
Drug type	**Action**	**Examples**
Tricyclic antidepressants	Block reuptake of serotonin and noradrenaline	Imipramine
MAO inhibitors	Block activity of monoamine oxidase	Iproniazid
Selective serotonin reuptake inhibitors (SSRIs)	Block reuptake of serotonin	Fluoxetine (Prozac)
		Sertraline (Zoloft)
		Paroxetine (Paxil)

Anxiety Disorders

Animals normally become anxious at times, especially when they are in obvious danger. But anxiety disorders are different. They are characterized by intense feelings of fear or anxiety that are not appropriate for the circumstances. People with an anxiety disorder have persistent and unrealistic worries about impending misfortunes. They also tend to suffer multiple physical symptoms attributable to hyperactivity of the sympathetic nervous system.

G. B.'s case is a good example. He was a 36-year-old man with two college degrees who began to experience severe spells that were initially diagnosed as some type of heart condition. He would begin to breathe heavily, sweat, experience heart palpitations, and sometimes suffer pains in his chest and arms. During these attacks, he was unable to communicate coherently and would lie helplessly on the floor until an ambulance arrived to take him to an emergency room.

Extensive medical testing and multiple attacks in a period of about 2 years eventually led to the diagnosis of **generalized anxiety disorder.** Like most of the 5 percent of the U.S. population who suffer an anxiety disorder at some point in their lives, G. B. was unaware that he was overly anxious.

The cause of generalized anxiety is difficult to determine, but one likely explanation is that these attacks are related to the cumulative effect of general stress. Although G. B. appeared outwardly calm most of the time, he had been a prodemocracy activist in communist Poland, a dangerous position to adopt. Because of the dangers, he and his family eventually had to escape from Poland to Turkey, and from there they went to Canada. G. B. may have had continuing worries about the repercussions of his political activities—worries (and stress) that eventually found expression in generalized anxiety attacks.

The most common and least disabling type of anxiety disorders are **phobias.** A phobia pertains to a clearly defined dreaded object (such as spiders or snakes) or some greatly feared situation (such as enclosed spaces or crowds). Most people have mild aversions to some types of stimuli.

Such an aversion becomes a phobia only when a person's feelings toward a disliked stimulus lead to overwhelming fear and anxiety. The incidence of disabling phobias is surprisingly high, being estimated to affect at least one in ten people. For most people with a phobia, the emotional reaction can be controlled by avoiding what they dread.

Panic disorder has an estimated incidence on the order of 3 percent of the population. The symptoms of panic disorder include recurrent attacks of intense terror that come on without warning and without any apparent relation to external circumstances. Panic attacks usually last only a few minutes, but the experience is always terrifying. There is sudden activation of the sympathetic nervous system, leading to sweating, a wildly beating heart, and trembling.

Although panic attacks may occur only occasionally, the victim's dread of another episode may be continual. Consequently, many people with panic disorders also experience *agoraphobia,* a fear of public places or situations in which help might not be available. This phobia makes some sense because a person with a panic disorder may feel particularly vulnerable to having an attack in a public place.

Freud believed that anxiety disorders were psychological in origin and treatable with talking therapies in which people confronted their fears. But anxiety disorders are now known to have a clear biological link. These disorders are most effectively treated with benzodiazepines, of which diazepam (Valium) is the best known. Alprazolam (Xanax) is the most commonly prescribed drug for panic attacks. Benzodiazepines act by augmenting GABA's inhibitory effect and are believed to exert a major influence on neurons in the amygdala.

The most widely prescribed anxiolytic (antianxiety) drugs, which are detailed in Chapter 7, are the benzodiazepines, such as Valium, Librium, and Xanax. These drugs are thought to be effective because of their agonistic action on the $GABA_A$ receptor (see Figure 7-8). Although $GABA_A$ receptors are found throughout the brain, the amygdala has an especially high concentration. The infusion of benzodiazepines into the amygdala blocks fear, suggesting that the amygdala may be the site of their action.

Why would the brain have a mechanism for benzodiazepine action? It certainly did not evolve to allow us to take Valium. Probably this mechanism is part of a system that both increases and reduces anxiety levels. The mechanism for raising anxiety seems to entail a compound known as diazepam-binding inhibitor. This compound appears to bind antagonistically with the $GABA_A$ receptor, resulting in greater anxiety.

There are times when such an increase in anxiety is beneficial, especially if we are drowsy and need to be alert to deal with some kind of crisis. Impairment of this mechanism or the one that reduces anxiety can cause serious emotional problems, even anxiety disorders (Chapter 15).

In Review

Emotion and motivation have common autonomic responses (sweating and rapid heartbeat), subjective feelings (fear or trust, joy or pain), and a cognitive component—what we think about the arousing situation. The autonomic responses result from the activity of the hypothalamus and related structures. Psychologists have proposed that, when the body experiences an autonomic reaction and intense feelings, the brain creates a story to explain those experiences. The amygdala and the orbitofrontal-cortex circuits contribute to our feelings and our motives. Our emotional thoughts and thinking that motivates us both likely result from activity throughout the cerebral hemispheres. Abnormalities in the neural circuits that produce emotional and motivated behavior are responsible for society's most pervasive behavioral disorders—the anxiety disorders and depression.

CONTROL OF REGULATORY BEHAVIOR

Feeding behaviors are central to our existence. After all, we must eat and drink to live. But there is more to feeding behavior than sustenance alone. We also derive great pleasure from eating and drinking.

In fact, for many people, eating is a focus of daily life, if not for survival, for its centrality to social activities, from get-togethers with family and friends to business meetings and even to identification with a group. Are you a gourmet, a vegetarian, or a snack-food junkie? Do you diet? In this section, we focus mainly on the control of eating in humans, but we also consider how homeostatic mechanisms control our intake of fluids.

Controlling Eating

Control over eating is a source of frustration and even grief for many people in the developed world. In 2000, the World Health Organization identified **obesity,** the excessive accumulation of body fat, as a worldwide epidemic. The United States is a case in point. From 1990 to 2000, the percentage of overweight people has increased from about 50 percent to 60 percent of the population. The proportion of people considered obese has increased from about 12 percent to 20 percent.

The increasing numbers of overweight and obese children and adults persist despite a substantial decrease in fat intake in American diets. What behaviors might cause persistent weight gain? One key to understanding weight gain in the developed world is evolutionary.

Generalized anxiety disorder. Persistently high levels of anxiety often accompanied by maladaptive behaviors to reduce anxiety; thought to be caused by chronic stress.

Phobia. Fear of a clearly defined object or situation.

Panic disorder. Recurrent attacks of intense terror that come on without warning and without any apparent relation to external circumstances.

Obesity. Excessive accumulation of body fat.

For more information on obesity and obesity-related health risks, visit the Chapter 11 Web links on the *Brain and Behavior* Web site (**www.worth publishers.com/kolb**).

Weight-Loss Strategies

Focus on Disorders

Among the wide range of diets and weight-loss strategies on the market, none have stopped the obesity epidemic. Diets range widely in their recommended proportions and types of fats, carbohydrates, and proteins allowed. In the past few years, low-carbohydrate diets have become popular—Atkins, Zone, and South Beach among them.

Proponents of these plans claim significant weight loss and good health, without hunger. The accompanying charts profile the dietary proportions recommended for the beginning phase of the Atkins plan, for the Zone diet, and for a diet high in nonsaturated fats and low in carbohydrates. Shown for comparison is the dietary composition that the American Heart Association recommended in 2000.

What scientific evidence supports the claims made by these diets? Are they fads or do they really work? The difficulty in reaching scientific conclusions about a diet's effectiveness is that studies need random samples of individuals on different diets to compare over a period of at least 1 year. Few such studies have been designed, and the conclusion of a recent review by Arne Astrup and colleagues (2004) is that weight loss is associated with the restriction of energy intake and the duration of the diet but *not* with carbohydrate restriction.

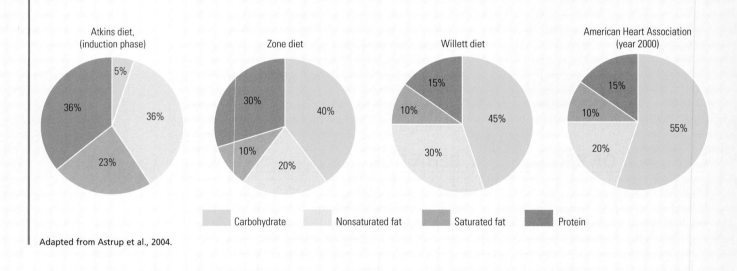

Adapted from Astrup et al., 2004.

Even 40 years ago, much of our food was only seasonally available. In a world with uncertain food availability, it makes sense to store excess body calories in the form of fat to be used later when food is scarce. Down through history and in many cultures today, plumpness is desirable as a standard of beauty and a sign of health and wealth.

In a postindustrial society where food is continuously and easily available, as it is today, being overweight may not be the healthiest strategy. People eat as though food will be scarce and fail to burn off the extra calories by exercising, and the result is apparent. About half of the U.S. population has dieted at some point in their lives. At any given time, at least 25 percent report that they are currently on a diet. For a comparison of how some well known diets perform, see "Weight-Loss Strategies."

Eating disorders entail being either underweight or overweight. Most Americans are overweight but live in a culture obsessed with slimness. The human control system for feeding has multiple neurobiological inputs, including cognitive factors such as

For example, in one study, 63 participants followed either of two diets in which the proportions of nutrients are essentially reversed (Foster et al., 2003). In the low-carbohydrate–high-protein Atkins plan, the percentage of carbohydrates allowed ranges from 5 percent in the induction phase to a maximum of 19 percent in the maintenance phases. Protein is at least 36 percent and fat as much as 59 percent of the menu, depending on the phase. In an energy-restricted diet that is high in carbohydrates and low in protein, the allowable percentages are 60 percent carbohydrate and only 15 percent protein and 25 percent fat. After 6 months, the low-carbohydrate group on Atkins had lost a larger percentage of body weight on average (7 percent versus 3 percent); but, after 1 year, the difference was no longer significant (4.4 percent versus 2.5 percent).

Thus, the low-carbohydrate diet was superior in the short run but not in the long run, a finding supported by those of two other studies reviewed by Astrup's group. Two problems with all studies are that drop-out rates tend to be high and it is difficult to ensure compliance with the diets. Therefore, to date, there is no evidence that, in the long term, the low-carbohydrate diets are superior.

What mechanisms might cause weight loss? The greater weight loss in the short term on the low-carbohydrate diets appears to be a result of increased loss of stored fat. There is no evidence that any diet affects the expenditure of energy, a claim made by the Atkins diet. Crankiness due to low car-bohydrate intake, which lowers serotonin levels, has been reported.

Another possible explanation, but not proved, for the short-term success of the low-carbohydrate diet is the combination of restricted food choices and enhanced feeling of satiety produced by its high protein content. The drop-out rate may be related to a long-term dissatisfaction with the restricted food choices, but that possibility, too, needs to be confirmed. Astrup concludes that, at present, the only certain solution to weight loss appears to be a permanent switch to a diet reduced in *calories* and fat combined with increased physical activity. One of the largest sources of calories is sugar (a carbohydrate) in highly refined foods.

Finally, although not specifically related to dieting, there is increasing evidence of the health-protective effects of diets that are high in fruits, vegetables, legumes, and whole grains and that include fish, nuts, and low-fat dairy products. Perhaps the best known of such diets is the Mediterranean diet, which has well-documented benefits in reducing the risk of heart disease as well as obesity (Panagiotakos et al., 2004). Such diets need not be restricted in fat intake as long as people are active and energy intake does not exceed energy expenditure. Although there has been some debate about whether the effects of such diets on health are partly biased by genetics or culture, systematic clinical trials of people at risk for cardiovascular disease elsewhere in the world have shown clear reductions in cardivascular disease and death.

thoughts about food. These cognitive factors also include the association between environmental cues (e.g., watching television or studying) and the act of eating. The constant pairing of such cues with eating can result in the cues alone becoming a motivation, or incentive, to eat. We return to this phenomenon in the discussion of rewards and addictions at the end of the chapter.

Anorexia nervosa is a disorder with a huge cognitive component—namely, self-image. Anorexia is especially identified with adolescent girls. A person's body image is highly distorted in anorexia. This misperception leads to an exaggerated concern with being overweight, spiraling to excessive dieting, compulsive exercising, and severe, potentially life threatening weight loss.

The neurobiological control of feeding behavior in humans is not as simple as it is in the fly described earlier in the chapter. The multiple inputs to the human control system for feeding come from three major sources: the cognitive factors already introduced, the hypothalamus, and the digestive system.

Anorexia nervosa. Exaggerated concern with being overweight that leads to inadequate food intake and often excessive exercising; can lead to severe weight loss and even starvation.

Visit the Chapter 11 Web links on the *Brain and Behavior* Web site (**www.worthpublishers.com/kolb**) to learn more about eating disorders.

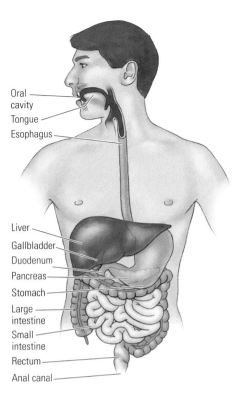

Oral cavity
Tongue
Esophagus

Liver
Gallbladder
Duodenum
Pancreas
Stomach
Large intestine
Small intestine
Rectum
Anal canal

Figure 11-25

The Digestive System

Aphagia. Failure to eat; may be due to an unwillingness to eat or to motor difficulties, especially with swallowing.

Hyperphagia. Disorder in which an animal overeats, leading to significant weight gain.

THE DIGESTIVE SYSTEM AND THE CONTROL OF EATING

The digestive tract, illustrated in **Figure 11-25**, begins in the mouth and ends at the anus. Food travels from the oral cavity to the stomach through the esophagus. The stomach, which is a storage reservoir, secretes hydrochloric acid, which starts to break food into smaller particles, and pepsin, an enzyme that breaks proteins down into amino acids.

The partly broken down food then moves to the upper part of the small intestine through the duodenum, where digestive enzymes produced in the gall bladder and pancreas further break the food down to allow the absorption of amino acids, fats, and simple sugars into the bloodstream. Most of the remaining water and electrolytes in food are absorbed by the large intestine, and the waste passes out of the body through the anus.

The digestive system extracts three types of nutrients for the body: lipids (fats), amino acids (the building blocks of proteins), and glucose (sugar). Each is a specialized form of energy reserve. Because we require varying amounts of these reserves, depending on what we are doing, the body has detector cells to keep track of the level of each nutrient in the bloodstream.

Glucose is the body's primary fuel and is virtually the only energy source for the brain. Because the brain requires glucose even when the digestive tract is empty, the liver acts as a short-term reservoir of glycogen, a starch that acts as an inert form of glucose. When blood-sugar levels fall, as when we are sleeping, detector cells tell the liver to release glucose by converting glycogen into glucose.

Thus the digestive system functions mainly to break down food, and the body needs to be apprised of how well this breakdown is proceeding. Feedback mechanisms provide such information. When food reaches the intestines, it interacts with receptors there to trigger the release of at least 10 different peptide hormones, including one known as cholecystokinin (CCK).

The released peptides inform the brain (and perhaps other organs in the digestive system) about the nature and quality of the food in the gastrointestinal tract. The level of CCK appears to play a role in satiety, or the feeling of having eaten enough. For example, if CCK is infused into the hypothalamus of an animal, the animal's appetite diminishes.

THE HYPOTHALAMUS AND THE CONTROL OF EATING

Feeding behavior is influenced by hormones including insulin, growth hormone, and sex steroids. These hormones stimulate and inhibit feeding, and they aid in the conversion of nutrients into fat and the conversion of fat into glucose. Not surprisingly, the hypothalamus, which controls hormone systems, is the key brain structure in feeding.

Investigation into the role of the hypothalamus in the control of feeding began in the early 1950s, when researchers discovered that damage to the lateral hypothalamus in rats caused the animals to stop eating, a symptom known as **aphagia** (from the Greek *a*, signifying "absent," and *phagein*, "to eat"). In contrast, damage to the ventromedial hypothalamus (VMH), caused the animals to overeat, a symptom known as **hyperphagia.** A VMH-lesioned rat that overate to the point of obesity is shown in the Procedure section of **Experiment 11-1**. The Results section reveals that the VMH-lesioned rat weighed more than a kilogram, three times the weight of her normal sister, which was 340 grams.

At about the same time, researchers also found that electrical stimulation of the lateral hypothalamus elicits feeding, whereas stimulation of the ventromedial hypothalamus inhibits feeding. The opposing effects of injury and stimulation to these two hypothalamic regions led to the idea that the lateral hypothalamus signals "eating on," whereas the VMH signals "eating off." This model quickly proved to be too simple, however.

The lateral hypothalamus contains not only cell bodies but also fiber bundles passing through it, and damage to either can produce aphagia. Similarly, damage to fibers passing through the VMH often causes injury as well to the paraventricular nucleus of the hypothalamus. And damage to the paraventricular nucleus alone is now known to produce hyperphagia. Clearly, then, there is more to the hypothalamus's role in the control of feeding than the activities of the lateral and ventromedial hypothalamus alone.

In the half-century since the first studies on the hypothalamus's role in feeding, researchers have learned that damage to the lateral and ventromedial hypothalamus and to the paraventricular nucleus has multiple effects. These effects include changes in hormone levels (especially that of insulin), in sensory reactivity (the taste and attractiveness of food is altered), in glucose and lipid levels in the blood, and in metabolic rate. The general role of the hypothalamus is to act as a sensor for the levels of lipids, glucose, hormones, and various peptides. For example, groups of hypothalamic neurons sense the level of glucose (so-called glucostatic neurons) as well as the level of lipids (so-called lipostatic neurons).

The sum of the activity of all such hypothalamic neurons creates a very complex homeostat controlling feeding. **Figure 11-26** shows that this homeostat receives inputs from three sources: from the digestive system (such as information about blood-glucose levels), from hormone systems (such as information about the level of CCK), and from parts of the brain that process cognitive factors. We turn to these cognitive factors next.

COGNITIVE FACTORS AND THE CONTROL OF EATING

Cognitive factors are especially important for the control of eating in humans. Just thinking about a favorite food is often enough to make us feel hungry. The cognitive aspect to feeding includes not only the images of food that we pull from memory but also external sensations, especially food-related sights and smells. In addition, learned associations, such as learned taste aversions discussed earlier, are related to feeding.

The neural control of cognitive factors probably originates in multiple brain regions. Two structures are clearly important: the amygdala and the inferior prefrontal cortex. Damage to the amygdala alters food preferences and abolishes taste-aversion learning. These effects are probably related to the amygdala's efferent connections to the hypothalamus.

The amygdala's role in regulating species-typical behaviors is well established, but the role of the inferior prefrontal cortex is more

---

EXPERIMENT 11-1

Question: Does the hypothalamus play a role in eating?

Procedure

The ventromedial hypothalamus (VMH) of the rat on the right was damaged, and her body weight was monitored for a year. Her sister on the left is normal.

Intact brain of sister rat   Rat brain with lesion

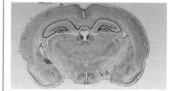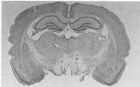

Results:

The VMH-lesioned rat showed a dramatic increase in food intake and body weight.

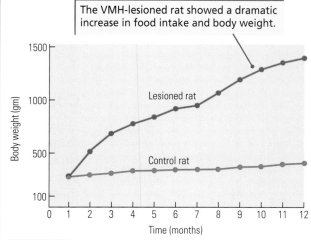

Conclusion

The VMH plays a role in controlling the cessation of eating. Damage to the VMH results in prolonged and dramatic weight gain.

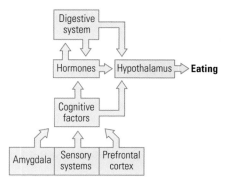

Figure 11-26

Simple Model of Control of Feeding Behavior

difficult to pin down. Rats and monkeys with damage to the orbital cortex lose weight, in part because they eat less. Humans with orbital injuries are invariably slim, but we know of no formal studies on their eating habits. The inferior prefrontal cortex receives projections from the olfactory bulb, and cells in this region do respond to smells. Because odors influence the taste of foods, damage to the inferior prefrontal cortex likely decreases eating because of diminished sensory responses to food odor and perhaps to taste.

An additional cognitive factor in the control of eating is the pleasure that we derive from it, especially from eating foods with certain tastes, such as chocolate. What pleasure is and how the brain produces it are topics discussed at the end of this chapter in the context of reward. At this point, simply keep in mind that pleasure and its absence are cognitive factors in the control of eating.

Finally, Randy Seeley and Stephen Woods (2003) have noted that, in spite of the problem that people now appear to have with weight gain, adult mammals do a masterful job of matching their caloric intake to caloric expenditure. Consider that a typical man eats 900,000 calories per year. To gain just one extra pound requires him to eat 4000 calories more than are burned in that year. This increase amounts to only 11 calories per day, or one potato chip. According to Seeley and Woods, the average weight gain in the U.S population is less than 1 pound per year. This weight gain corresponds to an error in homeostasis of less than 0.5 percent, which is a rather small error. Seeley and Woods conjectured that the nervous sytem must juggle two competing challenges in weight control. The first is to maintain adequate stores of fuel and the second is to provide fuel for current cellular functions. They noted that the current obesity "epidemic" could be the result of factors that alter the sensing of stored fuel, the sensing of ongoing fuel availability, or the integration of these two types of signal. Treatment strategies for obesity will require an understanding of what these factors are and how they operate.

Controlling Drinking

About 70 percent of the human body is composed of water that contains a range of chemicals that participate in the hundreds of chemical reactions of bodily functions. Homeostatic mechanisms control water levels (and hence chemical concentrations) within rather narrow limits. These mechanisms are essential because the rate of a chemical reaction is partly determined by how concentrated the supplies of participating chemicals are.

As with eating, we drink for many reasons. We consume some beverages, such as coffee, wine, beer, and juice, as part of social activities or just because they taste good. We drink water for its health benefits, to help wash down a meal or to intensify the flavor of dry foods. On a hot day, we drink water because we are thirsty, presumably because we have lost significant moisture through sweating and evaporation.

Although we think of thirst as a single phenomenon, there are actually two kinds of thirst. **Osmotic thirst** results from an increase in the concentrations of dissolved chemicals, known as *solutes,* in the body fluids. **Hypovolemic thirst** results from a loss of overall fluid volume from the body. Here we consider each kind briefly.

OSMOTIC THIRST

The solutes found inside and outside cells in the body have an ideal concentration for the body's chemical reactions. This concentration requires a kind of thermostat, much like the one for body temperature. Deviations from the ideal solute concentration activate systems to reestablish that concentration.

Consider what happens when we eat salty foods, such as potato chips. The salt (NaCl) spreads through the blood and enters the extracellular fluid that fills the spaces

---

Osmotic thirst. Results from an increased concentration of dissolved chemicals, or *solutes,* in body fluids.

Hypovolumic thirst. Produced by a loss of overall fluid volume from the body.

between our cells. This produces a shift away from the ideal solute concentration. Receptors in the hypothalamus along the third ventricle detect the altered solute concentration and relay this message to various hypothalamic areas that, in turn, stimulate us to drink in response to osmotic thirst. In addition, other messages are sent to the kidneys to reduce water excretion.

HYPOVOLEMIC THIRST

Unlike osmotic thirst, hypovolemic thirst arises when the total volume of body fluids declines, motivating us to drink more and replenish their supplies. In contrast with osmotic thirst, however, hypovolemic thirst encourages us to choose something other than water, because water would dilute the solute concentration in the blood. Rather, we prefer to drink flavored beverages that contain salts and other nutrients.

Hypovolemic thirst and its satiation are controlled by a different hypothalamic circuit from the one that controls osmotic thirst. When fluid volume drops, the kidneys send a hormone signal (angiotensin) that stimulates midline hypothalamic neurons. These neurons, in turn, stimulate drinking.

In Review

Feeding is a regulatory behavior that has a large cognitive component in humans. The hypothalamus is the principal brain structure in the control of eating. Three of its regions—the lateral hypothalamus, the ventromedial hypothalamus, and the paraventricular nucleus— play especially important roles. Groups of neurons in the hypothalamus act as sensors to detect the levels of glucose, lipids, and peptides in the blood. Neural control of the cognitive factors in eating probably includes multiple brain regions. The brain also motivates us to drink whenever solutes in the blood deviate from ideal levels or whenever there is a significant drop in the body's volume of fluids. In either case, receptors detect the shifts, and neurons in the hypothalamus stimulate the experience of thirst.

CONTROL OF NONREGULATORY BEHAVIOR

Unlike feeding, which organisms must repeatedly do to survive, sexual behavior— notwithstanding procreation, which is essential to the survival of the species—is not essential for an individual organism's survival. Yet sexual activity is of enormous psychological importance to humans. Sexual themes repeatedly appear in our art, literature, and films. They also bombard us in the advertising that we create to help sell products.

Indeed, in Sigmund Freud's psychodynamic theory of human behavior, sexual drives are central. Such significance makes it all the more important to understand how human sexual behavior is controlled. The answer lies in both gonadal hormones and brain circuits.

Effects of Sex Hormones on the Brain

In Chapter 6, we encountered the influence of gonadal hormones on the brain when we considered how a male's Y chromosome controls the differentiation of embryonic gonad tissue into testes, which in turn secrete testosterone. Testosterone masculinizes both the sex organs and the brain during development. This process is an *organizing effect* of gonadal hormones. A major organizing effect that gonadal hormones have on the brain is in the hypothalamus, especially the preoptic area of the medial hypothalamus. But organizing effects also operate in other nervous system regions, notably the amygdala, the prefrontal cortex, and the spinal cord.

These sex-related differences in the nervous system make sense behaviorally. After all, animal courtship rituals differ between the sexes, as do copulatory behaviors, with females engaging in sexually receptive responses and males in mounting ones. The production of these sex differences in behaviors depends on the action of gonadal hormones on the brain both during development and during adulthood.

The actions of hormones on the adult brain are referred to as *activating effects,* in contrast with the developmental organizing effects. Here we consider organizing and activating effects separately.

ORGANIZING EFFECTS OF SEX HORMONES

During fetal development, as you know, a male's testes produce male hormones, the androgens. In the developing rat (the species in which the organizing effects of gonadal hormones have been most extensively studied), androgens are produced during the last week of fetal development and the first week after birth. The androgens produced at this time greatly alter both neural structures and later behavior. For example, the hypothalamus and prefrontal cortex of a male rat differ structurally both from those of female rats and from those of males that were not exposed to androgens during their development.

Furthermore, in adulthood, males with little exposure to the androgen testosterone during development behave like genetic female rats. If given estrogen and progesterone, they become sexually "receptive" and display typical female behaviors when mounted by males. Male rats that are castrated in adulthood do not act in this way.

Sexual dimorphism, the differential development of brain areas in the two sexes (see Chapter 6), arises from a complex series of steps. Cells in the brain produce aromatase, an enzyme that converts testosterone into estradiol, one of the female sex hormones called estrogens. Therefore a female hormone, estradiol, actually masculinizes a male brain.

Females are not masculinized by the presence of estrogens, because the fetuses of both sexes produce a liver enzyme *(alpha fetoprotein)* that binds to estrogen, rendering it incapable of entering neurons. Testosterone is unaffected by alpha fetoprotein, and so it enters neurons and is converted into estradiol.

The organizing effects of testosterone are clearly illustrated in the preoptic area of the hypothalamus, which plays a critical role in the copulatory behavior of male rats. Comparing this area in males and females, Roger Gorski and his colleagues found a nucleus about five times as large in the males as in the females (Gorski, 1984). Significantly, the sexual dimorphism of the preoptic area can be altered by manipulating gonadal hormones during development. The castration of male rats at birth leads to a smaller preoptic area, whereas treating infant females with testosterone increases the preoptic area's size.

The organizing effects of gonadal hormones are more difficult to study in humans. The work of John Money and Anke Ehrhardt (1972), however, revealed an important role of these hormones in human development (see "Androgen-Insensitivity Syndrome and the Androgenital Syndrome").

ACTIVATING EFFECTS OF SEX HORMONES

The sexual behavior of both males and females also depends on the actions that gonadal hormones have on the *adult* brain. In most vertebrate species, female sexual behavior varies in the course of an estrous cycle during which the levels of hormones that the ovaries produce fluctuate. The rat's estrous cycle is about 4 days long, with

Testosterone

Estradiol

Sexual dimorphism. Differential development of brain areas in the two sexes.

Androgen-Insensitivity Syndrome and the Androgenital Syndrome

Focus on Disorders

After the testes of a male fetus have formed, sexual development depends on the actions of testicular hormones. This dependence is made extremely clear by studying people with *androgen-insensitivity syndrome*. In this syndrome, an XY (male) fetus produces androgens, but the body is not able to respond to them.

Such a genetic male therefore develops a female appearance, or phenotype, as shown in the top photograph. Because their estrogen receptors are not affected by the syndrome, these people are still responsive to estrogen produced both by the adrenal gland and by the testes. As a result, they develop female secondary sexual characteristics during puberty, even without additional hormone treatment. A person with androgen-insensitivity syndrome is therefore a genetic male who appears to be female.

If no Y chromosome is present to induce the growth of testes, a fetus develops ovaries and becomes a female. In some cases, however, the female fetus is exposed to androgens, producing a syndrome known both as *congenital adrenal*

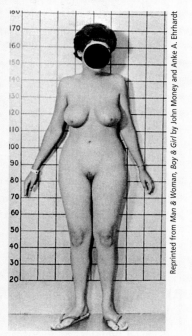

Reprinted from *Man & Woman, Boy & Girl* by John Money and Anke A. Ehrhardt

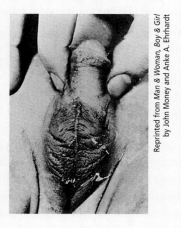

Reprinted from *Man & Woman, Boy & Girl* by John Money and Anke A. Ehrhardt

hyperplasia and as the *androgenital syndrome*. This exposure to androgens can occur if the adrenal glands of either the mother or the infant produce an excessive amount of androgens.

The effects vary, depending on when the androgens are produced and how much exposure there is. In extreme cases, an enlarged clitoris develops that can be mistaken for a small penis, as shown in the bottom photograph. In less severe cases, there is no gross abnormality in genital structure, but there is a behavioral effect: these girls show a high degree of tomboyishness. In early childhood, they identify with boys and prefer boys' clothes, toys, and games. One explanation for this behavioral effect is that the developing brain is masculinized, thus changing later behavior.

(*Top*) In androgen-insensitivity syndrome, a genetic male (XY) is insensitive to gonadally produced androgens but remains sensitive to estrogens, leading to the development of a female phenotype. (*Bottom*) In congenital adrenal hyperplasia, a genetic female (XX) is exposed to androgens produced by the adrenal gland embryonically, leading to the partial development of male external genitalia.

sexual receptivity being only in the few hours during which the production of the ovarian hormones estrogen and progesterone peaks. These ovarian hormones alter brain activity, which in turn alters behavior. Furthermore, in female rats, various chemicals are released after mating, and these chemicals inhibit further mating behavior.

The activating effect of ovarian hormones can be seen clearly in cells of the hippocampus. **Figure 11-27** compares hippocampal pyramidal neurons taken from female rats at two points in the estrous cycle: one when estrogen levels are high and the other when they are low. When estrogen levels are high, more dendritic spines and, presumably, more synapses emerge. These neural differences during the estrous cycle are all the more remarkable when we consider that cells in the female hippocampus are continually changing their connections to other cells every 4 days throughout the animal's adulthood.

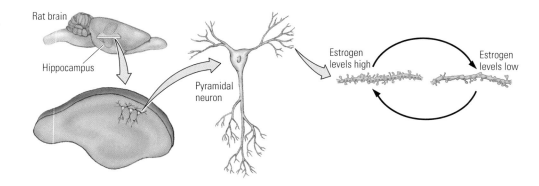

Figure 11-27

Hormonal Effects

A comparison of the dendrites of hippocampal pyramidal neurons at high and low levels of estrogen in the rat's (4-day) estrous cycle reveals that there are many fewer dendritic spines in the low period. Adapted from "Naturally Occurring Fluctuation in Dendritic Spine Density on Adult Hippocampal Pyramidal Neurons," by C. S. Woolley, E. Gould, M. Frankfurt, and B. McEwen, 1990, *Journal of Neuroscience, 10,* p. 1289.

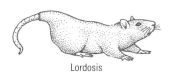

Lordosis

Figure 11-28

Studying Sexual Motivation and Mating   In this experiment, a male rat is required to press the bar 10 times to gain access to a receptive female who "drops in" through a trap door. The copulatory behavior of the male rat illustrates mating behavior, whereas the bar pressing for access to a female rat illustrates sexual motivation. Adapted from "Sexual Motivation: A Neural and Behavioral Analysis of the Mechanisms Underlying Appetitive and Copulatory Responses of Male Rats," by B. J. Everitt, 1990, *Neuroscience and Biobehavioral Reviews, 14,* p. 227.

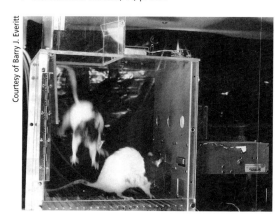

In males, testosterone activates sexual behavior in two distinctly different ways. First, the actions of testosterone on the amygdala are related to the motivation to seek sexual activity. Second, the actions of testosterone on the hypothalamus are needed to produce copulatory behavior. In the next section, we look at both processes.

The Hypothalamus, the Amygdala, and Sexual Behavior

The hypothalamus is the critical structure controlling copulatory behaviors in both males and females. The ventromedial hypothalamus controls the female mating posture, which in quadrapedal animals is called *lordosis* and consists of an arching of the back and an elevation of the rump while the female otherwise remains quite still. Damage to the VMH abolishes lordosis. The role of the VMH is probably twofold: it controls the neural circuit that produces lordosis, and it influences hormonal changes in the female during coitus.

In males, the neural control of sexual behavior is somewhat more complex. The medial preoptic area, which is larger in males than in females, controls copulation. Damage to the medial preoptic area greatly disrupts mating performance, whereas electrical stimulation of this area activates mating, provided that testosterone is circulating in the bloodstream. Curiously, however, although destruction of the medial preoptic area stops males from mating, they continue to show interest in receptive females. For instance, monkeys with lesions in the medial preoptic area will not mate with receptive females, but they will masturbate while watching them from across the room.

Barry Everitt (1990) studied this phenomenon in an ingenious way. He designed an apparatus, shown in **Figure 11-28,** that allowed male rats to press a bar to deliver receptive females. After males were trained in the use of this apparatus, lesions were made in their medial preoptic areas. Immediately, their sexual behavior changed. They would still press the bar to obtain access to females, but they would no longer mate with them.

Apparently, the medial preoptic area controls mating, but it does not control sexual motivation. The brain structure controlling sexual motivation appears to be the amygdala. When Everitt trained male rats in his apparatus and then lesioned their amygdalae, they would no longer press the bar to gain access to receptive females, but they would mate with receptive females that were provided to them.

In summary, the hypothalamus controls copulatory behavior in both males and females. In males, the amygdala influences sexual motivation, and it may do the same among females of species in which sexual activity is not tied to fluctuations in ovarian hormones, which includes the human species. In other words, it is likely that the amygdala plays a key role in sexual motivation for human females as well as for males.

Sexual Orientation, Sexual Identity, and Brain Organization

An interesting question about human sexual behavior has to do with **sexual orientation** —a person's sexual attraction to the opposite sex or to the same sex. Does sexual orientation have a neural basis? Although research to answer this question has been limited in scope, it now appears that differences in the structure of the hypothalamus may form a basis not only for sexual orientation but also for **sexual identity**—a person's feeling either male or female.

Like rats, humans have sex-related differences in the structure of the hypothalamus. The preoptic area of male humans can have twice as many neurons as does that of females, and a region known as the bed nucleus of the stria terminalis is 2.5 times as large in males (Swaab & Hofman, 1995). Similarly, a hypothalamic region known as INAH3 is two times as large in males, and a region known as the suprachiasmatic nucleus (SCN) contains twice as many cells in males as in females.

One hypothesis is that the hypothalamus of homosexual men should be more similar to the norm for females than for males. This hypothesis turns out to be incorrect, however. First, no difference between heterosexual and homosexual men is observed in the size of the preoptic area. Second, the SCN is twice as large in homosexual men as in heterosexual men.

Some evidence suggests a role for the SCN in sexual behavior in both male and female rats, and there is strong evidence that manipulating gonadal hormones alters the structure of the SCN. In contrast with the larger SCN in homosexual men, the INAH3 is twice as large in the heterosexual brain as in the homosexual brain. These findings suggest that homosexual men form, in effect, a "third sex" because their hypothalami differ from those of either females or heterosexual males (Swaab & Hofman, 1995).

No research has been published on the hypothalami of homosexual women. Paul Vasey (2002) described homosexual behavior in Japanese macaque monkeys. He compared the hypothalami of this species to data collected in purely heterosexual monkey species. To date, he has found no unique pattern of hypothalamic organization in homosexual female Japanese macaques, but we must wonder, Does the homosexual behavior of these monkeys and human females have a similar basis?

In contrast with homosexuals, transsexuals feel strongly that they have been born the wrong sex. Their desire to be the opposite sex can be so strong that they undergo sex-change surgery. Little is known about the causes of transsexuality, but it is generally assumed to result from a disturbed interaction between brain development and circulating hormones.

Swaab and Hofman (1995) found that the bed nucleus of the stria terminalis was female sized in a small group of five male-to-female transsexuals. This finding suggests the possibility of a biological basis for transsexuality. We must, however, be wary of drawing cause-and-effect conclusions, especially in such a small sample of people.

If differences in brain organization do exist in people with nontraditional sexual orientations and sexual identities, what might give rise to these brain differences? Dean Hamer and his colleagues (1993) studied the incidence of homosexuality in the families of 114 homosexual men. They recorded a higher-than-average incidence of male homosexuality on the maternal side of the men's families but not on the paternal side.

This maternal–paternal difference is most easily explained if a gene on the mother's X chromosome is implicated. Further investigation revealed that a large percentage of homosexual brothers had in common one small area at the tip of the X chromosome (known as area Xq28). This finding suggests that at least one subtype of male sexual orientation may be genetically influenced.

Sexual orientation. A person's sexual attraction either to the opposite sex or to the same sex.

Sexual identity. A person's feeling either male or female.

We must be cautious in drawing this conclusion, however. William Byne (1994) argued that, even if certain configurations of genes and neurotransmitters are correlated with homosexuality, correlation does not prove causation. After all, genes specify proteins, not sexual behavior.

Conceivably, particular sequences of DNA might cause the brain to be wired in ways that lead to a particular sexual orientation. But it is equally possible that these genes could influence the development of certain personality traits that in turn influence the way in which social experiences contribute to learning a certain sexual orientation. Clearly, establishing the cause-and-effect connections is not an easy task.

Cognitive Influences on Sexual Behavior

People think about sex. People dream about sex. People make plans about sex. These behaviors may include activity in the amygdala or the hypothalamus, but they must certainly also include the cortex. This is not to say that the cortex is essential for sexual motivation and copulation.

In studies of rats whose entire cortices have been removed, both males and females still engage in sexual activity, although the males are somewhat clumsy. Nevertheless, the cortex must play a role in certain aspects of sexual behavior. For instance, imagery about sexual activity must include activity in the ventral visual pathway of the cortex. And thinking about sexual activity and planning for it must require the participation of the frontal lobes.

As you might expect, these aspects of sexual behavior are not easily studied in rats, and they remain uncharted waters in research on humans. However, changes in the sexual behavior of people with frontal-lobe injury are well documented. And recall J. P.'s case, described in "Agenesis of the Frontal Lobes" on page 414.

Although J. P. displayed a loss of inhibition about sexual behavior, frontal-lobe damage is just as likely to produce a loss of libido (sexual interest). The wife of a man who, 5 years earlier, had a small tumor removed from the medial frontal region, complained that she and her husband had since had no sexual contact whatsoever. He was simply not interested, even though they were both still in their 20s.

The husband said that he no longer had sexual fantasies or sexual dreams and, although he still loved his wife, he did not have any sexual urges toward her or anyone else. Such cases clearly indicate that the human cortex has an important role in controlling sexual behaviors. The exact nature of that role is still poorly understood.

In Review

Sexual behavior is controlled by a combination of gonadal hormones, neurons in the hypothalamus and limbic system, and cognitive factors. The hypothalamus controls the details of copulation in both males and females, whereas the motivation for sexual behavior is controlled by the amygdala. In contrast with a regulatory behavior such as feeding, nonregulatory neural control of sexual behavior is affected by the organizing effects of hormones in the course of development and by their activating effects in adulthood. These hormones influence the size of subregions and the structure of cells in the hypothalamus, as well as in the cerebral hemispheres. These anatomical differences presumably account for some of the differences in sexual behavior, orientation, and identity between males and females and among individual organisms.

REWARD

Survival for most animals depends on minimizing contact with certain stimuli and maximizing contact with others. Contact is minimized when an animal experiences fear or anxiety, but sometimes an animal *avoids* a stimulus that is not fear arousing. Why? And why do animals *maintain* contact with other stimuli?

A simple answer is that animals maintain contact with stimuli that they find rewarding in some way and ignore or avoid stimuli that they find neutral or aversive. According to this view, reward is a mechanism that evolved to help increase the adaptive fitness both of entire species and of individual members of a species.

But what exactly is reward? One rather circular definition is that reward is the activity of neural circuits that function to maintain an animal's contact with certain environmental stimuli, either in the present or in the future. Presumably, an animal perceives the activity of these circuits as pleasant. This pleasantness would explain why reward can help maintain not only adaptive behaviors such as feeding and sexual activity but also potentially nonadaptive behaviors such as drug addiction. After all, evolution would not have prepared the brain specifically for the eventual development of psychoactive drugs.

The first clue to the presence of a reward system in the brain came with an accidental discovery by James Olds and Peter Milner in 1954. They found that rats would perform behaviors, such as pressing a bar, to administer a brief burst of electrical stimulation to specific sites in their brains. This phenomenon is called *intracranial self-stimulation* or *brain-stimulation reward.*

Typically, rats will press a lever hundreds or even thousands of times per hour to obtain this brain stimulation, stopping only when they are exhausted. Why would animals engage in such a behavior when it has absolutely no value to their survival or to that of their species? The simplest explanation is that the brain stimulation is activating the system underlying reward (Wise, 1996).

After 50 years of research on brain-stimulation reward, investigators now know that dozens of sites in the brain will maintain self-stimulation. Significantly, however, some regions, including the lateral hypothalamus and medial forebrain bundle, are especially effective. Stimulation there activates fibers that form the ascending pathways from dopamine-producing cells of the midbrain tegmentum, shown in **Figure 11-29**. This pathway, as you learned in Chapters 5 and 7, is the mesolimbic dopamine pathway that sends dopamine-containing terminals to various sites, including especially the nucleus accumbens and the prefrontal cortex.

Neuroscientists believe that the mesolimbic dopamine system is central to circuits mediating reward for several reasons:

1. Dopamine release shows a marked increase when animals are engaged in intracranial self-stimulation.
2. Drugs that enhance dopamine release increase self-stimulation, whereas drugs that decrease dopamine release decrease self-stimulation. It seems that the amount of dopamine released somehow determines how rewarding an event is.
3. When animals engage in behaviors such as feeding or sexual activity, the release of dopamine rapidly increases in locations such as the nucleus accumbens.
4. Highly addictive drugs such as nicotine and cocaine increase the level of dopamine in the nucleus accumbens.

Even opiates appear to affect at least some of an animal's actions through the dopamine system. Animals quickly learn to press a bar to obtain an injection of opiates directly into the midbrain tegmentum or the nucleus accumbens. The same animals do not work to obtain the opiates if the dopaminergic neurons of the mesolimbic system are inactivated. Apparently, then, animals engage in behaviors that increase dopamine release.

◉ On the *Foundations* CD, you can watch a video showing self-stimulation in a rat in the section on electrical brain stimulation in the module on research methods.

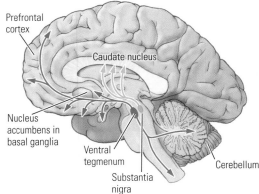

Figure 11-29

Mesolimbic Dopamine System Axons emanating from the ventral tegmentum (blue arrows) project diffusely through the brain to synapse on their targets. Dopamine release in the mesolimbic pathways has a role in feelings of reward and pleasure. The nucleus accumbens is a critical structure in this "reward system." [Recall from Chapter 5 that the nigrostriatial pathway (orange arrows) is active in maintaining normal motor function.]

Note, however, that dopamine is not the only reward compound in the brain. For example, Rainer Spanagel and Friedbert Weiss (1999) stressed that drugs can be rewarding in the absence of dopamine, and Keith Trujillo and his colleagues (1993) found that the reinforcing actions of opiates take place through activation of both dopaminergic and nondopaminergic systems. These findings suggest the existence of more than one reward-related system in the brain.

In Chapter 7, we encountered the idea that reward has multiple parts in our consideration of Robinson and Berridge's incentive-sensitization theory of addiction. These researchers proposed that reward contains separable psychological components, corresponding roughly to "wanting," which is often called *incentive,* and "liking," which is equivalent to an evaluation of pleasure (Robinson & Berridge, 1993, 2003). This idea can be applied to discovering why we increase contact with a stimulus such as chocolate.

Two independent factors are at work: our desire to have the chocolate (wanting) and the pleasurable effect of eating the chocolate (liking). This distinction is important. If we maintain contact with a certain stimulus because dopamine is released, the question becomes whether the dopamine plays a role in the wanting or the liking aspect of the behavior. Robinson and Berridge proposed that wanting and liking processes are mediated by separable neural systems and that dopamine is the transmitter in wanting. Liking, they hypothesize, entails opioid and benzodiazepine–GABA systems.

According to Robinson and Berridge, wanting and liking are normally two aspects of the same process; so rewards are usually wanted and liked to the same degree. However, it is possible, under certain circumstances, for wanting and liking to change independently. Consider rats with lesions of the ascending dopaminergic pathway to the forebrain.

These rats do not eat. Is it simply that they do not desire to eat (a loss of wanting) or has food become aversive to them (a loss of liking for it)? To find out which factor is at work, the animals' facial expressions and body movements in response to food can be observed to see how liking is affected. After all, when animals are given various foods to taste, they produce different facial and body reactions, depending on whether they perceive the food as pleasant or aversive.

For example, when a normal person tastes something sweet, he or she usually responds by licking the fingers or the lips, as shown at the top of **Figure 11-30**. In contrast, if the taste is unpleasantly salty, say, as shown in the bottom panel, the reaction is often spitting, grimacing, or wiping the mouth with the back of the hand. Rats, too, show distinctive positive and negative responses to pleasant and unpleasant tastes.

So, by watching these responses when food is squirted into the mouth of a rat that otherwise refuses to eat, we can tell to what extent a loss of liking for food is a factor in the animal's food rejection. Interestingly, rats that do not eat after receiving lesions to the dopamine pathway act as though they still like food.

Now consider a rat with a self-stimulation electrode in the lateral hypothalamus. This rat will often eat heartily while the stimulation is on. The obvious inference is that the food must taste good—presumably even better than it does usually. But what if we squirt food into the rat's mouth and observe its behavior when the stimulation is on versus when it is off?

If the brain stimulation primes eating by evoking pleasurable sensations, we would expect that the animal would be more positive in its facial and body reactions toward foods when the stimulation is turned on. In fact, the opposite is found. During stimulation, rats react more aversively to tastes such as sugar and salt than when stimulation is off. Apparently, the stimulation increases wanting but not liking.

Figure 11-30

Human Reactions to Taste　Positive (hedonic) reactions are elicited by sucrose and other palatable tastes. Hedonic reactions include licking the fingers and licking the lips. Negative (aversive) reactions are elicited by quinine and other nonpalatable tastes. Aversive reactions include spitting, making a face of distaste, and wiping the mouth with the back of the hand.

Adapted from "Food Reward: Brain Substrates of Wanting and Liking," by K. C. Berridge, 1996, *Neuroscience and Biobehavioral Reviews, 20,* p. 6

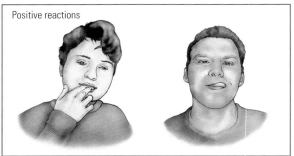

Positive reactions

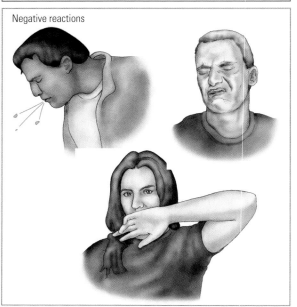

Negative reactions

In conclusion, experiments of this sort show that what appears to be a single event—reward—is actually composed of at least two independent processes. Just as our visual system independently processes "what" and "how" information in two separate streams, our reward system appears to include independent processes of wanting and liking. Reward is not a single phenomenon any more than the processes of perception or memory are.

⊙ For more information on the brain's reward system, visit the Chapter 11 Web links on the *Brain and Behavior* Web site (**www.worthpublishers.com/kolb**).

In Review

Rewards are the effects that events have on the behavior of animals. Neural circuits maintain contact with rewarding environmental stimuli in the present or in the future through liking and wanting subsystems. The challenge for researchers, as well as their reward, lies in separating the neural subsystems that take part in reward and in accounting for how the rewarding effects of environmental events influence liking or wanting.

SUMMARY

■ *How do we experience emotions and motives?* Our inner, subjective feelings and thoughts influence how we behave. We interpret these subjective feelings cognitively as a range of emotion, as love at one end and hate at the other. Motivation is the cause of behavior that seems purposeful. As with emotion, we describe motivation in subjective terms such as hunger and curiosity. Both emotions and motivations are inferred states that can be without awareness or intent. Unconscious emotions and motives make it difficult to conclude that our behavior is controlled by the state that we call free will.

■ *What controls the behaviors in which animals will engage at any given time?* Animals are motivated to engage in behavior for its reward. Rewards range from sensory stimulation to the activity of hormones to the activity of dopamine cells in the brainstem. Neural circuits controlling species-typical behaviors such as mouse killing by cats are organized in the brainstem and manifest the evolutionary advantage for these active circuits: they are rewarding. If animals did not want to engage in motivated behaviors, their species would become extinct.

■ *How do evolution and experience interact with neurobiology to produce behavior?* Behavior is controlled by its consequences as well as by its biology. Consequences may affect the evolution of the species or the behavior of an individual animal. Behaviors that are selected by evolution are often triggered by innate releasing mechanisms. Behaviors that are selected only in an individual animal are shaped by that animal's environment and are learned.

■ *What are the chemical senses and how do they function?* Smell and taste are based on the detection of chemical signals by the olfactory and gustatory senses. Chemical neuroreceptors interact with chemosignals, leading to neural activity in cranial nerve 1 for olfaction and cranial nerves 7, 9, and 10 for taste. The cranial nerves enter the brain and, through a series of synapses, pass to brainstem and forebrain areas. Smell and taste input merges in the orbitofrontal cortex to produce our perception of flavor.

■ *What principal neural circuit operates in emotional and motivated behavior?* The neural structures that initiate emotional and motivated behaviors are the hypothalamus, the pituitary gland, the amygdala, the dopamine and noradrenaline pathways from nuclei in the lower brainstem, and the frontal lobes.

■ *What stimulates emotional and motivated behavior?* The experience of both emotion and motivation is controlled by activity in the ANS, hypothalamus, and forebrain,

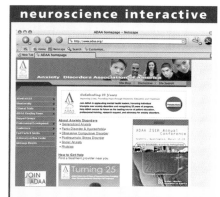

neuroscience interactive

Many resources are available for expanding your learning online:

■ **www.worthpublishers.com/kolb**

Try the Chapter 11 quizzes and flashcards to test your mastery of the chapter material. You'll also be able to link to other sites that will reinforce what you've learned.

■ **www.adaa.org**

Link to this Web site to learn more about anxiety disorders.

■ **www.nationaleatingdisorders.org**

Learn more about the research and treatment of eating disorders at this Web site of the National Eating Disorders Association.

On your *Foundations* CD-ROM, in the module on the Central Nervous System, you can review some of the anatomical structures that are important to understanding what causes behaviors.

especially the amygdala and frontal cortex. Emotional and motivated behavior may be an unconscious response to internal or external stimuli and be controlled by the activity of innate releasing mechanisms or be a cognitive response to events or thoughts.

■ *What is the difference in the neural control of regulatory and nonregulatory behaviors?* The two distinctly different types of motivated behaviors are (1) regulatory (homeostatic) behaviors that maintain vital body-system balance and (2) nonregulatory behaviors, basically consisting of all other behaviors. These nonregulatory behaviors are not controlled by a homeostatic mechanism and are not reflexive. Feeding is a regulatory behavior controlled by the interaction of the digestive and hormonal systems and the hypothalamic and cortical circuits. Sexual activity is a nonregulatory behavior motivated by the amygdala. Copulatory behavior is controlled by the hypothalamus (the ventromedial hypothalamus in females and the preoptic area in males).

■ *Why do we find certain behaviors rewarding?* Survival depends on maximizing contact with some environmental stimuli and minimizing contact with others. Reward is a mechanism for controlling this differential. Two independent features of reward are wanting and liking. The wanting component is thought to be controlled by dopaminergic systems, whereas the liking component is thought to be controlled by opiate–benzodiazepine systems.

KEY TERMS

amygdala, p. 411
androgen, p. 393
anorexia nervosa, p. 423
aphagia, p. 424
drive, p. 393
emotion, p. 390
evolutionary psychology, p. 396
generalized anxiety disorder, p. 421
hippocampus, p. 411
homeostatic mechanism, p. 405
hyperphagia, p. 424
hypovolumic thirst, p. 426

innate releasing mechanism (IRM), p. 395
Klüver-Bucy syndrome, p. 416
learned taste aversion, p. 402
medial forebrain bundle (MFB), p. 406
motivation, p. 390
nonregulatory behavior, p. 405
obesity, p. 421
osmotic thirst, p. 426
panic disorder, p. 421

pheromone, p. 399
phobia, p. 421
pituitary gland, p. 406
prefrontal cortex, p. 412
preparedness, p. 402
psychosurgery, p. 418
regulatory behavior, p. 405
reinforcer, p. 400
releasing hormone, p. 408
sensory deprivation, p. 391
sexual dimorphism, p. 428
sexual identity, p. 431
sexual orientation, p. 431
somatic marker hypothesis, p. 416

REVIEW QUESTIONS

1. What are some causes of behavior?

2. Compare the evolutionary and environmental influences on behavior.

3. What key brain structures control motivated behavior? How does each contribute to this control?

4. Contrast the organizing and activating effects of hormones.

5. Contrast the roles of the hypothalamus and the amygdala in sexual behavior and sexual motivation.

6. Compare the organization and operation of the chemical senses with those of vision.

7. Consider the similarities and differences between the brain's control of emotional pain and physical pain.

FOR FURTHER THOUGHT

1. Why do cats kill birds? Use the same logic to account for a specific human behavior of your choice.

2. How could a concept such as preparedness explain racism?

3. What can you infer about brain and behavior relations from the finding that stimulation of the hypothalamus elicits complex behaviors such as feeding, digging, and sexual activity?

4. What are the social and moral implications of evidence that sexual orientation is associated with brain organization?

RECOMMENDED READING

Barondes, S. H. (1993). *Molecules and mental illness.* New York: Scientific American Library. A very readable summary of the neurochemical bases of various forms of psychiatric disease. The Scientific American Library series has excellent illustrations and is written for an educated lay audience.

Becker, J. B., Breedlove, S. M., & Crews, D. (2002). *Behavioral endocrinology* (2nd ed.). Cambridge, MA: MIT Press. What is behavioral endocrinology and why study it? This book provides the answers. It is a broad survey of the effects of hormones on the behavior of humans and other animals. The topics range from sexual behavior to cognitive and motor behaviors.

Damasio, A. R. (1999). *The feeling of what happens: Body and emotion in the making of consciousness.* New York: Harcourt Brace. Damasio argues that emotions are curious adaptations that are part and parcel of the neural machinery that we have evolved for our survival. Damasio's ideas have developed from his study of people with frontal-lobe injuries who have abnormal emotional control and a parallel abnormality in other cognitive activities. This interesting book has influenced thinking about the role of emotion in the brain's daily activities.

Eibl-Eibesfeldt, I. (1989). *Human ethology.* New York: Aldine de Gruyter. One of the first ethologists to study human behavior, Eibl-Eibesfeldt has written a thorough book in which he summarizes what is known about the species-typical behavior of people. This book provides a wealth of photographic examples of human behaviors that are genetically programmed and found throughout the world's cultures.

Lane, R. D., & Nadel, L. (Eds.). (2000). *Cognitive neuroscience of emotion.* New York: Oxford University Press. This book is a showcase for the newly emerging ideas of the cognitive neuroscience of emotion. The chapters range from heavily theoretical accounts to strongly empirical ones, but all focus on the role of emotion in cognition.

Robinson, T. E., & Berridge, K. C. (1993). The neural basis of drug craving: An incentive-sensitization theory of addiction. *Brain Research Reviews, 18,* 247–291. The Robinson-Berridge theory of drug addiction and craving is a thorough analysis of the evidence that wanting and liking drugs are two different things that likely have different neural bases.

Woods, S. C., Seeley, R. J., Porte, D., & Schwartz, M. W. (1998). Signals that regulate food intake and energy homeostasis. *Science, 280,* 1378–1382. Obesity is an increasingly prevalent and important health problem. Naturally, those who wish to lose weight are hoping that a magic bullet will be found to treat obesity. This article is one in a special issue of *Science* that looks at the regulation of body weight. The authors review the signals that tell us when to eat (or not) and conclude that a single magic bullet is unlikely but that treatments aimed at multiple targets may be realistic.

Why Do We Sleep and Dream?

Left: **Bob Thomas/Tony Stone.** *Middle:* **Dr. Dennis Kunkel/Phototake.** *Right:* **Hank Morgan/Photo Researchers.**

The Variety of Biological Rhythmns

As winter approaches in Northern latitudes, many Arctic animals prepare their escape. Arctic terns fly 15,000 kilometers to Antarctica, where it is summer. Lemmings, mice, and ground squirrels cannot travel long distances; these rodents spend the winter in burrows in a sleeplike state called *hibernation.*

Polar bears, in contrast, congregate to go out onto the pack ice. They migrate *toward* the Arctic as the days grow ever shorter. Some travel thousands of kilometers. In the continuous darkness of the Arctic winter, polar bears (also known as sea bears, *Ursus maritimus*) hunt seals, walrus, and whales. They take time to sleep on the ice but, because their world is continuously dark, their sleep cannot be called either nighttime or daytime sleep.

When summer comes again, the birds return and the rodents emerge from their burrows. The sea bears return from the ice, dig beds in the earth, and spend the entire summer in shallow **torpor**—a condition resembling sleep except that the decline in body temperature is greater than during sleep. If the bears have access to food throughout the year, they do not enter torpor. Even if you find torpor somehow appealing, it remains hard to imagine spending all summer unconscious.

David Myers/Tony Stone

Sea-bear behavior is remarkable to us humans. We are **diurnal animals** (from the Latin *dies,* meaning "day"): we are active during daylight, and we sleep when it is dark. Our recent evolutionary history places early modern humans in Africa at equatorial latitudes, where day and night are almost equal in length. Because we are adapted for daylight vision and have difficulty seeing well at night, we humans are not adapted by natural selection for darkness. That animals seek out darkness and flourish in it seems strange to us.

We sleep for about 8 hours each night on average. Our sleep is characterized by a decline in body temperature and a loss of awareness of our surroundings. Sea bears sleep in the winter, as mentioned, but their summer torpor seems related to hibernation. The strategy used by rodents to extend body-fat supplies as long as possible is similar to shallow torpor except that declines in body temperature are so extreme that the animals expend almost no energy.

Despite the great differences among human, bear, and rodent behaviors, all are adaptations that maximize obtaining food and that minimize spending or losing energy stores obtained from food. Humans evolved to be active during the day—we see best then to obtain food—and inactive at night—to conserve body resources. Sea bears hunt all winter and so build up fat supplies. They enter torpor and so extend the period during which they live on those fat stores when resources are scarce.

Sea bears are clearly prepared to go out on the ice well in advance of its formation. They walk along the Arctic shores for weeks before the ice forms; they also leave the ice before it melts. Birds migrate before food resources are depleted and winter arrives. Rodents gorge themselves, build nests, and store food in their burrows before winter and hibernation set in. The migratory behavior of birds also is a strategy used to maximize food acquisition and minimize energy loss, except the objective is achieved by moving to a habitat where food is abundant.

Torpor. Inactive condition resembling sleep but with a greater decline in body temperature.

Diurnal animal. Organism that is active chiefly during daylight.

Biorhythm. Inherent rhythm that controls or initiates various biological processes.

W e are similar to sea bears, rodents, and birds in one other way. Their behaviors and ours evolved to respond not simply to immediate environmental changes but also to longer-term changes that result in food abundance or shortages. Today, with humans controlling more of their environment, food abundance or shortage may be a matter of the distance to the nearest pizzeria.

We live by the clock, too, retiring to sleeping sites in preparation for sleep and frequently arising before it is fully light to prepare for our daily activities. But we, along with other animals, still appear to have warning of impending winter or impending changes in the day–night cycle. There are environmental signals to which we all respond. These signals prime us to anticipate daily and seasonal changes. But, even in the absence of obvious signals, we and other animals can anticipate daily and seasonal changes. It follows that we have a biological clock that regulates our behavior in concert with the rhythmic changes of our world.

In this chapter, we seek answers to questions related to biological rhythms and sleep:

■ How is our behavior modified to cope with the day–night cycle?
■ Why has sleep evolved as a strategy for waiting out the night?
■ What neural mechanisms regulate sleep and waking?
■ How do disorders of the natural rhythms of sleep occur?

A CLOCK FOR ALL SEASONS

We first consider evidence for the existence of a biological clock, how that clock keeps time, and how it regulates our behavior. Because environmental cues themselves are not always consistent, we examine the role of biological clocks in interpreting environmental cues in an intelligent way.

Origins of Biological Rhythms

Biorhythms, the inherent rhythms that control or initiate various biological processes, are linked to the rhythmic cycle of days and seasons produced by Earth's rotation on its axis and by its progression in orbit around the sun (**Figure 12-1**). Earth rotates on

Figure 12-1

Origins of Biorhythms
Each part of the earth faces the sun for part of its daily rotation cycle (daytime) and faces away from the sun for the other part (nighttime). Seasonal changes in temperature and in the amount of daylight are related to the annual revolution of the earth around the sun and the tilt of its axis.

Seasons change as the earth revolves around the sun. Each revolution takes 1 year.

Northern winter

Northern summer

Sun

The tilt of the earth on its axis determines seasons.

Day and night result from rotation of the earth on its axis every 24 hours.

its axis once every 24 hours, producing a 24-hour cycle of day and night. Earth's axis is tilted slightly, and so, as Earth orbits the sun once each year, the North and South Poles incline slightly toward the sun for part of the year and slightly away from the sun for the rest of the year.

When inclined toward the sun, the Southern Hemisphere experiences summer and gets more direct sunshine for more hours each day, and the climate is warmer. At the same time, the Northern Hemisphere, inclined away from the sun, receives less direct sunlight, making the days shorter and the climate colder. Tropical regions, being near the equator, undergo little seasonal change as Earth progresses around the sun.

The seasonal differences in polar and equatorial regions cause animals living near the poles to be relatively more affected by seasonal changes and animals living near the equator to be relatively more affected by day-and-night changes. Seasonal and daily changes may have combined effects on organisms as well, inasmuch as the onset and duration of daily changes depend on the season and latitude. Animals living in polar regions also have to cope with greater fluctuations in daily temperature, light, and food availability than do animals living near the equator.

We humans are equatorial animals in that our behavior is governed more by daily cycles than by seasonal cycles. Our behavior is dominated by a rhythm of daylight activity and nocturnal sleep. Not only does human waking and sleep behavior cycle daily, so also do pulse rate, blood pressure, body temperature, rate of cell division, blood-cell count, alertness, urine composition, metabolic rate, sexual drive, and responsiveness to medications.

Biorhythms are not unique to animals. Plants display rhythmic behavior, exemplified by species in which leaves or flowers open during the day and close at night. Even unicellular algae and fungi display rhythmic behaviors related to the passage of the day. Some animals, including lizards and crabs, change color in a rhythmic pattern. The Florida chameleon, for example, turns green at night, whereas its coloration matches its environment during the day. In short, almost every organism and every cell display changes of some sort that are related to daily or seasonal changes.

Biological Clocks

If the behavior of animals were affected only by seasonal and daily changes, the neural mechanisms that account for changes in behavior would be much simpler to study than they are. Behavior would be driven by external cues, which would be easy to identify, and, accordingly, the neural processes that respond to those cues also would be easy to identify.

That behavior is not driven simply by external cues was first recognized in 1729 by French geologist Jean Jacques D'Ortous de Mairan (see Raven, Evert, & Eichorn, 1992). In an experiment similar to that illustrated in the Procedure section of **Experiment 12-1**, de Mairan isolated a plant from daily light and dark cues and from temperature cues and noted that the rhythmic movements of its leaves continued,

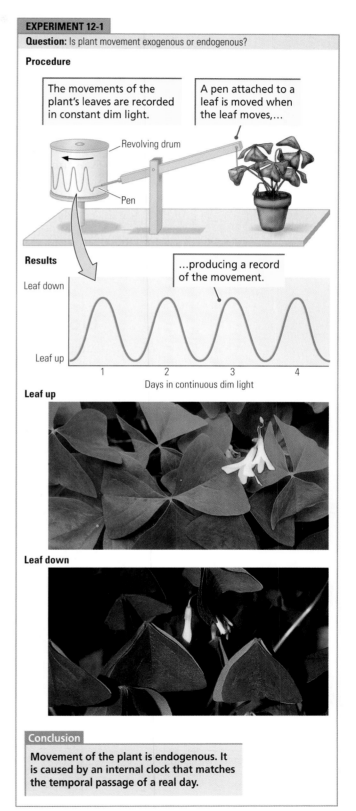

EXPERIMENT 12-1

Question: Is plant movement exogenous or endogenous?

Procedure

The movements of the plant's leaves are recorded in constant dim light.

A pen attached to a leaf is moved when the leaf moves,...

Revolving drum

Pen

Results

Leaf down

Leaf up

...producing a record of the movement.

1   2   3   4
Days in continuous dim light

Leaf up

Leaf down

Conclusion

Movement of the plant is endogenous. It is caused by an internal clock that matches the temporal passage of a real day.

Biological clock. Neural system that times behavior.

as graphed in the Results section of the experiment. What concerned de Marain's followers was the possibility that some undetected external cue stimulated the rhythmic behavior of the plant.

Such cues could include changes in gravity, changes in electromagnetic fields, and even changes in the intensity of rays from outer space. Nevertheless, further experiments showed that the daily fluctuations are endogenous—they come from within the plant. In fact, experiments show that most organisms have an internal **biological clock** that matches the temporal passage of a real day.

Your clock and calendar enable you to plan and schedule your time. Your biological clock performs these functions, too. An endogenous biological clock allows an animal, in effect, to anticipate events: to migrate before it gets cold rather than waiting until it gets cold and to mate at the correct time of the year. The clock allows animals to arrive at the same place at the same time if they are to mate or to begin a migration. Most important, a biological clock signals to an animal that, if daylight lasts for about 12 hours today, it will last for about 12 hours tomorrow but, if it lasts for 4 hours today, it will last for about 4 hours tomorrow.

Plants and animals evolved internal clocks through natural selection to avoid being tricked into displaying maladaptive behavior. Plant bulbs that begin to grow during a January thaw only to be killed by a subsequent cold spell exemplify such maladaptive behavior.

Biological Rhythms

Although the existence of endogenous biological clocks was demonstrated more than 200 years ago, the detailed study of biorhythms had to await the development of procedures that could analyze ongoing behavior over a long period of time. Behavior analysis requires a method for counting behavioral events and a method for displaying those events in a meaningful way. For example, the behavior of a rodent can be measured by giving the animal access to a running wheel, such as that illustrated in **Figure 12-2A**, in which it can exercise.

A chart recorder or a computer records each turn of the wheel and displays the result (Figure 12-2B). Because most rodents are nocturnal, sleeping during light hours and becoming active during dark hours, their wheel-running activity takes place in the dark (Figure 12-2C). If each day's activity is plotted under the preceding day's activity in a column, we can observe a pattern of activity over a period of time. Various details of the chart can then be examined, including when the animal was active and how active it was.

Figure 12-2

Recording the Daily Activity Cycle of a Rat Adapted from *Biological Clocks in Medicine and Psychiatry* (pp. 12–15), by C. P. Richter, 1965, Springfield, IL: Charles C Thomas.

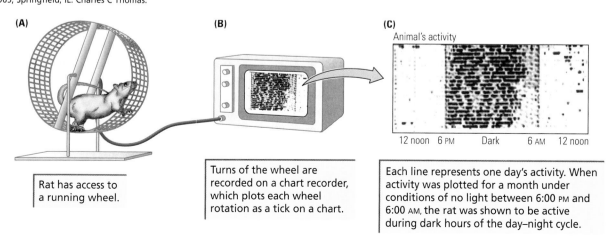

(A) Rat has access to a running wheel.

(B) Turns of the wheel are recorded on a chart recorder, which plots each wheel rotation as a tick on a chart.

(C) Animal's activity

12 noon   6 PM   Dark   6 AM   12 noon

Each line represents one day's activity. When activity was plotted for a month under conditions of no light between 6:00 PM and 6:00 AM, the rat was shown to be active during dark hours of the day–night cycle.

Perhaps the most important piece of information charted by an activity record is the cycle of activity. The time required to complete a cycle of activity is called a **period.** The activity period of most rodents is about 24 hours in an environment in which the lights go on and off with regularity. Our own sleep–wake period also is about 24 hours. Many other kinds of behaviors, however, have periods that are more or less than 24 hours.

Animals have a surprising number of biological clocks, and those clocks have varying periods. Two kinds of rhythms typical of most animals are *circannual rhythms* (Latin *circa,* meaning "about," plus *annum,* meaning "year"), of which the migratory cycles of sea bears and Arctic terns are examples, and **circadian rhythms** (from Latin for "about a day"), which are the day–night rhythms found in almost all animals and cellular processes. These two are not the only kinds of rhythms, however.

Infradian (Latin *infra,* meaning "within") *rhythms* are those that have a period of less than one day. Our eating behavior, which takes place about every 90 minutes to 2 hours, including snacks, is an example of an infradian rhythm. Rodents, although active throughout the night, are most active at the beginning and end of the dark period.

Many sea-dwelling animals' rhythms are about 12 hours, which matches the twice-daily changes in tides produced by the pull of the moon on the earth and its oceans. Therefore, an infradian rhythm is embedded within their circadian rhythm. Our eye-blink rate, our heart rate, and even the rhythmic action potentials of some of our neurons are other examples of infradian rhythms.

Biological rhythm	Time frame	Example
Circannual	Yearly	Migratory cycles of birds
Ultradian	Less than a year	Human menstrual cycle
Circadian	Daily	Human sleep cycle
Infradian	Less than a day	Human eating cycles

Other biorhythms have periods greater than a day and less than a year. These are *ultradian* (meaning "beyond a day") *rhythms.* The menstrual cycle of female humans, with an average period of about 28 days, is an ultradian biorhythm.

We focus in this chapter on the circadian rhythm, which is central to our sleep–waking behavior. Note, however, that the fact that a behavior appears to be rhythmic does not mean that it is ruled by a biological clock. There is evidence that sea bears will remain on the ice as long as the ice pack and food supplies last, and many migrating birds will postpone their migrations as long as they have a food supply. Therefore, whether a rhythmic behavior is produced by a biological clock must be demonstrated experimentally. A definitive experiment to support the conclusion that the sea bear does have a clock would be methodologically difficult to conduct, but such demonstrations are not difficult to make with other animals, including ourselves.

Free-Running Rhythms

To determine if a rhythm is produced by a biological clock, researchers must design a test in which they remove all external cues. If light is proposed to be a major cue, the experiment can be set up in three ways: a test can be given in continuous light, it can be given in continuous darkness, or the selection of light or darkness can be left to the subject.

That the human sleep–waking rhythm is governed by a biological clock was first demonstrated by Jurgen Aschoff and Rutger Weber (see Kleitman, 1965), who allowed subjects to select their light–dark cycle. The experimenters placed individual subjects in an underground bunker where no cues signaled when day began or ended. Thus, the subjects selected the periods when their lights were on or off, when they were active, and when they slept. In short, they selected their own day and night length. By measuring ongoing behavior and recording sleeping periods with sensors on the beds,

Period. Time required to complete a cycle of activity.

Circadian rhythm. Day–night rhythm.

○ To learn more about biological clocks, biological rhythms, or circadian rhythms, go to the Chapter 12 Web links on the *Brain and Behavior* Web site (**www.worthpublishers.com/kolb**).

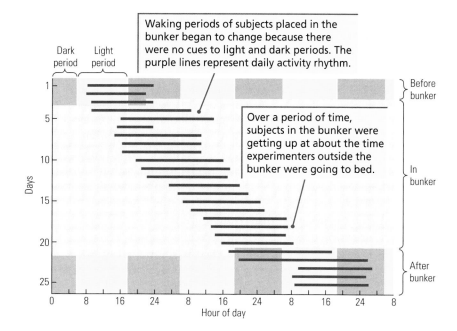

Figure 12-3

Free-Running Rhythm in a Human Subject The record for days 1 through 3 shows the daily sleep period under normal day–night conditions. That for days 4 through 20 shows the free-running rhythm that developed while the subject was isolated in a bunker and allowed to control day and night length. The daily activity period shifts from 24 hours to 25.9 hours. On days 21 through 25, the period returns to 24 hours when the subject is again exposed to a normal light-and-dark cycle. Adapted from *Sleep* (p. 33), by J. A. Hobson, 1989, New York: Scientific American Library.

Aschoff and Weber found that the subjects continued to show daily sleep-activity rhythms. This finding demonstrated that humans have an endogenous biological clock that governs sleep–waking behavior.

Figure 12-3 shows, however, that the biorhythms recorded by Aschoff and Weber were peculiar when compared with the rhythms before and after isolation. Although the period of the subjects' sleep–wake cycles approximated a normal period of 24 hours before and after the test, during the test they progressively deviated away from clock time. Rather than being 24 hours, the activity period in the bunker was about 25 to 27 hours, depending on the subject.

The subjects were choosing to go to bed from 1 to 2 hours later every "night." A shift by an hour or so of sleeping time is not remarkable for a few days, but its cumulative effect quickly became dramatic: soon the subjects were getting up at about the time the experimenters outside the bunker were going to bed. Clearly, the subjects were displaying their own personal cycles. A rhythm that runs at a frequency of the body's own devising when environmental cues are absent is called a **free-running rhythm.**

The period of free-running rhythms depends on the way in which external cues are removed. When hamsters, a nocturnal species, are tested in constant darkness, their free-running periods are a little shorter than 24 hours; when they are tested in constant light, their free-running periods are a little longer than 24 hours. This test dependency in hamsters is typical of nocturnal animals.

As **Figure 12-4** shows, the opposite free-running periods are typical of diurnal animals (Binkley, 1990). When sparrows, which are diurnal birds, are tested in constant darkness, their free-running periods are a little longer than 24 hours; when they are tested in constant light, their free-running periods are a little shorter than 24 hours. Why periods change in different lighting conditions is not clear, but a rule of thumb is that animals expand and contract their sleep periods as the sleep-related lighting period expands or contracts.

Understanding this point enables you to predict how artificial lighting influences human circadian periods, and you can offer an explanation of why Aschoff and Weber's subjects displayed periods that were longer than 24 hours. Endogenous rhythmicity is not the only factor that contributes to circadian periods, however. An endogenous

Free-running rhythm. Rhythm of the body's own devising in the absence of all external cues.

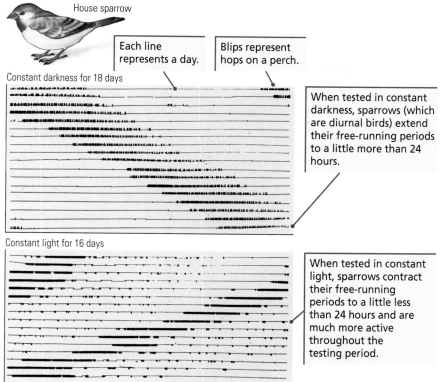

House sparrow

Each line represents a day.

Blips represent hops on a perch.

Constant darkness for 18 days

When tested in constant darkness, sparrows (which are diurnal birds) extend their free-running periods to a little more than 24 hours.

Constant light for 16 days

When tested in constant light, sparrows contract their free-running periods to a little less than 24 hours and are much more active throughout the testing period.

Figure 12-4

Free-Running Rhythms of a Diurnal Animal Adapted from *The Clockwork Sparrow* (p. 16), by S. Binkley, 1990, Englewood Cliffs, NJ: Prentice Hall.

rhythm that is just a little slow or a little fast would be useless because the error would accumulate, and so there must also be a mechanism for setting rhythms to correspond to environmental events.

Zeitgebers

Because Aschoff and Weber's subjects had a sleep–wake cycle of 24 hours before and after they entered the experiment and because hamsters usually have a 24-hour rhythm, we might wonder how normal rhythms are maintained. The biological clock must keep to a time that matches changes in the day–night cycle. If a biological clock is like a slightly defective wristwatch that runs either too slow or too fast, it will eventually provide times that are inaccurate by hours and so become useless.

If we reset the wristwatch each day, however—say, when we awaken—it would then provide useful information even though it is not perfectly accurate. There must be an equivalent way of resetting a free-running biological clock. In experiments to determine how clocks are set, researchers have found that cues such as sunrise and sunset, eating times, and other activities can all set the circadian clock.

Normally, light is the most potent stimulus. Aschoff and Weber called such a cue a *Zeitgeber* (German for "time giver"). When a clock is reset by a Zeitgeber, it is said to be **entrained.** The importance of light in entraining circadian rhythms is explained in "Seasonal Affective Disorder."

Biological clocks are flexible. They can be reset each day so that they accurately correspond to the season. In polar regions, you'll recall, the time of onset and the length of day and night are changing as the seasons progress. At the higher latitudes, daylight begins very early in the morning in summer and very late in the morning in winter. To adjust to these changes, an animal responds both to daylight and to how long the day will last.

Zeitgeber. Environmental event that entrains biological rhythms; a "time giver."

Entrainment. Determination or modification of the period of a biorhythm.

Seasonal Affective Disorder

In diurnal species, the perception of longer nights by the circadian pacemaker most likely stimulates pressure for more sleep. If not satisfied, cumulative sleep deprivation can result. In *seasonal affective disorder* (SAD), the light phase of the circadian rhythm is too short to entrain the circadian rhythms. Consequently, a person's biorhythm probably becomes a free-running rhythm.

People vary in the duration of their free-running rhythm phases relative to the actual day–night cycle. Some are phase retarded, with sleep time coming earlier each day; some are phase delayed, with sleep time coming later each day. Common symptoms are observed in or reported by more than

two-thirds of people who report that they are depressed during the winter months in northern latitudes, including

Sadness	Later waking
Anxiety	Increased sleep time
Irritability	Interrupted, not
Decreased physical	refreshing sleep
sleep activity	Daytime drowsiness
Increased appetite	Decreased libido
Carbohydrate craving	Menstrual difficulties
Increased weight	Work difficulties
Earlier sleep onset	Interpersonal difficulties

Researchers consistently report that light is capable of ameliorating the depression of SAD, and one treatment for SAD symptoms, *phototherapy,* uses light to entrain the circadian rhythm. The basic idea is to increase the short winter photoperiod by exposing a person to artificial bright light. Typical room lighting is not sufficiently bright.

A person undergoing phototherapy for SAD sits in front of a bank of bright lights. Some manufacturers recommend exposure in the morning, others in the evening. Still others recommend bracketing the day with morning and evening exposure. There may be merit to all these recommendations. Recent evidence suggests that there may be two pacemaking neural oscillators, one regulating activity and one regulating other body rhythms. Each may be related to different Zeitgebers.

Exposure to a bright light each winter morning and/or evening entrains the circadian rhythm. Courtesy of Bio-Light by Enviro-Med, 800-222-3296, www.bio-light.com

Hamster

A biological clock that is reset each day tells an animal that daylight will begin tomorrow at approximately the same time that it began today and that tomorrow will last approximately as long as today did. But when should the clock be reset? The current research opinion is that light Zeitgebers work best when exposure occurs near the beginning or the end of the light segment of the cycle.

The very potent entraining effect of light Zeitgebers is illustrated by laboratory studies of Syrian hamsters, perhaps one of the most compulsive animals with respect to timekeeping. When given access to running wheels, these hamsters exercise during the night segment of the laboratory day–night cycle. A single brief flash of light is an effective Zeitgeber for entraining their biological clocks. (If a hamster happens to blink during this Zeitgeber, the light will still penetrate its closed eyelids and entrain its biological clock.)

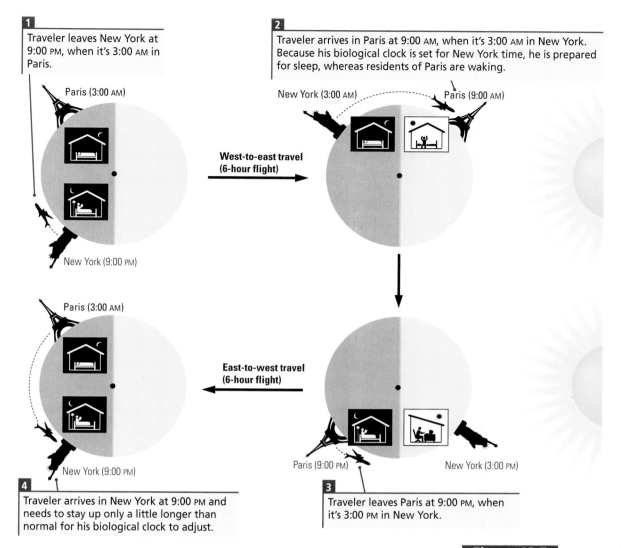

1 Traveler leaves New York at 9:00 PM, when it's 3:00 AM in Paris.

Paris (3:00 AM)

New York (9:00 PM)

West-to-east travel (6-hour flight)

2 Traveler arrives in Paris at 9:00 AM, when it's 3:00 AM in New York. Because his biological clock is set for New York time, he is prepared for sleep, whereas residents of Paris are waking.

New York (3:00 AM)　　　Paris (9:00 AM)

East-to-west travel (6-hour flight)

Paris (3:00 AM)

New York (9:00 PM)

4 Traveler arrives in New York at 9:00 PM and needs to stay up only a little longer than normal for his biological clock to adjust.

Paris (9:00 PM)　　　New York (3:00 PM)

3 Traveler leaves Paris at 9:00 PM, when it's 3:00 PM in New York.

Figure 12-5

Jet Lag Disruption in the entrainment of a person's biological clock that may be brought on by jet travel is likely more pronounced in west-to-east travel, because the disruption in the person's circadian rhythm is dramatic. On the return journey, the traveler's biological clock has a much easier adjustment to make.

Considering the somewhat less compulsive behavior that most of us display, we should shudder at the way in which we entrain our own clocks when we stay up late in artificial light, sleep late some days, and get up early by using an alarm clock on other days. Such inconsistent behavior with respect to the human biological clock has been associated with accidents and daytime fatigue.

Entrainment also works best if the adjustment to the biological clock is not too large. People who work shifts are often subject to huge adjustments, especially when they work the graveyard shift (11:00 PM to 7:00 AM), the period when they would normally sleep. The results of studies show that adapting to such a change is difficult and stressful. Adaptations to shift work are better if people first work the evening shift (3:00 PM to 11:00 PM) for a time before beginning the graveyard shift.

Long-distance air travel—say, from North America to Europe or Asia—also demands a large and difficult time adjustment. For example, travelers flying east from New York to Paris will begin their first European day just when their biological clocks are prepared for sleep (**Figure 12-5**). The difference between a person's circadian rhythm and the daylight cycle in a new environment can produce the feeling of disorientation called jet lag. The west-to-east traveler generally has a more difficult adjustment than does the east-to-west traveler, who needs to stay up only a little longer than normal.

In Review

Many behaviors occur in a rhythmic pattern in relation to time. These biorhythms may display a yearly cycle (circannual rhythms) or a daily cycle (circadian rhythms). Biological rhythms are timed internally by regions of the nervous system that serve as biological clocks to regulate most of our circadian rhythms, especially our sleep–wake cycles. Although biological clocks keep fairly good time, their periods may be slightly shorter or longer than a 24-hour day unless they are reset each day. Their spontaneous periods are called free-running rhythms. Zeitgebers are environmental cues that reset the biological clock.

NEURAL BASIS OF THE BIOLOGICAL CLOCK

Curt Richter (1965) was the first researcher to attempt to locate biological clocks in the brain. In the 1930s, he captured wild rats and tested them in activity wheels. He found that the animals ran, ate, and drank when the lights were off and were relatively quiescent when the lights were on. Richter's hypothesis was that the rats' behavior and the biological clock that was responsible for rhythmicity were separate.

Richter proposed that the biological clock acted as a pacemaker to instruct other neural structures when they should produce the behaviors for which they were responsible. Thus, behaviors such as running, eating, drinking, and changes in body temperature occur when the pacemaker tells their relevant neural areas that it is time to begin.

Richter further proposed that this biological clock is localized in the brain, rather than being a property of all body or all brain cells. By inserting an electrode into the brain to damage brain tissue with electric current, he found that animals lost their circadian rhythms after damage to the hypothalamus. Subsequently, by making much more discrete lesions, experimenters have shown that a region called the **suprachiasmatic nucleus** (SCN) acts as a biological clock (Ralph & Lehman, 1991). As illustrated in **Figure 12-6**, the SCN is located in the hypothalamus, just above (*supra*) the optic chiasm—hence its name.

The SCN receives information about light through its own special visual pathway, the **retinohypothalamic pathway.** This pathway consists of a subset of cone receptors in the retina that are connected to a subset of optic-tract fibers and use glutamate as their primary neurotransmitter in the SCN. Light signals are carried by this pathway to the suprachiasmatic nucleus to excite and to entrain it. Visual fibers carrying information about light also go to an area of the thalamus (the intergeniculate leaflet), but we will limit our consideration of rhythms to the role of the SCN.

Scientists have also found pacemakers in the retina and in the pineal gland. Some behaviors may be paced by widely distributed pacemaker brain cells. Among the other possible pacemakers, the pineal gland has received the most study. It acts as a pacemaker in some species of birds. It is excited by light that enters the brain not through the visual system but through the skull. When the heads of such birds are painted black, the pineal gland's pacemaker activities are blocked. Because the pineal gland can respond directly to light, it has been called the "third eye." In most animals, however, the suprachiasmatic nucleus is the main pacemaker.

Suprachiasmatic Rhythms

Further evidence for the role of the SCN in circadian rhythms comes from a remarkable series of experiments demonstrating that some neurons of the nucleus have intrinsic rhythmic activity (Earnest et al., 1999). Following up on Richter's original experiments,

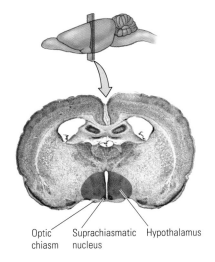

Optic   Suprachiasmatic   Hypothalamus
chiasm   nucleus

Figure 12-6

Suprachiasmatic Nucleus in a Rat Brain

Suprachiasmatic nucleus (SCN).
Main pacemaker of circadian rhythms located just above the optic chiasm.

Retinohypothalamic pathway.
Neural route from a subset of cone receptors in the retina to the suprachiasmatic nucleus of the hypothalamus; allows light to entrain the rhythmic activity of the SCN.

investigators have found that, if the suprachiasmatic nuclei are selectively lesioned in rodents, the animals still eat, drink, exercise, and sleep a normal amount, but at haphazard times.

By itself, disorganized behavior does not definitively demonstrate that the SCN is the clock that gives instructions about when these activities should take place. The SCN could just be a way station between receptors in the eye and a clock located elsewhere in the brain. Three other lines of evidence do show, however, that the suprachiasmatic nucleus is indeed a biological clock:

1. The metabolic activity of the SCN is higher during the light period of the day–night cycle than it is during the dark period of the cycle. If 2-deoxyglucose—a form of glucose that is taken up by metabolically active cells but is not used by them and cannot escape from them—is tagged with a radioactive label, cells that are more active will subsequently give off more radioactivity. When 2-deoxyglucose is injected into rodents, its accumulation by the SCN should be relative to the animal's daily rhythm if the neurons in the nucleus are responsible for the rhythm. More tracer is found in the SCN after injections given in the light period of the light–dark cycle than after injections given in the dark period. This experiment demonstrates that suprachiasmatic cells have rhythmic metabolic activity and that the SCN is special in this respect.
2. Recording electrodes placed in the SCN confirm that neurons in this region are more active during the light period of the cycle than during the dark period.
3. If all the pathways into and out of the SCN are cut, the neurons of the suprachiasmatic nucleus maintain their rhythmic electrical activity.

Together, the results of these experiments show that the suprachiasmatic neurons have a rhythmic pattern of activity that is intrinsic.

Evidence for Dual Clocks

After scientists had demonstrated that the SCN is rhythmically active, the question of how that rhythmicity is generated became central. When the SCN was removed from the brain, maintained in a laboratory dish, and subjected to electrical recording, the neurons were found to maintain their rhythmic activity. Furthermore, if the neurons were isolated from one another, each one was rhythmic. Individual cells did seem to have slightly different rhythms, however. This cellular individuality suggests either that, collectively, the cells express average rhythm or that the SCN has components that are able to produce rhythms with different periods or both. For example, findings from studies on the genes that control rhythms in fruit flies suggest that two separate groups of circadian neurons may control the rhythm of a fly's evening and morning locomotor peaks (Stoleru et al., 2004).

Evidence for two oscillators within the SCN have been obtained in the rat (de la Iglesia et al., 2004). One of the oscillators receives direct projections from the retina, whereas the other does not. The presence of dual oscillators might explain why all of the body's rhythms do not change together in response to temporal changes in Zeitgebers.

For example, rat activity levels change rapidly in response to changes in the onset of light, whereas change in body temperature rhythm is slower. Applied to humans, this finding might mean that sleep cycles adapt rapidly for a traveler arriving in Europe from North America, whereas the body-temperature cycle that accompanies the sleep–wake period lags behind. The traveler might get a good night's sleep but feel tired because his body temperature is low and remains set to accompany pretravel sleep time.

Immortal Time

How do suprachiasmatic cells develop their rhythmic activity? One possibility is that the endogenous rhythm is learned. That is, the cells may initially have no rhythm but, after they receive their first exposure to rhythmic stimulation from environmental Zeit-gebers, they become rhythmic.

One way of examining whether rhythmicity is learned is to maintain animals from birth in an environment without Zeitgebers. In experiments in which animals are raised in constant darkness, their behavior still becomes rhythmic. It is possible that the animals' fetal suprachiasmatic cells acquired rhythmicity from the mother, but, in experiments in which animals have been maintained without entraining cues for a number of generations, each generation continues to display rhythmic behavior. Even if the mother has received a lesion of the SCN so that her behavior is not rhythmic, the behavior of the offspring is rhythmic. Thus, it seems that rhythmicity is not learned.

A line of evidence supporting the idea that suprachiasmatic cells are genetically programmed for rhythmicity comes from studies performed in Canada by Martin Ralph and his coworkers with the use of transplantation techniques (Ralph & Lehman, 1991). The general design of the experiments is illustrated in **Figure 12-7**. First, hamsters are tested in constant dim light or in constant darkness to establish their free-running rhythm. They then receive a suprachiasmatic lesion, followed by another test to show that the lesion has abolished their rhythmicity. Finally, the hamsters receive transplants of suprachiasmatic cells obtained from hamster embryos. About 60 days later, the hamsters again show rhythmic activity, demonstrating that the transplanted cells have become integrated into the host brain and are responsible for reestablishing rhythmic behavior.

In further experiments, Ralph and his coworkers identified and selectively bred hamsters that displayed a 20-hour rhythm. They named the gene that was responsible for the short rhythm *tau*. If they destroyed the SCN in a genetically normal hamster with a 24-hour period and then transplanted cells from a fetal 20-hour hamster into the cavity, the former 24-hour hamster exhibited the 20-hour period of the hamster having the *tau* gene.

David Earnest and his coworkers (1999) carried the transplantation methodology one step further. They harvested cells from the rat SCN and used them to produce an immortalized cell line. By treating each generation of cells with 2-deoxyglucose, they were able to demonstrate that the cells' rhythm was passed on from one generation of cells to the next.

They then transplantated the cells from the immortal cell line into rats that had received suprachiasmatic lesions and restored the circadian rhythm in the rats. Thus, the rhythmic behavior of the suprachiasmatic neurons is immortal in that it is passed from one hamster generation to the next or from one cultured suprachiasmatic neuron to the next and from hamster to culture and visa versa.

(A) Normal

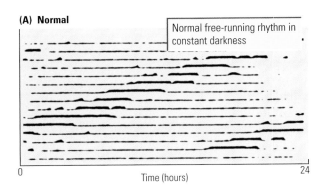

Normal free-running rhythm in constant darkness

0   Time (hours)   24

(B) Suprachiasmatic lesion

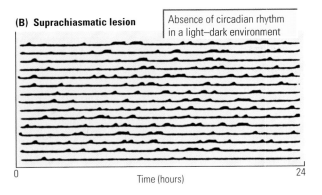

Absence of circadian rhythm in a light–dark environment

0   Time (hours)   24

(C) Suprachiasmatic transplant

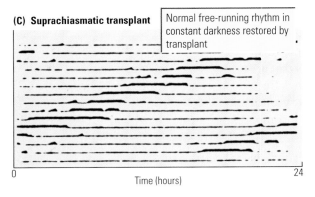

Normal free-running rhythm in constant darkness restored by transplant

0   Time (hours)   24

Figure 12-7

Circadian Rhythms Restored by Neural Transplantation Adapted from "Transplantation: A New Tool in the Analysis of the Mammalian Hypothalamic Circadian Pacemaker," by M. R. Ralph and M. N. Lehman, 1991, *Trends in Neurosciences, 14,* p. 363.

What Ticks?

Considerable research is being directed toward determining what genes control the ticking of the circadian clock. Because a single suprachiasmatic neuron displays a circadian rhythm, the timing device must be in the neuron itself, possibly entailing an increase and decrease of one or more proteins made by the cell. Just as the back-and-forth swing of a pendulum makes a grandfather clock tick, the increase and decrease in the amount of the protein makes the cell tick once each day.

According to this notion, a protein is made until it crests at a certain level, at which point it inhibits its own production; when its level falls to a critical point, production again rises. In turn, the electrical activity of the cell is linked to protein oscillation, allowing the cell to control other cells during a part of the oscillation. (The actual way that the oscillation is produced is a little more complex than this description suggests.)

Findings from studies on mutant and knockout mice suggest that at least a half dozen genes and the proteins produced by them form two interlocking loops to produce the circadian rhythm of suprachiasmatic cells in mammals (Coogan & Piggins, 2004). Although the mechanism is not fully worked out, the excitation of suprachiasmatic cells through the retinohypothalamic pathway can presumably degrade one of the proteins to entrain the sequence of biochemical steps in the interlocking loops.

Pacemaking Circadian Rhythms

The suprachiasmatic nucleus is of itself not responsible for directly producing rhythmic behavior. For example, after the SCN has been damaged, the behavioral activities of drinking and eating and of sleeping and wakefulness still occur. They no longer occur at appropriate times, however.

One proposal for how the SCN controls behavioral rhythms is illustrated in **Figure 12-8**. In this model, light entrains the SCN, and the pacemaker in turn drives a number of "slave" oscillators. Each slave oscillator is responsible for the rhythmic occurrence of one behavior. In other words, drinking and eating, body temperature, and sleeping and waking are each produced by a separate slave oscillator.

The signal, or "chime," that synchronizes slave oscillators may be both hormonal and a neurotransmitter signal from axons of suprachiasmatic neurons. Evidence that a hormone takes part comes from findings that transplanted suprachiasmatic neurons still send the signal, although they do not make axonal connections with distant neurons. Because motor-activity cycles can be restored by transplants in rodents, activity may be driven hormonally. As "Synchronizing Biorhythms at the Molecular Level" explains, a protein made and secreted by suprachiasmatic cells may be one chime. Other rhythms may be driven by neural connections to slave oscillators.

Shortly, we will consider some of the events of sleeping and waking behavior and the neural mechanisms that control them. Understanding circadian rhythms is important

Figure 12-8

Organization of the Circadian Timing System

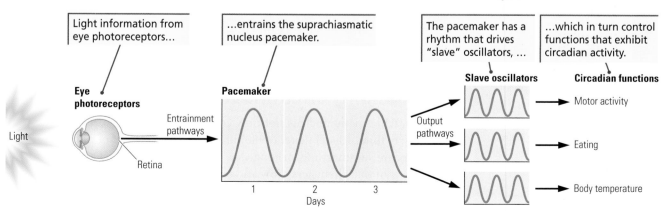

Synchronizing Biorhythms at the Molecular Level

To be effective, a biological clock needs an input signal that tracks light changes during cycles of day and night, the oscillator for timekeeping, and an output signal that can drive slave oscillators. As you know, the input signal is carried by the retinohypothalamic pathway, which projects from special retinal receptors through ganglion neurons. These neurons have excitatory glutaminergic synapses onto the cells of the suprachiasmatic nucleus.

In the rodent, this pathway stimulates SCN neurons to be active during the light part of the cycle. Findings from molecular-genetic studies into the clockwork show that a number of genes and their protein products take part in timing the SCN oscillation. The genes *Period* and *Cryptochrome* encode the oscillator.

Period and *Cryptochrome* are switched on by the proteins Clock and Bmal and switched off by the protein complex of Per and Cry so that gene turn-on follows gene turn-off in an inexorable daily loop. Mutations either in *Period* or *Cryptochrome* can lead to inherited sleep disorders. In addition, investigations into the sleeping habits of people suggest that modifications in genes that produce other proteins, such as Clock, can influence whether an individual will be "early to bed and early to rise" or "late to bed and late to rise" (Archer et al., 2003).

How does the SCN signal the slave oscillators in the rest of the brain to synchronize body temperature, metabolic activity, growth-hormone release, sleep activity, and so forth,

with the light–dark cycle? A puzzling anatomical feature of SCN neurons is that they do not all form major pathways from the SCN to other nuclei in the brain over which the "chime" that signals circadian activity can be sent. In addition, if transplanted SCN neurons are grafted in place of a damaged SCN, the new SCN chime is sufficient to signal other brain regions even though the grafted neurons do not form axons that project to the SCN's usual targets.

These findings suggest that one chime from the SCN is chemical. Michelle Cheng and her colleagues (2003) described six lines of evidence suggesting that a protein called prokineticin 2 (PK2) may be a SCN chime in mice:

1. PK2 levels are approximately 50 times as high in SCN neurons during the light (inactive) part of the cycle as in the dark (active) part of the cycle.
2. The production of PK2 is controlled by *Clock* genes.
3. In mice with deficient *Clock* genes, the expression of PK2 in SCN neurons was extremely low.
4. After mice maintained in constant darkness were exposed to light, the level of PK2 increased rapidly.
5. Receptors for PK2 are found in a number of brain regions that that are thought to serve as slave oscillators.
6. The administration of PK2 by injection into the brain by a cannula during the dark period of the circadian cycle resulted in a suppression of the expected increase of locomotor activity displayed by the mice.

for understanding sleeping and waking. If the circadian pacemaker function of the SCN is disrupted, sleep is disrupted. Consequently, some sleep disorders may be due not to the mechanisms that control sleep but to a malfunction of the pacemaker.

Pacemaking Circannual Rhythms

The suprachiasmatic nucleus not only controls daily rhythms, it can also control circannual rhythms. Russel Reiter (1980) illustrated this form of pacemaking in hamsters. Hamsters are summertime, or long-day, breeders. As the days lengthen in springtime, the gonads of male hamsters grow and release hormones that stimulate the males' sexual behavior. As the days shorten in the winter, the gonads shrink, the amount of the

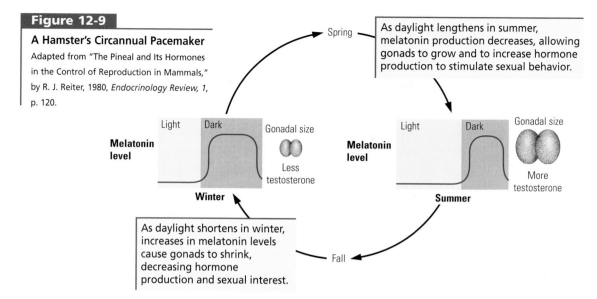

Figure 12-9

A Hamster's Circannual Pacemaker

Adapted from "The Pineal and Its Hormones in the Control of Reproduction in Mammals," by R. J. Reiter, 1980, *Endocrinology Review, 1,* p. 120.

As daylight lengthens in summer, melatonin production decreases, allowing gonads to grow and to increase hormone production to stimulate sexual behavior.

As daylight shortens in winter, increases in melatonin levels cause gonads to shrink, decreasing hormone production and sexual interest.

hormones produced by the gonads decreases, and the males stop being interested in sexual behavior.

During the dark phase of the day–night cycle, the pineal gland secretes the hormone **melatonin.** This hormone influences daily and seasonal biorhythms. **Figure 12-9** shows that, when a hamster's melatonin level is low, gonads enlarge and, when it is high, gonads shrink. The control that the pineal gland exerts over the gonads is in turn controlled by the suprachiasmatic nucleus. Through a rather indirect pathway, the SCN drives the pineal gland as a slave oscillator.

During the daylight period of the circadian cycle, the SCN inhibits melatonin secretion by the pineal gland. Thus, as the days become shorter, the period of inhibition becomes shorter and thus the period in which melatonin is released becomes longer. When the period of daylight is shorter than 12 hours, melatonin release becomes sufficiently long to inhibit the hamster's gonads so that they shrink.

Melatonin also influences the testes of animals that are short-day breeders, such as sheep and deer, which mate in the fall and early winter. Its effect on reproductive behavior in these species is the reverse of that in the hamster: their reproductive activities begin as melatonin release increases.

The origins of many biorhythms are not yet understood. In his book titled *Biological Clocks in Medicine and Psychiatry,* Curt Richter (1965) summarized a lifetime of recording various normal and abnormal rhythms. Richter recorded rhythmic activity in many bodily functions—including body temperature, hormone levels, eating, and drinking.

Richter hypothesized that many physical and behavioral disorders might be caused by "shocks," either physical or environmental, that upset the timing of biological clocks. For example, the record of psychotic attacks suffered by English writer Mary Lamb, illustrated in **Figure 12-10,** is one of many rhythmic records that Richter thought represented the action of an abnormally functioning biological clock.

Melatonin. Hormone secreted by the pineal gland during the dark phase of the day–night cycle; influences daily and seasonal biorhythms.

Figure 12-10

Dysfunctional Clock? Attacks of mental illness displayed by the English writer Mary Lamb through her adult life appear to have had a cyclical component. Such observations would be difficult to obtain today, because the drugs used to treat psychiatric disorders can mask abnormal biorhythms. Adapted from *Biological Clocks in Medicine and Psychiatry* (p. 92), by C. P. Richter, 1965, Springfield, IL: Charles C Thomas.

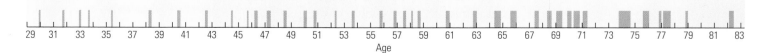

29 31 33 35 37 39 41 43 45 47 49 51 53 55 57 59 61 63 65 67 69 71 73 75 77 79 81 83

Age

In Review

A number of nuclei in the brain serve as diurnal biological clocks, including the suprachiasmatic nucleus of the hypothalamus and the pineal gland of the thalamus. Cues from the environment called Zeitgebers entrain the suprachiasmatic nucleus so that it can accurately control daily rhythms. Damage to the suprachiasmatic nucleus disrupts the rhythm of daily behaviors. We know that the pacemaking produced by the suprachiasmatic nucleus is a product of its cells because, if removed and cultured in a dish, the cells continue their rhythmic behavior and even pass on their rhythms to offspring cells cultured in a dish. If such immortal cells are transplanted back into a brain from which the suprachiasmatic nucleus has been removed, they restore the animal's rhythmic behavior.

SLEEP STAGES AND DREAMING

Most of us are awake during the day and asleep at night. Both behavioral states are more complex than our daily experiences suggest. *Waking* behavior encompasses some periods in which we are relatively still, other periods in which we are still but mentally active, and still other periods in which we are physically active. Our *sleeping* behavior is similarly variable in that it consists of periods of resting, napping, long bouts of sleep, and various sleep-related events including snoring, dreaming, thrashing about, and even sleepwalking. In this section, we describe some of the behavioral events of waking and sleeping and some of the neural processes that underlie them.

Measuring How Long We Sleep

A crude measure of sleeping and waking behavior is the self-report; that is, people record in a diary when they wake and when they retire to sleep. These diaries show considerable variation in sleep–waking behavior. People sleep more when they are young than when they are old. Most people sleep about 7 to 8 hours per night, but some people sleep much more or less than that, even as little as 1 hour each day.

Some people nap for a brief period in the daytime, and others never nap. Benjamin Franklin is credited with the aphorism, "Early to bed and early to rise makes a man healthy, wealthy, and wise," but measures of sleep behavior indicate that the correlation that Franklin made does not actually exist. Apparently, variations in sleeping times are quite normal.

Measuring Sleep in the Laboratory

In contrast with self-reports, laboratory sleep studies allow researchers to record physiological changes associated with sleep. The electrical activity in the brain and body is measured with a polygraph, as described in Chapter 4. **Figure 12-11** illustrates a typical polygraph setup in a sleep laboratory and some commonly used measures.

Electrodes are pasted onto a number of standard locations on the skull's surface for an electroencephalogram (EEG), a record of brain-wave activity; onto muscles of

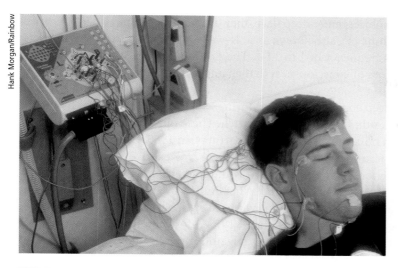

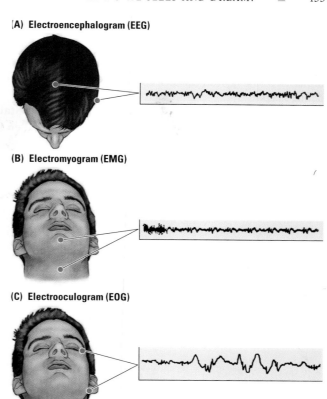

(A) Electroencephalogram (EEG)

(B) Electromyogram (EMG)

(C) Electrooculogram (EOG)

Figure 12-11

Setup in a Sleep Laboratory   Electronic equipment records readouts from the electrodes attached to the sleeping subject. **(A)** Electroencephalogram made from a point on the skull relative to a neutral point on the ear. **(B)** Electromyogram made between two muscles, such as those on the chin and throat. **(C)** Electrooculogram made between the eye and a neutral point on the ear.

the neck for an electromyogram (EMG), a record of muscle activity; and above the eyes for an electrooculogram (EOG), a record of eye movements. A thermometer also may be used to measure body temperature. Together, these measures provide a comprehensive physiological measure of sleeping–waking states.

The EEG recording traces distinct patterns of brain-wave activity and is the primary measure of sleep states. The neocortex generates rhythmic patterns from states categorized as awake, drowsy, sleeping, and dreaming.

Waking State   When a person is awake, the EEG pattern consists of small-amplitude (height) waves with a fast frequency. This pattern, the **beta rhythm** (β), is also called fast activity, activated EEG, or waking EEG. The waves of the beta rhythm have a frequency (repetition period) ranging from 15 to 30 Hz (times per second).

Drowsy State   When a person becomes drowsy, the fast-wave activity of the neocortex slows down and deepens concurrently. The amplitude of the waves increases, and the frequency of the waves becomes slower. When subjects relax and close their eyes, they may produce the *alpha rhythm,* large, extremely regular brain waves that have a frequency ranging from 7 to 11 Hz (review Figure 4-25).

In humans, you may recall, alpha rhythms are generated in the region of the visual cortex at the back of the brain, and they abruptly stop if a relaxed person is disturbed or opens his or her eyes. Recall, too, that not everyone displays alpha rhythms, and some people display them much better than others.

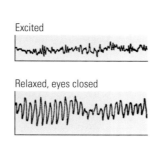

Excited

Relaxed, eyes closed

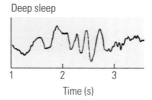

Deep sleep

1   2   3
Time (s)

Beta rhythm. Fast brain-wave activity pattern associated with a waking EEG.

Delta rhythm. Slow brain-wave activity pattern associated with deep sleep.

REM sleep. Fast brain-wave pattern displayed by the neocortical EEG record during sleep.

NREM (non-REM) sleep. Slow-wave sleep associated with delta rhythms.

Slow-wave sleep. NREM sleep.

⊙ To learn more about the EEG and the stages of sleep and waking, visit the EEG section in the module on research methods on your *Foundations of Behavioral Neuroscience* CD. (See the Preface for more information about this CD.)

Sleeping State   As subjects enter deep sleep, they produce yet slower, wider EEG waves known as **delta rhythms** (δ), also known as slow-wave activity or resting activity. Delta rhythm waves have a frequency of 1 to 3 Hz. The slowing of brain-wave activity is also associated with the loss of consciousness that characterizes sleep.

Dreaming State   Sleep consists of periods during which a sleeper is relatively still and periods when the mouth, fingers, and toes twitch. These opposite aspects of sleep are readily observable in household pets and bed partners. In 1955, Eugene Aserinsky and Nathaniel Kleitman (Lamberg, 2003), working at the University of Chicago, observed that the twitching periods are also associated with rapid eye movements (REMs).

Rapid eye movements coincide with distinct brain-wave patterns recorded on the EEG that suggest that the subject is awake, with the eyes flickering back and forth behind the sleeper's closed eyelids (see Dement, 1972). By accumulating and analyzing REMs recorded on EEGs, the Chicago investigators were the first to identify **REM sleep,** the fast-wave pattern displayed by the neocortical EEG record, and their association with vivid dreams. The EEG record suggested that dreaming subjects were awake, even though Aserinsky and Kleitman confirmed that the subjects really were asleep.

A Typical Night's Sleep

Because fast-wave activity is associated with REM sleep, the phase of sleep associated with delta rhythms on the EEG recording is called **NREM** (for non-REM) **sleep** and sometimes **slow-wave sleep.** With this distinction between sleep phases in mind, we now turn to comparing the EEG patterns associated with the course of a typical night's sleep.

Figure 12-12A displays the EEG patterns associated with waking, sleeping, and dreaming. Non-REM sleep is divided into four stages on the basis of EEG records. Notice that the main change characterizing these stages is that brain waves become larger and slower in a progression from stage 1 sleep through stage 4 sleep.

The designation of these stages assumes that the sleeper moves from relatively shallow sleep in stage 1 to deeper sleep in stage 4. Self-reports from subjects who are awakened from sleep at different times suggest that stage 4 is the deepest sleep, and subjects act groggy when disturbed during these periods. A remarkable feature of sleep is that

---

Figure 12-12

Sleep Recording and Revelations
(A) Electroencephalograph patterns associated with waking, with the four NREM sleep stages, and with REM sleep. **(B)** In a typical night's sleep, a person undergoes a number of sleep-state changes, roughly in 90-min periods. Non-REM sleep dominates the early sleep periods, and REM sleep dominates later sleep. The duration of each stage of sleep is indicated by the thickness of each bar, which is color-coded to the corresponding stage in part A, with the dark purple REM sleep bars labeled. The depth of each stage is graphed as the relative length of the bar. Adapted from "Sleep and Dreaming," by D. D. Kelley, in E. R. Kandel, J. H. Schwartz, and T. M. Jessell (Eds.), *Principles of Neuroscience*, 1991, New York: Elsevier, p. 794.

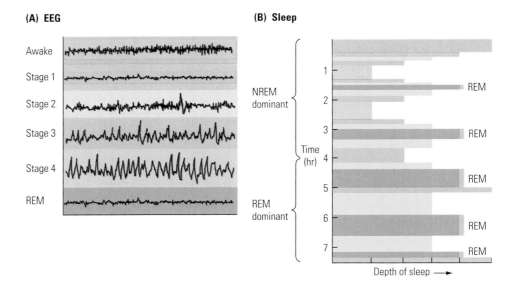

the EEGs of waking, of stage 1 sleep, and of REM sleep are similar. In all three conditions, the brain waves have an active, beta-rhythm pattern. Other unique physiological events occur in REM. The oculograph, for example, indicates that the subject's eyes are moving, revealing that it is recording REM sleep.

On the basis of a record of brain activity from one subject during a typical night's sleep, Figure 12-12B graphs when these different sleep stages actually occur and how long they last in the course of a night's sleep. Notice that the depth of sleep changes several times. The subject cycles through the four stages of NREM sleep and then enters REM sleep. This NREM–REM sequence lasts approximately 90 min and is typically repeated about four times in the course of the sleep period.

You can see by the labels indicating REM sleep in Figure 12-12B that the durations of the different sleep stages roughly divide the sleep period into two parts, the first dominated by NREM sleep and the second dominated by REM sleep. Body temperature is lowest (about 1.5 degrees below a normal temperature of 37.7°C) during the first part of the sleep period and rises during the second part. When subjects are awakened in REM sleep, they appear more alert and attentive than they are when awakened at other times, and they report that they have been vividly dreaming.

Findings from studies of sleep in the laboratory confirm that the sleep of individual people is highly variable; they also confirm that REM sleep takes up a substantial proportion of sleep time. Adults who typically sleep about 8 hours spend about two of those hours in REM sleep. A person's REM durations may also vary at different times of life. Periods of REM sleep increase during growth spurts, in conjunction with physical exertion, and, for women, during pregnancy.

The time spent in REM sleep also changes dramatically over the life span. As is illustrated in **Figure 12-13**, most people sleep less as they grow older. Furthermore, in the first 2 years of life, REM sleep makes up nearly half of sleep time, but it declines proportionately until, in middle age, it constitutes little more than 10 percent of sleep time.

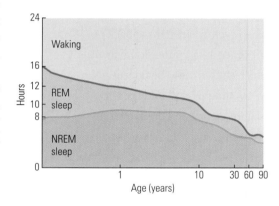

Figure 12-13

Sleeping and Waking over the Life Span The amount of time that humans spend sleeping decreases with age. The amount of REM sleep is especially high in the first few years of life. Adapted from "Ontogenetic Development of the Human Sleep-Dream Cycle," by H. P. Roffward, J. Muzio, and W. C. Dement (1966), *Science, 152.*

Non-REM Sleep

Although many people may think that sleep is an inactive period, a remarkable range of activities take place during sleep (see "Restless Legs Syndrome" on page 458). During NREM sleep, body temperature declines, heart rate decreases, blood flow decreases, we perspire and lose body weight owing to water loss, and our levels of growth hormone increase.

It was once thought that we do not dream during NREM sleep, but findings from recent studies show that, when subjects are aroused from NREM sleep, they do report dreams. These dreams lack the vividness of dreams reported by subjects aroused from REM sleep, however. Non-REM sleep is also the time during which we toss and turn in bed, pull on the covers, and engage in other movements. If we talk in our sleep, we will do so during NREM sleep. If we make flailing movements of the limbs, such as banging with an arm or kicking with a foot, we will usually do so in NREM sleep.

Some people even get up and walk while asleep, and this "sleepwalking" takes place in NREM sleep. Children may experience brief, very frightening dreams called *night terrors,* which also occur in NREM sleep. All these conditions are inconsistent with a period that is often described as quiet and inactive.

◉ For more information on Restless Legs Syndrome and night terrors, and to learn about current research to help people suffering from these disorders, visit the Chapter 12 Web links on the *Brain and Behavior* Web site (**www.worth publishers.com/kolb**).

Restless Legs Syndrome

I've always been a fairly untalented sleeper. Even as a child, it would take me some time to fall asleep, and I would often roll around searching for a comfortable position before going under. But my real difficulties with sleeping did not manifest themselves until early adulthood. By that time, my father had been diagnosed with Restless Legs Syndrome (RLS) and I was suffering the same symptoms.

Initially, my symptoms consisted of a mild tingling in my legs. It caused me to be fidgety and made it hard to fall asleep. Eventually, I went through a number of days without much sleep and reached a point where I simply could not function. I went to a doctor who prescribed a small course of sleeping medication (a benzodiazepine). I was able to get good sleep and my sleep cycle seemed to get back on track. Over the next decade I had periodic bouts of tingling in my legs which caused me to be fidgety and interfered with sleep. As time passed, the bouts occurred with increasing frequency and the symptoms became more noticeable and uncomfortable. I would simply suffer through these bouts, sleeping poorly and paying the consequences, or I would seek medical help. Being a student, I did not have a regular doctor. Unfortunately, most physicians I met did not know about RLS, and thought I was "drug seeking" or merely stressed out. I received a variety of patronizing responses and found these experiences insulting and demeaning. It would have been easy to give up and try to deal with it on my own, but because of my father's diagnosis, I knew the true source of the problem and was determined to get help.

Bill Aron/PhotoEdit

When I took my current position, I started seeing a doctor on a regular basis. By this time, my sleep was being seriously affected by RLS. The sensations in my legs were something like a combination of an ache in my muscles (much like one gets after exercising) and an electrical, tingling sensation. They would be briefly relieved with movement, such as stretching, rubbing, contracting my muscles, or changing position, but would return within seconds. In fact, my wife says my cycle is about 13 to 15 seconds between movements. I do this either when awake or during sleep. Trying not to move greatly increases the discomfort—much like trying to not scratch a very bad itch. The symptoms get worse in the evening and at night. Most nights, I have trouble falling asleep. Other nights, I

REM Sleep and Dreaming

REM sleep is no less exciting and remarkable than NREM sleep. During REM sleep, our eyes move and our toes, fingers, and mouths twitch, and males have penile erections. Still, we are paralyzed, as indicated by **atonia** (no tone), the absence of muscle tone due to the inhibition of motor neurons. Atonia is recorded on an EMG by the absence of muscle activity.

Atonia. No tone; condition of complete muscle inactivity produced by the inhibition of motor neurons.

wake up after an hour or so and then have trouble going back under.

Now my doctor takes me seriously. We exchanged research articles and thoroughly discussed treatment options. As part of this process, my wife met with my physician to relate her experiences. I was stunned to learn how severely my RLS was interfering with her sleep. I think she was being compassionate and not complaining so I wouldn't feel any more upset than I already was about my sleeping difficulties. My doctor started me on a regular course of sleeping medication (again, a benzodiazepine) and encouraged me to stay on it. This was a life-changing event. For the first time in my adult life, I was getting good sleep on a regular basis. My wife and I also got separate beds.

On the down side, RLS is a chronic and progressive condition. Over the years I've had to slowly increase dosages, switch to new medicines, and am now on two medications. I have always communicated openly and honestly with my physician, and we have worked together to monitor issues such as tolerance and medication dosages. I have gone for consultation with a neurologist experienced with RLS. I still get good sleep, but I have had to make many significant adjustments.

I am very up front about the fact that I have RLS. In fact, whenever I teach the topic of sleep and sleep disorders in my brain and behavior classes, I always make some time to talk about my experiences with RLS. Occasionally, students approach me with their own difficulties, and I try to provide them with information and resources.

—Stuart Hall, Ph.D., University of Montana

Restless legs syndrome (RLS) is a sleep disorder in which a person experiences unpleasant sensations in the legs described as creeping, crawling, tingling, pulling, or pain. The sensations are usually in the calf area but may be felt anywhere from the thigh to the ankle. One or both legs may be affected; for some people, the sensations are also felt in the arms.

People with RLS describe an irresistible urge to move the legs when the sensations occur. Many people with RLS have a related sleep disorder called *periodic limb movement in sleep* (PLMS). It is characterized by involuntary jerking or bending leg movements in sleep that typically occur every 10 to 60 s. Some people experience hundreds of such movements per night, which can wake them, disturb their sleep, and annoy bed partners. People with these disorders get less sleep at night and may feel sleepy during the day.

These symptoms affect both sexes, and symptoms can begin at any time but are more severe among older people. Young people who experience symptoms are sometimes thought to have "growing pains" or may be considered hyperactive because they cannot easily sit still in school.

There is no laboratory test for these disorders, and a doctor cannot detect anything abnormal in a physical examination. The disorder may also be of central nervous system origin because the syndrome has been reported in a patient who had no legs (Estivill et al., 2004). In mild cases, massage, exercise, stretching, and hot baths may be helpful. For more severe cases, patients can restrict their intake of caffeine, take benzodiazepines to help them get to sleep, and take L-dopa, a drug that is also used to treat Parkinson's disease. These treatments reduce symptoms, but at present there is no cure for the condition.

You can get an idea of what REM sleep is like by observing a cat or dog. At the onset of REM sleep, the animal usually subsides into a sprawled posture as the paralysis of its muscles sets in. **Figure 12-14** illustrates the sleep postures of a horse. Horses can sleep while standing up by locking their knee joints, and they can sleep while lying down with their heads held slightly up. At these times, they are in NREM sleep; when they are completely sprawled out, they are in REM sleep.

Figure 12-14

Nap Time Horses usually seek an open, sunny area in which to take brief periods of sleep. I. W.'s horse, Lady Jones, illustrates three sleep postures. At left, she displays NREM sleep, standing with legs locked and head down, and, at center, she displays NREM sleep lying down with head up. At right, she is in REM sleep, in which all postural and muscle tone is lost.

During REM sleep, mammals' limbs twitch visibly, and, if you look carefully at the face of a dog or cat, you will also see the skin of the snout twitch and the eyes move behind the eyelids. It might seem strange that an animal that is paralyzed can make small twitching movements, but the neural pathways that mediate these twitches are presumably spared the paralysis. One explanation for the twitching movements of the eyes, face, and distal parts of the limbs is that such movements may help to maintain blood flow in those parts of the body.

An additional change resulting from atonia during REM sleep is that mechanisms that regulate body temperature stop working and body temperature moves toward room temperature. The sleeper may wake up from REM sleep feeling cold or hot, depending on the temperature of the room.

The most remarkable aspect of REM sleep—dreaming—was discovered by William Dement and Nathaniel Kleitman in 1957 (Dement, 1972). When subjects were awakened from REM sleep, they reported that they had been having vivid dreams. In contrast, subjects aroused from NREM sleep were much less likely to report that they had been dreaming, and the dreams that they did report were much less vivid. The technique of electrical recording from a sleeping subject in a sleep laboratory made it possible to subject dreams to experimental analysis, and such studies provided some objective answers to a number of interesting questions concerning dreaming.

The first question that studies of dreaming answered was, How often do people dream? Reports by people on their dreaming behavior had previously suggested that dreaming was quite variable, with some people reporting that they dreamed frequently and others reporting that they never dreamed. Waking subjects up in periods of REM showed that everyone dreams, that they dream a number of times each night, and that dreams last longer as a sleep session progresses. Those who claimed not to dream were presumably forgetting their dreams. Perhaps people forget their dreams because they do not wake up in the course of a dream or immediately afterward, thus allowing subsequent NREM sleep activity to erase the memory of the dream.

Another interesting question that objective measures answered was, How long do dreams last? There had been suggestions that dreams last but an instant. By waking people up at different intervals after the onset of a REM period and matching the reported dream content to the previous duration of REM sleep, researchers were able to show that dreams appear to take place in real time. That is, an action that a person performed in a dream lasts about as long as it would take to perform while awake.

What We Dream About

The study of dreaming in sleep laboratories also allows researchers to study some of the questions that have always intrigued people. Why do we dream? What do we dream about? What do dreams mean?

Past explanations of dreaming have ranged from messages from the gods to indigestion. The first modern treatment of dreams was described by the founder of psychoanalysis, Sigmund Freud, in *The Interpretation of Dreams,* published in 1900. Freud reviewed the early literature on dreams, described a methodology for studying them, and provided a theory to explain their meaning. We briefly consider Freud's theory because it remains popular in psychoanalysis and in the arts.

Freud suggested that the function of dreams was the symbolic fulfillment of unconscious wishes. His theory of personality was that people have both a conscious and an unconscious. Freud proposed that the unconscious contains unacknowledged desires and wishes, which are sexual. He further proposed that dreams have two levels of meaning. The *manifest content* of a dream consists of a series of often bizarre images and actions that are only loosely connected. The *latent content* of the dream contains its true meaning, which, when interpreted by a psychoanalyst, provides a coherent account of the dreamer's unconscious wishes.

Freud provided a method for interpreting manifest symbols and reconstructing the latent content of dreams. For example, he pointed out that a dream usually begins with an incident from the previous day, incorporates childhood experiences, and includes ongoing unfulfilled wishes. He also identified a number of types of dreams, such as those that deal with childhood events, anxiety, and wish fulfillment. The content of the dream was important to Freud and other psychoanalysts in clinical practice because, when interpreted, dreams served as a source of insight into a patient's problems.

Other psychoanalysts, unhappy with Freud's emphasis on sexual desire, developed their own methods of interpretation. Psychoanalyst Carl Jung, a contemporary of Freud, proposed that the symbolism of dreams signifies distant human memories encoded in the brain but long since lost to conscious awareness. Jung proposed that dreams allow a dreamer to relive the history of the human race, our "collective unconscious." As more theories of dream interpretation developed, their central weakness became apparent: it was difficult, if not impossible, to know which interpretation was correct.

The dream research of Freud and his contemporaries was impeded by their reliance on a subject's memory of a dream and by the fact that many of their subjects were patients. This situation unquestionably resulted in the selection of the unusual by both the patient and the analyst. Now that researchers study dreams more objectively by waking subjects and questioning them, one might think that the meaning of dreams might be better understood. Certainly, knowledge of the content of dreams has improved.

Research suggests that most dreams are related to events that happened quite recently and concern ongoing problems. Colors of objects, symbols, and emotional content most often relate to events taking place in a person's recent waking period. Calvin Hall and his colleagues (1982) documented more than 10,000 dreams of normal people and found that more than 64 percent are associated with sadness, anxiety, or anger. Only about 18 percent are happy. Hostile acts against the dreamer outnumber friendly acts by more than two to one. Surprisingly, in regard to Freud's theory, only about 1 percent of dreams include sexual feelings or acts.

Contemporary dream hypotheses fall into two groups: those stating that dreams have no meaning and those stating that dreams are meaningful. The views of a major proponents of each position are described next.

J. Allan Hobson (2004), a scientist who has devoted his life to the scientific study of sleep and dreaming, proposed in his *activation–synthesis* hypothesis that, during a dream, the cortex is bombarded by signals from the brainstem, and these signals produce the pattern of waking (or activated) EEG. The cortex, in response to this excitation, generates images, actions, and emotion from personal memory stores. In the absence of external verification, these dream events are fragmented and bizarre and reveal nothing more than that the cortex has been activated. Furthermore, Hobson proposed, on the

● Visit the Chapter 12 Web links on the *Brain and Behavior* Web site (**www.worthpublishers.com/kolb**) to investigate more about research on dreams.

basis of PET-imaging results, that part of the frontal cortex is less active in dreaming than in waking. Because the frontal cortex controls working memory, memory for events that have just happened, and attention, the dreamer has difficulty both in remembering and linking dream events as they take place and in deciding what dream events should follow other events.

According to Hobson's hypothesis, dreams are nevertheless personal in that memories and experiences are activated, but they have no meaning. So, for example, the following dream, with its bizarre, delusional, and fragmented elements, would be representative of images that are synthesized to accompany brain activation. According to Hobson's hypothesis, any meaning that the dream might seem to have is created by the dreamer after the fact, as was perhaps done by the middle-aged dreamer who recounted this dream:

> I found myself walking in a jungle. Everything was green and fresh and I felt refreshed and content. After some time I encountered a girl whom I did not know. The most remarkable thing about her was her eyes, which had an almost gold color. I was really struck by her eyes not only because of their unique color but also because of their expression. I tried to make out other details of her face and body but her eyes were so dominating that was all I could see. Eventually, however, I noticed that she was dressed in a white robe and was standing very still with her hands at her side. I then noticed that she was in a compound with wire around it. I became concerned that she was a prisoner. Soon, I noticed other people dressed in white robes and they were also standing still or walking slowly without swinging their arms. It was really apparent that they were all prisoners. At this time I was standing by the fence that enclosed them, and I was starting to feel more concerned. Suddenly it dawned on me that I was in the compound and when I looked down at myself I found that I was dressed in a white robe as well. I remember that I suddenly became quite frightened and woke up when I realized that I was exactly like everyone else. The reason that I remembered this dream is the very striking way in which my emotions seemed to be going from contentment, to concern, to fear as the dream progressed. I think that this dream reflected my desire in the 1970s to maintain my individuality. (Recounted by A. W.)

Anttio Revonsuo (2000) of Finland agrees with Hobson about the content of dreams but uses content analysis to argue that dreams are biologically important in that they lead to enhanced performance in dealing with threatening life events. In his *evolutionary hypothesis of dreams,* Revonsuo argues that this enhanced performance would have been especially important for early humans, whose environment included frequent dangerous events that constituted extreme threats to their reproductive success. He notes that dreams are highly organized and are significantly biased toward threatening images (as, e.g., in the preceding dream). People seldom dream about reading, writing, and calculating, even though these behaviors may occupy much of their day.

The threatening events of dreams are the same ones that are threatening in real life (**Figure 12-15**). For example, animals and strange men who could be characterized as "enemies" figure prominently in dreams. Revonsuo cites overwhelming evidence that dream content incorporates the current emotional problems of the dreamer. He also reviews evidence to suggest that depressed dreamers who dream about their focal problems are better adjusted than those who do not.

Revonsuo also notes that recurrent dreams and nightmares generally begin in childhood, when a person is most vulnerable, and are associated with anxiety, threats, and pursuit. In them, the dreamer is usually watching, hiding, or running away. Revonsuo

Figure 12-15

Dream Content The terrifying visions that may persist even after awakening from a frightening dream are represented in this painting titled *The Night,* by Swiss artist Ferdinand Hodler. *The Night,* by Ferdinand Hodler (1853–1918), oil on canvas, 116 × 299 cm, Kunstmuseum, Berne, Switzerland.

therefore proposes that the experience of dealing with threats in dreams is adaptive because it can be applied to dealing with real-life threats. To illustrate, a student provided the following account of a dream from childhood that she had dreamed subsequently a few times:

> When I was five years old, I had a dream that at the time frightened me but that I now find somewhat amusing. It took place in the skating rink of my small hometown. There was no ice in the rink, but instead the floor consisted of sod. The women, my mother included, were working in the concession booth, and the men were in the arena, dressed in their work clothes. I was among the children of the town who were lined up in the lobby of the rink. None of the children, including myself, knew why we were lined up. The adults were summoning the children two at a time. I decided to take a peek through the window, and this is what I saw. There was a large circus-ride type metal chair that was connected to a pulley, which would raise the chair to about 20 feet into the air. The seat would be lowered and two children at a time would be placed in it. A noose was then placed around the neck of each and the chair was again raised. Once the chair reached its greatest height, the bottom would drop out of the chair and the children would be hanged (I did not see this but I thought that is what happened to them). At this point, I turned to a friend and said, "Here, Ursula, you can go ahead of me" and I went to my mother and told her what was going on. She smiled as if I were just being difficult and told me that I was to get back in the line. At this point I thought, "Forget it," and I found a place to hide underneath the big wooden bleachers in the lobby. It was dark and I could hear everyone out looking for me. (Recounted by N. W.)

When asked what she thought this dream meant, this student said that she really did not know. When told that it could be an anxiety dream, something common in children, that might represent an activity that she considered stressful, such as competing in figure skating and failing, she said that she did not think that was it. She volunteered, however, that her community's skating rink was natural ice and that it was bitterly cold whenever there was enough ice to go skating. When she had to skate, her feet got cold and her mother almost had to lift her up and drag her out onto the ice. Being dropped out of the chair may have been a symbolic representation of being pushed out onto the ice.

Elements of the dream did represent what went on at the skating rink. Men did prepare the ice and the women did run a concession booth, and she did resist being sent out to skate. The recurrence of the dream could be due to the conflict that she felt about having to do something that exposed her to the cold and her solution in hiding.

In Review

The average length of a night's sleep is from 7 to 8 hours, but some people sleep much less or much more. Sleep consists of two states, rapid eye movement, or REM, sleep and non-REM, or NREM, sleep. Non-REM sleep is divided into four stages on the basis of the EEG record. Brain waves in stage 1 sleep resemble waking patterns and REM sleep. Those in stages 2 through 4 are characterized by progressive slowing of the EEG record. People may have less-vivid dreams in non-REM sleep and will toss and turn. There are about four REM sleep periods each night, with each period getting longer as sleep progresses. REM sleep is also marked by muscle paralysis and dreams that are more vivid than those of NREM sleep. Among the various interpretations of the function of dreams, the activation–synthesis hypothesis suggests that they are simply a by-product of the brain's activity and so have no meaning, whereas the evolutionary hypothesis suggests that dreams help people to work out solutions to threatening problems and events.

WHAT DOES SLEEP ACCOMPLISH?

The simplest question that we can ask about sleep is, Why do we sleep? Any satisfactory explanation has a lot to account for. As we have seen, sleep is complex and progresses through periodic stages.

Sleep's rhythmic component lasts about 90 min in the course of which brain-wave activity gradually slows and then speeds up again. In REM sleep, the sleeping brain has a waking EEG, the motor system is paralyzed except for twitching movements, and people have more-vivid dreams than those in other stages of sleep. An adequate theory of sleep must account for all these phenomena. This section summarizes four theories of why we sleep.

Sleep As a Passive Process

One of the earliest explanations views sleep as a passive process that takes place as a result of a decrease in sensory stimulation. According to the theory, as evening approaches, there are fewer stimuli to maintain alertness, and so sleep sets in. This theory does not account for the complexity of sleep, nor is it supported by direct experimental investigations.

It predicts that, if subjects are deprived of all stimulation, they will go to sleep. Recall from Chapter 11, however, that findings from sensory-deprivation research fail to bear out this prediction. And the results of sleep experiments reveal that, when subjects are isolated in quiet bedrooms, they spend less, not more, time asleep. These results do not support the idea that sleep sets in because there is nothing else to do.

Shimon Amir   Jane Stewart

The passive-process theory of sleep originally did not consider biological rhythms as a contributing factor to sleep, but what we now know about biological rhythms provides some support for a weak version of this idea. Shimon Amir and Jane Stewart (1996) showed that initially neutral stimuli can be conditioned to be Zeitgebers, which entrain more-regular circadian rhythms and thus more-

Basic rest–activity cycle (BRAC). Recurring cycle of temporal packets, about 90-min periods in humans, during which an animal's level of arousal waxes and wanes.

regular periods of sleep. In other words, the activities in which we engage before we sleep and after we wake up will become Zeitgebers by being associated with light–dark changes. Therefore, exposure to darkness and quiet in the evening and to light and other kinds of stimulation in the morning is one way of synchronizing biological rhythms.

Sleep As a Biological Adaptation

Another explanation holds that sleep is a biologically adaptive behavior influenced by the many ways in which a species adapts to its environment:

■ Sleep is designed as an energy-conserving strategy to cope with times when food is scarce, as you learned in this chapter's first Focus. Each animal species gathers food at optimal times and conserves energy the rest of the time. If the nutrient value of the food that a species eats is high, the species can spend less time foraging and more time sleeping.

■ An animal's behavior is influenced by whether the species is predator or prey. The predator can sleep at its ease; the prey's sleep time is reduced because it must remain alert and ready to fight or flee at unpredictable times (**Figure 12-16**).

■ An animal that is strictly nocturnal or diurnal will likely sleep when it cannot travel easily. Dement has stated this idea as follows: "We sleep to keep from bumping into things in the dark."

The sleep patterns of most animal species are consistent with the adaptive explanation. **Figure 12-17** charts the average sleep time of a number of common mammals. Herbivores, including donkeys, horses, and cows, spend a long time collecting enough food to sustain themselves, which reduces their sleep time. Because they are also prey, their sleep time is further reduced as they watch for predators. Carnivores, including domestic cats and dogs, eat nutrient-rich foods and usually consume most of a day's or even a week's food at a single meal. Thus, because they do not need to eat constantly and because by resting they can conserve energy, carnivores spend a great deal of time each day sleeping.

The behavior of some animals does appear odd, however. Opossums, which spend much of their time asleep, may have specialized in energy conservation as a survival strategy. We humans are average among species in our sleep time, which is presumably indicative of an evolutionary pattern in which food gathering was not an overwhelming preoccupation and predation was not a major concern.

Sleep can contribute to energy conservation in a number of ways. During sleep, energy is not being expended in moving the body or supporting posture. The brain is a major user of energy, and so switching off the brain during sleep, especially NREM sleep, is another good way to conserve energy. The drop in body temperature that typically accompanies sleep slows metabolic activity, and so it, too, contributes to energy conservation.

A good explanation of sleep must explain not only sleep but also NREM and REM sleep. Before the discovery of REM sleep, Kleitman suggested that animals have a **basic rest–activity cycle** (BRAC) that, for humans, has a period of about 90 min (see Dement, 1972).

Figure 12-16

Do Not Disturb Biological theories of sleep suggest that sleep is an energy-conserving strategy and serves other functions as well, such as staying safe during the night.

Figure 12-17

Average Sleep Time Sleep time is affected both by the amount of time required to obtain food and by the risk of predation.

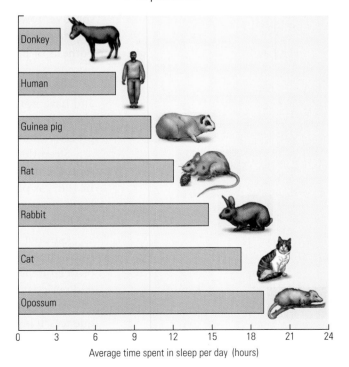

Average time spent in sleep per day (hours)

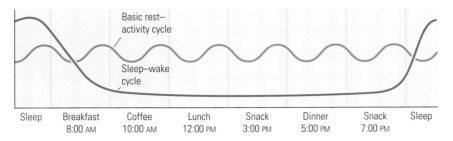

Figure 12-18

Behavioral Rhythms Our behavior is dominated by a basic rest–activity cycle (red) in which our activity levels change in the course of the day and by an NREM–REM sleep cycle (purple) during the night.

He based his hypothesis on the observation that human infants have frequent feeding periods between which they sleep.

As is illustrated in **Figure 12-18**, the behavior of adult humans also suggests that activity and rest are organized into temporal packets. School classes, work periods, meal times, coffee breaks, and snack times appear to be divided into intervals of 90 min or so. The later discovery that REM sleep occurs at intervals of about 90 min added support to Kleitman's hypothesis, because the REM periods could be considered a continuation into sleep of the 90-min BRAC cycle. The hypothesis now assumes that periods of eating are periods of high brain activity, just as are periods of REM.

Kleitman proposed that the BRAC rhythm is so fundamental that it cannot be turned off. Accordingly, in order for a night's sleep to be uninterrupted by periodic waking (and perhaps snacking), the body is paralyzed and only the brain is active. To use an analogy, rather than turning off your car's engine when you're stopped at a red light, you apply the brakes to keep the idling car from moving.

Sleep As a Restorative Process

The idea that sleep has a restorative function is widely held among poets, philosophers, and the public, as illustrated by Shakespeare in Macbeth's description of sleep:

> Sleep that knits up the ravell'd sleave of care,
> The death of each day's life, sore labour's bath,
> Balm of hurt minds, great nature's second course,
> Chief nourisher in life's feast.

Sleep as a restorative is also an idea that we can understand from a personal perspective. Toward the end of the day, we become tired, and, when we awaken from sleep, we are refreshed. If we do not get enough sleep, we often become irritable. One hypothesis of how sleep is restorative proposes that chemical events that provide energy to cells are reduced during waking and are replenished during sleep.

Nevertheless, fatigue and alertness may simply be aspects of the circadian rhythm and have nothing at all to do with wear and tear on the body or depletion of essential bodily resources. To evaluate whether sleep is essential for one or another bodily process, studies of sleep deprivation have been conducted.

Sleep-deprivation studies have not identified any function for which sleep is essential. One case study on sleep deprivation described by Dement illustrates this point. In 1965, as part of a science-fair project, a student named Randy Gardner planned to break the world record of 260 hours (almost 11 days) of consecutive wakefulness with the help of two classmates, who would keep him awake.

Gardner did break the record and then slept for 14 hours and reported no ill effects. The world record now stands at a little more than 18 days. A number of reviews of sleep-deprivation research are consistent in concluding that, at least for these limited periods of sleep deprivation, no marked physiological alterations ensue.

Although sleep deprivation does not seem to have adverse physiological consequences, it is associated with poor cognitive performance. Decreased performance contributes to accidents at work and on the road. The sleep-deprivation deficit does not manifest itself in an inability to do a task, because sleep-deprived subjects can perform even very complex tasks. Rather, the deficit is revealed when sustained attention is required and when a task is repetitive or boring.

Even short periods of sleep deprivation, amounting to the loss of a few hours of sleep, can increase errors on tasks requiring sustained attention. A confounding factor in cognitive performance is that sleep-deprived subjects will take **microsleeps,** brief sleeps lasting a few seconds. During microsleep, subjects may remain sitting or standing, but their eyelids droop briefly and they become less responsive to external stimuli. Many people who have driven a car while tired have experienced a microsleep and awakened just in time to prevent themselves from driving off the road.

Some studies have focused on the selective contributions of REM sleep. To deprive a subject of REM sleep, researchers allow subjects to sleep but awaken them as they start to go into REM sleep. REM-sleep deprivation has two effects:

1. Subjects show an increased tendency to go into REM sleep in subsequent sleep sessions, and so awakenings must become more and more frequent.
2. Subsequent to REM deprivation, subjects experience "REM rebound," showing more than the usual amount of REM sleep in the first available sleep session.

Some early reports of REM-deprivation studies stated that subjects could begin to hallucinate and display other abnormalities in behavior, but these reports have not been confirmed.

Two kinds of observations, however, suggest no adverse effects of prolonged or even complete deprivation of REM sleep. Virtually all antidepressant drugs, including MAO inhibitors, tricyclic antidepressants, and SSRIs, suppress REM sleep either partly or completely. The clinical effectiveness of these drugs may in fact derive from their REM-suppressant effects (Vogel et al., 1990). There are no reports of adverse consequences from prolonged REM deprivation as a consequence of treatment with antidepressants.

In a number of reported cases, lower-brainstem damage resulted in a complete loss of REM sleep. Some of these people suffered from **locked-in syndrome:** they were fully conscious, alert, and responsive but quadriplegic and mute. Five of seven patients with locked-in syndrome were reported to have no REM sleep, without apparent ill effects (Markand & Dyken, 1976). Patients with more-selective brainstem lesions reportedly remained ambulatory and verbally communicative, but their REM was abolished. They lived quite satisfactorily without REM sleep (Osorio & Daroff, 1980).

Sleep and Memory Storage

A fourth explanation of sleep proposes that sleep plays a role in solidifying and organizing events in memory. One group of experimenters proposes that events are stored in permanent memory in NREM sleep, whereas another group proposes that REM sleep fulfills this function.

To examine whether rats dream, Matthew Wilson and Bruce McNaughton (1994) made use of the finding that many hippocampal cells fire when a rat is in a certain location in an environment. These **place cells** are relatively inactive until the rat passes through a particular place in its environment, then they display a high rate of discharge.

The experimenters trained rats to look for food in a circular container or to search for food on a four-arm maze. Recordings were made from as many as 100 cells at the same time in three conditions: during NREM sleep, during a session in the food-searching task,

Microsleep. Brief period of sleep lasting a second or so.

Locked-in syndrome. Lower brainstem damage that results in a fully conscious, alert, and responsive condition, but the patient is quadriplegic and mute.

Place cell. Hippocampal neuron that fires when a rat is in a certain location in an environment.

○ To learn more about the role sleep plays in memory storage and retrieval, visit the Chapter 12 Web links on the *Brain and Behavior* Web site (**www.worthpublishers.com/kolb**).

Figure 12-19

Neural Replay? The activity of hippocampal cells suggests that rats dream about previous experiences. The dots on the periphery of the circles represent the activity of 42 hippocampal cells recorded at the same time during (1) slow-wave sleep before a food-searching task, (2) the food-searching task, and (3) slow-wave sleep after the task. No strong correlations between cells emerged during the slow-wave sleep that preceded the food-searching task, but correlations between cells during the food search and during the subsequent slow-wave sleep were strong. Adapted from "Reactivation of Hippocampal Ensemble Memories During Sleep," by M. A. Wilson and B. L. McNaughton, 1994, *Science, 165,* p. 678.

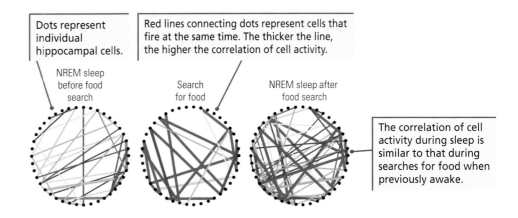

Dots represent individual hippocampal cells.

Red lines connecting dots represent cells that fire at the same time. The thicker the line, the higher the correlation of cell activity.

NREM sleep before food search

Search for food

NREM sleep after food search

The correlation of cell activity during sleep is similar to that during searches for food when previously awake.

and during NREM sleep after a session in the food-searching task. The experimenters then used computer methodology to look for cells whose discharge was correlated—that is, cells that discharged in a consistent temporal relation.

As is illustrated in **Figure 12-19**, the activity of only a few cells was strongly correlated in the sleep session that preceded the food-searching task. In the course of food searching, quite a number of cells discharged at the same time as a rat visited different locations in the apparatus. In the sleep session that followed the food-searching experience, correlations that were remarkably similar to those observed in food searching were observed.

Wilson and McNaughton proposed that, during NREM sleep, the memory of the previous food-searching experience is stored. Thus, if given another foraging opportunity, the animal knows where to look for the food.

To determine whether humans' dreams are related to memory, Pierre Maquet and his coworkers in Belgium trained subjects on a serial reaction task and observed regional blood flow in the brain with PET scans during training and during REM sleep on the subsequent night (Maquet et al., 2000). The subjects faced a computer screen on which six positional markers were displayed. The subjects were to push one of six keys when a corresponding positional marker was illuminated. The subjects did not know that the sequence in which the positional markers were illuminated was predetermined.

Consequently, as training progressed, the subjects indicated that they were learning because their reaction time improved on trials on which one positional marker was correlated with a preceding marker. On the PET-scan measures of brain activation, a similar pattern of neocortical activation was found during task acquisition and during REM sleep (**Figure 12-20**). On the basis of this result, Maquet and coworkers suggest, first, that the subjects were dreaming about their learning experience and, second, that the replay during REM strengthened the memory of the task.

Figure 12-20

Do We Store Memories During REM Sleep? Adapted from "Experience Dependent Changes in Cerebral Activation During Human REM Sleep," by P. Maquet et al., 1998, *Nature Neuroscience, 3,* p. 832.

(A) Reaction-time task

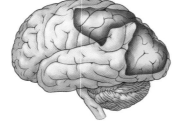

Subjects are trained on a reaction-time task, and brain activity is recorded with PET.

(B) REM sleep that night

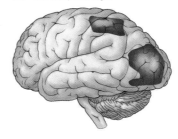

Subjects display a similar pattern of brain activity during subsequent REM sleep.

The results of some natural experiments raise questions about the memory-storing functions of sleep. There are many documented cases of people who sleep less than a couple of hours each day yet remain active and healthy, presumably with normal memory. These cases raise the question of why most people need much longer periods of sleep.

Consider the case reported of a 33-year-old man who suffered a head injury at age 20 and subsequently displayed little REM sleep, as documented in sleep-recording sessions in a sleep laboratory (Lavie et al., 1984). The lack of REM sleep did not appear to cause serious effects: the subject completed high school, attended law school, and subsequently practiced law.

Human infants spend a great deal of time sleeping in their first year or so but remember nothing of this period of life, although they are amassing motor skills. And the sloth is one of nature's great sleepers but is not noted among its great learners. Perhaps sleep facilitates plastic changes in the brain more generally and facilitates memory because memory depends on brain plasticity. Nevertheless, memory-storing explanations of sleep are extremely interesting and are being hotly debated (e.g., see Vertes, 2004, versus Walker & Stickgold, 2004). Sleep may also facilitate the normal function of the immune system, which also undergoes changes in its function in defense against disease.

Sloth

In Review

Among the explanations put forward concerning why we sleep, the biological explanation—that sleep is an adaptive strategy for conserving energy during times when food resources are hard to obtain—has replaced the passive explanation—that sleep results from lack of sensory stimulation. Scientists are examining the ideas that sleep is a restorative process and that sleep has a role in storing and sorting memory, but so far the evidence in favor of these ideas is not conclusive.

NEURAL BASIS OF SLEEP

The idea that the brain contains a sleep-inducing substance has long been popular and is reinforced by knowledge that a variety of chemical agents induce sleep. Such substances include sedative-hypnotics and morphine (Chapter 7). A twist on this idea held that the body secretes a chemical that induces sleep and that can be removed only by sleeping.

The hormone melatonin, secreted from the pineal gland during the dark phase of the light–dark cycle, causes sleepiness and is taken as an aid for sleep, and so it might be thought to be the sleep-producing substance. Sleep, however, survives the removal of the pineal gland. Thus, melatonin, and many other chemical substances, may only contribute to sleep, not cause it. If any chemical actually regulates sleep, it has not yet been identified (see "Synchronizing Biorhythms at the Molecular Level" on page 452).

In fact, experimenters have obtained evidence that sleep is *not* produced by a compound circulating in the bloodstream. When dolphins and birds sleep, only one hemisphere sleeps at a time. This ability presumably allows an animal's other hemisphere to remain behaviorally alert. This observation also strongly suggests that sleep is produced by the action of some region within each hemisphere.

In this section, we consider two points about the neural basis of sleep. First, we examine evidence that sleep is produced by the activity of a slave oscillator of the

Reticular activating system (RAS).
Large reticulum (mixture of cell nuclei and nerve fibers) that runs through the center of the brainstem.

Coma. Prolonged state of deep unconsciousness resembling sleep.

suprachiasmatic nucleus (see Figure 12-8). Second, we look at evidence that the various events associated with sleep, including events associated with REM and NREM sleep, are controlled by a number of different brainstem nuclei.

Reticular Activating System and Sleep

A dramatic experiment and a clever hypothesis by Giuseppe Moruzzi and Horace Magoun (1949) provide the beginnings of an answer to the question of which areas of the brain regulate sleep. Moruzzi and Magoun were recording the cortical EEG from anesthetized cats while electrically stimulating the cats' brainstems. They discovered that, in response to the electrical stimulation, the large, slow cortical EEG typical of the condition of anesthesia was dramatically replaced by the low-voltage, fast-wave EEG typical of waking.

The waking pattern of EEG activity outlasted the period of stimulation, demonstrating that the pattern was produced by the activity of neurons in the region of the stimulating electrode. During the "waking period," the cat did not become behaviorally aroused, because it was anesthetized, but its cortical EEG appeared to indicate that it was awake. This EEG pattern is referred to as a *desynchronized EEG,* meaning that the large, synchronized waves of sleep are replaced by low-voltage, fast activity brain waves of waking.

Findings from subsequent experiments by Moruzzi and Magoun and by others showed that a desynchronized EEG could be induced from a large area running through the center of the brainstem. Anatomically, this area is composed of a mixture of cell nuclei and nerve fibers that form a *reticulum* (from the Latin word *rete,* meaning "net"; described in Chapter 2). Moruzzi and Magoun named this brainstem area the **reticular activating system** (RAS) and proposed that it is responsible for sleep–waking behavior. The location of the RAS is illustrated in **Figure 12-21.**

We know that, if someone disturbs us when we are asleep, we usually wake up. To explain how sensory stimulation and the RAS are related, Moruzzi and Magoun proposed that sensory pathways entering the brainstem have collateral axons that synapse with neurons in the RAS. They proposed that sensory stimulation is conveyed to RAS neurons by these collaterals, and then RAS neurons produce the desynchronized EEG by axons that project to the cortex.

The results of subsequent experiments with sleeping cats show that electrical stimulation produces waking EEG activity and behavioral arousal in animals, just as if sensory stimulation had been used to wake them up. Moruzzi and Magoun further proposed that the cortex sends axons to the RAS, providing a route for people to stimulate their own reticular activating systems to stay awake. In sum, both sensory stimulation and conscious effort could activate the RAS to maintain waking.

Two other lines of experimental evidence support the idea that the RAS is responsible for desynchronized EEGs. Because Moruzzi and Magoun could possibly have stimulated various sensory pathways passing through the brainstem, it was necessary to demonstrate that brainstem neurons and not sensory-pathway stimulation produced the waking EEG. When experimenters cut the brainstem just behind the RAS, thereby severing incoming sensory pathways, RAS stimulation still produced a desynchronized EEG.

This result strengthened the argument that RAS neurons, not sensory pathways running through the region, are responsible for producing a desynchronized EEG. Furthermore, if the cut was made through the brainstem just in front of the RAS, the desynchronized EEG was no longer obtained in response to electrical stimulation of the

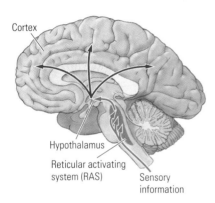

Cortex

Hypothalamus

Reticular activating
system (RAS)

Sensory
information

Figure 12-21

Sleep–Wake Controller   The reticular activating system, a region in the middle of the brainstem, is characterized by a mixture of cell bodies and fiber pathways. Stimulation of the RAS produces a waking EEG, whereas damage to it produces a slow-wave, sleeplike EEG.

RAS. Together these experiments demonstrate that RAS neurons acting through axons projecting to the cortex produce the waking EEG.

A different line of evidence obtained from humans who have suffered brainstem injury supports this conclusion. Damage that affects the RAS results in **coma,** a state of deep unconsciousness resembling sleep. In a well-publicized case, after taking a minor tranquilizer and having a few drinks at a birthday party, a 21-year-old woman named Karen Ann Quinlan sustained RAS damage that put her in a coma (Quinlan & Quinlan, 1977). She was hospitalized, placed on a respirator to support breathing, and fed by tubes. Her family fought a protracted legal battle to have her removed from life support, which was finally won before the Supreme Court of New Jersey. Even after having been removed from life support, however, Quinlan lived for 10 more years in a perpetual coma.

Despite substantial evidence that the RAS has a role in sleep–waking behavior, attempts to localize sleep to a particular structure or group of neurons within the RAS have not been successful. Findings from many studies demonstrate that discrete lesions at various locations within the RAS can produce periods of sleep that last for days; but, with care, animals in the laboratory and human brain-injured patients recover from these acute symptoms. These findings suggest that sleep–waking behavior is due to the activity of a diffuse network of fibers and cells rather than to regulation by a single nucleus. As described in the next section, patterns of a waking EEG are produced through at least two routes.

Neural Basis of EEG Changes Associated with Waking

A series of experiments performed on rats by Case Vanderwolf and his coworkers (Vanderwolf, 1988) suggested that nuclei in the midbrain and forebrain are responsible for producing the waking EEG pattern of the neocortex. **Figure 12-22** illustrates the location of these structures. Both send neural pathways into the neocortex, where they make diffuse connections with cortical neurons.

The basal forebrain contains large cholinergic cells. These neurons secrete acetylcholine (ACh) from their terminals onto neocortical neurons to stimulate a waking EEG (beta rhythm). The midbrain structure, the median raphé, contains serotonin (5-HT) neurons whose axons also project diffusely to the neocortex, where they also stimulate neocortical cells to produce a beta rhythm, recorded as a waking EEG.

Although both pathways produce a very similar pattern of waking EEG activity, the relations of the two types of desynchronized EEG to behavior are different. If the activity of the cholinergic projection is blocked by drugs or by lesions to the cells of the basal forebrain, the waking EEG that is normally recorded from an immobile rat is replaced by EEG activity resembling that of NREM sleep. If the rat walks or is otherwise active, a waking EEG is obtained from the neocortex. These findings suggest that the cholinergic EEG is responsible for the waking EEG when the rat is still and alert, whereas the serotonergic activation is additionally responsible for the waking EEG when the animal moves.

It is important to note that neither the basal forebrain system nor the median raphé system is responsible for behavior. In fact, if both structures are pharmacologically or surgically destroyed, a rat can still stand and walk around. Its neocortical EEG, however, resembles that of a sleeping animal.

Figure 12-22

Brain Activators In the rat, basal forebrain ACh neurons produce an activated EEG pattern when a rat is alert but immobile. The 5-HT raphé neurons of the midbrain produce an activated EEG pattern when the rat moves.

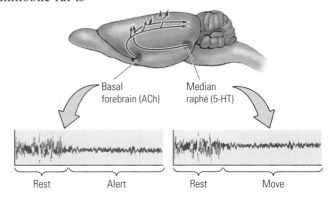

Basal forebrain (ACh)   Median raphé (5-HT)

Rest   Alert   Rest   Move

Peribrachial area. Cholinergic nucleus in the dorsal brainstem having a role in REM sleep behaviors; projects to medial pontine reticulum.

Medial pontine reticular formation (MPRF). Nucleus in the pons participating in REM sleep.

As long as one of the activating systems is producing a waking EEG, rats can learn simple tasks. If both systems are destroyed, however, an animal, although still able to walk around, is no longer able to learn or display intelligent behavior. In a sense, the cortex is like a house in which the lights are powered by two separate power sources: both must fail for the house to be left in darkness, but, if at least one source is operating, the lights will be on.

We do not know if the basal forebrain and median raphé produce the same two desynchronized EEG patterns in humans as they do in rats, but they likely do. Consequently, when we are alert, the cholinergic neurons are likely to be active and, when we move, the serotonin neurons are likely to be additionally active. You may have had the experience, when you felt sleepy in a class or behind the wheel of a car, of being able to wake yourself up by moving—shaking your head or stretching. Presumably, your arousal level decreased as your cholinergic neurons became inactive; but, when you moved, your serotonergic neurons became active and restored your level of arousal. When we enter sleep, both cholinergic and serotonergic neurons become less active, allowing slow waves to emanate in the cortex.

Neural Basis of REM Sleep

Barbara Jones

When we were looking at evidence related to the function of REM sleep, we considered a number of clinical cases in which people who had suffered brainstem damage no longer displayed REM sleep. This observation suggests that REM sleep is produced by the action of a neural area distinct from the RAS, which produces NREM sleep.

Barbara Jones (1993) and her colleagues described a group of cholinergic neurons known as the **peribrachial area,** which appears to be implicated in REM sleep. This area is located in the dorsal part of the brainstem just anterior to the cerebellum **(Figure 12-23)**.

Jones selectively destroyed these cells by spraying them with neurotoxin kainic acid and found that REM sleep in her experimental animal subjects was drastically reduced. This result suggests that the peribrachial area is responsible for producing REM sleep and REM-related behaviors. The peribrachial area extends into a more ventrally located nucleus called the **medial pontine reticular formation** (MPRF). Lesions of the MPRF also abolish REM sleep, and injections of cholinergic agonists (drugs that act like ACh) into the MPRF induce REM sleep. Thus, both the peribrachial area and the MPRF, illustrated in Figure 12-23, take part in the production of REM sleep.

If these two brain areas are responsible for producing REM sleep, how do other events related to REM sleep take place? Such events include:

▪ EEG pattern similar to waking EEG;
▪ rapid eye movements, or REM;
▪ sharp EEG spikes that are recorded from the pons, the lateral geniculate nucleus, and the visual cortex and are called *PGO* (pons, geniculate, occipital) *waves* after the structures in which they are found; and
▪ atonia, or absence of muscle tone due to the inhibition of motor neurons.

These REM-related activities are likely to be found in humans, although, at present, PGO waves have not been confirmed in humans.

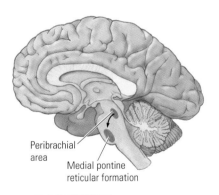

Peribrachial area

Medial pontine reticular formation

Figure 12-23

Brainstem Nuclei Responsible for REM Sleep Damage to either the peribrachial area or the medial pontine formation will reduce or abolish REM sleep.

One explanation of how other REM-related activities take place is illustrated in **Figure 12-24**. The MPRF sends projections to basal forebrain cholinergic neurons to activate them, resulting in the production of the activated EEG of the cortex. The MPRF area also excites the PGO pathway to produce PGO waves and eye movements. Finally, the atonia of REM sleep is produced by the MPRF through a pathway that sends input to the *subcoerulear nucleus,* located just behind it. The subcoerulear nucleus excites the *magnocellular nucleus of the medulla,* which sends projections to the spinal motor neurons to inhibit them so that paralysis is achieved during the REM-sleep period.

French researcher Michael Jouvet (1972) observed that cats with lesions in the subcoerulear nucleus display a remarkable behavior when they enter REM sleep. Rather than stretching out in the atonia that typically accompanies REM sleep, they stood up, looked around, and made movements of catching an imaginary mouse or running from an imaginary threat. If cats dream about catching mice or dream about escaping from a threat, then these cats appear to have been acting out their dreams.

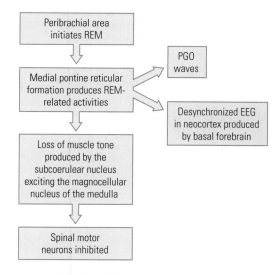

Figure 12-24

Neural Control of REM Sleep

In Review

Separate neural regions are responsible for sleep. The reticular activating system (RAS) in the central region of the brainstem is responsible for NREM sleep, whereas the peribrachial area and the medial pontine reticular formation (MPRF) are responsible for REM sleep. The last two areas, through activating pathways to the neocortex and spinal cord, are responsible for producing the waking EEG and the muscular paralysis that are associated with REM sleep.

SLEEP DISORDERS

Occasional disturbances of sleep are annoying and may result in impaired performance during the following day. About 15 percent of people complain of ongoing sleep problems; an additional 20 percent complain of occasional sleep problems. As people age, the incidence of complaints about sleep problems increases. In this section, we consider abnormalities of NREM sleep and REM sleep.

Disorders of Non-REM Sleep

The two most common sleep disorders are **insomnia,** prolonged inability to sleep, and **narcolepsy** (from Greek words meaning "numbness," and "to be seized"), uncontrollably falling asleep at inconvenient times. Both are considered disorders of slow-wave sleep. Insomnia and narcolepsy are related, as anyone who has stayed up late at night can confirm: a short night's sleep is often accompanied by a tendency to fall asleep at inconvenient times the next day.

Our understanding of insomnia is complicated by a large variation in how much time people spend asleep. Some short sleepers may think that they should sleep more, and some long sleepers may think that they should sleep less; yet, for each, the sleeping pattern may be appropriate. It is also possible that, for some people, circadian rhythms are disrupted by subtle life-style choices. Staying up late, for example, may set

Insomnia. Disorder of slow-wave sleep resulting in prolonged inability to sleep.

Narcolepsy. Slow-wave sleep disorder in which a person uncontrollably falls asleep at inappropriate times.

Drug-dependency insomnia.
Condition resulting from continuous use of "sleeping pills"; drug tolerance also results in deprivation of either REM or NREM sleep, leading the user to increase the drug dosage.

Sleep apnea. Inability to breathe during sleep; person has to wake up to breathe.

⊙ Visit the Chapter 12 Web links on the *Brain and Behavior* Web site (**www.worthpublishers.com/kolb**) to learn more about narcolepsy.

a person's circadian rhythm forward, encouraging a cascade of late sleep followed by still later staying up.

Some sleep problems are brought on by shift work or by jet lag, situations described earlier in the chapter. Other common causes of sleep disorders are stress, long hours of work, and irregular life styles. Just worrying about insomnia is estimated to play a major role in 15 percent of insomnia cases.

Sleep disorders are a complicating factor in other conditions, including depression. People who are depressed may sleep too much or too little. Anxiety and depression may account for about 35 percent of insomnias. There are also quantitative differences in the sleep of depressed patients, because they enter REM sleep very quickly. Entering REM sleep quickly, however, may be secondarily related to sleep deprivation, rather than being related directly to depression, because people who are sleep deprived also enter REM very quickly. Irregular sleeping patterns are also common in schizophrenia.

Insomnia may be brought on by sedative-hypnotic drugs, including seconal, sodium amytal, and many minor tranquilizers. These "sleeping pills" do help people get to sleep, but they cause additional problems. People may sleep under one of these drugs, but they are likely to feel groggy and tired the next day, which defeats the purpose of taking the drug. In addition, people develop tolerance to these medications, become dependent on them, and display rebound insomnia when they stop taking them. A person may increase the dose of the drug each time the drug fails to produce the desired effect. The syndrome in which patients unsuccessfully attempt to sleep by increasing their dosage of a drug is called **drug-dependency insomnia.**

Like many other people, you may have had the experience of being suddenly overcome by an urge to sleep at an inconvenient time, such as while attending a lecture. For some people, such experiences with narcolepsy are common and disruptive. J. S., a junior in college, sat in the front row of the classroom for his course on the brain; within a few minutes of the beginning of each class, he dropped off to sleep. The instructor became concerned about his abilities as a lecturer, but one day he heard another instructor describe the sleeping behavior of a student who turned out to be J. S. The instructor then asked J. S. to stay after class to discuss his sleeping behavior.

J. S. reported that sleeping in classes was a chronic problem. Not only did he sleep in class, but he fell asleep whenever he tried to study. He even fell asleep at the dinner table and in other inappropriate locations. His sleeping problem had made it a challenge to get through high school and was making it very difficult for him to pass his college courses.

About 1 percent of people suffer from narcolepsy, which takes a surprising number of forms. One cause of narcolepsy maybe be mutations in a gene that produces hypocretin/orexin peptides. Mutations in this gene or in the gene that makes the receptors for these compounds have been related to narcolepsy (Mignot, 2004).

J. S. had a form of narcolepsy in which he fell asleep while sitting still, and his sleeping bouts consisted of brief bouts of NREM sleep lasting from 5 to 10 min. This pattern was very similar to napping and to dropping off to sleep in class after a late night, but it was distinguishable as narcolepsy by its frequency and by the disruptive effect that it had on his academic career. J. S. eventually discussed his problem with his physician and received a prescription for Ritalin, an amphetamine-like drug that stimulates dopamine transmission (Chapter 7). The treatment proved very helpful.

Some people who suffer from daytime sleepiness attend sleep clinics to get help in sleeping better at night. Studies of narcoleptic people in sleep clinics have resulted in one surprising discovery concerning one of the causes of narcolepsy. "Sleep Apnea" describes a person who had to wake up to breathe; his **sleep apnea** left him extremely tired and caused him to nod off in the daytime.

Sleep Apnea

The first time I went to a doctor for my insomnia, I was twenty-five—that was about thirty years ago. I explained to the doctor that I couldn't sleep; I had trouble falling asleep, I woke up many, many times during the night, and I was tired and sleepy all day long. As I explained my problem to him, he smiled and nodded. Inwardly, this attitude infuriated me—he couldn't possibly understand what I was going through. He asked me one or two questions: Had any close friend or relative died recently? Was I having any trouble in my job or at home? When I answered no, he shrugged his shoulders and reached for his prescription pad. Since that first occasion I have seen I don't know how many doctors, but none could help me. I've been given hundreds of different pills—to put me to sleep at night, to keep me awake in the daytime, to calm me down, to pep me up—have even been psychoanalyzed. But still I cannot sleep at night. (In Dement, 1972, p. 73).

This patient went to the Stanford University Sleep Disorders Clinic in 1972. Recording electrodes were attached to him so that brain, muscle, eye, and breathing activity could be recorded while he slept (see Figure 12-11). The experimenters were amazed to find that he had to wake up to breathe.

They observed that he would go for more than a minute and a half without breathing, wake up and gasp for breath, and then return to sleep, at which time the sequence was repeated. Such sleep apnea (*a*, "not," and *pnea*, "breathing") may be produced by a central problem, such as a weak command to the respiratory muscles, or it may be obstructive,

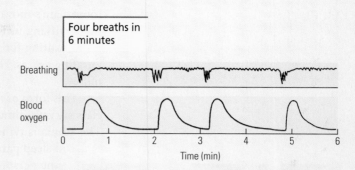

Breathing rate and blood-oxygen level recorded from a person with sleep apnea during REM sleep. Blood oxygen increased after each breath but then continued to fall until another breath was taken. This person inhaled only 4 times in the 6-min period; a normal sleeper would breathe more than 60 times in the same interval.

caused by collapse of the upper airway. When people suffering from sleep apnea stop breathing, they either wake up completely and have difficulty getting back to sleep or they have repeated partial awakenings throughout the night to gasp for breath.

Because sufferers are apparently unaware of their sleep apnea, it must be diagnosed by someone who watches them sleep. Sleep apnea affects all ages and both sexes, and 30 percent of people older than 65 years of age may have some form of it. Sleep apnea can even occur in children, in whom it has been associated with daytime behavioral disorder (Rosen et al., 2004). Sleep apnea is thought to be more common among people who are overweight and who snore, conditions in which air flow is restricted.

Treatments for sleep apnea include surgery or appliances that expand the upper airway, weight loss, and face masks that deliver negative pressure to open the airway. Sleep apnea may also be related to *sudden infant death syndrome* (SIDS), or crib death, in which otherwise healthy infants inexplicably die in their sleep.

Disorders of REM Sleep

Recall from the description of REM sleep that it is associated with muscular atonia and dreaming. REM-sleep atonia can occur when a person is not asleep, which happened to L. M., a college senior who, after hearing a lecture on narcoleptic disorders, recounted the following experience.

She had just gone to sleep when her roommate came into their room. She woke up and intended to ask her roommate if she wanted to go skating the next morning but found herself completely unable to speak. She tried to turn her head to follow her roommate's movements across the room but found that she was paralyzed. She had the terrifying feeling that some kind of monstrous creature was hiding in the bathroom waiting for her roommate. She tried to cry out but could produce only harsh, gurgling noises. Her roommate knocked her out of her paralysis by hitting her with a pillow.

This form of narcolepsy, called **sleep paralysis,** is extremely common. In informal class surveys, almost a third of students report that they have had such an experience. The atonia is typically accompanied by a feeling of dread or fear. It seems likely that, in sleep paralysis, a person has entered REM sleep and atonia has occurred, but the person remains partly conscious or has partly awakened.

The atonia of REM sleep may also occur while a person is awake; this form is called **cataplexy** (from *kataplessein,* a Greek word meaning "to strike down"). In cataplexy, an awake, alert person suddenly falls to the floor, atonic. Cataplexy is frequently reported to be triggered by excitement or laughing. Suddenly, the jaw drops, the head sinks, the arms go limp, the legs buckle, and the person falls down. The collapse can be so sudden that there is a real risk of injury.

While in an atonic condition, the person may see imaginary creatures or hear imaginary voices, called **hypnogogic** (Greek *hypnos,* "sleep," and *agogos,* "leading into") **hallucinations.** People who fall into a state of cataplexy with hypnogogic hallucinations give every appearance of having fallen into REM sleep while remaining conscious.

Conditions in which REM-sleep atonia occurs frequently may have a genetic basis. In 1970, William Dement was given a litter of Doberman pinscher dogs and, later, a litter of Labrador retrievers, all of whom had cataplexy. The disease is transmitted as a recessive trait; so, to develop it, a dog must inherit the gene from both its mother and its father. The descendants of those dogs provide animal models for investigating the neural basis of the disease as well as its treatment.

When a dog with cataplexy is excited, such as when it is running for a piece of food, it may suddenly collapse, as is illustrated on the left in **Figure 12-25**. Jerome Siegel (2004) investigated the cause of narcolepsy in dogs and found that

Figure 12-25

Cataplexy In both dog and human, an attack of cataplexy causes the head to droop and the back and legs to sag and can progress to a complete loss of muscle tone while the person or dog is awake and conscious. Cataplexy is distinct from the sleep attacks in that people hear and remember what is said around them, and dogs can track a moving object with their eyes. James Aronovsky (dog sequence), Joel Deutsch (human sequence), Slim Films.

neurons in the subcoerulear nucleus become inactive and neurons in the magnocellular nucleus of the medulla become active during attacks of cataplexy, just as they do during REM sleep. For some reason, the neurons responsible for paralysis during REM were producing paralysis during waking.

On the basis of anatomical examinations of the brains of narcoleptic dogs, Siegel suggested that the death of neurons in the amygdala and adjacent forebrain areas is a one-time event just before the onset of the disease early in life. Presumably, the loss of these neurons somehow results in the loss of inhibition in the brainstem areas that produce paralysis. It is important to note that, although a genetic basis for cataplexy has been identified in dogs, there is as yet no evidence that all cases of human cataplexy are genetic. Like some forms of narcolepsy, cataplexy is treatable with Ritalin.

Recall Jouvet's experiment, in which he reported that cats with lesions to the subcoerulear region of the brainstem entered REM sleep without the accompanying atonia and apparently acted out their dreams. A similar condition has been reported in people and may either have a genetic basis or be caused by brain damage. The condition has been named *REM without atonia*. The behavior of people who have REM without atonia suggests that they are acting out their dreams. The following two accounts are those of a 67-year-old patient (Schenck et al.,1986):

> I was on a motorcycle going down the highway when another motorcyclist comes up alongside me and tries to ram me with his motorcycle. Well, I decided, I'm going to kick his motorcycle away and at that point my wife woke me up and said, "What in heavens are you doing to me?" because I was kicking the hell out of her.

> I had a dream where someone was shooting at me with a rifle and it was in a field that had ridges in it, so I decided to crawl behind a ridge—and I then had a gun too—and I look over the ridge so when he showed up I would shoot back at him and when I came to [i.e., awakened] I was kneeling alongside the bed with my arms extended like I was holding the rifle up and ready to shoot.

In both dreams the patient had vivid pictorial images, but he heard nothing and he felt afraid. Although a large number of patients who have had such experiences have been described, most are elderly and suffer from brain injury or other brain-related disorders. REM without atonia can be treated with benzodiazepines, which block REM sleep.

Sleep and Consciousness

Many scientists interested in the neural basis of consciousness study sleep and sleep-related disorders. Clearly, the many different qualities and stages of waking and sleeping suggest that consciousness is not a unitary condition, either neurally or behaviorally. Rather, we experience a variety of "states of consciousness," some of which can occur simultaneously.

René Descartes, whose theory of the duality of body and mind is described in Chapter 1, conceived of his idea of a mind through a dream. He dreamed that he was interpreting the dream as it occurred. Later, when awake, he reasoned that, if he could think and analyze a dream while asleep, the mind must be able to function during both waking and sleeping. Therefore it must be independent of the body that undergoes sleeping and waking transitions.

Sleep paralysis. Inability to move during deep sleep owing to the brain's inhibition of motor neurons.

Cataplexy. Form of narcolepsy linked to strong emotional stimulation in which an animal loses all muscle activity or tone, as if in REM sleep, while awake.

Hypnogogic hallucination. Dreamlike event at the beginning of sleep or while a person is in a state of cataplexy.

More-recent research sheds additional light on consciousness. For example, what we colloquially refer to as waking comprises at least two different states: alert consciousness and consciousness with movement. People attempting to go to sleep or attempting to stay awake appear to realize that they can take advantage of these different conditions to achieve their objective.

People who are tired and wish to fall asleep usually seek out a dark, quiet room, where they lie still. In doing so, they are removing themselves from a condition of "moving consciousness." People who want to stay awake, especially if they are tired, can apparently do so as long as they keep moving. By walking around and otherwise remaining active, they can stay awake indefinitely.

Similarly, sleep consists of a number of NREM conditions and a REM condition. People in both NREM sleep and REM sleep are at least in some sense conscious when they dream. Dream consciousness can also occur in conjunction with waking consciousness, as witnessed by reports that people who fall into a state of cataplexy are conscious of being awake while experiencing the visual and emotional features of dreams when they have hypnogogic hallucinations.

Allan Hobson reported the peculiar symptoms that he suffered after a brainstem stroke (Hobson, 2002). For the first 10 days after the lesion he suffered from complete insomnia and experienced neither REM nor non-REM sleep. He did experience sudden visual hallucinations that had a dreamlike quality whenever he closed his eyes, however. This experience suggested that eye closure is sufficient to produce the visual components of REM sleep but with neither loss of consciousness nor paralysis. He eventually recovered normal sleeping patterns and the hallucinations stopped.

Besides being a source of insight into the neural basis of consciousness, the study of sleep states and events may help to explain some psychiatric and drug-induced conditions. For example, among the symptoms of schizophrenia are visual and auditory hallucinations. Are these hallucinations dream events that occur unexpectedly during waking? Many people who take hallucinogenic drugs such as LSD report that they have visual hallucinations. Does the drug initiate the visual features of dreams? People who have panic attacks suffer from very real fright that has no obvious cause. Are they experiencing the fear attacks that commonly occur during sleep paralysis and cataplexy? The answers to these questions are incomplete, but the similarities in symptoms between some waking and some sleeping conditions do suggest that some waking disturbances may be sleep events that occur when a person is awake.

In Review

Disorders of NREM sleep include insomnia, in which a person has difficulty falling asleep at night, and narcolepsy, in which a person falls asleep involuntarily in the daytime. Treating insomnia with sleeping pills, usually sedative hypnotics, may cause drug-dependent insomnia, in which progressively higher doses must be taken to achieve sleep. Disorders of REM sleep include sleep paralysis, in which a person awakes but is paralyzed and experiences a sense of fear, and cataplexy, in which a person may lose muscle tone and collapse in the daytime. Cataplexy may be associated with hypnogogic hallucinations, in which a person experiences dreams while paralyzed but awake. The study of sleep suggests that consciousness is not unitary but can take various forms.

SUMMARY

■ *What are biological rhythms?* Biorhythms are cyclic behavior patterns of varying length displayed by animals, plants, and even single-celled organisms. Mammals display a number of biological rhythms including circadian, or daily, rhythms and circannual, or yearly, rhythms. In the absence of environmental cues, circadian rhythms are free running, lasting a little more or a little less than their usual period of 24 hours, depending on the individual organism or the environmental conditions. Cues that reset a biological clock to a 24-hour rhythm are called Zeitgebers.

■ *What is a biological clock?* A biological clock is a neural structure responsible for producing rhythmic behavior. Among the biological clocks in the brain are the suprachiasmatic nucleus and the pineal gland. The suprachiasmatic nucleus is the mammalian biological clock responsible for circadian rhythms, and it has its own free-running rhythm with a period that is a little more or a little less than 24 hours. Stimuli from the environment such as sunrise and sunset entrain the free-running rhythm so that its period is 24 hours.

■ *How does a biological clock keep time?* Neurons of the suprachiasmatic nucleus are active in the daytime and inactive at night. These neurons display their rhythmicity when disconnected from other brain structures, when removed from the brain and cultured in a dish, and after having been cultured in a dish for a number of generations. When reimplanted into a brain without a suprachiasmatic nucleus, they restore the animal's circadian rhythms. The different aspects of circadian rhythms of neurons, including their period, are under genetic control.

■ *How is sleep measured?* Sleep events are measured by recording the brain's activity to produce an electroencephalogram, or EEG; muscular activity to produce an electromyogram, or EMG; and eye movements to produce an electrooculogram, or EOG. A typical night's sleep consists of four stages, as indicated by physiological measures, which take place in a number of cycles in the course of the night. During REM sleep, the EEG has a waking pattern, and the sleeper displays rapid eye movements. Stages of sleep in which the EEG has a slower rhythm are called non-REM (NREM) sleep. Intervals of NREM sleep and REM sleep alternate four or five times each night; the duration of NREM sleep is longer in the early part of sleep, whereas the duration of REM sleep is longer in the later part of sleep period. These intervals also vary with age.

■ *What events are associated with REM sleep?* A sleeper in slow-wave sleep has muscle tone, may toss and turn, and has dreams that are not especially vivid. A sleeper in REM sleep has no muscle tone and so is paralyzed and has vivid dreams whose duration coincides with the duration of the REM period. The activation–synthesis hypothesis proposes that dreams are not meaningful and are only a by-product of the brain's state of excitation during REM. The evolutionary hypothesis suggests that dreams evolved as a mechanism to cope with real threats and fears posed by the environment.

■ *Why do we sleep?* Several theories of sleep have been advanced, including the propositions that sleep results from the absence of sensory stimulation, that it is a biological adaptation that conserves energy resources, and that it is a restorative process that fixes wear and tear in the brain and body. Sleep may also organize and store each day's memories.

■ *What is the neural basis of sleep?* Separate neural regions of the brain are responsible for NREM and REM sleep. The reticular activating system (RAS) located in the central

neuroscience interactive

Many resources are available for expanding your learning online:

■ **www.worthpublishers.com/kolb**
Try the Chapter 12 quizzes and flashcards to test your mastery of the chapter material. You'll also be able to link to other sites that will reinforce what you've learned.

■ **www.sleepapnea.org**
This site from The American Sleep Apnea Association is a good place to learn more about the causes of, and treatments for, this disorder.

■ **www.sleepfoundation.org**
The headquarters of the National Sleep Foundation can be a fascinating starting point for investigation about sleep disorders and normal sleep patterns.

On your *Foundations* CD-ROM, you can review some of the research methods useful to understanding sleep in the three-dimensional research laboratory.

area of the brainstem is responsible for NREM sleep. If it is stimulated, a sleeper awakes; if it is damaged, a person may enter a condition of coma. The peribrachial area and the medial pontine reticular formation of the brainstem are responsible for REM sleep. If these areas are damaged, REM sleep may no longer occur. Pathways from these areas project to the cortex to produce the cortical activation of REM and to the brainstem to produce the muscular paralysis of REM.

■ *What disorders are associated with sleep?* Disorders of NREM sleep include insomnia, the inability to sleep at night, and narcolepsy, inconveniently falling asleep in the daytime. The administration of sedative hypnotics to induce sleep may induce drug-dependency insomnia, a sleep disorder in which progressively larger doses of the drug are required to produce sleep. Disorders of REM sleep include sleep paralysis, in which a dreaming person awakens but remains unable to move and sometimes feels fear and dread. Cataplexy is a disorder in which an awake person collapses into a state of paralysis. At the same time, the person may remain awake and have hypnogogic hallucinations similar to dreaming.

KEY TERMS

atonia, p. 458
basic rest–activity cycle
  (BRAC), p. 464
beta rhythm, p. 455
biological clock, p. 442
biorhythm, p. 440
cataplexy, p. 477
circadian rhythm, p. 443
coma, p. 470
delta rhythm, p. 456
diurnal animal, p. 439
drug-dependency
  insomnia, p. 474
entrainment, p. 445
free-running rhythm, p. 444

hypnogogic hallucination,
  p. 477
insomnia, p. 473
locked-in syndrome,
  p. 467
medial pontine reticular
  formation (MPRF),
  p. 472
melatonin, p. 453
microsleep, p. 467
narcolepsy, p. 473
non-REM (NREM) sleep,
  p. 456
peribrachial area, p. 472
period, p. 443

place cell, p. 467
REM sleep, p. 456
reticular activating system
  (RAS), p. 470
retinohypothalamic
  pathway, p. 448
sleep apnea, p. 474
sleep paralysis, p. 477
slow-wave sleep, p. 456
suprachiasmatic nucleus
  (SCN), p. 448
torpor, p. 439
Zeitgeber, p. 445

REVIEW QUESTIONS

1. Why are circadian and circannual rhythms such prominent rhythms in mammals?

2. Describe some of the details of the circadian clock that allow it to be easily studied.

3. In what ways are NREM sleep and REM sleep organized differently in the brain?

4. Describe the various theories of sleep.

5. What are some of the most common sleep disorders, and what are their causes and treatments?

FOR FURTHER THOUGHT

What ways can you suggest to combine the different theories of why we sleep into a unified theory?

RECOMMENDED READING

Dement, W. C. (1972). *Some must watch while some must sleep.* Stanford CA: Stanford Alumni Association. This short book is written in an engaging style for the beginning student of sleep. Nevertheless, instructors and even experts in sleep find it to be an excellent introduction by one of the pioneers of sleep research.

Hobson, J. (1989). *Sleep.* New York: Scientific American Library. This book covers most of the main ideas that have developed from research into sleep. It also covers areas of psychology, ethology, neuroscience, and molecular biology, and it provides an overview of the disorders of sleep. Hobson presents his own activation synthesis theory of dreams.

Kleitman, N. (1965). *Sleep and wakefulness.* Chicago: University of Chicago Press. This book is an exhaustive description of research into sleep and covers all the major findings produced by the first decades of sleep research.

How Do We Learn and Remember?

Left: **Oliver Meckes/Ottawa/Photo Researchers.** *Middle:* **Dimitri Messinis/AP Photo.** *Right:* **ADEAR/RDF/Visuals Unlimited.**

Movement, Learning, and Neuroplasticity

As we travel through life, we are constantly changing the organization of our brains by learning new things. The neural basis for learning and memory resides at the synapse, as detailed in Chapter 5. So, to learn anything new, we must change the connections in the nervous system, and, to do so, we keep adding new synapses.

What are the implications of all these changes? After all, stated in Chapter 2, neural connections take up space. Is there a limit to what we can learn? Does learning one thing affect how we learn something else? If so, is the effect good or bad? It can be both.

Many lines of research show that practicing motor skills, such as playing a musical instrument, induces the organization of the somatosensory and motor maps in the cortex to change, as described in Chapter 10. The mental maps generally become larger, at least for the finger and hand representations. Presumably, musical skill improves, but are other abilities enhanced, too?

Patrick Ragert and colleagues (2003) showed that professional pianists have not only better motor skills but enhanced somatosensory perception in their fingers as well. When the researchers measured the ability to detect subtle sensory stimulation of the fingertips, they found that the pianists were more sensitive than controls.

They also found that the enhancement in tactile sensitivity was related to the hours per day that the musicians spent practicing. The investigators then asked whether the enhanced perceptual ability precluded further improvement in the musicians. Surprisingly, when both the musicians and controls were given a 3-hour training session designed to improve tactile sensitivity, the musicians showed more improvement than did the controls, and, again, the extent of improvement correlated with daily practice time.

This result implies that well-practiced musicians not only learn to play music but also develop a greater capacity for learning. Rather than using up all the available synapses, they had developed a capacity to make even more.

Not all motor learning is good, however. Many musicians develop *focal hand dystonia,* a condition in which the person develops abnormal finger and hand positions, cramps, and difficulty in coordinating hand and finger movements. Dystonia can be so disabling that some musicians must give up their occupation.

Typically, dystonia afflicts musicians who practice trying to make perfect finger movements on their instruments. Musicians at high risk include string players, who receive vibratory stimulation at their fingertips. The constant practice has been suggested to lead not only to improved musical ability but also to distortion or disordering of the motor maps in the cortex. Synchronous activation of the digits by the vibration leads to this unwanted side effect.

Victor Candia and colleagues (2003) reasoned that the dystonia was likely an example of disordered learning and could be treated by retuning the motor map. The authors used a neuroimaging technique known as magnetoencephalography to measure changes in sensory-evoked magnetic fields in the cortex.

At the beginning of the study, the musicians with dystonia had a disordered motor map in which the fingers overlapped one another, rather than being distinct. In training, each subject used a hand splint tailored to his or her individual hand anatomy. The splint allowed for the immobilization of different fingers while the subjects made independent movements of the others.

After 8 days of training for about 2 hours per day, the subjects showed marked alleviation in the dystonic symptoms, and the neuroimaging showed a normalization of the cortical map with distinct fingers. Thus, training was able to reverse the learned changes in the motor map and provide a treatment for the dystonia. The musicians actually "learned" a disorder, and they were able to "unlearn" it. In view of the study by Ragert and colleagues, we can only wonder whether the musicians' unlearning was actually faster because of the enhanced capacity to learn.

Most people tend to regard the brain as a relatively static structure that controls behavior, but the brain changes throughout life, and these changes allow us to modify our behavior, to adapt and learn, and to remember. In Chapter 5, we introduced the term *neuroplasticity* to describe the nervous system's potential for changes that enhance its adaptability to environmental change and its ability to compensate for injury. If we reflect on our own lives, we can easily compile a list of experiences that must change the brain:

- the profound changes during development discussed in Chapter 6;
- the acquisition of culture;
- preferences for certain foods or beverages or for art or other experiences; and
- the ability to cope with neurodegeneration in the aging process and, for many, to accommodate neurological injury or disease.

A characteristic common to all these examples is some form of learning. Understanding how the brain supports learning is a fundamental question of neuroscience. In Chapter 5, we analyzed different types of learning including habituation, sensitization, and associative learning, at the level of the neuron. We noted in Experiment 5-4, for example, that synapses change with events such as those observed in long-term potentiation (LTP). Such changes can take place anywhere in the brain.

Exactly where in the brain might such changes take place when we learn specific types of information? We can investigate the nature of the neural changes that support learning by describing the changes in neurons exposed to specific sensory experiences. Another strategy is to look at the neural changes that accompany various forms of brain plasticity, such as recovery from brain injury or addiction to drugs. The overriding goal of this chapter, however, is to generalize beyond learning to understand the nature of behavior and the changing brain.

CONNECTING LEARNING AND MEMORY

Learning, as you know, is a change in an organism's behavior as a result of experience. **Memory** refers to the ability to recall or recognize previous experience. Memory thus implies a mental representation of the previous experience. This hypothetical mental representation is sometimes referred to as a *memory trace*, and neuroscientists presume that a memory trace corresponds to some type of physical change in the brain.

At the macro level, however, what we know about the process of learning and the formation of memories is inferred from changes in behavior, not observed directly. The study of learning and memory therefore requires behavioral measures that evaluate such behavioral changes. We begin here by looking at the ways that learning and memory researchers study animals in the laboratory. We then look at what general types of learning and memory can be identified from the results obtained in such studies.

Studying Learning and Memory in the Laboratory

A challenge for psychologists studying memory in laboratory animals (or people) is to get the subjects to reveal what they can remember. Because laboratory animals do not talk, investigators must devise ways for a subject to show its knowledge. Different species can "talk" to us in different ways, and so the choice of test must be matched to the capabilities of the species.

In the study of rats, mazes or swimming pools are typically used because rats live in tunnels and near water. Studies of monkeys have taken advantage of the monkeys' sharp vision and avid curiosity by requiring them to look under objects for

---

Memory. The ability to recall or recognize previous experience.

Pavlovian conditioning. Learning procedure whereby a neutral stimulus (such as a tone) comes to elicit a response because of its repeated pairing with some event (such as the delivery of food); also called *classical conditioning* or *respondent conditioning*.

Eye-blink conditioning. Commonly used experimental technique in which subjects learn to pair a formerly neutral stimulus to a defensive blinking response.

Conditioned stimulus (CS). In Pavlovian conditioning, an originally neutral stimulus that, after association with an unconditioned stimulus (UCS), triggers a conditioned response.

Unconditioned stimulus (UCS). A stimulus that unconditionally—naturally and automatically—triggers a response.

Unconditioned response (UCR). In classical conditioning, the unlearned, naturally occurring response to the unconditioned stimulus, such as salivation when food is in the mouth.

Conditioned response (CR). In Pavlovian conditioning, the learned response to a formerly neutral conditioned stimulus (CS).

Fear conditioning. Learned association, a conditioned emotional response, between a neutral stimulus and a noxious event such as a shock.

food or at television monitors. When birds are the subjects, natural behaviors such as singing are used. And, for human subjects, there is a tendency to use paper-and-pencil tests.

Consequently, psychologists have devised hundreds of different tests in the past century and, in doing so, have shown that there are many types of learning and memory, each of which appears to have its own neural circuitry. Let us first consider some classic examples of how animals can be trained to "talk" to investigators. A century ago, two very different traditions emerged for studying learning and memory, one based on the work of Edward Thorndike in the United States and the other on experiments conducted by Ivan Pavlov in Russia.

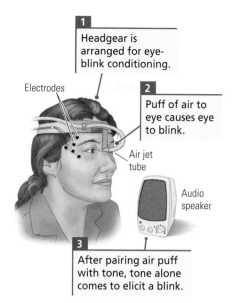

1 Headgear is arranged for eye-blink conditioning.

Electrodes

2 Puff of air to eye causes eye to blink.

Air jet tube

Audio speaker

3 After pairing air puff with tone, tone alone comes to elicit a blink.

Figure 13-1

Eye-Blink Conditioning A subject wears headgear containing an apparatus that delivers a puff of air to the eye, which causes the subject to blink. When the air puff is paired with a tone, the subject learns the association and subsequently blinks to the tone alone. Circuits in the cerebellum mediate this form of learning.

PAVLOVIAN CONDITIONING

In the early years of the twentieth century, Russian physiologist Ivan Pavlov discovered that, when a food reward accompanied some stimulus, such as a tone, dogs learned to associate the stimulus with the food. Then, whenever they heard the tone, they would salivate even though no food was present. This type of learning has many names, including **Pavlovian conditioning,** *respondent conditioning,* and *classical conditioning,* and its characteristics have been documented by many studies.

A key feature of Pavlovian conditioning is that animals learn the association between two stimuli (such as the presentation of the food and the tone) and tell us that they have learned it by giving the same response (such as salivation) to both stimuli. Pet owners are familiar with this type of learning: to a cat or dog, the sound of a can opener is a clear stimulus for food. Experimentally, two forms of Pavlovian conditioning are commonly used today: eye-blink conditioning and fear conditioning. These forms have proved especially useful because they are associated with neural circuits in discrete brain regions.

Eye-blink conditioning has been used to study Pavlovian learning in rabbits and people (**Figure 13-1**). In these studies, a tone (or some other stimulus) is associated with a painless puff of air to the eye of the subject. The tone, which is the **conditioned stimulus** (CS), comes to elicit a blink that is initially produced by the air puff, which is the **unconditioned stimulus** (UCS), because blinking is the normal reaction—the **unconditioned response** (UCR)—to a puff of air. Thus, the subject tells us that it has learned that the signal stimulus predicts the puff by blinking in response to the signal alone—a **conditioned response** (CR).

This form of learning is mediated by circuits in the cerebellum (see Figure 10-14). The cerebellum does not have special circuits just for eye-blink conditioning, which is an artificial situation. Rather, the cerebellum has circuits designed to pair various motor responses with environmental events. Eye-blink conditioning experiments simply take advantage of this biological predisposition.

In **fear conditioning,** a noxious stimulus is used to elicit fear, an emotional response. A rat or other animal is placed in a box that has a grid floor through which a mild but noxious electric current can be passed. As shown in **Experiment 13-1,** a tone (the CS) is presented just before a brief, unexpected, mild electric shock. (This shock is roughly equivalent to the static-electrical shock that we get when we rub our feet on a carpet and then touch a metal object or another person.)

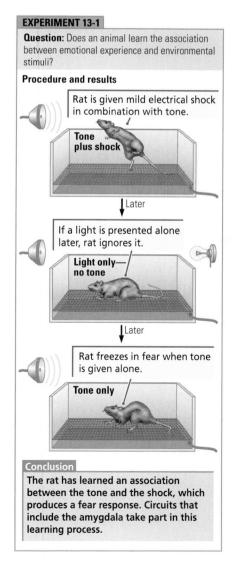

EXPERIMENT 13-1

Question: Does an animal learn the association between emotional experience and environmental stimuli?

Procedure and results

Rat is given mild electrical shock in combination with tone.

Tone plus shock

↓ Later

If a light is presented alone later, rat ignores it.

Light only— no tone

↓ Later

Rat freezes in fear when tone is given alone.

Tone only

Conclusion

The rat has learned an association between the tone and the shock, which produces a fear response. Circuits that include the amygdala take part in this learning process.

Instrumental conditioning. Learning procedure in which the consequences (such as obtaining a reward) of a particular behavior (such as pressing a bar) increase or decrease the probability of the behavior occurring again; also called operant conditioning.

Visuospatial learning. Using visual information to identify an object's location in space.

When the tone is later presented without the shock, the animal will act afraid. It may become motionless and may urinate in anticipation of the shock. Presentation of a novel stimulus, such as a light, in the same environment has little effect on the animal. Thus, the animal tells us that it has learned the association between the tone and the shock.

Because the CR is emotional, circuits of the amygdala, rather than the cerebellum, mediate fear conditioning. Although both eye-blink and fear conditioning are Pavlovian, different parts of the brain mediate the learning.

INSTRUMENTAL CONDITIONING

The second tradition of studying learning and memory was begun in the United States by Edward Thorndike (1898). Thorndike was interested in how animals solve problems. In one series of experiments, Thorndike placed cats in a box with a plate of fish outside it **(Figure 13-2)**. The only way for a hungry cat to get to the fish was to figure out how to get out of the box.

The solution was to press on a lever, which activated a system of pulleys that opened the box's door. The cat gradually learned that its actions had consequences: on the initial trial, the cat touched the releasing mechanism only by chance as it restlessly paced inside the box. The cat apparently learned that something that it had done opened the door, and it tended to repeat the behaviors that had occurred just before the door opening. After a few trials, the cat took just seconds to get the door open so that it could devour the fish.

Later studies by B. F. Skinner (e.g., 1938) used a similar strategy of reinforcement to train rats to press bars or pigeons to peck keys to obtain food (Chapter 11). Many animals will learn to bar press or key peck if they are simply placed into the apparatus and allowed to discover the response necessary to obtain the reward, just as Thorndike's cats learned to escape his puzzle boxes. This type of learning is **instrumental conditioning,** or *operant conditioning.* The subject demonstrates that it has learned the association between its actions and the consequences by the increasing speed at which it can perform the task.

The variety of such instrumental associations is staggering, as we are constantly learning the association between our behavior and its consequences. It should be no surprise, therefore, that instrumental learning is not localized to any particular circuit in the brain. The circuits needed vary with the actual requirements of the task, as is demonstrated by the following examples.

Richard Morris devised a task in 1980 that has become popular in research in learning and memory. He placed rats in a large swimming pool in which an escape platform was invisible to the rats because it was just under the water's surface. **(Figure 13-**

Figure 13-2

Thorndike's Puzzle Box

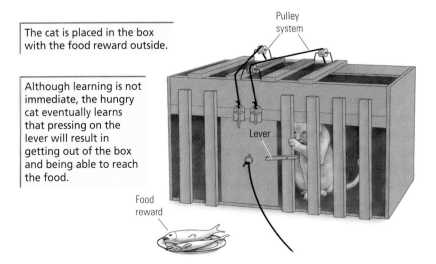

The cat is placed in the box with the food reward outside.

Although learning is not immediate, the hungry cat eventually learns that pressing on the lever will result in getting out of the box and being able to reach the food.

Pulley system

Lever

Food reward

3A shows the setup.) The task for the rat was to discover that there was an escape from the water and then to figure out where the platform was.

In one version of the test, illustrated in Figure 13-3B, the only available cues were distal ones—that is, external to the pool. Because no single cue would identify the location of the platform, the rats had to learn the relation between several cues in the room and the platform's location. To do so obviously requires **visuospatial learning,** the use of visual information to identify an object's location in space.

Rats normally learn the Morris task in just a few trials such that, when placed anywhere in the pool, they can swim directly to the hidden platform. We can infer that a rat that is able to swim but is unable to learn this task has some disturbance in the neural circuits underlying visuospatial learning.

In a variation of the task, after rats have been trained to find the platform, its location is changed (Figure 13-3C). The platform is moved to a new position every day; the rats must find the platform on the first trial in the pool and then go to that location for the remainder of that day's trials. In this case, the rats' task is to learn not only the platform's location with respect to the visual world but also its new location each day.

 For more information on learning through conditioning, visit the Chapter 13 Web links on the *Brain and Behavior* Web site (**www.worthpublishers. com/kolb**). On the site you can also go to the PsychSim Tutorials for an interactive demonstration of operant conditioning.

(A)

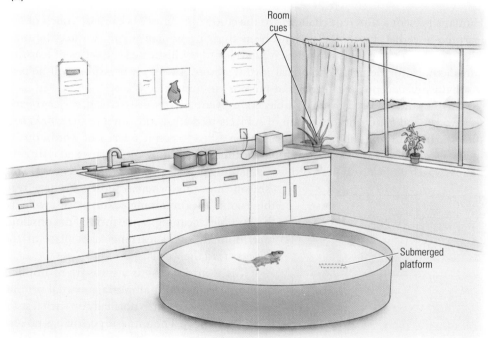

Room cues

Submerged platform

(B) Place learning

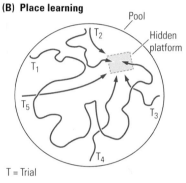

Pool

Hidden platform

T = Trial

(C) Matching-to-place learning

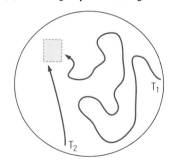

(D) Landmark learning

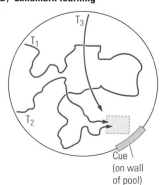

Cue (on wall of pool)

Figure 13-3

Instrumental Conditioning   **(A)** General arrangement of the swimming pool used in three different visuospatial learning tasks for rats. The red lines in parts B, C, and D mark the rat's swimming path on each trial (T). **(B)** In a *place-learning task* (Morris, 1981), a rat is put into the pool at various starting locations and must learn the location of a hidden platform, which can be done only by considering the configuration of visual cues in the room—windows, wall decorations, potted plants, and the like. **(C)** In a *matching-to-place task* (Whishaw, 1989), the rat is again put in the pool at random locations, but the hidden platform is in a new location each test day. The animal must learn that the location where it finds the platform on the first trial of each day is the location of the platform for all that day's trials. **(D)** In a *landmark-learning task* (Kolb & Walkey, 1987), the rat is required to ignore the room cues and to learn that only the cue on the wall of the pool signals the location of the platform. The platform and cue are moved on each trial so that the animal is penalized for trying to use room cues to solve the problem.

Learning set. An understanding of how a problem can be solved with a rule that can be applied in many different situations.

Implicit memory. Memory in which subjects can demonstrate knowledge but cannot explicitly retrieve the information.

Amnesia. Partial or total loss of memory.

Explicit memory. Memory in which a subject can retrieve an item and indicate that he or she knows that the retreived item is the correct item (i.e., conscious memory).

Rats quickly learn this puzzle and form what is known as a **learning set,** an understanding of how a problem can be solved through the use of a rule that can be applied in many different situations. In the current example, the rule is that the successful solution (finding the platform) requires a shift in strategy when the old strategy fails. Well-trained animals need only a single trial to learn the platform's location each day, and they will swim flawlessly to that location on subsequent trials. This type of task, in which the rat must keep track of a specific piece of information on a given day, places demands on the brain that are clearly different from the simpler Morris version, in which the learning is gradual, much like that in Thorndike's cats.

In yet another variation, a cue can be placed on the wall of the pool (Figure 13-3D). The rat's task is to learn that the cue, and only the cue, indicates the approximate location of the platform. In this case, the platform moves on every trial but always maintains the same relation to the cue, which also moves. The brain therefore is learning that all the distal cues are irrelevant and only the local cue is relevant. This task is very different, and, once again, different neural circuitry is required to solve it.

Two Categories of Memory

Humans present a different challenge to the study of memory because so much of our learning is verbal. Psychologists have been studying human memory since the mid-1800s, and cognitive psychologists have developed sophisticated measures of learning and memory for neuropsychological investigations. Two such measures will help us distinguish between two categories of memory in humans.

In one kind of task, a group of subjects are given a list of words to read, such as *spring, winter, car,* and *boat.* Another group of subjects read a list consisting of the words *trip, tumble, run,* and *sun.* All the subjects are then asked to define a series of words, one of which is *fall.* The word *fall* has multiple meanings, including the season and a tumble. People who have just read the word list containing names of seasons are likely to give the "season" meaning, whereas those who have read the second list, containing action words, will give the "tumble" meaning. Some form of unconscious (and unintentional) learning takes place as the subjects read the word lists.

This word-list task is a measure of **implicit memory.** People with **amnesia,** a partial or total loss of memory, perform normally on such tests of implicit memory. The amnesic person has no recollection of having read the word list yet acts as though some neural circuit has been influenced by it. Thus, there is a dissociation between the memory of the unconscious (or implicit) learning and the conscious recollection of training, which is referred to as **explicit memory.**

This implicit–explicit distinction is not restricted to verbal learning but is true of visual learning and motor learning tasks as well. For example, subjects can be shown the top panel of the Gollin figure test in **Figure 13-4** and asked what it shows. They are unlikely to be able to identify an image, and so they are presented with a succession of more nearly complete sketches until they can identify the picture.

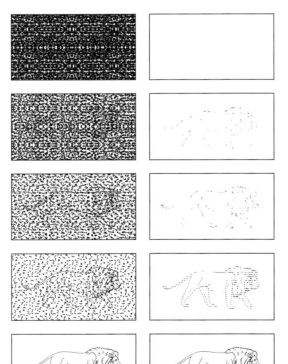

Figure 13-4

Gollin Figure Test
Subjects are shown a series of drawings in sequence, from least to most clear, and asked to identify the image. The object cannot be identified in the first sketch, and most people must see several of the panels before they can identify it. On a retention test some time later, however, subjects identify the image sooner than they did on the first test, indicating some form of memory for the image. Amnesic subjects also show improvement on this test, even though they do not recall taking the test before.

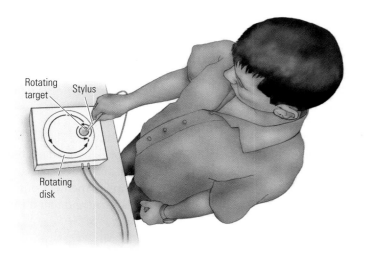

Rotating target
Stylus
Rotating disk

Figure 13-5

Pursuit-Rotor Task The subject must keep the stylus in contact with the metal disc that is moving in a circular pattern on a turntable, which also is moving in a circular pattern. Although the task is difficult, most people show significant improvement after a brief period of training. When given a second test at some later time, both normal subjects and amnesics show retention of the task. The amnesics typically do not recall learning the task before.

When control subjects and amnesics are later shown the same sketch, both groups are able to identify the figure sooner than they could the first time. Even though the amnesic subjects may not recall having seen the sketches before, they behave as though they had.

A second kind of measure reveals implicit learning of motor skills. For instance, a person can be taught a motor skill, such as the pursuit-rotor task shown in **Figure 13-5**. A small metal disc moves in a circular pattern on a turntable that also is moving. The task is to hold a stylus on the small disc as it spins. This task is not as easy as it looks, especially when the turntable is moving quickly.

Nonetheless, with an hour's practice, most people become reasonably proficient. If they are presented with the same task a week later, both normal subjects and amnesics will take less time to perform it. Here, too, the amnesics will fail to recall having ever performed the task before. We can see, therefore, that the distinction between tests of implicit and explicit memory is consistent and must provide some key to how the brain stores information.

The implicit–explicit distinction is just one way in which psychologists have categorized different memory processes. Many researchers prefer to distinguish between **declarative memory,** which refers to the specific contents of specific experiences that can be verbally recalled, such as times, places, or circumstances, and **procedural memory,** which is the ability to to do something. Although some theorists may make subtle distinctions between the implicit–explicit and declarative–procedural dichotomies, as applied to humans there is really little practical difference and we will use the explicit–implicit dichotomy.

Table 13-1 lists other commonly used dichotomies, with the general distinction being that one memory category requires the recollection of specific information whereas the other refers to knowledge of which we are not consciously aware. We can include Pavlov's classical conditioning, Thorndike's instrumental learning, and Skinner's operant learning in this analysis, too, because all of them are types of implicit learning.

Nonspeaking animals can display explicit memory. One of us owned a cat that loved to play with a little ball. One day the ball was temporarily put on a high shelf to keep

Declarative memory. Ability to recount what one knows, to detail the time, place, and circumstances of events; often lost in amnesia.

Procedural memory. Ability to recall a movement sequence or how to perform some act or behavior.

Table 13-1	Terms Describing Two Categories of Memory
Term for conscious memory	**Term for unconscious memory**
Explicit	Implicit
Declarative	Procedural
Fact	Skill
Memory	Habit
Knowing that	Knowing how
Locale	Taxon
Cognitive mediation	Semantic
Conscious recollection	Skills
Elaboration Integration	
Memory with record	Memory without record
Autobiographical	Perceptual
Representational	Dispositional
Episodic	Semantic
Working	Reference

Note: These paired terms have been used by various theorists to differentiate conscious from unconscious forms of memory. This list is intended to help you relate other discussions of memory that you may encounter to the one in this book, which favors the explicit–implicit distinction.

it away from an inquisitive 1-year-old boy. For weeks afterward, the cat would sit and stare at the location where the ball had been placed—an example of explicit memory.

Animals also display explicit memory when they learn psychological tasks. Recall that, in one variant of the Morris task, rats were given a new platform location on each day of training. The task therefore was to go to the platform's last location. This piece of information is explicit and can be demonstrably forgotten.

Suppose that a well-trained rat is given one trial with the platform at a new location and then not given a second trial for an hour, a day, 3 days, or a week. The rat has no difficulty with a delay of an hour or even a day. Some rats are flawless at 3 days, but most have forgotten the location by the time a week has elapsed. Instead, they swim around looking for the platform. This behavior illustrates their implicit memory of the learning set, or the "rules of the game"—namely, that there is a platform and that it can be found with a certain type of search strategy.

What Makes Explicit and Implicit Memory Different?

One reason that explicit and implicit memories differ is that each type of memory is housed in a different set of neural structures. Another reason that they differ is that explicit and implicit information are processed differently.

ENCODING MEMORIES

Implicit information is encoded in very much the same way as it is perceived and can be described as data-driven, or "bottom up," processing. The idea is that information enters the brain through the sensory receptors and is then processed in a series of subcortical and cortical regions. For example, recall from Chapter 8 that visual information about an object goes from the visual receptors (the "bottom") to the lateral geniculate nucleus, the occipital cortex, and then through the ventral stream to the temporal lobe, where the object is recognized.

Explicit memory, in contrast, depends on conceptually driven, or "top down," processing, in which the subject reorganizes the data. For example, if you were searching for a particular object such as your set of keys, you would ignore other objects. This is a top-down process because circuits in the temporal lobe (the "top") form an image that influences how incoming visual information (the "bottom") is processed, which in turn greatly influences the recall of information later.

Because a person has a relatively passive role in encoding implicit memory, he or she will have difficulty recalling the memory spontaneously but will recall the memory more easily when **primed** by the original stimulus or some feature of it. Because a person plays an active role in processing information explicitly, the internal cues that were used in processing can also be used to initiate spontaneous recall.

Findings from studies of eyewitness testimony demonstrate the active nature of recalling an explicit memory and its potential fallibility (e.g., Loftus, 1997). In a typical experiment, people are shown a video clip of an accident in which a car collides with another car stopped at an intersection. One group of subjects is asked to estimate how fast the car was going when it "smashed" into the other car. A second group is asked how fast the car was going when it "bumped" into the other car.

Later questioning indicates that the memory of how fast the first car was moving is biased by the instruction: subjects looking for "smashing" cars estimate faster speeds than those estimated by subjects looking for "bumping" cars. In other words, the instruction causes the information to be processed differently. In both cases, the subjects were certain that their memories were accurate.

⊙ To test your own memory, visit the Chapter 13 Web links on the *Brain and Behavior* Web site (**www.worth publishers.com/kolb**).

Priming. Using a stimulus to sensitize the nervous system to a later presentation of the same or a similar stimulus.

Other experiments show that implicit memory also is fallible. For example, subjects are read the following list of words: *sweet, chocolate, shoe, table, candy, horse, car, cake, coffee, wall, book, cookie, hat.* After a delay of a few minutes, the subjects hear another list of words that includes some of the words from the first list and some that are new. Subjects are asked to identify which words were present on the first list and to indicate how certain they are of the identification.

One of the words on the second list is *sugar.* Most subjects indicate not just that *sugar* was on the first list but that they are *certain* that it was. Although other sweet things were, *sugar* was not. This type of demonstration is intriguing, because it shows the ease with which we can form "false memories" and defend their veracity with certainty.

PROCESSING MEMORIES

Although memories can be distinguished generally as implicit or explicit, the brain does not process all implicit or all explicit memories in the same way. Memories can be divided according to categories that are different from those listed in Table 13-1. For example, we can make a distinction between memories for different types of sensory information.

We have seen that visual and auditory information is processed by different neural areas, and so it is reasonable to assume that auditory memories are stored in different brain regions from those in which visual memories are stored. We can also make a distinction between information stored in so-called *short-term memory* and information held for a longer time in *long-term memory.* In short-term memory, information—such as the telephone number of a restaurant that we have just looked up in the Yellow Pages—is held in memory only briefly, for a few minutes at most, and then is discarded. In long-term memory, information—such as a close friend's name—is held in memory indefinitely, perhaps for a lifetime.

The frontal lobes play an important role in short-term memory, whereas the temporal lobe plays a central role in long-term storage of verbal information. The crucial point is that no single place in the nervous system can be identified as the location for memory or learning. Virtually the entire nervous system can be changed with experience, but different parts of an experience change different parts of the nervous system. One challenge for the experimenter is to devise ways of manipulating experience to demonstrate change in different parts of the brain.

STORING MEMORIES

Acceptance of the idea that every part of the brain can learn influences our view of the nature of the neural circuits that mediate memory. For one thing, we could expect that areas that process information also house the memory of that information. Areas that process visual information, for example, likely house visual memory. Because the temporal lobe has specialized regions for processing color, shape, and other visual information regarding an object's characteristics, we can predict that the memory for various visual attributes of objects will be stored separately.

This prediction has been confirmed by a series of PET studies by Alex Martin and colleagues (1995) at the U.S. National Institute of Mental Health. In one of these studies, subjects were shown black-and-white line drawings of objects and asked to generate words denoting either colors or actions of the objects. The idea was that the processing of color and motion is carried out in different locations in the temporal lobe, and thus the activity associated with the memories of color and motion also might be dissociated.

In fact, just such a dissociation was demonstrated. **Figure 13-6** shows that recall of colors activates a region in the ventral temporal lobe, just anterior to the area controlling color perception, whereas recall of action words activates a region in the middle

Figure 13-6

Memory Distribution Lateral view of the left hemisphere shows regions of increased blood flow when subjects generate color words (red) and action words (blue) to describe objects shown to them in static, black-and-white drawings. Purple indicates areas of overlap. The red region extends under the lateral part of the temporal lobe. These data suggest that object memory is organized as a distributed system in which the attributes of an object are stored close to the regions of the cortex that mediate the perception of those attributes. Activation in the parietal lobe is likely related to the movements associated with actions, and in the frontal lobe to the spontaneous generation of behavior. Adapted from "Discrete Cortical Regions Associated with Knowledge of Color and Knowledge of Action," by A. Martin, J. V. Haxby, F. M. Lalonde, C. L. Wiggs, and L. G. Ungerleider, 1995, *Science, 270,* p. 104.

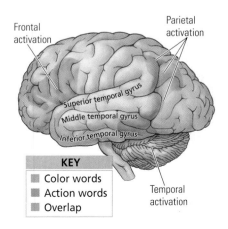

Frontal activation

Parietal activation

Superior temporal gyrus

Middle temporal gyrus

Inferior temporal gyrus

Temporal activation

KEY
- ■ Color words
- ■ Action words
- ■ Overlap

Episodic memory. Autobiographical memory for events pegged to specific place and time contexts.

○ For additional information on episodic amnesia, visit the Chapter 13 Web links on the *Brain and Behavior* Web site (**www.worthpublishers. com/kolb**).

temporal gyrus, just anterior to the area controlling the perception of motion. This distribution of neural activation shows not only that object memory is at least partly located in the temporal lobe but also that it is found in regions associated with the original perception of the objects.

What Is Special about Personal Memories?

One aspect of memory that is unique to each of us is our personal, or autobiographical, memory. This **episodic memory** includes not only a record of events (episodes) that took place but also our presence there and our role in the events. Our personal experiences form the basis of who we are and the rules by which we live. That is, we have memories not only for events but also for their context at a particular time in a particular place. We thus have a concept of time and a sense of our personal role in a changing world.

Imagine what would happen if we lost our personal memory? We would still recall events that took place, but we would be unable to see our role in them. People with frontal-lobe injuries sometimes exhibit such symptoms, as illustrated in a case described by Endel Tulving (2002).

K. C. had a serious traumatic brain injury in a motorcycle accident that produced multiple cortical and subcortical lesions. What is remarkable about K. C., however, is that his cognitive abilities are intact and indistinguishable from most normal healthy adults. He can still play chess and the organ, and his short-term memory is intact. He knows who he is, when his birthday is, the names of schools that he attended, the location of the family cottage, and so on.

What K. C. cannot do is recall any personally experienced events. This episodic amnesia covers his entire life, from birth until the present. Thus, whereas he knows facts about himself, he has no memory for events that included him personally. For example, he is unable to describe an event that took place in school that specifically included him, while at the same time recalling going to school and the knowledge that he gained there.

Findings from neuroimaging studies of people with episodic amnesia suggest that they consistently have frontal-lobe injuries (Lepage et al., 2000), but exactly why these lesions produce episodic amnesia is still unclear. Nonetheless, Tulving made the interesting proposal that episodic memory is a marvel of nature: it transforms the brain into a kind of time machine that allows us to dwell on the past and make plans for the future. He goes further to suggest that this ability may be unique to humans and is presumably due to some novel evolutionary development of the frontal lobe.

Not all people with episodic amnesia have brain injury, however. Many case reports describe patients with massive memory disturbances resulting from some sort of "psychiatric" or "psychogenic" disorder. Such cases have been fodder for numerous movie plots.

Hans Markowitsch (2003) noted that the amnesia reported in some of these cases is remarkably similar to episodic amnesia seen in neurological patients. Neuroimaging of patients with psychogenic amnesia shows a massive reduction in brain activity in frontal regions that is remarkably similar to that seen in neurological patients with episodic amnesia (**Figure 13-7**). Therefore patients with psychogenic amnesias can be assumed to have a dysfunction of frontal-brain activity that acts to block the retrieval of autobiographical memory.

Figure 13-7

Lost Episodes Horizontal images through the brains of two patients with selective retrograde amnesia for autobiographical information. The section on the left is from an amnesic patient who had a brain infection (herpes simplex encephalitis). The right frontal and temporal lobes are dark, owing to a metabolic reduction in the right temporofrontal region (arrow). The section on the right shows the brain of a patient with psychogenic amnesia. Again, a significant metabolic reduction is visible in the right temporofrontal area (arrow). From "Functional Neuroimaging Correlates of Functional Amnesia," by H. J. Markowitsch, 1999, *Memory 7*, Plate 2. Reprinted by permission of Psychology Press Ltd., Hove.

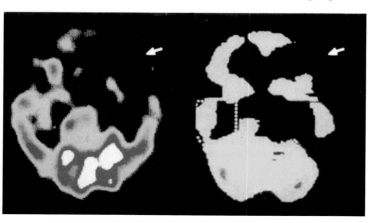

In Review

Among the multiple forms of learning, a process that results in a relatively permanent change in behavior as a result of experience, a primary distinction can be made between Pavlovian conditioning, in which some environmental stimulus (such as a tone) is paired with a reward, and operant conditioning, in which a response (such as pushing a button) is paired with a reward. The demands on the nervous system are different in the two types of learning, and so we can expect that the regions of the brain related to each learning form will be different.

Memory is the ability to recall or recognize previous experience; this definition implies the existence of a memory trace, or a mental representation of a previous experience. There are many forms of memory, each related to mental representations in different parts of the brain. One useful distinction is between implicit memory, in which information is unconsciously learned, and explicit memory, which is conscious memory for specific information. The mental representations of implicit and explicit memory are held in different regions of the brain. Another form of memory, episodic memory, is autobiographical and unique to each person.

DISSOCIATING MEMORY CIRCUITS

Beginning in the 1920s and continuing until the early 1950s, American psychologist Karl Lashley looked for the neural circuits underlying memory for the solutions to mazes learned by laboratory rats and monkeys. Lashley's working hypothesis was that memories must be represented in the perceptual and motor circuitry used to learn solutions to problems. He believed that, if he removed bits of this circuitry or made knife cuts that disconnected it, amnesia should result.

In fact, however, neither procedure produced amnesia. Lashley found that the severity of the memory disturbance was related to the size of the injury rather than to its location. In 1951, after 30 years of searching, Lashley concluded that he had failed to find the location of the memory trace, although he did believe that he knew where it was *not* located (Lashley, 1960).

Ironically, just two years later William Scoville made a serendipitous discovery that had not been predicted by Lashley's studies. On August 23, 1953, Scoville performed a bilateral medial-temporal-lobe resection on a young man who became known as Case H. M. H. M. had severe epilepsy that was not controlled by medication. Like Wilder Penfield (see Chapter 9), Scoville was a neurosurgeon who was attempting to rid people of seizures by removing the abnormal brain tissue that was causing them.

H. M.'s seizures were originating in the medial temporal region, which includes the amygdala, hippocampal formation, and associated cortical structures, and so Scoville removed them bilaterally, leaving the more lateral temporal lobe tissue intact. As shown in **Figure 13-8**, the removal included the anterior part of the hippocampus,

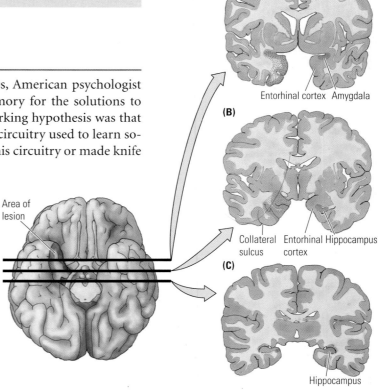

Figure 13-8

Extent of H. M.'s Surgery H. M.'s brain viewed ventrally, with the right-hemisphere lesion highlighted. The left side of the brain has been left intact to show the relative location of the medial temporal structures. Because the lesion runs along the wall of the medial temporal lobe, it can be seen in several cross sections of the brain. Parts A, B, and C, based on MRI scans, depict such sections of H. M.'s brain. Adapted from "H. M.'s Medial Temporal Lobe Lesion: Findings from Magnetic Resonance Imaging," by S. Corkin, D. G. Amaral, R. G. Gonzalez , K. A. Johnson, and B. T. Hyman, 1997, *Journal of Neuroscience, 17*, p. 3966.

For additional information about the role played by the hippocampus in memory function, visit the Chapter 13 Web links on the *Brain and Behavior* Web site (**www.worthpublishers. com/kolb**).

the amygdala, and the adjacent cortex. The behavioral symptoms that Scoville noted after the second surgery were completely unexpected, and so he invited Brenda Milner, one of Penfield's associates, to study H. M. Milner and her colleagues have studied H. M. for more than 50 years, making him the most studied case in neuroscience (e.g., Corkin, 2002).

H. M.'s most remarkable symptom is severe amnesia: he is unable to recall anything that has happened since his surgery in 1953. H. M. still has an above-average I.Q. score (118 on the Wechsler Adult Intelligence Scale; 100 is average), and he performs normally on perceptual tests. Furthermore, his recall of events from his childhood and school days is intact. Socially, H. M. is well mannered, and he can engage in sophisticated conversations. However, he cannot recall events that have just happened. H. M. has no explicit memory.

In one study by Suzanne Corkin, H. M. was given a tray of hospital food, which he ate. A few minutes later, he was given another tray. He did not recall having eaten the first meal and proceeded to eat another. A third tray was brought, and this time he ate only the dessert, complaining that he did not seem to be very hungry.

To understand the implications and severity of H. M.'s condition, one need only consider a few events in his postsurgical life. His father died, but H. M. continued to ask where his father was, only to experience anew the grief of hearing that his father had passed away. (Eventually H. M. stopped asking about his father, suggesting that some type of learning had taken place.)

Similarly, when in the hospital, he typically asks, with many apologies, if the nurses can tell him where he is and how he came to be there. He remarked on one occasion, "Every day is alone in itself, whatever enjoyment I've had, and whatever sorrow I've had." His experience is that of a person who perceives his surroundings but cannot comprehend the situation that he is in because he does not remember what has gone before.

Formal tests of H. M.'s memory show what one would expect: he cannot recall specific information just presented. In contrast, his implicit-memory performance is nearly intact. He performs normally on tests such as the incomplete-figure or pursuit-rotor tasks illustrated in Figures 13-4 and 13-5. Whatever systems are required for implicit memory must therefore be intact, but those systems crucial to explicit memory are misssing or dysfunctional. Another case, similar to that of H. M., is discussed in "Patient Boswell's Amnesia." Curiously, H. M. can recognize faces, including his own face, and he recognizes that he has aged. Face recognition depends on the parahippocampal gyrus, which is partly intact on H. M.'s right side.

There are probably several reasons why Lashley did not find a syndrome like that shown by H. M. Most important, Lashley did not use tests of explicit memory, and so his animal subjects would not have shown H. M.'s deficits. Rather, Lashley's tests were mostly measures of implicit memory, with which H. M. has no problems. The following case illustrates that Lashley probably should have been looking in the basal ganglia for deficits revealed by his tests of implicit memory.

J. K. was born on June 28, 1914. He was above average in intelligence and worked as a petroleum engineer for 45 years. In his mid-70s, he began to show symptoms of Parkinson's disease, and, at about age 78, he started to have memory difficulties. (Recall that, in Parkinson's disease, the projections from the dopaminergic cells of the brainstem to the basal ganglia die.)

Curiously, J. K.'s memory disturbance was related to tasks that he had done all his life. On one occasion, he stood at the door of his bedroom frustrated by his inability to recall how to turn on the lights. He remarked, "I must be crazy. I've done this all my life and now I can't remember how to do it!" On another occasion, he was seen trying to turn the radio off with the television's remote control. This time he explained, "I don't recall how to turn off the radio so I thought I would try this thing!"

Patient Boswell's Amnesia

Focus on Disorders

Boswell is a man who, at the age of 48, developed a brain infection known as herpes simplex encephalitis. Before his illness, Boswell had had 13 years of schooling and had worked for nearly 30 years in the newspaper advertising business. By all accounts, he was successful in his profession and was a normal, well-adjusted person.

Boswell recovered from the acute symptoms of the disease, which included seizures and a 3-day coma. His post-disease intelligence was low average, probably owing to the neurological damage caused by the disease. Nonetheless, his speech and language remained normal in every respect, and he suffered no defects of sensory perception or of movement.

But Boswell was left with a severe amnesic syndrome. If he hears a short paragraph and is asked to describe its main points, he routinely gets scores of zero. He can only guess the day's date and is unable even to guess what year it is. When asked what city he is in, he simply guesses. He does know his place of birth, and he can correctly recall his birth date about half the time. In sum, Boswell has a severe amnesia for events both before and since his encephalitis. He does show implicit memory, however, on tests such as the pursuit-rotor task (see Figure 13-5).

Boswell's amnesia has been extensively investigated by Antonio Damasio and his colleagues (1989), and his brain pathology is now well documented. The critical damage is a bilateral destruction of the medial temporal regions and a loss of the basal forebrain and the posterior part of the orbital frontal cortex. In addition, Boswell has lost the insular cortex, which is found in the lateral fissure and not visible in the adjoining illustration.

In contrast, his sensory and motor cortices are intact, as are his basal ganglia. Boswell's injury is thus more extensive than H. M.'s. Like H. M., he has a loss of new memories, but, unlike H. M., he also has a severe loss of access to old information, probably because of his insular and prefrontal injuries. Nonetheless, again like H. M., Boswell has an intact procedural memory, a fact that illustrates the dissociation between neural circuits underlying explicit and implicit forms of memory.

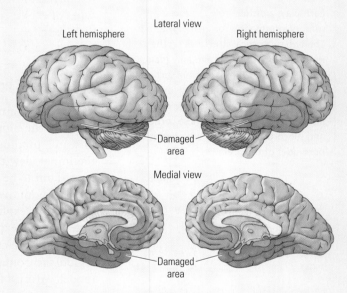

After a herpes simplex encephalitis infection, patient Boswell has severe amnesia and has difficulty remembering events before and after his illness. This model highlights the areas of damage in the medial temporal region, the basal forebrain, and the posterior orbital frontal cortex. Compare Figure 13-7.

J. K. clearly had a deficit in implicit memory. In contrast, he was aware of daily events and could recall explicit events as well as most men his age. He could still speak intelligently on issues of the day that he had just read about. Once when we visited him, one of us entered the room first and he immediately asked where the other was, even though it had been 2 weeks since we told him that we would be coming to visit.

This intact long-term memory is very different from the situation of H. M., who would not have remembered that anybody was coming, even 5 min after being told. Because Parkinson's disease primarily affects the basal ganglia, J. K.'s deficit in implicit memory was likely related to his basal ganglia dysfunction.

In Review

To identify the circuits responsible for memory, it is important to separate explicit memory from implicit memory. Explicit memory relies on the anterior part of the hippocampus, the amygdala, and the adjacent cortex. These areas were damaged in H. M.'s brain, and so he had no explicit memory. An implicit-memory deficit indicates deterioration of the basal ganglia characteristic of Parkinson's disease, as seen in patients such as J. K.

NEURAL SYSTEMS UNDERLYING EXPLICIT AND IMPLICIT MEMORIES

Findings from laboratory studies, largely on rats and monkeys, have shown that the symptoms of patients such as H. M. and J. K. can be reproduced in animals by injuring the medial temporal region and basal ganglia, respectively. Other structures, most notably in the frontal and temporal lobes, also have been found to play roles in certain types of explicit memory. We now consider the systems for explicit and implicit memory separately.

Neural Circuit for Explicit Memories

The dramatic amnesic syndrome discovered in H. M. in the 1950s led investigators to focus on the hippocampus, which at the time was regarded as a large brain structure in search of a function. However, because H. M. has damage to other structures, too, the initial view that the hippocampus is the location of explicit-memory processing turned out to be incorrect. It took several decades of anatomical and behavioral studies to sort out the complexities, but, by the mid-1990s, a consensus began to emerge on a theory for explicit memory. Note that, if you consult books or reviews published before then, the explanation may be quite different (see Gazzaniga, 2000).

The prime candidates for a role in explicit memory include the medial temporal region, the frontal cortex, and structures closely related to them. Before considering the model, we must first revisit the anatomy of the medial temporal region. As we do so, it is important to keep in mind the studies by Martin and colleagues, discussed earlier (look again at Figure 13-6). Findings from those studies showed that memories of the color and motion characteristics of objects reside in separate locations in the temporal lobe and thus that the medial temporal region must have multiple sensory inputs.

The macaque monkey has been the principal subject of anatomical study on the medial temporal region, and there are likely few differences between macaques and humans in this respect. Three medial temporal cortical regions, in addition to the hippocampus and amygdala, take part in explicit memory. As illustrated in **Figure 13-9**, these regions, which lie adjacent to the hippocampus, are the **entorhinal cortex,** the **parahippocampal cortex,** and the **perirhinal cortex** (from the Greek *para*, meaning "beside," and *rhinal*, from the rhinal, or nasal, sulcus on the bottom of the brain).

A sequential arrangement of connections, charted in **Figure 13-10,** shows that the major cortical regions project to the perirhinal and parahippocampal cortices, which in turn project to the entorhinal cortex. The prominent input

Figure 13-9

Medial Temporal Cortex and Subcortical Structures The brain of a rhesus monkey viewed ventrally, showing the medial temporal regions on the left. Each plays a distinct role in processing sensory information for memory storage. The two subcortical structures on the right, the hippocampus and amygdala, are not directly visible from the surface of the brain, because they lie within the medial temporal cortical regions illustrated on the left. All these cortical and subcortical structures are present on both sides of the brain.

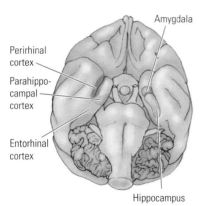

Figure 13-10

Reciprocal Medial Temporal Connections Input from the sensory cortices flows to the parahippocampal and perirhinal regions, then to the entorhinal cortex, and, finally, to the hippocampus, which then feeds back to the medial temporal regions that connect to the neocortical regions.

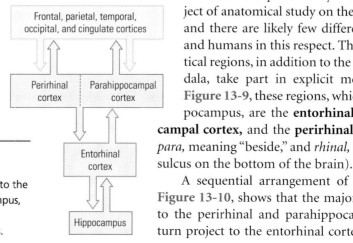

from the neocortex to the perirhinal region is from the visual regions of the ventral stream coursing through the temporal lobe. The perirhinal region is thus a prime candidate for visual object memory.

Similarly, the parahippocampal cortex has a strong input from regions of the parietal cortex believed to take part in visuospatial processing. Thus, the parahippocampal region likely has a role in visuospatial memory. Because both the perirhinal and the parahippocampal regions project to the entorhinal cortex, this region likely participates in more-integrative forms of memory. Indeed, the entorhinal cortex is the first to show cell death in Alzheimer's disease. Recall from Chapter 5 that Alzheimer's disease is a form of dementia characterized by severe deficits in explicit memory (see "Alzheimer's Disease" on page 498).

Entorhinal cortex. Located on the medial surface of the temporal lobe; provides a major route for neocortical input to the hippocampal formation; often degenerates in Alzheimer's disease.

Parahippocampal cortex. Cortex located along the dorsal medial surface of the temporal lobe.

Perirhinal cortex. Cortex lying next to the rhinal fissure on the base of the brain.

THE HIPPOCAMPUS AND SPATIAL MEMORY

We are left with a conundrum. If the hippocampus is not the key structure in explicit memory yet is the recipient of the entorhinal connections, what does it do? The answer is that the hippocampus is probably engaged in processes requiring the memory for places, such as recalling the location of an object. This idea was first advanced by John O'Keefe and Lynn Nadel in 1978.

Certainly, both laboratory animals and human patients with selective hippocampal injury have severe deficits in various forms of spatial memory. Rats with hippocampal damage have great difficulty solving spatial-navigation tasks such as those shown in Figure 13-3. Similarly, monkeys with hippocampal lesions have difficulty learning the location of objects, as can be demonstrated in tasks such as those illustrated in **Figure 13-11**.

Monkeys are trained to displace objects to obtain a food reward (Figure 13-11A). After they have learned how to do so, they are given one of two tasks. In the *visual-recognition task* shown in Figure 13-11B, the animal displaces a sample object to obtain a food reward. After a short delay, the animal is presented with two objects, one of which is novel. The task is to learn that the novel object must be displaced to obtain a food reward. This task is a test of explicit visual object memory. Monkeys with perirhinal lesions are impaired at the visual-recognition task.

In the *object-position task* in Figure 13-11C, the monkey is shown one object, which is displaced for a food reward. Then the monkey is shown the same object along with a second, identical one. The task is to learn that the object that is in the same position as it was in the initial presentation must be displaced. Monkeys with hippocampal lesions are selectively impaired at this object-position task.

From the results of these studies on the hippocampus, we would predict that animals with especially good spatial memories should have bigger hippocampi than do species with poorer spatial memories. David Sherry and his colleagues (1992) tested this hypothesis in birds. Many birds are cachers: they take foods, such as sunflower seeds, and hide (cache) them for later consumption. Some birds can find hundreds of items that they have cached. To evaluate whether the hippocampus

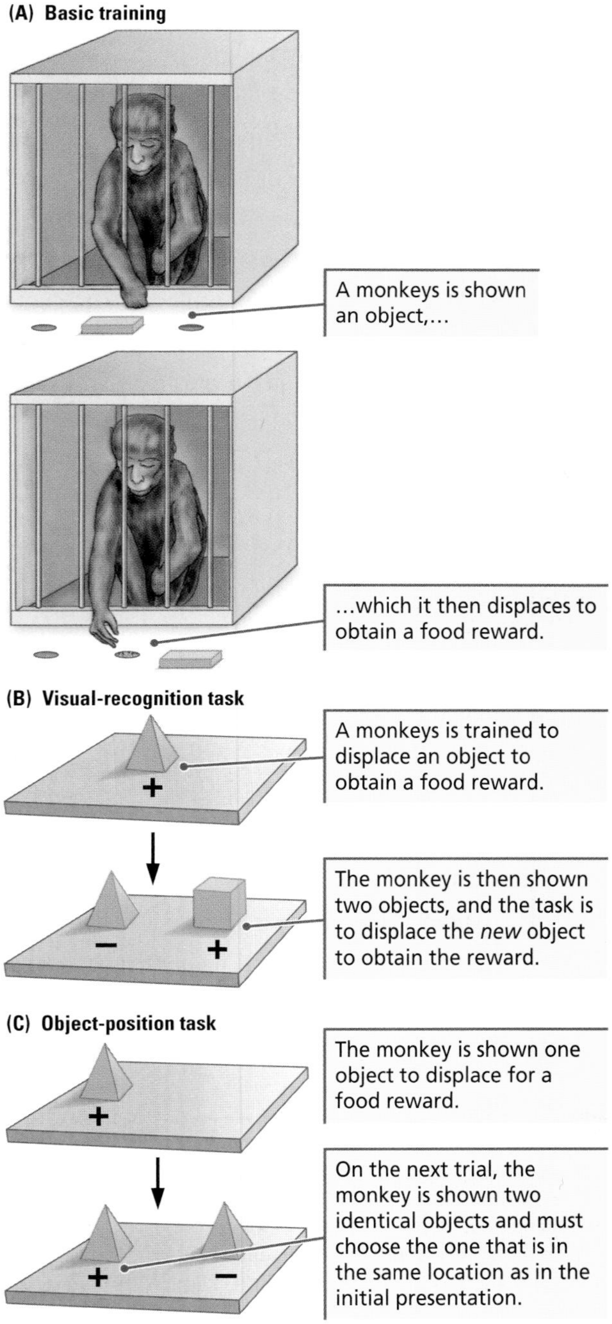

(A) Basic training

A monkeys is shown an object,...

...which it then displaces to obtain a food reward.

(B) Visual-recognition task

A monkeys is trained to displace an object to obtain a food reward.

The monkey is then shown two objects, and the task is to displace the *new* object to obtain the reward.

(C) Object-position task

The monkey is shown one object to displace for a food reward.

On the next trial, the monkey is shown two identical objects and must choose the one that is in the same location as in the initial presentation.

Figure 13-11

Two Memory Tasks for Monkeys (A) In "basic training," a monkey learns to displace an object to obtain a food reward. (B) and (C) The plus and minus signs indicate whether the object is (+) or is not (−) associated with food.

Focus on Disorders

Alzheimer's Disease

That the brain undergoes atrophy with aging was noted in the 1880s, but the reason was not really understood until German physician Alois Alzheimer published a landmark study in 1906. Alzheimer reported on a 51-year-old woman for whom he described a set of behavioral symptoms and associated neuropathology. In particular, the woman was demented and had various abnormalities in the cellular structure of the cerebral cortex, including both the neocortex and the limbic cortex.

An estimated 1 million people are now affected by Alzheimer's disease in the United States, although the only certain diagnostic test remains postmortem examination of cerebral tissue. The disease progresses slowly, and many people with Alzheimer's disease probably die from other causes before the cognitive symptoms become incapacitating. We knew of a physics professor who continued to work until he was nearly 80 years old, at which time he succumbed to a heart attack. Postmortem examination of his brain revealed significant Alzheimer's pathology. His slipping memory had been attributed by his colleagues to "old timer's disease."

The cause of Alzheimer's disease remains unknown, although it has been variously attributed to genetic predisposition, abnormal levels of trace elements (e.g., aluminum), immune reactions, and slow viruses. Two principal neuronal changes take place in Alzheimer's disease:

1. *Loss of cholinergic cells in the basal forebrain.* One treatment for Alzheimer's disease, therefore, is to provide medication to increase acetylcholine levels in the forebrain. An example is Cognex, which is the trade name for tacrine hydrochloride, a cholinergic agonist that appears to provide temporary relief from the progression of the disease.

2. *Development of neuritic plaques in the cerebral cortex.* A **neuritic plaque** consists of a central core of homogeneous protein material *(amyloid)*, surrounded by degenerative cellular fragments. The cortical plaques, illustrated here, are not distributed evenly throughout the cortex but are concentrated especially in the temporal-lobe areas related to memory. The plaques are often associated with another abnormality, neurofibrillary tangles, which are paired helical filaments found in both the cerebral cortex and the hippocampus.

Cortical neurons begin to deteriorate as the cholinergic loss and plaques develop. The first cells to die are in the entorhinal cortex, and significant memory disturbance ensues.

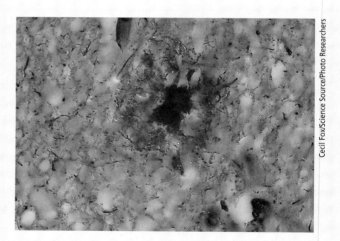

Neuritic plaque, as often found in the cerebral cortices of Alzheimer patients. The amyloid is the dark spot in the center of the image, which is surrounded by the residue of degenerated cells.

Cecil Fox/Science Source/Photo Researchers

Neuritic plaque. Area of incomplete necrosis (dead tissue) consisting of a central protein core (amyloid) surrounded by degenerative cellular fragments; often seen in the cortex of people with senile dementias such as Alzheimer's disease.

plays a role in this activity, Sherry and his coworkers measured hippocampal size in bird species that are closely related, but only one of which is a food cacher.

As shown in **Figure 13-12**, the hippocampal formation is larger in birds that cache food than in birds that do not. In fact, the hippocampus of food-storing birds is more than twice as large as expected for birds of their brain size and body weight. Sherry found a similar relation when he compared different species of food-storing rodents.

Rodents such as Merriam's kangaroo rat, which stores food in various places through-out its territory, have larger hippocampi than those of rodents such as the bannertail kangaroo rat, which stores food only in its burrow. Hippocampal size in both birds and mammals appears to be related to the cognitive demands of foraging and food storing, which are highly spatial activities.

One prediction that we might make from the Sherry experiments is that people who have jobs with high spatial demands might have large hippocampi. Taxi drivers in London fit this category. To qualify for a cab driver's license in London, candidates must pass an extensive examination demonstrating that they know the location of every street in that huge and ancient city.

Eleanor Maguire and her colleagues (2000), using magnetic resonance imaging (MRI), found the posterior region of the hippocampus in London taxi drivers to be significantly larger than in the control subjects. This finding presumably explains why this select group is able to pass a spatial-memory test that most of us would fail miserably.

RECIPROCAL CONNECTIONS FOR EXPLICIT MEMORY

A key feature of the medial temporal pathway of explicit memory is that it is reciprocal. That is, the connections from the neocortex run to the entorhinal cortex and then back to the neocortex (see Figure 13-10). These reciprocal connections have two benefits:

1. Signals that the medial temporal regions send back to the cortical sensory regions keep the sensory experience alive in the brain. Therefore the neural record of an experience outlasts the actual experience.
2. The pathway back to the cortex means that the neocortex is kept apprised of information being processed in the medial temporal regions. We shall see that such feedback does not happen in the basal ganglia systems taking part in implicit memory, which may help to explain the unconscious nature of implicit memory.

Although we have focused on the role of the medial temporal regions, other structures also are important in explicit memory. People with frontal-lobe injuries are not amnesic like H. M. or J. K., but they do have difficulties with memory for the temporal order of events. Imagine that you are shown a series of photographs and asked to remember them. A few minutes later, you are asked whether you recognize two photographs and, if so, to indicate which one you saw first.

H. M. would not remember the photographs. People with frontal-lobe injuries would recall seeing the photographs but would have difficulty recalling which one they had seen most recently. The role of the frontal lobe in explicit memory is clearly more subtle than that of the medial temporal lobe. But just what is that role?

All the sensory systems in the brain send information to the frontal lobe, as do the medial temporal regions. This information is not used for direct sensory analysis, and so it must have some other purpose. In general, the frontal lobe appears to have a role in many forms of short-term memory.

Joaquin Fuster (e.g., Fuster, Bodner, & Kroger, 2000) studied single-cell activity in the frontal lobe during short-term-memory tasks. For example, if monkeys are shown an object that they must remember for a short time before being allowed to make a response, neurons in the prefrontal cortex will show a sustained firing during the delay. Consider the tests illustrated in **Figure 13-13:**

■ A monkey is shown a light, which is the cue, and then must make a response after a delay.

■ In the *delayed-response task,* the monkey is shown two lights in the choice test and must choose the one that is in the same location as the cue.

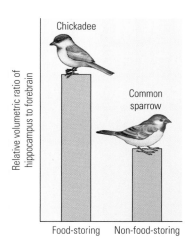

Figure 13-12

Inferring Spatial Memory This graph relates hippocampal volume to forebrain volume in 3 food-storing (left) and 10 non-food-storing (right) families of songbirds. The hippocampi of birds that cache food, such as the black-capped chickadee, are about twice as large as the hippocampi of birds, such as the sparrow, that do not. Data from "Spatial Memory and Adaptive Specialization of the Hippocampus," by D. F. Sherry, L. F. Jacobs, and S. J. C. Gaulin, 1992, *Trends in Neuroscience, 15,* pp. 298–303.

■ In the *delayed-alternation task,* the monkey is again shown two lights in the choice tests but now must choose the light that is *not* in the same location as the cue.

■ Finally, in the *delayed-matching-to-sample task,* the monkey is shown, say, a red light, and then, after a delay, is shown a red and a green light. The task is to choose the red light, irrespective of its new location.

Fuster has found that, in each task, certain cells in the prefrontal cortex will fire throughout the delay. Animals that have not learned the task show no such cell activity. Curiously, if a trained animal makes an error, the activity of the cells corresponds to it: the cells stop responding before the error occurs. In a real sense, the cells have "forgotten" the cue.

People who have chronically abused alcohol can develop an explicit-memory disturbance known as **Korsakoff's syndrome.** Such people have severe deficits in explicit memory and, in some cases, in implicit memory as well. This syndrome is caused by a thiamine (vitamin B_1) deficiency that results from poor nutrition (alcohol abusers often neglect to eat) and the fact that alcohol inhibits the body's ability to absorb vitamin B_1.

The effect of the B_1 deficiency is to produce cell death in the medial part of the diencephalon (the "between brain"; see Chapter 2), including the medial thalamus and mammillary bodies of the hypothalamus. In addition, 80 percent of Korsakoff patients have atrophy (loss of cells) of the frontal lobes. The memory disturbance is probably so severe in many Korsakoff patients because the damage includes not only the frontal lobe but medial temporal structures as well (see "Korsakoff's Syndrome" on page 502).

Mortimer Mishkin and his colleagues (Mishkin, 1982; Murray, 2000) at the U.S. National Institute of Mental Health proposed a circuit for explicit memory that incorporates the evidence from both humans and laboratory animals having injuries to the temporal and frontal lobes. **Figure 13-14** presents a modified version of the Mishkin model that includes not only the frontal and temporal lobes but also the medial thalamus, which is implicated in Korsakoff's syndrome, and the activating systems from the basal forebrain, which are implicated in Alzheimer's disease:

In the following tests, a monkey is shown a light, which is the cue, and then it makes a response after a delay.

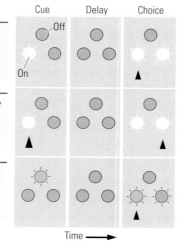

Delayed-response task: The monkey must choose the light that is in the same location as the cue.

Delayed-alternation task: The monkey must choose the light that is not in the same location as the cue.

Delayed-matching-to-sample task: The monkey must choose the light that is the same color as the cue.

Cue   Delay   Choice

Time ⟶

Figure 13-13

Testing Short-Term Memory (*Top*) A monkey performing a short-term memory task responds by pressing the disc to get a fruit juice reward. (*Bottom*) The correct disc varies, depending on the requirements of the task. The correct choice for each task is indicated by an arrow. Adapted from *Memory in the Cerebral Cortex* (p. 178), by J. Fuster, 1995, Cambridge, MA: MIT Press.

■ The sensory neocortical areas send their connections to the medial temporal regions, which are in turn connected to the medial thalamus and prefrontal cortex.

■ The basal forebrain structures are hypothesized to play a role in the maintenance of appropriate levels of activity in the forebrain structures so that they can process information.

■ The temporal-lobe structures are hypothesized to be central to the formation of long-term explicit memories.

■ The prefrontal cortex is central to the maintenance of temporary (short-term) explicit memories as well as memory for the recency (chronological order) of explicit events.

Neural Circuit for Implicit Memories

Hypothesizing that the basal ganglia are central to implicit memory, Mishkin and his colleagues (Mishkin, 1982; Mishkin et al., 1997) also proposed a circuit for implicit memories. As **Figure 13-15** shows, the basal ganglia receive input from the entire neocortex and

(A)

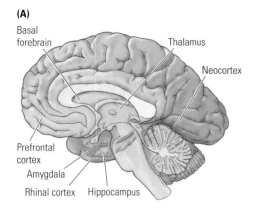

Basal forebrain
Thalamus
Neocortex
Prefrontal cortex
Amygdala
Rhinal cortex   Hippocampus

(B)

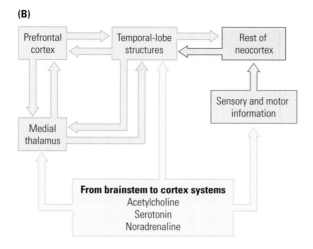

From brainstem to cortex systems
Acetylcholine
Serotonin
Noradrenaline

Figure 13-14

Neural Circuit Proposed for Explicit Memory
(A) General neuroanatomical areas controlling explicit memory. **(B)** Circuit diagram showing the flow of information, beginning with inputs from the sensory and motor systems, which are not considered part of the memory circuit.

(A)

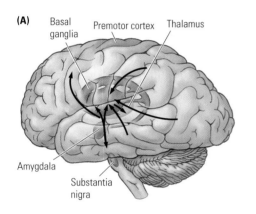

Basal ganglia   Premotor cortex   Thalamus
Amygdala
Substantia nigra

(B)

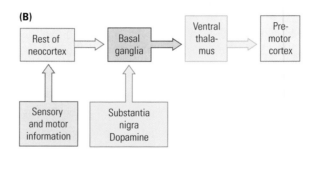

Rest of neocortex → Basal ganglia → Ventral thalamus → Premotor cortex
Sensory and motor information
Substantia nigra Dopamine

Figure 13-15

Unidirectional Neural Circuit Proposed for Implicit Memory
(A) General anatomical areas controlling implicit memory. **(B)** Circuit diagram showing the unidirectional flow of information, beginning with inputs from the sensory and motor systems, which are not considered part of the memory circuit.

send projections to the ventral thalamus and then to the premotor cortex. The basal ganglia also receive widely and densely distributed projections from dopamine-producing cells in the substantia nigra. Dopamine appears to be necessary for circuits in the basal ganglia to function, and so it may indirectly participate in implicit-memory formation.

The connection from the cortex to the basal ganglia in the implicit-memory system is unidirectional. Thus, most of the neocortex receives no direct information regarding the activities of the basal ganglia, which Mishkin believes accounts for the unconscious nature of implicit memories. In order for memories to be conscious, there must be direct feedback to the neocortical regions involved. (Recall that, in the explicit-memory system, the medial temporal regions send connections back to the neocortical regions.)

Mishkin's model shows why people with dysfunction of the basal ganglia, as occurs in Parkinson's disease, have deficits in implicit memory, whereas people with injuries to the frontal or temporal lobes have relatively good implicit memories, even though they may have profound disturbances of explicit memory. In fact, some people with Alzheimer's disease are able to play games expertly, even though they have no recollection of having played them before. Daniel Schacter (1983) wrote of a golfer with Alzheimer's disease who retained his ability to play golf, despite some impairment of his explicit knowledge of the events of having played a round, as indexed by his inability to find shots or to remember his strokes on each hole. This man's medial temporal system was severely compromised by the disease, but his basal ganglia were unaffected.

○ To review the locations of the basal ganglia, visit the section on subcortical structures on your *Foundations of Behavioral Neuroscience* CD. (See the Preface for more information about this CD.)

Korsakoff's syndrome. Permanent loss of the ability to learn new information (anterograde amnesia) and to retrieve old information (retrograde amnesia) caused by diencephalic damage resulting from chronic alcoholism or malnutrition that produces a vitamin B_1 deficiency.

Korsakoff's Syndrome

Focus on Disorders

Over the long term, alcoholism, especially when accompanied by malnutrition, produces defects of memory. Joe R. was a 62-year-old man who was hospitalized because his family complained that his memory had become abysmal. His intelligence was in the average range, and he had no obvious sensory or motor difficulties. Nevertheless, he was unable to say why he was in the hospital and usually stated that he was actually in a hotel.

When asked what he had done the previous night, he typically said that he "went to the Legion for a few beers with the boys." Although he had, in fact, been in the hospital, it was a sensible response because that is what he had done on most nights in the preceding 30 years. Joe R. was not certain of what he had done for a living but believed that he had been a butcher. In fact, he had been a truck driver for a local delivery firm. His son was a butcher, however, and so, once again, his story was related to something in his life.

Joe's memory for immediate events was little better. On one occasion, we asked him to remember having met us, and then we left the room. On our return 2 or 3 minutes later, he had no recollection of ever having met us or of having taken psychological tests that we administered.

Joe R. had Korsakoff's syndrome, a condition named after Sergei Korsakoff, a Russian physician who in the 1880s first called attention to a syndrome that accompanies chronic alcoholism. The most obvious symptom is severe loss of memory, including amnesia for both information learned in the past (**retrograde amnesia**) and information learned since the onset of the memory disturbance (**anterograde amnesia**). One unique characteristic of the amnesic syndrome in Korsakoff patients is that they tend to make up stories about past events, rather than admit that they do not remember. Like those of Joe R., however, these stories are generally plausible because they are based on actual experiences.

Curiously, Korsakoff patients have little insight into their memory disturbance and are generally indifferent to suggestions that they have a memory problem. In fact, such patients are generally apathetic to things going on around them. Joe R. was often seen watching television when the set was not turned on.

The cause of Korsakoff's syndrome is a thiamine (vitamin B_1) deficiency resulting from prolonged intake of large quantities of alcohol. Joe R. had a long history of drinking a 26-ounce bottle of rum every day, in addition to a "few beers with the boys." The thiamine deficiency results in the death of cells in the midline diencephalon, including especially the medial regions of the thalamus and the mammillary bodies of the hypothalamus.

Most Korsakoff patients also show cortical atrophy, especially in the frontal lobe. With the appearance of the Korsakoff symptoms, which can happen quite suddenly, prognosis is poor. Only about 20 percent of patients show much recovery after a year on a vitamin B_1–enriched diet. Joe R. has shown no recovery after several years and will spend the rest of his life in a hospital setting.

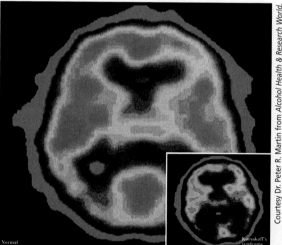

Courtesy Dr. Peter R. Martin from *Alcohol Health & Research World*, Spring 1985, 9, cover.

These PET scans, from a normal patient (larger image) and a Korsakoff patient (inset), demonstrate reduced activity in the frontal lobe of the diseased brain. (The frontal lobes are at the bottom center of each scan.) Red and yellow represent areas of high metabolic activity versus the lower level of activity in the darker areas.

Neural Circuit for Emotional Memories

We now consider a third type of memory, **emotional memory.** Whether emotional memories are implicit or explicit is not altogether clear; in fact, they seemingly could be both. Certainly people can react with fear to specific stimuli that they can identify, and we have seen that they can also fear situations for which they do not seem to have specific memories.

Indeed, a common pathology is a panic disorder in which people show marked anxiety but cannot identify a specific cause. For this reason, emotional memory can be seen as a special form of memory. Emotional memory also has a unique anatomical component—namely, the amygdala—discussed in detail in Chapter 11 and mentioned earlier in the present chapter in regard to fear conditioning, in which the amygdala seems to be responsible for our feelings of anxiety toward stimuli that by themselves would not normally produce fear.

Emotional memory has been studied most thoroughly in fear conditioning by pairing noxious stimuli, such as foot shock, with a tone (see Experiment 13-1). Michael Davis (1992) and Joseph LeDoux (1995) used this type of experiment to demonstrate that the amygdala is critical to emotional memory. Damage to the amygdala abolishes emotional memory but has little effect on implicit or explicit memory.

The amygdala has close connections with the medial temporal cortical structures, as well as with the rest of the cortex. It sends projections to structures controlling the production of autonomic responses—namely, the hypothalamus and periaqueductal gray matter (PAG) of the brainstem (**Figure 13-16**). In addition, the amygdala is connected to the implicit-memory system through its connections with the basal ganglia. The amygdala has connections to systems that control autonomic functions (e.g., blood pressure and heart rate) as well as connections to the hypothalamus and its control of hormonal systems.

Fear is not the only type of emotional memory that is coded by the amygdala. A study of severely demented patients by Bob Sainsbury and Marjorie Coristine (1986) nicely illustrates this point. The patients were believed to have severe cortical abnormalities but intact amygdalar functioning.

The researchers first established that the ability of these patients to recognize photographs of close relatives was severely impaired. The patients were then shown four photographs, one of which depicted a relative (either a sibling or a child) who had visited in the past 2 weeks. The task was to identify the person whom they liked better than the others. Although the subjects were unaware that they knew anyone in the group of photographs, they consistently preferred the photographs of their relatives. This result suggests that, although the explicit, and probably implicit, memory of the

Retrograde amnesia. Inability to remember events that took place before the onset of amnesia.

Anterograde amnesia. Inability to remember events subsequent to a disturbance of the brain such as head trauma, electroconvulsive shock, or certain neurodegenerative diseases.

Emotional memory. Memory for the affective properties of stimuli or events.

(A)

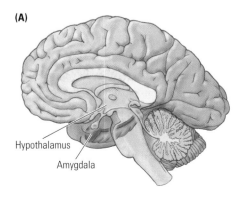

Hypothalamus

Amygdala

(B)

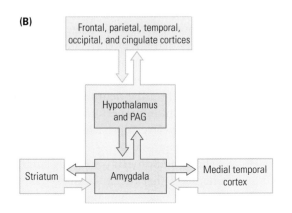

Figure 13-16

Neural Circuit Proposed for Emotional Memory   (A) The key structure in emotional memory is the amygdala. **(B)** Circuit diagram showing the flow of information in emotional memory.

relative was gone, each patient still had an emotional memory that guided his or her preference.

Emotionally arousing experiences tend to be vividly remembered, a fact confirmed by findings from both animal and human studies. James McGaugh (2004) concluded that emotionally significant experiences, both pleasant and unpleasant, must activate hormonal and brain systems that act to "stamp in" these vivid memories.

He noted that many neural systems likely take part, but the basolateral part of the amygdala is critical. The general idea is that emotionally driven hormonal and chemical systems (likely cholinergic and noradrenergic) stimulate the amygdala, which in turn modulates the laying down of memory circuits in the rest of the brain, especially in the medial temporal and prefrontal regions and basal ganglia. People with amygdala damage would thus not be expected to have enhanced memory for emotion-laden events, and they do not (Cahill et al., 1995).

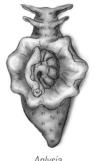

To learn more about the connection between emotionally arousing experiences and memory, visit the Chapter 13 Web links on the *Brain and Behavior* Web site (**www.worth publishers.com/kolb**).

In Review

Certain neural structures and circuits are associated with different types of learning and memory. One system, consisting of the prefrontal cortex and the medial temporal lobe and regions related to them, is the likely neural location of explicit memory. A second system, consisting of the basal ganglia and neocortex, forms the neural basis for implicit memory. A third system, which includes the amygdala and its associated structures, forms the neural basis for emotional memory. Presumably, when we learn different types of information, changes take place in synapses in these systems, and these changes produce our memories of the experiences. We now turn to the question of what these synaptic changes might be.

STRUCTURAL BASIS OF BRAIN PLASTICITY

We have encountered three different categories of memory and the different brain circuits that underlie each type. Our next task is to consider how the neurons in these circuits change to store the memories. The consensus among neuroscientists is that the changes take place at the synapse, in part because that is where neurons influence one another.

This idea dates back to 1928, when Spanish anatomist Santiago Ramón y Cajal suggested that the process of learning might produce prolonged morphological changes in the efficiency of the synapses activated in the learning process. This idea turned out to be easier to propose than to study. The major challenge that researchers still encounter as they investigate Cajal's suggestion is knowing where in the brain to look for synaptic changes that might correlate with memory for a specific stimulus.

This task is formidable. Imagine trying to find the exact location of the neurons responsible for storing your grandmother's name. You would face a similar challenge in trying to find the neurons responsible for the memory of an object in a monkey's brain as the monkey performs the visual-recognition task illustrated in Figure 13-11B. Investigators have approached the problem of identifying synaptic change in two distinctly different ways.

The first approach is to study simple neural systems. Recall from the experiments in Chapter 5 that the study of *Aplysia* revealed that changes in the properties of the synapse take place when animals learn the association between a noxious stimulus and a cue signaling the onset of the stimulus. We saw as well that synaptic changes take

Aplysia

place in hippocampal slices in which long-term potentiation (LTP) is induced. The identification of synaptic change is possible in *Aplysia* and in LTP because we know where in the nervous system to look. But we have little information about where to look for memory-storing synapses in mammals.

Accordingly, a second approach to finding the neural correlates of memory aims to determine that synaptic changes are correlated with memory in the mammalian brain. The next step is to localize the synaptic changes to specific neural pathways. Then the task is to analyze the nature of the synaptic changes themselves.

The goal of this section is to describe the studies that have identified the presence of synaptic changes correlated with various types of experience. We first consider the general research strategy. We then look at the gross neural changes correlated with different forms of experience, ranging from living in specific environments to learning specific tasks or having specific experiences to the chronic administration of trophic factors, hormones, and addictive drugs. We shall see that the general synaptic organization of the brain is modified in a strikingly similar manner by each of these diverse forms of experience.

Measuring Synaptic Change

In principle, experience could cause the brain to change in either of two ways: by modifying existing circuitry or by creating novel circuitry. In actuality, the plastic brain uses both strategies.

MODIFYING EXISTING CIRCUITS

The simplest way to find synaptic change is to look for gross changes in the morphology of dendrites, which are essentially extensions of the neuron membrane that allow more space for synapses. Because complex neurons, such as pyramidal cells, have 95 percent of their synapses on the dendrites, measurement of the changes in dendritic extent can be used to infer synaptic change.

Cells that have few or no dendrites have limited space for inputs, whereas cells that have complex dendritic structure may have space for tens of thousands of inputs. More dendrites mean more connections, and fewer dendrites mean fewer connections. Change in dendritic structure, therefore, implies change in synaptic organization.

A striking feature of dendrites is that their shape is highly changeable. Dale Purves and his colleagues (Purves & Voyvodic, 1987) labeled cells in the dorsal-root ganglia of living mice with a special dye that allowed them to visualize the cells' dendrites. When they examined the same cells at intervals ranging from a few days to weeks, they identified obvious qualitative changes in dendritic extent, as represented in **Figure 13-17**. We can assume that new dendritic branches have new synapses and that lost branches mean lost synapses.

An obvious lesson from the Purves studies is that the morphology of neurons is not static. Instead, neurons change their structure in response to their changing experiences. As they search for neural correlates of memory, researchers can take advantage of this changeability by studying the changes in dendritic morphology that are correlated with specific experiences, such as the learning of some task.

What do changes in dendritic morphology reveal? Let us consider the case in which a given neuron generates more synaptic space. The new synapses that are formed can be either additional synapses between neurons that were already connected with the neuron in question or synapses between neurons that were not formerly connected. Examples of these distinctly different synapse types are illus-

Figure 13-17

Dendritic Plasticity   Reconstructions of parts of the dendrites of three mouse superior cervical ganglion cells observed at an interval of 3 months. Changes in both the extension and the retraction of particular dendritic branches are evident.
Adapted from "Imaging Mammalian Nerve Cells and Their Connections over Time in Living Animals," by D. Purves and J. T. Voyvodic, 1987, *Trends in Neuroscience, 10*, p. 400.

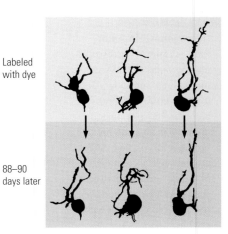

Labeled with dye

88–90 days later

(A) Before experience

Single synapse on dendritic spine

Axon 1

Axon 2

Axon 3

(B) After experience

New axon

Axon 1
New axon
Axon 2

New axon collateral

Axon 3

Formation of new synapses from new axon terminals

Formation of new synapses from original terminals

(C) Various observed shapes of new dendritic spines

Figure 13-18

Effects of Experience **(A)** Three inputs to a dendrite of a pyramidal cell. Each axon forms a synapse with a different dendritic spine. **(B)** Formation of multiple spine heads. Either the original axons may divide and innervate two spine heads or new axons or axon collaterals (dotted outlines) may innervate the new spine heads. **(C)** Single dendritic spines may sprout multiple synapses.

trated in **Figure 13-18** (see also "Dendritic Spines, Small but Mighty" on page 181).

New synapses can result either from the growth of new axon terminals or from the formation of synapses along axons as they pass by dendrites. In both cases, however, the formation of new synapses corresponds to changes in the local circuitry of a region and not to the development of new connections between distant parts of the brain. The formation of new connections between widely separated brain regions would be very difficult in a fully grown brain because of the dense plexus of cells, fibers, and blood vessels that lies in the way. Review "Optimizing Connections in the Brain" on page 35.

Thus, the growth of new synapses indicates modifications to basic circuits that are already in the brain. This strategy has an important implication for the location of synaptic changes underlying memory. During development, the brain forms circuits to process sensory information and to produce behavior. These circuits are most likely to be modified to form memories, just as in the Martin study discussed earlier (see Figure 13-6).

CREATING NOVEL CIRCUITS

Before the mid-1990s, the general assumption was that the mammalian brain did not make new neurons in adulthood. The unexpected discovery in the 1970s that the brains of songbirds such as canaries grow new neurons to produce songs in the mating season led researchers to reconsider the possibility that the adult mammalian brain, too, might be capable of generating new neurons. This possibility can be tested directly by injecting animals with a compound that is taken up by cells when they divide to produce new cells, including neurons.

When such a compound, bromode-oxyuridine (BrdU), is injected into adult rats, dividing cells incorporate it into their DNA. In later analysis, a specific stain can be used to identify the new neurons. **Figure 13-19** shows such an analysis in the rat olfactory bulb and hippocampus.

This technique has now yielded considerable evidence that the mammalian brain, including the primate brain, can generate neurons destined for the olfactory bulb, hippocampal formation, and possibly even the neocortex of the frontal and temporal lobes (Eriksson et al., 1998; Gould et al., 1999). The reason is not yet clear, but adult neurogenesis may enhance brain plasticity, particularly with respect to processes underlying learning and memory. For example, Elizabeth Gould and her colleagues (1999) showed that the generation of new neurons in the hippocampus is enhanced when animals learn explicit-memory tasks such as the Morris water task (see Figure 13-3). Furthermore, as we shall see, the generation of these new neurons appears to be increased by experience.

Figure 13-19

Neurogenesis in Adult Rats Confocal microscopic photographs: cells stained red with an antibody (called NeuN) to neurons are neurons; cells stained green with an antibody to bromode-oxyuridine (BrdU) are new cells including both neurons and glia; cells stained yellow are positive for both red and green and are new neurons.

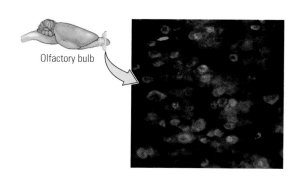

Olfactory bulb

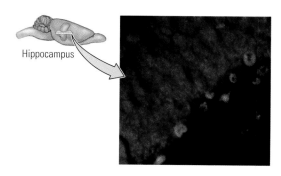

Hippocampus

Enriched Experience and Plasticity

One way to stimulate the brain is to house animals in environments that provide some form of generalized sensory or motor experience. Such an experiment is described in Chapter 6: Donald Hebb took laboratory rats home and let them have the run of his kitchen. After an interval, Hebb compared the "enriched" rats with another group of rats that had remained in cages in his laboratory at McGill University, training both groups to solve various mazes.

The enriched animals performed better, and Hebb concluded that one effect of the enriched experience was to enhance later learning. This important conclusion laid the foundation for the initiation of Head Start in the United States. This program provides academic experiences for disadvantaged pre-school-aged children.

When subsequent investigators have worked with rats, they have opted for a more constrained enrichment procedure that uses some type of "enriched enclosure." For example, in our own studies, we place groups of six rats in enclosures. These enclosures give animals a rich social experience as well as extensive sensory and motor experience.

The most obvious consequence of such experience is an increase in brain weight that may be on the order of 10 percent relative to cage-reared animals, even though the enriched rats typically weigh less, in part because they get more exercise. The key question is, What is responsible for the increased brain weight? A comprehensive series of studies by Anita Sirevaag and William Greenough (1988) used light- and electron-microscopic techniques to analyze 36 different aspects of cortical synaptic, cellular, and vascular morphology in rats raised either in cages or in complex environments. The simple conclusion was that there is a coordinated change not only in the extent of dendrites but also in glial, vascular, and metabolic processes in response to differential experiences (**Figure 13-20**).

Animals with enriched experience have not only more synapses per neuron but also more astrocytic material, more blood capillaries, and higher mitochondrial volume. (Higher mitochondrial volume means greater metabolic activity.) Therefore, clearly, when the brain changes in response to experience, the expected neural changes take place, but there are also adjustments in the metabolic requirements of the larger neurons.

Gerd Kempermann and his colleagues (1998) sought to determine whether experience actually alters the number of neurons in the brain. To test this idea, they compared the generation of neurons in the hippocampi of mice housed in complex environments with that of mice reared in laboratory cages. They located the number of new neurons by injecting the animals with BrdU several times in the course of their complex-housing experience.

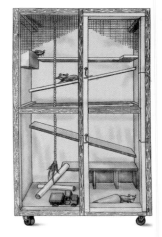

Enriched rat enclosure

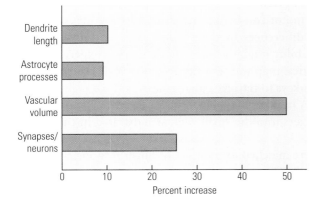

Figure 13-20

Consequences of Enrichment Schematic summary of some cortical changes that take place in response to experience. Note that such changes are found not only in neurons but also in astrocytes and vasculature. Based on data from "Differential Rearing Effects on Rat Visual Cortex Synapses. I. Synaptic and Neuronal Density and Synapses per Neuron," by A. Turner and W. T. Greenough, 1985, *Brain Research, 329*, pp. 195–203; "Differential Rearing Effects on Rat Visual Cortex Synapses. III. Neuronal and Glial Nuclei," by A. M. Sirevaag and W. T. Greenough, 1987, *Brain Research, 424*, pp. 320–332; and "Experience-Dependent Changes in Dendritic Arbor and Spine Density in Neocortex Vary with Age and Sex," by B. Kolb, R. Gibb, and G. Gorny, 2003, *Neurobiology of Learning and Memory, 79*, pp. 1–10.

The BrdU was incorporated into new neurons that were generated in the brain during the experiment. When they later looked at the hippocampi, they found more new neurons in the complex-housed rats than in the cage-housed rats. Although the investigators did not look in other parts of the brain, such as the olfactory bulb, similar changes can reasonably be expected to have taken place in other structures. This result is exciting because it implies that experience not only can alter existing circuitry but also can influence the generation of new neurons and thus new circuitry.

Sensory or Motor Training and Plasticity

The studies showing neuronal change in animals housed in complex environments demonstrate that large areas of the brain can be changed with such experience. This finding leads us to ask whether specific experiences would produce synaptic changes in localized cerebral regions. One way to approach this question is to give animals specific experiences and then see how their brains have been changed by those experiences. Another way is to look at the brains of people who have had a lifetime of some particular experience. We will consider each of these research strategies separately.

MANIPULATING EXPERIENCE EXPERIMENTALLY

Perhaps the most convincing study of this sort was done by Fen-Lei Chang and William Greenough (1982). They took advantage of the fact that the visual pathways of the laboratory rat are about 90 percent crossed. That is, about 90 percent of the connections from the left eye to the cortex project through the right lateral geniculate nucleus to the right hemisphere, and vice versa for the right eye.

Chang and Greenough placed a patch over one eye of each rat and then trained the animals in a maze. The visual cortex of only one eye would receive input about the maze, but the auditory, olfactory, tactile, and motor regions of both hemispheres would be equally active as the animals explored the maze. (Chang and Greenough also severed the corpus callosum so that the two hemispheres could not communicate and share information about the world.)

A comparison of the neurons in the two hemispheres revealed that those in the visual cortex of the trained hemisphere had more extensive dendrites. The researchers concluded that some feature associated with the encoding, processing, or storage of visual input from training was responsible for the formation of new synapses, because the hemispheres did not differ in other respects.

Complementary studies have been conducted by Randy Nudo and his colleagues on the motor systems of monkeys. In the discussions of both the sensory and the motor systems in Chapters 8 through 11, you learned that the sensory and motor worlds are represented by cortical maps. For example, in the motor system are maps of the body that represent discrete muscles and movements (see Experiment 10-4).

In the course of mapping the motor cortex of monkeys, Nudo and his colleagues (1997) noted striking individual differences in their topography. The investigators speculated that the individual variability might be due to each animal's experiences up to the time in life at which the cortical map was derived. To test this idea directly, they trained two groups of squirrel monkeys to retrieve banana-flavored food pellets either from a small or a large food well. A monkey was able to insert its entire hand into the large well but only one or two fingers into the small well, as illustrated in the Procedures section of **Experiment 13-2**.

Monkeys in the two groups were matched for number of finger flexions, which totaled about 12,000 for the entire study. The monkeys trained on the small well improved with practice, making fewer finger flexions per food retrieval as training proceeded. Maps of forelimb movements were produced by microelectrode stimulation of the cortex. The maps showed systematic changes in the animals trained with the small, but not the large, well. Presumably, these changes are due to the more demanding motor requirements of the small-well condition. The results of this experiment demonstrate that the functional topography of the motor cortex is shaped by learning new motor skills, not simply by repetitive motor use.

Most studies demonstrating plasticity in the motor cortex have been performed on laboratory animals in which the cortex has been mapped by microelectrode stimulation. Now the development of new imaging techniques, such as transcranial magnetic stimulation (TMS) and functional magnetic resonance imaging (fMRI), makes it possible to show parallel results in humans who have special motor skills. For example, there is an increased cortical representation of the fingers of the left hand in musicians who play string instruments and an increased cortical representation of the reading finger in Braille readers. (We return to the details of these imaging techniques in Chapter 14.)

Thus, the functional organization of the motor cortex is altered by skilled use in humans. It can also be altered by chronic injury in humans and laboratory animals (see Figure 10-26). Jon Kaas (2000) showed that, when the sensory nerves from one limb are severed in monkeys, large-scale changes in the somatosensory maps ensue. In particular, in the absence of input, the relevant part of the cortex no longer responds to stimulation of the limb, which is not surprising.

This cortex does not remain inactive, however. Rather, the deafferented cortex begins to respond to input from other parts of the body. The region that formerly responded to the stimulation of the hand now responds to stimulation on the face, whose area is normally adjacent to the hand area.

Similar results can be found in the cortical maps of people who have had limbs amputated. For example, Vilayanur Ramachandran (1993) found that, when the face of a limb amputee is brushed lightly with a cotton swab, the person has a sensation of the amputated hand being touched. **Figure 13-21** illustrates the rough map of the hand that Ramachandran was actually able to chart on the face. The likely explanation is that the face area in the motor cortex has expanded to occupy the deafferented limb cortex, but the brain circuitry still responds to the activity of this cortex as representing input from the limb. This response may explain the "phantom limb" pain often experienced by amputees.

The idea that experience can alter cortical maps can be demonstrated with other types of experience. For example, if animals are trained to make certain digit movements over and over again, the cortical representation of those digits expands at the expense of the remaining motor areas. Similarly, if animals are trained extensively to discriminate among different sensory stimuli such as tones, the auditory cortical areas responding to those stimuli increase in size.

As indicated in the Focus on New Research at the beginning of this chapter, one effect of musical training is to alter the motor representations of the digits used to play different instruments, and we can speculate that musical training is also likely to alter the auditory representations of specific sound frequencies. Both changes are essentially forms of memory, and the underlying synaptic changes are likely to take place on the appropriate sensory or motor cortical maps.

EXPERIMENT 13-2

Question: Does the learning of a fine motor skill alter the cortical motor map?

Procedures

Difficult task	Simple task
One group of monkeys was trained to retrieve food from a small well.	Another group of monkeys was trained to retrieve food from a large well.

Both groups were allowed 12,000 finger flexions. The small-well task was more difficult and required the learning of a fine motor skill in order to match performance of the simpler task.

Results

The motor representation of digit, wrist, and arm was mapped.

KEY

■ Digit   ■ Wrist/forearm   ■ Digit, wrist, and forearm

Conclusion

The digit representation in the brain of the animal with the more difficult task is larger, corresponding to the neuronal changes necessary for the acquired skill.

Adapted from "Adaptive Plasticity in Primate Motor Cortex as a Consequence of Behavioral Experience and Neuronal Injury," by R. J. Nudo, E. J. Plautz, and G. W. Milliken, 1997, *Seminars in Neuroscience, 9,* p. 20.

(A)

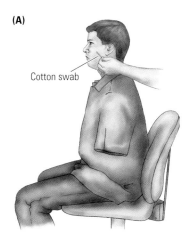

Cotton swab

(B)

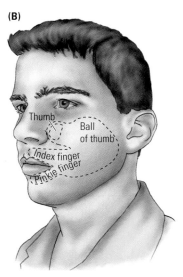

Thumb
Ball of thumb
Index finger
Pinkie finger

Figure 13-21

Cortical Reorganization When the face of an amputee is stroked lightly with a cotton swab **(A)**, the person experiences the touch as the missing hand being lightly touched **(B)** as well as experiencing touch to the face. The deafferented cortex forms a representation of the amputated hand on the face. As in the normal map of the somatosensory cortex, the thumb is disproportionately large. Adapted from "Behavioral and Magnetoencephalographic Correlates of Plasticity in the Adult Human Brain," by V. S. Ramachandran, 1993, *Proceedings of the National Academy of Sciences, USA, 90,* p. 10418.

EXPERIENCE-DEPENDENT CHANGE IN THE HUMAN BRAIN

According to the Ramachandran amputee study, the human brain appears to change with altered experience. This study did not directly examine neuronal change, however; neuronal change was inferred from behavior. The only way to directly examine synaptic change is to look directly at brain tissue. Although the experimental manipulation of experiences in people followed by an examination of their brains is not an option, the brains of people who died from nonneurological causes can be examined and the structure of their cortical neurons can be related to their experiences.

One way to test this idea is to look for a relation between neuronal structure and education. Arnold Scheibel and his colleagues conducted many such studies in the 1990s (Jacobs & Scheibel, 1993; Jacobs, Scholl, & Scheibel, 1993). In one study, they found a relation between the size of the dendrites in Wernicke's area (a cortical language area) and the amount of education. The cortical neurons from the brains of deceased people with a college education had more dendritic branches than did those from people with a high-school education, which, in turn, had more dendritic material than did those from people with less education. People who have more dendrites may be more likely to go to college, but that possibility is not easy to test.

Another way to look at the relation between human brain structure and behavior is to correlate the functional abilities of people with their neuronal structure. For example, one might expect to find differences in language-related areas between people with high and low verbal abilities. This experiment is difficult to conduct, because it presupposes behavioral measures taken before death and such measures are not normally available.

However, Scheibel and his colleagues took advantage of the now well-documented observation that, on average, the verbal abilities of females are superior to those of males. When they examined the structure of neurons in Wernicke's area, they found that females have more extensive dendritic branching there than males do. Furthermore, in a subsequent study, they found that this sex difference was present as early as age 9, suggesting that such sex differences emerge within the first decade. In fact, on average, young girls tend to have significantly better verbal skills than young boys do.

Finally, these investigators approached the link between experience and neuronal morphology in a slightly different way. They began with two hypotheses. First, they suggested that there is a relation between the complexity of dendritic branching and the nature of the computational tasks performed by a brain area.

To test this hypothesis, they examined the dendritic structure of neurons in different cortical regions that handle different computational tasks. For example, when they compared the structure of neurons corresponding to the somatosensory representation of the trunk with those for the fingers, they found the latter to have more-complex cells. They reasoned that the somatosensory inputs from receptive fields on the chest wall would constitute less of a computational challenge to cortical neurons than would those from the fingers and that the neurons representing the chest would therefore be less complex.

This hypothesis was shown to be correct (**Figure 13-22**). Similarly, when Scheibel's group compared the cells in the finger area with those in the supramarginal gyrus (SMG), a region of the parietal lobe that is associated with higher cognitive processes (that is, thinking), they found the SMG neurons to be more complex.

The group's second hypothesis was that dendritic branching in all regions is subject to experience-dependent change. As a result, the researchers hypothesized that predominant life experience (e.g., occupation) should alter the structure of dendrites. Although they did not test this hypothesis directly, they did make an interesting observation.

In their study comparing cells in the trunk area, the finger area, and the SMG, they found curious individual differences. For example, especially large differences in trunk and finger neurons were found in the brains of people who had a high level of finger dexterity maintained over long periods of time (e.g., career word processors). In contrast, no difference between trunk and finger neurons was found in a sales representative. One would not expect a good deal of specialized finger use in this occupation, which would mean less-complex demands on the finger neurons.

In summary, although the studies showing a relation between experience and neural structure in humans are based on correlations rather than on actual experiments, the findings are consistent with those observed in experimental studies of other species. We are thus led to the general conclusion that specific experiences can produce localized changes in the synaptic organization of the brain. Such changes likely form the structural basis of memory.

Plasticity, Hormones, Trophic Factors, and Drugs

Articles in newspapers and popular magazines often report that drugs can damage your brain. Some drugs certainly do act as toxins and can selectively kill brain regions, but a more realistic mode of action of drugs is to *change* the brain. Although not many studies have looked at drug-induced morphological changes, there is evidence that some compounds can greatly change the synaptic organization of the brain. These compounds include hormones, neurotrophic factors, and psychoactive drugs. We will briefly consider each category.

HORMONES

As stated in earlier chapters, the levels of circulating hormones play a critical role both in determining the structure of the brain and in eliciting certain behaviors in adulthood. Although the structural effects of hormones were once believed to be expressed only in the course of development, current belief is that adult neurons also can respond to hormonal manipulations with dramatic structural changes. We will consider the actions of two types of hormones detailed in Chapter 7, gonadal hormones and stress-related hormones.

We encountered the gonadal hormones in Chapters 6, 7, and 11. Research findings have established that there are differences in the structure of neurons in the cortices of male and female rats and that these differences depend on gonadal hormones. What is more surprising, perhaps, is that gonadal hormones continue to influence cell structure and behavior in adulthood.

Elizabeth Hampson and Doreen Kimura (1988) showed that the performance of women on various cognitive tasks changes throughout the menstrual cycle as their estrogen levels fluctuate. Changes in estrogen level appear to alter the structure of neurons and astrocytes in the neocortex and hippocampus, which likely account for at least part of the behavioral fluctuation. **Figure 13-23** illustrates changes in the dendritic spines in the hippocampal cells of female rats at different phases of their 4-day estrous cycle. As the estrogen level rises, the number of synapses rises; as the estrogen level drops, the number of synapses declines (Chapter 11).

Curiously, the influence of estrogen on cell structure may be different in the hippocampus and neocortex. Jane Stewart found, for example, that, when the ovaries of middle-aged female rats are removed, estrogen levels drop sharply, producing an increase in the number of spines on pyramidal cells throughout the neocortex but a decrease in spine

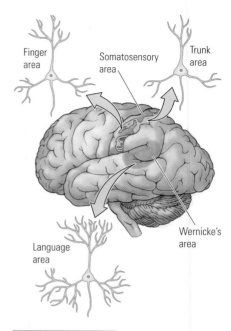

Figure 13-22

Experience and Neural Complexity
Confirmation of Scheibel's hypothesis that cell complexity is related to the computational demands required of the cell. Neurons that represent the trunk area of the body have relatively less computational demand than do cells representing the finger region. In turn, cells engaged in more-cognitive functions (such as language, as in Wernicke's area) have greater computational demand than do those engaged in finger functions.

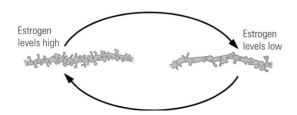

Estrogen levels high
Estrogen levels low

Figure 13-23

Hormones and Neuroplasticity   Sections of dendrites from hippocampal cells during times of high and low levels of estrogen during the rat's 4-day estrous cycle reveal many more dendritic spines during the period when estrogen levels are high. Adapted from "Naturally Occurring Fluctuation in Dendritic Spine Density on Adult Hippocampal Pyramidal Neurons," by C. S. Woolley, E. Gould, M. Frankfurt, and B. S. McEwen, 1990, *Journal of Neuroscience, 10,* p. 4038.

density in the hippocampus (Stewart & Kolb, 1994). How these synaptic changes might influence processes such as memory is not immediately obvious, but the question is reasonable—especially because menopausal women also experience sharp drops in estrogen levels and a corresponding decline in verbal memory ability.

This question is also relevant to middle-aged men, who show a slow decline in testosterone levels that is correlated with a drop in spatial ability. Rats that are gonadectomized in adulthood show an increase in cortical spine density, much like the ovariectomized females, although we do not know how this change is related to spatial behavior. Nonetheless, a reasonable supposition is that testosterone levels might influence spatial memory throughout life.

When the body is stressed, the pituitary gland produces adrenocorticotrophic hormone (ACTH), which stimulates the adrenal cortex to produce steroid hormones known as *glucocorticoids* (see Figure 7.20). Important in protein and carbohydrate metabolism, controlling sugar levels in the blood and the absorption of sugar by cells, glucocorticoids have many actions on the body, including the brain. Robert Sapolsky (1992) proposed that glucocorticoids can sometimes be neurotoxic.

In particular, he found that, with prolonged stress, cells in the hippocampus appear to be killed by glucocorticoids. Elizabeth Gould and her colleagues (1998) showed that even brief periods of stress can reduce the number of new granule cells produced in the hippocampus in monkeys, presumably through the actions of stress hormones. Evidence of neuron death and reduced neuron generation in the hippocampus has obvious implications for the behavior of animals, especially for processes such as spatial memory.

In sum, hormones can alter the synaptic organization of the brain and even the number of neurons in the brain. Little is known today about the behavioral consequences of such changes, but hormones can likely alter the course of plastic changes in the brain.

NEUROTROPHIC FACTORS

In the discussion on the origins of neurons in Chapter 6 you learned about *neurotrophic factors,* chemical compounds that signal stem cells to develop into neurons or glia. Neurotrophic compounds, listed in **Table 13-2**, also act to reorganize neural circuits. The first neurotrophic factor was discovered in the peripheral nervous system more than a generation ago; it is known as **nerve growth factor** (NGF). Nerve growth factor is trophic (i.e., having to do with the process of nutrition) in the sense that it stimulates neurons to grow dendrites and synapses, and, in some cases, it promotes the survival of neurons.

Trophic factors are produced in the brain by neurons and glia. Trophic factors can affect neurons both through cell-membrane receptors and by actually entering the neuron to act internally on its operation. For example, trophic factors may be released postsynaptically to act as signals that can influence the presynaptic cell. Recall from Chapter 5 that the Hebb synapse, a synapse that changes with use so that learning takes place, is hypothesized to employ just such a mechanism.

Experience stimulates their production, and so neurotrophic factors have been proposed as agents of synaptic change. For example, brain-derived neurotrophic factor (BDNF) is increased when animals solve specific problems such as mazes. This finding has led to speculation that the release of BDNF may enhance plastic changes, such as the growth of dendrites and synapses.

Unfortunately, although many researchers would like to conclude that BDNF has a role in learning, this conclusion does not necessarily follow. The behavior of animals when they solve mazes differs from their behavior when they remain in cages, and so we must first demonstrate that changes in BDNF, NGF, or any other trophic factor are actually related to the formation of new synapses.

Table 13-2	Molecules Exhibiting Neurotrophic Activities

Proteins initially characterized as neurotrophic factors

   Nerve growth factor (NGF)

   Brain-derived neurotrophic factor (BDNF)

   Neurotrophin 3 (NT-3)

   Ciliary neurotrophic factor (CNTF)

Growth factors with neurotrophic activity

   Fibroblast growth factor, acidic (aFGF or FGF-1)

   Fibroblast growth factor, basic (bFGF or FGF-2)

   Epidermal growth factor (EGF)

   Insulin-like growth factor (ILGF)

   Transforming growth factor (TGF)

   Lymphokines (interleukin 1, 3, 6 or IL-1, IL-3, IL-6)

   Protease nexin I, II

   Cholinergic neuronal differentiation factor

Nevertheless, if we assume that trophic factors do act as agents of synaptic change, then we should be able to use the presence of increased trophic factor activity during learning as a marker of where to look for changed synapses associated with learning and memory.

PSYCHOACTIVE DRUGS

Many people commonly use stimulant drugs such as caffeine, and some use more psychoactively stimulating drugs such as nicotine, amphetamine, or cocaine. The long-term consequences of abusing psychoactive drugs are now well documented, but the question of why these drugs cause problems remains to be answered. One explanation for the behavioral changes associated with chronic psychoactive drug abuse is that the brain is changed by the drugs.

One experimental demonstration of these changes is **drug-induced behavioral sensitization,** often referred to simply as *behavioral sensitization*. Drug-induced behavioral sensitization is the progressive increase in behavioral actions in response to repeated administration of a drug, even when the amount given in each dose does not change. Behavioral sensitization occurs with most psychoactive drugs, including amphetamine, cocaine, morphine, and nicotine.

As the Results section in Experiment 5-3 shows, *Aplysia* becomes more sensitive to a stimulus after repeated exposure to it. Psychoactive drugs appear to have a parallel action: they lead to increased behavioral sensitivity to their actions. For example, a rat given a small dose of amphetamine may show an increase in activity. When the rat is given the same dose of amphetamine on subsequent occasions, the increase in activity is progressively larger. If no drug is given for weeks or even months, and then the amphetamine is given in the same dose as before, behavioral sensitization continues, which means that some type of long-lasting change must have taken place in the brain in response to the drug. Drug-induced behavioral sensitization can therefore be viewed as a memory for a particular drug.

The parallel between drug-induced behavioral sensitization and other forms of memory leads us to ask if the changes in the brain after behavioral sensitization are similar to those found after other forms of learning. They are. For example, there is evidence of increased numbers of receptors at synapses and of more synapses in sensitized animals.

In a series of studies, Terry Robinson and his colleagues found a dramatic increase in dendritic growth and spine density in rats that were sensitized to amphetamine, cocaine, or nicotine relative to rats that received injections of a saline solution (Robinson & Kolb, 2004). **Experiment 13-3** compares the effects of amphetamine and saline treatments on cells in the nucleus accumbens. Neurons in the amphetamine-treated brains have more dendritic branches and increased spine density. Repeated exposure to psychoactive stimulant drugs thus alters the structure of cells in the brain. These changes in turn may be related to "learned addictions."

These plastic changes were not found throughout the brain. Rather, they were localized to such regions as the prefrontal cortex and nucleus accumbens, both of which receive a large dopamine projection. Recall from Chapters 7 and 11 that dopamine is believed to play a significant role in the rewarding properties of drugs (Wise, 2004). Other psychoactive drugs also appear to alter neuronal

Nerve growth factor (NGF)
Neurotrophic factor that stimulates neurons to grow dendrites and synapses and, in some cases, promotes the survival of neurons.

Drug-induced behavioral sensitization. Escalating behavioral response to the repeated administration of a psychomotor stimulant such as amphetamine, cocaine, or nicotine; also called *behavioral sensitization*.

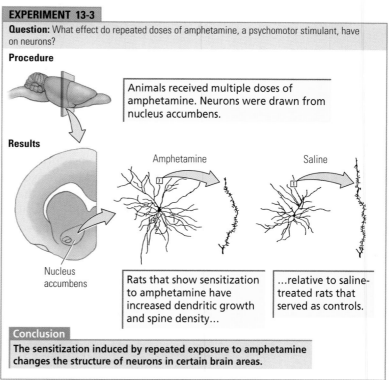

EXPERIMENT 13-3

Question: What effect do repeated doses of amphetamine, a psychomotor stimulant, have on neurons?

Procedure

Animals received multiple doses of amphetamine. Neurons were drawn from nucleus accumbens.

Results

Amphetamine

Saline

Nucleus accumbens

Rats that show sensitization to amphetamine have increased dendritic growth and spine density...

...relative to saline-treated rats that served as controls.

Conclusion

The sensitization induced by repeated exposure to amphetamine changes the structure of neurons in certain brain areas.

Adapted from "Persistent Structural Adaptations in Nucleus Accumbens and Prefrontal Cortex Neurons Produced by Prior Experience with Amphetamine," by T. E. Robinson and B. Kolb, 1997, *Journal of Neuroscience, 17,* p. 8495.

structure: marijuana, morphine, and certain antidepressants change dendritic length and spine density, although in somewhat different ways from those of stimulants. For example, morphine produces a decrease in dendritic length and spine density in the nucleus accumbens and prefrontal cortex (Robinson & Kolb, 2004).

What do changes in synaptic organization induced by drugs mean for later experience-dependent plasticity? If rats are given amphetamine, cocaine, or nicotine for 2 weeks before being placed in complex environments, the expected increases in dendritic length and spine density in the cortex do not happen (Kolb et al., 2003). This is not because the brain can no longer change: giving the animals additional drug doses can still produce change. Rather, something about prior drug exposure alters the way in which the brain later responds to experience. Why prior drug exposure has this effect is not yet known but, obviously, drug taking can have long-term effects on brain plasticity.

In Review

Experience produces plastic changes in the brain, including the growth of dendrites, the formation of synapses, and the production of new neurons. Further, like environmental stimulation, hormones, neurotrophic factors, and psychoactive drugs appear to be able to produce long-lasting effects on brain morphology that are strikingly similar to those observed when animals show evidence of memory for sensory events. These structural changes include not only changes in synaptic organization, as inferred from the dendritic analyses, but also changes in the numbers of neurons, at least in the hippocampus. Thus, the neural changes that correlate with memory are similar to those observed in other situations of behavioral change.

RECOVERY FROM BRAIN INJURY

The nervous system appears to be conservative in its use of mechanisms related to behavioral change. This message is important: it implies that, if we wish to change the brain, such as after injury or disease, then we should look for treatments that will produce the types of neural changes that we have found to be related to learning, memory, and other forms of behavioral change.

Partial recovery of function is common after brain injury, and the average person would probably say that the process of recovery requires that the injured person relearn lost skills, whether walking, talking, or using the fingers. But what exactly does recovery entail? After all, a person with brain trauma or brain disease has lost neurons, and so the brain may be missing critical structures that are needed for learning or memory.

Recall, for example, that H. M. has shown no recovery of his lost memory capacities, even after 50 years of practice in trying to remember information. The requisite neural structures are no longer there, and so relearning is simply not possible. In H. M.'s case, the only solution would be to replace his lost medial temporal structures, a procedure that at present is not feasible. But other people, such as Donna, whom we meet next, do show some recovery.

Donna's Experience with Brain Injury

Donna began dancing lessons when she was 4 years old, and she was a "natural." By the time she finished high school she had the training and skill necessary for a career with a major dance company. Donna remembers vividly the day that she was chosen to play a leading role in *The Nutcracker*. She had marveled at the costumes as she watched the popular Christmas ballet as a child, and now she would dance in those costumes!

Although her career as a dancer was interrupted by the births of two children, Donna never lost interest in dancing. In 1968, when both her children were in school, she began dancing again with a local company. To her amazement, she could still perform most of the movements, although she was rusty on the classic dances that she had once memorized so meticulously. Nonetheless, she quickly relearned. In retrospect, she should not have been so surprised, because she had always had an excellent memory.

One evening in 1990, while on a bicycle ride, Donna was struck by a drunk driver. Although she was wearing a helmet, she suffered a traumatic brain injury that put her in a coma for several weeks. As she regained consciousness, she was confused and had difficulty talking and understanding others. Her memory was very poor, she had spatial disorientation and often got lost, she had various motor disturbances, and she had difficulty recognizing anyone but her family and closest friends.

In the ensuing 10 months, Donna regained most of her motor abilities and language skills, and her spatial abilities improved significantly. Nonetheless, she was short-tempered and easily frustrated by the slowness of her recovery, symptoms that are typical of people with brain trauma. She suffered periods of depression.

She also found herself prone to inexplicable surges of panic when doing simple things. On one occasion early in her rehabilitation, she was shopping in a large supermarket and became overwhelmed by the number of salad dressing choices. She ran from the store, and only after she sat outside and calmed herself could she go back inside to continue shopping.

Two years later, Donna was dancing once again, but she now found it very difficult to learn new steps. Her emotions were still unstable, which was a strain on her family, but her episodes of frustration and temper outbursts became much less frequent. A year later, they were gone and her life was not obviously different from that of other middle-aged women.

Some cognitive changes persisted, however. Donna seemed unable to remember the names or faces of new people she met and was unable to concentrate if there were distractions such as a television or radio playing in the background. She could not dance as she had before her injury, although she did work at it diligently. Her balance on sudden turns gave her the most difficulty. Rather than risk falling, she retired from her life's first love.

Donna's experiences demonstrate the human brain's capacity for continuously changing its structure and ultimately its function throughout a lifetime. On the basis of what we have learned in this chapter, we can identify three different ways in which Donna could recover from her brain injury: she could learn new ways to solve problems, she could reorganize the brain to do more with less, and she could generate new neurons to produce new neural circuits. We will briefly examine these three possibilities.

The brain changes to correspond to the new experiences and new abilities of these dancers. When Donna returned to dancing after a 10-year break, she retained much of her skill, even though she had not practiced at all. After her accident, Donna had to relearn how to talk, walk, and dance. She did not go through the same learning process that she had experienced as a child, but her brain had to change in some way to allow her to regain her lost abilities. That change had limits, however, because she never recovered the ability that these young women have—that is, to learn new dances.

Three-Legged Cat Solution

The simplest solution to recovery from brain injury is to compensate in a manner that we call the "three-legged cat solution." Cats that lose a leg to accident (and subsequent veterinary treatment) quickly learn to compensate for the missing limb and once again become mobile; they can be regarded as having shown recovery of function. The limb is still gone, but the behavior has changed in compensation.

A similar explanation can account for many instances of apparent recovery of function after brain injury. Imagine a right-handed person who has a stroke that leads

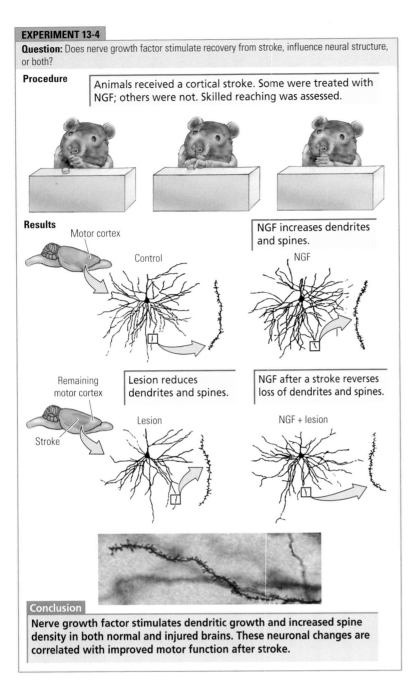

EXPERIMENT 13-4

Question: Does nerve growth factor stimulate recovery from stroke, influence neural structure, or both?

Procedure

Animals received a cortical stroke. Some were treated with NGF; others were not. Skilled reaching was assessed.

Results

Motor cortex

Control

NGF increases dendrites and spines.

NGF

Remaining motor cortex

Lesion reduces dendrites and spines.

Lesion

NGF after a stroke reverses loss of dendrites and spines.

NGF + lesion

Stroke

Conclusion

Nerve growth factor stimulates dendritic growth and increased spine density in both normal and injured brains. These neuronal changes are correlated with improved motor function after stroke.

Adapted from "Nerve Growth Factor Treatment Prevents Dendritic Atrophy and Promotes Recovery of Function after Cortical Injury," by B. Kolb, S. Cote, A. Ribeiro-da-Silva, and A. C. Cuello, 1997, *Neuroscience, 76,* p. 1146.

Bryan Kolb

to the loss of the use of the right hand and arm. Unable to write with the affected limb, she switches to her left hand. This type of behavioral compensation is presumably associated with some sort of change in the brain. After all, if a person learns to use the opposite hand to write, some changes in the nervous system must underlie this new skill.

New-Circuit Solution

A second way to recover from brain damage is for the brain to change its neural connections to overcome the neural loss. This way is most easily accomplished by processes that are similar to those that we considered for other forms of plasticity. That is, the brain forms new connections that allow it to "do more with less."

Although this change in the brain would seem to be logical, such changes appear to be fairly small. As a result, there is relatively modest recovery in most instances of brain injury, *unless there is some form of intervention*. Stated differently, recovery from brain damage can be increased significantly if the person engages in some form of behavioral or pharmacological therapy. The therapy must play a role in stimulating the brain to make new connections and to do more with less.

Behavioral therapy, such as speech therapy or physiotherapy, presumably increases brain activity, which facilitates the neural changes. In a pharmacological intervention, the patient takes a drug known to influence brain plasticity. An example is nerve growth factor. When NGF is given to animals with strokes that damaged the motor cortex, there is an improvement in motor functions, such as reaching with the forelimb to obtain food (**Experiment 13-4**).

The behavioral changes are correlated with a dramatic increase in dendritic branching and spine density in the remaining, intact motor regions. The morphological changes are correlated with improved motor functions, such as reaching with the forelimb to obtain food, as illustrated in Experiment 13-2 (Kolb et al., 1997). Recovery is by no means complete, which is not surprising, because brain tissue is still missing.

In principle, we might expect that any drug that stimulates the growth of new connections would help people recover from brain injury. There is one important constraint, however. The neural growth must be in regions of the brain that could influence a particular lost function. For example, if a drug stimulated the growth of synapses on cells in the visual cortex, we would not expect to find enhanced recovery of hand use. The visual neurons play no direct role in moving the hand.

Rather, we would need a drug that stimulates the growth of synapses on neurons that can control hand use, such as neurons in the premotor or prefrontal cortex. As mentioned earlier, amphetamine has this action, and so we might predict that amphetamine will stimulate motor recovery. This possibility is now undergoing clinical trials.

Lost-Neuron-Replacement Solution

The idea that brain tissue could be transplanted from one animal to another goes back to the beginning of the twentieth century. There is now good evidence that tissue from fetal brains can be transplanted and will grow and form some connections in the new brain. Unfortunately, in contrast with transplanted hearts or livers, transplanted brain tissue functions poorly. The procedure seems most suited to conditions in which a small number of functional cells are required, such as in the replacement of dopamine-producing cells in Parkinson's disease or in the replacement of superchiasmatic cells to restore circadian rhythms.

In fact, by 2004, dopamine-producing cells had been surgically transplanted into the striata of many Parkinson patients. Although the disease has not been reversed, some patients, especially the younger ones, have shown functional gains that justify the procedure. Nonetheless, the fact that the tissue is taken from aborted human fetuses raises serious ethical issues that will not be easily resolved.

There is a second way to replace lost neurons. Because experience can induce the brain to generate new neurons, we know that the brain is capable of making neurons in adulthood. The challenge is to get the brain to do it after an injury.

The first breakthrough in this research was made by Brent Reynolds and Sam Weiss (1992). Cells lining the ventricle of adult mice were removed and placed in a culture medium. The researchers demonstrated that, if the correct trophic factors are added, the cells begin to divide and can produce new neurons and glia. Furthermore, if the trophic factors—particularly **epidermal growth factor** (EGF)—are infused into the ventricle of a living animal, the subventricular zone generates cells that migrate into the striatum and eventually differentiate into neurons and glia.

In principle, it ought to be possible to use trophic factors to stimulate the subventricular zone to generate new cells in the injured brain. If these new cells were to migrate to the site of injury and essentially to regenerate the lost area, then it might be possible to restore at least some lost function. It seems unlikely that all lost behaviors could be restored, however, because the new neurons would have to establish the same connections with the rest of the brain that the lost neurons once had. This task would be daunting, because the connections would have to be formed in an adult brain that already had billions of connections. Nonetheless, there is at least reason to hope that such a treatment might someday be feasible.

There may be another way to use trophic factors to stimulate neurogenesis and enhance recovery. Recall that regions such as the hippocampus and olfactory bulb normally produce new neurons in adulthood and that the number of neurons in these areas can be influenced by experience. It is possible, therefore, that we could stimulate the generation of new neurons in intact regions of the injured brains and that these neurons could help the brain develop new circuits to restore partial functioning. Thus, experience and trophic factors are likely to be used in studies of recovery from brain injury in the coming years.

Epidermal growth factor (EGF). Neurotrophic factor that stimulates the subventricular zone to generate cells that migrate into the striatum and eventually differentiate into neurons and glia.

In Review

Learning to recover from brain injury poses a special problem, because the brain may lose large areas of neurons and their associated functions. Three ways to compensate for the loss of neurons are: learn new ways to solve problems, reorganize the brain to do more with less, and replace the lost neurons. Although complete recovery is not currently practical, all three strategies can be used to enhance recovery from injury. Moreover, rehabilitation programs will likely begin to look at the possibility of combining these three ways to further enhance recovery. In each case, however, recovery entails taking advantage of the brain's capacity to change.

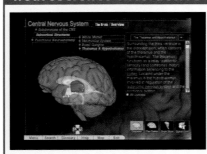

neuroscience interactive

Many resources are available for expanding your learning online:

◼ www.worthpublishers.com/kolb

Try the Chapter 13 quizzes and flashcards to test your mastery of the chapter material. You'll also be able to link to other sites that will reinforce what you've learned.

◼ www.alz.org

Learn more about what happens when memory function deteriorates in Alzheimer's disease.

On your *Foundations* CD-ROM, you can review the brain anatomy that underlies learning and memory in the module on the Central Nervous System.

SUMMARY

◼ *How does the brain learn and remember?* Two distinctly different forms of learning and memory may be referred to as implicit and explicit. The neural circuits underlying them are distinctly different: the reciprocal system for explicit (conscious) memory includes medial temporal structures; the unidirectional system for implicit (unconscious) memory includes the basal ganglia. Multiple subsystems within the explicit and implicit systems control different aspects of memory. Emotional memory, a third form, has characteristics of both implicit and explicit memory. The neural circuits for emotional memory are unique in that they include the amygdala. Finally, episodic memory includes not only a record of events (episodes) that occurred but also our presence there and our role in the events. The frontal lobe likely plays a unique role in this autobiographical memory.

◼ *What changes take place in the brain in response to experience?* The brain has the capacity for structural change, which is presumed to underlie functional change. The brain changes in two fundamental ways in response to experience. First, changes take place in existing neural circuits. Second, novel neural circuits are formed, both by new connections among existing neurons and by the generation of new neurons.

◼ *What stimulates plastic change in the brain?* The key to brain plasticity is neural activity. Through such activity, synapses are formed and changed. Neural activity can be induced by general or specific experience, as well as by electrical or chemical stimulation of the brain. Chemical stimulation may range from hormones to neurotrophic compounds to psychoactive drugs. Much of the brain is capable of plastic change with experience. Different experiences lead to changes in different neural systems.

◼ *How might brain plasticity stimulate recovery from injury?* Plastic changes after brain injury parallel those seen when the brain changes with experience. Changes related to recovery do not always occur spontaneously, however, and must be stimulated either by behavioral training or by the stimulating effects of psychoactive drugs or neurotrophic factors. The key to stimulating recovery from brain injury is to produce an increase in the plastic changes underlying the recovery.

KEY TERMS

amnesia, p. 488
anterograde amnesia, p. 503
conditioned response (CR), p. 484
conditioned stimulus (CS), p. 484
declarative memory, p. 489
drug-induced behavioral sensitization, p. 513
emotional memory, p. 503
entorhinal cortex, p. 497
epidermal growth factor (EGF), p. 517
episodic memory, p. 492

explicit memory, p. 488
eye-blink conditioning, p. 484
fear conditioning, p. 484
implicit memory, p. 488
instrumental conditioning, p. 486
Korsakoff's syndrome, p. 501
learning set, p. 488
memory, p. 484
nerve growth factor (NGF), p. 513
neuritic plaque, p. 498

parahippocampal cortex, p. 497
Pavlovian conditioning, p. 484
perirhinal cortex, p. 497
priming, p. 490
procedural memory, p. 489
retrograde amnesia, p. 503
unconditioned response (UCR), p. 484
unconditioned stimulus (UCS), p. 484
visuospatial learning, p. 486

REVIEW QUESTIONS

1. How does experience change the brain?

2. What are the critical differences between the studies of learning conducted by Pavlov and those conducted by Thorndike?

3. Distinguish among explicit, implicit, and emotional memory: What are the circuits for each?

4. What is the structural basis of neuroplasticity, and what are various methods for studying its relation to behavior?

5. Why are there changes in sensory representations after amputation of a limb?

6. What mechanisms might account for recovery from brain injury?

FOR FURTHER THOUGHT

1. Imagine that a person has a stroke and loses a large part of the left hemisphere, rendering him unable to speak. Imagine further that a treatment has been devised in which new neurons can be generated to replace the lost brain regions. What would be the behavioral consequences of this brain regeneration? Would the person be the same as he was before the stroke? (Hint: The new cells would have no experiences.)

2. How do we learn from experience?

3. Our life is filled with experiences that alter brain organization. How might different experiences interact with one another?

RECOMMENDED READING

Florence, S. L., Jain, N., & Kaas, J. H. (1997). Plasticity of somatosensory cortex in primates. *Seminars in Neuroscience, 9,* 3–12. Jon Kaas and his colleagues are leaders in the study of brain plasticity. This very readable review introduces the reader to the exciting discoveries that Kaas and his colleagues are making in the study of cortical plasticity in monkeys.

Fuster, J. M. (1995). *Memory in the cerebral cortex.* Cambridge, MA: MIT Press. Joaquin Fuster has summarized the evidence on how the cortex codes information for storage and retrieval, and he presents a cogent theory of how the cortex allows us to learn and to remember.

Gazzaniga, M. S. (Ed.). (2000). *The new cognitive neurosciences.* Cambridge, MA: MIT Press. This edited book spans the entire field of cognitive neuroscience. There is something for everyone in this broad and well-written collection of chapters.

Hebb, D. O. (1949). *The organization of behavior.* New York: Wiley. Although this book was written 50 years ago, it remains the clearest introduction to the fundamental questions about how the brain can learn.

Kolb, B., & Whishaw, I. Q. (1998). Brain plasticity and behavior. *Annual Review of Psychology, 49,* 43–64. The authors provide a general review of the field of brain plasticity and behavior. Any student writing a paper on this topic would do well to start with this article and its extensive bibliography.

Sapolsky, R. M. (1992). *Stress, the aging brain, and the mechanisms of neuron death.* Cambridge, MA: MIT Press. Robert Sapolsky is a leading researcher and theorist interested in the role of hormones and brain function. This very readable text not only introduces the reader to the basic facts but also provides a provocative broth of ideas.

Squire, L. (1987). *Memory and brain.* New York: Oxford University Press. Larry Squire is perhaps the most visible cognitive neuroscientist studying brain mechanisms underlying memory. This monograph is the best single volume describing what is known about the organization of the brain and memory.

Wise, R. A. (2004). Dopamine, learning and motivation. *Nature Neuroscience Reviews, 5,* 483–494. A provocative review that leads to the conclusion that dopamine is necessary not only for reward but even for learning.

How Does the Brain Think?

Animal Intelligence

Focus on Comparative Biology

A fundamental characteristic of intelligent animals is that they think. We begin to explore how the brain thinks and where thinking takes place in the brain by examining thought in an intelligent nonhuman animal—an African gray parrot named Alex, pictured here with Irene Pepperberg (1990, 1999), who has been studying Alex's ability to think and use language for nearly three decades.

A typical session with Alex and Pepperberg might proceed as follows (Mukerjee, 1996): Pepperberg shows Alex a tray with four corks. "How many?" she asks. "Four," Alex replies. She then shows him a metal key and a green plastic one.

"What toy?"
"Key."
"How many?"
"Two."
"What's different?"
"Color."

Alex does not just have a vocabulary; the words have meaning to him. He can correctly apply English labels to numerous colors (red, green, blue, yellow, gray, purple, orange), shapes (two-, three-, four-, five-, six-corner), and materials (cork, wood, rawhide, rock, paper, chalk, wool).

Alex, an African gray parrot, and Irene Pepperberg, along with items of various shapes and colors, which Alex can count, describe, and answer questions about.

He can also label various items made of metal (chain, key, grate, tray, toy truck), wood (clothespin, block), and plastic or paper (cup, box). Most surprising of all, he can use words to identify, request, and refuse items and to respond to questions about abstract ideas, such as the color, shape, material, relative size, and quantity of more than 100 different objects.

Alex's thinking is often quite complex. Suppose he is presented with a tray that contains the following seven items: a circular rose-colored piece of rawhide, a piece of purple wool, a three-corner purple key, a four-corner yellow piece of rawhide, a five-corner orange piece of rawhide, a six-corner purple piece of rawhide, and a purple metal box. If he is then asked, "What shape is the purple hide?" he will answer correctly, "Six-corner." To come up with this answer, Alex must comprehend the question, locate the correct object of the correct color, determine the answer to the question about that object's shape, and encode his answer into an appropriate verbal response.

This task is not easy to do. After all, there are four pieces of rawhide and three purple objects, so Alex cannot respond to just one attribute. He has to mentally combine the concepts of rawhide and purple and find the object that possesses them both. Then he has to figure out the object's shape. Clearly, considerable mental processing is required, but Alex succeeds at such tasks time and again.

Alex also demonstrates that he understands what he is saying. If he requests one object and is presented with another, he is likely to say no and repeat his original request. In fact, when given incorrect objects on numerous occasions in formal testing, he said no and repeated his request 72 percent of the time, said no without repeating his request 18 percent of the time, and made a new request the other 10 percent of the time. Such responses suggest that Alex's requests lead to an expectation in his mind. He knows what he is asking for, and he expects to get it.

Alex's cognitive abilities are unexpected in a bird. We all know that parrots can talk, but most of us assume that there is no real thought behind their words. Alex proves otherwise. In the past 30 years, there has been great interest in the intellectual capacities of chimpanzees and dolphins, but Alex's mental life appears to be just as rich as those two large-brained mammals. The fact that birds such as Alex are capable of forms of "thought" is a clue to the neural basis of thinking. At first, a logical presumption may be that thinking, which humans are so good at, must be due to some special property of the massive human neocortex. But birds do not possess a neocortex. Rather, birds evolved specific brain nuclei that function much as the layers of the cortex do. This difference in organization of the forebrain between birds and mammals implies that think-

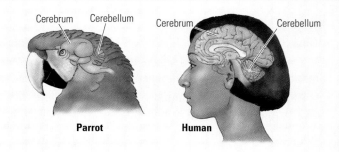

ing must be an activity of complex neural circuits and not of some particular region in the brain.

The idea of neural circuits is the essence of Donald Hebb's concept that **cell assemblies** (networks of neurons) represent objects or ideas, and the interplay among those networks results in complex mental activity. As you have seen in the last few chapters, connections among neurons are not random but rather are organized into systems (e.g., the visual, auditory, and motor systems) and subsystems (such as the dorsal and ventral streams of vision). Thinking, therefore, must be due to the activity of many different systems, which in the mammalian brain are in the cortex.

This chapter examines the organization of the neural systems and subsystems that control thinking. Our first task is to define the mental processes that we wish to study. In other words, What is the nature of thought? We then consider the cortical regions that play the major roles in thinking. You have encountered all these regions before in the course of studying vision, audition, and movement. Here we examine how these same regions may function to produce thought.

One characteristic of how the cortex is organized to produce thought is that fundamentally different types of thinking are carried out in the left and right cerebral hemispheres. As a result, this chapter also explores the asymmetrical organization of the brain. Another distinguishing feature of human thought is that there are individual differences in the ways that people think. We consider several sources of these differences, including those related to sex and to what we call intelligence. Finally, we address consciousness and how it may relate to the neural control of thought.

Cell assembly. Hypothetical group of neurons that become functionally connected because they receive the same sensory inputs. Hebb proposed that cell assemblies were the basis of perception, memory, and thought.

Psychological construct. Idea, resulting from a set of impressions, that some mental ability exists as an entity; examples include memory, language, and emotion.

THE NATURE OF THOUGHT

The study of thought, language, memory, emotion, and motivation is tricky because these mental processes are abstract. They cannot be seen. They can be inferred from behavior and are best thought of as **psychological constructs,** ideas that result from a set of impressions. The mind *constructs* the idea as being real, even though it is not a tangible thing. Thought is a psychological construct built from the impression that people are constantly monitoring events and behaviors in their minds.

We have the impression that people are good or bad at forming these things that we call thoughts, even though thoughts do not really exist as things. We run into trouble, however, when we try to locate constructs such as thought or memory in the brain. The fact that we have English words for these constructs does not mean that the brain is organized around them. Indeed, it is not.

For instance, although people talk about memory as a unitary thing, the brain does not treat memory as something unitary that is localized in one particular place (Chapter 13). In fact, there are many forms of memory, each of which is treated differently by quite widely distributed brain circuits. Thus, this psychological construct of memory that we think of as being a single thing turns out not to be unitary at all.

Even though making assumptions about psychological constructs such as memory and thought is risky, we should certainly not give up searching for how the brain produces them. The assumption of a neurological basis for psychological constructs has perils, but it does not mean that we should fail to consider brain locations for these constructs. After all, thought, memory, emotion, motivation, and other constructs are the most interesting activities performed by the brain.

Psychologists typically use the term **cognition** to describe the processes of thought. The term *cognition* means "knowing." It refers to the processes by which we come to know about the world.

For behavioral neuroscientists, cognition usually entails the ability to pay attention to stimuli, whether external or internal, to identify these stimuli, and to plan meaningful responses to them. External stimuli are those that stimulate neural activity in our sensory receptors. Internal stimuli include cues from the autonomic nervous system as well as from neural processes related to constructs such as memory and motivation.

Cognition. Act or process of knowing or coming to know; in psychology, used to refer to the processes of thought.

Syntax. Ways in which words are put together to form phrases, clauses, or sentences; proposed to be a unique characteristic of human language.

Characteristics of Human Thought

Although human cognition is widely believed to have unique characteristics, in what ways, exactly, is it unique? Many may answer that human thought is verbal, whereas the thought of other animals is nonverbal. Language is presumed to give humans an edge in thinking, and in some ways it does:

■ Language provides the brain with a way to categorize information, allowing us to easily group together objects, actions, and events that have factors in common.
■ Language provides a means of organizing time, especially future time. It enables us to plan our behavior around time (such as "Monday at 3:00 PM") in ways that nonverbal animals cannot.
■ Perhaps most important, human language has **syntax**—sets of rules about how words are put together to create meaningful utterances (Chapter 9).

Linguists argue that, although other animals, such as chimpanzees, can use and recognize a large number of sounds (about three dozen for chimps), they do not arrange these sounds in different orders to produce new meanings. Because of this lack of syntax, chimpanzee language is literal and inflexible (but see "The Origins of Spoken Language" on page 11). Human language, in contrast, has enormous flexibility, which enables us to talk about virtually any topic, even highly abstract ones. In this way, our thinking is carried beyond a rigid here and now.

The importance of syntax to human thinking is illustrated by Oliver Sacks's description of Joseph, an 11-year-old deaf boy who was raised without sign language for his first 10 years, and so was never exposed to syntax. According to Sacks:

> Joseph saw, distinguished, used; he had no problems with perceptual categorization or generalization, but he could not, it seemed, go much beyond this, hold abstract ideas in mind, reflect, play, plan. He seemed completely literal—unable to juggle images or hypotheses or possibilities, unable to enter an imaginative or figurative realm. . . . He seemed, like an animal, or an infant, to be stuck in the present, to be confined to literal and immediate perception. . . . (Sacks, 1989, p. 40)

As stated in Chapter 9, language, including syntax, develops innately in children because the brain is programmed to use words in a form of universal grammar. However, in the absence of words—either spoken or signed—there can be no development of grammar. And, without the flexibility of language that grammar allows, there can also be no "higher level" thought.

Without syntactical language, thought is stuck in the world of concrete, here-and-now perceptions. Syntactical language, in other words, influences the very nature of our thinking. We will return to this idea when we consider the differences between the thought processes of the left and right hemispheres.

In addition to arranging words in syntactical patterns, the human brain appears to have a passion for stringing together events, movements, and thoughts. For example, we combine notes into melodies, movements into dances, and images into movies. We design elaborate rules for games and governments. To conclude that the human brain is organized to structure events, movements, and thoughts into chains seems reasonable. Syntax is merely one example of this innate human way of thinking about the world.

We do not know how this propensity to string things together evolved, but one possibility is that there is natural selection for stringing movements together. Stringing movements together into sequences can be highly adaptive. For instance, it would allow for building houses or weaving fibers into cloth.

William Calvin (1996) proposed that the most important motor sequences to ancient humans were those used in hunting. Throwing a rock or a spear at a moving target is a complex act that requires much planning. Sudden ballistic movements, such as throwing, last less than an eighth of a second and cannot be corrected by feedback. The brain has to plan every detail of these movements and then spit them out as a smooth-flowing sequence.

A modern-day football quarterback does so when he throws a football to a receiver who is running a zigzag pattern to elude a defender. A skilled quarterback can hit the target on virtually every throw, stringing his movements together rapidly in a continuous sequence with no pauses or gaps. This skill is unique to humans. Although chimpanzees can throw objects, their throws are not accurate. No chimpanzee could learn to throw a ball to hit a moving target.

The human predisposition to sequence movements may have encouraged our development of language. Spoken language, after all, is a sequence of movements of the tongue and mouth. Viewed in this way, the development of language is a by-product of a brain that was already predisposed to operate by stringing movements, events, or even ideas together.

A critical characteristic of human motor sequencing is that we are able to create novel sequences with ease. We constantly produce new sentences, and composers and choreographers earn a living creating new sequences in music and dance. Creating novel sequences of movements or thoughts is a function of the frontal lobes. People with damaged frontal lobes have difficulty generating novel solutions to problems, and they are described as lacking imagination. As you know, the frontal lobes are critical to the organization of behavior; it turns out that they are critical to the organization of thinking as well. One of the major differences between the human brain and the brains of other primates is the size of the frontal lobes.

The Neural Unit of Thought

What exactly goes on within the brain to produce what we call thinking? In the discussion of Alex the parrot, we concluded that thinking must result from the activity of complex neural circuits rather than being the property of some particular region in the brain. One way to identify the role of neural circuits is to consider the responses of individual neurons during cognitive activity.

William Newsome and his colleagues (1995) took this approach in training monkeys to identify the presence of apparent motion in a set of moving dots on a television screen. **Experiment 14-1** shows their procedure. The researchers varied the difficulty of the task by manipulating the number of dots that moved in the same direction. For instance, if all the dots are made to move in the same direction, perceiving the whole array of dots as moving in that direction is very easy. If only a small percentage of the dots are

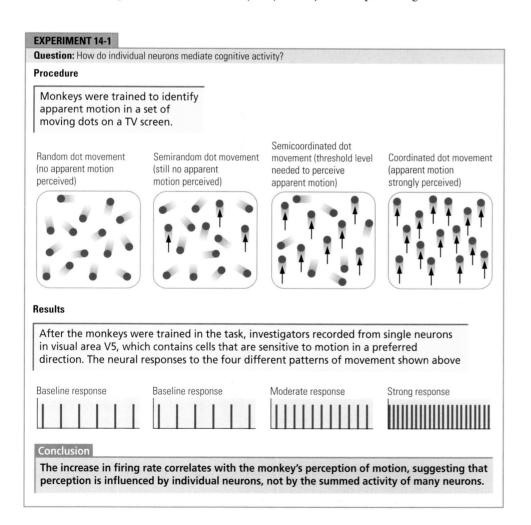

EXPERIMENT 14-1

Question: How do individual neurons mediate cognitive activity?

Procedure

Monkeys were trained to identify apparent motion in a set of moving dots on a TV screen.

Random dot movement (no apparent motion perceived)

Semirandom dot movement (still no apparent motion perceived)

Semicoordinated dot movement (threshold level needed to perceive apparent motion)

Coordinated dot movement (apparent motion strongly perceived)

Results

After the monkeys were trained in the task, investigators recorded from single neurons in visual area V5, which contains cells that are sensitive to motion in a preferred direction. The neural responses to the four different patterns of movement shown above

Baseline response

Baseline response

Moderate response

Strong response

Conclusion

The increase in firing rate correlates with the monkey's perception of motion, suggesting that perception is influenced by individual neurons, not by the summed activity of many neurons.

made to move in the same direction, however, perceiving apparent motion in that direction is much more difficult.

In fact, a threshold number of dots moving together is required to create apparent motion. If the number of dots moving in the same direction is too small, the viewer gets an impression of random movement. Apparently, on the basis of the proportion of dots moving in the same direction, the brain decides whether dots are moving in a consistent direction.

After the monkeys had been trained in the task, the investigators recorded from single neurons in visual area V5, which contains cells that are sensitive to movement in a preferred direction. Consider a neuron that is sensitive to motion in the vertical direction. Such a neuron responds with a vigorous burst of action potentials when there is vertical movement in its receptive field. But, just as the observer has a threshold for the perception of coherent motion in one direction, so, too, does the neuron. In other words, if at some point random activity of the dots increases to a level at which it obscures movement in a neuron's preferred direction, that neuron will stop responding because it does not detect any consistent pattern.

So the question becomes: How does the activity of any given neuron correlate with the perceptual threshold for apparent motion? On the one hand, if our perception of apparent motion results from the summed activity of many dozens, or even thousands, of neurons, there should be little correlation between the activity of any one neuron and that perception. On the other hand, if our perception of apparent motion is influenced by individual neurons, then there should be a strong correlation between the activity of a single cell and that perception.

The results of the experiment were unequivocal: the sensitivity of individual neurons was very similar to the perceptual sensitivity of the monkeys to apparent motion. In other words, if individual neurons failed to respond to the stimulus, the monkeys behaved as if they did not perceive any apparent motion. This finding is curious. Given the large number of V5 neurons, one would think that perceptual decisions are based on the responses of a large pool of neurons. But Newsome's results show that the activity of individual cortical neurons is correlated with perception.

Still, there must be some way of converging the inputs of individual neurons to arrive at a consensus. This convergence of inputs can be explained by Hebb's idea of a cell assembly—an ensemble of neurons that represents a complex concept. In this case, the ensemble of neurons represents a sensory event (apparent motion), which the activity of the ensemble detects.

Such cell assemblies could be distributed over fairly large regions of the brain or they could be confined to smaller areas, such as cortical columns. Cognitive scientists have developed computer models of these circuits and have demonstrated that they are capable of sophisticated statistical computations with reasonably high efficiency. The performance of other complex tasks, such as Alex the parrot's detection of an object's color, also are believed to entail ensembles of neurons. These cell assemblies provide the basis for cognition. Different ensembles combine together, much like words in language, to produce coherent thoughts.

What is the contribution of individual neurons to a cell assembly? Each neuron acts as a computational unit. As Experiment 14-1 shows, even one solitary neuron is capable of deciding on its own when to fire if its summed inputs indicate that movement is taking place. Neurons are the only elements in the brain that combine evidence and make decisions. They are the foundation of thought and cognitive processes.

The combination of these individual neurons into novel neural networks produces complex mental representations, such as ideas. Our next step is to determine where the cell assemblies for various complex cognitive processes are located in the human brain.

In Review

Thought is the act of attending to, identifying, and making meaningful responses to stimuli. Many animals, probably including all mammals and birds, are capable of thought. Unlike thought in other animals, human thought has the added flexibility of language, which influences the nature of human thinking. Human thought is also characterized by the ability to generate strings of ideas, many of which are novel. The basic unit of thought is the neuron. The cell assembly is the vehicle by which neurons interact to influence behavior and to produce cognitive processes.

Association cortex. Neocortex outside the primary sensory and motor cortices that functions to produce cognition.

⊙ You can review the regions of the cortex on your *Foundations of Behavioral Neuroscience* CD. Visit the section on subdivisions of the central nervous system for a three-dimensional model of the cortex. (See the Preface for more information about this CD.)

COGNITION AND THE ASSOCIATION CORTEX

In Chapters 8 through 11, we considered the regions of the cortex responsible for deciphering inputs from sensory receptors and for executing movements. These regions together occupy about a third of the cortex (**Figure 14-1**). The remaining cortex, located in the frontal, temporal, and parietal lobes, is often referred to as the **association cortex,** which functions to produce cognition.

A fundamental difference between the association cortex and the primary sensory and motor cortex is that the association cortex has a distinctive pattern of connections. Recall that a major source of input to all cortical areas is the thalamus. The primary sensory cortex receives inputs from thalamic areas that receive information from the sense organs. In contrast, the association cortex receives its inputs from regions of the thalamus that receive their inputs from other regions of the cortex.

As a result, the inputs to the association cortex have been highly processed before they get to the association regions. This information must therefore be fundamentally different from the information reaching the primary sensory and motor cortex. The association regions contain knowledge, either about our external or internal world or about movements. To understand the types of knowledge that the association areas contain, we consider different forms of cognitive behavior and then trace these behaviors to different parts of the association cortex.

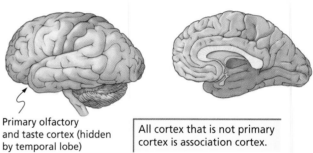

Primary olfactory and taste cortex (hidden by temporal lobe)

All cortex that is not primary cortex is association cortex.

KEY (cortical areas)	
■ Primary motor	■ Primary auditory
■ Primary sensory	■ Primary olfactory
■ Primary visual	and taste

Figure 14-1

Cortical Functions Lateral and medial views of the left and right hemisphere, respectively, showing the primary motor and sensory areas. All remaining cortical areas are collectively referred to as association cortex, which functions in thinking.

Knowledge about Objects

Imagine looking at a cardboard milk carton sitting on a counter directly in front of you. What do you see? Now, imagine moving the carton off to one side. What do you see now? Next, tilt the carton toward you at a 45° angle. Again, what do you see? Probably you answered that you saw the same thing in each situation: a white rectangular object with colored lettering on it.

Intuitively, you probably feel that the brain must "see" the object much as you have perceived it. As you learned in Chapter 8, however, the brain's "seeing" is more compartmentalized than are your perceptions. This compartmentalizaton is revealed in people who suffer damage to different regions of the occipital cortex. They often lose one particular aspect of visual perception. For instance, those with damage to visual area V4 can no longer perceive color, whereas those with damage to area V5 can no longer see movement (when the milk carton moves, it becomes invisible to them).

Moreover, your perception of the milk carton's rectangular shape is not always a completely accurate interpretation of the forms that your visual system is processing.

When the carton is tipped toward you, you still perceive it as rectangular, even though it is no longer presenting a rectangular shape to your eyes. Your brain has somehow ignored the change in information about shape that your retinas have sent it and concluded that this shape is still the same milk carton.

This example demonstrates many properties of visual perception. But there is more to your conception of the milk carton than merely processing its physical characteristics. For example, you know what a milk carton is, what it contains, and where you can get one. This knowledge about milk cartons that you have acquired is represented in the temporal association cortex that forms the ventral stream of visual processing. If the temporal association regions are destroyed, a person loses visual knowledge not only about milk cartons but also about all other objects. Like D. F., whose case is discussed in Chapter 8, the person becomes agnosic.

Knowledge about objects includes even more than simply knowing what they are and what they are used for. Two cases described by Martha Farah (1995) illustrate this point. Case 1 was unable to localize visual stimuli in space and to describe the location of familiar objects from memory. He was, however, good at both identifying objects and describing their appearance from memory. In other words, Case 1 could both perceive and imagine objects, but he could not perceive or imagine their location.

Case 2 was the opposite of Case 1. Case 2 could localize objects and describe their locations from memory, but he could not identify objects or describe them from memory. Case 1 had a lesion in the parietal association cortex, whereas Case 2's lesion was in the temporal association cortex. Knowledge about objects is thus found in more than one location, depending on the nature of the knowledge. Knowledge of *what* things are is temporal; knowledge of *where* things are is parietal.

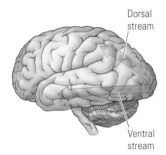

Dorsal stream

Ventral stream

Spatial Cognition

The location of objects is just one aspect of what we know about space. *Spatial cognition* refers to a whole range of mental functions that vary from navigational ability (the ability to go from point A to point B) to the mental manipulation of complex visual arrays like those shown in **Figure 14-2**.

Imagine traveling to an unfamiliar park for a walk. As you walk about the park, you need to proceed in an organized, systematic way. You do not want to go around and around in circles. You also need to be able to find your way back to your bus stop. These abilities require a representation of the physical environment in your mind's eye.

Now let's presume that, at some time in the walk, you are uncertain of where you are (a common problem). One solution is to create a mental image of your route, complete with various landmarks and turns. It is a small step from mentally manipulating these kinds of navigational landmarks and movements to manipulating other kinds of images in your mind. Therefore, the ability to mentally manipulate visual images seems likely to have arisen in parallel with the ability to navigate in space.

The evolution of skill at mentally manipulating things is also closely tied to the evolution of physical movements. In the course of evolution, animals likely first moved by using whole-body movements (such as the swimming motion of a fish), then developed coordinated limb movements (quadrupedal walking), and finally became capable of discrete limb movements, such as the reaching movements of human arms. As the guidance strategies for controlling movements became more sophisticated, cognitive abilities increased as well to support those guidance systems.

It seems unlikely that more sophisticated cognitive abilities evolved on their own. For instance, why would a fish be able to manipulate an object in its mind that it could

Figure 14-2

Spatial Cognition These two figures are the same, but they are oriented differently in space. Researchers test spatial cognition by giving subjects pairs of stimuli like this pair and asking if the shapes are the same or different.

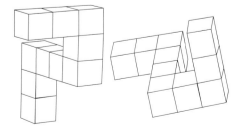

not manipulate in the real world? In contrast, a human who can manipulate objects by hand might be expected to be able to imagine such manipulations. After all, we are constantly observing our hands manipulating things, and so we must have many mental representations of such activity. Alex the parrot, although not having hands, manipulates objects with his beak.

Once the brain can process the manipulation of objects that are physically present, it seems a small step to picturing the manipulation of objects that are only imagined. This ability enables us to solve problems like the one depicted in **Figure 14-3**. The ability to manipulate an object in the mind's eye probably flows from the ability to manipulate tangible objects with the hands.

Which parts of the brain take part in the various aspects of spatial cognition? Some clues related to spatial navigation come from the study of how children develop navigational skills. People navigate by using several kinds of information to guide them. They may take note of single cues or landmarks (a pine tree, a park bench), they may keep track of their movements (turned left, walked 30 meters), and they may relate observed landmarks to their own movements (turned right *at* the bench), thus creating a spatial representation known as a *place response*.

Research findings show a progressive change in the type of navigational information that children use at different ages. In one study, Linda Acredolo (1976) brought children into a small, nondescript room that had a door at one end, a window at the other end, and a table along one wall. The children were walked to a corner of the table and blindfolded. While blindfolded, they were walked in a circuitous route back to the door. Then the blindfold was removed and they were asked to return to the point at which they had been blindfolded.

Unbeknown to the children, the table had sometimes been moved. If children used a place response, they returned to the correct place, even though the table had been moved. If children used a cue or landmark response, they walked directly to the table, regardless of where it was positioned. And, if children used a movement response, they turned in the direction in which they had originally turned when first entering the room.

Acredolo found that 3-year-olds tend to use a movement response, whereas children a few years older used a cue or landmark response, and, by age 7, children had begun to use a place response to find the correct location. This developmental progression probably mimics the evolutionary progression of spatial cognition. Because the cortex matures so late in children, it is likely that the cortex controls the more sophisticated place response in spatial navigation.

Research findings have also provided clues to the brain regions participating in other aspects of spatial cognition. For instance, the dorsal stream in the parietal lobes plays a central role in the control of vision for action (Chapter 8). Discrete limb movements are made to points in space, and so a reasonable supposition is that the evolutionary development of the dorsal stream provided a neural basis for such spatial cognitive skills as the mental rotation of objects. In fact, people with damage to the parietal association regions, especially in the right hemisphere, have deficits in the processing of complex spatial information, both in the real world and in their imaginations.

If we trace the evolutionary development of the human brain, we find that the parietal association regions expanded considerably more in humans than in other primates. This expanded brain region functions, in part, to perform complex spatial operations such as those just discussed. Humans have a capacity for constructing things that far exceeds that of our nearest relative, the chimpanzee. A long leap of logic may be required in making the assertion, but perhaps our increased capacity for building and manipulating objects played an important role in the evolutionary development of our spatial cognitive abilities.

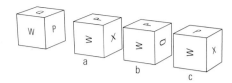

Figure 14-3

Mental Manipulation Try this sample test item used to measure spatial orientation. Compare the three cubes on the right with the one on the left. No letter appears on more than one face of a given cube. Which cube—*a, b,* or *c*— could be a different view of the cube on the left? You can find the correct answer below.

The answer to the mental manipulation in Figure 14-3 is *a*.

Pay Attention!

The brain is clearly capable of processing chemical, mechanical, and electrical energy and generating a rich experience of the world that we take for granted. This personal experience of the world is not simply a matter of registering the presence of particular stimuli but includes subjective features, too, such as what it is like to feel happy versus what it is like to feel surprised.

Such experiences all form what we think of as the "mind." Until recently there did not appear to be any simple way to examine the neurological basis of the mind, and much of our mental life appeared to be beyond the study of nosy neuroscientists. But recent advances in cognitive psychology and cognitive neuroscience have made it possible to derive some inkling of the nature of our mental life.

One way to approach the problem is to consider how our experience of the same world changes. For instance, our subjective experience varies with our frame of mind (e.g., whether we are happy or sad), our motivational state (e.g., food or sexual activity), and our awareness of different features of the environment (e.g., color or movement). Marisa Carrasco and her colleagues (Carrasco, Ling, & Read, 2004) asked a simple question: Does attention alter the appearance of visual information?

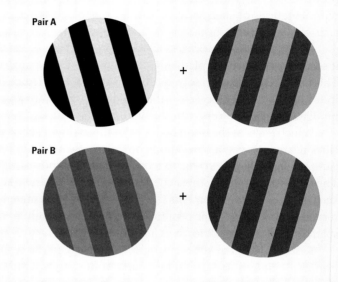

This question seems simple, but psychologists have debated it for more than 100 years. Does simply paying attention to information change how we perceive the information? Or does attention simply intensify our perception of the information?

Carrasco and her colleagues developed a method for assessing phenomenological correlates of attention directly. Participants were presented with pairs of oriented gratings—for example, pairs A and B shown here—and asked to report the orientation of the grating having the higher light–dark

Attention

Imagine going to a football game where you intend to meet some friends. You search for them as you meander through the crowd in the stadium. Suddenly, you hear the distinctive laugh of one friend, and you turn to scan in that direction. You see your group and rush to join them.

This common experience demonstrates the nature of **attention,** selective narrowing or focusing of awareness to part of the sensory environment or to a class of stimuli. Even when you are bombarded by sounds, smells, feelings, and sights, you can still detect a familiar laugh or spot a familiar face. In other words, you can direct your attention. "Pay Attention!" describes researchers' efforts to understand how attention operates.

More than 100 years ago, William James (1890) defined attention in the following way: "It is the taking possession by the mind in clear and vivid form of one out of what seem several simultaneous objects or trains of thought." James's definition goes beyond our example of locating friends in a crowd, inasmuch as he notes that we can attend selectively to thoughts as well as to sensory stimuli. Who hasn't at some time been so preoccupied with a thought as to exclude all else from mind? So attention can be directed inward as well as outward.

Attention. Selective narrowing or focusing of awareness to part of the sensory environment or to a class of stimuli.

contrast. In some trials, as in pair A, the gratings have large differences in contrast, whereas in others, as in pair B, they appear to have less or no difference. Thus, the task was to identify orientation by using information about contrast.

The authors manipulated attention by briefly preceding one of the two choices with a dot that automatically attracted a subject's attention. When the dot was shown in trials with large differences in contrast, the dot failed to influence perception. However, when the dot was flashed on trials in which the contrast difference was small or absent, the observer's perception was altered: he or she now believed that the grating preceded by the dot had higher contrast.

Thus, attention increased the subjective experience of contrast. What is intriguing about the study is that the enhanced attention was covert and not intentional, yet it nonetheless altered sensory impression. As we learned in Chapter 2, the brain is creating the sensory world, but our fantasy world clearly is not static and is influenced by our unconscious awareness.

Another way to think about our mental world is to measure brain activity as we experience different sensory stimuli. For example, changes in cerebral blood flow are correlated with specific visual or auditory stimuli (Chapter 9). But what about more private mental feelings? Recall

that social exclusion activates specific limbic cortical areas (see "The Pain of Rejection" on page 389). And what about individual differences in subjective experience and brain activity?

Stephan Hamann and his colleagues (2004) measured the brain activity of males and females to sexually arousing visual stimuli. Men are generally more interested than women in sexually arousing visual stimuli and are more responsive to it. In this study, men and women showed similar brain activity across most brain regions, but there were large differences in the amygdala: men showed higher activation than women to the same stimuli, the difference being larger in the left amygdala than in the right.

Surprisingly, women actually showed no more activation in the amygdala for sexually arousing scenes than for neutral scenes. The difference was not because the women were not aroused by the stimuli; they reported the stimuli to be just as arousing as did the men. The mental experience of the same visual stimulus appears to show a sex-related difference, which may provide a basis for the greater role of visual stimuli in male sexual arousal. The results obtained in the Hamann study do not tell us whether the basis of the sex difference was experiential or genetic, but they do show that large individual differences in brain activity can be related to the same stimulus.

SELECTIVE ATTENTION

Like the neural basis of many other mental processes, the neural basis of attention is particularly difficult to study. However, research findings on monkeys have identified neurons in the cortex and midbrain that show enhanced firing rates to particular locations or visual stimuli to which the animals have been trained to attend. Significantly, *the same stimulus* can activate a neuron at one time but not at another, depending on the monkey's learned focus of attention.

In the study shown in **Experiment 14-2**, James Moran and Robert Desimone (1985) trained monkeys to hold a bar while gazing at a fixation point on a screen. A sample stimulus (e.g., a vertical red bar) appeared briefly at one location in the visual field, followed about 500 ms later by a test stimulus at the same location. When the test stimulus was identical with the initial sample stimulus, an animal was rewarded if it immediately released the bar that it held in its hand. Each animal was trained to attend to stimuli presented in one particular area of the visual field and to ignore stimuli in any other area. In this way, the same visual stimulus could be presented to different regions of a neuron's receptive field to test whether the cell's response varied with stimulus location.

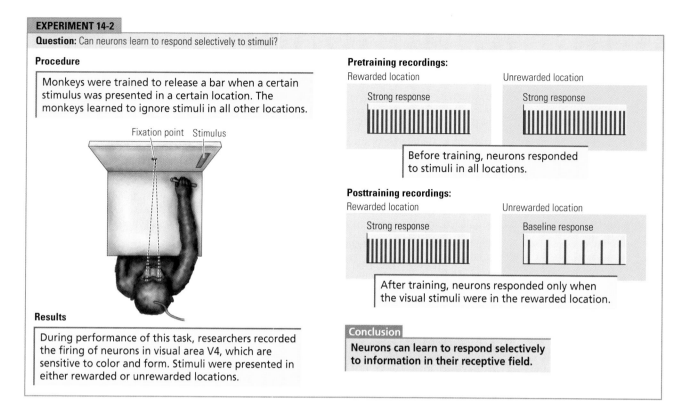

EXPERIMENT 14-2

Question: Can neurons learn to respond selectively to stimuli?

Procedure

Monkeys were trained to release a bar when a certain stimulus was presented in a certain location. The monkeys learned to ignore stimuli in all other locations.

Fixation point   Stimulus

Pretraining recordings:

Rewarded location | Unrewarded location
Strong response | Strong response

Before training, neurons responded to stimuli in all locations.

Posttraining recordings:

Rewarded location | Unrewarded location
Strong response | Baseline response

After training, neurons responded only when the visual stimuli were in the rewarded location.

Results

During performance of this task, researchers recorded the firing of neurons in visual area V4, which are sensitive to color and form. Stimuli were presented in either rewarded or unrewarded locations.

Conclusion

Neurons can learn to respond selectively to information in their receptive field.

As the animals performed the task, the researchers recorded the firing of neurons in visual area V4. Neurons in area V4 are sensitive to color and form, with different neurons responding to different combinations of these two variables (e.g, a red vertical bar or a green horizontal bar). Visual stimuli were presented either in the correct location for a reward or in an incorrect location for no reward.

As diagrammed in the Results section of Experiment 14-2, neurons responded only when a visual stimulus was in the correct location, even though *the same stimulus* was presented in the incorrect location. Before training, the neurons responded to all stimuli in both locations. This finding tells us that the ability to attend to specific parts of the sensory world is a property of single neurons. Once again, we see that the neuron is the computational unit of cognition.

DEFICITS OF ATTENTION

Attention is likely a property of neurons throughout the brain, with some regions playing a more central role in attention than others. The frontal lobes, for instance, play a very important part. People with frontal-lobe injuries tend to become overly focused on environmental stimuli. They seem to selectively direct their attention to an excessive degree or have difficulty in shifting attention.

The results of studies of these people suggest that the frontal association cortex plays a critical role in the ability to flexibly direct attention where it is needed. Indeed, the formation of plans, which you know to be a frontal-lobe function, *requires* this ability. In addition, the parietal association cortex plays a key role in other aspects of attention. This role is perhaps best illustrated by studying the attention deficit referred to as *neglect*.

Neglect is a condition in which a person ignores sensory information that should be considered important. Usually the condition affects only one side of the body, in which case it is called **contralateral neglect. Figure 14-4** shows contralateral neglect in a dog that would eat food only from the right side of its dish. Neglect is a fascinating

Contralateral neglect. Ignoring a part of the body or world on the side opposite (i.e., contralateral) that of a brain injury.

Extinction. In neurology, neglect of information on one side of the body when it is presented simultaneously with similar information on the other side of the body.

symptom because it often entails no damage to sensory pathways. Rather, the problem is a failure of attention.

People with damage to the parietal association cortex of the right hemisphere may have particularly severe neglect of objects or events in the left side of their world. For example, one man dressed only the right side of his body, shaved only the right side of his face, and read only the right side of a page (if you can call that reading). He was capable of moving his left limbs spontaneously, but, when asked to raise both his arms, he would raise only the right. When pressed, he could be induced to raise the left arm, but then he would quickly drop it to his side again.

As people with contralateral neglect begin to recover, they show another interesting symptom, **extinction.** This symptom refers to the neglect of information on one side of the body when it is presented simultaneously with similar information on the other side of the body. **Figure 14-5** shows a common clinical test for extinction.

The patient is asked to keep his or her eyes fixed on the examiner's face and to report objects presented in one or both sides of the visual field. When presented with a single object (a fork) to one side or the other, the patient orients himself or herself toward the appropriate side of the visual field, and so we know that he or she cannot be blind on either side. But now suppose that two forks are presented, one on the left and one on the right. Curiously, the patient ignores the fork on the left and reports that there is one on the right. When asked about the left side, the patient is quite certain that nothing appeared there and that only one fork was presented, on the right.

Perhaps the most curious aspect of neglect is that people with it fail to pay attention not only to one side of the physical world around them but also to one side of the world that they represent in their minds. We studied one woman who had complete neglect for everything on her left side. She complained that she could not use her kitchen, because she could never remember the location of anything on her left.

We asked her to imagine standing at the kitchen door and to describe what was in the various drawers on her right and left. She could not recall anything on her left. We then asked her to imagine walking to the end of the kitchen and turning around.

We now asked her what was on her right, which had previously been on her left. She broke into a big smile and tears ran down her face as she realized that she now knew what was on that side of the room. All she had to do was reorient her body in her mind's eye. She later wrote and thanked us for changing her life, because she was now able to cook again. Clearly, neglect can exist in the mind as well as in the physical world.

Although complete contralateral neglect is normally associated with parietal-lobe injury, specific forms of neglect can arise from other injuries. Ralph Adolphs and his colleagues (2005) described case S. M., a woman with bilateral amygdala damage, who could not recognize fear in faces. On further study, the reason was shown to be that S. M. failed to look at the eyes when she looked at faces; instead, she looked at other facial features such as the nose. Because fear is most clearly identified in the eyes and not the nose, she did not identify the emotion. When she was specifically instructed to look at the eyes, her recognition of fear became entirely normal. Thus, the amygdala plays a role in directing attention to the eyes to identify facial expressions.

Dennis O'Brien

Figure 14-4

Contralateral Neglect in a Dog This dog had a right hemisphere brain tumor and would eat the food in the right side of its dish but ignore food in the left side.

Figure 14-5

Testing for Extinction A stroke patient who shows neglect for information presented to his left responds differently, depending on whether objects in the left and right visual fields are similar or different.

When shown two identical objects

Patient's right visual field

Patient's left visual field

Patient sees only the object in his right visual

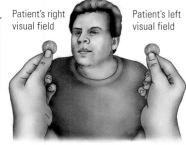

When shown two different objects

Patient sees the object in both visual fields.

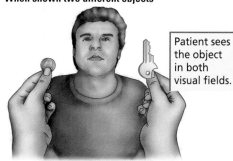

When shown two kinds of an object

Patient sees only the object in his right visual field.

Planning

Imagine the following scenario. It's Friday noon and one of your friends proposes that you go to a nearby city for the weekend to attend a concert. She will pick you up at 6:00 PM and you will drive there together.

Because you are completely unprepared for this invitation and because you are going to be busy until 4:00, you must rush home at 4:00 and get organized. En route you stop at a fast food restaurant so that you won't be hungry on the 2-hour drive. You also need money, and so you zoom to the nearest ATM. When you get home, you grab various pieces of clothing appropriate for the concert and the trip. You also pack your toiletries. You somehow manage to get ready by 6:00, when your friend arrives.

Although the task of getting ready in a hurry may make us a bit harried, most of us can manage to do it, but people with frontal-lobe injury cannot. To learn why, let's consider what the task requires.

1. You have to plan your behavior, which requires selecting from many options. What do you need to take with you? Money? Then which bank machine is closest and what is the quickest route to get there? Do you also need something to eat? Then what is the fastest way to get food on a Friday afternoon?
2. In view of your time constraint, you have to ignore irrelevant stimuli. For instance, if you pass a sign advertising a sale in your favorite music store, you have to ignore it and persist with the task at hand.
3. You have to keep track of what you have done already, a requirement especially important while you are packing. You do not want to forget items or to duplicate items. You do not want to take four pairs of shoes but no toothbrush, for example.

The general requirements of this task can be described as the temporal (or time) organization of behavior. You are planning what you need to do and when you need to do it. Such planning is the general function of the frontal lobes.

But note that, to perform this task, you also need to recognize objects (an occipital- and temporal-lobe function) and to make appropriate movements with respect to them (a parietal-lobe function). You can therefore think of the frontal lobes as acting like an orchestra conductor. The frontal lobes make and read some sort of motor plan (a kind of motor "score," analogous to the musical score of a conductor) to organize behavior in space and time. People with frontal-lobe injuries are simply unable to organize their behavior.

Performance on the Wisconsin Card Sorting Task provides an example of the kinds of deficits that frontal-lobe injury creates. **Figure 14-6** shows the testing materials. The subject is presented with the four stimulus cards arrayed at the top. These cards bear designs that differ in color, form, and number of elements, thus creating three possible sorting categories to be used in the task.

The subject must sort a deck of cards into piles in front of the various stimulus cards, depending on the sorting category called for. The correct sorting category is never stated. The subject is told after placing each card whether the choice that he or she has made is correct or incorrect.

For example, in one trial, the first correct sorting category is color. Then, after the subject has sorted a number of cards by color, the correct solution switches, without warning, to form. When the subject has started to sort by form, the correct solution again changes unexpectedly, this time to the number of items on each card. The sorting rule later becomes color again, and so on, with each change in rule coming unannounced.

Shifting response strategies is particularly difficult for people with frontal-lobe lesions, who may continue responding to the original stimulus (color) for as

---

Figure 14-6

Wisconsin Card Sorting Test The subject's task is to place each card in the bottom pile under the appropriate card in the top row, sorting by one of three possible categories: color, number, or form. Subjects are never explicitly told what the corrrect sorting category is, only whether their responses are correct or incorrect. After subjects have begun using one sorting category, the tester unexpectedly changes to another category.

many as 100 cards until the test ends. They may even comment that they know that color is no longer the correct category, but they continue to sort on the basis of it. As one such person stated: "Form is probably the correct solution now so this [sorting by color] will be wrong, and this will be wrong, and wrong again." Curiously, then, despite knowing what the correct sorting category is, the frontal-lobe patient is unable to shift behavior in response to the new external information.

Imitation and Understanding

In all communication—both verbal and nonverbal—the sender and receiver must have a common understanding of what counts. If a person speaks a word or makes a gesture, it will be understood only if another person interprets it correctly. To accomplish this coordination in communication, the processes of producing and perceiving a message must have some kind of representation common to the brain of the sender and that of the receiver.

How is this common representation achieved? How do both the sender and the receiver of a potentially ambiguous gesture, such as a raised hand or a faint smile, have a common understanding of what that gesture means? Giacomo Rizzolatti and Michael Arbib (1998) proposed an answer to these questions.

In the frontal lobes of monkeys, they identified neurons that discharge during the production of active movements of the hand or mouth or both. These neural discharges do not precede the movements but instead occur in synchrony with them. Because it would take time for a neural message to go from a frontal lobe to a hand, we would predict that, if these cells are controlling the movements, they will discharge before the movements take place. The cells must therefore be recording that the movement is taking place.

In the course of his studies, Rizzolatti also made the remarkable finding that many of these neurons discharge when a monkey sees other monkeys make the same movements. They also discharge when the monkey sees the experimenter make the movements. Rizzolatti called these "mirror neurons." A **mirror neuron** does not respond to an object, only to a specific observed action. The researchers proposed that mirror neurons represent actions, whether one's own or those of others. Such neural representations could be used both for imitating others' actions and for understanding the meaning of those actions, thus enabling appropriate responses. Mirror neurons therefore provide the link between the sender and the receiver of communication.

Rizzolatti and his colleagues used PET to look for these same neuron populations in humans. Subjects were asked to watch a movement, to make the same movement, or to imagine the movement. In each case, a region of the lateral frontal lobe in the left hemisphere, including Broca's area, was activated.

Taken together with those of the monkey studies, this finding suggests that primates have a fundamental mechanism for action recognition. People apparently recognize actions made by others because the neural patterns produced when the actions are observed are similar to those produced when they themselves make those same actions. According to Rizzolatti, the human capacity to communicate with words may have resulted from a progressive evolution of the mirror-neuron system observed in the monkey brain. After all, the ability to mimic behaviors, such as dancing and singing, is central to human culture. The evolution of this capacity was perhaps the precursor to the evolution of language. For language, the same neurons would recognize words spoken by others and would produce those same words in speech.

A major difference between humans and monkeys is that the mirror neurons are localized to the left hemisphere in humans. Although the reason is not immediately clear, the existence of a unilateral representation may be significant for understanding

Mirror neuron. Nerve cell that fires when a monkey observes a specific action being made by another monkey.

how language is organized in the brain. If the abilities to mimic and to understand gestures were present before language developed and if the neural circuits for these abilities became lateralized, then language would also have become lateralized because the system on which it is based already existed in the left hemisphere.

In Review

The association cortex contains knowledge about both our external and our internal worlds and functions to produce the many different forms of cognitive behavior in which we engage. As a general rule, the temporal lobes generate knowledge about objects, whereas the parietal lobes produce various forms of spatial cognition. In addition, neurons in both the temporal and the parietal lobes seem to contribute to our ability to selectively attend to particular sensory information. The frontal lobes function not only to make movements but also to plan movements and to organize our behavior over time. In humans, an area of the left frontal lobe interprets the behavior of others so that the information can be used to plan appropriate actions.

STUDYING THE HUMAN BRAIN AND COGNITION

Historically, the functions of the association cortex have been inferred largely from the study of neurological patients. In recent years, however, many new technologies have been developed to study cognition in the normal brain. So, in addition to traditional neuropsychological studies of brain-damaged patients, researchers now have a rich array of more-modern methods to help them analyze the neural correlates of human thought. Here we consider some of these research techniques. Using them to study the neural basis of cognition is often referred to as **cognitive neuroscience.**

Methods of Cognitive Neuroscience

Beginning in the mid-1800s, physicians such as Paul Broca began to make clinical observations about the mental activity of people with specific brain injuries. In the twentieth century, this clinical approach developed into the discipline now called **neuropsychology.** Neuropsychological studies consist of analysis of the behavioral symptoms of people with circumscribed, usually unilateral brain lesions due to stroke, illness, surgery, or trauma.

Presumably, if a patient shows impairment on some behavioral test, the damaged area must play a role in that particular behavior. To conclude that the area in question has a special function, however, requires showing that lesions in other parts of the brain do not produce a similar deficit. For example, if a temporal-lobe patient is impaired on a test of verbal memory, we would need to demonstrate that someone with frontal- or parietal-lobe injury does not have a similar impairment. Neuropsychological studies typically compare the effects that injuries to different brain regions have on particular tasks, as illustrated in "Neuropsychological Assessment."

A second approach to examining human brain function is to measure brain activity and correlate this measurement with the cognitive activity inferred to be taking place at the same time. One method of measuring brain activity is to use electrical recordings, such as the event-related potentials (ERPs) discussed in Chapter 4 (see Figures 4-27 and 4-28).

Cognitive neuroscience. Study of the neural basis of cognition.

Neuropsychology. General term used to refer to the study of the relation between brain function and behavior.

Neuropsychological Assessment

Beginning in the late 1940s and continuing today, neuropsychologists have devised a battery of behavioral tests designed to evaluate the functional capacities of different cortical areas, especially association areas. Although "high tech" procedures such as PET, fMRI, and ERP also have been developed, "low tech" behavioral assessment continues to be one of the best and simplest ways to measure cognitive function.

To illustrate the nature and power of neuropsychological assessment, we will compare the test performance of three patients on five of the tests used in a complete neuropsychological assessment. The first two are tests of delayed memory—one verbal, the other visual. The patients were read a list of words and two short stories. They were also shown a series of simple drawings. Their task was to repeat the words and stories immediately after hearing them and to draw the simple figures. Then, without warning, they were asked to do so again 30 min later. Their performances on these delayed tests yield the delayed verbal and visual memory scores.

The third test is verbal fluency, in which patients were given 5 min to write down as many words as they could think of that start with the letter *s*, excluding people's names and numbers. Next is the Wisconsin Card Sorting Test, which assesses abstract reasoning (see Figure 14-6). Finally, the patients were given a reading test. For all these tests, performance was compared with that of a normal control subject.

The first patient, J. N., was a 28-year-old man who had developed a tumor in the anterior and medial part of the left temporal lobe. Preoperative psychological tests showed this man to be of superior intelligence, with his only significant deficits being on tests of verbal memory. When we saw him, 1 year after surgery that successfully removed the tumor, he had returned to his job as a personnel manager. His intelligence was still superior, but, as the accompanying score summary shows, he was still impaired on the delayed verbal

Subjects' Scores				
Test	Control	J. N.	E. B.	J. W.
Delayed verbal memory	17	9*	16	16
Delayed visual memory	12	14	8*	12
Verbal fluency	62	62	66	35*
Card-sorting errors	9	10	12	56*
Reading	15	21	22	17

* Abnormally poor score

memory test, recalling only about 50 percent as much as the other subjects did.

The second patient, E. B., was a college senior majoring in psychology. An aneurysm in her right temporal lobe had burst, and the anterior part of that lobe had been removed. E. B. was of above-average intelligence and completed her bachelor of arts degree with good grades. Her residual deficit was clearly shown on her delayed visual memory test, where she recalled just a little more than half of what the other subjects did.

The third patient, J. W., was a 42-year-old police detective who had a college diploma and also was of above-average intelligence. He had a benign tumor in the left frontal lobe. We saw him 10 years after his surgery, at which time he was still working in the police force, although at a desk job. His verbal fluency was markedly reduced, as was his ability to solve the card-sorting task. His reading skill, however, was unimpaired, which was also true of the other patients.

Two points can be made from the results of these neuropsychological assessments. First, damage to different parts of the brain produces different symptoms, which allows functions to be localized to different cerebral regions. Second, brain organization is asymmetrical. Left-hemisphere damage preferentially affects verbal functions, whereas right-hemisphere damage preferentially affects nonverbal functions.

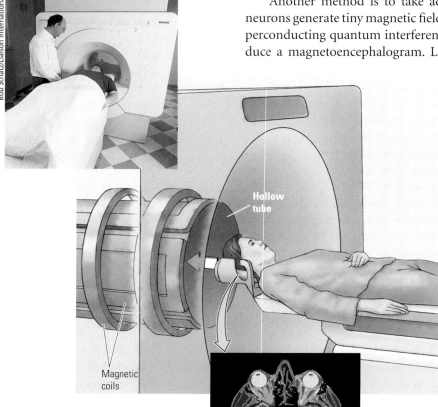

Another method is to take advantage of the fact that the electrical currents of neurons generate tiny magnetic fields. A special recording device known as a SQUID (superconducting quantum interference device) can record these magnetic fields and produce a magnetoencephalogram. Like the ERP procedure, **magnetoencephalography** (MEG) requires that many measurements be taken and averaged.

A third approach to the study of human brain function is to measure brain metabolism, as in a PET scan, described in Chapter 8. A more recent, less-invasive alternative is **magnetic resonance imaging** (MRI), illustrated in **Figure 14-7**. MRI is based on the principle that hydrogen atoms behave like spinning bar magnets in the presence of a magnetic field.

Normally, hydrogen atoms point randomly in different directions but, when placed in a magnetic field, they line up in parallel as they orient themselves with respect to the field's lines of force. In MRI, radio pulses are applied to a brain whose atoms have been aligned in this manner, and the radio pulses form a second magnetic field. This second field causes the spinning atoms to wobble irregularly, thus producing a tiny electrical current that the MRI measures.

When the currents are recorded, images of the brain based on the density of the hydrogen atoms in different regions can be made. For example, areas of the brain with a high water (H_2O) content (neuron-rich areas) will stand out from areas with a lower water content (axon-rich areas). Figure 14-7 shows such a magnetic resonance image. When a region of the brain is active, the amount of blood flow and oxygen to it increases. A change in the oxygen content of the blood alters the spin of the blood's hydrogen atoms. This alteration, in turn, affects the MRI signal.

In 1990, Segi Ogawa and his colleagues showed that MRI could accurately match these changes in magnetic properties to specific locations in the brain (Ogawa et al., 1990), a process known as **functional magnetic resonance imaging** (fMRI). **Figure 14-8** illustrates changes in the fMRI signal in the visual cortex of a person who is being stimulated visually. Manipulation of the characteristics of the stimulus (color, motion, spatial orientation) allows the dissociation of the activity of the various visual areas of the occipital lobes (the areas shown in Figure 8-17). In other words, fMRI can show that different visual areas are differentially activated when different types of visual stimuli are presented.

A major advantage over PET is that fMRI allows the anatomical structure of each subject's brain to be identified, and brain activity can then be related to localized anatomical regions on the brain image. Functional MRI also has better spatial resolution than does PET. And the actual change in the oxygen signal caused by changes in blood flow can be monitored.

On the negative side, however, fMRI is expensive. The resolution of standard hospital MRI is generally insufficient for research purposes, and so neuroscientists need to buy even more expensive equipment to conduct their specialized research. In addition, fMRI can be very difficult for subjects to endure. They are required to lie motionless

Figure 14-7

Magnetic Resonance Imaging
The subject is placed in a long metal cylinder that has two sets of magnetic coils arranged at right angles to each other. An additional coil, known as a radio frequency coil, surrounds the head (not shown) and is designed to perturb the static magnetic fields to produce the magnetic resonance image.

Hollow tube

Magnetic coils

Bob Schatz/Liaison International

On your *Foundations* CD, you can further investigate magnetic resonance imaging. In the module on research methods, visit the area on MRI technology to see scans of different brain sections.

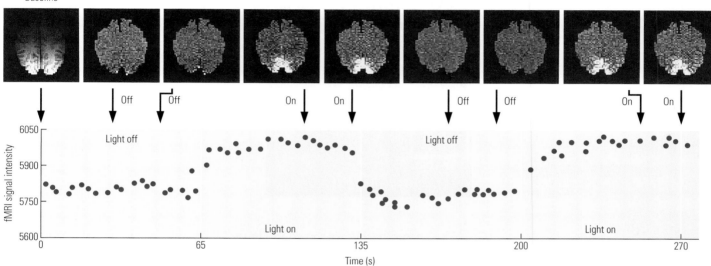

Figure 14-8

Functional MRI Functional magnetic resonance images showing V1 activation in a normal human brain during visual stimulation. The occipital pole is at the bottom. A baseline acquired in darkness (*far left*) was subtracted from the subsequent images (see Figure 9-22). The subject wore tightly fitting goggles containing light-emitting diodes that were turned on and off as a rapid sequence of scans was obtained in a period of 270 s. The images show prominent activity in the visual cortex when the light is on and rapid cessation of activity when the light is off. The graph (*bottom*) illustrates that the on-line fMRI measure can be quantified. Adapted from "Dynamic Magnetic Resonance Imaging of Human Brain Activity During Primary Sensory Stimulation," by K. K. Kwong et al., 1992, *Proceedings of the National Academy of Sciences, USA, 89*, p. 5678.

in a long, noisy tube, an experience that can be quite claustrophobic. The confined space also restricts the types of behavioral experiments that can be performed.

Yet another way to study human brain function is to disrupt brain activity briefly while a person is performing some task to observe the results. Wilder Penfield used this procedure when he electrically stimulated the brains of patients who were about to undergo neurosurgery (Chapter 9). Although much has been learned by using brain stimulation, it has a major drawback: it can be carried out only on subjects whose brains are exposed. This requirement makes it impractical as a laboratory research tool.

More recently, a procedure has been developed that can be used on normal subjects. This technique is called **transcranial magnetic stimulation** (TMS). A low-frequency magnetic stimulus placed next to the skull causes a disruption of brain function in the region immediately adjacent to the magnet. Thus, by placing a small coil over the skull and using repetitive TMS (rTMS), one can interfere with the neural activity of the brain regions under the coil.

One reason for this interference is a drop in blood flow in the stimulated area, resulting in disturbed functioning. In a typical experiment, a region of brain is located first on an image obtained by MRI. When the coordinates of the region are identified, the magnetic coil for TMS is put in place.

The Power of Cognitive Neuroscientific Analysis

Thomas Paus and colleagues (1997) combined TMS, PET, and fMRI to produce a very powerful investigative tool, illustrated in **Figure 14-9**. Paus first located the motor cortex by using fMRI. Then a magnetic coil was positioned over that region. The subject was next placed in a PET scanner, and PET activity was recorded while magnetic stimulation was applied.

Magnetoencephalography (MEG). Recording of the changes in tiny magnetic fields generated by the brain.

Magnetic resonance imaging (MRI). Imaging procedure in which a computer draws a map from the measured changes in the magnetic resonance of atoms in the brain; allows the production of a structural map of the brain without actually opening the skull.

Functional magnetic resonance imaging (fMRI). Type of magnetic resonance imaging that takes advantage of the fact that changes in the distribution of elements such as oxygen alter the magnetic properties of the brain. Because oxygen consumption varies with behavior, changes that are produced by behavior can be mapped and measured.

Transcranial magnetic stimulation (TMS). Procedure in which a low-frequency magnetic coil is placed over the skull to stimulate the underlying brain tissue; can be used either to induce behavior or to disrupt ongoing behavior.

Figure 14-9

Integrated Imaging Technique
Transcranial magnetic stimulation (TMS) can be used in combination with other imaging techniques, such as PET or fMRI, to study cortical functioning. Researchers such as Tomas Paus use this integrated technique to locate and to study brain regions in healthy subjects.

1 Brain region is located with the use of MRI.

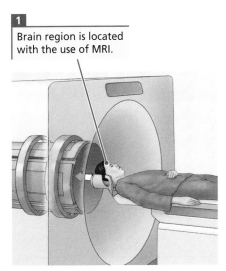

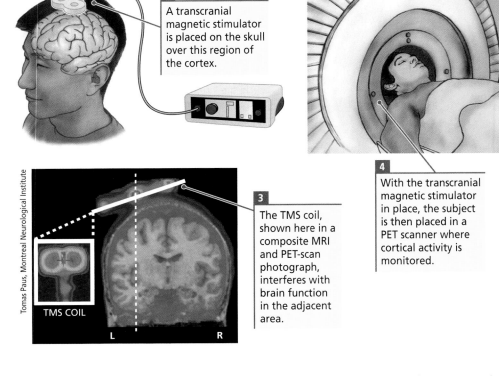

2 A transcranial magnetic stimulator is placed on the skull over this region of the cortex.

3 The TMS coil, shown here in a composite MRI and PET-scan photograph, interferes with brain function in the adjacent area.

TMS COIL

L   R

Tomas Paus, Montreal Neurological Institute

4 With the transcranial magnetic stimulator in place, the subject is then placed in a PET scanner where cortical activity is monitored.

The imaged results are shown in **Figure 14-10**. The drop in neural activity in the motor cortex as a result of the magnetic stimulation also affected regions connected with the motor cortex. When Paus stimulated the frontal eye fields in the premotor area, he found a decline in blood flow in parietal regions in the dorsal stream that are presumably connected to the frontal eye fields.

The combination of these three technologies thus allows a novel procedure for mapping connectivity in the human brain as well as for measuring the effect of TMS on the performance of particular cognitive activities. Studies using TMS to record cognitive activity have not yet been reported, but the technique is powerful and will certainly be used for this purpose in the near future.

The power of cognitive neuroscientific analysis can also be illustrated in an fMRI study by Dirk Wildgruber and his colleagues (1999). This study was based on the clinical observation that people with damage to the frontal lobe of either hemisphere often have difficulty reversing the serial order of items such as digits, the days of the week, or the months of the year. For instance, when these patients are asked to count or to list the days or months in a forward direction, they do so with ease but, when asked for the same information in reverse order (Sunday, Saturday, Friday, and so on), they have difficulty. The frontal lobes seem to be active during the reverse-serial-order task but not during the forward task.

To evaluate this hypothesis, fMRI was conducted on normal subjects who silently recited the names of the months either forward or backward. **Figure 14-11** summarizes

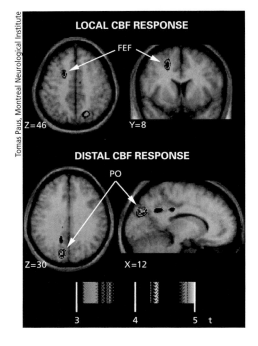

LOCAL CBF RESPONSE

FEF

Z=46   Y=8

DISTAL CBF RESPONSE

PO

Z=30   X=12

3   4   5   t

Tomas Paus, Montreal Neurological Institute

Figure 14-10

Brain Mapping   In this example, TMS was used to stimulate the premotor cortex region that controls eye movements and is called the frontal eye field (FEF). A TMS coil was then positioned over that area. Measurement of cerebral blood flow (CBF), by using PET, showed that the TMS altered blood flow, both at the site of stimulation (the local CBF response) and in the parietal occipital cortex (PO, the distal CBF response), which reveals the connections between the frontal and posterior cortical regions. Adapted from "Transcranial Magnetic Stimulation During Positron Emission Tomography: A New Method for Studying Connectivity of the Human Cerebral Cortex," by T. Paus, R. Jech, C. J. Thompson, R. Comeau, T. Peters, and A. Evans, 1997, *Journal of Neuroscience, 17*, pp. 3178–3184.

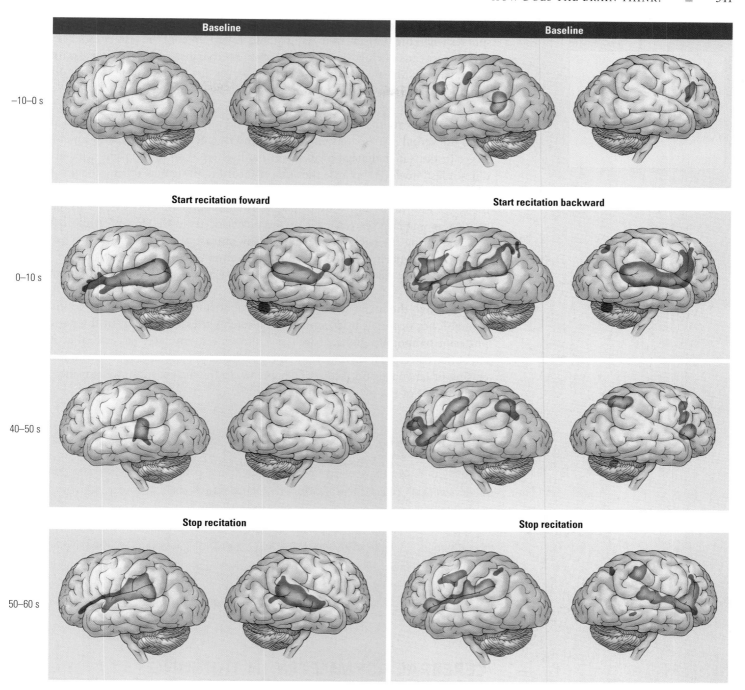

Figure 14-11

Hypothesis Testing with fMRI Summary illustrations of fMRI-measured cerebral activation when normal subjects were asked to mentally recite the names of the months either forward (*shown on the left*) or backward (*shown on the right*). (*Top row*) During the 10-s period preceding the beginning of the task, but after instructions were given, there is some fMRI signal in the frontal lobe and posterior temporal region in the "recite backward" condition, possibly because subjects are rehearsing. During the verbal command to begin (*second row*), the subjects show activation of the temporal auditory areas bilaterally, with greater activation on the left in the "recite forward"

condition and greater activation in the frontal lobe in the "recite backward" condition. When the instructions are completed (*third row*), activation is seen only in the left posterior temporal region in the "recite forward" condition, but, in the "recite backward" condition, it is also seen in the frontal and posterior parietal regions, especially on the left. (*Bottom row*) When the subjects hear the instruction to stop, the temporal auditory areas are once again activated. Adapted from "Dynamic Pattern of Brain Activation During Sequencing of Word Strings Evaluated by fMRI," by D. Wildgruber, U. Kischka, H. Ackermann, U. Klose, and W. Grodd, 1999, *Cognitive Brain Research, 7*, pp. 285–294.

the major findings of the study. The top row shows scans from the right and left hemispheres when the subjects were lying quietly for 10 s before the task began. The second row shows scans during the first 10 s after the verbal instructions to start reciting were given, whereas the third row shows scans during the next 40 to 50 s while the silent recitation was going on. The bottom row shows scans during the 10 s after the subjects were told to stop reciting.

Two major results emerge from the study. First, when the subjects heard and analyzed the verbal instructions, increased blood flow to the temporal auditory areas was larger in the left (language-processing) hemisphere than in the right. This activation did not last, however, because the subjects heard nothing new during the task.

Second, reciting the months activated the brain differently, depending on whether the recitation was in a forward or backward direction. During the forward recitation, activation was largely restricted to the posterior temporal cortex in the left hemisphere. During the backward recitation, in contrast, there was bilateral activation of the frontal and parietal cortex, although activation was greater on the left side. Clearly, fMRI is a highly valuable method for analyzing changes in brain activity as they take place.

Although the major goal of the Wildgruber study was to examine the role of the frontal lobes in serial-ordering tasks, it also showed involvement of the parietal and posterior temporal regions, as well as a left–right asymmetry in cerebral activity. We encountered cerebral asymmetry before, particularly in reference to the auditory processing of language and music in Chapter 9. In the next section, we consider the differential role of the two hemispheres in thinking.

In Review

Analysis of the behavioral symptoms of brain-injured patients began in the late 1800s. In the twentieth century, this approach developed into the field of neuropsychology. Until the 1990s, neuropsychological assessment was the primary source of insights into how the human brain thinks. In recent years, however, the development of sophisticated imaging techniques, including ERP, PET, fMRI, MEG, and TMS, has allowed the development of cognitive neuroscience, the study of brain activity while subjects perform various cognitive tasks. By using multiple methods, contemporary researchers can gather converging evidence on the nature of neural activity during human thought.

CEREBRAL ASYMMETRY IN THINKING

A fundamental discovery in behavioral neuroscience was the finding by Broca and his contemporaries in the mid-1800s that language is lateralized to the left hemisphere. But the implications of this finding were not really understood until the 1960s, when Roger Sperry (1968) and his colleagues began to study people who had undergone surgical separation of the two hemispheres as a treatment for intractable epilepsy. That the two cerebral hemispheres were more specialized in their functions than researchers had previously realized soon became apparent.

Popular authors in the 1980s seized on this idea and began to write about "left brained" and "right brained" people and how left-brained people's right-hemisphere skills could supposedly be improved by training to use nonverbal strategies to solve cognitive problems. Although this type of popularized discussion has declined in recent years, the concept of cerebral asymmetry is still important to understanding how the human brain thinks. So, before considering how the two sides of the brain cooperate in generating cognitive activity, we look at the anatomical differences between the left and right hemispheres.

Anatomical Asymmetry

As you learned in Chapter 9 in examining brain asymmetries related to audition, the language- and music-related areas of the left and right temporal lobes differ anatomically. In particular, the primary auditory area is larger on the right, whereas the secondary auditory areas are larger on the left in most people. Other regions also are asymmetrical. For instance, the posterior parietal cortex of the right hemisphere is larger than the corresponding region of the left hemisphere.

Figure 14-12 shows that the lateral fissure, which partly separates the temporal and parietal lobes, has a sharper upward course in the right hemisphere relative to the left. The result is that the posterior part of the right temporal lobe is larger than the same region on the left side of the brain, as is the left parietal lobe relative to the right.

There are also anatomical asymmetries in the frontal lobes. For example, the region of the sensory–motor cortex representing the face is larger in the left hemisphere than in the right, a difference that presumably corresponds to the special role of the left hemisphere in talking. Furthermore, Broca's area (the frontal operculum) is organized differently on the left and right. The area visible on the surface of the brain is about one-third larger on the right than on the left, whereas the area of cortex buried in the sulci of this region is greater on the left than on the right.

Not only do these gross anatomical differences between the two hemispheres exist but so, too, do hemispheric differences in the details of cellular and neurochemical structure. For example, the neurons in Broca's area on the left have larger dendritic fields than do the corresponding neurons on the right. The discovery of these structural asymmetries and others tells us little about why such differences exist. Ongoing research is now beginning to show that they are due to underlying differences in cognitive processing by the two sides of the brain.

Although many anatomical asymmetries in the human brain are related to language, such asymmetries are not unique to humans. Most, if not all, mammals have brain asymmetries, as do many species of birds. Cerebral asymmetry therefore cannot simply be present for the processing of language. Rather, human language more likely evolved after the brain had become asymmetrical. Language simply took advantage of processes that had already been lateralized by natural selection in earlier members of the human lineage.

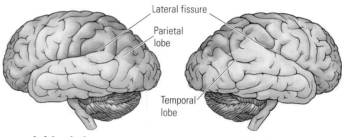

Left hemisphere Right hemisphere

Figure 14-12

Cerebral Asymmetry   The lateral fissure in the left hemisphere has a flatter course compared with the lateral fissure on the right, which takes a more upward course. As a result, the posterior part of the right temporal lobe is larger than the same region on the left side, and the inferior parietal region is larger on the left than on the right.

Functional Asymmetry in Neurological Patients

That the two hemispheres of the human brain sometimes specialize in different functions is shown by studying people with damage to the left or right side of the brain. To see these functional differences clearly, compare the cases of G. H. and M. M.

When G. H. was 5 years old, he went on a hike with his family and was hit on the head by a large rock that rolled off an embankment. He was unconscious for a few minutes and had a severe headache for a few days, but he quickly recovered. By age 18, however, he had started having seizures.

Figure 14-13

Contrasting Parietal-Lobe Injuries

Case G. H.

Injury to this area of the right hemisphere caused difficulties in copying drawings, assembling puzzles, and finding the way around a familiar city.

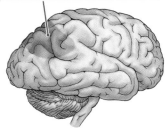

Case M. M.

Injury to this area of the left hemisphere caused difficulties in language, copying movements, reading, and generating names of objects or animals.

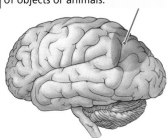

Neurosurgical investigation revealed that G. H. had suffered a right posterior parietal injury from the rock accident. The drawing at the top of **Figure 14-13** shows the area affected. After surgery to remove this area, G. H. had weakness of the left side of his body and showed contralateral neglect. But these symptoms lessened fairly quickly and, a month after the surgery, they had completely cleared.

Nevertheless, G. H. suffered chronic difficulties in copying drawings and, 4 years later, he still performed this task at about the level of a 6 year old. He also had trouble assembling puzzles, which he found disappointing because he had enjoyed doing puzzles before his surgery. When asked to do tasks such as the one in Figure 14-3, he became very frustrated and refused to continue.

Finally, he had difficulty finding his way around the city in which he lived. The general landmarks that he had used to guide his travels before the surgery no longer seemed to work for him. G. H. now has to learn street names and use a verbal strategy to go from one place to another.

M. M.'s difficulties were quite different. M. M., a 16-year-old girl, had a meningioma, which is a tumor of the brain's protective coverings, the meninges (see "Brain Tumors" on page 83). The tumor was surgically removed, but it had placed considerable pressure on the left parietal region, causing damage to the area shown on the bottom drawing in Figure 14-13.

After the surgery, M. M. experienced a variety of problems. For one thing, she suffered aphasia, or impairment in the use of language (Chapter 9), although this condition lessened over time. A year after the surgery, she was able to speak quite fluently. Unfortunately, her other difficulties persisted.

In solving arithmetic problems, in reading, and even in simply calling objects or animals by name, M. M. performed at about the level of a 6 year old. When asked to copy a series of arm movements, such as those illustrated in **Figure 14-14**, she had great difficulty. She seemed unable to figure out how to make her arm move to match the example.

She had no difficulty in making movements spontaneously, however, which means that she was able to move her limbs. Rather, she had a general impairment in copying movements, which is a symptom of apraxia, a general impairment in making voluntary movements in the absence of paralysis or a muscular disorder (Chapter 10).

What can we learn about brain function by comparing these two patients? Their lesions were in approximately the same location but in opposite hemispheres, and their

Series 1

Figure 14-14

Two Arm-Movement Series Subjects observe the tester perform each sequence and then copy it as accurately as they can. People with left-hemisphere injury, especially in the posterior parietal region, are impaired at copying such movements.

Series 2

symptoms were very different. Judging from the difficulties that G. H. had, the right hemisphere plays a role in the control of spatial skills, such as drawing, assembling puzzles, and navigating in space. In contrast, M. M.'s condition reveals that the left hemisphere seems to play some role in the control of language functions, as well as in various cognitive tasks related to schoolwork—namely, reading and arithmetic. In addition, the left hemisphere plays a role in controlling sequences of voluntary movement that differs from the role of the right hemisphere.

To some extent, therefore, the left and right hemispheres think about different types of information. The question is whether these differences in function can be observed in a normal brain.

Functional Asymmetry in the Normal Brain

In the course of studying the auditory capacities of people with temporal-lobe lesions, Doreen Kimura (1967) came upon an unexpected finding in her normal control subjects. She presented people with two strings of digits, one played into each ear, a procedure known as **dichotic listening.** The subjects' task was to recall as many of the digits as possible.

Kimura found that her normal controls recalled more digits presented to the right ear than to the left. This result is a bit surprising because the auditory system is repeatedly crossed, beginning in the midbrain. Nonetheless, information coming from the right ear seems to have preferential access to the left (speaking) hemisphere.

In a later study, Kimura (1973) played two pieces of music, one to each ear. She then gave subjects a multiple-choice test in which she played four bits of musical selections and asked the subjects to pick out those that they had heard before. In this test, she found that normal subjects were more likely to recall the music played to the left ear than that played to the right ear. This result implies that the left ear has preferential access to the right (musical) hemisphere.

The demonstration of this functional asymmetry in the normal brain provoked much interest in the 1970s, leading to demonstrations of functional asymmetries in the visual and tactile systems as well. Consider the visual system. If we fixate on a target, such as a dot, all the information to the left of the dot goes to the right hemisphere and all the information to the right of the dot goes to the left hemisphere, as shown in **Figure 14-15**.

If information is presented for a relatively long time—say, 1 s—we can easily report what was in each visual field. If, however, the presentation is brief—say, only 40 ms—then the task is considerably harder. This situation allows us to reveal a brain asymmetry.

Words presented briefly to the right visual field, and hence sent to the left hemisphere, are more easily reported than are words presented briefly to the left visual field. Similarly, if complex geometric patterns or faces are shown briefly, those presented to the left visual field, and hence sent to the right hemisphere, are more accurately reported than are those presented to the right visual field. Apparently, the two hemispheres are processing information differently. The left hemisphere seems to be biased toward processing language-related information, whereas the right hemisphere seems to be biased toward processing nonverbal, especially spatial, information.

A word of caution: Although asymmetry studies are fascinating, what they tell us about the differences between the two hemispheres is not entirely clear. They tell us that *something* is different, but it is a long leap to conclude that the two hemispheres house entirely different kinds of skills.

Dichotic listening. Experimental procedure for simultaneously presenting a different auditory input to each ear through stereophonic earphones.

Figure 14-15

Visual Pathways to the Two Hemispheres When fixating at a point, each eye sees both visual fields but sends information about the right visual field only to the left hemisphere and information about the left visual field only to the right hemisphere. In normal subjects given short exposures to stimuli (well under 1 s), the left hemisphere is more accurate at perceiving words, whereas the right hemisphere is more accurate at perceiving objects, such as faces.

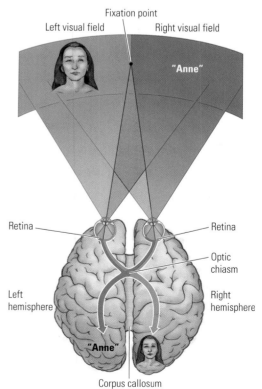

Fixation point
Left visual field — Right visual field
"Anne"
Retina — Retina
Optic chiasm
Left hemisphere — Right hemisphere
"Anne"
Corpus callosum

Split brain. Surgical disconnection of the two hemispheres in which the corpus callosum is cut.

Yet this dichotomy was a common thread in popular "left-brain–right-brain" articles written in the late 1970s and the 1980s. These reports ignored the fact that the two hemispheres have many functions in common, such as the control of movement in the contralateral hand and the processing of sensory information through the thalamus. Still, there *are* differences in the cognitive operations of the two hemispheres. These differences can be better understood by studying people whose cerebral hemispheres have been surgically separated for medical treatment.

EXPERIMENT 14-3

Question: Will severing the corpus callosum affect the way in which the brain responds?

Procedure

The split-brain subject fixates on the dot in the center of the screen while an image is projected to the left or right visual field. He is asked to identify verbally what he sees.

Screen   Projector

Results

If the spoon is presented to the right visual field, the subject verbally answers, "Spoon."

If the spoon is presented to the left visual field, the subject verbally answers, "I see nothing."

Left visual field   Right visual field   Left visual field   Right visual field

Severed corpus callosum

Conclusion

When the left hemisphere, which can speak, sees the spoon in the right visual field, the subject responds correctly. When the right hemisphere, which cannot speak, sees the spoon in the left visual field, the subject does not respond.

The Split Brain

Epileptic seizures may begin in a restricted region of one hemisphere and then spread through the fibers of the corpus callosum to the corresponding location in the opposite hemisphere. To prevent the spread of seizures that cannot be controlled through medication, neurosurgeons sometimes cut the 200 million nerve fibers of the corpus callosum. The procedure is medically beneficial for many patients, leaving them virtually seizure-free with only minimal effects on their everyday behavior.

In special circumstances, however, the results of a severed corpus callosum become more readily apparent, as demonstrated through extensive psychological testing by Roger Sperry, Michael Gazzaniga, and their colleagues (Sperry, 1968; Gazzaniga, 1970). On close inspection, these **split-brain** patients can be shown to have a unique behavioral syndrome that can serve as a source of insight into the nature of cerebral asymmetry.

Before a consideration of the details of split-brain studies, let us make some predictions on the basis of what we already know about cerebral asymmetry. First, we would expect that the left hemisphere has language, whereas the right hemisphere does not. Second, we would expect that the right hemisphere might be better at certain types of nonverbal tasks, especially those concerning visuospatial skills.

We might also ask how a severed corpus callosum affects the way in which the brain thinks. After all, after the corpus callosum has been cut, the two hemispheres have no way of communicating with each other. The left and right hemispheres would therefore be free to think about different things. In a sense, a split-brain patient has two different brains.

One way to test the cognitive functions of the two hemispheres in a split-brain patient is to take advantage of the fact that information in the left visual field goes to the right hemisphere, whereas information in the right visual field goes to the left hemisphere. Because the corpus callosum is cut in these patients, information presented to one side of the brain has no way of traveling to the other side. It can be processed only in the hemisphere that receives it.

Experiments 14-3 and **14-4** show some basic testing procedures that use this approach. The split-brain subject fixates on the dot in the center of the screen while information is presented to the left or right visual field. The person must make responses with the left hand (controlled by the right hemisphere), with the right hand (controlled

EXPERIMENT 14-4A

Question: How can the right hemisphere of a split-brain subject show that it knows information?

Procedure

The split-brain subject is asked to use his left hand to pick out the object shown on the screen to the left visual field (right hemisphere).

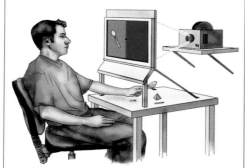

Results

The subject chooses the spoon with his left hand because the right hemisphere sees the spoon and controls the left hand. If the right hand is forced to choose, it will do so by chance because no stimulus is shown to the left hemisphere.

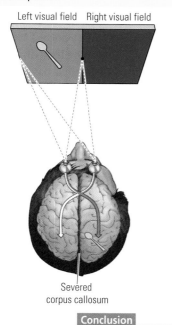

Left visual field   Right visual field

Severed
corpus callosum

EXPERIMENT 14-4B

Question: What happens if both hemispheres are asked to respond to competing information?

Procedure

Each visual field is shown a different object—a spoon to the left and a pencil to the right. The split-brain subject is asked to use both hands to pick up the object seen.

Results

In this case, the right and left hands do not agree. They may each pick up a different object, or the right hand may prevent the left hand from performing the task.

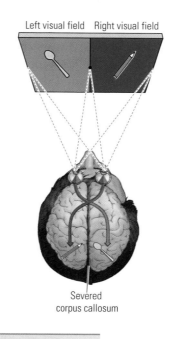

Left visual field   Right visual field

Severed
corpus callosum

Conclusion

Each hemisphere is capable of responding independently. The left hemisphere may dominate in a competition, even if the response is not verbal.

by the left hemisphere), or verbally (which also is a left-hemisphere function). In this way, researchers are able to observe what each hemisphere knows and what it is capable of doing.

As illustrated in Experiment 14-3, for instance, a subject might be flashed a picture of an object—say, a spoon—and asked to state what he or she sees. If the picture is presented to the right visual field, the person will answer, "Spoon." If the picture is presented to the left visual field, however, the person will say, "I see nothing." The patient responds in this way for two reasons:

1. The right hemisphere (which receives the visual input) does not talk, and so it cannot respond verbally, even though it sees the spoon in the left visual field.
2. The left hemisphere does talk, but it does not see the spoon, and so it answers—quite correctly, from its own perspective—that no picture is present.

Now suppose that the task changes. In Experiment 14-4A, the picture of a spoon is still presented to the left visual field, but the subject is asked to use the left hand to pick out the object shown on the screen. In this case, the left hand, controlled by the right hemisphere, which sees the spoon, readily picks out the correct object. Can the right hand also choose correctly? No, because it is controlled by the left hemisphere, which cannot see a spoon on the left. If the person is forced in this situation to select an object with the right hand, the left hemisphere does so at random.

Now let's consider an interesting twist. The Procedure for Experiment 14-4B is to show each hemisphere a different object—say, a spoon to the right hemisphere and a pencil to the left. The subject is asked to use both hands to pick out the object seen. The problem here is that the right hand and left hand do not agree. While the left hand tries to pick up the spoon, the right hand tries to pick up the pencil or tries to prevent the left hand from performing the task.

This conflict between the hemispheres can be seen in the everyday behavior of some split-brain subjects. One woman, P. O. V., reported frequent interhemispheric competition for at least 3 years after her surgery. "I open the closet door. I know what I want to wear. But as I reach for something with my right hand, my left comes up and takes something different. I can't put it down if it's in my left hand. I have to call my daughter."

We know from Experiment 14-3 that the left hemisphere is capable of using language, but what functions does the right hemisphere control? Other split-brain studies have attempted to answer this question. Investigations into the visuospatial capacities of the two hands were sources of some of the first insights.

For example, one split-brain subject was presented with several blocks, each having two red sides, two white sides, and two half-red and half-white sides, as illustrated in the Procedure section of **Experiment 14-5**. The task was to arrange the blocks to form patterns identical with those shown on cards. When the subject used his right hand to perform the task, he had great difficulty. His movements were slow and hesitant. In contrast, when he did the task with his left hand, his solutions were not only accurate but quick and decisive.

Findings from other studies of split-brain patients have shown that, as tasks of this sort become more difficult, the left-hand superiority increases. Normal subjects perform equally well with either hand, indicating the connection between the two hemispheres. But, in split-brain subjects, each hemisphere must work on its own. Apparently, the right hemisphere has visuospatial capabilities that the left hemisphere does not.

Once again, however, some caution is needed. Although findings from studies of split-brain patients in the past 35 years have shown that the two hemispheres process information differently, there is more overlap in function between them than was at first suspected. For instance, the right hemisphere does have some language functions, and the left hemisphere does have some spatial abilities. Nonetheless, the two sides are undoubtedly different.

EXPERIMENT 14-5

Question: How does each hemisphere perform on a visuospatial construction task?

Procedure

The subject is asked to arrange the blocks so that they duplicate the pattern shown on the card.

Sample card

Blocks

Results

The split-brain patient is unable to duplicate the pattern by using his right hand...

...but, with his left hand, he performs the task correctly.

Conclusion

The right hemisphere is superior at visuospatial processing.

Adapted from *Cognitive Neuroscience: The Biology of the Mind* (p. 323), by M. S. Gazzaniga, R. B. Ivry, and G. R. Mangun, 1999, New York: Norton.

Explaining Cerebral Asymmetry

Various hypotheses have been proposed to explain hemispheric differences. One idea, which dates back a century, is that the left hemisphere plays an important role in the control of fine movements. Recall M. M., the meningioma patient with left-parietal-lobe damage who suffered apraxia. Although that condition subsided, she was left with a chronic difficulty in copying movements.

So perhaps one reason that the left hemisphere has a role in language is that the production of language requires fine motor movements of the mouth and tongue. Significantly, damage to the language-related areas of the left hemisphere almost always interferes with both language and movement, regardless of whether the person uses oral language or sign language. Reading Braille, however, may not be so affected by left-hemisphere lesions. People use the left hand to read Braille, which is essentially a spatial pattern, and so processes related to reading Braille may reside in the right hemisphere.

h ou s e

Braille

Another clue that the left hemisphere's specialization for language may be related to its special role in controlling fine movements comes from the study of where certain parts of speech are processed in the brain. Recall that cognitive systems for representing abstract concepts are likely to be related to systems that produce more-concrete behaviors. Consequently, we might expect that the left hemisphere would have a role in forming concepts related to fine movements.

Concepts that describe movements are the parts of speech that we call verbs. Interestingly, a fundamental difference between left- and right-hemisphere language abilities is that verbs seem to be processed only in the left hemisphere, whereas nouns are processed in both hemispheres. In other words, not only does the left hemisphere have a special role in controlling the production of actions, but it also controls the production of mental representations of actions in the form of words.

If the left hemisphere excels at language because it is better at controlling fine movements, what is the basis of the right hemisphere's abilities? One idea is that the right hemisphere has a special role in controlling movements in space. In a sense, this role is an elaboration of the functions of the dorsal visual stream.

Once again, we can propose a link between movement at a concrete level and at a more abstract level. If the right hemisphere is producing movements in space, then it is also likely to produce mental images of such movements. We would therefore predict that right-hemisphere patients would be impaired both at making spatially guided movements and at thinking about such movements. Significantly, they are.

Bear in mind that theories about the reasons for hemispheric asymmetry are highly speculative. Because the brain has evolved to produce movement and to create a sensory reality, the observed asymmetry must be somehow related to these overriding functions. In other words, more recent functions, such as language, are likely to be extensions of preexisting functions. The fact that language is represented asymmetrically does not mean that the brain is asymmetrical *because* of language. After all, brains are asymmetrically organized in other species that do not talk.

The Left Hemisphere, Language, and Thought

We end our examination of brain asymmetry by considering one other provocative idea. Michael Gazzaniga (1992) proposed that the superior language skills of the left hemisphere are important in understanding the differences in thinking between humans and other animals. He called the speaking hemisphere the "interpreter."

◉ For links to more sites about split-brain patients, visit the Chapter 14 Web links on the *Brain and Behavior* Web site (**www.worthpublishers.com/kolb**).

◉ To learn more about the role of the brain's hemispheres in language function, visit the section on language in the module on the central nervous system on your *Foundations* CD.

What he meant is illustrated in the following experiment, using split-brain patients as subjects.

Each hemisphere is shown the same two pictures, such as a picture of a match followed by a picture of a piece of wood. A series of other pictures is then shown, and the task is to pick out a third picture that has an inferred relation to the other two. In our example, the third picture might be a bonfire. The right hemisphere is incapable of making the inference that a match struck and held to a piece of wood could create a bonfire, whereas the left hemisphere can easily arrive at this interpretation.

An analogous task uses words. For example, one or the other hemisphere might be shown the words *pin* and *finger* and then be asked to pick out a third word that is related to the other two. In this case, the correct answer might be *bleed.*

The right hemisphere is not able to make this connection. Although it has enough language ability to pick out close synonyms for *pin* and *finger* (*needle* and *thumb,* respectively), it cannot make the inference that pricking a finger with a needle will result in bleeding. Again, the left hemisphere has no difficulty with this task. Apparently, the language capability of the left hemisphere gives it a capacity for interpretation that the right hemisphere lacks. One reason may be that language serves to label and express the computations of other cognitive systems.

Gazzaniga goes even farther. He suggests that the addition of the language abilities possessed by the left hemisphere makes humans a "believing" species. That is, humans can now make inferences and have beliefs about sensory events.

In contrast, Alex, the gray parrot, would not be able to make inferences or hold beliefs about things, because he does not have a system analogous to our left-hemisphere language system. Alex can use language but does not make inferences about sensory events with language. Gazzaniga's idea is certainly intriguing. It implies a fundamental difference in the nature of cerebral asymmetry, and therefore in the nature of cognition, between humans and other animals because of the nature of human language.

In Review

The two cerebral hemispheres process information differently, which means that they think differently. In particular, the right hemisphere plays a role in spatial movements and spatial cognition as well as in music. The left hemisphere plays a role in the control of voluntary movement sequences and in language. The addition of verbal mediation to left-hemisphere thinking may confer a fundamental advantage to the left hemisphere because language can label the computations of the brain's various cognitive systems. As a result, the left hemisphere is able to make inferences that the right hemisphere cannot.

VARIATIONS IN COGNITIVE ORGANIZATION

No two brains are identical. Brains differ in gyral patterns, cytoarchitectonics, vascular patterns, and neurochemistry, among other things. Some of these differences are genetically determined, whereas others are due to plastic changes such as those created by experience and learning. Some brain differences are idiosyncratic, or unique to a particular person, whereas many other variations are systematic and common to whole categories of people. In this section, we consider two systematic variations in brain organization, those related to sex and handedness, and one idiosyncratic variation.

Sex Differences in Cognitive Organization

Popular media are rife with the idea that men and women think differently, and there seems to be some scientific basis to this view. Books, such as one by Doreen Kimura (1999), compile considerable evidence for the existence of marked sex differences in the way in which men and women perform on many cognitive tests. For example, paper-and-pencil tests consistently show that, on average, females have better verbal fluency than males do, whereas males do better on tests of spatial reasoning, as illustrated in **Figure 14-16**. Our focus here is on how such differences relate to the brain.

NEURAL BASIS OF SEX DIFFERENCES

Many investigators have searched without success for gross differences in the structures of the male and female cortices. If such differences exist, they must be subtle. There is stronger indication, however, that gonadal hormones influence the structure of cells in the brain, including cortical cells.

For example, the structures of neurons in the prefrontal cortices of rats were found to be influenced by gonadal hormones (Kolb & Stewart, 1991). The cells in one prefrontal region, located along the midline, have larger dendritic fields (and presumably more synapses) in males than in females, as shown in the top row of **Figure 14-17**. In contrast, the cells in the orbitofrontal region have larger dendritic fields (and presumably more synapses) in females than in males, as shown in the bottom row. These sex differences are

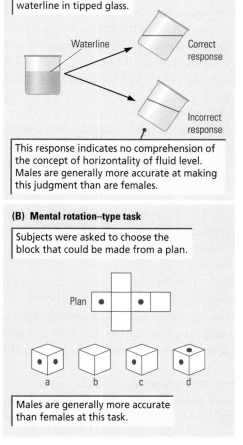

(A) Spatial relation–type task

Subjects were asked to draw a line to indicate waterline in tipped glass.

Waterline → Correct response

Incorrect response

This response indicates no comprehension of the concept of horizontality of fluid level. Males are generally more accurate at making this judgment than are females.

(B) Mental rotation–type task

Subjects were asked to choose the block that could be made from a plan.

Plan

a b c d

Males are generally more accurate than females at this task.

(C) Short-term-memory–type task

Subjects were asked to fill in the empty boxes with the appropriate symbols from the top row.

When given a larger number of boxes to fill in and a time limit, females complete from 10 to 20 percent more items than males do.

(D) Verbal-fluency–type task

Subjects were asked to fill in each blank to form words that make a sentence.

1. F_____ M_____ A_____ J_____

2. C_____ B_____ E_____ S_____

3. D_____ I_____ J_____ K_____

Females are generally faster at this type of test than males are.

Figure 14-16

Tasks That Reliably Show Sex-Related Cognitive Differences **(A)** On this spatial-relations task, the incorrect response was given by about two-thirds of female subjects. **(B)** Men typically find mental rotation tasks much easier than women do. **(C)** In tests of short-term memory with a time limit, women typically complete from 10 percent to 20 percent more items than men do. **(D)** As a rule, women are faster at verbal fluency tests than men are.

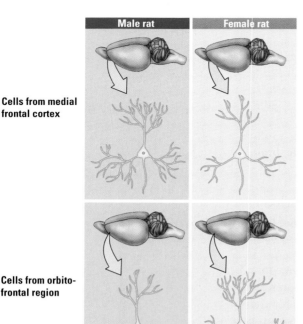

Figure 14-17

Sex Differences in the Architecture of Neurons In the frontal cortices of male and female rats, cells in the midline frontal region (*shown by arrows in the top two drawings*) are more complex in males than in females, whereas the opposite is true of the orbitofrontal region (*shown by arrows in the bottom two drawings*).

not found in rats that have had their gonads or ovaries removed at birth. Presumably, sex hormones somehow change the brain's organization and ultimately its cognitive processing.

Findings from a second study showed that the presence or absence of gonadal hormones affects the brain not only in early development but also in adulthood. In the course of this study, which focused on how hormones affect recovery from brain damage, the ovaries of middle-aged female rats were removed (Stewart & Kolb, 1994). When the brains of these rats and those of control rats were examined some months later, the cortical neurons (especially the prefrontal neurons) of rats whose ovaries had been removed had undergone structural changes. Specifically, the cells had grown 30 percent more dendrites and their spine density increased compared with the cells in control rats. Clearly, gonadal hormones can affect the neural structure of the brain at any point in an animal's life.

What do these hormonal effects mean in regard to how neurons process information and, ultimately, how the brain thinks? One possibility is that gonadal hormones may influence the way in which experience changes the brain. Evidence in support of this possibility came from a study by Robbin Gibb and her colleagues (Gibb, Gorny, & Kolb, 2005).

These investigators placed male and female rats in complex environments like those described in Chapter 13. After 4 months, they examined the animals' brains and found a sex difference in the effects of experience. Both sexes showed experience-dependent changes in neural structure, but the details of those changes were different.

Females exposed to the enriched environment showed a greater increase in dendritic branching in the cortex, whereas males housed in the same environment showed a greater increase in spine density. In other words, although the brains of both sexes were changed by experience, they were changed *in different ways*, which were presumably mediated by the animals' exposure to different gonadal hormones. These differences almost certainly affect cognitive processing in one sex relative to the other, although exactly how is a matter for speculation.

Another way to investigate the effects of sex hormones on how neurons process information is to relate differences in hormone exposure to particular human cognitive abilities. This type of study presents obvious problems, because we cannot control hormone types and levels in people. We can, however, take advantage of naturally occurring hormone variations within a single sex.

Using these naturally occurring variations is rather simple to do in women. We can use the age of onset of the first menstrual cycle (known as *menarche*) as a marker for the presence of female gonadal hormones. Because this age varies considerably (from as early as 8 years old to as late as 18), there is ample opportunity to relate the presence of female hormones to women's cognitive abilities.

In a study by Sharon Rowntree (2005), girls had been recruited at age 8 to take part in a 10-year longitudinal study of the relation between age at menarche and body type. The age at which each started to menstruate was known to within 1 month. At age 16, all the subjects were given tests of verbal fluency (such as writing in 5 min as many words as possible that start with the letter *d*) and of spatial manipulation (such as the one illustrated in Figure 14-3).

Rowntree reasoned that, if hormones alter cortical neurons, then the age at which the neurons are changed may influence cognitive processing, which is exactly what she found evidence for, as summarized in **Figure 14-18**. Specifically, girls who reached menarche earlier (age 12 or younger) were generally better at the verbal tasks than were

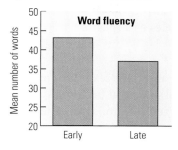

Early-maturing girls show higher verbal fluency than later-maturing girls.

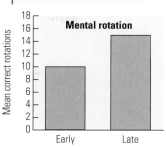

Late-maturing girls show higher spatial ability than earlier-maturing girls.

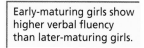

Figure 14-18

Effects of Sex Hormones   Girls who reach menarche early (before age 12) have better verbal skills but weaker spatial skills than do girls who reach menarche late (after age 14). Data courtesy of S. Rowntree, from "Spatial and Verbal Ability in Adult Females Vary with Age at Menses," by S. Rowntree, 2005, manuscript in preparation.

girls who began to menstruate later, whereas girls who reached menarche later were generally better at the spatial tasks. In short, the age at which gonadal hormones affect the brain may be the critical factor in the development of cognitive skills.

This idea has been examined in another way by Deborah Waber (1976). She did a retrospective study in which age at puberty was estimated in both boys and girls. She found that, regardless of sex, early-maturing adolescents performed better on tests of verbal abilities than they did on tests of spatial abilities, whereas late-maturing subjects showed the opposite pattern.

Waber argued that sex differences in mental abilities are due to differences in the organization of cortical function that are related to differential rates of physical maturation. Because boys usually mature later than girls, they show a different pattern of cognitive skills from that of girls.

The advantage of using same-sex subjects in such studies is to reduce the probability that different experiences before puberty account either for the girls' age differences at menarche or for their different cognitive abilities. Rather, the gonadal hormones of puberty seem more likely to influence the structure of cortical neurons and, ultimately, cognitive processing.

The postpubertal experiences of the girls could have affected the brains of early maturers differently from those of late maturers, but gonadal hormones would still have played an important mediating role. Interestingly, boys reach puberty later than girls, and boys, on average, do better at spatial tasks and worse on verbal tasks than girls do. Perhaps the age at which hormones affect the brain is the critical factor here.

An additional way to consider the neural basis of sex differences is to look at the effects of cortical injury in men and women. If there are sex differences in the neural organization of cognitive processing, there ought to be differences in the effects of cortical injury in the two sexes. In fact, Doreen Kimura (1999) conducted this kind of study and showed that the pattern of cerebral organization within each hemisphere may differ between the sexes.

Investigating people who had sustained cortical strokes in adulthood, Kimura tried to match the location and extent of injury in her male and female subjects. She found that, although men and women were almost equally likely to be aphasic subsequent to left-hemisphere lesions of some kind, men were more likely to be aphasic and apraxic after damage to the left posterior cortex, whereas women were far more likely to be aphasic and apraxic after lesions to the left frontal cortex. These results, summarized in **Figure 14-19**, suggest a difference in intrahemispheric organization between the two sexes.

Figure 14-19

Evidence for Intrahemispheric Differences in Cortical Organization of Men and Women   Apraxia is associated with frontal damage to the left hemisphere in women and with posterior damage in men. Aphasia occurs most often when damage is to the front of the brain in women but in the rear of the brain in men. Adapted from *Sex and Cognition*, by D. Kimura, 1999, Cambridge, MA: MIT Press.

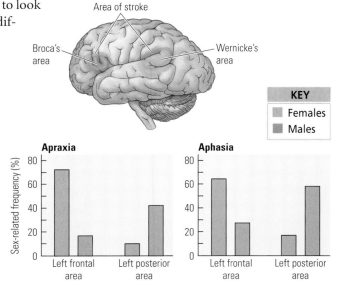

To learn more about sex-related cognitive differences, read the articles on gender and cognition in the Chapter 14 Web links on the *Brain and Behavior* Web site (**www.worthpublishers. com/kolb**).

EVOLUTION OF SEX-RELATED COGNITIVE DIFFERENCES

Although emphasis has been on the role of gonadal hormones to explain sex differences in cognitive function, we are still left with the question of how these differences arose in the first place. To answer this question, we must look back at human evolution. Ultimately, males and females of a species have virtually all their genes in common. Mothers pass their genes to both sons and daughters, and fathers do the same.

The only way in which a gene can affect one sex preferentially is for that gene's activities to be influenced by the animal's gonadal hormones, which in turn are determined by the presence or absence of the Y chromosome. The Y chromosome carries a gene called the *testes-determining factor* (TDF). This gene stimulates the body to produce testes, which then manufacture androgens, which subsequently influence the activities of other genes.

Like other body organs, the brain is a potential target of natural selection. We should therefore expect to find sex-related differences in the brain whenever the two sexes differ in the adaptive problems that they have faced in the evolutionary history of the species. The degree of aggressive behavior produced by the brain is a good example.

Males are more physically aggressive than females in most mammalian species. This trait presumably improved males' reproductive success, reinforcing natural selection for greater aggressiveness in males. Producing higher levels of aggression entails male hormones. We know from studies of nonhuman species that aggression is related directly to the presence of androgens and to the effects of these hormones on gene expression both during brain development and later in life. In this case, therefore, natural selection has worked on gonadal hormone levels to favor aggressiveness in males.

Explaining sex-related differences in cognitive processes, such as language or spatial skills, is more speculative than explaining sex-related differences in aggressive behavior. Nevertheless, some hypotheses come to mind. For instance, we can imagine that, in the history of mammalian evolution, males have tended to range over larger territories than females have. This behavior requires spatial abilities, and so the development of these skills would have been favored in males.

Support for this hypothesis comes from comparing spatial problem-solving abilities in males of closely related mammalian species—one in which the males range over large territories versus one in which the males do not have such extensive ranges. For example, pine voles have restricted ranges and no sex-related difference in range, whereas meadow voles have ranges about 20 times as large as those of pine voles, with the males ranging more widely than the females.

When the spatial skills of pine voles and meadow voles are compared, meadow voles are far superior. Furthermore, among meadow voles, there is a sex difference in spatial ability that favors males, but no such sex difference exists among pine voles. Recall from Chapter 13 that the hippocampus is implicated in spatial navigation skills. Significantly, the hippocampus is larger in meadow voles than in pine voles, and it is larger in meadow vole males than in females (Gaulin, 1992). A similar logic could help explain sex-related differences in spatial abilities between human males and females.

Explaining sex-related differences in language skills also is speculative. One hypothesis holds that, if males were hunters and often away from home, the females left behind in social groups would be favored to develop tools for social interaction, one of which is language. It might also be argued that females were selected for fine motor skills (such as foraging for food and making clothing and baskets). Because of the relation between language and fine motor skills, enhanced language capacities might have evolved as well in females.

Although such speculations are interesting, they are not testable. We will probably never know with certainty why sex-related differences in brain organization developed.

Handedness and Cognitive Organization

Nearly everyone prefers one hand over the other for writing or throwing a ball. Most people prefer the right hand. In fact, left-handedness has historically been viewed as odd. Left-handedness, however, is not rare. An estimated 10 percent of the human population worldwide is left-handed. This proportion represents the number of people who write with the left hand. When other criteria are used to determine left-handedness, estimates range from 10 percent to 30 percent of the population.

Because the left hemisphere controls the right hand, right-handedness has generally been assumed to be somehow related to the presence of speech in the left hemisphere. If this were so, then language would be located in the right hemispheres of left-handed people. This hypothesis is easily tested, and it turns out to be false.

In the course of preparing epileptic patients for surgery to remove the abnormal tissue causing their seizures, Ted Rasmussen and Brenda Milner (1977) injected the left or right hemisphere with sodium amobarbital (see "The Sodium Amobarbital Test" on page 556). This drug produces a short-acting anesthesia of the entire hemisphere, making possible a determination of where speech is located. For instance, if a person becomes aphasic when the drug is injected into the left hemisphere but not when the drug is injected into the right, then speech must be in that person's left hemisphere.

Rasmussen and Milner found that virtually all right-handed people had speech in the left hemisphere, but the reverse was not true for left-handed people. About 70 percent of left-handers also had speech in the left hemisphere. Of the remaining 30 percent, about half had speech in the right hemisphere and half had speech in both hemispheres.

Findings from anatomical studies have subsequently shown that left-handers with speech in the left hemisphere have anatomical asymmetries similar to those of right-handers. In contrast, left-handers with speech located in the right hemisphere or in both hemispheres—known as **anomalous speech representation**—have either a reversed anatomical asymmetry or no obvious anatomical asymmetry at all.

Sandra Witelson and Charlie Goldsmith (1991) asked whether there might be any other gross differences in the structure of the brains of right- and left-handers. One possibility is that the connectivity of the cerebral hemispheres may differ. To test this idea, the investigators studied the hand preference of terminally ill subjects on a variety of one-handed tasks.

They later did postmortem studies of the brains of these patients, paying particular attention to the size of the corpus callosum. They found that the corpus callosum's cross-sectional area was 11 percent greater in left-handed and ambidextrous (no hand preference) people than in right-handed people. Whether this enlarged callosum is due to a greater number of fibers, to thicker fibers, or to more myelin remains to be seen. If the larger corpus callosum is due to a greater number of fibers, the difference would be on the order of 25 million more fibers. Presumably, such a difference would have major implications for the organization of cognitive processing in left- and right-handers.

Synesthesia

Some systematic variations in brain organization are idiosyncratic. **Synesthesia** is the capacity to join sensory experiences across sensory modalities, as discussed in "A Case of Synesthesia" on page 557. Examples of this rare capacity include the ability to hear

Anomalous speech representation. Condition in which a person's speech zones are located in the right hemisphere or in both hemispheres.

Synesthesia. Ability to perceive a stimulus of one sense as the sensation of a different sense, such as when sound produces a sensation of color.

Focus on Disorders

The Sodium Amobarbital Test

Guy, a 32-year-old lawyer, had a vascular malformation over the region corresponding to the posterior speech zone. The malformation was beginning to cause neurological symptoms, including epilepsy. The ideal surgical treatment was removal of the abnormal vessels.

The problem was that the removal of vessels sitting over the posterior speech zone poses a serious risk of permanent aphasia. Because Guy was left-handed, his speech areas could be in the right hemisphere. If so, the surgical risk would be much lower.

To achieve certainty in such doubtful cases, Jun Wada and Ted Rasmussen (1960) pioneered the technique of injecting sodium amobarbital, a barbiturate, into the carotid artery to produce a brief period of anesthesia of the ipsilateral hemisphere. (Injections are now normally made through a catheter inserted into the femoral artery.) This procedure enables an unequivocal localization of speech, because injection into the speech hemisphere results in an arrest of speech lasting as long as several minutes. As speech returns, it is characterized by aphasic errors.

Injection into the nonspeaking hemisphere may produce no or only brief speech arrest. The amobarbital procedure has the advantage of allowing each hemisphere to be studied separately in the functional absence of the other (anesthetized) hemisphere. Because the period of anesthesia lasts several minutes, a variety of functions, including memory and movement, can be studied to determine a hemisphere's capabilities.

The sodium amobarbital test is always performed bilaterally, with the second cerebral hemisphere being injected

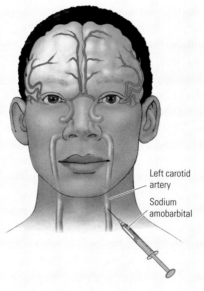

Left carotid artery

Sodium amobarbital

To avoid damaging the speech zones of patients about to undergo brain surgery, surgeons inject sodium amobarbital into the carotid artery. The sodium amobarbital anesthetizes the hemisphere where it is injected (in this case, the left hemisphere), allowing the surgeon to determine if that hemisphere is dominant for speech.

several days after the first one to make sure that there is no residual drug effect. In the brief period of drug action, the patient is given a series of simple tasks requiring the use of language, memory, and object recognition. Speech is tested by asking the patient to name some common objects presented in quick succession, to count and to recite the days of the week forward and backward, and to spell simple words.

If the injected hemisphere is nondominant for speech, the patient may continue to carry out the verbal tasks, although there is often a period as long as 30 s during which he or she appears confused and is silent but can resume speech with urging. When the injected hemisphere is dominant for speech, the patient typically stops talking and remains completely aphasic until recovery from the anesthesia is well along, somewhere in the range of 4 to 10 min.

Guy was found to have speech in the left hemisphere. During the test of his left hemisphere, he could not talk. Later, he said that, when he was asked about a particular object, he wondered just what that question meant. When he finally had some vague idea, he had no idea of what the answer was or how to say anything. By then he realized that he had been asked all sorts of other questions to which he had also not responded.

When asked which objects he had been shown, he said he had no idea. However, when given an array of objects and asked to choose with his left hand, he was able to identify the objects by pointing, because his nonspeaking right hemisphere controlled that hand. In contrast, his speaking left hemisphere had no memory of the objects, because it had been asleep.

A Case of Synesthesia

Michael Watson tastes shapes. He first came to the attention of neurologist Richard Cytowic when they were having dinner together. After tasting a sauce that he was making for roast chicken, Watson blurted out, "There aren't enough points on the chicken."

When Cytowic quizzed him about this strange remark, Watson said that all flavors had shape for him. "I wanted the taste of this chicken to be a pointed shape, but it came out all round. Well, I mean it's nearly spherical. I can't serve this if it doesn't have points" (Cytowic, 1998, p. 4).

Watson has synesthesia, which literally means "feeling together." All his life Watson has experienced the feeling of shape when he tastes or smells food. When he tastes intense flavors, he reports an experience of shape that sweeps down his arms to his fingertips. He experiences the feeling of weight, texture, warmth or cold, and shape, just as though he was grasping something.

The feelings are not confined to his hands, however. Some taste shapes, such as points, are experienced over his whole body. Others are experienced only on the face, back, or shoulders. These impressions are not metaphors, as other people might use when they say that a cheese is "sharp" or that a wine is "textured." Such descriptions make no sense to Watson. He actually feels the shapes.

Cytowic systematically studied Watson to determine whether his feelings of shape were always associated with particular flavors and found that they were. Cytowic devised the set of geometric figures shown here to allow Watson to communicate which shapes he associated with various flavors.

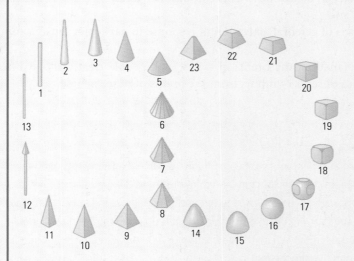

Neurologist Richard Cytowic devised this set of figures to help Michael Watson communicate the shapes that he senses when he tastes food.

colors and to taste shapes. Richard Cytowic (1998) estimated that the incidence of synesthesia is about 1 in every 25,000 people.

Synesthesia runs in families, the most famous case being the family of Russian novelist Vladimir Nabokov. As a toddler, Nabokov complained to his mother that the letter colors on his wooden alphabet blocks were "all wrong." His mother understood what he meant, because she too perceived letters and words in particular colors. Nabokov's son is synesthetic in the same way. Perhaps one example of synesthesia that is quite common is the "shivering" sensation on one's back produced by certain sounds.

Such sensory blendings are difficult for most of us to imagine. We wonder how sounds or letters could possibly produce colors, but there is little doubt that synesthesia exists. Studies of people with this sensory ability show that the same stimuli always elicit the same synesthetic experiences for them.

The most common form of synesthesia is colored hearing. For many synesthetics, colored hearing means that they hear both speech and music in color, the experience being a visual melange of colored shapes, movement, and scintillation. The fact that colored hearing is more common than other types of synesthesia is curious.

To experience some simulations of synesthesia, visit the Chapter 14 Web links on the *Brain and Behavior* Web site (**www.worthpublishers.com/kolb**).

There are five primary senses (vision, hearing, touch, taste, and smell), and these generate synesthetic pairings. Most pairings, however, are in one direction. For instance, whereas synesthetic people may see colors when they hear, they do not hear sounds when they look at colors. Furthermore, some sensory combinations occur rarely, if at all. In particular, taste or smell rarely triggers a synesthetic response.

The neurological basis of synesthesia is difficult to study because each case is so idiosyncratic. Few studies have related synesthesia directly to brain function or brain organization, and different people may experience synesthesia for different reasons. Various hypotheses have been advanced to account for synesthesia, including:

■ extraordinary neural connections between the different sensory regions that are related in a particular synesthetic person,
■ increased activity in areas of the frontal lobes that receive inputs from more than one sensory area, and
■ unusual patterns of cerebral activation in response to particular sensory inputs.

Whatever the explanation, the brains of synesthetic people clearly think differently about certain types of sensory inputs from the brains of other people.

In Review

No two brains are alike, and no two people think the same. Nevertheless, although many individual differences in brain structure and thinking are idiosyncratic, there are also systematic variations, such as those related to sex and handedness. The reasons for these differences in the cerebral organization of thinking are not known; they are undoubtedly related to differences in the synaptic organization of the neural circuits that underlie different types of cognitive processing.

INTELLIGENCE

Most people would probably say that one of the biggest influences on anyone's thinking ability is intelligence. We consider intelligence easy to identify in people, and even easy to observe in other animals. Yet intelligence is not at all easy to define. Despite years of studying human intelligence, researchers are not yet in agreement about what intelligence entails. We therefore begin this section by reviewing some hypotheses of intelligence.

The Concept of General Intelligence

In the 1920s, Charles Spearman proposed that, although there may be different kinds of intelligence, there is also some sort of underlying general intelligence, which he called the "g" factor. Consider for a moment what a general factor in intelligence might mean for the brain. Presumably, brains with high or low "g" would have some general difference in brain architecture.

This difference could not be something as simple as size, because human brain size (which varies from about 1000 to 2000 grams) correlates poorly with intelligence. Another possibility is that "g" is related to some special characteristic of cerebral connectivity or even to the ratio of neurons to glia. Still another possibility is that "g" is related to the activation of specific brain regions, possibly in the frontal lobe (Duncan et al., 2000; Gray & Thompson, 2004).

The results of preliminary studies of Albert Einstein's brain imply that cerebral connectivity and glia-to-neuron ratio may play important roles. Sandra Witelson and her colleagues (Witelson, Kigar, & Harvey, 1999) found that, although Einstein's brain was the same size and weight as the average male brain, the lateral fissure was short in Einstein's brain, as illustrated in **Figure 14-20** (compare Figure 14-12), and both the left and the right lateral fissures had a particularly striking upward deflection. This arrangement essentially fuses the inferior parietal area with the posterior temporal area.

The inferior parietal cortex is known to have a role in mathematical reasoning, and so it is tempting to speculate that Einstein's mathematical abilities were related to re-arrangements of this area. But there may be another important difference in Einstein's brain. Marion Diamond and her colleagues (1985) looked at the glia-to-neuron ratio in Einstein's brain versus the mean for a control population. They found that Einstein's inferior parietal cortex had a higher glia-to-neuron ratio than average, meaning that each of his neurons in this region had an unusually high number of glial cells supporting them.

The glia-to-neuron ratio was not unusually high in any other cortical areas of Einstein's brain measured by these researchers. Possibly, then, certain types of intelligence could be related to differences in cell structure in localized regions of the brain. But, even if this hypothesis proves to be correct, it still offers little neural evidence in favor of a general factor in intelligence.

A neuropsychological possibility is that the "g" factor is related to language processes in the brain. Recall that language ability qualitatively changes the nature of cognitive processing in humans. So perhaps people with very good language skills also have an advantage in general thinking ability.

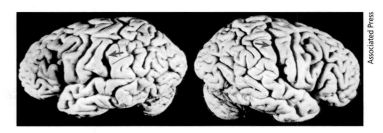

Associated Press

Figure 14-20

Einstein's Brain The lateral fissure (*at arrows*) takes an exaggerated upward course relative to its course in typical brains, essentially fusing the posterior temporal regions with the inferior parietal regions. Reprinted with the permission of S. Witelson, D. Kigar, T. Harvey, and *The Lancet*, June 19, 1999.

Multiple Intelligences

There have been many other hypotheses of intelligence since Spearman's, but few have considered the brain directly. One exception is a proposal by Howard Gardner, a neuropsychologist at Harvard. Gardner (1983) considered the effects of neurological injury on people's behavior. He concluded that there are seven distinctly different forms of intelligence and that each form can be selectively damaged by brain injury. This view that there are multiple kinds of human intelligence should not be surprising, given the many different types of cognitive operations that the human brain is capable of performing.

Gardner's seven categories of intelligence are: linguistic, musical, logical-mathematical, spatial, bodily-kinesthetic, intrapersonal, and interpersonal. Linguistic and musical intelligence are straightforward concepts, as is logical-mathematical intelligence. Spatial intelligence refers to the spatial abilities discussed in this chapter, especially the ability to navigate in space, and the ability to draw and paint. Bodily-kinesthetic intelligence refers to superior motor abilities, such as those exemplified by skilled athletes and dancers.

The two types of "personal" intelligence are less obvious. They refer to operations of the frontal and temporal lobes that are required for success in a highly social environment. The intrapersonal aspect is an awareness of one's own feelings, whereas the extrapersonal aspect is the ability to recognize the feelings of others and to respond appropriately. Gardner's definition of intelligence has the advantage not only of being quite inclusive but also of acknowledging forms of intelligence not typically recognized in industrialized cultures.

One prediction stemming from Gardner's analysis of intelligence is that brains ought to differ in some way when people have more of one form of intelligence and less of another. Logically, we could imagine that, if a person were higher in musical intelligence and lower in interpersonal intelligence, then the regions of the brain for music (especially the temporal lobe) would differ in some fundamental way from the "less efficient" regions for interpersonal intelligence. Unfortunately, we do not know what that difference might be.

Divergent and Convergent Intelligence

One of the clearest differences between lesions in the parietal and temporal lobes and lesions in the frontal lobes is in the way in which they affect performance on standardized intelligence tests. Posterior lesions produce reliable, and often large, decreases in intelligence test scores, whereas frontal lesions do not. One thing is puzzling, however. If frontal-lobe damage does not diminish a person's score on an intelligence test, why do people with this kind of damage often do such "stupid" things? The answer lies in the difference between two kinds of intelligence referred to as divergent and convergent.

According to J. P. Guilford (1967), traditional intelligence tests measure what is called **convergent thinking**—that is, thinking that applies a person's knowledge and reasoning skills so as to narrow the range of possible solutions to a problem, zeroing in on one correct answer. Typical intelligence test items using vocabulary words, arithmetic problems, puzzles, block designs, and so forth, all require convergent thinking. They demand a single correct answer that can be easily scored.

In contrast, **divergent thinking** reaches outward from conventional knowledge and reasoning skills to explore new, more unconventional kinds of solutions to problems. Divergent thinking assumes a variety of possible approaches and answers to a question, rather than a single "correct" solution. A task that requires divergent thinking is to list all the possible uses for a coat hanger that you can imagine. Clearly, a person who is very good at divergent thinking might not necessarily be good at convergent thinking, and vice versa.

The distinction between divergent and convergent intelligence is useful because it helps us to understand the effects of brain injury on thought. Frontal-lobe injury is believed to interfere with divergent thinking rather than with the convergent thinking measured by standardized I.Q. tests. The convergent intelligence of people with damage to the temporal and parietal lobes is often impaired.

Injury to the left parietal lobe, in particular, causes devastating impairment of the ability to perform cognitive processes related to academic work. These people may be aphasic, alexic, and apraxic. They often have severe deficits in arithmetic ability. All such impairments would interfere with school performance or, in fact, performance at most jobs.

Our patient M. M., discussed earlier, had left-parietal-lobe injury and was unable to return to school. In contrast with people like M. M., those with frontal-lobe injuries seldom have deficits in reading, writing, or arithmetic and show no decrement in standardized I.Q. tests. C. C.'s case is a good example.

C. C. had a meningioma along the midline between the two frontal lobes; extracting it required the removal of brain tissue from both hemispheres. C. C. had been a

Convergent thinking. Form of thinking that searches for a single answer to a question (such as 2 + 2 = ?); contrasts with divergent thinking.

Divergent thinking. Form of thinking that searches for multiple solutions to a problem (such as, how many different ways can a pen be used?); contrasts with convergent thinking.

prominent lawyer before his surgery; afterward, although he still had a superior I.Q. and superior memory, he was unable to work, in part because he no longer had any imagination. He could not generate the novel solutions to legal problems that had characterized his career before the surgery. Thus, both M. M. and C. C. suffered problems that prevented them from working, but their problems differed because different kinds of thinking were affected.

Intelligence, Heredity, Environment, and the Synapse

Another way of categorizing human intelligence was proposed by Donald Hebb. He, too, thought of people as having two forms of intelligence, which he called intelligence A and intelligence B. **Intelligence A** refers to innate intellectual potential, which is highly heritable. That is, it has a strong genetic component. **Intelligence B** is observed intelligence, which is influenced by experience as well as other factors, such as disease, injury, or exposure to environmental toxins, especially in development.

Hebb understood that the structure of brain cells can be significantly influenced by experience. In his view (Hebb, 1980), experiences influence brain development and thus observed intelligence because they alter the brain's synaptic organization. It follows that people with lower-than-average intelligence A can raise their intelligence B by appropriate postnatal experiences, whereas people with higher-than-average intelligence A can be negatively affected by a poor environment. The task is to identify what is a "good" and a "bad" environment in which to stimulate people to reach their highest potential intelligence.

One implication of Hebb's view of intelligence is that the synaptic organization of the brain plays a key role. This synaptic organization is partly directed by a person's genes, but it is also influenced by experience. Variations in the kinds of experiences to which people are exposed, coupled with variations in genetic patterns, undoubtedly contribute to the individual differences in intelligence that we observe—both quantitative differences (as measured by I.Q. tests) and qualitative differences (as in Gardner's view).

The effects of experience on intelligence may not be simply due to differences in synaptic organization. Experience changes not only the number of synapses in the brain but also the number of glia. Remember that Einstein's brain was found to have more glia per neuron in the inferior parietal cortex than control brains did. Intelligence, then, may be influenced not only by the way in which synapses are organized but also by glial density.

Intelligence A. Hebb's term for innate intellectual potential, which is highly heritable and cannot be measured directly.

Intelligence B. Hebb's term for observed intelligence, which is influenced by experience as well as other factors in the course of development and is measured by intelligence tests.

In Review

Researchers have proposed many different forms of human intelligence, including Spearman's concept of general intelligence, Gardner's idea of multiple intelligences, Guilford's concepts of convergent and divergent thinking, and Hebb's intelligence A and intelligence B. Each form of intelligence that humans possess is likely related to particular structural organizations in the brain. To date, we know little about the structural differences that account for the significant individual variations in intelligence that we observe. Preliminary findings from studies of Einstein's brain suggest some provocative possibilities, however.

CONSCIOUSNESS

Conscious experience is familiar to all of us, yet it remains a largely mysterious product of the brain. Everyone has an idea of what it means to be conscious, but, like thinking and intelligence, consciousness is easier to identify than to define. Definitions range from the view that consciousness is merely a manifestation of complex processes of thought to more-slippery notions that see consciousness as being the subjective experience of awareness or of "the inner self." Despite the difficulty of saying exactly what consciousness is, scientists generally agree that it is a process, not a thing. And consciousness is probably not a single process but a collection of several processes, such as those associated with seeing, talking, thinking, emotion, and so on. Recall that Descartes defined consciousness as the ability to speak and to reason by using past memories (Chapter 1).

Consciousness is also not unitary but can take various forms. A person is not necessarily equally conscious at all stages of life. We don't think of a newborn baby as being conscious in the same way that a healthy older child or adult is. Indeed, we might say that part of the process of maturation is becoming fully conscious. Recall from Chapter 12 that the level of consciousness even changes across the span of a day as we pass through various states of drowsiness, sleep, and waking. One trait that characterizes consciousness, then, is its constant variability.

Why Are We Conscious?

Countless people, including neuroscience researchers, have wondered why we have the experience that we call **consciousness,** which we define here as the level of responsiveness of the mind to impressions made by the senses. The simplest explanation is that we are conscious because it provides an adaptive advantage. Either our creation of the sensory world or our selection of behavior is enhanced by being conscious. Consider visual consciousness as an example.

According to Francis Crick and Christof Koch (1998), an animal such as a frog acts a bit like a zombie when it responds to visual input. Frogs respond to small, preylike objects by snapping and to large, looming objects by jumping. These responses are controlled by different visual systems and are best thought of as being reflexive rather than conscious. These visual systems work well for the frog. So why do we need to add consciousness?

Crick and Koch suggested that reflexive systems are fine when the number of such systems is limited, but, as their number grows, reflexive arrangements become inefficient, especially when two or more systems are in conflict. As the amount of information about an event increases, it becomes advantageous to produce a single, complex representation and make it available for a sufficient time to the parts of the brain (such as the frontal lobes) that make a choice among many possible plans of action. This sustained, complex representation is consciousness.

We must still have the ability to respond quickly and unconsciously when we need to. This ability exists alongside our ability to process information consciously. Recall from the discussion of the visual system in Chapter 8 that the ventral stream is conscious, but the dorsal stream, which acts more rapidly, is not. The action of the unconscious, on-line dorsal stream can be seen in athletes. To hit a baseball or tennis ball traveling at more than 100 miles per hour requires athletes to swing before they are consciously aware of actually seeing the ball. The conscious awareness of the ball comes just after hitting it.

In a series of experiments, Marc Jeannerod and his colleagues (Castiello, Paulignan, & Jeannerod, 1991) found a similar dissociation between behavior and awareness

Consciousness. Level of responsiveness of the mind to impressions made by the senses.

in normal volunteers as they make grasping movements. **Experiment 14-6** illustrates the results of a representative experiment. Subjects were required to grasp one of three rods as quickly as possible. The correct target rod on any given trial was indicated by a light on that rod.

On some trials, unbeknown to the subjects, the light jumped from one target to another. Subjects were asked to report if such a jump had occurred. As shown in the Results section of the experiment, although subjects were able to make the trajectory correction, they were sometimes actually grasping the correct target before they were aware that the target had changed. On some trials, there was a dissociation between motor and vocal responses such that, to their surprise, subjects had already grasped the target some 300 ms before they emitted the vocal response. Like baseball players, they experienced conscious awareness of the stimulus event only after their movements had taken place. No thought was required to make the movement, just as frogs catch flies without having to think about it.

Such movements are different from those consciously directed toward a specific object, as when we reach into a bowl of jellybeans to select a candy of a certain color. In this case, we must be aware of all the different colors surrounding the color that we want. Here the conscious ventral stream is needed to discriminate among particular stimuli and respond differentially to them. Consciousness, then, allows us to select behaviors that correspond to an understanding of the nuances of sensory inputs.

What Is the Neural Basis of Consciousness?

Consciousness must be related in some way to the activity of neural systems in the brain, particularly in the forebrain. One way to investigate these systems is to contrast two kinds of neurological conditions. The first is the condition in which a person lacks conscious awareness about some subset of information, even though he or she processes that information unconsciously.

Examples include blindsight (see D. B.'s case in Chapter 8), form agnosia (see D. F.'s case, also in Chapter 8), implicit learning in amnesia (discussed in Chapter 13), and visual neglect (discussed in this chapter). Another example is obsessive-compulsive disorder, in which people persist in some behavior, such as checking to see that the stove is off, even though they have already checked a great many times.

All these examples show that stimuli can be highly processed by the brain without entering conscious awareness. These phenomena are quite different from the neurological condition in which people experience conscious awareness of stimuli that are not actually there. Examples include phantom limbs (discussed in Chapter 13) and the hallucinations of schizophrenia. In both these cases, there is consciousness of specific events, such as pain in a missing limb or the perception of voices, even though these events are clearly not "real."

Two conclusions can be drawn from these contrasting examples. First, the representation of a visual object or event is likely to be distributed over many parts of the visual system and probably over parts of the frontal lobes as well. Damage to different areas not only produces different specific symptoms, such as agnosia or neglect, but can also produce a specific loss of visual consciousness. Second, because visual consciousness can be lost, it follows that parts of the neural circuit must produce this awareness.

At the beginning of this chapter, we considered the idea that the unit of thinking is the neuron. It is unlikely, however, that the neuron can be the unit of conscious

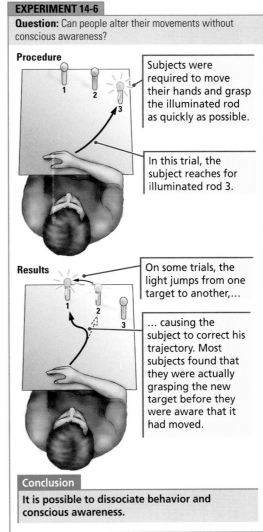

EXPERIMENT 14-6

Question: Can people alter their movements without conscious awareness?

Procedure

Subjects were required to move their hands and grasp the illuminated rod as quickly as possible.

In this trial, the subject reaches for illuminated rod 3.

Results

On some trials, the light jumps from one target to another,...

... causing the subject to correct his trajectory. Most subjects found that they were actually grasping the new target before they were aware that it had moved.

Conclusion

It is possible to dissociate behavior and conscious awareness.

Adapted from "The Neural Correlates of Conscious Experience," by C. Frith, R. Perry, and E. Lumer, 1999, *Trends in Cognitive Sciences, 3,* pp. 105–114.

experience. Instead, consciousness is presumably a process that somehow emerges from neural circuits, with greater degrees of consciousness being associated with increasingly complex circuitry.

For this reason, humans, with their more complex brain circuits, are often suggested to have a greater degree of consciousness than other animals do. Simple animals such as worms are assumed to have less consciousness (if any) than dogs, which in turn are assumed to have less consciousness than humans. Brain injury may alter self-awareness in humans, as in contralateral neglect, but, unless a person is in a coma, he or she still retains some conscious experience.

Some people have argued that language makes a fundamental change in the nature of consciousness. Recall Gazzaniga's belief that the left hemisphere, with its language capabilities, is able to act as an interpreter of stimuli. This ability, he felt, is an important difference between the functions of the two hemispheres. Yet people who are aphasic are not considered to have lost consciousness. In short, although language may alter the nature of our conscious experience, any one brain structure seems unlikely to be equated with consciousness. Rather, viewing consciousness as a product of all cortical areas, their connections, and their cognitive operations makes more sense.

We end this chapter on an interesting, if speculative, note. David Chalmers (1995) proposed that consciousness includes not only the information that the brain experiences through its sensory systems but also the information that the brain has stored and, presumably, the information that the brain can imagine. In his view, then, consciousness is the end product of all the brain's cognitive processes.

An interesting implication of such a notion is that, as the brain changes with experience, so does the state of consciousness. As our sensory experiences become richer and our store of information greater, our consciousness may become more complex. From this perspective, there may indeed be some advantage to growing old.

In Review

In the course of human evolution, sensory experience has become increasingly complex as the brain has expanded the analyses performed by sensory systems. It is hypothesized that this informational complexity must be organized in some fashion and that consciousness is a property of the nervous system that emerges as a result. Viewed in this way, consciousness allows the brain to produce a single representation of experience at any given moment and to make a choice among the many different and sometimes conflicting possible plans of action. As relative human brain size has increased in our evolution, so, too, has our degree of consciousness. But not all behavior needs to be controlled consciously. In fact, it is better that we are able to make rapid movements, such as batting a ball, without conscious thought. In such cases, speed is critical, and it would be impossible to respond quickly enough if there were conscious analysis of the movements.

SUMMARY

■ *What is thinking?* One of the products of brain activity in both humans and nonhumans is the generation of complex processes that we refer to as thinking or cognition. Various cognitive operations are described by English words such as *language* and *memory.* These operations, however, are not physical things, but rather psychological constructs. They are merely inferred and are not to be found in discrete places in the brain. The brain carries out multiple cognitive operations including perception, action for perception, imagery, planning, spatial cognition, and attention. These operations require the widespread activity of many cortical areas.

■ *What is the neural basis of cognition?* The unit of cognition is the neuron. Neurons in the association cortex specifically take part in most forms of cognition. Various syndromes result from association-cortex injury, including agnosia, apraxia, aphasia, and amnesia. Each syndrome includes the loss or disturbance of a form of cognition.

■ *What is cerebral asymmetry?* The cognitive operations of the brain are organized asymmetrically in the cerebral hemispheres, with the two hemispheres carrying out complementary functions. The most obvious functional difference in the two hemispheres is language, which is normally housed in the left hemisphere. Cerebral asymmetry is manifested in anatomical differences between the two hemispheres and can be inferred from the differential effects of injury to opposite sides of the brain. Asymmetry can also be seen in the normal brain and in the brain that is surgically split for the relief of intractable epilepsy.

■ *What might account for individual differences in cognition?* Unique brains produce unique thought patterns. Marked variations in brain organization exist among individual people, as exhibited by idiosyncratic differences such as synesthesia. Systematic differences exist as well, as in the performance of females and males on various cognitive tests, especially on tests of spatial and verbal behavior. Sex differences result from the action of gonadal hormones on the organization of the cerebral cortex, possibly on the formation of the architecture of cortical neurons. Not only is the action of the hormones important but also the timing of those actions. Differences also appear in the organization of the cerebral hemispheres in right- and left-handers. Rather than being a single group, however, left-handers constitute at least three different groups: one whose members appear to have speech in the left hemisphere, as right-handers do, and two that have anomalous speech representation, either in the right hemisphere or in both hemispheres. The reason for these organizational differences remains unknown.

■ *What is the neural basis of intelligence?* Intelligence is difficult to define. In fact, we find various forms of intelligence among humans within our own culture and in other cultures. There are obvious differences in intelligence across species, as well as within a species. Intelligence is not related to differences in brain size within a species or to any obvious gross structural differences between different members of the species. It may be related to differences in synaptic organization or to the ratio of glia to neurons.

■ *What methods are used to study how the brain thinks?* Neuropsychological studies, which began in the late 1800s, examine the behavioral capacities of people and laboratory animals with localized brain injuries. The development of different types of brain-recording systems, such as EEG, ERP, and MEG, has led to new ways of measuring brain activity while subjects are engaged in various cognitive tasks. Brain metabolism can also be measured by using imaging techniques such as PET and fMRI. An alternative to correlating metabolic activity with behavior is to stimulate the brain during cognitive activity, a technique that disrupts behavior. The original studies by Penfield used direct electrical stimulation, but more recently transcranial magnetic stimulation has been used to disrupt activity. With the use of multiple methods, it is possible to gather converging evidence on the way in which the brain thinks.

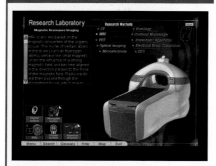

neuroscience interactive

Many resources are available for expanding your learning online:

■ **www.worthpublishers.com/kolb**
Try the Chapter 14 quizzes and flashcards to test your mastery of the chapter material. You'll also be able to link to other sites that will reinforce what you've learned.

■ **www.apraxia-kids.org**
Learn more about apraxia and how it affects children from this Web site from the headquarters of the Childhood Apraxia of Speech Association.

■ **www.web.mit.edu/synesthesia/www**
Work through some interactive demonstrations of what it might be like to have synesthesia at this Web site from the Massachusetts Institute of Technology.

On your *Foundations* CD-ROM, you can review the brain anatomy that underlies cognition in the module on the Central Nervous System. You can also learn more about magnetic resonance imaging technology in the module on Research Methods.

■ *What is consciousness, and how does it relate to brain organization?* The larger a species' brain is relative to its body size, the more knowledge the brain creates. Consciousness is a property that emerges from the complexity of the nervous system.

KEY TERMS

anomalous speech
 representation, p. 555
association cortex, p. 527
attention, p. 530
cell assembly, p. 522
cognition, p. 523
cognitive neuroscience,
 p. 536
consciousness, p. 562
contralateral neglect,
 p. 532
convergent thinking, p. 560

dichotic listening, p. 545
divergent thinking, p. 560
extinction, p. 532
functional magnetic
 resonance imaging
 (fMRI), p. 539
intelligence A, p. 561
intelligence B, p. 561
magnetic resonance
 imaging (MRI), p. 539
magnetoencephalography
 (MEG), p. 539

mirror neuron, p. 535
neuropsychology, p. 536
psychological construct,
 p. 522
split brain, p. 546
synesthesia, p. 555
syntax, p. 523
transcranial magnetic
 stimulation (TMS),
 p. 539

REVIEW QUESTIONS

1. What are the characteristics of thinking? How do these characteristics relate to the brain?

2. Summarize the role of the association cortex in thinking.

3. In what ways is the function of the cerebral hemispheres asymmetrical? In what ways is its functioning symmetrical?

4. Identify the key variations in cerebral asymmetry.

5. How does intelligence relate to brain organization?

FOR FURTHER THOUGHT

1. Contrast the ideas of syntax, mirror neurons, and the integrative mind with respect to the neural control of thinking.

2. What types of studies are necessary to identify a neural basis of consciousness?

RECOMMENDED READING

Barlow, H. (1995). The neuron doctrine in perception. In M. Gazzaniga (Ed.), *The cognitive neurosciences* (pp. 415–435). Cambridge, MA: MIT Press. Barlow introduces the reader to the fascinating question of what the basic neural unit of cognition might be. He traces the history of thinking about the problem and provides a nice summary of the evidence that the neuron is the basic unit of cognition.

Calvin, W. H. (1996). *How brains think.* New York: Basic Books. This delightful book ties together information from anthropology, evolutionary biology, linguistics, and the neurosciences to deliver an entertaining account of how intelligence evolved and how it may work. This little book would be a wonderful springboard for a group discussion at the undergraduate level and beyond.

Cytowic, R. E. (1998). *The man who tasted shapes.* Cambridge, MA: MIT Press. Cytowic gives us an inside look at the cases that led him to study synesthesia. Reading about "pointed tastes" is better than science fiction, especially for the majority of us who can barely imagine such sensory experiences.

Kimura, D. (1999). *Sex and cognition.* Cambridge, MA: MIT Press. Kimura has written a short yet comprehensive monograph on what is known about sex differences in brain organization and function. She is critical but fair in her analysis of the literature. The book is nicely spiced with ideas about what sex differences in brain organization might mean.

Kolb, B., & Whishaw, I. Q. (2003). *Fundamentals of human neuropsychology* (5th ed.). New York: Worth Publishers. For those who want to read more about the organization of the human brain and the ways in which brain injury alters cognition, this book provides a broad introduction. Indeed, the authors, who incidentally are the authors of the book that you are reading, also provide more extensive discussions of the material that you read in Chapters 8 through 11, 13, and 14.

CHAPTER

15

What Happens When the Brain Misbehaves?

Left: **Dr. Dennis Kunkel/Phototake.** *Middle:* **Randy Faris/CORBIS.**
Right: **ISM/Phototake.**

Neuropsychoanalysis

Identifying the neural basis of brain disorders and abnormal behavior has suffered from the lack of a unifying theory. Among the questions that a unifying theory of neuropsychology would answer is, How does the brain produce our concept of *self,* our beliefs about who we are as individuals?

The first coherent attempt at a theory of self is found in the writings of Sigmund Freud and other psychiatrists, beginning a century ago. Freud's theories were based on his observations of his patients and were made without the help of the anatomical or imaging data available today. The underlying tenet of Freud's theory is that our motivations remain largely hidden in our unconscious minds.

Freud posited that these motivations, largely our sexual and aggressive urges, are actively withheld from conscious awareness by a mysterious repressive force. He believed that mental illness results from the failure of repressive processes. Freud proposed three components of mind, illustrated in **Figure 15-1A**:

1. Primitive functions, including "instinctual drives" such as sex and aggression, are located in the part of the mind that Freud thought to be operating on an unconscious level and called the *id.*
2. The rational part of the mind he called the *ego.* Much of the activity of the ego Freud also believed is unconscious, although experience (to him, our perceptions of the world) is conscious.
3. The *superego* aspect of mind acts to repress the id and to mediate the ongoing interaction between the ego and the id.

For Freudians, abnormal behaviors result from the emergence of unconscious drives into voluntary, conscious behavior. The aim of *psychoanalysis,* the original talking therapy, is to trace the symptoms back to their unconscious roots and thus expose them to rational judgment.

By the 1960s, the notion of id-ego-superego seemed antiquated and without much relevance to the emerging

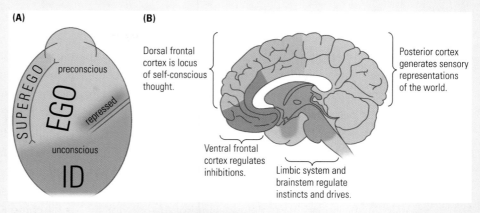

(A) SUPEREGO — preconscious — EGO — repressed — unconscious — ID

(B) Dorsal frontal cortex is locus of self-conscious thought. Posterior cortex generates sensory representations of the world. Ventral frontal cortex regulates inhibitions. Limbic system and brainstem regulate instincts and drives.

Figure 15-1

Mind Models **(A)** Freud based his model of the mind, drawn in 1933, solely on clinical observations (color added). Dotted lines mark the border between conscious and unconscious processing. **(B)** Contemporary brain-imaging and lesioning studies map a "mind" model comparable to the one developed by Freud. The brainstem and limbic system correlate with Freud's depiction of the id, the ventral frontal and posterior cortex with the ego, and the dorsal frontal cortex with the superego. Part A from A. W. Freud et al., by arrangement with Paterson Marsh Ltd, London; coloring added by Oliver Turnbull. Part B adapted from a drawing by Oliver Turnbull.

discipline of neuroscience. But, as neurobehavioral studies became more sophisticated, it became clear that people do engage in a lot of unconscious processing. Recall the evidence that we are largely unaware of our dorsal visual stream (Chapter 8) or the operations of the systems underlying implicit memory (Chapter 13).

What about repressing unpalatable thoughts or behaviors? People with contralateral neglect deny that they have any problems (Chapter 14). A woman with contralateral neglect is beautifully illustrated in a case described by Vilayanur Ramachandran (1995). He irrigated her left ear canal with cold water.

The technique temporarily stimulates the vestibular system and removes the neglect. The woman suddenly became aware of her paralyzed arm and knew that it had been paralyzed continuously since her stroke 8 days earlier. She was thus capable of recognizing both her deficit and that she had unconsciously registered the deficit.

Remarkably, when the stimulation wore off, the woman once again showed neglect. She reverted to the belief that her arm was normal. She was even unable to recall that she had acknowledged that the arm was abnormal, even though she could recall most other details of what had happened during the cold-water therapy.

It was obvious to Ramachandran that memories can be selectively repressed. Patients rationalize away unwanted facts, a behavior also described in Chapter 14 with patients given sodium amytal. Such patients experience a period of aphasia and hemiparalysis yet deny that they had any difficulties during the drug administration. Mark Solms (2004) thus wondered if repression, the cornerstone of Freud's theories, might indeed be a central feature of the normal human mind.

But what is being repressed normally? Remember that the organization of the human brain is not much different from that of other primates or even from mammals more generally. If you have pets (or if you have read Chapter 11), you know that much of what seems to drive animal behavior is directed toward pleasurable reward, whether it is attention or food from their owners or the chance to hunt or chase a Frisbee.

Freud argued that human behavior is similarly governed by the *pleasure principle.* People cling to false notions of who they are, and, though our behavior is hardly driven by "sex," sexual and other pleasurable behaviors play a major role in everyday life. Recall that the neurotransmitter dopamine has been associated with seeking pleasurable rewards such as drugs, sexual activity, and food.

Dopamine could certainly fit into Freud's model of the mind. Similarly, the behavior of frontal-lobe patients (Chapter 11) is what one might expect from a damaged mind in which inhibitory (repressive) functions are impaired. Such people may act impulsively and seemingly without concern for the social consequences of their actions. Recall from Chapter 13 that people with psychogenic amnesia have drastically reduced metabolic activity in the frontal lobe.

Figure 15-1B is Solms's simple model of how brain activity could be related to Freud's model. We do not wish to push the Freudian perspective too far, and certainly debate about its merit continues among neuroscientists, but we want to introduce you to these ideas. In the final analysis, understanding abnormal behavior will require some unified theory of how the brain produces the mind, and a reinvention of Freudian theory in a modern context provides an example of how such a model might operate.

I nvestigating the origins and treatment of abnormal behavior is perhaps the most fascinating pursuit in the study of the brain and behavior. We have explored brain systems and encountered brain disorders throughout this book. Our task now is synthesis, to consider the neural basis of behavioral disorders systematically, in regard to research, diagnosis, and treatment strategies.

Consider first the established distinction between the diagnosis and the treatment of "neurological" and "psychiatric" disorders. Once a single discipline, today neurological and psychiatric disorders tend to be treated by two different medical specialists: neurologists and psychiatrists. Neurologists identify and treat brain pathology medically. Since Freud, in contrast, psychiatrists have embraced psychoanalysis along with their medical training. Psychiatrists treat patients with pharmacological and other medical treatments in combination with behavioral therapies, and clinicians offer behavioral treatments ranging from counseling to psychotherapy.

Neurology and psychiatry became quite separate in the twentieth century. But, as researchers learn more about the neurological basis of psychiatric disorders, the disciplines are growing more similar once again. At present, however, neurologists treat organic disorders of the nervous system such as Parkinson's disease and stroke. Psychiatrists treat behavioral disorders such as schizophrenia and depression.

With the organic-neurological and behavioral-psychiatric distinction in mind, we look next at how researchers investigate the neurobiology of organic and psychiatric disorders. We then examine how disorders are classified and distributed in the population. After surveying general treatment categories, we review established and emerging treatments for representative disorders that you have encountered throughout the book.

RESEARCH ON BRAIN AND BEHAVIORAL DISORDERS

The rich history and multidisciplinary nature of neuroscience research makes studying and understanding the brain relevant to all fields of human endeavor and no less relevant to our own personal understanding of our selves.

Multidisciplinary Research Methods

From the ideas of Aristotle in antiquity to Descartes and to Darwin presented in Chapter 1, you have seen how fields as diverse as philosophy, biology, and even robotics shape our contemporary view of the brain. In the century and a half since Darwin articulated the biological foundation for the study of the brain, brain research has become still more multidisciplinary, ranging from clinical observation to the tools of molecular biology and quantum physics.

One way to summarize the methods of studying the link between brain and behavior is to consider them from the macro level of the whole organism down to the molecular level, as shown in **Table 15-1**. Behavioral studies by their very nature are investigations of the whole organism. Those conducted by Broca and others nearly 150 years ago, in which they examined the relation between language disorders and brain damage, were in many ways the starting point of systematic studies of brain–behavior relations.

Later, behavioral studies used groups of patients or laboratory animals with brain injuries. In the development of the modern science of behavioral analysis since the 1950s, more elaborate measures have been used both to analyze mental activity and to relate behavior to brain states in intact, active animals and humans. The emergence of molecular biology through the 1990s and continuing today has enabled neuroscientists to breed strains of animals, usually mice, with either a gene knocked out (deleted or inactivated) or a gene inserted. Today, neuroscientists are using knockout technology both to create animal models of human disorders and to generate treatments for neurobehavioral disorders (Chapter 3).

Improvements in brain-imaging techniques in the past decade have made it possible for changes in brain activity to be measured without direct access to the brain. Recall, for example, the dissociation of linguistic and musical abilities both between and within hemispheres that we examined in Chapter 9, where we analyzed the procedures used in producing and interpreting PET scans.

Table 15-1	Summary of Methods of Studying Brain and Behavior	
Technique		**Chapter in which an example is discussed**
Behavioral studies		
Clinical investigations of individual cases		11, 15
Neurosurgical studies of patients at surgery		9
Neuropsychological analyses of groups of patients		14
Neuropsychological analyses of laboratory animals		13
Ethological studies of behavior		6
Cognitive psychology and psychophysics		14
Developmental studies		6
Behavioral genetics		6
Brain imaging		
Positron emission tomography (PET)		8
Functional magnetic resonance Imaging (fMRI)		14
Magnetic resonance spectroscopy (MRS)		15
Brain stimulation		
Electrical stimulation		10
Transcranial magnetic stimulation (TMS)		14
Brain recording		
Electroencephalography		5
Magnetoencephalography		14
Event-related potentials		5
Long-term enhancement		5
Single-cell recording		4
Brain anatomy		
Cytological measures (i.e., measuring cell morphology)		3
Histological measures (i.e., measuring cell characteristics)		3
Tracing neural connections		4
Synaptic measures		13

Causes of Abnormal Behavior

Neuroscientists presume that abnormal behavior can result from abnormal brain functioning. Evidence for brain abnormalities is relatively straightforward in neurological disorders, and the causes are largely known, at least in a general sense:

1. *genetic errors,* as in Huntington's disease
2. *progressive cell death* resulting from a variety of neurodegenerative causes, as in Parkinson's or Alzheimer's disease
3. *rapid cell death,* such as in stroke or traumatic brain injury
4. *loss of neural connections* seen in disorders such as multiple sclerosis

In contrast with neurological disorders, far less is known about the causes of psychiatric disorders. To date, no large-scale neurobiological studies have been done of either postmortem pathology or biochemical pathology in the population at large. Still, clues to possible causes of psychiatric behaviors have been uncovered throughout the preceding chapters. In each case, some abnormality of the brain's structure or activity must be implicated. The questions asked by neuropsychologists are, What is that particular brain abnormality? What is its cause?

Table 15-2 lists the most likely categories of causes underlying behavioral disorders, micro to macro. At the microscopic level of causes is genetic error, such as that responsible for Tay-Sachs disease. Genetic error is probably linked to some of the other proposed causes, such as hormonal or developmental anomalies, as well.

Genes may be the source not only of anatomical, chemical, or physiological defects but also of susceptibility to other factors that may cause behavioral problems. A person may have a genetic predisposition to be vulnerable to stress, infection, or pollution, which is the immediate cause of some abnormal conditions listed in Table 15-2. In other cases, no genetic predisposition is needed, and abnormal behavior arises strictly from environmental factors.

The triggering environmental factor may be poor nutrition or exposure to toxic substances, including naturally occurring toxins, manufactured chemicals, and infectious agents. Other disorders are undoubtedly related to negative experiences. Negative experience ranges from developmental deprivation, the extreme psychosocial neglect

Table 15-2	Causes of Certain Behavioral Disorders
Cause	**Disorder (chapter discussed)**
Genetic error	Tay-Sachs disease (3)
Hormonal anomaly	Androgenital syndrome (11)
Developmental anomaly	Schizophrenia (7)
Infection	Encephalitis (2)
Injury	Traumatic brain injury (1)
Natural environmental toxins	Shellfish poisoning (7)
Manufactured toxins	MPTP poisoning (5)
Poor nutrition	Korsakoff's syndrome (13)
Stress	Anxiety disorders (11)
Negative experience	Developmental delays among Romanian orphans (6)

of Romanian orphans in the 1980s and 1990s detailed in Chapter 6 being one example, to traumas or chronic stress in later life, such as experiences implicated in anxiety disorders.

Investigating the Neurobiology of Behavioral Disorders

That a single brain abnormality can cause a behavioral disorder, explaining everything about that disorder and its treatment, is well illustrated. A defect in the gene for phenylalanine hydroxylase, an enzyme that breaks down phenylalanine, causes **phenylketonuria** (PKU). Babies with PKU have elevated levels of the amino acid phenylalanine in their blood.

Left untreated, PKU causes severe mental retardation, but PKU can be easily treated, just by restricting the dietary intake of phenylalanine. If other behavioral disorders were as simple and well understood as PKU is, research in neuroscience could quickly yield cures for them. Many disorders do not result from a single genetic abnormality, however, and the causes of most disorders are still largely conjectural.

The major problem is that a psychiatric diagnosis of developmental disability is based mainly on behavioral symptoms, and behavioral symptoms give few clues to specific neurochemical or neurostructural causes. This problem also can be seen in treating PKU. Table 15-3 lists what is known about PKU at different levels of analysis: genetic, biochemical, histological, neurological, behavioral, and social.

The underlying problem in PKU becomes less apparent with the procession of entries in the table. In fact, it is not possible to predict the specific biochemical abnormality from information at the neurological, behavioral, or social levels. But the primary information available *is* at the neurological, behavioral, and social levels.

For most psychiatric diseases, the underlying pathology is unknown. For PKU, elevated phenylpyruric acid levels in the urine of a single patient was the organic clue

Phenylketonuria (PKU). Behavioral disorder caused by elevated levels of the amino acid phenylalanine in the blood and resulting from a defect in the gene for the enzyme phenylalanine hydroxylase; the major symptom is severe mental retardation.

Table 15-3	Phenylketonuria: A Behavioral Disorder for Which the Neurobiological Pathogenesis Is Known
Level of analysis	**Information known**
Genetic	Inborn error of metabolism; autosomal recessive defective gene
Biochemical pathogenesis	Impairment in the hydroxylation of phenylalanine to tyrosine, causing elevated blood levels of phenylalanine and its metabolites
Histological abnormality	Decreased neuron size and dendritic length, and lowered spine density; abnormal cortical lamination
Neurological findings	Severe mental retardation, slow growth, abnormal EEG
Behavioral symptoms	For 95 percent of patients, IQ below 50
Social disability	Loss of meaningful, productive life; significant social and economic cost
Treatment	Restrict dietary intake of phenylalanine

Source: Adapted from "Special Challenges in the Investigation of the Neurobiology of Mental Illness," by G. R. Heninger, 1999, in *The Neurobiology of Mental Illness* (p. 90), edited by D. S. Charney, E. J. Nestler, and B. S. Bunney, New York: Oxford University Press.

needed to understand the behavioral disorder. The task for future study and treatment of most behavioral disorders is to identify the biological markers that will lead to similar understandings.

CHALLENGES TO DIAGNOSIS

Knowledge about behavioral disorders is also hampered by its very nature. Most diagnostic information gathered is about a patient's behavior, which comes both from patients and from their families. Unfortunately, people are seldom objective observers of their own behavior or that of a loved one. We tend to be selective in noticing and reporting symptoms. If we believe that someone has a memory problem, for example, we often notice memory lapses that we might ordinarily ignore.

Furthermore, we are often not specific in identifying symptoms. Simply identifying a memory problem is not really helpful. Treatment requires knowing exactly what type of memory deficit is the basis of the problem. Loss of memory for words, places, or habits implies very different underlying pathologies and brain systems.

Not only do patients and their loved ones make diagnosis difficult, but those who do the diagnosing do so as well. Behavioral information about patients may be interpreted by general physicians, psychiatrists, neurologists, psychologists, or social workers, as well as by others. Evaluators with different conceptual biases shape and filter the questions that they ask and the information that they gather differently.

One evaluator believes that most behavioral disorders are genetic in origin, another believes that most result from a virus, and a third believes that many can be traced to repressed sexual experiences during childhood. Each makes quite different types of observations and gives very different kinds of diagnostic tests. In contrast, the diagnosis of nonbehavioral disorders is not so dependent on subjective observations made by an evaluator but rather depends on experimental methods.

RESEARCH CHALLENGES

Even if the problems of psychiatric diagnosis were solved, major obstacles to investigating behavioral disorders would still exist. For organizational complexity, the nervous system far outstrips other body systems. The brain has a wider variety of cell types than does any other organ, and the complex connections among neurons add a whole new dimension to understanding normal and abnormal functioning.

As our understanding of brain and behavior has progressed, it has become apparent that multiple receptor systems serve many different functions. As George Heninger (1999) pointed out, there is as yet no clear demonstration of a single receptor system with a specific relation to a specific behavior. For example, the neurotransmitter GABA (Chapter 7) affects some 30 percent of the synapses in the brain. When GABA agonists such as benzodiazepines are given to people, multiple effects on behavior become apparent. It is difficult to administer enough of a benzodiazepine to reduce anxiety to a "normal" level without producing sedative side effects as well.

Other receptor systems detailed in Chapter 5, such as those involving acetylcholine, dopamine, and serotonin, are equally diffuse, with little specificity between biochemistry and behavior. One example of a close relation between a receptor system and behavior is seen in the dopaminergic system and its relation to Parkinson's disease. But even here it is impossible to tie dopamine depletion to a consistent behavioral syndrome. Two people with Parkinson's disease can have quite different symptoms even though the basis of the disease is known to be a loss of neurons in the substantia nigra.

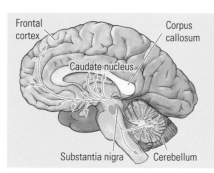

Frontal cortex

Corpus callosum

Caudate nucleus

Substantia nigra

Cerebellum

Dopaminergic system
Active in maintaining normal motor behavior. Loss of dopamine is related to Parkinson's disease, in which muscles are rigid and movements are difficult to make. Increases in dopamine activity may be related to schizophrenia.

Even if a patient has actual neuropathology, such as lesions in the nervous system, determining the cause of a behavioral disorder may still be difficult. Magnetic resonance imaging may show that a person with multiple sclerosis has many nervous system lesions, yet the person displays very few outward symptoms. Similarly, only when the loss of dopamine neurons exceeds about 60 to 80 percent do investigators see clinical signs of Parkinson's disease.

This is not to suggest that most of our brain cells are not needed. It simply shows that the brain is capable of considerable plasticity. When diseases progress slowly, the brain has a remarkable capacity for adapting.

Just as obvious brain lesions do not always produce behavioral symptoms, behavioral symptoms are not always linked to obvious neuropathology. For instance, some people have notable behavioral problems after suffering brain trauma, yet no obvious signs of brain damage appear on an MRI scan. The pathology may be subtle, such as a drop in dendritic-spine density, or so diffuse that it is hard to identify.

Given the current diagnostic methods for both behavioral disorders and neuropathology, identifying disorders and their causes is seldom an easy task. A major avenue for investigating the causes of behavioral disorders is to develop and study animal models. For example, rats with specific lesions of the nigrostriatal dopamine system are used as a model of Parkinson's disease. This model has led to significant advances in our understanding of how specific dopaminergic agonists and cholinergic antagonists act in the treatment of Parkinsonism.

One problem with the use of animal models, however, is the oversimplified view that they provide of the neurobiology of behavioral abnormalities. The fact that a drug reduces symptoms does not necessarily mean that it is acting on a key biochemical aspect of the pathology. Aspirin can get rid of a headache, but that does not mean that the headache is caused by the receptors on which aspirin acts.

Similarly, antipsychotic drugs block D-2 receptors, but that does not mean that schizophrenia is caused by abnormal D-2 receptors. It quite possibly results from a disturbance in glutamatergic systems, and, for some reason, dopamine antagonists are effective in rectifying the abnormality.

This is not to imply that animal models are unimportant. We have seen throughout this book that they *are* important. But modeling human disorders is a complex task, and so caution is needed when you read news stories about studies using animal models that point toward possible cures for human behavioral diseases.

Such caution especially applies to psychiatric disorders in which causes are still unknown. Furthermore, many symptoms of disorders such as schizophrenia and anxiety are largely cognitive. The objective identification of any cognitive processes mimicked by a laboratory model is difficult.

In Review

Neurobiological investigations of behavioral disorders are based on the assumption that a direct link ought to exist between brain abnormalities and disorders in behavior. In most cases, however, this relation is far from direct. Discrete biological markers are difficult to identify, except in the most well studied disorders. Surprisingly, we encounter instances of brain pathology without obvious clinical symptoms and of clinical symptoms without obvious pathology. Still, the general causes of behavioral disorders range from genetic factors to negative experiences, including injuries, toxins, and stress. It will be some time, however, before a science of brain and behavior can fully explain the disordered mind.

CLASSIFYING AND TREATING BRAIN AND BEHAVIORAL DISORDERS

Behavioral disorders afflict millions every year. **Figure 15-2** summarizes the lifetime rates of psychiatric disorders among people in the United States of America. Nearly one-half of the sample had met the criteria for a psychiatric disorder at some point in their lives. Of these people, only a minority had received treatment of any kind, and an even smaller percentage had received treatment from a mental-health specialist.

Large-scale surveys of neurological disorders show a similar pattern of prevalence, as summarized in **Table 15-4**. Acute disorders happen suddenly. Many of those afflicted do not survive. They are represented in "short term" statistics. Statistics for chronic disorders represent the survivors, people who have a disorder for a prolonged period.

If you are surprised to find hearing disorders among the neurological, remember that many disorders of hearing are related to a deficit either in the transduction of sound into neural activity or in the eighth cranial nerve itself. Looking at the statistics presented in Figure 15-2 and Table 15-4, we can only marvel that most people are relatively normal most of the time.

Figure 15-2

Distribution of Psychiatric Disorders in the United States Adapted from "Lifetime and 12-Month Prevalence of DSM-III-R Psychiatric Disorders in the United States," by R. C. Kessler, K. A. McGonagle, S. Zhao, D. B. Nelson, M. Hughes, S. Eshleman, H. Wittchen, and K. S. Kendler, 1994, *Archives of General Psychiatry, 51,* pp. 8–19.

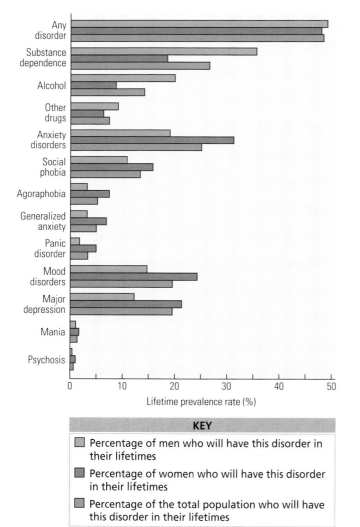

Lifetime prevalence rate (%)

KEY

☐ Percentage of men who will have this disorder in their lifetimes

☐ Percentage of women who will have this disorder in their lifetimes

☐ Percentage of the total population who will have this disorder in their lifetimes

Table 15-4	Prevalence of Major Neurological and Communicative Disorders in the United States
Disorder	**Estimated number of cases**
Acute disorders (per year)	
Trauma: head and spinal cord	500,000/yr
Stroke	500,000/yr
Infectious disorders	25,000/yr
TOTAL ACUTE	1,025,000/yr
Chronic disorders (cumulative survivors)	
Nervous system	
Stroke	2,000,000+
Traumatic brain injury	10,000,000+
Spinal-cord injury	500,000
Epilepsy	2,000,000
Hearing and speech	
Deafness	2,000,000
Partial deafness	11,600,000
Speech	8,400,000
Language	6,600,000
Movement disorders (e.g., Parkinson's, Huntington's, Tourette's)	800,000
Demyelinating diseases (MS, ALS)	200,000
Disorders of early life (e.g., cerebral palsy)	1,000,000
Neuromuscular disorders	1,000,000
Other neurological disorders (e.g., chronic pain, insomnia, neuro-AIDS)	9,000,000
TOTAL CHRONIC	55,100,000+

Identifying and Classifying Mental Disorders

Epidemiology is the study of the distribution and causes of diseases in human populations. A major contribution of epidemiological studies has been to help define and assess behavioral disorders, especially those that we are labeling as psychiatric disorders.

The first set of criteria for diagnoses in psychiatry was developed in 1972. Since that time, two parallel sets of criteria have been developed. One is the World Health Organization's International Classification of Diseases (ICD-10 being the most recent version), and the other is the most recent edition of the American Psychiatric Association's *Diagnostic and Statistical Manual of Mental Disorders*, the DSM-IV, published in 1994. In 2000, the APA revised the text to include research information developed since publication in 1994. The classification scheme used in this most recent revision, **DSM-IV-TR,** is summarized in **Table 15-5.**

DSM-IV-TR. Text revision of the fourth, and most recent, edition of the American Psychiatric Association's classification of psychiatric disorders, the *Diagnostic and Statistical Manual of Mental Disorders.*

⊙ To explore the DSM-IV online, visit the Chapter 15 Web links on the *Brain and Behavior* Web site (**www.worth publishers.com/kolb**).

Table 15-5	**Summary of DSM-IV-TR Classification of Abnormal Behaviors**
Diagnostic category	**Core features and examples of specific disorders**
Disorders usually first diagnosed in infancy, childhood, and adolescence	Tend to emerge and sometimes dissipate before adult life: pervasive developmental disorders (such as autism), learning disorders, attention-deficit hyperactivity disorder, conduct disorder, separation-anxiety disorder
Delirium, dementia, amnesia, and other cognitive disorders	Dominated by impairment in cognitive functioning: Alzheimer's disease, Huntington's disease
Mental disorders due to a general medical condition	Caused primarily by a general medical disorder: mood disorder due to a general medical condition
Substance-related disorders	Brought about by the use of substances that affect the central nervous system: alcohol-use disorders, opioid-use disorders, amphetamine-use disorders, cocaine-use disorders, hallucinogen-use disorders
Schizophrenia and other psychotic disorders	Functioning deteriorates toward a state of psychosis, or loss of contact with reality
Mood disorders	Severe disturbances of mood resulting in extreme and inappropriate sadness or elation for extended periods of time: major depressive disorder, bipolar disorders
Anxiety disorders	Anxiety: generalized anxiety disorder, phobias, panic disorder, obsessive-compulsive disorder, acute stress disorder, posttraumatic stress disorder
Somatoform disorders	Physical symptoms that are apparently caused primarily by psychological rather than physiological factors: conversion disorder, somatization disorder, hypochondriasis
Fictitious disorders	Intentional production or feigning of physical or psychological symptoms
Dissociative disorders	Significant changes in consciousness, memory, identity, or perception, without a clear physical cause: dissociative amnesia, dissociative fugue, dissociative identity disorder (multiple personality disorder)
Eating disorders	Abnormal patterns of eating that significantly impair functioning: anorexia nervosa, bulimia nervosa
Sexual disorders and sexual-identity disorder	Chronic disruption in sexual functioning, behavior, or preferences: sexual dysfunctions, paraphilias, sexual-identity disorder
Sleep disorders	Chronic sleep problems: primary insomnia, primary hypersomnia, sleep-terror disorder, sleepwalking disorder
Impulse-control disorders	Chronic inability to resist impulses, drives, or temptations to perform certain acts that are harmful to the self or others: pathological gambling, kleptomania, pyromania, intermittent explosive disorder
Adjustment disorders	A maladaptive reaction to a clear stressor, such as divorce or business difficulties, that first occurs within 3 months after the onset of the stressor
Other conditions that may be a focus of clinical attention	Conditions or problems that are worth noting because they cause significant impairment, such as relational problems, problems related to abuse or neglect, medication-induced movement disorders, and psychophysiological disorders

Source: Adapted from *Diagnostic and Statistical Manual of Mental Disorders* (4th ed.), 1994, Washington, DC: American Psychiatric Association.

Figure 15-3

Early-Onset Schizophrenia A comparison of three-dimensional maps derived from MRI scans reveals that, compared with healthy teenagers aged 13 to 18 (map shown at left), patients with childhood onset schizophrenia (map shown at right) have widespread loss of gray matter across the cerebral hemispheres. Courtesy of Paul Thompson and Arthur W. Toga, University of California Laboratory of Neuro Imaging, Los Angeles, and Judith L. Rapoport, National Institute of Mental Health.

Average annual loss (%)

0 −1 −2 −3 −4 −5

Normal adolescents   Schizophrenic subjects

As already stated, any classification of psychiatric disorders is to some extent arbitrary and unavoidably depends on prevailing cultural views. A good example is the social definition of abnormal sexual behavior. From its inception, the DSM listed homosexual behavior as pathological. Since 1980, however, the *Manual* has omitted this "disorder." The revision is due to changed cultural beliefs about what sexual abnormality is as much as it is to new findings from research on the neurological bases of sexual preference (Chapter 11).

One continually emerging means of looking for indicators of behavioral disorders is brain imaging, including MRI and PET (Chapters 9 and 14). These imaging tools are not currently used clinically, but they may soon be used both to classify disorders and to monitor the effectiveness of treatment.

To be useful, imaging tests must be sensitive enough to detect unique features of brain disorders but specific enough to rule out similar conditions. The latter feature is problematic, inasmuch as many behavioral disorders display similar abnormalities. Enlarged ventricles may appear in schizophrenia, Alzheimer's disease, alcoholism, or head trauma, for example. Nonetheless, neuroscientists have begun using imaging technology to shed light on behavioral disturbances.

In an impressive example, research teams led by Judith Rapoport, Paul Thompson, and Arthur Toga compared the brains of healthy adolescents with those diagnosed with childhood-onset schizophrenia (see review by Sowell et al., 2004). **Figure 15-3** shows that, between the ages of 13 and 18, the children who developed schizophrenia showed a remarkable loss of gray matter in the cerebral cortex. This loss was correlated with the onset of a variety of behavioral disturbances characteristic of the disease. Such analyses could provide an important aid to treatment because early detection of schizophrenia ought to provide a rationale for proper drug treatment that may slow down the progress of the disease.

Not all disorders will show such obvious loss of tissue, but they may show abnormal blood flow or metabolism that can be detected either by fMRI or PET. The PET images in **Figure 15-4** illustrate the metabolic changes in adult-onset schizophrenia, showing an obvious abnormality in activity in the prefrontal cortex. Note that this area does not show loss of gray matter in the early-onset-schizophrenia MRI study reproduced in Figure 15-3. Therefore the two diseases seem likely to have different origins.

Combining behavioral diagnoses with neuroimaging may enable movement beyond symptom checklists like those published in the DSM to more-objective medical diagnoses. Further, imaging analyses may provide treatments to reduce the severity of such serious disorders as schizophrenia and Alzheimer's disease. Remember, however, that not all brain pathology will be detected by using current imaging techniques. Part of the challenge for the future is to improve current techniques and to develop others that can identify more-subtle molecular abnormalities in the nervous system.

Figure 15-4

Adult-Onset Schizophrenia PET scans of the brains of (*left*) an adult schizophrenia patient and (*right*) a person who does not have schizophrenia. Note the abnormally low blood flow in the prefrontal cortex at the top of the left-hand scan.

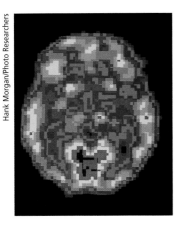
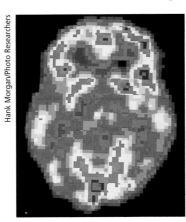

Hank Morgan/Photo Researchers

Treatments for Disorders

We have encountered disorders of brain and behavior in every chapter of this book, especially in the Focus boxes. Indexed in Table 1-1 on page 6, the variety of disorders is broad, but an inclusive list would consist of some 2000 entries. The long-term prospects for curing organic or behavioral disorders on the macro level depend on the ability to treat structural and biochemical abnormalities at the micro level.

On the organic side, the unifying characteristic is some underlying nervous system abnormality. Organic abnormalities include genetic disorders (such as Huntington's chorea), developmental disorders (such as autism), infectious diseases (such as meningitis), nervous system injuries (such as brain or spinal-cord trauma), and degenerative conditions (such as Alzheimer's disease). On the structural side, organic disorders include the congenital absence of neurons or glia, the presence of abnormal neurons or glia, the death of neurons or glia, and neurons or neural connections with unusual structures. Similarly, abnormalities may appear in the biochemical organization or operation of the nervous system. Biochemical abnormalities include disordered proteins in cell-membrane channels, low or high numbers of neuroreceptors, low or high numbers of molecules, especially neurotransmitters or hormones, and any improper balances.

The ultimate clinical problem for behavioral neuroscience is to apply its knowledge to generate treatments that can restore a disordered brain (and mind) to the range of normalcy. This challenge is daunting because the first task is so difficult: learning the cause of a particular behavioral disturbance. Few behavioral disorders have as simple a cause as PKU does. Most, like schizophrenia, are extremely complex. Still, a variety of more or less effective treatments for a range of behavioral disorders have been developed, as summarized in **Table 15-6**.

Treatments fall into four general categories: neurosurgical, pharmacological, electrophysiological, and behavioral. In very invasive neurosurgical treatment, the skull is opened and some intervention is performed on the brain. Pharmacotherapy is less invasive. A chemical that affects the brain is either ingested or injected. Noninvasive physiological and behavioral treatments manipulate the body or the experience, which in turn influences the brain. As you will see, each treatment category has a specific objective.

NEUROSURGICAL TREATMENTS

Historically, neurosurgical manipulations of the nervous system with the goal of directly altering it have been largely reparative, such as when tumors are removed or arteriovenous malformations are corrected. More recently, however, neurosurgical approaches aim at altering brain activity to alleviate some behavioral disorder. The surgery either damages some dysfunctional area of the brain or stimulates dysfunctional areas with electrodes.

The treatment of Parkinson's disease can employ both neurosurgeries (Boucai, Cerquetti, & Merello, 2004). In the first technique, an electrode is placed into the motor thalamus and an electric current is used to damage neurons that are responsible for producing the tremor characteristic of Parkinson's. In the second neurosurgery, **deep brain stimulation** (DBS), an electrode fixed in place in the globus pallidus or subthalamic nucleus is connected to an external electrical stimulator that can be activated by the patient to facilitate normal movements.

Another neurosurgical strategy is highly experimental, as well as controversial. In Chapter 6, you learned that the brain develops in a fixed sequence: from cell division to cell differentiation to cell migration to synaptogenesis. If a region of the brain is

Deep brain stimulation (DBS). Neurosurgery to facilitate normal movements, in which an electrode is fixed in place in the globus pallidus or subthalamic nucleus and connected to an external electrical stimulator controlled by the patient.

Table 15-6	Summary of Treatments of Brain and Behavior	
Treatment		**Chapter in which an example is discussed**
Neurosurgical		
Damage to dysfunctional area (e.g., Parkinson's disease)		10
Implantation of embryonic or endogenous stem cells to regenerate lost tissue		13
Deep brain stimulation (e.g., implantation of stimulation electrode to control tremor in Parkinson's disease)		10
Removal of abnormal tissue (e.g., epilepsy, tumor)		9
Repair of abnormality (e.g., arteriovenous malformations)		9
Pharmacological		
Antibiotic or antiviral agents or both (e.g., encephalitis)		2
Drugs to alter neurochemistry		7
Neurotrophic factors		13
Nutritional		11
Electrophysiological		
Direct electrical brain stimulation		15
Electroconvulsive therapy (ECT)		15
Transcranial magnetic stimulation (TMS)		14
Behavioral		
Behavioral training (e.g., speech therapy, cognitive therapy)		13
Psychotherapy		15

functioning abnormally or if it is diseased or dead, it should be possible to return this region to the embryonic state and regrow a normal region.

This technique has a science-fiction ring to it, but it may someday be feasible. In laboratory rats, for example, stem cells can be induced by neurotrophic factors to generate new cells that can migrate to the site of an injury (Chapter 6). This process may not be practical in a large brain such as that possessed by humans, but the principle of using stem cells to generate new neurons still holds. Stem cells might be placed directly into a dysfunctional region and then supplied with different growth factors that would stimulate them to generate a functional region.

Where would the stem cells come from? In the 1980s, surgeons experimented with implanting fetal cells into adult brains (see "The Case of the Frozen Addict "on page 171), but this approach has had limited success. Another idea comes from the discovery that multipotent stem cells in other body regions, such as in bone marrow, appear to be capable of manufacturing neural stem cells.

If the use of multipotent stem cells proves to be a practical way of generating neural stem cells, it should be possible to take bone marrow cells from a person, place them in a special culture medium to generate thousands or millions of stem cells, and then place these stem cells into the damaged brain. The challenge is to get the cells to differentiate appropriately and develop the correct connections. At present, this challenge is still formidable, but meeting it is well within the realm of possibility.

Transplanting stem cells is being seriously talked about today as a treatment for disorders such as stroke. In fact, Douglas Kondziolka and his colleagues (2000) tried cell transplants with a sample of 12 stroke victims. They harvested progenitor cells from a rare tumor known as a teratocarcinoma. The tumor cells were chemically altered to develop a neuronal phenotype, and then between 2 million and 6 million cells were transplanted into regions around the stroke.

The patients were followed for a year, and, for 6 of them, PET scans showed an increase in metabolic activity in the areas that had received the transplanted cells, indicating that the transplants were having some effect on the host brain. Behavioral analyses also showed some improvement in these patients. This study is only the first of its type, and the behavioral outcome was modest, but it does show that such a neurosurgical treatment may be feasible.

ELECTROPHYSIOLOGICAL TREATMENTS

Treating the mind by treating the body is an ancient notion. In the 1930s, researchers used insulin to lower blood sugar and produce seizures as a treatment for depression. By the 1950s, insulin therapy had been replaced by electroconvulsive therapy (ECT), the first electrical brain-stimulation treatment.

Electroconvulsive therapy was developed as a treatment for depression and, although its mode of action was not understood, it did prove useful in some patients. Although rarely used today, ECT is still sometimes the only treatment that works for people with severe depression. One reason may be that ECT stimulates the production of a variety of neurotrophic factors, especially BDNF (brain-derived neurotrophic factor).

Significant problems with ECT include the massive convulsions caused by the electrical stimulation. These convulsions normally require large doses of medications to prevent them. Another problem is that ECT leads to memory loss, a symptom that can be quite troublesome with repeated ECT treatments.

A newer research technique described in Chapter 14, transcranial magnetic stimulation (TMS), uses magnetic rather than electrical stimulation. To date, the only widespread clinical application of TMS is as a treatment for depression. Clinical applications for TMS are growing, as reviewed in "Treating Behavioral Disorders with TMS."

Transcranial magnetic stimulation is a far less drastic treatment than ECT and will probably become a far more widely used treatment in the coming decade (Rossi &

For more information on the use of TMS in research and in the treatment of mental illness, visit the Chapter 15 Web links on the *Brain and Behavior* Web site (**www.worthpublishers.com/kolb**).

Treating Behavioral Disorders with TMS

In transcranial magnetic stimulation, a magnetic field is placed over the scalp to affect the underlying brain regions. The advantage of TMS is that it can be applied to localized brain regions, or focal areas, thought to be implicated in specific disorders. If the magnetic field is sufficiently strong, an area of cortex as small as a quarter can be activated with the use of this technique.

The primary clinical use of TMS is for depression. Findings from brain-imaging studies show that depression is associated with reduced metabolic activity in the dorsolateral prefrontal cortex. Stimulation of the region might help to resolve the depression.

The results of controlled clinical studies of drug-resistant patients show that daily stimulation of the left dorsolateral prefrontal cortex may produce significant reductions in depressive symptoms compared with sham TMS treatment (e.g., George et al., 1997). One difficulty is that the relief may be transient, possibly because the stimulation does not reach deeper regions of the hemisphere, such as the limbic cortex.

Recent experiments are attempting to induce controlled seizures with TMS to create an ECT-like effect. With the energy transfer so much weaker in TMS, researchers reason that TMS would not produce the drastic side effects of ECT (Sporn et al., 2004).

Schizophrenia also may also be a good candidate for TMS therapy (Haraldsson et al., 2004). The clear pathology in the frontal lobe, for example, would be relatively easy to target. Similarly, auditory hallucinations originate in the auditory cortex and this region, too, would be an accessible target for TMS. Studies have been done on both targets.

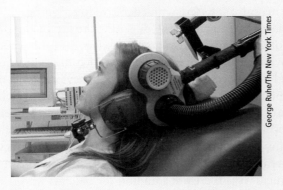

In clinical therapy for depression, transcranial magnetic stimulation influences action potentials in a localized brain area.

George Ruhe/The New York Times

High-frequency TMS to the prefrontal cortex has been promising, at least for negative symptoms. Several studies using TMS to specifically treat auditory hallucinations are ongoing. The general finding is that daily TMS for only about 20 min produces significant reduction in hallucination frequency in most, but not all, schizophrenia patients studied (e.g., Hoffman et al., 2003). Other symptoms were unchanged. Long-term follow-ups showed a slow return of the hallucinations.

One TMS study of schizophrenia patients is especially intriguing. Paul Fitzgerald and colleagues (2004) wondered if repeated stimulation might make the brain more plastic. If so, would there be a difference in schizophrenic subjects?

The authors stimulated the motor cortex of control subjects and found that a 15-min train of TMS produced a change in the excitability of the motor cortex to later short pulses of TMS. They concluded that the train of TMS had produced a plastic change in the brain, likely by reducing cortical inhibition.

Curiously, the same procedure induced no similar plastic change when used with schizophrenia subjects. Two implications of this finding are:

1. The failure to record a persisting change in the schizophrenia subjects suggests that TMS is having somewhat different effects in the controls and patients. The difference in effects may explain why the effects of TMS are apparently not permanent. To produce persisting changes in cortical excitability, schizophrenia patients may require much longer courses of stimulation than do control subjects.

2. The reduced plasticity in the patients may account for the memory problems of schizophrenia patients. If the brain is less plastic, producing the neural changes necessary for learning will be more difficult.

TMS has not yet been used clinically in anxiety disorders, in large part because neuroimaging studies have not yet identified specific targets. There is optimism that such targets will be found with more-sensitive PET and fMRI analyses, and TMS could then be tried as a way to influence activity in such regions (Boland & Keller, 2004).

Rossini, 2004). One advantage that contributes to reduced side effects is the precision of TMS. The magnetic stimulation can be applied narrowly, to a focal area, rather than diffusely, as in ECT. And the prospective range of applications for TMS is broad.

Electrical stimulation may also have a role in treating certain neurological diseases. As noted earlier, Parkinson's disease can be treated with the implantation of electrodes into the putamen. In both animal studies and preliminary studies in human stroke patients, focal electrical stimulation of the regions next to tissue damaged by stroke is now being used. The electrical activation of these adjacent regions appears to increase the production of synapses and to enhance function (Teskey et al., 2003).

PHARMACOLOGICAL TREATMENTS

Two developments in the 1950s led to a pharmacological revolution in the treatment of behavioral disorders:

1. A drug used to premedicate surgical patients was discovered to have antipsychotic properties. This finding led to the development of phenothiazines as a treatment for schizophrenia, and, in the next 40 years, these neuroleptic drugs became increasingly more selective and effective.
2. A new class of antianxiety drugs was invented—namely, the anxiolytics—and medications such as Valium quickly became the most widely prescribed drugs in the United States.

The power of these two classes of drugs to change disordered behavior revolutionized the pharmaceutical industry. That revolution is just now reaping major rewards with the development of the second-generation, or so-called atypical, antidepressants such as Prozac (Chapter 7). These SSRIs (selective serotonin reuptake inhibitors) hold promise in the restoration of more-normal behavior in people with a wide range of disorders. Another revolutionary pharmaceutical, L-dopa, provided the first treatment for a serious motor dysfunction in Parkinson's disease (Chapter 5). L-Dopa's effectiveness led to optimism that drugs might be developed as "magic bullets" to correct the chemical imbalances found in Alzheimer's disease and other disorders.

Neuroscientists now know that most behavioral disorders cannot be reduced to a single chemical abnormality. Pharmacological treatments need considerable refinement; they are no panacea for neurobiological dysfunctions. Nonetheless, for many people, drug treatment provides relief from a host of mental and motor problems.

Pharmacological treatments have their downsides. Significant side effects top the list, and long-term effects may create new problems. Consider a person who receives antidepressant medication. Although the drug may ease the depression, it may produce unwanted side effects, including decreased sexual desire, fatigue, and sleep disturbance. These last two effects may also interfere with cognitive functioning.

Thus, although the medication is useful for getting the person out of the depressed state, it may produce other symptoms that are themselves disturbing and may complicate the person's recovery. Furthermore, in cases in which the depression is related to life events, a drug does not provide a person with the behavioral tools needed to cope with an adverse situation. As some psychologists say, "A pill is not a skill."

A second example of drug treatments' negative side effects can be seen in many people being treated for schizophrenia with neuroleptics. These antipsychchotic drugs act not only on the mesolimbic dopamine system, which is likely to be functioning abnormally in the schizophrenia patient, but also on the nigrostriatal dopaminergic system, which controls movement. It is therefore common for patients who take neuroleptics for a prolonged period to begin having motor disturbances. **Tardive dyskinesia,** an inability to stop the tongue from moving, is a motor symptom.

To learn more about the drugs used to treat mental disorders, visit the *Brain and Behavior* Web site and go to the Web links for Chapter 15 (**www.worth publishers.com/kolb**).

Tardive dyskinesia. Inability to stop the tongue from moving; motor side effect of neuroleptic drugs.

Movement-disorder side effects often persist long after the medication has been stopped. Taking drugs for behavioral disorders, then, does carry some risk. Rather than acting like "magic bullets," these medications can sometimes act like "magic shotguns."

BEHAVIORAL TREATMENTS

Although all psychiatric disorders are ultimately related to the nervous system, environmental factors often contribute to them as well. The influence of environmental factors on behavior is illustrated by the simple fact that our behavior in the context of a formal social gathering is quite different from that in the company of our closest friends. Social and cultural factors affect how the brain operates to produce behaviors, normal as well as abnormal ones. We are a long way from understanding exactly how environmental factors influence brain activity or promote pathological behaviors at specific times and places.

Treatments for behavioral disorders need not be direct biological or medical interventions. Just as the brain can alter behavior, behavior can alter the brain (Chapter 11). Therefore, behavioral treatments often focus on key environmental factors that influence how a person acts.

As behavior changes in response to these treatments, the brain is affected as well. An example is the treatment of generalized anxiety disorders, as illustrated by the case of G. B. in Chapter 11. Although G. B. required immediate treatment with antianxiety medication, the long-term treatment entailed changing his behavior. His anxiety disorder was not simply a problem of abnormal brain activity. It was also a problem of experiential and social factors that fundamentally altered his perception of the world.

In the past 40 years, psychologists have developed two general ways to change behavior, behavioral therapies and cognitive therapies. **Behavioral therapies** apply well-established learning principles to eliminate unwanted behaviors. For example, if a person is debilitated by a fear of insects, there is little point in looking for inner causes. Rather, the behavioral therapist will try to replace the maladaptive behaviors with more constructive ways of behaving, which might include training to relax or systematic exposure to unthreatening insects (butterflies) and then gradual exposure to more-threatening insects (bees), the latter technique being called *systematic desensitization.*

Cognitive therapies take the perspective that thoughts intervene between events and emotions. Consider responses to losing a job. One thought could be that "I am a loser, life is hopeless." An alternate thought is that "the boss is a jerk and he did me a favor."

You can imagine that the former cognitions might lead to depression, whereas the latter would not. Cognitive therapies challenge a person's self-defeating attitudes and assumptions. Such therapy can be quite important for people with brain injuries, too, because it is easy for people to think that they are "crazy" or "retarded" after brain injury.

If one of your relatives or friends were to have a stroke and become aphasic, you would expect the person to receive speech therapy, which is a form of behavioral treatment for an injured brain. The logic in speech therapy is that, by practicing (relearning) the basic components of speech and language, the patient should be able to regain at least some of the lost function. The same logic can be applied to other types of behavioral disorders, whether motor or cognitive.

Therapies for cognitive disorders resulting from brain trauma or dysfunction aim to retrain people in the fundamental cognitive processes that they have lost. Although cognitive therapy seems as logical as speech therapy after a stroke, the difficulty is that such therapy assumes that we know what fundamental elements of cognitive activity are meaningful to the brain. Cognitive scientists are far from understanding these elements well enough to generate optimal therapies. Still, neuropsychologists such as George Prigatano and Catherine Mateer and their respective colleagues are developing

Behavioral therapy. Treatment that applies learning principles, such as conditioning, to eliminate unwanted behaviors.

Cognitive therapy. Psychotherapy based on the perspective that thoughts intervene between events and emotions, and thus the treatment of emotional disorders requires changing maladaptive patterns of thinking.

Ⓞ You can learn more about cognitive and behavioral therapies by visiting the Chapter 15 Web links on the *Brain and Behavior* Web site (**www.worth publishers.com/kolb**).

Psychotherapy. Talking therapy derived from Freudian psychoanalysis and other psychological interventions.

neurocognitive programs that are able to improve functional outcomes following traumatic brain injury and stroke (Prigatano, 1986; Sohlberg & Mateer, 1989).

In addition to disturbances in cognitive activities such as language and memory, people's emotions may be disturbed. In the 1920s, Sigmund Freud developed the idea that talking about such emotional problems enables people to have insights into their causes that can serve as treatments, too. These "talking cures," as well as other forms of psychological intervention, may be broadly categorized as **psychotherapies.**

Since Freud's time, many ideas have been put forth about the best type of behavioral therapy for emotional disorders. The key point here is that, for many disorders, whether neurological or psychiatric, medical treatments may be ineffective unless patients also receive psychotherapy. Indeed, in many cases, the only effective treatment lies in treating the unwanted behaviors directly.

Consider a 25-year-old woman pursuing a promising career as a musician who suffered a traumatic brain injury in an automobile accident. After the accident, she found that she was unable to read music. Not surprisingly, she soon became depressed. Part of her therapy required that she confront her disabling cognitive loss by talking about it rather than by simply stewing about it. Only when she pursued psychotherapy did she begin to recover from her intense depression.

For many people with cognitive impairments resulting from brain disease or trauma, the most effective treatment for their depression or anxiety is to help them adjust by encouraging them to talk about their difficulties. In fact, group therapy, which provides such encouragement, is standard treatment in brain-injury rehabilitation units. In this regard, Fred Linge, whose case history begins Chapter 1 of this book, has played a major role in establishing support groups for people with head trauma. These groups serve as a form of group therapy.

You may be thinking that, although behavioral therapies may be of some help in treating brain dysfunction, the real solution must lie in altering the brain and its activities. This notion may be valid, but remember a key fact: because every aspect of behavior is the product of brain activity, it can be argued that behavioral therapies *do* act by changing brain function. That is, not only does altering the brain change our behavior, but altering our behavior also changes the brain.

If people can change the way that they think and feel about themselves or some aspect of their lives, this change has taken place because "talking about their problems" has altered the way in which their brains function. In a sense, then, behavioral therapies can be viewed as "biological interventions." These interventions may sometimes be helped along by drug treatments that make the brain more receptive to change through behavioral therapies. In this way, drug treatments and behavioral therapies may have synergistic effects, each helping the other to be more effective.

In Review

Epidemiological studies have been used to identify and classify behavioral disorders, but little is known about the relation between these disorders and specific biological pathologies. Rather, the classification schemes such as the DSM-IV are essentially checklists of likely symptoms. Therapies for brain and behavioral disorders range from the very invasive (neurosurgery), moderately invasive ((pharmacological or electrophysiological brain stimulation), to indirect, noninvasive cognitive rehabilitation and other behavioral therapies. Today, none of these therapies are completely effective, but, as more is learned about the details of brain–behavior relations, we can look forward to improved recovery from a wide range of behavioral dysfunctions that affect a large percentage of the population.

UNDERSTANDNG AND TREATING NEUROLOGICAL DISORDERS

We now review in more detail several common neurological disorders: brain trauma, stroke, epilepsy, multiple sclerosis, and neurodegenerative disorders. In our lifetimes, each of us likely will have at least one close friend or relative develop one of these disorders, even if we ourselves escape them. Their causes are understood, at least in a general sense, although, for most, development of rehabilitative treatments remains, unfortunately, primitive.

Traumatic Brain Injury

As detailed in Chapter 1, traumatic brain injury is a common result of head impacts with other objects—as can occur in automobile and industrial accidents—and of sporting injuries. Cerebral trauma, or injury from a blow to the head, is the most common form of brain damage in people under age 40. In one telephone survey in Sweden, cerebral concussion, defined as an injury resulting from a violent blow or shock producing at least brief unconsciousness, was reported by 5 percent of those interviewed. In addition, another estimated 5 percent of the general population are likely to have suffered concussion without obvious unconsciousness, although they would have experienced some confusion about the events before and after the blow to the head.

The two most important factors in the incidence of head trauma are age and sex. Children and elderly people are more likely to suffer head injuries from falls than are others, and males between 15 and 30 are very likely to incur brain injuries, especially from automobile and motorcycle accidents (**Figure 15-5**). A child's chance of suffering significant traumatic brain injury before he or she is old enough to drive is 1 in 30.

SYMPTOMS AND OUTCOME OF BRAIN TRAUMA

Traumatic brain injury can affect brain function by causing direct damage to the brain. Trauma can disrupt the brain's blood supply; induce bleeding, leading to increased intracranial pressure; cause swelling, leading to increased intracranial pressure; expose the brain to infection; and scar brain tissue (the scarred tissue becomes a focus for later epileptic seizures).

Traumatic brain injuries are commonly accompanied by a loss of consciousness that may be brief (minutes) or prolonged (coma). The duration of unconsciousness can serve as a measure of the severity of damage, because it correlates directly with mortality, intellectual impairment, and deficits in social skills. The longer the coma lasts, the greater the possibility of serious impairment and death.

Two kinds of behavioral effects result from traumatic brain injuries: (1) impairment of the specific functions mediated by the cortex at the coup (the site of impact) or countercoup (opposite side) lesion and (2) more-generalized impairments from widespread trauma throughout the brain. Discrete impairment is most commonly associated with damage to the frontal and temporal lobes, the brain areas most susceptible to traumatic brain injuries.

More-generalized impairment results from minute lesions and lacerations scattered throughout the brain. Tears due to movement of the hemispheres in relation to each other are characterized by a loss of complex cognitive functions, including reductions in mental speed, concentration, and overall cognitive efficiency. Patients generally complain of poor concentration or lack of ability.

They fail to do things as well as they could before the injury, even though their intelligence rating may still be well above average. In fact, in our experience, bright people seem to be the most affected by traumatic brain injuries, in large part because they

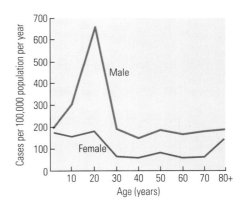

Figure 15-5

Incidence Rates of Head Trauma
These statistics were collected from 1965 through 1974 in Olmsted County, Minnesota. Nationwide, the proportions remain remarkably consistent a generation later. Adapted from Annegers et al., 1980.

are acutely aware of any loss of cognitive skill that prevents them from returning to their former competence level.

Traumatic brain injuries that damage the frontal and temporal lobes also tend to have significant effects on personality and social behavior. According to Muriel Lezak (2003), few victims of traffic accidents who have sustained severe head injuries ever resume their studies or return to gainful employment. If they do reenter the work force, they do so at a lower level than before their accidents.

One frustrating problem with traumatic brain injuries is misdiagnosis: their chronic effects often are not accompanied by any obvious neurological signs or abnormalities in CT or MRI scans, and the patients may therefore be referred for psychiatric or neuropsychological evaluation. A new imaging technique, **magnetic resonance spectroscopy** (MRS) is promising for accurate diagnosis of traumatic brain injuries. Magnetic resonance spectroscopy, a modification of MRI, can identify changes in specific markers of neuronal function.

One such marker is N-acetylaspartate (NAA), the second most abundant amino acid in the human brain (Tsai & Coyle, 1995). The level of NAA expression assesses the integrity of neurons, and deviations from normal levels (up or down) can be taken as a marker of abnormal brain function. People with traumatic brain injuries show a chronic decrease in NAA, which correlates with the severity of the injury (Brooks, Friedman, & Gasparovic, 2001). Although not widely used clinically yet, MRS promises to be a useful tool not only in identifying brain abnormalities but also in monitoring the cellular response to therapeutic interventions.

RECOVERY FROM TRAUMATIC BRAIN INJURY

Although it is often stated that recovery from head trauma may continue for 2 to 3 years, there is little doubt that the bulk of the cognitive recovery occurs in the first 6 to 9 months. Recovery of memory functions appears to be somewhat slower than recovery of general intelligence, and the final level of memory performance is lower than for other cognitive functions. Harvey Levin and his colleagues (1982) suggested that people with brainstem damage, as inferred from oculomotor disturbance, have a poorer cognitive outcome, and this poorer outcome is probably true of people with initial dysphasias or hemipareses as well.

Although the prognosis for significant recovery of cognitive functions is good, there is less optimism about the recovery of social skills or normal personality, areas that often show significant change. Findings from numerous studies support the conclusions that the quality of life—in regard to social interactions, perceived stress levels, and enjoyment of leisure activities—is significantly reduced after traumatic brain injury and that this reduction is chronic. There have been few attempts to develop tools to measure changes in psychosocial adjustment in brain-injured people; so we must rely largely on subjective descriptions and self-reports, which provide little information about the specific causes of these problems.

Stroke

In Chapter 2, we described the symptoms and aftereffects of *stroke,* an interruption of blood flow either from the blockage of a vessel or from the bleeding of a vessel. Although we may be able to point to a specific immediate cause of a stroke, this initial event merely sets off a sequence of damaging events that progresses even if the blood flow is restored. Stroke results in a lack of blood, called **ischemia,** followed by a cascade of cellular events that wreak the real damage. Changes at the cellular level can seriously compromise not only the injured part of the brain but other brain regions as well.

EFFECTS OF STROKE

Consider what happens after a stroke that interrupts the blood supply to one of the cerebral arteries. In the first seconds to minutes after ischemia, as illustrated in **Figure 15-6**, changes begin in the ionic balance of the affected regions, including changes in pH and in the properties of the cell membrane. These ionic changes result in a variety of pathological events, such as the release of massive amounts of glutamate and the prolonged opening of calcium channels.

The open calcium channels in turn allow toxic levels of calcium to enter the cell, not only producing direct toxic effects but also instigating various second-messenger pathways that can prove to be harmful to the neurons. In the ensuing minutes to hours, mRNA is stimulated, altering the production of proteins in the neurons and possibly proving to be toxic to the cells.

Next, brain tissues become inflamed and swollen, threatening the integrity of cells that may be far removed from the stroke site. Finally, a form of neural shock, referred to as **diaschisis,** occurs. Thus, not only is localized neural tissue and its function lost but areas related to the damaged region also suffer a sudden withdrawal of excitation or inhibition. Such sudden changes in input can lead to a temporary loss of neural function, both in areas adjacent to an injury and in regions that may be quite distant in the nervous system.

A stroke may also be followed by changes in the metabolism of the injured hemisphere, its glucose utilization, or both, which may persist for days. Like diaschisis, these metabolic changes can have severe effects on the functioning of otherwise normal tissue. For example, after a cortical stroke, metabolic rate has been shown to decrease about 25 percent throughout the rest of the hemisphere.

TREATMENTS FOR STROKE

The ideal treatment is to restore blood flow in blocked vessels before the cascade of nasty events begins. One such clot-busting drug, described in Chapter 2, is tissue plasminogen activator (t-PA). The difficulty with t-PA is that it must be administered within 3 hours to be effective. Only a small percentage of stroke patients currently arrive at the hospital soon enough, in large part because stroke is often not considered to be an emergency.

Other drugs called **neuroprotectants** can be used to try to block the cascade of postinjury events, but to date these drugs have not proved to be as helpful as was hoped. When the course of the stroke has led to dead brain tissue, the only treatments that can be beneficial are those that facilitate plastic changes in the brain. Examples are speech therapy or physical therapy. Although it would seem logical that therapies would be beneficial, there is surprisingly little evidence regarding which poststroke treatments are actually helpful or what timing or duration is most beneficial.

Epilepsy

In epilepsy, a person suffers recurrent seizures that register on an EEG and are associated with disturbances of consciousness (Chapter 4). The character of epileptic episodes can vary greatly, and seizures are common; 1 person in 20 will experience at least one seizure in his or her lifetime. The prevalence of multiple seizures is much lower, however: about 1 in 200.

Epileptic seizures are classified as **symptomatic** if they can be identified with a specific cause, such as infection, trauma, tumor, vascular malformation, toxic chemicals, very high fever, or other neurological disorders. Seizures are **idiopathic** if they appear spontaneously and in the absence of other diseases of the central nervous system.

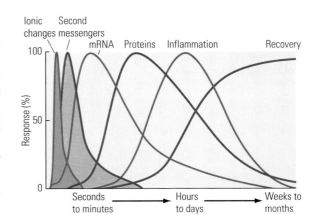

Figure 15-6

Results of Ischemia A cascade of events takes place after blood flow is blocked as a result of stroke. Within seconds, ionic changes at the cellular level spur changes in second-messenger molecules and RNA production. Changes in protein production and inflammation follow and resolve slowly, in hours to days. Recovery begins within hours to days and continues from weeks to months or years.

Diaschisis. Neural shock that follows brain damage in which areas connected to the site of damage show a temporary arrest of function.

Neuroprotectant. Drug used to try to block the cascade of poststroke neural events.

Symptomatic seizure. Identified with a specific cause, such as infection, trauma, tumor, vascular malformation, toxic chemicals, very high fever, or other neurological disorders.

Idiopathic seizure. Appears spontaneously and in the absence of other diseases of the central nervous system.

⊙ You can read the latest news about epilepsy on the *Brain and Behavior* Web site (**www.worthpublishers.com/kolb**). Visit the Web links for Chapter 15.

Table 15-7 **Factors That May Precipitate Seizures in Susceptible Persons**

Hyperventilation	Trauma	Emotional stress
Sleep	Hormonal changes	Drugs
Sleep deprivation	Menses	Phenothiazines
Sensory stimuli	Puberty	Analeptics
Flashing lights	Adrenal steroids	Tricyclic antidepressants
Reading, speaking, coughing	Adrenocorticotrophic hormone (ACTH)	Alcohol
Laughing		Excessive anticonvulsants
Sounds: music, bells	Fever	

Source: Adapted from *Behavioral Neurobiology* (p. 5), by J. H. Pincus and G. J. Tucker, 1974, New York: Oxford University Press.

Table 15-7 summarizes the great variety of circumstances that appear to precipitate seizures. The range of circumstances is striking, but seizures do have a consistent feature: the brain is most epileptogenic when it is inactive and the patient is sitting still.

Although epilepsy has long been known to run in families, its incidence is lower than a one-gene model would predict. More likely, certain genotypes carry a predisposition to seizure, given certain environmental circumstances. The most remarkable clinical feature of epileptic disorders is the widely varying intervals between attacks—from minutes to hours to weeks or even years. In fact, it is almost impossible to describe a basic set of symptoms to be expected in all, or even most, people with epilepsy. Nevertheless, three particular symptoms *are* found within the variety of epileptic episodes:

1. An *aura,* or warning, of impending seizure may take the form of a sensation—an odor or a noise—or it may simply be a "feeling" that the seizure is going to occur.
2. *Loss of consciousness* ranges from complete collapse in some people to simply staring off into space in others. The period of lost consciousness is often accompanied by amnesia, including the victim forgetting the seizure itself.
3. Seizures commonly have a *motor component,* but, as noted, the movement characteristics vary considerably. Some people shake; others exhibit automatic movements, such as rubbing the hands or chewing.

In Chapter 4, we described a diagnosis of epilepsy, confirmed by EEG. Some seizures, however, are difficult to document except under special circumstances (e.g., an EEG recorded during sleep). Moreover, not all persons with an EEG suggestive of epilepsy actually have seizures. Some estimates suggest that as many as 4 people in 20 simply have abnormal EEG patterns, many more than the 1 in 200 thought to suffer from epilepsy (see Table 15-4). Among the many types of epileptic seizures, we compare only two here: focal and generalized seizures.

FOCAL SEIZURES

Focal seizures begin in one place and then spread out. John Hughlings-Jackson hypothesized in 1870 that focal seizures probably originate from the point (focus) in the neocortex representing the region of the body where the movement is first seen. He was later proved correct. In *Jacksonian focal seizures,* for example, the attack begins with jerking movements in one part of the body—a finger, a toe, or the mouth—and then spreads to adjacent parts. If the attack begins with a finger, the jerks might spread to other fingers, then the hand, the arm, and so on, producing so-called "Jacksonian marches."

Focal seizure. Category of seizure that begins locally (at a focus) and then spreads out to adjacent areas.

Complex partial seizures, another focal type, originate most commonly in the temporal lobe and somewhat less frequently in the frontal lobe. Complex partial seizures are characterized by three common manifestations:

1. subjective experiences that presage the attack—for example, forced, repetitive thoughts, alterations in mood, feelings of deja vu, or hallucinations;
2. **automatisms**—repetitive stereotyped movements such as lip smacking or chewing or activities such as undoing buttons; and
3. postural changes, such as when the person assumes a **catatonic,** or frozen, **posture.**

GENERALIZED SEIZURES

Generalized seizures lack focal onset and often occur on both sides of the body. The **grand mal** ("big bad") attack is characterized by loss of consciousness and stereotyped motor activity. Patients typically go through three stages: (1) a tonic stage, in which the body stiffens and breathing stops; (2) a clonic stage, in which there is rhythmic shaking; and (3) a postseizure **postictal depression** during which the patient is confused. About 50 percent of grand mal seizures are preceded by an aura.

The **petit mal** ("little bad") attack is a loss of awareness with no motor activity except for blinking, turning the head, or rolling the eyes. Petit mal attacks are of brief duration, seldom exceeding about 10 s. The typical EEG recording of a petit mal seizure has a 3/s spike-and-wave pattern.

TREATMENT OF EPILEPSY

The treatment of choice for epilepsy is an anticonvulsant drug such as diphenylhydantoin (DPH, Dilantin), phenobarbital, or one of several others (Rogawski & Loscher, 2004). These drugs are anesthetic agents when given in low doses, and patients are advised not to drink alcohol. Although the mechanism by which these drugs act is uncertain, they presumably inhibit the discharge of abnormal neurons by stabilizing the neuronal membrane, especially in inhibitory neurons.

If medication fails to alleviate the seizure problem satisfactorily, surgery can be performed to remove the focus of abnormal functioning in patients with focal seizures. The abnormal tissue is localized by the surgeon both by EEG and cortical stimulation (Chapter 9). It is then removed with the goal of eliminating the cause of the seizures. Many patients show complete recovery and are seizure free, although some must remain on anticonvulsants after the surgery to ensure that the seizures do not return.

Multiple Sclerosis

Recall from Chapter 3 that, in *multiple sclerosis* (MS), myelin is damaged and the functions of the neurons whose axons it encases are disrupted. Multiple sclerosis is characterized by the loss of myelin, largely in motor tracts but also in sensory nerves. The myelin sheath and, in some cases, the axons are destroyed. Brain imaging with MRI, as shown in **Figure 15-7**, allows areas of sclerosis (Greek for "hardness") to be identified in the brain and spinal cord.

Remissions and relapses are a striking feature of MS: in many cases, early symptoms are initially followed by improvement. The course varies, running from a few years to as long as 50 years. Paraplegia, however, the classic feature of MS, may eventually confine the affected person to bed.

Automatism. Unconscious, repetitive, stereotyped movement characteristic of seizure.

Catatonic posture. Rigid or frozen pose resulting from a psychomotor disturbance.

Grand mal seizure. Characterized by loss of consciousness and stereotyped motor activity.

Postictal depression. Postseizure state of confusion and reduced affect.

Petit mal seizure Of brief duration, a seizure characterized by loss of awareness with no motor activity except for blinking, turning the head, or rolling the eyes.

Figure 15-7

Diagnosing MS Imaged by MRI, discrete multiple sclerosis lesions appear around the lateral ventricles and in the white matter of the brain. Adapted from Ciccarelli et al., 2000.

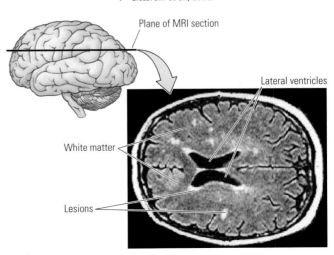

Plane of MRI section

Lateral ventricles

White matter

Lesions

Autoimmune disease. Illness resulting from the immune system's loss of the ability to discrimininate between foreign pathogens in the body and the body itself.

Dementia. Acquired and persistent syndrome of intellectual impairment characterized by memory and other cognitive deficits and impairment in social and occupational functioning.

⊙ Visit the Chapter 15 Web links on the *Brain and Behavior* Web site (**www.worthpublishers.com/kolb**) for additional information about autoimmune diseases like multiple sclerosis and myasthenia gravis.

Worldwide, about 1 million people are afflicted with MS; women outnumber men about two to one. Multiple sclerosis is most prevalent in northern Europe, somewhat less prevalent in North America, and rare in Japan and in more southerly or tropical countries. The overall incidence of of MS is 50 per 100,000 people, making it one of the most common structural diseases of the nervous system.

The cause of MS is still not known. Proposed causes include bacterial infection, a virus, environmental factors including pesticides, and an immune response of the central nervous system. Often a number of cases will be seen in a single family, but there is no clear evidence that MS is inherited or that it is transmitted from one person to another.

ROLE OF THE IMMUNE SYSTEM IN MULTIPLE SCLEROSIS

The ability to discriminate between a foreign pathogen in the body and the body itself is a central feature of the immune system. In **autoimmune diseases** such as myasthenia gravis, the immune system makes antibodies to a person's own body (Chapter 4). Recent research has focused on the possible relation of the immune system to MS.

As the genomes of various organisms have been sequenced in recent years, it has become apparent that all biological organisms have many genes in common, and thus the proteins found in different organisms are surprisingly similar. And here is the problem for the human immune system: a foreign microbe may have proteins that are very similar to the body's own proteins. If the microbe and human have a common gene sequence, the immune system can mistakenly attack itself, a process known as *horror autotoxicus.* Many microbial protein sequences are homologous with structures found in myelin, which leads to an attack against the microbe and a person's own myelin.

The work showing the important role of the immune system in MS has led to intense research to develop new treatments (Steinman et al., 2002). One strategy is to build up tolerance in the immune system by the injection of DNA encoding myelin antigens as well as DNA encoding specific molecules that are in the cascade of steps that leads to the death of myelin cells.

Neurodegenerative Disorders

Demographics such as those now developing in North America and Europe have never been experienced by human societies. Since 1900, the percentage of older people has been steadily increasing. In 1900, about 4 percent of the population had attained 65 years of age. By 2030, about 20 percent of the population will be older than 65—about 50 million in the United States alone. Dementias affect from 1 to 6 percent of the population older than age 65 and from 10 to 20 percent older than age 80. It has been estimated that, for every person diagnosed with dementia, several others suffer undiagnosed cognitive impairments that affect their quality of life (Larrabee & Crook, 1994).

Projections over the next 35 years estimate that between 10 and 20 million elderly people in the United States will have mild to severe cognitive impairments. When this projection is extended across the rest of the developed world, the social and economic costs are truly staggering. Not every person who grows old also becomes depressed, forgetful, or demented. Many people live to very old age and enjoy active, healthy, productive lives. The question for most of us is how to ensure that we are in this latter group; at present, however, there are depressingly few answers.

Table 15-8	Degenerative and Nondegenerative Dementias	
Degenerative	**Nondegenerative**
Alzheimer's disease	Vascular dementias (e.g., multi-infarct dementia)
Extrapyramidal syndromes (e.g., progressive supernuclear palsy)	Infectious dementia (e.g., AIDS dementia)
Wilson's disease	Neurosyphillis
Huntington's disease	Posttraumatic dementia
Parkinson's disease	Demyelinating dementia (e.g., multiple sclerosis)
Frontal temporal dementia	
Corticobasal degeneration	Toxic or metabolic disorders (e.g., vitamin B_{12} and niacin deficiencies)
Leukodystrophies (e.g., adrenoleukodystrophy)	Chronic alcohol or drug abuse (e.g., Korsakoff's syndrome)
Prion-related dementias (e.g., Creutzfeld-Jakob disease)	

Source: Adapted from "Diagnostic Classifications: Relationship to the Neurobiology of Dementia," by D. I. Kaufer and S. T. DeKosky, 1999, in *The Neurobiology of Mental Illness* (p. 642), edited by D. S. Charney, E. J. Nestler, and B. S. Bunney, New York: Oxford University Press.

TYPES OF DEMENTIA

Dementia refers to an acquired and persistent syndrome of intellectual impairment. The DSM-IV-TR defines the two essential diagnostic features of dementia as (1) memory and other cognitive deficits and (2) impairment in social and occupational functioning. Daniel Kaufer and Steven DeKosky (1999) divide dementias into two broad categories: degenerative and nondegenerative (**Table 15-8**).

Nondegenerative dementias are a heterogeneous group of disorders with diverse etiologies, including diseases of the vascular or endocrine systems, inflammation, nutritional deficiency, and toxic conditions, as summarized in the right-hand column of Table 15-8. In contrast, many *degenerative dementias* listed in the left-hand column are presumed to have a degree of genetic transmission. Here we review two in detail, Parkinson's disease and Alzeimer's disease. Both pathological processes are primarily intrinsic to the nervous system and tend to affect certain neural systems selectively.

PARKINSON'S DISEASE

Parkinson's disease is fairly common; estimates of its incidence vary from 0.1 percent to 1.0 percent of the population, and the incidence rises sharply in old age. In view of the increasingly aging population in western Europe and North America, the incidence of Parkinson's disease is certain to rise in the coming decades. As detailed in Chapter 5, Parkinsonism is also of interest for a number of other reasons:

■   Parkinson's disease seems related to the degeneration of the substantia nigra and to the loss of the neurotransmitter dopamine, which is produced there and released in the striatum. The disease, therefore, is the source of an important insight into the role of this brainstem nucleus and its dopamine in the control of movement.

■   Although Parkinson's disease is described as a disease entity, symptoms vary enormously among people, thus illustrating the complexity in understanding a behavioral disorder. Parkinson's disease has a well-defined set of cells that degenerate, yet the symptoms are not the same in every sufferer.

■ Many symptoms of Parkinson's disease strikingly resemble changes in motor activity that take place as a consequence of aging. Thus the disease is a source of indirect insight into the more general problems of neural changes in aging.

The symptoms of Parkinson's disease begin insidiously, often with a tremor in one hand and with slight stiffness in the distal parts of the limbs. Movements may then become slower, the face becoming masklike with loss of eye blinking and poverty of emotional expression. Thereafter the body may become stooped, and the gait becomes a shuffle with the arms hanging motionless at the sides. Speech may become slow and monotonous, and difficulty in swallowing may cause drooling.

Although the disease is progressive, the rate at which the symptoms worsen is variable, and only rarely is progression so rapid that a person becomes disabled within 5 years; usually from 10 to 20 years elapse before symptoms cause incapacity. A most curious aspect of Parkinson's disease is its on-again–off-again quality: symptoms may appear suddenly and disappear just as suddenly.

Partial remission may also occur in response to interesting or stimulating situations. Oliver Sacks has recounted an incident in which a stationary Parkinson patient leaped from his wheelchair at the seaside and rushed into the breakers to save a drowning man, only to fall back into his chair immediately afterward and become inactive again. Although remission of some symptoms in activating situations is common, remission is not usually as dramatic as this case.

The four major symptoms of Parkinson's disease are tremor, rigidity, loss of spontaneous movement *(akinesia)*, and disturbances of posture. Each symptom may be manifest in different body parts in different combinations. Because some of the symptoms entail the appearance of abnormal behaviors (positive symptoms) and others the loss of normal behaviors (negative symptoms), we consider the symptoms in these two major categories.

To review, positive symptoms are behaviors not seen in normal people or seen only so rarely—and then in such special circumstances—that they can be considered abnormal. Negative symptoms are marked not by any particular behavior but rather by the absence of a behavior or by the inability to engage in an activity.

Positive Symptoms   Because positive symptoms are common in Parkinson's disease, they are thought to be held in check, or inhibited, in normal people but released from inhibition in the process of the disease. The most common positive symptoms are:

■ *Tremor at rest.* Tremor consists of alternating movements of the limbs when they are at rest; these movements stop during voluntary movements or during sleep. The tremors of the hands often have a "pill rolling" quality, as if a pill were being rolled between the thumb and forefinger.

■ *Muscular rigidity.* Muscular rigidity consists of increased muscle tone simultaneously in both extensor and flexor muscles. It is particularly evident when the limbs are moved passively at a joint; movement is resisted, but, with sufficient force, the muscles yield for a short distance and then resist movement again. Thus, complete passive flexion or extension of a joint occurs in a series of steps, giving rise to the term *cogwheel rigidity.* The rigidity may be severe enough to make all movements difficult, like moving in slow motion but being unable to speed up the process.

■ *Involuntary movements.* These small movements or changes in posture, sometimes referred to as **akathesia** or "cruel restlessness," may be concurrent with general inactivity to relieve tremor and sometimes to relieve stiffness but often for no apparent reason. Other involuntary movements are distortions of posture, such as occur during *oculogyric crisis* (involuntary turns of the head and eyes to one side), which last for periods of minutes to hours.

Akathesia. Small, involuntary movements or changes in posture; motor restlessness.

Negative Symptoms   After detailed analysis of negative symptoms, Jean Prudin Martin (1967) divided patients severely affected with Parkinson's disease into five groups:

Festination. Tendency to engage in a behavior, such as walking, at faster and faster speeds.

1. *Disorders of posture.* These disorders include those of fixation and of equilibrium. A *disorder of fixation* presents as an inability, or difficulty, in maintaining a part of the body (head, limbs, and so forth) in its normal position in relation to other parts. A person's head may droop forward or a standing person may gradually bend forward until he or she ends up on the knees. *Disorders of equilibrium* create difficulties in standing or even sitting unsupported. In less severe cases, people may have difficulty standing on one leg, or, if pushed lightly on the shoulders, they may fall passively without taking corrective steps or attempting to catch themselves.

2. *Disorders of righting.* In these disorders, a person has difficulty in achieving a standing position from a supine position. Many advanced patients have difficulty even in rolling over.

3. *Disorders of locomotion.* Normal locomotion requires support of the body against gravity, stepping, balancing while the weight of the body is transferred from one limb to another, and pushing forward. Parkinson patients have difficulty initiating stepping, and, when they do walk, they shuffle with short footsteps on a fairly wide base of support because they have trouble maintaining equilibrium when shifting weight from one limb to the other. Often, Parkinson patients who have begun to walk demonstrate **festination:** they take faster and faster steps and end up running forward.

4. *Disturbances of speech.* One of the symptoms most noticeable to relatives is the almost complete absence of prosody in the speaker's voice.

5. *Akinesia.* A poverty or slowness of movement may also manifest itself in a blankness of facial expression or a lack of blinking, swinging of the arms when walking, spontaneous speech, or normal movements of fidgeting. It is also manifested in difficulty in making repetitive movements, such as tapping, even in the absence of rigidity. People who sit motionless for hours show akinesia in its most striking manifestation.

Cognitive Symptoms   Although Parkinson's disease is usually thought of as a motor disorder, changes in cognition occur as well. Psychological symptoms in Parkinson patients are as variable as the motor symptoms. Nonetheless, a significant percentage of patients show cognitive symptoms that mirror their motor symptoms.

Oliver Sacks, for example, reports the negative effects of Parkinsonism on cognitive function: an impoverishment of feeling, libido, motive, and attention; people may sit for hours, apparently lacking the will to begin or continue any activity. In our experience, thinking seems generally to be slowed and is easily confused with dementia because patients do not appear to be processing the content of conversations. In fact, they are simply processing very slowly.

The cognitive slowing in Parkinson patients has some parallels to changes in Alzheimer's disease. Findings from postmortem studies show clear Alzheimer-like brain abnormalities in most Parkinson patients, even if they did not have obvious signs of dementia. We return to these parallels later.

Causes of Parkinsonism   As stated in Chapter 5, the ultimate cause of Parkinson's disease is the loss of cells in the substantia nigra. This loss may be due to disease, such as encephalitis or syphillis, to drugs such as MPTP (see "The Case of the Frozen Addict" on page 171), or to unknown causes that are referred to as idiopathic. Idiopathic causes may be familial or may be part of the aging process.

Idiopathic causes may also include environmental pollutants, insecticides, and herbicides. Demographic studies of patient admission in the cities of Vancouver and

You can learn more about the brain structures involved in Parkinson's disease in the model on control of movement on your *Foundations of Behavioral Neuroscience* CD. You can also view a video of a man suffering from this disorder in the section on the basal ganglia. (See the Preface for more information about this CD.)

Helsinki show an increase in the incidence of patients getting the disease at ages younger than 40. This finding has prompted the suggestion that water and air might contain environmental toxins that work in a fashion similar to MPTP.

Treatment of Parkinson's Disease No known cure for Parkinson's disease exists, and none will be in sight until the factors that produce the progressive deterioration of the substantia nigra are known. Thus, treatment is symptomatic and directed toward support and comfort. The major symptoms of Parkinsonism are influenced by psychological factors, a person's outcome being affected by how well he or she copes with the disability.

As a result, patients should seek behaviorally oriented treatment early, including counseling on the meaning of symptoms, the nature of the disease, and the potential for most to lead long and productive lives. Physical therapy should consist of simple measures such as heat and massage to alleviate painful muscle cramps and training and exercise to cope with the debilitating changes in movement. Pharmacological treatment has two main objectives:

1. to increase the activity in whatever dopamine synapses remain and
2. to suppress the activity in structures that show heightened activity in the absence of adequate dopamine action.

L-Dopa, which is converted into dopamine in the brain, enhances effective dopamine transmission, as do drugs such as amantadine, amphetamine, monoamine oxidase inhibitors, and tricyclic antidpressants. Naturally occurring anticholinergic drugs, such as atropine and scopolamine, and synthetic anticholinergics, such as benztropine (Cogentin), and trihexyphenidyl (Artane), are used to block the cholinergic systems of the brain that seem to show heightened activity in the absence of adequate dopamine activity.

A drawback of drug therapies is that, as the disease progresses, they become less effective and produce an increased incidence of side effects. Some drug treatments in which dopamine receptors are directly stimulated have been reported to result in increased sexuality and an increased incidence of compulsive gambling.

A number of treatments of Parkinson's disease focus on treating its positive symptoms. Two surgical treatments described earlier in the chapter are based on the idea that an increase in the activity of globus pallidus neurons inhibits motor function. Lesioning the internal part of the globus pallidis (GP_i) has been found to reduce rigidity and tremor. Hyperactivity of GP_i neurons can also be reduced by electrically stimulating the neurons, a neurosurgical treatment called deep brain stimulation (DBS), permanently implanting a stimulating electrode in the GP_i or an adjacent brain area, the subthalamic nucleus. Patients carry a small electrical stimulator that they can turn on to produce DBS and so reduce the symptoms of rigidity and tremor. These two treatments may be used sequentially: when DBS becomes less effective as the disease progresses, a GP_i lesion may be produced.

A promising treatment is to try to increase the number of dopamine-producing cells. The simplest way to do so is to transplant embryonic dopamine cells into the basal ganglia and, in the 1980s and 1990s, this treatment was used to varying degrees of success. A newer course of treatment proposes to increase the number of dopamine cells either by transplanting stem cells that could then be induced to take a dopaminergic phenotype or by stimulating the production of endogenous stem cells and their migration to the basal ganglia.

The advantage of stem cells is that they do not have to be derived from embryonic tissue but can come from a variety of sources including the person's own bone marrow. Another source of dopamine cells is retinal endothelial cells that can be harvested from neonatal tissue. The advantage of these cells is that a single retina can generate enough cells to treat hundreds of patients.

All these treatments are highly experimental. At present, neonatal retinal cells have probably been the most successful. Curiously, perhaps because this treatment is the least controversial, the media have basically ignored it and have focused on the more contentious issue of using embrological tissue. The retinas can be harvested from newborn infants who die and, as noted, a single retina can generate cells for thousands of patients, meaning that very few donors are necessary.

ANATOMICAL CORRELATES OF ALZHEIMER'S DISEASE

The most prevalent dementia is Alzheimer's disease, which accounts for about 65 percent of all dementias. At present the cause of Alzheimer's disease is unknown. Given the increasing population of elderly people and thus of Alzheimer's disease, research is being directed toward potential causes, including genetic predisposition, environmental toxins, high levels of trace elements such as aluminum in the blood, an autoimmune response, a slow-acting virus, and reduced blood flow to the cerebral hemispheres.

Until a decade ago, the only way to identify and to study Alzheimer's disease was to study postmortem pathology. This approach was less than ideal, however, because a determination of which brain changes came early in the disease and which followed as a result of the early changes was impossible. Nonetheless, it became clear that widespread changes take place in the neocortex and limbic cortex and associated changes take place in a number of neurotransmitter systems, none of which alone can be correlated simply with Alzheimer's clinical symptoms. Interestingly, most of the brainstem, cerebellum, and spinal cord are relatively spared its major ravages.

The principal neuroanatomical change in Alzheimer's disease is the emergence of neuritic (amyloid) plaques, chiefly in the cerebral cortex (see "Alzheimer's Disease" on page 498). Increased plaque concentration in the cortex has been correlated with the magnitude of cognitive deterioration. Neuritic plaques are generally considered nonspecific phenomena in that they can be found in non-Alzheimer patients and in dementias caused by other known events.

Another anatomical correlate of Alzheimer's disease is neurofibrillary tangles—paired helical filaments that are found in both the cerebral cortex and the hippocampus. The posterior half of the hippocampus is affected more severely than the anterior half. Light-microscopic examination has shown that the filaments have a double-helical configuration. They have been described mainly in human tissue and have also been observed in patients with Down's syndrome, Parkinson's disease, and other dementias.

Finally, neocortical changes that correlate with Alzheimer's disease are not uniform. Although the cortex shrinks, or atrophies, losing as much as one-third of its volume as the disease progresses, some areas are relatively spared. **Figure 15-8** shows lateral and medial views of the human brain; color shading indicates the areas of degeneration. The darker the shading, the more severe the degeneration.

As is clearly shown in Figure 15-8A, the primary sensory and motor areas of the cortex, especially the visual cortex and the sensory–motor cortex, are spared. The frontal lobes are less affected than the posterior cortex, but the areas of most extensive change are the posterior parietal areas, inferior temporal cortex, and limbic cortex. The limbic system undergoes the most severe degenerative changes in Alzheimer's disease, and, of the limbic structures, the entorhinal cortex is affected earliest and most severely (Figure 15-8B).

A number of investigators agree that the entorhinal cortex shows the clearest evidence of cell loss. This loss has important implications for understanding some of the

Figure 15-8

Cortical Degeneration in Alzheimer's Disease   Representative distribution and severity of degeneration in an average Alzheimer case shown in **(A)** lateral and **(B)** medial views. The darker the area, the more pronounced the degeneration. Areas in white are largely spared, with only basic changes discernible. Adapted from Brun, 1983.

(A)   Posterior parietal cortex

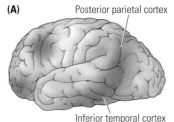

Inferior temporal cortex

(B)   Limbic cortex

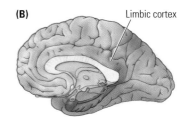

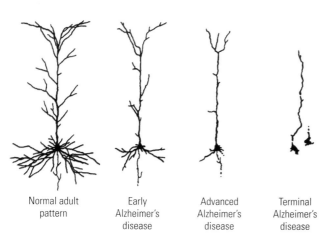

Normal adult
pattern

Early
Alzheimer's
disease

Advanced
Alzheimer's
disease

Terminal
Alzheimer's
disease

As their neurons degenerate, patients with Alzheimer's disease experience worsening symptoms, including memory loss and personality changes. Neurons drawn from Golgi-stained sections in "Age-Related Changes in the Human Forebrain," by A. Scheibel, *Neuroscience Research Program Bulletin*, 1982, 20, pp. 577–583.

disease symptoms. The entorhinal cortex is the major relay through which information from the neocortex gets to the hippocampus and related structures and is then sent back to the neocortex. Damage to the entorhinal cortex is associated with memory loss. Given that memory loss is an early and enduring symptom of Alzheimer's disease, it is most likely caused by the degenerative changes that take place in this area of the cortex.

Many studies describe loss of cells in the cortices of Alzheimer patients, but this finding is disputed. There seems to be a substantial reduction in large neurons, but these cells may shrink rather than disappear. The more widespread cause of cortical atrophy, however, appears to be a loss of dendritic arborization.

In addition to a loss of cells are changes in the neurotransmitters of the remaining cells. In the 1970s, researchers believed that a treatment for Alzheimer's disease could be found to parallel the L-dopa treatment of Parkinson's disease, and the prime candidate neurotransmitter was acetylcholine. Unfortunately, the disease has proved to be far more complex, because other transmitters clearly are changed as well. Noradrenaline, dopamine, and serotonin are reduced, as are the NMDA and AMPA receptors for glutamate.

Are Parkinson's and Alzheimer's Aspects of One Disease?

Striking similarities in the pathologies of Parkinson's and Alzheimer's diseases led Donald Calne to ask whether these diseases are syndromes resulting from various neurodegenerative processes in the brain (Calne & Mizuno, 2004). Their pathologies are far more similar than was previously recognized.

One apparent difference that we have seen already is that all cases of Parkinson's disease have in common a loss of cells in the substania nigra. The Parkinsonian brain suffers a larger loss, but the brains of Alzheimer patients also have nigral cell loss. There are other anatomical correlates between the diseases.

The best studied of these correlates is the **Lewy body,** a circular fibrous structure that forms within the cytoplasm of neurons and is thought to correspond to abnormal neurofilament metabolism (**Figure 15-9**). Until recently, the Lewy body was believed to be a hallmark of Parkinson's disease, and it was most often found in the brainstem in the region of the substantia nigra. It is now clear, however, that Lewy bodies are found in several neurodegenerative disorders, including Alzheimer's disease. There are even reports of people with Alzheimer's-like dementias who do not have plaques and tangles but have extensive Lewy bodies in the cortex.

Calne noted that, when investigators went to Guam at the end of the Second World War to investigate a report of widespread dementia described as similar to Alzheimer's disease, they did indeed report a high incidence of Alzheimer's disease. Many years later, Calne and his colleagues, experts in Parkinson's disease, examined the same general group of people and found that they had Parkinson's disease. Calne noted that, if you look for Alzheimer symptoms in these people, you find them and miss the Parkinson symptoms. And vice versa.

Indeed, as we age, all of us will show a loss of cells in the substantia nigra, but only after we have lost about 60 percent of them will we start to show Parkinson symptoms. From this perspective, we begin to understand Calne's powerful argument and its important implications for treating both syndromes.

Figure 15-9

Lewy Body Lewy bodies are characteristic of Parkinson's disease and are found in the brains of patients with other disorders as well. Courtesy of J. T. Stewart, MD, University of South Florida College of Medicine.

Midbrain Lewy body

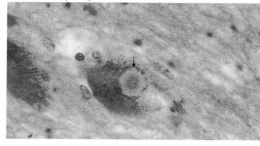

Lewy body. Circular fibrous structure, found in several neurodegenerative disorders, that forms within the cytoplasm of neurons and is thought to result from abnormal neurofilament metabolism.

In Review

We have considered five common neurological disorders: traumatic brain injury, stroke, epilepsy, multiple sclerosis, and two neurodegenerative diseases. Each of us in our lifetimes will likely know a person who has one of these disorders, and chances are that we will know of an example of each disorder. The cause of traumatic brain injuries is obvious—namely, a blow to the head—but the pathology is far more difficult to identify, even with fancy imaging techniques. The pathology of the other neurological disorders is equally elusive, the causes are poorly understood, and some disorders, such as Parkinson's and Alzheimer's, may actually be syndromes of a single disease. Effective treatments must wait until the causes are far better understood than they are today.

UNDERSTANDING AND TREATING PSYCHIATRIC DISORDERS

The DSM-IV-TR summarizes a wide range of psychiatric disorders. We focus on three general types that are the best studied and understood and are summarized in **Table 15-9**: psychosis, mood disorders, and anxiety disorders. Added together, the prevalences of these disorders total to between 40 and 50 percent of the U.S. population. This is true even when we account for those who aquire more than one disorder.

Table 15-9	The Spectrum of Psychiatric Illness	
Disorder	**Prevalence (%)**	**Common Symptoms**
Psychotic disorders		
Schizophrenia	1.3	Characterized by delusions, hallucinations, disorganized speech, inappropriate or blunted emotional responses, loss of motivation and cogntive effects
Mood disorders		
Major depression	5.3	Episodes during which the patient feels sad or empty nearly every day; loses interest or pleasure in hobbies and activities, experiences changes in appetite, weight, energy levels or sleeping patterns; harbors thoughts of death or suicide
Dysthymia	1.6	Similar to major depression but the symptoms are less severe and more chronic (years). Also includes low self-esteem, fatigue, and poor concentration
Bipolar	1.1	Episodes of abnormally elevated or irritable mood during which the person feels inflated self-esteem, needs less sleep, talks more than usual; or engages excessively in pleasurable but unwise activities. These manic periods alternate with depressive episodes.
Anxiety disorders		
Generalized anxiety	5	Unrealistic, excessive and long-lasting worry, motor tension, restlessness, irritability, difficulty sleeping
Panic disorder	3	Brief, recurrent, unexpected episodes of terror, sympathetic crises, shortness of breath
Post-traumatic stress	3	Recurrent episodes of fear triggered by reminders of a previous extremely stressful event
Social phobia	13	Aversion, fear, autonomic arousal in unfamiliar social settings
Specific phobias	11	Aversion, fear, autonomic arousal in specific situations (exposure to animals, blood, and so on)
Obsessive-compulsive	2	Recurrent obsessions and compulsions: obsessions are persistent, intrusive, inappropriate thoughts that cause anxiety; compulsions are repetitive acts that are performed to reduce anxiety

Source: Adapted from Gross and Hen, 2004; Hyman, 2003.

Type I schizophrenia. Characterized predominantly by positive symptoms (behavioral excesses, such as hallucinations and agitated movements); likely due to a dopaminergic dysfunction and associated with acute onset, good prognosis, and a favorable response to neuroleptics.

Type II schizophrenia. Characterized by negative symptoms (behavioral deficits) and associated with chronic affliction, poor prognosis, poor response to neuroleptics, cognitive impairments, enlarged ventricles, and cortical atrophy, particularly in the frontal cortex

Psychotic Disorders

Psychotic disorders are psychological disorders in which a person loses contact with reality, experiencing irrational ideas and distorted perceptions. Although there are many psychotic disorders (among which are schizophrenia, schizoaffective disorder, and schizophreniform disorder), schizophrenia is the most common and best understood. It has become clear in the past 25 years that the complexity of behavioral and neurobiological factors that characterize schizophrenia make it especially difficult to diagnose and classify. Understanding schizophrenia is an evolving process that is far from complete.

DIAGNOSING SCHIZOPHRENIA

The DSM-IV-TR lists six diagnostic symptoms of schizophrenia:

1. delusions, or beliefs that distort reality;
2. hallucinations, or distorted perceptions, such as hearing voices;
3. disorganized speech, such as incoherent statements or senselessly rhyming talk;
4. disorganized behavior or excessive agitation;
5. the opposite extreme, catatonic behavior; and
6. negative symptoms, such as blunted emotions or loss of interest and drive, all characterized by the absence of some normal response.

The DSM-IV-TR criteria for schizophrenia are subjective. They are more helpful in clinical diagnoses than in relating schizophrenia to measurable brain abnormalities.

CLASSIFYING SCHIZOPHRENIA

Timothy Crow addressed this problem by looking for a relation between brain abnormalities and specific schizophrenia symptoms. He proposed two distinct syndromes, which he called type I and type II (Crow, 1980, 1990).

■ **Type I schizophrenia** is characterized predominantly by positive symptoms, those that manifest behavioral excesses, such as hallucinations and agitated movements. Type 1 schizophrenia is likely due to a dopaminergic dysfunction. It is also associated with acute onset, good prognosis, and a favorable response to neuroleptics (antipsychotic drugs; see Chapter 7).

■ **Type II schizophrenia,** in contrast, is characterized by negative symptoms, those that entail behavioral deficits. Type II schizophrenia is associated with chronic affliction, poor prognosis, poor response to neuroleptics, cognitive impairments, enlarged ventricles, and cortical atrophy, particularly in the frontal cortex (see Figure 15-4).

Crow's analysis had a major effect on clinical thinking about schizophrenia. Between 20 percent and 30 percent of patients, however, show a pattern of mixed type I and type II symptoms. The types may actually represent points along a continuum of biological and behavioral manifestations of schizophrenia.

NEUROANATOMICAL CORRELATES OF SCHIZOPHRENIA

Another approach to investigating schizophrenia is to deemphasize typing and to focus instead on individual psychotic symptoms. Alan Breier (1999) stated that findings from a growing number of brain-imaging studies suggest a neuroanatomical basis for some diagnostic symptoms described by the DSM. For example, researchers found abnormalities in the auditory regions of the temporal lobe and in Broca's area among patients with auditory hallucinations (McGuire, Shah, & Murray, 1993).

Ⓞ Read the latest research into the causes of schizophrenia on the *Brain and Behavior* Web site (**www.worth publishers.com/kolb**). Go to the Web links for Chapter 15.

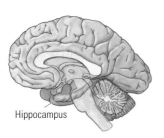

(A)

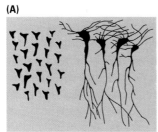

Organized (normal) pyramidal neurons

(B)

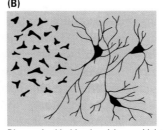

Disorganized (schizophrenic) pyramidal neurons

Hippocampus

Rather than the consistently parallel orientation of hippocampal neurons characteristic of normal brains **(A)**, hippocampal neurons in the schizophrenic brain have a haphazard organization **(B)**. Adapted from "A Neurohistologic Correlate of Schizophrenia," by J. A. Kovelman and A. B. Scheibel, 1984, *Biological Psychiatry, 19,* p. 1613.

Similarly, structural abnormalities in Wernicke's area are often found among patients with thought disorders (Shenton et al., 1992). The schizophrenic brain also generally has large ventricles and thinner cortex in the medial temporal regions, and the dendritic fields of cells in the dorsal prefrontal regions and hippocampus are abnormal (Cho Gilbert, & Lewis, 2004), as are those in the entorhinal cortex (Arnold, Rushinsky, & Han, 1997). These regions participate in various forms of memory. Deficits in verbal and spatial memory among people with schizophrenia will quite possibly turn out to be correlated with these medial temporal abnormalities.

Another correlation is frequently seen in schizophrenia between an abnormally low blood flow in the dorsolateral prefrontal cortex and deficits in executive functions, such as those measured by the Wisconsin Card Sorting Test (for a review, see Berman & Weinberger, 1999). Interestingly, when Daniel Weinberger and Barbara Lipska (1995) studied pairs of identical twins in which only one twin had been diagnosed as having schizophrenia, they found that the twin with schizophrenia always had a lower blood flow in the prefrontal cortex while taking this card-sorting test (see Figure 15-3).

NEUROCHEMICAL CORRELATES OF SCHIZOPHRENIA

Neuroscientists also consider the neurochemical correlates of brain–behavior relations in schizophrenia. As discussed in Chapter 7, dopamine abnormalities were the first to be linked to schizophrenia, and the fact that most neuroleptic drugs act on the dopamine synapse was taken as evidence that schizophrenia is a disease of ventral tegmental dopamine system. Similarly, drugs that enhance dopaminergic activity, such as amphetamine, can produce psychotic symptoms reminiscent of schizophrenia.

The dopamine theory of schizophrenia now appears to be too simple, however, because many other neurochemical abnormalities, summarized in **Table 15-10,** also have

Table 15-10	**Biochemical Changes Associated with Schizophrenia**
Decreased dopamine metabolites in cerebrospinal fluid	
Increased striatal D_2 receptors	
Decreased expression of D_3 and D_4 mRNA in specific cortical regions	
Decreased cortical glutamate	
Increased cortical glutamate receptors	
Decreased glutamate uptake sites in cingulate cortex	
Decreased mRNA for the synthesis of GABA in prefrontal cortex	
Increased $GABA_A$-binding sites in cingulate cortex	

Source: Adapted from "The Neurochemistry of Schizophrenia," by W. Byne, E. Kemegther, L. Jones, V. Harouthunian, and K. L. Davis, 1999, in *The Neurobiology of Mental Illness* (p. 242), edited by D. S. Charney, E. J. Nestler, and B. S. Bunney, New York: Oxford University Press.

Mania. Disordered mental state characterized by excessive euphoria.

Bipolar disorder. Mood disorder characterized by alternating periods of depression and mania.

been associated with schizophrenia. In particular are abnormalities in dopamine and dopamine receptors, glutamate and glutamate receptors, and GABA and GABA binding sites. Considerable variability exists among patients in the extent of each of these abnormalities, however. How these neurochemical variations might relate to the presence or absence of specific symptoms is not yet known.

To summarize, schizophrenia is a complex disorder associated with both positive and negative symptoms, abnormalities in brain structure and metabolism (especially in the prefrontal and temporal cortex), and neurochemical abnormalities in regard to dopamine, glutamate, and GABA. Given the complexity of all these behavioral and neurobiological factors, it is not surprising that schizophrenia is so difficult to characterize and to treat.

Mood Disorders

In the past 50 years, researchers have debated whether mood disorders are psychological or biological in origin. Now, in those with genetic predispositions to stress, environmental factors seem likely to act on the brain to produce biological changes related to people's moods and emotions. Although the precise nature of a genetic reactivity to stress is not fully understood, several genes have been implicated (Sanders, Detera-Wadleigh, & Gershon, 1999).

The DSM-IV-TR identifies a continuum of mood disorders, but the ones of principal interest here—depression and mania—represent the extremes of affect (see Table 15-9). The main symptoms of major depression are prolonged feelings of worthlessness and guilt, disruption of normal eating habits, sleep disturbances, a general slowing of behavior, and frequent thoughts of suicide (Chapter 7).

Mania, the opposite affective extreme from depression, is characterized by excessive euphoria. The affected person often formulates grandiose plans and behaves in an uncontrollably hyperactive way. Periods of mania often change, sometimes abruptly, into states of depression and back again to mania. This condition is called **bipolar disorder.** Little is known about the neurobiology of bipolar disorder.

Our emphasis here is on extending your knowledge about depression. Findings from clinical studies suggest that monoamine systems, particularly both the norepinephrine and the serotonin systems, have roles in depression. Many monoamine theories of depression have been proposed (review Chapter 7). To date, however, no unifying theory fully explains either the development of depression in otherwise normal people or how antidepressant medications treat it.

NEUROBIOLOGY OF DEPRESSION

Neuroscientists have known for more than 30 years that antidepressant drugs acutely increase the synaptic levels of norepinephrine and serotonin. This finding led to the idea that depression results from a decrease in the availability of one or both neurotransmitters. Lowering their levels in normal subjects does not produce depression, however. Recall, too, that antidepressant medications increase the level of norepinephrine and serotonin within days, but it takes weeks for drugs to start relieving depression.

Various explanations for these results have been suggested, none completely satisfactory. Ronald Duman (2004) reviewed evidence to suggest that antidepressants act, at least in part, on signaling pathways, such as on cAMP, in the postsynaptic cell. Neurotrophic factors appear to affect the action of antidepressants and, furthermore, neurotrophic factors may underlie the neurobiology of depression. Investigators know, for example, that brain-derived neurotrophic factor is down-regulated by stress and up-regulated by antidepressant medication (Chapter 13).

Given that BDNF acts to enhance the growth and survival of cortical neurons and synapses, BDNF dysfunction may adversely affect noreprinephrine and serotonin systems through the loss of either neurons or synapses. Antidepressant medication may increase the release of BDNF through its actions on cAMP signal transduction. The key point here is that the cause is most likely not just a simple decrease in transmitter levels. Rather, explaining both the biochemical abnormalities in depression and the actions of antidepressants is likely far more complex than it seemed a generation ago.

MOOD AND REACTIVITY TO STRESS

A significant psychological factor in understanding depression is reactivity to stress. When we are stressed, the hypothalamic-pituitary-adrenal system (**HPA axis**) is stimulated to produce stress hormones—steroids such as cortisol (hydrocortisone). Monoamines modulate the secretion of hormones by the HPA axis, as illustrated in **Figure 15-10**.

The best-established abnormality in the HPA-axis modulation is an oversecretion of cortisol from the adrenal gland. As explained in Chapter 7, normally, when you are stressed, the hypothalamus secretes corticotropin-releasing hormone, which stimulates the pituitary to produce adrenocorticotropic hormone (ACTH). The ACTH circulates through the blood and stimulates the adrenal medulla to produce cortisol.

The hypothalamic neurons that begin this cascade are regulated by norepinephrine neurons in the locus coeruleus. If the cortisol release is too large, the norepinephrine neurons fail to regulate the cortisol. High levels of cortisol are bad for neurons, and chronic increases lead to the death of neurons in the hippocampus.

Moreover, Charles Nemeroff (2004) showed that, during critical periods in early childhood, abuse or other severe environmental stress can permanently disrupt the reactivity of the HPA axis. Chronic stress can lead to the oversecretion of cortisol, an imbalance associated with depression in adulthood. Nemeroff found, for example, that

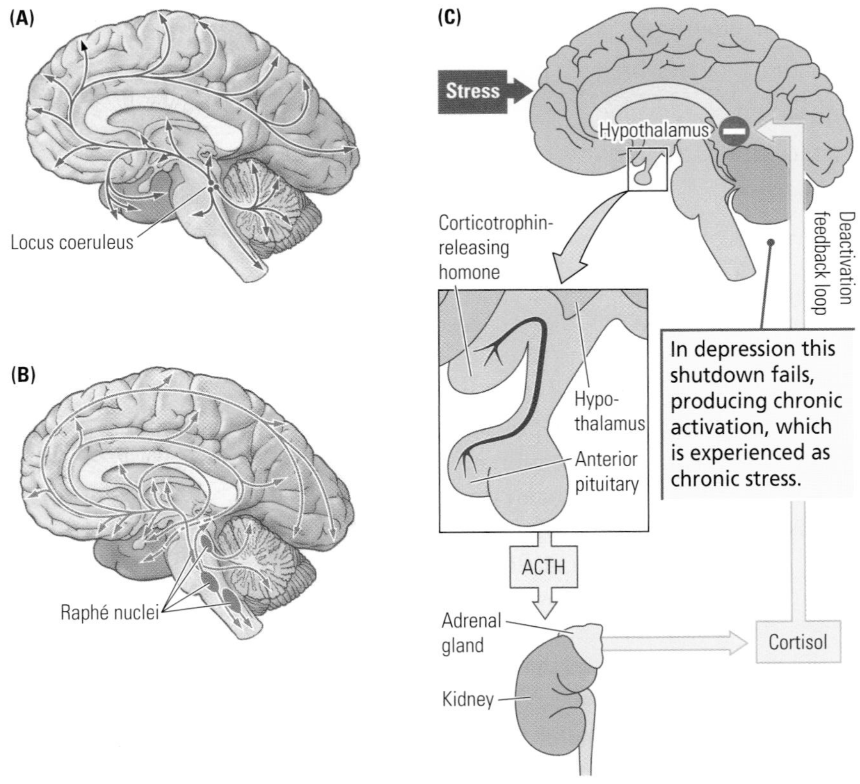

HPA axis. Hypothalamic-pituitary-adrenal circuit that controls the production and release of hormones related to stress.

Figure 15-10

HPA axis **(A)** In this medial view of the stress activating system, the locus coeruleus contains the cell bodies of norepinephrine neurons, the hypothalamus contains corticotrophin-releasing hormone, and dopamine cell bodies reside in the ventral tegmentum. **(B)** Cell bodies of the serotonergic activating system emanate from the Raphé nuclei. **(C)** When activated, the HPA system affects mood, thinking, and, indirectly, the secretion of cortisol by the adrenal glands. HPA deactivation begins when cortisol binds to hypothalamic receptors

Antidepressant Action in Neurogenesis

Focus on New Research

A puzzle in treating depression is that, even though there is an almost immediate increase in monoamines in the brains of people who begin taking antidepressant drugs, patients typically must wait from 3 to 4 weeks for the medication to take effect. If low levels of monoamines cause depression, then why does it take so long to see and feel improvement? One explanation is that the increased monoamine levels initiate a slow reparative process in their target areas in the brain.

In fact, findings from postmortem studies of the brains of depressed people show cell loss in the prefrontal cortex and hippocampus, and some of this loss may be reversed by the antidepressants' actions. Furthermore, exposure to chronic stress can cause cell death and dendritic shrinkage in the hippocampus, changes that likely result from high levels of cortisol. The possibility arises, therefore, that antidepressant drugs act to reverse cell loss, at least in the hippocampus. In fact, there is good evidence that fluoxetine (Prozac) and other SSRIs stimulate neurogenesis in the hippocampi of rats and mice.

Luca Santarelli and colleagues (2003) conducted an experiment to test whether antidepressants are capable of reversing the behavioral symptoms when neurogenesis is prevented in depressed animals. They used a mouse bred with a genetic knockout manipulation that omitted a specific serotonin receptor (5-HT-1A). This receptor is thought to be stimulated by antidepressants such as fluoxetine.

The mice were tested in two behavioral procedures, including one that the investigators proposed as a model of depression. In this test, animals exposed to chronic unpredictable stress develop a general deterioration in the state of their fur coat and this deterioration can be reversed by chronic, but not acute, treatment with antidepressants.

Santarelli's team hypothesized that, if the action of fluoxetine on depression was to increase neurogenesis in the hippocampus, then mice without the necessary 5-HT-1A receptor would not respond to the drug treatment. In contrast, those animals with the serotonin receptor would show both a reversal in cell loss in the hippocampus and in the associated behavioral changes, which is exactly what the researchers found. Importantly, the effect of the drug was not seen after only 5 days of drug treatment, but it was seen after 11 or 28 days of treatment.

Santarrelli and his team concluded that the hippocampus has a role in mood regulation and that interfering with hippocampal neurogenesis impairs this mood regulation. They proposed that antidepressants act, at least in part, to increase neurogenesis and thus relieve the impairment in hippocampal mood regulation. It is important to note that humans with hippocampal damage are not typically depressed, and so the way in which neurogenesis in the hippocampus might relieve depression remains puzzling.

This study demonstrates how environmental factors such as chronic stress may alter the human brain's homeostatic regulator. Santarelli's animal model further explains how a class of drugs (in this case, antidepressants) act at the cellular level to reverse both anatomical and behavioral symptoms.

45 percent of adults with depression lasting 2 years or more had experienced abuse, neglect, or parental loss as children.

Fluoxetine (Prozac), a major drug for treating depression, is an SSRI that effectively increases the amount of serotonin in the cortex (Chapter 7). But independent of serotonin production, fluoxetine stimulates both BDNF production and neurogenesis in the hippocampus, resulting in a net increase in the number of granule cells (see "Antidepressant Action in Neurogenesis").

To summarize, the fact that noreprinephrine- and serotonin-activating systems are so diffusely distributed makes relating depression to a single brain structure impossible. Findings from neuroimaging studies show that depression is accompanied by an increase in blood flow and glucose metabolism in the orbital frontal cortex, the anterior cingulate cortex, and the amygdala. This elevated blood flow drops as the symptoms of depression remit when a patient takes antidepressant medication (Drevets, Kishore, & Krishman, 2004). The participation of these brain structures in affect should not be surprising, given their role in emotional behavior (Chapter 11).

For additional information about anxiety and mood disorders, visit the Chapter 15 Web links on the *Brain and Behavior* Web site (**www.worth publishers.com/kolb**).

Anxiety Disorders

We all experience anxiety at some time, usually acutely as a response to a stressful stimulus or, less commonly, as a chronic reactivity, an increased anxiety response, even to seemingly minor stressors. Anxiety reactions certainly are not pathological and are likely an evolutionary adaptation by which organisms cope with adverse conditions. But anxiety can become pathological to the point of making life miserable.

As you discovered in Chapter 11, anxiety disorders are among the most common. The DSM-IV lists six classes of anxiety disorders, which are summarized in Table 15-9. Together, the six disorders affect more than 20 percent of the U.S. population at some point in their lifetimes with an annual estimated cost of about $44 billion (Gross & Hen, 2004).

Imaging studies of people with anxiety disorders record increased baseline activity in the cingulate cortex and parahippocampal gyrus and an enhanced response to anxiety-provoking stimuli in the amygdala and prefrontal cortex. The likely culprit is excessive excitatory neurotransmission in the anterior cingulate cortex, prefrontal cortex, amygdala, and parahippocampal region. Researchers hypothesize that, because drugs that enhance the inhibitory transmitter GABA are particularly effective in reducing anxiety, excessive excitatory neurotransmission may enhance anxiety. But what is the cause?

In the past decade, considerable interest has developed in investigating why some people show a pathological level of anxiety to stimuli to which others have a much-attenuated response. One hypothesis, just covered in the section on depression, is that stressful experiences early in life increase a person's susceptibility to a variety of behavioral abnormalities, especially anxiety disorders. Findings from studies on laboratory animals confirm that early experience can alter the stress response in adulthood.

Michael Meaney and his colleagues (e.g., Weaver et al., 2004) demonstrated a range of maternal licking-and-grooming behavior among rat mothers. Pups raised by mothers that display low levels of licking and grooming show more anxiety-related behaviors, including an enhanced corticosterone response in response to mild stressors, than do pups raised by mothers displaying high levels of licking and grooming.

What is particularly intriguing in these studies is that rat pups raised by low or high lickers and groomers themselves show the same behavior toward their own infants. This link is not a direct genetic one, however, because pups raised by adoptive mothers show the behaviors of their adoptive mothers rather than their biological mothers.

Meaney's group showed that the licking-and-grooming behaviors alter the expression of certain genes, thus showing that early experiences can alter the phenotype. More exciting, the researchers have reversed the adverse effects of early experience with chemical treatments. This promising line of inquiry will likely lead to new forms of treatment for anxiety disorders in coming years.

Although anxiety disorders used to be treated primarily with benzodiazepines such as Valium, now they are effectively treated with SSRIs such as Prozac, Paxil, Celexa, and Zoloft. Antidepressant drugs do not act immediately, however, suggesting that SSRI treatment must stimulate some gradual type of change in brain structure, much as in the actions of these drugs in treating depression.

Cognitive-behavior therapy (CBT)
Treatment that challenges the reality of patients' obsessions and the behavioral necessity for their compulsions.

Finally, simply giving medications does not give people the coping skills that they may need to get better, as stated earlier. This statement is especially true for anxiety disorders. The treatment of obsessive-compulsive disorders in particular requires an integrated approach, including both medications and **cognitive-behavior therapy** (CBT). This therapy focuses on challenging the reality of the patients' obsessions and the behavioral necessity for their compulsions. The most effective behavioral therapies expose and reexpose the patients to their fears. For example, treating a fear of germs requires that the patient be exposed repeatedly to potentially germy environments, such as public washrooms, until the discomfort abates (Abramowitz, 1998).

In Review

Our knowledge of psychiatric disorders such as psychosis, mood disorders, and anxiety disorders is best viewed as work in progress. Significant progress has been made in understanding the neurobiology of these disorders. Schizophrenia is correlated with abnormalities in dopamine, GABA, and glutamate systems. Structural abnormalities and low blood-glucose utilization are observed in both the prefrontal cortex and the temporal cortex. Treatments emphasize normalizing the dopaminergic abnormalities. In contrast, the monoamine systems are abnormal in mood disorders, particularly in signal transduction in postsynaptic cells. And, in depression, abnormally high levels of blood flow and glucose utilization show up in the prefrontal and anterior cingulate cortex and in the amygdala. Antidepressant treatments aim largely at normalizing the monoaminergic systems, which in turn normalizes glucose utilization. Anxiety disorders are likely related to GABA systems and abnormally high levels of blood flow in the cingulate cortex, amygdala, and parahippocampal cortex. Treatments are aimed at reversing the GABAergic abnormalities and helping people learn to modify their behaviors.

IS MISBEHAVIOR ALWAYS BAD?

You know the movie plot in which a person has some sort of blow to the head and becomes a different (and better) person. You might wonder whether pathological changes in the brain and behavior sometimes lead to improvement. A report by Jim Giles (2004) on Tommy McHugh's case is thought provoking.

McHugh, a heroin addict, had committed multiple serious crimes and had spent a great deal of time in jail. He suffered a cerebral hemorrhage (bleeding into the brain) from an aneurysm. His bleeding was repaired surgically by placing a metal clip on the leaking artery. After he recovered from the injury, McHugh showed a dramatic change in personality, took up painting, which he had never done before, and has become a successful artist. His life of crime is now only for the record books.

His injury-induced brain changes appear to have been beneficial. The exact nature of McHugh's brain injury is not easy to identify, because the metal clip in his brain precludes the use of MRI. Aspects of his cognitive behavior suggest that he may have frontal-lobe damage.

Bruce Miller has studied a larger group of 12 patients who, like Tommy McHugh, have frontal or temporal injury or both. All developed new musical or artistic talents after their injuries (Miller et al., 2000). Miller speculates that loss of function in one brain area sometimes can release new functions elsewhere.

The general idea that manipulating the brain might be beneficial is clearly a slippery slope. The idea behind psychosurgery was based on this general idea (Chapter 11). Today, it might be possible to influence brain function more scientifically through a strategy loosely described as **neurocognitive enhancement.** The general idea is that, by using our knowledge of pharmacology, brain plasticity, brain stimulation, neurogenetics, and so on, it will one day be possible to manipulate brain functioning.

Many people already use drugs to alter brain function. But what about treatments such as genetic manipulation? In the studies undertaken by Michael Meaney and his collaborators, they were able to show that specific behavioral manipulations can alter the expression of genes in rats. Serious moral and ethical issues certainly need discussion before neuroscientists begin to offer routes to neurocognitive enhancement. (See reviews of these issues by Caplan, 2003, and Farah et al., 2004).

Neurocognitive enhancement. Brain-function enhancement by pharmacological, physiological, or surgical manipulation.

SUMMARY

■ *What are the prospects for creating a unified theory of the bain and behavior?* Freud's theories have been out of favor in behavioral neuroscience for about 50 years, but modern neuroimaging studies are reviving a Freudian-type theory of the self, a theory more in keeping with current scientific knowledge about brain organization and function. As a new, unifying model of the self develops, researchers and practitioners may begin to identify the neural basis of diseases now labeled as "mental" or "psychiatric."

■ *What research methods do neuroscientists use to investigate the neurobiology of behavioral disorders?* Most behavioral disorders have multiple causes—genetic, biochemical, anatomical, and social–environmental variables—all interacting. Research methods directed toward these causes include family studies designed to find a genetic abnormality that might be corrected, biochemical anomolies that might be reversed by drug or hormone therapy, anatomical pathologies that might account for behavioral changes, and social–environmental variables. Investigators rely increasingly on neuroimaging (MRI, PET, TMS, ERP) to examine brain–behavior relations in vivo in normal subjects as well as in those having disorders. Interest is growing in the use of more-refined measurements of behavior, especially cognitive behavior, to better understand behavioral symptoms.

■ *How are disorders classified?* Disorders can be classified according either to presumed etiology (i.e., cause), to symptomatology, or to pathology. The primary etiological classification, neurological versus psychiatric, is artificial, because it presupposes that two classifications accommodate all types of disorders. In fact, as more is learned about etiology, more disorders fall into the neurological category. The symptomatological classification requires a checklist, such as the DSM-IV. The problem in such diagnosis is that symptoms of psychiatric disorders overlap. The checklist of likely symptoms for disorders is thus open to interpretation. Symptoms may appear more or less prominent, depending on the perceptions of the classifier. The pathological classification of behavioral disorders may be possible with MRI or other scans but often requires postmortem examination. In either event, it is becoming clear that disorders have more overlap in pathology than was previously recognized.

■ *How are general treatment categories deployed to combat disorders of brain and behavior?* The treatment of behavioral disorders is usually tied to the presumed causes. If a disorder is presumed to be primarily one of biochemical imbalance, such as depression, the treatment is likely to be pharmacological. If the disorder has a suspected anatomical cause, the treatment may include the removal of pathological tissue (e.g., epilepsy) or the use of implanted electrodes to activate underactive regions (e.g.,

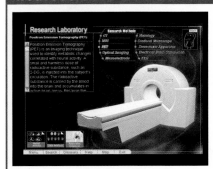

neuroscience interactive

Many resources are available for expanding your learning online:

■ **www.worthpublishers.com/kolb**
Try the Chapter 15 quizzes and flashcards to test your mastery of the chapter material. You'll also be able to link to other sites to reinforce what you've learned.

On your *Foundations* CD you can review the major concepts and anatomical fundamentals in the modules on the Central Nervous System and Neural Communication. You can also see demonstrations of brain imaging technologies such as EEG, MRI, fMRI, and PET in the module on Research Methods.

■ **www.nmss.org**
Link to this site to learn more about the role of the immune system in multiple sclerosis.

■ **www.neuroskills.com**
Read the latest news about traumatic brain injury at the Traumatic Brain Injury Resource Guide.

Parkinson's disease, stroke). Brain activation with TMS is promising and noninvasive. Many disorders, however, require medical treatment concurrent with behavioral therapy, including physiotherapy or cognitive rehabilitation for stroke or trauma and behavioral or cognitive therapies for anxiety disorders.

■ *What is the neurological plague of the twenty-first century?* The aging population of the Western world will increase the number of people with hidden diseases of behavior, especially the neurodegenerative disorders and stroke. Like other plagues in human history, this one will affect not only the person who has the disease but also the caregivers. About half of the caregivers for people with disorders linked to aging will seek psychiatric care themselves.

■ *Can brain dysfunction or alteration ever lead to positive outcomes?* The logic of psychosurgery is that, by altering brain organization, it might be possible to influence abnormal behavior. The history of psychosurgery has not been a good one, but the general principle could be applied to genetic manipulations, transplants, and brain stimulation. There is also evidence that, in some cases, people with abnormal behaviors may inadvertently benefit from neurological disease, although this outcome is certainly not common.

KEY TERMS

akathesia, p. 592
autoimmune disease, p. 590
automatism, p. 589
behavioral therapy, p. 583
bipolar disorder, p. 600
catatonic posture, p. 589
cognitive-behavior therapy (CBT), p. 604
cognitive therapy, p. 583
deep brain stimulation (DBS), p. 579
dementia, p. 590

diaschisis, p. 587
DSM-IV-TR, p. 577
festination, p. 593
focal seizure, p. 588
grand mal seizure, p. 589
HPA axis, p. 601
idiopathic seizure, p. 587
ischemia, p. 586
Lewy body, p. 596
magnetic resonance spectroscopy (MRS), p. 586
mania, p. 600

neurocognitive enhancement, p. 605
neuroprotectant, p. 587
petit mal seizure, p. 589
phenylketonuria (PKU), p. 573
postictal depression, p. 589
psychotherapy, p. 584
symptomatic seizure, p. 587
tardive dyskinesia, p. 582
type I schizophrenia, p. 598
type II schizophrenia, p. 598

REVIEW QUESTIONS

1. What are the difficulties in developing a unifying theory of the neurobiology of abnormal behavior?

2. What are the causes of abnormal behavior?

3. What are the treatments for abnormal behavior?

4. What are the methods of studying brain and behavior?

5. In what sense is behavioral therapy a biological intervention?

FOR FURTHER THOUGHT

1. What type of studies will be required to establish the basis of mental disorders and their treatments?

2. Why would abnormalities in the anterior cingulate and prefrontal cortex produce so many different behavioral syndromes?

RECOMMENDED READING

Barondes, S. M. (1993). *Molecules and mental illness.* New York: Scientific American Library. Like the other books in the Scientific American Library, this one is beautifully written and illustrated and is easily accessible. It provides a good general discussion of the neurobiology of mental disorders.

Charney, D. S., & Nestler, E. J. (Eds.). (2004). *The neurobiology of mental illness* (2nd ed.). New York: Oxford University Press. This is a serious book for those interested in the latest information on the neurobiology of mental illness. Coverage includes the entire spectrum of mental disorders with thorough reference lists and clear discussions.

Sacks, O. (1998). *The man who mistook his wife for a hat: And other clinical tales.* New York: Touchstone. This collection of short essays provides interesting reading about some strange relations between brain and behavior. Sacks is an excellent writer, and his accounts are not only entertaining but thought provoking as well.

Solms, M., & Turnbull, O. (2002). *The brain and the inner world.* New York: Other Press/Karnac Books. An introduction to the issues concerning the organization of the mind and the brain.

Epilogue

What Have We Learned and What Is Its Value?

Neuroscience in an Evolutionary Context

Revisiting the Principles of Nervous System Function

Principle 1: Information-Processing Sequence in the Brain Is "In → Integrate → Out"

Principle 2: Sensory and Motor Functions Throughout the Nervous System Are Separated

Principle 3: Inputs and Outputs to the Brain Are Crossed

Principle 4: Brain Anatomy and Function Display Both Symmetry and Asymmetry

Principle 5: The Nervous System Works Through Excitation and Inhibition

Principle 6: The Nervous System Functions on Multiple Levels

Principle 7: Brain Components Operate Both Hierarchically and in Parallel

Principle 8: Functions in the Brain Are Both Localized in Specific Regions and Distributed

Neuroscience in the Twenty-first Century

Throughout this book, we examined the nervous system with a focus on function, on how our behavior and our brains interact. We began with Fred Linge, who met the challenge of brain trauma sustained in a car accident by learning to compensate for his changed abilities. The brain injuries suffered by Tan, D. B., Roger, Donna, and other patients proved to be sources of insight into brain function.

We met Alex the parrot, Kamala the elephant, puffins, sea bears, butterflies, sea snails, fruit flies, and nematodes whose behavior also proved to be a source of insight into brain function. We examined car engines, robots, and prehistoric flutes. Each teaches a different lesson about the organization and functioning of the brain.

As we reflect on the many topics that we have covered, an important question emerges: What basic concepts about the brain does all this information suggest? To answer this question, we retrace our path from brain to behavior all the way back to Chapter 2, to revisit the principles of nervous system function set out there.

You have seen that these big ideas apply equally at the micro and macro levels of nervous system neurobiology, as well as to the broader picture of behavior that emerges. In fact, however, most of the themes that have been introduced span more than a single chapter in this book. Our goal here is to bind those themes together to produce a set of key concepts about brain function and its links to behavior. The real task is to learn how the brain produces behavior, including consciousness.

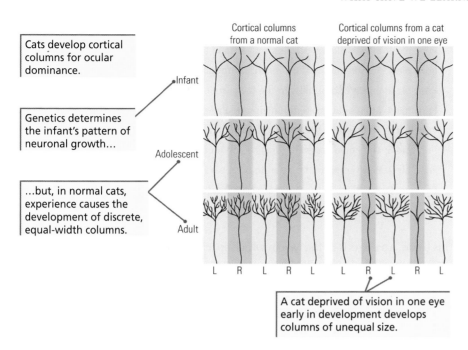

Cats develop cortical columns for ocular dominance.

Genetics determines the infant's pattern of neuronal growth...

...but, in normal cats, experience causes the development of discrete, equal-width columns.

Cortical columns from a normal cat

Cortical columns from a cat deprived of vision in one eye

Infant

Adolescent

Adult

L R L R L L R L R L

A cat deprived of vision in one eye early in development develops columns of unequal size.

Figure E-1

Critical Experience As detailed in Chapter 6, beginning at a critical period in its development, a kitten was deprived of vision in its right eye. Whereas the pattern of neural growth, determined by genetic inheritance, is normal in the left eye, the cortical dominance columns in the right eye are abnormal, showing the effect of experience.

NEUROSCIENCE IN AN EVOLUTIONARY CONTEXT

Evolution results from the complex interplay of biology and environment, of genes and experience. This ongoing interplay influences how humans and other animals behave and learn from earliest infancy through old age. Experience can influence the messages that genes produce, and genes, in turn, can influence an organism's environment and experience.

Our bodies and our behaviors stem in part from the activity of the 20,000 or so genes that we inherit from our parents. Each gene encodes a protein, and each protein can be modified or combined with one or many others to produce the hundreds of thousands of molecules that build our brains. Predictable developmental stages are initiated by this genetic code, but the details of development can be influenced by chance, by experience, and by the environment (**Figure E-1**).

Experience does not just mean events in the outside world. It encompasses the internal environment, too: the action of hormones and other neurochemicals, the progress of a disease or recovery from an injury, and reactions to stress. Internal experience includes our own thoughts (Chapter 14) and dreams (Chapter 12). Both processes result from changes in our brains, and they cause neural changes as well.

The dance of genetic and experiential influences continues throughout our lives just as it does in the continuing evolution of our species. Experiences can turn the genes in neurons on, and the way in which genes are turned on influences experience. The influence of genes and experience is not simply to form neurons and place them in appropriate relations with one another but also to eliminate excess or faulty neurons and connections, analogously to the sculpting of a statue from an unshaped block of marble.

REVISITING THE PRINCIPLES OF NERVOUS SYSTEM FUNCTION

Determining the relative contributions that genes and environment make to the brain and behavior has so far eluded science. But watching their interplay suggests general principles, summarized in **Table E-1**, that form the basis for many discussions throughout

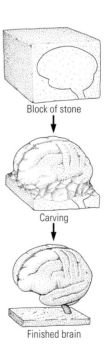

Block of stone

Carving

Finished brain

In the first months of life, our brains overproduce neurons and connections and then prune away unnecessary neurons and incorrect connections, analogously to a sculptor chiseling a statue from a block of stone.

Table E-1	Eight Principles of Nervous System Function
Principle 1: Information-processing sequence in the brain is "in → integrate → out."
Principle 2: Sensory and motor functions throughout the nervous system are separated.
Principle 3: Inputs and outputs to the brain are crossed.
Principle 4: Brain anatomy and function display both symmetry and asymmetry.
Principle 5: The nervous system works through excitation and inhibition.
Principle 6: The nervous system functions on multiple levels.
Principle 7: Brain components operate both parallelly and hierarchically.
Principle 8: Functions in the brain are both localized in specific regions and distributed.

this book. Analogous to the way in which species evolve by reacting to the interplay of nature and nurture, principles of nervous system function evolve from the interaction of science and research. Thus the selection of these concepts is somewhat arbitrary; we could have chosen more or different principles.

The reason for extracting guiding principles is just as important as their content or wording. You reviewed the methods and treatments of neuropsychology in Chapter 15. We invite you now to revisit the functional principles that you first studied in Chapter 2, knowing what you know now about neuropsychology, brain and behavior, and how they work together.

Your task is to synthesize the large body of information that you have learned into an integrated theory of how the brain works. Perhaps the overriding message that emerges from this effort is that mental activity results from brain activity. Through research, we can eventually understand how this process takes place.

Principle 1: Information-Processing Sequence in the Brain Is "In → Integrate → Out"

Most neurons have afferent (incoming) connections with tens or sometimes hundreds or thousands of other neurons, as well as efferent (outgoing) connections to neurons and many other cell types, such as muscle cells. The parts of the nervous system make a great many connections with one another. Sensory and motor systems interact constantly to control the organism's interaction with its environment.

The entire brain receives inputs, creates information, and produces behavior, as charted in **Figure E-2**. To the animal whose brain is engaged in this process, the creation of information from inputs represents reality. The more complex the brain circuitry, the more complex the reality created and, subsequently, the more complex the thought. The emergence of thought that enables consciousness may be the brain's ultimate act of integration.

THE NEURON IS THE BASIC UNIT OF ANATOMY, PHYSIOLOGY, AND COGNITION

Neurons are remarkably similar in all species, no matter where they are found in the nervous system. The three basic parts of the neuron are the cell body, the dendrites, and the axon, including the axon terminal, or end foot (**Figure E-3**). The neuron is the basic unit of information processing, of brain plasticity, and even of cognition.

Drugs, for example, act at the level of individual neurons, and individual neurons are what an animal's experiences change. Individual neurons also communicate with one another to generate sensation and perception and to create behavior. Differences

For a closer look at the structure of a neuron, visit the module on neural communication on your *Foundations of Behavioral Neuroscience* CD. (See the Preface for more information about this CD.)

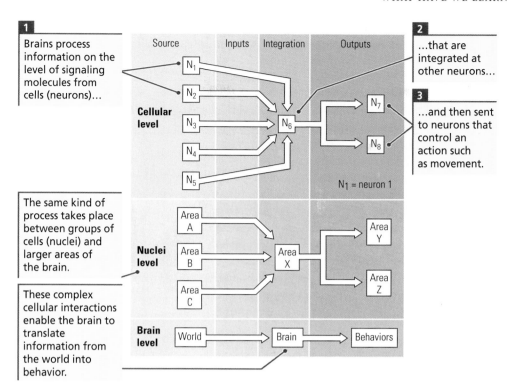

1 Brains process information on the level of signaling molecules from cells (neurons)...

2 ...that are integrated at other neurons...

3 ...and then sent to neurons that control an action such as movement.

The same kind of process takes place between groups of cells (nuclei) and larger areas of the brain.

These complex cellular interactions enable the brain to translate information from the world into behavior.

N_1 = neuron 1

Figure E-2

Levels of Neural Processing   The brain integrates and makes decisions about information at increasingly complex levels of organization.

among brains are due to differences in how individual neurons are distributed, organized, and connected.

As brains have evolved to be larger and much harder to build to an exact blueprint, nature's solution has been to create extra neurons that duplicate the function of other neurons. The strategy in developing a brain with many neurons is to shed unused and unnecessary neurons, sculpting the brain to the organism's current needs and experiences.

Not only does this strategy prevent dependency on the survival of each individual neuron, it also allows great flexibility in adapting to specific environmental conditions. An organism can spend its energy in maintaining neurons required in daily life. Allowing unneeded neurons to die does not result in the loss of any essential mental or behavioral function. Because the neuron is the functional unit of the brain, investigating what a neuron looks like, how it conducts information, and how it works with other neurons to produce behavior remains a focus for studying the function of the brain and understanding how the brain produces behavior.

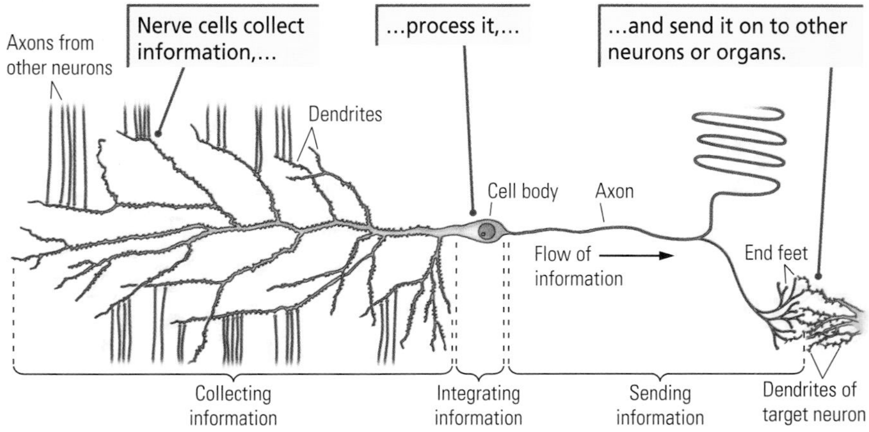

Nerve cells collect information,...   ...process it,...   ...and send it on to other neurons or organs.

Axons from other neurons

Dendrites

Cell body   Axon

Flow of information

End feet

Collecting information

Integrating information

Sending information

Dendrites of target neuron

Figure E-3

Processing Unit   A neuron is made up of dendrites, which collect information from other cells; a cell body, which processes the information and provides the energy required to keep the operation going; and an axon, which communicates this information to other neurons.

THE SYNAPSE IS THE KEY SITE OF NEURAL COMMUNICATION AND LEARNING

Dendrites, which are essentially extensions of the cell body's surface, allow a neuron to collect information from other cells, whereas the axon provides a pathway for passing that information along. Although the dendrites and axon both handle messages, the business site for communication is the synapse (**Figure E-4**).

Figure E-4

Synaptic Connections

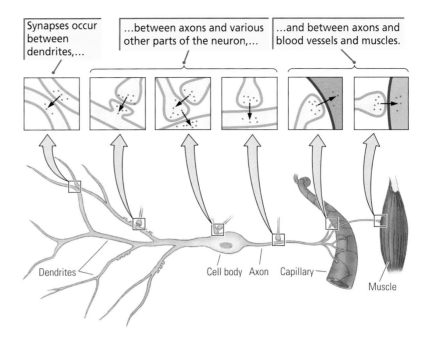

Synapses occur between dendrites,...

...between axons and various other parts of the neuron,...

...and between axons and blood vessels and muscles.

Dendrites   Cell body   Axon   Capillary   Muscle

Synapses occur most often between an axon terminal of one neuron and a dendrite, cell body, or axon of another neuron. The primary mode of communication across most synapses is chemical. The chemical either alters channels on the receiving (postsynaptic) neuron or initiates postsynaptic events through second messengers (Chapter 5).

Synaptic activity can be influenced in several ways. The most direct route is either to increase or decrease the amount of chemical transmitter released into the synaptic cleft or to enhance or attenuate that chemical's action on its postsynaptic receptor. This route is the primary route of action of most drugs (Chapter 7).

There are less-direct routes, too. One effect of repeated exposure to drugs is either to change characteristics of the postsynaptic membrane (such as the number of receptor sites on it) or to alter the number of synapses. The number of synapses may be increased by the addition of new synapses to the existing neurons; the synaptic space may be increased by the addition of dendritic spines.

Drugs, hormones, neurotrophic factors, experiences

Synaptic change

Behavioral change

Changes in receptors or in the number of synapses are likely events in processes such as learning and drug addiction. Indeed, synaptic change is required for virtually any behavioral change, whether the change is related to learning, to development and aging, or to recovery from brain injury. Because synaptic change is the key to behavioral change, it follows that factors that enhance or diminish synaptic change (such as neurotrophic factors, drugs, hormones, or experiences) will stimulate or retard behavioral change. Many new treatments for behavioral disorders are designed to maximize synaptic change.

CONSCIOUSNESS ORGANIZES BRAIN PROCESSING AND THE BEHAVIOR PRODUCED BY THE BRAIN

We take for granted that we are conscious but debate whether other animals are. Consciousness implies that we act not simply in relation to immediate circumstances but also on the basis of memory and further implies the ability to communicate the reasons for our actions to others. Simply stated, we think about our actions and articulate our reasons. Clearly, other animals have memory and, clearly, they have communication systems. But are they conscious in the way that humans are?

Presumably, consciousness provides an adaptive advantage when a large amount of information must be processed before we decide how to behave in a particular situation. But behaviors that depend on conscious processing are slower than automatic behaviors. As a result, conscious analysis is usually applied to tasks where speed is not critical, such as discriminating between the various colors of socks in a drawer.

In contrast, rapid automatic movements, such as swinging a baseball bat at a ball, are usually performed without conscious control. As you learned in the discussion of the ventral and dorsal streams of the visual system (Chapter 8), the distinction between conscious and unconscious processing is fundamental to the difference between thinking about objects and moving in relation to objects. Very likely, the conscious processing of sensory information was enhanced by the emergence of language, which, may have evolved in part to categorize information.

Many other animals have brains that are similar to ours, they have memory, and they can communicate. These are reasons to believe that animals are in some sense also conscious. But, because consciousness appears to be a specialized function of only certain regions of the brain, many kinds of consciousness may have evolved and we may be unique among animal species in having a self-aware consciousness not common to other animals.

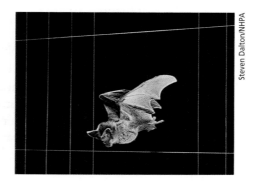

Ezra Shaw/Getty Images

Some neural processing happens so quickly that we cannot be aware of it. The ball coming out of the pitcher's hand will travel too fast for Hideki Matsui to consciously see it, but he may still get a hit.

Principle 2: Sensory and Motor Functions Throughout the Nervous System Are Separated

The segregation of sensory and motor functions exists throughout the nervous system (review the law of Bell and Magendie in Chapter 2). Distinctions between motor and sensory functions become subtler in the forebrain.

THE BRAIN CREATES A REPRESENTATION OF THE EXTERNAL WORLD AND PRODUCES BEHAVIOR IN RESPONSE TO THAT WORLD

Most animals with a multicellular brain have a common problem. They must move from place to place to eat and to reproduce. These movements, which are controlled by the nervous system, cannot be random. Rather, they must be made in response to the external world where food and mates are found. This external world is created by the nervous system through inputs from various sensory receptors. An animal's perception of what the external world is like therefore depends on the complexity and organization of its nervous system.

Recall that different animals, such as dogs, bats, and chimpanzees, have developed different "views" of the external world. For a dog, the world is dominated by odors; for a bat, it is largely a world of sounds; and, for a chimpanzee, colors are in the forefront of perception. None of these representations of the external world are more "correct" than the others. They are simply different perspectives on what is "out there" to be perceived.

Each representation creates a unique picture that suits the behavioral repertoire of the animal species. The behavior of dogs is driven by smells, whether it is the smell of a strange dog, a potential mate, or a possible prey. The flight of bats is

○ To review the sensory systems of the brain, investigate the modules on the central nervous system and the visual system on the *Foundations* CD.

Steven Dalton/NHPA

Even though bats create a world largely through sound rather than sight, they manage to move from place to place without much trouble. Employing echolocation, this bat ably navigates through a mesh screen in the dark.

guided by auditory information, as when bats use sound to locate insects to eat. And the behavior of chimpanzees is driven by color, the best example being to spot ripe fruit in trees.

The brains of animals do something else as well: they create knowledge about the world. They keep track of where objects are, where food may be found, where safe sleeping places are located. As brains evolved into larger and larger organs, the amount of knowledge processed and stored grew so big that some mechanism for organizing it was needed.

One solution to the problem of categorizing information is to create some form of coding system, of which human language is the ultimate example. In essence, the earliest function of language may have been to organize the brain's information. Language, in other words, evolved for the brain to talk to itself. Later, language also provided a way to share knowledge *between* brains.

Given the achievements of the human species in all these behavioral functions—representing the world and moving about in it, acquiring and organizing knowledge—our brain's evolutionary development has clearly been very successful indeed. Still, the human nervous system is not special: many kinds of coding and language likely allow each animal species to succeed at its specialized mode of life.

BRAIN ORGANIZATION SEGREGATES SENSORY INFORMATION USED FOR ACTION AND FOR KNOWLEDGE

In the ordinary course of our daily lives, we operate under the illusion that our behavior is conscious. We believe that we give conscious commands to produce purposeful movements. Usually, we are unaware that many of our actions, even very complex actions, are performed without conscious control. We are unaware that we shape our fingers to the objects that we are about to grasp (Chapter 10). We are surprised to learn that, subsequent to temporal-lobe injury, we can reach for objects that we cannot consciously see and that, subsequent to parietal-cortex damage, we can misreach for objects that we can see.

This dichotomy between conscious action and unconscious action shows us that the brain segregates actions that require conscious reflection from those that require only action. Reaching for a handrail on a moving bus would not be an effective protective action if we had to think about it for any length of time before doing it.

Much of our behavior can be divided into categories of knowledge and action. For example, basketball is a complex sport, and knowledge of rules and strategies is required to understand the game. But an experienced player probably gives little attention to rules and strategies and catches, throws, and shoots the ball almost automatically.

Shooting a basketball can be learned in a single trial, but shooting it accurately takes many thousands of trials. Many skills can similarly be divided into these action and knowledge categories. Because the brain segregates action and knowledge, complex behavior also can be segregated into categories of largely more conscious and largely more automatic, as can brain regions.

ANIMALS ENGAGE IN BEHAVIORS FOR MULTIPLE REASONS

One of the most difficult questions to answer is why animals engage in behaviors, especially why they perform particular behaviors at particular times. To address this question, in Chapter 11 we considered the story of Roger, who seemed to have strange, indiscriminate eating preferences. We also considered the housefly and learned that what appears to be purposeful behavior is really a response to stimuli coming from its feet and esophagus (**Figure E-5**).

In addition, we examined why cats kill birds, factors that affect the annual cycle of polar bears, and ideas about why we sleep and dream. We found it helpful to classify

Figure E-5

Prewired Behavior A housefly's taste receptors are on its feet. Stretch receptors in its foregut tell it when it is full.

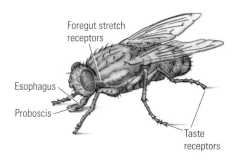

Foregut stretch receptors

Esophagus

Proboscis

Taste receptors

the many different kinds of animal behaviors as either regulatory or nonregulatory. Regulatory behaviors maintain basic body functions, such as constant body temperature or circadian patterns of sleeping and waking. Most regulatory behaviors require little brainpower and are largely controlled by the hypothalamus and associated brainstem structures.

It is more difficult to say why we engage in nonregulatory behaviors. We seek stimulation, finding an absence of sensory input intolerable. We also seek mates, orienting much of our lives around this behavior and activities associated with it. In addition, we make plans and organize our behaviors temporally. Searching for the reasons behind these nonregulatory behaviors led us to investigate the anatomical structures that control each of them.

Although we still do not know much about the reasons for many of our nonregulatory behaviors, we can draw several conclusions. Above all, behavior is controlled by its consequences. These consequences may shape the behavior of a species or the behavior of an individual organism. Behaviors that are adaptive and brains that are likely to engage in adaptive behaviors are selected in the course of evolution.

We learned that cats kill birds because neural circuits in the brainstem control these behaviors. Activation of these circuits is presumably rewarding, and so, in a sense, animals engage in many behaviors because the behaviors feel good. We learned, too, that animals do not need to actually engage in a rewarded behavior to experience this positive feeling. Electrical stimulation of the attendant neural circuits appears to be just as rewarding (perhaps even more so) than actually using the circuits.

Because objects can take on different meanings, there are different reasons for our actions. This difference is illustrated in Chapters 7 and 11, with the use of the terms *wanting* and *liking*. Wanting is thought to be controlled by systems related to need, such as primary hunger and primary thirst, whereas liking is thought to be controlled by other neural structures that are sensitive to experience.

Principle 3: Inputs and Outputs to the Brain Are Crossed

Most of the brain's input and output pathways are crossed. Each hemisphere receives sensory stimulation from the opposite (contralateral) side of the body and controls muscles on the opposite side as well. Crossed organization explains why people who experience strokes in the left cerebral hemisphere may have difficulty sensing stimulation to the right side of the body or moving body parts on the right side. The opposite is true of people with strokes in the right cerebral hemisphere.

The human visual system is crossed in a more complicated way than are sensory and motor systems for other parts of the body or for animals with eyes on the sides of their head, such as rats (Chapter 8). The human brain divides each eye's visual field into a left half and a right half. The information that either eye receives from the left visual field is sent to the right side of the brain, and the information that either eye receives from the right visual field is sent to the left side of the brain.

A crossed nervous system must join the two sides of the perceptual world together somehow. To do so, innumerable neural connections link the left and right sides of the brain. The most prominent connecting cable is the corpus callosum, which joins the left and right cerebral hemispheres with about 200 million nerve fibers.

An important exception to the crossed-circuit principle is in the olfactory system. Olfactory information does not cross but rather projects directly into the same (ipsilateral) side of the brain.

Principle 4: Brain Anatomy and Function Display Both Symmetry and Asymmetry

Even though the left and right hemispheres appear anatomically similar and share many functions, some, such as the articulation of speech, are lateralized to a single hemisphere in most people. One reason that functions are lateralized may be the greater efficiency of having a single neural network control a complex behavior that depends on multiple sources of sensory input, knowledge, or both. For instance, language or birdsong produced by a brain that has bilateral control of the sound-producing apparatus is hard to imagine. After all, an organism cannot simultaneously make two different sounds, one produced by each hemisphere.

A single control system therefore makes more sense. This concept can be easily applied to other functions. For example, although we can move our limbs independently, many of our movements, such as eating or dressing, require limb cooperation. Control of such behaviors clearly necessitates the integration of multiple sources of sensory input and multiple movements. The nervous system has evolved lateralized networks to oversee these functions.

It is tempting to overemphasize the asymmetrical organization of the brain, especially the cerebral hemispheres. In fact, however, both sides of the brain undertake most brain functions. Both sides process sensory inputs from all the sensory domains, and both sides produce movements of one side of the body. The brain, in other words, has both symmetrical and asymmetrical organization (Figure E-6).

Even a language function, which we think of as lateralized, has both symmetrical and asymmetrical aspects (Chapter 9). It is the *output* apparatus for language that must be controlled unilaterally. There is no obvious reason why the receptive aspects of language must be unilaterally controlled, and, in fact, the right hemisphere does have receptive functions, especially for nouns.

Because functions are both symmetrically and asymmetrically organized, our brains can, in a sense, operate as two different brains. In fact, the hemispheres actually do act separately if the corpus callosum is severed (Chapter 14).

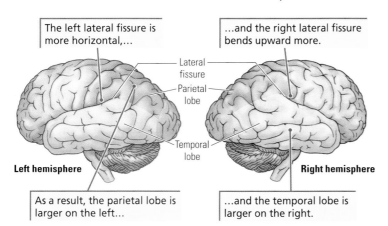

The left lateral fissure is more horizontal,...

...and the right lateral fissure bends upward more.

Lateral fissure

Parietal lobe

Temporal lobe

Left hemisphere

Right hemisphere

As a result, the parietal lobe is larger on the left...

...and the temporal lobe is larger on the right.

Figure E-6

Superficial Differences   Although at first glance the brain's hemispheres appear identical on the right and the left sides, closer inspection reveals that they are asymmetrical. The brain's functions, however, are both symmetrical and asymmetrical.

Principle 5: The Nervous System Works Through Excitation and Inhibition

The juxtaposition of excitation and inhibition is central to nervous system functioning. The same principle that governs the production of behavior governs the activity of individual neurons. The activity of neurons and neural systems is literally a balancing act between the forces of inhibition and excitation.

The human nervous system is designed to balance excitation and inhibition. To function, we maintain homeostatic balances of our regulatory systems (Chapters 7, 11, and 12). We also maintain homeostasis with our external world, either by changing the world or adapting to it (Chapters 13, 14, and 15).

As you have progressed through this book, you have seen that there is an interplay of excitation and inhibition at many levels of nervous system function. At the level of the cell and its components, single neurons can be either excited or inhibited, and, through their neurotransmitters, cells act to stimulate or inhibit one another (Figure E-7). An example in vision is how the activity of single retinal ganglion neuron can

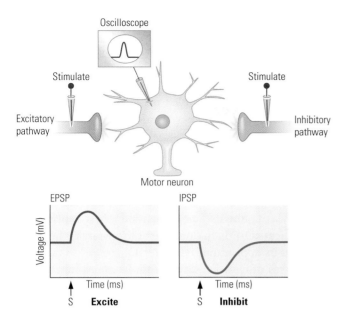

EPSP

IPSP

Voltage (mV)

Time (ms)

Time (ms)

S **Excite**

S **Inhibit**

Figure E-7

Neural Integration   Researcher John C. Eccles used the experimental setup shown here to demonstrate information integration at the neural level (Chapter 4). Stimulation of a neuron's excitatory pathway produces a membrane depolarization called an excitatory postsynaptic potential (EPSP). Stimulation of the inhibitory pathway produces a membrane hyperpolarization called an inhibitory postsynaptic potential (IPSP).

be excited or inhibited by stimulation to its different parts, as shown in **Figure E-8**.

Beyond the level of the cell, the dual processes of excitation and inhibition continue to apply. For instance, systems in the reticular formation controlling sleep–wake cycles essentially balance the inhibition and activation of forebrain systems (Chapter 12). Similarly, motor control includes the inhibition of some movements while other movements are being activated (Chapter 10).

Many diseases can be thought of as disorders of excitatory and inhibitory signals. Huntington's chorea, for example, is the loss of the ability to inhibit choreiform (convulsive) movements, whereas depression is an inability to activate many kinds of behaviors (Chapter 15). Some diseases are characterized by changes in both inhibition and excitation. Parkinson's disease features both an uncontrollable tremor *and* difficulty in initiating movement, and schizophrenia may feature both flattened emotions *and* sensory hallucinations. The release of behaviors such as tremor or hallucination represents a loss of inhibition, whereas the absence of behaviors such as movement or facial expression represents a loss of excitation.

Figure E-8

Play of Light   The receptive field of a retinal ganglion cell with an on-center and off-surround responds to the presence or absence of light. A spot of light in the center receptive field excites the neuron but, when the light shines on the surround, the cell is inhibited (Chapter 8).

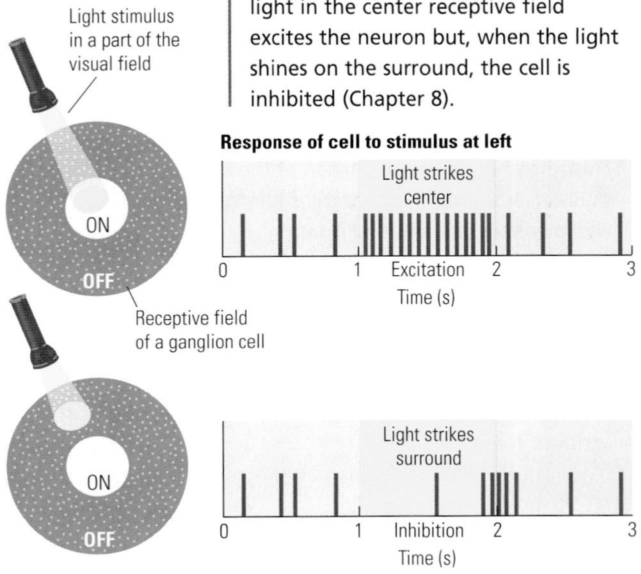

Light stimulus in a part of the visual field

Response of cell to stimulus at left

Light strikes center

0   1   Excitation   2   3
Time (s)

Receptive field of a ganglion cell

Light strikes surround

0   1   Inhibition   2   3
Time (s)

Principle 6: The Nervous System Functions on Multiple Levels

Similar sensory and motor functions are carried out in various parts of the central nervous system: the spinal cord, brainstem, and forebrain. But why are multiple areas with overlapping functions needed? Putting all the controls for a certain function in a single place seems simpler. Why bother with duplication? It turns out that, as the brain evolved, new areas were added, but old ones were retained. The simplest solution has been to add new structures on top of existing ones.

Among the millions of animal species that inhabit our planet, very few have nervous systems. Of those that do, still fewer have brains, and very few have large brains. The nervous system and the brain likely began with a single cell that first became more complex by incorporating new organelles and then, by dividing, organized into a primitive nervous system and eventually into a brain.

To review the basics of excitation and inhibition, go to the section on synaptic transmission in the module on neural communication on your *Foundations* CD.

In short, all brain cells descended from a first brain cell, all nervous systems evolved from a first nervous system, and all brains evolved from a first brain. Brain cells, nervous systems, and the brain did not evolve in isolation, however. Brain cells and muscle cells evolved together to form more-complex networks, suggesting that the primary evolutionary force sculpting these organs was and is the production of movement.

We have seen that true cells, those with nuclei and other organelles, evolved from simpler forms, and multicellular organisms evolved from single-celled organisms. We have also seen that muscles and neurons are the distinguishing feature in only one of the five kingdoms of living organisms, the animals. And we have seen that, across the 15 phyla of animals, a nervous system first appears and then becomes more complicated until, in only one of these phyla, the chordates, the first brain makes its appearance (Chapter 1).

Among the seven classes of chordates, the brain becomes more complex; but, in only two of these classes, birds and mammals, does the brain become especially large and complex. Only in mammals has a true neocortex evolved, and the neocortex becomes large in only a few orders, including whales and primates. Among the primates, the cortex becomes especially large in the apes and reaches its largest size in the human family.

In the only remaining member of the human family, we modern humans, the cortex has evolved its largest and most complex form (**Figure E-9**).

Because brain cells, the nervous system, and the brain evolved gradually and because representative animals having nervous systems of various complexities still exist, neuroscientists are able to use a wide range of species of living organisms and animals to study functions of the human brain. Because we have an evolutionary history in common with other animals, we are not special, but we are specialized.

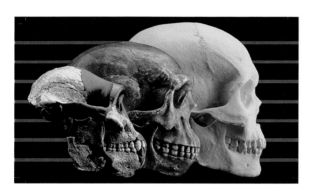

Figure E-9

Containing the Brain   In the course of human evolution, the relative size of the brain has increased threefold, as illustrated here by a comparison of the skulls of *Australopithecus afarensis* (*left*), *Homo erectus* (*center*), and *Homo sapiens* (*right*).

Principle 7: Brain Components Operate Both Hierarchically and in Parallel

The brain and spinal cord are semiautonomous areas organized into functional levels. Even within a single level, more than one area may take part in a given function. With these different systems and levels, how do we eventually obtain a unified conscious experience?

This question focuses on the binding problem: how the brain ties together its various activities into a whole perception or behavior. The solution must somehow be related to how the parts of the nervous system are connected. The two alternative possibilities for "wiring" the nervous system are serial circuits and parallel circuits.

THE PRINCIPLE OF COMMON DESCENT RESULTS IN A HIERARCHY OF COMPLEXITY IN THE EVOLUTION OF THE BRAIN

In the evolution of complex nervous systems, simpler and evolutionarily more primitive forms have not been discarded and replaced but rather have been added to. As a result, all anatomical and functional features of simpler nervous systems are present in the most complex nervous systems, including ours.

The bilaterally symmetrical nervous system of simple worms is common to complex nervous systems. Indeed, the spinal cord that constitutes most of the nervous system of the simplest fishes is recognizable in humans, as is the brainstem of more-complex fishes, amphibians, and reptiles. The neocortex, although particularly complex in dolphins and humans, is nevertheless clearly the same organ found in other mammals.

Hierarchy is manifest in the complex behavior of adult humans, in that it is a mixture of many behaviors that are clearly recognizable in other animals, including regulatory behaviors, emotional behavior, cognitive functions, and more specialized, nonregulatory behaviors seen only prominently in humans. The addition and integration of new levels of complexity in the hierarchical organization of the brain is seen not only in adult behavior but also in the development of the human brain from infancy into adulthood. Hierarchical organization accounts for the increasingly more complex behavior that characterizes development as well.

The increasing complexity of movement and cognitive functions are manifestations of the maturation of successive levels of a hierarchally organized brain (see Figure E-2). In addition, the abnormalities associated with brain injury and brain disease that seem bizarre when considered in isolation are only the normal manifestation of parts of a hierarchically organized brain. Through the principle of hierarchy, we can see that our evolutionary history, our developmental history, and our own personal history are integrated at the various anatomical and functional "levels" of the nervous system.

PATTERNS OF NEURAL ORGANIZATION ARE PLASTIC

The brain is plastic in two fundamental ways:

1. Although we tend to think of regions of the brain as having fixed functions, the brain has a capacity to adapt to different experiences by changing where specific functions are represented. For example, a person with an amputated arm has an increased representation of the face in the somatosensory cortex, as shown in **Figure E-10**. In the absence of the limb, the face becomes more sensitive (Chapter 10).
2. The brain is also plastic in the sense that the connections among neurons in a given functional system are constantly changing in response to experience. This type of plasticity is manifested in our capacity for learning from experience and for subsequently recalling learned material (Chapter 13).

One result of brain plasticity is that animals can acquire culture, patterns of behavior that are not easy to predict simply by studying brain anatomy and function. Many species of animals display behaviors that differ, depending on a specific group of animals of that species. Different pods of killer whales have different diets and different groups of chimpanzees use different kinds of tools. Nevertheless, we humans are specialized in the extent to which culture plays a role in our lives.

We have learned to read, to calculate, to compose and play music, and to develop the sciences. Clearly, the human nervous system evolved long before we mastered these achievements. In turn, culture now plays a dominant role in shaping our behavior. Because we drive cars, use computers, and watch television, we and our nervous systems must be different from those of our ancestors who did not engage in these activities.

Figure E-10

Brain Plasticity   When their faces are lightly touched, amputees feel as if their missing hands are being touched.

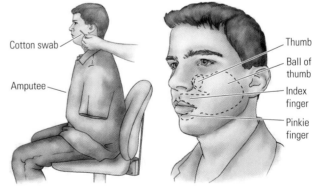

Cotton swab

Amputee

Thumb

Ball of thumb

Index finger

Pinkie finger

Principle 8: Functions in the Brain Are Both Localized in Specific Regions and Distributed

The parts of the brain make a great many connections with one another. This connectivity is the key to its functioning. Sensory information, knowledge, and the control of movement are all represented at multiple levels in the nervous system, beginning at the spinal cord and ending in the association cortex (**Figure E-11**).

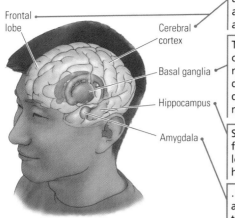

Frontal lobe
Cerebral cortex
Basal ganglia
Hippocampus
Amygdala

Specific areas of the cortex are part of circuits for motor activity, vision, memory, and other functions.

The basal ganglia are part of circuits for voluntary movement, and movement disorders such as Parkinson's disease result from neural malfunction in that area.

Some memory and spatial functions are partly localized in the hippocampus,...

...and other processes, such as emotion, rely on circuits that include the amygdala.

Figure E-11

Neural Connectivity Functions are localized in specific parts of the brain, but different aspects of a function—types of memory, for example—may be localized in more than one area.

For a review of brain anatomy, visit the module on the central nervous system on your *Foundations* CD. You can rotate the three-dimensional models for a closer look at the brain structures.

These multiple levels of representation imply that functions can be only partly localized to specific regions in the brain. In fact, functions and controls are both localized and distributed. You have seen such an example of localized and distributed function in the organization of the sensory and motor systems.

Clearly, there are sensory pathways into the brain and, just as clearly, there are motor pathways out of the brain. Although sensory impressions and motor actions can occur in isolation one from the other, neither can ever be truly normal without the other. For every function, there are parallel and distributed systems of control. For the somatosensory system, the different body senses have the same anatomical pathways to some extent and can function in isolation, but their conjoint operation provides us with our normal body image.

A key problem in studying the brain is the extent to which functions can be thought to reside in specific locations. A fundamental difficulty in localizing functions begins with the problem of defining what a function is. Consider motivation. In Chapter 11, we used the psychological construct of motivation as a shorthand way to describe the processes that initiate various behaviors. But motivated behavior ranges from basic needs, such as maintaining a constant body temperature, to lusting after an abstract concept, such as wealth. The neural systems underlying such disparate behaviors are clearly going to be segregated.

Similarly, wanting sexual activity and engaging in it are two types of behavior organized by different neural pathways. Apparently, the function that we call sexual behavior has many aspects, and these aspects reside in widely separated areas of the brain. A similar analysis may be applied to most other behaviors, a prime example being memory. Memories are often extremely rich in detail and may include sensory detail, emotions, words, and movement. As described in Chapter 13, there are many types of memory processing, including the implicit–explicit distinction. As with sexual behavior, one simple incident may be encoded in different places in the brain to form a "memory" of the event.

An implication of the concept of localized and distributed functions is that damage to a small area of the brain produces focal symptoms, but it takes massive brain damage to destroy a function completely. A relatively small injury can destroy some aspect of memory, but it takes a very widespread injury to destroy *all* memory capability. Thus, a brain-injured person may be amnesic for the explicit recall of new information, but he or she can still recall a lot of explicit information from the past and may retain *implicit* recall of new information.

NEUROSCIENCE IN THE TWENTY-FIRST CENTURY

As you reflect on what you have learned in this book, you might wonder what we will learn about the brain in the twenty-first century. It is often said that most of what we now know about brain function was discovered in the 1990s, the so-called "decade of the brain." There is some truth in this statement. At the beginning of the 1860s, investigators such as John Hughlings-Jackson were just starting to develop a vague idea of how the brain is organized. And the brain's chemical synapses were unknown until the 1950s.

With the research technology of recent years, however, many new insights have come to light. Investigators have now begun to understand the important process of how genes control neural activity. The development of new imaging techniques such as fMRI and ERP have opened up the normal brain to cognitive neuroscientists, allowing them to investigate brain activity in laboratory subjects. As we reflect on the study of brain and behavior in the past 150 years, we can only marvel at how far it has advanced and how much potential for future discoveries lies just at our doorstep.

Studies of brain and behavior have also begun to capture the public imagination. Whereas explanations of events in regard to brain function were unknown to the general public 25 years ago, today, the media usually report new discoveries in neuroscience and their possible applications weekly.

If we really understood the brain, we could build a robot behaviorally indistinguishable from ourselves, but this possibility exists today only in the realm of science fiction. As scientists have uncovered the complexities of emergent properties of genes, proteins, and neurons, the possibility of building a "humanoid robot" appears to be receding rather than growing closer. Most see the more short term goal of neuroscience as restoring normal behavior by repairing a damaged nervous system.

One day we will likely be able to stimulate processes of repair not only in malfunctioning brains but in injured spinal cords as well. These advances will come about through the efforts of neuroscientists to understand how the brain produces and organizes consciousness and, ultimately, overt behavior.

Along the way, we will learn how the brain stores and retrieves information, why we engage in the behaviors that we do, and how we are able to read the lines on this page and generate ideas and thoughts. The coming decades will be exciting times for the study of brain and behavior. They offer an opportunity for us to broaden our understanding of what makes us human.

For the latest information on research and advancements in the field of neuroscience, visit the Epilogue Web links on the *Brain and Behavior* Web site (**www.worthpublishers.com/kolb**).

Appendix

Why Do Scientists Use Animals in Research?

Ethics and Animal Research

Focus on Comparative Biology

In the 1970s, Edward Taub, a scientist at the Institute for Behavioral Research, a private facility in Silver Spring, Maryland, was conducting research on the role that sensory information plays in motor control. Taub was interested in the extent to which the motor system could produce movement in the absence of sensory information. His research was relevant to the question of whether training could be expected to stimulate the recovery of function in people who had suffered a loss of sensory information due to peripheral nerve injury.

Taub's studies required cutting the dorsal roots of the spinal cords in monkeys, thus severing the sensory fibers from the arms (see Figure 2-28). The lesion given to the monkeys was analogous to one that a person who had damage to the dorsal cervical roots of the spinal cord would suffer—a common traumatic injury.

In 1981, one of Taub's laboratory technicians, Alex Pacheco, accused him of inflicting unnecessary pain on the monkeys and failing to provide them with adequate food and veterinary care. Pacheco convinced the local police to confiscate the animals. In the next several years, an organization called People for the Ethical Treatment of Animals (PETA), cofounded by Pacheco, carried on a legal battle against the Institute for Behavioral Research over the animals' fate.

Arguing that humans do not have the moral right to use animals for research purposes, PETA attempted to terminate Taub's Silver Spring experiment. The scientists at the Institute for Behavioral Research sought to continue their research on the grounds that it was conducted according to accepted laboratory and legal standards and that research on animals provides benefits to humans (Guillermo, 1994).

Whereas the duration of Taub's experiments would have been relatively short, the legal dispute with PETA kept the Silver Spring project and its monkeys in limbo for years. In 1987, a group of scientists led by Mortimer Mishkin, a neuroscientist at the National Institute of Mental Health (NIMH), suggested that the monkeys provided a unique opportunity to look at what happens to parts of the brain that have been deprived of sensory input for a long period of time. The scientists received permission to map the somatosensory cortex of an old monkey that would shortly have to be sacrificed because of ill health.

They found that the somatosensory cortex had undergone a massive reorganization: the area that formerly represented the arm now represented the face (this result is described in Chapter 10). The face area of the somatosensory cortex had encroached into the arm area over a distance of 10 to 14 mm, a full order of magnitude greater than what findings from earlier studies had suggested might occur (Pons et al., 1991). This result demonstrated that the adult brain is capable of undergoing enormous plastic changes even well into old age. The findings also contributed to an understanding of some aspects of "phantom limbs" experienced by human amputees (discussed in Chapter 14).

Taub continued his research on monkeys at the University of Alabama in Birmingham. He subsequently applied to humans his discovery that the cortex can reorganize. He developed a widely acclaimed technique, extremity constraint induced therapy (EXCITe) on the basis of observations obtained from his monkeys (Taub & Crago, 1995).

Through this technique, patients who have lost the use of limbs owing to stroke, spinal-cord injury, or hip fracture work with robots or human therapists to exercise the disabled muscles (Alberts, Butler, & Wolf, 2004). EXCITe promotes enlargement of the muscle-output area in the affected hemisphere as well as greatly improved motor performance of the paretic limb. Taub's discovery is but one recent example of a scientific breakthrough leading to a treatment that owes its success to experiments with animal subjects.

The dispute between the scientists and the animal-rights group at Silver Spring is not an isolated incident but part of a much larger controversy regarding the experimental use of animals by humans. On one side are people who approve of such use of animals; on the other side are people who disapprove, in varying degrees. The debate centers on issues of law, morals, custom, and biology.

Because researchers in many branches of science experiment with animals to understand the functions of the body, the brain, and behavior, the issues in this debate are important to them. Because many people benefit from this research, including those who have diseases of the nervous system or nervous system damage, this debate is important to them. And, because you, as a student, encounter many experiments on animals in this book, these issues are important to you as well.

We first consider the terminology relevant to the debate on animal research. Next, we examine the arguments for and against the use of animals in experimental research. We then consider the legal and administrative rules used by scientific organizations and government bodies to regulate academic research and to guide commercial experimentation and the treatment of laboratory animals.

FRAMING THE ANIMAL RESEARCH CONTROVERSY

Inasmuch as this debate centers on animals, let us begin by determining which organisms we consider to be animals. As stated in Chapter 1, the biological definition of an animal includes approximately 1 million species belonging to the 15 phyla of the animal kingdom. When we speak of animal rights, however, we are far more likely to think of mammals such as monkeys, dogs, cats, and mice than of fruit flies, flatworms, and jellyfish.

Thus, we can already glimpse the complexity of defining the issue: when it comes to animal rights, people have widely divergent views on what they mean by an animal and, by implication, which of the 1 million species of animals should be accorded "rights." As we will see later, scientific organizations and government bodies have focused on higher vertebrates as "animals" for purposes of establishing regulations for their use in research.

Narrowly defining the many groups who have an interest in animal welfare is equally difficult. Humane societies are interested in the welfare of pets. The number of pets abandoned or destroyed each year in North America roughly equals the number of animals used for research. Many groups promote the sterilization of pets, rescue abandoned pets, and promote educational programs to improve the welfare of pets.

Other groups are interested in the welfare of all animals—pets, wild animals, and animals used for agriculture and research. These groups promote the welfare of animals through conservation, promote education for those who use animals, and support laws that offer protection to animals from excessive exploitation and abuse. Other groups are antivivisectionists, who oppose the use of animals in research. Still others, "animal rights" groups, oppose the use of animals by humans for some or all purposes.

That brings us directly to how we define the "use" of animals. Humans make use of animals in many ways quite apart from scientific experiments. Since prehistoric times, we have hunted animals for food, domesticated them as workers and companions, and raised them not only for meat but also for milk, eggs, clothing, and shelter.

Dogs were first domesticated more than 12,000 years ago, and people have bred them ever since for work and for show. Dogs are valued today for their skills, in herding, search and rescue, drug detection, and homeland security; for assisting the blind and deaf, wheelchair bound, and those prone to epileptic seizures; for their aid in research on diagnosing certain diseases; and for their unconditional love as our pets. Some groups oppose some of these uses or even any uses of dogs by humans.

In societies that use animals for food, there are widely divergent practices. In some societies, people eat dogs; in other societies, people eat pigs; and, in still others, they eat horses. Animal activists and others may oppose hunting, protest the treatment of animals by the commercial agriculture industry, or advocate a vegetarian diet. Clearly, attitudes toward the use of animals are widely divergent between cultures and even within a single culture.

Most of us would agree that animals should not be subjected to "needless pain and suffering," but what do we mean by that phrase? Psychologists have argued that pain and suffering are subjective experiences. Because humans have language, we can to some extent describe to one another our experiences. We can surmise on the basis of similar neuroanatomy and outward appearances that other mammals' experiences might be similar to our own, but we cannot know what they are actually feeling.

As you can see from this brief attempt to define the basic arguments in the animal-rights debate, the points of view are far ranging and diverse and the conclusions—including precise definitions of terms—very sparse. We would do well to acknowledge at this point that considering the contrasting viewpoints on the animal research controversy will yield no simple right or wrong answer.

ARGUMENTS THAT FAVOR THE USE OF ANIMALS IN RESEARCH

If paleolithic cave paintings are any indication, humans have always observed and studied animals. Some of the oldest surviving scientific texts were written about animal behavior. The only Nobel Prize ever given for the study of behavior was awarded jointly to three scientists for their studies on animal behavior.

Recall from Chapter 1 that Descartes made important contributions to the understanding of anatomy and physiology by dissecting animals. When we consider the in-

If you would like additional information about this Nobel Prize winning study of animal behavior, visit the Web site of the Nobel Foundation at **http://nobelprize.org/medicine/ laureates/1973/presentation-speech. html**.

formation contained in this book, we see that the scientific community has acquired much of its knowledge about the nervous system and its relation to behavior through observing, studying, and performing experiments on animals. Generations of students have learned basic biology by dissecting frogs and administering injections to hatchlings. Most of the treatments for both human and animal diseases originated in studies with animals.

People are also interested in the marvelous abilities of animals. We are amazed at the complexity of the songs of birds and whales, the navigational capabilities of migratory geese and butterflies, and the accuracy of dogs in identifying a scent. We humans were mystified that birds can fly and that bats use echolocation until we were able to understand the principles underlying these behaviors and to reproduce them mechanically for our own use. Divers and shipbuilders continue to be astonished that sperm whales can dive to depths in the ocean that would crush a submarine.

People have a wide spectrum of reasons for studying animals. The arguments in favor of conducting research with animals can be classified among three general benefits: health, insight, and the progress of science.

Argument 1. The Health and Well-being of Animals and Humans

The benefits to humans of animal research are well documented. Indeed, in a 1988 paper, the American Medical Association (AMA) asserted that research using animals is essential for medical advances. The publication provides a long list of diseases for which there are treatments, from the treatment of rabies and anthrax in the 1800s to the development of monoclonal antibodies for cancer at the end of the twentieth century, as examples of the benefits of animal experimentation. The AMA also points out that more that 7 of every 10 Nobel Prizes in medicine have been awarded for discoveries and advances made through the use of experimental animals in research.

Looking toward the future, the report states that biomedical research using animals is essential to continued progress in clinical medicine. Progress on AIDS, heart disease, aging, and congenital defects depends to a great extent on animal research. The AMA's viewpoint is shared by a host of patient groups, including those that advocate for sufferers of Parkinson's disease, Huntington's chorea, multiple sclerosis, Alzheimer's disease, spinal-cord injury, heart disease, and stroke (Feeney, 1987).

Humans also benefit from animal research in many nonmedical ways. Farmers, fishermen, and aboriginal groups who have a hunter-gatherer life style depend on thriving animal populations for their livelihoods. In the past century, people, governments, and other organizations have become increasingly aware of the economic and ecological value of wildlife as well as of domestic animals and have invested in projects designed to preserve animals and their habitats.

On an individual level, people who enjoy the company of animals, use them for work, or raise them for food have a keen interest in seeing that their animals are healthy. Insofar as all of us eat, each of us has a vital interest in the quality of the food supply and the integrity of the food chain. To attain and maintain these goals requires that humans understand the biology and behavior of animals.

Less obvious, perhaps, are the benefits that animals themselves derive from being studied by humans. Biologists in general and behavioral neuroscientists in particular seek to understand the functions of the body and the brain, as well as behavior. These findings are no less applicable to animals than to humans.

Because our lives are connected to the lives of animals in so many ways, the more that we humans learn about animal behavior, physiology, genetics, health, and disease, the better we are able to care for them. As already noted, animal research in the 1800s led to the discovery of cures for rabies and anthrax. As you may be aware, these diseases are devastating to animals as well as humans.

In 1999, a mosquito-borne organism called the West Nile virus was identified as the cause of death of a number of birds in the New York City area. Although public concern centered on the health risks to humans and the spread of the virus, measures to control it continue to benefit birds and other animals susceptible to the disease. Horses, for example, are prone to die from West Nile virus and are now innoculated.

Domestication and captivity convey broader benefits to animals. Biologists believe that, if not for its domestication, which began in Asia about 12,000 years ago, the horse might be an extinct species today. Selective breeding has made today's horses, dogs, cattle, and other animals healthier than their ancestors were. Domestication also allows many animals to receive good vetenairy care, enabling them to live much longer than they would under feral conditions.

The world's major zoos, in addition to providing opportunities for the public to observe and learn about animals, are dedicated to developing the best possible habitat, diet, and health care for the animals in their charge. Zoo care has enabled a number of endangered species to survive and even to increase their numbers. Animal research in zoos and laboratories has enabled farmers and pet owners to improve the food that they give to their animals and to give their animals advanced veterinary care.

> ⊙ For the latest information on the facilities, laboratories, research, and programs at the Smithsonian National Zoological Park, visit their Web site at **http://nationalzoo.si.edu/ ConservationAndScience**.

Argument 2. Insights into the Evolution of the Human Body

As described in Chapter 1, all animals, including humans, descend from a common founding ancestor. The study of the anatomy, physiology, genetics, ecology, and behavior of various animals provides the primary information about how natural selection occurs and how we humans evolved. A number of branches of science including biology, genetics, psychology, neuroscience, sociology, and anthropology have a primary interest in the evolution of animals and their physical and behavioral traits. The theory of natural selection, which states that humans descended from an animal lineage through an evolutionary process, is one of the most important unifying theories in all science.

Allied to the study of evolution is the study of the development of behavior. Extremely interesting questions can be answered by combining the two. For example, because development in some respects recapitulates evolution, the study of the development of the brain and behavior can be a source of insight into the neural organization of behavior. In addition, some animals are extremely precocious when born, whereas the maturation of other animals is greatly delayed. The study of rates of maturation can be a source of insight into evolutionary processes that influence brain development and behavior.

Argument 3. Restricted Experimentation on Humans

The study of animals is especially important to branches of medical science that deal with genetic bases of disease, including neuroscience and psychology. Animals that have large numbers of offspring, have short reproductive cycles, and are inexpensive to maintain are useful for genetic experiments. In fact, many animals used for research are small and can be housed in laboratories at a reasonable cost.

In regard to ethics—which is where the animal-rights debate is centered—the use of humans for certain experiments that can provide answers to important research questions is widely considered to be morally unacceptable. As mentioned in Chapter 1, in past centuries, experiments on humans, especially the retarded or mentally ill, were justified on the grounds that impaired persons were unable to feel pain in the way that "normal" people do.

Throughout the twentieth century, people throughout the world became increasingly intolerant of this justification, and the scientific community developed a stringent code of ethics for experiments on human subjects requiring, among other things, informed consent. Thus, most of today's experiments that are performed on animals cannot be performed on humans and would not otherwise be possible.

Scientists interested in brain function and behavior are especially dependent on animals for such information. Perhaps the earliest study that illustrates the dependence of humans on animals for insights into the function of the nervous system was that performed by François Magendie (Finger, 1994). In 1807, Scottish anatomist Charles Bell described the dorsal and ventral roots of the spinal cord. He proposed that the dorsal roots subserve motor functions and the ventral roots subserve sensory functions.

In adult humans, the roots are fused, making it difficult to conclude anything about their function from studying, say, human spinal-cord-injury victims. However, in 1821, Magendie observed that, in puppies, the dorsal and ventral roots are separate. He was able to selectively cut the roots and determine, contrary to Bell's hypothesis, that the dorsal roots are sensory and the ventral roots are motor.

Magendie's discovery of the "law of the spinal roots" has been described as the most important discovery in clinical neurology. We list it as Principle 2 in Chapter 2 and the Epilogue: Sensory and motor functions throughout the nervous system are separated. The Bell and Magendie law allows neurologists to precisely locate an injury to the spinal cord from the symptoms presented by the patient. It also led investigators to search for other locations in the nervous system where sensory and motor functions are separated.

Many other types of experiments must be performed on animals or not at all. Behavioral neuroscientists cannot damage a part of the human brain as part of a study to determine what that area of the brain does. They cannot implant electrodes into the cells of a human brain to study how those cells mediate perceptual, motor, or cognitive functions.

Scientists cannot experiment on humans with most new treatments for diseases. Before they are tested in humans in clinical trials, drugs must first be tested on animals in preclinical trials. Scientists cannot use humans to explore many potential cures for the 2000 known genetic diseases that affect the nervous system or explore cures for such common conditions as anxiety disorders, schizophrenia, Alzheimer's disease, and the behavioral disorders that are secondary to diseases such as AIDS.

◉ To learn more about the life and work of François Magendie, as well as the Bell and Magendie law, visit the following Web sites at **www.whonamedit. com/doctor.cfm/2104.html** and **www.whonamedit.com/synd. cfm/2383.html**

◉ Learn more about preclinical trials and the drug approval process at **www. wyeth.com/education/approval.asp**.

ARGUMENTS AGAINST THE USE OF ANIMALS IN RESEARCH

For as long as animals have been used for scientific study, people have voiced concern about such use and their opposition to it. The American Society for the Prevention of Cruelty to Animals (ASPCA), founded in New York City in 1866, was the first organization in North America with the goal of protecting animals from abuse. Today, however, the ASPCA focuses on rescuing stray animals and does not take an official stand on the question of their use in research.

In the early part of the twentieth century, a movement arose against vivisection—performing surgical operations on living animals to study living organs or the effects of diseases. The Humane Society of the United States, founded in 1954, supports legal sanctions against animal cruelty and worked to pass the Laboratory Animal Welfare Act in 1966. More recently, it established a program of humane alternatives to animal dissection in schools and a goal of eliminating animal pain and distress in laboratories by 2020 (Humane Society of the United States, 2000).

PETA, founded in 1980, seeks to ban the use of animals for food, clothing, entertainment, and research. Since the Silver Spring lawsuit described in the Focus on Comparative Biology at the beginning of this appendix, PETA has engaged in many undercover investigations, lobbying efforts, and court cases to stop uses of animals that violate its views. Many other groups and individual persons also oppose animal use, for widely different reasons and to widely different degrees. This broad variation notwithstanding, the reasons for opposing animal research can be classified as either scientific or philosophical.

○ For more information about the ASPCA, the Human Society, or PETA, you can visit their Web sites at **www.aspca.org**, **www.hsus.org**, or **www.peta.org**.

The Scientific Arguments

Scientific arguments against the use of animals in research reject the contention that animal research yields improvements for humans. Some proponents of this argument claim that animals are too different from humans to provide useful biological information about human diseases. Others observe that widespread improvements in human health and longevity have been brought about by improvements in public hygiene and changes in diet and life style rather than by research using animals.

Some also point out that, despite the number of experiments conducted by scientists, many diseases remain uncured. Ingrid Newkirk, cofounder (with Alex Pacheco) and president of PETA, said on the *Today* show in 1985: "If [animal experimentation] were such a valuable way to gain knowledge, we should have eternal life by now." Her view fails to recognize the complexity of the disease conditions from which humans and other animals can suffer.

Harold A. Herzog, Jr., compiled the views of animal-rights activists. Among the statements that he collected, the following quotation and others similar to it have been widely used in the animal-rights literature and in arguments made by animal-rights activists.

> I can't find any substantial data to indicate that anything has been discovered from animals that could not have been gathered from some other source. Thalidomide was a drug that was found to be safe on experimental animals and given to the human population. It was a total disaster. They say that vaccines were discovered from animal research. But the Chinese had vaccines before the time of Christ, and they were not found from animal research. They were discovered from actual clinical trials and human patients (Herzog, 1993).

There is abundant data indicating that animal research has led to new discoveries. And, despite the many thousands of studies performed each year with new drugs, the occurrence of tragedies such as the deformities caused by thalidomide is not surprising. No human enterprise, including science, can guarantee that there will be no errors or oversights.

Herzog also reported that some activists took a blame-the-victim stance toward persons suffering from chronic diseases, particularly illnesses associated with life style and diet. Opponents of experimentation on animals frequently told him that, if people would simply give up eating meat, diseases such as cancer and heart disease would disappear.

Bioethicist Michael W. Fox takes the view that scientific advances create problems of their own for animals and people alike. In a book focusing on genetic engineering (M. W. Fox, 1999), he condemns as unethical and unnecessary such advances as cloning, pigs bioengineered to produce human hemoglobin, and transgenic plants that secrete their own insecticides. In Fox's view, all life on Earth will eventually suffer from "genetic pollution" as genetically altered animals, plants and other organisms spread their engineered genes throughout the environment.

The Philosophical Arguments

Two of the several philosophical arguments made against the use of animals in research are the utilitarian argument and the life argument. Both conclude that all use of animals should end.

UTILITARIAN PHILOSOPHY

Perhaps the most widely publicized argument against the use of animals is that made by Peter Singer, a professor of philosophy at Princeton University (Singer, 1990). Singer holds that, because animals have in common with humans the capacity to experience pain and suffering, they are worthy of the same degree of moral consideration that is proposed to be granted to humans. Singer follows the utilitarian philosophy that ethical decisions should be made by adding up all the pleasures and pains that would result from different choices and choosing the option that yields the greatest aggregate pleasure and the least pain.

The pleasures and pains of nonhuman animals must be included in this tally, Singer argues. If they were, people would become vegetarians and otherwise adopt a life style that avoids the use of animals in the service of human purposes. Singer also coined the term *speciesism* to describe a prejudice or attitude of bias in favor of the interests of members of one's own species and against those of members of other species. Thus, Singer argues that, just as one should not be racist or sexist, one should not be speciesist.

○ For the latest information and articles from Peter Singer, visit his Web site at **http://utilitarian.net/singer**.

THE LIFE ARGUMENT

Tom Regan, a professor of philosophy at North Carolina State University, also advocates a vegetarian life style but rejects the utilitarian philosophy (Regan, 1996). Regan argues that there are many ways to sum up pain and pleasure, and one of these ways might include support for the use of animals by humans. For example, most animals used for scientific research do not suffer any pain, and on average a person will suffer approximately 10 years of discomfort and pain in a lifetime.

Regan argues that, by virtue of being alive, animals possess inherent value equal to that of humans. Their lives are equal in importance to ours. Thus, one species (humans) does not have the right to end the lives of the other species (animals) for any purpose, including research or food.

Bioethicist Michael A. Fox also supports vegetarianism (M. A. Fox, 1999). He postulates that, if animal experimentation were to stop, the human species would doubtless continue to exist just as it did before such experimentation began, albeit with a diminished life span and quality of life.

○ To visit the Tom Regan Animal Rights Archive, go to **www.lib.ncsu.edu/ arights**. Clicking the link to "Manuscript Holdings," will give you access to the Tom Regan Collection which includes his personal papers as well as books documenting his role in the animal rights movement.

EVALUATING THE ARGUMENTS AGAINST ANIMAL USE

One might ask about the results of carrying these arguments to their logical extremes. Doing so would require not only universal vegetarianism but also allowing animals to "live free" and not killing them or harming them under any circumstances. We might conclude that, if this were to happen, there would quickly be chaos.

Consider this: Anthropologists have found that humans have always used animals for food. What changes in human societies does an adherence to the rights philosophy forecast? On the economic front, many industries would shut down, and many areas of biological research would cease to acquire new knowledge. Domesticated animals would require vegetarian feed. Wild and feral animals, from gophers to elephants, would invade and consume crops planted by humans. Mice, cockroaches, ants, and other creatures would overrun human homes.

Some animal activists have even argued that humans should take responsibility for regulating the conduct of animals in nature, supplying food for predators so that they have no need to kill and eat prey. Because most animals are prey to some animals and predators to other animals, this argument would require regulating and feeding every animal on Earth. Given the difficulties that humans have in preserving at-risk species, regulating the behavior of every animal species would be impossible. One might also ask whether this animal-rights position would require that knowledge gained through animal experimentation should no longer be used.

LEGISLATION AND PROFESSIONAL GUIDELINES FOR THE USE OF ANIMALS IN RESEARCH

Just as the scientific community has established ethical standards for research on human subjects, it has also developed regulations governing experimentation on animals. The governments of most industrialized nations have legislation regulating the use of animals in research; most states and provinces have additional legislation. Universities and other organizations engaged in research also have rules governing animal use. Finally, professional societies to which scientists belong and journals in which scientists publish have rules governing animal use.

For example, in Canada, 20 organizations interested in the care and use of research animals have formed the Canadian Council on Animal Care (see accompanying table). The Council is dedicated to enhanced animal care and use through education, voluntary compliance, and codes of ethics. It is organized so that it can flexibly respond to the concerns of both the scientific community and the general public through rapid and frequent amendments to its guidelines.

The Canadian Council endorses four principles as guidelines for reviewing protocols for experiments that will use animals:

1. That the use of animals in research, teaching, and testing is acceptable only if it promises to contribute to the understanding of environmental principles or issues, fundamental biological principles, or development of knowledge that can reasonably be expected to benefit humans, animals, or the environment.
2. That optimal standards for animal health and care result in enhanced credibility and reproducibility of experimental results.
3. That acceptance of animal use in science critically depends on maintaining public confidence in the mechanisms and processes used to ensure necessary, humane, and justified animal use.
4. That animals should be used only if the researcher's best efforts to find an alternative have failed. Those using animals should employ the most humane methods on the smallest number of appropriate animals required to obtain valid information.

Legislation concerning the care and use of laboratory animals in the United States is set forth in the Animal Welfare Act, which includes laws passed by Congress in 1966, 1970, 1976, and 1985. Legislation in other countries is similar and in some cases

○ For additional information on the Canadian Council on Animal Care, visit **www.ccac.ca**.

○ To learn more about how the United States has legislated the care and use of laboratory animals, read the full text of the Laboratory Animal Welfare Act at this Web page from the United States Department of Agriculture and the National Agricultural Library **www.nal.usda.gov/awic/ legislat/usdaleg1.htm**. You can also visit Web sites for the Animal and Plant Health Inspection Service at **www. aphis.usda.gov/ac** and the Office of Human Research Protections at **www. hhs.gov/ohrp**. To read the full text of *The Guide for the Care and Use of Laboratory Animals* go to **www.nap.edu/reading room/books/labrats**.

more strict. The U.S. Act covers mammals, including rats, mice, and birds, but excludes farm animals that are not used in research. It is administered by the U.S. Department of Agriculture through inspectors in the Animal and Plant Health Inspection Service, Animal Care.

In addition, the Health Research Extension Act (passed in 1986) covers all animal uses conducted or supported by the U.S. Public Health Service and applies to any live vertebrate animal used in research, training, or testing. The Office of Human Research Protections of the National Institutes of Health administers this Act. It requires that each institution provide acceptable assurance that it meets all minimum regulations and conforms with *The Guide for the Care and Use of Laboratory Animals* (National Research Council, 1996) before conducting any activity that includes animals. The typical method for demonstrating conformance with the *Guide* is to seek voluntary accreditation from the Association for Assessment and Accreditation of Laboratory Animal Care International.

All U.S. universities that are accredited and receive government grant support are required to provide adequate treatment for all vertebrates. Reviews and specific protocols for fish, reptiles, mice, dogs, or monkeys to be used in research, teaching, or testing are administered through the same process. Anyone using animals in a U.S. university submits a protocol to that university's institutional Animal Care and Use Committee, composed of researchers, veterinarians, persons who have some knowledge of science, as well as laypersons from the university and the community.

Companies that use animals for research are not required to follow this process. In effect, however, if they do not, they will be unable to publish the results of their research, because research journals require that research conforms with national guidlines on animal care. In addition, discoveries made with the use of animals would not be recognized by goverment agencies that approve drugs for clinical trials with humans. Companies therefore use standards described as Good Laboratory Practice (GPL) that are as rigorous as those used by government agencies.

U.S. regulations specify that researchers consider alternatives to procedures that may cause more than momentary or slight pain or distress to animals. Most of the attention on alternatives has focused on the use of animals in testing and stems from high public awareness of some tests for pharmacological compounds, especially toxic compounds. The testing of such compounds is now regulated by the National Institute of Environmental Health Sciences.

Membership in the Canadian Council on Animal Care, a Society Dedicated to Enhanced Animal Care and Use Through Education, Voluntary Compliance, and Codes of Ethics

Agriculture Canada

Association of Canadian Faculties of Dentistry

Association of Canadian Medical Colleges

Association of Universities and Colleges of Canada

Canadian Association for Laboratory Animal Medicine

Canadian Association for Laboratory Animal Science

Canadian Federation of Humane Societies

Canadian Institute for Health Research

Canadian Society of Zoologists

Committee of Chairpersons for Departments of Psychology

Confederation of Canadian Faculties of Agriculture and Veterinary Medicine

Department of National Defense

Environment Canada

Fisheries and Oceans Canada

Health and Welfare Canada

Heart and Stroke Foundation of Canada

National Cancer Institute

National Research Council

Natural Sciences and Engineering Research Council

Canada's Research-Based Pharmaceutical Companies (Rx&D)

◉ For a wealth of information regarding Good Laboratory Practice (GPL), go to **http://pharmacos.eudra.org/F2/ eudralex/vol-7/A/7AG4a.pdf** (PDF format).

POLICIES OF PROFESSIONAL SOCIETIES ON THE USE OF ANIMALS IN RESEARCH

To comply with and reinforce the standards mandated by government bodies, scientific societies, too, have established procedures and policies for ensuring the proper handling of research animals. Most of these organizations hold annual meetings for members so that they may discuss their research findings. Many societies also publish journals that facilitate the dissemination of research results.

Both presentations and publication are important to scientists and hence provide means for administering such procedures and policies. Universities and agencies that employ scientists use presentations and publications as evidence of productivity. Granting agencies and councils use evidence of productivity to decide whether to fund a scientist's research. Thus, scientists must conform to the procedures and policies to conduct and publish their research.

The Society for Neuroscience is one of the largest professional organizations in the world, with almost 40,000 members from many scientific disciplines and many different countries. Presentation at Society meetings and publication in the Society's *Journal of Neuroscience* are governed by its "Policy on the Use of Animals in Neuroscience Research." The Policy requires that research be performed in compliance with the Health Research Extension Act and *The Guide for the Care and Use of Laboratory Animals.* The Society also requires a local committee review of the research that conforms to the following guidelines:

> An important element of the Society Policy is the establishment of a local committee that is charged with reviewing and approving all proposed animal care and use procedures. In addition to scientists experienced in research involving animals and a veterinarian, the membership of this local committee should include an individual who is not affiliated with the member's institution in any other way. In reviewing a proposed use of animals, the committee should evaluate the adequacy of institutional policies, animal husbandry, veterinary care, and the physical plant. Specific attention should be paid to proposed procedures for animal procurement, quarantine and stabilization, separation by species, disease diagnosis and treatment, anesthesia and analgesia, surgery and postsurgical care, and euthanasia. The review committee also should ensure that procedures involving live vertebrate animals are designed and performed with due consideration of their relevance to human or animal health, the advancement of knowledge, or the good of society. This review and approval of a member's use of live vertebrate animals in research by a local committee is an essential component of the Society Policy. (Society for Neuroscience Policies on the Use of Animals and Human Subjects in Neuroscience Research)

From the regulations and laws described in this section, we can see that research in which animal subjects are used is not undertaken without serious consideration for the proper care and handling of the animals.

THE FUTURE OF RESEARCH WITH ANIMALS

Attitudes and policies concerning the use of animals in all domains undergo constant revision. There was a time when virtually all people gave little consideration to the loss of species through extinction, to how domestic animals were housed, or to how scientific experiments were conducted.

There have been changes in all these areas, and many of the changes now carry the force of law. These changes have been stimulated in large part by improvements in our knowledge of animals, our world, and ourselves. It is also important to note that research on animals is self-limiting: when an answer to a problem has been obtained, the experiment need not be redone, which is not to say that the use of animals in research will quickly end. As noted elsewhere in this book, in the light of research progress, the brain appears to be more complex than has been thought.

○ You can visit the Web site for the Society for Neuroscience at **www.sfn.org** and browse their online journal at **www.jneurosci.org**.

Still, the use of animals in research raises important questions. The debate between groups who support the use of animals in research and groups who oppose their use is often heated and strident. In a 1992 article, Martin L. Stephens, Humane Society Vice President for Laboratory Animals, argued that it does not need to be so.

In his view, the debate has a substantial middle ground, bordered on one side by scientists who are proponents of experimentation and who see no room for improvement in the treatment of laboratory animals and on the other by detractors who see all animal researchers as sadists. In the middle are a great many responsible and reasonable people who, to varying degrees, are willing to work for some reforms and to recognize the value of some animal research.

In his book titled *The Origins of Virtue* (1997), Matt Ridley argued that questions that are posed as moral dilemmas can also be posed as biological ones. As a biological question, the use of animals in scientific research can be addressed as a question of the exploitation by one species (humans) of other species in much the same way that exploitation by nonhuman species of each other can be studied. Presumably, just as human knowledge of other animals and ourselves improves, so too will there be continued improvements in the way in which humans interrelate with other animals.

Glossary

absolutely refractory. Refers to the state of an axon in the repolarizing period during which a new action potential cannot be elicited (with some exceptions), because gate 2 of sodium channels, which is not voltage-sensitive, is closed.

acetylcholine (ACh). The first neurotransmitter discovered in the peripheral and central nervous systems; activates skeletal muscles.

action potential. Large, brief, reversal in polarity of an axon.

activating system. Neural pathways that coordinate brain activity through a single neurotransmitter; cell bodies are located in a nucleus in the brainstem and axons are distributed through a wide region of the brain.

addiction. Desire for a drug manifested by frequent use of the drug, leading to the development of physical dependence in addition to abuse; often associated with tolerance and unpleasant, sometimes dangerous, withdrawal symptoms on cessation of drug use. Also called *substance dependence.*

afferent. Conducting toward a central nervous system structure.

agonist. Substance that enhances the function of a synapse.

akathesia. Small, involuntary movements or changes in posture; motor restlessness.

alcohol myopia. "Nearsighted" behavior displayed under the influence of alcohol: local and immediate cues become prominent, and remote cues and consequences are ignored.

allele. Alternate form of a gene; a gene pair contains two alleles.

alpha rhythm. Rhythmical EEG wave with a frequency of 11 cycles per second.

Alzheimer's disease. Degenerative brain disorder; first appears as progressive memory loss and later develops into generalized dementia.

amblyopia. A condition in which vision in one eye is reduced as a result of disuse; usually caused by a failure of the two eyes to point in the same direction.

amnesia. Partial or total loss of memory.

amphetamine. Drug that releases the neurotransmitter dopamine into its synapse and, like cocaine, blocks dopamine reuptake.

amplitude. Intensity of a stimulus; in audition, roughly equivalent to loudness, graphed by increasing the height of a sound wave.

amygdala. Almond-shaped collection of nuclei located within the limbic system; plays a role in emotional and species-typical behaviors.

androgen. Male hormone related to level of sexual interest.

anencephaly. Failure of the forebrain to develop.

anomalous speech representation. Condition in which a person's speech zones are located in the right hemisphere or in both hemispheres.

anorexia nervosa. Exaggerated concern with being overweight that leads to inadequate food intake and often excessive exercising; can lead to severe weight loss and even starvation.

antagonist. Substance that blocks the function of a synapse.

anterograde amnesia. Inability to remember events subsequent to a disturbance of the brain such as head trauma, electroconvulsive shock, or certain neurodegenerative diseases.

antianxiety agent. Drug that reduces anxiety; minor tranquillizers such as benzodiazepines and sedative-hypnotic agents are of this type.

aphagia. Failure to eat; may be due to an unwillingness to eat or to motor difficulties, especially with swallowing.

aphasia. Inability to speak or comprehend language despite the presence of normal comprehension and intact vocal mechanisms; *Broca's aphasia* is the inability to speak fluently despite the presence of normal comprehension and intact vocal mechanisms; *Wernicke's aphasia* is the inability to understand or to produce meaningful language even though the production of words is still intact.

apoptosis. Cell death that is genetically programmed.

apraxia. Inability to make voluntary movements in the absence of paralysis or other motor or sensory impairment, especially an inability to make proper use of an object.

association cortex. Neocortex outside the primary sensory and motor cortices that functions to produce cognition.

associative learning. Linkage of two or more unrelated stimuli to elicit a behavioral response.

astrocyte. Glial cell with a star-shaped appearance that provides structural support to neurons in the central nervous system and transports substances between neurons and capillaries.

atonia. No tone; condition of complete muscle inactivity produced by the inhibition of motor neurons.

attention. Selective narrowing or focusing of awareness to part of the sensory environment or to a class of stimuli.

autism. Cognitive disorder with severe symptoms including greatly impaired social interaction, a bizarre and narrow range of interests, marked abnormalities in language and communication, and fixed, repetitive movements.

autoimmune disease. Illness resulting from the immune system's loss of the ability to discrimininate between foreign pathogens in the body and the body itself.

automatism. Unconscious, repetitive, stereotyped movement characteristic of seizure.

autonomic nervous system (ANS). Part of the PNS that regulates the functioning of internal organs and glands.

autoreceptor. "Self-receptor" in a neural membrane that responds to the transmitter that neuron releases.

axon collateral. Branch of an axon.

axon hillock. Juncture of soma and axon where the action potential begins.

axon. "Root," or single fiber, of a neuron that carries messages to other neurons.

barbiturate. Drug that produces sedation and sleep.

basal ganglia. Group of nuclei in the forebrain that coordinates voluntary movements of the limbs and the body; located just beneath the neocortex and connected to the thalamus and to the midbrain.

basic rest–activity cycle (BRAC). Recurring cycle of temporal packets, about 90-min periods in humans, during which an animal's level of arousal waxes and wanes.

basilar membrane. Receptor surface in the cochlea that transduces sound waves into neural activity.

behavioral therapy. Treatment that applies learning principles, such as conditioning, to eliminate unwanted behaviors.

beta rhythm. Fast brain-wave activity pattern associated with a waking EEG.

bilateral symmetry. Body plan in which organs or parts present on both sides of the body are mirror images in appearance. For example, the hands are bilaterally symmetrical, whereas the heart is not.

binding problem. A theoretical problem with the integration of sensory information. Because a single sensory event is analyzed by multiple parallel channels that do not converge on a single region, there is said to be a problem in binding together the segregated analyses into a single sensory experience.

biological clock. Neural system that times behavior.

biorhythm. Inherent rhythm that controls or initiates various biological processes.

bipolar disorder. Mood disorder characterized by alternating periods of depression and mania.

bipolar neuron. Neuron with one axon and one dendrite.

blind spot. Region of the retina where axons forming the optic nerve leave the eye and where blood vessels enter and leave; this region has no photoreceptors and is thus "blind."

blob. Region in the visual cortex that contains color-sensitive neurons, as revealed by staining for cytochrome oxidase.

brainstem. Central structures of the brain including the hindbrain, midbrain, thalamus, and hypothalamus.

Broca's area. Anterior speech area in the left hemisphere that functions with the motor cortex to produce the movements needed for speaking.

carbon monoxide (CO). Acts as a neurotransmitter gas in the activation of cellular metabolism.

cataplexy. Form of narcolepsy linked to strong emotional stimulation in which an animal loses all muscle activity or tone, as if in REM sleep, while awake.

catatonic posture. Rigid or frozen pose resulting from a psychomotor disturbance.

cell assembly. Hypothetical group of neurons that become functionally connected because they receive the same sensory inputs. Hebb proposed that cell assemblies were the basis of perception, memory, and thought.

cell body (soma). Core region of the cell containing the nucleus and other organelles for making proteins.

cell-adhesion molecule (CAM). A chemical to which specific cells can adhere, thus aiding in migration.

central nervous system (CNS). The brain and spinal cord.

cerebellum. Major structure of the hindbrain specialized for motor coordination. In large-brained animals, it may also have a role in the coordination of other mental processes.

cerebral cortex. Outer layer of brain-tissue surface composed of neurons; the human cerebral cortex contains many folds.

cerebral palsy. Group of brain disorders that result from brain damage acquired perinatally.

cerebrospinal fluid (CSF). Clear solution of sodium chloride and other salts that fills the ventricles inside the brain and circulates around the brain and spinal cord beneath the arachnoid layer in the subarachnoid space.

cerebrum. Major structure of the forebrain, consisting of two virtually identical hemispheres (left and right).

channel. Opening in a protein embedded in the cell membrane that allows the passage of ions.

chemical synapse. Junction where messenger molecules are released when stimulated by an action potential.

chemoaffinity hypothesis. Proposal that neurons or their axons and dendrites are drawn toward a signaling chemical that indicates the correct pathway.

cholinergic neuron. Neuron that uses acetylcholine as its main neurotransmitter.

chordates. Group of animals that have both a brain and a spinal cord.

circadian rhythm. Day–night rhythm.

cladogram. Phylogenetic tree that branches repeatedly, suggesting a classification of organisms based on the time sequence in which evolutionary branches arise.

cochlea. Inner-ear structure that contains the auditory receptor cells.

cochlear implant. Electronic device implanted surgically into the inner ear to transduce sound waves into neural activity and allow deaf people to hear.

cognition. Act or process of knowing or coming to know; in psychology, used to refer to the processes of thought.

cognitive neuroscience. Study of the neural basis of cognition.

cognitive therapy. Psychotherapy based on the perspective that thoughts intervene between events and emotions, and thus the treatment of emotional disorders requires changing maladaptive patterns of thinking.

cognitive-behavior therapy (CBT) Treatment that challenges the reality of patients' obsessions and the behavioral necessity for their compulsions.

color constancy. Phenomenon whereby the perceived color of an object tends to remain constant relative to other colors, regardless of changes in illumination.

coma. Prolonged state of deep unconsciousness resembling sleep.

common ancestor. Forebear from which two or more lineages or family groups arise and so is ancestral to both groups.

concentration gradient. Differences in concentration of a substance among regions of a container that allows the substance to diffuse from an area of higher concentration to an area of lower concentration.

conditioned response (CR). In Pavlovian conditioning, the learned response to a formerly neutral conditioned stimulus (CS).

conditioned stimulus (CS). In Pavlovian conditioning, an originally neutral stimulus that, after association with an unconditioned stimulus (UCS), triggers a conditioned response.

cone. Photoreceptor specialized for color and high visual acuity.

consciousness. Level of responsiveness of the mind to impressions made by the senses.

contralateral neglect. Ignoring a part of the body or world on the side opposite (i.e., contralateral) that of a brain injury.

convergent thinking. Form of thinking that searches for a single answer to a question (such as $2 + 2 = ?$); contrasts with divergent thinking.

corpus callosum. Fiber system connecting the two cerebral hemispheres.

cortical column. Cortical organization that represents a functional unit six cortical layers deep and approximately 0.5 mm square and that is perpendicular to the cortical surface.

corticospinal tract. Bundle of nerve fibers directly connecting the cerebral cortex to the spinal cord, branching at the brainstem into a same-side lateral tract that informs movement of limbs and digits and an opposite-side ventral tract that informs movement of the trunk; also called pyramidal tract.

cranial nerve. One of a set of 12 nerve pairs that control sensory and motor functions of the head, neck, and internal organs.

critical period. Developmental "window" during which some event has a long-lasting influence on the brain; often referred to as a *sensitive period.*

cross-tolerance. Response to a novel drug is reduced because of tolerance developed in response to a related drug.

culture. Learned behaviors that are passed on from one generation to the next through teaching and learning.

current. The flow of electrons from a region of higher negative charge to a region of lower negative charge; the flow of various ions across the neuron membrane.

cytoarchitectonic map. Map of the neocortex based on the organization, structure, and distribution of the cells.

deafferentation. Loss of incoming sensory input usually due to damage to sensory fibers; also loss of any afferent input to a structure.

declarative memory. Ability to recount what one knows, to detail the time, place, and circumstances of events; often lost in amnesia.

deep brain stimulation (DBS). Neurosurgery to facilitate normal movements, in which an electrode is fixed in place in the globus pallidus or subthalamic nucleus and connected to an external electrical stimulator controlled by the patient.

delta rhythm. Slow brain-wave activity pattern associated with deep sleep.

dementia. Acquired and persistent syndrome of intellectual impairment characterized by memory and other cognitive deficits and impairment in social and occupational functioning.

dendrite. Branch of a neuron that consists of an extension of the cell membrane, thus greatly increasing the area of the cell.

dendritic spine. Protrusion from a dendrite that greatly increases its surface area and is the usual point of dendritic contact with axons.

depolarization. Decrease in electrical charge across a membrane, usually due to the inward flow of sodium ions.

dermatome. Area of the skin supplied with afferent nerve fibers by a single spinal-cord dorsal root.

diaschisis. Neural shock that follows brain damage in which areas connected to the site of damage show a temporary arrest of function.

dichotic listening. Experimental procedure for simultaneously presenting a different auditory input to each ear through stereophonic earphones.

diencephalon. The "between brain" that contains the hypothalamus, thalamus, and epithalamus; thought to coordinate many basic instinctual behaviors, including temperature regulation, sexual behavior, and eating.

diffusion. Movement of ions from an area of higher concentration to an area of lower concentration through random motion.

disinhibition theory. Explanation holding that alcohol has a selective depressant effect on the cortex, the region of the brain that controls judgment, while sparing subcortical structures responsible for more-primitive instincts, such as desire.

dissolution. Hypothetical condition whereby disease or damage in the highest levels of the nervous system would produce not just loss of function but a repertory of simpler behaviors as seen in animals that have not evolved that particular brain structure.

diurnal animal. Organism that is active chiefly during daylight.

divergent thinking. Form of thinking that searches for multiple solutions to a problem (such as, how many different ways can a pen be used?); contrasts with convergent thinking.

dopamine (DA). Amine neurotransmitter that plays a role in coordinating movement, in attention and learning, and in behaviors that are reinforcing.

dopamine hypothesis of schizophrenia. Proposal that schizophrenic symptoms are due to excess activity of the neurotransmitter dopamine.

dorsal spinothalamic tract. Pathway that carries fine-touch and pressure fibers.

Down's syndrome. Chromosomal abnormality resulting in mental retardation and other abnormalities, usually caused by an extra chromosome 21.

drive. Hypothetical state of arousal that motivates an organism to engage in a particular behavior.

drug-dependency insomnia. Condition resulting from continuous use of "sleeping pills"; drug tolerance also results in deprivation of either REM or NREM sleep,

leading the user to increase the drug dosage.

drug-induced behavioral sensitization. Escalating behavioral response to the repeated administration of a psychomotor stimulant such as amphetamine, cocaine, or nicotine; also called *behavioral sensitization.*

DSM-IV-TR. Text revision of the fourth, and most recent, edition of the American Psychiatric Association's classification of psychiatric disorders, the *Diagnostic and Statistical Manual of Mental Disorders.*

dualism. Philosophical position that holds that both a nonmaterial mind and the material body contribute to behavior.

echolocation. Ability to identify and locate an object by bouncing sound waves off the object.

efferent. Conducting away from a central nervous system structure.

electrical potential. An electrical charge; the ability to do work through the use of stored potential electrical energy.

electrical stimulation. Passing an electrical current from the tip of an electrode through tissue, resulting in changes in the electrical activity of the tissue.

electrical synapse. Fused presynaptic and postsynaptic membrane that allows an action potential to pass directly from one neuron to the next.

electricity. The flow of electrons.

electrode. An insulated wire or a saltwater-filled glass tube that is used to stimulate or record from neurons.

electroencephalogram (EEG). Graph that records electrical activity through the skull or from the brain and represents graded potentials of many neurons.

emotion. Cognitive interpretation of subjective feelings.

emotional memory. Memory for the affective properties of stimuli or events.

encephalization quotient (EQ). Jerison's measure of brain size obtained from the ratio of actual brain size to the expected brain size, according to the principle of proper mass, for an animal of a particular body size.

end foot. Knob at the tip of an axon that conveys information to other neurons; also called a terminal button.

end plate. On a muscle, the receptor–ion complex that is activated by the release of the neurotransmitter acetylcholine from the terminal of a motor neuron.

endorphin. Peptide hormone that acts as a neurotransmitter and may be associated with feelings of pain or pleasure; mimicked by opioid drugs such as morphine, heroin, opium, and codeine.

entorhinal cortex. Located on the medial surface of the temporal lobe; provides a major route for neocortical input to the hippocampal formation; often degenerates in Alzheimer's disease.

entrainment. Determination or modification of the period of a biorhythm.

ependymal cell. Glial cell that makes and secretes cerebral spinal fluid; found on the walls of the ventricles of the brain.

epidermal growth factor (EGF). Neurotrophic factor that stimulates the subventricular zone to generate cells that migrate into the striatum and eventually differentiate into neurons and glia.

epinephrine (EP, or adrenaline). Chemical messenger that acts as a hormone to mobilize the body for fight or flight during times of stress and as a neurotransmitter in the central nervous system.

episodic memory. Autobiographical memory for events pegged to specific place and time contexts.

event-related potential (ERP). Brief change in slow-wave brain activity in response to a sensory stimulus.

evolutionary psychology. Discipline that seeks to apply principles of natural selection to understand the causes of human behavior.

excitation. A process by which the activity of a neuron or brain area is increased.

excitatory postsynaptic potential (EPSP). Brief depolarization of a neuron membrane in response to stimulation, making the neuron more likely to produce an action potential.

explicit memory. Memory in which a subject can retrieve an item and indicate that he or she knows that the retrieved item is the correct item (i.e., conscious memory).

extinction. In neurology, neglect of information on one side of the body when it is presented simultaneously with similar information on the other side of the body.

extrastriate (secondary visual) cortex. Visual cortical areas outside the striate cortex.

eye-blink conditioning. Commonly used experimental technique in which subjects learn to pair a formerly neutral stimulus to a defensive blinking response.

fear conditioning. Learned association, a conditioned emotional response, between a neutral stimulus and a noxious event such as a shock.

festination. Tendency to engage in a behavior, such as walking, at faster and faster speeds.

fetal alcohol syndrome (FAS). Pattern of physical malformation and mental retardation observed in some children born of alcoholic mothers.

filopod. Process at the end of a developing axon that reaches out to search for a potential target or to sample the intercellular environment.

focal seizure. Category of seizure that begins locally (at a focus) and then spreads out to adjacent areas.

forebrain. Evolutionarily the newest part of the brain; coordinates advanced cognitive functions such as thinking, planning, and language; contains the limbic system, basal ganglia, and the neocortex.

fovea. Region at the center of the retina that is specialized for high acuity; its receptive fields are at the center of the eye's visual field.

free-running rhythm. Rhythm of the body's own devising in the absence of all external cues.

frequency. Number of cycles that a wave completes in a given amount of time.

frontal lobe. Cerebral cortex anterior to the central sulcus and beneath the frontal bone of the skull.

functional magnetic resonance imaging (fMRI). Type of magnetic resonance imaging that takes advantage of the fact that changes in the distribution of elements such as oxygen alter the magnetic properties of the brain. Because oxygen consumption varies with behavior, changes that are produced by behavior can be mapped and measured.

G proteins. Family of guanyl nucleotide–binding proteins coupled to metabotropic receptors that, when activated, bind to other proteins.

gamma-aminobutyric acid (GABA). Amino acid neurotransmitter that inhibits neurons.

ganglia. Collection of nerve cells that function somewhat like a brain.

gate. Protein embedded in a cell membrane that allows substances to pass through the membrane on some occasions but not on others.

generalized anxiety disorder. Persistently high levels of anxiety often accompanied by maladaptive behaviors to reduce anxiety; thought to be caused by chronic stress.

geniculostriate system. Projections from the retina to the lateral geniculate nucleus to the visual cortex.

glabrous skin. Skin that does not have hair follicles but contains larger numbers of sensory receptors than do other skin areas.

glial cell. Nervous system cell that provides insulation, nutrients, and support, as well as aiding in the repair of neurons.

glioblast. Product of a progenitor cell that gives rise to different types of glial cells.

glucocorticoid. One of a group of steroid hormones, such as cortisol, secreted in times of stress; important in protein and carbohydrate metabolism.

glutamate. Amino acid neurotransmitter that excites neurons.

gonadal (sex) hormone. One of a group of hormones, such as testosterone, that control reproductive functions and bestow sexual appearance and identity as male or female.

graded potential. Small voltage fluctuation in the cell membrane restricted to the vicinity on the axon where ion concentrations change to cause a brief increase (hyperpolarization) or decrease (depolarization) in electrical charge across the cell membrane.

grand mal seizure. Characterized by loss of consciousness and stereotyped motor activity.

gray matter. Areas of the nervous system composed predominantly of cell bodies and blood vessels.

growth cone. Growing tip of an axon.

growth spurt. Sproradic period of sudden growth that lasts for a finite time.

gyrus (pl. gyri). A groove in brain matter, usually a groove found in the neocortex or cerebellum.

habituation. Learning behavior in which a response to a stimulus weakens with repeated stimulus presentations.

hair cell. Sensory neurons in the cochlea tipped by cilia; when stimulated by waves in the cochlear fluid, outer hair cells generate graded potentials in inner hair cells, which act as the auditory receptor cells.

hapsis. Perceptual ability to discriminate objects on the basis of touch.

head-direction cell. A neuron in the hippocampus that discharges when an animal faces in a particular direction.

hemisphere. Literally, half a sphere, referring to one side of the cerebral cortex or one side of the cerebellum.

hertz (Hz). Measure of frequency (repetition rate) of a sound wave; one hertz is equal to one cycle per second.

heterozygous. Having two different alleles for the same trait.

hindbrain. Evolutionarily the oldest part of the brain; contains the pons, medulla, reticular formation, and cerebellum structures that coordinate and control most voluntary and involuntary movements.

hippocampus. Distinctive, three-layered subcortical structure of the limbic system lying in the medial region of the temporal lobe; plays a role in species-specific behaviors, memory, and spatial navigation and is vulnerable to the effects of stress.

homeobox gene cluster. A group of genes that specify the segmental organization of the nervous system of insects and vertebrates and so are thought to have arisen in a common ancestor to these lineages.

homeostasis. State of internal metabolic balance and regulation of physiological systems in an organism.

homeostatic mechanism. Process that maintains critical body functions within a narrow, fixed range.

hominid. General term referring to primates that walk upright, including all forms of humans, living and extinct.

homonymous hemianopia. Blindness of an entire left or right visual field.

homozygous. Having two identical alleles for a trait.

homunculus. Representation of the human body in the sensory or motor cortex; also any topographical representation of the body by a neural area.

HPA axis. Hypothalamic-pituitary-adrenal circuit that controls the production and release of hormones related to stress.

Huntington's chorea. Autosomal genetic disorder that results in motor and cognitive disturbances; caused by an increase in the number of CAG (cytosine-adenine-guanine) repeats on chromosome 4.

hydrocephalus. Buildup of pressure in the brain and, in infants, swelling of the head caused if the flow of CSF is blocked; can result in retardation.

hyperkinetic symptom. Symptom of brain damage that results in excessive involuntary movements, as seen in Tourette's syndrome.

hyperphagia. Disorder in which an animal overeats, leading to significant weight gain.

hyperpolarization. Increase in electrical charge across a membrane, usually due to the inward flow of chloride ions or the outward flow of potassium ions.

hypnogogic hallucination. Dreamlike event at the beginning of sleep or while a person is in a state of cataplexy.

hypokinetic symptom. Symptom of brain damage that results in a paucity of movement, as seen in Parkinson's disease.

hypothalamus. Diencephalon structure that contains many nuclei associated with temperature regulation, eating, drinking, and sexual behavior.

hypovolumic thirst. Produced by a loss of overall fluid volume from the body.

idiopathic seizure. Appears spontaneously and in the absence of other diseases of the central nervous system.

implicit memory. Memory in which subjects can demonstrate knowledge but cannot explicitly retrieve the information.

imprinting. Process that predisposes an animal to form an attachment to objects or animals at a critical period in development.

incentive salience. Quality acquired by drug cues that become highly desired and sought-after incentives in their own right.

incentive-sensitization theory. When a drug is associated with certain cues, the cues themselves elicit desire for the drug; also called *wanting-and-liking theory*.

inhibition. A process by which the activity of a neuron or brain area is decreased or stopped.

inhibitory postsynaptic potential (IPSP). Brief hyperpolarization of a neuron membrane in response to stimulation, making the neuron less likely to produce an action potential.

innate releasing mechanism (IRM). Hypothetical mechanism that detects specific sensory stimuli and directs an organism to take a particular action.

insomnia. Disorder of slow-wave sleep resulting in prolonged inability to sleep.

instrumental conditioning. Learning procedure in which the consequences (such as obtaining a reward) of a particular behavior (such as pressing a bar) increase or decrease the probability of the behavior occurring again; also called operant conditioning.

insula. Located within the lateral fissure, multifunctional cortical tissue that contains regions related to language, to the perception of taste, and to the neural structures underlying social cognition.

intelligence A. Hebb's term for innate intellectual potential, which is highly heritable and cannot be measured directly.

intelligence B. Hebb's term for observed intelligence, which is influenced by experience as well as other factors in the course of development and is measured by intelligence tests.

interneuron. Association neuron interposed between a sensory neuron and a motor neuron; thus, in mammals, interneurons constitute most of the neurons of the brain.

ionotropic receptor. Embedded membrane protein with two parts: a binding site for a neurotransmitter and a pore that regulates ion flow to directly and rapidly change membrane voltage.

ischemia. Lack of blood to the brain as a result of stroke.

Klüver-Bucy syndrome. Behavioral syndrome, characterized especially by hypersexuality, that results from bilateral injury to the temporal lobe.

Korsakoff's syndrome. Permanent loss of the ability to learn new information (anterograde amnesia) and to retrieve old information (retrograde amnesia) caused by diencephalic damage resulting from chronic alcoholism or malnutrition that produces a vitamin B_1 deficiency.

lateralization. Process whereby functions become localized primarily on one side of the brain.

law of Bell and Magendie. The general principle that sensory fibers are located dorsally and ventral fibers are located ventrally.

learned taste aversion. Acquired association between a specific taste or odor and illness; leads to an aversion to foods having that taste or odor.

learning set. An understanding of how a problem can be solved with a rule that can be applied in many situations.

learning. Relatively permanent change in behavior that results from experience.

Lewy body. Circular fibrous structure, found in several neurodegenerative disorders, that forms within the cytoplasm of neurons and is thought to result from abnormal neurofilament metabolism.

limbic system. Disparate forebrain structures lying between the neocortex and the brainstem that form a functional system controlling affective and motivated behaviors and certain forms of memory; includes cingulate cortex, amygdala, hippocampus, among other structures.

locked-in syndrome. Lower brainstem damage that results in a fully conscious, alert, and responsive condition, but the patient is quadriplegic and mute.

long-term potentiation (LTP). In response to stimulation at a synapse, changed amplitude of an excitatory postsynaptic potential that lasts for hours to days or longer and plays a part in associative learning.

luminance contrast. The amount of light reflected by an object relative to its surroundings.

magnetic resonance imaging (MRI). Imaging procedure in which a computer draws a map from the measured changes in the magnetic resonance of atoms in the brain; allows the production of a structural map of the brain without actually opening the skull.

magnetic resonance spectroscopy (MRS). Modification of MRI in which changes in specific markers of neuronal function can be identified; promising for accurate diagnosis of traumatic brain injuries.

magnetoencephalography (MEG). Recording of the changes in tiny magnetic fields generated by the brain.

magnocellular (M) cell. Large-celled visual-system neuron that is sensitive to moving stimuli.

major tranquilizer (neuroleptic). Drug that blocks the D2 receptor; used mainly for treating schizophrenia.

mania. Disordered mental state characterized by excessive euphoria.

masculinization. Process by which exposure to androgens (male hormones) alters the brain, rendering it identifiably male.

materialism. Philosophical position that holds that behavior can be explained as a function of the nervous system without explanatory recourse to the mind.

medial forebrain bundle (MFB). Tract that connects structures in the brainstem with various parts of the limbic system; forms the activating projections that run from the brainstem to the basal ganglia and frontal cortex.

medial geniculate nucleus. Major thalamic region concerned with audition.

medial pontine reticular formation (MPRF). Nucleus in the pons participating in REM sleep.

melatonin. Hormone secreted by the pineal gland during the dark phase of the day–night cycle; influences daily and seasonal biorhythms.

memory. The ability to recall or recognize previous experience.

meninges. Three layers of protective tissue—dura mater, arachnoid, and pia mater—that encase the brain and spinal cord.

mentalism. Of the mind; an explanation of behavior as a function of the nonmaterial mind.

metabotropic receptor. Embedded membrane protein, with a binding site for a neurotransmitter but no pore, linked to a G protein that can affect other receptors or act with second messengers to affect other cellular processes.

microglia. Form of glial cell that scavenges debris in the nervous system.

microsleep. Brief period of sleep lasting a second or so.

midbrain. Central part of the brain that contains neural circuits for hearing and seeing as well as orienting movements.

mind. Proposed nonmaterial entity responsible for intelligence, attention, awareness, and consciousness.

mind–body problem. Quandary of explaining a nonmaterial mind in command of a material body.

mirror neuron. Nerve cell that fires when a monkey observes a specific action being made by another monkey.

monoamine oxidase (MAO) inhibitor. Antidepressant drug that blocks the enzyme monoamine oxidase from degrading neurotransmitters such as dopamine, noradrenaline and serotonin.

monosynaptic reflex. Reflex requiring one synapse between sensory input and movement.

motivation. State inferred from behavior that seems purposeful and goal-directed.

motor neuron. Neuron that carries information from the spinal cord and brain to make muscles contract.

motor sequence. Movement modules preprogrammed by the brain and produced as a unit.

multiple sclerosis (MS). Nervous system disorder that results from the loss of myelin (glial-cell covering) around neurons.

mutation. Alteration of an allele that yields a different version of that allele.

myelin. Glial coating that surrounds axons in the central and peripheral nervous systems.

narcolepsy. Slow-wave sleep disorder in which a person uncontrollably falls asleep at inappropriate times.

narcotic analgesic. Drug like morphine, with sleep-inducing (narcotic) and pain-relieving (analgesic) properties.

natural selection. Darwin's theory for explaining how new species evolve and existing species change over time. Differential success in the reproduction of different characteristics (phenotypes) results from the interaction of organisms with their environment.

negative pole. The source of electrons.

neocortex (cerebral cortex). Newest, outer layer (new bark) of the forebrain and composed of about six layers of gray matter that creates our reality.

neoteny. Process in which maturation is delayed, and so an adult retains infant characteristics; idea derived from the observation that newly evolved species resemble the young of their common ancestors.

nerve growth factor (NGF). Neurotrophic factor that stimulates neurons to grow dendrites and synapses and, in some cases, promotes the survival of neurons.

nerve impulse. Propagation of an action potential on the membrane of an axon.

nerve net. Simple nervous system that has no brain or spinal cord but consists of neurons that receive sensory information and connect directly to other neurons that move muscles.

nerve. Large collection of axons coursing together outside the central nervous system.

netrins. The only class of tropic molecules yet isolated.

neural Darwinism. Hypothesis that the processes of cell death and synaptic pruning are, like natural selection in species, the outcome of competition among neurons for connections and metabolic resources in a neural environment.

neural plate. Thickened region of the ectodermal layer that gives rise to the neural tube.

neural stem cell. A self-renewing, multipotential cell that gives rise to any of the different types of neurons and glia in the nervous system.

neural tube. Structure in the early stage of brain development from which the brain and spinal cord develop.

neuritic plaque. Area of incomplete necrosis (dead tissue) consisting of a central protein core (amyloid) surrounded by degenerative cellular fragments; often seen in the cortex of people with senile dementias such as Alzheimer's disease.

neuroblast. Product of a progenitor cell that gives rise to any of the different types of neurons.

neurocognitive enhancement. Brain-function enhancement by pharmacological, physiological, or surgical manipulation.

neuron. A specialized cell engaged in information processing.

neuropeptide. A multifunctional chain of amino acids that acts as a neurotransmitter; synthesized from mRNA on instructions from the cell's DNA.

neuroplasticity. The nervous system's potential for neurophysical or neurochemical change that enhances its adaptability to environmental change and its ability to compensate for injury.

neuroprotectant. Drug used to try to block the cascade of poststroke neural events.

neuropsychology. General term used to refer to the study of the relation between brain function and behavior.

neurotransmitter. Chemical released by a neuron onto a target with an excitatory or inhibitory effect.

neurotrophic factor. A chemical compound that acts to support growth and differentiation in developing neurons and may act to keep certain neurons alive in adulthood.

nicotinic ACh receptor (nAChr). Ionotropic receptor at which acetylcholine and the drug nicotine act as ligands to activate the flow of ions through the receptor pore.

nitric oxide (NO). Acts as a chemical neurotransmitter gas—for example, to dilate blood vessels, aid digestion, and activate cellular metabolism.

nocioception. Perception of pain and temperature.

node of Ranvier. The part of an axon that is not covered by myelin.

nonregulatory behavior. Behavior not required to meet the basic needs of the animal.

noradrenergic neuron. From *adrenaline,* (epinephrine); a neuron containing norepinephrine.

norepinephrine (NE, or noradrenaline). Neurotransmitter found in the brain and in the parasympathetic division of the autonomic nervous system.

NREM (non-REM) sleep. Slow-wave sleep associated with delta rhythms.

nucleus (pl. nuclei). A group of cells forming a cluster that can be identified with special stains to form a functional grouping.

obesity. Excessive accumulation of body fat.

obsessive-compulsive disorder (OCD). Behavioral disorder characterized by compulsively repeated acts (such as hand washing) and repetitive, often unpleasant, thoughts (obsessions).

occipital lobe. Cerebral cortex at the back of the brain and beneath the occipital bone.

ocular-dominance column. Functional column in the visual cortex maximally responsive to information coming from one eye.

oligodendroglia. Glial cell in the central nervous system that myelinates axons.

opponent-process theory. Explanation of color vision that emphasizes the importance of the opposition of pairs of colors: red versus green and blue versus yellow.

optic ataxia. Deficit in the visual control of reaching and other movements.

optic chiasm. Junction of the optic nerves from each eye at which the axons from the nasal (inside—nearer the nose) halves of the retinas cross to the opposite side of the brain.

organizational hypothesis. Proposal that actions of hormones during development alter tissue differentiation; for example, testosterone masculinizes the brain.

orienting movement. Movement related to sensory inputs, such as turning the head to see the source of a sound.

oscilloscope. A device that measures the flow of electrons to measure voltage.

osmotic thirst. Results from an increased concentration of dissolved chemicals, or *solutes,* in body fluids.

ossicles. Bones of the middle ear: malleus (hammer), incus (anvil), and stapes (stirrup).

pain gate. Hypothetical neural circuit in which activity in fine-touch and pressure pathways diminishes the activity in pain and temperature pathways.

panic disorder. Recurrent attacks of intense terror that come on without warning and without any apparent relation to external circumstances.

parahippocampal cortex. Cortex located along the dorsal medial surface of the temporal lobe.

paralysis. Loss of sensation and movement due to nervous system injury.

paraplegia. Paralysis of the legs due to spinal-cord injury.

parasympathetic system. Part of the autonomic nervous system; acts in opposition to the sympathetic system—for example, preparing the body to rest and digest by reversing the alarm response or stimulating digestion.

parietal lobe. Cerebral cortex posterior to the central sulcus and beneath the parietal bone at the top of the skull.

parvocellular (P) cell. Small-celled visual-system neuron that is sensitive to form and color differences.

Pavlovian conditioning. Learning procedure whereby a neutral stimulus (such as a tone) comes to elicit a response because of its repeated pairing with some event (such as the delivery of food); also called *classical conditioning* or *respondent conditioning.*

peptide hormone. Chemical messenger synthesized by cellular DNA that acts to affect the target cell's physiology.

periaqueductal gray matter (PAG). Nuclei in the midbrain that surround the cerebral aqueduct joining the third and fourth ventricles; PAG neurons contain circuits for species-typical behaviors (e.g., female sexual behavior) and play an important role in the modulation of pain.

peribrachial area. Cholinergic nucleus in the dorsal brainstem having a role in REM sleep behaviors; projects to medial pontine reticulum.

period. Time required to complete a cycle of activity.

peripheral nervous system (PNS). All the neurons in the body located outside the brain and spinal cord.

perirhinal cortex. Cortex lying next to the rhinal fissure on the base of the brain.

petit mal seizure Of brief duration, a seizure characterized by loss of awareness with no motor activity except for blinking, turning the head, or rolling the eyes.

phenylketonuria (PKU). Behavioral disorder caused by elevated levels of the amino acid phenylalanine in the blood and resulting from a defect in the gene for the enzyme phenylalanine hydroxylase; the major symptom is severe mental retardation.

pheromone. Odorant biochemical released by one animal that acts as a chemosignal and can affect the physiology or behavior of another animal.

phobia. Fear of a clearly defined object or situation.

pituitary gland. Endocrine gland attached to the bottom of the hypothalamus; its secretions control the activities of many other endocrine glands; known to be associated with biological rhythms.

place cell. Hippocampal neuron that fires when a rat is in a certain location in an environment.

positive pole. Location to which electrons flow.

positron emission tomography (PET). Imaging technique that detects changes in blood flow by measuring changes in the uptake of compounds such as oxygen or glucose.

postictal depression. Postseizure state of confusion and reduced affect.

postsynaptic membrane. Membrane on the transmitter-input side of a synapse.

posttraumatic stress disorder (PTSD). Syndrome characterized by physiological arousal symptoms related to recurring memories and dreams related to a traumatic event—for months or years after the event.

prefrontal cortex. The cortex lying in front of the motor and premotor cortex of the frontal lobe; the prefrontal cortex is particularly large in the human brain.

preparedness. Predisposition to respond to certain stimuli differently from other stimuli.

presynaptic membrane. Membrane on the transmitter-output side of a synapse.

primary auditory cortex (area A1). Asymmetrical structures, found within Heschl's gyrus in the temporal lobes, that receive input from the ventral region of the medial geniculate nucleus.

primary visual cortex (V1). Striate cortex that receives input from the lateral geniculate nucleus.

priming. Using a stimulus to sensitize the nervous system to a later presentation of the same or a similar stimulus.

procedural memory. Ability to recall a movement sequence or how to perform some act or behavior.

progenitor cell. Precursor cell derived from a stem cell; it migrates and produces a neuron or a glial cell.

proprioception. Perception of the position and movement of the body, limbs, and head.

prosody. Melodical tone of the spoken voice.

psyche. Synonym for mind, an entity once proposed to be the source of human behavior.

psychedelic drug. Drug that can alter sensation and perception; lysergic acid dielthylmide, mescalin, and psilocybin are examples.

psychoactive drug. Substance that acts to alter mood, thought, or behavior and is used to manage neuropsychological illness.

psychological construct. Idea, resulting from a set of impressions, that some mental ability exists as an entity; examples include memory, language, and emotion.

psychomotor activation. Increased behavioral and cognitive activity; at certain levels of consumption, the drug user feels energetic and in control.

psychopharmacology. Study of how drugs affect the nervous system and behavior.

psychosurgery. Any neurosurgical technique intended to alter behavior.

psychotherapy. Talking therapy derived from Freudian psychoanalysis and other psychological interventions.

pump. Protein in the cell membrane that actively transports a substance across the membrane.

Purkinje cell. Distinctive neuron found in the cerebellum.

pyramidal cell. Distinctive neuron found in the cerebral cortex.

quadrantanopia. Blindness of one quadrant of the visual field.

quadriplegia. Paralysis of the legs and arms due to spinal-cord injury.

quantum (pl. quanta). Quantity, equivalent to the contents of a single synaptic vesicle, that produces a just observable change in postsynaptic electric potential.

radial glial cell. Path-making cell that a migrating neuron follows to its appropriate destination.

radiator hypothesis. Idea that selection for improved brain cooling through increased blood circulation in the brains of early hominids enabled the brain to grow larger.

rapidly adapting receptor. Body sensory receptor that responds briefly to the onset of a stimulus on the body.

rate-limiting factor. Any enzyme that is in limited supply, thus restricting the pace at which a chemical can be synthesized.

receptive field. Region of the visual world that stimulates a receptor cell or neuron.

referred pain. Pain felt on the surface of the body that is actually due to pain in one of the internal organs of the body.

regulatory behavior. Behavior required to meet the basic needs of the animal.

reinforcer. In operant conditioning, any event that strengthens the behavior that it follows.

relatively refractory. Refers to the state of an axon in the later phase of an action potential during which increased electrical current is required to produce another action potential; a phase during which potassium channels are still open.

releasing hormones. Peptides that are released by the hypothalamus and act to increase or decrease the release of hormones from the anterior pituitary.

REM sleep. Fast brain-wave pattern displayed by the neocortical EEG record during sleep.

resting potential. Electrical charge across the cell membrane in the absence of stimulation; a store of energy produced by a greater negative charge on the intracellular side relative to the extracellular side.

reticular activating system (RAS). Large reticulum (mixture of cell nuclei and nerve fibers) that runs through the center of the brainstem.

reticular formation. Midbrain area in which nuclei and fiber pathways are mixed, producing a netlike appearance; associated with sleep–wake behavior and behavioral arousal.

retina. Light-sensitive surface at the back of the eye consisting of neurons and photoreceptor cells.

retinal ganglion cells. Neural cells of the retina that give rise to the optic nerve.

retinohypothalamic pathway. Neural route from a subset of cone receptors in the retina to the suprachiasmatic nucleus of the hypothalamus; allows light to entrain the rhythmic activity of the SCN.

retrograde amnesia. Inability to remember events that took place before a disturbance of the brain.

reuptake. Deactivation of a neurotransmitter when membrane transporter proteins bring the transmitter back into the presynaptic axon terminal for subsequent reuse.

rod. Photoreceptor specialized for functioning at low light levels.

saltatory conduction. Propagation of an action potential at successive nodes of Ranvier; saltatory means "jumping" or "dancing."

schizophrenia. Behavioral disorder characterized by delusions, hallucinations, disorganized speech, blunted emotion, agitation or immobility, and a host of associated symptoms.

Schwann cell. Glial cell in the peripheral nervous system that forms the myelin on sensory and motor axons.

scotoma. Small blind spot in the visual field caused by a small lesion or migraines of the visual cortex.

scratch reflex. Automatic response in which the hind limb reaches to remove a stimulus from the surface of the body.

second messenger. Activated by a neurotransmitter (the first messenger), a chemical that carries a message to initiate a biochemical process.

second-generation antidepressant. Drug whose action is similar to tricyclics (first-generation antidepressants) but more selective in its action on the serotonin re-uptake transporter proteins; also called *atypical antidepressant*.

segmentation. Division into a number of parts that are similar; refers to the idea that many animals, including vertebrates, are composed of similarly organized body segments.

selective serotonin reuptake inhibitor (SSRI). Antidepressant drug that blocks the reuptake of serotonin into the presynaptic terminal.

sensitization. Learning behavior in which the response to a stimulus strengthens with repeated presentations of that stimulus because the stimulus is novel or because the stimulus is stronger than normal—for example, after habituation has occurred.

sensory deprivation. Experimental setup in which a subject is allowed only restricted sensory input; subjects generally have a low tolerance for deprivation and may even display hallucinations.

sensory neuron. Neuron that carries incoming information from sensory receptors into the spinal cord and brain.

sexual dimorphism. Differential development of brain areas in the two sexes.

sexual identity. A person's feeling either male or female.

sexual orientation. A person's sexual attraction either to the opposite sex or to the same sex.

sleep apnea. Inability to breathe during sleep; person has to wake up to breathe.

sleep paralysis. Inability to move during deep sleep owing to the brain's inhibition of motor neurons.

slowly adapting receptor. Body sensory receptor that responds as long as a sensory stimulus is on the body.

slow-wave sleep. NREM sleep.

small-molecule transmitters. Class of quick-acting neurotransmitters synthesized in the axon terminal from products derived from the diet.

somatic marker hypothesis. Posits that "marker" signals arising from emotions and feelings act to guide behavior and decision making, usually in an unconscious process.

somatic nervous system (SNS). Part of the PNS that includes the cranial and spinal nerves to and from the muscles, joints, and skin that produce movement, transmit incoming sensory input, and inform the CNS about the position and movement of body parts.

somatosensory neuron. Brain cell that brings sensory information from the body into the spinal cord.

sound wave. Undulating displacement of molecules caused by changing pressure.

spatial summation. Graded potentials that occur at approximately the same location on a membrane are summated.

species. Group of organisms that can interbreed.

species-typical behavior. Behavior that is characteristic of all members of a species.

spinal cord. Part of the central nervous system encased within the vertebrae or spinal column.

split brain. Surgical disconnection of the two hemispheres in which the corpus callosum is cut.

steroid hormone. Fat-soluble chemical messenger synthesized from cholesterol.

storage granule. Membranous compartment that holds several vesicles containing a neurotransmitter.

stretch-sensitive channel. Ion channel on a tactile sensory neuron that activates in response to stretching of the membrane, initiating a nerve impulse.

striate cortex. Primary visual cortex in the occipital lobe; its striped appearance when stained gives it this name.

stroke. Sudden appearance of neurological symptoms as a result of severe interruption of blood flow.

substance abuse. Use of a drug for the psychological and behavioral changes that it produces aside from its therapeutic effects.

sulcus (pl. sulci). A small cleft formed by the folding of the cerebral cortex.

supplementary speech area. Speech-production region on the dorsal surface of the left frontal lobe.

suprachiasmatic nucleus (SCN). Main pacemaker of circadian rhythms located just above the optic chiasm.

sympathetic system. Part of the autonomic nervous system; arouses the body for action, such as mediating the involuntary fight or flight response to alarm by increasing heart rate and blood pressure.

symptomatic seizure. Identified with a specific cause, such as infection, trauma, tumor, vascular malformation, toxic chemicals, very high fever, or other neurological disorders.

synapse. Junction between one neuron and another neuron, usually between an end foot of the axon of one neuron and a dendritic spine of the other neuron.

synaptic cleft. Gap that separates the presynaptic membrane from the postsynaptic membrane.

synaptic vesicle. Organelle consisting of a membrane structure that encloses a quantum of neurotransmitter.

synergy. Innate pattern of movement coded by the motor cortex.

synesthesia. Ability to perceive a stimulus of one sense as the sensation of a different sense, such as when sound produces a sensation of color.

syntax. Ways in which words are put together to form phrases, clauses, or sentences; proposed to be a unique characteristic of human language.

tardive dyskinesia. Inability to stop the tongue from moving; motor side effect of neuroleptic drugs.

Tay-Sachs disease. Inherited birth defect caused by the loss of genes that encode the enzyme necessary for breaking down certain fatty substances; appears 4 to 6 months after birth and results in retardation, physical changes, and death by about age 5.

tectopulvinar system. Projections from the retina to the superior colliculus to the pulvinar (thalamus) to the parietal and temporal visual areas.

tectum. Roof (area above the ventricle) of the midbrain; its functions are sensory processing, particularly visual and auditory, and producing orienting movements.

tegmentum. Floor (area below the ventricle) of the midbrain; a collection of nuclei with movement-related, species-specific, and pain-perception functions.

temporal lobe. Cortex lying below the lateral fissure, beneath the temporal bone at the side of the skull.

temporal summation. Graded potentials that occur at approximately the same time on a membrane are summated.

thalamus. Diencephalon structure through which information from all sensory systems is integrated and projected into the appropriate region of the neocortex.

threshold potential. Voltage on a neural membrane at which an action potential is triggered by the opening of Na^+ and K^+ voltage-sensitive channels; about -50 millivolts relative to extracellular surround.

tolerance. Lessening of response to a drug over time.

tonotopic representation. Property of audition in which sound waves are processed in a systematic fashion from lower to higher frequencies.

topographic map. A spatially organized neural representation of the external world.

topographic organization. Neural spatial representation of the body or areas of the sensory world perceived by a sensory organ.

torpor. Inactive condition resembling sleep but with a greater decline in body temperature.

tract. Large collection of axons coursing together within the central nervous system.

transcranial magnetic stimulation (TMS). Procedure in which a low-frequency magnetic coil is placed over the skull to stimulate the underlying brain tissue; can be used either to induce behavior or to disrupt ongoing behavior.

transmitter-activated receptor. Protein embedded in the membrane of a cell that has a binding site for a specific neurotransmitter.

transmitter-sensitive channel. Receptor complex that has both a receptor site for a chemical and a pore through which ions can flow.

transporter. Protein molecule that pumps substances across a membrane.

trichromatic theory. Explanation of color vision based on the coding of three primary colors: red, green, and blue.

tricyclic antidepressant. First-generation antidepressant drug, with a chemical structure characterized by three rings, that blocks serotonin reuptake transporter proteins.

tropic molecule. Signaling molecule that attracts or repels growth cones.

tumor. Mass of new tissue that grows uncontrolled and independent of surrounding structures.

type I schizophrenia. Characterized predominantly by positive symptoms (behavioral excesses, such as hallucinations and agitated movements); likely due to a dopaminergic dysfunction and associated with acute onset, good prognosis, and a favorable response to neuroleptics.

type II schizophrenia. Characterized by negative symptoms (behavioral deficits) and associated with chronic affliction, poor prognosis, poor response to neuroleptics, cognitive impairments, enlarged ventricles, and cortical atrophy, particularly in the frontal cortex.

unconditioned response (UCR). In classical conditioning, the unlearned, naturally occurring response to the unconditioned stimulus, such as salivation when food is in the mouth.

unconditioned stimulus (UCS). A stimulus that unconditionally—naturally and automatically—triggers a response.

ventral spinothalamic tract. Pathway from the spinal cord to the thalamus that carries information about pain and temperature.

ventricle. A cavity in the brain that contains cerebral spinal fluid.

ventricular zone. Lining of neural stem cells surrounding the ventricles in adults.

ventrolateral thalamus. Part of the thalamus that carries information about body senses to the somatosensory cortex.

vertebrae. The bones, or segments, that form the spinal column.

vestibular system. A set of receptors in the middle ear that indicate position and movement of the head.

visual field. Region of the visual world that is seen by the eyes.

visual-form agnosia. Inability to recognize objects or drawings of objects.

visuospatial learning. Using visual information to identify an object's location in space.

volt. A measure of a difference in electrical potential.

voltmeter. A device that measures the difference in electrical potential between two bodies.

voltage gradient. Difference in charge between two regions that allows a flow of current if the two regions are connected.

voltage-sensitive channel. Gated protein channel that opens or closes only at specific membrane voltages.

Wernicke's area. Secondary auditory cortex (planum temporale) lying behind Heschl's gyrus at the rear of the left temporal lobe that regulates language comprehension; also called posterior speech zone.

white matter. Areas of the nervous system rich in fat-sheathed neural axons.

wild type. Refers to a normal (most common in a population) phenotype or genotype.

withdrawal symptoms. Physical and psychological behaviors displayed by an addict when drug use ends.

zeitgeber. Environmental event that entrains biological rhythms; a "time giver."

References

Chapter 1

Benkman, C. W., & Lindholm, A. K. (1990). The advantages and evolution of morphological novelty. *Nature, 349*, 519–520.

Blumer, D., & Benson, D. F. (1975). Personality changes with frontal and temporal lobe lesions. In D. F. Benson & D. Blumer (Eds.), *Psychiatric aspects of neurologic disease* (pp. 151–170). New York: Grune & Stratton.

Brain Injury Association. (2002). The costs and causes of traumatic brain injury (http://www.biausa.org).

Bronson, R. T. (1979). Brain weight–body weight scaling in dogs and cats. *Brain, Behavior and Evolution, 16*, 227–236.

Campbell, N. A. (1996). *Biology.* Menlo Park, CA: Benjamin Cummings.

Cassidy, J. D., Carroll, L. J., Peloso, P. M., Borg, J., von Holst, H., Holm, L., Kraus, J., & Coronado, V. G.; WHO Collaborating Centre Task Force on Mild Traumatic Brain Injury. (2004). Incidence, risk factors and prevention of mild traumatic brain injury: Results of the WHO Collaborating Centre Task Force on Mild Traumatic Brain Injury. *Journal of Rehabilitation Medicine, 43*(Suppl.), 28–60.

Coren, S. (1994). *The intelligence of dogs.* Toronto: The Free Press.

Darwin, C. (1963). *On the origin of species by means of natural selection, or the preservation of favored races in the struggle for life.* New York: New American Library. (Original work published 1859)

Darwin, C. (1965). *The expression of the emotions in man and animals.* Chicago: University of Chicago Press. (Original work published 1872)

Dawkins, R. (1976). *The selfish gene.* Oxford: Oxford University Press.

Descartes, R. (1972). *Treatise on man* (T. S. Hall, Trans.). Cambridge, MA: Harvard University Press. (Original work published 1664)

Eibl-Eibesfeldt, I. (1970). *Ethology: The biology of behavior.* New York: Holt, Rinehart and Winston.

Falk, D. (1990). Brain evolution in *Homo:* The "radiator" theory. *Behavioral and Brain Sciences, 13*, 344–368.

Geshwind, N., & Galaburda, A. M. (1985). *Cerebral lateralization.* Cambridge, MA: MIT Press.

Goodall, J. (1986). *The chimpanzees of Gombe.* Cambridge, MA: Harvard University Press.

Gould, S. J. (1981). *The mismeasure of man.* New York: Norton.

Hebb, D. O. (1949). *The organization of behavior: A neuropsychological theory.* New York: Wiley.

Heron, W. (1957). The pathology of boredom. *Scientific American, 196*(1), 52–56.

Jacobsen, E. (1932). Electrophysiology of mental activities. *American Journal of Psychology, 44*, 677–694.

Johnson, D., & Blake, E. (1996). *From Lucy to language.* New York: Simon & Schuster.

Kolb, B., & Whishaw, I. Q. (2003). *Fundamentals of human neuropsychology* (5th ed.). New York: W. H. Freeman and Company.

Linge, F. R. (1990). Faith, hope, and love: Nontraditional therapy in recovery from serious head injury, a personal account. *Canadian Journal of Psychology, 44*, 116–129.

Lorenz, K. Z. (1981). *The foundations of ethology.* New York: Springer Verlag.

MacMillan, M. (2000). *An odd kind of fame: Stories of Phineas Gage.* Cambridge, MA: MIT Press.

Martin, R. D. (1990). *Primate origins and evolution: A phylogenetic reconstruction.* Princeton, NJ: Princeton University Press.

McKinney, M. L. (1998). The juvenilized ape myth: Our "overdeveloped" brain. *Bioscience, 48*, 109–116.

Milton, K. (1993). Diet and primate evolution. *Scientific American, 269*(2), 86–93.

Morwood, M. J., Soejono, R. P., Roberts, R. G., Sutikna, T., Turney, C. S. M., Westaway, K. E., Rink, W. J., Zhao, J.-X., van den Bergh, G. D., Due, R. A., Hobbs, D. R., Moore, M. W., Bird, M. I., & Fifield, L. K. (2004). Archaeology and age of a new hominin from Flores in eastern Indonesia. *Nature, 431*, 1092–1095.

Murdock, G. P. (1965). *Culture and society: Twenty-four essays.* Pittsburgh: University of Pittsburgh Press.

Penfield, W., & Roberts, L. (1959). *Speech and brain mechanisms.* Princeton, NJ: Princeton University Press.

Schuiling, G. A. (2003). The cook, the thief, his wife and her lover: On the evolution of the human reproductive strategy. *Journal of Psychosomatic Obstetrics and Gynaecology, 24*(4), 273–277.

Stedman, H. H., Kozyak, B. W., Nelson, A., Thesier, D. M., Su, L. T., Low, D. W., Bridges, C. R., Shrager, J. B., Minugh-Purvis, N., & Mitchell, M. A. (2004). Myosin gene mutation correlates with anatomical changes in the human lineage. *Nature, 428*, 415–418.

Taglialatela, J. P., Savage-Rumbaugh, S., & Baker, L. A. (2003). Vocal production by a language-competent *Pan paniscus. International Journal of Primatology, 24*, 1–17.

Terkel, J. (1995). Cultural transmission in the black rat: Pinecone feeding. *Advances in the Study of Behavior, 24*, 119–154.

Weiner, J. (1995). *The beak of the finch.* New York: Vintage.

Wilson, E. O. (1980). *Sociobiology.* Cambridge, MA: Belknap Press of Harvard University Press.

Chapter 2

Axel, R. (1995). The molecular logic of smell. *Scientific American, 273*(4), 154–159.

Brodmann, K. (1909). *Vergleichende Lokalisationlehr der Grosshirnrinde in ihren Prinzipien dargestellt auf Grund des Zellenbaues.* Leipzig: J. A. Barth.

Chiu, D., Krieger, D., Villar-Cordova, C., Kasner, S. E., Morgenstern, L. B., Bratina, P. L., Yatsu, F. M., & Grotta, J. C. (1998). Intravenous tissue plasminogen activator for acute ischemic stroke: Feasibility, safety, and efficacy in the first year of clinical practice. *Stroke, 29*, 18–22.

Chklovskii, D. B., Schikorski, T., & Stevens, C. F. (2002). Wiring optimization in cortical circuits. *Neuron, 34*, 341–347.

Diamond, M. C., Scheibel, A. B., & Elson, L. M. (1985). *The human brain coloring book.* New York: Barnes & Noble.

Elliott, H. (1969). *Textbook of neuroanatomy.* Philadelphia: Lippincott.

Everett, N. B. (1965). *Functional neuroanatomy.* Philadelphia: Lea & Febiger.

Felleman, D. J., & van Essen, D. C. (1991). Distributed hierarchical processing in the primate cerebral cortex. *Cerebral Cortex, 1*, 1–47.

Frackowiak, R. S. J., Friston, K. J., Frith, C. D., Dolan, R. J., & Mazziotta, J. C. (1997). *Human brain function.* New York: Academic Press.

Hamilton, L. W. (1976). *Basic limbic system anatomy of the rat.* New York and London: Plenum.

Heimer, L. (1995). *The human brain and spinal cord: Functional neuroanatomy and dissection guide* (2d ed.). New York: Springer Verlag.

Herrick, C. J. (1926). *Brains of rats and men.* Chicago: University of Chicago Press.

Jerison, H. J. (1991). *Brain size and the evolution of mind.* New York: American Museum of Natural History.

Kandel, E. R., Schwartz, J. H., & Jessell, T. M. (Eds.). (1995). *Essentials of neural science and behavior.* East Norwalk, CT: Appleton & Lange.

Klyachko, V. A., & Stevens, C. F. (2003). Connectivity optimization and the positioning of cortical areas. *Proceedings of the National Academy of Sciences, USA, 100*, 7937–7941.

Luria, A. R. (1973). *The working brain.* Harmondsworth, UK: Penguin.

Netter, F. H. (1962). *The Ciba collection of medical illustrations: Vol 1. Nervous system.* New York: Ciba.

Papez, J. W. (1937). A proposed mechanism of emotion. *Archives of Neurology and Psychiatry, 38*, 724–744.

Penfield, W., & Jasper, H. H. (1954). *Epilepsy and the functional anatomy of the human brain.* Boston: Little, Brown.

Purves, D., Augustine, G. J., Fitzpatrick, D., Katz, L. C., LaMantia, A.-S., & McNamara, J. O. (1997). *Neuroscience.* Sunderland, MA: Sinauer.

Ranson, S. W., & Clark, S. L. (1959). *The anatomy of the nervous system.* Philadelphia: Saunders.

Shepherd, G. M. (1990). *The synaptic organization of the brain* (3rd ed.). New York: Oxford University Press.

Sporns, O., Tononi, G., & Edelman, G. M. (2002). Theoretical neuroanatomy and the connectivity of cerebral cortex. *Behavioural Brain Research, 135*, 69–74.

Teasell, R., Foley, N., Bhogal, S. K., Jutai, J., & Speechley, M. (2003). *Evidence-based review of stroke rehabilitation.* Report to Heart and Stroke Foundation of Ontario.

Truex, R. C., & Carpenter, M. B. (1969). *Human neuroanatomy.* Baltimore: Williams & Wilkins.

Whiting, B. A., & Barton, R. A. (2003). The evolution of cortico-cerebellar complex in primates: Anatomical connections predict patterns of correlated evolution. *Journal of Human Evolution, 44,* 3–10.

Zeki, S. (1993). *A vision of the brain.* London: Blackwell Scientific.

Chapter 3

Alberts, B., Johnson, A., Lewis, J., Raff, M., Roberts, K., & Walter, P. (2002). *Molecular biology of the cell* (4th ed.). New York: Garland.

Ashrafi, K., Chang, F. Y., Watts, J. L., Fraser, A. G., Kamath, R. S., Ahringer, J., & Ruvkun, G. (2003). Genome-wide RNAi analysis of *Caenorhabditis elegans* fat regulatory genes. *Nature, 421,* 268–272.

Balaban, F., Teillet, M. A., & LeDouarin, N. (1988). Application of the quail-chick chimera system to the study of brain development and behavior. *Science, 241,* 1339–1342.

de Duve, C. (1996). The birth of complex cells. *Scientific American, 274*(4), 50–57.

Eells, J. B. (2003). The control of dopamine neuron development, function and survival: Insights from transgenic mice and the relevance to human disease. *Current Medical Chemistry, 10,* 857–870.

Kamath, R. S., Fraser, A. G., Yan, D., Poulin, G., Durbin, R., Gotta, M., Kanapin, A., Le Bot, N., Moreno, S., Sohrmann, M., Welchman, D. P., Zipperlen, P., & Ahringer, J. (2003). Systematic functional analysis of the *Caenorhabditis elegans* genome using RNAi. *Nature, 421,* 231–237.

Levitan, I. B., & Kaczmarek, L. K. (1997). *The neuron: Cell and molecular biology* (2nd ed.). Oxford: Oxford University Press.

Niemann, H., Rath, D., & Wrenzycki, C. (2003). Advances in biotechnology: New tools in future pig production for agriculture and biomedicine. *Reproduction in Domestic Animals, 38,* 82–89.

Nottebohm, F., O'Loughlin, B., Gould, K., Yohay, K., & Alvarez-Buylla, A. (1994). The life span of new neurons in a song control nucleus of the adult canary brain depends on time of year when these cells are born. *Proceedings of the National Academy of Sciences, USA, 91,* 7849–7853.

Parker, H. G., Kim, L. V., Sutter, N. B., Carlson, S., Lorentzen, T. D., Malek, T. B., Johnson, G. S., DeFrance, H. B., Ostrander, E. A., & Kruglyak, L. (2004). Genetic structure of the purebred domestic dog. *Science, 304,* 1160–1164.

Rubinsztein, D. C. (2002). Lessons from animal models of Huntington's disease. *Trends in Genetics, 18,* 202–209.

Wahlsten, D., & Ozaki, H. S. (1994). Defects of the fetal forebrain in acallosal mice. In M. Lassonde & M. A. Jeeves (Eds.), *Callosal agenesis* (pp. 125–132). New York: Plenum.

Webb, B. (1996). A cricket robot. *Scientific American, 275*(6), 94–99.

Chapter 4

Bartholow, R. (1874). Experimental investigation into the functions of the human brain. *American Journal of Medical Sciences, 67,* 305–313.

Descartes, R. (1972). *Treatise on man* (T. S. Hall, Trans.). Cambridge, MA: Harvard University Press. (Original work published 1664)

Eccles, J. (1965). The synapse. *Scientific American, 212*(1), 56–66.

Hodgkin, A. L., & Huxley, A. F. (1939). Action potentials recorded from inside nerve fiber. *Nature, 144,* 710–711.

Jiang, Y., Ruta, V., Chen, J., Lee, A., & MacKinnon, R. (2003). The principle of gating charge movement in a voltage-dependent K⁺ channel. *Nature, 423,* 42–48.

Penfield, W., & Jasper, H. H. (1954). *Epilepsy and the functional anatomy of the human brain.* Boston: Little, Brown.

Posner, M. I., & Raichle, M. E. (1994). *Images of mind.* New York: W. H. Freeman and Company.

Przedborski, S. (2004). Programmed cell death in amyotrophic lateral sclerosis: A mechanism of pathogenic and therapeutic importance. *Neurologist, 10,* 1–7.

Ranck, J. B. (1973). Studies on single neurons in dorsal hippocampal formation and septum in unrestrained rats: I. Behavioral correlates and firing repertoires. *Experimental Neurology, 41,* 461–531.

Ruta, V., Jiang, Y., Lee, A., Chen, J., & MacKinnon, R. (2003). Functional analysis of an archaebacterial voltage-dependent K⁺ channel. *Nature, 422,* 180–185.

Valenstein, E. S. (1973). *Brain control.* New York: Wiley.

Chapter 5

Bailey, C. H., & Chen, M. (1989). Time course of structural changes at identified sensory neuron synapses during long-term sensitization in *Aplysia. Journal of Neuroscience, 9,* 1774–1780.

Ballard, A., Tetrud, J. W., & Langston, J. W. (1985). Permanent human Parkinsonism due to 1-methyl-4-phenyl-1,2,3,6-tetrahydropyridine (MPTP). *Neurology, 35,* 949–956.

Barbeau, A., Murphy, G. F., & Sourkes, T. L. (1961). Les catecholamines dans la maladie de Parkinson. Bel-Air Symposium on Monoamines and the Central Nervous System, Georg et Cie, Geneva.

Birkmayer, W., & Hornykiewicz, O. (1961). Der L-3,4-Dioxyphenylalanin (L-DOPA) Effekt bei der Parkinson A Kinase. *Wiener Klinische, 73,* 787–789.

Bliss, T. V. P., & Lømø, T. (1973). Long lasting potentiation of synaptic transmission in the dentate area of the anesthetized rabbit following stimulation of the perforant path. *Journal of Physiology (London), 232,* 331–356.

Cooper, J. R., Bloom, F. E., & Roth, R. H. (1991). *The biochemical basis of neuropharmacology.* New York: Oxford University Press.

Ehringer, H., & Hornykiewicz, O. (1960/1974). Distribution of noradrenaline and dopamine (3-hydroxytyramine) in the human brain and their behavior in the presence of disease affecting the extrapyramidal system. In J. Marks (Ed.), *The treatment of Parkinsonism with L-dopa* (pp. 45–56). Lancaster, UK: MTP Medical and Technical Publishing.

Engert, F., & Bonhoeffer, T. (1999). Dendritic spine changes associated with hippocampal long-term synaptic plasticity. *Nature, 399,* 66–70.

Fischer, M., Kaech, S., Knutti, D., & Matus, A. (1998). Rapid actin-based plasticity in dendritic spines. *Neuron, 20,* 847–854.

Galef, B. G., Jr., Attenborough, K. S., & Wishin, E. E. (1990). Responses of observer rats *(Rattus norvegicus)* to complex, diet-related signals emmitted by demonstrator rats. *Journal of Comparative Psychology, 104,* 11–19.

Hebb, D. O. (1949). *The organization of behavior.* New York: Wiley.

Kandel, E. (1976). *Cellular basis of behavior.* San Francisco: W. H. Freeman and Company.

Kandel, E. R., Schwartz, J. H., & T. M. Jessell. (Eds.). (2000). *Principles of neural science* (4th ed.). New York: McGraw-Hill.

Parkinson, J. (1817/1989). An essay on the shaking palsy. In A. D. Morris & F. C. Rose (Eds.), *James Parkinson: His life and times* (pp. 151–175). Boston: Birkhauser.

Sacks, O. (1976). *Awakenings.* New York: Doubleday.

Sulzer, D., Joyce, M. P., Lin, L., Geldwert, D., Haber, S. N., Hatton, T., & Rayport, S. (1998). Dopamine neurons make glutamatergic synapses in vitro. *Journal of Neuroscience, 18,* 4588–4602.

Tashiro, A., & Yuste, R. (2003). Structure and molecular organization of dendritic spines. *Histology and Histopathology, 18,* 617–634.

Tréatikoff, C. (1974). Thesis for doctorate in medicine, 1919. In J. Marks (Ed.), *The treatment of Parkinsonism with L-dopa* (pp. 29–38). Lancaster, UK: MTP Medical and Technical Publishing.

Ungerstedt, U. (1971). Adipsia and aphagia after 6-hydroxydopamine induced degeneration of the nigrostriatal dopamine system in the rat brain. *Acta Physiologica (Scandinavia), 82*(Suppl. 367), 95–122.

Widner, H., Tetrud, J., Rehngrona, S., Snow, B., Brundin, P., Gustavii, B., Bjorklund, A., Lindvall, O., & Langston, J. W. (1992). Bilateral fetal mesencephalic grafting in two patients with Parkinsonism induced by 1-methyl-4-phenyl-1,2,3,6-tetrahydropyridine (MPTP). *New England Journal of Medicine, 327,* 1556–1563.

Chapter 6

Agate, R. J., Grisham, W., Wade, J., Mann, S., Wingfield, J., Schanen, C., Palotie, A., & Arnold, A. P. (2003). Neural, but not gonadal, origin of brain sex differences in a gynandromorphic finch. *Proceedings of the National Academy of Sciences, USA, 100,* 4873–4878.

Ames, E. W. (1997). *The development of Romanian orphanage children adopted to Canada.* Final report to Human Resources Development, Canada.

Bunney, B. G., Potkin, S. G., & Bunney, W. E. (1997). Neuropathological studies of brain tissue in schizophrenia. *Journal of Psychiatric Research, 31,* 159–173.

Changeux, J.-P., & Danchin, A. (1976). Selective stabilization of developing synapses as a mechanism for the specification of neuronal networks. *Nature, 264,* 705–712.

Constantine-Paton, M., & Law, M. I. (1978). Eye specific termination bands in tecta of three-eyed frogs. *Science, 202,* 639–641.

Curtis, S. (1978). *Genie: A psycholinguistic study of a modern-day "wild-child."* New York: Academic Press.

Dawson, G., & Fischer, K. W. (1994). *Human behavior and the developing brain.* New York: Guilford Press.

Edelman, G. M. (1987). *Neural darwinism: The theory of neuronal group selection.* New York: Basic Books.

Epstein, H. T. (1979). Correlated brain and intelligence development in humans. In M. E. Hahn, C. Jensen, & B. C. Dudek (Eds.), *Development and evolution of brain size: Behavioral implications* (pp. 111–131). New York: Academic Press.

Galaburda, A. M., & Christen, Y. (1997). *Normal and abnormal development of the cortex.* Berlin: Springer Verlag.

Gershon, E. S., & Rieder, R. O. (1992). Major disorders of mind and brain. *Scientific American, 267*(3), 126–133.

Goldstein, J. M., Seidman, L. J., Horton, N. J., Makris, N., Kennedy, D. N., Caviness, V. S., Jr., Faraone, S. V., & Tsuang, M. T. (2001). Normal sexual dimorphism of the adult human brain assessed by in vivo magnetic resonance imaging. *Cerebral Cortex, 11,* 490–497.

Greenough, W. T., & Chang, F. F. (1988). Plasticity of synapse structure and pattern in the cerebral cortex. In A. Peters and E. G. Jones (Eds.), *Cerebral cortex, Vol. 7: Development and maturation of the cerebral cortex* (pp. 391–440). New York: Plenum.

Harlow, H. F. (1971). *Learning to love.* San Francisco: Albion.

Hebb, D. O. (1947). The effects of early experience on problem solving at maturity. *American Psychologist, 2,* 737–745.

Hebb, D. O. (1949). *The organization of behavior.* New York: Wiley.

Horn, G., Bradley, P., & McCabe, B. J. (1985). Changes in the structure of synapses associated with learning. *Journal of Neuroscience, 5,* 3161–3168.

Huttenlocher, P. R. (1994). Synaptogenesis in human cerebral cortex. In G. Dawson & K. W. Fischer (Eds.), *Human behavior and the developing brain* (pp. 137–152). New York: Guilford Press.

Jacobsen, M. (1991). *Developmental neurobiology* (3rd ed.). New York: Plenum.

Juraska, J. M. (1990). The structure of the cerebral cortex: Effects of gender and the environment. In B. Kolb & R. Tees (Eds.), *The cerebral cortex of the rat* (pp. 483–506). Cambridge, MA: MIT Press.

Kennedy, H., & Dehay, D. (1993). Cortical specification of men and mice. *Cerebral Cortex, 3,* 171–186.

Kolb, B., & Fantie, B. (1997). Development of the child's brain and behavior. In C. R. Reynolds & E. Fletcher-Janzen (Eds.), *Handbook of clinical child neuropsychology* (2nd ed., pp. 17–41). New York: Plenum.

Kolb, B., Forgie, M., Gibb, R., Gorny, G., & Rowntree, S. (1998). Age, experience, and the changing brain. *Neuroscience and Biobehavioral Reviews, 22,* 143–159.

Kolb, B., & Gibb, R. (1993). Possible anatomical basis of recovery of function after neonatal frontal lesions in rats. *Behavioral Neuroscience, 107,* 799–811.

Kolb, B., & Whishaw, I. Q. (1998). Brain plasticity and behavior. *Annual Review of Psychology, 49,* 43–64.

Kolb, B., Wilson, B., & Taylor, L. (1992). Developmental changes in the recognition and comprehensional expression: Implications for frontal lobe function. *Brain and Cognition, 20,* 74–84.

Korsching, S. (1993). The neurotrophic factor concept: A reexamination. *Journal of Neuroscience, 13,* 2739–2748.

Kovelman, J. A., & Scheibel, A. B. (1984). A neurohistologic correlate of schizophrenia. *Biological Psychiatry, 19,* 1601–1621.

Lenneberg, E. H. (1967). *Biological foundations of language.* New York: Wiley.

Levitt, P. (1995). Experimental approaches that reveal principles of cerebral cortical development. In M. Gazzaniga (Ed.), *The cognitive neurosciences* (pp. 147–163). Cambridge, MA: MIT Press.

Lorenz, K. (1970). *Studies on animal and human behavior* (Vols. 1 and 2). Cambridge, MA: Harvard University Press.

Malanga, C. J., & Kosofsky, B. E. (2003). Does drug abuse beget drug abuse? Behavioral analysis of addiction liability in animal models of prenatal drug exposure. *Developmental Brain Research, 147,* 47–57.

Marin-Padilla, M. (1988). Early ontogenesis of the human cerebral cortex. In A. Peters & E. G. Jones (Eds.), *Cerebral cortex, Vol. 7: Development and maturation of the cerebral cortex* (pp.1–34). New York: Plenum.

Marin-Padilla, M. (1993). Pathogenese of late-acquired leptomeningeal heterotopias and secondary cortical alterations: A Golgi study. In A. M. Galaburda (Ed.), *Dyslexia and development: Neurobiological aspects of extraordinary brains* (pp. 64–88). Cambridge, MA: Harvard University Press.

Michel, G. F., & Moore, C. L. (1995). *Developmental psychobiology.* Cambridge, MA: MIT Press.

Moore, K. L. (1988). *The developing human: Clinically oriented embryology* (4th ed.). Philadelphia: Saunders.

Morshead, C. M., & van der Kooy, D. (2004). Disguising adult neural stem cells. *Current Opinion in Neurobiology, 14,* 125–131.

Myers, D. G. (1998). *Psychology* (5th ed.). New York: Worth Publishers.

National Institute on Drug Abuse. (1995). NIDA survey provides first national data on drug use during pregnancy. *NIDA Research Findings, 10*(1), 1–2.

National Institute on Drug Abuse. (1998). *Research report series: Nicotine addiction* (pp. 1–8). NIH Publ. 01-4342.

National Institute on Drug Abuse. (1999). Prenatal cocaine exposure costs at least $352 million per year. *NIDA Research Findings, 13*(5), 1–2.

Overman, W., Bachevalier, J., Schuhmann, E., & Ryan, P. (1996). Cognitive gender differences in very young children parallel biologically based cognitive gender differences in monkeys. *Behavioral Neuroscience, 110,* 673–684.

Overman, W., Bachevalier, J., Turner, M., & Peuster, A. (1992). Object recognition versus object discrimination: Comparison between human infants and infant monkeys. *Behavioral Neuroscience, 106,* 15–29.

Piaget, J. (1952). *The origins of intelligence in children.* New York: Norton.

Purpura, D. P. (1974). Dendritic spine "dysgenesis" and mental retardation. *Science, 186,* 1126–1127.

Purpura, D. P. (1975). Normal and abnormal development of cerebral cortex in man. *Neurosciences Research Program Bulletin, 20,* 569–577.

Purves, D., & Lichtman, J. W. (1985). *Principles of neural development.* Sunderland, MA: Sinauer.

Rakic, P. (1995). Corticogenesis in human and nonhuman primates. In M. Gazzaniga (ed.), *The cognitive neurosciences* (pp. 127–145). Cambridge, MA: MIT Press.

Riesen, A. H. (1975). *The developmental neuropsychology of sensory deprivation.* New York: Academic Press.

Riesen, A. H. (1982). Effects of environments on development in sensory systems. In W. D. Neff (Ed.), *Contributions to sensory physiology* (Vol. 6, pp. 45–77). New York: Academic Press.

Rutter, M. (1998). Developmental catch-up, and deficit, following adoption after severe global early privation. *Journal of Child Psychology and Psychiatry, 39,* 465–476.

Salm, A. K., Pavelko, M., Drouse, E. M., Webster, W., Kraszpulski, M., & Birkle, D. L. (2004). Lateral amygdala nucleus expansion in adult rats is associated with exposure to prenatal stress. *Developmental Brain Research, 148,* 159–167.

Sherman, S. M., & Spear, P. D. (1982). Organization of visual pathways in normal and visually deprived cats. *Physiological Reviews, 62,* 738–855.

Shingo, T., Gregg, C., Enwere, E., Fujikawa, H., Hassam, R., Geary, C., Cross, J. C., & Weiss, S. (2003). Pregnancy-stimulated neurogenesis in the adult female forebrain mediated by prolactin. *Science, 299,* 117–120.

Snowdon, D. A. (1997). Aging and Alzheimer's disease: Lessons from the nun study. *Gerontologist, 37,* 150–156.

Sodhi, M. S., & Sanders-Bush, E. (2004). Serotonin and brain development. *International Review of Neurobiology, 59,* 111–174.

Sperry, R. W. (1963). Chemoaffinity in the orderly growth of nerve fiber patterns and connections. *Proceedings of the National Academy of Sciences, USA, 50,* 703–710.

Spreen, O., Tupper, D., Risser, A., Tuokko, H., & Edgell, D. (1984). *Human developmental neuropsychology.* New York: Oxford University Press.

Twitchell, T. E. (1965). The automatic grasping response of infants. *Neuropsychologia, 3,* 247–259.

Volpe, J. J. (1987). *Neurology of the newborn* (2nd ed.). Philadelphia: Saunders.

Weiss, S., Reynolds, B. A., Vescovi, A. L., Morshead, C., Craig, C. G., & van der Kooy, D. (1996). Is there a neural stem cell in the mammalian forebrain? *Trends in Neurosciences, 19*(9), 387–393.

Werker, J. F., & Tees, R. C. (1992). The organization and reorganization of human speech perception. *Annual Review of Neuroscience, 15,* 377–402.

Wiesel, T. N. (1982). Postnatal development of the visual cortex and the influence of environment. *Nature, 299,* 583–591.

Yakolvlev, P. E., & Lecours, A.-R. (1967). The myelogenetic cycles of regional maturation of the brain. In A. Minkowski (Ed.), *Regional development of the brain in early life.* Oxford: Blackwell.

Chapter 7

Anglin, M. D., Burke, C., Perrochet, B., Stamper, E., & Dawud-Noursi, S. (2000). History of the methamphetamine problem. *Journal of Psychoactive Drugs, 32,* 137–141.

Becker, J. B., Breedlove, S. M., & Crews, D. (1992). *Behavioral endocrinology.* Cambridge, MA: MIT Press.

Becker, J. B., Breedlove, S. M., Crews, D., & McCarthy, M. M. (2002). *Behavioral endocrinology* (2nd ed.). Cambridge, MA: Bradford.

Castañeda, E., Becker, J., & Robinson, T. E. (1988). The long-term effects of repeated amphetamine treatment in vivo on amphetamine, KCl, and electrical stimulation evoked striatal dopamine release in vitro. *Life Sciences, 42,* 2447–2457.

Comer, R. J. (2004). *Abnormal psychology.* New York: W. H. Freeman and Company.

Comings, D. E., Rosenthal, R. J., Lesieur, H. R., Rugle, L. J., Muhleman, D., Chiu, C., Dietz, G., & Gade, R. (1996). A study of the dopamine D_2 receptor gene in pathological gambling. *Pharmacogenetics, 6,* 223–234.

Cooper, J. R., Bloom, F. E., & Roth, R. H. (1998). *The biochemical basis of neuropharmacology.* New York: Oxford University Press.

Feldman, R. S., Meyer, J. S., & Quenzer, L. F. (1997). *Principles of neuropsychopharmacology.* Sunderland, MA: Sinauer.

Fraioli, S., Crombag, H. S., Badiani, A., & Robinson, T. E. (1999). Susceptibility to amphetamine-induced locomotor sensitization is modulated by environmental stimuli. *Neuropsychopharmacology, 20,* 533–541.

Freud, S. (1974). *Cocaine papers* (R. Byck, Ed.). New York: Penguin.

Gilbertson, M. W., Shenton, M. E., Ciszewski, A., Kasai, K., Lasko, N. B., Orr, S. P., & Pitman, R. K. (2002). Smaller hippocampal volume predicts pathologic vulnerability to psychological trauma. *Nature Neuroscience, 5,* 1242–1247.

Hampson, E., & Kimura, D. (1992). Sex differences and hormonal influences on cognitive function in humans. In J. B. Becker, S. M. Breedlove, & D. Crews (Eds.), *Behavioral endocrinology* (pp. 357–398). Cambridge, MA: MIT Press.

Henquet, C., Krabbendam, L., Spauwen, J., Kaplan, C., Lieb, R., Wittchen, H. U., & van Os, J. (2004). Prospective cohort study of cannabis use, predisposition for psychosis, and symptoms in young people. *British Medical Journal,* 10.1126 on-line (5 pp.).

Hynie, I., & Todd, E. C. D. (1990). Domoic acid toxicity. *Canada Diseases Weekly Report, 16.*

Inturrisi, C. E. (2002). Clinical pharmacology of opioids for pain. *Clinical Journal for Pain, 18*(Suppl.), S3–S13.

Isbell, H., Fraser, H. F., Wikler, R. E., Belleville, R. E., & Eisenman, A. J. (1955). An experimental study of the etiology of "rum fits" and delirium tremens. *Quarterly Journal of Studies on Alcohol, 16,* 1–35.

Julien, R. M. (1995). *A primer of drug action.* New York: W. H. Freeman and Company.

Khan, A., Khan, S., Kolts, R., & Brown, W. A. (2003). Suicide rates in clinical trials of SSRIs, other antidepressants, and placebo: Analysis of FDA reports. *American Journal of Psychiatry, 160,* 790–792.

Kosterlitz, H. W., & Hughes, J. (1977). Peptides with morphine-like action in the brain. *British Journal of Psychiatry, 130,* 298–304.

Liberzon, I., & Phan, K. L. (2003). Brain-imaging studies of posttraumatic stress disorder. *CNS Spectroscopy, 8,* 641–650.

MacAndrew, C., & Edgerton, R. B. (1969). *Drunken comportment: A social explanation.* Chicago: Aldine.

MacDonald, T. K., Zanna, M. P., & Fong, G. T. (1998). Alcohol and intentions to engage in risky health-related behaviours: Experimental evidence for a casual relationship. In J. Adair & F. Craik (Eds.), *Advances in psychological science: Vol. 2. Developmental, personal, and social aspects* (pp. 12–59). East Sussex, UK: Psychology Press.

McCann, U. D., Lowe, K. A., & Ricaurte, G. A. (1997). Long-lasting effects of recreational drugs of abuse on the central nervous system. *The Neurologist, 3,* 399–411.

Medwar C., & Hardon, A. (2004). *Medicines out of control: Antidepressants and the conspiracy of goodwill.* New York: Aksant, Transaction.

Morgan, M. S. (1999). Memory deficits associated with recreational use of "ecstasy." *Psychopharmacology, 141,* 30–36.

Morrow, A. L., Janis, G. C., VanDoren, M. J., Matthews, D. B., Samson, H. H., Janak, P. H., & Grant, K. A. (1999). Neurosteroids mediate pharmacological effects of ethanol: A new mechanism of ethanol action? *Alcohol and Clinical and Experimental Research, 23,* 1933–1940.

Olney, J. W., Ho, O. L., & Rhee, V. (1971). Cytotoxic effects of acidic and sulphur-containing amino acids on the infant mouse central nervous system. *Experimental Brain Research, 14,* 61–67.

Pert, C. B., & Snyder, S. H. (1973). Properties of opiate-receptor binding in rat brain. *Proceedings of the National Academy of Sciences, USA, 70,* 2243–2247.

Piazza, P. V., Deminiere, J. M., LeMoal, M., & Simon, H. (1989). Factors that predict individual vulnerability to amphetamine self-administration. *Science, 29,* 1511–1513.

Phillips, P. E. M., Stuber, G. D., Helen, M. L. A. V., Wightman, R. M., & Carelli, R. M. (2003). Subsecond dopamine release promotes cocaine seeking. *Nature, 422,* 614–818.

Robinson, T. E., & Becker, J. B. (1986). Enduring changes in brain and behavior produced by chronic amphetamine administration: A review and evaluation of animal models of amphetamine psychosis. *Brain Research Reviews, 11,* 157–198.

Robinson, T. E., & Berridge, K. C. (1993). The neural basis of drug craving: An incentive-sensitization theory of addiction. *Brain Research Reviews, 18,* 247–291.

Santarelli, L., Saxe, M., Gross, C., Surget, A., Battaglia, F., Dulawa, S., Weisstaub, N., Lee, J., Duman, R., Arancio, O., Belzung, C., & Hen, R. (2003). Requirement of hippocampal neurogenesis for the behavioral effects of antidepressants. *Science, 301,* 805–809.

Sapolsky, R. M. (1992). *Stress, the aging brain, and the mechanisms of neuron death.* Cambridge, MA: MIT Press.

Sapolsky, R. M. (1994). *Why zebras don't get ulcers.* New York: W. H. Freeman and Company.

Sapolsky, R. M. (2003). Stress and plasticity in the limbic system. *Neurochemical Research, 28,* 1735–1742.

Teitelbaum, J. S., Zatorre, R. J., Carpenter, S., Gendron, D., Evans, A. C., Gjedde, A., & Cashman, N. R. (1990). Neurologic sequelae of domoic acid intoxication due to the ingestion of contaminated mussels. *New England Journal of Medicine, 322,* 1781–1787.

Thompson, P. M., Hayashi, D. M., Simon, S. L., Gheaga, J. A., Hong, M. S., Sui, Y., Lee, J. Y., Toga, A. W., Ling, W., & London, E. D. (2004). Structural abnormalities in the brains of human subjects who use methamphetamine. *Journal of Neuroscience, 24,* 6028–6036.

Wenger, J. R., Tiffany, T. M., Bombardier, C., Nicholls, K., & Woods, S. C. (1981). Ethanol tolerance in the rat is learned. *Science, 213,* 575–577.

Whishaw, I. Q., Mittleman, G., & Evenden, J. L. (1989). Training-dependent decay in performance produced by the neuroleptic *cis(Z)*-flupentixol on spatial navigation by rats in a swimming pool. *Pharmacology, Biochemistry, and Behavior, 32,* 211–220.

Zink, C. F., Pagnoni, G., Martin-Skurski, M. E., Chappelow, J. C., & Berns G. S. (2004). Human striatal responses to monetary reward depend on saliency. *Neuron, 42,* 509–517.

Chapter 8

Balint, R. (1909). Seelenlähmung des Schauens optiche ataxie, räumlielie Störung der Aufmerksamkeit. *Monatschrift fuer Psychiatrie und Neurologie, 25,* 51–81.

Farah, M. J. (1990). *Visual agnosia.* Cambridge, MA: MIT Press.

Geschwind, N. (1972). Language and the brain. *Scientific American, 226*(4), 78–83.

Goodale, M. A., Milner, D. A., Jakobson, L. S., & Carey, J. D. P. (1991). A kinematic analysis of reaching and grasping movements in a patient recovering from optic ataxia. *Nature, 349,* 154–156.

Held, R. (1968). Dissociation of visual function by deprivation and rearrangement. *Psychologische Forschung, 31,* 338–348.

Hubel, D. H. (1988). *Eye, brain, and vision.* New York: Scientific American Library.

Kline, D. W. (1994). Optimizing the visibility of displays for older observers. *Experimental Aging Research, 20,* 11–23.

Kuffler, S. W. (1952). Neurons in the retina: Organization, inhibition and excitatory problems. *Cold Spring Harbor Symposia on Quantitative Biology, 17,* 281–292.

Lashley, K. S. (1941). Patterns of cerebral integration indicated by the scotomas of migraine. *Archives of Neurology and Psychiatry, 46,* 331–339.

Merbs, S. L., & Nathans, J. (1992). Absorption spectra of human cone pigments. *Nature, 356,* 433–435.

Milner, A. D., & Goodale, M. A. (1995). *The visual brain in action.* Oxford: Oxford University Press.

Posner, M. I., & Raichle, M. E. (1997). *Images of the mind.* New York: Scientific American Library.

Prusky, G., & Douglas, R. (2004). Rapid quantification of adult and developing mouse spatial vision using a virtual optomotor system. Manuscript submitted for publication.

Purves, D., Augustine, G. J., Fitzpatrick, D., Katz, L. C., LaMantia, A.-S., & McNamara, J. O. (Eds.). *Neuroscience.* Sunderland, MA: Sinauer.

Sacks, O., & Wasserman, R. (1987). The case of the colorblind painter. *The New York Review of Books, 34,* 25–33.

Szentagothai, J. (1975). The "module-concept" in cerebral cortex architecture. *Brain Research, 95,* 475–496.

Tanaka, K. (1993). Neuronal mechanisms of object recognition. *Science, 262,* 685–688.

Tanaka, K. (1996). Inferotemporal cortex and object vision. *Annual Review of Neuroscience, 19,* 100–139.

Weizkrantz, L. (1986). *Blindsight: A case study and implications.* Oxford: Oxford University Press.

Winderickx, J., Lindsey, D. T., Sanocki, E., Teller, D. Y., Motulsky, B. G, & Deeb, S. S. (1992). Polymorphism in red photopigment underlies variation in colour matching. *Nature, 356,* 431–433.

Wong-Riley, M. T. T., Hevner, R. F., Cutlan, R., Earnest, M., Egan, R., Frost, J., & Nguyen, T. (1993). Cytochrome oxidase in the human visual cortex: Distribution in the developing and the adult brain. *Visual Neuroscience, 10,* 41–58.

Zeki, S. (1993). *A vision of the brain.* Oxford: Blackwell Scientific.

Zihl, J., von Cramon, D., & Mai, N. (1983). Selective disturbance of movement vision after bilateral brain damage. *Brain, 106,* 313–340.

Chapter 9

Belin, P., Zatorre, R. J., Lafaille, P., & Pike, B. (2000). Voice-selective areas in the human auditory cortex. *Nature, 403,* 309–312.

Chomsky, N. (1965). *Aspects of the theory of syntax.* Cambridge, MA: MIT Press.

Drake-Lee, A. B. (1992). Beyond music: Auditory temporary threshold shift in rock musicians after a heavy metal concert. *Journal of the Royal Society of Medicine, 85,* 617–619.

Fiez, J. A., Raichle, M. E., Balota, D. A., Tallal, P., & Petersen, S. E. (1996). PET activation of posterior temporal regions during auditory word presentation and verb generation. *Cerebral Cortex, 6,* 1–10.

Fiez, J. A., Raichle, M. E., Miezin, F. M., & Petersen, S. E. (1995). PET studies of auditory and phonological processing: Effects of stimulus characteristics and task demands. *Journal of Cognitive Neuroscience, 7,* 357–375.

Frackowiak, R. S. J., Friston, K. J., Frith, C. D., Dolan, R. J., & Mazziotta, J. C. (1997). *Human brain function.* San Diego: Academic Press.

Gazzaniga, M. S. (1992). *Nature's mind.* New York: Basic Books.

Geissmann, T. (2001). Gibbon songs and human music from an evolutionary perspective. In N. L. Wallin, B. Merker, & S. Brown (Eds.), *The origins of music* (pp. 103–124). Cambridge, MA: MIT Press.

Heffner, H. E., & Heffner, R. S. (1990). Role of primate auditory cortex in hearing. In W. C. Stebbins & M. A. Berkeley (Eds.), *Comparative perception: Vol. 2. Complex signals* (pp. 279–310). New York: Wiley.

Hirsh, I. J. (1966). Audition. In J. B. Sidowsky (Ed.), *Experimental methods and instrumentation in psychology* (pp.247–272). New York: McGraw-Hill.

Knudsen, E. I. (1981). The hearing of the barn owl. *Scientific American, 245*(6), 113–125.

Lewis, D. B., & Gower, D. M. (1980). *Biology of communication.* New York: Wiley.

Loeb, G. E. (1990). Cochlear prosthetics. *Annual Review of Neuroscience, 13,* 357–371.

Luria, A. R. (1972). *The man with a shattered world.* Chicago: Regnery.

Marler, P. (1991). The instinct to learn. In S. Carey and R. German (Eds.), The Epigenesis of mind: Essays on biology and cognition (p. 39), Hillsdale, NJ: Lawrence Erlbaum.

McFarland, D. (1985). *Animal behaviour.* Bath, UK: Pitman Press.

Neuweiler, G. (1990). Auditory adaptations for prey capture in echolocating bats. *Physiological Reviews, 70,* 615–641.

Nottebohm, F., & Arnold, A. P. (1976). Sexual dimorphism in vocal control areas of the songbird brain. *Science, 194,* 211–213.

Penfield, W., & Rasmussen, T. (1950). *The cerebral cortex of man.* New York: Macmillan.

Penfield, W., & Roberts, L. (1959). *Speech and brain mechanisms.* Princeton, NJ: Princeton University Press.

Peretz, I., Kolinsky, R., Tramo, M., Labrecque, R., Hublet, C., Demeurisse, G., & Belleville, S. (1994). Functional dissociations following bilateral lesions of auditory cortex. *Brain, 117,* 1283–1301.

Pinker, S. (1997). *How the mind works.* New York: Norton.

Posner, M. I., & Raichle, M. E. (1997). *Images of mind.* New York: W. H. Freeman and Company.

Purves, D., Augustine, G. J., Fitzpatrick, D., Katz, L. C., LaMantia, A.-S., & McNamara, J. O. (1997). *Neuroscience.* Sunderland, MA: Sinauer.

Rauschecker, J. P., Tian, B., & Hauser, M. (1995). Processing of complex sounds in the macaque nonprimary auditory cortex. *Science, 268,* 111–114.

Romanski, L. M., Tian, B., Fritz, J., Mishkin, M., Goldman-Rakic, P. S., & Rauschecker, J. P. (1999). Dual streams of auditory afferents target multiple domains in the primate prefrontal cortex. *Nature Neuroscience, 2,* 1131–1136.

Shepherd, G. M. (1994). *Neurobiology* (3rd ed.). New York: Oxford University Press.

Trehub, S., Schellenberg, E. G., & Ramenetsky, G. B. (1999). Infants' and adults' perception of scale structures. *Journal of Experimental Psychology: Human Perception and Performance, 25,* 965–975.

Winter, P., & Funkenstein, H. (1971). The auditory cortex of the squirrel monkey: Neuronal discharge patterns to auditory stimuli. *Proceedings of the Third Congress of Primatology, Zurich, 2,* 24–28.

Yost, W. A. (1991). Auditory image perception and analysis: The basis for hearing. *Hearing Research, 56,* 8–18.

Zatorre, R. J., Evans, A. C., & Meyer, E. (1994). Neural mechanisms underlying melodic perception and memory for pitch. *Journal of Neuroscience, 14,* 1908–1919.

Zatorre, R. J., Evans, A. C., Meyer, E., & Gjedde, A. (1992). Lateralization of phonetic and pitch discrimination in speech processing. *Science, 256,* 846–849.

Zatorre, R. J., Meyer, E., Gjedde, A., & Evans, A. C. (1995). PET studies of phonetic processing of speech: Review, replication, and reanalysis. *Cerebral Cortex, 6,* 21–30.

Chapter 10

Aldridge, J. W. (2005). Grooming. In I. Q. Whishaw and B. Kolb (Eds.), *Analysis of behavior of the laboratory rat* (pp. 141–149). New York: Oxford University Press.

Alexander, R. E., & Crutcher, M. D. (1990). Functional architecture of basal ganglia circuits: Neural substrates of parallel processing. *Trends in Neurosciences, 13,* 266–271.

Asanuma, H. (1989). *The motor cortex.* New York: Raven Press.

Bauman, M. L., & Kemper, T. L. (1994). *The neurobiology of autism.* Baltimore: Johns Hopkins University Press.

Blakemore, S.-J., Wolpert, D. M., & Frith, C. D. (1998). Central cancellation of self-produced tickle sensation. *Nature Neuroscience, 1,* 635–640.

Brinkman, C. (1984). Supplementary motor area of the monkey's cerebral cortex: Short- and long-term deficits after unilateral ablation and the effects of subsequent callosal section. *Journal of Neuroscience, 4,* 918–992.

Bucy, P. C., Keplinger, J. E., & Siqueira, E. B. (1964). Destruction of the "pyramidal tract" in man. *Journal of Neurosurgery, 21,* 385–398.

Corkin, S., Milner, B., & Rasmussen, T. (1970). Somatosensory thresholds. *Archives of Neurology, 23,* 41–58.

Courchense, E., Carper, R., & Akshoomoff, N. (2003). Evidence of brain overgrowth in the first year of life in autism. *Journal of the American Medical Association, 290,* 337–344.

Critchley, M. (1953). *The parietal lobes.* London: Arnold.

Crowe, D. A., Chafee, M. V., Averbeck, B. B., & Georgopoulos, A.P. (2004). Participation of primary motor cortical neurons in a distributed network during maze solution: Representation of spatial parameters and time-course comparison with parietal area 7a. *Experimental Brain Research, 158,* 28–34.

Evarts, E. V. (1968). Relation of pyramidal tract activity to force exerted during voluntary movement. *Journal of Neurophysiology, 31,* 14–27.

Fadiga, L., & Craighero, L. (2004). Electrophysiology of action representation. *Journal of Clinical Neurophysiology, 21,* 100–106.

Friedhoff, A. J., & Chase, T. N. (1982). Gilles de la Tourette syndrome. *Advances in Neurology, 35,* 1–17.

Galea, M. P., & Darian-Smith, I. (1994). Multiple corticospinal neuron populations in the macaque monkey are specified by their unique cortical origins, spinal terminations, and connections. *Cerebral Cortex, 4,* 166–194.

Georgopoulos, A. P., Kalaska, J. F., Caminiti, R., & Massey, J. T. (1982). On the relations between the direction of two-dimentional arm movements and cell discharge in primate motor cortex. *Journal of Neuroscience, 2,* 1527–1537.

Georgopoulos, A. P., Pellizzer, G., Poliakov, A. V., & Schieber, M. H. (1999). Neural coding of finger and wrist movements. *Journal of Computational Neuroscience, 6,* 279–288.

Georgopoulos, A.P., Taira, M., & Lukashin, A. (1993). Cognitive neurophysiology of the motor cortex. *Science, 260,* 47–52.

Hess, W. R. (1957). *The functional organization of the diencephalon.* London: Grune & Stratton.

Hughlings-Jackson, J. (1931). *Selected writings of John Hughlings-Jackson* (Vols. 1 and 2, J. Taylor, Ed.). London: Hodder.

Kaas, J. H. (1987). The organization and evolution of neocortex. In S. P. Wise (Ed.), *Higher brain functions* (pp. 237–298). New York: Wiley.

Kandel, E. R., Schwartz, J. H., & Jessell, T. M. (Eds.). (2000). *Principles of neural science* (4th ed.). New York: McGraw-Hill.

Keele, S. W., & Ivry, R. (1991). Does the cerebellum provide a common computation for diverse tasks? A timing hypothesis. *Annals of the New York Academy of Sciences, 608,* 197–211.

Komar & Melamid. (2004). *When elephants paint: The quest of two Russian artists to save the elephants of Thailand.* New York: HarperCollins.

Kuypers, H. G. J. M. (1981). Anatomy of descending pathways. In V. B. Brooks (Ed.), *Handbook of Physiology, Vol. 7: The nervous system* (pp. 579–666). Bethesda, MD: American Physiological Society.

Lang, C. E., & Schieber, M. H. (2004). Reduced muscle selectivity during individuated finger movements in humans after damage to the motor cortex or corticospinal tract. *Journal of Neurophysiology, 91,* 1722–1733.

Lashley, K. S. (1951). The problem of serial order in behavior. In L. A. Jeffress (Ed.), *Cerebral mechanisms and behavior* (pp. 112–136). New York: Wiley.

Leonard, C. M., Glendinning, D. S., Wilfong, T., Cooper, B. Y., & Vierck, C. J., Jr. (1991). Alterations of natural hand movements after interruption of fasciculus cuneatus in the macaque. *Somatosensory and Motor Research, 9,* 61–75.

Levitt, J. J., Blanton, R. E., Smalley, S., Thompson, P. M., Guthrie, D., McCracken, J. T., Sadoun, T., Heinichen, L., & Toga, A. W. (2003). Cortical sulcal maps in autism. *Cerebral Cortex, 7,* 728–735.

Melzack, R. (1973). *The puzzle of pain.* New York: Basic Books.

Melzack, R., & Wall, P. D. (1965). Pain mechanisms: A new theory. *Science, 150,* 971–979.

Mountcastle, V. B. (1978). An organizing principle for cerebral function: The unit module and the distributed system. In G. M. Edelman & V. B. Mountcastle (Eds.), *The mindful brain* (pp. 7–50). Cambridge, MA: MIT Press.

Napier, J. (1980). *Hands.* Princeton NJ: Princeton University Press.

Nudo, R. J., Wise, B. M., SiFuentes, F., & Milliken, G. W. (1996). Neural substrates for the effects of rehabilitative training on motor recovery after ischemic infarct. *Science, 272,* 1791–1794.

Onodera, S., & Hicks, T. P. (1999). Evolution of the motor system: Why the elephant's trunk works like a human's hand. *The Neuroscientist, 5,* 217–226.

Penfield, W., & Boldrey, E. (1958). Somatic motor and sensory representation in the cerebral cortex as studied by electrical stimulation. *Brain, 60,* 389–443.

Pons, T. P., Garraghty, P. E., Ommaya, A. K., Kaas, J. H., Taum, E., & Mishkin, M. (1991). Massive cortical reorganization after sensory deafferentation in adult macaques. *Science, 252,* 1857–1860.

Porter, R., & Lemon, R. (1993). *Corticospinal function and voluntary movement.* Oxford: Clarendon Press.

Roder, P. M. (2000). The early origins of autism. *Scientific American, 282*(2), 56–63.

Roland, P. E. (1993). *Brain activation.* New York: Wiley-Liss.

Rothwell, J. C., Taube, M. M., Day, B. L., Obeso, J. A., Thomas, P. K., & Marsden, C. D. (1982). Manual motor performance in a deafferented man. *Brain, 105,* 515–542.

Sacks, O. (1974). *Awakenings.* New York: Vintage.

Sacks, O. W. (1998). *The man who mistook his wife for a hat: And other clinical tales.* New York: Touchstone Books.

Schieber, M. H., & Hibbard, L. S. (1993). How somatotopic is the motor cortex hand area? *Science, 261,* 489–492.

Thatch, W. T., Goodkin, H. P., & Keating, J. G. (1992). The cerebellum and the adaptive coordination of movement. *Annual Reviews of Neuroscience, 15,* 403–442.

Twitchell, T. E. (1965). The automatic grasping response of infants. *Neuropsychologia, 3,* 247–259.

von Holst, E. (1973). *The collected papers of Erich von Holst* (R. Martin, Trans.). Coral Gables, FL: University of Miami Press.

Wallace, P. S., & Whishaw, I. Q. (2003). Independent digit movements and precision grip pattern in 1–5-month old human infants: Hand-babbling, including vacuous then self-directed hand and digit movements, precedes targeted reaching. *Neuropsychologia, 41,* 1912–1918.

Woolsey, T. A., & Wann, J. R. (1976). Areal changes in mouse cortical barrels following vibrissal damage at different postnatal ages. *Journal of Comparative Neurology, 170,* 53–66.

Chapter 11

Ackerly, S. S. (1964). A case of paranatal bilateral frontal lobe defect observed for thirty years. In J. M. Warren & K. Akert (Eds.), *The frontal granular cortex and behavior* (pp. 192–218). New York: McGraw-Hill.

Adelmann, P. K., & Zajonc, R. B. (1989). Facial efferents and the experience of emotion. *Annual Review of Psychology, 40,* 249–280.

Astrup, A., Larsen, T. M., & Harper, A. (2004). Atkins and other low-carbohydrate diets: Hoax or an effective tool for weight loss? *Lancet, 364,* 897–899.

Barondes, S. H. (1993). *Molecules and mental illness.* New York: Scientific American Library.

Bartoshuk, L. M. (2000). Comparing sensory experiences across individuals: Recent psychophysical advances illuminate genetic variation in taste perception. *Chemical Senses, 25,* 447–460.

Bartoshuk, L. M., Duffy, V. B., Lucchina, L. A., Prutkin, J., & Fast, K. (1998). PROP (6-*n*-propylthiouracil) supertasters and the saltiness of NaCl. *Annals of the New York Academy of Sciences, 855,* 793–796.

Beatty, J. (1995). *Principles of behavioral neuroscience.* Dubuque, IA: Brown & Benchmark.

Becker, J. B., Breedlove, S. M., & Crews, D. (1992). *Behavioral endocrinology.* Cambridge, MA: MIT Press.

Berridge, K. C. (1996). Food reward: Brain substrates of wanting and liking. *Neuroscience and Biobehavioral Reviews, 20,* 1–25.

Butler, R. A., & Harlow, H. F. (1954). Persistence of visual exploration in monkeys. *Journal of Comparative and Physiological Psychology, 47,* 257–263.

Byne, W. (1994). The biological evidence challenged. *Scientific American, 270*(5), 50–55.

Daly, M., & Wilson, M. (1988). *Homicide.* New York: Aldine.

Damasio, A. R. (1994). *Descartes' error: Emotion, reason, and the human brain.* New York: Plenum.

Damasio, A. R. (1999). *The feeling of what happens: Body and emotion in the making of consciousness.* New York: Harcourt Brace.

Davis, M., Walker, D. L., & Myers, K. M., (2003). Role of the amygdala in fear extinction measured with potentiated startle. *Annals of the New York Academy of Sciences, 985,* 218–232.

Dethier, V. G. (1962). *To know a fly.* San Francisco: Holden-Day.

Eibl-Eibesfeldt, I. (1989). *Human ethology.* New York: Aldine de Gruyter.

Eisenberger, N. I., Lieberman, M. D., & Williams, K. D. (2003). Does rejection hurt? An fMRI study of social exclusion. *Science, 302,* 290–292.

Everitt, B. J. (1990). Sexual motivation: A neural and behavioral analysis of the mechanisms underlying appetitive and copulatory responses of male rats. *Neuroscience and Biobehavioral Reviews, 14,* 217–232.

Field, T. M., Woodson, R., Greenberg, R., & Cohen, D. (1982), Discrimination and imitation of facial expression by neonates. *Science, 218,* 179–181.

Flegal, K. M., Carroll, M. D., Kuczmarski, R. J., & Johnson, C. L. (1998). Overweight and obesity in the United States: Prevalence and trends, 1960–1994. *International Journal of Obesity and Related Metabolic Disorders, 22,* 39–47.

Foster, G. D., Wyatt, H. R., Hill, J. O., McGuckin, B. G., Brill, C., Mohammed, B. S., Szapary, P. O., Rader, D. J., Edman, J. S., & Klein, S. (2003). A randomized trial of a low-carbohydrate diet for obesity. *New England Journal of Medicine, 348,* 2082–2090.

Garcia, J., & Koelling, R. A. (1966). Relation of cue to consequences in avoidance learning. *Psychonomic Science, 4,* 123–124.

Glickman, S. E., & Schiff, B. B. (1967). A biological theory of reinforcement. *Psychological Review, 74,* 81–109.

Gorski, R. A. (1984). Critical role for the medial preoptic area in the sexual differentiation of the brain. *Progress in Brain Research, 61,* 129–146.

Hamer, D. H., Hu, S., Magnuson, V. L., Hu, N., & Pattatucci, M. L. (1993). A linkage between DNA markers on the X chromosome and male sexual orientation. *Science, 261,* 321–327.

Hebb, D. O. (1955). Drives and the C.N.S. (conceptual nervous system). *Psychological Review, 62,* 243–254.

Heron, W. (1957). The pathology of boredom. *Scientific American, 196*(1), 52–56.

Insel, T. R., & Fernald, R. D. (2004). How the brain processes social information: Searching for the social brain. *Annual Review of Neuroscience, 27,* 697–722.

Jacob, S., Kinnunen, L. H., Metz, J., Cooper, M., & McClintock, M. K. (2001). Sustained human chemosignal unconsciously alters brain function. *Neuroreport, 12,* 2391–2394.

Jacobsen, C. F. (1936). Studies of cerebral function in primates. *Comparative Psychology Monographs, 13,* 1–68.

Klüver, H., & Bucy, P. C. (1939). Preliminary analysis of the temporal lobes in monkeys. *Archives of Neurology and Psychiatry, 42,* 979–1000.

Kolb, B., & Nonneman, A. J. (1975). The development of social responsiveness in kittens. *Animal Behavior, 23,* 368–374.

Kolb, B., & Taylor, L. (2000). Facial expression, emotion, and hemispheric organization. In L. Nadel & R. D. Lane (Eds.), *Cognitive neuroscience of emotion* (pp. 62–83). New York: Oxford University Press.

Lane, R. D., & Nadel, L. (Eds.). (2000). *Cognitive neuroscience of emotion.* New York: Oxford University Press.

LeDoux, J. (1996). *The emotional brain.* New York: Simon & Schuster.

MacLean, P. D. (1949). Psychosomatic disease and the "visceral brain": Recent developments bearing on the Papez theory of emotion. *Psychosomatic Medicine, 11,* 338–353.

Money, J., & Ehrhardt, A. A. (1972). *Man and woman, boy and girl.* Baltimore: Johns Hopkins University Press.

Nieuwenhuys, R., Voogd, J., & van Huijzen, C. (1981). *The human central nervous system: A synopsis and atlas* (2nd ed.). Berlin: Springer Verlag.

Olds, J., & Milner, P. (1954). Positive reinforcement produced by electrical stimulation of septal area and other regions of rat brain. *Journal of Comparative and Physiological Psychology, 47,* 419–427.

Panagiotakos, D. B., Pitsavos, C., Polychronopoulos, E., Chrysohoou, C., Zampelas, A., & Trichopoulou, A. (2004). Can a Mediterranean diet moderate the development and clinical progression of coronary heart disease? A systematic review. *Medical Science Monitor, 10,* RA193–RA198.

Robinson, T. E., & Berridge, K. C. (1993). The neural basis of drug craving: An incentive-sensitization theory of addiction. *Brain Research Reviews, 18,* 247–291.

Robinson, T. E., & Berridge, K. C. (2003). Addiction. *Annual Review of Psychology, 54,* 25–53.

Seeley, R. J., & Woods, S. C. (2003). Monitoring of stored and available fuel by the CNS: Implications for obesity. *Nature Reviews Neuroscience, 4,* 885–909.

Skinner, B. F. (1938). *The behavior of organisms.* New York: Appleton-Century-Crofts.

Smith, D. V., & Shepherd, G.M. (2003). Chemical senses: Taste and olfaction. In L. R. Squire, F. E. Bloom, S. K. McConnell, J. L. Roberts, N. C. Spitzer, & M. J. Zigmond (Eds.), *Fundamental neuroscience* (2nd ed., pp. 631–667). New York: Academic Press.

Spanagel, R., & Weiss, F. (1999). The dopamine hypothesis of reward: Past and current status. *Trends in Neurosciences, 22,* 521–527.

Stern, K., & McClintock, M. K. (1998). Regulation of ovulation by human pheromones. *Nature, 392,* 177–179.

Swaab, D. F., Gooren, L. J., & Hofman, M. A. (1995). Brain research, gender and sexual orientation. *Homosexuality, 28,* 283–301.

Swaab, D. F., & Hofman, M. A. (1995). Sexual differentiation of the human hypothalamus in relation to gender and sexual orientation. *Trends in Neurosciences, 18,* 264–270.

Trujillo, K. A., Herman, J. P., & Schafer, M.-H. (1993). Drug reward and brain circuitry: Recent advances and future directions. In S. G. Korenman & J. D. Barchas (Eds.), *Biological bases of substance abuse* (pp. 119–142). New York: Oxford University Press.

Vasey, P. L. (2002). Sexual partner preference in female Japanese macaques. *Archives of Sexual Behavior, 31,* 51–62.

Wise, R. A. (1996). Addictive drugs and brain stimulation reward. *Annual Review of Neuroscience, 19,* 319–340.

Woods, S. C., Seeley, R. J., Porte, D., & Schwartz, M. W. (1998). Signals that regulate food intake and energy homeostasis. *Science, 280,* 1378–1382.

Woolley, C. S., Gould, E., Frankfurt, M., & McEwen, B. (1990). Naturally occurring fluctuation in dendritic spine density on adult hippocampal pyramidal neurons. *Journal of Neuroscience, 10,* 4035–4039.

World Health Organization. (2000). Obesity: Preventing and managing the global epidemic. WHO Technical Report Series, No. 894, 1–253.

Chapter 12

Amir, S., & Stewart, J. (1996). Resetting of the circadian clock by a conditioned stimulus. *Nature, 8,* 542–545.

Archer S. N., Robilliard, D. L., Skene, D. J., Smits, M., Williams, A., Arendt, J., & von Schantz, M. (2003). A length polymorphism in circadian clock gene *Per3* is linked to delayed sleep phase syndrome and extreme diurnal preference. *Sleep, 26,* 413–415.

Binkley, S. (1990). *The clockwork sparrow.* Englewood Cliffs, NJ: Prentice Hall.

Cheng, M. Y., Bullock, C.. M., Li, C., Lee, A. G., Bermak, J. C., Belluzzi, J., Weaver, D. R., Leslie, F. M., & Zou, W.-Y. (2003). Prokineticin 2 transmits the behavioural circadian rhythm of the suprachiasmatic nucleus. *Nature, 417,* 405–410.

Cohen, D. B. (1979). *Sleep and dreaming: Origins, nature and functions.* Oxford: Pergamon.

Coogan, A. N., & Piggins, H. D. (2004). MAP kinases in the mammalian circadian system: Key regulators of clock function. *Journal of Neurochemistry, 90,* 769–775.

de la Iglesia, H. O., Cambras, T., Schwartz, W. J., & Diez-Noguera, A. (2004). Forced desynchronization of dual circadian oscillators within the rat suprachiasmatic nucleus. *Current Biology, 14,* 796–800.

Dement, W. C. (1972). *Some must watch while some must sleep.* Stanford, CA: Stanford Alumni Association.

Earnest, D. J., Liang, E. Q., Ratcliff, M., & Cassone, V. M. (1999). Immortal time: Circadian clock properties of rat suprachiasmatic cell lines. *Science, 283,* 693–695.

Estivill, E., de la Fuente-Panell, V., Segarra-Isern, F., & Albares-Tendero, J. (2004). Restless legs syndrome in a patient with amputation of both legs. *Revista de Neurologia, 39,* 536–538.

Hall, C. S., Domhoff, G. W., Blick, K. A., & Weesner, K. E. (1982). The dreams of college men and women in 1950 and 1980: A comparison of dream contents and sex differences. *Sleep, 5,* 188–194.

Hobson, J. A. (1989). *Sleep.* New York: Scientific American Library.

Hobson J. A. (2002). Sleep and dream suppression following a lateral medullary infarct: A first-person account. *Consciousness and Cognition, 11,* 377–390.

Hobson, J. A. (2004). *13 dreams Freud never had: A new mind science.* New York: Pi Press.

Jones, B. E. (1993). The organization of central cholinergic systems and their functional importance in sleep-waking states. *Progress in Brain Research, 98,* 61–71.

Jouvet, M. (1972). The role of monoamines and acetylcholine-containing neurons in the regulation of the sleep–waking cycle. *Ergebnisse der Physiologie, 64,* 166–307.

Kleitman, N. (1965). *Sleep and wakefulness.* Chicago: University of Chicago Press.

Lamberg, L. (2003). Scientists never dreamed finding would shape half-century of sleep research. *Journal of the American Medical Association, 290,* 2652–2654.

Lavie, P., Pratt, H., Scharf, B., Peled, R., & Brown, J. (1984). Localized pontine lesion: Nearly total absence of REM sleep. *Neurology, 34,* 118–120.

Maquet, P., Laureys, S., Peigneux, P., Fuchs, S., Petiau, C., Phillips, C., Aerts, J., Del Fiore, G., Degueldre, C., Meulemaqns, T., Luxen, A., Franck, G., Ven Der Linden, M., Smith, C., & Cleermans, A. (2000). Experience dependent changes in cerebral activation during human REM sleep. *Nature Neuroscience, 3,* 831–836.

Markand, O. N., & Dyken, M. L. (1976). Sleep abnormalities in patients with brain stem lesions. *Neurology, 26,* 769–776.

Mignot, E. (2004). A year in review: Basic science, narcolepsy, and sleep in neurological diseases. *Sleep, 27,* 1209–1212.

Moruzzi, G., & Magoun, H .W. (1949). Brain stem reticular formation and activation of the EEG. *Electroencephalography and Clinical Neurophysiology, 1,* 455–473.

Osorio, I., & Daroff, R. B. (1980). Absence of REM and altered NREM sleep in patients with spinocerebellar degeneration and slow saccades. *Annals of Neurology, 7,* 277–280.

Quinlan, J., & Quinlan, J. (1977). *Karen Ann: The Quinlans tell their story.* Toronto: Doubleday.

Ralph, M. R., & Lehman, M. N. (1991). Transplantation: A new tool in the analysis of the mammalian hypothalamic circadian pacemaker. *Trends in Neurosciences, 14,* 363–366.

Raven, P. H., Evert, R. F., & Eichorn, S. E. (1992). *Biology of plants.* New York: Worth Publishers.

Revonsuo, A. (2000). The reinterpretation of dreams: An evolutionary hypothesis of the function of dreaming. *Behavioral and Brain Sciences, 24,* 277–299.

Reiter, R. J. (1980). The pineal and its hormones in the control of reproduction in mammals. *Endocrinology Review, 1,* 109–131.

Richter, C. P. (1965). *Biological clocks in medicine and psychiatry.* Springfield, IL: Charles C Thomas.

Roffward, H. P., Muzio, J., & Dement, W. C. (1966). Ontogenetic development of the human sleep-dream cycle. *Science, 152,* 604–619.

Rosen, C. L., Storfer-Isser, A., Taylor, H. G., Kirchner, H. L., Emancipator, J. L., & Redline, S. (2004). Increased behavioral morbidity in school-aged children with sleep-disordered breathing. *Pediatrics, 114,* 1640–1648.

Schenck, C. H., Bundlie, S. R., Ettinger, M. G., & Mahowald, M. W. (1986). Chronic behavioral disorders of human REM sleep: A new category of parasomnia. *Sleep, 9,* 293–308.

Siegel, J. (2004). Brain mechanisms that control sleep and waking. *Naturwissenschaften, 91,* 355–365.

Stoleru, D., Peng, Y., Agosto, J., & Rosbash, M. (2004). Coupled oscillators control morning and evening locomotor behavior of *Drosophila. Nature, 431,* 862–868.

Vanderwolf, C. H. (1988). Cerebral activity and behavior: Control by central cholinergic and serotonergic systems. *International Review of Neurobiology, 30,* 225–340.

Vertes, R. P. (2004). Memory consolidation in sleep: Dream or reality. *Neuron, 44,*135–148.

Vogel, G. Q., Buffenstein, A., Minter, K., & Hennessey, A. (1990). Drug effects on REM sleep and on endogenous depression. *Neuroscience and Behavioral Reviews, 14,* 49–63.

Walker, M. P., & Stickgold, R. (2004). Sleep-dependent learning and memory consolidation. *Neuron, 44,*121–133.

Wilson, M. A., & McNaughton, B. L. (1994). Reactivation of hippocampal ensemble memories during sleep. *Science, 265,* 676–679.

Chapter 13

Cahill, L., Babinsky, R., Markowitsch, H. J., & McGaugh, J. L. (1995). The amygdala and emotional memory. *Nature, 377,* 295–296.

Candia, V., Wienbruch, C., Elbert, T., Rockstroh, B., & Ray, W. (2003). Effective behavioral treatment of focal hand dystonia in musicians alters somatosensory cortical organization. *Proceedings of the National Academy of Sciences, USA, 100,* 7942–7946.

Chang, F.-L. F., & Greenough, W. T. (1982). Lateralized effects of monocular training on dendritic branching in adult split-brain rats. *Brain Research, 232,* 283–292.

Corkin, S. (2002). What's new with the amnesic patient H. M.? *Nature Reviews Neuroscience, 3,* 153–160.

Corkin, S., Amaral, D. G., Gonzalez, R. G., Johnson, K. A., & Hyman, B. T. (1997). H. M.'s medial temporal lobe lesion: Findings from magnetic resonance imaging. *Journal of Neuroscience, 17,* 3964–3979.

Damasio, A. R., Tranel, D., & Damasio, H. (1989). Amnesia caused by herpes simplex encephalitis, infarctions in basal forebrain, Alzheimer's disease and anoxia/ischemia. In F. Boller & J. Grafman (Eds.), *Handbook of neuropsychology* (Vol. 3, pp. 149–166). New York: Elsevier.

Davis, M. (1992). The role of the amygdala in fear and anxiety. *Annual Review of Neuroscience, 15,* 353–375.

Eriksson, P. S., Perfilieva, E., Bjork-Eriksson, T., Alborn, A. M., Nordborg, C., Peterson, D. A., & Gage, F. H. (1998). Neurogenesis in the adult human hippocampus. *Nature Medicine, 4,* 1313–1317.

Florence, S. L., Jain, N., & Kaas, J. H. (1997). Plasticity of somatosensory cortex in primates. *Seminars in Neuroscience, 9,* 3–12.

Fuster, J. M. (1995). *Memory in the cerebral cortex.* Cambridge, MA: MIT Press.

Fuster, J. M., Bodner, M., & Kroger, J. K. (2000). Cross-modal and cross-temporal association in neurons of frontal cortex. *Nature, 405,* 347–351.

Gazzaniga, M. S. (Ed.). (2000). *The new cognitive neurosciences.* Cambridge, MA: MIT Press.

Gibb, R., Gorny, G., & Kolb, B. (2005). Experience-dependent changes in dendritic arbor and spine density in neocortex vary with age and sex. *Neurobiology of Learning and Memory.* Manuscript submitted.

Gould, E., Tanapat, P., Hastings, N. B., & Shors, T. J. (1999). Neurogenesis in adulthood: A possible role in learning. *Trends in Cognitive Sciences, 3,* 186–191.

Gould, E., Tanapat, P., McEwen, B. S., Flugge, G., & Fuchs, E. (1998). Proliferation of granule cell precursors in the dentate gyrus of adult monkeys is diminished by stress. *Proceedings of the National Academy of Sciences, USA, 95,* 3168–3171.

Hampson, E., & Kimura, D. (1988). Reciprocal effects of hormonal fluctuations on human motor and perceptual-spatial skills. *Behavioral Neuroscience, 102,* 456–459.

Hebb, D. O. (1947). The effects of early experience on problem solving at maturity. *American Psychologist, 2,* 737–745.

Hebb, D. O. (1949). *The organization of behavior.* New York: Wiley.

Jacobs, B., Schall, M., & Scheibel, A. B. (1993). A quantitative dendritic analysis of Wernicke's area in humans: II. Gender, hemispheric, and environmental factors. *Journal of Comparative Neurololgy, 327,* 97–111.

Jacobs, B., & Scheibel, A. B. (1993). A quantitative dendritic analysis of Wernicke's area in humans: I. Lifespan changes. *Journal of Comparative Neurololgy, 327,* 83–96.

Kaas, J. (2000). The reorganization of sensory and motor maps after injury in adult mammals. In M. S. Gazzaniga (Ed.), *The cognitive neurosciences* (pp. 223–236). Cambridge, MA: MIT Press.

Kempermann, G., Kuhn, H. G., & Gage, F. H. (1998). Experience-induced neurogenesis in the senescent dentate gyrus. *Journal of Neuroscience, 18,* 3206–3212.

Kolb, B. (1999). Towards an ecology of cortical organization: Experience and the changing brain. In J. Grafman & Y. Christen (Eds.), *Neuropsychology: From lab to the clinic* (pp. 17–34). Paris: Springer Verlag.

Kolb, B., Gorny, G., Cote, S., Ribeiro-da-Silva, & Cuello, A. C. (1997). Nerve growth factor stimulates growth of cortical pyramidal neurons in young adult rats. *Brain Research, 751,* 289–294.

Kolb, B., Gorny, G., Li, Y., Samaha, A. N., & Robinson, T. E. (2003). Amphetamine or cocaine limits the ability of later experience to promote structural plasticity in the neocortex and nucleus accumbens. *Proceedings of the National Academy of Science, USA, 100,* 10523–10528.

Kolb, B., & Walkey, J. (1987). Behavioral and anatomical studies of the posterior parietal cortex of the rat. *Behavioural Brain Research, 23,* 127–145.

Kolb, B., & Whishaw, I. Q. (1998). Brain plasticity and behavior. *Annual Review of Psychology, 49,* 43–64.

Lashley, K. H. (1960). In search of the engram. Symposium No. 4 of the Society of Experimental Biology. In F. A. Beach, D. O. Hebb, C. T. Morgan, & H. T. Nissen (Eds.), *The neuropsychology of Lashley* (pp. 478–505). New York: McGraw-Hill. (Reprinted from *Physiological mechanisms of animal behavior,* pp. 454–482, 1951. Cambridge: Cambridge University Press.)

LeDoux, J. E. (1995). In search of an emotional system in the brain: Leaping from fear to emotion and consciousness. In M. S. Gazzaniga (Ed.), *The cognitive neurosciences* (pp. 1047–1061). Cambridge, MA: MIT Press.

Lepage, M., McIntosh, A. R., & Tulving, E. (2001). Transperceptual encoding and retrieval process in memory: A PET study of visual and haptic objects. *Neuroimage, 14,* 572–584.

Loftus, E. F. (1997). Creating false memories. *Scientific American, 277*(3), 70–75.

Maguire, E. A., Gadian, D. G., Johnsrude, I. S., Good, C. D., Ashburner, J., Frackowiak, R. S., & Frith, C. D. (2000). Navigation-related structural change in the hippocampi of taxi drivers. *Proceedings of the National Academy of Sciences, USA, 97,* 4398–4403.

Markowitsch, H. J. (2003). Psychogenic amnesia. *Neuroimage, 20*(Suppl. 1), S132–S138.

Martin, A., Haxby, J. V., Lalonde, F. M., Wiggs, C. L., & Ungerleider, L. G. (1995). Discrete cortical regions associated with knowledge of color and knowledge of action. *Science, 270,* 102–105.

McGaugh, J. (2004). The amygdala modulates the consolidation of memories of emotionally arousing experiences. *Annual Review of Neuroscience, 27,* 1–28.

Milner, B., Corkin, S., & Teuber, H. (1968). Further analysis of the hippocampal amnesic syndrome: 14 year follow-up study of HM. *Neuropsychologia, 6,* 215–234.

Mishkin, M. (1982). A memory system in the brain. *Philosophical Transactions of the Royal Society of London, Biological Sciences, 298,* 83–95.

Mishkin, M., Suzuki, W. A., Gadian, D. G., & Vargha-Khadem, F. (1997). Hierarchical organization of cognitive memory. *Philosophical Transactions of the Royal Society of London, Biological Sciences, 352,* 1461–1467.

Morris, R. G. M. (1981). Spatial localization does not require the presence of local cues. *Learning and Motivation, 12,* 239–260.

Murray, E. (2000). Memory for objects in nonhuman primates. In M. S. Gazzaniga (Ed.), *The new cognitive neurosciences* (pp. 753–763). Cambridge, MA: MIT Press.

Nudo, R. J., Plautz, E. J., & Milliken, G. W. (1997). Adaptive plasticity in primate motor cortex as a consequence of behavioral experience and neuronal injury. *Seminars in Neuroscience, 9,* 13–23.

O'Keefe, J., & Nadel, L. (1978). *The hippocampus as a spatial map.* New York: Oxford University Press.

Purves, D., & Voyvodic, J. T. (1987). Imaging mammalian nerve cells and their connections over time in living animals. *Trends in Neurosciences, 10,* 398–404.

Ragert, P., Schmidt, A., Altenmuller, E., & Dinse, H. R. (2003). Superior tactile performance and learning in professional pianists: Evidence for meta-plasticity in musicians. *European Journal of Neuroscience, 19,* 473–478.

Ramachandran, V. S. (1993). Behavioral and magnetoencephalographic correlates of plasticity in the adult human brain. *Proceedings of the National Academy of Sciences, USA, 90,* 10413–10420.

Ramón y Cajal, S. (1928). *Degeneration and regeneration of the nervous system.* London: Oxford University Press.

Reynolds, B., & Weiss, S. (1992). Generation of neurons and astrocytes from isolated cells of the adult mammalian central nervous system. *Science, 255,* 1707–1710.

Riesen, A. H., Dickerson, G. P., & Struble, R. G. (1977). Somatosensory restriction and behavioral development in stumptail monkeys. *Annals of the New York Academy of Sciences, 290,* 285–294.

Robinson, T. E., & Kolb, B. (1997). Persistent structural adaptations in nucleus accumbens and prefrontal cortex neurons produced by prior experience with amphetamine. *Journal of Neuroscience, 17,* 8491–8498.

Robinson, T. E., & Kolb, B. (1999). Alterations in the morphology of dendrites and dendritic spines in the nucleus accumbens and prefrontal cortex following repeated treatment with amphetamine or cocaine. *European Journal of Neuroscience, 11,* 1598–1604.

Robinson, T. E., & Kolb, B. (2004). Structural plasticity associated with drugs of abuse. *Neuropharmacology, 47*(Suppl. 1), 33–46.

Sainsbury, R. S., & Coristine, M. (1986). Affective discrimination in moderately to severely demented patients. *Canadian Journal on Aging, 5,* 99–104.

Sapolsky, R. M. (1992). *Stress, the aging brain, and the mechanisms of neuron death.* Cambridge, MA: MIT Press.

Schacter, D. L. (1983). Amnesia observed: Remembering and forgetting in a natural environment. *Journal of Abnormal Psychology, 92,* 236–242.

Scheibel, A. (1982). Age-related changes in the human forebrain. *Neurosciences Research Program Bulletin, 20,* 577–583.

Sherry, D. F., Jacobs, L. F., & Gaulin, S. J. C. (1992). Spatial memory and adaptive specialization of the hippocampus. *Trends in Neurosciences, 15,* 298–303.

Sirevaag, A. M., & Greenough, W. T. (1987). Differential rearing effects on rat visual cortex synapses: III. Neuronal and glial nuclei, boutons, dendrites, and capillaries. *Brain Research, 424,* 320–332.

Sirevaag, A. M., & Greenough, W. T. (1988). A multivariate statistical summary of synaptic plasticity measures in rats exposed to complex, social and individual environments. *Brain Research, 441,* 386–392.

Skinner, B. F. (1938). *The behavior of organisms.* New York: Appleton-Century-Crofts.

Squire, L. (1987). *Memory and brain.* New York: Oxford University Press.

Stewart, J., & Kolb, B. (1994). Dendritic branching in cortical pyramidal cells in response to ovariectomy in adult female rats: Suppression by neonatal exposure to testosterone. *Brain Research, 654,* 149–154.

Thorndike, E. L. (1898). Animal intelligence: An experimental study of the associative processes in animals. *Psychological Review Monograph Supplements, 2,* 1–109.

Tulving, E. (2002). Episodic memory: From mind to brain. *Annual Review of Psychology, 53,* 1–25.

Turner, A., & Greenough, W. T. (1985). Differential rearing effects on rat visual cortex synapses: I. Synaptic and neuronal density and synapses per neuron. *Brain Research, 329,* 195–203.

Whishaw, I. Q. (1989). Dissociating performance and learning deficits in spatial navigation tasks in rats subjected to cholinergic muscarinic blockade. *Brain Research Bulletin, 23,* 347–358.

Wise, R. A. (2004). Dopamine, learning and motivation. *Nature Neuroscience Reviews, 5,* 483–494.

Woolley, C. S., Gould, E., Frankfurt, M., & McEwen, B. S. (1990). Naturally occurring fluctuation in dendritic spine density on adult hippocampal pyramidal neurons. *Journal of Neuroscience, 10,* 4035–4039.

Chapter 14

Acredolo, L. P. (1976). Frames of reference used by children for orientation in unfamiliar spaces. In G. Moore & R. Gooledge (Eds.), *Environmental knowing* (pp. 165–172). Stroudsburg, PA: Dowden, Hutchinson, and Ross.

Adolphs, R., Gjosselin, F., Buchanan, T. W., Tranel, D., Schyns, P., & Damasio, A. R. (2005). A mechanism for impaired fear recognition after amygdala damage. *Nature, 433,* 68–72.

Barlow, H. (1995). The neuron doctrine in perception. In M. Gazzaniga (Ed.), *The cognitive neurosciences* (pp. 415–435). Cambridge, MA: MIT Press.

Calvin, W. H. (1996). *How brains think.* New York: Basic Books.

Carrasco, M., Ling, S., & Read, S. (2004). Attention alters appearance. *Nature Neuroscience, 7,* 308–313.

Castiello, U., Paulignan, Y., & Jeannerod, M. (1991). Temporal dissociation of motor responses and subjective awareness. *Brain, 114,* 2639–2655.

Chalmers, D. J. (1995). *The conscious mind: In search of a fundamental theory.* Oxford: Oxford University Press.

Crick, F., & Koch, C. (1998). Consciousness and neuroscience. *Cerebral Cortex, 8,* 97–107.

Cytowic, R. E. (1998). *The man who tasted shapes.* Cambridge, MA: MIT Press.

Diamond, M. C., Scheibel, A. B., Murphy, G. M., Jr., & Harvey, T. (1985). On the brain of a scientist: Albert Einstein. *Experimental Neurology, 88,* 198–204.

Duncan, J., Seitz, R. J., Kolodny, J., Bor, D., Herzog, H., Ahmed, A., Newell, F. N., & Emslie, H. (2000). A neural basis for general intelligence. *Science, 289,* 457–459.

Farah, M. J. (1995). The neural bases of mental imagery. In M. Gazzaniga (Ed.), *The cognitive neurosciences* (pp. 2963–2975). Cambridge, MA: MIT Press.

Frith, C., Perry, R., & Lumer, E. (1999). The neural correlates of conscious experience: An experimental framework. *Trends in Cognitive Sciences, 3,* 105–114.

Gardner, H. (1983). *Frames of mind.* New York: Basic Books.

Gaulin, S. J. (1992). Evolution of sex differences in spatial ability. *Yearbook of Physical Anthropology, 35,* 125–131.

Gazzaniga, M. S. (1970). *The bisected brain.* New York: Appleton-Century-Crofts.

Gazzaniga, M. S. (1992). *Nature's mind.* New York: Basic Books.

Gazzaniga, M. S., Ivry, R. B., & Mangun, G. R. (1999). *Cognitive science: The biology of the mind.* New York: Norton.

Gibb, R., Gorny, G., & Kolb, B. (2005). The therapeutic effects of complex rearing after frontal lesions in infancy are sex dependent. Manuscript submitted for publication.

Gray, J. R., & Thompson, P. M. (2004). Neurobiology of intelligence: Science and ethics. *Nature Reviews Neuroscience, 5,* 471–482.

Guilford, J. P. (1967). *The nature of human intelligence.* New York: McGraw-Hill.

Hamann, S., Herman, R. A., Nolan, C. J., & Wallen, K. (2004). Men and women differ in amygdala response to visual sexual stimuli. *Nature Neuroscience, 7,* 411–416.

Hebb, D. O. (1980). *Essay on mind.* Hillsdale, NJ: Lawrence Erlbaum.

James, W. (1890). *Principles of psychology.* New York: Henry Holt.

Kimura, D. (1967). Functional asymmetry of the brain in dichotic listening. *Cortex, 3,* 163–178.

Kimura, D. (1973). The asymmetry of the human brain. *Scientific American, 228*(3), 70–78.

Kimura, D. (1992). Sex differences in the brain. *Scientific American, 367*(3), 119–125.

Kimura, D. (1999). *Sex and cognition.* Cambridge, MA: MIT Press.

Kolb, B., & Stewart, J. (1991). Sex-related differences in dendritic branching of cells in the prefrontal cortex of rats. *Journal of Neuroendocrinology, 3,* 95–99.

Kolb, B., & Whishaw, I. Q. (2003). *Fundamentals of human neuropsychology* (5th ed.). New York: W. H. Freeman and Company.

Kwong, K. K., Belliveau, J. W., Chesler, D. A., Goldberg, I. E., Weisskiff, R. M., Poncelet, B. P., Kennedy, D. N., Hoppel, B. E., Cohen, M. S., Turner, R., Cheng, H. M., Brady, T. J., & Rosen, B. R. (1992). Dynamic magnetic resonance imaging of human brain activity druing primary sensory stimulation. *Proceedings of the National Academy of Sciences, USA, 89,* 5675–5679.

Moran, J., & Desimone, R. (1985). Selective attention gates visual processing in the extrastriate cortex. *Science, 229,* 782–784.

Mukerjee, M. (1996). Interview with a parrot [field note]. *Scientific American, 274*(4), 24.

Newsome, W. T., Shadlen, M. N., Zohary, E., Britten, K. H., & Movshon, J. A. (1995). Visual motion: Linking neuronal activity to psychophysical performance. In M. Gazzaniga (Ed.), *The cognitive neurosciences* (pp. 401–414). Cambridge, MA: MIT Press.

Ogawa, S. J., Lee, L. M., Kay, A. R., & Tank, D. W. (1990). Brain magnetic resonance imaging with contrast dependent on blood oxygenation. *Proceedings of the National Academy of Sciences, USA, 87,* 9868–9872.

Paus, T., Jech, R., Thompson, C. J., Comeau, R., Peters, T., & Evans, A. (1997). Transcranial magnetic stimulation during positron emission tomography: A new method for studying connectivity of the human cerebral cortex. *Journal of Neuroscience, 17,* 3178–3184.

Pepperberg, I. M. (1990). Some cognitive capacities of an African grey parrot (*Psittacus erithacus*). In P. J. B. Slater, J. S. Rosenblatt, & C. Beer (Eds.), *Advances in the study of behavior* (Vol. 19, pp. 357–409). New York: Academic Press.

Pepperberg, I. M. (1992). Proficient performance of a conjunctive, recursive task by an African grey parrot (*Psittacus erithacus*). *Journal of Comparative Psychology, 106,* 295–305.

Pepperberg, I. M. (1999). *The Alex studies.* Cambridge, MA: Harvard University Press.

Rasmussen, T., & Milner, B. (1977). The role of early left brain injury in determining lateralization of cerebral speech functions. *Annals of the New York Academy of Sciences, 299,* 355–369.

Rizzolatti, G., & Arbib, M. A. (1998). Language within our grasp. *Trends in Neurosciences, 21,* 188–194.

Rowntree, S. (2005). Spatial and verbal abilities in adult females vary with age at menses. Manuscript submitted for publication.

Sacks, O. (1989). *Seeing voices.* Los Angeles: University of California Press.

Sperry, R. (1968). Mental unity following surgical disconnection of the cerebral hemispheres. *Harvey Lectures, 62,* 293–323.

Stewart, J., & Kolb, B. (1994). Dendritic branching in cortical pyramidal cells in response to ovariectomy in adult female rats: Suppression by neonatal exposure to testosterone. *Brain Research, 654,* 149–154.

Waber, D. P. (1976). Sex differences in cognition: A function of maturation rate? *Science, 192,* 572–574.

Wada, J., & Rasmussen, T. (1960). Intracarotid injection of sodium amytal for the lateralization of cerebral speech dominance: Experimental and clinical observations. *Journal of Neurosurgery, 17,* 266–282.

Warren, D. K., Patterson, D. K., & Pepperberg, I. M. (1996). Mechanisms of American English vowel production in a grey parrot (*Psittacus erithacus*). *Auk, 11,* 41–58.

Wildgruber, D., Kischka, U., Ackermann, H., Klose, U., & Grodd, W. (1999). Dynamic pattern of brain activation during sequencing of word strings evaluated by fMRI. *Cognitive Brain Research, 7,* 285–294.

Witelson, S. F., & Goldsmith, C. H. (1991). The relationship of hand preference to anatomy of the corpus callosum in men. *Brain Research, 545,* 175–182.

Witelson, S. F., Kigar, D. L., & Harvey, T. (1999). The exceptional brain of Albert Einstein. *Lancet, 353,* 2149–2153.

Chapter 15

Abramowitz, J. S. (1998). Does cognitive-behavior therapy cure obsessive-compulsive disorder? A meta-analytic evaluation of clinical significance. *Behavior Therapy, 29,* 339–355.

American Psychiatric Association. (1994). *Diagnostic and statistical manual of mental disorders* (4th ed.). Washington, DC: American Psychiatric Association.

Andreasen, N. C., & Olsen, S. A. (1982). Negative versus positive symptoms in schizophrenia: Definition and validation. *Archives of General Psychiatry, 39,* 789–794.

Annegers, J. F., Grabow, J. D., Groover, E. R., Laws, E. R., Elveback, L. R., & Kurland, L. T. (1980). Seizures after head trauma: A population study. *Neurobiology, 30,* 683–689.

Arnold, S. E., Rushinsky, D. D., & Han, L. Y. (1997). Further evidence of abnormal cytoarchitecture in the entorhinal cortex in schizophrenia using spatial point analyses. *Biological Psychiatry, 142,* 639–647.

Barondes, S. M. (1993). *Molecules and mental illness.* New York: Scientific American Library.

Berman, K. F., & Weinberger, D. R. (1999). Neuroimaging studies of schizophrenia. In D. S. Charney, E. J. Nestler, & B. S. Bunney (Eds.), *The neurobiology of mental illness* (pp. 246–257). New York: Oxford University Press.

Boland, R. J., & Keller, M. B. (2004). Diagnostic classification of mood disorders: Historical context and implications for neurobiology. In D. S. Charney & E. J. Nestler (Eds.), *Neurobiology of Mental Illness* (2nd ed., pp. 357–379). New York: Oxford University Press.

Boucai, L., Cerquetti, D., & Merello, M. (2004). Functional surgery for Parkinson's disease treatment: A structured analysis of a decade of published literature. *British Journal of Neurosurgery, 18,* 213–222.

Breier, A. (1999). Diagnostic classification of the psychoses: Historical context and implications for neurobiology. In D. S. Charney, E. J. Nestler, & B. S. Bunney (Eds.), *The neurobiology of mental illness* (pp. 195–202). New York: Oxford University Press.

Brooks, W. M., Friedman, S. D., & Gasparovic, C. (2001). Magnetic resonance spectroscopy in traumatic brain injury. *Journal of Head Trauma and Rehabilitation, 16,* 149–164.

Brun, A. (1983). An overview of light and electron microscopic changes. In B. Reisberg (Ed.), *Alzheimer's disease* 127–143. New York: The Free Press.

Calne, D. B., & Mizuno, Y. (2004). The neuromythology of Parkinson's disease. *Parkinsonism and Related Disorders, 10,* 319–322.

Caplan, A. L. (2003). Is better best? *Scientific American, 289*(3), 104–105.

Charney, D. S., & Nestler, E. J. (Eds.). (2004). *Neurobiology of mental illness* (2nd ed.). New York: Oxford University Press.

Cho, R. Y., Gilbert, H., & Lewis, D. A. (2004). The neurobiology of schizophrenia. In D. S. Charney & F. J. Nestler (Eds.), *Neurobiology of Mental Illnes* (2nd ed., pp. 299–310). New York: Oxford University Press.

Ciccarelli, P. A., Brex, A. J., Thompson, A. J., & Miller, D. H. (2000). Disability and lesion load in MS: A reassessment with MS functional composite score and 3D fast flair. *Journal of Neurology, 249,* 18–24.

Crow, T. J. (1980). Molecular pathology of schizophrenia: More than one disease process? *British Medical Journal, 280,* 66–68.

Crow, T. J. (1990). Nature of the genetic contribution to psychotic illness: A continuum viewpoint. *Acta Psychiatrica Scandinavia, 81,* 401–408.

Drevets, W. C., Gadde, K. M., & Krishnan, K. R. (1999). Neuroimaging studies of mood disorders. In D. S. Charney, E. J. Nestler, & B. S. Bunney (Eds.), *The neurobiology of mental illness* (pp. 394–418). New York: Oxford University Press.

Drevets, W. C., Kishore, M. G., & Krishman, K. R. R. (2004). Neuroimaging studies of mood disorders. In D. S. Charney & E. J. Nestler (Eds.) *Neurobiology of mental illness* (2nd ed., pp. 461–490). New York: Oxford University Press.

Duman, R. S. (1999). The neurochemistry of mood disorders. In D. S. Charney, E. J. Nestler, & B. S. Bunney (Eds.), *The neurobiology of mental illness* (pp. 333–347). New York: Oxford University Press.

Duman, R. S. (2004). The neurochemistry of depressive disorders. In D. S. Charney & E. J. Nestler (Eds.). *Neurobiology of mental illness* (2nd ed., pp. 421–439). New York: Oxford University Press.

Farah, M. J., Illes, J., Cook-Deegan, R., Gardner, H., Kandel, E., King, P., Parens, E., Sahakian, B., & Wolpe, P. R. (2004). Neurocognitive enhancement: What can we do and what should we do? *Nature Reviews Neuroscience, 5,* 421–425.

Fitzgerald, P. B., Brown, T. L., Marston, N. A. U, Oxley, T., de Castella, A., Daskalakis, Z. J., & Kulkarni, J. (2004). Reduced plastic brain responses in schizophrenia: A transcranial magnetic stimulation study. *Schizophrenia Research, 71,* 17–26.

George, M. S., Wasserman, E. M., Kimbrell, T. A., & Little, I. T. (1997). Mood improvements following daily left prefrontal repetitive transcranial magnetic stimulation in patients with depression: A placebo-controlled crossover study. *American Journal of Psychiatry, 154,* 1752–1756.

Giles J. (2004). Neuroscience: Change of mind. *Nature, 430,*14.

Gross, C., & Hen, R. (2004). The developmental origins of anxiety. *Nature Reviews Neuroscience, 5,* 545–552.

Haraldsson, H. M., Ferrarelli, F., Kalin, N. H., & Tonomi, G. (2004). Transcranial magnetic stimulation in the investigation and treatment of schizophrenia: A review. *Schizophrenia Research, 71,* 1–16.

Heninger, G. R. (1999). Special challenges in the investigation of the neurobiology of mental illness. In D. S. Charney, E. J. Nestler, & B. S. Bunney (Eds.), *The neurobiology of mental illness* (pp. 89–98). New York: Oxford University Press.

Hoffman, R. E., Hawkins, K. A., Gueorguieva, R., Boutros, N. N., Rachid, F., Carroll, K., & Krystal, J. H. (2003). Transcranial magnetic stimulation of left temporoparietal cortex and medication-resistant auditory hallucinations. *Archives of General Psychiatry, 60,* 49–56.

Hyman, S. E. (2003). Diagnosing disorders. *Scientific American, 289*(3), 97–103.

Kessler, R. C., McGonagle, K. A., Zhao, S., Nelson, C. B., Hughes, M., Eshleman, S., Wittchen, H., & Kendler, K. S. (1994). Lifetime and 12-month prevalence of DSM-III-R psychiatric disorders in the United States. *Archives of General Psychiatry, 51,* 8–19.

Kondziolka, D., Wechsler, L., Goldstein, S., Meltzer, C., Thulborn, K. R., Gebel, J., Jannetta, P., DeCesare, S., Elder, E. M., McGrogan, M., Reitman, M. A., & Bynum, L. (2000). Transplantation of cultured human neuronal cells for patients with stroke. *Neurology, 55,* 565–569.

Larrabee, G. J., & Crook, T. H. (1994). Estimated prevalence of age-related memory impairment derived from standardized tests of memory function. *International Psychogeriatrics, 6,* 95–104.

Levin, H. S., Benton, A. L., & Grossman, R. G. (1982). *Neurobehavioral consequences of closed head injury.* New York: Oxford University Press.

Lezak, M. (2004). *Neuropsychological assessment* (4th ed.). New York: Oxford University Press.

Martin, J. P. (1967). *The basal ganglia and posture.* London: Ritman Medical Publishing.

Matser, J. T., Kessels, A. G., Jordan, B. D., Lezak, M. D., & Troost, J. (1998). Chronic traumatic brain injury in professional soccer players. *Neurology, 51,* 791–796.

McGuire, P. K., Shah, G. M. S., & Murray, R. M. (1993). Increased blood flow in Broca's area during auditory hallucinations in schizophrenia. *Lancet, 342,* 703–706.

Merikangas, K. R., & Swendsen, J. D. (1999). Contributions of epidemiology to the neurobiology of mental illness. In D. S. Charney, E. J. Nestler, & B. S. Bunney (Eds.), *The neurobiology of mental illness* (pp. 100–107). New York: Oxford University Press.

Miller, B. L., Boone, K., Cummings, J. L., Read, S. L., & Mishkin, F. (2000). Functional correlates of musical and visual ability in frontotemporal dementia. *British Journal of Psychiatry, 176,* 458–463.

Nemeroff, C. B. (2004). Early-life adversity, CRF dysregulation, and vulnerability to mood and anxiety disorders. *Psychopharmacology Bulletin, 38,*14–20.

Post, J. R. M., & Weiss, R. B. (1999). Neurobiological models of recurrence in mood disorder. In D. S. Charney, E. J. Nestler, & B. S. Bunney (Eds.), *The neurobiology of mental illness* (pp. 365–393). New York: Oxford University Press.

Prigatano, G. (1986). *Neuropsychological rehabilitation after brain injury.* Baltimore: Johns Hopkins University Press.

Ramachandran, V. S. (1995). Anosognosia in parietal lobe syndrome. *Conscious Cognition, 4,* 22–51.

Rogawski, M. A., & Loscher, W. (2004). The neurobiology of antiepileptic drugs. *Nature Reviews Neuroscience, 5,* 553–564.

Rossi, S., & Rossini, P. M. (2004). TMS in cognitive plasticity and the potential for rehabilitation. *Trends in Cognitive Sciences, 8,* 273–279.

Sacks, O. (1998). *The man who mistook his wife for a hat: And other clinical tales.* New York: Touchstone.

Sanders, A. R., Detera-Wadleigh, & Gershon, E. S. (1999). Molecular genetics of mood disorders. In D. S. Charney, E. J. Nestler, & B. S. Bunney, *The neurobiology of mental illness* (pp. 299–316). New York: Oxford University Press.

Santarelli, L., Saxe, M., Gross, C., Surget, A., Battaglia, F., Dulawa, S., Weisstaub, N., Lee, J., Duman, R., Arancio, O., Belzung, C., & Hen, R. (2003). Requirement of hippocampal neurogenesis for the behavioral effects of antidepressants. *Science, 301,* 805–809.

Shenton, M. E., Kikinis, R., Jolesz, F. A., Pollak, S. D., LeMay, M., Wible, C. G., Hokama, H., Martin, J., Metcalf, D., Colemen, M., & McCarley, R. W. (1992). Abnormalities of the left temporal lobe and thought disorder in schizophrenia: A quantitative magnetic resonance imaging study. *New England Journal of Medicine, 327,* 604–611.

Sohlberg, M. M., & Mateer, C. (1989). *Introduction to cognitive rehabilitation.* New York: Guilford Press.

Solms, M. (2004). Freud returns. *Scientific American, 290*(5), 83–89.

Sowell, E. R., Thompson, P. M., & Toga, A. W. (2004). Mapping changes in the human cortex through life span. *The Neuroscientist, 10,* 372–392.

Sporn, J., Belanoff, J. K., Schatzberg, A., & Charney, D. S. (2004). Principles of the pharmacotherapy of depression. In D. S. Charney & E. J. Nestler (Eds.), *Neurobiology of Mental Illness* (2nd ed., pp. 491–511). New York: Oxford University Press.

Steinman, L., Martin, R., Bernard, C., Conlon, P., & Oksenberg, J. R. (2002). Multiple sclerosis: Deeper understanding of its pathogenesis reveals new targets for therapy. *Annual Review of Neuroscience, 25,* 491–505.

Teskey, G. C., Flynn, C., Goertzen, C. D., Monfils, M. H., & Young, N. A. (2003). Cortical stimulation improves skilled forelimb use following a focal ischemic infarct in the rat. *Neurological Research, 25,* 794–800.

Tsai, G., & Coyle, J. T. (1995). *N*-Acetylaspartate in neuropsychiatric disorders. *Progress in Neurobiology, 46,* 531–540.

Weaver, I. C., Cervoni, N., Champagne, F. A., D'Alessio, A. C., Sharma, S., Seckl, J. R., Dymov, S., Szyf, M., & Meaney, M. J. (2004). Epigenetic programming by maternal behavior. *Nature Neuroscience, 7,* 847–854.

Weinberger, D. R., & Lipska, B. K. (1995). Cortical maldevelopment, anti-psychotic drugs and schizophrenia: A search for common ground. *Schizophrenia Research, 16,* 87–110.

Appendix

Alberts, J. L., Butler, A. J., & Wolf, S. L. (2004). The effects of constraint-induced therapy on precision grip: A preliminary study. *Neurorehabilitation and Neural Repair, 18,* 250–258.

American Medical Association. (1989). *Use of animals in biomedical research: The challenge and response.* American Medical Association white paper, Chicago.

Feeney, D. M. (1987). Human rights and animal welfare. *American Psychologist, 42,* 593–599.

Finger, S. (1994). *Origins of neuroscience: A history of explorations into brain function.* New York: Oxford University Press.

Fox, M. A. (1986). *The case for animal experimentation: An evolutionary and ethical perspective.* Berkeley: University of California Press.

Fox, M. A. (1996). Animal experimentation is not justified. In D. Bender & B. Leone (Eds.), *Animal rights: Opposing viewpoints* (pp. 82–89). San Diego: Greenhaven Press.

Fox, M. A. (1999). *Deep vegetarianism.* Philadelphia: Temple University Press.

Fox, M. W. (1999). *Beyond evolution.* New York: Lyons Press.

Guillermo, K. S. (1994). *Monkey business: The disturbing case that launched the animal rights movement (People for the Ethical Treatment of Animals).* Bethesda, MD: National Press Books.

Herzog, H. A., Jr. (1993). The movement is my life: The psychology of animal rights activism. *Journal of Social Issues, 49,* 103–119.

Humane Society of the United States. (2000). Animal research issues. (http://www.hsus.org/about/history.html)

National Research Council. (1996). *The guide for the care and use of laboratory animals.* Washington, DC: National Research Council.

Palca, J. (1991). Famous monkeys provide surprising results. *Science, 254,* 1789.

Pons, T. P., Garraghty, T. E., Ommaya, A. K., Kaas, J. H., Taub, E., & Mishkin, M. (1991). Massive cortical reorganization after sensory deafferentation in adult macaques. *Science, 254,* 1857–1860.

Regan, T. (1983). *The case for animal rights.* Berkeley: University of California Press.

Regan T. (1996). The case for strong animal rights. In D. Bender and B. Leone (Eds.). *Animal rights: Opposing viewpoints* (pp. 34–40). San Diego: Greenhaven Press.

Ridley, M. (1997). *The origins of virtue: Human instincts and the evolution of cooperation.* New York: Viking.

Singer, P. (1990). *Animal liberation* (2nd ed.). New York: New York Review of Books.

Stephens, M. L. (1992). The middle ground. *The Scientist, 6*(17), 12.

Taub, E., & Crago, J. E. (1995). Behavioral plasticity following central nervous system damage in monkeys and man. In B. Julesz and I. Kovacs (Eds.), *SFI studies in the sciences of complexity* (Vol. 23, pp. 201–215). Redwood City, CA: Addison-Wesley.

Name Index

Subject Index

Note: Page numbers followed by f indicate figures; those followed by t indicate tables.